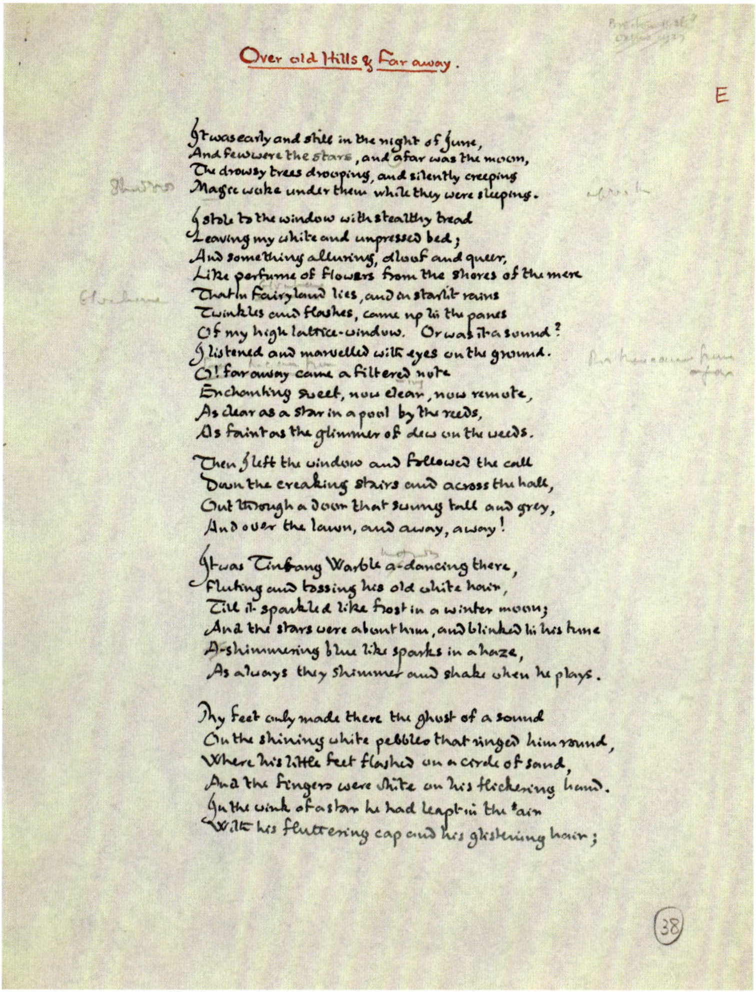

Over old Hills & Far away.

E

It was early and still in the night of June,
And few were the stars, and afar was the moon,
The drowsy trees drooping, and silently creeping
Magic woke under them while they were sleeping.

I stole to the window with stealthy tread
Leaving my white and unpressed bed;
And something alluring, aloof and queer,
Like perfume of flowers from the shores of the mere
That in Fairyland lies, and on starlit rains
Twinkles and flashes, came up to the panes
Of my high lattice-window. Or was it a sound?
I listened and marvelled with eyes on the ground.
O! far away came a filtered note
Enchanting sweet, now clear, now remote,
As clear as a star in a pool by the reeds,
As faint as the glimmer of dew on the weeds.

Then I left the window and followed the call
Down the creaking stairs and across the hall,
Out through a door that swung tall and grey,
And over the lawn, and away, away!

It was Tinfang Warble a-dancing there,
Fluting and tossing his old white hair,
Till it sparkled like frost in a winter moon;
And the stars were about him, and blinked to his tune
A-shimmering blue like sparks in a haze,
As always they shimmer and shake when he plays.

My feet only made there the ghost of a sound
On the shining white pebbles that ringed him round,
Where his little feet flashed on a circle of sand,
And the fingers were white on his flickering hand.
In the wink of a star he had leapt in the air
With his fluttering cap and his glistening hair;

(38)

I

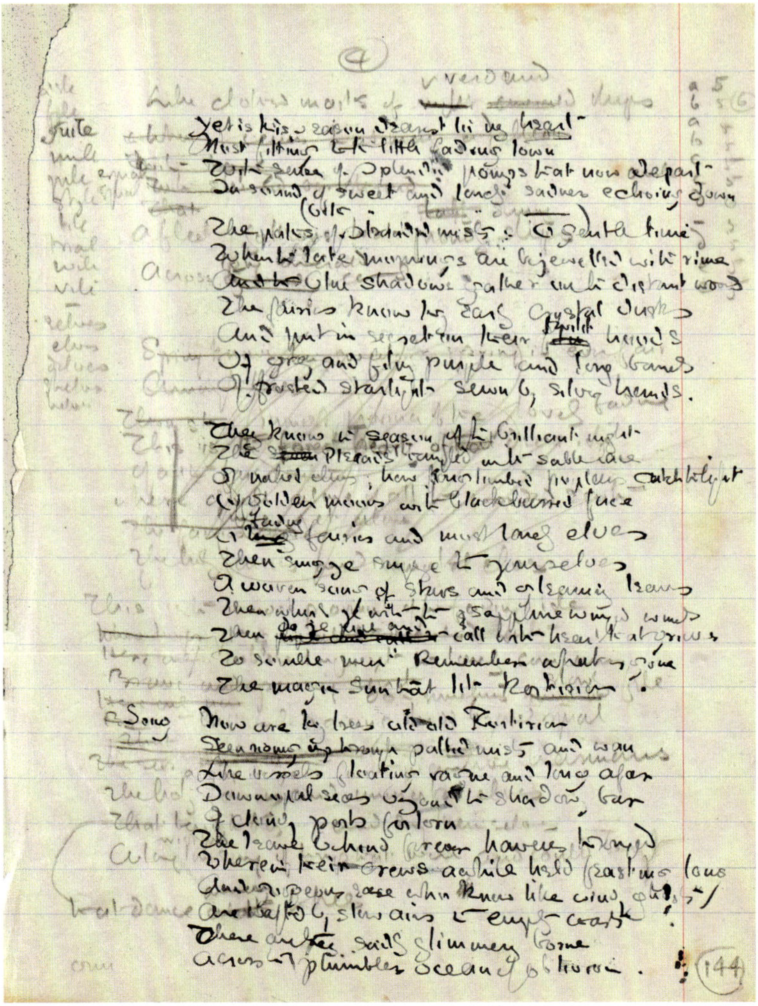
Yet is this season dearest to my heart
Most fitting to the little fading town
With secret of splendid songs that now depart
In sound of sweet and lonely sadness echoing down
The paths of sodden mists: O gentle time
When the late mornings are bejewelled with rime
And the blue shadows gather on the distant woods
The fairies know thy early crystal dusks
And put in secret on their twilit hoods
Of grey and filmy purple and long bands
Of frosted starlight sewn by silver hands.
They know the season of the brilliant night
The [illegible] Pleiads tangled with sable lace
Of naked elms, [illegible] catch the light
Of golden moons with blackbarred face
[illegible] fairies and most lonely elves
Then [illegible] to yourselves
A woven song of stars and gleaming leaves
Then whirl ye with the sapphire winged winds
Then [illegible] call with heart that grieves
To sombre men "Remember what is gone
The magic sun that lit Kortirion!"
Song
Now are the trees all old Kortirion
Seen [illegible] through pallid mists and wan
Like vessels floating vague and long afar
Down unpathed seas beyond the shadowy bar
Of cloudy ports forlorn
They leave behind forever havens loved
Wherein their crews a while held feasting long
[illegible]
Are wafted by slow airs to empty coasts
There are the sails glimmering borne
Across the plumbless ocean [illegible]
144

The Collected Poems of J. R. R. Tolkien

Works by J.R.R. Tolkien

THE HOBBIT · LEAF BY NIGGLE · ON FAIRY-STORIES
FARMER GILES OF HAM · THE HOMECOMING OF BEORHTNOTH
THE LORD OF THE RINGS · THE ADVENTURES OF TOM BOMBADIL
THE ROAD GOES EVER ON (WITH DONALD SWANN)
SMITH OF WOOTTON MAJOR

*Works Published Posthumously (*edited by Christopher Tolkien)*

SIR GAWAIN AND THE GREEN KNIGHT, PEARL AND SIR ORFEO*
LETTERS FROM FATHER CHRISTMAS · THE SILMARILLION*
PICTURES BY J.R.R. TOLKIEN* · UNFINISHED TALES*
THE LETTERS OF J.R.R. TOLKIEN*
FINN AND HENGEST · MR. BLISS
THE MONSTERS AND THE CRITICS AND OTHER ESSAYS*
ROVERANDOM · THE CHILDREN OF HÚRIN*
THE LEGEND OF SIGURD AND GUDRÚN* · THE FALL OF ARTHUR*
BEOWULF: A TRANSLATION AND COMMENTARY*
THE STORY OF KULLERVO · THE LAY OF AOTROU AND ITROUN
BEREN AND LÚTHIEN* · THE FALL OF GONDOLIN*
THE NATURE OF MIDDLE-EARTH · THE FALL OF NÚMENOR

The History of Middle-earth – by Christopher Tolkien

I THE BOOK OF LOST TALES, PART ONE
II THE BOOK OF LOST TALES, PART TWO
III THE LAYS OF BELERIAND
IV THE SHAPING OF MIDDLE-EARTH
V THE LOST ROAD AND OTHER WRITINGS
VI THE RETURN OF THE SHADOW
VII THE TREASON OF ISENGARD
VIII THE WAR OF THE RINGS
IX SAURON DEFEATED
X MORGOTH'S RING
XI THE WAR OF THE JEWELS
XII THE PEOPLES OF MIDDLE-EARTH

Also by Christina Scull & Wayne G. Hammond

J.R.R. TOLKIEN: ARTIST AND ILLUSTRATOR
THE LORD OF THE RINGS: A READER'S COMPANION
THE J.R.R. TOLKIEN COMPANION AND GUIDE
THE ART OF THE HOBBIT BY J.R.R. TOLKIEN
THE ART OF THE LORD OF THE RINGS BY J.R.R. TOLKIEN

The Collected Poems of J.R.R. Tolkien

Edited by

Christina Scull

Wayne G. Hammond

VOLUME ONE

HarperCollins*Publishers*

HarperCollins*Publishers* Ltd
1 London Bridge Street
London SE1 9GF

HarperCollins*Publishers*
Macken House, 39/40 Mayor Street Upper
Dublin 1, D01 C9W8, Ireland

www.tolkien.co.uk · www.tolkienestate.com

Published by HarperCollins*Publishers* 2024

1

Further acknowledgements appear on pp. 1471–2. Every effort has been made to trace all owners of copyright. The editors and publishers apologise for any errors or omissions and would be grateful if notified of any corrections.

A CIP catalogue record for this book is available from the British Library

ISBN 978-0-00-862882-6

Printed and bound in Italy by Rotolito S.p.A.

Contents

VOLUME ONE

VOLUME THREE

Illustrations

Introduction

IN THE days of J.R.R. Tolkien's youth, at the turn of the twentieth century, it was still recommended that young men acquire what used to be called 'polite arts', so that they might behave like gentlemen even if, like Tolkien, the recipient was not born to wealth. These pursuits included, among other things, music, art, and the writing of poetry. Tolkien loved music, enjoyed singing on occasion, but never composed or learned to play an instrument. He could, however, draw and paint passably well, and for most of his life he wrote poems which are skilful and highly inventive. It is this latter talent which is the subject of our book.

Because his most commercially successful writings, *The Hobbit* and *The Lord of the Rings*, have had so many readers, and because they include between them nearly one hundred poems (depending on how one counts), Tolkien's skill as a poet ought to be already well known. In fact, there is ample anecdotal evidence that many who enjoy his stories of Middle-earth pass over their poems very quickly or avoid them altogether, either in haste to get on with the prose narrative or because they dislike poetry in general, or think they do. It is their loss, for they are missing elements integral to the stories which help to drive their plots and contribute to character and mood. Those who hurry past Tolkien's poems are also forgoing the simple emotional pleasure one often finds in the reading of verse.

As it happens, Tolkien admitted that as a child he himself was 'insensitive to poetry, and skipped it if it came in tales. Poetry I discovered much later in Latin and Greek, and especially through being made to try and translate English verse into classical verse' (*On Fairy-Stories*, in *Tree and Leaf* (2001 edn.), p. 42). The ancient Greek poet Homer, Tolkien would tell his friend Father Robert Murray, was the source of his first discovery of 'the sensation of literary pleasure' (2 December 1953, *The Letters of J.R.R. Tolkien* (rev. edn. 2023, hereafter *Letters*), p. 258). Classical poetry had been an important part of his education at King Edward's School, Birmingham, indeed it was essential for boys planning, as Tolkien did, to go on to Oxford or Cambridge, where Latin and Greek remained ascendant. A pupil was taught the elements of grammar and applied them in translation, learning vocabulary, literature, and ancient history in the process. But Tolkien also became aware of a rich heritage of poetry in English. This extended back to *Beowulf* and the *Canterbury Tales*, and yet also included works which were relatively recent, even current. Alfred, Lord Tennyson had died only in 1892, the year of Tolkien's birth. Algernon Charles Swinburne lived to 1909, Thomas Hardy to 1928, and Rudyard Kipling to 1936, while the Georgian poets were just beginning to emerge during Tolkien's years as an Oxford undergraduate – Rupert Brooke, John Masefield, and James Elroy Flecker among them. Another Georgian, Lascelles Abercrombie, would become an academic colleague of Tolkien at Leeds.

Tolkien and his friends read poems, and plays and essays, memorized, declaimed, and debated them, and used them as models of language and moral behaviour. They did so in the context of schoolwork, but also privately, because they found it interesting and uplifting. Nor did they feel confined to a set curriculum: witness, for example, Tolkien's discovery of the writings of William Morris – looking to the North, not to the Classical South – and W.F. Kirby's translation of the Finnish *Kalevala* in its distinctive metre. Closest to Tolkien among like-minded pupils at King Edward's School were Christopher Wiseman, whose special artistic interest was music; Robert Quilter 'Rob' Gilson, the headmaster's son, who liked to sketch churches and planned to become an architect; and Vincent Trought, a poet, artist, and scholar who died tragically young in 1912. Together with a few more light-hearted friends they formed the 'Tea Club, Barrovian Society' ('Barrovian' because they met in Barrow's Stores in Birmingham), or TCBS for short. As Humphrey Carpenter puts it, Tolkien 'delighted his friends with recitations from *Beowulf*, the *Pearl*, and *Sir Gawain and the Green Knight*, and recounted horrific episodes from the Norse *Völsunga Saga*, with a passing jibe at [Richard] Wagner whose interpretation of the myths he held in contempt' (*J.R.R. Tolkien: A Biography* (1977, hereafter *Biography*), p. 46). After Tolkien left King Edward's School, a younger pupil was taken into the TCBS, G.B. (Geoffrey Bache) Smith, a lover of English literature and an amateur poet of merit.

Tolkien himself composed verse now and then, as inspiration struck. When he was six or seven he wrote, or tried to write, a poem or story about a 'green great dragon', only to be told by his mother that he would have to say 'great green dragon'. Later this philological point was all he could recall about the work. When he was twelve, he wrote a limerick (see Appendix I) for his guardian, Father Francis Morgan. It is his earliest poem to survive, as far as we are aware. After this there are none in his papers – though we do not suppose for a moment that he wrote no poetry between the ages of twelve and eighteen – before he included *Morning* (poem no. 1 below) in a letter to his beloved, Edith Bratt, dated 28 March 1910. Two months earlier, Father Francis had forbidden him to have further contact with Edith until he came of age, lest she distract him from his schoolwork.

Tolkien followed *Morning* in 1910 with four further poems: *Spring*, *Evening*, *Wood-Sunshine*, and *The Sirens Feast* (nos. 2–5). He would return to all of these in coming years, revising and retitling each two or three times – much of his poetry received similar treatment. He wrote his first published poem, *The Battle of the Eastern Field* (no. 6), a parodic account of a school rugby football match cast in the style of Macaulay's 'Battle of Lake Regillus', for the King Edward's School magazine for March 1911. That autumn, he matriculated at Exeter College, Oxford, where at first he read Greats (Classics) and immersed himself in social activities, perhaps too many for the sake of his studies. But he did not forget Edith: at the stroke of 3 January 1913, when he became twenty-one, he wrote to her after nearly three years' enforced absence. Within the month, they were engaged. That spring, after receiving a Second Class result in Greats in the Oxford examination called Honour Moderations, Tolkien changed his course of study to English and gave shape to his career.

In 1913 Gilbert Murray, then Oxford's Regius Professor of Greek, tried to summarize the state of undergraduate poetry at the university as represented in the collection *Oxford Poetry 1910–1913*, a reprint of four volumes of the *Oxford Poetry* annual. Its twenty-five authors, Murray felt, were 'free and individual', but 'in touch with almost all the moving impulses of contemporary poetry' and in rebellion against the previous generation of poets, Tennyson in particular. 'Very few indeed of the new poets who have lately stirred the pulses of our generation have failed to find their way to some undergraduate's room' (*Oxford Poetry 1910–1913*, pp. xiv–xv). By 'new poets' Murray seems to have meant the Georgians: he mentions the first volume of *Georgian Poetry*, published in 1912, and that he admired it. Modernists such as T.S. Eliot and Ezra Pound, who eventually eclipsed earlier poets at least for a time, had not yet made their mark.

A reading of the Oxford volume, however, shows that most of its poets in fact followed stylistically their Victorian predecessors, only a few daring to be adventurous. There was no sea-change in British literary culture merely because the century had turned. A writer of poetry of around 1910, like almost any reader of poems of that day, typically would have been more familiar with the sensuality of Swinburne or the narrative verse of Kipling, or with the Classical poetry of their education, than with anything written in the twentieth century, and this is evident among the Oxonians. Whatever Murray may have supposed them to be reading – and they were certainly reading the Georgians by 1913, the end of the period of the Oxford anthology – it had little effect on their own compositions. Tolkien makes an interesting contrast: an eccentric poet, he did not hew to any era, school, or movement, but tried his hand at different forms and metres because he was pleased to do so or thought it appropriate for a subject. Nor did he hesitate to vary the subject of his poems, whether serious or comic.

Shortly after he became an undergraduate in 1911, he wrote *A Fragment of an Epic* (no. 7), a long poem about King Richard I of England in the Third Crusade, almost certainly because 'Richard I before Jerusalem' was the announced topic for Oxford's Newdigate Prize for undergraduate poetry to be awarded in 1912. For this work he adopted, not for the last time, a deliberately antiquated style, heavily weighted with archaic words:

> Now round him throngéd bravely that array all fair harness'd
> and proudly bear'd and flauntéd gallant pennon plume and crest,
> and where he tower'd golden were the stoutest men of heart
> 'neath spear and spear rais'd heavenward, whence glistering
> did start
> the gilded morning sunlight; and lo! headpiece and hauberk
> to shield, to greave, and corslet gave it silversparkling back.

We do not know if *A Fragment of an Epic* was, in fact, ever sent to the Newdigate jury. At any rate, it did not win the prize, which went to a work much less vigorous and wholly unmemorable.

Still later in 1911, Tolkien composed three relatively conventional poems, among them the short but beautiful *From Iffley* (no. 10), which begins 'From the many-willowed margin of the immemorial Thames', but also two parodic accounts of train journeys by 'Lemminkainen' told in the style of Kirby's *Kalevala* (nos. 8–9). The *Kalevala* would later, in 1914, also inspire a straightforward adaptation by Tolkien, *The Story of Kullervo* (no. 17). By then, he had written as well the earliest of his poems which were the literary beginnings of his private mythology broadly called 'The Silmarillion': *The Grimness of the Sea* (no. 13, ?early 1912) which evolved into *The Horns of Ylmir*, and *The Voyage of Éarendel the Evening Star* (no. 16, September 1914).

As its members left King Edward's School for university, the TCBS effectively thinned to a core group of Tolkien, Wiseman, Gilson, and Smith. Gilson and Wiseman went to Cambridge, Tolkien and Smith to Oxford (at different colleges). All four were able to meet again in person only twice, and three of them – without Tolkien – once more, in 1914 and 1915. The First World War, or Great War, having begun in August 1914, one by one the friends enlisted and duties limited their movements. Their future was now unclear, but they agreed on a collective purpose to be put into effect once the war was over. Through their personal artistic achievements – poetry, music, architecture – the TCBS would

> drive from life, letters, the stage and society that dabbling in and hankering after the unpleasant sides and incidents in life and nature which have captured the larger and worser tastes in Oxford, London and the world . . . to reestablish sanity, cleanliness, and the love of real and true beauty in everybody's breast. [G.B. Smith, letter to Tolkien, 24 October 1915, Bodleian Library]

It was a bold plan, but naïve, and quickly dashed by the war. Gilson was killed on the first day of the Somme, 1 July 1916, and Smith died that December after being wounded by an exploding shell. Wiseman, a naval officer, luckily escaped harm. Tolkien, serving as an Army signals officer with the Lancashire Fusiliers, was posted to France in June and himself saw action on the Somme. In November 1916 he was invalided home with 'trench fever', a bacterial disease which almost certainly saved his life: before the war's end, his battalion was all but annihilated.

On 12 August 1916 Tolkien wrote to Smith about 'the hope and ambitions (inchoate and cloudy I know) that first became conscious at the Council of London', the first of the wartime meetings of the TCBS, in December 1914. 'That Council was as you know followed in my own case with my finding a voice for all kinds of pent up things and a tremendous opening up of everything for me: – I have always laid that to the credit of the inspiration that even a few hours with the four always brought to all of us' (*Letters*, pp. 6–7). In the present book one can see clearly what he meant by a 'tremendous opening up'. Within a year, by the end of 1915, he composed at least twenty-five poems, including *You and Me and the Cottage of Lost Play* (no. 28), *Kôr: In a City Lost and Dead* (no. 30), and *The Shores of Faery* (no. 31), which among others were early expressions of his mythology.

He was now twenty-three, and embraced poetry as a favoured mode of expression. Poetry of course had long been considered the highest form of art in literature, and to be a poet was to be notably accomplished. Many in Tolkien's generation, indeed many hundreds if not thousands, wrote poems – for better or worse, for pleasure if not for publication. At the start of the First World War, as an aid to recruitment and morale, poets did their part to promote patriotism and self-sacrifice. The violence of battle, and the pessimism a lengthy war generates, were also evident in poems early on, but uncommon until soldier-poets came to know the horrors of the trenches, especially after the events of the Somme. G.B. Smith wrote a fine and, for him, prophetic verse on the declaration of war, 'Anglia Valida in Senectute', which includes the lines (*A Spring Harvest* (1918), p. 50):

We are old, we are old, and worn and school'd with ills,
    Maybe our road is almost done,
Maybe we are drawn near unto the hills
    Where rest is and the setting sun . . .

Much later, distant echoes of Smith's poem, or at least similar sentiments, would appear in verses by Tolkien, among them *Bilbo's Last Song* (no. 127):

Shadows long before me lie,
beneath the ever-bending sky,
but islands lie behind the Sun
that I shall raise ere all is done;
lands there are to west of West,
where night is quiet and sleep is rest.

If we widen our scope of view, we see that Tolkien wrote more than forty poems during the years 1914–18. And yet, only one, *Companions of the Rose* (no. 55), directly incorporates the imagery of war. In the first instance it is a memorial to the Battle of Minden, fought in 1759 by the predecessor of Tolkien's regiment, the Lancashire Fusiliers, but it is also a personal lament for Gilson and Smith, who died at La Boisselle and Warlencourt respectively:

O! God Boisselle and Warlencourt to me
Are names more full of mourning than the sea,
Their poignant glory shines with clearer flame
Than even Minden's ancient valiance . . .

This is not to say that the effects of war are not reflected in other poems by Tolkien in this period. His personal experience of combat was limited to only a few months, but that was enough. Many of his wartime verses are concerned with loneliness and loss, on the poet's distance from home and wife, on his inability to master his own fate, on darkness and profound sadness – feelings common among soldiers on active duty, whether or not they are in harm's way. Even Tolkien's earliest works after the declaration of war, *Dark* (no. 20) and *Ferrum et Sanguis* (no. 21, four lines quoted below), written months before he caught sight of the trenches, reflect a sinking of spirits which he projected onto the whole of the Earth and even the heavens:

> The earth and all that dwell thereon are dark in a great gloom —
> — a vast black hand has dared its frightful shade across the sun,
> and, lest the stars come out and still do light us in its room,
> has fouled the heavens with his touch, or plucked them
> one by one . . .

He was fortunate, however, to be able to meet one last time with G.B. Smith in late August 1916, together with their mutual Oxford friend H.T. Wade-Gery, when their paths crossed in Bouzincourt. Immediately afterward, his spirits lifted, Tolkien wrote *The Thatch of Poppies* (no. 49) and *The Forest Walker* (no. 50), in the latter referring obliquely to his feelings on the death of Rob Gilson.

A nearly equal number of poems in the war years were, or became, related to Tolkien's mythology. As John Garth has said, 'the anxieties of war stoked [his] creative fires'. His 'mind wandered through the world that had started to evolve at Oxford and in the training camps, in his lexicon, and in his poems' (*Tolkien and the Great War* (2003), p. 187). No doubt it helped to keep him sane, in the face of battle or boredom, to be able to escape from time to time, if only into a world of his imagination. In addition to poetry, he had long been interested in the invention of languages, eventually sophisticated languages based on historical principles. By late 1914 he seems to have begun work on Qenya (later Quenya), influenced by Finnish. He also invented Gnomish (or Goldogrin, or Noldorissa, through later development Noldorin and Sindarin), influenced by his study of Welsh. The 'lexicon' referred to by Garth is the *Qenyaqetsa*, a phonology and lexicon of Qenya, begun around 1915 (published as *Parma Eldalamberon* 12 in 1998). Later in life, Tolkien said that his 'Middle-earth' stories were made to provide a world in which his invented languages could be spoken; in practice, both pursuits were simultaneous, and each influenced and reinforced the other. Languages such as Qenya and Gnomish are of underappreciated importance in

Tolkien's works; in the present book they are represented by several complete poems, such as *Nieninque* (no. 65), and even in verse composed in English by frequent words and names.

In many respects, poems related to 'The Silmarillion' often evoke the same emotions as other of Tolkien's wartime verses. In *Habbanan* (later *Eruman*) *beneath the Stars* (no. 45), for example, the men gathered 'into rings | Round their red fires, while one voice sings — | And all about is night' were surely no different, except in geography, from those Tolkien knew in army camps. And in *Tol Eressea* (later *The Lonely Isle*, no. 46), dedicated 'For England', he expressed his thoughts while crossing the English Channel to France, as he watched the white cliffs of his home fade into the distance:

> Never shall I forget this farewell gaze,
> Or cease to hear the sorrow of these seas
> To think thee crowned in glory of thy summer days,
> Thy shores all full of music and thy lands of ease . . .

Tolkien's best known poem from this time is probably *Goblin Feet* (no. 27). Written while still an undergraduate, it was the first of his works to be published in a book, the 1915 number of *Oxford Poetry*. He seems to have submitted it to the editors with *You and Me and the Cottage of Lost Play*, but only *Goblin Feet* was accepted. He wrote it, he said, to please Edith, who liked 'spring and flowers and trees, and little elfin people' (quoted in *Biography*, p. 74) – *You and Me*, and *Tinfang Warble* (no. 29), both written within days of *Goblin Feet*, are also of this sort. Much later, after he had abandoned in his writings the idea of diminutive fairies or elves, he wished that the poem could be forgotten. Instead, it has been reprinted numerous times, and was twice praised by the literary historian Geraldine E. Hodsgon. In her immediately post-war *Criticism at a Venture* (1919) she included it in a review of early twentieth-century poetry, placing it among work by the likes of John Masefield and Walter de la Mare – fine company. When *Oxford Poetry 1915* was published, however, Tolkien was happy to have his work in print, especially alongside a poem by Smith (who also had submitted two and had only one chosen) and three by Wade-Gery.

Not a few Oxford undergraduates were published poets. There were then many more newspapers and magazines which regularly printed poetry than there are today. Some students, such as Wilfred Childe, H.R. Freston, and Sherard Vines, were even able to publish small books of their verse. Tolkien himself desired to have his poems in such a book, from at least the summer of 1915; by then he had written enough he thought of worth to make up a volume. He sent some of his verses, at least *You and Me*, *The Shores of Faery*, *Kôr*, and *The Princess Nî* (no. 32), to a former master at King Edward's School, one-time professional literary critic R.W. 'Dickey' Reynolds. Reynolds replied:

> You ask for criticisms, but really I have none to make. . . . There are one or two loose endings knocking about appealing for their companion rhymes and somewhat spoiling the finish. Occasionally you have left awkwardnesses of construction and order unpurged away, and sometimes your joy in the sheer beauty of words seems in danger of running away with you. . . .
>
> I don't know which I should select as the best, but the two which took my fancy most were 'Goblin Feet' and 'You and Me'. They are both quite charming and almost perfect. [letter to Tolkien, 11 July 1915, Bodleian Library]

Near the end of July, Tolkien asked his old teacher for advice about publishing. Reynolds told him that in normal times, it would have been best for him first to publish single poems, to establish his name before trying for a book; but as the times were not normal, he could not follow the usual course. It might have occurred to both Reynolds and Tolkien that as the life expectancy of junior officers at the front was said to be (and, at certain periods during the war, was) very brief, this could be Tolkien's only chance for publication. But Reynolds added:

> The poems are there, and you and your friends – among whom I hope I may count myself – would naturally like to see them put into a more permanent and accessible form than scattered sheets of typescript. On the whole I think I should advise you to accept your friends' offer. Though it is hardly necessary to warn you that you must be prepared for the book to fall very very flat. Neither readers nor reviewers have any attention to give to poetry just now, nor are likely to for some time to come. [2 August 1915, Bodleian Library]

It is not known what 'offer' might have been made by Tolkien's friends – presumably by Gilson, Wiseman, and Smith, or some combination thereof – unless it was that they would lend critical and moral support in pursuing publication.

In January 1916 Tolkien was asked to allow *Goblin Feet* to appear in a collection of 'fairy' poetry. In response, he sent the compiler, Dora Owen, several other poems to consider as well – he had no lack of works in the genre. Probably for lack of space, Owen chose to include only *Goblin Feet* in her *Book of Fairy Poetry*, and that was not published until 1920. Nonetheless, she praised Tolkien's work as a whole, saying that his poems gave her 'a great deal of pleasure; they seem to me to have imagination, freshness, and a certain haunting quality in their music. All your fairy poems have the right fairy ring. I feel covetous, but I refrain, for I think you certainly ought to publish.' 'Messrs. Sidgwick & Jackson', she added, 'have published a good deal of modern verse' – indeed, they were its leading publisher. But Elkin Matthews and John Lane were 'always on the look-out for new-comers' and should be considered (2 February 1916, Bodleian Library). G.B. Smith had already recommended Sidgwick & Jackson, as well as another London publisher, Hodder & Stoughton, the previous October. On 3 February 1916 Smith, now with the Army in France, wrote again: 'Yes, publish – write to Sidgwick and Jackson or who you will. You I am sure are chosen, like Saul among the Children of Israel. Make haste, before you come out to this orgy of death and cruelty' (Bodleian Library).

Tolkien wanted to publish, as much to improve his income as to validate himself as a poet. He pinned his hopes on Sidgwick & Jackson, choosing them perhaps because their name was always mentioned among reputable firms. (Foremost at the time, they published Rupert Brooke, one of the most successful of the war poets, though he achieved his fame posthumously.) On 15 February 1916 Tolkien wrote to Edith: 'I sent my "mess" off to Sidgwick and Jackson. . . . Do pray about it darling – it means a lot to me' (Bodleian Library). It was a forlorn desire. At the end of March he received the reply: 'We have now received our reader's report upon the MS. [manuscript] which you kindly submitted to us, "The Trumpets of Faerie", and regret to say that we are not advised to undertake publication' (Sidgwick & Jackson archive, Bodleian Library). Tolkien appears to have had their letter on 3 April, when he told Edith: 'My poems were returned rejected this morning to add to the general gloom!'

He was now a newlywed, only recently returned from a week's honeymoon before duty called him back to camp. The 'gloom' of renewed separation from Edith dimmed the joy of marriage, and Tolkien's disappointment in having his poems rejected added another layer of darkness. And yet it was no shame for him to have failed in the attempt. Many soldiers wrote poetry, far more than could be accommodated in print by all of Britain's publishers put together. Looking at the situation today, and at the thickness of their letter file for 1916, filled with similar rejections, one cannot help but feel sympathy for Sidgwick & Jackson's staff, depleted by the war and overworked.

Gloomy as he was, Tolkien did not dwell on the matter. He was not like the friend he had yet to meet, C.S. Lewis, who found as a young man that in trying to write great poetry, in fact aching to be acclaimed as a great poet, he hoped on too slim a chance, and in the process focused too much on himself and too little on his work. Lewis was also concerned to expound a theory or philosophy of poetry, and to analyse his feelings when he was rejected. Tolkien, in contrast, seems to have been little inclined to self-searching, though he did fill pages with notes on different kinds of metres, and later, as a don, he lectured on fine points of prosody and versification by the Anglo-Saxons. (Extracts from these lectures are included in Peter Grybauskas's edition of Tolkien's *Battle of Maldon* (2023). Extracts from a 1938 radio broadcast by Tolkien on Old English verse were printed by Christopher Tolkien as an appendix to *The Fall of Arthur* in 2013.)

Despite his envisioned role in the later TCBS as a poet whose verse would help to lift up the world, Tolkien appears to have been more concerned, in his final years as an undergraduate, to qualify for a career as an academic. He wanted to write poetry, to have it published, and to be acknowledged as a poet, but it was not his priority: probably he had few illusions about being able to support himself and a family with so financially fragile a pursuit.

We cannot be sure which of his poems he assembled for his proposed book, or in what order, but an early list is suggestive (see Appendix III). As first written, it seems to have included twenty-eight titles (one is a duplicate), all works first composed between 1910 and July 1915. Tolkien probably compiled the list in late summer 1915, following R.W. Reynolds' comments that August. Most likely in early 1916, after his friends praised one of his then recent poems, the complex *Kortirion* (no. 40), Tolkien added to the top of his list four more titles, all verses composed towards the end of the previous year. He struck through one earlier title, 'Sirens' (*The Sirens Feast*), bracketed others once or twice as a code we are at a loss to explain, and placed dots next to twenty-five titles we suspect comprised his final selection: *Kortirion* (no. 40), *The Pool of the Dead Year* (no. 42), *Dark Are the Clouds about the North* (no. 38), *A Song of Aryador* (no. 37), *The Happy Mariners* (no. 33), *The Horns of Elfland* (i.e. *The Trumpets of Faërie*, no. 34), *The Princess Nî* (no. 32), *The Shores of Faery* (no. 31), *Morning Song* (no. 1), *Darkness on the Road* (no. 11), *The Mermaid's*

Flute (no. 19), *The Lay of Earendel* (no. 18), *Tinfang Warble* (no. 29), *You and Me and the Cottage of Lost Play* (no. 28), *Kôr: In a City Lost and Dead* (no. 30), *Goblin Feet* (no. 27), *May Day* (no. 26), *The Two Riders* (no. 25), *Why the Man in the Moon Came Down Too Soon* (no. 24), *Dark* (no. 20), *Sea-Song of an Elder Day* (no. 13), *The Voyage of Éarendel the Evening Star* (no. 16), *Outside* (no. 14), and *Wood-Sunshine* (no. 4).

Tolkien seems already to have decided to call the collection *The Trumpets of Faërie* in summer 1915. On 2 August that year, R.W. Reynolds told him: 'I am not altogether in love with your title. It sounds to me just a trifle precious, but I may be a little morbid on that point; and it is certainly descriptive. I think the fairy poems are your strongest and most original vein.' On 19 September Reynolds asked again if Tolkien had thought of a different title for his book. 'It is a pity "faerie" has got rather spoiled of late. Otherwise your first suggestion would have been so good, as it really does hit off what is, I think, the really characteristic note of your work' (Bodleian Library). Reynolds' objection is not clear. The sense of 'homosexual' for *faerie*, or rather *fairy*, does not seem to have been common in Britain until the 1920s; perhaps Reynolds found the word, in its usual folkloric sense, too frivolous in a time of war. And yet, as John Garth explains in *Tolkien and the Great War*, fairy-tales and fairy art were popular with the British soldier: Faërie – that is, the fairy folk tradition – allowed him 'to recover a sense of beauty and wonder, escape mentally from the ills confining him, and find consolation for the losses afflicting him' (p. 78). In any event, it seems possible that it was because of Reynolds' criticism that Tolkien substituted in his list of poems the title 'Horns of Elfland' for 'The Trumpets of Faërie', as he did also in a draft of that poem before restoring the earlier title.

In her letter of 2 February 1916 Dora Owen wrote: 'Why not put "The Trumpets" first? It seems to me stronger than the poems to which you have given the precedence' (Bodleian Library). From this it is clear that at least at this time, *The Trumpets of Faërie* was not the first poem among the contents of Tolkien's proposed book of the same title. On 2 August 1915, R.W. Reynolds had written to Tolkien that he liked the 'introductory poem' to his book, and thought 'it would be very suitable' (Bodleian Library). If Tolkien's manuscript list of poems offers any guide – it is not necessarily definitive – the first title (before the later four were added) was *The Happy Mariners*, followed by *The Swallow and the Traveller on the Plains* (no. 35), then *Horns of Elfland* (*The Trumpets of Faërie*). *Swallow* is a series of rather dark thoughts, earlier called *Thoughts on Parade*, composed by Tolkien at his first training camp in 1915, while reflecting on his loss of freedom to come and go as he pleased, and to be with Edith:

O swallow, black swallow, I gazed up at thee
out of heat and dust and a great weariness;
bravely thou wert beating far aloft
under the sunless clouds in those great spaces
where thunder sits enchained and the winds
are cavernously penned.

It was one of several poems initially on his list he did not mark with a dot, for the most part works of a more personal nature, choosing in the end (as it seems) not to include them in a collection primarily of fairy poems such as *Goblin Feet* or poems related to his mythology set in an invented Faërie. He did, however, retain *As Two Fair Trees*, a love-poem without a 'fairy' element.

It seems possible that the poems from Tolkien's mythology, including two concerning Earendel, and not to mention *Tinfang Warble* (delightfully musical though it is), confused Sidgwick & Jackson's reader in 1916 as much as the *Lay of Leithian* (no. 92), a long 'Silmarillion' poem, puzzled a different reader (Edward Crankshaw) when Tolkien sent it to the publisher George Allen & Unwin in 1937; that critic thought it an authentic Celtic *geste* and did not know what to do with it. Most of Tolkien's poems, at this or any other stage of his life, were unlike most that could be encountered in the mainstream of English literature. Another factor for Sidgwick & Jackson, though, may have been Tolkien's tendency towards an excess of words and a love of long lines, what one might call a lavishness of space. He was criticized for this feature by his TCBS friends, especially G.B. Smith, to whom he circulated his verse. On 22 March 1915, Smith wrote:

> I have discovered several interesting things about you. The first is, that your syntax occasionally tends to become obscure. The 'Sea-Song' [*Sea-Song of an Elder Day*, no. 13] has this one fault in some slight degree, though it does not matter much in so vigorous a work. Here is a better example [from *Outside*, no. 14]:

It calls from the river of Night, where
the ghosts of the people of day —
Of the whispering dreaming trees,
of the leaves and the listening grass,

Float thin on the many-lunged
heaving of the breath of the slumbering world.

It is the penalty of using long sentences in so very luxurious a style. One meets with such a lot of different tropes and adjectives in about half a sentence, that if the sentence is long, one is apt to lose oneself before the end of it. I think you can afford to prune a very little here. But don't knock the words out, they are good. I should try some shorter metres and try to make shorter sentences.

Smith's illustration divided the long lines Tolkien had preferred:

It calls from the river of night, where the ghosts of the
people of day —
of the whispering dreaming trees, of the leaves and
listening grass —
float thin on the many-lunged heaving of the breath of the
slumbering world.

This, however, remained the form of *Outside*, for which there were no further versions. Smith apologized in the same letter: 'However, I am here advising where angels should fear to tread, because I only know one sort of poetry really well, and that is the lyric.' He praised *As Two Fair Trees*, but 'cut out the word "*a*" in the last line: this improves the metre.' In that poem, the final line of its second and third versions is 'binds us with a golden strength of many centuries', but in the final manuscript the indefinite article is omitted – 'with golden strength' – following Smith's suggestion. Also in the same letter, Smith praised *Why the Man in the Moon Came Down Too Soon*, but commented: 'I am sure with a little more command over the small technical details, such as pleasant rhythm and so on, which can be obtained by practice and the reading of good authors, your things will be quite the best stuff. They are amazingly good now' (Bodleian Library).

A few days later, Smith suggested that Tolkien's verse was 'very apt to get complicated and twisted and to be most damned difficult to make out'. He mentioned the 'Earendel' poems, but gave an example from the end of *The Mermaid's Flute* (no. 19):

And winding through weed-roots there pallidly shimmers
Dim, tremulous blowing of ammonite horns.

I don't know now what that means. I think it contains at least two most delightful visions – winding through weed-roots, and tremulous blowing – did you *mean* blowing? – of ammonite horns. Perhaps you meant glowing, which makes it much easier, and not less pleasant. But even so the sentence is exhausting, partly because of 'dim', partly because of 'there pallidly shimmers'. You *must* tone this kind of thing down, or people will never bother to get at your meaning. If I were you, I should revise everything with elaborate care, making 'a child can read it' your aim and motto. I am afraid the 'Mermaid' is rather bad in this respect. The palace I can understand with some slight effort ['they dreamt of a palace | Where crooning old mere-songs a maiden abode | Clad in sapphire and green with enchanted sea-chalice'], but after that I really got rather lost. The palace by the way is very good. 'Bended reflections of star-glimmer stand' quite nonplusses me, I am afraid.

Smith also suggested, tongue in cheek, that 'even if you were set down by a hard task-master to write out "Mary had a little lamb" or "We are seven" every morning for three years, it would not be wasted if this requisite lucidity were coupled with the luxuriance of your verse' (27 March 1915, Bodleian Library). He thought that his friend should read William Blake, at least his shorter poems such as the *Songs of Innocence* – the longer works being extraordinarily obscure – and that he should write more lyric verse as a 'safer' form for a young poet, rather than lays.

To briefly digress: it strikes us as ironic that Tolkien survived the war but, until *The Adventures of Tom Bombadil and Other Verses from the Red Book* in 1962, had no published book of his poetry, while Smith was killed but fairly soon had a posthumous collection in print, *A Spring Harvest*. After Smith's death his mother wrote to R.W. Reynolds, whom Smith also had as a master at King Edward's School, in regard to her son's wish that a book of his poems be published. Reynolds in turn contacted Tolkien, and Tolkien consulted Christopher Wiseman. The latter, critical of Reynolds in letters to Tolkien – neither Wiseman nor Rob Gilson kept a good opinion of Reynolds from their school days – felt that the book should be in the hands of Tolkien and Wiseman himself as the surviving members of the TCBS. Reynolds in fact seems to have been happy to play only a supporting role. Wiseman suggested an arrangement of Smith's poems, while Tolkien wrote a brief prefatory note. Reynolds then submitted the edited text to Sidgwick & Jackson, and possibly because he was known in the literary community, he received more polite consideration than Tolkien had for *The Trumpets of Faërie*, if in the end the same result.

> We have given very careful consideration to the poems by the late Lieut. Geoffrey Bache Smith which you kindly sent us, and have taken several opinions upon them. They are undoubtedly the work of a writer of promise, and had he lived we might have expected excellent things from him, but we feel that he had hardly yet come to his full power of independent expression. We fear that the poems are unlikely to appeal to a sufficient number of readers to render publication remunerative, and we are therefore returning the MS. to you, with our best thanks for letting us see it. [R.B. McKerrow, letter to Reynolds, 8 January 1918, Bodleian Library; McKerrow was a director of the firm]

Smith's poems appeared instead, in June or July 1918, under the imprint of Erskine Macdonald, Ltd. 'Erskine Macdonald', whose real name was Galloway Kyle, issued numerous books of poetry during the war, taking advantage of the many soldier-poets who wished to publish, but (according to reports) did so at the expense of the author or the author's family or friends, and then avoided payment of royalties. In the case of *A Spring Harvest*, one wonders if Smith's mother, a widow who had lost both sons in the war, was able to foot a printing bill, and if not – allowing that it was beyond the means of Tolkien or Wiseman – it is not unlikely that R.W. Reynolds lent the book his financial as well as moral support.

The importance of Smith in particular among his friends cannot be overstated in regard to Tolkien's work as a poet. In a letter of 6–8 March 1941 to his son Michael, then with the armed forces, Tolkien recalled that he 'never expected to survive' his own military service; 'and the intense emotion of regret, the vivid (almost raw) perception of the young man who feels himself doomed to die before he has "said his word", is with me still: a cloud, a patch of sun, a star, were often more than I could bear. I was, of course, a poet (and might have been a recognized one, but for exam-papers and you chaps: J. M. & C. and the chains of Christian matrimony!); but each man has his own modes.' Here he refers to his sons John, Michael, and Christopher, curiously omitting his daughter Priscilla (then a girl of eleven); surely his words are meant to be taken with a wink, and his desire to be an academic, father, and husband understood to be greater than any literary hopes.

'I said,' he continued, 'outside Lichfield Cathedral, to a friend of my youth – long since dead of gas-gangrene (God rest his soul: I grieve still) – "Why is that cloud so beautiful?" He said: "Because you have begun to write poetry, John Ronald." He was wrong. It was because Death was near, and all was intolerably fair, lost ere grasped. That was why I began to write poetry' (*Letters*, p. 71; this note does not appear in the original (1981) edition). The friend was G.B. Smith, who died quickly and unexpectedly after being shelled; the occasion recalled was surely the TCBS 'Council of Lichfield', 25–6 September 1915, when Tolkien, Smith, Wiseman, and Gilson met all together for the last time. Tolkien demonstrably did not begin to write poetry only with the outbreak of war and from a sense that Death was close at hand, but the peculiar combination of fear in the face of beauty does seem to have been an impetus for him to write, as it was for so many other poets in or out of the trenches.

Smith had been Tolkien's chief critic, and although Wiseman continued to read his friend's work and offer opinions, these tended to be of less utility than Smith's, which had been from a fellow practising poet. Nor was Wiseman's enthusiasm for Tolkien's poetry, though genuine, of the same degree that Smith had expressed. This loss, or lessening, of positive criticism following Smith's death, and of the TCBS 'inspiration' Tolkien had found so important, may be one reason why he composed fewer than a dozen poems between the end of 1916 and the early 1920s. Another, surely, was that he had begun to write 'The Silmarillion' in prose, initially in the form of *The Book of Lost Tales*, and at the same time continued his hobby of language invention in connection with his mythology. Wiseman in fact urged him to pursue his 'epic'. He thought it a mistake to suppose that poems such as *Kortirion*, or *The Voyage of Éarendel the Evening Star*, or *The Pool of the Dead Year* could stand by themselves; instead, 'I want you to connect all these up properly, & make their meaning & context tolerably clear' (letter to Tolkien, 4 March 1917, Bodleian Library; quoted in our *J.R.R. Tolkien Companion and Guide: Chronology*, hereafter *Chronology* (2017), p. 106).

More immediately, late in 1916 and early in 1917, Tolkien was anxious to make a memorial to Smith. His *G.B.S.* (no. 53) is a whirlwind of emotions, and was clearly a challenge to write. Only a short while earlier, a few weeks before Smith was struck by shrapnel, Tolkien had composed the playful *To Early Morning Tea* (no. 52), celebrating his evacuation, suffering from trench fever, to the friendly Red Cross hospital at Le Touquet:

Most precious distillation of the herbs
Of Ind or of Cathay
And all those sunny lands most far away,
Bearing within your stream the fragrances
And all the subtle odours
Of strange flowers . . .

Back in England, Tolkien received medical treatment and was examined regularly by doctors to judge if he was fit to return to fighting. Part of the time, he was allowed to convalesce at home with Edith. But his illness recurred, and he was assigned to a reserve battalion in Yorkshire. One cannot be surprised that his mood was clouded, a circumstance reflected in *Companions of the Rose*, *I Stood upon an Empty Shore* (no. 57), and *Build Me a Grave* (no. 58), and in two poems related to his mythology, *Ye Laggard Woodlands* (no. 54) and *The Grey Bridge of Tavrobel* (no. 56). In November 1917, however, there was a ray of light: the birth of a son, John. Tolkien was inspired to write *A Rime for My Boy* (no. 59) probably in May or June the following year. We have speculated that *The Cat and the Fiddle* (later *The Man in the Moon Stayed Up Too Late*, no. 60) and *The Ruined Enchanter* (no. 62), both from 1919, were also composed with young John in mind.

In late 1918, with the war winding down, Tolkien was released from army duties to find work in Oxford. There he joined the staff of the *Oxford English Dictionary* and became a freelance tutor of university students. He was formally demobilized in 1919. That was another lean year for his poetry, but it was probably then that he wrote *A Rhyme Royal on Easter Morning* (no. 61), trying on a type of rhyming stanza which had been introduced by Chaucer, and also *The Motorcyclists* (no. 63), not the last of his protests against modern noise and pollution, though in style it looked back to a fourteenth-century satire about a blacksmith's forge. The beautiful *Light as Leaf on Lind* (no. 64), which evolved into Strider's 'tale of Tinúviel' in *The Lord of the Rings*, also dates from around this time. In mid-1919 Tolkien largely abandoned work on *The Book of Lost Tales*, probably because he was asked to prepare the glossary for Kenneth Sisam's *Fourteenth Century Verse and Prose* (*A Middle English Vocabulary*, published in 1922).

In October 1920 he took up a Readership in the new English School at the University of Leeds; four years later, he became Professor of English Language. In connection with his teaching, but also out of personal enjoyment, he translated in verse Old and Middle English works such as *Beowulf* (no. 88), *Sir Gawain and the Green Knight* (no. 70), and *Pearl* (no. 90). He placed individual poems in local journals

– *The Gryphon*, *The Microcosm*, *Yorkshire Poetry* – and three in each of two collections of verse by members of the Leeds University English School Association, *A Northern Venture* (1923: *The Nameless Land*, no. 74; *Why the Man in the Moon Came Down Too Soon*, no. 24; and *Enigmata Saxonica Nuper Inventa Duo*, no. 71) and *Leeds University Verse 1914–24* (1924: *An Evening in Tavrobel*, no. 48; *The Lonely Isle*, no. 46; and *The Princess Ní*, no. 32). In connection with his Leeds colleague E.V. Gordon, he encouraged students to sing verses in Old, Middle, and Modern English, Gothic, Old Norse, and Latin at social gatherings, at which they also read sagas and drank beer. Collectively known as the 'Leeds Songs' and printed by mimeograph, these poems for the most part were written by Tolkien or Gordon, or drawn from Icelandic student songbooks. Thirteen of those known to be by Tolkien (nos. 76–85, 97–99) were published, without permission and with not a few changes and inaccuracies, in 1936 in the collection *Songs for the Philologists*, edited by a former Leeds student. It is not known how many of the 'Leeds Songs' Tolkien wrote altogether, but it was certainly more than thirteen. In fact, he composed some of them even after he returned to Oxford, continuing to help E.V. Gordon, who had succeeded to Tolkien's Leeds chair.

Probably in 1921 Tolkien began a new poem related to his mythology, *The Lay of the Fall of Gondolin* (no. 66), following his prose treatment of the tale of Tuor in *The Book of Lost Tales*. This was one of five 'Silmarillion' poems written while at Leeds (they were not all completed); the others were *The Children of Húrin* (no. 67), the *Lay of Leithian* in octosyllabic couplets (no. 92), *The Flight of the Noldoli*, and a lay of Earendel. We have omitted the final two from our book, but they are published in full in *The Lays of Beleriand* (1985), one of the twelve invaluable volumes of *The History of Middle-earth* edited by Tolkien's youngest son, Christopher. The lay ultimately called *The Children of Húrin* was the earliest major work by Tolkien in alliterative verse, and was also the longest of his alliterative poems, that is, in the principal metrical form of Old English poetry. Later, in 1931 or 1932, he also began, but did not complete, a version of the Húrin tale in rhyming couplets (no. 130).

On 22 July 1925 Tolkien wrote to his friend H.F.B. Brett-Smith, who had congratulated him on his election the previous day to Oxford's Rawlinson and Bosworth Chair of Anglo-Saxon. He had 'a yet greater need to pose as a minim poet [the slightest of poets] in your gentle eyes', now that he was returning to Oxford where Brett-Smith was a don. 'You see the slim virtues of philology have not eradicated the vice, or if you like the virtues of verse have not yet quite been stifled by the fumes of philology. . . . I enclose one of the latest acts of virtue', a poem 'purely philological in inspiration' (quoted in David J. Holmes Autographs catalogue, 1991, item 161). In a second letter to Brett-Smith, dated 10 August, Tolkien referred to the poem he sent as a 'torn and tattered page of an unknown periodical', which together with his 'philological' comment suggests that the work was *Iúmonna Gold Galdre Bewunden* (no. 69, the precursor to *The Hoard*), published in *The Gryphon* for January 1923; its title is based on a line in *Beowulf*, 'the gold of bygone men was wound about with spells'. (A torn leaf of this poem is in the Bodleian Library.) He evidently also sent his friend some of his poems in typescript, as in the later letter he apologized for claiming them back. He did so only because

> I was still then nursing the fond fancy that someone would publish a collection of this sort of stuff for me – since I could not & cannot afford to pay [for it] myself. That notion being now abandoned, since I can't find anyone that will, you can keep anything I send you!
>
> . . . It is probably as well as it is [that Brett-Smith shows an 'isolated' appreciation of his poetry] – & I trust you are discreet – for if I were foolishly to publish a volume of such moonshine both philologists and literatudinarians would (for different reasons) consider me to suffer from softening of the brain. [quoted in David J. Holmes Autographs catalogue, 1991, item 161, corrected]

According to Douglas A. Anderson, Tolkien offered his collection *The Trumpets of Faërie* to the Swan Press of Leeds, 'and again was turned down. . . . In the spring of 1926 the Oxford publisher Basil Blackwell turned it down [as well]' (Anderson, 'Publishing History' (2006), p. 549). We cannot confirm these further attempts, but one at least is suggested by a new, enlarged list of his poetry Tolkien made around this time (see list F, Appendix III), and the Swan Press would have seemed ideal since they had published the two Leeds English School poetry books mentioned above, as well as the journal *Yorkshire Poetry*. Basil Blackwell would have been worth approaching also, as he was an established publisher of amateur work (such as the annual volumes of *Oxford Poetry*) and, from January 1926, Tolkien's Oxford neighbour in Northmoor Road. Two other lists among Tolkien's papers suggest that he still hoped to publish a collection of his verse even later, perhaps in the early 1930s.

Mention of Tolkien's poems occasionally entered into his discussions with Stanley or Rayner Unwin at George Allen & Unwin, publisher of *The Hobbit* and eventually other works of Tolkien's fiction. In 1946, hoping that Allen & Unwin would take his story *Farmer Giles of Ham* while his work on *The Lord of the Rings* dragged on, and knowing that *Farmer Giles* was thought too short to stand on its own, Tolkien recalled that he had 'once planned a volume of "Farmer Giles" with (say) three other probably shorter stories interleaved with such verse as would consort with them from the *Oxford Magazine*: *Errantry* [no. 128], *Tom Bombadil* [*The Adventures of Tom Bombadil*, no. 121], and possibly *The Dragon's Visit* [no. 107]' (letter to Stanley Unwin, 30 September 1946, Tolkien–George Allen & Unwin archive, HarperCollins). In 1952 Tolkien wrote to Rayner Unwin, with whom he was discussing *Errantry*: 'I have *tried* often to get "Errantry" and such things published, but unsuccessfully. The O.M. [*Oxford Magazine*] used at one time . . . to accord me space; but no one else. I should, of course, be very pleased to submit a collection to you when I have a moment' (22 June 1952, *Letters*, p. 235). Unwin replied on 1 July that if *Errantry* was 'at all typical of your bottom drawer of MSS [manuscripts] (and I suspect it is) some of them should certainly see the light of day' (Tolkien–George Allen & Unwin archive, HarperCollins). But publication of *The Lord of the Rings* soon became a priority, and it was not until 1961 that a collection of Tolkien's poems again came up for discussion (*The Adventures of Tom Bombadil and Other Verses from the Red Book*; see poem no. 24).

Even before he left for Leeds in 1920, Tolkien published two works in the *Stapeldon Magazine* of Exeter College, Oxford, *From Iffley* and *The Happy Mariners*; he had been a member of the Stapeldon Society as an undergraduate. Now, after his return to Oxford in autumn 1925 to take up his new professorial chair, magazines again offered outlets for his verse. Two 'bestiary' poems appeared in the *Stapeldon Magazine* in 1927, the original *Fastitocalon* (no. 95) and *Iumbo* (no. 96). Still more poems went to the *Oxford Magazine* between 1931 and 1937, such as *Progress in Bimble Town* (no. 103), *The Adventures of Tom Bombadil*, and *Errantry*, whose history is intertwined with that of Bilbo Baggins' song of Eärendil in *The Lord of the Rings* (no. 128). The late 1920s and early 1930s were the period also of *The Lay of Aotrou and Itroun* (no. 116), based on Breton lays, of two 'New Lays' which continued the *Völsunga Saga* (no. 131), of the verse-drama *The Homecoming of Beorhtnoth Beorhthelm's Son* (no. 129), of *The Fall of Arthur* (no. 140), and of *Mythopoeia* (no. 136) which is at the heart of Tolkien's thoughts about creativity.

Most notably, from as early as 1928 to as late as 1936 (the dates are disputed), Tolkien wrote twenty-four poems as part of *The Hobbit*. The birth of John, Michael, Christopher, and Priscilla inspired him to tell stories; these were chiefly in prose, but Tolkien did not overlook the love children naturally have of rhythm and rhyme. (Still, he included only one poem, the *Rhyme* of 1938 (no. 172), in the series of letters he wrote to his sons and daughter as by 'Father Christmas'.) *The Hobbit* was his longest and most ambitious story for children, and his turning point as an author. Its success led to a sequel, *The Lord of the Rings*, completed only after long labour between 1937 and 1955. For this, Tolkien wrote seventy-three poems as we have counted them, a remarkable number for a book which, as we have said, is read by many for its prose narrative, with its verse often passed over. Space has allowed us to include only a selection of poems from *The Hobbit* and *The Lord of the Rings*, but these are representative of the whole.

For many years *The Lord of the Rings* was Tolkien's primary focus in his writing of poetry, though he still found time for unrelated, even lengthy works of verse such as *King Sheave* (no. 146) and *The Death of St. Brendan* (later *Imram*, no. 175), the latter contained in another, abandoned work of fiction, *The Notion Club Papers*. Concurrently, he had academic and administrative tasks to perform at Oxford University, whose younger staff were depleted during the Second World War, as well as duties to his wife and children, who had periods of illness. Tolkien had complaints too, most debilitatingly rheumatism and arthritis, which made him sometimes unable to hold a pen. But he set none of these responsibilities aside for the sake of his poetry or fiction (his scholarly writings, on the other hand, tended to be delayed or abandoned). It is a wonder he did so much, having had so much to do; he had remarkable energy, though that could not last. Towards the end of 1955 he commented to his friend Lord Halsbury that

> since the publishers [of *The Lord of the Rings*, the final volume of which had then just appeared] are now pressing for the *Silmarillion* &c. . . . , I do intend as soon as I can find time to try to set the material in order for publication. Though I am rather tired, and no longer young enough to pillage the night to make up for the deficit of hours in the day. [10 November 1955, *Letters*, p. 331]

In 1959 Tolkien reached the age of sixty-seven, and by university policy took compulsory retirement that June. After five years at Leeds and thirty-four at Oxford, it would not have been odd if he felt at sea removed from the familiar structure of university life he had lived for so long. At the least, he was cynical. In *To the University of Oxford* (no. 183), composed probably at the end of 1959, he wrote:

So here we are, so far so good,
though elementarily posed in hood,
with cows in clover, pigs in fat,
while complimentarily raising hat.
It looks like thunder, smells like cheese,
and automatically charges fees.
It's round the corner, underground,
but axiomatically can't be found.

He was not without work. His edition of the Middle English *Ancrene Wisse* (see no. 186) was long overdue. From 1961 to 1962 he revisited decades of his poetry in order to produce *The Adventures of Tom Bombadil and Other Verses from the Red Book* as an adjunct to *The Lord of the Rings*; for this he developed, out of an earlier 'germ', the poem *Bombadil Goes Boating* (no. 186), and he refashioned other work into some of his most intriguing verse, such as *The Sea-Bell* from earlier *Looney* (no. 134). The success of the *Bombadil* collection led Tolkien to comment to his son Michael that the book 'sold nearly 8,000 copies before publication . . . and that, even on a minute initial royalty, means more than is at all usual for anyone but [beloved poet, later Poet Laureate, John] Betjeman to make on verse!' (19 December 1962, *Letters*, p. 456).

Then there was *The Silmarillion*, which Tolkien had promised to complete for his publisher George Allen & Unwin, to follow *The Lord of the Rings*, which continued to gain in popularity. But he was unclear what he should do to consolidate for publication the many parts and versions of his mythology, in prose and verse, and make it consistent with *The Lord of the Rings* behind which 'The Silmarillion' lay as 'history'. At his death in 1973 he left the further book unfinished, indeed in disarray, for his son Christopher to complete or discard as he chose. The difficulty he faced in attempting to complete it himself was reflected, maybe, in *Though All Things Fail* (no. 190) from *c.* 1964:

Though all things fail & come to naught,
and all in vain is vainly wrought;
though Time's long lanes stretch lagging on
without a turn, till they are gone,
and all things that must walk that way

have nothing accomplished that shall stay
or be remembered — once all thought
is nothing, of nothing, unto naught . . .

Tolkien could be prone to such thoughts. Humphrey Carpenter described him as 'by nature a cheerful almost irrepressible person with a great zest for life', but after the death of his mother in November 1904 'there was to be a second side . . . capable of bouts of profound despair' (*Biography*, p. 31). This may be an exaggeration – all human spirits have their dark corners – though we have seen in Tolkien's earlier poetry that he could be dispirited, and this was still true at the end of the 1950s. Addressing a gathering of Tolkien enthusiasts in Rotterdam in 1958, he read a poem in Quenya, with the translation:

> Twenty years have flowed away down the Long River, that never in my life will return from the Sea. Ah years in which looking far away, I saw ages long-passed, when still trees grew free in a wide country. Alas for now all begins to wither in the breath of cold-hearted wizards: to know things they break them, and their lordship is in the fear of death.

Carpenter reports that after the death of C.S. Lewis in 1963, Tolkien began a diary which indicates 'the appalling depths of gloom to which he could sink, albeit only for short periods. "Life is grey and grim," he wrote at one such moment. "I can get nothing done, between staleness and boredom . . . and anxiety and distraction"' (*Biography*, p. 242). By then, he had lived through two wars, and society had changed profoundly from the one he knew in childhood.

The poems Tolkien wrote in his final years were relatively few and miscellaneous. Some were *jeux d'esprit*, such as *Rosalind Ramage* (no. 187), composed after hearing from a young *Hobbit* enthusiast and budding poet. In *Three Children* (no. 188) Tolkien again wrote a poem based on a nursery rhyme, while *As You Must Admit* (no. 193) seems to exist solely for the pleasure of its words and rhymes. And there were limericks, clerihews, and adages (Appendixes I and II), in which Tolkien delighted in shorter forms. But then there is *Though All Things Fail*, and *Where the Riming Rune Tree Blows* (no. 189) which conveys the sadness of some kind of temporary estrangement between Tolkien and his daughter Priscilla, and *My Heart Is Not in This Land Where I Live* (no. 192) which recalls the longing he expressed years earlier when in camp or with the army in France:

My heart is not in this land where I live:
I am far from home.
I have friends that are dear to me; but
under their voices are echoes, and
beyond their faces are shadows of the
land that was my home.
Longing is on me, for those that I have
lost; and for fields that I shall not
see again: they have been destroyed,
but I cannot forget my home.

For his final recorded poem, however – *For W.H.A.*, published in the journal *Shenandoah* in 1967 (no. 195) – Tolkien returned to form, and returned a favour. Writing in both Old and Modern English, he honoured the work of the renowned poet W.H. Auden, a long-time correspondent and enthusiastic promoter of *The Lord of the Rings*. Five years earlier, Auden had contributed 'A Short Ode to a Philologist' in *English and Medieval Studies Presented to J.R.R. Tolkien on the Occasion of His Seventieth Birthday*.

When he read the selection of poems Tolkien sent him in 1915, R.W. Reynolds thought that he detected echoes in them of Francis Thompson, John Keats, Rudyard Kipling, Walter de la Mare, and William Ernest Henley, as well as one borrowing which seemed obvious to Reynolds, the phrase 'East of the Sun and West of the Moon' which appears in *The Earthly Paradise* by William Morris (1868–70). Tolkien seems to have objected to one or more of these thoughts; perhaps he pointed out that 'East of the Sun and West of the Moon' is the title of a Norwegian fairy-story pre-dating Morris's book by some years. Reynolds apologized, explaining that he was merely testing his 'literary instinct' (19 July 1915, Bodleian Library); and yet, he was not entirely wrong.

Tolkien was probably familiar with the work of all of the poets Reynolds mentioned, certainly so in the case of Morris. He was widely read, as were his friends at King Edward's School. When Tolkien was preparing to begin his army training, G.B. Smith recommended books for him to bring to camp, heavily weighted towards poetry:

> O, get '1914 and other poems' by Rupert Brooke, and read the first six. In fact, get all R.B. [Rupert Brooke], and also Georgian Verse [i.e. *Georgian Poetry*], also [Sir Thomas] Browne's Religio Medici, and 'Urn Burial' [i.e. Browne's *Hydriotaphia, or Urne Buriall*], also [Sir Philip] Sidney's 'Defense of Poesie' – but you will have all these. Get the old spelling, preferably Clarendon Press Editions – there are some quite nice ones. Get Bacon's essays as they were writ, and bring 'em here. [letter to Tolkien, 9 July 1915, Bodleian Library]

John Garth has said that 'all of Tolkien's friends were capable of intellectual seriousness. They dominated every school debate and play, and they formed the backbone of the Literary Society' (*Tolkien and the Great War*, p. 5). Tolkien himself spoke to the Literary Society, in February 1911, about the Norse sagas, Smith in November 1911 (after Tolkien had left school for Oxford) on early English ballads, and Smith again in February 1913 on King Arthur. Others in the Society dealt with Morris, Browning, Ruskin, Arnold, Lamb, Kipling, Tennyson, Keats, Swinburne – an array which suggests something of the conservative cultural atmosphere of King Edward's in Tolkien's time at the school and just beyond. It is also instructive that in February 1913 his friend Sidney Barrowclough spoke to the Society about modern poets such as William Butler Yeats, John Masefield, and John Drinkwater, but was dubious about the lasting quality of their work.

From his reading, Tolkien created lists of 'magnificent words (and phrases)', and of 'delightful dialectal words' and 'more dialectals etc., words delightful but not grand' (see Appendix IV). The first of these cites Tennyson, Sidney, Chaucer, Shelley, Milton, Spenser, Keats, Patmore, Compton Mackenzie, 'Johnson' (presumably Samuel), 'Browning' (presumably Robert), and 'Lodge' (probably the Elizabethan Thomas Lodge), as well as the French linguist Antoine Meillet (an expert in Indo-European languages), John Earle's translation of *Beowulf*, and the generic categories 'Elizabethan' and 'scientific'. In a subsidiary list are also found Byron and Wordsworth. Many of the listed words, however, come from Shakespeare, that grandmaster of the English language whom Tolkien later claimed to dislike, while the vast majority are credited to Tolkien's contemporary, Francis Thompson, who had died only in 1907.

These word lists date probably from Tolkien's final undergraduate years, and mirror the lavishness of vocabulary in his early poems his friends found a point of concern. Christopher Wiseman commented in April 1915 that he could not think where Tolkien got his many amazing words, and along with Rob Gilson feared that they would carry him away. Smith seems to have been more concerned with his friend's syntax, as mentioned earlier; he himself used unusual words in verse, such as *gramarye* and *threnodie*. Tolkien was indeed carried away, until he learned to rein in his tendency towards elaboration. In the course of preparing this book we have been fascinated to see this process at work in the development of his poems, not entirely one of simplification in his use of words (as the lengthy glossary in this book attests), but of increasing ease of comprehension without sacrificing style or beauty.

In fact, one finds only a few of the 'magnificent' or 'delightful' words when reading Tolkien's poems, and chiefly in his earliest works. Over time his tastes and manner of writing evolved. His word lists do provide a glimpse into what he was reading in his youth, and at least at the level of some individual words, into works which may have inspired his poems. Still, when he wrote *enrondured*, or *galleon*, or *plenilune*, all of which are credited in his lists to Francis Thompson, was he necessarily thinking of one of Thompson's poems? None of these words was coined by Thompson, and as Megan N. Fontenot has cautioned ('"No Pagan Ever Loved His God": Tolkien, Thompson, and the Beautification of the Gods', 2018), we must not overlook the fact that Thompson also wrote prose essays, which may have been more influential than his poetry on Tolkien's writings.

In 1914, full of enthusiasm, Tolkien read a paper about Thompson to the Exeter College Essay Club. He had bought Thompson's collected works, in three volumes, published only the previous year. He spoke of Thompson as one of the greatest of poets, skilled with metre and a master of language drawn from the Liturgies and the Vulgate more so than from Classical sources, and combining a knowledge of the Elizabethans with an acquaintance of the technicalities of modern science (something which may explain some of the categorization of words in Tolkien's lists). John Garth has said that Thompson 'appears to have influenced the content of one of Tolkien's first attempts at poetry', *Wood-Sunshine*, comparing it to Thompson's 'Sister Songs' with its 'sylvan vision of fairies' (*Tolkien and the Great War*, p. 14) and echoing a thought earlier expressed by Humphrey Carpenter.

Garth has also suggested that 'an obscure reference to "the land of Luthany"' in Thompson's poem 'The Mistress of Vision' ('In the land of Luthany, and the tracts of Elenore') 'seems to have prompted Tolkien to adopt *Luthany* as the name for his mythological Britain when it was ruled by the Elves (an important though temporary concept in his legendarium)' (*Tolkien at Exeter College* (2022), p. 32), and that

'Thompson's influence may be seen in the Latinate vocabulary and metrical variety of Tolkien's early poems, such as *Kortirion among the Trees* (1915), in which "the seven lampads" derives from *To My Godchild*' ('"Francis Thompson": Article for Exeter College Essay Club' (2006), p. 221). A borrowing of *Luthany* seems likely; and certainly, Thompson's imagery in 'To My Godchild' is similar to Tolkien's in *Kortirion*, both referring to the stars. Tolkien also may have known, however, of Samuel Taylor Coleridge's use of *lampads* in his 'Ode to the Departing Year' ('wheeling round the throne the Lampads seven') and 'Ne Plus Ultra' ('the Lampads seven | That watch the Throne of Heaven'), though these allude instead to the seven lamps of fire said in the Book of Revelation to burn before the throne of God. (*Lampad* does not appear in Tolkien's word lists.)

As we have seen, R.W. Reynolds too thought that Thompson had influenced Tolkien. Christopher Wiseman disagreed, however, saying in a letter of December 1916 that he could not see any obvious connection between Tolkien's poems and Thompson's, though his friend Tolkien had studied Thompson deeply. More recently, the critic Allan Turner found

> little in Tolkien of the introspection and the late Victorian sentimentality which characterise Thompson, except perhaps in the poem about the Cottage of Lost Play [*You and Me and the Cottage of Lost Play*]. Even here, though, there is a significant difference in the treatment of childhood and adulthood; Thompson is concerned with the pain of lost innocence, but Tolkien voices gentle nostalgia for a wholly imaginary scene of bliss in a never-never land. In terms of style and language, there is nothing in Tolkien's early poems, or at least in those which have been published, that reflects either the personal viewpoint or the aureate vocabulary, the deliberately striking metaphors, the Classical and Christian references, in fact the whole highly-wrought diction that are habitual to Thompson. Even in the descriptive poems in which Tolkien paints the strong sensory effects of nature, such as 'Kôr' . . . or 'Sea Chant of an Elder Day' . . . the evocative vocabulary is still less self-consciously 'arty' than anything to be found in Thompson, and the whole viewpoint is more distanced, with the poetic persona disappearing into the background. ['Early Influences on Tolkien's Poetry' (2013), pp. 207–8]

It seems best to say that Tolkien chose not to adopt Thompson's eccentricities of style, instead creating his own, but gladly borrowed from Thompson's words. When, for example, Thompson writes in 'The Hound of Heaven', the work for which he is best known:

I said to dawn: Be sudden — to Eve: Be soon;
    With thy young skiey blossoms heap me over
        From this tremendous Lover —
Float thy vague veil about me, lest He see!

or describes, in the same poem,

        Banqueting
    With her in her wind-walled palace,
    Underneath her azured daïs,
    Quaffing, as your taintless way is,
        From a chalice
Lucent-weeping out of the dayspring.

we do not find a precursor of Tolkien's poetry in its character or structure, but we do recognize words, or alternate forms of words, used by both poets: *skiey*, *azure*, *quaff*, *chalice*, *lucent*.

Allan Turner has examined Francis Thompson as one of four possible influences, or categories of influences, on Tolkien's earliest poems. Another is William Morris, an early poetic model 'more apparent' than Thompson 'although still fairly indirect' ('Early Influences on Tolkien's Poetry', p. 208). Despite Morris not being cited in the word lists, there is no doubt that Tolkien was drawn to his works. In October 1914 he wrote to Edith that he was 'trying to turn one of the stories' of the *Kalevala* 'into a short story somewhat on the lines of Morris' [prose] romances with chunks of poetry in between' (*Letters*, p. 3). Turner points out, as Verlyn Flieger did earlier in her edition of Tolkien's *Story of Kullervo*, that the work by Morris which fits this description best is *The House of the Wolfings*. Tolkien bought a copy of *The House of the Wolfings* in spring 1914, with money from Oxford's Skeat Prize, simultaneously acquiring Morris's *Life and Death of Jason* and his translation of the *Völsunga Saga*. Turner argues that *Jason* is pertinent as an example of a longer poem containing a related poem in a contrasting metre, like the second version of Tolkien's *Children of Húrin* (no. 67), a work in alliterative verse which includes a rhyme of Beren and Lúthien in iambic tetrameter (see *Light as Leaf on Lind*, no. 64).

Carl Phelpstead has written about this form of mixed prose and verse, noting that Morris naturally linked its composition to the Icelandic sagas. But since Tolkien himself read Old Norse literature, in translation and in the original, he could have come across the form directly in the sagas as well as indirectly through Morris. Phelpstead promotes the sagas as an influence on *The Lord of the Rings*, itself a prose narrative incorporating verse:

> [A]lthough the verses in Tolkien's fiction are all his own, they are presented as either composed or recited from memory by the characters within the narrative. This puts Tolkien in a position analogous to that of a saga-writer who composed his own verses to satisfy readers' expectations of the genre (the difference being that in Tolkien's case the idea that the verses were composed by anyone other than the author of the narrative prose is a transparent fiction). ['"With Chunks of Poetry in Between": *The Lord of the Rings* and Saga Poetics' (2008), p. 25]

In his 'William Morris and Tolkien: Some Unexpected Connections' (2019) Tom Shippey convincingly compares lines from *Kôr* (as *The City of the Gods*) with Morris's book-length poem *The Earthly Paradise*, and illustrates the popularity in Victorian times and later – notably among soldiers in the First World War – of long narrative poems, also citing Tennyson's *Idylls of the King* and Robert Browning's *The Ring and the Book*. This, Shippey argues, was why Tolkien himself wrote long narrative works such as *The Children of Húrin* and *The Lay of Leithian*. He also suggests that 'in writing his *Legend of Sigurd and Gudrún* [i.e. the 'New Lays'], Tolkien may well have been hoping to emulate Morris's extremely successful poem *The Story of Sigurd the Volsung* (1876)', and 'in writing *The Fall of Arthur*' Tolkien 'surely was responding both to Tennyson's *Idylls of the King* and Morris's own "Defence of Guenevere" (and other Arthurian poems, 1858)' (pp. 233–4).

Turner's third category of influence on Tolkien's early poems is Georgianism. As we have seen, G.B. Smith encouraged his friend to read the Georgians in a letter of 1915; and if Gilbert Murray was right that they were part of the Oxford undergraduate culture by 1913, Tolkien would have known of them already (if perhaps not intimately) before Smith's recommendation. Their works, especially those of Rupert Brooke, were indeed widely popular at that time. According to Turner, and as it is generally oversimplified, Georgianism was

> part of a reaction against the over-wrought sentiment of the Victorians and the decadence of the *fin de siècle*, so to this extent it was related to the stirrings of modernism. However, in contrast to modernism it was intended to be based on tradition and to appeal to a wider public rather than a small elite, which was to give it the taint of mediocrity as its rival gained ground after the war. ['Early Influences on Tolkien's Poetry', p. 212]

Turner concludes that if Tolkien 'were to be associated with any literary movement, it would have to be this, with its emphasis on readability, together with close ties to the native soil and its past; in essence it is not far removed from the ideals of William Morris, although the poetry that it produced was quite different' (p. 213).

If there is a quibble to be made of this, it is that 'Georgianism' was less a movement than a critical concept. Its name derives from a label meant to distinguish the verse Edward Marsh chose for his five *Georgian Poetry* anthologies (the first was published in 1912), composed under the new king, George V, from that produced in the previous era, the Edwardian, which had followed the Victorian. Many of the new poems had a fresh outlook on the natural world and rural living, but by no means all. Their binding characteristic was that Marsh (and to differing degrees the publisher Harold Monro) found in them a special strength and beauty, a characteristic both vague and personal. Another difficulty is that the Georgians – that is, the poets who have been grouped under that name by critics – did not necessarily think of themselves as 'Georgian', nor did they agree on what made a Georgian a 'Georgian'. Robert H. Ross explores this question at considerable length in *The Georgian Revolt, 1910–1922: Rise and Fall of a Poetic Ideal* (1965):

> To be Georgian in 1912–15 . . . connoted several things. It meant to be 'modern', in the sense that the Georgian shared with most prewar poets the prevailing spiritual euphoria and the confidence that poetry was being infused with a new, vital release of creative energy. It meant also to be anti-Victorian, to write poetry which, in tone, form, and diction, was free of both fin de siècle weariness and Victorian 'painted adjectives'. But above all, Georgianism in 1912–15 was synonymous with realism [i.e. truth to life]. [p. 125]

Looking at Tolkien's earliest poems, or even some not so early, one would be hard put to argue that they were without ornateness of description or diction, and thus 'anti-Victorian'. Pointing especially to *Goblin Feet*, Bradford Lee Eden ('Strains of Elvish Song and Voices: Victorian Medievalism, Music, and Tolkien', 2010) describes how Tolkien made use of musical language and symbolism arising from a Victorian tradition, as in works by Tennyson, Swinburne, and Morris. Some of Tolkien's early poems are also continuations of the 'fairy' tradition in literature beloved of the Victorians and Edwardians, which John Garth explores in the fourth chapter of *Tolkien and the Great War*. As Garth comments, 'G.B. Smith admired [Rupert] Brooke's poetry and thought Tolkien should read it, but the poems Tolkien wrote' at the end of April 1915, when he returned to Oxford for his final term, such as *Goblin Feet* and *You and Me and the Cottage of Lost Play*, 'could hardly have been more different' (p. 72).

One does find 'Georgian' pastoralism and sentimentality in Tolkien's poems – *From Iffley* and *May Day* (no. 26) come to mind – but it is not predominant. Nor is it necessarily Georgian: equally, even preferably, it could be called Romantic – allowing that this label, no less than that of Georgianism, may be defined differently from critic to critic. Julian Eilmann devotes an entire book to Tolkien as a Romantic (*J.R.R. Tolkien: Romanticist and Poet*, 2017), pointing out in his writings common motifs of Romantic poetry such as nostalgia, and images which 'illustrate the poetry of the moment' (p. 306) such as twilight on a lawn (as in *Tinfang Warble*) or the movement of trees (as in *Over Old Hills and Far Away*, no. 43). 'A typical element of Romantic longing', Eilmann writes, is 'the unattainability of the poetic magic', as found in *Tinfang Warble*:

> He pipes not to me,
> He pipes not to thee,
> He whistles for none of you.
> Dancing all alone,
> His music is his own,
> The tunes of Tinfang Warble!

This also illustrates what Eilmann calls the 'lyrical I enchanted by the marvellous' (p. 307) – the tale of a poet, told in the first person, of a marvellous experience. Another example is provided by *The Happy Mariners*, where 'the Romantic longing of the lyrical I remains sorely unfulfilled' (p. 311):

> Ye follow Earendel through the West,
> The shining mariner, to Islands blest;

While only from beyond that sombre rim
A wind returns to stir these crystal panes
And murmur magically of golden rains
That fall for ever in those spaces dim.

Eilmann takes a particularly German point of view of what Romanticism entails (in origin, his book was a German dissertation). The British variety of Romanticism was as broad and varied as those we call the British Romantic poets of the early nineteenth century. It is hard to define as a movement or period, but in general was characterized by spontaneity and freedom, by the importance of emotion and individuality, and by Nature ascendant over the works of Man. Today we tend to think of the Romantics mainly as nature poets, idealizing rural life and extolling natural wildness, but they were also interested in myth and legend, folklore (including fairy-lore), the supernatural, and the divine. Foremost among many were Wordsworth, Coleridge, Byron, Shelley, and Keats, with Blake often added as a proto-Romantic. The popularity of their works endured through the Victorian era, notably influencing the poems of William Morris and the art and writings of the Pre-Raphaelites.

Tolkien read all of these poets, as we know from his word lists or various works – for example, Coleridge's *Biographia Literaria* lies behind thoughts about the imagination Tolkien expresses in *On Fairy-Stories*, and Tolkien's drawing *Xanadu* (?1913; see our *J.R.R. Tolkien: Artist and Illustrator* (1975), hereafter *Artist and Illustrator*, fig. 37) illustrates the setting of Coleridge's poem 'Kubla Khan'. In his *Biography* Humphrey Carpenter states that R.W. Reynolds at King Edward's School 'tried to instil into his pupils some idea of taste and style. He was not particularly successful with Ronald Tolkien, who preferred Latin and Greek poetry to Milton and Keats' (p. 47). We wonder if that was so only as Reynolds saw it in the classroom, and a different matter within Tolkien's circle. In November 1910, Tolkien's close friend Vincent Trought read a paper on Romanticism to the school Literary Society; as reported in the *King Edward's School Chronicle*, he

> began by giving a sketch of the history of the movement. Beginning with Thomson, he dealt with Goldsmith, Gray, Collins, Cowper, Burns, and Blake. The work of all these poets [of the eighteenth century] led up in different degrees to that of Wordsworth and Coleridge [authors of the seminal *Lyrical Ballads* of 1798]. Next came [Sir Walter] Scott, who popular-

> ised the movement, and Byron. They were followed by the culmination of romantic splendour in the work of Shelley and Keats. By the help of this history and of some very interesting comparative readings, the lecturer showed what romanticism really means. First, he read two epitaphs from Milton and Gray respectively, poems from Gray and Swinburne, and from Milton and Keats. From these some general conclusions were drawn. The romantic poet more or less subordinates self-control to emotion. The classical poet [against whom the Romantics were set in opposition] is noticeable for his firm grasp of the images which fill his mind; the romantic poet for their fervour and glow. Finally, the romantic poet is more human. [December 1910, p. 92]

There is no mention in the report of Tolkien in attendance, but he and his friends were at the heart of the Society.

After the lecture, Christopher Wiseman responded by speaking of 'Romanticism in music', and Rob Gilson 'showed that there was a romantic revival in painting contemporaneous with that in literature' (p. 92). A few years later, on 9 February 1916, G.B. Smith wrote to Tolkien:

> I never knew you until I went to Oxford: we have really seen but little of each other. I suppose it is our love of poetry. But even so, I am all the conservative: I love classic forms, and comfort, here as everywhere else I am conservative utterly, and romanticist hardly at all. And Romance is of your nature. I remember how your first verses perplexed me: I am glad to say I see now [that Smith has read *Kortirion*] that my criticism of them was just. [Bodleian Library]

While reading Tolkien's poems for this collection, we were reminded sometimes of the work of Keats, probably because of emotions Keats expressed (chiefly melancholy) and occasional subject matter which Tolkien shared, at least after a fashion. William Sherwood has argued in *The 'Romantic Faëry': Keats, Tolkien, and the Perilous Realm* (2019) that 'Keats and Tolkien share a conception of Faërie as the national heritage of England and Britain', and that there is a 'Keatsian aesthetic' in the *Lay of Leithian* and *The Lord of the Rings* (pp. 1, 28). Tolkien borrowed Sidney Colvin's 1887 biography of Keats from the Exeter College library in May 1915, which suggests that he had more than a passing interest in the poet, and Keats is cited four times in Tolkien's list of 'magnificent words', for *antre* (an archaic word for 'cave'), *gloom*, *impearled*, and *nectarous*, all of them in Keats's *Endymion*. Tolkien seems never to have used the first and last of these words in his poems, but *gloom* appears frequently, and *impearled* is in *Kôr* ('Under an azure sky, on whose dark ground | Impearled as 'gainst a floor of porphyry').

For his final category of early influences on Tolkien, Allan Turner mentions the Classical poetry Tolkien encountered in school, as well as nineteenth-century English poems by writers, such as Tennyson and Swinburne, who 'often experimented with classical metres'. Tolkien was interested in metre, Turner comments, but 'the specific forms that he set out to master and utilise as a medium for his own creative ideas were those of Old and Middle English and Old Norse, his professional study' ('Early Influences on Tolkien's Poetry', p. 217). In fact, all forms of metre were of interest to Tolkien, and well before he became a professional scholar. Around the time he compiled his word lists, he also filled two pages describing 'Metres to try things in':

· The 'Alison' ('Alysoun') metre, from the anonymous thirteenth- or fourteenth-century lyric poem, rhyming ABABBBBC, with a refrain DDDC.

· The common sonnet, evidently well known to Tolkien, as he did not bother to define it.

· The 'ottava rima', with stanzas of eight lines, '5 beat iambic, ABABABCC' (an *iamb* being a metrical 'foot' or unit, consisting of one short, or unstressed, syllable followed by one long, or stressed, syllable, as *da-DUM*).

· The Chaucerian 'roundel' (or rondel), which 'consists of lines of 5 beat iambs (with plenty of feminine endings)', which Tolkien analysed in twelve- and thirteen-line variants (a 'feminine ending' being a metrical foot which ends on an unstressed syllable).

· The 'ballade' (not to be confused with the ballad metre), which 'consists of 3 stanzas & 7 or 8 lines, in which the last line *though integral to the stanza* is same in each stanza. The rhyming system must be same in each stanza; *also the rhymes*' (emphasis in the original).

· The complex 'Epithalamion' stanza in eighteen lines, after the poem by that name by Edmund Spenser.

· The 'metabolic stanza', as in Chaucer's 'Anelida and Arcite' and 'Sir Thopas', in which the rhyme pattern changes from line to line.

Tolkien also described stanzas in six, seven, eight, nine, and ten lines with different schemes, and included his own 'Earendel metre', probably referring (in advance of composition) to *The Lay of Earendel* (no. 18), described as 'with *2nd* line long or the long's [longs ?] only sporadic'. In the event, he did not 'try things' in all of the metres he described, and did try others he did not think to list, such as the octosyllabic couplets of the *Lay of Leithian*, the trochaic tetrameter of the *Kalevala*, and the quantitative metre (common in Greek and Latin poetry, based on the quantity, or length, of syllables rather than on stresses) he adopted for *Earendel at the Helm* (no. 124), written in Qenya. Then, too, there was the metre he invented for *Errantry*, which he described as 'depending on trisyllabic assonances or near-assonances' (letter to Rayner Unwin, 22 June 1952, *Letters*, p. 235).

We have not analysed every poem in this collection according to its metre, lest our book become overly technical. No doubt there will be readers eager to do that work for themselves. It has already been done for selected poems: for example, by Geoffrey Russom in 'Tolkien's Versecraft in *The Hobbit* and *The Lord of the Rings*' (2000), and comprehensively for the poems in *The Lord of the Rings* by Thomas Kullmann in *Tolkien as a Literary Artist: Exploring Rhetoric, Language and Style in* The Lord of the Rings (2021). Kullmann identifies several of the *Lord of the Rings* poems as in iambic tetrameter, others in iambic dimeter, trimeter, pentameter, heptameter, or octameter, some in dactyls rather than iambs, a few in the ballad metre (see below), some in alliterative verse, and a number in still other forms, including those Kullmann describes only as 'irregular' or 'complex'. (In poetry, *dimeter* indicates a line with two metrical feet, *trimeter* one of three feet, *tetrameter* four, *pentameter* five, *heptameter* six, and *octameter* eight. A *dactyl* is a metrical foot with one stressed followed by two unstressed syllables.)

Russom focuses on only a few of the poems, and differs from Kullmann in his descriptions – thus illustrating the difficulty of describing metre when there are differences of opinion as to how various forms are to be defined. In *The Keys of Middle-earth: Discovering Medieval Literature through the Fiction of J.R.R. Tolkien* (2nd edn., 2015), Stuart

D. Lee and Elizabeth Solopova provide a useful explanation of the complicated rules of alliterative verse, a form found often in the present book, and also a brief introduction to other metres used by Tolkien, such as the ballad metre 'where a longer line with four stresses is followed by a shorter line with three stresses' (p. 58; see *An Elven-maid There Was of Old*, no. 160).

Russom is correct in stating that

> Tolkien offers [in *The Lord of the Rings*] a varied assortment of archaic and folkloric meters, sometimes realized with unusual strictness, sometimes with unusual freedom. These metrical preferences may express the yearning for a vanished past that permeates Tolkien's writing, yet they also register dissatisfaction with the predominance of a single form in the English literary canon [iambic pentameter]. ['Tolkien's Versecraft in *The Hobbit* and *The Lord of the Rings*', p. 53]

Kathy Cawsey has called *The Lord of the Rings* (under which she includes *The Hobbit*) a 'poetic project' in which Tolkien 'makes a claim about the value of older poetic *forms*, as well as their content and subject-matter'. The poems and songs in these works, she says, 'demonstrate the worth of out-of-date, non-trendy, de-valued poetic forms – medieval and traditional forms which may no longer glitter, but which are still gold' ('Could Gollum Be Singing a Sonnet?: The Poetic Project of *The Lord of the Rings* (2017), p. 53). She notes, as others have done, how Tolkien used poems to convey meaning and emotion, each according to its speaker. 'In terms of form Tolkien was a virtuoso poet: the verses in *The Lord of the Rings* demonstrate his mastery of an astonishing variety and range of poetic structures', which she discusses in detail. 'They also show extreme care with, and attention to rhyme, rhythm, and overall sound' (p. 54).

Also in relation to this body of poems, referring to the characters who recite them, Carl Phelpstead has observed that

> particular metrical forms are associated with certain kinds of speaker. The hobbit songs use rhyming verse forms such as ballad metre, whereas the poetry of the Anglo-Saxon-like Rohirrim is in alliterative metre like that of Old English poetry. The antiquity of that metre no doubt also explains its use in the Entish catalogue poem that fails to mention hobbits until Treebeard composes additional lines. ['"With Chunks of Poetry in Between": *The Lord of the Rings* and Saga Poetics', p. 29]

(Treebeard's verse beginning 'Learn now the lore of Living Creatures', in Book III, Chapter 4 of *The Lord of the Rings*, is not included in the present book.)

Later in the same essay, Phelpstead compares Tolkien's use of poetry in *The Lord of the Rings* with 'Icelandic sagas, particularly the *Íslendingasögur*', where 'situational verses are typically represented as being extemporized by characters. . . . Middle-earth resembles saga Iceland in being populated by characters who are able to compose verse on the spur of the moment', such as Tom Bombadil, Frodo, Sam, Legolas, Aragorn, and Éomer (p. 29). The 'stylistic contrast between verse and prose' in *The Lord of the Rings* is significant, Phelpstead argues:

> Tolkien employs a much greater variety of verse forms than is found in Icelandic sagas (in which the vast majority of the verse is in *dróttkvætt* metre): rhyming couplets, ballad metre, a variety of other stanza patterns (some unusual or unique), alliterative verse, free verse modelled on the Psalms, even sonnets. This formal variety is in accord with Tolkien's desire to represent the Third Age of Middle-earth as one . . . that resembled that of the Icelandic skald in its appreciation of metrical virtuosity. In *The Lord of the Rings*, stylistic contrast between verse and prose is taken even further than in Icelandic sagas when a poem is in a different language from the surrounding prose. The most substantial passages in Elvish (both Quenya and Sindarin) in the text are in verse. . . . [pp. 30–1]

Tolkien himself used *dróttkvætt*, or 'court metre', in *The Derelicts* (no. 119). This is a strict and complex form, explained in our discussion of the poem. For his 'New Lays' he used another Old Norse form, *fornyrðislag* – 'old story metre' or 'old lore metre' – one of three found in the Elder Edda. 'The norm of the strophe [stanza] for *fornyrðislag*', he explained, 'is four lines (eight half-lines) with a complete pause at the end, and also a pause (not necessarily so marked) at the end of the fourth half-line' (*The Legend of Sigurd and Gudrún* (2009), p. 48).

Tolkien is reported to have said that 'his typical response upon reading a medieval work was to desire not so much to make a philological or critical study of it as to write a modern work in the same tradition' (related by the Thomas Malory scholar Eugene Vinaver, as recalled by Richard C. West in 'The Interlace Structure of *The Lord of the Rings*' (1975), p. 80). We see this tendency in many of Tolkien's poems, drawing from or translating works such as *Beowulf*,

The Battle of Maldon, 'The Fight at Finnesburg', *Crist I* (*Advent*) and riddles from the Exeter Book, bestiary poems, *Sir Gawain and the Green Knight*, *Pearl*, *Sir Orfeo*, *The Owl and the Nightingale*, *Piers Plowman*, the *Völsunga Saga*, and writings by Geoffrey Chaucer. John D. Rateliff makes a related comment in 'Inside Literature: Tolkien's Exploration of Medieval Genres' (2014):

> Just as inventing his own languages gave Tolkien insights into language itself that most of his contemporaries lacked, so too his predilection not just for translating medieval works . . . but for writing new works in a variety of medieval genres . . . gave him insights into medieval literature not accessible to critics and authors who approached such works only from the outside, as museum specimens, fossils from an array of extinct genres. [p. 133]

Many of Tolkien's poems inspired by medieval works are alliterative in form, as are some of his original works mentioned earlier in our Introduction. Convenient discussions of these are 'Alliterative Verse by Tolkien' (2006) and 'Tolkien's Development as a Writer of Alliterative Poetry in Modern English' (2013), both by Tom Shippey. 'Tolkien's alliterative compositions', Shippey writes,

> were quite various in date, intention, and even literary model. Alliterative poetry is an old form, extending from at least the seventh century to the sixteenth, and it changed markedly from the Old English period (i.e., before 1066) to the later Middle English period of *Pearl*, *Sir Gawain*, and *Piers Plowman*. ['Alliterative Verse by Tolkien', p. 10]

Because of changes to the language over time, Modern English contains more unstressed syllables and 'filler-words', such as articles and prepositions, than did Old English, thus

> translations from Old to Modern English always come out longer. [And] since alliterative poetry is based overwhelmingly on stress, this makes its older formats hard to imitate. In between, Middle English poets, and even the late Old English *Battle of Maldon*, Tolkien's model for 'Beorhtnoth' [*The Homecoming of Beorhtnoth Beorhthelm's Son*], allowed themselves metrical liberties at which the *Beowulf*-poet would have shaken his head disapprovingly. ['Alliterative Verse by Tolkien', p. 10]

Tolkien's original poems based on Old English models, such as *The Children of Húrin*, are 'inevitably somewhat slack or unorthodox metrically', Shippey says, and the demands of metre result in Tolkien adopting 'frequent archaic word-order patterns', since 'Old English was much more flexible in this respect than Modern English' ('Alliterative Verse by Tolkien', p. 11). When it came to Middle English, Tolkien called *Pearl* 'about as difficult a task as any translator could be set. It is impossible to make a version in the same metre close enough to serve as a "crib". But I think anyone who reads my version, however learned a Middle English scholar, will get a more direct impression of the poem's impact (on one who knew the language)' (letter to Michael George Tolkien, 5 January 1965, *Letters*, p. 493). In *The Nameless Land* he took up the challenge of writing an original poem in the *Pearl* metre, scholars having judged it 'almost impossibly difficult to write in', though he did not attempt to equal the length of the original (101 stanzas; letter to Jane Neave, 18 July 1962, *Letters*, p. 448).

Soon after publication of the first part of *The Lord of the Rings* (*The Fellowship of the Ring*), Tolkien complained to an early enthusiast of his work, Miss F.L. Perry, that not one review of his book mentioned that it contains verse. In another letter to Miss Perry later that year, after publication of *The Two Towers*, Tolkien remarked more broadly: 'I have written a good deal of verse (of very varying merit), and some of it has been published here and there. But I have never collected it. I think I am best at the kind of thing seen in the present book [*The Lord of the Rings*] – verses arising from the emotions of a story, and written to represent the feelings of other 'characters' than myself. The very long narrative poems, I do not suppose will be ever published. They may!' (22 November 1954, Bonhams, New York sale of 22 June 2023, lot 152).

In October 1968 Tolkien wrote to his son Michael that his poetry had received 'little praise – comment even by some admirers being as often as not contemptuous (I refer to reviews by self-styled literary blokes)'. He felt that this had something to do with 'the contemporary atmosphere – in which "poetry" must only reflect one's personal agonies of mind or soul, and exterior things are only valued by one's own "reactions"' (*Letters*, p. 555). Around the same time, he used similar words to thank a reader who had sent him some of his own poems, for saying that he enjoyed Tolkien's poetry in *The Lord of the Rings* immensely. His own verse, Tolkien replied, 'has been (even by admirers) usually the target of dispraise. I like it not so much because I wrote it, as because I like that kind (or those kinds) of verse and am warmed to find others that still do so too' (14 January 1969, Christie's, London sale of 12 July 2023, lot 92).

Speaking about her father's poetry in 1988, Priscilla Tolkien suggested that it received so little critical interest because of changing fashion, 'a reaction against story telling, the "poetic", the mysterious, fantasy and romance: i.e. romantic love is seen as embarrassing. The prevailing mood is for subjectivity and often political and social realism. Obscurity is often regarded as a virtue' (Christina Scull, 'Tolkien's Poetry' (1988), p. 22). Reappraisals of any kind of art – poetry, painting, sculpture, music – are always occurring; so too are reversals of opinion. Pre-Raphaelite art, for example, was long derided or ignored, but today is broadly admired. Nor does the wider public always hew to the views of professional critics: the music of Vaughan Williams drew critical scorn after his death, compared with newer modes of composition, but has never ceased to be popular, at least in Britain.

Melanie A. Rawls has said that 'to review the body of critical commentary on the poetry and verse of J.R.R. Tolkien is to discover a wild variety of critical opinion. For some critics, his poetry is well-crafted and beautiful. Other critics announce that the verse is excruciatingly bad. At times two critics with opposite opinions are referring to the same poem.' She cites, for example, Randal Helms in 1974 (*Tolkien's World*) referring to *Errantry* as 'stunningly skillful . . . with smooth and lovely rhythms', but also Alan Bold in 1983 ('Hobbit Verse versus Tolkien's Poem') arguing that the same poem displayed 'all the sentimental silliness of the early Tolkien with its relentlessly contrived internal rhyming'. Bold, Rawls points out, 'does not think highly of *any* of Tolkien's verse' except for *The Homecoming of Beorhtnoth Beorhthelm's Son*; he praised Tolkien as 'a man who was capable of writing superlative narrative and descriptive prose' but 'virtually incapable of understanding the linguistic point of post-medieval poetry' ('The Verse of J.R.R. Tolkien', *Mythlore*, Winter 1993, p. 4).

Although she is concerned in her article mainly with the poems of *The Hobbit* and *The Lord of the Rings*, Rawls also mentions *You and Me and the Cottage of Lost Play*, *Kortirion among the Trees*, *Tinfang Warble*, and the *Lay of Leithian*, picking at aspects she finds unsuccessful: metre which in her view provides no source of interest, mawkish tone, words which call too much attention to themselves, predictable rhyme, excessive length. That such points are in the eye, or ear, of the beholder is shown by a strong response to Rawls by Paul Edwin Zimmer ('Another Opinion of "The Verse of J.R.R. Tolkien"', *Mythlore*, Spring 1993). Zimmer took issue with any attempt to judge Tolkien's early poems, like *You and Me* and the others Rawls cites, according to current standards, which themselves might seem ludicrous decades from now. Tolkien in fact – one must keep in mind that he was a Victorian by birth, and by education Edwardian – did not necessarily meet the general standards of taste in poetry as they were found when his earlier poems were composed, as he tended to prefer earlier forms. Rawls later replied to Zimmer (letter, *Mythlore*, Summer 1993) that she had meant in her article to demonstrate a restrained praise for Tolkien's poetry, and had examined his earlier work in order to show his improvement over time.

It is not hard to find negative criticism of Tolkien's poetry. The most prominent example may be in Brian Rosebury's *Tolkien: A Critical Assessment* (1992), where Tolkien's early poems are described as 'highly derivative', showing 'beyond doubt that Humphrey Carpenter's assertion that "for [Tolkien] English literature ended with Chaucer" is an overstatement' – an assertion since discredited, most notably by Holly Ordway. 'Among a number of post-medieval, mainly nineteenth-century, influences', Rosebury continues, 'the shadows of Keats and early Tennyson, and of Milton's "Lycidas", fall particularly heavily across them.' Quoting from *Kortirion among the Trees*, he argues that 'winter (personified) comes in with "icy shears" and "blue-tipped spears", and the melodious phrasing ranges from Tennysonian sonorousness ("sunlight dripping on long lawns") to Keatsian airiness ("whirl ye with the sapphire-winged winds")' (p. 82). Clearly a matter of opinion, neither of these seems to us an especially bad quality in verse.

Speaking in general of Tolkien's early poems – in so far as they were known some thirty years ago – Rosebury finds even the better poems, as he regards them, derivative, 'and their proneness to romantic cliché ("to thee my spirit dances oft in sleep" [from *The Town of Dreams and the City of Present Sorrow*]) means that they can only be regarded as immature works, by a writer whose genuine but limited talent for verse was destined never to be reconciled with twentieth-century taste' (p. 84). When he turns to Tolkien's poetry later than the *Lay of Leithian*, Rosebury declares that the best of it, and some of the worst, is contained in *The Lord of the Rings* – for Rosebury, Tolkien's only important achievement, with *The Hobbit* and 'The Silmarillion' ranked among 'Minor Works'. (In Rosebury's second edition, *Tolkien: A Cultural Phenomenon* (2003), this label becomes 'Fiction and Poetry', but the criticisms remain.) He dismisses the poems of the *Adventures of Tom Bombadil* collection except for *The Sea-Bell*, finds *Mythopoeia* 'at least [a] semi-pastiche' (p. 110) with echoes of

Alexander Pope, admires *The Lay of Aotrou and Itroun* though it too is a pastiche, and regards *The Homecoming of Beorhtnoth Beorhthelm's Son* 'almost literally, an academic exercise', belonging 'rather among the monuments of [Tolkien's] distinctively humane scholarship than among his important works as a creative artist' (p. 113).

That Tolkien could be critical of his own work is shown by his revision of some of his poems many times – the record seems to be the more than twenty versions of the related *Errantry* and *Eärendil Was a Mariner* – and even then he was not always satisfied. He was encouraged when friends or readers affirmed the quality of his work, though doubts lingered. Perhaps the greatest affirmation of the worth of his poetry he received was from recordings. In late August 1952 he read some of his poems from *The Hobbit* and *The Lord of the Rings*, as well as some of his prose, into a tape recorder owned by his friend George Sayer. According to Sayer, the experiment gave Tolkien confidence, in his texts and in his ability to recite them. In 1954 he made a private recording of *The Homecoming of Beorhtnoth Beorhthelm's Son*, speaking all of the voices and making sound effects. In 1967 he made a commercial recording for Caedmon Records, *Poems and Songs of Middle Earth*, of selections from the *Adventures of Tom Bombadil* poetry, together with a performance by pianist Donald Swann and baritone William Elvin of Swann's settings of some of Tolkien's poems, *The Road Goes Ever On: A Song Cycle* (1967). Caedmon later released selections from Tolkien's 1952 recordings as *J.R.R. Tolkien Reads and Sings His The Hobbit and The Fellowship of the Ring* and *J.R.R. Tolkien Reads and Sings His The Lord of the Rings: The Two Towers / The Return of the King* (both 1975). These have since been reissued, with additional material, for instance in *The J.R.R. Tolkien Audio Collection* (Harper Audio/Caedmon, 2001). Tolkien's 1954 recording of *Beorhtnoth* was privately released in 1992, with supporting material read by his son Christopher, and commercially issued by HarperCollins in 2023.

As we have said, and it bears repeating, there are those who pass by the poems in *The Hobbit* and *The Lord of the Rings* when reading those works, to their loss. Professor Michael D.C. Drout has told of asking the students in his Tolkien course if they themselves do so, at which 'a large percentage . . . raise their hands' while 'a much smaller proportion gasps in shock' ('Reading Tolkien's Poetry' (2013), p. 1). It has also been a loss that scholars have tended to focus on that same sub-set of poems, evidently a zone of comfort, even after other verse was published by Christopher Tolkien in *The History of Middle-earth* to document the growth of 'The Silmarillion', or identified in miscellaneous (admittedly obscure) publications by bibliographers.

One notable, relatively early exception to such treatments is 'Niggle's Leaves: The Red Book of Westmarch and Related Minor Poetry of J.R.R. Tolkien' by Steven M. Deyo (1986). We hope that the present book, providing a far larger body of work than was previously available, will aid a broader and deeper consideration of Tolkien's poetry than we have seen so far. Existing studies are listed in our bibliography at the end of Volume 3: these include several entries in the *J.R.R. Tolkien Encyclopedia: Scholarship and Critical Assessment* (2006), edited by Michael D.C. Drout; the essay collection *Tolkien's Poetry* (2013), edited by Julian Eilmann and Allan Turner; Eilmann's *J.R.R. Tolkien: Romanticist and Poet* (2017); our own article 'Poetry' in *The J.R.R. Tolkien Companion and Guide* (2017); and Corey Olsen's 'Poetry' in *A Companion to J.R.R. Tolkien*, edited by Stuart D. Lee (2nd edn. 2022), as well as Olsen's *Exploring J.R.R. Tolkien's* The Hobbit (2012) in which the *Hobbit* poems are discussed more extensively than anywhere else. We must also mention here, in a general context, an ambitious doctoral thesis by Penelope Anne Holdaway, *An Exploration of Changing Visions of Faërie through His Non-Middle-earth Poetry* (2021).

At Tolkien's request, George Sayer wrote a blurb to be used as publicity for *The Lord of the Rings*, then in production. 'He surprised me', Tolkien told Rayner Unwin. 'I did not think he would be overheated! But though "greatest living poet" is absurd, at least I am comforted in the thought that the verses are up to standard, and are (as I think) adequate and in place; though C.S. Lewis regards them as on the whole poor, regrettable, and out of place' (11 April 1953, *Letters*, p. 245). Sayer's comments seem to have been lost, and were not used. We ourselves make no claim to greatness for Tolkien as a poet, and yet there is much in his poetry that is good, occasionally superb, and the whole is consistently interesting, if sometimes puzzling. This was the view Tolkien's TCBS friends took of his poems, and we hope it will be the largely sympathetic response of readers to the present book.

In April 2016 we were invited to meet with Chris Smith and David Brawn of the publisher HarperCollins to discuss the feasibility of a volume or volumes of Tolkien's collected poems. We learned that the Tolkien Estate was eager to bring more of Tolkien's unpublished poems into print, and that Christopher Tolkien wished to have his father's talent for poetry known by a wider public. As an initial task, we agreed to review files of poems that would be sent us, and to suggest to Christopher ways to present them. He knew that the work would raise many editorial questions, but preferred not to dictate an approach; instead, he left it to us to consider the issues involved and propose the best solutions. We had already done something of the sort, on a relatively small scale, with our edition of *The Adventures of Tom Bombadil and Other Verses from the Red Book* (2014), which includes historical notes and early versions, and otherwise had proven ourselves to Christopher as editors and critics of his father's writings.

Near the end of August 2016 we received high-resolution scans of more than one thousand pages – prodigious imaging work by Bodleian Library staff – ranging from almost illegible draft manuscripts in soft pencil to professional typescripts. With these were fifty-three pages of notes about the files by Christopher, which have proved invaluable. We began to make lists and analyses of the poems that autumn, but at the same time, needed to produce a new, expanded edition of our *J.R.R. Tolkien Companion and Guide*, commissioned at the same April meeting at HarperCollins; the latter project occupied us for the following year. In December 2016 we sent an initial report to Christopher, remarking that his father's poetry was

> part of his creative life no less than his prose, his languages, and his art. Some of his poems indeed are related to his art, some are integral to his *legendarium* ['The Silmarillion'], and some include names related to his invented languages (or are in the languages themselves). Although his readers are aware that he wrote poetry, if only from verses in *The Hobbit* and *The Lord of the Rings*, its extent is not well known and its qualities are underappreciated. He aspired to be a poet in the first instance. Within his larger works of fiction, poems help to establish character and place as well as further the story; as individual works, they delight with words and rhyme. They express his love of trees and the sea, of nature and the seasons, of landscape and music, and of language. They convey his humour and sense of wonder. His wartime poems are concerned not with trenches and battle, but with life, loss, faith, and friendship, and his longing for England and [his wife] Edith.

We estimated the number of poems Tolkien wrote, and determined that some sixty of those included in the files we received had not been published. Since the project had first been described to us as 'collected poems', we considered whether to make a comprehensive collection, rather than a selection of only 'best' or representative poems, or only those Tolkien thought to collect together, or which were only unpublished or obscure. But Christopher had not envisioned a book of his father's 'entire and vast poetic *opus*', as he put it to us, and recognized the amount of work it would take to address that larger body. He was concerned, rather, with his father's 'early poetry'. This in fact was the label applied to the files we received; but those did not contain only poems from an early period, or even all of Tolkien's early poems, but also unpublished work from the 1950s and 1960s.

What, in any case, was meant by 'early'? We gave this question no little thought. Should the term apply to any poems written by Tolkien prior to, say, the publication of *The Hobbit* in 1937 – to suggest only one arbitrary, but meaningful, date? Or should the division be still earlier? There were many poems by Tolkien composed around the time of the First World War, but also work from the 1930s, which had never been published, and poems such as *Noel* (*c.* 1936, no. 148) which were published but largely unknown. There was also the important point that not a few demonstrably early poems had later evolved – *Vestr um Haf* (?1931, no. 127), for example, became *Bilbo's Last Song* (*c.* 1960) – and arguably, one could not be fully appreciated without also considering the other.

We granted that Tolkien's poems, taken all together, amounted to a substantial number, and for a time – acknowledging Christopher's focus on earlier material – we considered whether to include only poems the first versions of which pre-dated *The Hobbit.* The verses included with that work, and those in *The Lord of the Rings*, are so well known that their omission might be excused; and yet, some of these are among Tolkien's best poetry, and many other interesting verses he conceived *after* 1937 had not yet been published. We considered that there were already volumes in print partly or wholly devoted to his longer poems, such as *The Lays of Beleriand*, *The Legend of Sigurd and Gudrún*, and *The Fall of Arthur*, works which as a practical matter could not be included whole in a *Collected Poems*. We thought, however, that brief, representative extracts from longer works ought to be included if a book of Tolkien's poetry were to show fully his development and, in some cases, verse forms he did not use elsewhere.

We were of two minds about incomplete poems, such as *Empty Chapel* (no. 36), a haunting work with a Pre-Raphaelite air which in manuscript unfortunately tails off into illegibility. Nor were we certain about Tolkien's translations or adaptations of poems such as *Beowulf* and *Sir Gawain and the Green Knight*, or whether we should restrict our collection by omitting works in Old and Middle English, for example, or in Tolkien's invented languages.

We continued to develop ideas through 2017 and 2018, as other work called for our attention and Christopher, on his part, was occupied with his final book, *The Fall of Gondolin* (2018), and with the continuing business of his father's literary properties. As may be supposed, it was no short or easy task to read and organize hundreds of pages of Tolkien's texts, but essential to do so in order to propose most responsibly what to do with them. In the end, we felt that it would be a lost opportunity not to collect together as many of Tolkien's poems as possible, regardless of their date of composition, language, or circumstance, and we recommended that the collection be modelled after Christopher's *History of Middle-earth* series, combining original texts with editorial notes and commentary tailored to the particular purpose. To illustrate this, we prepared a draft of thirty-six poems, shown in different versions and with comments, and in February 2019 sent it to Christopher with notes for a general introduction and a sample glossary. He replied a month later, approving our concept and execution, without change, and finding the work 'remarkable and immensely desirable'.

That, unfortunately, was our last contact with Christopher. At his death in January 2020, much remained to be done with the book if it was to proceed. Christopher had approved our plan, but it had yet to be presented to the trustees of the Tolkien Estate (Christopher had retired as a trustee in 2017, but remained his father's literary executor), and to HarperCollins. The Covid-19 pandemic complicated the matter, but at last all was agreed and we continued our work. From February 2022, when Wayne retired from his long career as a rare books librarian, we were able to complete this book more readily if not immediately. We regret that it could not be completed sooner, and that Christopher did not live to see the final product. There are more questions we had wanted to ask him, and were always glad of his advice.

A few words are in order about the files we initially received for this project, which represent the bulk of Tolkien's poetry papers. These comprise two notebooks, called by Christopher from their blue wrappers Blue Poetry Books I and II, and two miscellaneous groups of papers, Verse Files I and II. The Blue Poetry Books are handwritten, and both include versions of some of the same poems. Blue Poetry Book I begins with *Morning* (no. 1) and ends with *Sea-Song of an Elder Day* (no. 13) and *Build Me a Grave beside the Sea* (no. 58). Blue Poetry Book II also begins with *Morning* (no. 1) and ends with *The Lonely Harebell* (no. 39) and parts of *Kortirion* and *The Pool of the Dead Year*. The versions in Blue Poetry Book I, however, are later than those in Blue Poetry Book II: Christopher gave the notebooks numbers evidently before he completed an analysis of the contents of both together. The notebooks also contain dozens of poems on individual leaves, placed there probably most often by Tolkien himself, but occasionally by Christopher; some are next to poems of which they are earlier or later versions, while others are single or multiple texts of poems which appear in neither notebook, but are contemporary with other poems contained within, and a few are poems written subsequent to those in the notebook. In addition, a leaf was sometimes removed from a notebook and placed elsewhere.

The two Verse Files preserve additional loose sheets, for poems not recorded in the Blue Poetry Books. Their contents extend from revised texts of earlier works through the 1930s, often with later rewriting, to original poems composed through the 1960s, some in response to special occasions or requests; and here one finds many of the works in typescript. As we have seen, Tolkien circulated copies of early poems to the TCBS and to R.W. Reynolds, and to Edith Bratt; by March 1915 some of these were typewritten, possibly by Tolkien himself. (On 22 March G.B. Smith advised him that 'typewriting is always useful because it shows up one's faults better than anything else. Things always look as silly as they can in that medium'; Bodleian Library.) In May that year Tolkien had typescripts of twelve of his poems made professionally by the Oxford Copying Office, and continued to use a typewriting service as far as he was able. Once he was employed at Leeds, he seems to have had access to a typewriter which used a distinctive purple ribbon; later, at Oxford, from around 1927, he owned or had access to several typewriters, including one, a 'Hammond', with interchangeable fonts.

Altogether, the two Blue Poetry Books and the two Verse Files include a substantial number of Tolkien's poems. Some are found in a single manuscript or typescript, but most are in multiple versions, and many of the typescripts have both ribbon and carbon copies. Tolkien also preserved cuttings of some of his poems published in magazines or journals, some of which he marked with revisions. He did not preserve, however, every version of every poem, contrary to the myth that he kept every scrap of everything he wrote. Nor do the four files contain all of Tolkien's known poems, or all versions of them, as we soon realized. The Bodleian Library, University of Oxford, subsequently provided scans of other poetry we identified in its Tolkien papers. Relevant material also came from the Tolkien papers in the Archival Collections and Institutional Repository of Marquette University, Milwaukee, Wisconsin, and from the E.V. and Ida Gordon archive at the University of Leeds. (Citations to these materials are given in greater detail at the end of our third volume.) The Blue Poetry Books and Verse Files are in the care of the Bodleian Library, but as of this writing have not yet been processed. Other papers, still in Christopher Tolkien's care when he died and which might contain additional versions of some of his father's poems, regrettably could not be consulted for this book.

We should make it clear that *The Collected Poems of J.R.R. Tolkien* is not a *Complete Poems*, though it represents most of the works of poetry Tolkien is known to have written, at least 240 discrete poems depending on how one distinguishes titles and versions. Also, even with three volumes allowed to us, we have had to impose some economies of space. We have made a generous selection of the poems written for *The Hobbit* and *The Lord of the Rings*, but omitted the greater part; of course there will be few, if any, readers of this book who do not own a copy of those works. We have also omitted a few shorter poems from 'The Silmarillion', which however are readily available in *The History of Middle-earth*. As explained, we have included only extracts from Tolkien's longer poems, generally from the final version transcribed from an existing printing. We have included some verses which Tolkien left incomplete but developed to an extent, but not a few poems which for one reason or another are problematic, such as the late verse which begins

> There is no room for Stories in this hall
> the room is far too great and full of men
> of sound of voices saying many things

but immediately descends into a short text of workings too rough to interpret (see no. 183). Finally, we excluded the majority of poems Tolkien composed in languages other than Modern English, while admitting a few examples in Old and Middle English, Latin, Gothic, Qenya (Quenya), and Sindarin. More of Tolkien's verses in Elvish have been printed and analysed in the linguistic journals *Parma Eldalamberon* and *Vinyar Tengwar*.

❦

We have chosen to present Tolkien's poems in 195 entries (and appendices), in order of the earliest text of each; and each entry itself typically contains a chronological sequence, from the earliest version of a work to its latest, as far as we can determine its history. It is not a perfect approach – there can be none which all readers would judge perfect – since few of the poems can be dated with absolute confidence. Even so, we feel that a chronological order, even one after a fashion, best serves to illustrate Tolkien's development as a poet, rather than, say, arranging his works by subject or theme.

We have had to judge the accuracy of dates of composition or revision Tolkien inscribed on his poems, only some of which were (apparently) written contemporary with the manuscript or typescript. Many were added long after the event, and Tolkien's memory for dates has been shown time and again to be questionable. We have also judged the dates of manuscripts by his handwriting, or of typescripts by the typewriter he used, or either form by its paper or some other physical feature: for example, particular papers were used for examination purposes at Leeds or Oxford, the use of a purple typewriter ribbon can be dated to Tolkien's years at Leeds (nominally 1920–5, though he continued to teach there part of the time into 1926), and 'miniature' fonts are associated with Tolkien's 'Hammond' typewriter which he seems to have begun to use around 1927. His correspondence has also been useful, when it mentions a poem or poems.

The result is an order of works which we believe to be as correct as can be made with the evidence available, but in places has been formed by editorial decision. In certain periods – the Leeds years in the 1920s, parts of the 1930s, and the 1950s – the dating of Tolkien's poems approaches guesswork, and the order of works is close to arbitrary, if in the right chronological vicinity. To illustrate: Tolkien translated at least 200 lines of *Sir Gawain and the Green Knight* from Middle English to Modern English by mid-November 1923, and his *Enigmata Saxonica Nuper Inventa Duo* was published in June 1923. We do not have precise dates for the beginning of either. Should *Enigmata* appear in sequence before *Sir Gawain*, because June precedes November? Or was Tolkien more likely to have worked from an earlier date on *Sir Gawain*, since it was part of his teaching curriculum? We judged the latter, and thus *Sir Gawain* is no. 70, and *Enigmata* no. 71; but both were begun in ?1923. As is our general practice, we have tried to be conservative in our statements, using queries (?), *circa* ('around, about', abbreviated *c.*), 'between', 'no later than', and so forth.

For most of the poems selected from *The Hobbit* and *The Lord of the Rings*, it has been convenient to group those related verses in two sub-sequences (nos. 108–115 and 149–171) according to the spans of years in which the books were written and revised, and in the order the poems appear in the stories. We have assumed that poems in *The Hobbit* were written in the order in which they appear in the published text, but we cannot date them precisely. Although scholars can agree that Tolkien began to write *The Hobbit* no later than 1929, opinions vary as to when he substantially completed it, either by January 1933, when he lent the story to C.S. Lewis, or October 1936, when he sent it to George Allen & Unwin for publication. With only a few exceptions, it is also difficult to date the poems written for *The Lord of the Rings*, in part because the development of that work, especially in its earlier stages, was circuitous. Some poems for *The Lord of the Rings* stand apart because they developed from earlier, independent works: *The Man in the Moon Stayed Up Too Late* (Frodo's song at the Prancing Pony, no. 60), for example, is a later version of *Nursery Rhymes Undone, or Their Scandalous Secret Unlocked* (1919).

Another exception to strict chronological order applies to ten of the thirteen poems by Tolkien published in the unauthorized *Songs for the Philologists* in 1936. We surmise that these were composed at Leeds, have given them the arbitrary date *c.* 1924, and present them in the order they appear in the booklet – we do not know in what order they were actually written. The three remaining songs, known to have been composed in Oxford, appear together with the date ?1928, determined by a letter Tolkien wrote to his friend E.V. Gordon.

Readers who find that the occasional date, or other statement, given here conflicts with one we gave in our *J.R.R. Tolkien Companion and Guide* will appreciate that we have had much greater access to Tolkien's poetry for the present book than we did earlier, and this has sometimes led us to different conclusions.

Each entry is identified by number, and each version given in detail within an entry is identified by letter. The heading of each entry includes its most significant titles, or first lines when there is no formal title, and a span of dates from composition to final revision or publication. By *version* we mean the original form of a text or a development from an earlier text. With a few exceptions, we have included the earliest and latest versions of each poem, if extant and legible, as well as any significant intermediate texts, either in full or in summary, as seemed best for each individual work. By 'earliest' text we mean the earliest that survives; sometimes it is clear that an earlier version still once existed but has been lost. In our description of a poem we account for all versions, and for all known copies (manuscript, typescript, and printed), though we do not fully describe, or transcribe, every version, some being identical to others and some showing little development. Since each poem has its own characteristics, we have sometimes varied our approach as to its description, as seemed best under particular circumstances. To better illustrate Tolkien's method of composition, we have transcribed selected poems or versions (such as no. 40A) in greater detail, showing changes, additions, and deletions.

A few examples will illustrate our method. The relatively straightforward *Morning* (no. 1) is shown in four versions (from more than four copies, manuscript and typescript), written and revised over only some five years; versions C and D evolved from A and B, though with different wording and changes of title (*Morning*, to *Morning-Song*, to *Morning Song*), indeed there are significant differences between the original versions and the latest.

Compare, however, the greater number of texts presented as no. 13: these too evolved in only about five years, but between the twelve lines of *The Grimness of the Sea* to the seventy-four-line song made by Tuor in 'The Silmarillion', *The Horns of Ylmir*, only one half of one line of the original version survived. Or compare the curious sequence of related verses presented as no. 48, with *A Dream of Coming Home*, *A Memory of July in England*, *July*, *Two Eves in Tavrobel* (*July*, *May*), *An Evening in Tavrobel*, and *Once upon a Time*, a line of development which spanned 1916 to 1964.

For even greater length and complexity, see poem no. 40, *Kortirion among the Trees*, later *The Trees of Kortirion*, composed and revised between 1915 and ?1962, whose description required eight texts and heavy commentary, or the most complex of Tolkien's poems in terms of evolution, *Errantry* and *Eärendil Was a Mariner* (no. 128). The two poems named *Fastitocalon* (no. 95), written far apart in time (?1927 and 1961 or 1962), could be considered distinct works which happen to share a title, though one is clearly derived from the other. Against these, though, a comparison may be made with *Iumbo* (no. 96) and *Grey as a House*, i.e. *Oliphaunt* (no. 167), which have a few elements in common – they are both about elephants – but in most respects are entirely distinct, and therefore are given separate entries.

A few further aspects of our method must also be mentioned. Entries are numbered, and versions are lettered, for ease of reference only; one cannot count solely from these the total number of poems included, nor the total number of versions. Each entry had its own needs for reference and description, as we judged them, and we worked accordingly. Some poems have only one version, and for those it did not seem necessary to call it 'A', which would have implied the existence at least of B; for these, the entry number is sufficient. We have always lettered first and final versions, but we did not think it essential to assign a letter to every quotation from every intermediate text, that is, between versions fully described: examples of this can be seen in no. 33, among numerous others. We have also used letters to denote texts which are not versions, strictly speaking: a poem Tolkien wrote in a language other than Modern English, such as Old English or Quenya, receives a letter designation to distinguish it from its translation, the latter supplied by ourselves or another scholar when Tolkien did not do so himself.

For some of the poems, it seemed most appropriate to quote additional, related verses in discussion, rather than give them separate entries: for example, versions of nursery rhymes Tolkien wrote in Middle English and Latin, which we provide in relation to *Éadig Béo Þu* (no. 80); *Elvish Song in Rivendell*, which may related to the *Hobbit* verse *Sing All Ye Joyful, Now Sing All Together* (no. 114); and Théoden's poetic cry before the battle of the Pelennor Fields, 'Arise, arise, Riders of Théoden!' in conjunction with *From Dark Dunharrow in the Dim Morning* (no. 169) from *The Lord of the Rings*.

In his manuscripts, and in notes added to typescripts, Tolkien's handwriting is sometimes beautifully clear, indeed calligraphic, but on occasion it presents difficulties in reading, even to the point when an editor regretfully has to admit defeat. Much of Tolkien's drafting and many of his early manuscripts are in soft pencil, sometimes rubbed or overwritten with ink. Now and then he erased his pencil text after writing over it, but not always. When he edited his poems, the process could be confusing, with replacement words or phrases written in any vacant spot on a page, on a facing page, or on a rider (a separate piece of paper). Sometimes he indicated that text, even entire sections, was to be moved with a hasty arrow whose destination is not always clear. On occasion, he marked revisions on a later version, then marked some or all of them as well on an earlier text. Some of his initial workings of a poem appear only as miscellaneous phrases, as he tried out combinations of words, sometimes (as for no. 18) too rough and incoherent to transcribe accurately and meaningfully. In these varied circumstances, we have done the best we can.

For some of Tolkien's poems, the earliest extant version is a fair copy, a term which means a manuscript of a text made following the correction of a previous copy or, alternatively, a fresh copy written in a more legible hand. For simpler texts, it is possible that Tolkien had the poem clear and complete in his head before setting it down, but given that he most often scribbled at least the first version of a work, a clean copy is most likely a fair copy in the technical sense. For more complex poems, it is nearly certain that one or more working copies preceded a fair copy.

We have transcribed Tolkien's texts as found, and to the extent we can decipher them. His punctuation was not consistent from draft to draft, moving indiscriminately between comma, semi-colon, and colon, and between full stop, colon, and semi-colon, to say nothing of sometimes indistinguishable marks made half an inch from the relevant position. Early drafts especially have little or no punctuation, and the ampersand (&) often used for 'and', as Tolkien rapidly set his thoughts on paper.

Nor was he consistent with capitalization, variously at the beginning of each line or only at the beginning of a sentence, and between, say, 'sun' and 'Sun' or 'earth' and 'Earth', which may or may not suggest significant differences of meaning. Also in our transcriptions of manuscripts, we have retained Tolkien's indentations, as they appear to us; sometimes it can be hard to know for sure what he intended. Invented personal and place names, which sometimes varied in Tolkien's works over time (such as *Éarendel*, *Eärendel*, *Earendel*, *Eärendil*), have been transcribed, or used in comments, as they appear in the particular text under discussion.

Tolkien variously used single and double quotation marks; we have standardized these, preferring single marks. Sometimes we have had to take our best judgement as to whether a word is capitalized, whether a mark is a full stop or a comma, and whether Tolkien intended two words to be conjoined, set apart, or hyphenated. Writing a draft for his eyes only, of course not thinking of the poor editor decades later, he did not need to be concerned about such niceties. Here and there we have silently corrected the odd error, and occasionally, when needed for clarity, we have added missing marks of punctuation in square brackets. Where we have presented lines of poetry not set off as block quotations, the vertical (|) is used to indicate a line break in the original work, and a double vertical (| |) a caesura, or pause. Omissions of text are indicated by the ellipsis (. . .), except for a complete line or lines of a poem, which is shown by a line of spaced full stops. Ornaments of various sorts, inserted by Tolkien between stanzas or sections in some of his texts, are reproduced in this book uniformly as asterisks.

For lines of poetry too long to fit within our text measure, we have used turnovers; that is, we have carried words which extend beyond the measure onto a second line, with an indent beyond the deepest indent found in the original poem. For example:

> Its organ whose stops are the piping of gulls and the
>   thunderous swell;

In this example, from no. 13, there are no indents in the original, thus we have used a single indent in carrying over.

In our discussion and notes we have omitted mention of most changes in punctuation, etc. between versions, leaving their illustration to the texts themselves. Some changes of this sort almost always occurred copy to copy, according to Tolkien's preference of the moment. Readers should also understand that in publishing some of his father's poems in *The History of Middle-earth*, for the sake of clarity Christopher Tolkien occasionally, and silently, added marks of punctuation and modestly regularized. This suited his purpose, which was not to trace the development of texts to the granular degree we have followed, but to document the history of his father's mythology and tales.

We have used notes following individual poems mainly to point out important textual changes between versions, changes Tolkien considered but did not execute, and other textual issues. We have also used them sometimes to explain points, often fine and miscellaneous, which could not be expressed easily in our main discussions; see, for example, poems 6 through 9. In notes as well as in our discussion proper, we have occasionally commented on the meanings of words when it seemed appropriate to raise them within the entry, in addition to, and more fully than, we have done in the glossary of archaic, unusual, or potentially unfamiliar words at the end of this book.

In addition to the appendices we have already mentioned, we have transcribed lists Tolkien made of his poems for reference and, probably, when planning to publish collections.

When referring to a particular poem, we have often used its most familiar title, not necessarily its latest title, for example *The Happy Mariners* rather than *Tha Eadigan Saelidan*. We have followed the usual convention in Tolkien studies whereby 'The Silmarillion', with the title in quotation marks, refers to Tolkien's mythology in general, and *The Silmarillion*, in italics, indicates both the work Tolkien intended to publish and that which, edited by Christopher Tolkien, was first published in 1977. Otherwise, we have italicized the titles of Tolkien's works, regardless of length or form, but have followed standard scholarly practice when citing titles by other authors.

We are grateful to Christopher Tolkien, to his wife Baillie, and to the Tolkien Estate for their confidence in our ability to undertake this project. Chris Smith at HarperCollins has shown infinite patience as we worked with Christopher to determine the scope of the book and agree on many details, and then produced a work longer than any of us at first imagined. Cathleen Blackburn, solicitor for the Tolkien Estate, has been an invaluable advisor and point of contact. Catherine McIlwaine, Tolkien Archivist in the Bodleian Library, Oxford, arranged for scans to be made and answered many difficult questions. We are grateful also more generally to the staff of the Bodleian Library, which we visited directly for research. William Fliss, Archivist in the Archival Collections and Institutional Repository of Marquette University, Milwaukee, Wisconsin, similarly provided scans from its collection of Tolkien papers, and helped in other ways, both remotely and in person on our visits to Marquette. At Wheaton College, Wheaton, Illinois, Archivist Laura Schmidt Stanifer assisted us with research into Tolkien papers held by the Marion E. Wade Center. We send thanks as well to the staff of Special Collections & Galleries, Leeds University Library, for providing scans from their E.V. and Ida Gordon archive.

Special thanks go to Tolkien linguist Arden R. Smith, for reading our poetry entries and saving us from multiple errors typographical, substantive, and linguistic, and for translations from Old English. (Other translations are largely our own.) We would also like to thank Jessica Yates for telling us long ago about the link between Tolkien's 'Leeds songs' (*Songs for the Philologists*) and the collections *What the Children Sing* and *The Scottish Students' Song Book*; Brian Sibley for pointing out to us the Tolkien poems in the Walter Hooper archive now in the Bodleian Library, and Andoni Cossio for his comments on Chaucer and 'little Louis', both at the eleventh hour; and Christopher Gilson for permission to include his translation of *Narqelion* (no. 41) from the journal *Vinyar Tengwar*. Finally, we are grateful to scholars who earlier commented on Tolkien's poetry, especially Douglas A. Anderson, Julian Eilmann, John Garth, Carl Phelpstead, John D. Rateliff, Tom Shippey, and Allan Turner. Other sources for the present book are listed in our bibliography.

Christina Scull & Wayne G. Hammond
Williamstown, Massachusetts
April 2024

Chronology

Here we have attempted to show in concise form the history of the writing, revision, and publication of poems included in this book, during the span of Tolkien's life, the better to appreciate the periods in which he was most prolific as a poet and those in which his work was relatively fallow. Our chronology also illustrates how often he revisited his poems across the months and years. As noted in our general introduction, evidence is usually lacking for a certain date of a poem, and – avoiding guesswork as much as possible – some dates can be assigned only in broad spans. This issue has been particularly acute when dating, or attempting to date, the poems of *The Lord of the Rings*, the history of which even Christopher Tolkien, with access to the full range of his father's papers, could not trace with precision. In regard to *The Lord of the Rings*, readers should keep in mind our choice, explained in our general introduction, to present, and number, most of our selection of its poems in the order they appear in the published book, excepting only those Tolkien adapted from earlier work; for it will be seen here that the order of publication of the poems is not always the same as the order of their writing.

Some titles are abbreviated. Selected events in Tolkien's life, and in world history, are included to provide context. Actions described in the entries (e.g. 'writes [a poem]', 'visits Switzerland') are generally to be understood as performed by Tolkien.

3 January 1892 John Ronald Reuel Tolkien is born in Bloemfontein, Orange Free State (now a province of the Republic of South Africa).

15 February 1896 Arthur Tolkien, Ronald's father, dies while Ronald, his mother Mabel, and his brother Hilary are on home-leave in England. Mother and sons will remain there, making their home in and around Birmingham.

1898 or 1899 Tolkien writes a poem or story about a 'green great dragon'. He will claim to be insensitive to poetry as a child, but to discover it later through studies of Latin and Greek.

1900 Mabel Tolkien converts to Roman Catholicism and instructs her sons in the faith.

Autumn 1900 Tolkien begins to attend King Edward's School in Birmingham, where he will read Classical poetry and also be exposed to poems in English. Except for brief periods, he will be a student of

King Edward's School until summer 1911. With his friends Robert Q. 'Rob' Gilson, Vincent Trought, and Christopher Wiseman, among others, forms the 'TCBS' (Tea Club, Barrovian Society), later to include G.B. (Geoffrey Bache) Smith.

8 August 1904 Tolkien writes a limerick ('There was an old priest naméd Francis') about Father Francis Morgan, a priest of the Birmingham Oratory who has become a good friend of the family.

14 November 1904 Mabel Tolkien dies. Father Francis becomes guardian of the Tolkien boys.

Beginning of 1908 Ronald and Hilary become boarders of Mr and Mrs Louis Faulkner. Ronald will fall in love with another lodger, Edith Bratt.

Between ?1908 and 1910 Tolkien writes a limerick in one of his early invented languages, Nevbosh ('Dar fys ma vel gom co palt "hoc"').

Autumn 1909 Learning that Ronald and Edith have been meeting clandestinely, Father Francis demands that their relationship cease.

January 1910 Father Francis moves Ronald and Hilary to new lodgings.

21 January 1910 Having learned that Ronald has continued to meet with Edith, Father Francis forbids him to have contact with her until he comes of age.

28 March 1910 Tolkien writes the poem *Morning* [1] with a letter to Edith, who has moved to Cheltenham, but does not give it to her until they are reunited in 1913.

Between March 1910 and September 1911 Revises *Morning* [1].

?Between May and July 1910 Writes *The Dale-Lands* [2].

June 1910 Writes *Evening* [3].

July 1910 Writes *Wood-Sunshine* [4] and *The Sirens Feast* [5].

?July 1910 Revises *Wood-Sunshine* [4].

Autumn 1910–summer 1911 Discovers the Finnish *Kalevala* in the translation by W.F. Kirby.

February or March 1911 Writes *The Battle of the Eastern Field* [6], published in the March number of the *King Edward's School Chronicle*.

June–July 1911 Writes *A Fragment of an Epic* [7].

?Late July–early September 1911 Visits Switzerland.

September 1911 Writes *The New Lemminkainen* [8].

15 October 1911 Matriculates at Exeter College, University of Oxford, where he will read Greats (Classics). His friends Gilson and Wiseman attend the University of Cambridge.

Late October 1911 Writes *Lemminkainen Goeth to the Ford of Oxen* [9]. Possibly this early, writes *From Iffley* [10].

6 November 1911 Writes *Darkness on the Road* [11].

7 November 1911 Writes *Sunset in a Town* [12].

Late 1911 or 1912 Revises *Darkness on the Road* [11] and *Sunset in a Town* [12].

Between 1911 and 1915 Revises *Morning* [1].

20 January 1912 Vincent Trought dies.

?Early 1912 Possibly visits his aunt Jane Neave in St Andrews, Scotland and is inspired to write *The Grimness of the Sea* [13]; a revision follows.

3 January 1913 As soon as he turns twenty-one, writes to Edith Bratt. Later in the month, she will agree to marry him.

First part of 1913 Edith moves to Warwick. Tolkien will visit her there as often as he can, and Warwick will come to figure in his private mythology.

February 1913 Sits the First Public Examination for the Honour School of Greek and Latin Literature (Honour Moderations), achieving only a Second Class, though his paper on Comparative Philology is marked 'alpha'. With the next term, he will change his course of study to the English Honour School.

October 1913 G.B. Smith matriculates at Corpus Christi College, Oxford. He will respond with enthusiasm to Tolkien's poetry and encourage his literary ambitions.

December 1913 Writes *Outside* [14]. *From Iffley* [10] is published in the *Stapeldon Magazine* (Exeter College, Oxford) for this month, but the editor loses (and does not print) its second stanza.

1913–14 Purchases the collected *Works* of Francis Thompson, a writer whose vocabulary Tolkien finds attractive.

?1914 Revises *From Iffley* [10].

8 January 1914 Betrothed to Edith, and she is received into the Catholic Church. On or around this date, writes *Magna Dei Gloria* [15].

26 January 1914 Revises *A Fragment of an Epic* [7].

4 March 1914 Reads a paper on Francis Thompson to the Exeter College Essay Club.

Spring 1914 Wins the Skeat Prize for English; with the award, buys two works by William Morris, *The Life and Death of Jason* and *The House of the Wolfings*, Morris's translation of the *Völsunga Saga*, and *A Welsh Grammar* by Sir John Morris-Jones. Morris will remain an inspiration for Tolkien as a writer.

?May 1914 Revises *The Sirens Feast* [5] as *The Sirens*.

11 May 1914 Revises *Wood-Sunshine* [4].

18 May 1914 Revises *The Dale-Lands* [2]; will recast the poem later this year.

August 1914 Explores the Lizard Peninsula in Cornwall.

4 August 1914 Great Britain declares war on Germany, bound by treaty to reply to Germany's invasion of Belgium. Tolkien determines to complete his degree course rather than enlist at once, as many other Oxford students have done.

24 September 1914 While on a visit to his aunt Jane Neave and his brother Hilary at Phoenix Farm, Gedling, writes *The Voyage of Éarendel the Evening Star* [16], with the earliest appearance of a figure connected with Tolkien's private 'Silmarillion' mythology; further drafting follows.

Between ?October 1914 and ?April 1915 Writes *The Story of Kullervo* [17].

Late 1914 Begins to create, or continues to work on, an invented 'fairy' language (Qenya, later Quenya), influenced by Finnish. As he does so, also develops another language, Gnomish (or Goldogrin, or Noldorissa, later through further development Noldorin and Sindarin), influenced by Welsh.

October 1914 Joins the Oxford University Officer Training Corps.

22 November 1914 Reads a paper on the *Kalevala* to the Sundial Society, Corpus Christi College, Oxford.

By 27 November 1914 Revises *The Voyage of Éarendel the Evening Star* [16] as *The Voyage of Earendel.*

27 November 1914 Revises *The Grimness of the Sea* [13]. Reads *The Voyage of Earendel* [16] to the Exeter College Essay Club.

December 1914 Revises *Outside* [14].

4 December 1914 Revises *The Grimness of the Sea* as *The Tides* [13]; revisions follow, one as *Sea Chant of an Elder Day*.

6 December 1914 Tells Edith: 'I am always wanting to write things of my own now-a-days and they will come into my head just when I have settled down opposite a good book.'

12–13 December 1914 Attends the TCBS 'Council of London', inspiring him to find his voice as a poet.

?Winter 1914 Writes *The Minstrel Renounces the Song* [18] and *The Mermaid's Flute* [19].

21 December 1914 Writes *Dark* (*Copernicus v. Ptolemy*) [20].

22 December 1914 Writes and revises *Ferrum et Sanguis*. Writes *The Sparrow's Morning Chirp to a Lazy Mortal* [22]; a revision follows.

Late 1914 or early 1915 Revises *Outside* [14].

January 1915 Writes *As Two Fair Trees* [23]; a revision follows.

?Early 1915 Revises *The Dale-lands* [2] and *Wood-Sunshine* [4].

?March 1915 Revises *Outside* [14].

March 1915 Revises *Sea Chant of an Elder Day* [13] and reads it to members of the Exeter College Essay Club; a further revision follows, as *A Sea-Song of an Elder Day*. Revises *The Sparrow's Morning Chirp to a Lazy Mortal* [22] as *Bilink* and *Sparrow-song*. Possibly at this time, paints in a sketch-book entitled *The Book of Ishness* a watercolour, *Water, Wind and Sand*, connected with *A Sea-Song of an Elder Day*.

8 March 1915 Revises *Dark* [20]; a further revision follows, with the added title *Copernicus and Ptolemy*.

10–11 March 1915 Writes *Why the Man in the Moon Came Down Too Soon: An East Anglian Phantasy* [24]; a revision follows, as *A Faërie: Why the Man in the Moon Came Down Too Soon*.

12 March 1915 Tells Edith of his 'sudden hopes of really writing some day soon more than ordinarily good things'.

Easter vacation 1915 Probably during this time, paints *Tanaqui* in *The Book of Ishness*, later connected with *Kôr: In a City Lost and Dead* [30].

By mid-March 1915 Sends Smith a handwritten copy of (at least) *The Minstrel Renounces the Song* [18].

17 March 1915 Smith asks Tolkien to send him typewritten copies of his poems, which he could then forward to Rob Gilson.

17–18 March 1915 Revises *The Mermaid's Flute* [19]. He will send a manuscript copy to G.B. Smith before 27 March.

Between 17 and 22 March 1915 Has eleven poems professionally typed: *The Dale-Lands* [2], revised; *Wood-Sunshine* [4], revised; *From Iffley* [10], revised on some copies as *Valedictory*; *Darkness on the Road* [11]; *Sea-Song of an Elder Day* [13]; *Outside* [14], revised; *The Voyage of Earendel* [16], revised as *The Last Voyage of Éarendel* (or *Ëarendel*) and *Éalá! Éarendel Engla Beorhtast*; *Dark* (*Copernicus and Ptolemy*) [20]; *Sparrow-Song* [22], now *Sparrow Song*; *As Two Fair Trees* [23], revised; and *A Faërie: How* [*sic*] *the Man in the Moon Came Down Too Soon* [24].

?Spring 1915 Begins to keep a systematic record of his invention of Qenya, *Qenyaqetsa*, eventually including a phonology and lexicon.

22 March 1915 G.B. Smith comments on *A Sea-Song of an Elder Day* [13], *Outside* [14], *As Two Fair Trees* [23], and *A Faërie: Why the Man in the Moon Came Down Too Soon* [24].

25 March 1915 G.B. Smith sends Tolkien praise by their mutual friend H.T. Wade-Gery for *Why the Man in the Moon Came Down Too Soon* [24], *As Two Fair Trees* [23], *Sea-Song of an Elder Day* [13], and *Dark* (*Copernicus and Ptolemy*) [20].

April 1915 Revises *Evening* [3].

15–16 April 1915 Writes *Courage Speaks to a Child of Earth* [25]; a revision follows, as *Now and Ever.*

?Mid-April 1915 Writes *May Day* [26].

20–21 April 1915 Revises *May Day* [26], one version as *May Day in a Backward Year.*

22 April 1915 Revises *Evening* [3] and *Magna Dei Gloria* [15].

27–28 April 1915 Writes *Goblin Feet* [27] and *You and Me and the Cottage of Lost Play* [28].

29–30 April 1915 Writes *Tinfang Warble* [29].

30 April 1915 Writes *Kôr: In a City Lost and Dead* [30].

Late April 1915 Revises *Evening* (*Completorium*) [3].

2 May 1915 Revises *Evening* (*Completorium*) [3], *Darkness on the Road* [11], and *The Mermaid's Flute* [19].

3 May 1915 Revises *Morning* as *Morning-Song* [1].

10 May 1915 Paints *West of the Moon, East of the Sun*, which will inspire the poem *The Shores of Faery* [31].

Mid- to late May 1915 Engages the Oxford Copying Office to make typescripts of ten of his poems, bound in this order, with a cover and title-leaf reading 'Poems': *Sparrow Song* [22]; *Now and Ever* [25]; *May Day in a Backward Year* [26]; *Goblin Feet* [27]; *Kôr: In a City Lost and Dead* [30]; *You and Me and the Cottage of Lost Play* [28]; *Tinfang Warble* [29]; *The Mermaid's Flute* [19]; *Darkness on the Road* [11]; and *Morning Song* [1]. A revision of *Sparrow Song* follows.

10–15 June 1915 Sits his final examinations at Oxford, achieving First Class Honours.

28 June 1915 Applies for a commission as a second lieutenant in the Army. Gilson and Smith have already enlisted in the Army, and Wiseman in the Navy.

8–9 July 1915 Writes *The Shores of Faery* [31]; a revision follows.

9 July 1915 Writes *Princess Ní* [32].

c. 11 July 1915 Writes *The Happy Mariners* [33], following workings in the *Book of Ishness* sketch-book; a revision follows.

13–14 July 1915 Writes *The Trumpet of Faery* [34], following workings in *The Book of Ishness*; a revision follows, as *The Trumpets of Faery* (*Horns of Elfland*).

19 July 1915 Begins training at Bedford, the first of a series of Army camps to which he is posted. R.W. Reynolds comments on *You and Me and the Cottage of Lost Play* [28], *Kôr: In a City Lost and Dead* [30], *The Shores of Faery* [31], and *The Princess Ní* [32].

After 19 July 1915 Writes *Thoughts on Parade* [35].

24 July 1915 Revises *The Happy Mariners* [33].

?Late July–early September 1915 Writes (fragments of) *Empty Chapel* [36].

4 August 1915 Revises *Thoughts on Parade* [35] as *The Swallow and the Traveller on the Plains.*

9 September 1915 Revises *The Happy Mariners* [33].

By 12 September 1915 Writes *The Pines of Aryador* [37].

12 September 1915 Revises *The Pines of Aryador* [37] as *A Song of Aryador.*

14 September 1915 Writes *Dark Are the Clouds about the North* [38]; revisions follow.

25–6 September 1915 Tolkien, Gilson, Smith, and Wiseman meet in the TCBS 'Council of Lichfield'.

?Late September 1915 Writes *The Lonely Harebell* [39]; a revision follows.

?October 1915 Has six poems professionally typed: *The Shores of Faery* [31], *Princess Nî* [32], *The Happy Mariners* [33], *The Trumpets of Faery* [34], *A Song of Aryador* [37], and *Dark Are the Clouds about the North* [38]. A revision of *The Happy Mariners* follows.

November 1915 Writes *Kortirion among the Trees* [40].

21–28 November 1915 Revises *Kortirion among the Trees* [40].

Between November 1915 and March 1916 Writes *Narqelion* [41].

Between 28 November and 4 December 1915 Writes *The Pool of the Dead Year* [42]; revisions follow, ultimately as *The Pool of the Dead Year (and the Passing of Autumn).*

December 1915 Posted to Brocton Camp in Staffordshire. His experiences there will inspire *Habbanan beneath the Stars* [45].

1 December 1915 *Goblin Feet* [27] is published in *Oxford Poetry 1915.*

?Late 1915 Revises *Morning Song* [1].

?1916 Writes out the last half of *Goblin Feet* [27] on military paper.

***c.* 19 January 1916** Sends several poems to Dora Owen to consider for publication in *The Book of Fairy Poetry* (1920).

Late January–February 1916 Writes and revises *Over Old Hills and Far Away* [43].

By 9 February 1916 Proposes to Sidgwick & Jackson, London, that they publish a book of his poems, *The Trumpets of Faerie.*

16 March 1916 Attends delayed degree ceremony at Oxford.

16–18 March 1916 Writes *The Town of Dreams and the City of Present Sorrow* [44]; a revision follows, as *The Wanderer's Allegiance,* later *The Sorrowful City.*

22 March 1916 Marries Edith in Warwick.

31 March 1916 Sidgwick & Jackson reject Tolkien's book of poems. He will receive word on 3 April.

6 June 1916 Crosses the English Channel as part of the British Expeditionary Force in France, encamps at Étaples for further training. He has qualified as a Signalling Officer for his battalion, the 11th Lancashire Fusiliers.

After 6 June 1916 Writes *Habbanan beneath the Stars* [45] and revises it as *Eruman beneath the Stars*. Writes *Tol Eressea* [46] and revises it as *For England: The Lonely Isle*. Writes *Two-Lieut* [47].

1 July 1916 Battle of the Somme begins. Rob Gilson is killed.

4–8 July 1916 Writes *A Dream of Coming Home* [48]; a revision follows.

7–8 July 1916 Writes *A Memory of July in England* [48]; a revision follows.

10–14 August 1916 While billeted at Bus-lès-Artois, on two evenings visits a wood to think about Rob Gilson's death and its effect on the TCBS.

22 August 1916 Tolkien, G.B. Smith, and H.T. Wade-Gery meet at Bouzincourt. It will be the last time Tolkien sees Smith.

24–26 August 1916 While with his battalion at Thiepval Wood, revises part of *Kortirion among the Trees* [40].

24–25 August 1916 Writes *The Thatch of Poppies* [49].

25–26 August 1916 Writes *The Forest Walker* [50].

Late August or early September 1916 Revises *The Thatch of Poppies* [49] and *The Forest Walker* [50].

12–24 September 1916 While with his battalion at Franqueville for a long training session, writes *O Lady Mother* [51] and revises *The Mermaid's Flute* [19] and *The Forest Walker* [50].

28–29 October 1916 Suffering from trench fever, he is admitted to hospital at Gézaincourt, then transferred to another hospital at Le Touquet.

30 October–7 November 1916 While in hospital at Le Touquet, writes *To Early Morning Tea* [52], and revises it as *Morning Tea*.

9 November 1916 Invalided home to England, he is admitted to hospital in Birmingham.

November 1916 Revises *The Lonely Harebell* [39]; further revisions follow. Revises *Over Old Hills and Far Away* [43], and *The Town of Dreams and the City of Present Sorrow* [44] titled thus.

3 December 1916 G.B. Smith dies from shell wounds. Later this month, his mother will write to R.W. Reynolds about publishing her son's poetry; Reynolds in turn will defer to Tolkien and Wiseman.

Between 9 December 1916 and ?27 February 1917 Spends leave with Edith in Great Haywood, and with relatives in Birmingham, though still subject to Medical Board examinations.

Christmas 1916–?April 1917 Writes *G.B.S.* [53]; revisions follow.

End of 1916–first half of 1917 Begins to write the first prose version of his mythology, *The Book of Lost Tales*, and begins work on a grammar and a lexicon of his invented language Gnomish.

?1917 Subdivides from *The Town of Dreams and the City of Present Sorrow*, and revises, *The Town of Dreams* [44], and *The City of Present Sorrow* as *Wínsele Wéste, Windge Reste Réte Berofene.*

1917 *Goblin Feet* [27] is reprinted in *Oxford Poetry 1914–1916*. In the latter part of the year, Tolkien writes much of the remainder of *The Book of Lost Tales*, but will not fully abandon it until 1919.

18 January 1917 Christopher Wiseman comments on *The Pool of the Dead Year* [42] and *The Forest Walker* [50].

27 February–28 March 1917 In hospital at Harrogate, Yorkshire. From 28 March Tolkien will have three weeks' sick leave with Edith.

?March 1917 Writes *Ye Laggard Woodlands* [54]; revisions follow.

4 March 1917 Christopher Wiseman urges Tolkien to start his 'epic', connecting related poems.

19 April 1917 Posted to the Holderness peninsula, Yorkshire.

?June 1917 Lives with Edith in a 'lonely house' near Roos, Holderness. She dances for him, inspiring the dancing Elf Lúthien Tinúviel in his mythology.

August 1917 Revises part of *Kortirion among the Trees* [40].

1 August 1917 Writes *Companions of the Rose* [55] on Minden Day.

Mid-August–16 October 1917 In hospital in Hull.

28–29 August 1917 Revises *Companions of the Rose* [55].

August or September 1917 Writes *The Grey Bridge of Tavrobel* [56].

31 August–2 September 1917 Revises *A Sea-Song of an Elder Day* [13].

September 1917 Revises *The Mermaid's Flute* [19] as *The Mermaid's Flute from 'The Lay of Earendel'.*

After 2 September 1917 Revises *A Sea-Song of an Elder Day* as *The Horns of Ulmo* [13].

16 November 1917 Birth of the Tolkiens' first child, John.

?November 1917 Writes *I Stood upon an Empty Shore* [57].

Mid-November 1917–late February or early March 1918 With the Royal Defence Corps at Easington, Yorkshire. During this period, severs and revises the Prelude from *The Town of Dreams and the City of Present Sorrow* [44] as *The Song of Eriol.*

?January–March 1918 Revises *The Lonely Harebell* [39] as *Elf-alone* (*Elfalone*).

?April 1918 Writes *Build Me a Grave beside the Sea* [58].

?May or June 1918 Writes *A Rime for My Boy* [59].

June or July 1918 *A Spring Harvest* by G.B. Smith, edited by Tolkien and Christopher Wiseman, is published.

?Summer 1918 Revises *Build Me a Grave beside the Sea* [58]; revisions follow.

November 1918 Declared temporarily unfit for military duty, Tolkien returns to Oxford to apply for sedentary employment.

11 November 1918 The Armistice is signed.

?1919 Writes verses which may be connected with *G.B.S.* [53]. Writes *Nursery Rhymes Undone, or Their Scandalous Secret Unlocked* [60] (a revision follows) and *The Motor-cyclists* [63].

?1919 or 1920 Writes *Light as Leaf on Lind* [64].

January 1919 Begins work on the staff of the *Oxford English Dictionary.*

?20 April 1919 Writes *A Rhyme Royal upon Easter Morning* [61].

15 July 1919 Demobilized from the Army.

Summer–autumn 1919 Probably during this period, Tolkien is commissioned to write the glossary (*A Middle English Vocabulary*) for *Fourteenth Century Verse and Prose*, edited by his former tutor, Kenneth Sisam. He will continue to work on it in coming years (it will published on 11 May 1922).

c. November 1919 Writes and revises *The Ruined Enchanter* (*The Ruined Enchanter: A Fairy Ballad*) [62].

c. 1920 Revises *The Pool of the Dead Year* [42] as *The Pool of Forgetfulness.*

1920 *Goblin Feet* [27] is reprinted in *The Book of Fairy Poetry*, edited by Dora Owen.

?1920 or ?1921 Revises *The Minstrel Renounces the Song* [18] as *The Lay of Earendel.*

Between ?1920 and ?1923 Revises *Tinfang Warble* [29].

June 1920 *The Happy Mariners* [33] is published in the *Stapeldon Magazine* for this month.

Between autumn 1920 and October 1923 Revises *Nursery Rhymes Undone, or Their Scandalous Secret Unlocked* [60] as *The Cat and the Fiddle, or, A Nursery Rhyme Undone and Its Scandalous Secret Unlocked*, and as *The Cat and the Fiddle, Being A Nursery Rhyme Undone and Its Scandalous Secret Unlocked.*

1 October 1920 Takes up the Readership of English Language at the University of Leeds. He will be concerned with Old and Middle English verse, including works such as *Beowulf* and Chaucer's *Canterbury Tales*.

22 October 1920 Birth of the Tolkiens' second child, Michael.

?1921 Writes *Nieninqe* [65]; more versions follow. Begins *The Lay of the Fall of Gondolin* [66] and *The Golden Dragon* (*Túrin Son of Húrin and Glórund the Dragon*) [67].

Between ?1921 and ?1925 Revises *The Lay of the Fall of Gondolin* [66] in multiple versions. Abandons the first version of *Túrin Son of Húrin and Glórund the Dragon* [67] and begins a second, as *Túrin* or *The Children of Húrin*. Revises *The Last Voyage of Éarendel* [16]; *The Lay of Earendel* [18] as *The Bidding of the Minstrel from The Lay of Earendel*; *Now and Ever* (*Two Riders*) [25]; *Goblin Feet* [27]; *You and Me and the Cottage of Lost Play* [28] as *Mar Vanwa Tyaliéva: The Cottage of Lost Play*; *Princess Nî* [32] as *The Princess Ní*; *Elfalone* [39]; *Over Old Hills and Far Away* [43]; *Wínsele Wéste, Windge Reste Réte Berofene* [44]; *For England: The Lonely Isle* [46] as *The Lonely Isle*; *Build Me a Grave* [58] as *The Brothers-in-Arms*; and *The Ruined Enchanter* [62].

Between ?1921 and November 1931 Revises *Nieninqe* as *Nieninque* [65].

?1922 Writes *The Clerkes Compleinte* [68].

12 January 1922 E.V. Gordon takes up the post of Assistant Lecturer in English at Leeds. He and Tolkien will form a club for students of Old Icelandic, and produce a standard edition of *Sir Gawain and the Green Knight* in Middle English.

December 1922 *The Clerkes Compleinte* [68] is published in *The Gryphon* for this month.

?Late 1922 Writes and revises *Iumonna Gold Galdre Bewunden* [69].

?Early 1923 Writes *Enigmata Saxonica Nuper Inventa Duo* [71]. Revises *A Faërie: Why the Man in the Moon Came Down Too Soon* [24] as *Why the Man in the Moon Came Down Too Soon*; another version follows. Revises *May-Day* [26]. Revises *Kôr: In a City Lost and Dead* [30] as *The City of the Gods*.

Between ?1923 and 1925 Corrects a copy of *The Clerkes Compleinte* [66] as it appeared in *The Gryphon*, a Leeds magazine, and makes a revised typescript.

1923 Writes and revises *Moonshine* [73]. Revises *Light as Leaf on Lind* [64] as *As Light as Leaf on Lindentree*.

January 1923 *Iumonna Gold Galdre Bewunden* [69] is published in *The Gryphon* for this month.

Spring 1923 *The City of the Gods* [30] is published in *The Microcosm* (Leeds) for this season.

?Summer 1923 Writes obituary of Henry Bradley (editor of the *Oxford English Dictionary*, *d.* 23 May), including *Úþwita Sceal Ealdgesægenum* [72].

June 1923 *Why the Man in the Moon Came Down Too Soon* [24], *Tha Eadigan Saelidan: The Happy Mariners* [33], and *Enigmata Saxonica Nuper Inventa Duo* [71] are published in *A Northern Venture: Verses by Members of the Leeds University English School Association*.

October 1923 *Úþwita Sceal Ealdgesægenum* [72] is published with Tolkien's obituary of Henry Bradley in the *Bulletin of the Modern Humanities Research Association* for this month.

October–November 1923 *The Cat and the Fiddle: A Nursery Rhyme Undone and Its Scandalous Secret Unlocked* [60] is published in *Yorkshire Poetry* for this date.

By mid-November 1923 Begins translation of *Sir Gawain and the Green Knight* [70].

c. 1924 Writes poems or songs for the amusement of English School students at Leeds; these include *From One to Five* [76]; *Ruddoc Hana* [77]; *Ides Ælfscýne* [78]; *Bagmē Blōma* [79]; *Éadig Béo Þu* [80]; *Ofer Wídne Gársecg* [81]; *I Sat upon a Bench* [82]; *Pēro & Pōdex* [83], revised as *The Root of the Boot*; *Frenchmen Froth* [84]; and *Lit' and Lang'* [85]. A further poem, *All Hail* [86] probably belongs with these works, as well as another, *Smakkabagms*. Also writes *Two Eves in Tavrobel: July*, reduced from *A Memory of July in England* [48], and *Two Eves in Tavrobel: May*, adapted from the 'Prelude' of *A Dream of Coming Home* [48], and reconceives *May* as *An Evening in Tavrobel*; and writes *The Lion Is Loud and Proud* [87]. Revises *The Horns of Ulmo* [13] as *The Horns of Ylmir*, *Eruman beneath the Stars* [45], *The Thatch of Poppies* [49], *The Forest Walker* [50], *G.B.S.* [53], *Companions of the Rose* [55], and *The Cat & the Fiddle, or, A Nursery Rhyme Undone & Its Scandalous Secret Unlocked* [60] as *The Cat & the Fiddle, being, A Nursery Rhyme Undone & Its Scandalous Secret Unlocked*. Types, or has typed, eleven poems possibly as the basis of a collection he proposes to the Swan Press, Leeds: *The Horns of Ylmir* [13], *The Mermaid's Flute* [19], *Kortirion among the Trees* [40], *Eruman beneath the Stars* [45], *A Dream of Coming Home* [48], *Two Eves in Tavrobel: July* and *May* [48], *The Thatch of Poppies* [49], *The Forest Walker* [50], *O! Lady Mother Throned amid the Stars* (titled thus) [51], *G.B.S.* [53], and *Companions of the Rose* [55].

?1924 Revises *The Minstrel Renounces the Song* [16], with this title added; further revisions follow, as *The Lay of Earendel* and *The Bidding of the Minstrel from The Lay of Earendel.*

?1924 or ?1925 Revises *The Lay of the Fall of Gondolin* [66].

1924 Revises *Dark* [20], *The Shores of Faery* [31] twice, and *As Light as Leaf on Lindentree* [64].

May 1924 Writes *The Nameless Land* [74]. *The Princess Ní* [32], *The Lonely Isle* [46], and *An Evening in Tavrobel* [48] are published in *Leeds University Verse 1914–24*.

August 1924 Writes *Ave atque Vale: Farewell to the Rural Pleasures of Vacation* [75], possibly now also revises it as *Lines Composed on an Evening of Extraordinary Liquid Beauty in a Village Inn (at End of a Summer Holiday)*. Revises *The Nameless Land* [74]; further revisions follow.

***c.* 21 August 1924** Revises *The Trumpets of Faery* [34] as *The Trumpets of Faërie* and *The Horns of the Host of Doriath*.

1 October 1924 Tolkien becomes Professor of English Language at Leeds.

21 November 1924 Birth of the Tolkiens' third child, Christopher.

***c.* 1925** Begins, but does not complete, a translation of *Beowulf* in alliterative verse, *The Song* (or *Tale*) *of Beewolf Son of Echgethew* [88], and a translation of *The Owl and the Nightingale* [89].

?1925–6 Translates *Pearl* [90].

23 April 1925 *Sir Gawain and the Green Knight*, an edition in Middle English by Tolkien and E.V. Gordon, is published.

June 1925 *Light as Leaf on Lindentree* (omitting *As*) [64] is published in *The Gryphon* for this month.

Summer 1925–September 1931 Writes, but does not complete, the first incarnation of the *Lay of Leithian* [92].

By 23 August 1925 Writes *Gawain's Leave-Taking* [91].

Late August–mid-September 1925 With his family, spends a holiday in Filey on the Yorkshire coast, possibly an influence on his future 'Bimble Bay' poems. A storm during this visit inspires his story *Roverandom*.

1 October 1925 Takes up the Rawlinson and Bosworth Professorship of Anglo-Saxon at Oxford, attached to Pembroke College. For the next academic year he will do double duty, with teaching duties at both Oxford and Leeds. His teaching of works such as *Beowulf* and the *Völsunga Saga* is balanced against the examining of postgraduate theses and administrative duties.

Late 1925 or after Revises *The Clerkes Compleinte* [68] according to Oxford (rather than Leeds) conditions.

?1926 Writes *Shadowland* [93].

First part of 1926 Sends poems to R.W. Reynolds for comment, including the *Lay of Leithian* [92].

Spring 1926 Reportedly proposes a collection of his poetry to Oxford publisher Basil Blackwell, without success.

April 1926 Sends his translation of *Pearl* [90] to Kenneth Sisam at Oxford University Press.

11 May 1926 Meets C.S. Lewis.

***c.* 1927** Revises *The Lonely Isle* [46], *Morning Tea* as *An Ode Inspired by Intimations of the Approach of Early Morning Tea* [52], *The Ruined Enchanter* [62], *Moonshine* [71], and his translation of *The Owl and the Nightingale* [89].

?1927 Writes *Fastitocalon* [95] in its original version, *Iumbo, or Ye Kinde of ye Oliphaunt* [96], and *Knocking at the Door* [94]. Revises *Tinfang Warble* [29], *Over Old Hills and Far Away* [43], and *The Nameless Land* [74].

1927 *The Nameless Land* [74] is published in *Realities: An Anthology of Verse*.

Early 1927 Revises *The Grey Bridge of Tavrobel* [56].

May 1927 *Tinfang Warble* [29] and *The Grey Bridge of Tavrobel* [56] are published in *Inter-University Magazine* for this month.

June 1927 *Fastitocalon* [95] and *Iumbo, or Ye Kinde of ye Oliphaunt* [96] are published in the *Stapeldon Magazine* for this month.

?1928 Writes *Syx Mynet* [97], *La Húru* [98], *Natura Apis* [99], *The Hills Are Old* [100], *A Song of Bimble Bay* [102], *The Progress of Bimble* [103], and *Glip* [104]. Writes *Natura Formice* [101]; revisions follow. Writes *Poor Old Grabbler* [106] and revises it as *Old Grabbler*. Writes and revises *The Dragon's Visit* [107].

Early 1928 Writes *The Bumpus* [105]; revisions follow.

18 June 1929 Birth of the Tolkiens' fourth child, Priscilla.

Between November 1929 and 23 September 1930 Writes two poems entitled *The Corrigan* [116].

Late November or early December 1929 Tolkien lends a typescript of the *Lay of Leithian* [92] to C.S. Lewis.

***c.* 1929** Begins to write *The Hobbit*, ultimately with twenty-four poems (including our selection [108]–[115]). Tolkien will continue to write the story until at least 1932 (see our discussion for no. 108), and to circulate it in typescript to friends.

c. 1930 Writes *The Lay of Beowulf* [117], *Hengest* [118], and *The Derelicts* [119]. Revises *The Horns of the Host of Doriath* [34] and *Kortirion among the Trees* [40]. Translates Lewis Carroll's 'Jabberwocky' as *Bealuwérig* [App. V].

30 July 1930 E.V. Gordon marries Ida Pickles; in celebration, Tolkien writes *Brydleoþ* [120].

?Autumn 1930 Revises the second *Corrigan* poem, as *Aotrou and Itroun ('Lord and Lady'), a Breton Lay* [116].

c. 1931 Writes *The Adventures of Tom Bombadil* [121]; a revision follows. Writes *Errantry* [128]. Revises *O! Lady Mother* as *Consolatrix Afflictorum* and *Stella Vespertina* [51].

c. 1931–4 Writes *Monday Morning* [122].

?1931 Writes *The Last of the Old Gods* [126] and *Vestr um Haf* [127]. Writes and revises *Oilima Markirya* [123], *Earendel* (*Earendel at the Helm, Éarendel at the Helm*) [124], *Dir Avosaith a Gwaew Hinar* [125], and *The Home-coming of Beorhtnoth Beorhthelm's Son* [129]. Revises *A Rhyme Royal upon Easter Morning* [61], and *The Progress of Bimble* [102] as *Progress in Bimble Town.*

?1931 or ?1932 Begins, but does not complete, *The Children of Húrin* in rhyming couplets [130]. Writes *Völsungakviða en nýja*, or *The New Lay of the Völsungs*, and *Guðrúnarkviða en nýja*, *The New Lay of Gudrún* [131], and *The Prophecy of the Sibyl* [132].

15 October 1931 *Progress in Bimble Town* [102] is published in the *Oxford Magazine* for this date.

29 November 1931 Delivers *A Secret Vice*, a lecture on the invention of languages, to the Johnson Society of Pembroke College, Oxford, including *Nieninque* [65], *Oilima Markirya* [123], *Earendel at the Helm* [124], and *Dir Avosaith a Gwaew Hinar* [125].

c. 1932 Writes *Bleak Heave the Billows* [133]. Writes *Looney* [134]; revisions follow. Revises *Iumonna Gold Galdre Bewunden* [69]; further revisions follow.

?January 1932 Writes *Quare Fremunt Omnes Gentes* [135].

8 April 1932 C.S. Lewis recommends to his brother Tolkien's translation of *The Owl and the Nightingale* [89].

?Between June 1932 and June 1933 Writes *Mythopoeia* [136]; multiple versions follow.

Between August 1932 and October 1935 Tolkien recites *Iumonna Gold Galdre Bewunden* in Oxford lectures on *Beowulf.*

c. 1933 Writes *The Merryman* [137], *A Cherry with No Stone* [138], and *Hit Was an Olde Mon fro Pimbilmere* [138].

?1933 Writes *Doworst* [139]. Begins to write *The Fall of Arthur* [140]. Writes or revises *Firiel* [141].

?1933 or ?1934 Possibly writes *The Shadow Man* [147].

15 January 1933 Lends the typescript of *The Hobbit* to C.S. Lewis. If John D. Rateliff is correct in his argument for dating *The Hobbit*, it is now complete as later published; but see below for ?Early 1936.

?Autumn 1933 With C.S. Lewis, forms an informal literary club, the Inklings.

9 November 1933 *Errantry* [128] is published in the *Oxford Magazine* for this date.

21 December 1933 Gives *Doworst* [139] to R.W. Chambers.

?1934 Revises *The Adventures of Tom Bombadil* [121].

1934 *Firiel* [141] is published in the annual *Chronicle of the Convents of the Sacred Heart.*

18 January 1934 *Looney* [125] is published in the *Oxford Magazine* for this date.

15 February 1934 *The Adventures of Tom Bombadil* [121] is published in the *Oxford Magazine* for this date.

By 9 December 1934 Lends *The Fall of Arthur* [140] to R.W. Chambers.

c. 1935 Writes and revises *The Wanderers* [142].

After 26 June 1935 Writes *When Little Louis Came to Stay* [143].

?November 1935 or later Revises *Mythopoeia* [136].

?1936 Writes *The Shadow Man* [147] and *Noel* [148].

?1936 or ?1937 Writes *Monað Modes Lust mid Mereflode* [144], *Ilu Ilúvatar en Káre Eldain a Firimoin* [145], and *King Sheave* [146] as part of *The Lost Road.* Revises *The Nameless Land* [74] as *Ælfwine's Song Calling upon Eärendel* and *The Song of Ælfwinë (on Seeing the Uprising of Eärendel)*, and *The Dragon's Visit* [107].

1936 Thirteen poems by Tolkien [76–85, 97–99] are published in *Songs for the Philologists*, without permission, and with many editorial alterations and typographical errors. *The Shadow Man* [147] and *Noel* [148] are published in the *'Annual' of Our Lady's School, Abingdon* for this year.

?Early 1936 Asked to produce a revised edition of John R. Clark Hall's *Beowulf and the Finnesburg Fragment*, Tolkien comes into contact with Susan Dagnall of the book's publisher, George Allen & Unwin. Dagnall reads *The Hobbit* in its circulating typescript and urges Tolkien to publish it. If Humphrey Carpenter's account in *Biography* is correct, Tolkien now writes the final chapters of *The Hobbit*, including its final poems [112–115].

By summer 1936 Offers his translation of *Pearl* [90] to the publisher J.M. Dent.

August 1936 *Pearl* [90] is read on the BBC's London region radio.

October 1936 Submits a complete typescript of *The Hobbit* to George Allen & Unwin.

25 November 1936 Delivers his lecture *Beowulf: The Monsters and the Critics* to the British Academy, emphasizing the work as poetry. It will be published on 1 July 1937.

?1937 Revises *Knocking at the Door* [94].

1937 Revises *Kortirion among the Trees* [40].

4 February 1937 *The Dragon's Visit* [107] is published in the *Oxford Magazine* for this date.

18 February 1937 *Knocking at the Door* [94] is published in the *Oxford Magazine* for this date.

Late February 1937 Revises *Down the Swift Dark Stream You Go* [111] while reading proof of *The Hobbit.*

4 March 1937 *Iumonna Gold Galdre Bewunden* [69] is published in the *Oxford Magazine* for this date.

August 1937 Works on *The Fall of Arthur* [140], but leaves it incomplete.

21 September 1937 *The Hobbit* is published. Its success will lead George Allen & Unwin to request a sequel.

December 1937 Begins to write *The Lord of the Rings*, a task which will occupy him on and off until its publication in 1954–5. In the process, he will return to earlier text to make revisions even while writing later portions of the story.

Between ?late February and 4 March 1938 In *The Lord of the Rings*, writes *The Road Goes Ever On and On* (bk. I, ch. 3 version) [115]. Writes *Upon the Hearth the Fire Is Red* [150]; revisions follow. Writes early versions of *Snow-White! Snow-White! O Lady Clear!* [151]; further versions follow. Writes *O Water Warm and Water Hot!* [152].

3 August 1938 At the Summer Diversions in Oxford, recites from memory, and in character as a fourteenth-century poet, Chaucer's 'Nun's Priest's Tale' from the *Canterbury Tales*.

End of August 1938 In *The Lord of the Rings*, writes *Hey! Come Merry Dol* [154] and *Hop Along, My Little Friends* [154]; revisions follow. Writes the Barrow-wight's chant [155], revised as *Cold Be Hand and Heart and Bone*. Probably at this time, writes *Get Out, You Old Wight!* [155].

First half of September 1938 In *The Lord of the Rings*, revises *The Root of the Boot* [83] as Bingo's song at Bree, but rejects that and revises for the purpose *The Cat and the Fiddle, Being A Nursery Rhyme*

Undone and Its Scandalous Secret Unlocked [60] as *They Say There's a Little Crooked Inn*. Revises *As Light as Leaf on Lindentree* [64] as Trotter/Aragorn's tale of Tinúviel.

Between ?late September and ?early October 1938 In *The Lord of the Rings*, writes *The Road Goes Ever On and On* (bk. I, ch. 1 version) [115]. Writes versions of the Ring verse, ultimately *Three Rings for the Elven-kings under the Sky* [149]. Writes *Sing Hey! for the Bath at Close of Day* [152]; revisions follow. Writes *Farewell We Call to Hearth and Hall* [153]; revisions follow. Revises *Hey! Come Merry Dol* [154]. Revises *The Tale of Tinúviel* [64].

Between ?mid-October and December 1938 In *The Lord of the Rings*, writes *Elbereth Gilthoniel sir evrin pennar oriel* [151].

By 25 December 1938 Writes *Rhyme* [172] as his annual letter from 'Father Christmas', now addressed specifically to Priscilla.

28 July 1939 At the Summer Diversions in Oxford, recites Chaucer's 'Reeve's Tale' in character as Chaucer.

?Summer 1939 Tolkien's version of Chaucer's *Reeve's Tale*, in Middle English verse prepared for recitation, is published.

Between August and autumn 1939 In *The Lord of the Rings*, revises *They Say There's a Little Crooked Inn* [60] as *There Is an Inn, a Merry Old Inn*, now Frodo's song at Bree. Writes and revises *All That Is Gold Does Not Glitter* [156] in Gandalf's letter to Frodo at Bree. Writes and revises *Gil-galad Was an Elven King* [157]. Revises *The Tale of Tinúviel* [64]. Further revises *The Root of the Boot* [83], now as Sam's song in the trolls' wood (*The Stone Troll*); more revisions follow. Adapts *Errantry* [128] as Bilbo's song at Rivendell; many revisions follow. Writes *Seek for the Sword that Was Broken* [156].

3 September 1939 Britain declares war, following Germany's attack on Poland two days earlier. Tolkien will serve as an Air Raid Warden in Oxford, and will shoulder more academic and administrative duties while younger dons are in war service.

4 September 1939 Charles Williams moves to Oxford with the staff of the London offices of Oxford University Press.

?1940 Revises *The Happy Mariners* [33].

16 July 1940 Tolkien's *Prefatory Remarks on Prose Translation of 'Beowulf'* in John R. Clark Hall's *Beowulf and the Finnesburg Fragment* is published, including a portion of his alliterative verse translation of *Beowulf* [88] with further polish.

Between late August 1940 and ?autumn 1941 In *The Lord of the Rings*, further revises Bilbo's song at Rivendell [128]. Writes *A Elbereth Gilthoniel* (bk. II, ch. 1) [151], replacing *Elbereth Gilthoniel sir evrin pennar oriel*. Writes *When Winter First Begins to Bite* [158].

Writes *I Sit beside the Fire* [158]; revisions follow. Writes Gimli's song of Durin, ultimately *The World Was Young, the Mountains Green* [159]; revisions follow. Writes Legolas's song of Nimrodel, ultimately *An Elven-maid There Was of Old* [160]; revisions follow. Writes *When Evening in the Shire Was Grey* [163].

Late 1941 Revises *Aotrou and Itroun* [116]. Writes Galadriel's song of farewell, ultimately *I Sang of Leaves* [161], and her lament, ultimately *Ai! Laurië Lantar Lassi Súrinen* [162], also known as *Namárië*; revisions follow for both.

Between ?December 1941 and ?January 1942 In *The Lord of the Rings*, writes the lament for Boromir [163], ultimately *Through Rohan over Fen and Field*; revisions follow. Writes Treebeard's song of his journeying, ultimately *In the Willow-Meads of Tasarinan* [164]; revisions follow. Writes Treebeard's song of the Ent and the Entwife, ultimately *When Spring Unfolds the Beechen Leaf* [165]; revisions follow. Writes *O Orofarnë* [165].

Between ?February and ?midsummer 1942 In *The Lord of the Rings*, writes first thoughts for *Where Now the Horse and the Rider?* [166]; revisions follow. Writes *Elfstone, Elfstone, Bearer of My Green Stone* [168], revised as *Where Now Are the Dúnedain, Elessar, Elessar?*

By August 1942 Lends his translation of *Pearl* [90] to Basil Blackwell. Blackwell will have it in hand for many years, even setting it in type, but relinquish the rights when Allen & Unwin agree to publish it with Tolkien's translation of *Sir Gawain and the Green Knight* [70].

1943 or 1944 Prepares edition of *Sir Orfeo* for military cadets at Oxford; this will be typed by the Oxford Copying Office in 1944. Probably at the same time, Tolkien makes a translation of the Middle English poem [173]. From the start of 1943 until the end of the programme in 1945, Tolkien served as lecturer and administrator for series of courses offered at Oxford to Navy and Air Force cadets.

Late 1943 Writes *A Closed Letter to Andrea Charicoryides, etc.* [174].

By 30 April 1944 In *The Lord of the Rings*, writes and revises *Grey as a Mouse* (*Oliphaunt*) [167].

c. 13 December 1944 In *The Lord of the Rings*, continues to revise Bilbo's song at Rivendell [128]; further revisions follow.

c. 1945 Revises *As Two Fair Trees* [23].

?1945 or ?1946 (or c. 1955) Revises *The Song of Ælfwine* [74].

15 May 1945 Charles Williams dies.

June 1945 *The Lay of Aotrou and Itroun* [116] is published in the *Welsh Review* for this month.

15 August 1945 Second World War ends.

Between the end of 1945 and mid-1946 In *The Notion Club Papers*, writes *The Ballad of St. Brendan's Death* [175] and revises it as *The Death of St. Brendan*; further revisions follow. Also in *The Notion Club Papers*, revises *Monað Modes Lust mid Mereflode* [144] and *King Sheave* [146].

10 October 1945 Takes up the Merton Professorship of English Language and Literature at Oxford.

Between *c.* 23 September 1946 and ?October 1947 In *The Lord of the Rings*, writes Aragorn's prophecy in several versions, ultimately *Over the Land There Lies a Long Shadow* [168]. Writes and revises *From Dark Dunharrow in the Dim Morning* [169]. Writes *Arise, Arise, Riders of Théoden* [169]. Writes the poem that becomes *We Heard of the Horns in the Hills Ringing* [170]; revisions follow. Writes *Out of Doubt, Out of Dark, to the Day's Rising* (bk. V, ch. 5) [170], *Mourn Not Overmuch!* [170], and *Faithful Servant Yet Master's Bane* [170].

By 30 September 1946 Revises *Iumonna Gold Galdre Bewunden* [69] as *The Hoard.*

30 September 1946 Sends *The Hoard* [69], *The Bumpus* [105], *The Dragon's Visit* [107], *The Lay of Aotrou and Itroun* [116], *The Adventures of Tom Bombadil* [121], *Errantry* [128], and one of his 'Man in the Moon' poems, probably *Why the Man in the Moon Came Down Too Soon* [24], to George Allen & Unwin for possible publication with his story *Farmer Giles of Ham* (published without other work by Tolkien in 1949).

By January 1947 Lends his translation of *Sir Gawain and the Green Knight* [70] to his friend Gwyn Jones.

Between 14 August and 14 September 1948 In *The Lord of the Rings*, writes *I Sit upon the Stones Alone* [171] and revises it as *In Western Lands beneath the Sun*. Writes *Out of Doubt, Out of Dark, to the Day's Rising* (bk. VI, ch. 6) [170]. Writes variants of *The Road Goes Ever On and On* (bk. VI, ch. 6) [115], part of *Upon the Hearth the Fire Is Red* (bk. VI, ch. 9) [150], and *A! Elbereth Gilthoniel!* (bk. VI, ch. 9) [151].

***c.* 1949 or 1950** Returns to the *Lay of Leithian* [92], creating a new incarnation.

October 1949 Completes initial writing of *The Lord of the Rings*.

20 October 1949 His story *Farmer Giles of Ham* is published.

?1950s or earlier Revises *Lines Composed on an Evening . . .* [75] as *Lines Composed in a Village Inn on an Evening of Extraordinary Liquid Beauty*.

?1950s or later Revises *O! Lady Mother Throned amid the Stars* as *Mother! O Lady Throned beyond the Stars* [51] and *A Rhyme Royal upon Easter Morning* [61].

c. 1950 Revises *The Horns of Ylmir* [13], *The New Lay of the Völsungs* [131], and *The New Lay of Gudrún* [131].

August 1950 Refers to his translation of *Sir Gawain and the Green Knight* [70] as far advanced.

c. 1951 Writes *Be He Foe or Friend, Be He Foul or Clean* [176] as part of the *Annals of Aman*.

Late August 1952 While staying with his friends George and Moira Sayer, privately tape-records selected poems (and some prose passages) from *The Hobbit* as published and *The Lord of the Rings* in manuscript.

Between 30 August and 10 September 1952 Reworks Bilbo's song at Rivendell [128] as *Eärendil Was a Mariner*; revisions follow.

24 October 1952 Is busy producing a contribution to the journal *Essays and Studies*, i.e. *The Homecoming of Beorhtnoth Beorhthelm's Son* [129], due by 2 December.

February or March 1953 Completes his translation of *Sir Gawain and the Green Knight* [70]. Completes a revision of *The Homecoming of Beorhtnoth Beorhthelm's Son* [129], titled thus and with editorial additions.

15 April 1953 Delivers the W.P. Ker Memorial Lecture in the University of Glasgow, on *Sir Gawain and the Green Knight*.

Summer 1953 Revises *Doworst* [139].

1953–6 Lectures on *The Owl and the Nightingale*, and conceivably revisits his translation [89].

October 1953 *The Homecoming of Beorhnoth Beorhthelm's Son* [129] is published in *Essays and Studies 1953*.

December 1953 Tolkien's translation of *Sir Gawain and the Green Knight* [70] is broadcast on the BBC Third Programme (radio) in four parts.

c. 1954 Writes *Scatha the Worm* [177].

?1954 Writes *Wilt Thou Learn the Lore* [178].

29 July 1954 *The Fellowship of the Ring*, the first volume of *The Lord of the Rings*, is published.

11 November 1954 *The Two Towers*, the second volume of *The Lord of the Rings*, is published.

3 December 1954 *The Homecoming of Beorhtnoth Beorhthelm's Son* [129], adapted for small cast, is broadcast on the BBC Third Programme. The recording will be broadcast again in June 1955.

c. 1955 Revises *The Song of Ælfwinë (on Seeing the Uprising of Eärendel)* as *The Song of Ælfwine on Seeing the Uprising of Earendel* [74]; further revisions follow. Revises *Shadowland* [93].

?1955 Revises *The Death of St. Brendan* [175] as *Imram.*

20 October 1955 *The Return of the King*, the third volume of *The Lord of the Rings*, is published.

3 December 1955 *Imram* is published in *Time and Tide* for this date.

?1956 Writes *Cat* [179], *You Walk on Grass* [180], and *The Wind So Whirled a Weathercock* [181].

?March 1958 For a 'Hobbit' dinner with fans of *The Lord of the Rings* to be held in Rotterdam, Tolkien prepares brief remarks, including a poem in Quenya and English, developed in three drafts.

28 March 1958 Reads his speech in Rotterdam, with the final poem *Loä Yukainen avar Anduinë Sí Valútier*, or *Twenty Years Have Flowed Away* [182].

c. 1959 Writes *To the University of Oxford* [183].

June 1959 Retires from the Merton Professorship.

5 June 1959 Delivers his *Valedictory Address* in Oxford.

1960 Writes *Gardeners' Secrets* and revises it as *Utch! A Gardener's Secrets* [184].

1961 or 1962 Writes and revises *The Complaint of Mîm the Dwarf* [185].

First half of November 1961 Revises *Why the Man in the Moon Came Down Too Soon* as *The Man in the Moon Came Down Too Soon* [24], *The Hoard* [69], *The Bumpus* as *Perry-the-Winkle* [105], *The Dragon's Visit* [107], and *Looney* as *Sea-Bell* (*The Sea-Bell*) [135]

15 November 1961 Sends *The Man in the Moon Came Down Too Soon* [24], *The Hoard* [69], *Perry-the-Winkle* [105], *The Dragon's Visit* [107], *Errantry* [128], and *The Sea-Bell* [135] to George Allen & Unwin as candidates to include in *The Adventures of Tom Bombadil and Other Verses from the Red Book.*

?Late 1961 or ?early 1962 Revises *The Voyage of Earendel* [16] as *Éala! Éarendel Engla Beorhtast!* and *The Cottage of Lost Play: Mar Vanwa Tyaliéva* (or *Mar Vanwa Tyaliéva: The Cottage of Lost Play*) [28] as *The Little House of Lost Play: Mar Vanwa Tyaliéva*. Possibly revises *Vestr um Haf* [127] as *Bilbo's Last Song*; the poem is certainly in final form by October 1968.

Late 1961 or early 1962 Writes *The Fliting of Tom Bombadil* [186] and revises it as (after other titles) *Bombadil Goes Boating*, based on a 'germ' of uncertain (but late) date. Revises *The Princess Ní* [32] as *Princess Mee*, *Kortirion among the Trees* as *The Trees of Kor-*

tirion [40], *Fastitocalon* [95], *The Adventures of Tom Bombadil* [121], *Oilima Markirya* [123], and *The Shadow Man* as *Shadow-Bride* [147]. Possibly revises *The Last Voyage of Éarendel* as *Éala! Éarendel Engla Beorhtast!* [16], and *The Hills Are Old* [100]. Possibly considers *A Rhyme Royal upon Easter Morning* [61] for revision.

5 February 1962 Sends *The Trees of Kortirion* [40], *Knocking at the Door* [94], *Firiel* [141], and *Shadow-Bride* [147] to George Allen & Unwin as candidates to include in *The Adventures of Tom Bombadil and Other Verses from the Red Book*.

After 5 February 1962 Revises *Knocking at the Door* [94] as *The Mewlips*, and *Firiel* [141] as *The Last Ship*.

Michaelmas Term 1962 Teaches *Beowulf* at Oxford while his friend C.L. Wrenn is on sabbatical.

22 November 1962 *The Adventures of Tom Bombadil and Other Verses from the Red Book* is published, including *The Man in the Moon Came Down Too Soon* [24], *Princess Mee* [32], *The Man in the Moon Stayed up Too Late* [60], *The Hoard* [69], *The Stone Troll* [83], *The Mewlips* [94], *Fastitocalon* [95], *Perry-the-Winkle* [105], *The Adventures of Tom Bombadil* [121], *Errantry* [128], *The Sea-Bell* [135], and *The Last Ship* [141], *Shadow-Bride* [147], *Oliphaunt* [167], *Cat* [179], *Bombadil Goes Boating* [186], and part of *The Wind So Whirled a Weathercock* [181].

Hilary Term 1963 Teaches *The Freswæl* (the 'Frisian tragedy' of the fight at Finnesburg as told in *Beowulf* and separately) at Oxford while C.L. Wrenn is on sabbatical.

22 November 1963 C.S. Lewis dies.

December 1963 Writes *Rosalind Ramage* [187].

1964 Writes and revises *Once upon a Time* [48] and *Three Children* [188]. Revises *The Dragon's Visit* [107].

c. 1964 Writes and revises *Where the Riming Rune-Tree Blows* [189].

c. 1964 or 1965 Writes and revises *Though All Things Fail and Come to Naught* [190].

28 May 1964 *Tree and Leaf* (his essay *On Fairy-Stories* and story *Leaf by Niggle*) is published.

Late 1964 Revises *Rosalind Ramage* [187].

March 1965 Composer Donald Swann by now has begun to set songs from *The Lord of the Rings* to music (culminating in 1967 as *The Road Goes Ever On: A Song Cycle*).

October 1965 *Once upon a Time* [48] and *The Dragon's Visit* [107] are published in *Winter's Tales for Children 1*, edited by Caroline Hillier.

1966 Writes and revises *No Longer Fear Champagne* [191].

?1966 Writes and revises *My Heart Is Not in This Land Where I Live* [192], *As You Must Admit* [193], and *'At Last the Time Has Come' He Said* [194].

?1967 Writes *For W.H.A.* [195].

28 April 1967 Tells a former student that he has given up his translation of *The Owl and the Nightingale* [89] 'at present'.

Autumn 1967 The recording *Poems and Songs of Middle Earth* is released.

31 October 1967 *The Road Goes Ever On: A Song Cycle* is published.

9 November 1967 His story *Smith of Wootton Major* is published.

Winter 1967 *For W.H.A.* [194] is published in a special number of the journal *Shenandoah* for this season.

July 1968 Tolkien and Edith move to Poole, Dorset.

29 November 1971 Edith Tolkien dies.

January 1972 Tolkien returns to Oxford.

2 September 1973 Tolkien dies after a brief illness.

The Collected Poems of J.R.R. Tolkien

is dedicated to the memory of

CHRISTOPHER TOLKIEN

whose encouragement and trust
have meant so much to us

· CS & WH ·

FOR "LITTLE ONE":

Lo! morning gilds the skies:
Come, come, my darling rise!
for the blackbird thrills his call
in the silvery poplar tall,
and with passing whisper brief
the breeze has wakened now
each gently sleeping leaf
on every quivering bough.
Lo! the gloomy hush of night
from the Sun has taken flight,
and the mist that did enshroud
the wan ghostly birth of dawn
in the mystery of its cloud
faded from has ~~fled before~~ the morn.
But wake, dear sweet grey eyes:
for, though a song of ~~joy~~ day doth rise
from glad Earth to God above
for me drear night is o'er
only when in joy once more
I clasp thee to me little one
and the day again's begun
in thy morning kiss of love.

——" ——.

R.T.
to
E.B.

I

Morning · *Morning Song* (1910–15)

Morning is the earliest dated poem by Tolkien to survive in his papers, apart from a limerick in a picture-letter dated 1904 (see Appendix I). Its first extant version, transcribed here as A as amended by Tolkien, seems to be that which he wrote in a letter to his beloved, Edith Bratt, on 28 March 1910.

He had met Edith in 1908 when both were lodgers in the home of Mr and Mrs Louis Faulkner, in the Birmingham suburb of Edgbaston. By summer 1909 they were in love. But Tolkien's guardian, Father Francis Morgan of the Birmingham Oratory, was concerned that the boy's relationship would distract him from study; and indeed, in December 1909 Tolkien failed his first attempt to win an Oxford scholarship. In late January 1910, having continued to meet with Edith against his guardian's wishes, he was moved to other lodgings and forbidden to have further contact with her until he came of age in January 1913. He was permitted, however, on Holy Saturday, 26 March 1910, to write a long letter to Edith, who by now had moved to Cheltenham. Two days later, he composed a shorter message, together with the poem *Morning* (then untitled), but did not post it to Edith until April 1913, after they had reunited. He inscribed the verse 'For "Little One"' and 'RT [Ronald Tolkien] to EB'. Writing it 'cheered me up', he said, though it was 'nonsense' and only for Edith, as it 'would not seem nice to anyone else' (Bodleian Library).

[A]

Lo! morning gilds the skies:
Come, come, my darling rise!
for the blackbird thrills his call
in the silvery poplar tall,
and with passing whisper brief
the breeze has wakened now
each gently sleeping leaf
on every quivering bough.
Lo! the gloomy hush of night
from the Sun has taken flight,
and the mist that did enshroud
the wan ghostly birth of dawn
in the mystery of its cloud

has faded from the morn.
But wake, dear sweet grey eyes:
for, though a song of day doth rise
from glad Earth to God above
for me drear night is o'er
only when in joy once more
I clasp thee to me little one
and the day again's begun
in thy morning kiss of love.

'Gilds the skies' suggests the sky becoming golden with the rising of the sun. Compare the 'gilded morning sunlight' in poem no. 7, line 26. In later versions, Tolkien became less colourful ('dawn awakes the skies') and then less exuberant ('dawn goes palely up the skies').

A subsequent manuscript (B, as below before further changes) has the title *Morning*, though the heading is in a different ink than the text proper, and may have been added later. Tolkien inscribed the sheet 'March 1910', but also 'Attempts before Oct. 1911', suggesting that he may have set down the text at or around the later date. On the facing page in the notebook in which he wrote the poem is a dedication, 'To EMB' (Edith Mary Bratt), and a curious note by Tolkien that an earlier version from 1909 was 'sent to EMB' but 'lost'. In an early list of his poems (see Appendix III) he recorded similarly that *Morning* was composed in 1909 and 1910 but lost in 'autumn [1909]', while on a later typescript he dated its origin to '1909 or earlier'. The poem and message in his note to Edith of 28 March 1910 seem, however, to have been composed concurrently. There he said: 'To day I wrote this little poem which you will understand for you have watched the sunrise with me once in a long past happy time' (Bodleian Library).

[B]

Lo, dawn awakes the skies!
Come sleeping one arise,
For our blackbird thrills his call
From his silver poplar tall;
And on every quivering bough
With passing whisper brief
A breeze is waking now
Each gently sleeping leaf.

The dead dim hush of night
The sun has put to flight,

And the mist which did enshroud
In its chill and mystic cloud
The ghostly dawning day
Has faded from the morn.
Come sleeping one arise
And ope thine eyes of grey.

The poem was now more concise and, relative to text A, had many changes. Although in setting it down Tolkien appears not to have had the version of 28 March in hand, he does seem to have had at least one other, intermediary working in memory if not on paper. Near the foot of manuscript B he noted that the final two lines ('Come sleeping one arise | And ope thine eyes of grey') had earlier read 'And from the Earth's bright array | Bursts the Song of Love reborn' – a more developed reading than that given in A.

He made a fair copy of this text with only minor differences of punctuation, also dated 'March 1910' and with the title *Morning* possibly added later, as well as the inscription 'æsp & ósle', Old English 'aspen-tree and blackbird'. The 'poplar tall' with 'quivering bough' of texts A and B is the quaking or common aspen, a species of poplar (*Populus tremula*). Tolkien first made specific mention of an 'aspen' in the body of the poem only when he re-cast it as *Morning-Song* in a new manuscript (C, before further revision), dated 'May 3 1915' (later struck through, but with every appearance of having been added at the time of writing). By this time, the word *ousel* (or *ouzel*) was archaic; earlier (A3, B3) Tolkien preferred *blackbird*, but *ousel* would remain in text D.

[C] Come, dawn goes palely up the skies!
Come, O my sleeping one arise!
Come, heark our ousel thrill a call
Warbling in the poplar tall,
Where slender herald breezes rouse,
Passing, murmuring to the boughs,
The rainy voice of aspen leaves;
And swallows twitter in the eaves
'Come, O my sleeping one arouse'!

The hush and dimness of the night
Grows strange with creeping strands of light,
And all the pale mists, that did enshroud
Coldly in a breathless cloud

The earth that greyly swathéd lies,
Like ghostly smoke along the skies
The coming sun will roll away,
And bid thee ope thine eyes of grey;
And bid thee 'sleeping one arise'.

On this manuscript Tolkien also wrote the Old English word *Morgenléoþ* 'Morningsong' and deleted an earlier title, *Madrigal.* 'Madrigal' would not have been inapt: the word means 'a short lyrical poem of amatory character', especially as would be suitable for setting as a part-song. And it is in this context that one finds similar poems by other writers, such as 'Frühlingsmorgen' ('Spring Morning') by Richard Leander, with its linden-tree tapping on a window and the refrain 'Wake up!' ('Steh' auf!'), set to music by Mahler in his *Lieder und Gesänge*, and the verse beginning 'Hark, hark, the lark in heaven's blue!' in Shakespeare's *Cymbeline*, which bids the 'sweet maid, arise!' Tolkien's most immediate inspiration, however, may have been the hymn 'Laudes Domini' ('Beim frühen Morgenlicht' or 'In the Early Morning Light'), which begins:

When morning gilds the skies,
My heart awaking cries,
    May Jesus Christ be praised.
When evening shadows fall,
This rings my curfew call,
    May Jesus Christ be praised.

Tolkien had a professional typescript made from text C, inscribed it '1910', and revised the poem further. A second professional typescript followed in mid- to late May 1915, with the title now *Morning Song* (without a hyphen); to a carbon copy only, leaving the ribbon copy untouched, Tolkien made two small alterations. These were carried into a fifth manuscript and final text, transcribed here as D.

[D]

Come, dawn goes palely up the skies!
O! come from shadowed sleep arise
For, hark, our ousel thrills a call
Warbling in the poplar tall,
Where slender herald breezes rouse,
Passing, murmuring to the boughs,

The rainy voice of aspen leaves;
And swallows twitter in the eaves
'Come from thy silver dreams arise!'

The hush and dimness of the night
Grows strange with creeping strands of light,
And those pale mists that did enshroud
Coldly in a breathless cloud
The earth that greyly swathéd lies,
Like ghostly smoke along the skies
The coming sun will roll away,
And bid thee ope thine eyes of grey;
And from thy golden dreaming rise!'

With expanded text C, Tolkien introduced a slightly altered rhyme pattern: AABBCCDDC for each stanza. This scheme continued in the final version, except that D9 rhymes A rather than C.

By the time he recast *Morning* in May 1915 Tolkien was engaged to Edith and more experienced as a poet, having written much in the intervening years while an Oxford undergraduate. Relative to text B, version C (and thus D) has more sophisticated imagery and vocabulary ('The dead dim hush of night | The sun has put to flight' > 'The hush and dimness of the night | Grows strange with creeping strands of light'). Now also more confident in the quality of his poems, Tolkien had engaged the Oxford Copying Office (William Hunt, 18 Broad Street) to make typescripts of selected works – including the penultimate version of *Morning Song* – which by late 1915 he hoped to publish.

A14: 'Faded from the morn' originally read 'fled before the morn'. The handwriting of the alteration appears to be later than that of the main text, perhaps from 1913, when the letter was sent to Edith at last, rather than 1910.

B12: Tolkien marked 'mystic' to be changed to 'breathless'. He also considered the adjectives 'trailing' and 'pallid'.

B13: Tolkien marked this line to be changed to 'The ghostly dawning day'.

B14: Tolkien marked 'morn' to be changed to 'skies'.

C5: For 'slender herald' Tolkien also considered 'restless wingéd', 'half-awakened', and 'slender fingered'.

C12: For 'And all the mists' Tolkien also considered 'The mists of sleep', and for 'that did enshroud' he considered 'yet still enshroud'.

C13: For this line Tolkien also considered 'Clinging in a ghostly cloud'.

2

The Dale-Lands (1910–14)

The Dale-Lands is inscribed 'May 1910' in the earliest of its four manuscripts. But as the text of this version (A) appears on a sheet below the deleted words 'Also in June and July 1910 "A Fragment of an Epic" herein infixed' (i.e. inserted; see poem no. 7), it may be that Tolkien composed the work in May 1910 but did not write it out until later, perhaps as a fair copy of a still earlier working. Two other manuscripts of the poem are likewise inscribed 'May 1910'. On manuscript A Tolkien first called the poem *Spring*, but changed its title to *Deep in the Vales* and then to *The Dale-Lands*. In a later text he also considered, but did not adopt, the title *Valley-Lands*. A variation, *The Dale Lands*, appears on yet another of the manuscripts.

[A]

Deep in the vale where the bluebells ring
neath the young gay trees that heavenward spring;
down in the dale where the marsh-gold spreads
mid the long lush grasses' waving heads;
steep'd in the warmth and lull'd by the hum
of the winged workers that go and come;
whither only the drowsiest breezes fare
mid the steamy scents of summer air,
there are the beds and the leaf-veil'd bowers
whereon to dream the flitting hours.

The *marsh-gold* (or *marshgold*) is the marsh marigold, *Caltha palustris*, a showy yellow flower in northern wetlands. The 'winged workers' are bees.

Following this text, Tolkien noted that he revised lines 3 and 4 at the time of writing to 'down in the dale, where the emerald spreads | Round the prouder grasses with flaunting heads'. 'Emerald' presumably refers to low grass or vegetation, distinct from the 'prouder [i.e. taller] grasses'. At some early moment he also altered the final line of the poem to read 'whereon odorous dreams enchant the hours'. Another note on this sheet, dated 18 May 1914, records that Tolkien added a couplet after line 4: 'Buckled with marsh gold brave their shoon, | And they nod to the eye of the daisy-moon'. This change was carried into a new manuscript, with minor differences of punctuation, headed 'Recast 1914'. Two other manuscripts largely follow the same revised text, but with the heading 'On néolum dalum', Old English 'In deep dales'.

The final version is a professional typescript, inscribed by Tolkien in a later hand (and from uncertain memory) '1907?' but is similar to others made from his poems in March 1915. We give its text as B.

[B]

Deep in the vale where the bluebells ring
'Neath the young gay trees that heavenward spring;
Down in the dale where the emerald spreads
Round the prouder grasses flaunting heads: —
Buckled with marshgold brave their shoon,
And they nod to the eye of the daisy moon: —
Steeped in the warmth and lulled by the hum
Of the wingéd workers that go and come;
Whither only the drowsiest breezes fare
Mid the steamy scents of summer air, —
There are the beds and the leaf-veiled bowers
Whereon odorous dreams enchant the hours.

With lines 5–6 in B, and with other revisions, Tolkien made the poem impressionistic compared with the more straightforward version A. *Buckled* is used presumably in the sense of 'girded', and *brave* as 'splendid, showy' (compare *braw*). *Shoon* as the obsolete form of 'shine' seems more likely than *shoon* as the archaic plural of 'shoes' (e.g. 'The Man in the Moon had silver shoon' in *The Man in the Moon Came Down Too Soon*, see poem no. 24). The marsh marigold grows to one to two feet in height, not like a (low) 'shoe' in relation to the 'daisy-moon' (or moon daisy, the ox-eye daisy, *Leucanthemum vulgare*) at one to three feet.

In his poetry Tolkien used a wide variety of words to refer to a hollow or depression in the ground: *vale* and *dale* as here, also *dell*, *dingle*, and *hollow*. Concise dictionaries unhelpfully cross-define these: a dale is a valley or hollow, a vale is a dale or valley, and so on. But even the full *Oxford English Dictionary* struggles, defining *vale* as 'a dale or valley, especially one which is comparatively wide and flat'; *dale* as a valley or hollow, noting that the word is used especially in northern England; *dell* as 'a deep natural hollow or vale of no great extent, the sides usually clothed with trees or foliage'; and *dingle* as a deep dell or hollow, or a deep narrow cleft between hills, noting its use in Yorkshire dialect. *Valley* and *hollow* are more general terms, respectively suggesting larger and smaller natural features. For the purposes of Tolkien's poems, one does not need to pay attention to strict definitions of these words, but may take them to mean roughly the same and suppose that they were chosen for aesthetic effect or for the sake of rhyme.

B4: Tolkien considered whether to change 'flaunting' to 'tossing'.

3

Evening · Completorium (1910–15)

Tolkien inscribed the date of composition 'June 1910' on the earliest of five manuscripts of *Evening*, as the poem was first called; we give this version below as A. On two later manuscripts, however, he indicated that he wrote the poem originally in March 1910 (compare the date of *Morning*, poem no. 1), before rewriting it on 22 April 1915. For the purpose of ordering the poems in this book, we have accepted the date on the first manuscript of *Evening*, which Tolkien appears to have written contemporary with the text, as closer to the original composition of the poem, while the March 1910 dates on other manuscripts were inscribed apparently five years later.

[A]

Daylong strife is o'er at last
    And the toiling yearning tears
    As of hopeless lonely years
Fade and vanish in the past.
Lo! the clouds that once did lower
    Glooming o'er the purer skies
    Now with wondrous glowing dyes
Drape the sun's far evening bower;
And no more a chant does thrill
    Upward from life's war below,
    But a hymn with half-heard flow
Deeply swells; and sweet and still
Sinks a peace too great to bear,
    And a joy beyond all life
    Lulling all the lust of strife
Bathes the burning brow of care:
And 'tis evening come at last,
    And though other pains will grieve
    Glad the morrow's ill we leave
Unto God; for day is past.

A very different and slightly longer version of the poem, given here as B, is inscribed 'April 1915' and 'To EMB' (Edith Mary Bratt).

[B]

The dusty war of day is past;
  Its uncompanioned lonely fears
  Of yearning toil and hopeless tears
Grow mellow as they fade at last.
The vapour that despondent lowers
  Cloudbarred over purer skies
  Does now in Evening's memory rise
To burning heights and golden towers.
No more tumultuous war songs thrill
  From Life's embattled heat below,
  But a mighty hymn with half-heard flow
Deeply swells; and sweet and still
An organ peals too great to bear
  In mighty music deep compound
  Of all transformèd human sound
Distilled in slender doméd air;
Till Even droops her limpid hands
  And cool with laving dew allay
  The fevered eyelids of the day
Or smooth a lingering silver bands
Of fading sunset hair away.

Text B includes a few alterations in the course of writing, notably a reversal in line 16 of 'doméd slender' to 'slender doméd', as well as alternate readings written in the margins which would come into later versions. Some of these readings also appear as marginalia in a third manuscript, again with the title *Evening*, and inscribed 'March 1910 rewritten April 22 1915'. Tolkien developed this in turn in yet a fourth manuscript, with the title *Evening* changed (probably at some later date) to *Completorium*, the Latin name for the last service of the day in Catholic ritual, more often known as Compline; this text also is inscribed 'March 1910 | Rewritten Ap[ril] 22 1915', but Tolkien struck through the earlier date and 'Rewritten', and ultimately the entire page.

The final manuscript of the poem, with further revisions, is dated 'May 2', indicating that Tolkien wrote it not long after the penultimate version of April 1915. We give this text as C. Again, the title *Evening* was altered at some point to *Completorium*. The same text, and title change, also appears in a typescript later dated '1915'. Tolkien added the word 'far' at the start of line 16 in both the final manuscript and the typescript.

[C]

The dusty afternoon is past
 By all the gathered unshed tears
 Of all the day, as Even nears,
Grown mellow, till it fade at last.
The vapour that despondent lowers
 In cloudy bars o'er purer skies
 Does now in Evening's memory rise
To burning heights and golden towers.
No more tumultuous war-songs smoke
 From Life's embattled heated maze,
 But all the long white homing ways
Are murmurous with many folk,
Whose mingled voices blending bear
 A mighty music deep, compound
 Of all transforméd human sound
Far up the slender doméd air:
Then Even droops her limpid hands
 That, cool with dewy sleep, allay
 The fevered eyelids of the day,
And smooth the lingering silver bands
Of fading sunset hair away.

Text A consistently follows the rhyme scheme ABBA, but the final five lines of later versions (with twenty-one lines) are rhymed ABBAB. The revised versions incorporate much of the imagery of text A but express it differently. Every line is reworked, and the whole suggests a more positive outlook despite the war and strife Tolkien had described metaphorically in 1910 having become real, in the Great War, by 1915. By then, he was engaged to Edith and able to visit her in Warwick, where she was living with her cousin Jennie Grove.

B17: 'Even', i.e. Evening.

B20: The article 'a', despite plural 'bands', appeared in two versions before being changed to 'the'.

C6: In the sequence of manuscripts preceding C, this line progressed: 'Cloudbarred over purer skies' (text B) > 'Cloud-barred over purer skies' > 'In cloudy bars o'er purer skies'.

4

Wood-Sunshine (1910–14)

Tolkien wrote the earliest manuscript of *Wood-Sunshine*, transcribed here as A, on one page together with *The Sirens Feast* (later *The Sirens*, see poem no. 5), but later struck it through. He dated it 'July 1910' apparently at the time of composition.

[A] Come sing ye light fairy things tripping so gay,
Like visions like glinting reflections of joy
All fashion'd of radiance careless of grief,
O'er this green and brown carpet; nor hasten away
Neath the gold and green arras of sun-broider'd leaf.
And ye that do work in the forest's employ
For the weaving of leafage and framing of bough
Or in cleansing the morn from the soiling of night
And that labouring rustle down dell and o'er howe
Till when ye with eventide's reddening light
Faint-whispering pensive by rivulet brood
And drooping in slumber do dream in some glade,
O! come to me! Dance for me! Sprites of the wood,
O! Come to me! Sing to me once ere ye fade!

Probably not long after writing text A, Tolkien made a second, revised, but untitled manuscript of the work (B), but struck this through as well.

[B] Come! sing ye light fairy things tripping so gay,
all fashioned of radiance careless of grief,
o'er this magical carpet: nor hasten away
neath the gold and green arras of sun-broidered leaf,
like visions like glinting reflections of joy:
And ye that do work in the forest's employ
for the weaving of leafage and building of bole,
and when cleansed in the morn from the fingers of night
go with labouring rustle o'er dell and o'er knoll
Till when ye with eventide's reddening light
faint whispering pensive by rivulet brood
and drooping in slumber bring dreams of the wood —

O come to me! dance for me! sprites of the glade
O Come to me! sing to me once ere ye fade.

Two later manuscripts are marked as 'recast'; one, written on the same sheet as a revision of *The Dale-Lands* (poem no. 2), is dated only to the year 1914, the other to 11 May 1914. These differ from text B primarily in a few word changes – 'tripping' in line 1 giving way to 'lilting', and 'sprites' in line 13 to 'fays' and then to 'elves' – and in the reordering of lines. Yet another manuscript, inscribed 'July 1910' (later, and struck through), has an added title, *Wood-Elves Dance*, in Modern English and the equivalent in Old English, 'Wealdielfa geláe'. Each of these three manuscripts is textually identical to the others except for minor differences of punctuation.

A few further changes of punctuation occur in the typescript given here as C; otherwise, this follows from the 'recast' manuscripts. The typescript was made almost certainly in early 1915, as Christopher Wiseman saw it that April (see below). On this Tolkien wrote, in a later hand, its date of original composition as '1908 or earlier'.

[C] Come, sing ye light fairy things lilting so gay
On this magical carpet; nor hasten away
All fashioned of radiance, careless of grief
Like visions, like glinting reflections of joy
'Neath the sun-broidered arras of green and gold leaf:
And ye that do work in the forest's employ
For the weaving of leafage and building of bole;
That in cleansing the morn from the fingers of night
Go with labouring rustle down dell and o'er knoll,
Till when ye with eventide's reddening light
Faint-whispering pensive by rivulet brood,
And drooping in slumber bring dreams to the wood —
O! come to me! sing to me! elves of the glade,
O! come to me! dance to me! once ere ye fade.

In his biography of Tolkien, Humphrey Carpenter quotes the first four and final two lines of *Wood-Sunshine*, misleadingly as if they were consecutive. He comments that 'fairy sprites dancing on a woodland carpet seem a strange choice for a rugger-playing youth of eighteen who had a strong taste for Grendel [in *Beowulf*] and the dragon Fafnir [in the story of Sigurd]' (*Biography*, p. 47), and suggests that Tolkien was influenced by J.M. Barrie's play *Peter Pan*, which he saw performed in Birmingham in April 1910 and which culminates famously with a plea to the audience to believe in fairies. Carpenter also finds in *Wood-Sunshine* 'a distinct resemblance to an episode in the first part of [Francis] Thompson's "Sister Songs"' (p. 48). In Thompson's work the speaker hears 'a dainty dubious sound, | As of goodly melody' and spies 'elfin swarms' among the flowers; Thompson describes their dancing and music at some length. 'It may be', Carpenter writes, 'that this was the source of Tolkien's interest in such things' (p. 48). If so, Tolkien must have known Francis Thompson's poetry by 1910; but we can be sure only that he bought a copy of Thompson's *Works* on its publication in 1913–14 and delivered a talk about Thompson to the Exeter College Essay Club in Oxford on 4 March 1914.

In his *Tolkien and the Great War* John Garth repeats the thought that *Wood-Sunshine*, like *Sister Songs*, 'dealt with a sylvan vision of fairies' (p. 14). And yet, English literature and English culture have a long 'fairy' tradition, such that Tolkien need not have been influenced by Thompson's work in particular. Garth also perceives that the fairies of Tolkien's poem 'may have been nothing more, on one level, than wood-sunshine itself: the imaginative embodiment of light dappling the leaves on tree-branch and forest floor' (p. 36). We would add that the poem is indeed as much, or more, about nature as it is about wood-sprites.

Probably in April 1915, Tolkien sent some of his poems to Christopher Wiseman. His friend was inspired to set *Wood-Sunshine* to music, but thought at first that it was about night-time, when 'weaving of leafage and building of bole' are conducted in the best fairy-stories. On 25 April 1915 Wiseman remarked in a letter that among the poems Tolkien sent to him he liked *Wood-Sunshine* second-best (see further, *As Two Fair Trees*, poem no. 23).

A4: A note in the margin, referenced to 'green and brown', reads 'magic-' followed by what appears to be 'inspired'.

A8: Tolkien amended 'cleaning' to 'cleansing'. He also marked 'soiling' to be changed to 'soil' followed by another short word we cannot make out.

A9: In this line, added in the course of writing, Tolkien first wrote 'knowe' (a northern English or Scottish form of *knoll* 'hillock', cf. C9), but changed it to 'howe' (another word for 'small hill'), the better to rhyme with 'bough'.

5

The Sirens Feast · *The Sirens* (1910–?14)

Tolkien wrote the first of two manuscripts of this poem on the same page as the first version of *Wood-Sunshine* (no. 4). The date 'July 1910' is inscribed at the top (next to the title for *Wood-Sunshine*), and the title '*The Sirens Feast*' appears in the margin next to the second poem. Given here as A, the latter text includes minor changes made by Tolkien in the course of writing.

[A] Clawed by the frothy fingers of the hungry deeps,
  That moan'd in restless agony around,
Stood darkly once, its cruel and unrelenting steeps
  Tower'd high, an isle by no man living found.
While but the weary wailing of some circling gulls
  Echoed the seething surge's wind-flung cry,
As it gnawed and tore the noisome weed-swathed hulls
  Of long forgotten ships now rotting nigh,
Still faint upon the sigh of heaven's labouring breath
  Was raised anon a pale alluring song
Most sweet, but shuddering hollow as a cry of death
  And laden with horror of o'erhanging wrong.
'Twas the Sirens, as the stricken Sun gan weary sink
  Who summon'd from the shivering depths below
Dim Dread and Shapeless Fear that night with them to drink,
  And taste th' unhallowed feast of nameless woe.

The second manuscript too bears the date July 1910, with the note '(pract[ically] unaltered)', that is, little altered from text A, though there are a few further workings, included below in the final text (B). This sheet is also inscribed 'Before untitled', which could mean that manuscript A was given its title only later, not at the time of writing. Here Tolkien wrote the title in shorter form as *The Sirens*, but also 'Meremenna Symbel', 'The Sirens Feast' in Old English. There is no indication in his papers when he revised the poem, but it seems possible that he did so in May 1914, when he revised (and dated manuscripts of) *The Dale-Lands* (no. 2) and *Wood-Sunshine*.

[B] Clawed by the frothy fingers of the hungry deep
That moaned in restless agony around
Stood darkly once, its cruel and unrelenting steep
Towered high, an isle by no man living found.
Only the weary wailing of some circling gulls
Echoed the seething surge's wind-flung cry,
As it gnawed and tore the weed-swathed noisome hulls
Of long-forgotten ships now rotting nigh,
When faint upon the sigh of heaven's labouring breath
Was raised aloft a pale alluring song
Most sweet, that shuddered hollow, as a cry of death.
The air grew loaden with o'erhanging wrong:
The Sirens as the stricken Sun would weary sink
Did summon from the shivering depths below
Horror and Shapeless Fear that night with them to drink
And taste the unhallowed feast of nameless woe.

In Greek mythology Sirens used music to lure sailors to shipwreck and death on rocky coasts. They were not mermaids, but generally depicted as women combined with birds. In later popular image they are sometimes shown with fish tails, and are at least connected with the sea (Old English *mere*).

A13: *Gan* is an obsolete form of *gone*, cf. Old English *gān* 'to go'. Compare 'would' in B13.

6

The Battle of the Eastern Field (1911)

Tolkien's first published poem, *The Battle of the Eastern Field*, appeared on pp. 22–6 in the March 1911 number of the *King Edward's School Chronicle*, the magazine of the school Tolkien attended in Birmingham (with interruptions) from 1900 to 1911. We give the text below as printed, including 'omitted' portions marked with lines of asterisks. No preliminary workings appear to have survived. At the date of publication, and probably of composition, Tolkien was nineteen. He was in the First (upper) Class at King Edward's School, and through activities such as the Debating Society had demonstrated a skill with words and a ready wit. Among his friends he was sometimes called 'Gabriel', or 'Gab' for short – hence, we suppose, the 'author's notes' signed 'G.A.B.' within *The Battle of the Eastern Field*. The poem is otherwise not signed, but in Tolkien's papers there is a marked and further amended copy of the printed work, with his manuscript initials 'JRRT'.

We have described Tolkien's annotations on his marked copy in line-specific notes at the end of the entry. Our line numbering below does not include fully 'deleted' lines or sections (i.e. except for line 87), or interjections by 'G.A.B.' The varying use of square and rounded brackets reflects the original.

[On Friday March 31st I came across this curious fragment in the waste paper basket, in the Prefects' room. Much of it was so blotted that I could not decipher it. I publish it with emendations of my own. G.A.B.]

I

Ho, rattles sound your warnote!
Ho, trumpets loudly bray!
The clans will strive and gory writhe
Upon the field to-day.
To-day the walls and blackboards
Are hung with flaunting script,
From Atlas on the staircase
To Bogey's darkling crypt.

Each knight is robed in scarlet,
Or clad in olive green;
A gallant crest upon each breast
Is proudly heaving seen.
While flows our Yellow River,
While stands the great Pavil,
That Thursday in the Lenten Term
Shall be a beanfeast still.

II

Thus spake the Green-clad Chieftain
To the foe in Scarlet dight,
'Shall no one wrest the silver grail
'Nor dare another fight!'
And the doughty foeman answer'd —
'Ay, the goblet shall be won,
'And on a famous field of war
'Great deeds of prowess done!'
So hard by Brum's great river
They bade the hosts to meet,
Array'd upon the Eastern Field
For victory or defeat.

III

Now greyly dawns that fatal day
Upon the Eastern Field,
That Thursday in the Lenten Term
With honour ever sealed.

*　　*　　*　　*　　(!! G.A.B.)

Nor without secret trouble
Does the bravest mark his foes,
For girt by many a vassal bold
Each mighty leader shows.
Around the Green-clad Chieftain
Stands many a haughty lord,
From Edgbastonia's ancient homes,
From Mosli's emerald sward;
Towers Ericillus of the sands;
Glowers Falco of the Bridge.

But noblest stands that Chiefest Lord
From the Fountain's lofty ridge.
Among the blood-red ranks were seen
'Midst many an honour'd name
Great Sekhet and those brethren
The Corcii of fame.

IV

Now straight the shrill call sounded
That heralds in the fray,
And loud was heard the clamour
Of the watchers far away.

*   *   *   (bother ! ! ! G.A.B.)

Swiftly rushed out that Chiefest Lord,
And fiercely onward sped,
His corslet girt about his waist,
His close helm on his head.
Now round in thickest throng there pressed
These warriors red and green,
And many a dashing charge was made,
And many a brave deed seen.
Full oft a speeding foeman
Was hurtled to the ground,
While forward and now backward,
Did the ball of fortune bound:
Till Sekhet mark'd the slaughter,
And toss'd his flaxen crest
And towards the Green-clad Chieftain
Through the carnage pressed;
Who fiercely flung by Sekhet,
Lay low upon the ground,
Till thick wall of liegemen
Encompassed him around.
His clients from the battle
Bare him some little space,
And gently rubbed his wounded knee,
And scanned his pallid face.

*   *   *   *

(The rest of this touching scene and most of the remainder of the battle are blotted out. I had'nt [*sic*] time to put in any of my own. G.A.B.)

XIII

*   *   *   *

. . . meanwhile in the centre
Great deeds of arms were wrought,
Where Cupid ran on cunning foot,
And where the Hill-lord fought.
But Cupid lo! outrunning
The fleetest of the hosts,
Sped to where beyond the press,
He spied the Great Twin Posts;
He crossed the line . . . . [he scored a try? G.A.B.]
And . . . . then . . . .

*   *   *   fly

(bother these blots, G.A.B.)

XX

Then tenfold from the watchers
The shouts and din arose,
Like the roar of the raucous signal
When the dinner-hour bull blows.   (! ! ! G.A.B.)
Now backward and now forward,
Rocked furious the fray,
When sudden came the last shrill call
Which marked the close of play.

[G.A.B. This is unworthy of the poet; I emend to –
'when sudden from the midmost host
The clarion called for peace.'

Ed. It was'nt [*sic*] a clarion, and 'peace' does NOT rhyme with 'fray.']

XXI

Then cried the king Mensura,
'Ho, henchman lade the board,
'With tankards and with viands rare
'From out thy toothsome hoard;
'For never, I ween, shall warriors,
'Who have fought a noble fight,
'All thirsty and a hungering,
'Depart without a bite.
'So let the war-worn clansmen
'Of banner green or red,
'Sip my steaming cup of peace,
'And friendly break my bread.'
So at Mensura's bidding,
Was straight a feast array'd
And thither limped the men of war,
And thirst and hunger stay'd.
When so, they put forth from them
The lust of meat and drink, (! ! Homer)
Tough ne'er from food or foemen,
Did any ever shrink,
Before them many a king and lord
Held speech, and many a cheer
Was raised for all those men of heart,
To whom brave war is dear.

* * * *

(The Ed. won't let me put any more in. Most of them then went home to bed. G.A.B.)

The Battle of the Eastern Field is a parody primarily of 'The Battle of Lake Regillus', one of the *Lays of Ancient Rome* by Thomas Babington Macaulay, first published in 1842. The earlier work begins:

Ho, trumpets, sound a war-note!
  Ho, lictors, clear the way!
The Knights will ride, in all their pride,
  Along the streets to-day.
To-day the doors and windows
  Are hung with garlands all,

From Castor in the Forum,
    To Mars without the wall.
Each Knight is robed in purple,
    With olive each is crown'd;
A gallant war-horse under each
    Paws haughtily the ground.
While flows the Yellow River,
    While stands the Sacred Hill,
The proud Ides of Quintilis
    Shall have such honor still.

The historical battle of Lake Regillus, *c.* 496 BC, was fought by the newly established Roman Republic and the confederation known as the Latin League. According to legend, the demigod brothers Castor and Pollux, the 'Great Twin Brethren', took the side of the Romans. Macaulay's account was well known to schoolboys of Tolkien's day – he and Christopher Wiseman, great friends, referred to themselves as the 'Twin Brethren'. Also well known was Macaulay's 'Horatius', which tells of a (possibly legendary) Roman soldier who held a bridge alone against invading Etruscans. Both poems celebrate martial ideals of bravery and perseverance – values often associated also with sport – and were among the texts assigned to pupils at Tolkien's school for annual poetry recital competitions at least as early as 1906. Jessica Yates was the first to explore Tolkien's debt to Macaulay, in '"The Battle of the Eastern Field": A Commentary' (1979). Much later, Birmingham historian Maggie Burns made a closer analysis of the poem, with reference to Tolkien's marked copy ('*The Battle of the Eastern Field*', 2008).

The subject of Tolkien's poem, beneath its 'epic' language, is a rugby football match between two houses of King Edward's School: Richards', whose players wore green, and Measures', clothed ('dight') in red. The winner would have the Football Cup ('the silver grail', line 19). Tolkien recorded in one of his poetry notebooks that the work is 'a celebration of a sanguinary housematch', that is, one which draws blood, figuratively speaking. Maggie Burns suggests that the match in question is that described by G.F. Cottrell in the *King Edward's School Chronicle* for June 1911:

> The 1st XV. House matches produced good games and, as Measures' and Richards' each won five of their six matches, it was necessary to play a deciding match, which was won by Richards' by 11 points to 3. This match produced one of the

> finest games ever seen on the School ground and will long be remembered by those who had the good fortune to play or to be spectators. ['Football Retrospect', p. 42]

Cottrell does not give a date for the event, but the editorial in the February 1911 *Chronicle* notes that 'the House Competition has provided some excellent games, and the matches . . . have been very keenly contested' (p. 2). Tolkien mentions Friday, 31 March in his prefatory note, a date almost certainly later than when he would have needed to submit his poem to appear in the *Chronicle* for March 1911, and 'Thursday in the Lenten Term' on line 32. Maggie Burns assigns a February date from the language of line 29, in which the day of the match 'greyly dawns'.

Throughout the poem Tolkien includes references to King Edward's School, fellow students, staff, and Birmingham itself. The 'Eastern field' of the poem's title is the playing field used by the school off the Eastern Road, south of the city centre. 'Yellow River' in line 13 repeats the sobriquet in Macaulay for the river Tiber, discoloured by yellow sand, but Tolkien undoubtedly refers to Bourn Brook, a muddy waterway adjoining the Eastern Road field, from which errant balls sometimes had to be fetched. 'Edgbastonia' with its 'ancient homes' refers to Edgbaston, a fashionable suburb of central Birmingham, and 'Mosli's emerald sward' to the southern suburb of Moseley; as a boy, Tolkien lived in both. Among those on Richards' team, 'the Green-clad Chieftain' was presumably E.B. Alabaster, team captain (he is not named among Tolkien's annotations); 'Ericillus of the sands' was L.K. Sands; 'Falco of the bridge' was F.T. Faulconbridge; 'that Chiefest Lord' was G.F. Cottrell, school Football Captain; 'Cupid' was H.L. Higgins; and 'the Hill-lord' was E.L. Hill. On Measures' team were 'Great Sekhet', fair-haired C.L. Wiseman, who 'toss'd his flaxen crest'; 'the Corcii of fame', brothers W.H. and R.S. Payton; and Tolkien himself, team captain, 'the doughty foeman'. A.E. Measures, a classicist and Assistant Master, figures as 'the king Mensura'.

Maggie Burns observes that the final stanza of *The Battle of the Eastern Field* ('XXI'), in which 'Mensura' bids both 'clans' in the conflict to feast together, is not modelled on 'The Battle of Lake Regillus', which ends with the victory of the Romans. Line 100, 'For never, I ween, shall warriors', recalls, however, a line from Macaulay's 'Horatius', and 'G.A.B.' acknowledges that line 113, 'The lust of meat and drink', is taken from Homer. (Burns notes similar lines in the *Odyssey*, but such words are also in the *Iliad*.) Tolkien closes his poem by departing from heroism in battle to declare the blessings of peace after 'a noble fight' (line 101). None at the time could know that within five years at least three of those who played the game (Cottrell, R.S. Payton, and Sands) would die on an actual battlefield in France.

In her 1979 article Jessica Yates argues 'that Tolkien "'Saxonised" the Roman world of Macaulay in the preferred use of English vocabulary and the more barbaric tone of his diction', using words such as *clan*, *grail*, *corslet*, *helm*, *flaxen*, *liegemen*, and *henchmen* to 'evoke the Germanic heroic tradition' (p. 5).

7: In regard to 'Atlas on the staircase', Maggie Burns notes ('*The Battle of the Eastern Field*', p. 17) that 'photos of the old King Edward's [School] in New Street show . . . a globe standing at the top of the Masters' staircase'.

8: Maggie Burns states that 'Bogey' was almost certainly a porter who stoked the furnace and did other work in the lower parts of King Edward's School as it stood in Tolkien's day, before moving from New Street in central Birmingham to the suburb of Edgbaston.

Asterisks following 32: On his personal copy of the printed poem Tolkien struck through this line and wrote: '(apparently the foes assemble) but a lacuna occurs here in [?mss, i.e. manuscripts]'. The revision is relatively early, to judge by the handwriting, and in both ink and pencil.

35: The Bourn Brook is by no means a 'great river'. Neither is the Rea, a short distance to the east in Birmingham (popularly 'Brum') and largely redirected beneath the city through culverts.

47: *Sekhet* (or *Sekhmet*) is the name of an Egyptian female deity, a goddess of war as well as healing. We cannot explain why it was applied to Christopher Wiseman, unless his golden hair, combined with a fierce performance on the football pitch, were related to Sekhet's traditional depiction as a lioness. Maggie Burns suggests that the nickname might 'have derived from a school joke' (p. 18). John Garth in *Tolkien and the Great War*, who had not seen Tolkien's marked copy, wrote that 'Wiseman surely lurks behind *Sekhet*, a nod to his fair hair and his passion for ancient Egypt'. Tolkien, he thinks, may not have known that Sekhet is a female deity, and perhaps met the name only in *She* by H. Rider Haggard, 'which lists "Sekhet, the lion-headed" among the Egyptian powers, but does not specify her gender' (Garth, p. 20).

48: In *Acta Senatus*, a report of a Latin debate written, in Latin, anonymously by Tolkien and published immediately following *The Battle of the Eastern Field* in the March 1911 *King Edward's School Chronicle*, W.H. Payton is given the invented Latin name 'M. [Marcus] Corcius Pato', while the younger R.S. Payton is 'Q. [Quintus] Corcius Pato Iunior'. *Corcii* is the plural of *Corcius*.

Asterisks following 52: On his personal copy Tolkien struck through the parenthetical comment here and wrote across the asterisks: 'an hiatus in which app[arently] the early scenes of the battle were described'.

Parenthetical comment following 76: On his personal copy Tolkien struck through the second sentence and the initials 'G.A.B.'

84: Maggie Burns interprets 'the Great Twin Posts' as a reference to the 'Great Twin Brethren' of Macaulay's poem, that is, Castor and Pollux, presumably in addition to its more direct reference to goal posts.

85: On his personal copy Tolkien deleted the question mark and initials from the parenthetical note in this line. In rugby, 'scoring a try' means touching the ball to the ground beyond the opponents' goal line.

Note after 87: On his personal copy Tolkien struck through the parenthetical note and wrote: 'another large lacuna occurs'.

91: On his personal copy Tolkien, apparently now unhappy with the phrase, underlined 'bull blows' and struck through and replaced the parenthetical note with 'poetic indignum' and a large exclamation mark. 'Bull' is perhaps local slang for 'whistle'. *Indignum* is literally 'unworthy'.

'Editorial note' preceding 96: On his personal copy Tolkien struck this through.

113: On his personal copy Tolkien struck through the parenthetical note.

7

A Fragment of an Epic (1911–14)

The first page of the sole text of this poem, a manuscript of eight pages on eight leaves, includes three phrases which could be considered its title, or in combination, title and subtitle (or subtitles): *A Fragment of an Epic*, *Before Jerusalem*, and *Richard Makes an End of Speech*. None is obviously consecutive with another. The words 'A fragment of an epic' are underlined, 'Before Jerusalem' is written separately near the edge of the sheet, and 'Richard makes an end of speech' immediately precedes the start of the poem, as if its introduction, though Tolkien did not count it within the sequence of line numbers he added in the margin. 'Richard' is King Richard I of England (lived 1157–1199), popularly known as Richard the Lionheart (Coeur de Lion), a leader in the Third Crusade (1189–92).

Thus by these words of speeding enhearten'd for the Cross
dight then themselves the riders of the realms of western kings
in grimly gleaming armour; and there mid the tokenings
of olden-founded kindreds, which unrecking of the loss
had sped the gayest blossom of their garland to the strife,
spread glowing its mystic crimson, holy torch of hallow'd war
the sacred cherish'd emblem, living Tree of Death and Life.

And high midst all the thronging there stood he who noblest bore
that Sign, the king most kingly, the north-born warrior
with golden locks emprison'd in the glorious glinting helm
which fram'd his face was harden'd in the anxious gaze of care.
Yet in his eyes there gleameth that awful war-fain glare
with which his northern fathers erst mark'd in colder realm
the garnering of the balefield by ruddy-handed Tyr;
while by his side huge-looming hangs the thrice-forg'd leaping brand,
the blood-fain sword of battles, Bane of Hell, and Evil's fear,
first heav'd to smite the loathsome destroyer of that dim land,
the Worm of Greed slow creeping in its slot of icy slime,
and never to fail until with its most utter dint it quell

warring beneath the Cross in this outer burning clime
the marshaller of all the vast vassal hordes of Hell.

Now round him throngéd bravely that array all fair harness'd
and proudly bear'd and flauntéd gallant pennon plume and crest,
and where he tower'd golden were the stoutest men of heart
'neath spear and spear rais'd heavenward, whence glistering did start
the gilded morning sunlight; and lo! headpiece and hauberk
to shield, to greave, and corslet gave it silversparkling back.
There glimmer'd gaily over steel and cloth of skilful work
the hues and myriad glamour of their western blazonry,
while slowly the Lamp beloved in the days of dearth and lack,
and in the wan-lit seasons of drear winter's misery,
by all the northern kindreds, ever waxing hotter rose,
and turn'd to scourge and weapon of the burning Lord of Woes.

Thus shone the sun on that arming, and o'er the fateful field,
and kindled all the shadows of the bleak-embattled town,
which greyly loomed behind; and straight quiver'd and dazéd reel'd
the lift beneath that piercing hail of radiance sent down
vibrant with death to conquer and to melt and quell to nought
the swart stark crags which raised the Sainted Burg aloft.
And soon the beams illumin'd in the welkin's sudden blaze
before the expectant glances of the serried Christian host
their mystic floating banner on the height; and by the Grace
down-flowing crimson from the deep-crimson'd Tree, it toss'd
emblazon'd on its cloth, were all the weary anxious hearts
and wavering spirits stirréd. With good courage for good fight
they turn'd to abide the countless oncoming of the darts,
which like an evil cloud-gloom foreshow'd by their darkling flight
the sudden blast of fury and assault. Lo! all the horde
and armies from the wasteland of trackless yellow thirst,
the foes of Christ and Christendom, in burning madness roar'd
'gainst where the Lionhearted mid the bristling pennon'd hurst
of spears shone proudly golden from the close-knit knightly throng.

The lustful wolfish clamour of relentless speeding hate
rais'd by the mightiest wielders of the bitter brands of Wrong
surg'd from the resistless clust'ring and the swarms of that foul brood,
which like a rout of the dwellers in the noisome murky fears,
and empty cavernous sorrows of Hell, did execrate
with turmoil of vainshrieking venom'd tongues the Sacred Rood,
as they swept about the shining array of Christian peers.
Undaunted by that outpour from the sudden sluice of Dread
following their gold-clad leader all the squadron cloth'd in awe
loud calling on the Cross as fell tearing lightning sped
with the clanging wrathful thunder of God anger'd; and like straw
were the thronging tribes unnumber'd cleft as cleft will be the damn'd
on the latest Day of Dooming by the Angels of God's Ire
in flashing holy onslaught. Yet ever a mightier band
still living strove demented with their brandish'd blades afire
in rank on rank to sully neath their foul-hewn pagan blows
the red-cross warriors' armour glinting fair; to smite and hew
with ill-curvéd blades of cunning the Holy Badge which rose
ever before the loathing of their madden'd blood-fain view.
And many a knight met bane thus beneath those strokes of dread,
and dew'd with the living purple of his warrior's martyrdom
the war-torn purple token of his Master's Death, Who shed
His Blood in that same holy often violated home.

Then one gigantic paynim espied where flash'd and fell
the wasting arm of Richard on the vassal swarms of Hell,
and strow'd the wither'd sands with their hate-enkindled blood
Lo! he wielded some strange lordship amid the mingled flood
of reckless battling; and as some lofty billow-crest
hissing with fiendish lusting for utter wrack, upwhirls
and flings in shattering thunder a huge o'erwhelming breast
of watery might, in agony of frenzy-lashéd swirls
to shiver against some bitter cliff or many-pinnacléd
escarpment of the landwall all grey panoplied;
so hurl'd he all his gruesome esquadrons 'gainst the light
of that golden-gleaming beacon of the ardent western might.

Now torn, as by ravening whirlpools round the Ocean's teeth,
in that fell rush of horror but few cross-clad knights there clave anigh
to lionhearted Richard; yet awhile they smote and drave
and reapéd for the burning the foul fruit of Mahmoud's lie,
till on the sick earth bestrowéd in loathly piles there lay
all weltering the deftly wrought gear of Araby.
Still ever flash'd and fell that grim arm more listlessly,
while thicker ever swarméd the banesmen to the fray,
and thinner grew the circle of the leaping swords which rose
and hew'd but now about him. Down scorch'd the awful sun,
and the main host of the steel-lapp'd avengers of Christendom
were sunder'd, wrapp'd in battle by a sea of hungry foes.

His heart wax'd dark and sullen, and all the battle-lust
forsook his soul; for round him his gallant liegemen died
mid the howls of Mahmoud's werewolves, and stain'd was the bloody dust,
which to his feet all iron-shod scorch'd deep, as with a stride
he spann'd his dastard-stricken steed: and though he hew'd and cleft
amain the towering banewall of foemen, they but hemm'd
more fiercely in the dinted and sore batter'd crush now left
of that equipage unrivall'd. E'en now but hardly stemm'd
the balesheen of that mighty one, the ploughshare of the press,
the rush of that death-fraught torrent, and already gashes gaped
amid the golden cunning of his matchless fair harness.
Lo! sudden, as oft in direst of tidings the doom escaped
full long is dreadly ended by one utmost stroke of bale,
as though to daunt the spirit, when the weary body flagg'd
a muttering of foul portent arose, like distant gale
swift rushing to destroy some unhappy bark sore dragg'd
and labour'd by the waveswell, till 'neath the dripping cloud
the driven waters bellow before the wind. So now
the murmur to a shout and a resounding roar wax'd loud,
and louder as of Hell triumphant and the Holy Cross laid low.

Behold the hosts divided and left wide a steel-hedg'd lane
before the mighty marshaller, the vassal Lord of Hell,
now hasting to the weird and the latest utter bane

of dauntless golden Richard, and the warflame none might quell.
And when along he passéd, the press clang'd to again
and as a mighty sea-swathe rush'd boiling in his train,
till where he faced emprison'd in a steelwall'd ring of doom
the weary king undaunted in his golden framéd ploom.
Then as it sang the balesong all lusting in its sheath
for its draught of woeful ruin, and the endless ill of death,
he lightly drew his scimitar and forth it leapéd fain,
unmatchéd blade of wronging of whose fellow none had told.
Before that gleaming moon-blade, crookéd symbol of Hell's pain,
from its evil magic glimmer shrank the boldest of the bold
from all the green-rob'd kingdoms and hale lands of tree and rill;
for in its deadly glinting they beheld with sudden hate
the dim faint perfum'd cruelty, and the lustful hidden ill
and the immemorial horror of the Orient's moveless fate.
And they sicken'd as though they gazéd o'er the very brink of Hell,
but of Hell grown sickly loathsome in a foully fair attire.
There mid the death-bound stillness rested Richard a brief spell,
though he read the gleam of aweing, and his heart had burst with ire
in his body sick and weary; and the smoothly utter'd word
of that deadly foe he deemed but the purring of a beast
o'er its prey desired and captured, nor sign'd as if he heard
the offers of peace and treason. But with a wrathful hand he seiz'd
the cross-wrought hilt, and calling on the glory of the Right
and the Holy Tree uplifted o'er the darkness of the world
he flung on high the warflame that had smitten for the Right
in the days of Eld; and like an enragéd lion he hurl'd
his might against the scornful enharnessment of Wrong.
And as he smote it seeméd that all the mighty throng
waited fearful through long ages for the falling of the blow.
Now flicker'd before the burning eye of heaven blade 'gainst blade
and awful was the dint of that combat. None might know
the ending but they markéd how the Christian King 'gan fade,
and ever off the seeming soft robes of his swart foe

turn'd by the hidden strength of fiend-hammer'd vest of steel
his mightiest hewings slipped. Then with a laugh of fiendish bale
the darkling foe triumphant did his bitt'rest dinting deal,
and as the kingly champion sank 'neath that biting hail
he smote the helm uncloven, and its golden glory twinn'd
nigh the proud head of kingship; and the world went blind and dimm'd.
Yet ever evil vaunteth its victory too soon
and rouseth all unwitting failing Good to one last stroke;
so to the dazéd soul of great Richard in his swoon
came words of blasphemous taunting as his foe rejoicing spoke.

Lo all his dim mind fillèd with the memory of his fame
and the Faith for which he warréd. Like sudden lion he sprang,
and uttering the Word most sainted cast against the deadly flame
of the blazing sky the blood-ice, the blade which grimly sang
of the wrath of ancient races; how it smote for good long ere
the Light fared northward to the longers after light,
and shed its radiance widely, and bloom'd exceeding fair,
and will bide till It lights for ever the blind groping in the night;
how it travailed down the ages, in this fair undaunted land
where the Light was first enkindled, to smite the Light's fell foe.
Aye raiséd golden Richard with his latest strength that brand,
— lo! it falleth, ghastly, wonderful, and lo! it cleaves atwo
the scimitar of evil, and has ploughéd in its ire
through that neck snakelike and lovely, and has driven to the heart.
There it bursts in countless fragments as of leaping sparks of fire,
and thus in that dread battle-hour has slain, and played its part.

Fell'd with the frozen scorning still graven on his face
the marshaller of all the vast vassal hordes fell dead,
and men seem'd a mighty moaning rose and ever wax'd apace
of awful hate and terror; and the Lamp of heaven fled,
and it was as if a night-time of heavy speechless spell
sank down, and the air grew loadéd and thick, as with some dim wrong
in its last mad throes defeated and cast back to lightless Hell,

But now the light returned and still stood a batter'd throng
around their wounded king; but men fear'd and wonder'd sore,
for there were the glistering fragments of the shiver'd Bloom of
Strife,
and there the gruesome staining of an evil pool of gore,
where the champion of evil had spilt his bitter life,
but the body had been wafted by that awful fleeting night.
Behold! the ravening wolfthrongs fled like leaves wide
scattering
before the vengeful wind of the enhearten'd Christian might;
And with awe and joy and sorrow they stoop'd and rais'd their
king.

This manuscript, unusually, includes Tolkien's signature, with the date 'July 1911', in handwriting probably contemporary with the composition. On the verso of its final leaf Tolkien wrote 'JRRT' and 'Ronald Tolkien' with 'R.E.S. 1911', the latter initials perhaps an abbreviation for 'Richard [Makes an] End [of] Speech', one of the phrases inscribed at the head of the text. The date 'June and July 1910' referring to *A Fragment of an Epic* on the manuscript of text A of *The Dale-Lands* (poem no. 2) is evidently incorrect at least to its year. On a page of one of his poetry notebooks, Tolkien referred to the work as '"Fragment of Epic" (Crusades)' and dated it 'June and July 1911'.

It is probably no coincidence that the subject of poems to be entered for the 1912 Newdigate Prize for English verse, offered to undergraduates at the University of Oxford, was 'Richard I before Jerusalem'; and this must be considered in light of Tolkien's dating of the *Fragment* to July, or June and July, 1911. Although this subject may have been announced by summer 1911 – after the Newdigate Prize for 1911 was presented at Encaenia, the annual university event held typically towards the end of June – Tolkien did not matriculate at Exeter College, Oxford until that October. It seems more likely that he heard of it before he arrived and wrote a verse for possible entry, than that he had a poem on the subject already written. The inscription 'Before Jerusalem', though apparently written later than the text proper, in smaller script and off to the side of the page, would seem to tie the *Fragment* firmly to the competition. It is also suggestive that Tolkien numbered the (198) lines of the poem as if to ensure that its length did not exceed the limit of 300 specified for the prize entry.

In an early list of his poems (list A, Appendix III) Tolkien included the title 'Richeard Englenacyning maþeleþ fore fyrdum', Old English for 'Richard, King of England, Speaks before the Army'. This is curious, in that Richard makes no speech in the *Fragment*, unless Tolkien intended actually to create a longer 'epic' of which the poem surviving in his papers was truly a fragment. At the start of the poem Richard has literally 'made an end of [a] speech', that is, has finished speaking his 'words of speeding', or encouragement; now would come the arming of his men and their prowess in battle.

It is also curious that their action appears to take place before Jerusalem, 'the bleak-embattled town', 'the Sainted Burg' on 'the swart stark crags' – Jerusalem is built upon a plateau in the Judean Mountains. The city was taken in 1099 by soldiers of the First Crusade, who killed most of its Muslim and Jewish inhabitants, but in 1187 seized from the Crusaders by Saladin. Richard was involved with the driving of Muslim forces from Acre, and in other operations in the Holy Land, but only came within sight of Jerusalem, hindered by weather, illness, and intrigue, never to the city itself. In 1192 he negotiated a treaty with Saladin and returned to England. Tolkien seems either to have imagined what a battle outside Jerusalem would have been like for Richard, or he drew upon another action (or actions) in the Crusade, perhaps the event of 1191 known as the Battle of Arsuf (or Arsur). A passage from the thirteenth-century *Itinerarium Regis Ricardi* ('Travels of King Richard') shares with the *Fragment* the image of Richard as a remarkable heroic figure that was traditional as late as Tolkien's day:

> There the king, the fierce, the extraordinary king, cut down the Turks in every direction, and none could escape the force of his arm, for wherever he turned, brandishing his sword, he carved a wide path for himself; and as he advanced and gave repeated strokes with his sword, cutting them down like a reaper with his sickle, the rest, warned by the sight of the dying, gave him more ample space, for the corpses of the dead Turks which lay on the face of the earth extended over half a mile. [anonymous translation from the Latin, in *Chronicles of the Crusades* (1848), pp. 239–40]

The Middle English romance *Richard Coer de Lyon* is even more militant, portraying the Crusaders as relentlessly seeking out Muslim foes, who are described as evil; but it is said that Richard, exceedingly great in battle, could be found among the fray by the blood that had been spilled upon the grass. Tolkien follows in this vein, emphasizing the Crusaders' forest of spears and especially sword upon sword, though the Christians made much use also of the crossbow. The historical Richard – born in Oxford, perhaps a factor in the choice of the Newdigate subject – was, at least, a gifted soldier, expert at strategy and tactics and skilled at command. At the time of the Third Crusade he was thirty-three, and his warrior's reputation preceded him as he travelled East.

It is not known if Tolkien further revised his *Fragment* and entered it for the Newdigate Prize; no later workings have survived. In any event, the 1912 prize was won by William Chase Greene, a Rhodes Scholar from Massachusetts. In Greene's text (*Harvard Graduates' Magazine* 21 (1912–13), p. 41), Richard speaks in the first person of his regret that Jerusalem could not be taken:

> The Holy City sleeps; and yet to-day
> I cannot bear to lift mine eyes and look
> Upon the fairness of her walls and towers.
> O living Lord, Whose empery doth lie
> Amid and far beyond these outward signs,
> Long have I toiled, enduring pain of peace
> And pain of battle; cities have I sacked
> A score, from grassy plain of Picardy
> To Ajalon reverberant of war:
> But in this land mine armies waste away,
> Vanquished in victory. Wherefore, O Lord,
> Dost Thou deny Thy blessing to Thy host?

Curiously, on 26 January 1914, so dated in the manuscript, Tolkien revisited the *Fragment*, changing line 75 first to 'His Blood the Fount unstinted whither all athirst may come', then to 'His Blood in that Land most holy where God's great Doom will come', still referring to the sacrifice of Jesus in the Holy Land.

5–7: The 'crimson . . . sacred cherish'd emblem . . . Tree of Death and Life' is the red cross worn by the Crusaders. Compare 'deep-crimson'd Tree', l. 43.

13: The 'northern fathers' are the Norse ancestors of the Normans. Richard was the great-great-grandson of William the Conqueror, the first Norman king of England.

14: In Norse mythology Tyr is a god of war, typically portrayed as one-handed (or one-armed) after his encounter with the wolf Fenrir. Here the image is of a hand red (*ruddy*) with blood *garnering* (collecting, as if harvesting) dead men on the *balefield* or battlefield, a field of death (*bale*).

17–21: 'The loathsome destroyer of that dim land, | . . . the vast vassal hordes of Hell', i.e. the Muslims in the Holy Land, the forces of Saladin. Saladin himself is not named in the poem, and may or may not have been meant as the 'marshaller' of the 'vassal hordes'. See note for l. 184.

18: 'Worm of Greed slow creeping in its slot of icy slime' is an allusion to a crawling dragon, like Fáfnir in the story of Sigurd. Tolkien later used 'Worm of Greed' as an epithet for the dragon Glórund in his *Children of Húrin* (begun *c.* 1921, poem no. 67).

19: 'Utter dint', i.e. the final stroke.

22: 'Bravely' originally read 'gaily'.

24: 'He tower'd golden': Richard was indeed tall and fair-haired.

30: 'The Lamp', i.e. the light of Jesus Christ.

33: The 'Lord of Woes' is Satan.

35, 39: 'The bleak-embattled town', 'the Sainted Burg', i.e. Jerusalem.

38: For 'vibrant with death to conquer and to melt and quell to nought' Tolkien added in pencil 'as' before 'to conquer', and appears to have considered whether to change 'and to melt' to 'or to melt'.

43–44: 'The Grace | down-flowing crimson from the deep-crimson'd Tree' is a reference to the blood of Christ crucified, related here to the Crusaders' red cross; compare ll. 5–7.

51: 'Lionhearted', i.e. Richard the Lionheart (*Coeur de Lion*).

51–2: 'Bristling pennon'd hurst of spears', i.e. a group of spear-carrying men with banners or pennants (*pennon*), by appearance like a small hill (*hurst*).

58: 'Vainshrieking', i.e. shrieking in vain, without success. The 'Sacred Rood' is the Holy Cross, on which Jesus was crucified.

70: 'Ill-curvéd blades', i.e. scimitars. The 'Holy Badge' is the sign of the Cross.

74: 'Master's Death', i.e. the death of Jesus Christ.

79–88: Here and later in the poem Tolkien indulges in sea-imagery, of floods and great waves, which would become more prominent in poems such as *The Grimness of the Sea* (no. 13).

91: 'Mahmoud', i.e. the prophet Muhammad.

98: 'Steel-lapp'd', i.e. armoured. Tolkien presumably meant chain mail, or should have, as the twelfth century was too early for plate armour of the sort generally associated with knights (in the popular imagination).

102: 'Werewolves' is presumably meant figuratively, i.e. warriors as fierce as wild, even supernatural animals, but with a satanic overtone. Compare 'wolf-throngs' in l. 196.

108: 'The ploughshare of the press', i.e. a body of men cutting through another by force of arms and numbers, like a plough cutting through soil.

125: 'Sea-swathe', i.e. like a great wave.

132: 'Moon-blade', i.e. a scimitar, curved like a crescent moon.

134: 'From all' originally read 'out of'.

157: 'Fiend-hammer'd vest of steel', i.e. chain mail.

170ff.: Tolkien gives Richard's sword a heroic history before its final victory and shattering.

171: 'Long ere' originally read 'before'.

174: 'It', capitalized in the manuscript, presumably refers to 'Light' in l. 172.

184: If, as we wonder earlier in these notes, the 'marshaller' is to be equated with Saladin, as a matter of history Saladin did not die at Richard's hand, but from illness soon after Richard's departure. The 'marshaller' is perhaps intended as some other commander representing the Muslim leadership.

192: The 'Bloom of Strife' is Richard's sword, cf. l. 173, 'bloom'd exceeding fair'.

8

The New Lemminkainen (1911)

Tolkien discovered the *Kalevala* in his final year as a pupil at King Edward's School (1910–11). One of the most significant works of literature written in Finnish, it was first published (in its longest form of fifty *runos*) in 1849 by its compiler-author, Elias Lönnrot. It has been called the national epic of Finland, though it is not an epic in the usual sense, but 'essentially a conflation and concatenation . . . of traditional songs, narrative, lyric, and magic, sung by unlettered singers . . . living to a great extent in northern Karelia [the eastern province of Finland]', as Francis Peabody Magoun, Jr. comments in his prose translation, *The Kalevala, or Poems of the Kaleva District* (1963, p. xiii).

Lönnrot had collected tales and songs to which he added linking material of his own. In doing so he approximated the distinctive metre of his sources: trochaic tetrameter, with four beats and usually eight syllables per line, in which a stressed syllable is followed by an unstressed syllable. Translators of the *Kalevala* into English poetry have followed suit, including William Forsell Kirby, whose rendering was the second complete translation of the work into English, but the first made directly from the Finnish: his *Kalevala: The Land of the Heroes*, was published in 1907 in Dent's Everyman's Library. Lines 9–20 from Runo XI, in which Lemminkäinen is introduced under two of his by-names, are a useful example of Kirby's text:

> Kauko fed himself on fishes,
> Ahti was reared up on perches,
> And he grew a man most handsome,
> Very bold and very ruddy,
> And his head was very handsome,
> And his form was very shapely,
> Yet he was not wholly faultless,
> But was careless in his morals,
> Passing all his time with women,
> Wandering all around at night-time,
> When the maidens took their pleasure
> In the dance, with locks unbraided.

Henry Wadsworth Longfellow adopted the same metre for his *Song of Hiawatha* (1855), a poem to which Tolkien referred in a paper, *On 'The Kalevala' or Land of Heroes*, first delivered in Oxford in 1914:

> It is of course the unrhymed trochaic metre of 'Hiawatha'. This was pirated as was the idea of the poem and much of the incident (though none of its spirit at all) by Longfellow. . . . 'Hiawatha' is not a genuine storehouse of Indian [Native American] folklore, but a mild and gentle bowdlerising of the Kalevala coloured I imagine with disconnected bits of Indian lore and perhaps a few genuine names. [*The Story of Kullervo*, ed. Flieger (2015), pp. 77–8]

John D. Rateliff in 'Hiawatha Earendil' (2010), and John Garth in '"The Road from Adaptation to Invention": How Tolkien Came to the Brink of Middle-earth in 1914' (2014), suggest similarities between Longfellow's *Hiawatha* and Tolkien's writings, with Garth in particular discussing *The Story of Kullervo* (poem no. 17). Lewis Carroll called the *Kalevala* metre, perhaps with tongue in cheek and Longfellow in mind, one in which 'any fairly practised writer, with the slightest ear for rhythm, could compose, for hours together', as he himself did in his 1887 parody 'Hiawatha's Photographing'.

It was not long after Tolkien read Kirby's *Kalevala* that he was moved to devise his own parody of that work. On the first page of the single manuscript of *The New Lemminkainen* he wrote a general 'argument', 'Lemminkainen goeth to his brother in the Southlands'; and in one of his poetry notebooks he dated the poem to September 1911, calling it 'Lemminkainen goeth to the Lands of Ilma the Smith and Kemi the Brook (being some lost runos of the Kálevalá) (parody on Kirby's translation in "Everyman" series)'.

Runo I

Argument: Lemminkainen boards the fire-consumer, known as Puffpuff the million-footed.

Then the skittish Lemminkainen,
He the handsome Grecian hero,
He whose other name was Hermes,
Thus did speak and burbled thiswise,
Thus endeavoured to express him,
To express his grief and anger

To address the iron dragon.
'Dragon thou of many sections,
'Thou of many hundred sections,
'Of compartments several thousand,
'Wherefore art thou full to bursting,
'Art thou thuswise overflowing?
' I have not yet got a ticket,
'Have not purchased yet a billet,
'Wherefore snortest so impatient?'
But the much-dissected dragon
In his coal-consuming fury
In his water-wasting anger
Answered not, nor yet responded,
Only shrieked and shrilly squirkling
Started with a sudden jerking,
Nearly left the Greek behind him.
Leapt the lithe and active Grecian,
Like a rabbit like a reindeer
Like a turnip or potato,
For he would not be deserted.
So the dragon bore him onward.
Onward then the dragon bore him
Through the noisome murk of Kalma,
Through the dusky realms of Ahto,
Grimes beloved of Manalainen,
Past the wastes of Hiitola
and the meads of Väinämöinen;
Bore him from the land of Pohja
Even Pohja's northern regions;
Bore him to the southern countries,
As before without a ticket.

Runo II

Arg[ument]: Lemminkainen dines.

Lemminkainen rather startled
Thus consider'd and reflected,
cogitated and bethought him,
ponder'd much and calculated —
'Inexpensive 'tis to travel
'Ticketless without a ticket

'Unprovided with a billet —
'Inexpensive and exciting
'Hazardous and rather cheaper —
'Leaves some cash to pay for luncheon'
Thus beminded Kaukomieli
(Same old chap as Lemminkainen)
Gat him down the quaking pathway
He the famished Saarelainen
(Just a name for dear old Kauko)
wandered clutching on the railing
Down the many-jointed gangway
In the dragon's littlemary.
Then rejoiced in cheese and mutton,
Bread and gingerale and melon
Coffee, butter, and potatoes,
In the inside of the dragon.
On that dragon's littlemary,
In the special dining section.
Thence replenish'd and repleted
Sought he then the steaming bathroom,
Sought in vain or tub or water
Could'nt [*sic*] find the bath or bath whisk
So return'd unwash'd but peaceful
And reflected on his dinner.
Onward sped the speeding dragon
Millionfooted Pufpuffainen
He the firedevouring pufpuf,
while the drowsy Lemminkainen
While the peaceful sated Kauko
Also known as Saarelainen
Still reflected on his dinner.

Runo III

Argument: Lemminkainen changeth dragons, and singeth him a sledge on which he traverseth the great town of the Southlands – for the moderate sum of 2/–.

From his slumber and reflection
from his after-dinner dreaming
Lemminkainen was arouséd,

Was most impolitely waken'd
By a fiendish howling porter.
Much incensed and rather startled,
Straight the skittish Saarelainen
Bounded from the quaking dragon,
Dragging all his goods and chattels.
Then he spoke and thus addressed him
Thus addressed him just as follows
To a very haughty porter
To a high and noble porter.
'O thou porter, beery porter,
'(If you please no pun intended)
'O thou scum, thou arrant scoundrel
'O thou wasp thou scavenge insect,
'Well I wot thy pa and mother
'All thy lineage and ancestors
'(Everyone kept public houses)
'Wherefore standest monumental
'Wherefore posest as a statue.
'I command you and conjure you
'Order thee and bid thee soothly
'Catch a wandering sledge and pile me
'All my goods and chattels on it,
'Whispering the word of magic
'That shall cause him to propel me
'On the sledge across the city
'To the dread and gloomy caverns
'To the smoky smelly burrows
'Where there lives the Dirty Dragon
'He the rover of the South Coast.'
Then the noble porter yawning,
He the gaping statuesque one,
He the corduroy-adorned one,
Grasped the goods of Lemminkainen,
Seized the chattels and upraised them,
Piled them on the handsome sledge then,
Spoke the word of whisper'd magic.
Straight the sledge it got a move on
Passed beyond the looming portals
Of the Northern Dragon's mansion,
Speeding on with Lemminkainen,
Over road and over asphalt

Over squares and narrow highways
Past the shops hotels and theatres.
Through the mighty town of Southland,
Sped the sledge with Lemminkainen;
Brought the weary Kaukomieli
Even to the grimmest portal
Even to the gate forbidding
Of the Dirtdevouring monster,
He that traverseth the South coast.
Lightly Lemminkainen bounded
From the sledge and gladly stretched him.
To the driver with a red nose
(Yes with quite a red proboscis)
Gave to him the skilful pilot
Gave him silver by the handful
Gave ungrudgingly his silver
To the sum of perhaps two shillings
— Generoushearted Lemminkainen.

Runo IV

Argument: Lemminkainen changeth his dragon for a roadhop and arriveth at the mansion of Kemi the Brook and Ilmarinen the smith where he spieth his brother amid the kine (— pedigreed alderneys).

Saarelainen all amazéd
All distraught and rather mither'd
In a country rather strangish
Though he'd once or twice before this
Visited the Southland Dragon —
Was so cowed, so push'd & hustled,
That he felt he'd better purchase
Felt in fear constrain'd to buy him
Just for once a little ticket.
—Though it came somewhat expensive
— thus reflected Lemminkainen —
When one planks down 4 bob coolly
For a piece of greenish cardboard.
Natheless he plank'd his 4 bob
He the economic Kauko

Planked it for a piece of cardboard,
And provided with this tit-bit
Sallied forth to meet the dragon
To encounter dragon second.
But the dragon took no notice,
Neither snorted neither snarkled
Neither shook nor quaked nor trembled
Nor show'd any signs of movement.
Whereupon encourag'd Kauko
(One of Lemminkainen's nicknames)
Enter'd this most filthy dragon,
Chose its least disgusting section,
Sat in this select compartment.
There he spent two hours or morish
Seeing that the beast was sluggish;
There he tried to breathe and gaspéd
Stifléd squash'd and suffocated
Not to say asphyxiated;
Till at last in grief and anguish
Quite enraged and very angry
Really positively wrathful
Spoke he to that horrid dragon
To that despicable creature.
What he said would spoil the poetry,
Make it quite unfit for reading,
So we leave our Lemminkainen
On the platform gazing madly
Gazing furious and sadly
At the disappearing tailpiece
Of that nauseating serpent
Of that most annoying beastlet.
Then sang Ahti Saarelainen,
Sang a humming buzzing roadhop,
Sang a driver and an engine.
Then he grasped his goods and chattels,
Rescued from the dragon's inside,
Lightly cast them on the roadhop
And was wafted through the country,
Through the meadows and pastures
Through the greenwood and the heathland
To the blooming brook of Kemi
To the land of Ilmarinen

Of the smith of Ilmatola.
There he saw amid the pastures
By the blooming brook of Kemi
Mid the land of Ilmarinen
Of the smith of Ilmatola.
Saw and recognised immediate

Here the manuscript ends abruptly. At the foot of its final page Tolkien wrote 'see scrap for end', but the 'scrap' in question appears to have been lost. A further line written on this page, but struck through heavily, begins 'His brother with the'; we are unable to make out more.

In the *Kalevala* Lemminkäinen is an adventurer, a rogue, a ladies' man, a powerful singer, skilled in magic. Francis Magoun suggests that his name means 'lover, lover boy'. Lönnrot made him one of the principal figures in the *Kalevala*, combining different characters from his source material; these also contribute to Lemminkäinen's several by-names. In his 1914 *Kalevala* paper Tolkien called him 'a confirmed villain of loose morals and wife-beating propensities' who nonetheless 'shows only his best and most affectionate feeling for his mother' (Bodleian Library). In one sequence Lemminkäinen journeys north to Pohjola (or Pohja) to woo the daughter of Louhi. There he is set three tasks: to capture the Elk of Hiisi while on snowshoes, to bridle the fiery steed of Hiisi (literally on fire, with smoke and flames), and to shoot a swan on the river of Tuonela, the realm of the dead. He succeeds in the first two, but is killed before he can complete the third. His mother, however, restores him to life. Tolkien's 'new Lemminkainen' (he omits the umlaut) is similarly handsome and lively, though without the loose morals of his namesake – travelling by rail without a ticket notwithstanding. He too confronts a fiery creature, though it is only a locomotive, and his journey, 'to his brother in the Southlands', is comparatively mundane if not without incident.

As a parody derived from the *Kalevala*, Tolkien's *New Lemminkainen* contains words, passages, and features in direct imitation of his source. But it is not far-fetched to read the poem also as autobiography, following the course of an actual journey Tolkien made in summer 1911. Of this we have no direct evidence; but from ?late July to early September that year, before he went up to Oxford as an undergraduate in October, Tolkien joined his aunt Jane Neave, her friends the Brookes-Smith family, and others on a walking tour of Switzerland. The destination of his poem's hero, made explicit in the argument of Runo IV – the home of 'Kemi the Brook and Ilmarinen the smith' – surely refers to the farm of the Brookes-Smiths at Hurst Green in Sussex. Tolkien and his brother Hilary had met the family through their aunt, and Jane had come to know James and Ellen Brookes-Smith while she was Lady Warden of University Hall at the University of St Andrews. Jane later purchased a farm near Nottingham in partnership with Mrs Brookes-Smith.

Following this line of supposition, *The New Lemminkainen* suggests that after he left King Edward's School in Birmingham, Tolkien went by train ('Puffpuff') to London, there '[traversed] the great town of the Southlands' by 'sledge' (taxi, one supposes), changed to another 'dragon' (train), and finally engaged a 'roadhop' (a vehicle of some sort) to take him to Hurst Green and the Brookes-Smiths' farm, where Hilary Tolkien had recently gone to work 'amid the kine [cows]'. In our notes we assume that this journey occurred, and speculate accordingly in regard to finer details.

Kalma (or Tuoni, or Manalainen, or Mana) in the *Kalevala* is the personification of Death, whose domain is Tuonela. Ahto is the God of the Sea and the Waters, Hiitola the domain of Hiisi (Finnish 'demon'), and Väinämöinen an eternal sage who lives on a farm. If, again, *The New Lemminkainen* does reflect an actual journey Tolkien made, his mention of lands associated in the *Kalevala* with darkness, dreariness, gloom, save for the last ('the meads of Väinämöinen'), may be a comment on centres of industry he passed through, including Birmingham itself, and perhaps Coventry. On the other hand, it may be fruitless to associate these lines overmuch with the route a train of 1911 would have taken between Birmingham and London: where, exactly, would be the 'realms of Ahto', in the *Kalevala* including lakes or rivers (as this route would not pass through, say, the Lake District or the Fens)? But here compare 'the clouded wastes of Ahto' in poem no. 9. In any event, there is an analogous passage in the *Kalevala* (Runo XIII, ll. 149–54, Kirby translation) in which Lemminkäinen travels to the north:

> O'er the hills and dales he glided,
> Through the lands beyond the ocean,
> Over all the wastes of Hiisi,
> Over all the heaths of Kalma,
> And before the mouth of Surma,
> And behind the house of Kalma.

Surma is the beast that guards the gates of Tuonela.

Runo I, Argument: A *runo* (rune) is a poem, or part of a longer poem. *Puffpuff* is slang, especially a nursery-name, for a locomotive, by extension a train, at this time a 'fire-consumer' or rather a consumer of coal burnt to produce steam (cf. 'coal-consuming' and 'water-wasting', ll. 17, 18). 'Million-footed' suggests the nature of a train as a lengthy conveyance for the multitude.

1: Tolkien prefers to call his Lemminkainen 'skittish'; Kirby frequently describes *Kalevala* Lemminkäinen as 'lively', while Magoun uses 'reckless'.

2–3: 'He the handsome Grecian hero, | He whose other name was Hermes' almost certainly alludes to Tolkien's performance as the Greek god Hermes in Aristophanes' play *Peace* at King Edward's School on 26 July 1911.

7: 'Iron dragon', i.e. the train. Later (l. 182) Tolkien uses *serpent* with the same meaning. On 1 January 1938, Tolkien would say to an audience at Oxford's Natural History Museum: 'Coming on an express train lit up at night – very likely an Englishman of long ago would have been alarmed, and possibly have thought that he saw a lot of wizards or devils being dragged to perdition by a smoking dragon' (lecture on dragons, in Scull and Hammond, *The Hobbit, 1937–2017* (2018), p. 62).

14: *Billet* in English is not synonymous with *ticket*, but is French 'ticket'.

20: *Squirkling* seems to be a kind of laughing, perhaps from *squirk* 'half-suppressed laugh, sharp squeaking sound'.

34: Tolkien appears to equate Pohja (Pohjola, Finnish 'north'), in the *Kalevala* a northern farm presided over by Louhi (and itself cold and gloomy), with Birmingham in the English Midlands.

36: The 'southern countries' are equivalent to the home counties around London, especially Sussex on the south coast of England.

48–52: As Tolkien remarks, *Kaukomieli* (shortened to *Kauko*) and *Saarelainen* are other names for Lemminkainen. In his translation of the *Kalevala* Magoun glosses *Kaukomieli* as '(handsome) man with a far-roving mind'; *Saarelainen* 'man of the island' pertains to the island Saari, where Lemminkäinen woos the maiden Kyllikki in Runo XI.

54–5: 'Down the many-jointed gangway | In the dragon's littlemary': Lemminkainen enters the dining car. *Littlemary* (or *little Mary*) is a colloquialism for 'stomach', from J.M. Barrie's play *Little Mary* (1903).

63–5: A sauna, or 'steaming bathroom', with a 'bath or bath whisk', is an unlikely feature on a train, but a traditional aspect of Finnish culture. In Runo XXIII of the *Kalevala* (ll. 351–4, Kirby translation) a bride is instructed: 'When the evening bath is wanted, | Fetch the water and the bath-whisks, | Have the bath-whisks warm and ready, | Fill thou full with steam the bathroom'.

64: In 'Sought in vain or tub or water' the first *or* is not a misprinted *for*. The combination *or . . . or* in early usage means 'either . . . or', thus here, 'sought in vain [for] either tub or water'.

69: 'Pufpuffainen' combines *pufpuff* (alternatively in the poem *puffpuff*, *pufpuf*) 'locomotive, train' with the Finnish denominative suffix *-(a)inen*, making a name of the whole.

Runo III, Argument: Trains from Birmingham to London in 1911, operated by the London and North Western Railway, terminated at London's Euston Station. From there Tolkien would have needed to cross London ('the great town of the Southlands') to another station serving the southern region for Hurst Green in Sussex. '2/–' is an abbreviation for two shillings in pre-decimal British currency. 'Singeth . . . a sledge' refers to the power of song to effect magic, in which Lemminkäinen is skilled. The northern land of the *Kalevala* was not a place of paved roads where one would find a taxi, but rather would have a sledge, though in Tolkien's poem it travels 'over road and over asphalt'.

88–107: Tolkien's Lemminkainen is as rude to the porter as his namesake in the *Kalevala* is to others, notably the Master of Pohjola in Runo XXVII; and he likewise uses an innate power of song to conjure someone to do his bidding, 'whispering the word of magic'.

88–9: 'Beery porter' plays on *porter* in the sense of someone employed to carry luggage and *porter* 'dark brown bitter beer'. Tolkien writes, 'If you please no pun intended', but it was.

91: A porter's duties included keeping the railway cars tidy: hence, presumably, Tolkien's reference to *scavenge* 'pick up discarded items'.

92: 'I wot', i.e. 'I know'.

110: The 'corduroy-adorned' porter is in the standard uniform for railway porters.

116: 'The looming portals | Of the Northern Dragon's mansion' are probably the Euston Arch, the original neo-classical entrance to the station, an imposing sandstone structure with four Doric columns and bronze gates built in 1837 but demolished in 1961.

Runo IV, Argument: We can find no recorded use of the slang or colloquial *roadhop* in the sense evidently meant here, a hired vehicle such as a taxi; it may be a coinage by Tolkien, perhaps from *road* + *hop* 'to obtain a lift on (a vehicle)'. Kemi (Kemijoki) is a river in northern Finland, mentioned in *Kalevala* Runo XX. Ilmarinen in the *Kalevala* is a craftsman, an eternal smith. Here Kemi is made a 'brook' to pair with Ilmarinen's 'smith', playing on the name of Tolkien's friends the Brookes-Smiths. Alderneys are a breed of dairy cattle originating on the Channel Island of Alderney.

141–2: 'Though he'd once or twice before this | Visited the Southland Dragon' suggests (if the poem is truly autobiographical) that there are journeys made by the young Tolkien which we have not seen recorded.

149: *Plank* is a dialect word for 'put or set down' (now more commonly *plonk* or *plunk*). '4 bob' is slang for four shillings, British pre-decimal currency.

158: *Snarkled* may be related to the dialect word *snark* 'to snore', or perhaps is only a nonsense word suggesting a sound made by a locomotive.

166–7: The 'sluggish' train presumably made many stops. In the earlier part of the twentieth century the rail network in Britain was more extensive than it is now, with more stations, branch lines, and local services. The nearest rail station to Hurst Green, then as now, would have been Etchingham.

184–6: *Ahti* is another by-name of Lemminkäinen in the *Kalevala*, often used as a sort of title before *Saarelainen*. Once more Lemminkainen sings, producing 'a humming buzzing roadhop', presumably another taxi obtained at the rail station. In Runo XXVI of the *Kalevala*, when his mother warns him of the dangers he would face on a journey to Pohjola, Lemminkäinen replies variously 'I'll create, by songs of magic | Both a man and horse of alder . . . | And a man of snow I'll sing me . . . | For the wolf's mouth sing a muzzle, | For the bear sing iron fetters' (Kirby translation, ll. 139–40, 169, 209–10).

191–2: 'The meadows and pastures . . . the greenwood and the heathland' are still to be found at Hurst Green, on the borders of East Sussex and Kent.

195: *Ilmatola* from its construction presumably means 'land of Ilmarinen'.

9

Lemminkainen Goeth to the Ford of Oxen (1911)

In one of his poetry notebooks, on a page on which he also wrote *From Iffley* (poem no. 10), Tolkien dated a second 'Lemminkainen' poem to October 1911 and described it as 'a spurious interpolation of the Kálevalá rightly rejected by W.H. [*sic*] Kirby in his translation (A freshman from Birmingham school goes up to Oxford)'. See our discussion of W.F. Kirby's translation of the Finnish *Kalevala* in connection with Tolkien's earlier poem of this nature (no. 8).

Runo MDCCCCXI

Argument: Lemminkainen having to depart from Pohja goes again in search of the dragon PufK, who refuses to take him. Honka the road-hop however takes him on his back and puts him down on the banks of the Is-Is. He makes his way to the halls of Kol and there remains.

Lo! thc lively Kaukomieli
Also known as Lemminkainen
(More familiarly as Kauko)
Got him from the lands of Pohja;
Forth did fare and hasten onwards
Through the gloomy mists of autumn
In the very bluest spirits,
Till he came to where is station'd
In the reek of serpents hundred,
In the noisome smoke of reptiles,
Looming dim and arching upwards
All the vast expanse and cavern'd
Lair of mighty dragon-farers.
There he ventured, and accosted,
And address'd a fair-sized reptile.
'Serpent black and subterranean
'Thou who farest shrilly shrieking
'Through the clouded wastes of Ahto,

'Mid the smoking stacks of Pohja,
'To the distant lands of learning;
'To the Southlands and the dwellings
'Of the Don and lurking Prokta;
'Bear me to the Ford of Oxen;
'Bear me in thy quaking tumtum
'Waft me from the lands of Pohja;
'Dump me by the stream of Is-Is'.
Nought the dragon-farer answer'd
Nought replied, and spake him nothing.
Impolitely did not deign to;
Seem'd to scorn him and despise him.
So the lively Lemminkainen
Left the dragons' smoke fill'd cavern,
Very cross and rather poorer,
Seeing they had swallowed quickly
Every morsel of his luggage!
As he wander'd much bewilder'd
All distraught and not good temper'd
From the twilight to the daylight
From the gloom into the sunshine.
Lo! he spied a honking roadhop
Rooting up the road towards him.
Swiftly Lemminkainen mounted
On the monster; whereupon it
After prefatory snortings
Bounded forward like an arrow
—well, a rather rummy arrow;
quite impossible projectile—.
Never stopped it loudly tooting;
Creaking all its many jointings;
Rattling up its oily tumtum;
Droning down the dusty roadways;
Roaring through the scattered hamlets;
Till it found amid the lowlands
In the many-willow'd meadows,
Crumbling in the drip and dankness,
Many-mansion'd many-pillar'd
All the city of the fording.

There the roadhop duly dump'd him,
Dump'd him and returnéd heedless;

But the lively Lemminkainen
Much subdued and somewhat awestruck
Spoke soliloquising thuswise:
'Lemminkainen Kaukomieli,
'Ahti Saarelainen likewise,
'Wherefore hast thou wander'd hither?
'For there will be no returning
'To the ancient homes of Pohja
'To the playing fields of Selli;
'Till a sojourn full of labour,
'Full of strangeness be completed
'By the willow'd bank of Is-Is'.
Quaking thus he tapp'd the portal
Of a hugely-looming mansion
Crown'd with tower of crumbled stonework,
And embattled walls with windows
Darkly peeping at the stranger:
Then the portal yawnéd grimly,
And he enter'd and was swallow'd
In the darkness as it loudly
Crashed behind him as he passed it.
Yet they say that after sojourn
There of many days and nighttimes
Back will whirl the dragon-farer,
And in clash and roar and clangour
Bear him once again to Pohja;
To the dwellings once familiar;
To the domiciles and mansions
Down in Pohja of the murk-land.
But his name for ever changéd
Shall be alter'd and mutated,
And the lively Lemminkainen,
Shall be never more call'd Kauko,
Nor address'd as Saarelainen.
Old Ed then his appellation,
Nomination, designation,
Sole cognominal notation.
Thus adieu to Saarelainen
E'en to handsome Kaukomieli
Let his hidden names be whatso
Boasted each one once that faréd
From his well-belovéd Pohja

To the realms of Don and Prokta
In the southlands; in the lowly
Many willow'd water-meadows
By the thronging banks of Is-Is.

Following this text Tolkien wrote: 'Having promis'd another production I felt I must send one. I do (with all apologies). You may consign it to the wagger-pagger-tagger (Oxonese [Oxford student slang] for waste paper basket) if you like. [*signed*] R.' It seems likely that he was addressing one of his friends from King Edward's School.

The title of this poem at once marks it as a description of a journey to Oxford ('the Ford of Oxen'), and given its date, one inevitably looks to connect it with Tolkien's own journey when he went up to university as a freshman. As with the earlier *Kalevala* parody, the present work sacrifices history for comedy. It suggests that Lemminkainen attempted to travel by train from Pohja (Birmingham) to the Ford of Oxen (Oxford) but was unable to do so; and a train having carried away his luggage without him, he resorted to a 'roadhop', a 'monster', noisy and dirty, to take him to 'the city of the fording'. By his own recollection, Tolkien 'was brought up to Oxford by car (then a novelty), together with L.K. Sands [also of King Edward's School], by Dickie [R.W. Reynolds, one of the School masters]: in the October of that astonishing hot year 1911, and we found every one in flannels boating on the river' (letter to the Rev. Denis Tyndall, another 'old boy' of King Edward's School, 9 January 1964, *Letters*, p. 480). Much would depend on the size of Reynolds' car, if it was largely filled already with a driver and two passengers, but perhaps Tolkien sent his luggage on ahead by rail, and it is this which the poem describes in its parodic manner. At any rate, the latter part of the present work is notably autobiographical, presenting more or less as it occurred Tolkien's sense of a profound change in his life, and the whole served as a second, much briefer exercise in writing the *Kalevala* metre.

For further writing by Tolkien inspired by the *Kalevala* and W.F. Kirby's translation, see poem no. 17.

Title: The roman numerals 'MDCCCCXI' suggest that the runo is part of an enormously longer poem, but in fact merely translate to the date of composition, 1911.

Argument: As in the earlier *Kalevala* parody, 'Pohja' stands in for Birmingham, in the north relative to Oxford. 'Is-Is' is the Isis, the name of the river Thames at Oxford. The 'halls of Kol' are the college (*kol*-lege) halls of the University. We are at a loss to explain the capital letter at the end 'PufK'; 'Puf' is presumably short for 'Puffpuff', used in the earlier poem for a locomotive or train. Following his wordplay of poem no. 8, he calls a train a 'dragon', a 'reptile', a 'serpent'.

18–19: For 'Through the clouded wastes of Ahto, | Mid the smoking stacks of Pohja', compare ll. 29–30 of the earlier poem, 'Through the noisome murk of Kalma, | Through the dusky realms of Ahto', and see our notes pertaining to these. It is easy to relate 'the smoking stacks of Pohja' to the heavy industry of Birmingham, but less so to explain the reference to Ahto, the Finnish god of waters. Again, Tolkien may have been concerned to describe a journey in the manner of one in the *Kalevala*.

22: A *don* is a university teacher. 'Prokta' is a play on *proctor*, a university official especially concerned with discipline.

23: 'Ford of Oxen' refers to Oxford, originally *Oxenford*, a place where oxen could ford a shallow river. Compare 'city of the fording', l. 57.

24: *Tumtum* is a child's word for *stomach* ('tummy').

54–6: Compare 'the many-willow'd meadows' and 'many-mansion'd many-pillar'd' with 'the many-willowed margin' and 'many-mansioned tower-crownéd' in the contemporaneous *From Iffley* (no. 10).

68: 'Playing fields of Selli' probably refers to the recreation ground at Selly Park in Birmingham. Cricket and football were played there.

94: 'Old Ed' is short for 'Old Edwardian', that is, a former pupil at King Edward's School.

10

From Iffley · Valedictory (1911–?15)

Tolkien wrote this brief poem as early as his first term at university, Michaelmas Term 1911. In its extant manuscript and typescript copies, before alteration, he called it *From Iffley*. In all of these its text is substantially the same (A).

[A] From the many-willowed margin of the immemorial Thames
Standing in a vale outcarven in a world-forgotten day
There is dimly seen uprising through the greenly veiléd stems
Many-mansioned tower-crownéd in its dreamy robe of grey
That strange city by the river agéd in the lives of men
Proudly wrapt in mystic memory overpassing human ken.

In December 1913 the poem was published in the *Stapeldon Magazine* of Exeter College, Oxford, as by 'J.' (p. 11); we give this text as B. Changes to punctuation and accents, relative to A, were made in the printed version probably at an editor or compositor's discretion.

[B] From the many-willowed margin of the immemorial Thames,
Standing in a vale outcarven in a world-forgotten day,
There is dimly seen uprising through the greenly veilèd stems,
Many-mansioned, tower-crownèd in its dreamy robe of grey,
All the strange city by the fording: agèd in the lives of men,
Proudly wrapt in mystic mem'ry overpassing human ken.

Tolkien inscribed each of the poem's two manuscripts 'Oct[ober] 1911', but on a separate page of one of his poetry notebooks recorded its date more vaguely as 'After Oct[ober] 1911, till 1913'. One of the manuscripts, from at least 1914, labels the six lines with the numeral '1' and follows them with '2', suggesting that there should be a second stanza; and indeed, Tolkien added: 'Second stanza lost by ed[itor] of Stap[eldon] Mag[azine]' and '1st stanza appeared in Stapeldon Magazine, Exeter Coll[ege] Oxford [June >] Dec[ember]. [1914 >] 1913'. There do not seem to be any extant workings for a second stanza, and remarkably, Tolkien seems never to have reconstructed it from memory.

At the head of the second manuscript, Tolkien also wrote 'Oxenaford (of Gifeteslage gesewen)', Old English for 'Oxford (Seen from Iffley)'. As noted for poem no. 9, Oxford was once called Oxenford, a place where oxen could ford the river Isis (the Thames); Oxford is therefore, as in the manuscript versions of this poem, the 'city by the fording'. The village of Iffley, with a small Norman parish church, stands about two miles south-east of the centre of Oxford and affords views from its higher ground. It is recorded in Domesday Book as 'Givetelei', with elements suggesting a bird and a glade or clearing, but in medieval times the name had many different spellings, and eventually evolved into its present form.

The two manuscripts of the poem were followed by a ribbon typescript and two carbon copies, made probably in spring 1915. Tolkien circulated one to Christopher Wiseman, who wrote on 25 April that he was annoyed to see his friend address the Thames as 'immemorial', a word which sounded good but was thin in meaning. Wiseman also warned that Tolkien would be seen to have borrowed the word from another poem, possibly *The Princess* by Tennyson: 'Myriads of rivulets hurrying thro' the lawn, | The moan of doves in immemorial elms, | And murmuring of innumerable bees'. Borrowed or not, *immemorial* is perfectly apt in context, meaning 'ancient beyond memory, extremely old'; at any rate, Tolkien let it stand.

He did, however, revise the first words in the penultimate line of each of the carbon typescripts, changing 'All the city by the fording' to 'That strange city by the river'. We give this final text as C.

[C] From the many-willowed margin of the immemorial Thames
Standing in a vale outcarven in a world-forgotten day
There is dimly seen uprising through the greenly veiléd stems
Many-mansioned tower-crownéd in its dreamy robe of grey
That strange city by the river agéd in the lives of men
Proudly wrapt in mystic memory overpassing human ken.

The revised phrase also appears as a later pencil note on one of the manuscripts. One of the carbon copies is inscribed '1912 [*sic*] see Exeter College Stapeldon Mag[azine]'. Both carbon copies include (with a strike-through or erasure) a change of title, to *Valedictory*. It seems likely that, by now, Tolkien looked ahead to the end of his undergraduate years at university and to his entry into the war, having delayed army service until he completed his studies. The poem, then, could be read as a melancholy farewell to his beloved Oxford, the 'city of dreaming spires' ('tower-crownéd in its dreamy robe of grey').

Willows are prominent on the banks of Oxford's rivers. Compare 'many-willowed' here with 'the many-willow'd meadows' in *Lemminkainen Goeth to the Ford of Oxen* (no. 9), also written in October 1911. Compare, too, 'Many-mansioned tower-crownéd' with 'Many-mansion'd many-pillar'd' in poem no. 9.

John Garth has described Tolkien's poem as 'grandiloquent', 'with a long line probably inspired by William Morris'. It suggests, he feels, 'that the enduring character of Oxford predated the arrival of its inhabitants, as if the university were *meant* to emerge in this valley. Here is an early glimpse of the spirit of place that pervades much of Tolkien's work: human variety is partly shaped by geography, the work of a divine hand' (*Tolkien and the Great War*, p. 35).

A3: As typed, there is no accent in 'veiled'. Tolkien added it by hand ('veiléd') on the carbon copies.

11

Darkness on the Road (1911–15)

Tolkien dated the writing of this strongly emotional poem to 6 November 1911 on both the first and third of its three manuscripts. Near the end of the second stanza of the first version (A), he inscribed a dedication, 'To EMB' (Edith Mary Bratt); in autumn 1911 he had still over a year to wait before he came of age in January 1913 and could resume contact with Edith (see our comments to poem no. 1).

[A]

Lonely, lonely o'er the wasteland
  Dimly lighted by the moon
Slowly slowly I am toiling
  All my heart in weary swoon.
And the moan of wailing breezes
  Stirring in the silver'd heath
Coldly weeping its own sorrow
  To the bowing shrubs beneath
Whispers round me without recking
  Aught of any alien grief.

Only only o'er the wasteland
  Comes a radiant relief;
One warm beckoning beam of comfort
  In the wide expanse of night.
Yonder are the glowing windows
  Of the house of love and light
Distant, welcoming the wanderer,
  If with but a slender ray,
Calling onward and portending
  All the gladness of the day.

The second manuscript of the poem is on the same sheet as the later manuscript of *Sunset in a Town* (poem no. 12). It is largely a copy of the first version, with a few minor differences of punctuation and capitalization. In the third manuscript, however, inscribed 'Nov[ember] 6 1911 re[vised] May 2 1915', Tolkien altered *Darkness on the Road* more extensively, notably in the second stanza. We give the final text as B.

[B]

Lonely, lonely, o'er the wasteland
    Dimly lighted by the moon
I was slow unhappy toiling
    With my heart in weary swoon:
And the moan of wailing breezes
    Stirring in the silvered heath
Coldly weeping their own sorrow
    To the bowing shrubs beneath
Whispered round me without caring
    That I fainted on the dune.

Only, only, o'er the wasteland
    Dimly lighted by the moon
Gleamed a little glowing window
    With a sudden slender beam
Twinkling through the dark like sunlight
    Filters through a sunless dream.
Then I fancied cheer and gladness;
    Strains of far-off fireside tune
Seemed to tremble in the voices
    Of the winds upon the dune.

By now, Tolkien and Edith were engaged, and the poem, perhaps accordingly, has a more optimistic tone.

At the head of the third manuscript, Tolkien wrote 'Nihthelm ofer wegas', literally 'night-covering over [the] ways' in Old English. Probably in March or April 1915, Tolkien made, or had made, a typescript of the poem, preserved as ribbon and two carbon copies, with no changes to the text; later he inscribed one of the carbon copies '1909–13'. In mid- to late May that year, he had the revised *Darkness on the Road* professionally typed by the Oxford Copying Office, without change.

12

Sunset in a Town (1911)

The first of two manuscripts of *Sunset in a Town* (A) is inscribed 'Nov[ember] 7 1911', dated one day after Tolkien wrote *Darkness on the Road* (poem no. 11). Yet again he was inspired by Oxford, now entwined with a sense of the vastness of time and the insignificance of Man.

[A]

In a pale and saffron sweetness
    Shadows o'er the city flow:
Bluely dark its spires and mansions
    Grimly loom against the glow.

Where has shed the sun in sinking
    All his glory like to blood,
There the day-worn world a-weary
    Drinks refreshment from its flood,

And where soft and boundless radiance
    Meets the rugged crags of gloom,
One may gaze down sunlit ages
    On Earth's endless birth and doom.

Toss'd against the shining stillness
    Lightless, grimy-robed, and blind,
Rear the fruitless fruit of labour,
    Narrow dens of human kind;

But beyond the golden yearning
    of that evensong of flame
Stretch eternities of splendour,
    Ardent ages without name.

The second, slightly revised manuscript of the poem (B) is on a page with the second manuscript of *Darkness on the Road.*

[B]

In a pale saffron sweetness
    Shadows o'er the city flow:
Bluely dark its spires and mansions
    Grimly loom against the glow.

Where has shed the sun in sinking
    All his glory like to blood,
There the day-worn world a-thirsty
    Drinks refreshment from its flood,

And where soft and boundless radiance
    Meets the rugged crags of gloom,
One may gaze down sunlit ages
    On Earth's endless birth and doom.

Toss'd against the shining stillness,
    Lightless, grimy-robed, and blind,
Rear the fruitless fruit of labour,
    Narrow dens of human kind;

But beyond the golden yearning
    of that evensong of flame
Stretch eternities of splendour
    Ardent ages without name.

Compare 'Bluely dark its spires and mansions' with 'Many-mansioned tower-crownéd in its dreamy robe of grey' in *From Iffley* (poem no. 10), line 4.

A7: Tolkien replaced 'a-weary' with 'a-thirsty', but wrote 'a-weary?' in the margin as if uncertain of the change.

13

The Grimness of the Sea · The Tides · Sea Chant of an Elder Day · Sea-Song of an Elder Day · The Horns of Ylmir (1912–17)

This complex poem, which in its final state Tolkien called *The Horns of Ylmir*, evolved from a twelve-line impression of the wild, storm-tossed British coast into the song of seventy-four lines that Tuor made for his son Eärendel in Tolkien's private 'mythology' – 'The Silmarillion', as it came to be called, after the Elvish jewels whose theft precipitates many events. The earliest incarnation of the poem, *The Grimness of the Sea*, survives in two manuscripts; we give the earlier of these, before revision, as A. It is inscribed '1912 (sometime)'. As written in one of Tolkien's poetry notebooks, this first text falls between poems dated 1911 and 1913. Above the ink title *The Grimness of the Sea* there was once a title in pencil, *The Tides* (see below), but this has been mostly erased, and may have been added (and removed) later. Marginal notes ('sit', 'gaze', 'muse') indicate that Tolkien considered whether the poem should be in the present rather than the past tense.

[A] I sat on the magic margin twixt the music of the sea
With its endless dirging sorrow of what was, and is to be,
And the land with warring sunder'd, and rent with myriad scars,
Into ghostly towers unnumber'd that seem pleading to the stars.
I gazed on the crush'd and battered litter of rocky bones
Torn from the storm-flay'd shoreland, while the wounded Ocean moans,
His bitter hurts, and spuming around the riven jags
Of the overwhelméd outpost of the embattled host of crags,
Seems with remorse half-sicken'd, to gloat o'er the fleshless frame
As of some huge vanquish'd carcase in his watery warring slain;
And I mused on the eternal conflict of the changeful changeless sea
With the warworn weary bulwarks of the land which may not flee.

Tolkien marked up this text and carried his revisions into a second manuscript, making further alterations in the process. In addition to changes of words such as 'twixt' to ''tween' in line 1 and 'unnumber'd' to 'uncounted' in line 4, he expanded examples of elision (such as 'sunder'd' to 'sundered' in line 3) and he revised punctuation – a common process in his future work as a poet., The second text, given below as B, is also entitled *The Grimness of the Sea*, and has two inscriptions: 'Original nucleus of "The Sea-song of an Elder Day" (1912)' and 'St Andrews'. At least the first of these notes must have been written no earlier than 1917, when the poem had 'Sea-song' in its title (see below). Tolkien's aunt Jane Neave lived for several years in St Andrews, a seaside university town north of Edinburgh, where she was Lady Warden of University Hall. At the end of 1911 she resigned to take up farming at Gedling, Nottinghamshire, but was not able to move until 6 April 1912 at the earliest. Tolkien may have visited her in St Andrews in the early part of 1912 and written *The Grimness of the Sea* at that time; or if he was not there in 1912, it may be that his inscription 'St Andrews' indicates only that in writing *The Grimness of the Sea* he was recalling an earlier visit.

[B] I sat on the magic margin 'tween the music of the Sea
With its endless dirging sorrow of what was, and is to be,
And the land with warring sundered and torn with myriad scars
Into ghostly towers uncounted that seem pleading to the stars:
I gazed on the crushed and battered litter of rocky bones
Rent from the storm-flayed shoreland, while the wounded Ocean moans
His bitter hurts, and spuming around the riven jags
Of the overwhelméd outpost of th'embattled host of crags
Seems, with remorse half sickened, to gloat o'er the fleshless frame
Of some huge vanquished carcase in his watery warring slain;
Then I mused on the eternal conflict of the changeless changeful sea
With the war-worn weary bulwarks of the Land which may not flee.

In his account of *The Horns of Ylmir* in *The Shaping of Middle-earth* (1986, see text F) Christopher Tolkien begins with *The Tides* (see text D); at that time, he was unaware of *The Grimness of the Sea*. 'I have found nothing earlier than this text [*The Tides*]', he wrote, though 'it is clear from my father's notes to subsequent versions that he remembered the origin of the poem to be earlier than that time' (p. 214).

In August 1914 Tolkien made a walking tour of Cornwall's Lizard peninsula, the southern-most point of England. On 8 August he wrote to Edith Bratt: 'The sun beats down on you and a huge Atlantic swell smashes and spouts over the snags and reefs. The sea has carved weird wind-holes and spouts into the cliffs which blow with trumpety noises or spout foam like a whale, and everywhere you see black and red rock and white foam against violet and transparent sea-green' (quoted in Carpenter, *Biography*, p. 70). He also made drawings of the rocky coast and churning waves (Hammond and Scull, *Artist and Illustrator*, figs. 20, 21). On 27 November 1914, according to the date he inscribed above the text, he used the same sheet in one of his poetry notebooks on which he wrote text A to draft a sixteen-line addition (C) to *The Grimness of the Sea*.

[C] The immeasurable hymn of the Ocean I heard as it rose and fell:
Its organ whose stops are the piping of gulls and the thunderous swell;
The burden of the waters and the surging of the waves
Whose voices come on for ever and go rolling to the caves
Where an endless fugue of echoes splashes against wet stone
And rise and mingle in unison into a murmurous drone.
Down in an awful dark which has gulped the driven wind,
His yells and great white spoutings from the cavern where he's pinned
Burst from some turbulent fissure, and a leaping jet of froth
Spits into the sunlight, and the sea chant ends in wrath.
Drowned in water and music I lie on a dripping rock
Hearkening still but a-slumbering to the roar of the land ward shock
But the suck and suck of green eddies and the slap of ripples are all
That reach to my sheltered rock and I dream till the seamews call
Till the tide go out and the wind die and the organ of ocean cease
And I wake to silent caverns and empty sands and peace.

A few days later, Tolkien reworked and extended this addition, taking up earlier elements from *The Grimness of the Sea*, into a poem of forty lines which he now called *The Tides*. Its single extant (full) manuscript is inscribed with the date 4 December 1914 and 'On the Cornish Coast', evidently referring to Tolkien's visit there earlier in the year. Another manuscript of the poem once existed, written in the poetry notebook opposite the earliest text of *The Grimness of the Sea* and its extension, but this leaf was largely excised, leaving a stub with a fragment of text which is clearly that of *The Tides*, and was clearly a working document rather than a fair copy.

For its full manuscript, Tolkien wrote *The Tides* first in pencil on two pages, then in ink over pencil, obscuring most of his initial workings. To the ink text he made a few pencilled alterations, often without deleting the existing words, and on pages of his poetry notebook facing the manuscript proper he made further trials. Here we give, as D, the ink text as written before Tolkien applied revisions.

[D] I sat on the ruined margin of the deep-voiced echoing sea
whose roaring foaming music crashed in endless cadency
on the land besieged for ever (and) in an æon of assaults
torn into towers and pinnacles and caverned in great vaults;
that arch over trampled wreckage and the litter of rock-hewn shapes
riven in old sea-warfare from the black crags and the capes
by ancient battailous tempest and primeval mighty tide.
Then the trumpet of the Westwind shouted, and the grey sea sang, and cried,
white with the spume of anger to his armies and his powers
to array their billowed cavalry 'gainst the worn and drenchéd towers,
and the high wind-bannered fortalice of the unsurrendered coast.
then his long white restless feelers in the van of the clangorous host
leaping and creeping coil onward like the arms of a tentacled thing;
and the outriders of the tumult rustle and suck and cling,
till the plumed troops came galloping from the anger-driven sea
in ceaseless clamorous onslaught on the land's grim panoply;
and the foam-haired waterhorses, green rolling volumes, came;
and the full mad tide swarmed onward, and its warsong burst to flame.

Then the immeasurable hymn of the Ocean was heard as it rose and fell
to its organ whose stops are the piping of gulls and the thunderous swell;
and the burdon of the waters and the singing of the waves
whose voices come on for ever and go rolling to the caves
where an endless fugue of echoes splash against wet stone
and arise and mingle in unison into a murmurous drone;
while from down in a bellowing dark which has gulped the driven wind
his yell and great white spoutings from the cavern where he's pinned
burst out of a turbulent fissure, and a leaping jet of froth
spits into the sunlight — and the sea-chant ends in wrath;
as a chaos of splintered water hits a dripping black façade
like a fountain up to heaven and to earth as a cascade.
But drowned in water and music I find sleep in the infinite hymn,
and the song of the movement of Ocean as I lie on the streaming brim,
while the wet air is salt with the foam of the surge round mine isléd rock
and I hearken yet but aslumber to the roar of the landward shock.
Then the waters pour off and the reefs thrust their glistening shoulders again
naked up into the airs and the sun-rifts and seagoing rain,
and the suck and suck of green eddies and the slap of ripples are all
that reach to my sheltered stone; and I dream till the sea-mew call,
and the tide go out, and the wind die, and the Organ of Ocean cease,
and I wake to silent caverns, and empty sands, and peace.

Clangorous 'repeated clanging, uproar' in line 12 suggests the repeated noise of the waves, which in line 16 make an 'onslaught' against a 'grim panoply' – the land, as if clad in armour (*panoply*). The 'foam-haired waterhorses' of line 17 are white-capped breakers (heavy waves). *Mine* in the construction 'mine isléd' (D33) is the archaic form of *my* used before a word beginning with a vowel.

Tolkien reworked *The Tides* heavily, often struggling to achieve a desired vocabulary and order of lines. Especially concerned with the end of the poem, on the page facing its second manuscript page he reworked more fully, and significantly abridged, lines 29 through 40:

but drowned in water & music I lie on a dripping rock
hearkening still but aslumber in the [roar of the >] roaring
 landward shock
and the suck and suck of green eddies and the slap of ripples are all
that reach to [my > mine isléd >] my sheltered stone, and I dream
 till the seamew call,
and the tide go out, and the wind die, and the organ of Ocean cease
and I wake to silent caverns and empty sands, and peace.

Also opposite the first page of this manuscript are the first fourteen lines of the next stage of the poem, *Sea Chant of an Elder Day*; and because these are partly overwritten by some of his revisions to *The Tides*, it is evident that Tolkien returned to *The Tides* even as he worked on its successor.

In full, the *Sea Chant* exists in two manuscripts. On the earliest, the beginning of its title is spelled *Seachant* – there is no appreciable space between the words as written, though this may have been accidental. On the later of the two manuscripts (E) he wrote at its head '(Jan[uary] 1915 < Dec[ember] 1914 < 1912)', then altered 'Jan' to 'Mar[ch]', and at its end he inscribed 'Essay Club | March 1915'. He read the *Sea Chant* to the Essay Club of Exeter College, Oxford, of which he was a member, in March of his penultimate term as an undergraduate.

[E] In a dim and perilous region, down whose great tempestuous
 ways
I heard no sound of men's voices; in those eldest of the days,
I sat on the ruined margin of the deep voiced echoing sea
Whose roaring foaming music crashed in endless cadency
On the land besieged for ever in an aeon of assaults
And torn in towers and pinnacles and caverned in great vaults:
And its arches shook with thunder and its feet were piled with
 shapes
Riven in old sea-warfare from the crags and sable capes
By ancient battaillous tempest and primeval mighty tide.
When the trumpet of the first winds shouted and the grey sea
 sang and cried;

When a new white wrath woke in him, and his armies rose to war,
And swept in billowed cavalry to the walled and moveless shore,
When the windy-bannered fortalice of the high and virgin coasts
Flung back the first thin feelers of those elder tidal hosts;
But while the torrents gathered, and the leaping waters ran,
There came the long restless streamers of the stealthy-whispering van,
The outriders of the tumult: — like the arms of a tentacléd thing
That coiling and creeping onward did rustle and suck and cling;
Then the pluméd troops came galloping from the anger-driven sea
In gigantic clamorous onslaught on the Earth's grim panoply;
And the foam-haired water horses in green rolling volumes came
And the full mad tide swarmed landward, and its warsong burst to flame.

* * *

Then the immeasurable hymn of Ocean I heard as it rose and fell
To its organ whose stops were the piping of gulls, and the thunderous swell;
And the burdon of the waters and the singing of the waves
Whose voices came on for ever and went rolling to the caves,
Where an endless fugue of echoes splashed against wet stone
And arose and mingled in unison into a murmurous drone;
Till from down in a bellowing dark which had gulped the driven wind
His yell and great white spoutings, from the abyss where he was pinned,
Burst out of a turbulent fissure a leaping tower of froth
Splintered in the sunlight: — and the sea-music broke in wrath:
While the thunder of great battles shook the World beneath my rock,
And the landwall crashed in Chaos; and the Earth tottered at the shock

Where a dome of shouting waters smote a dripping black façade,
And its catastrophic fountains smashed in deafening cascade.
Then again through that giant welter the great organ pealed anew
While the voices of the flood sang deeply, and the voice of the High Wind grew,
And his breath blew the bitter tresses of the sea in the land's dark face,
And the wild air thick with spindrift fled on a whirling race
From battle unto battle: — till at length the seas abate
And draw back for a season and nurse their endless hate:
Then the waters pour off and the Earth heaved its glistening shoulders again
Naked up into the airs and sun-rifts and sea-going rain:
And the suck and suck of green eddies and the slap of ripples is all
That reach to mine isléd stone where I dream, till the seamew call;
And the tide go out; and the Wind die; and the Organ of Ocean cease,
And I waken to silent caverns, and empty sand, and peace —
In a lonely sunlit region down whose old chaotic ways
Yet no sound of men's voices echoed in those eldest of all days.

'Tresses of the sea' in line 39 refers to seaweed, here being blown upon the shore. In line 44, *sunrifts* presumably refers to breaks in clouds or mist through which the sun shines; compare *cloudrifts* in F44.

Dissatisfied with the final ten lines of text E (41–50), Tolkien replaced them, in the process expanding the poem to fifty-six lines:

From battle unto battle — till at length did the seas abate
And draw back for a season and nurse their endless hate;
Then the waters poured off and the Earth heaved its glistening shoulders again,
Naked up into the airs and the sunrifts and seagoing rain.
And the suck and suck of green eddies and the slap of ripples was all
That reached to mine isléd stone save the old unearthly call
Of sea-birds long forgotten and the grating of ancient wings.

Then I fell to a murmurous slumber mid these far off elder things
In a lonely sunlit region whose incalculable days
No man saw rise in splendour and go down the doméd ways,
As the world reeled with new vigour and strange things held the Earth,
And there was day and night and tempest in great cycles ere our birth.
The aeons roll like legions and the infantry of years
Go by in song and battle until the Oceans wane to meres
And the tides go out and the Winds die and all sea-musics cease
And I waken to the silent caverns, and empty sands, and peace.

There is also a typescript of this stage of the poem, identical with text E with only minor exceptions, and including the new ending, but now entitled *A Sea-Song of an Elder Day* and, unusually, signed 'J.R.R.T.' G.B. (Geoffrey Bache) Smith, a friend from King Edward's School, had written on 17 March 1915, asking Tolkien to send typewritten copies of his poems, which Smith offered to forward, after reading, to their schoolmate R.Q. (Robert Quilter 'Rob') Gilson. On 22 March Smith observed 'that typewriting is always useful because it shows up one's faults better than anything else. Things always look as silly as they can in that medium. Hence I have discovered several interesting things about you. The first is, that your syntax occasionally tends to become obscure. The "Sea-song" has this one fault in some slight degree, though it does not matter much in so vigorous a work' (Bodleian Library). H.T. Wade-Gery, a friend of Smith (and future Oxford colleague of Tolkien) who was shown the poem, thought it exaggerated, but found some lines to be good. In the event, the *Sea-Song* remained complex and retained its character as Tolkien continued to revise it, despite his readers' criticisms.

At this point it is important to mention one of Tolkien's paintings, *Water, Wind and Sand* (Hammond and Scull, *Artist and Illustrator*, fig. 42), found in a sketch-book he called *The Book of Ishness*. We wrote in *Artist and Illustrator* that the picture, inscribed 'Illustration to Sea Song of an Elder Day',

> captures very well the emotional flavour of rock and wave on the Cornish coast when the sea is rough, but as in a dream-vision, stylized and in extraordinarily bright colours. . . . Tolkien must have had in mind the idea of someone transported to the sea in his thoughts and soul but not in body. The small

> figure in the painting, enclosed in a white sphere, is in the midst of the elements yet set apart from them. Perhaps it is meant to be Tolkien himself, experiencing at close hand the sea's 'deafening cascade'. . . . [p. 46]

We wonder now, though, if the figure that appeared to us to be in 'a white sphere' is not the speaker of the poem on his 'isléd stone'. The position of *Water, Wind and Sand* in the sketch-book suggests that it may be dated to early 1915, which would accord with Tolkien's reading of the poem at Exeter College that March; but this is not certain.

Tolkien entered the army in June 1915, as soon as he completed his final Oxford examinations, and in summer 1916 fought on the Somme. He returned to England that November with trench fever, a highly infectious disease carried by lice, and began a long series of hospital treatments and periods of recuperation as his illness recurred. In April 1917 he was posted to a reserve battalion on the Holderness peninsula near Withernsea, and probably from early June was able to live with his wife in officer's quarters near the village of Roos; then, in mid-August, he was admitted to hospital in Hull, where he stayed for nine weeks. The final versions of his sea poem date from this later period, from spring and summer 1917, according to notes Tolkien later wrote on two further manuscripts. The first note reads 'Remodelled from No. 4 Aug[ust] 31 [to] Sep[tember] 2 1917 Hospital Hull', and the second '1910–11–12 rewr[itten] & recast after. Present shape due to rewriting and adding introd[uction] & ending in a lonely house near Roos Holderness (Thirtle Bridge Camp) Spring 1917'. In fact, the 'Spring 1917' manuscript contains a later stage of textual development than the pages marked as from August and September. 'No. 4' refers to a numeral written at the head of the second manuscript of the *Sea Chant*. The 'lonely house' was presumably the officer's quarters Tolkien shared with Edith.

Opposite the beginning of the second manuscript of the *Sea Chant*, Tolkien wrote:

> This is the song that Tuor told to Eärendel his son what time the Exiles of Gondolin dwelt awhile in Dor Tathrin the Land of Willows after the burning of their city. Now Tuor was the first of Men to see the Great Sea, but guided by Ulmo towards Gondolin he had left the shores of the Ocean and passing through the Land of Willows became enamoured of its loveliness, forgetting both his quest and his former love of the sea. Now Ulmo lord of the Vai [the great ocean] coming in his

> deep-sea car sat at twilight in the reeds of Sirion and played to him on his magic flute of hollow shells. Thereafter did Tuor hunger ever after the sea and had no peace in his heart did he dwell in pleasant inland places.

This could be the 'introduction' to which he refers in his 'Spring 1917' inscription, but it seems more likely that he was referring to the three lines beginning 'Tuor recalleth' in text F below, which introduce a new frame and link the poem to Tolkien's developing 'Silmarillion' mythology. The 'ending' he refers to is presumably lines 67–74 in text F, which follow on the close of the *Sea-Song* ('empty sands, and peace').

Christopher Tolkien comments in *The Shaping of Middle-earth* (p. 215) that the paragraph concerning Tuor ('This is the song . . .') 'very evidently belongs with the tale of *The Fall of Gondolin* . . . , and was no doubt added at the time of the composition of the tale . . . since the *Sea Chant* has no point of contact with the Tuor legend, nor indeed with any feature of the mythology'. Tolkien wrote *The Fall of Gondolin*, one of the earliest tales of 'The Silmarillion', while he was convalescing at the end of 1916 or early in 1917. In this, Tuor, having made his way to the sea,

> set up his abode, dwelling in a cove sheltered by great sable rocks, whose floor was of white sand, save when the high flood partly overspread it with blue water; nor did foam or froth come there save at times of the direst tempest. There long he sojourned alone and roamed about the shore or fared over the rocks at the ebb, marvelling at the pools and the great weeds, the dripping caverns and the strange sea-fowl that he saw and came to know; but the rise and fall of the water and the voice of the waves was ever to him the greatest wonder and ever did it seem a new and unimaginable thing. [*The Book of Lost Tales, Part Two* (1984), p. 151]

The poem, or song, is not, however, one of Tuor's direct experiences with the sea, but of visions sent by Ulmo to Tuor in his place of exile: there Tuor and his companions 'abode very long indeed, and Eärendel was a grown boy ere the voice of Ulmo's conches drew the heart of Tuor, that his sea-longing returned with a thirst the deeper for years of stifling; and all that host arose at his bidding, and got them down Sirion to the Sea' (*The Book of Lost Tales, Part Two*, p. 196).

Tolkien achieved the final text of the poem through these two manuscripts ('August to September' and 'Spring') and a further typescript. The 'August to September' manuscript, written in ink over erased pencil, has two titles, *Sea-Song of an Elder Day* and, above this, *The Horns of Ulmo*. The 'Spring' (i.e. later) manuscript is entitled only *The Horns of Ulmo*. The title of the typescript, made *c.* 1924, from which we have taken the text below (F, which excludes Tolkien's few late revisions recorded in our notes), was originally *The Horns of Ulmo*, but was changed by Tolkien to *The Horns of Ylmir* 'from "The Fall of Gondolin"'. *Ulmo* is the name of the Lord of Waters in Tolkien's invented language Qenya (later Quenya), while *Ylmir* is the name of the same being, one of the Ainur or angelic powers, in another Elvish language, Gnomish (Goldogrin, Noldorissa; by later evolution, Noldorin, Sindarin). Christopher Tolkien published this version in *The Shaping of Middle-earth*, pp. 215–17.

[F] 'Tuor recalleth in a song sung to his son Earendel the visions that Ylmir's conches once called before him in the twilight in the Land of Willows.'

''Twas in the Land of Willows where the grass is long and green —
I was fingering my harp strings, for a wind had crept unseen
And was speaking in the tree-tops, while the voices of the reeds
Were whispering reedy whispers as the sunset touched the meads,
Inland musics subtly magic that those reeds alone could weave —
'Twas in the Land of Willows that once Ylmir came at eve.

In the twilight by the river on a hollow thing of shell
He made immortal music, till my heart beneath his spell
Was broken in the twilight, and the meadows faded dim
To great grey waters heaving round the rocks where sea-birds swim.

I heard them wailing round me where the black cliffs towered high
And the old primeval starlight flickered palely in the sky.
In that dim and perilous region down whose great tempestuous ways
I heard no sound of men's voices, in those eldest of the days,
I sat on the ruined margin of the deep-voiced echoing sea

Whose roaring foaming music crashed in endless cadency
On the land besieged for ever in an æon of assaults
And torn in towers and pinnacles and caverned in great vaults;
And its arches shook with thunder and its feet were piled with shapes
Riven in old sea-warfare from those crags and sable capes.

Lo! I heard the embattled tempest roaring up behind the tide
When the trumpet of the first winds sounded, and the grey sea sang and cried
As a new white wrath woke in him, and his armies rose to war
And swept in billowed cavalry toward the walled and moveless shore.
There the windy-bannered fortress of those high and virgin coasts
Flung back the first thin feelers of the elder tidal hosts;
Flung back the restless streamers that like arms of a tentacled thing
Coiling and creeping onward did rustle and suck and cling.
Then a sigh arose and a murmuring in that stealthy-whispering van,
While, behind, the torrents gathered and the leaping billows ran,
Till the foam-haired water-horses in green rolling volumes came —
A mad tide trampling landward — and their war-song burst to flame.

Huge heads were tossed in anger and their crests were towers of froth
And the song the great seas were singing was a song of unplumbed wrath,
For through that giant welter Ossë's trumpets fiercely blew,
That the voices of the flood yet deeper and the High Wind louder grew;
Deep hollows hummed and fluted as they sucked the sea-winds in;
Spumes and great white spoutings yelled shrilly o'er the din;
Gales blew the bitter tresses of the sea in the land's dark face
And wild airs thick with spindrift fled on a whirling race
From battle unto battle, till the power of all the seas
Gathered like one mountain about Ossë's awful knees,

And a dome of shouting water smote those dripping black façades
And its catastrophic fountains smashed in deafening cascades.

* * *

Then the immeasurable hymn of Ocean I heard as it rose and fell
To its organ whose stops were the piping of gulls and the thunderous swell,
Heard the burden of the waters and the singing of the waves
Whose voices came on for ever and went rolling to the caves,
Where an endless fugue of echoes splashed against wet stone
And arose and mingled in unison into a murmurous drone —
'Twas a music of uttermost deepness that stirred in the profound
And all the voices of all oceans were gathered to that sound;
'Twas Ylmir, Lord of Waters, with all-stilling hand that made
Unconquerable harmonies, that the roaring sea obeyed,
That its waters poured off and Earth heaved her glistening shoulders again
Naked up into the airs and the cloudrifts and sea-going rain,
Till the suck and suck of green eddies and the slap of ripples was all
That reached to mine isléd stone save the old unearthly call
Of sea-birds long-forgotten and the grating of ancient wings.

Thus murmurous slumber took me mid those far-off eldest things
(In a lonely twilit region down whose old chaotic ways
I heard no sound of men's voices, in those the eldest of the days
When the world reeled in the tumult as the Great Gods tore the Earth,
In the darkness, in the tempest of the cycles ere our birth),
Till the tides went out, and the Wind died, and did all sea-musics cease,
And I woke to silent caverns and empty sands and peace.

Then the magic drifted from me and that music loosed its bands —
Far, far-off, conches calling — lo! I stood in the sweet lands,

And the meadows were about me where the weeping willows grew,
Where the long grass stirred beside me, and my feet were drenched with dew.
Only the reeds were rustling, but a mist lay on the streams
Like a sea-roke drawn far inland, like a shred of salt sea-dreams.
'Twas in the Land of Willows that I heard th'unfathomed breath
Of the Horns of Ylmir calling — and shall hear them till my death.'

Tolkien set down 'Ulmo' in all three iterations of F, but changed the name to 'Ylmir' in the second manuscript and in the typescript. Ulmo, or Ylmir, in 'The Silmarillion' 'dwells in the outer ocean and controls the flowing of all waters and the courses of rivers, the replenishment of springs and the distilling of rains and dews throughout the world. At the bottom of the sea he bethinks him of music deep and strange yet full ever of a sorrow' (*The Book of Lost Tales, Part One* (1983), p. 58). Ossë in line 42 is one of the lesser powers ('gods') in the pantheon of 'The Silmarillion', and one of those subordinate to Ulmo/Ylmir: 'Salmar there was with him [Ulmo], and Ossë and Ónen to whom he gave the control of the waves and lesser seas, and many another' (*The Book of Lost Tales, Part One*, p. 58). The 'tumult as the Great Gods tore the Earth, | In the darkness, in the tempest of the cycles ere our birth' (F63–64) is described in *The Chaining of Melko* in *The Book of Lost Tales*: 'Vaporous storms and a great roaring of uncontrolled sea-motions burst upon the world, and the forests groaned and snapped. The sea leapt upon the land and tore it, and wide regions sank beneath its rage or were hewn into scattered islets, and the coast was dug into caverns', etc. (*The Book of Lost Tales, Part One*, p. 100).

In the long evolution from poem to poem discussed in this entry, only about one-half of one line survived from *The Grimness of the Sea* to *The Horns of Ylmir* – 'I sat on the ruined margin of the deep-voiced echoing sea', originally 'I sat on the magic margin twixt the music of the sea' – while other imagery variously entered and was omitted or further developed. This series of verses is one of the most illustrative of Tolkien's growth as a poet in his early years, as his work expanded in length and complexity of thought. His developing use of vocabulary is also notable, as some archaic or poetic words such as *battailous* ultimately gave way to more familiar forms (in this case, *embattled*).

Images of the sea were prominent in Tolkien's imagination, and expressed often in his writings. Though his personal experience was gained largely from visits to the English coast, his understanding of the sea and of its emotional effect upon men was profound. Apart from Tuor in an early prose story, Ælfwine 'knew not and had never seen the sea, yet he heard its great voice speaking deeply in his heart, and its murmurous choirs sang ever in his secret ear between wake and sleep' (*The Book of Lost Tales, Part Two*, p. 314). Legolas in *The Lord of the Rings* likewise feels the 'sea-longing' to which he eventually succumbs, while Aldarion in the Númenórean tale of Aldarion and Erendis cannot be kept from the sea even for the sake of his family or royal duties. Images of great waters early became a significant element in Tolkien's mythology, but are seen perhaps most notably in the later tale of Númenor, the land of Men drowned, as a punishment, when the world was remade at the end of the Second Age. In this there was a personal connection: Tolkien had a recurring 'dream of the ineluctable Wave, either coming out of the quiet sea, or coming in towering over the green inlands. . . . It always ends by surrender, and I awake out of deep water. I used to draw it or write bad poems about it' (letter to Christopher Bretherton, 16 July 1964, *Letters*, pp. 486–7).

A1: Tolkien considered whether to change 'magic' to 'rended' ('torn apart'); compare 'ruined' in texts D, etc. 'Rent' in A3 became 'torn' in text B.

D2: On the facing page of his notebook, Tolkien changed this line to 'with its long long sorrow of things that are and were to be'.

D3: The word '(and)' is in parentheses as written; presumably Tolkien was unsure whether to include it. On the facing page, he changed this line to: 'and the land in a million sieges and an æon of assaults'.

D6: On the facing page of his notebook, Tolkien considered but struck through 'torn down in an ancient slaughter', presumably as a revision to 'riven in old sea-warfare'.

D7: On the facing page of his notebook, Tolkien changed this line to 'embattled against the tempest and the legions of the tide'.

D11: Tolkien considered whether to change 'unsurrendered' to 'riven and drenchéd' (compare D10), then struck through 'and'.

D12: On the facing page of his notebook, Tolkien wrote that 'clangorous' should be changed to 'clamorous'; but compare 'clamorous' in D16.

E39: 'Tresses of the sea', i.e. seaweed.

F Introduction: The quotation marks are in the original.

F1: Much later, in red biro (ballpoint pen) and thus no earlier than the mid-1940s, Tolkien marked ''Twas' to be changed to 'It was'. Because this and other markings on the typescript are much later, and seem to be musings rather than revisions intended to create yet another text, we have recorded them in notes rather than incorporate them in version E.

F3: Reeds are commonly said to have 'voices', here 'reedy whispers', or (at F71) 'rustling', or (poem no. 37, D4) 'murmurous': that is, the sound of reed-grasses brushing against one another in the breeze.

F7: Tolkien changed 'shells' to 'shell' in the typescript. In *The Fall of Gondolin* he describes Ulmo's

> great instrument of music; and this was of strange design, for it was made of many long twisted shells pierced with holes. Blowing therein and playing with his long fingers he made deep melodies of a magic greater than any other among musicians hath ever compassed on harp or lute, on lyre of pipe, or instruments of the bow. Then coming along the river he sate among the reeds at twilight and played upon his thing of shells; and it was nigh to those places where Tuor tarried. [*The Book of Lost Tales, Part Two*, p. 155]

F13: Much later in the typescript (in red) Tolkien changed 'down' to 'in'.

F16: Much later in the typescript (in red) Tolkien considered whether to change 'roaring foaming music crashed in endless cadency' to 'endless roaring music crashed in foaming cadency'.

F21: Much later in the typescript (in red) Tolkien marked 'roaring' to change to 'rolling'. In the first manuscript, this line reads 'By ancient battailous tempest and primeval mighty tide', and is followed by a line of asterisks indicating a break, struck through. The next line followed: 'Lo! the trumpet of the first winds sounded, and the grey sea sang and cried'.

F25: 'Fortalice' survived in both manuscripts until replaced with 'fortress' in the second.

F28: In the typescript this line is marked with an 'X' (in red ballpoint ink, therefore much later). Christopher Tolkien feels that this was 'probably primarily on account of the use of *did*' (*The Shaping of Middle-earth*, p. 218); and in this regard, compare l. 65.

F37–44: In the first manuscript these lines were significantly different:

> Its breath blew the bitter tresses of the sea in the land's dark face,
> And wild airs thick with spindrift fled on a whirling race
> From battle unto battle:—Then vast thunders rove the rocks;
> And the landwall crashed in chaos; Earth tottered neath the shocks;
> Great domes of shouting water smote her dripping black façades
> And their catastrophic fountains smashed in deafening cascades.

F41–2: In the second manuscript the lines read originally 'From battle unto battle:—till the thunder rove the rock | And the landwall crashed in chaos, and Earth tottered neath the shock'. Tolkien changed them there to the final form, in the process writing and deleting a line presumably meant at one stage to replace l. 41, 'Till the last thundering thunder o'erwhelmed the riven rock'.

F47: 'Burden' is spelled thus in the second manuscript, but still 'burdon' in the first.

F51–2: The two lines following 'murmurous drone—' were new in the second manuscript, replacing four lines in the first:

Deep hollows hummed and fluted as they sucked the [*deleted:* deep]
    sea-winds in;
Spumes and great white spoutings yelled shrilly o'er the din —
A music of uttermost deepness seemed to stir in the profound,
All the bellowing of Oceans was gathered in that sound;

F65: Much later in the typescript (in red) 'died' is marked to be changed to 'ceased', and 'cease' to 'died', and 'did' is struck through. In *The Shaping of Middle-earth* Christopher Tolkien observes that these alterations would have destroyed the rhyme. Also, an 'X' is written (in red) against this line in the margin; see Christopher Tolkien's comment on 'did' for l. 28, above.

14

Outside (1913–14)

Tolkien recorded, but later struck through, on the first manuscript of *Outside* (A), that he composed the poem in December 1913 at Barnt Green, and that it was 'suggested by a tune heard in 1912'. Barnt Green, south-east of Birmingham, was the home of his relatives, the Incledons.

[A] We sit in a magic oasis of gold in a desert of blue,
when out of the lull of a many voices grown suddenly still
I hear outside in the dimness, in the night inexplorably vague
a voice that pipes to my heart with a shrill bitter fluting of ill.
It calls from the river of night, where the ghosts of the people of day
— of the whispering dreaming trees, of the leaves and listening grass —
— float thin on the many-lunged heaving of the breath of the slumbering world.
An unbearable wandering wisp of a melody cloudy and vast,
but paler than image of starlight be-mirror'd in tear-grey dew,
is borne on the winds of loneliness out of some lightless place.
'Tis a fragment of tune clear as moonlight but equally woven with gloom;
a thread that the knife of the wind has torn from a fabric of space,
from a myriad music of mists that is fashion'd of silver and black
with a burden of desperate blue as a nightmare of hopeless skies:
And the light seems to wane and the fire-song is frozen to whispering ash,
And the chill of the fear of the darkness sits by my shoulder and cries
of terror primeval and helpless, of the dreads of the children of Earth,
of dim altars and magic unfathom'd that in shadow-wrapt forests abide.

I hear it; it lures and repels me, and wanly it wails in my ears;
It pipes and it tells me of lurking, of wizardry pale — and
outside.

A second, revised manuscript followed, dated December 1914, achieved after Tolkien filled two pages with rough workings. At first he was uncertain whether to retain the original first line, in which 'we' are comfortably 'in a magic oasis of gold in a desert of blue', or immediately to create a sinister mood, so that the poem would begin as well as end with unease. At this stage *Outside* comprised twenty-four lines, ending:

Only the Pines were ancient or evil enough to believe
For they come from an æon unelfin, and of things long before us it
cried
Before us now scattered and haunting: — there wanly I hear it
again
As it luringly pipingly tells me of — I know not, but calls me
outside.

But Tolkien omitted these in a third manuscript, which otherwise is largely a fair copy of the second. On this he wrote again its dates of original composition and recasting, and the Old English words 'Se nihtstapa' ('The Night-walker').

The final text of the poem was reached in a typescript (of which ribbon and carbon copies are extant) slightly revised from the third manuscript. Before giving it a few further revisions at some later date (included in B, below), Tolkien circulated it to friends.

[B] We crouch by the islandéd firelight in a circling ocean of dark,
When out of the lull of a many voices grown suddenly still
I hear outside in the dimness in the night inexplorably vague
A voice that pipes to my heart, with a shrill hollow fluting of ill.
It calls from the river of Night where the ghosts of the people of
day —
Of the whispering dreaming trees, of the leaves and the
listening grass —
Float thin on the many-lunged heaving of the breath of the
slumbering world.
An unbearable wandering wisp of a melody slender as glass
And pale as an image of starlight mirrored in tear-grey dew,
Is borne on the winds of loneliness out of some lightless place:

There's Something unelfin, inhuman, goes haunting and stopping out there,
Down the hill with the two moonlit woods, up the path — and I daren't see its face —
Up the path — to the gate — to the window — no! over the shadowy hedge
The thin hooting fluting voice calls, and I listen with ears and with eyes,
While the light seems to wane and the fire-song is frozen to whispering ash,
And the chill of the fear of the darkness sits by my shoulder and cries
Of terror primeval and empty and the dreads of the children of earth;
Of things that are ancient and nameless, unelfin, inhuman, and old,
That cling to the gloom of great forests and go piping about in the dark
With a thin hooting fluting voice calling and calling outside in the cold.

On 22 March 1915 G.B. Smith pointed to this as an example of Tolkien the poet using long sentences in a 'very luxurious' style: 'One meets with such a lot of different tropes and adjectives in about half a sentence, that if the sentence is long, one is apt to lose oneself before the end of it. I think you can afford to prune a very little here. But don't knock the words out, they are good. I should try [to] save shorter metres and try to make shorter sentences' (Bodleian Library). Instead of lines 5–8 as Tolkien fashioned them, Smith suggested that they be broken thus:

It calls from the river of Night, where
the ghosts of the people of day —
Of the whispering dreaming trees,
of the leaves and the listening grass,
Float thin on the many lunged
heaving of the breath of the slumbering world.

The 'thin hooting fluting voice' may be compared to the music of Timpinen (Tinfang, Tinfang Warble) in an early text in Tolkien's mythology, if with a different aspect: 'Then slept Eriol, and through his dreams there came a music thinner and more pure than any he heard before, and it was full of longing. Indeed it was as if pipes of silver or flutes of shape most slender-delicate uttered crystal notes and threadlike harmonies beneath the moon upon the lawn; and Eriol longed in his sleep for he knew not what' (*The Book of Lost Tales, Part One*, p. 46; see also poem no. 29).

A2: The construction 'a many' is a dialectal form meaning 'very many'.

B7: 'Many-lunged', which persisted in all versions of the poem (in the third manuscript as 'many-lungéd'), was corrected in the typescript from 'many-hinged', evidently a typist's error. G.B. Smith quotes the latter in writing to Tolkien, probably in March 1915, suggesting that he read a copy of the typescript before Tolkien made final changes.

15

Magna Dei Gloria (1914–15)

Edith Bratt was received into the Roman Catholic Church in Warwick, where she was living, and she and Tolkien were formally betrothed, on 8 January 1914, the first anniversary of their reunion once Tolkien came of age. *Magna Dei Gloria* almost certainly was written in response to these events. It exultantly conveys the strength of Tolkien's love for Edith and of his religious faith, so intensely and personally, perhaps, that he cancelled both of its versions and did not include it in any proposed collection of his poems.

Its first manuscript, of two, is dated to January 1914, dedicated 'to EMB' (Edith Mary Bratt), and inscribed '(Warwick)'. Striking this draft through, Tolkien wrote a second manuscript, inscribed '1915 Ap[ril] 22', near the end of the short vacation between Hilary and Trinity terms at Oxford. We give these versions as A and B.

[A]

Love hath breath'd upon me and I live!
Love shineth in its deep.
Love hath lived within me and I breathe!
Lo now I wake from sleep.

★

I have a lover and the world is fair,
    And night departs the sun;
I see her eyes a-mist with love,
    And every fight is won.
Life standeth forth reveal'd, and its veil it falleth down;
My body leapeth sudden heal'd touched by the spirit's crown.
The mystery of endless worlds and innumerable hearts' desire
In a perfect moment's vision lit by flicker of Eternal Fire
    Sees my soul, and sings rejoicing,
    Life and Death and All re-voicing,
    In God, Eternal Love, rejoicing
        Ad Magnam Dei Gloriam.

★

The body loveth and the flesh is blest,
For love doth it renew:
The spirit loveth, and the being all,
Soul and its raiment too,
Is glorified beyond all song, and beyond all gaze is led
To the Fount of Love, to the Heart of God, one fathomless mystic Red.
Beyond these opalescent shades, and dimness of just dawning sight
To where no vision wanly fades; to the one great Blazing Light
If smallest soul love smallest being
Down eternities to God 'tis seeing,
To Love Eternal, Aim of Being
Et Magnam Dei Gloriam.

★

Love hath breath'd upon me and I live!
Love shineth in its deep.
Love hath lived within me and I breathe!
Lo! Lo! I wake from sleep.

[B] Love hath breathed upon me and I live!
Love shineth in its deep.
Love hath lived within me and I breathe!
Lo, now I wake from sleep.

★

Are other eyes a-mist with love?
Then every fight is won.
Has love aroused my dull heart too?
Then 'tis but just begun.
Life standeth forth revealed and casts its one veil down;
My body leapeth sudden healéd touched by the spirit's crown.
The mystery of endless worlds and innumerable hearts' desire
In a perfect moment's vision lit by flicker of Eternal Fire
Sees my soul, and sings rejoicing,
Life and Death and All re-voicing,

In God, Eternal Love, rejoicing
In magna Dei gloria.

*

The body loveth and the flesh is blest
For love doth it renew
The spirit loveth and the being all.
Soul and its raiment too
Is glorified beyond all song,
And beyond all gaze is led
To the Fount of Love, to the Heart of God
Unfathomed mystic Red:
Beyond these opalescent shades,
Huge dimness of just dawning sight
To where no vision wanly fades
To that great Blazing Light.
If least of souls love smallest being
Through eternity to God 'tis seeing,
To Love Unending, Aim of Being
et Magnam Dei Gloriam.

*

Love hath breathed upon me and I live:
Love shineth in its deep.
Love hath lived within me and I breathe
—And lo! I wake from sleep.

B7: Tolkien considered whether to change 'dull' to 'blind'.

B10: Tolkien considered whether to change 'the spirit's crown' to 'this spirit-crown'.

16

The Voyage of Éarendel the Evening Star · *The Last Voyage of Éarendel* · *Éala! Éarendel Engla Beorhtast!* (1914–?1961 or ?62)

In 1914, during the Oxford long (summer) vacation, Tolkien visited his aunt Jane Neave and his brother Hilary at Phoenix Farm, Gedling. There, on 24 September, he composed *The Voyage of Éarendel the Evening Star*, as it was first called. Its earliest extant version, given here as A, was written in ink over a pencil text Tolkien later erased; it is impossible to know if the erased text was the original version, or if there was an even earlier manuscript. Above the title, Tolkien wrote the word 'English', presumably to distinguish the text from an alternate, 'Classical' version (see below). Its date of composition, 'Sep[tember] 1914 24', written by Tolkien in the upper left corner of the first page, appears to be contemporary with the rest of the manuscript. In the upper right corner, Tolkien wrote 'EMB' (Edith Mary Bratt) followed by a cross above a bar.

[A] I

Éarendel sprang up from the Ocean's cup
    In the gloom of the mid-world's rim;
From the door of Night as a ray of Light
    Leapt over the twilight brim,
And launching his bark like a silver spark
    From the golden-fading sand
Down the sunlit breath of Day's fiery Death
    He sped from Westerland.

II

He threaded his path o'er the aftermath
    Of the glory of the Sun,
And went wandering far past many a star
    In his gleaming galleon.
On the gathering tide of darkness ride
    The argosies of the sky

And spangle the night with their sails of light
    As the Evening star goes by;

III

But unheeding he dips past these twinkling ships,
    By his wandering spirit whirled
On a magic quest through the darkling West
    Toward the margent of the World:
And he fares in haste o'er the jewelled waste
    To the dusk from whence he came
With his heart afire with bright desire
    And his face in silver flame.

IV

For the Ship of the Moon from the East comes soon,
    From the Haven of the Sun,
Whose white gates gleam in the coming beam
    Of the mighty Silver One.
Lo! with bellying clouds as his vessel's shrouds
    He weighs anchor down the dark
And on shimmering oars leaves the blazing shores
    In his argent-orbéd bark.

V

And Éarendel fled from that Shipman dread
    Beyond the dark Earth's pale,
Back under the rim of the Ocean dim,
    And behind the world set sail;
And he heard the mirth of the folk of Earth
    And hearkened to their tears,
As the world dropped back in a cloudy wrack
    On its journey down the years.

VI

Then he glimmering passed to the starless vast
    As an isléd lamp at sea
And out of the ken of mortal men
    Set his lonely errantry
Tracking the sun in his galleon
    And voyaging the skies

Till his splendour was shorn by the birth of Morn
And he died with the Dawn in his eyes.

Humphrey Carpenter states in *Biography* (p. 71) that Tolkien's poem, by implication the original version, 'was headed with the line from Cynewulf's *Crist* that had so fascinated him: *Eala Earendel engla beorhtast!*' This is true, however, only of the final manuscript, and by revision of the later typescripts. 'The Ocean's cup' recalls *ofer ȳða ful* ('over the cup of waves') in *Beowulf.* Christopher Tolkien has noted (*The Book of Lost Tales, Part Two*, p. 269) that the image of a 'Ship of the Moon' coming forth from the white gates of 'the Haven of the Sun' later appeared in his father's 'Silmarillion' tale *The Hiding of Valinor*, and that in *The Tale of the Sun and Moon* the Moon likewise has 'shimmering oars'.

Opposite manuscript A, on two pages of one of Tolkien's poetry notebooks, are the pencilled bones of an alternate version of the poem (given here, in truncated form, as B), headed 'Classical', with different names substituted for 'Éarendel' and 'Westerland' in the first and fifth stanzas.

[B] Sprang Phosphorus up from the Ocean's cup
Into the gloom of the mid-world's rim

. . . .

6 On the lucent fading sea,
Down the sunlit breath of Day's fiery death
He sped from Hesperie.

. . . .

29 Lo! with bellying clouds as [her > the] vessel's shrouds
She weighs anchor down the dark
And on shimmering oars leaves the skiey shores
In his argent-orbéd bark.

33 But Phosphorus fled from that blazing dread

. . . .

In Greek mythology *Phosphorus* was a name for the morning star; the evening star was called Hesperus, and was long considered a separate celestial body. Phosphorus and Hesperus were, appropriately, half-brothers, both sons of the dawn goddess Eos, or Aurora. *Hesperie* in line 8 is a variant of *Hesperia* 'western land'.

On the same page immediately following these workings are ten further lines in pencil, as below, but it is not clear if Tolkien intended them for his 'Classical' version or as revisions to his 'English' text (A): they would suit either. The first three are bracketed, and the fourth and seventh are marked as if of special importance; none, however, was carried into later texts.

Then to depth unknown he sped alone
    To the lightless void of space,
And beyond the ken of Earthborn men
    He turned his radiant face

Then he sped alone to the deeps unknown —
    Of his faring [*written above:* journey] none can tell
How far afloat in his glimmering boat
    He reached the gates of Hell
Then tracked the sun in his galleon
    And voyaged up the skies

Tolkien made another version, based on A, with only minor differences, of which the most substantive is in line 16, 'even-star' for 'Evening star'. This text is entitled more simply (and without accented *E*) *The Voyage of Earendel*, with the original, fuller title rendered in Old English, 'Scipfæreld Éarendeles Æfensteorran'. The manuscript is dated 'Sep[tember] 1914', for its first invention, but may have been made for reading to the Essay Club of Exeter College later that year, on 27 November. At the foot of its second page Tolkien wrote 'Ex[eter] Coll[ege] Essay Club Dec[ember]. [*sic*] 1914'.

This was followed in turn by a typescript, which survives in a ribbon copy and two carbon copies, each with manuscript annotations. On two of its three sheets Tolkien altered the Modern English title of the poem to *The Last Voyage of Éarendel* – on a second copy, *The Last Voyage of Ëarendel* – and the Old English title to 'Éalá! Éarendel Engla Beorhtast' ('Hail! Éarendel, Brightest of Angels'). One of the carbon copies is inscribed 'Gedling Notts. [Nottinghamshire] Sept[ember] 1913 [*sic*] & later'. The typescript text is largely the same as that in the earlier ('English') manuscripts, except for minor differences of punctuation and readings in the third, fifth, and sixth stanzas. The ribbon copy contains a few pencilled, disconnected, and mostly illegible or erased workings which do not seem to be of significance. Tolkien also tried alternate readings on one of the carbon copies, notably 'endless quest' for 'magic quest' in line 19 and 'timbered' for 'orbéd' in line 32, both carried into the final text; 'As a lamp on an isle' for 'As an isléd lamp at sea' in line 42, which was not adopted; and for lines 45–48, also rejected, 'Following the Sun in his galleon | He sailed to unknown skies | And when golden Morn in the East was born | New flame was in his eyes.'

A subsequent typescript was made with a purple ribbon while Tolkien was employed at Leeds in the early 1920s. In this at first he retained the revised Old and Modern English titles, but struck through the latter. Again, the text was little changed, except that the revisions Tolkien wrote on two copies of the earlier typescript were incorporated.

He now marked the poem with many further, indeed substantial, changes, including some which had appeared on the third copy of the earlier typescript; and in a final manuscript (C, below), entitled only *Éala! Éarendel Engla Beorhtast!* (adding a second exclamation mark), he took up all of the changes of the second typescript. Christopher Tolkien included this version in *The Book of Lost Tales, Part Two*, pp. 267–9. Its date, he says there, 'cannot be determined, though the handwriting shows it to be substantially later than the original composition' (p. 267). It seems possible that Tolkien revisited the work in late 1961 or early 1962, while considering poems to include in *The Adventures of Tom Bombadil and Other Verses from the Red Book*.

[C] Éarendel arose where the shadow flows
  At Ocean's silent brim;
Through the mouth of night as a ray of light
  Where the shores are sheer and dim
And launched his bark like a silver spark
  From the last and lonely sand;
Then on sunlit breath of day's fiery death
  He sailed from Westerland.

He threaded his path o'er the aftermath
  Of the splendour of the Sun,
And wandered far past many a star
  In his gleaming galleon.

On the gathering tide of darkness ride
    The argosies of the sky,
And spangle the night with their sails of light
    As the streaming star goes by.

Unheeding he dips past these twinkling ships,
    By his wayward spirit whirled
On an endless quest through the darkling West
    O'er the margin of the world;
And he fares in haste o'er the jewelled waste
    And the dusk from whence he came
With his heart afire with bright desire
    And his face in silver flame.

The Ship of the Moon from the East comes soon
    From the Haven of the Sun,
Whose white gates gleam in the coming beam
    Of the mighty silver one.
Lo! with bellying clouds as his vessel's shrouds
    He weighs anchor down the dark,
And on shimmering oars leaves the blazing shores
    In his argent-timbered bark.

Then Éarendel fled from that Shipman dread
    Beyond the dark earth's pale,
Back under the rim of the Ocean dim,
    And behind the world set sail;
And he heard the mirth of the folk of earth
    And the falling of their tears,
As the world dropped back in a cloudy wrack
    On its journey down the years.

Then he glimmering passed to the starless vast
    As an isléd lamp at sea,
And out of the ken of mortal men
    Set his lonely errantry
Tracking the Sun in his galleon
    Through the pathless firmament,
Till his light grew old in abysses cold
    And his eager flame was spent.

The word, or name, *Éarendel* is found in the Old English *Crist I*, also known as *Advent*, preserved in the medieval Exeter Book (Exeter Cathedral Library MS 3501). *Crist I* is part of a triad, often considered a single poem attributed wholly to Cynewulf, now treated as three poems on the Advent, Ascension, and Last Judgement of Christ, with Cynewulf arguably the author of only the second. Lines 104–5 of the poem read 'Eálá Earendel engla beorhtast | Ofer middangeard monnum sended', in Tolkien's translation 'Hail Earendel, brightest of angels, above the Middle-earth sent unto men' (*Sauron Defeated* (1992), p. 236). Bosworth and Toller's dictionary of Old English defines *earendel* as 'a shining light, ray'. The word also appears, with a variant spelling, in the Old English Blickling Homilies, in which St John the Baptist is described as 'the new dawn' ('si niwa eorendel') heralding the arrival of the Sun (Christ). In 1967 Tolkien wrote that

> when first studying A-S [Anglo-Saxon, i.e. Old English] professionally (1913–) [when, as a student at Oxford, he changed his course from Classics to the English School] – I had done so as a boyish hobby when supposed to be learning Greek and Latin – I was struck by the great beauty of his word (or name) [Éarendel], entirely coherent with the normal style of A-S, but euphonic to a peculiar degree in that pleasing but not 'delectable' language. Also its form strongly suggests that it is in origin a proper name and not a common noun. . . . To my mind the A-S uses [in *Crist* and the Blickling Homilies] seem plainly to indicate that it was a star presaging the dawn (at any rate in English tradition): that is what we now call *Venus*: the morning-star as it may be seen shining brilliantly in the dawn, before the actual rising of the Sun. That is at any rate how I took it. Before 1914 [*sic*] I wrote a 'poem' upon Earendel who launched his ship like a bright spark from the havens of the Sun. I adopted him into my mythology – in which he became a prime figure as a mariner, and eventually as a herald star, and a sign of hope to men. [draft letter to Mr Rang, August 1967, *Letters*, pp. 542–3]

Eärendil (variously spelled) did eventually become important in the 'Silmarillion' mythology, as a human transformed with his ship into the 'star' Venus. He is the chief figure, or mentioned, in several of the poems in this book.

Just as significantly, in 1946 Tolkien referred to *Éarendel* in his unfinished *Notion Club Papers*:

There's little to be found out about [*Éarendel*] in Anglo-Saxon, though the name is there all right. Some guess [in relation to the Prose Edda] that it was really a star-name for Orion, or for Rigel. A ray, a brilliance, the light of dawn: so run the glosses [comments on Old English words].

Éalá Éarendel engla beorhtost
ofer middangeard monnum sended!'

he chanted. '"Hail Earendel, brightest of angels, above the middle-earth sent unto men!" When I came across that citation in the dictionary I felt a curious thrill, as if something had stirred in me, half wakened from sleep. There was something very remote and strange and beautiful behind those words, if I could grasp it, far beyond ancient English.

'I know more now, of course. The quotation comes from the *Crist*; though exactly what the author meant is not so certain. It is beautiful enough in its place. But I don't think it is any irreverence to say that it may derive its curiously moving quality from some older world.' [*Sauron Defeated*, p. 236]

This was in a fictional context, in the persona of Lowdham, but the sentiment was surely Tolkien's own, and indeed, Humphrey Carpenter quotes (*Biography*, p. 64) some of the words as Tolkien's, without identifying their source.

In his draft letter to Mr Rang and in the original title of the present poem, Tolkien variously refers to Éarendel, that is, to the very bright planet Venus, as a morning star and an evening star. Most of the time Venus is one or the other, depending on the point of its orbit around the Sun. As a 'morning star' it is visible in the east before sunrise, and as an 'evening star' in the west after sunset. In the *Voyage* Éarendel (Venus), as the evening star, becomes visible at 'the mid-world's rim' (low in the west) after sunset ('the sunlit breath of Day's fiery Death'), and proceeds below the horizon ('back under the rim of the Ocean dim'). It may appear to be 'chased' by the Moon, as both bodies move through the heavens, and it 'dies' when the glare of the Sun, which Venus follows closely, makes it impossible to see.

According to John Garth in *The Worlds of J.R.R. Tolkien* (2020), the evening star 'had been very visible on clear evenings at the Lizard in August 1914', when Tolkien made his walking tour in Cornwall (see poem no. 13). 'Venus had sprung from the western horizon to vanish again due west after an hour and a half of brilliance.' Tolkien's poem, composed a few weeks later, was therefore 'a myth made from observation' (p. 64). David Haden states in *Tolkien and the Lizard: J.R.R. Tolkien in Cornwall, 1914* (2021), however, that Tolkien could have seen the same celestial display on 24 September in Gedling, provided that he was at a sufficiently high elevation, such as on a ridge or in a church tower. Kristine Larsen explores this and other astronomical aspects of Eärendil thoroughly in '"Following the Star": Eärendil, Númenor, and the Star of Bethlehem' (2023).

Humphrey Carpenter called *The Voyage of Éarendel the Evening Star* the beginning of Tolkien's private mythology (*Biography*, p. 71). It is, at least, the first appearance of the name of an important figure in 'The Silmarillion' (see further, poem no. 18). But when Tolkien wrote the *Voyage* his mythology was only on the brink of conception, and Éarendel was no more than a personification of the evening (or morning) star, if with an angelic aspect. (John Garth, in *Tolkien and the Great War*, p. 45, characterized Éarendel as 'the steersman of Venus, the planet that presages the dawn'.) Carpenter recounts that Tolkien showed the poem to his friend G.B. Smith, who asked what it was 'really about', to which Tolkien replied: 'I don't know. I'll try to find out' (*Biography*, p. 75). His 'search' for the answer to Smith's question is seen as integral to the subsequent invention of 'The Silmarillion'. Since we do not know Carpenter's source for the exchange, neither can we know what Smith hoped to learn; but Tolkien's response, that he would 'try to find out', akin to Picasso's 'I do not seek, I find' or Michelangelo's statement that his sculpture was already present in the marble, is telling in regard to Tolkien's organic creative method.

In *The Road to Middle-earth*, Tom Shippey holds that Tolkien 'no doubt' looked for 'Earendel' in the 1900 edition of the *Crist* by A.S. Cook, and in Jakob Grimm's *Teutonic Mythology*. The latter would have told him that an analogue of the name, 'Aurvandill', appears in the Prose Edda, and that 'Orendel' in the German poem of that name (*c.* 1200) is a king's son, shipwrecked in the Holy Land, who returns home 'to convert his heathen countrymen', thus 'a messenger of hope' (1992 edn., pp. 218, 219). John Garth, however, points out in '"The Road from Adaptation to Invention": How Tolkien Came to the Brink of Middle-earth in 1914' that Tolkien had at hand when he read of Earendel in the *Crist* an article by Barend Symons on *Heldensage* (hero-sagas) in *Grundriss der germanischen Philologie* (1893), which he had borrowed for the summer from the Exeter College library. Symons writes there of the 'Orendelsage' in which the hero is 'a wanderer upon the waters, a seafarer, the central figure in a

Germanic mariner myth, now lost, corresponding to (but not deriving from) the classical myth of Ulysses/Odysseus; he certainly belongs among the oldest Germanic heroes' (Garth, p. 14). Tolkien had also borrowed *Bibliothek der angelsächsischen Poesie,* edited by Christian W.M. Grein and Richard Paul Wülcker (1883–98), which contains the *Crist.*

Allan Turner suggests in his essay 'Early Influences on Tolkien's Poetry' (2013) 'that Eärendil's setting sail "O'er the margin of the world" sounds like an echo of Francis Thompson's "Across the margent of the world I fled"' from 'The Hound of Heaven', and that Tolkien's use of 'margent' in the draft we have given as A 'helps to confirm the similarity' of the phrases (p. 206). In fuller form, Thompson wrote:

> Across the margent of the world I fled,
> And troubled the gold gateways of the stars,
> Smiting for shelter on their clangèd bars;
> Fretted to dulcet jars
> And silvern chatter the pale ports o' the moon.

In his '"Road from Adaptation to Invention"', examining the earliest version of *The Voyage of Éarendel the Evening Star*, John Garth, drawing upon a suggestion by Hugh Brogan, argues that Tolkien is indebted to the poem 'Arethusa' by Percy Bysshe Shelley:

> Arethusa arose
> From her couch of snows
> In the Acroceraunian mountains,—
> From cloud and from crag,
> With many a jab,
> Shepherding her bright fountains.

'Shelley's poem retells the Greek myth', Garth explains,

> in which the nereid Arethusa flees from the Alpheus down the Acroceraunian mountains . . . and thence under earth and sea until she finds a new home as a fountain on the island of Ortygia. Tolkien's poem tells of a mariner sailing off the edge of the world, being hunted by the Moon, and finding his place among the heavenly bodies as the Evening Star (the planet Venus).

'The closest similarities' between the poems are, however, in their metre; in their rhyme scheme, AABCCB (provided that Tolkien's lines with internal rhyme, such as 'Éarendel sprang up from the Ocean's cup', are considered as half-lines – 'Éarendel sprang up || from the Ocean's cup'); in 'the structural organisation of their narratives'; and in some 'verbal echoes' of vocabulary (pp. 15–16). Garth acknowledges, though, that there are also differences, such as 'in some of the B-rhymed lines, where Shelley prefers anapaests (two unstressed syllables followed by one stressed syllable . . .) while Tolkien often prefers iambs (two syllables, unstressed–stressed . . .)' (p. 16).

The merits of this argument notwithstanding, if an inspiration from Shelley were needed, 'The Cloud' would seem in some respects a better candidate, with its images of the heavens and sailing among them:

> The sanguine Sunrise, with his meteor eyes,
>   And his burning plumes outspread,
> Leaps on the back of my sailing rack,
>   When the morning star shines dead;
> As on the jag of a mountain crag,
>   Which an earthquake rocks and swings,
> An eagle alit one moment may sit
>   In the light of its golden wings.

Not only does 'The Cloud' share with *The Voyage of Éarendel the Evening Star* its metre and rhyme scheme – here ABCBDEFE in long lines – compared with 'Arethusa' it is the more widely known and revered of Shelley's works. Indeed, it was praised above all others as 'more purely and typically Shelleian', sprung 'from the faculty of make-believe', by Francis Thompson in an essay ('Shelley') first published in 1909 and which leads off the third volume of Thompson's 1913 collected *Works*, the latter purchased by Tolkien in 1913–14. The same metre and rhyme scheme would soon appear again in Tolkien's *Why the Man in the Moon Came Down Too Soon* (1915, poem no. 24).

It is also interesting to note, though in regard to Tolkien probably irrelevant, that Charles William Stubbs, Dean of Ely Cathedral and later Bishop of Truro, published a poem in his book *Bryhtnoth's Prayer and Other Poems* (1899), 'The Carol of the Star', in which *Earendel* is mentioned throughout in refrains: 'Hail Earendel, | Brightest of Angels!' and 'Godlight be with us, | Hail Earendel!' The first verse reads:

They came three Kings who rode apace,
To Bethlem town by God's good grace:
    Hail Earendel,
    Brightest of Angels!
Pardie [i.e. verily]! It was a duteous thing,
Wise men to worship childë King:
    Godlight be with us,
    Hail Earendel!

Stubbs understood that *Earendel* was the 'mythic name' of the Star of Bethlehem ('Bethlem'), but this seems to be nowhere else attested.

A5: Tolkien considered 'sun-born', 'argent', and 'ardent' as alternatives to 'silver'.

A5–8: Kris Swank has described the similiarity between these lines by Tolkien and four by G.B. Smith in his poem 'Legend' (published in *A Spring Harvest*, 1918). In the latter 'a sweet bird'

Sang of blessed shores and golden
Where the old, dim heroes be,
Distant isles of sunset glory,
Set beyond the western sea.

Swank does not seek to claim borrowing between Tolkien and Smith, in either direction, noting that the death-imagery of going into the west was conventional. In 'The Poetry of Geoffrey Bache Smith with Special Note of Tolkienian Contents' (2021) she points out other instances of shared vocabulary and ideas in verses by the two friends, while rightly cautioning that 'similarity is not proof of influence' (p. 13).

A8: 'Sped from Westerland', i.e. the evening star is setting in the West.

A14: Tolkien is picturing stars as sailing vessels; *argosies* are large merchant ships.

A18: 'His wandering spirit': to the ancients, planets (like Venus) were celestial bodies that wandered among the 'fixed' stars. English *planet* is from the Greek for 'wanderer'.

A19: 'Darkling' originally read 'darkening'.

A29: *Bellying* 'swelling', presumably as if the clouds were sails; here Tolkien seems to equate *shrouds* with sails rather than lines which support rigging. Tolkien considered 'blazing' as an alternative to 'vessel's'.

A31: 'Blazing' originally read 'skiey'.

A32: Tolkien considered 'golden-hornéd' as an alternative to 'argent-orbéd'.

A45: *Galleon* is typically applied to a large, especially Spanish, ship of war, but here, as elsewhere, Tolkien is using it poetically for 'ship', and for the rhyme.

B31: 'Skiey' originally read 'blazing'.

17

The Story of Kullervo (1914–?15)

As noted for poem no. 8, Tolkien discovered the Finnish *Kalevala* while at King Edward's School, in the English translation by W.F. Kirby. He was inspired first to write his 'Lemminkainen' parodies, but later embraced the *Kalevala* tale of Kullervo, which was to become a seminal influence on his story of Túrin Turambar in 'The Silmarillion'; each is a tale of revenge which ends in tragedy. Tolkien's brief, unfinished *Story of Kullervo* is chiefly in prose, but portions are in verse. Altogether the work comprises just over twenty-one foolscap pages, in addition to three pages with a list of names and draft plot synopses. Verlyn Flieger has published its text in *Tolkien Studies* 7 (2010) and in book form as *The Story of Kullervo* (2015), together with Tolkien's paper on the *Kalevala* mentioned earlier (see poem no. 8); here space allows for only an extract from the poem, in our transcription made from the manuscript in the Bodleian Library.

Prior to the following passage by Tolkien, near the end of the manuscript, Kullervo and a fair maiden, Wanōna, have met in the forest and become lovers. When at last he speaks of his family, she realizes that she is his long-lost sister. Because they have committed incest, however unwittingly, she will seek death by casting herself over a waterfall:

To the wood I went for berries
And forsook my tender mother
Over plains and neath the mountains
Wandered two days and a third one
Till the pathway home I found not
For the paths led ever deeper
Deeper deeper into darkness
Deeper deeper into sorrow
Into woe and into horror.
O thou sunlight O thou moonbeam
O thou dear unfettered breezes
Never never will I see thee
Never feel thee on my forehead
For I go in dark and terror
Down to Tuoni to the River.

In Finnish mythology, Tuoni is the goddess of Tuonela, the realm of the dead.

Most of the poetry in Tolkien's *Kullervo* is based closely on Kirby's translation, sometimes for several lines together, much of the alteration being simple rewording. For the passage quoted, Tolkien condensed a longer corresponding text (Runo 35, ll. 217–56) while keeping its flavour and metre. The Kirby text begins:

> 'When I was a little infant,
> Living with my tender mother,
> To the wood I went for berries,
> 'Neath the mountain sought for raspberries.
> On the plains I gathered strawberries,
> Underneath the mountain, raspberries,
> Plucked by day, at night I rested,
> Plucked for one day and a second,
> And upon the third day likewise.
> But the pathway home I found not,
> In the woods the pathways led me,
> And the footpath to the forest.

In a letter to the poet W.H. Auden in 1955 Tolkien wrote that the Finnish language 'set the rocket off in story [i.e. inspired him to write]. I was immensely attracted by something in the air of the Kalevala, even in Kirby's poor translation', though he 'never learned Finnish well enough to do more than plod through a bit of the original, like a schoolboy with Ovid' (*Letters*, p. 313). He borrowed C.N.E. Eliot's *Finnish Grammar* (1870) at least twice from the Exeter College Library, in 1911 and 1914.

In a note to his 1914/15 paper on the *Kalevala* he describes Kirby

> sometimes seem[ing] to plunge unnecessarily for [the] prosy and verbally preposterous, though the great difficulty of course of the original style [of the *Kalevala*] it is hard to exaggerate. As far as I can see he seems to have tried as nearly as possible the task of making each line correspond to each line in the original which hasn't improved things, but occasionally he is very good indeed. [Bodleian Library]

Iwona Piechnik has said, however, that Kirby showed 'great respect for the archaic spirit of the poem and its form' ('Finnic Tetrameter in J.R.R. Tolkien's *The Story of Kullervo* in Comparison to W.F.

Kirby's English Translation of the *Kalevala*' (2021), p. 205) but that some adaptation was inescapable.

In Finnish, primary stress falls on the first syllable of a word, while stress in English varies but is often on the final syllable. And whereas the distinctive *Kalevala* metre is usually accompanied by parallels of sounds between nearby words, such as alliteration (the repetition of initial sounds) and assonance (the repetition of vowel sounds), features natural to Finnish, it is more difficult to achieve in English in a long form. Tolkien comments in his essay that 'the reason why translations [of the *Kalevala*] are not all good is that we are dealing with a language separated by quite an immeasurable gulf in method of expression from English' (Bodleian Library). Kirby in translating, and Tolkien in his turn, compensates through the repetition of words or phrases with the same rhythm.

Tolkien wrote further to Auden that his discovery of a Finnish grammar at Exeter College occurred 'when I was supposed to be reading for Honour Mod[eration]s', the first public examination for Classics students, 'say 1912 to 1913' (*Letters*, pp. 312, 313; Tolkien sat 'Hon. Mods.' in late February 1913); and in his essay he confessed that 'when H. Mods. should have been occupying all my forces I once made a wild assault on the stronghold of the original language and was repulsed at first with heavy losses' (Bodleian Library). From this, Verlyn Flieger argues that 1912 is the earliest possible date for *The Story of Kullervo*. But Tolkien's statements point to his extracurricular study of Finnish, not necessarily to his version of *Kullervo*, while more specifically in October 1914 he wrote to Edith Bratt: 'Amongst other work I am trying to turn one of the stories [of *Kalevala*, i.e. *Kullervo*] . . . into a short story somewhat on the lines of [William] Morris' romances with chunks of poetry in between' (*Letters*, p. 3). The phrase 'I am trying' implies that Tolkien was only then writing *Kullervo*; there is no suggestion that the work was already begun one or two years earlier. See further, our *J.R.R. Tolkien Companion and Guide: Reader's Guide* (2017, hereafter *Reader's Guide*), p. 594.

It is not known precisely when Tolkien abandoned *The Story of Kullervo*, but it may be significant that one page of the manuscript contains early workings of the poem *May Day* (no. 26), which is dated (in two other copies) to 20–21 April 1915. It seems reasonable to suppose that Tolkien set *Kullervo* aside in order to pursue other work, probably that spring, which was for him a period of remarkable creativity – several poems date from this time – as well as his final term at Oxford, leading to examinations in June.

Iwona Piechnik's essay referenced above compares at length Tolkien's translation from the *Kalevala* with Kirby's, noting in particular that apart from their similarity, Tolkien's has (on balance) more archaic vocabulary, while Kirby's includes more repetition of words.

2, 5, 13: In her edition, Verlyn Flieger inserts at the end of each of these lines a full stop, required by sense but not present in the manuscript.

18

The Minstrel Renounces the Song · The Lay of Earendel · The Bidding of the Minstrel (1914–?25)

Tolkien wrote the earliest draft of this work on three pages, quickly and for the most part very roughly. Occasional phrases, such as 'a jewelled bird that goes gallantly', 'a measureless journey', and 'gallantly bent on an albatross flight', can be deciphered and compared with finished texts. Most importantly, before revision the draft began 'Now listen to a song of immortal sea-yearning', line 5 of version A transcribed below.

Tolkien had promised G.B. Smith that he would 'try to find out' what his September 1914 poem *The Voyage of Éarendel the Evening Star* (no. 16) was 'really about', but he seems to have returned to the wandering mariner only after composing the first workings of his new poem. Nowhere in the draft, only in the first lines of the first coherent version (A), do we find the name *Éarendel.* On the back of one leaf, however, Tolkien wrote, often without pause or capitalization:

> Earendel's boat goes through North [*added:* back of N[orth] Wind]. Iceland Greenland and the wild islands: a mighty wind and crest of great wave carry him to hotter climes on back of West Wind. Land of strange men land of magic. The home of Night *the Spider.* He escapes from the meshes of Night with a few comrades sees a great mountain island and a golden city – wind blows him southward tree men. Sun dwellers spices fire-mountains red sea: mediterranean: loses his boat (travels afoot through wilds of Europe?) or Atlantic. Home. waxes aged. has a new boat builded. bids adieu to his north land sails west again to the lip of the world: just as the sun is diving into the sea. He set sail upon the sky and returns no more to Earth.

Around 1916–17 Tolkien added to this statement an explanation that 'the golden city was Kôr' (see poem no. 30), and that Éarendel 'had caught the music of the Solosimpe and returns to find it only to find that the fairies have departed from Eldamar' – their dwelling place in the distant West of the world – incorporating elements of the developing 'Silmarillion' mythology. But in winter 1914, if indeed he composed his poem at that time (as noted on one of its manuscripts, see below), Tolkien appears to have conceived of Éarendel only as a great mariner sailing earthly seas, not yet a fixture of the sky or connected with fairies (elves).

The version of the present poem following the draft is preserved again as a rough manuscript, though much less rough than the initial workings. The poem as conceived at this point was much longer than before, but here it is relevant to give only its first forty lines.

[A] Sing me yet more of Éarendel the wanderer
Chant me a lay of his white-oared ship —
marvellous cunning imagineless gondola
foamily musical out on the deep!
Then listen to a song of immortal sea-yearning
Tale to make hearts beat wild with delight,
weaving a winelike spell, and a burning
Wonder from spray and the odours of night
Velvety murmurous out on far oceans
Tossing at anchor off islets forlorn
Full of the joy of intoxicate motions
Of bellying sails when a wind is born
And the gurgling bubble of tropical water
Tinkles from under the ringed stem,
— thousands of miles is the ship from those wrought her
A petrel, a sea bird a white-wingéd gem
Gallantly bent on a measureless faring
Ere she came homing in sea laden flight
Circuitous lingering restlessly daring
Coming to haven, unlooked for, at night.
Slender the boat and of glimmering timber —
Her sails were all silvern and taper her mast
Silver her throat with foam and her limber
Flanks when she swanlike floated past —
Who can tell (or what harp can accompany
melodies strange enough, rich enough tunes
pale with the magic of cavernous harmony,
loud with shore-music of beaches and dunes).
How she would strain as the North wind summoned her
Or slide into harbourless fjords alone
by intricate channels and portals columnar
Pillared and lintelled with cavernous stone

There was the dwelling of monster and nicer
Walruses bright and narwhal and seal
In grottos vast under wavering flicker
Whiles would be seen and a shivering peal
Of ghostly sea laughter would rise with a shudder
billowing echoed on stalagmite bars
or it felt as were unbidden hands at her rudder
as the ship was half lifted with tremular jars.

The manuscript containing text A, which occupies one and a half pages, continues on its second page and two further sheets. At first Tolkien seems to have meant the whole to comprise a single work, but later split off the remainder, after line 40, as *The Mermaid's Flute*; and this being so, we have discussed the additional workings with poem no. 19. Tolkien appears to have come very soon to conceive of both the present work and *The Mermaid's Flute* as two parts of a longer *Lay of Earendel*. By mid-March 1915 he gave handwritten copies of both parts to G.B. Smith, who commented on the earlier poem that 'the bits about the boat coming home, and about the music, were very good indeed' (17 March 1915, Bodleian Library; see further, poem no. 19).

Tolkien wrote a second manuscript on paper removed from an examination booklet, probably from the years he was on the English faculty at Leeds. At its head is a title added in pencil, *The Minstrel Renounces the Song*. Its text (B) is a revision of the first twenty-eight lines of A, with a few lines new to the version; lines 29–40 of A were abandoned. By now Éarendel had become part of a mythology in which his 'tale of immortal sea-yearning' was made by fairies (later, elves) 'ere the change of the light', long ago, before their ships foundered and rotted, and 'the fire and wonder in men's hearts' had grown cold.

[B] Sing me yet more of Éarendel the wandering,
chant me a lay of his white-oared ship,
more marvellous cunning than mortal men's pondering,
foamily musical out on the deep!
Then harken — a tale of immortal sea-yearning
the fairies once made ere the change of the light,
weaving a wine-like spell and a burning
wonder of spray, and the odours of night,
of murmurous gloamings out on far oceans
of his tossing at anchor off islets forlorn,

to the unsleeping waves never-ending sea-motions
of bellying sails when a wind was born
and the gurgling bubble of tropical water
tinkled from under the ringéd stem
and thousands of miles was his ship from those wrought her
a petrel, a sea-bird, a white-wingéd gem,
gallantly bent on a measureless faring
ere she came homing in sea-laden flight,
circuitous, lingering, restlessly daring
coming to haven unlooked for, at night.
But the music is broken, the words half-forgotten,
the sunlight is faded the moon has grown old,
the fairy ships foundered or weed-swathed and rotten
the fire and the wonder in men's hearts are cold.
Who now can tell (and what harp can accompany
(with) melodies strange enough, rich enough tunes
pale with the magic of cavernous harmony,
loud with shore-music of beaches and dunes)
how slender his boat; of what glimmering timber;
how her sails were all silvern and taper her mast,
and silver her throat with foam and her limber
flanks as she swan-like floated past.
And the song I can sing is as shreds one remembers
of golden imaginings fashioned in sleep;
as a whispered tale told by the withering embers
of old things far off that but few hearts keep.

The first of three extant typescripts of the poem, now entitled *The Lay of Earendel*, was derived from B, with little further revision. On the back of its second sheet is typed, as if a draft greeting, 'John Francis Reuel Tolkien AND MICHAEL HILARY REUEL send love to mummy', indicating that the version cannot be earlier than Michael's birth in October 1920 – one could reasonably date it to 1920 or 1921. A second typescript in turn was derived from the first, marked by Tolkien that it was composed originally in winter 1914 (i.e. the winter of 1914–15) in St John Street, Oxford – during the academic year 1914–15 Tolkien shared rooms at 59 St John Street with his fellow undergraduate Colin Cullis. This version includes only minor alterations, but also two lines which break off abruptly: 'Songs have been sung in Elfland since the hills were green and young | Of the deeds that were done i'. This is not an abandoned continuation of the present poem, but a few words which may have been the intended opening to *The*

Lay of the Fall of Gondolin (poem no. 66), another work which can be dated to around 1921 in its earliest form.

With the third and final typescript, incorporating revisions to the second, Tolkien changed the title of the work to *The Bidding of the Minstrel from The Lay of Earendel*. This version (C, below) was typed with the purple ribbon associated with Tolkien's years at Leeds. Our transcription includes his final alterations, notably 'Eldar' for 'fairies' in line 6 and 'Elven' for 'fairy' in line 23.

[C] 'Sing us yet more of Éarendel the wandering,
Chant us a lay of his white-oared ship,
More marvellous-cunning than mortal men's pondering,
Foamily musical out on the deep.
Sing us the tale of immortal sea-yearning
The Eldar once made ere the change of the light,
Weaving a winelike spell, and a burning
Wonder of spray and the odours of night;
Of murmurous gloamings out on far oceans;
Of his tossing at anchor off islets forlorn
To the unsleeping waves never-ending sea-motions;
Of bellying sails when a wind was born,
And the gurgling bubble of tropical water
Tinkled from under the ringéd stem,
And thousands of miles was his ship from those wrought her
A petrel, a sea-bird, a white-wingéd gem,
Gallantly bent on a measureless faring
Ere she came homing in sea-laden flight,
Circuitous, lingering, restlessly daring,
Coming to haven unlooked for, at night.'

'But the music is broken, the words half-forgotten,
The sunlight is faded, the moon is grown old,
The Elven ships foundered or weed-swathed and rotten,
The fire and the wonder of hearts is acold.
Who now can tell, and what harp can accompany
With melodies strange enough, rich enough tunes,
Pale with the magic of cavernous harmony,
Loud with shore-music of beaches and dunes,
How slender his boat; of what glimmering timber;
How her sails were all silvern and taper her mast,
And silver her throat with foam and her limber
Flanks as she swanlike floated past!

The song I can sing is as shreds one remembers
Of golden imaginings fashioned in sleep,
A whispered tale told by the withering embers
Of old things far off that but few hearts keep.'

Christopher Tolkien included this last version in *The Book of Lost Tales, Part Two*, pp. 270–1.

By spring 1915 elements of the 'Silmarillion' mythology were a strong presence in Tolkien's thoughts, and it was probably early in that year when he began to write a lexicon of his invented Elvish language Qenya. In this is an entry for *Earendl*, so spelled, glossed as 'the wanderer, the greater sailor who sailed up into the sky in his ship Vingelot, which now is the morning or evening star. Voronwe was his faithful companion on earth, also Elwenillo, Voronwe's son.' The meaning of *ea*, *earen(-d)* is given as 'eagle'. In *The Silmarillion* (1977, p. 325) the name *Eärendil* is translated as 'Lover of the Sea'.

A3: A *gondola* is not only a flat-bottomed boat such as those used on the canals of Venice, but also a ship's boat, or a kind of small vessel designed for war. The pairing of 'wanderer' (A1) and 'gondola' is near-rhyme, i.e. similar but not exactly alike in their final sounds, depending on the pronunciation of final *-er*.

A9: 'Velvety murmurous', i.e. the smooth sound of the waves. Compare 'murmurous gloamings' in texts B and C.

A12: Compare 'bellying sails' with the 'bellying clouds' of *The Voyage of Éarendel the Evening-Star* (poem no. 16).

A16–20: Tolkien compares Éarendel and his wide-roving ship with the petrel, a seabird which flies far from land.

A22: 'Taper her mast': masts are typically tapered towards the top, to reduce weight and wind resistance, and to transfer strength to the base where stress is greatest.

A34: The male narwhal, an Arctic white whale, has a long fluted tusk, or tooth.

B9: 'Murmurous gloamings', i.e. the sound of the waves on multiple occasions at twilight.

C5: In *The Book of Lost Tales, Part Two*, p. 270, 'Sing us the tale' is misprinted 'Sing us a tale'.

C6: Here Tolkien seems to have intended *Eldar* in its strictest sense, of elves who left the Great Lands in Middle-earth and saw the light of Valinor at Kôr (see poem no. 30)

19

The Mermaid's Flute (1914–17)

As we have said, the poem ultimately called *The Bidding of the Minstrel from The Lay of Earendel* (no. 18) was originally, in its first text following a draft, only the first forty lines of a longer poem which Tolkien chose to divide in two. The remainder became, at last, *The Mermaid's Flute*, the first, much amended workings of which are transcribed below as text A. According to a note by Tolkien on one version of *Bidding*, the whole of the originally longer work was composed in winter 1914 in his rooms in St John Street, Oxford.

[A] White-days would wane slow and a far sun sink under
Globed and afire in some watery west
And twilight creep over the world's edge in wonder
Blue, robed in dreams, and all sleepily tressed.
A shivering breeze then would roughen the water
Darkling to indigo under the dusk
When out on a skerry, some last flicker caught her
May be or the moon, on a white-hollowed tusk
A deep-thronéd mereking's pale handed daughter
Made shimmering melody born of green deeps
Where in twilit and blue-shadowed sea grot was taught her
The fathomless magic the mere people keeps
As she piped would a cold thrill seize on all hearkened,
Their hearts would go blind with the murmurous spells
And the blossom'd Earth fade from desire as Night darkened
And dreams of white foam and of marvellous shells
Of phosphorous sheens and of pale pools pellucid
Of coral and polyp and tendrilous weed
Rhythmically swaying all tangled and noosëd
To submarine swells, wherein silver fish feed —
— Such dreams would arise; or they dreamt of a palace
Where crooning old mere-songs a maiden abode
Clad in sapphire and green with enchanted sea-chalice
To still their heart-longing: — alluring it glowed
All roofëd with magical scaly-tiled cupolas
Builded with faint-blushing coraline walls
Or of long sunken gold, while through many a loophole was

Fairy light gleaming: lo! conch-music calls
With sweet hollow sound from each wide-open casement
Whence in and out swimming and gliding there glints
A shoal of fish mail clad in woven enlacement
Anemones twining their myriad tints
Circle it round, and its gables shell-copéd
Are ringed with liquid and musical swirls
Of restless sea-motions and bannered with ropëd
Sea-tassels all knotted and wartëd with pearls:
They fancy their heavy feet wistfully wander
On darkening pathways of silver-grained sand
Whereon mirrored is dimly a moon wraith from yonder
Or bended reflections of star-glimmers stand.
Faint echoes go wavering down the sea-hollows
And silent things luminous sail by in gloom
As twilight fades slowly and sea darkness follows
And deeper and wider the weed-shadows loom
And night sinks the dream where the poolëd shades quiver
Till Dawn lift the slumbering Sun from the Seas
Far out at East and there runs a cold shiver
Through Ocean: a shuddering wisp of a breeze
Then over the white pavéd floor go grey glimmers
Of twisted light heralding fire handed morns
And winding through weed roots there pallidly shimmers
Dim tremulous blowing of ammonite horns.

Lines 11–30 and 32–6 of this version survive as well on a fragment of a fair copy manuscript.

Tolkien's description of life under the sea is accurate but dreamlike, with its 'marvellous shells | Of phosphorous sheens and of pale pools pellucid' (i.e. translucently clear). 'Coral and polyp' are naturally matched – *coral*, a marine invertebrate, is typically a colony of *polyps*, or smaller marine organisms with tubular bodies and stinging tentacles – an *anemone* is a polyp. 'Tendrilous weed' is seaweed, which waves like tendrils in the flow of water. The 'white-hollowed tusk' (later 'hollow white tusk') is the flute of the poem's title, presumably of the same unusual sort found in some museums, made from the horn (tusk) of a narwhal. An *ammonite* is an extinct marine mollusc with a flat spiral shell; ammonite fossils are plentiful at Lyme Regis, Dorset, where Tolkien took holidays.

On its face, *The Mermaid's Flute* has no evident connection with the tale of Éarendel, or with the earlier part of the original poem from which *The Mermaid's Flute* was divided, except, maybe, in so far as it follows thematically on lines in poem no. 18 in which 'a shivering peal | Of ghostly sea laughter would rise with a shudder' from the dwellings of sea-creatures. At the time of its composition, it seems that there was no connection sufficient to bind the two parts of the original poem. But by 1916–17, when Tolkien set down in one of his poetry notebooks ideas and suggestions, and possibly earlier as he gathered his thoughts, the figure of Éarendel (or Eärendel) became important to the developing mythology, and within the outline of the mariner's great tale – apparently never written in full – is a reference to a 'wreck' in the 'fiord of the Mermaid'. Still later, Tolkien both equated, and denied equation of, mermaids with the Oarni or Spirits of the Sea, and he told how the mermaids loved Eärendel, came to him, and rescued him after his ship foundered. (See *The Book of Lost Tales, Part Two*, ch. 5.)

Another manuscript of *The Mermaid's Flute* is dated 'Mar[ch] 17–18 and May 2' (1915), and beside this Modern English title the first page is inscribed *Séo Meremennen*, 'The Mermaid' or 'The Siren' in Old English. Tolkien made a few revisions to this version relative to text A, some of them only minor changes of punctuation, but most notably, lines 5–10 now read:

A shivering breeze then would roughen the water
    Dark under Eve, and on hollow white tusk
Far out on a skerry — a moon-flicker caught her
    Or homing sunbeam gone astray in the dusk
A deep-thronéd mere-king's pale-handéd daughter
    Did melodize musical songs of the deep

Still later, on a page marked 'Franqueville Sept[ember] 1916' – Tolkien was there with the army in France from 12 to 24 September – he replaced lines 5–10 as follows:

Far out on a skerry mid darkening water
    Touched by the moon in the gathering dusk
Maybe 'twas a gleam of thin starlight that caught her
    With long slender fingers on hollow white tusk
That deep-thronéd mereking's pale-handéd daughter
    Playing wizardrous songs of the untrodden deep

As noted for no. 17, Tolkien sent manuscript copies of *The Minstrel Renounces the Song* and *The Mermaid's Flute* to G.B. Smith. On 27

March 1915 Smith counselled Tolkien about 'the "Earendel" things', that he should 'move slowly'.

> Your verse is very apt to get complicated and twisted, and to be most damned difficult to make out. Look here, for instance [lines A51–52 as slightly revised]:
>
> > And winding through weed-roots there pallidly shimmers
> > Dim, tremulous blowing of ammonite horns.
>
> I don't know now what that means. I think it contains at least two most delightful visions – winding through weed-roots, and tremulous blowing – did you *mean* blowing? – of ammonite horns. Perhaps you meant glowing, which makes it much easier, and not less pleasant. But even so the sentence is exhausting, partly because of 'dim', partly because of 'there pallidly shimmers'. You *must* tone this kind of thing down, or people will never bother to get at your meaning. If I were you, I should revise everything with elaborate care, making 'a child can read it' your aim and motto. I am afraid the 'Mermaid' is rather bad in this respect. The palace I can understand with some slight effort, but after that I really got rather lost. The palace by the way is very good. 'Bended reflections of star-glimmer stand' quite nonplusses me, I am afraid. [Bodleian Library]

In his own poetry, which showed much promise before his death in France in 1916, Smith preferred decidedly less florid language: 'Out of the gathering darkness crashes a wind from the ocean, | Rushing with league-long paces over the plain of the waters, | Driving the clouds and the breakers before it in sudden commotion' ('Wind over the Sea', *A Spring Harvest*, p. 47).

In mid- to late May 1915 Tolkien had *The Mermaid's Flute*, with other poems (but not *The Minstrel Renounces the Song*), professionally typed by the Oxford Copying Office. Two copies survive in his papers, one of them a carbon copy on which he made several small revisions and replaced two passages, the first as given above for the Franqueville 1916 correction, the other lines 25–32. He inscribed the carbon copy 'Warwick Lent 1915 (night) with corrections devised hospital Cottingham Road 1917 Sept[ember]?' Lent in 1915 began on 17 February, with Easter on 4 April; Tolkien was in Warwick for most, possibly all, of the Oxford Easter vacation. 17–18 March, within Lent, may be the pertinent dates for revision of *The Mermaid's Flute*, as written on the second manuscript. The 'hospital' was Brooklands' Officers' Hospital in Hull, where Tolkien recuperated from mid-August 1917. The title of the poem was now more fully *The Mermaid's Flute from 'The Lay of Earendel'*.

This revised copy was itself typed in turn, probably late during Tolkien's years at Leeds. At some later date, he lightly marked the final typewritten text with thoughts for still more revisions, but as these are clearly tentative, we give here (as B) the poem as typed, incorporating only those changes which appear to be corrections to typist's errors. Two of Tolkien's further thoughts – those we can decipher from among his additions – are transcribed in our notes.

[B] White days would wane slow and a far sun sink under
Globed and afire in the watery west,
And twilight creep over the world's edge in wonder
Blue-robéd in dreams and all sleepily tressed.
Far out on a skerry mid darkening water
Touched by the moon in the gathering dusk
Maybe 'twas a gleam of thin starlight that caught her
With long slender fingers on hollow white tusk
That deep-thronéd mere-king[']s pale-handed daughter
Playing wizardrous tunes of the untrodden deep,
Of the twilit and blue-shadowed grot where she wrought her
Her pipe and its magic of fathomless sleep.
As she fluted a tremor would seize on all hearkened;
Their hearts would go blind with the murmurous spells,
And the blossomed earth fade from desire as night darkened,
And dreams of white foam and of marvellous shells;
Of glittering pools, pale, glassily lucid;
Of coral and polyp and tendrilous weed,
Rhythmically swaying all tangled and nooséd
To submarine swells, wherein silver fish feed:—
—Such dreams would arise; or they dreamt of her palace
Where crooning old mere-songs that maiden abode
Clad in sapphire and green with enchanted sea-chalice
To still their heart-longings — alluring it glowed,
Its silver domes tiléd with magic scales gleaming,
And buildèd of long-sunken gold were its walls;
Through faint-blushing coraline windows came streaming
Pale lights of sea-fairies. Hark! conch-music calls
Tremulous, hollow, from wide-open casements
Where mail-clad the fishes swim out and swim in,

Swim silent and slender through woven enlacements
    Of deep-hued anemones' tentacles thin.
O! Magic broods over its gables shell-copèd
    That, ringèd with liquid and musical swirls
Of restless sea-motions, are bannered with ropèd
    Sea-tassels all knotted and warted with pearls.
Then they fancy their heavy feet wistfully wander
    On darkening pathways of silver-grained sand
Whereon mirrored is palely a moon-wraith from yonder,
    Or bended reflections of star-glimmer stand.
Faint echoes go wavering down the sea-hollows,
    And silent things luminous sail by in gloom,
As twilight fades slowly and sea-darkness follows,
    And deeper and wider the weed-shadows loom:
While night sinks to dream where the poolèd shades quiver,
    Till Dawn list the slumbering Sun from the seas
Far out at east, and there runs a cold shiver
    Through Ocean, a shuddering wisp of a breeze:
Then over the white pavéd floor go grey glimmers
    Of twisted light heralding fire-handed morn,
And winding through weed-roots a pale fanfare shimmers,
    Dim tremulous blowing of ammonite horn.

A4: In the second manuscript, this line began 'Blue-robéd in dreams'.

B1: Tolkien considered whether to change this line to 'The white days waned slowly and a far sun sank under'.

B4: Tolkien considered whether to change this line to 'Blue-robéd and dreamlike and all shadowy tressed'.

20

Dark · Copernicus v. Ptolemy · Copernicus and Ptolemy (1914–?24)

The first version of *Dark* bears the date 21 December 1914, written in the same weight of pencil as the text proper, with a second date (8 March 1915) and an alternate title, *Copernicus v.* [*versus*] *Ptolemy*, added later in a lighter pencil. The text is heavily worked, with many, only partly illegible jottings in the margins; and for each of the first nine lines, Tolkien noted the number of feet (stresses). Here we give the underlying original text as A.

[A] The sun is gone; and all the Earth is dark,
the bow of whose great sable breast
stands curved against the farthest skirts
of that black canopy that roofs us in —
— its height is markéd only by the stars,
dim distant little things from where
still and sombre are the wide grey woods,
and the sweeping gables of some pallid hall
loom heavy, — . Yesternight I felt
the Earth a ball that wanders without light
through the unpath'd ways of globéd space
separated for ever and for ever from the stars
by distance untráversable and its own strange fate
that sets it from all Heaven's orbs apart;
and lo! the world tonight has opened all
its congregated glooms and great stark lines
into a spread Infinity: that I must cry
alone in this vast dark magnificence:
'Is there no mountainous catastrophic wall,
no chasmic gulf and end of things to bound
the endless stretch of Night's chaotic floor
on which the wide Earth resupine
gazes with folded arms behind her darkened head
upon the swinging pageantry of the sky,

whose sombre jewelry of adamants and jet
swept of the yellow gilt of day
sparkled with a huge wide wonder, and
its marvellous design is manifest —
— a spectacle gigantic — fraught with we know not what intent,
that we gaze for ever, and we comprehend — not yet!'

Adamant, in line 25 (as a plural), is an old word for 'diamond'. *Jet* is a very dark mineral in popular use in the nineteenth century for mourning jewellery. Here the jewels (celestial bodies, 'Heaven's orbs') are 'sombre' in the sense that they are not ostentatious. By text C, however, the celestial 'jewelry' is lit with 'adamantine fire', suggesting a diamond-like brilliance, the idea reinforced by 'stab[bing] with burning flame' and thus less 'sombre' in any sense of the word.

Possibly on 8 March 1915 (in accord with the second date on text A), Tolkien struck through this manuscript and wrote out a new, untitled version. We have transcribed this text as B, as it stood before Tolkien marked it for further revision.

[B] The Sun is gone and all the Earth is dark
And still, the bow of whose great sable breast
Stands curvëd huge against the farthest skirts
Of that black canopy that roofs us in —
— Its height is markëd only by the Stars
Dim distant little things from here below
Where still and sombre are the wide grey woods
And the sweeping gables of the pallid hall
Loom heavy. And thus twas yesternight I felt
The Earth a ball that wanders without light
Along the unpath'd ways of globéd space
Separated for ever and for ever from the stars
By distance untráversable and its own strange fate
That sets it from all Heaven's orbs apart;
And lo! the world tonight has opened all
Its congregated glooms and great stark lines
Into a spread Infinity that I must cry
Alone in this vast dark magnificence
'Is there no monstrous catastrophic wall
No chasmic gulf and end of things to bound
This utter stretch of Night's chaotic floor
On which the wide Earth resupine does gaze

With folded arms behind her darkened head
Upon the swinging pageantry of the sky
Whose sombre jewelry of adamants and jet
Kindles illuminous with silver flame
The uranian vesture of the firmament
Its domed and echoless expanse afire
— A spectacle gigantic — and we gaze
Forever, and we comprehend not yet. [']

A third manuscript again bore the title *Dark*, but now with the added title *Copernicus and Ptolemy*, a small but meaningful change of conjunction, *and* rather than *versus*. Also inscribed on the sheet is Old English *Þéostru* ('Darkness'), the title under which Tolkien entered the work in an early list of his poems. This version, too, is marked with the dates December 1914 and March 1915. Its text is moderately revised relative to B, with differences of punctuation and capitalization and two minor alterations: 'vast' for 'huge' in line 3, and 'only markëd' for 'markëd only' in line 5, possibly an accidental inversion as it is unique to this text.

Tolkien altered this version further, most thoroughly its final six lines:

Doth watch the domed and echoless expanse,
Whose sombre jewels with adamantine fire
Illuminous, now put to flame the dark
Uranian vesture of the firmament? ———"
— O Spectacle gigantic, we too gaze
For ever, and we comprehend — not yet.

Before doing so, however, he had the poem professionally typed. Two carbon copies survive, each with the titles *Dark* and *Copernicus of* [*sic*] *Ptolemy*. (Christopher Tolkien maintained that the typescript could not have been made by his father, who would not have mistaken an ampersand for 'of'.) In line 3 there is curiously a reversion to 'huge'; the typist was, perhaps, provided with a fair copy containing the earlier reading. Tolkien marked up one of the copies for revision, at some points as he did the third manuscript, but with still further changes. Now he also abandoned the title *Copernicus and Ptolemy*, striking it through on one of the copies after correcting 'of' to 'and'. At some later date, he wrote on the revised typescript '1912? often retouched, last touches 1924'.

The latest text of the poem, again entitled *Dark*, is a typescript made with a purple ribbon, which dates it to the period when Tolkien taught at the University of Leeds (early 1920s) and accords with his note 'last touches 1924'. Our transcription (C) incorporates two small alterations which Tolkien could have marked at a much later date, 'her' for 'whose' in line 2, and 'and' added before 'huge' in line 3.

[C]

The sun is gone, and all the Earth is dark
and hushed; the bow of her great sable breast
stands curvëd and huge against the farthest skirts
of that black canopy that roofs us in —
its height is markëd only by the Stars,
dim distant little things from here below,
where still and sombre are the wide grey woods
and the sweeping gable of the pallid hall
looms heavy. And thus 'twas yesternight I felt
the Earth a ball that wanders without light
along the unpath'd ways of globëd space,
separated for ever and for ever from the stars
by distance untráversable and its own strong fate:
and lo! tonight the world has open'd all
its congregated glooms and great stark lines
into a spread infinity, that I must cry
alone in this vast dark magnificence:
'Is there no monstrous catastrophic wall,
no chasméd gulf and end of things to bound
this utter stretch of Night's chaotic floor,
wherefrom the wide reclining Earth doth gaze
with folded arms behind her darken'd head
upon the swinging splendour of the sky,
whose sombre jewels, with adamantine fire
illumin'd, stab with burning flame the dark
uranian vesture of the firmament!'

As explained in our Introduction, while pupils at King Edward's School Tolkien and his friends came together socially as the 'TCBS', but it was only after they had gone to university, and the membership of the group had thinned to a core of Tolkien, Rob Gilson, Christopher Wiseman, and a late addition, G.B. Smith, that they became concerned to reform arts and society in England through their creative activities. Contact between the friends was energizing. After they met in London on 12–13 December 1914, Tolkien found 'a voice for all kinds of pent up things and a tremendous opening up of everything for me' (letter to Smith, 12 August 1916, *Letters*, p. 7). *Dark*, among other poems by Tolkien, followed closely the friends' so-called 'Council of London'. Of course, as we have seen, Tolkien wrote energetically also earlier in 1914, inspired especially by his reading, but his creative work was strengthened by sharing it with sympathetic, but honest, critics.

On 25 March 1915, having read *Dark*, Smith cautioned that Tolkien should 'beware of the word "dim", and do not make your things difficult to read by length and complication of sentences. Poetic licence exists to make things direct, simple and full of force' (Bodleian Library). Wiseman received a group of Tolkien's poems that spring after Smith and Gilson had read them, and was enthusiastic, wondering where his friend found so many amazing words. Along with Gilson, he feared that Tolkien would be carried away by them. Later, reflecting on Tolkien's use of light in his poems, Wiseman felt that the light in *Copernicus and Ptolemy*, as he referred to it, was like that of a cavern lit by arc lamps and magnesium wire. Tolkien reined in his vocabulary in the latest version of *Dark*, abandoning 'chasmic' for 'chasmëd' and replacing 'resupine' with the more straightforward 'reclining'; but altogether, his friends' criticism did little to change his preferences.

In regard to the poem's alternate title, Claudius Ptolemy of Alexandria was a scholar of the second century AD whose name was given to the geocentric view of the universe, whereby the Earth is at the centre of all things, and the Sun, Moon, planets, and stars revolve around the Earth on concentric crystalline spheres. This 'Ptolemaic' system, explained by Ptolemy in his *Almagest* ('The Greatest', a name given by admirers), was widely accepted for many centuries. Then in 1543, the Pole Nicolaus Copernicus, a canon of the church with an interest in mathematics and astronomy, described in his *De Revolutionibus Orbium Coelestium* a heliocentric universe, with the Earth only one of several planets orbiting a central sun. Each of these two great world systems had its adherents, the Ptolemaic by virtue of long acceptance, the Copernican due to a superior mathematical foundation and, increasingly, evidence from improved observation of the heavens that it reflected physical reality. Heliocentricism was not considered by religious authorities to be consonant with Church teachings, however, and was banned or restricted until the early nineteenth century. The title *Copernicus v. Ptolemy* reflects, then, an important debate in early science and a notable instance of censorship imposed by the Catholic Church, either of which, or both, Tolkien presumably found of interest. In *Dark* the poet sees the two points of view on successive nights. First, in heliocentrism, the Earth is indeed 'a ball that wanders . . . through the unpath'd ways of globéd space', a moving body speeding along its orbit around the Sun; and then, in the geocentric view, it is static, unmoving, as it seems to be while the heavens appear to revolve around us, 'the swinging pageantry of the sky'.

Tolkien's view of the night sky in the first quarter of the twentieth century would have been much clearer and more impressive than it is now in England, where light pollution tends to obscure its features. Astronomical imagery also appears in other of his poems, such as *Habbanan* (later *Eruman*) *beneath the Stars* (no. 45), and in his stories of Middle-earth.

A20: For 'chasmic' Tolkien considered 'chasméd' (as in C19) and 'm'strous' (monstrous). *Chasmed* 'having chasms' is in the original *Oxford English Dictionary*, as is *chasmy* 'abounding with chasms', but *chasmic* does not appear in the *OED* until the second supplement, which records the earliest instance of the word in a work by H.E. Bates, dated 1926. In *Dark* the word became 'chasmëd' in the final typescript.

21

Ferrum et Sanguis (1914)

The earliest manuscript of this poem is inscribed 'Ex umbris et loco tenebroso' and 'De Profundis', Latin for 'out of the shadows and the dark place' and 'out of the depths'. Below these, '1914' is centred as if a title, or part of a title. The same page contains two texts, both in pencil. The first (A) is written thus:

[A] The earth and all that dwell thereon are dark in a great gloom —
— a vast black hand has dared its frightful shade across the sun,
and, lest the stars come out and still do light us in its room,
has fouled the heavens with his touch, or plucked them one by one
— the faith and shining hopes of men and even orbéd Love —
and tramped them under his huge impious foot with great mire: —
This piteous damp — the blood that drips from his stark iron glove
wet with the life of men: O God! when will Thy blazing ire
rekindle us the sun, and break the unutterable fear
we bear in the abyss of dark! Have pity, O God, and hear!

In a second, slightly revised version, the long lines of text A are divided in two: 'The earth and all that dwell thereon | Are dark in a great gloom', and so forth. Next to the second text is written 'Ferrum et Sanguis', Latin for 'iron and blood'.

At length, Tolkien struck through both of these texts and made a new manuscript, again in pencil, with minor revisions and still with divided lines; this is inscribed 'Ferrum et Sanguis' followed by '1914', two lines divided by an ornament, perhaps (or perhaps not) meant to be conjoined as the poem's title. Yet another copy (B, below), with the same title, one further textual difference, and longer lines as in A, is written in ink on an oblong scrap of paper. (It is conceivable that the shape of the paper, wider than it is tall, dictated Tolkien's return to the poem's original format.)

[B] The earth and all that dwell thereon are dark in a great gloom:
A frightful hand has dared its shade across the blackened sun,
And, lest the stars come out and still do light us in its room,
Has fouled the heavens with his touch, or plucked them one by one
—The radiant faith and hopes of men and orbéd shining Love—
To tramp them under his huge feet in curdled impious mire,
In piteous damp, the blood that drips from iron inhuman glove.
'Tis wet with the life of men, O God! When will Thy blazing Ire
Rekindle us the sun and break the unutterable fear
We bear in this abyss of dark! Have pity, O God, and hear!

Tolkien seems to have composed *Ferrum et Sanguis*, to give it its simplest title, only one day after the initial version of *Dark* (poem no. 20). Its first text (A) includes the apparently contemporary date 22 December. Each of these works is concerned with darkness, but whereas one celebrates a night splendid with the light of stars, in the other a 'great gloom' and 'vast black hand' have settled on the Earth, crushing hope and love.

The subject of *Ferrum et Sanguis* is undoubtedly the Great War, which by December 1914 was in its fifth month. This appears to be the first of Tolkien's poems to touch upon it. The swift end to hostilities some had predicted with naïve optimism had not come, and the effects of the conflict were apparent even in Oxford as undergraduates left to enlist and buildings and streets filled with troops, convalescents, and refugees. Tolkien himself, continuing his studies, drilled in the University Parks with the Oxford Officers Training Corps.

'Iron and blood' is a familiar phrase from a speech by the nineteenth-century German leader Otto von Bismarck; it refers to the use of military power to unify Germany and extend its territory. 'De Profundis' are the first words of one of the penitential psalms ('Out of the depths I call to you, Lord; Lord, hear my cry!'), a prayer for the dead. In 'ex umbris et loco tenebroso' Tolkien may have had in mind the Tenebrae 'service of shadows' conducted by the Catholic Church in Holy Week, in which candles are gradually extinguished until the room is in total darkness.

A2: Among workings on the first manuscript, Tolkien considered for this line 'a frightful (or vast dark) hand has dared its shade across the (frightful) blackened sun'.

A6: In the first revised text Tolkien changed this line to 'And tramped them under his huge foot | In this deep impious mire'. In the final text, he changed 'foot' to 'feet'.

A7: 'This piteous damp — the blood' originally read 'O God, this mire is blood'.

B6: The third pencil manuscript has the reading 'impious curdled mire', the one in ink (as here) 'curdled impious mire'.

B7: The reading 'iron inhuman glove' entered in the later versions; 'iron inhuman' is written in the margin of the third pencil manuscript, though already in the line proper.

22

The Sparrow's Morning Chirp to a Lazy Mortal · Bilink, Bilink! · Sparrow Song (1914–15)

The earliest version of this *jeu d'esprit* is a rough manuscript (A) with the contemporary date 22 December (1914). Its title, *The Sparrow's Morning Chirp to a Lazy Mortal*, both explains its subject and conveys the playful mood in which it was written.

[A]

The sparrows in the morning cold
wash their little selves and groom,
— bilink! though not very old,
every puffy little plume

★

Bilink! in the winter's hold
Dressing's most uncommon cold

★

The sparrows just outside my room
bilink! bilink! to the Sun
Chirp till winter even's gloom —
'days are very quickly done'.

★

Bilink! we have but begun
Day when night is sudden come

★

Then bilink bilink
what do you think
It hardly pays these dreary days
Getting up to eat and drink?

Stop in bed and snooze instead!
bilink
bilink
What d'you think?

This text, which we have transcribed in its form before revision, was much altered by Tolkien in the course of writing or soon after, and finally struck through. The manuscript includes alternate readings as well as the beginning of a new first stanza. Evidently noticing conflicts of tense – is the speaker observing the sparrows, or are the birds themselves speaking? – Tolkien changed 'The sparrows' to 'We sparrows', 'their little selves' to 'our little selves', and 'my room' to 'your room'. But a second, untitled manuscript of the poem (B), probably close in date to the first, divides the work between 'M' and 'S' – perhaps the Mortal of the original title, or Man, and the Sparrows in reply. This too was ultimately cancelled.

[B]

M
Bilink, Bilink!
Just a wink —
Just one more — one more before
I barter for the icy brink
Of shave and bath this dreamy path
O bilink, bilink
How I shrink!
Bilink! In the winter's hold
Dressing's most uncommon cold

★

S
Pooh! sparrows in the morning cold
With early twitter wash and groom
Bilink! virtuous as gold
Ev'ry fussy little plume: —
And sparrows just outside your room
Bilink, bilink, to the Sun —
Chirp till winter-even's gloom.
'Days are very quickly done'.

★

Bilink! we have but begun
Day when night is sudden come!

*

M

Then! Bilink bilink
Don't you think
It hardly pays these dreary days
Getting up to eat and drink —
Stop in bed and snooze instead
Bilink bilink!
What d'you think?

In still further rough workings, Tolkien considered different rhyme schemes and made a list of rhyming words: *bees*, *please*, *breeze*, *freeze*, *keys*, *lees*, etc. From these followed two manuscripts, each dated 'March 1915'. One, entitled *Bilink* with 'Sparrow-Song' added at the side, is inscribed 'Another song for my little one' – Edith Bratt – and signed 'JRRT'. The other manuscript has the Modern English title *Sparrow-Song*, with a deleted extension 'and man's defiance' – but not 'Bilink' – and two titles in Old English, *Spearwansong* ('Song of the Sparrow, Sparrow-song') and *Spearwena Morgenswég* ('Morning-song of Sparrows'). On both copies, Tolkien amended lines 14 ('Sparrows in the morning cold' > 'Sparrows ere the morn is old') and 20 ('Don't you think' > 'Dost not think').

He made further changes to the second manuscript of this version, and to a professional typescript (inscribed '1914–15'), before a new typescript was made for him by the Oxford Copying Office in mid- to late May 1915, based on the earlier typescript as amended. The new version was now called *Sparrow Song*, without a hyphen.

Tolkien revised a copy of the later typescript to create the final text (C). He was particularly concerned to amend lines 4–5, which for a time read 'I barter for the icy brink | Of bath and shave this dream-white cave'.

[C]

Nay Bilink! Bilink!
Just a wink
Just one more — one more before
I barter for the trembling brink
Of icy bathe this dream-white cave;
This pillowed palace of fair ease
Where wine of slumber to the lees

I fain would drink
O, Bilink, Bilink!
Yea, I shrink,
For, Bilink, in the winter's hold
Uprising is too shudder-cold

⋆

Kilapee! come merry be
Sparrows ere the morn is old
Pipe and twitter silverly
Busily them lave and preen —
Bilink lo! the dawning gold
The gable-end with arrow-sheen
Has shot, and glistered glancing thence
To dapple on your window pane.
Come, kilapink, upon the fence
We chirping wait till even wane!
Kilapee! salaam the Sun!
Ah! days are but too quickly done:
Ah! bilink we have but begun
Morn, when night is sudden come!

⋆

Then Bilink! Bilink!
Dost not think
It little pays these dreary days
Rising up to eat and drink?
Come! Lie abed and dream instead
Ah Bilink, Bilink!
(What d'ye think).

'Bilink' and 'Kilapee' seem to be Tolkien's interpretation of the sparrow's chirping or trilling; we have not found these 'transcriptions' in any ornithological authority. T.A. Coward wrote in *The Birds of the British Isles and Their Eggs* of the common House Sparrow (*Passer domesticus*) that its 'short and incessant chirp needs no description, and its double note "phillip" . . . is as familiar. Whilst the young are in their nests, the old birds utter a long parental "churr."' At dusk in their winter roosts, 'each individual penetrating chirp' of a sparrow 'seems distinct, and yet the whole is a jumble of shrill notes' (1936 edn., p. 55). Well before Coward's book first appeared in 1920, sparrows were so abundant in England as to be considered a nuisance.

Tolkien's poem is a portrait, perhaps a self-portrait, of an unwilling riser, exchanging the comfort of bed for the chilly air of a bedroom, compared with the industry of a common little bird. It is an amusing picture of a common domestic matter, but as the poem develops it takes on a grander stance, with its 'dream-white cave' (presumably a warm space between the sheets) and 'pillowed palace of fair ease' where the speaker would drink the 'wine of slumber'.

A3: *Bilin(c)* is given as a linguistic element, meaning 'sparrow, small bird', in the Gnomish surname *Gwarbilin* 'Warble'. See *The Book of Lost Tales, Part One*, p. 268.

B4: 'Barter', i.e. exchange.

C7: 'To the lees': down to the sediment left in a bottle when it is almost empty. Compare in Tennyson's 'Ulysses', 'I will drink | Life to the lees'.

C16: 'Lave and preen', compare B11 'wash and groom'.

C17–20: 'Dawning gold', etc., is a rapturous description of the rising sun making light-patterns on walls, like the brightness of arrows ('arrow-sheen') shot from bows.

C23: 'Salaam' is an expression of respectful compliments.

23

As Two Fair Trees (1915–*c.* 1945)

The earliest text of *As Two Fair Trees* (A) has no date or title. Tolkien wrote it in pencil, in twenty-five lines, then, with alterations, in ink over the first eighteen. The final seven lines remained in pencil only and were omitted in later texts.

[A]

Lo! young we are and yet have stood
like planted hearts in the great Sun
of Love so long (as two fair trees
in woodland or in open dale
stand utterly entwined, and breathe
the airs and suck the very light
together) — that we have become
as one, deep-rooted in the soil
of Love, and tangled in sweet growth: —
and even so have shared the days,
and laughed the laughs, and drunk the hours,
tasted each other's tears, and known grey rain
and lonely winds and night: — we two;
that now although our years not yet
are heavy on us still has Love
a great immeasurable sweet chain
wrought us of linkéd days whose good or ill
binds us with a golden strength of many centuries.

O happy we that have both youth and older love:
O happy we with eyes undimmed by age
To gaze upon this terrible sweet land
That is too often as seen by wild young eyes
Uncomprehending or unseen till age
which battered and polluted by the world
Keepeth no longer its clear vision true.

Tolkien slightly revised the poem in a second manuscript, probably not long after writing the initial text; this is reproduced in McIlwaine, *Tolkien: Maker of Middle-earth*, p. 146. The only significant difference with text A was that 'soil of Love' became 'soil of Life' in lines 8–9. The work now had its Modern English title as well as an equivalent in Old English, *Swá Twégen Fægre Béamas*, and the date January 1915. In poetry list A in Appendix III, its Old English title is *Uncer Lufu* ('Our Love').

One of three professional typescript copies of the poem is inscribed 'Warwick 1913? 14?', and another '1914?', all in a later hand. But the placement of the first manuscript in one of Tolkien's poetry notebooks, and the similarity of its script to that of the second manuscript, suggest that January 1915 is the correct date of composition. The typescript, extant in a ribbon copy and two carbon copies and evidently made from the earliest manuscript (with 'Love' in line 9), probably dates from early 1915 as well. Tolkien circulated the poem to friends early that year. On 22 March 1915 G.B. Smith praised it in a letter to Tolkien, calling it 'very good' and 'much the best thing in your collection', but noting that he 'cut out the word "*a*" in the last line: this improves the metre' (Bodleian Library). The words 'with a golden strength' are altered to 'with golden strength' in both early manuscripts and two of the three typescript copies. In another letter, of 25 March, Smith reported that H.T. Wade-Gery agreed with him that *As Two Fair Trees* was 'fearfully good' (Bodleian Library).

A further manuscript of the poem, following after the typescripts, is in a substantially later hand and inscribed, also much later than the earlier versions, 'Warwick 1913'. It includes a few workings in pencil and ballpoint pen which cannot be earlier than the 1940s. In this Tolkien adopted a more grounded style, changing 'the soil of Love' or 'of Life' to 'the same rich soil', omitting a second use of 'sweet', and making the 'immeasurable' chain simply 'a long chain'. We give the text as B, with late suggested revisions indicated in notes.

[B]

Lo! young we are, and yet have stood
like planted hearts in the high sun
of love so long (as two fair trees
in woodland or upon a hill
stand utterly entwined, and breathe
the air, and suck the very light
together) that we have become
As one, deep-rooted in the same
rich soil, and tangled in sweet growth.
Thus we have shared our living days,
and laughed our laughter, drunk our hours,
tasted each other's tears, and born grey rain,
and lonely winds, and night: us two:

So now, although our years not yet
are heavy on us, still our love
has wrought already a sweet chain
of linkéd days whose good or ill
binds us with golden strength of many centuries.

The subject matter of the poem is surely Tolkien's love for Edith Bratt and the relationship he was able to resume with her in 1913, soon after he came of age that January; and perhaps it was his memory of reconnecting with Edith in Warwick, where she had gone to live, which led him to believe that he had written the poem closer to that time. That he returned to this early work long after its initial composition suggests the depth of feeling he had for the woman who became his wife. In a late letter to his son Christopher he wrote of 'the dreadful sufferings' of his childhood and Edith's, 'from which we rescued one another . . . ; the sufferings that we endured after our love began', but intervening events 'never touched our depths nor dimmed our memories of our youthful love' (11 July 1972, *Letters*, p. 590).

B9: Tolkien considered 'linkéd' as a possible revision for 'tangled'.
B10: Tolkien considered 'linkéd' in place of 'living'.
B16: Tolkien considered 'long' in place of 'sweet'.
B17: Tolkien considered 'living' in place of 'linkéd'.

24

Why the Man in the Moon Came Down Too Soon: An East Anglian Phantasy · A Faërie: Why the Man in the Moon Came Down Too Soon · The Man in the Moon Came Down Too Soon (1915–62)

Tolkien dated the writing of his first 'Man in the Moon' poem (see also no. 60) to 10 and 11 March 1915 in each of its two manuscripts, initially misdating one to 1914 before correcting the figure. The earlier of these, entitled *Why the Man in the Moon Came Down Too Soon: An East Anglian Phantasy*, is heavily worked, in pencil over pencil, with many revisions. It is impossible to know which of its changes were made in the course of composition and which (if any) after an initial text was in place, nor can we make out all of the words that are overwritten. The later manuscript, entitled *A Faërie: Why the Man in the Moon Came Down Too Soon* and with an additional title in Old English, *Se Móncyning* ('The Moon King'), for the most part is a fair copy of the first version as revised.

Here, as text A, we have transcribed the second manuscript, while substantive (and decipherable) workings in the first manuscript are described in our notes. For this, and for its later versions, Tolkien chose again the metre and rhyme scheme (ABCBDEFE) he had used in *The Voyage of Éarendel the Evening Star* (no. 16), composed the previous year.

[A]

The Man in the Moon had silver shoon
    And his beard was of silver thread;
He was girt with pale gold and inaureoled
    With gold about his head.
Clad in silken robe in his great white globe
    He opened an ivory door
With a crystal key, and in secrecy
    He stole down the lucent floor;

*

Down a filigree stair of spidery hair
    He slipped in gleaming haste,
And laughed with glee to be merry and free;
    And he faster earthward raced,
For he was tired of his pearls and diamond twirls;
    Of his pallid minaret
Dizzy and white at its lunar height
    In a world of silver set —

*

And adventured this peril for ruby and beryl
    And emerald and sapphire,
And all lustrous gems for new diadems,
    Or to blazon his pale attire.
He was lonely too with nothing to do
    But to stare at the golden world,
Or strain for the hum that would distinctly come
    As it gaily past him whirled;

*

And at plenilune in his argent moon
    He had wearily longed for Fire:
Not the limpid lights of wan selenites,
    But a red terrestrial pyre
With impurpurate glows of crimson and rose
    And leaping orange tongue;
For great seas of blues and the passionate hues
    When a dancing dawn is young;

*

For the meadowy ways like chrysoprase,
    At topaz eve: — and then
How he longed for the mirth of the populous Earth
    And the sanguine blood of men;
And coveted song and laughter long
    And viands hot, and wine —
Eating pearly cakes of light snow-flakes
    And drinking thin moonshine.

*

And he twinkled his feet as he thought of the meat,
Of the punch and the peppery brew,
Till he tripped unaware on his slanting stair,
And fell like meteors do;
As the whickering sparks in splashing arcs
Of stars blown down like rain
From his laddery path took a foamy bath
In the Ocean of Almain;

*

And began to think, lest he melt and sink,
What in the moon to do,
When a Yarmouth boat found him far afloat
To the mazement of the crew
Caught in their net all shimmering wet
In a phosphorescent sheen
Of bluey whites and opal lights
And delicate liquid green.

*

With the morning fish — 'twas his regal wish —
They packed him to Norwich town
To get warm on gin in a Norfolk inn,
And dry his watery gown:
Though canorous spells from the musical bells
Of the city's fifty towers
Shouted the news of his lunatic cruise
In the early morning hours,

*

No hearths were laid — not a breakfast made — ,
And no one would sell him gems;
He found ashes for fire, and his gay desire
For chorus and brave anthems
Met snores instead with all Norfolk abed;
And his round heart nearly broke,
More empty and cold than above of old,
Till he bartered his faerie cloak

*

For a kitchen nook by a smoky cook;
And his belt of gold for a smile,
And a priceless jewel for a bowl of gruel —
Ensample cold and vile
Of the proud plum porridge of Anglian Norwich —
He arrived so much too soon
For unusual guests on adventurous quests
From the mountains of the Moon.

The two manuscripts were followed by a professional typescript, with a few differences of punctuation relative to text A. This is entitled *A Faërie: How the Man in the Moon Came Down Too Soon*, the replacement of *Why* by *How* probably a typist's error. From this source, with still more punctuation changes, the poem was published in June 1923 in *A Northern Venture: Verses by Members of the Leeds University English School Association* (with an error in line 42, 'peppery stew' for 'peppery brew', perpetuated in our 2014 extended edition of *The Adventures of Tom Bombadil and Other Verses from the Red Book*).

On 22 March 1915 G.B. Smith wrote to Tolkien that '"The Man in the Moon" is excellent i' faith. I am sure with a little more command over the small technical details, such as pleasant rhythm and so on, which can be obtained by practice and the reading of good authors, your things will be quite the best stuff. They are amazingly good now' (Bodleian Library). On 25 April, Christopher Wiseman commented that, compared with the 'Eárendel' poem (presumably no. 18 in the present book) in which he and Rob Gilson felt that Tolkien had not succeeded, the 'magnificently gaudy' *Man in the Moon Came Down Too Soon* was much to be preferred (Bodleian Library).

A second professional typescript of the poem may have been made by the Oxford Copying Office in mid- to late May 1915, when ten other poems by Tolkien were similarly typed. This survives in a ribbon copy and a carbon copy; Tolkien inscribed the latter 'Oxford (March?) 1915, retouched 1923' and deleted '*A Faërie*' in the title. The words 'retouched 1923' may refer to minor changes of punctuation made to the poem for *A Northern Venture*, or to further changes Tolkien made to both copies of the second typescript. The latter were taken up into yet another typescript (B), made with a purple ribbon and thus from Tolkien's years on the English faculty at Leeds. Christopher Tolkien published this text, mistakenly described as the *Northern Venture* version, in *The Book of Lost Tales, Part One*, pp. 204–6.

[B] The Man in the Moon had silver shoon
And his beard was of silver thread;
He was girt with pale gold and inaureoled
With gold about his head.
Clad in silken robe in his great white globe
He opened an ivory door
With a crystal key, and in secrecy
He stole o'er a shadowy floor;

Down a filigree stair of spidery hair
He slipped in gleaming haste,
And, laughing with glee to be merry and free,
He swiftly earthward raced.
He was tired of his pearls and diamond twirls;
Of his pallid minaret
Dizzy and white at its lunar height
In a world of silver set;

And adventured this peril for ruby and beryl
And emerald and sapphire,
And all lustrous gems for new diadems,
Or to blazon his pale attire.
He was lonely too with nothing to do
But to stare at the golden world
Or strain for the hum that would distinctly come
As it gaily past him whirled;

And at plenilune in his argent moon
He had wearily longed for Fire —
Not the limpid lights of wan selenites,
But a red terrestrial pyre
With impurpurate glows of crimson and rose
And leaping orange tongue;
For great seas of blues and the passionate hues
When a dancing dawn is young;

For the meadowy ways like chrysoprase,
By winding Yare and Nen.
How he longed for the mirth of the populous Earth
And the sanguine blood of men;
And coveted song and laughter long
And viands hot, and wine,

Eating pearly cakes of light snow-flakes
    And drinking thin moonshine.

He twinkled his feet as he thought of the meat,
    Of the punch and the peppery brew,
Till he tripped unaware on his slanting stair,
    And fell like meteors do;
As the whickering sparks in splashing arcs
    Of stars blown down like rain
From his laddery path took a foaming bath
    In the Ocean of Almain;

And began to think, lest he melt and sink,
    What in the moon to do,
When a Yarmouth boat found him far afloat,
    To the mazement of the crew,
Caught in their net all shimmering wet
    In a phosphorescent sheen
Of bluey whites and opal lights
    And delicate liquid green.

With the morning fish — 'twas his regal wish —
    They packed him to Norwich town
To get warm on gin in a Norfolk inn,
    And dry his watery gown:
Though St. Peter's Knell waked many a bell,
    In the city's ringing towers
To shout the news of his lunatic cruise
    In the early morning hours,

No hearths were laid, not a breakfast made,
    And no one would sell him gems.
He found ashes for fire, and his gay desire
    For chorus and brave anthems
Met snores instead with all Norfolk abed;
    And his round heart nearly broke,
More empty and cold than above of old,
    Till he bartered his fairy cloak

With a half-waked cook for a kitchen nook;
    And his belt of gold for a smile;
And a priceless jewel for a bowl of gruel —
    A sample cold and vile
Of the proud plum-porridge of Anglian Norwich —
    He arrived so much too soon
For unusual guests on adventurous quests
    From the mountains of the Moon.

'Yare and Nen', introduced in the second typescript, are rivers: the Yare, which rises near Shipdham, Norfolk, and flows to the sea along the southern edge of Norwich, and the Nene (variously spelled, and pronounced *Nen*, with a short vowel), which flows from Northamptonshire to The Wash in East Anglia. 'St. Peter's' is the parish church of St Peter Mancroft in the centre of Norwich, with an important ring of bells.

The poem evolved further in two additional typescripts, nearly identical texts though made on different machines, one or both possibly by a professional service. This version (C), with the title now simply *The Man in the Moon Came Down Too Soon*, is revised substantially from the previous typescript, with many altered readings and eighteen additional lines. We have transcribed its text before Tolkien made still more revisions.

[C]

The Man in the Moon had silver shoon,
    and his beard was of silver thread;
With opals crowned and pearls all bound
    about his girdlestead,
In his mantle grey he walked one day
    across a shining floor,
And with crystal key in secrecy
    he opened an ivory door.

On a filigree stair of glimmering hair
    then lightly down he went,
And merry was he at last to be free
    on a mad adventure bent.
In diamonds white he had lost delight;
    he was tired of his minaret
Of tall moonstone that towered alone
    on a lunar mountain set.

He would dare any peril for ruby and beryl
to broider his pale attire,
For new diadems of lustrous gems,
emerald and sapphire.
He was lonely too with nothing to do
but stare at the world of gold,
And heark to the hum that would distantly come
as gaily round it rolled.

At plenilune in his argent moon
in his heart he longed for Fire:
Not the limpid lights of wan selenites,
but a blazing mountain-pyre
Whose hot heart glows with crimson and rose,
with leaping orange tongue;
Or the flaming skies in a swift sunrise
when the dawning day is young.

He'd have seas of blues, and the living hues
of forest green and fen;
How he yearned for the mirth of the populous earth
and the sanguine blood of Men!
He coveted song, and laughter long,
and viands hot, and wine,
Eating pearly cakes of light snowflakes
and drinking thin moonshine.

He twinkled his feet, as he thought of the meat,
of pepper, and punch galore;
And he tripped unaware on his slanting stair,
and fell like a meteor,
Like a starry spark in a flickering arc,
rippling down like rain
From his laddery path to a foaming bath
in the Ocean of Almain.

He began to think, lest he melt and sink,
what in the moon to do,
When a Yarmouth boat found him far afloat
to the amazement of the crew,

Caught in their net all shimmering wet
in a phosphorescent sheen
Of bluey whites and opal lights
and delicate liquid green.

Against his wish with the morning fish
they packed him to Norwich town:
'You had best get a bed in an inn,' they said,
'and dry your dripping gown!'
Only the knell of one slow bell
in tall St. Peter's tower
Announced the news of his lunatic cruise
at that unseemly hour.

Not a hearth was laid, not a breakfast made,
and dawn was cold and damp.
There were ashes for fire, and for grass the mire,
for the sun a smoking lamp
In a dim back-street; not a man did he meet,
no voice was raised in song.
There were snores instead, for all folk were abed
and still would slumber long.

He knocked as he passed on doors locked fast,
and called and cried in vain,
Till he came to an inn that had light within,
and tapped at a window-pane.
A drowsy cook gave a surly look,
and 'what do you want?' said he.
'I want fire and gold and songs of old
and red wine flowing free!'

'You won't get them here,' said the cook with a leer,
'but you may come inside.
'Silver I lack and silk to my back —
maybe I'll let you bide.'
A silver gift the latch to lift,
a pearl to pass the door.
For a seat by the cook in the ingle-nook
it cost him twenty more.

For hunger or drouth naught passed his mouth
    till he gave both crown and cloak;
And all that he got was an earthen pot,
    old and black with smoke,
Which the cook then filled with the leavings chilled,
    slopped from a broken spoon.
Of the good plum-porridge of Anglian Norwich:
    he arrived so much too soon
For unwary guests on adventurous quests
    from the Mountains of the Moon.

Tolkien amended the first of the later typescripts only slightly, a ribbon copy of the second even less so, but on a carbon copy of the latter he revised heavily. This work dates from late 1961, when Tolkien returned to some of his early poems to make a selection for *The Adventures of Tom Bombadil and Other Verses from the Red Book* (1962). In October 1961 his aunt Jane Neave had asked if he 'wouldn't get out a small book with Tom Bombadil at the heart of it, the sort of size of book that we old 'uns can afford to buy for Christmas presents' (quoted in Carpenter, *Biography*, p. 244). Bombadil by then was well known as a character in *The Lord of the Rings* (1954–5), but he had earlier featured in a poem published in 1934 (see no. 121), and Tolkien felt that that work might make a pretty booklet if illustrated by Pauline Baynes, the artist whose drawings had enhanced his *Farmer Giles of Ham* (1949). His publisher Rayner Unwin asked, however, that additional poems be added to the Bombadil verse to make up a book of a length reasonable for sales. Tolkien consequently 'raked up' and 'refurbished' poems from his files, in the process revising them as needed to fit the conceit that they had come from the same 'source' as *The Hobbit* and *The Lord of the Rings*, the 'Red Book of Westmarch', compiled by Hobbits. He sent Unwin a text of *The Man in the Moon Came Down Too Soon* for consideration on 15 November 1961.

It was because of this editorial fiction of a Hobbit poetry collection that Tolkien omitted references in *The Man in the Moon Came Down Too Soon* specific to Norwich or East Anglia. 'A Yarmouth boat' became 'a fisherman's boat'; 'to Norwich town' became 'back to land' (requiring also a change of line 60 for the sake of rhyme); 'in tall St. Peter's tower' became 'high in the Seaward Tower'; and in the final stanza, 'Anglian Norwich' was deleted in a larger revision. We give as D the final text of the poem, as published in *The Adventures of Tom Bombadil and Other Verses from the Red Book*, pp. 34, 36–8.

[D]

The Man in the Moon had silver shoon,
and his beard was of silver thread;
With opals crowned and pearls all bound
about his girdlestead,
In his mantle grey he walked one day
across a shining floor,
And with crystal key in secrecy
he opened an ivory door.

On a filigree stair of glimmering hair
then lightly down he went,
And merry was he at last to be free
on a mad adventure bent.
In diamonds white he had lost delight;
he was tired of his minaret
Of tall moonstone that towered alone
on a lunar mountain set.

He would dare any peril for ruby and beryl
to broider his pale attire,
For new diadems of lustrous gems,
emerald and sapphire.
He was lonely too with nothing to do
but stare at the world of gold
And heark to the hum that would distantly come
as gaily round it rolled.

At plenilune in his argent moon
in his heart he longed for Fire:
Not the limpid lights of wan selenites;
for red was his desire,
For crimson and rose and ember-glows,
for flame with burning tongue,
For the scarlet skies in a swift sunrise
when a stormy day is young.

He'd have seas of blues, and the living hues
of forest green and fen;
And he yearned for the mirth of the populous earth
and the sanguine blood of men.
He coveted song, and laughter long,
and viands hot, and wine,

Eating pearly cakes of light snowflakes
    and drinking thin moonshine.

He twinkled his feet, as he thought of the meat,
    of pepper, and punch galore;
And he tripped unaware on his slanting stair,
    and like a meteor,
A star in flight, ere Yule one night
    flickering down he fell
From his laddery path to a foaming bath
    in the windy Bay of Bel.

He began to think, lest he melt and sink,
    what in the moon to do,
When a fisherman's boat found him far afloat
    to the amazement of the crew,
Caught in their net all shimmering wet
    in a phosphorescent sheen
Of bluey whites and opal lights
    and delicate liquid green.

Against his wish with the morning fish
    they packed him back to land:
'You had best get a bed in an inn,' they said;
    'the town is near at hand.'
Only the knell of one slow bell
    high in the Seaward Tower
Announced the news of his moonsick cruise
    at that unseemly hour.

Not a hearth was laid, not a breakfast made,
    and dawn was cold and damp.
There were ashes for fire, and for grass the mire,
    for the sun a smoking lamp
In a dim back-street. Not a man did he meet,
    no voice was raised in song;
There were snores instead, for all folk were abed
    and still would slumber long.

He knocked as he passed on doors locked fast,
    and called and cried in vain,

Till he came to an inn that had light within,
and he tapped at a window-pane.
A drowsy cook gave a surly look,
and 'What do you want?' said he.
'I want fire and gold and songs of old
and red wine flowing free!'

'You won't get them here,' said the cook with a leer,
'but you may come inside.
Silver I lack and silk to my back —
maybe I'll let you bide.'
A silver gift the latch to lift,
a pearl to pass the door;
For a seat by the cook in the ingle-nook
it cost him twenty more.

For hunger or drouth naught passed his mouth
till he gave both crown and cloak;
And all that he got, in an earthen pot
broken and black with smoke,
Was porridge cold and two days old
to eat with a wooden spoon.

For puddings of Yule with plums, poor fool,
he arrived so much too soon:
An unwary guest on a lunatic quest
from the Mountains of the Moon.

The Man in the Moon Came Down Too Soon was inspired in the first instance by a familiar English nursery rhyme:

The man in the moon
Came down too soon,
And asked his way to Norwich;
He went by the south,
And burnt his mouth
With supping cold plum porridge.

Alternate words, with music, are given on p. 32 of the collection *What the Children Sing* (1915), edited by Alfred Moffat, a copy of which was owned by Edith Tolkien:

The Man in the Moon
Came tumbling down,
To ask his way to Norwich;
He went by the South
And burnt his mouth,
With eating cold plum porridge.

There is no evidence that Tolkien read a long poem by an unnamed Worcester College, Oxford undergraduate, *The Man in the Moon*, published in 1839–40, though the Tolkien scholar Thomas Honegger has suggested interesting parallels ('The Man in the Moon: Structural Depth in Tolkien', 1999). In the earlier work, the Man having become bored 'Of living so long in the land of dreams; | 'Twas a beautiful sphere, but nevertheless, | Its lunar life was passionless', he descends to Earth like a falling star and seeks the 'woes | And joys of human life'. It seems more likely that Tolkien recalled Chapter 24 of *At the Back of the North Wind* by George MacDonald (1870), in which the nursery rhyme 'Hey Diddle Diddle' is combined with the traditional 'Man in the Moon' rhyme:

But the man in the moon,
Coming back too soon
From the famous town of Norwich,
Caught up the dish,
Said, 'It's just what I wish
To hold my cold plum-porridge!'
Gave the cow a rat-tat,
Flung water on the cat,
And sent him away like a rocket.
Said, 'O Moon there you are!'
Got into her car,
And went off with the spoon in his pocket.

Hey ho! diddle, diddle!
The wet cat and wet fiddle,
They made such a caterwauling,
That the cow in a fright
Stood bolt upright
Bellowing now, and bawling;
And the dog on his tail,
Stretched his neck with a wail.

But 'Ho! ho!' said the man in the moon —
'No more in the South
Shall I burn my mouth,
For I've found a dish and a spoon.'

It also seems likely that the Man in the Moon of the traditional verse 'came down too soon' because 'soon' rhymes with 'moon', just as 'Norwich' pairs with 'porridge'. Tolkien, however, in the earlier versions of his poem 'explains' that the Man is 'too soon' because he arrives at night, 'with all Norfolk abed', before plum-porridge had been made for the day. In the final text, the Man instead comes down 'ere Yule' – in the context of Middle-earth, 'Yule' is a period of winter holidays, but the reader will interpret it as Christmas – when 'puddings of Yule with plums' are traditionally served. The *plum* in 'plum-porridge' or 'plum pudding' tends to refer to prunes (dried plums), or to any kind of dried fruit, such as currants, raisins, or sultanas. The plum-porridge (or plum-pottage) of old was a kind of spiced broth, liquid and savoury, unlike the sweet, firm plum pudding of today.

Possibly in mid-May 1915, Tolkien wrote four lines from *Why the Man in the Moon Came Down Too Soon* (from 'He was tired of his pearls . . .') in his *Book of Ishness* sketch-book, accompanied by a watercolour inscribed 'Illustr[ation]: To "Man in the Moon"' and depicting the Man sliding down to Earth on a spidery thread (Hammond and Scull, *Artist and Illustrator*, fig. 45). Both poem and picture are related to the appearance of the moon in *The Book of Lost Tales*: an island of glass, crystal, or silver, with a white turret from which an aged elf, a stowaway on 'the Ship of the Moon', 'watches the heavens, or the world beneath, and that is Uolë Kúvion who sleepeth never. Some indeed have named him the Man in the Moon . . .' (*The Book of Lost Tales, Part One*, p. 193). Christopher Tolkien has said that Uolë Kúvion 'seems almost to have strayed in from another conception', and that he was earlier called Uolë Mikúmi 'King of the Moon' (*The Book of Lost Tales, Part One*, p. 202).

Yet another version of the Man in the Moon appears, with a 'pallid minaret | Dizzy and white at its lunar height', in Tolkien's children's story *Roverandom*, conceived as an oral tale in 1925 and written down probably in 1927, though not published until 1998: 'It was white with pink and pale green lines in it, shimmering as if the tower were built of millions of seashells still wet with foam and gleaming; and the tower stood on the edge of a white precipice, white as a cliff of chalk, but shining with moonlight more brightly than a pane of glass far away on a cloudless night' (p. 22). In Tolkien's December 1927 letter to his children written in the guise of Father Christmas, the Man in the Moon visits the North Pole, 'as he gets lonely in the Moon, and we make him a nice little Plum Pudding' (*Letters from Father Christmas* (2023 edn.), p. 42).

In the preface to the *Tom Bombadil* collection, *The Man in the Moon Came Down Too Soon* is said to be one of two poems (with *The Last Ship*, no. 141) 'derived ultimately from Gondor. [These] are evidently based on the traditions of Men, living in shorelands and familiar with rivers running into the Sea. No. 6 [the present poem, no. 6 in the *Bombadil* collection] actually mentions *Belfalas* (the windy bay of Bel [the Bay of Belfalas, south of the kingdom of Gondor]) and the Sea-ward Tower, *Tirith Aear*, of Dol Amroth [the chief city and port of Belfalas] . . .' (p. 8).

Tolkien began to write a version of *The Man in the Moon Came Down Too Soon* in Old English, *Þa Mónan Cyning to Moldan Ság*, but abandoned it after only two lines:

> Ilc fyrn gefrægn on mónan fengel feaxhár wunian;
> his beardes brogdne þrǽdas beorhtum blandene seolfre

In 1967 he made a professional recording of the final version of his poem for *Poems and Songs of Middle Earth*. It was later reissued.

A3: 'Girt with pale gold' originally read 'girdled with gold' before Tolkien altered it in the first manuscript.

A12: In the first manuscript 'And he faster earthward raced' originally read 'As he wildly earthward raced'. In the first typescript this became 'And faster he earthward raced', in which form it was published in *A Northern Venture*, but reverted to 'And he faster earthward raced' with the second typescript, where Tolkien revised it again, to 'He swiftly earthward raced'. The line ultimately disappeared as the poem changed still further.

A14: The 'pallid minaret' is a slender tower, not the turret of a mosque.

A15: In the first manuscript 'at its lunar height' read 'at celestial height'.

A17: In the first manuscript this line began 'So adventured'. Tolkien changed it to 'And adventured' in the second manuscript.

A19: 'For new diadems' read 'to make new diadems' in the first manuscript. Tolkien altered it in the course of writing the second manuscript.

A20: Tolkien altered the original reading 'spangle' to 'blazon' in the first manuscript.

A25: Tolkien wrote to Jane Neave, to whom he had sent *The Man in the Moon Came Down Too Soon*, that the words *plenilune* (time of the full moon) and *argent* (silver) 'are beautiful . . . *before* they are understood – I wish I could have the pleasure of meeting them for the first time again! – and how is one to know them till one does meet them?' (22 November 1961, *Letters*, p. 440).

A27: *Selenite* (a variety of gypsum, usually colorless and transparent) contains the Greek element *selen-* 'moon'.

A33–34: 'Meadowy ways like chrysoprase, | At topaz eve': Tolkien presumably is relating the green of a meadow to the colour of the mineral chrysoprase, a variety of quartz also called chalcedony, and the yellow colour of the gem topaz to that of sunset. Apropos his use of *chrysoprase*, at a time when Tolkien tended to use unusual words lavishly in his poems and was taken to task for it by his TCBS friends, we find the critic Ivor Brown remarking (much later) on *chrysoprase*, as collected in his book *Random Words* (1971): 'I have in the past regretted the narrow and spare vocabulary of some recent poets. T.S. Eliot frankly admitted that he put the muse "on a lean diet" and he set a fashion in verbal austerity' (p. 41). He found, however, lines in 'an anthology of bad verse' by D.B. Chivers (*fl.* 1840):

> Like the sweet golden goblet found growing
> On the wild emerald cucumber-tree,
> Rich, brilliant, like chrysoprase glowing,
> Was my beautiful Rosalie Lee.

'High regard', says Brown, 'is due to a poet who was determined to save the muse from word-starvation' (p. 42).

A35–6: These lines remained unchanged from the first to the second manuscript, but Tolkien wrote an alternate reading on the opposite page of one of his poetry notebooks: 'For he had longed for the mirth of the populous Earth | When lonely above he hung'.

A39: 'Eating pearly cakes of light snow-flakes' read 'Fed many a year on cold lunar cheer' before Tolkien changed it in the first manuscript.

A41: 'He twinkled his feet as he thought of the meat' read 'So great was his hurry when he fancied curry' before Tolkien changed it in the first manuscript.

A48: The 'Ocean of Almain' is the North Sea. *Almain* is an older English name for Germany, and the North Sea has been called the 'German Ocean'.

A51: Yarmouth, i.e. Great Yarmouth, is a town south of Norwich, once a major fishing port.

A62: 'Fifty towers' refers to the city's many churches.

A63: 'Lunatic', with the Latin element *luna-* 'moon', reflects a folk belief that changes of the moon cause insanity.

A77: 'Anglian Norwich': Norwich is the capital of the English county of Norfolk in the region of East Anglia, so called because it was settled by Angles. Since medieval times, Norwich has been a major city in England, with many churches.

C15: *Moonstone* is a variety of the mineral feldspar. Its appearance, irridescent like pearl, and its name are both appropriate for this lunar setting.

C29–30: Before more thoroughly revising the poem for the *Tom Bombadil* collection, Tolkien changed 'Whose hot heart glows with crimson and rose' to 'With a hot heart that glows in crimson and rose', and 'with leaping orange tongue' to 'and leaping orange tongue'.

C79: In one of the typescripts, this line has the misreading 'I want a fire and gold', corrected in Tolkien's hand. The other typescript of this text has the correct reading. Both typescripts, however, misspell 'sapphire' in l. 20 (as 'saphhire'), which we have silently corrected.

25

Courage Speaks to a Child of Earth · *The Two Riders* (1915–?25)

The title of the first manuscript of this poem (given below as A) was originally *Courage Speaks to the Love of Earth*, briefly altered to *Courage Speaks to the Love of Life* before reverting. This was replaced in turn, possibly at once, by *Courage Speaks to a Child of Earth*, with an added extension, 'or a TCBSian to the TCBS'.

[A]

Tis a rhythmic course
On a strong-limbed horse
With the round earth fleeting under:
The wind in our ears
Is roaring years,
And his beating feet are thunder
His sweat is a-reek,
Yet the things we seek
Are a million miles out yonder
O good is speed,
And yet, more we need —
There is not one hour to squander.

O hold by my side
Lest he slacken his stride
And the shadows go about me,
And the wide green ways
Of our galloping days
Plunge in the gloom without me.

Yea! though mighty the Sun
when his course is run
And his beauty doth not blind us
O'er the world's pale rim
Till our days blow thin
And the stars are all behind us

In boundless course
On a wingéd horse
We'll dare the outer splendour
With the wind in our ears
Of the seven spheres
And the lost Earth faded slender.

'Seven spheres' refers to the concept in medieval astronomy (compare poem no. 20) in which seven concentric crystalline spheres were occupied by the Sun, the Moon, and the five planets visible to the naked eye (Mercury, Venus, Mars, Jupiter, and Saturn), all of which revolved around a central Earth.

Both this draft, signed 'RT' (Ronald Tolkien), and a second manuscript are inscribed 'Ap[ril] 15–16 1915'. The latter was first entitled *Courage Speaks with a Child of Earth*, but these words were struck through and *Now and Ever* written above, before that title too was deleted. Probably later, Tolkien wrote on this sheet a new title, *The Two Riders*, as well as the same in Old English, *Þá Twégen Rideras*. For this manuscript, he divided the lines into five groups of six, and slightly altered their punctuation. The first line gained an apostrophe (''Tis'), 'O good is speed' (line 10) became 'Most good is speed', and 'Yea! though mighty the sun' initially became 'Yea! though the mighty sun'. After writing out the text, Tolkien changed line 12 to 'With the round earth fleeting under', line 19 to 'Though the mighty sun' (omitting 'Yea!'), and line 21 to 'And no more his beauty blind us'.

The second manuscript, as revised, was typed by the Oxford Copying Office in mid- to late May 1915; two carbon copies survive in addition to a ribbon copy, one of them dated 'Spring 1915'. At this point, the title of the poem was still *Now and Ever*. On both carbon copies Tolkien altered this to *The Two Riders* and made a few other changes, notably the addition of quotation marks to indicate two speakers; but one of the copies has more revisions than the other, including added typewriting made with a purple ribbon such as Tolkien used at the University of Leeds. We give here, as B, the final text as revised.

[B]

'Come ride on my course
On my strong-limbed horse
With the round earth fleeting under:
The wind in our ears
Is roaring years,
And his beating feet are thunder

His sweat is a-reek,
Yet the things we seek
Are leagues uncounted yonder:
Great is his speed,
And, yet, more we need,
With the round earth fleeting under.'

*

'O hold by my side,
Lest he slacken his stride,
And the shadows go about me,
And the wide green ways
Of your galloping days
Plunge in the gloom without me!'

*

'When the mighty sun
Shall his day have run
And no more with his beauty blind us,
O'er the world's pale rim,
Till our days blow thin
And the stars are all behind us,

In boundless course
On wingéd horse
We'll dare the outer splendour,
With the wind in our ears
Of the seven spheres
And the lost Earth faded slender.'

On its surface, especially in its later versions, *The Two Riders* vividly describes the action of a horse, which Tolkien had experienced at Oxford as a member of the King Edward's Horse, a territorial cavalry regiment similar to the Officers Training Corps. On the first manuscript, however, he labelled the first and final stanzas 'TCBS', and the middle stanza '-ian', i.e. 'TCBSian'. These are of a piece with the inscription 'A TCBSian to the TCBS', and with the quotation marks added to the final text which present the poem more clearly as a dialogue. The TCBS, such as it had survived with its core members, was precious to Tolkien, but events were passing swiftly and the fellowship was in danger of breaking apart. Gilson, Smith, and Wiseman had already joined the war effort, and Tolkien was soon to follow, himself 'plunging into the gloom'.

And yet, one can only guess at the meaning of the changing titles. Was *Courage Speaks to the Love of Earth*, or *to the Love of Life*, meant to urge courage or steadfastness on his friends as combat neared? Was *Now and Ever* an expression of eternal friendship? The 'two' of *The Two Riders* suggests that Tolkien changed the title after Gilson and Smith were killed (in July and December 1916 respectively) and only Wiseman and Tolkien remained. This would also explain his late use of the singular 'my' in lines 1 and 2. In any case, the poem was written while the TCBS yet lived, and just after the members had been unable to meet in Oxford. With high hopes for their future achievements, Tolkien describes a 'boundless course' on which the members fly beyond the earthly sphere.

A3: Here, and in B3, Tolkien wrote 'earth', but in A30 and B30 capitalized 'Earth'.

A19–21: On the facing page of his poetry notebook, Tolkien wrote the alternate lines 'Yea though the mighty Sun | Shall his day have run | And his beauty no more blind us', with 'kingly?' also considered instead of 'mighty'.

26

May Day in a Backward Year · *May-Day* (1915–23)

As mentioned in our discussion of poem no. 17, the manuscript of *The Story of Kullervo* is accompanied by the earliest version of *May-Day* (as it was finally called). We have suggested that the writing of *Kullervo* was under way in October 1914, and may have continued into the early months of 1915; the contiguous manuscript of *May-Day* seems to have been conceived in the same period, most likely in the latter part, as Tolkien dated two later manuscripts of the poem to 20–21 April 1915, and another to May of that year.

The first version of the poem, not yet given a title, is in pencil, partly written over erasures, with alterations in both pencil and (later) ink. Here, as A, we give the text as it stood before revision.

[A] Trees are all blossomed, and swollen buds burst,
And silvern the orchards with sweet breathed snow
Laid in a night where the new-tasselled hurst
Was tufted with green; and the grass is a-glow
With the emerald flame of the year's early thirst
For the Sun; while the breezes that bending it blow
Fan its green fire till in flower-light it burst.
April's at ending; May is here now.
Many a silvan singer rejoices
    A-nest are their young:
    Be a love-carol sung,
    With quivering lung!
    Spring's in their voices.

Come wend to the woodland, come dance ye grey folk!
Come hatless — for pale tearful April is fled:
Come happy; come careless and carry no cloak
For the world doth not weep though pale April be dead.
Betimes is the chestnut with leaf, and the oak —
— That sluggard — is blushing a smoky bud-red
And the hawthorn a many gay weeks ago woke

When she caught the green spark that the meadow grass fed;
And the song of the children of men must be chanted
    By old and by young
    With May blossom hung
    With a carolling tongue;
    And the May-pole be planted.

Dance in the dingles and lilt in the dells
Or propped under feather-green larchés behold
The leafy-thrones ready for coming blue-bells
Mid the crozier fern fronds in warm matted mould.
Let the lutanist weave us a music of smells
Or the piper a tune of the silver and gold
Of May-dusk when far off is a tinkle of bells
Neath the little white moon and the shadows are cold
And the primrose pale-face is wan in the gloaming
    Come follow the Sun
    The May day is done
    Rest have we won
    And a sweet homing.

'Sweet-breathed snow' refers metaphorically to the fallen blossom of trees, as of the hawthorn; compare 'snow in summer' in *Once upon a Time* (no. 48). The 'silvan singers' are birds; compare 'merrily silvan the song-birds rejoice' in line 9 of text B (amended from 'Many a silvan songbird rejoices'). The 'grey folk' are not, surely, the trows (trolls) of folklore, but presumably those persons made dull or sad by winter. The European or common larch (*Larix decidua*) has clusters of needles Tolkien first described as 'feather-green' – evoking, maybe, a green plumage – but later as 'long-tasselled'. The larch is deciduous, growing new, bright green needles in spring and losing them in winter. The 'leafy-thrones' of line 29 are beds of shed needles – the fallen leaves of the larch – through which bluebells will grow, usually from April through June.

The common primrose (*Primula vulgaris*) is typically coloured a pale creamy yellow with a darker centre. To say that its 'pale-face' is 'wan' (i.e. pale) is redundant; thus 'The glimmering primroses faint in the gloam' in text B, and 'In the gloaming the primroses glimmering wan' in text C below. With 'crozier fern fronds' Tolkien is referring to the way fern *fronds* (leaves) gradually uncurl, and before fully extended resemble the hooked head of a bishop's staff, called a *crozier* (or *crosier*).

April in England is associated with rain ('tearful April'), preceding flowers in May. Apparently, at least as Tolkien observed it, certain plants greeted spring 1915 belatedly, though there is no suggestion of unusual rainfall or temperatures in Oxford weather records for that March and April. The May-pole in northern European cultures is an ancient fertility symbol representing a tree, now a cut pole but perhaps once an actual tree brought from the woods and set on the village green.

Tolkien heavily revised the manuscript of A and made a fresh copy, entitled *May Day*. This manuscript, too, underwent revision, gaining in a new fair copy the fuller title *May Day in a Backward Year* and an added title in Old English, *Þæt Ʒear Onʒinneþ Síðor Spréotan*, though there is not a great deal of difference between the two texts. In the latter form, given here as B, Tolkien had it typed in mid- to late May 1915 by the Oxford Copying Office.

[B] The earth is all blossomed and swollen buds burst,
    And silvern the orchards with sweet-breathéd snow
Laid in the night where the plum-trees were erst
    But tufted with green; and the grass is a-glow
With the emerald flame of the year's early thirst
    For the Sun, while the breezes that bending it blow
Fan its green fire till in flower-light it burst.
    Let May enter in, and let pale April go!
    For merrily silvan the song-birds rejoice —
            A-nest are their young;
            Be a love-carol sung
            With quivering lung!
        Spring's in their voice.

Come, wend to the woodland! Come, dance ye grey folk!
    Come hatless — for tearful pale April is fled:
Come happy, come careless, and carry no cloak,
    For May doth not weep, though pale April be dead.
Betimes is the chestnut with leaf, and the oak —
    That sluggard — is blushing a smoky bud-red,
And the hawthorn a many gay weeks ago woke,
    When she caught the green spark that the meadow grass
        fed.

’Tis a song of the sons of the earth we must chant,
We old, and we young
With a carolling tongue,
As all blossom-hung
The May-pole we plant.

Dance in the dingles, and lilt in the dells;
Or propped under long-tasselled larches behold
The leafy thrones ready for lazy blue-bells,
And the crozier fronds in the warm matted mould.
Let the lutanist weave us a music of smells,
Or the piper a tune from the silver and gold
Of a limpid May-dusk with its far-away bells
Neath the little white moon, as the shadows enfold
The glimmering primroses faint in the gloam.
Come May-day has fadéd,
And we flower-ladéd,
And sweetly dew-bathéd
Wend whispering home.

In B, ‘plum-trees’ may refer to the cherry plum (*Prunus cerasifera*), which in England is covered with white flowers as early as the beginning of March. Here the blossom had been on the trees *erst* (long ago, formerly) but is now on the ground. The final lines of the new version refer to another May Day tradition, in which, before sunrise, women would bathe their faces and eyes with dew found upon grass or in flower petals. There was a widespread folk belief that dew gathered on May Day morning was particularly good for the complexion.

Eight years later, if his dating is correct, Tolkien revised his poem again, now making several substantive changes and omitting the first stanza altogether. He made a new manuscript, entitled *May-Day* (now hyphenated), and inscribed it, at a still later date, ‘Part of 1st or 2nd, & 3rd verse out of 3 written at a house in Leamington Road (?) Warwick May 1915. Rewritten and arr[anged] 1923’ – the parenthetical query is Tolkien’s. In writing ‘May 1915’ he evidently forgot the 20–21 April dates he inscribed on earlier manuscripts of the poem, and that by May 1915 he had returned to Oxford for Trinity Term (begun 25 April). He had been in Warwick during the Easter 1915 vacation, to see Edith Bratt, who was living at 15 Victoria Road, while he himself stayed at 57 Emscote Road.

The final text survives also in a typescript (C) made with the purple ribbon associated with Tolkien’s years at Leeds. This differs from the preceding manuscript only in lines 5 ('its' amended from 'his') and 7 ('And' amended from 'But'). Tolkien's 'arrangement' of the poem in 1923 suggests that he may have offered it for publication that year in the Leeds collection *A Northern Venture: Verses by Members of the Leeds University English School Association* (see poem no. 24).

[C] Come away to the woods! Come and dance, ye grey folk!
Come hatless, for tearful pale April is fled:
Come happy, come careless, and carry no cloak,
For May doth not weep, though pale April be dead.
The chestnut is waking its leaves, and the oak,
Old sluggard, is blushing a smoky bud-red;
And the hawthorn is up: it is weeks since she woke
When she saw the green spark that the meadow-grass fed.
The copses are ringing with birds that rejoice:
A-nest are their young,
And their love-carols sung
With quivering lung.
Spring's in their voice.

O! Dance in the dingles and lilt in the dells,
Where the long-tasselled larches are singing, and rolled
At their feet are the carpets of misty bluebells
And the crozier fronds of the ferns in the mould.
Let the lutanist weave us a music of smells,
Or the piper a tune from the silver and gold
Of a limpid May-dusk with its far-away bells
Neath the little white moon, as the shadows enfold
In the gloaming the primroses glimmering wan.
The first star has twinkled;
The last bell has tinkled;
The grass is dew-sprinkled:
Come, May-day has gone!

May-Day is an early expression of Tolkien's interest in nature, in particular its flora, which engaged him throughout his life. In a letter to his son Christopher begun about 2 June 1971, Tolkien describes a holiday he and his wife recently took:

> . . . May was such a wonderful month – and we came in for a 'spring explosion' of glory, with Devon passing from brown to brilliant yellow-green, and all the flowers leaping out of dead

bracken or old grass. (Incidentally the oaks have behaved in a most extraordinary way. The old saw about the oak and the ash, if it has any truth, would usually need wide-spread statistics, since the gap between their wakening is usually so small that it can be changed by minor local differences of situation. But this year there seemed a month between them! The oaks were among the earliest trees to be leafed equalling or beating birch, beech and lime etc. Great cauliflowers of brilliant yellow-ochre tasselled with flowers, while the ashes (in the same situations) were dark, dead, with hardly even a visible sticky bud). [*Letters*, p. 573]

'Backward' in the title *May Day in a Backward Year* cannot be explained with certainty. The accompanying Old English title means 'The Year Begins to Sprout Late', but the chestnut is in leaf 'betimes' (early) and the hawthorn (*Crataegus monogyna*) has 'woken' already 'many gay weeks' before its time. (The hawthorn is also called the May-tree because it is usually in blossom by the first of May.) It may be significant that Tolkien returned to a simpler title, *May-Day*, and that in an early list of his poems by their Old English titles the work appears as *Þæt Ȝear Onȝinneþ Spréotan* ('The Year Begins to Sprout'), with no mention of lateness. (In a later list, the title became *Mayday*.) The poem is also curious in that it appears to have been written (or at least begun) during April, nine or ten days before May Day, but to the speaker the event has come and gone. At any rate, the subject of the poem is ultimately May Day itself, a festival as old as the Romans which marks the traditional start of summer, a season of warmth and new growth. To celebrate, flowers and greenery are gathered and 'blossoms hung' to decorate houses and buildings, thus the phrases 'going a-maying' and 'bringing in the May'.

A1: Another reading of this line, considered by Tolkien but abandoned, was 'O month of white blossom when swollen buds burst'.

B9: After the third manuscript was typed, Tolkien changed this line to 'Full-throated the song of the birds that rejoice', but did not carry the reading into text C.

B13: In the typescript this line is indented one further position, but in the preceding manuscript appears as we have transcribed it. Compare the final lines of the second and third stanzas.

B22: Tolkien changed the reading of text A, 'And the song of the children of men must be chanted', in the second manuscript (*May Day*) to ''Tis a song of the children of men must be chanted' > ''Tis a song of the children of earth we must chant', and in the third manuscript (*May Day in a Backward Year*) to ''Tis a song of the [children of > sons of the earth] we must chant'.

B36–39: In the second manuscript these lines originally read

Come May-day is done!
Let us follow the Sun
That to bedward has won [i.e. has gone to bed]
Sweet be our homing [i.e. coming home].

Tolkien wrote a version of this text in the margin of his first manuscript as well:

Come May-day is done
We follow the Sun
That bedward has won
And sweet be our homing.

Curiously, the first manuscript also includes among its revisions, in handwriting which appears to be contemporary with changes carried into the second manuscript, the reading ('Come May-day has fadéd', etc.) given only in the third (text B).

27

Goblin Feet (1915–*c.* 1923)

Goblin Feet is surely the best known of Tolkien's early poems. The first of his writings to appear in a book, it has also been a popular selection in anthologies. Its earliest extant manuscript (A) appears to be a fair copy, inscribed by Tolkien 'April 27–28 1915' and with an additional title in Old English, *Cumaþ þá Nihtielfas* ('The Night-Elves Come'). In this, the poem is divided into four parts.

[A] I am off down the road
Where the fairy lanterns glowed
And the little pretty flittermice are flying:
A slender band of grey
It runs creepily away
And the hedges and the grasses are a-sighing.
The air is full of wings,
And the blundering beetle-things
That warm you with their whirring and their humming.
O! I hear the tiny horns
Of enchanted leprechauns
And the padding feet of many gnomes a-coming!

*

O! the lights: O! the gleams: O! the little tinkly sounds:
O! The rustle of their noiseless little robes:
O! the echo of their feet — of their little happy feet:
O! their swinging lamps in little starlit globes.

*

I must follow in their train
Down the crooked fairy lane
Where the coney-rabbits long ago have gone,
And where silverly they sing
In a moving moonlit ring
All a-twinkle with the jewels they have on.
They are fading round the turn

Where the glow-worms palely burn
And the echo of their padding feet is dying!
O! it's knocking at my heart —
Let me go! O! let me start!
For the little magic hours are all a-flying.

★

O the warmth! O the hum! O the colours in the dark!
O the gauzy wings of golden honey-flies!
O the music of their feet — of their dancing goblin feet!
O the magic! O the sorrow when it dies.

On 1 December 1915 *Goblin Feet* was published in *Oxford Poetry 1915* (pp. 64–5), a collection of verse by Oxford University students edited by two of their own, G.D.H. Cole and T.W. Earp. The printed text of the poem follows manuscript A closely, with only a few exceptions. In the final printed lines (29–32) exclamation marks are more numerous, echoing Tolkien's practice earlier in the poem:

O! the warmth! O! the hum! O! the colours in the dark!
O! the gauzy wings of golden honey-flies!
O! the music of their feet — of their dancing goblin feet!
O! the magic! O! the sorrow when it dies.

Another exception is in line 9, where the second word is printed 'warn', but in the manuscript (not clearly) and a subsequent typescript (explicitly) it is 'warm'. In the context of winged noise-makers 'warn' seems the most appropriate, but as written in the manuscript the word is identical in its letterforms to the first part of 'warmth' in line 29, and indeed Tolkien may have intended 'warmth' to refer back, if in some sense which escapes us, to the 'whirring' and 'humming' of the 'beetle-things'. But 'warn' has persisted as the poem has been reprinted, following the original form of publication.

Also preserved in Tolkien's papers is a stray leaf of manuscript with the last half of the poem (from 'I must follow in their train', line 17). Relative to text A, this fragment has different punctuation, chiefly the presence, or absence, of exclamation marks (line 27, for example, reads 'Let me go — O let me start'), and two different readings: 'It is knocking at my heart', line 26; and 'little happy feet' rather than 'dancing goblin feet' in line 31, possibly an error, if Tolkien was recalling the 'little happy feet' of line 15. This text may well have been set down from memory, possibly in 1916, since it is written on a squared paper such as Tolkien would have had available for use in military service.

In mid- to late May 1915 he had *Goblin Feet* typed by the Oxford Copying Office; this instance survives in a ribbon copy and a carbon copy. In both, 'warm' is present in line 9, as are the numerous exclamation marks in the final stanza, but without the ornaments Tolkien used in his manuscript. It is not known which text was given to the editors of *Oxford Poetry 1915*. It seems that there had been a call for submissions by mid-May 1915, when G.B. Smith, busy with army training, asked Tolkien his opinion of *Oxford Poetry* and to show some of Smith's verses to its editors. In late July Smith wrote that two of his poems had been accepted for the volume (in the event, only one was published). Tolkien seems to have submitted both *Goblin Feet* and *You and Me and the Cottage of Lost Play* (poem no. 28), but only the first was chosen.

On the carbon copy of the professional typescript Tolkien later wrote: 'Oxford [*deleted:* end of 1914] spring 1915 (3 times published)'. The bracketed note of three publications probably refers to *Oxford Poetry 1915*, *The Book of Fairy Poetry* (edited by Dora Owen, 1920), and perhaps the direct reprint of *Oxford Poetry 1915* with two other volumes in the series as *Oxford Poetry 1914–1916* (1917); further reprints came soon after. Dora Owen evidently had seen *Goblin Feet* in *Oxford Poetry 1915* and, probably in January 1916, wrote to Tolkien for permission to reprint it in her *Book of Fairy Poetry*, then being planned. Tolkien sent her several of his 'fairy' poems, hopefully, but she too preferred to include only *Goblin Feet*.

Tolkien also marked a few alterations on the carbon copy, the most notable of which was a complete replacement of line 9, making the question of 'warm' or 'warn' moot. These revisions are reflected in a new typescript (B), made with the purple ribbon associated with Tolkien's years at Leeds.

[B]

I am off down the road
Where the fairy lanterns glowed
And the little pretty flittermice are flying:
A slender band of grey
It runs creepily away
And the hedges and the grasses are a-sighing.
The air is full of wings
Of the blundering beetle-things
That go droning by a-whirring and a-humming.

O! I hear the tiny horns
Of enchanted leprechauns
And the padding feet of many gnomes a-coming!

O! the lights: O! the gleams: O! the little tinkling sounds:
O! The rustle of their noiseless little robes:
O! the echo of their feet, of their little happy feet:
O! their swinging lamps in little starlit globes.

I must follow in their train
Down the crooked fairy lane
Where the coney-rabbits long ago have gone,
And where silverly they sing
In a moving moonlit ring
All a-twinkle with the jewels they have on.
They are fading round the turn
Where the glow-worms palely burn
And the echo of their padding feet is dying!
It is knocking at my heart —
Let me go! O! let me start!
For the little hours of magic are a-flying.

O! the warmth! O! the hum! O! the colours in the dark!
O! the gauzy wings of golden honey-flies!
O! the music of their feet, of their dancing goblin feet!
O! the magic! O! the sorrow when it dies.

According to Humphrey Carpenter, Tolkien wrote *Goblin Feet* to please Edith Bratt, 'who said that she liked "spring and flowers and trees, and little elfin people"' (*Biography*, p. 74). And yet, in a letter of 1 May 1915 Tolkien asked her: 'Why didn't you like the first of the "Goblin feet" verses darling? Too mothy and batty? Fairies especially some kinds are very mothy and batty' (Bodleian Library; the *flittermice* of line 3 are bats, compare German *Fledermaus*). G.B. Smith, however, congratulated Tolkien 'enormously on your contribution [to *Oxford Poetry*]. It reads most splendidly. . . .' As we have said, Smith himself had a poem in the collection ('Songs on the Downs'), and his friend H.T. Wade-Gery, who wrote in an older, lyric style, had three; both felt – modesty set firmly aside – that they, with Tolkien, were 'much the best' of the contributors. Smith wrote: 'I mean that we have really got the right ideals and conceptions' (22 December 1915, Bodleian Library). Today *Oxford Poetry 1915* is notable for including work by Tolkien, Naomi Mitchison (then Naomi Haldane), Aldous Huxley, and Dorothy L. Sayers (who composed an ambitious eight-page 'Lay'), while Smith and Wade-Gery are known only for their connection with Tolkien.

After receiving a copy of the book, Tolkien wrote to Edith on 17 December 1915 that '"Goblin Feet" is a little swamped and rather disappointing in print' (Bodleian Library), probably referring to its appearance. Set in small type across two pages, with as much white space as text, the poem typographically fails to impress.

In the journal *The New Age* for 30 March 1916, an anonymous reviewer of *Oxford Poetry 1915* read *Goblin Feet* as if it were syncopated ragtime music; and in the number for 11 July 1918, reviewing the collection *Oxford Poetry 1914–1916* incorporating the 1915 volume, Paul Selver felt that Tolkien's poem was 'rather too sing-song, even for lines which clearly run to a tune, actual or imagined; it is too "tinkly"' (p. 167). Even so, Tolkien's verse caught the attention of Geraldine E. Hodgson, whose review of then-recent poetry, *Criticism at a Venture* (1919), considered *Goblin Feet* one of the better contributions to *Oxford Poetry 1915*. She also included Tolkien's verse in her 1923 book, *English Literature: With Illustrations from Poetry and Prose*, where she compared it favourably to work by Walter de la Mare and Edith Sitwell.

Late in life, replying to yet another request to include *Goblin Feet* in an anthology, Tolkien wished that 'the unhappy little thing, representing all that I came (so soon after) to fervently dislike, could be buried for ever' (1971; quoted in *The Book of Lost Tales, Part One*, p. 32). By the time of this letter, he had long ago abandoned in his writings the idea of diminutive fairies or elves. One could argue how 'soon after' the publication of *Goblin Feet* Tolkien changed his thoughts. Certainly not at once: within days of writing *Goblin Feet*, he also composed *You and Me and the Cottage of Lost Play* (no. 28) and *Tinfang Warble* (no. 29) in much the same vein.

One aspect of *Goblin Feet* which Tolkien may well have come to dislike, as he began rigorously to develop his private mythology, is the poem's conflation of fairies, leprechauns, gnomes, and goblins as if the terms were synonymous. In his *c.* 1915–19 lexicon of Qenya, *Qenyaqetsa* (*Parma Eldalamberon* 12 (1998), p. 67), he glossed the word *Noldo* as 'Gnome', but there 'Gnome' is a change from 'Goblin'; and in the course of time, *Gnome* as a name of one of the second kindred of the Elves was itself abandoned, as it had associations in fairy-stories or folklore not consonant with Tolkien's fiction. Goblins, so called, appear in *The Book of Lost Tales* (as do Orcs) and in *The*

Hobbit (1937), the latter influenced by those in *The Princess and the Goblin* by George MacDonald (1872) and by the equally malicious goblins of folk and literary tradition. But the 'goblins' of *Goblin Feet* are not shown to be evil; neither, though, are they necessarily goblins in the usual sense, merely one kind of supernatural creature which haunts the landscape of Tolkien's poems.

In this he followed in a tradition of 'fairy poetry' centuries old, recently (in the late nineteenth century) brought again to the fore by writers such as William Allingham, William Butler Yeats, Walter de la Mare, and Christina Rossetti. *Goblin Feet* also contains a theme better known in later writings by Tolkien, that of a yearning to 'follow in their train | down the crooked fairy lane' into a world outside of normal life; but the speaker of the poem, like (say) Firiel in poem no. 141, does not follow after all. As Tolkien wrote in *On Fairy-Stories*, 'even upon the borders of Faërie we encounter [elves, and other creatures of the "Perilous Realm"] only at some chance crossing of the ways' (*Tree and Leaf* (2001), p. 10).

In *J.R.R. Tolkien: Romanticist and Poet* (2017) Julian Eilmann describes *Goblin Feet* as a Romantic work, with the lyrical call of longing 'O!' repeated fifteen times. 'Not only do the mythical creatures here embody the marvellous, for which the Romantic longs, but ultimately poetry itself' (p. 303). John Garth in *Tolkien and the Great War* similarly remarks that *Goblin Feet* 'turns in an instant from rising joy to loss and sadness, capturing once again a very Tolkienian yearning. The mortal onlooker wants to pursue the happy band, or rather he feels compelled to do so; but no sooner is the thought formed than the troop disappears around a bend' (pp. 74–5).

J.S. Ryan has observed that *Goblin Feet* 'possesses an undeniable sureness of rhythm, Georgian vocabulary, and a notion that the road that passes one's door embodies temptation and allure, particularly on summer nights' ('Homo Ludens: Amusement, Play and Seeking in Tolkien's Earliest Romantic Thought' (2009), p. 48; by 'Georgian vocabulary' we suppose that he meant words which evoke a rural or pastoral setting). He feels that the poem anticipates *The Road Goes Ever On and On* (no. 115) – 'The Road goes ever on and on, | Down from the door where it began', etc. It would be better to say, however, that *Goblin Feet* contains an early example of the Road in Tolkien's writings, an image which he would use frequently, most famously in *The Hobbit* and *The Lord of the Rings*, most immediately after *Goblin Feet* in *You and Me and the Cottage of Lost Play* with its 'warm and winding lane'. The appeal of the 'open road' is often found expressed in English literature known well by Tolkien's generation, by Robert

Louis Stevenson, John Masefield, and Edward Thomas, and especially by the influential George Borrow, in *Lavengro* and other works. (Tolkien himself did not admire Borrow, at least not as an undergraduate in 1914; see Scull and Hammond, *Chronology*, p. 59.)

B8: Tolkien makes it clear, by changing 'And' to 'Of', that the wings of l. 7 belong to the 'beetle-things'.

B13: 'Tinkling' of text A here became 'tinkling'.

B26: The amended reading 'It is knocking at my heart' appeared already in the partial pencil manuscript we have dated to 1916.

B28: Tolkien reordered the words of this line from 'For the little magic hours are all a-flying' to 'For the little hours of magic are a-flying', potentially a change in sense.

28

You and Me and the Cottage of Lost Play · *The Little House of Lost Play:* *Mar Vanwa Tyaliéva* (1915–?61 or ?62)

The earliest extant version of *You and Me and the Cottage of Lost Play*, as it was first called, is a manuscript, to all appearances a fair copy, dated 'Ap[ril] 27–28 [1915]' and with a second, Old English title, *Þæt Húsincel Ǣrran Ȝamenes* (literally 'The Small House of Former Play'). We give this text (A) incorporating revisions made in the course of writing, and with its original idiosyncratic indentation.

[A]

We know that land do you and I,
    And often have been there
In the long old days, old nursery days,
    A dark child and a fair.
Was it down the paths of firelight dreams
    In winter cold and white,
On the blue-spun twilit hours
Of little early tucked-up beds
    In drowsy summer night,
That You and I got lost in Sleep
    And met each other there —
Your dark hair on your white night-gown,
    And mine was tangled fair?

We wandered shyly hand in hand,
    Or rollicked in the fairy-sand
And gathered pearls and shells in pails,
    While all about the nightingales
        Were singing in the trees.
We dug for silver with our spades
    By little inland sparkling seas,
Then ran ashore through sleepy glades
    And down a warm and winding lane,
    We never never found again,
        Between high whispering trees.

The air was neither night nor day,
But faintly dark with softest light
When first there glimmered into sight
The Cottage of Lost Play: —
'Twas builded very very old,
White, and thatched with straws of gold,
And pierced with peeping lattices
That looked toward the sea;
And our own children's-garden plots
Were there — our own forgetmenots,
Red daisies, cress and mustard,
And blue nemophilë.
O! all the borders trimmed with box
Were full of favourite flowers — of phlox,
Of larkspur, pinks, and hollyhocks
    Beneath a red may-tree:
And all the paths were full of shapes,
Of tumbling happy white-clad shapes,
    And with them You and Me.

And some had silver watering-cans
    And watered all their gowns,
Or sprayed each other; some laid plans
    To build them houses, fairy towns,
        Or dwellings in the trees;
And some were clambering on the roof;
    Some crooning lonely and aloof;
And some were dancing fairy rings,
    And weaving pearly daisy-strings,
        Or chasing garden bees;
But here and there a little pair
With rosy cheeks and tangled hair
    Debated quaint old childish things —
        And we were one of these.

And why it was Tomorrow came
    And with his grey hand led us back;
And why we never found the same
    Old cottage, or the magic track
    That leads between a silver sea
And those old shores and gardens fair
Where all things are, that ever were —
    We know not — You and Me.

On this manuscript, Tolkien appears to have added the title only after the text proper was in place. Also at some later time, he struck through the first line and wrote 'You and me — we know that land' (incorporated in the text printed in *The Book of Lost Tales, Part One*, pp. 28–9). The manuscript originally included a further stanza, which Tolkien struck through:

O shall we go again to-night
   And wander silent there?
And will you, as once long ago,
   Let down your sweet dark hair?
O, let us go along the road
   Between a silver sea
And those old shores, and down the lane
   That winds through Memory;
That peep we in between the bars
   Of the golden cottage gates
And smell the flowers and see the stars —
   —: See little tangled pates,
   And hear a sound of little song,
   And catch a fragrance that has long
      Been faint to You and Me?

Tolkien's poem is an exaltation of nature, and of gardening. *Forget-menots* (forget-me-nots) are low-growing, brightly coloured flowers of the genus *Myosotis*. The daisy of course is well known (a common English variety is *Bellis perennis*); a *daisy-string*, or daisy chain, is a string of daisies whose stems have been threaded or braided together, for play. Cress and mustard are edible plants of the family *Brassicaceae*, often grown for salads. *Nemophilë* (*Nemophila*) is a low-growing flower, chiefly blue. Box (*Buxus*, U.S. *boxwood*) is a slow-growing evergreen shrub. *Phlox* is a showy perennial common in garden borders. *Larkspur* is a common name for perennial varieties of *Delphinium* and annual varieties of *Consolida*. *Pinks*, with sweet-smelling pink or white flowers, are also known by the name *Dianthus*. A *hollyhock* is a tall plant in the mallow family, of the genus *Alcea*, with large, showy flowers. The *lupin* (lupine), which enters the poem in version B, is part of the pea family, with tall, tapering spikes of flowers. The 'may-tree' is the hawthorn; see our comments for poem no. 26. A *fairy-ring* is a ring of grass darker in colour than surrounding grass, a phenomenon caused by fungi, but in folk-belief by fairies dancing.

On 1 May 1915 Tolkien wrote to Edith Bratt that he was glad she liked *You and Me*, and that he had 'altered' the final verse in his retained copy (presumably the manuscript given above; the copy Edith received seems not to have survived) 'because it was too intimate for anyone but you ever to see' (Bodleian Library). This surely confirms the identity of the 'You' of the poem, and Brian Rosebury's judgement that it is 'a homage, deliberately projected backwards in time and transformed into fairy-tale mode, to an aspect of Tolkien's adolescent romance with his fellow-orphan Edith Bratt' (*Tolkien: A Cultural Phenomenon*, p. 92).

Tolkien seems to have offered *You and Me* to the editors of *Oxford Poetry*, who chose to publish only *Goblin Feet* (no. 27). He also sent these two works to his former King Edward's School teacher, R.W. Reynolds, who replied (letter of 11 July 1915, Bodleian Library) that although he found both of them charming, if he were in the Oxford editors' shoes he himself would have chosen *Goblin Feet*, as it was less open to criticism than *You and Me*.

In mid- to late May 1915 Tolkien had the amended poem typed by the Oxford Copying Office; a ribbon copy and a carbon copy are in his papers. In this instance the first line reads 'You and me — we know that land'. On the carbon copy Tolkien later noted that the work had been composed at 59 St John Street, Oxford, in April 1915. He also indicated a few revisions, and specific indentations (by printer's measure) to certain lines in the third stanza, either in advance of or retrospectively after he made a further typescript with a purple ribbon, presumably during his years at Leeds. In the latter, line 1 reads 'You and I, we know that land', line 43 was changed to 'That laughed with You and Me', and the final stanza became:

And why it was Tomorrow came
    And with his grey hand led us back;
And why we never found the same
    Old cottage, or the magic track
    That leads between the sea and sky
To those old shores and gardens fair
Where all things are, that ever were,
    We know not, You and I.

The Leeds typescript is entitled *The Cottage of Lost Play: Mar Vanwa Tyaliéva*, but marked to indicate that the subtitle was to become the main title, and 'The Cottage of Lost Play' to read 'The House of Lost Play'; *Mar Vanwa Tyaliéva* is 'House of Lost Play' in

Qenya. The typescript is inscribed 'Oxford April 1915'. At some later point, Tolkien marked new changes on the Leeds version and drafted a replacement for the last lines of the poem (58–65):

> But why it was there came a time
> when we could take the road no more,
> though long we looked, and high would climb,
> or gaze from many a seaward shore
> to find the path between Sea and sky
> to those old gardens of delight;
> And how it is now in that land,
> if there the house and gardens stand,
> still filled with children clad in white —
> we know not, You and I.

These may have been in aid of the poem when Tolkien thought to include it in a collection of his work he hoped would be published at Leeds. In a working list of contents of the proposed book, he referred to the poem as *Mar Vanwa Tyaliéva: The Cottage of Lost Play.*

He largely abandoned these revisions, however, when he came to write a later, final version, now entitled *The Little House of Lost Play: Mar Vanwa Tyaliéva*, probably in late 1961 or early 1962 when he reviewed old poems to include in *The Adventures of Tom Bombadil and Other Verses from the Red Book* (see poem no. 24). This text, substantially different from earlier versions, exists in two typescripts, each surviving in ribbon and carbon copies. The second, given here as B, is slightly amended relative to the first.

[B]

> We knew that land once, You and I,
> and once we wandered there
> in the long days now long gone by,
> a dark child and a fair.
> Was it on the paths of firelight thought
> in winter cold and white,
> or in the blue-spun twilit hours
> of little early tucked-up beds
> in drowsy summer night,
>
> that you and I in Sleep went down
> to meet each other there,
> your dark hair on your white nightgown,
> and mine was tangled fair?

We wandered shyly hand in hand,
small footprints in the golden sand,
and gathered pearls and shells in pails,
while all about the nightingales
    were singing in the trees.
We dug for silver with our spades
and caught the sparkle of the seas,
then ran ashore to greenlit glades,
and found the warm and winding lane
that now we cannot find again,
    between tall whispering trees.

The air was neither night nor day,
an ever-eve of gloaming light,
when first there glimmered into sight
    the Little House of Play.
New-built it was, yet very old,
white, and thatched with straws of gold,
    and pierced with peeping lattices
    that looked toward the sea;
and our own children's garden-plots
were there: our own forgetmenots,
red daisies, cress and mustard,
    and radishes for tea.
There all the borders, trimmed with box,
were full of favourite flowers, with phlox,
with lupins, pinks, and hollyhocks,
    beneath a red may-tree;
and all the gardens full of folk
that their own little language spoke,
    but not to You and Me.

For some had silver watering-cans
    and watered all their gowns,
or sprayed each other; some laid plans
to build their houses, little towns,
    and dwellings in the trees.
And some were clambering on the roof;
some crooning lonely and aloof;
some dancing found the fairy-rings
all garlanded in daisy-strings,
    while some upon their knees

before a little white-robed king
crowned with marigold would sing
their rhymes of long ago.
But side by side a little pair
with heads together, mingled hair,
went walking to and fro
still hand in hand; and what they said,
ere Waking far apart them led,
that only we now know.

In *The Book of Lost Tales, Part One*, this text appears on pp. 30–1. If, indeed, Tolkien considered it for the *Bombadil* collection, it may have been rejected as too difficult to present as a poem written or compiled by hobbits (see our comments for poem no. 24).

As Christopher Tolkien has suggested, noting in particular lines A56–57, a possible influence on the poem may have been 'Daisy' by Francis Thompson: 'Where 'mid the gorse the raspberry | Red for the gatherer springs; | Two children did we stray and talk | Wise, idle, childish things'. Brian Rosebury sees in *You and Me* or *The Little House of Lost Play* (both versions are published in *The Book of Lost Tales, Part One*) elements of the poems of Christina Rossetti and William Allingham, 'but also a deeper resemblance in mood to the nostalgic nineteenth-century ballads of which [Thomas] Hood's "I remember, I remember" and [Thomas Love] Peacock's "Love and Age" . . . are examples' (*Tolkien: A Cultural Phenomenon*, p. 92). Certainly its 'fairy' imagery is of a piece with the contemporaneous *Goblin Feet* (no. 27) and *Tinfang Warble* (no. 29), and its atmosphere of joyful meeting and sad parting reflects Tolkien's relationship with Edith Bratt. John Garth, on his part, in *Tolkien and the Great War* discerns a debt to J.M. Barrie's Neverland, Tolkien having seen *Peter Pan* on stage at the age of eighteen.

In regard to Tolkien's private mythology, the poem is a precursor to *The Cottage of Lost Play*, the introduction to *The Book of Lost Tales*, a collection of prose stories Tolkien began to write near the end of 1916 or the beginning of 1917. In this, a story is told of a cottage in Valinor (the land of the Valar or 'gods'), near Kôr, visited by children in their dreams:

> Now in this place of gardens a high gate of lattice-work that shone golden in the dusk opened upon the lane of dreams, and from there led winding paths of high box to the fairest of all the gardens, and amidmost of the garden stood a white cottage. Of

> what it was built, nor when, no one knew, nor now knows, but it was said to me [Vairë] that it shone with a pale light, as it was of pearl, and its roof was a thatch, but a thatch of gold.

For the most part, the children 'did not often go into the house, but danced and played in the garden, gathering flowers or chasing the golden bees and butterflies'. But this was 'the Cottage of the Children, or of the Play of Sleep, and not of Lost Play, as has wrongly been said in song among Men' (*The Book of Lost Tales, Part One*, p. 19). Tolkien also wrote of a similar garden where children play, that of the Man-in-the-Moon, in his 1925/27 story *Roverandom.*

A 35: This line originally read 'Red daisies, mustard, radishes'; compare B36.
B26: The 'gloaming light' is twilight.

29

Tinfang Warble (1915–?27)

Written shortly after *Goblin Feet* (poem no. 27), *Tinfang Warble* is informed by the same enthusiasm for 'fairy' imagery ('O! the lights: O! the gleams: O! the little tinkly sounds'), but at first had only eight lines. Its earliest manuscript (A) is inscribed 'Ap[ril] 29–30 [1915]' and has an added title in Old English, *Tinfang Wearbela*.

[A]

O the hoot! O the hoot
Of his jolly little flute!
O the hoot of Tinfang Warble!
There! He's dancing all alone
    In the twilight on the lawn,
'Cause the little stars have grown:
O the dear old mad leprechaun
    And his name is Tinfang Warble.

The *Oxford English Dictionary* describes *hoot*, from Middle English *hūten* (*houten*), as 'perhaps echoic, representing an inarticulate sound like the hooting of owls or the "toot" of a horn or pipe'. By extension, if unusually, *hoot* may also apply to the sound of birds in general. Tolkien takes it further in connecting it to the flute, or musical pipe; apart from the convenient rhyme of *hoot* and *flute*, the flute since medieval times has been used to imitate bird sounds. Compare 'the thin hooting fluting voice' in *Outside* (poem no. 14).

The text of a typescript of *Tinfang Warble* made by the Oxford Copying Office in mid- to late May 1915 is identical to A; a carbon copy is inscribed 'Oxford 1914 [*sic*, for 1915] rewritten Leeds 1920–23'. Tolkien later changed 'leprechaun' in line 7 to 'leprawn', in both the manuscript and the typescript, but in the carbon copy of the latter he deleted the affected line, together with the line following, when otherwise revising and expanding the work (as B).

[B]

O the hoot! O the hoot
Of his jolly little flute!
O the hoot of Tinfang Warble!
There! He's dancing all alone
    In the twilight on the lawn,

Till the little stars have grown,
And their lamps are brightly blown
To flickering flames of blue
There he'll pipe to me and you,
    Dancing like a faun
In the twilight on the lawn —
And his name is Tinfang Warble.

Tolkien made a new typescript of the revised text, using the purple ribbon of his Leeds period, but probably around 1927 struck this through and typed below it on the same sheet a further version (C), using a 'Hammond' model typewriter with interchangeable, space-saving miniature (or 'midget') fonts. The latter was published in May 1927 in the *Inter-University Magazine* of the University Catholic Societies' Federation of Great Britain, with a comma misprinted for a full stop in line 11. Christopher Tolkien also included this text (correct) in *The Book of Lost Tales, Part One*, p. 108.

[C]

O the hoot! O the hoot!
How he trillups on his flute!
O the hoot of Tinfang Warble!

Dancing all alone,
Hopping on a stone,
Flitting like a faun,
In the twilight on the lawn,
And his name is Tinfang Warble!

The first star has shown
And its lamp is blown
To a flame of flickering blue.
He pipes not to me,
He pipes not to thee,
He whistles for none of you.
Dancing all alone,
His music is his own,
The tunes of Tinfang Warble!

In *The Book of Lost Tales* (begun late 1916 or early 1917, largely abandoned after June 1919) 'Tinfang Warble' is a name given by children to the piper Timpinen, who 'played and danced in summer dusks for joy of the first stars'.

> Now does he play about the gardens of the land; but Alalminórë [the Land of Elms, in Tol Eressëa; see poem no. 40] he loves the best, and this garden best of all. Ever and again we miss his piping for long months. . . . But on a sudden will his flute be heard again at an hour of gentle gloaming, or will he play beneath a goodly moon and the stars go bright and blue. [*The Book of Lost Tales, Part One*, pp. 94–5]

He is said to be 'neither wholly of the Valar [the 'gods'] nor of the Eldar [the Elves], but is half a fay of the woods and dells, one of the great companies of the children of Palúrien [Yavanna, one of the Valar], and half a Gnome or a Shoreland Piper' (p. 94; for the 'shoreland pipers', see poem no. 46). Among the host of the Valar, meanwhile, are 'brownies, fays, pixies, leprawns' with other 'sprites' (p. 66). As Tolkien's mythology grew, the 'pixie' element was abandoned.

The sound of Tinfang Warble's flute recalls the music of Pan, the ancient Greek god of the wild who plays a flute fashioned from lengths of hollow reed (a pan pipe). In *The Wind in the Willows* by Kenneth Grahame (1908, ch. 7), Pan creates a 'merry bubble and joy, the thin, clear happy call of the distant piping'. John Garth has suggested that Tinfang Warble 'had a contemporary visual counterpart in a painting that [as a commercial print] found a mass-market' among British soldiers in the First World War: Estella Canziani's *Piper of Dreams* 'depicts a boy sitting alone in a springtime wood playing to a half-seen flight of fairies' (*Tolkien and the Great War*, p. 77). In Greek and Roman mythology, the *faun* Tinfang is said to be like in his dancing (texts B and C) is half man, half goat, and Pan is represented in the same manner; but Tolkien does not describe Tinfang in such terms.

A3: In his ?1916–17 lexicon of Gnomish (*I·Lam na·Ngoldathon*), Tolkien glossed *Tinfang* as 'the fluter (surnamed *Gwarbilin* or Birdward)'. *Gwarbilin* echoes English *warble* 'sing with constantly changing notes'. *Timp*, as recurs in the Qenya name *Timpinen* (i.e. Tinfang Warble), is glossed in the Gnomish lexicon as 'hoot, note of a flute'. See *Parma Eldalamberon* 11 (1995), p. 70.

B7–9: As drafted in ink over erased pencil, these lines read 'Till the pale sky is o'ersown | With flickering lamps of blue. | There he pipes to me and you'.

30

Kôr: In a City Lost and Dead · The City of the Gods (1915–23)

There is only one extant manuscript of this poem, a fair copy in ink over erased pencil, dated 'Ap[ril] 30' and entitled *Kôr*, with its original subtitle *Sonnet to a City Dead and Lost* changed to *In a City Lost and Dead*. We give this text as A.

[A] A sable hill, gigantic, rampart-crowned
Stands gazing out across an azure sea
Under an azure sky, on whose dark ground
Impearled as 'gainst a floor of porphyry
Gleam marble temples white, and dazzling halls;
And tawny shadows fingered long are made
In fretted bars upon the ivory walls
By massy trees rock-rooted in the shade
Like stony chiselled pillars of the vault
With shaft and capital of black basalt.
There slow forgotten days for ever reap
The silent shadows counting out rich hours;
And no bird sings; and all the marble towers
White, hot and soundless, ever burn and sleep.

A typescript of the poem, with the altered title, was made by the Oxford Copying Office in mid- to late May 1915; this survives in both a ribbon copy and a carbon copy. Tolkien later inscribed the carbon copy 'St John Street Oxford April 1915', referring to his residence at the time. Also at its head he erased 'Kôr', typed in its place (with the purple ribbon of his Leeds period) a new title, *The City of the Gods*, and heavily struck through the subtitle. He made only one revision, to both the manuscript and the second typescript, presumably when he prepared the work for publication: in the penultimate line, he replaced 'no bird sings' with 'no voice stirs', possibly to avoid an echo of Keats' 'La Belle Dame sans Merci' ('The sedge has wither'd from the lake, | And no birds sing'). In this revised form (B), *The City of the Gods* was published in the Leeds journal *The Microcosm* for Spring

1923. Christopher Tolkien included this text, as *Kôr: In a City Lost and Dead*, in *The Book of Lost Tales, Part One*, on p. 136.

[B] A sable hill, gigantic, rampart-crowned
Stands gazing out across an azure sea
Under an azure sky, on whose dark ground
Impearled as 'gainst a floor of porphyry
Gleam marble temples white, and dazzling halls;
And tawny shadows fingered long are made
In fretted bars upon the ivory walls
By massy trees rock-rooted in the shade
Like stony chiselled pillars of the vault
With shaft and capital of black basalt.
There slow forgotten days for ever reap
The silent shadows counting out rich hours;
And no voice stirs; and all the marble towers
White, hot and soundless, ever burn and sleep.

It is arguable whether *Kôr* is a sonnet, as Tolkien first called it (*Sonnet to a City Dead and Lost*). It has the prescribed fourteen lines in two parts of a Italian (or Petrarchan) sonnet, though its first part, mainly descriptive, is in ten lines rather than the typical eight, and its second, on the passage of time and the emptiness of the city, is in four lines rather than six. Nor does the poem have the typical rhyme scheme of the Italian sonnet, or of the Shakespearean or Spencerian varieties. Joe R. Christopher, who analyzes *Kôr* in depth in his essay 'Tolkien's Lyric Poetry' (2000), comments that the poem

> begins as if it is going to be an English sonnet in rhyme scheme (ABAB CDCD), but then it has a couplet (EE), followed by an Italian style quatrain (FGGF) – or one could say it has an English 'octave' and a type of Italian sestet (EEF GGF). The irregularity . . . is related to the organization of the content of the poem. The first ten lines are one sentence, and the last quatrain is another. The first sentence describes the city externally; the second sentence emphasizes its having no inhabitants. [p. 144; a *couplet* is a unit of two lines, a *quatrain* of four, a *sestet* of six, and an *octave* of eight]

The name 'Kôr' is not original to Tolkien, but was first applied to a lost city in the novel *She* (1887) by H. Rider Haggard, a favourite of English boys. Haggard's Kôr, like Tolkien's, was made in antiquity and is splendid even in ruin. In Tolkien's *Book of Lost Tales* Kôr became the city of the Fairies (i.e. Elves), built on a hill of the same name in Eldamar (see poem no. 18). In these tales the folk of Kôr in time leave the city in pursuit of Melko (later Melkor, Morgoth), the evil Vala who has stolen their treasury of gems, including the greatest of jewels, the Silmarils. The present poem appears to describe Kôr as it is found by Eärendel (compare poem no. 18) in later days, when it is a dead city with 'silent shadows', after the Elves have departed for the Great Lands (Middle-earth) east of the sea. In his Qenya lexicon (*c.* 1915–19) Tolkien defined *Kôr* as 'the ancient town built above the rocks of Eldamar whence the fairies marched into the world' (*Qenyaqetsa*, p. 48). As Christopher Tolkien has remarked in discussing 'Kôr' and this poem in *The Book of Lost Tales, Part One*, although it can hardly be doubted that its author borrowed the name from Haggard, it was nonetheless absorbed into Tolkien's language invention and given new meaning and significance. In time, he came to prefer the name *Tûn* for the city (after Old English *tūn* 'town') and *Kôr* for the hill, and still later called the city *Tirion* and the hill *Túna*.

In his essay 'William Morris and Tolkien: Some Unexpected Connections' (2019) Tom Shippey suggests parallels between Tolkien's poem and lines early in Morris's *Earthly Paradise*:

> A nameless city in a distant sea,
> White as the changing walls of faërie,
> Thronged with much people clad in ancient guise
> I now am fain to set before your eyes;
> There, leave the clear green water and the quays,
> And pass betwixt its marble palaces . . .

Morris's work, Shippey argues, 'focused Tolkien's mind on the idea of an earthly paradise, not in the East where Mandeville located it [i.e. Sir John Mandeville, in his fourteenth-century *Travels*], but in the West, across the sea, and now inaccessible to us' (p. 242).

Tolkien later wrote in *The Book of Lost Tales*: 'Upon the hill-top the Elves built fair abodes of shining white – of marbles and stones quarried from the Mountains of Valinor that glistened wondrously, silver and gold and a substance of great hardness and white lucency', and 'a slender silver tower shooting skyward like a needle' – these are of a piece with the poem. But there the hill is 'sable' (black), 'gigantic, rampart-crowned', while in the later description it is 'covered only with a deep turf, and harebells grow atop of it ringing softly' (*The Book of Lost Tales, Part One*, p. 122).

A watercolour painting by Tolkien, *Tanaqui* (Hammond and Scull, *Artist and Illustrator*, fig. 43), is clearly a representation of Kôr as it is in the poem: there is the gleaming city upon a black hill, there the azure sky. Its position in *The Book of Ishness* suggests that it was made in early 1915; in our *Chronology* we make an educated guess that it dates from the 1915 Oxford Easter vacation (between 13 March and 25 April), much or all of which Tolkien spent in Warwick. If either assumption is correct, and the poem *Kôr* was composed on 30 April as Tolkien wrote on the manuscript, then he conceived the city of the Elves first in visual terms, before he wrote the words of the poem. The word or name *Tanaqui* appears nowhere else in Tolkien's works, and is not attested in the Qenya lexicon; it seems, however, to contain linguistic roots which mean 'high, lofty' and 'white'.

31

The Shores of Faery (1915–?24)

In addition to *Tanaqui* (see poem no. 30), *The Book of Ishness* contains a second watercolour view of Kôr, glistening white upon a black hill above golden sands. The city of the Elves is seen through an arch formed by the dying Trees of Valinor; from these grow a last silver blossom (the Moon) and a last golden fruit (the Sun), while a single bright star shines in the sky. In *Artist and Illustrator* (fig. 44) we gave this painting the title *The Shores of Faery*, because these words are written prominently on the facing page of the sketch-book, above a manuscript poem which seems to be a fair copy (no earlier workings appear to be extant); a reproduction of the page may be found in McIlwaine, *Tolkien: Maker of Middle-earth*, p. 205. Here, as A, we have transcribed the text of the poem in its original form, before revision.

[A] WEST of the MOON
EAST of the SUN

There stands a lonely Hill
Its feet are in the pale green Sea
Its towers are white & still
Beyond Taniquetil in Valinor.
No stars come there but one alone
That hunted with the Moon
For there the two Trees naked grow
That bear Night's silver bloom;
That bear the globéd fruit of noon
In Valinor.
There are the Shores of Faery
With their moonlit pebbled strand
Whose foam is silver music
On the opalescent floor
Beyond the great sea-shadows,
On the margent of the Sand
That stretches on for ever
From the golden feet of Kôr
Beyond Taniquetil
In Valinor.

O! East of the Sun, West of the Moon
Lies the Haven of the Star
The white town of the Wanderer,
and the rocks of Eglamar,
Where Wingelot is harboured
While Earéndel looks afar
On the magic and the wonder
'tween here and Eglamar
Out, out beyond Taniquetil
In Valinor — afar.

While writing the present book, we realized that the intended title of the painting is in fact *West of the Moon, East of the Sun*, written partly in capital letters on the page facing the art, a style Tolkien adopted for the titles of other pictures in this part of *The Book of Ishness*. *The Shores of Faery*, then, is not the title of the painting (as it now has been given in multiple accounts, alas, following our lead), but of the poem Tolkien wrote on the facing page, incorporating 'WEST of the MOON | EAST of the SUN' as its first lines. Later Tolkien marked these lines to be changed to 'East of the Moon | West of the Sun', but did not delete the original reading. He also changed 'East of the Sun, West of the Moon' in line 23 to 'West of the Sun, East of the Moon', and altered 'Wingelot' in line 27 to 'Vingelot'.

The title of the picture, and the first lines of the poem, are variations on 'East of the Sun and West of the Moon', the title of a Norwegian fairy-story included in George Webbe Dasent's *Popular Tales from the Norse* (1859), to which Tolkien refers in his Andrew Lang Lecture, *On Fairy-Stories* (delivered 1939, first published 1947) – Lang included the tale in his *Blue Fairy Book* (1890). The phrase was also used by other writers, among them William Morris in *The Earthly Paradise* (1868–70). In the context of 'The Silmarillion', *Faery* (or *Faëry*) is the name of a bay on the east coast of Valinor, the land of the 'gods' in the far West of the world, in or near which the Elves built their dwellings. Valinor was lit by the Two Trees, Silpion (later Telperion) and Laurelin, and it was their light that was caught in the Silmarils, the great jewels at the heart of 'The Silmarillion'; but the Trees were poisoned by the spider Ungwë Lianti (later Ungoliant) at the behest of the rebel Vala Melko. Among the Mountains of Valinor, Taniquetil is the loftiest, and the greatest of all the mountains in the world.

The 'one alone | That hunted with the Moon' (lines 7–8) is Earéndel, as the name is spelled in the manuscripts of this poem. A comparison may be made with *The Voyage of Éarendel the Evening Star* (poem no. 16): 'And Éarendel fled from that Shipman dread [the Moon] | Beyond the dark Earth's pale'. 'Night's silver bloom' in line 10 is the Moon, and 'the globéd fruit of noon' in line 11 is the Sun. In regard to (lines 19–20) 'the Sand | That stretches on for ever' and 'the golden feet', i.e. sands, of Kôr, in *The Book of Lost Tales* it is said that the Vala Aulë, a smith, brought to Kôr 'all the dust of magic metals that his great works had made and gathered, and he piled it about the foot of that hill, and most of this dust was of gold, and a sand of gold stretched way from the feet of Kôr out into the distance where the Two Trees blossomed' (*The Book of Lost Tales, Part One*, p. 122). In lines 24–25, the 'Haven of the Star' and 'the white town of the Wanderer' (i.e. Earéndel) are Kôr. Further explanation is given in the later 'prologue' (see below).

The painting, dated 'May 10 1915', evidently preceded composition of the poem, if the date Tolkien wrote on a revised manuscript of the work, 8–9 July 1915, is correct and was intended to be the date of original composition. The revised text incorporates the changes made to the *Book of Ishness* version, merges lines A1–2 as 'East of the Moon, West of the Sun', and divides line A6 as 'Beyond Taníquetil | In Valinôr' (thus keeping the poem to the same length).

Tolkien marked this second manuscript for revision in turn, notably changing the name 'Eglamar' in lines 26 and 30 to 'Eldamar'. (*Eldamar* is 'Elfhome' in Qenya. *Eglamar*, with the same meaning, was retained as a variant form in Gnomish.) Tolkien also asked himself ('W?') if the form 'Vingelot' should revert to 'Wingelot'. Besides the title *The Shores of Faery*, the second manuscript includes Old English *Ielfalandes Strand* ('Shores of Elf-land'); and facing it in one of Tolkien's poetry notebooks is a brief prose 'prologue' which describes the mariner and explains aspects of the poem:

> 'Ëarendel the Wanderer who beat about the Oceans of the World in his white ship Vingelot, and who sate [sat, resided] in old age upon the Isle of Seabirds in the Northern Waters set forth upon a last voyage.
>
> He passed Taníquetil and even Valinôr, and drew his bark over the bar at the margin of the World, and launched it on the Oceans of the Firmament. Of his ventures there no [one >] man has told save that hunted by the Orbed Moon he fled back to Valinôr, and mounting the towers of Kôr upon the rocks of Eglamar he gazed back upon the Oceans of the World. Thither does he come ever at plenilune when the moon sails a-harrying beyond Taníquetil and Valinôr.'

The enclosing quotation marks are in the original. The Isle of Seabirds is that place in Tolkien's mythology 'whither do all the birds of all waters come at whiles' (*The Book of Lost Tales, Part Two*, p. 253). On Earendel in northern waters and in the oceans of the sky, see our discussions for poems no. 16 and 18. *Bar* in this sense is a sandbank or shoal (compare Tennyson's poem 'Crossing the Bar', which treats metaphorically the passage from life to death). Here again, Tolkien marked 'Eglamar' to be altered to 'Eldamar'.

The two manuscript texts were followed by two typescripts, each including prologue and poem, and each with further changes marked. The first, which survives as both a ribbon copy and a carbon copy, is a professional typescript, made probably in October 1915. Later Tolkien inscribed the carbon copy 'Moseley & Edgb[aston]. July 1915 (walking & on bus). Retouched often since – esp[ecially]. 1924'. His Aunt Mabel and her husband, Tom Mitton, lived in Moseley, a suburb of Birmingham. The Birmingham Oratory, the centre of Tolkien's religious life as a boy and young man, was in the suburb of Edgbaston. Among other changes to this new text, the form 'Wingelot' was restored, the name 'Kôr' became 'Tún', and line 20 was replaced with three lines, 'To the dragonheaded door, | The gateway of the Moon | Beyond the towers of Tún'. The name 'Taníquetil' retained its acute accent (gained in the second manuscript), but 'Valinor' lost its circumflex. Despite being marked for revision in the preceding manuscript, 'Eglamar' remained in the typescript.

The second typescript contains the final text of *The Shores of Faery*, given here as B including Tolkien's alterations. Typed with a purple ribbon, it dates presumably from his years at Leeds, and therefore may be associated with the date 1924 mentioned above. Christopher Tolkien included this text in *The Book of Lost Tales, Part Two*, pp. 262 (prologue) and 271–2 (verse)

[B] 'Earendel the Wanderer who beat about the Oceans of the World in his white ship Wingelot sat long while in his old age upon the Isle of Seabirds in the Northern Waters ere he set forth upon a last voyage.

He passed Taníquetil and even Valinor, and drew his bark over the bar at the margin of the World, and launched it on the Oceans of the Firmament. Of his ventures there no man has told, save that hunted by the orbed moon he fled back to Valinor, and mounting the towers of Tún upon the rocks of Eglamar he gazed back upon the Oceans of the World. To Eglamar he comes ever at plenilune when the moon sails a-harrying beyond Taníquetil and Valinor.'

East of the Moon, west of the Sun
There stands a lonely hill;
Its feet are in the pale green sea,
Its towers are white and still,
Beyond Taníquetil
In Valinor.
There never comes but one lone star
That fled before the moon:
And there the two Trees naked are
That bore Night's silver bloom,
That bore the globed fruit of Noon
In Valinor.
There are the Shores of Faery
With their moonlit pebbled strand
Whose foam is silver music
On the opalescent floor
Beyond the great sea-shadows
On the marches of the sand
That stretches on for ever
To the dragonheaded door,
The gateway of the Moon,
Beyond Taníquetil
In Valinor.
West of the Sun, east of the Moon
Lies the haven of the star,
The white town of the Wanderer,
And the rocks of Eglamar.
There Wingelot is harboured,
While Earendel looks afar
O'er the darkness of the waters
Between here and Eglamar —
Out, out, beyond Taníquetil
In Valinor afar.

Here Tolkien very lightly marked the first, but not the second, instance of 'Eglamar' in the prologue, and the first, but not the second, instance in the text proper (lines 27, 31), to be changed to 'Eldamar'. Above 'Faery' in line 13 he wrote 'Elvenland', to rhyme with 'strand' and 'sand', but again the change is marked only in light pencil, and the affected word is not struck through. In regard to 'the dragonheaded door' of text B, in *The Book of Lost Tales* the Door of Night has pillars 'of the mightiest basalt and its lintel likewise, but great dragons of black stone are carved thereon, and shadowy smoke pours slowly from their jaws' (*The Book of Lost Tales, Part One*, pp. 215–16). As Christopher Tolkien points out, however, in that description the Door of Night is not 'the gateway of the Moon', 'for it is the Sun that passes through it into the outer dark, whereas "the Moon dares not the utter loneliness of the outer dark by reason of his lesser light and majesty, and he journeys still beneath the world"' (*The Book of Lost Tales, Part One*, p. 273). See also poem no. 33.

On the sheet with text B Tolkien also wrote the words 'Origin of my mythology', but struck them through and continued: 'First poem of | my mythology | Valinor | thought of about | 1910'. As we have seen, by mid-1915 several of Tolkien's poems contained elements which came to feature in 'The Silmarillion', but were written before the larger work was conceived, or while it was still in its earliest stages of conception. *The Voyage of Éarendel the Evening Star* (no. 16) is often called the 'beginning' of the mythology because it was in that poem that Tolkien first mentioned Éarendel, later a key figure in 'The Silmarillion'. Against this, one could say that *The Shores of Faery* was the 'first poem of [the] mythology' in the sense that it was the earliest of Tolkien's poems to be, from its origin, very substantially an integral part of 'The Silmarillion', naming in only a brief space Kôr (or Tún), Taniquetil, Valinor, the Two Trees, Eglamar (or Eldamar), Earendel, and Vingelot (or Wingelot), evidence that a wider context of invention was well in place. But to do so, one would need to overlook *Kôr: In a City Lost and Dead* (no. 30), written in April 1915 (not to mention the Qenya lexicon begun around this time), which likewise conveys the sense that Tolkien's mythology had now achieved a foundation of history, geography, and language.

It is unlikely that *The Shores of Faery* was conceived as early as 1910. It may be that Tolkien meant that he 'thought of' Valinor around ('about') that date, though if so it would be very remarkable. His friend George Sayer recalled (in 1992) that Tolkien 'had in a sense planned them ['The Silmarillion', though Sayer also seems to include *The Lord of the Rings*] before he went to school [presumably, Oxford, in 1911], and actually written one or two of the poems while he was still at school' ('Recollections of J.R.R. Tolkien', p. 23). Clyde Kilby, who visited Tolkien in Oxford and was allowed to read part of the draft 'Silmarillion', reported that Tolkien had 'told one of his closest friends that he had the whole of his mythic world in his mind as early as 1906. He told me that he was writing some of *The Silmarillion* (doubtless yet untitled) about 1910, and he wrote me that the story, meaning possibly the account as a whole, began in 1916–1917' (*Tolkien and The Silmarillion* (1976), p. 47). Such accounts are dubious, however – in 1906, Tolkien was only fourteen – and as far as we know are unsupported by anything in his papers. Nor have we seen any evidence for Humphrey Carpenter's claim (*Biography*, p. 76) that Tolkien intended *The Shores of Faery* to be the first of several poems comprising a 'Lay of Earendel'.

A8: Tolkien changed 'hunted with the Moon' to 'fled before the Moon' in his manuscript dated 8–9 July.

A10–11: 'Bear' in each of these lines continued into the manuscript dated 8–9 July, where each word was marked to become 'bore'; but 'bear', similarly marked for revision, is also in the first typescript.

A23: As mentioned above, Tolkien changed 'East of the Sun, West of the Moon' to 'West of the Sun, East of the Moon' in his earliest manuscript. He then marked the revised reading, in the manuscript dated 8–9 July, to 'West of the Sun, beyond the Moon', but this reading does not appear in later texts.

A27: Wingelot (or Vingelot, Qenya 'foamflower') is the name of Earéndel's boat.

B Prologue: On the ribbon copy of the first typescript Tolkien indicated (for a planned publication) that the prologue was to be set in small italics. Between the first and second typescripts, he changed the beginning of the final sentence of the prologue, 'Thither does he come ever', to 'To Eglamar he comes ever', presumably to avoid confusion as to which place 'thither' refers.

B7: In the first typescript Tolkien changed 'No stars come there but one alone' to 'Comes never there but one lone star', the reading of the second typescript; then in the latter, he marked the new text to read 'There never comes but one lone star'.

B20–3: On the carbon copy of the first typescript Tolkien changed 'From the golden feet of Kôr' to 'To the dragonheaded door, | The gateway of the Moon, | Beyond the towers of Tún'. The same revision appears on the ribbon copy, but 'Beyond the towers of Tún' is struck through, and does not appear in the later typescript.

32

Princess Nî · The Princess Ní · Princess Mee (1915–62)

The earliest manuscript of this poem, given here as A, is entitled *Princess Nî* (with a circumflex). It is a fair copy, inscribed 'July 9 1915', and has an added title in Old English, *Mægden Ní Owéne Dohtor* ('Maiden Nî, Daughter of Owen').

[A]

O! the Princess Nî
slender is she:
In gossamer shot with gold
and splintered pearls
on threaded curls
of elfin hair, 'tis told,
Is she wanly clad;
But with myriad
fireflies is she girdled
(Like garnets red
In an amber bed),
While her silver slippers, curdled
With opals pale,
Are of fishes' mail —
— How they slide on the coral floor! —
O! but over her frock
She wears a smock,
A feathery pinafore,
Of the down of eiders
With red money-spiders
Broidered here and there:
O! the Princess Nî
Most slender is she
But fairy-royal her wear.

Although the poem contains no explicit reference to the 'Silmarillion' mythology – and perhaps originally was not meant to have any connection – its Old English title, and the words 'Princess Nî daughter of Osse and Ônen' written by Tolkien on the page opposite text A in one of his poetry notebooks, tie it to his invented world. In

The Book of Lost Tales Ossë and his consort Ówen (later Ónen, Ui) are lesser spirits who control 'the waves and lesser seas' (*The Book of Lost Tales, Part One*, p. 58). In Tolkien's Qenya lexicon (*c.* 1915–19) Ô is defined as 'the sea', *Osse* as 'God of Sea', and *ōwen* as 'mermaid' (*Qenyaqetsa*, p. 70). If Nî is the 'daughter of Owen', presumably she too is of the sea, an aspect suggested by her slippers sliding 'on the coral floor'; but this is not borne out by the poem as a whole, which depicts a 'fairy' figure, and is more concerned with her manner of dress than with the princess herself.

The 'July 9' manuscript was followed, probably in October 1915, by a professional typescript which survives in both a ribbon copy and a carbon copy. Tolkien inscribed the former 'Moseley B'ham [Birmingham] Bus between Edgt. [Edgbaston] & Moseley July 1915', and amended the title to include the definite article. He marked both with revisions, all of which carried into a new typescript, made years later at Leeds using a purple ribbon. The resulting version, entitled *The Princess Ní* with an acute accent rather than a circumflex, is transcribed below as B.

[B]

O! the Princess Ní,
Slender is she:
In gossamer shot with gold
And splintered pearls
On threaded curls
Of elfin hair, 'tis told,
She is wanly clad;
But with myriad
Fireflies is she girdled,
Like garnets red
In an amber bed,
And her silver slippers, curdled
With opals pale,
Are of fishes' mail —
How they slide on the coral floor! —
And over her frock
She wears a smock,
A feathery pinafore,
Of the down of eiders
With red money-spiders
Broidered here and there.

O! the Princess Ní
Most slender is she,
And lighter than the air!

With small differences of punctuation, with its lines broken into groups of four (probably an editorial, not authorial, choice), and with line 12 reading instead 'While her silver slippers, curdled', this version was published in the collection *Leeds University Verse 1914–24* (1924), p. 58.

It seems possible that Tolkien chose 'Nî' as the subject's name simply because it rhymes with 'she', or because it has the same sound as the last syllable of 'Hermione', the name of the young daughter of Tolkien's former teacher R.W. Reynolds to whom Tolkien dedicated this poem. On 11 July 1915 Reynolds informed Tolkien that he had 'made a copy of the pretty little "Princess Nî" to keep for Hermione until she is of years to appreciate the dedication' (Bodleian Library). (Hermione, later Mrs Jolles, came to enjoy *The Lord of the Rings*.) *Nî* (or *Ní*) also, however, recalls the Irish feminine patronymic, as in the mythic *Caitlin Ní Uallacháin* (Cathleen Ni Houlihan). Qenya *nî* 'woman' appears in the Gnomish lexicon of ?1916–17.

Tolkien returned to *The Princess Ní* presumably in late 1961 or early 1962, when he considered poems to include in his *Adventures of Tom Bombadil* collection for George Allen & Unwin. In the course of two rough, almost illegible manuscripts and two heavily revised typescripts, none of them dated, he transformed the poem into a substantially new work, fifty lines longer than its predecessors, and gave it a new title. Princess Nî (in workings, again with a circumflex) at length became Princess Mee, and although still arrayed in an 'elven' manner, and explicitly an elf, she now had activity, dancing on a pool and observing her reflection. *Princess Mee*, the final version, is found in the Bodleian Library in three typescripts, only the last of which (made with Tolkien's Hammond typewriter and signed in pen 'JRRT') ends the final line with 'Shee!' Earlier typescripts conclude with a full stop rather than an exclamation mark.

We give here, as text C, the poem as it was printed in 1962 as the fourth poem in the *Tom Bombadil* volume, pp. 28–30.

[C]

Little Princess Mee
Lovely was she
As in elven-song is told:

She had pearls in hair
All threaded fair;
Of gossamer shot with gold
Was her kerchief made,
And a silver braid
Of stars about her throat.
Of moth-web light
All moonlit-white
She wore a woven coat,
And round her kirtle
Was bound a girdle
Sewn with diamond dew.

She walked by day
Under mantle grey
And hood of clouded blue;
But she went by night
All glittering bright
Under the starlit sky,
And her slippers frail
Of fishes' mail
Flashed as she went by
To her dancing-pool,
And on mirror cool
Of windless water played.
As a mist of light
In whirling flight
A glint like glass she made
Wherever her feet
Of silver fleet
Flicked the dancing-floor.

She looked on high
To the roofless sky,
And she looked to the shadowy shore;
Then round she went,
And her eyes she bent
And saw beneath her go
A Princess Shee
As fair as Mee:
They were dancing toe to toe!

She was as light
As Mee, and as bright;
But Shee was, strange to tell,
Hanging down
With starry crown
Into a bottomless well!
Her gleaming eyes
In great surprise
Looked up to the eyes of Mee:
A marvellous thing,
Head-down to swing
Above a starry sea!

Only their feet
Could ever meet;
For where the ways might lie
To find a land
Where they do not stand
But hang down in the sky
No one could tell
Nor learn in spell
In all the elven-lore.
So still on her own
An elf alone
Dancing as before
With pearls in hair
And kirtle fair
And slippers frail
Of fishes' mail went Mee:
Of fishes' mail
And slippers frail
And kirtle fair
With pearls in hair went Shee!

Within the 'editorial' frame of the *Tom Bombadil* collection *Princess Mee* is said to have been taken from 'marginalia' of the Hobbits' Red Book of Westmarch (as in *The Lord of the Rings*), some of which are 'nonsense'. The poem therefore is a hobbit's idea of an Elf-maiden, but in form is sophisticated as Tolkien plays with 'reflection' in the final eight lines. There was no longer any inkling of a connection between the princess of the poem and his mythology, though the imagery of the poem, silver and light, and especially dancing beneath the stars, recalls the dancing of Lúthien Tinúviel, a central figure in 'The Silmarillion'. More than one critic has suggested that *Princess Mee* was inspired by the myth of Narcissus, the youth doomed to love his own reflection but never to reach that other self mirrored in the water, but the princess seems more intrigued than transfixed.

In 1967 Tolkien made a professional recording of the final version of *Princess Mee* for Caedmon Records. This was withheld from the album *Poems and Songs of Middle Earth*, but issued in 2001 as part of *The J.R.R. Tolkien Audio Collection* (Harper Audio/Caedmon).

A6: Tolkien marked the ribbon copy of the first typescript that 'elfin' should be revised to 'elven'. This was not similarly done in the carbon copy, and not carried through to the *Leeds University Verse* text.

A7: 'Wanly clad': the princess is dressed in a pale garment, though with coloured decoration.

A14: Goldberry in *The Lord of the Rings* also wears shoes 'like fishes' mail' (bk. I, ch. 7).

A19: Eider down consists of the soft feathers of the eider duck.

A21: Tolkien gives an alternative reading for this line: 'Broidered up and down'.

A24: Tolkien gives an alternative reading for this line as well: 'But fairy-royal her gown'. Neither this nor the alternative for l. 21 was adopted in any later version.

C27: In two of Tolkien's typescripts of *Princess Mee*, including the last, the line 'Of windless water played' ends with a semi-colon; in the intermediate typescript, it ends with a comma. In the *Tom Bombadil* volume it ends with a full stop.

C43–54: In the intermediate and final typescripts of *Princess Mee*, these lines are joined to ll. 34–42, i.e. with no space after 'They were dancing toe to toe!'

33

The Happy Mariners · Tha Eadigan Saelidan: The Happy Mariners (1915–?40)

The earliest text of *The Happy Mariners* seems to be seven isolated lines of manuscript (A), written by Tolkien in his *Book of Ishness* sketch-book:

[A] I know a window in a tower
Opening on to oceans of the sky
And the wind that has been blowing round the stars
Nestles in its curtains up on high
It looks across grey Earth's great bowl
It stands upon the grey lips of the [*deleted:* great bowl]
[*added and deleted:* Earth]
Whence the stars go spouting up on high.

Here the poem was abandoned; but possibly not long after, Tolkien wrote a fuller version on the reverse side of a letter (never sent, or else a draft or retained copy) to A.B. How, the Bursar of Exeter College, Oxford, dated 11 July 1915. This manuscript is heavily worked, with changes in ink over initial writing in pencil, and with a column of words rhyming with 'seas' (*bees*, *breeze*, *cease*, etc.) jotted in the margin. We have transcribed, as B, the initial text before revision, except for seven lines (17–23) where the pencil manuscript is too badly obscured by overwriting.

[B] I know a window in a tower
That opens onto oceans of the sky
And wind that has been blowing round the stars
Comes and nestles in the curtains upon high
The tower stands on the grey lips of Earth
From whose great bowl constellate fountains leap
Spouted from the dragon gargoyles of the night
And they splinter on the jacinth wall of space
They burst and tangle and fall back into the deep
And out from beyond that sombre rim

The wind returns to stir the crystal panes
And murmur magically of golden rains
It is a white tower builded on the margin of the dawn
Out on the edge of nothing in the shades
And glimmers like a spike of lonely pearl
That mirrors rays forlorn when twilight fades

. . . .

But I alone look out behind the moon
Out from my windy bower
And find unmoving gazing here at me
The lonely star the silver watcher of the west

Tolkien continued to develop this poem through a further six manuscripts as well as scraps of workings, with minor or major changes between each text. He wrote, but did not complete, one of these drafts presumably soon after version B, on the back of a printed notice directing Exeter College students to notify officials and pay fees and expenses in advance of receiving degrees (hence Tolkien's letter to Mr How of 11 July; he had received his army commission on 28 June, and would not be in Oxford to receive his B.A. on 20 July). An inscription in one of his poetry notebooks dates the poem to 'Barnt Green July 1915 & Bedford (de Paris A[venue]) & later'; Tolkien had visited his Incledon relatives at Barnt Green in early July, and De Parys Avenue was the address at which he reported for duty on 19 July. Two of the manuscripts are dated 'July 24 [1915]', one with the added note 'rewritten Sep[tember] 9'; on 24 July Tolkien was training at Bedford (Bedfordshire), and by 9 September he had joined his battalion in Lichfield, Staffordshire.

The first of this middle sequence of manuscripts, following on the incomplete draft, is given here as C, in its form before revision. To the left of the poem, Tolkien recorded the number of metrical feet in each line.

[C] I know a window in a western tower
That opens on celestial seas
And wind that has been blowing through the stars
Comes to nestle in its tossing draperies.
The tower is on the grey lip of the Earth
From whose great bowl constellate fountains leap
Spouting from dragonheaded gargoyles of the night
Set wide upon the jacinth wall of space:

They tangle burst and interlace
Then fall back sparkling in the deep,
And still from out beyond that sombre rim
A wind returns to stir the crystal panes
And murmur magically of golden rains
That fall for ever in those spaces dim.
It is a white tower builded on the margin of dawn
Out on the edge of nothing in the shade;
It glimmers like a spike of lonely pearl
That mirrors beams forlorn and lights that fade,
And sea goes washing round the dark rock where it stands
And fairy boats go by to gloaming lands
All piled and twinkling in the gloom
With hoarded sparks of orient fire
That divers won in waters of the distant Sun:
And maybe 'tis a throbbing silver lyre
Or voices of grey sailors echo up,
For often is there sound of feet and tune
While I alone look out behind the moon
From in my white and windy tower
Set out upon the midworld's jewelled cup
And find unmoving silver-drest
Gazing straight on me Phospher Watcher of the West.

In line 15 Tolkien marked 'dawn' to be changed to 'eve', but in the next manuscript in this series the white tower was 'builded in the Twilit Isles'. Also in text C, line 23, Tolkien changed 'distant Sun' to 'unknown Sun'. 'Phospher Watcher of the West' in line 31 first appeared at this stage, though the idea of a bright star had already been suggested in text B, 'the lonely star the silver watcher of the west', and had an earlier parallel in the 'Classical' version of *The Voyage of Éarendel the Evening Star* (poem no. 16), in which Phosphorus 'sprang . . . up from the Ocean's cup'. With the next manuscript, inscribed 'Jul[y] 24', Tolkien altered the spelling of the name to 'Phosphor' and changed and extended the closing lines:

While I alone look out behind the moon
Upon the rim of midworld's jewelled cup
Within my white and windy tower
And see unmoving silver-drest
Far out at anchor on celestial seas
And gazing full on me Phosphor Watcher of the West.

On the back of this copy, possibly written later, is the Old English title *Þá Éadiȝan Sǽlidan*; see below.

Tolkien wrote yet another draft, apparently incomplete (it ends with 'white and windy tower'), opposite text C in one of his poetry notebooks. This is notable for the development of several lines from 'Or voices of grey sailors echo up' (C24):

Or voices of grey sailors echo up
Afloat among the shadows of the world
For often seems there ring of feet and song
Or the twilit twinkle of a trembling gong
O happy mariners upon a journey long
In oarless shallop and with canvas furled
To those great portals on the Western shores
Where far away constellate fountains leap
Against night's dragonheaded doors
And fall back sparkling in the deep
While I alone look out behind the moon
From my white and windy tower

The first six lines of this passage, however, are marked on the page for rearrangement, in the order given below in the next, penultimate manuscript of the middle sequence ('rewritten Sep[tember] 9'); we give this as D, incorporating, as best we can interpret their history, only those revisions concurrent with the writing of the text.

[D] I know a window in a western tower
That opens on celestial seas
And wind that has been blowing round the stars
Comes to nestle in its tossing draperies.
It is a white tower builded in the Twilit Isles
Where Evening sits for ever in the shade;
It glimmers like a spike of lonely pearl
That mirrors beams forlorn and lights that fade;
And sea goes washing round the dark rock where it stands
And fairy boats go by to gloaming lands
All piled and twinkling in the gloom
With hoarded sparks of orient fire
That divers drew from waters of the unknown Sun: —
And, maybe, 'tis a throbbing silver lyre,
Or voices of grey sailors echo up
Afloat among the shadows of the world

In oarless shallop and with canvas furled,
For often seems there ring of feet, and song,
Or twilit twinkle of a trembling gong.

O! happy mariners upon a journey long
To those great portals on Western Shores
Where far away constellate fountains leap,
And beat against Night's dragonheaded doors,
Then fall back sparkling in the deep,
As wide upon the jacinth wall of space
They tangle, burst, and interlace.
While I alone look out behind the moon
From in my white and windy tower.
Ye bide no moment and await no hour,
But chanting snatches of a mystic tune
Go through the shadows and the dangerous seas
Past sunless lands to fairy leas.
Ye follow ever Phosphor through the West —
The shining mariner — to Islands blest,
But still from out beyond that sombre rim
A wind returns to stir these crystal panes
And murmur magically of golden rains
That fall for ever in those spaces dim.

With this manuscript the poem was at last given a title, *The Happy Mariners*, as well as its equivalent in Old English, *Þá Éadiȝan Sǽlidan*. Tolkien marked manuscript D with several changes, including the relocation of two lines (25–26, to follow 'fairy leas'), and most notably changed 'Phosphor' (line 33) to 'Earendel'. These revisions carried into a professional typescript of the poem, made probably in October 1915, and this seems to have been the basis of *The Happy Mariners* as published in the June 1920 number of the *Stapeldon Magazine* of Exeter College, Oxford, pp. 69–70, with differences of punctuation and capitalization probably imposed by the *Stapeldon* editor. Here, as E, is the text of the typescript, incorporating Tolkien's further marked revisions.

[E] I know a window in a western tower
That opens on celestial seas,
And wind that has been blowing round the stars
Comes to nestle in its tossing draperies.
It is a white tower builded in the Twilit Isles,

Where Evening sits for ever in the shade;
It glimmers like a spike of lonely pearl
That mirrors beams forlorn and lights that fade;
And sea goes washing round the dark rock where it stands,
And fairy boats go by to gloaming lands
All piled and twinkling in the gloom
With hoarded sparks of orient fire
That divers won in waters of the unknown Sun: —
And, maybe, 'tis a throbbing silver lyre,
Or voices of grey sailors echo up
Afloat among the shadows of the world
In oarless shallop and with canvas furled,
For often seems there ring of feet and song
Or twilit twinkle of a trembling gong.

O! happy mariners upon a journey long
To those great portals on Western shores
Where far away constellate fountains leap
And dashed against Night's dragon-headed doors,
In foam of stars fall sparkling in the deep.
While I alone look out behind the Moon
From in my white and windy tower,
Ye bide no moment and await no hour,
But chanting snatches of a ghostly tune
Go through the shadows and the dangerous seas
Past sunless lands to fairy leas
Where stars upon the jacinth wall of space
Do tangle burst and interlace.
Ye follow Earendel through the West,
The shining mariner, to Islands blest;
While only from beyond that sombre rim
A wind returns to stir these crystal panes
And murmur magically of golden rains
That fall for ever in those spaces dim.

The published version prefers (or misprints) 'or song' for 'and song' in line 18, and 'Oh! happy mariners' for 'O! happy mariners' in line 20. Curiously, as printed there is an earlier reading in line 3, 'through the stars' rather than 'round the stars'. In line 28, the printed version has 'secret tune', which reflects a tentative change Tolkien marked to manuscript D, but the typescript seems to have retained 'mystic' before 'tune' (the typed word is obscured by correction), which

Tolkien marked for revision to 'ghostly'. In line 25 of the typescript he wrote 'Here' above 'While', but neither this nor 'ghostly tune' appear in later texts.

A curious fair copy manuscript, written by Tolkien in blue coloured pencil on squared paper torn from a small notebook of the sort he may have had for army duties, and entitled *Happ[y] Mariners*, clearly postdates D as revised. It includes all of the marked alterations of that text, except that the tune in line 28 is still 'mystic'.

The Happy Mariners was published a second time, in June 1923, in *A Northern Venture: Verses by Members of the Leeds University English School Association*. There its title is *Tha Eadigan Saelidan: The Happy Mariners*, set thus. The text follows the typescript E in most respects more closely than that of the *Stapeldon Magazine* appearance, though again there are probably editorial differences of punctuation and capitalization, 'Twilight Isles' in line 5 and 'murmer' in line 37 are misprints for 'Twilit Isles' and 'murmur', and an extraneous 'the' was inserted before 'twilit twinkle' in line 19. 'Mystic tune' remained in line 28. Christopher Tolkien included this text in *The Book of Lost Tales, Part Two*, pp. 273–4, silently correcting some of its printer errors.

Tolkien later revised *The Happy Mariners* still further, writing it out in neat calligraphy. He inscribed this 'revised 1940?' the date referring either to the text proper, much changed from the preceding versions, or to revisions he marked on the manuscript. His handwriting here is consistent with script from the 1940s, though it can be found also in earlier and later examples. Christopher Tolkien published this text in *The Book of Lost Tales, Part Two*, pp. 275–6, as it was first written out, with revisions traced in footnotes; we give it here (F) with Tolkien's final changes incorporated and earlier readings in our commentary and notes.

[F]

I know a window in a Western tower
that opens on celestial seas,
from wells of dark behind the stars
there ever blows a keen unearthly breeze.
It is a white tower builded in the Twilit Isles,
and springing from their everlasting shade
it glimmers like a house of lonely pearl,
where lights forlorn take harbour ere they fade.

Its feet are washed by waves that never rest.
There silent boats go by into the West
All piled and twinkling in the dark

with orient fire in many a hoarded spark
that divers won
in waters from the rumoured Sun.
There sometimes throbs below a silver harp,
touching the heart with sudden music sharp;
or far beneath the mountain high and sheer
the voices of grey sailors echo clear,
afloat among the shadows of the world
in oarless ships and with their canvas furled,
chanting a farewell and a solemn song:
for wide the sea is, and their journey long.

O happy mariners upon a journey far,
beyond the grey islands and past Gondobar,
to those great portals on the final shores
where far away constellate fountains leap,
and dashed against Night's dragon-headed doors
in foam of stars fall sparkling in the deep!
While I look out alone behind the moon
imprisoned in the white and windy tower,
you bide no moment and await no hour,
but go with solemn song and harpers' tune.

You follow Earendel without rest,
the shining mariner, beyond the West,
who passed the mouth of night and launched his bark
upon the seas of everlasting dark.
Here only long afar through window-pane
I glimpse the flicker of the golden rain
that falls for ever on those outer seas,
beyond the country of the shining Trees.

As in earlier poems, elements of *The Happy Mariners* prefigure aspects of *The Book of Lost Tales*. The Twilit Isles (D5, etc.) and a tower 'like a spike of lonely pearl' (B15, etc.) later appear in the tale *The Coming of the Valar and the Building of Valinor*:

> Now this was the manner of the Earth in those days. . . . Mightiest of regions are the Great Lands where Men do dwell and wander now, and the Lost Elves sing and dance upon the hills; but beyond their westernmost limits lie the Great Seas, and in that vast water of the West are many smaller lands and isles,

> ere the lonely seas are found whose waves whisper about the Magic Isles. Farther even than this, and few are the boats of mortal men that have dared so far, are set the Shadowy Seas whereon there float the Twilit Isles and the Tower of Pearl rises pale upon their most western cape. . . . [*The Book of Lost Tales, Part One*, p. 68]

For the 'twilit twinkle of a trembling gong' (D19) there is an analogue in *The Cottage of Lost Play*, which tells of 'Littleheart the Gong-warden', who 'sailed in Wingilot with Eärendel in that last voyage wherein they sought for Kôr. It was the ringing of this Gong on the Shadowy Seas that awoke the Sleeper in the Tower of Pearl that stands far out to west in the Twilit Isles' (*The Book of Lost Tales, Part One*, p. 15).

'The dragon gargoyles' (B7), later 'dragonheaded gargoyles', may be compared to the 'dragonheaded door' of poem no. 31, text C, and likewise with the Door of Night in the 'lost tale' *The Hiding of Valinor*:

> Thus came it that the Gods dared a very great deed, the most mighty of all their works; for making a fleet of magic rafts and boats with Ulmo's [the Lord of Waters] aid – and otherwise had none of these endured to sail upon the waters of Vai [the great ocean spanning the world] – they drew to the Wall of Things, and there they made the Door of Night (Moritarnon or Tarn Fui as the Eldar name it in their tongues). There it still stands, utterly black and huge against the deep-blue walls. Its pillars are of the mightiest basalt and its lintel likewise, but great dragons of black stone are carved thereon, and shadowy smoke pours slowly from their jaws. [*The Book of Lost Tales, Part One*, pp. 215–16]

The 'jacinth wall of space' (B and C, line 8) anticipates the deep blue Wall of Things, which enclosed the world. In regard to the 'sparks of orient fire | That divers won in waters of the distant [later unknown] Sun' (C22–23), it is said in *The Hiding of Valinor* that when the Valar sought to draw the Sun beneath the Earth, 'it was too frail and lissom; and much precious radiance was spilled in their attempts about the deepest waters, and escaped to linger as secret sparks in many an unknown ocean cavern. These have many elfin divers, and divers of the fays, long time sought beyond the outmost East, even as is sung in the song of the Sleeper in the Tower of Pearl' (*The Book of*

Lost Tales, Part One, p. 215). *The Happy Mariners* is evidently itself 'the song of the Sleeper in the Tower of Pearl'.

'Midworld', a name briefly found in earlier drafts, is not equivalent to 'Middle-earth' as used by Tolkien in his fiction from the 1930s, but to the Earth in early cosmology, between the sea and the heavens.

Christopher Tolkien was unable to explain the reference in F24 to the journey 'beyond the grey islands and past Gondobar'. *Gondobar*, Gnomish for 'City of Stone', was one of the seven names of Gondolin, the hidden city of the Elves in Tolkien's mythology (see poem no. 66). The name also appears, however, in a similar context in *The Nameless Land* (no. 74, begun in 1924; here we quote from the first version):

Of solemn surges on the bar
Beyond the world's edge waft to me;
In sleep I see a wayward star,
Than beacon-towers in Gondobar
More fair. . . .

The use of the name in this manner suggests that Tolkien at one time considered 'Gondobar' in association with Kôr (Tún), but did not record it.

Version F of *The Happy Mariners* as first written contained substantial references to the 'Silmarillion' mythology. It will be useful to quote here the final eighteen lines before Tolkien revised them:

While I, alone, look out behind the moon
from in my white and windy tower
ye bide no moment and await no hour,
but go with solemn song and harpers' tune
through the dark shadows and the shadowy seas
to the last land of the Two Trees,
whose fruit and flower are moon and sun,
where light of earth is ended and begun.

Ye follow Ëarendel without rest,
the shining mariner, beyond the West,
who passed the mouth of night and launched his bark
upon the outer seas of everlasting dark.
Here only comes at whiles a wind to blow,
returning darkly down the way ye go,
with perfume laden of unearthly trees.

Here only long afar through window-pane
I glimpse the flicker of the golden rain
that falls for ever on the outer seas.

We have mentioned the Shadowy Seas (as a proper noun). For the Two Trees and their 'last land' (Valinor), see poem no. 31. Before he struck through line 6 entirely, Tolkien changed it to 'to find the two fair trees'. In *The Book of Lost Tales* the Outer Sea(s) are dark waters beyond Valinor, where no boat or fish may pass except by the will of Ulmo; compare the 'outer seas' of text F, line 39.

On 24 October 1915 G.B. Smith wrote to Tolkien that *The Happy Mariners*, which his friend had sent to him for comment, was 'a magnificent effort: I could not wish to see it bettered' (Bodleian Library).

John Garth has suggested that the beginning of the poem 'reads like an opening-up of Keats's evocative lines in his "Ode to a Nightingale" about "magic casements, opening on the foam | Of perilous seas, in faery lands forlorn". But the faëry lands lie quite beyond reach, and the magic merely tantalizes' (*Tolkien and the Great War*, p. 89). Julian Eilmann (*J.R.R. Tolkien: Romanticist and Poet*, p. 311) relates the poem to aspects of German Romanticism, notably the 'Romantic longing of the lyrical I', or first person narrative ('While I alone look out behind the Moon').

C31: 'Phospher' is an obsolete spelling of *phosphor*. In this context, 'Phospher' is an abbreviated form of 'Phosphorus'.

D1: Above this line in the manuscript is the roman numeral 'I', apparently intended as a section number. But no second section is distinguished.

D13: 'That divers drew from' reverted to 'That divers won in' in E.

F3: 'From wells of dark' originally read 'and there from wells of dark'.

F4: 'There ever blows' originally read 'blows ever cold'.

F17: 'Beneath the mountain' originally read 'beneath the mountains'.

F29–40: For the original text before final revision, see our discussion above.

34

The Trumpet of Faery · *The Trumpets of Faery* · *The Horns of the Host of Doriath* (1915–*c.* 1930)

The earliest text of *The Trumpet of Faery*, as the poem was first called, is found in *The Book of Ishness*. We transcribe here, as A, its most complete part, as amended in the course of writing. Some of the initial text has been lost to erasure. Our transcription also reflects Tolkien's varying indentation of lines, as we interpret it: it is not clear from the manuscript, written quickly in pencil, if lines 17–24 are to be set to the left like lines 5–8, or indented halfway to the point of lines 1–4 and 9–16. From line 25, the text is far to the left on the sheet, with no indentation to the end. Tolkien distinctly drew an ornament only between lines 36 and 37. In line 1, Tolkien poetically compares the English elm (*Ulmus procera*), a tall, stately tree, to a (stone) pillar or column.

[A]

    From the pillared Elm columnar
    There rang a golden gong,
    And a sound of gates unlocking
    and a sound of golden song.
Then a silver fanfare trembled
And it shook the long moonbeams
And a thousand slender trumpets
Seemed to echo from old dreams.
    What a twinkle and a ringing
    What a shimmer and a singing
    As the long procession winding
    Down the alleys of the wood
    Came with banner pale a-streaming;
    Came with elfin mail a-gleaming —
    And their little horns were winding
    In the alleys of the wood.

O the elm its roots were twisted
In the white rays of the moon
In the sound of feet going inward

And of dying fading tune
Heark a clang of gates together
Through the eerie elfin night
As a thousand feet go homeward
In a crooked stream of light

What a fading and a dying
What a waning and a sighing
How those trumpets call for ever
From an endless long way off
O what echoes out from yonder
Down the dimming music wander
What a sound of sea for ever
And of foaming rocks far off.

More o more of Elfland's trumpets
Of their trembling peals of sound
Of their music silver air
That rings faintly from the ground!

⋆

O 'twas like old fir trees groaning
In great winds that are forgot
And like drowsy bees a-droning
In long noons that now are not;
Like the ring of roads in winter
Neath the creak of lumbering wains
Or the rustle of grey poplars
Like the silver plash of rains,
Or the flow of far off rivers
Where a rainbow distant quivers
Over many falling waters
And the wind is in the pines
Like the sea in rocky arches
Like the feathered voice of larches
Leaning out o'er falling waters
And a singing to the pines
Or it waned to long thin voices
As of stringéd violins,
Or the mellow autumn flutings
In the branches of the winds
Then like thunder in the mountains

Heard in uplands far away
Or like thunder on long shorelands
Of seas rolling in the bay
O the memories in its ringing
Like the great Earth quietly singing
Right out across the starlight
Little tunes of Elfinesse.

Also in *The Book of Ishness* are two pages of rough partial workings for the poem, including the following lines Tolkien considered for its final section:

What a murmur of old trees
On long afternoons forgot
What a drowsy drone of bees [*also:* What a drone
  of humming bees]
On old days that now are not.
O the ring of roads in winter
And the creaking of a wain,
And the rustle of high poplars
And the silver plash of rain,
And the flow of many waters
That go roaring to a fall
Like the mighty voice of forests
When the pines and larches call
O! the distant song of voices
And the wail of violins
And the mellow autumn flutings
In the branches of the winds
Mingle in that silver music
All the old regretful musics of the sad and [?weary] Earth
All the happy songs of laughter that go back to older mirth
Dying fading out of sound
With that ever calling longing
That in Fairy land is found

Droning bees enter into text B, below (line 35). Six further lines are also written on this page, partly unreadable, but it is not clear where, or if, they fit with the others:

For the pines have [?] sea voices
Like the breakers rolling in

But the larches slender singing
[*deleted:* Is like wind and dunes]
Is murmurous [*above:* feathery] and thin
[?] the murmurs [*above:* breezes] [?]

For *feathery* 'husky', compare 'feathered' below. Next to these lines is a column of words which rhyme with 'in' and 'thin'. Tolkien wrote similar lines in pencil next to the succeeding ink manuscript, not taken up into the text, beginning 'For the pines have great sea voices'.

Among other drafting, we can make out these (non-continuous) lines of interest:

It was mingled and was tangled
With a longing it was spangled
With the shimmer of a [?starlit] night
On the lakes of Elfinesse
In lagoons of Elfinesse

A version of this text reappears at the end of C, below.

Following on his drafts, Tolkien made a new manuscript of the poem, with alterations, which he dated 'July 13–14 1915' but also, on a second page in a later hand, 'July 14'. He first gave it the title *The Trumpets of Faery*, now with a plural noun, and above that wrote *Horns of Elfland*; later, he deleted these titles and again wrote *The Trumpets of Faery*. He also inscribed, on the first page of the manuscript, Old English *Ielfbíeman* ('Elf-horns'), and on a facing page, *Þa bíeman Ielfalandes* ('The Horns of Elfland'). We give as B this second text, as initially written (or amended in the course of writing, as far as we can judge) in ink over erased pencil, before further revision.

[B]

From the pillared Elm columnar
There rang a golden gong,
And a sound of gates unlocking,
And the sound of little song.
Then a silver fanfare trembled
And it shook the long moonbeams,
And a thousand slender trumpets
Seemed to echo from old dreams.
What a twinkle and a ringing;
What a shimmer and a singing
As the long procession winding

Down the alleys of the wood
Came with banners pale a-streaming;
Came with elfin mail a-gleaming;
With their little horns a-winding
Down the alleys of the wood.

⋆

O the Elm its roots were twisted
In the white rays of the moon;
In the sound of feet going inward
And of fading dying tune.
Hark! a clang of gates together
Through the eerie hush of night
As a thousand feet go homeward
Down the winding stream of light
O the hollow echo dying
O the waning and the sighing —
How those trumpets call for ever
From an endless long way off!
O! what echoes out from yonder
Down the dimming music wander;
What a sound of seas for ever
And of foaming rocks far off

O! 'twas like old fir trees groaning
In great winds that are forgot,
And like drowsy bees a-droning
In long noons that now are not;
Like the ring of roads in winter
Neath the creak of lumbering wains
Then the rustle of grey poplars
Like the silver plash of rains;
As the flow of far-off rivers
Where a rainbow distant quivers
Over many falling waters —
And the wind is in the pines
Like the sea in rocky arches
And the feathered voice of larches
Leaning out o'er falling waters
Is a-singing to the pines.

⋆

Then it waned to long thin voices
As of stringéd violins
Then to mellow autumn flutings
In the branches of the winds;
Then to thunder in the mountains
Heard on uplands far away
Or the thunder on long shorelands
Of seas rolling in the bay.
O the memories in its ringing
Like the great Earth quietly singing
Right out across the starlight
Little tunes of Elfinesse!
It was mingled and was tangled
With a longing: it was spangled
With the glimmer of the starlight
On lagoons in Elfinesse.

Three typescripts followed text B. The first of these, professionally typed probably in October 1915, was later inscribed by Tolkien 'Barnt Green 1915 July & Bedford Aug[ust]. — retouched and retitled Aug[ust]. 21st 1924'. On a preserved carbon copy he altered the title from *The Trumpets of Faery* to *The Trumpets of Faërie*, then to *The Horns of the Host of Doriath*, tying the work further to his mythology: in 'The Silmarillion' Doriath (called in *The Book of Lost Tales* Artanor) is a hidden kingdom of the Elves in Middle-earth, ruled by Thingol and Melian. The gates opening and closing in the poem must, therefore, be those of Thingol's underground stronghold, Menegroth, and the trumpet-sounding elves his host, or army, if somewhat fanciful. This version, incorporating changes marked on the second manuscript, is transcribed here as C, as the typescript stood before Tolkien revised it further.

[C] I

From the pillared Elm columnar
Rang a faintly golden gong,
And a sound of gates unlocking
And the sound of little song.
Then a silver fanfare trembled
And it shook the long moonbeams
As a thousand slender trumpets
Seemed to echo from old dreams.

What a twinkle and a ringing!
What a shimmer and a singing!
As the long procession winding
Down the alleys of the wood
Came with banners pale a-streaming,
Came with elfin mail a-gleaming,
With their little horns a-winding
Down the alleys of the wood.

II

The Elm its roots were twisted
In the white rays of the moon;
In the sound of feet going inward
And of fading dying tune.
Hark! a clang of gates together
Through the silent eerie night
As a thousand feet go homeward
Down the winding stream of light.
O! the blowing that is dying
With a hollow silver sighing:
How those trumpets call for ever
From an endless long way off!
What echoes out from yonder
Down the dimming music wander;
What a sound of seas for ever,
And of foaming rocks far off!

III

O! 'twas like old fir trees groaning
In great winds that are forgot,
And like drowsy bees a-droning
In long noons that now are not;
Like the ring of roads in winter
Neath the creak of lumbering wains
Then the rustle of grey poplars
Like the silver plash of rains;
As the flow of far-off rivers
Where a rainbow distant quivers
Over many falling waters —
And the wind is in the pines
Like the sea in rocky arches

Is the feathered voice of larches
Leaning out o'er falling waters
and a-singing to the pines.

Then it waned to long thin voices
As of stringéd violins;
Then to mellow autumn flutings
In the branches of the winds;
Then to thunder in the mountains
Heard on uplands far away,
Or to roaring of sea-voices
Piling shingle in the bay.
O! the memories in its ringing
Like the great Earth quietly singing
In the wide halls of the starlight
Olden tunes of Elfinesse.
It was mingled and was tangled
With a longing: it was spangled
With the glimmer of the starlight
On lagoons in Elfinesse.

Tolkien marked this text with numerous changes, which in turn were reflected in a second typescript. The latter was made with a purple ribbon, from Tolkien's period at the University of Leeds, but it can be more closely dated to *c.* 21 August 1924, if the inscription on the first typescript is correct. (On a list of Tolkien's poems from around this time – see Appendix III – the work appears as *The Trumpets of Faery*.) Tolkien marked alterations on the new copy also, but they are few and very minor. The final text of the poem, given below as D, is a third typescript, also called *The Horns of the Host of Doriath*, made by Tolkien on his Hammond typewriter.

[D]

In nightshade neath the Elmtree
A dimly ringing gong,
And a sound of gates unlocking,
And the welling forth of song.
Then a silver fanfare trembled
And it shook the long moonbeams
And a thousand slender trumpets,
As an echo heard in dreams.
What a twinkle and a ringing!
What a shimmer and a singing!
As the long procession winding

Down the alleys of the wood
Came with banners pale a-streaming;
Came with elfin mail a-gleaming;
With their haunting horns a-winding
Down the alleys of the wood.

The Elm, its roots were twisted
In the white rays of the moon,
In the sound of feet going inward
And the fading of a tune.
Hark! a clang of gates together
In the silence of the night,
As a thousand feet go homeward
Down a winding stream of light
O! the blowing that is dying
With a hollow silver sighing:
How those trumpets call for ever
From an endless long way off!
What echoes out from yonder
Down that melting music wander,
What a sound of seas for ever
And of foaming rocks far off!

I heard old fir-trees groaning
In great winds that are forgot,
And drowsy bees a-droning
In long noons that now are not;
The ring of roads in winter
Neath the creak of lumbering wains;
And the poplars grey were rustling
Like the silver plash of rains
Or the flow of far-off rivers
Where a rainbow distant quivers
Over many falling waters;
Then the wind was in the pines
Like the sea in rocky arches,
And the feathered voice of larches
Leaning out o'er falling waters
Was singing in the pines.

Then it waned to long thin voices
As of stringéd violins,
Then to mellow autumn flutings

In the branches of the winds,
Then to thunder in the mountains
Heard on uplands far away,
Or to roaring of sea-voices
Piling shingle in the bay.
O! the memories in its ringing
As of Niënor plaintive singing
In the wide halls of the starlight
Ancient tunes of Elfinesse.
It was twined and it was tangled
With all longing, it was spangled
With the glimmer of the starlight
On lagoons in Elfinesse.

Two of Tolkien's alterations to the final versions, both made in the second typescript (i.e. preceding D), are of special note. In line 33, the first person voice is given to the speaker; and in line 58, comparison is no longer to 'the great Earth quietly singing' but to the singing of Niënor, in 'The Silmarillion' the tragic sister of Túrin. The Elvish word *nienor* is translated as 'mourning' or 'lamentation', with the element *nie* 'tear'. And indeed, the poem laments that a pure experience of the Elves and their music cannot be attained, only 'an echo heard in dreams', emotions recalled from a distance. There is, however, a consolation in the sounds of nature, the voices of the trees and the waters, which remind the speaker of the 'ancient tunes of Elfinesse'.

As explained in our Introduction, Tolkien planned that the title *The Trumpets of Faërie* should serve both for this work and for a volume of his poetry he hoped to see published. To his former King Edward's School teacher R.W. Reynolds the phrase sounded 'just a trifle precious,' as he wrote to Tolkien on 2 August 1915; 'but', he continued, 'I may be a little morbid on that point; and it is certainly descriptive. I think the fairy poems are your strongest and most original vein' (Bodleian Library). Dora Owen, whose *Book of Fairy Poetry* included *Goblin Feet* (poem no. 27) and to whom Tolkien also sent the present work, felt much the same, that 'all your fairy poems have the right fairy ring' (Bodleian Library).

The Trumpets of Faërie (or *The Horns of the Hosts of Doriath*) and *Goblin Feet* in fact are similar in tone and subject, if not in length. In each, the speaker follows a fairy procession – not an uncommon occurrence in traditional literature – 'down the alleys of the wood' or 'down the crooked fairy lane', to the accompaniment of music. As we have seen, 'Fairy land' is mentioned in discarded workings for text A of the present poem. The use of 'little horns' in versions A, B, and C (changed in the second typescript to 'haunting horns') suggests that Tolkien was still thinking of diminutive fairies, as he had in *Goblin Feet*; and this would not be the last time he used such imagery, see *Kortirion among the Trees* (poem no. 40).

It may be worth noting that in the Middle English poem *Sir Orfeo*, which Tolkien knew well (see no. 173), Orfeo often sees 'the king of Faërie with his rout | . . . hunting in the woods about | with blowing far and crying dim', and at other times 'a mighty host . . . | ten hundred knights all fair arrayed | with many a banner proud displayed', 'or a sight more strange . . . | knights and ladies came dancing by | in rich array and raiment meet, | softly stepping with skilful feet; | tabour and trumpet went along, | and marvellous minstrelsy and song' (Tolkien's translation, *Sir Gawain and the Green Knight, Pearl and Sir Orfeo* (1975), ll. 281–302). 'The horns of Elfland' is a well known phrase from Tennyson's 'The Splendour Falls' in *The Princess*:

> O hark, O hear! how thin and clear,
>   And thinner, clearer, farther going!
> O sweet and far from cliff and scar
>   The horns of Elfland faintly blowing!
> Blow, let us hear the purple glens replying:
> Blow, bugle; answer, echoes, dying, dying, dying.

The blowing of horns – the horn of Boromir, the horns of Rohan, Merry's horn in the Shire – also figures dramatically in *The Lord of the Rings*.

A20: 'And of dying fading tune' read 'And of fading waning tune' before Tolkien changed it in the course of composition.

A22: 'Through the eerie elfin night' originally read 'Through the starlit fairy gloom'.

A45–47: These lines originally read 'Or the flow of far off waters | Where a distant rainbow quivers | Arched athwart a fall of waters'.

A52–54: These lines originally read 'And a calling to the pines | It tangled with thin voices | Like the wail of violins'. Tolkien also considered 'wailing' for 'calling'.

A64: 'Elfinesse' in the context of Tolkien's mythology is one name for the land of the Elves in the distant West of the world.

D1: 'Elmtree' read 'Elm-tree', with a hyphen, in the second typescript. Tolkien's manuscript revision to the first typescript reads either 'Elmtree' or 'Elm tree' – one cannot know for sure, in this example of his handwriting, if a space was intended.

D14: Tolkien marked 'elfin' to be changed to 'elvish', but did not strike through the typewritten word.

35

Thoughts on Parade · The Swallow and the Traveller on the Plains (1915)

Tolkien set this work down initially as prose, only afterward dividing it into lines as poetry. The first of its two manuscripts is not dated, but from its content must have been composed after Tolkien reported for army officer training at Bedford on 19 July 1915 and was no longer free to come and go, or to visit Edith, as he wished. Its title, *Thoughts on Parade*, may have a double meaning: that the poet's thoughts are parading through his consciousness, and that they are doing so while he is on parade, that is among an assembly of troops. Here we present the earlier text (A) broken into lines as Tolkien indicated, with revisions that seem concurrent with the writing, and with more substantive changes recorded in notes.

[A] O swallow black swallow I gazed up at thee
out of bitterness and servitude; bravely thou wert beating
far aloft under the sunless clouds in those great spaces
where thunder sits enchained and the winds are cavernously penned.
O swallow broad is the face of the Earth; the trees thereon
were ruffled and their leaves blown upward
for many vapours sped before the wind,
and thou went flying free in vastness
O tell me dost thou not fear the awful dome of heaven
as I do here upon the plains?
Doth not the sight of its blue seas
and white hills wake wonder in thy heart?
Thou plashest on the brink of oceans that are marginless —
art thou not afraid?
Thou gazest on vistas that are infinite
and art not stunned!
On the silence whose greatness exceeds all things thou lookest;
thou seest the towering shapes of vapour
before whose feet Everest becomes as a hillock
and is humbled.

Awful are the mountains of white foam,
they are girdled with black-stranded drift,
and footed in wind-strewn plains incalculable;
they are chasméd and rifted by the tempest and their knees are bowed.
They fall in precipices and grey slopes;
they burst and splinter in wild boulders and become
as immeasurable morasses and high beaches
to the untraversed oceans of the firmament.
There are the endless archipelagoes
piled and fretted in the waters of the sun
(whose outmost chain wanes from [the] eye
beyond the cincture of the world).
There are the chambers of the Brooding Dark.
Fumes and spoutings ray across the sky.
Some pitted crater unthinkable has blown to tatters a most mighty world
out there beyond the edge of this quiet Earth,
and the mirk of that huge turmoil
wreathes and hides the celestial mountains footed in the sea.
O swallow thou hast seen the gale come galloping from the windy walls
and blow the smokes back into that outer pit.
Then all the freezing waters of the sky did glister clear and endless
and the galleons of the stars set sail upon them
bound for the gloomy west:
most awful of all is then the sky
but these things thou hast not seen, for thou hast fled —
whither, o my swallow?
Thou knowest not all things;
thou knowest not the moon, the golden orb
before whom the starry boats founder and go out.
Thou hast fled to find the orient sun,
and left me on this plain, quailing and alone.
O chill the wind and bitter the glory of this cold heaven
and the pale cold majesty of the moon!
Infinite is the distance of the stars —
but thou O swallow at what gaze thou;
where is the flight of thy fleet wings?
Dread are the chasméd mountains and the fettered thunders of the sky:

terrible the oceans and the lofty isles, and the distances no eye may comprehend —
but not all the heavens seem so wide and chill
as the long white road from hence away.
O swallow it wanders up and down
the bosom of this our Mother Earth;
it is gone in the dusk
and I may not follow it
O swallow I have seen the grey rains
as they spill from an o'erflowing bowl of some far cloud
blown and tangled by the wind and silver tresséd by the slanting sun:
I have seen it plash and fall upon the bosom of the lands
and the blue shadows far away reek up in silver mist.
O swallow I do love these things
but at times do they speak too near to my heart
of things far off
and the long white road goes backward in the dusk
and I may not follow it.
Through the broad darkness arched under the long moonbeams it goes
and the night is murmuring
and it is odorous with old things till my heart must break.
O swallow at night is the Earth very wide and great
and the dread skies far away
and the thin clouds near and waning canopied
nor terrible as in the wide day.
In the night do I hope, though I see thee not
for these things thou dost not know
for thou hast fled along the pathways of the Sun
beating the golden spaces with thy dark wings my swallow.
O canst thou swallow swallow see the end of that homing road?
Dread are the mountains of the air and bottomless seas unplumbed
and in the day I long unquenchably.
Canst thou see?
The stars and the belated moon
the unutterable glory of the sun are nought to me
for I would follow that gloaming road
back home to her,
and I may not yet my swallow.
I may not flee as thou

tracking the splendour of the orient sun!
O swallow swallow swallow she is calling me
and the echo of her voice comes over the wide earth
along the white road home.
And the long road goes backward in the dusk
and I may not follow it.

Trial workings appear on pages facing this text in one of Tolkien's poetry notebooks. Of these, the most substantive is opposite lines 33 and following (compare lines 35–6 in text B):

And behold a pitted crater unthinkable beyond the edge of the tranquil Earth
doth seem to have blown to tattered steam a mighty world

Tolkien developed *Thoughts on Parade* further in a second manuscript, dated 4 August 1915. He was still in Bedfordshire, but before long would move to Lichfield in Staffordshire, to join the 13th Battalion of the Lancashire Fusiliers. The title of the poem now became *The Swallow and the Traveller on the Plains*. Tolkien set down this version with its lines already divided, and at first followed the order of text A; but then he made several deletions and insertions, and marked certain lines and sections to change position. In B below we have incorporated all of Tolkien's late alterations and present the poem in its final intended order.

[B] O swallow, black swallow, I gazed up at thee
out of heat and dust and a great weariness;
bravely thou wert beating far aloft
under the sunless clouds in those great spaces
where thunder sits enchained and the winds are cavernously penned.
O swallow, broad is the face of the Earth; the trees thereon
were ruffled and their leaves blown upward
for many vapours sped before the wind;
and thou went flying free in vastness.
O tell me dost thou not fear the awful dome of heaven,
as I do here upon the plain?
Doth not the sight of its blue seas
and white hills wake wonder in thy breast?
Thou plashest on the brink of oceans that are marginless:
art thou not afraid?

Thou gazest upon vistas that are infinite,
and art not stunned!
On the silence whose greatness exceeds all things thou lookest;
thou seest the towering shapes of vapour
before whose feet Everest becomes as a hillock
and is humbled;
awful are the mountains of white foam;
they are girdled with black stranded drift
and footed in wind-strewn plains incalculable;
they are chasmëd and rifted by the tempest, and their knees are
    bowed.
They fall in precipices and grey slopes;
they burst and splinter in wild boulders
and tangle in immeasurable morasses.
Untraversed are the oceans of the firmament
Where lie the endless archipelagoes piled and fretted in the
    waters of the Sun.
And their outmost chain wanes from the eye
Beyond the ramparts of the world.
O swallow, I have seen the grey rains, as they spill
from an o'erflowing bowl of some far cloud,
blown and tangled by the wind and silver-tressëd by the
    slanting sun:
I have seen them plash and fall upon the bosom of the lands,
and the blue shadows far away
reek up in silver mist.
O swallow, I do love these things,
and yet they speak too near my heart of things far off—
and the long white road goes backward in the dusk,
and I may not follow it.
Through the broad darkness arched beneath the long
    moonbeams it goes,
and the night is murmuring;
and it is odorous until my heart must break.
O ye chambers of the brooding Dark;
ye fumes and spoutings that are rayed across the sky—
What pitted crater out beyond the tranquil Earth
hath blown a world to tattered steam—
that and the mirk of that huge turmoil
wreathes and hides the celestial mountains footed in the sea?

O swallow! hast thou seen the gale come galloping from the windy walls,
and blow the smokes back into that far outer pit,
and all the freezing waters of the sky begin to glister clear and endless,
and the galleons of the stars set sail upon them
bound for the gloaming west.
Most awful of all is then the sky —
But not these things thou hast not abode to see, for thou hast fled —
— whither, O my swallow?
thou knowest not the moon — the golden orb
’fore whom the starry boats founder and go out.
Thou hast fled to find the orient sun,
beating the golden spaces with thy dark wings.
and left me on this plain, quailing and alone.
O chill the wind, and bitter the glory of this cold heaven,
and the pale cold majesty of the moon!
Infinite is the distance of the stars —
but thou, O swallow, at what gazest thou?
Where is the flight of thy fleet wings?
Dread are the mountains of the air, and the bottomless seas unplumbed,
terrible the oceans and the lofty isles,
and the distances no eye may comprehend —
but not all the heavens seem so wide and chill,
as the long white road from hence away.
It wanders up and down the bosom
of this our Mother Earth;
it is gone into the dusk —
and I may not follow it.
Dread are the mountains of the air,
and in the day I long unquenchably —
— O canst thou see?
O canst thou see the end of that long homing road?
The stars, and the belated moon;
The unutterable glory of the sun, are nought to me
for I would follow down that gloaming road
back home to her down paths behind the outer hills
and I may not yet, my swallow.

I may not flee, as thou,
tracking the splendour of the orient sun.
O swallow, swallow, who is calling me? —
and the echo of the voice comes over the wide earth
along the white road home —
and the long road goes backward in the dusk,
And I may not follow it.

It is probably wise not to take 'black swallow' in line 1 of both texts too literally. Although there is such a bird as a Black Swallow, it is not seen in England; the typical English swallow (*Hirundo rustica*) is predominately blue. But any swallow, or a related bird such as a martin, recognizable by its distinctive tail, will appear black silhouetted against the sky. Tolkien addresses a swallow because it is a familiar, and seemingly fearless, migratory bird, resident in the summer but wintering usually in southern Africa, a long journey twice each year ('broad is the face of the Earth', A5, B6). Flocks of swallows historically tended to arrive in England in March or April, and leave in September or October. Tolkien, in Bedford in July 1915, was only some sixty miles away from Edith Bratt in Warwick, but it was a 'long road' while he was bound by military law.

The language and nature of Tolkien's poem recall those of yet another verse he would have met within *The Princess* by Tennyson:

'O Swallow, Swallow, flying, flying South,
Fly to her, and fall upon her gilded eaves,
And tell her, tell her, what I tell to thee.

. . . .

'O Swallow, Swallow, if I could follow, and light
Upon her lattice, I would pipe and trill,
And cheep and twitter twenty million loves.

'O were I thou that she might take me in,
And lay me on her bosom, and her heart
Would rock the snowy cradle till I died.

Tennyson's poem was widely popular, inspiring art and musical adaptations. The English Romantic poet Samuel Taylor Coleridge had earlier composed lines with a similar sentiment, in 'Something Childish, but Very Natural':

If I had but two little wings
And were a little feathery bird,
To you I'd fly, my dear!
But thoughts like these are idle things,
And I stay here.

A19: Mount Everest, the world's tallest mountain, had not yet been climbed in 1915.

A32: Apparently later, Tolkien wrote 'ramparts' below 'cincture', but did not strike through the latter. 'Ramparts' is used in text B (l. 32).

A41: 'Waters of the sky did glister clear' originally read 'waters of the sky shimmered and glistened clear'.

A58: 'Lofty isles' originally read 'archipelagoes'.

A61: Tolkien marked this line to break at 'up and down | the bosom of this', but queried his decision. In text B, the line breaks at 'up and down the bosom | of this'.

A65–6: Tolkien marked the first of these lines to break at 'grey rains | as they spill', but queried his decision. In text B, the line breaks after 'spill'. Here 'as they spill from an o'erflowing bowl' was emended from '[tipped >] spilling from [the >] an o'erflowing bowl'.

B33–45: As first written, these lines were much later in the poem, after 'and I may not follow it' (l. 78).

B45: As written, this line is followed by five lines not included in our transcription. Tolkien struck through the final two of these; he did not strike through the first three, but omitted them from his numbering scheme, and therefore we have presumed that he meant them to be deleted from the final text. It will be illustrative to give here a portion of the manuscript, from final l. 45 (originally 78), as first constructed and with lines marked for the revised order:

45 and it is odorous until my heart must break.
At night, O swallow, is the Earth most wide and great,
and the dread skies far away,
yet in the night I hope, even though I see thee not,—
for these things thou canst not know
seeing thou hast fled along the pathways of the sun
63 beating the golden spaces with thy dark wings, [*deleted:* my swallow].
82 O canst thou, [*deleted:* swallow, swallow,] see the end of that long homing road?
70 Dread are the mountains of the air, and the bottomless seas unplumbed,
79 Dread are the mountains of the air,
80 and in the day I long unquenchably—
81 —O canst thou see?

B48–9: Tolkien wrote a stray manuscript of these lines on a page otherwise containing early workings for *The Pines of Aryador* (poem no. 37).

B85–7: These lines were written as follows, including line numbering:

85 for I would follow down that gloaming road
87 to paths behind the outer hills
88 and I may not yet, my swallow.

And on the facing page of Tolkien's poetry notebook is:

86 back home to her down paths etc.

We have interpreted Tolkien's intention to be that the addition marked as l. 86 was to replace the underlined words 'to paths' in the line marked '87'. On the preceding full page of manuscript, Tolkien marked '[83 >] 86' next to the line marked '81', '— O canst thou see?' but 'back home to her down paths' clearly does not fit the text at that point.

B90–1: Opposite these lines on the facing page of the notebook are 'she is calling' and 'echo of her voice'. We have taken these to be alternate readings for 'who is calling' ('who' is underlined in the manuscript) and 'echo of the voice' in the final text, but they are not clearly intended revisions. In text A the poem read 'she is calling' and 'her voice'; here Tolkien seems to have tried to focus more on a general longing for home than on his love of a woman.

36

Empty Chapel (?1915)

Written on four integral pages of one of Tolkien's poetry notebooks, and on both sides of an inserted leaf, are undated rough workings for a poem he did not complete, which are too interesting not to include in this collection. We have placed them here because they fall in the notebook between manuscripts of *The Swallow and the Traveller on the Plains* (poem no. 35) and *The Pines of Aryador* (no. 37). If the pages were filled in this order, the work in question would have been composed between late July and early September 1915; and in that case it would seem to be an early response by Tolkien to army life, beyond the drilling and manoeuvres he experienced as an Oxford undergraduate in the King Edward's Horse and the Officers Training Corps. It also seems influenced by a warlike attitude he saw in his fellow soldiers, as well as by his faith as a devout Roman Catholic. One may argue whether he gave the poem the title *Empty Chapel*, but these words are written, isolated from others, on the inserted sheet, and are part of what appears to serve as the poem's first line.

We have transcribed the most significant parts of these papers, in fragmentary form as written, and incorporating Tolkien's marked revisions. It is interesting to note also that on the page with fragment G, Tolkien jotted two columns of words, rhyming with *dark* and *bound*, and that on one page of the notebook he drew a stylized star, which on close examination appears to be a Christmas tree ornament.

[A] I knelt in a silent empty chapel
And a great wood lay around
And a forest filled with a tramping noise
And a mighty drumming sound

[B] O ye warriors of England that are marching dark
Can ye see no light before you but the courage in your heart

[C] O men of England marching in the dark
Most warlike of all peoples of the Earth
Is there no light before you on the land
Nor have ye seen a great star out at sea?
Nor does time shine heavy   o'er thee

[D] Ye children of the fair isles of the north
there your fathers named the dowry of the Queen
Lo war is in your nostrils and your heart
And burning with just anger as of old
Though stunted in dark places far from God
Though cheated and deluded and oppressed
Arise you O ye blind and dumb to war
Come open your eyes and glorify your God
Come sing a hymn of honour to your Queen

[E] I knelt in an empty chapel
and a great wood seemed around
and forest filled with a tramping noise
and throbbing sound of drums.
And wave after wave with rolling speed
I heard armies pass in dark.
The drum would grow in the distance like
a throb leaping from the ground
and come and come for ever
and go roaring on to war
Twas the sound of the armies of Britain
that marched by in the dark
They saw no light in the forest
With courage in their heart
And no one showed them the chapel
Where a simple soldier knelt
So they roared to war unhouseled
unaneled
O ye most mighty men of the island of the north
War is in your nostrils and courage in your heart
Though stunted in dark places
Ye have nigh forgotten God
The faith in your midmost
In the chapel in the wood
A silent empty chapel, that will
hold the world at prayer
Your kingdom grew and prospered and
Ye coltered o'er the Earth

The light of the faith it was in you in old days of [*illegible*]
But God's altars lie disfigured and
his churches desecrated

[F] Save the little empty chapel in the wood
Ye battle with the outlaws and ye pour your
island blood
For holiness and charity and ye knew not what ye do
Most warlike of all nations ye are blinded look to might
ye know not all your evil and still less ye know your good
Ye think not ill of foemen, but ye think ill of yourselves
Ye know not all your glory, yet ye know not what ye lack
O turn into the chapel and put by your unbelief
Or leave your sects and ugliness your dreary 'business' spirit
O think of what ye are the provider of all men
O weep for what ye have been blind foolish among men

[G] I kneel in an empty chapel and a great wood lies around
and before it fills with a tramping noise and a throbbing sound
of drums
that echoed from the distance and that rolls along the ground
and in long wave after long wave a countless army comes
and the drums and the drums they go rolling in the night
and the companies behind them

'The dowry of the Queen' in line D2 is England, and the Queen is the Virgin Mary, who in medieval times was given this title as England's special protectress. Tolkien himself was particularly devoted to Mary throughout his life. In lines E17–18, one who is *unhouseled* has not received the Eucharist, and one who is *unaneled* has died without receiving Extreme Unction, the sacrament of anointment in the Catholic Church. In Shakespeare's *Hamlet*, the ghost of Hamlet's murdered father tells him: 'Thus was I, sleeping, by a brother's hand | Of life, of crown, of queen at once dispatched, | Cut off, even in the blossoms of my sin, | Unhouseled, disappointed, unaneled'.

C5: Much of our transcription of this line is guesswork. The word (or words) we have read as 'o'er thee' is (or are) widely separated in the manuscript from the word we have read as 'heavy'.

E23: 'Midmost' is our best guess at the final word. Compare, for example, in Tennyson's *In Memoriam A.H.H.*, 'And in the midmost heart of grief | Thy passion clasps a secret joy'.

E28–9: These lines also have required some guesswork, and the final word or words of l. 29 have defeated us. If we are correct about 'coltered', Tolkien evidently is using *colter* (*coulter*), the cutting blade of a plough, metaphorically, i.e. that the kingdom of God has spread across the earth like seeds planted in the soil.

37

The Pines of Aryador · *A Song of Aryador* (1915)

In *The Book of Lost Tales, Part One* Christopher Tolkien states that *A Song of Aryador* (as the poem came to be called) is extant in two copies, one a manuscript dated 12 September 1915, the other a typescript with 'virtually no differences' (p. 138). At that time, he was not aware of other drafts which survive in his father's papers: altogether there are nine full or partial manuscripts, some of which share physical pages, as well as a typescript. The earliest of the texts, without date or title, comprises only ten lines in a rough hand, written on the same stray page as a few lines of a draft of *The Swallow and the Traveller on the Plains* (poem no. 35). We give the former here as A.

[A]

On the hills of Aryador
In the mountains by the shore
Lies a snowy silver floor
O [?manart]
And in the castle of the winds
Sounds the voice of violins

Where in the hills of Aryador
From the blue celestial shore
Sunward climb for ever more
O [?manart]

Only the first two lines of text A survive into later versions. We cannot explain the word we have transcribed as 'manart', but it is certainly one word, not 'man art'.

A longer version of the poem, also without title or date, is on a page of one of Tolkien's poetry notebooks, written over an earlier pencil text erased except for occasional words still faintly visible ('glooms', 'fumes', 'pines'). We give this as text B, as amended in the manuscript apparently at the time of writing. In one corner of the page is a column of words which rhyme with 'lights' (*fights*, *bites*, *whites*, etc.).

[B] In the hills of Aryador
Linger shadows of before.
Strange the murmurs and the song
Of a folk forgotten long.
Dwelling once in Aryador

When the Sun had fared abroad
Through great forests unexplored
And the woods were full of wandering silver lights
There were voices in the fells
And a sound of ringing bells
And a march of shadow-people on the heights
There were gleams of olden fire
And they sang in woodland choir
Amid the many odoured resin fumes

In the mountains by the shore
In forgotten Aryador
There was dancing and was singing
There were ancient footsteps ringing
In the pines of Aryador

And still there are the bells
And voices on the fells
Of homing men as lights begin to burn
In the dwellings of the folk
Down among the beech and oak
Where far below a many waters roar
But the great woods on the height
Look toward the westering light
And whisper in the wind of things of yore

In the hills of Aryador
Linger shadows of before
Strange the murmurs and the song
Of a folk forgotten long
Dwelling still in Aryador
When the valley
There the shadow folk

Here the draft ends, except for three stray lines: 'In the valley | Men are kindling [?tiny] lights | In the dwellings'.

Another text (C) is in the same notebook, on the page facing B, now entitled *The Pines of Aryador*.

[C]

On the hills of Aryador
Where the mountain waters pour
Soft the lights and warm the glooms,
Resin smells and odoured fumes
In the pines of Aryador

*

Do you hear the many bells
Of the goats upon the fells
Where the valley tumbles downward from the pines?
Do you hear the blue woods moan
When the Sun has gone alone
To hunt the mountain-shadows
In the pines

In the pines of Aryador
By the wooded inland shore
Green the lakeward bent and meadows
Fading into jewelled shadows
Of the dusk o'er Aryador

*

He is lost among the hills
And the upland slowly fills
With the shadow-folk that murmur in the fern;
And still there are the bells
And voices on the fells
And Eastward a few stars begin to burn
On the hills of Aryador
Twilight falls as long before
Men go homeward down the ways
Window lights with slender rays
Shine below in Aryador
In the dwellings of the folk
Down among the beech and oak
Where far below a many waters roar
But the great woods on the height

Watch the waning western light
And whisper to the wind of things of yore
When the valley was unknown
And the waters roared alone
And the shadow-folk danced downward all the night

From these first versions it will be seen that, although common elements recur, Tolkien found it hard to find a satisfactory construction; and the order of phrases and choice of words continued to vary as he produced additional manuscripts, some of them heavily worked, in many places indecipherable. The last of these is entitled *A Song of Aryador* in both Modern English and (on a facing page) the equivalent in Old English, *Ān lēoþ Éargedores*, and is dated 'Sep[tember] 12 1915'. Probably in October 1915, Tolkien used the *Song of Aryador* manuscript, further amended, as the basis of a professional typescript, with a few changes of punctuation. We give the typescript text here as D, incorporating two final revisions Tolkien made in manuscript; Christopher Tolkien published the same version in *The Book of Lost Tales, Part One*, p. 139.

[D]

In the vales of Aryador
By the wooded inland shore
Green the lakeward bents and meads
Sloping down to murmurous reeds
That whisper in the dusk o'er Aryador:

'Do you hear the many bells
Of the goats upon the fells
Where the valley tumbles downward from the pines?
Do you hear the blue woods moan
When the sun has gone alone
To hunt the mountain-shadows in the pines?

She is lost among the hills
And the upland slowly fills
With the shadow-folk that murmur in the fern;
And still there are the bells
And the voices on the fells —
And Eastward a few stars begin to burn.

Men are kindling tiny gleams
Far below by mountain-streams

Where they dwell among the beech-woods near the shore,
But the great woods on the height
Watch the waning western light
And whisper to the wind of things of yore,

When the valley was unknown,
And the waters roared alone,
And the shadow-folk danced downward all the night,
When the Sun had fared abroad
Through great forests unexplored
And the woods were full of wandering beams of light.

Then were voices on the fells
And a sound of ghostly bells
And a march of shadow-people o'er the height.
In the mountains by the shore
In forgotten Aryador
There was dancing and was ringing;
There were shadow-people singing
Ancient songs of olden gods in Aryador.'

When making his final revisions to the text, Tolkien also marked two belated changes to the preceding manuscript, as detailed in our notes.

A separate manuscript memo by Tolkien records that *A Song of Aryador* was composed at 'camp Whittington Heath (Lichfield) [*deleted:* Aug] Sept[ember] or Oct[ober]? 1915'. The date 12 September on the final manuscript version of the poem, however, accords with a letter written by Edith Tolkien to her husband on 14 September: having received a copy of the poem, she commented that it was her favourite (of her husband's poetry, or perhaps of poems recently sent to her). 'How can you compose such dainty things', she asked, 'while you're in that old Camp?' (Bodleian Library). In a letter of 2 February 1916, Dora Owen, to whom Tolkien sent some of his verses for her planned *Book of Fairy Poetry*, mentioned *A Song of Aryador* among those she particularly liked.

The name *Aryador* appears in Tolkien's *c.* 1915–19 Qenya lexicon, in the entry for *areandor* or *areanóre*, 'name of a mountainous district, the abode of the Shadow Folk'. But, he adds, the word was 'probably of Ilkorin origin [the language of Elves who in Tolkien's mythology had not migrated west and so were 'not of Kôr'], i.e. *Aryador*, which would be in Q[enya] *Aryar-* or *Aryandor*'. The word *aryan* in Qenya means 'shadow place' (*Qenyaqetsa*, p. 32). The name also appears in

Tolkien's ?1916–17 lexicon of Gnomish, as part of the entry 'Ariodor or Arion{dor}, (Ariador), (Aryador)'. These are glossed as 'names for the commoner *DorLòmin* or *Hithlum*. The name in this form is popularly connected with *armin* ['desert, waste']' but apparently belongs 'to one of [the] *Ilkorin* dialects & means [the] same as *dorlòmin*, etc. Land or Place of Shadow' (*I·Lam na·Ngoldathon*, p. 20).

In an annotated list of names accompanying his early tale *The Fall of Gondolin*, Tolkien wrote: '*Dor Lómin* or the "Land of Shadow" was that region named of the Eldar [the Elves] *hisilómë* (and this means "Shadowy Twilights") . . . and it is so called by reason of the scanty sun which peeps little over the Iron Mountains to the east and south of it' (*The Book of Lost Tales, Part One*, p. 112). In *The Book of Lost Tales* Tolkien wrote of the great migration of elves from Middle-earth, where they awoke, to Valinor in the west of the world:

> Grievous had been their march, and dark and difficult the way through Hisilómë the land of shade. . . . Indeed long after the joy of Valinor had washed its memory faint the Elves sang still sadly of it, and told tales of many of their folk whom they said and say were lost in those old forests and ever wandered there in sorrow. Still were they there long after when Men were shut in Hisilómë by Melko, and still do they dance there when Men have wandered far over the lighter places of the Earth. Hisilómë did Men name Aryador, and the Lost Elves did they call the Shadow Folk, and feared them. [*The Book of Lost Tales, Part One*, pp. 118–19]

We are inclined to think (though of course cannot be certain) that *The Pines of Aryador* or *A Song of Aryador* was originally an expression of various ideas and images which had occurred to Tolkien, proceeding maybe from the name *Aryador*, and which in turn informed the history of Elves and Men in his mythology. The earliest workings of the poem (A) are no more than a confusion of thoughts. Then in the first long text (B) Tolkien focused on the 'shadow-people on the height', their dancing and singing in the pines, while the 'homing men' of line 22 are evidently 'the folk' who dwell 'Down among the beech and oak' (in D20, only 'beech-woods'). But in C, although the 'shadow-folk' are present, the point of view has become that of men who 'go homeward down the ways'; and this persisted to the final version, by which point Tolkien emphasized the distance between Men, or of the man speaking in dialogue, and the mysterious, unseen shadow-folk in the hills 'singing | Ancient songs of olden gods'.

In line 12 of both the final manuscript and the typescript, 'She' is a late change from 'He', reflecting, perhaps, or anticipating, the association in Tolkien's mythology of the Sun with a female, Urwendi (earlier Urwen), one of the lesser 'gods'.

A5: There is an actual 'castle of the winds', Castell y Gwynt, a pinnacle of Glyder Fach in Snowdonia, north-west Wales.

B5: 'Once' originally read 'still'.

B12–14: Tolkien added these lines to the draft manuscript.

B14: 'Odoured resin' presumably refers to the smell of pine resin (but compare C4, 'Resin smells and odoured fumes', which separates 'smells' and 'fumes'). Tolkien omitted this imagery by text D.

B22: Tolkien wrote 'And' in the margin, presumably as a tentative revision for 'Of'.

B29: Tolkien seems to have considered whether to begin this line with 'Where' and 'For', both words struck through.

B32: 'Of a' appears (beneath a heavy strike-through) to have been a revision of 'Or of'.

B33: Near this line, not necessarily an alternate reading, is 'Sing the pines'.

B34: 'When' originally read 'How'.

C2: Written next to this line, apparently considered as a replacement (compare text D), is 'In the mountains by the shore'.

C12: Written next to this line is 'In the winds'. 'In the pines' originally read 'In the pines of Aryador'.

C13–17: Tolkien added these lines in revision.

C22: Following this line, but deleted, was 'of men that wend them homeward'. Following C24 are four lines too heavily struck through to decipher, except that one includes 'Men go homeward'; compare C26, 'Men go homeward down the ways'.

C27: 'And' is written in the margin next to the head of this line.

C29: 'In mountain' is written next to the head of this line.

C37: 'Then' is written next to the head of this line.

D6: In the preceding manuscript, this line read originally 'But do you hear the many bells'.

D9: In the preceding manuscript, 'blue woods' is spelled 'blue-woods', with a hyphen. We are inclined to think that Tolkien is referring, not to any particular species of pine, but to the blue appearance of woods seen from a distance.

D12: Tolkien marked 'He is lost' to be changed to 'She is lost' in both the typescript and the preceding manuscript.

D13: In the manuscript, this line read originally 'And the valley slowly fills'.

D17: The reading here, beginning 'And', is that of the manuscript as first written, but there Tolkien marked 'And' to be changed to 'While'.

D20: In this line, the manuscript has 'beechwoods', as one word without a hyphen.

D30: In the manuscript, 'Then' originally read 'There'.

D31: Tolkien altered this line in the typescript from 'And a mystic sound of bells', but marked no change to the manuscript.

D33: In the manuscript, 'In' originally read 'From'.

38

Dark Are the Clouds about the North (1915)

With this poem Tolkien again expressed (as in *Thoughts on Parade*, no. 35) the sorrow he felt at being separated from his beloved Edith. Lichfield, where he was billeted at the time of writing (probably September 1915) is in the north relative to Warwick, where Edith lived. The earliest manuscript of the work (A), given here as amended, has no title and is struck through. On the same sheet is a list of rhyming words (*one*, *sun*, *done*, *fun*, etc.).

[A]

The clouds are dark about the North,
a pale flare's in the sky;
Orion with his flaming belt
strides dazzlingly by —
and can you see the same far light
and swinging constellations bright
far off where you and I
sped swiftly once on silver streams
in a slender boat all oared with dreams
and golden in the sun
Dark are the lands 'tween you and me
and the upland air goes bitterly
and the Earth is wide and dim —
yet do I hear the whispering leaves
of poplars, or among the eaves
the swallows answer to the call
of our old morning blackbird singing
singing and at grey dawn winging
toward the murmuring poplars tall?
Do you hear him at the window
when the dawn goes up the skies
and remember other mornings
with the sunlight on your eyes,
now that days are all gone empty
and you wander all alone
where the poplar leaves are falling,
and the grey winds faintly calling
and the autumn swallows flown

Now that days are all gone lonely
do you stand beside the door
to watch the red sun sinking
and the eastern stars come winking
up the world's edge as of yore?
Here the clouds are round the North
and a glimmer's in the sky
and Orion is sloping slowly
from his splendour up on high
Dark and [*sic, for* are] the lands 'tween you and me
and the upland air goes bitterly

Four manuscripts of the poem and associated workings followed this initial version. They are not entirely consistent in the progression of texts, but on the whole we think we have determined their correct order. The second draft (i.e. the manuscript following on text A) was written out with more confidence, and with enough differences from text A that we give it here, as B, with notes regarding the third draft (which we will identify as text B[1]). Tolkien still had not given his poem a distinct title.

[B]

Dark are the clouds about the North
and a pale flare's in the sky:
Orion with his flaming belt
strides dazzlingly by: —
O can you see the same far light
and swinging constellations bright
afar where you and I
sped swiftly once on silver streams
in a slender boat all oared with dreams
and golden in the sun?
Dark are the lands 'tween you and me
and the upland air goes bitterly,
and the long night has begun —
yet do I hear the whispering leaves
of poplars and among the eaves
the swallows answer to the call
of our old morning blackbird singing,
singing and with grey dawn winging
toward the murmuring poplars tall?
Do you still hear him at the window
when the dawn creeps up the skies

and remember other mornings
with the sunlight on your eyes,
now that days are all gone empty
and you wander all alone
where the poplar leaves are falling
and the grey winds faintly calling
and the autumn swallows flown?
Now that days are all gone lonely
do you stand beside the door
and watch the red sun sinking
and the eastern stars come winking
up the world's edge as of yore?
Here to northward is all clouded
dark are the clouds about the North
and a glimmer's in the sky
and Orion's sloping slowly
from his splendour up on high —
Dark are the lands 'tween you and me
and the upland air goes bitterly.

Following the second and third drafts, Tolkien wrote out his poem again, with minor differences, most notably lines 8 and 9 which are marked to be reversed in order, but this text ends with line 24 ('with the sunlight on your eyes'). If it is not a fragment, it may be that Tolkien considered making his work shorter – probably the former, as the final manuscript of the poem, and two succeeding typescripts, continued to develop the longer text.

The final manuscript was the first to include a title, *Dark Are the Clouds about the North*, though Tolkien seems to have added it after writing out the poem proper. After the text was typed for the first time, he wrote the title on the ribbon copy and a carbon copy. The manuscript also has the inscription 'Sep[tember] 14 '15', and the ribbon copy of the penultimate, professional typescript 'Whittington Heath Lichfield Oct[ober] 1915'. Tolkien made several, identical revisions to the manuscript and to both copies of the typescript, described below in our notes. These were incorporated in a final typescript (C).

[C] Dark are the clouds about the North
    And a pale flare's in the sky,
As Orion with his flaming belt
    Strides dazzlingly by: —

O! can you see the same far light
And swinging constellations bright
    Afar, where you and I
Beyond the weir of silver streams
In a sunlit boat all oared with dreams
    Went gliding up the mere?
Dark are the lands 'tween you and me
And the upland air goes bitterly;
It sighs among the withered heath,
    And in its breath I seem to hear
Old voices, and the whispering leaves
Of poplars; while among the eaves
    The swallows answer to the call
Of our old morning blackbird singing,
Singing, and with grey dawn winging,
    Warbling us a madrigal.

Perhaps you hear him at the window
    Still when dawn goes up the skies,
And remember other mornings
    With the sunlight on your eyes,
Now that our days are all gone empty
    And you wander all alone
Where the poplar leaves are falling
And the grey winds sadly calling,
    And the autumn swallows flown.
Now that the days are all gone lonely
    Do you stand beside the door,
And watch the red sun sinking
And the Eastern stars come winking
    Up the world's edge as of yore?

Dark are the clouds about the North
    And a glimmer's in the sky,
And Orion slowly sloping
    From his splendour up on high:
Dark are the lands 'tween you and me
And the upland air goes bitterly.

The first line, 'Dark are the clouds about the North', entered as an alteration in the second manuscript (B), its first word now emphasizing darkness rather than clouds. Darkness and light recur throughout the poem, as contrasts: dark clouds, dark lands, dim Earth, starlight and sunlight. One instance came and went: in the second manuscript, Tolkien replaced 'And the Earth is wide and dim' (A13) with 'And the long night has begun', but in the next manuscript he deleted the new line and restored the earlier.

Orion is one of the most prominent of the winter constellations in the northern hemisphere. Named after a mythological hunter, its star-picture is predominantly imagined to be a man with a wide stance wearing a sword and carrying a club. Its most recognizable feature is a 'belt' of three stars in a short, straight line. In *The Lord of the Rings* (bk. I, ch. 3) Orion is called Menelvagor, 'the Swordsman of the Sky' with a 'shining belt', and in 'The Silmarillion' it is one of the signs set in the heavens by Varda, kindler of the stars: when the Swordsman first strode across the sky, the Elves woke in Middle-earth. In *Dark Are the Clouds about the North* Orion begins ('with his flaming belt | Strides dazzingly by') and ends ('sloping slowly | From his splendour up on high') a cycle of visibility, rising and then setting as the night passes.

Tolkien reworked lines 8–10 several times. In text A, lines 8–9, 'sped swiftly once on silver streams | in a slender boat all oared with dreams', were originally 'in a golden boat all oared with dreams | beneath a vanished sun', but were amended in the process of writing to accommodate 'golden' and 'sun' in line 10, 'and golden in the sun'. In the fourth, fragmentary manuscript, Tolkien altered and reordered lines 8–10 as 'In a slender boat all oared with dreams | Sped swiftly once o'er [silver >] golden streams | [And golden in the Sun? >] And down a silver weir'. Then in the fifth manuscript these reached the final text, with 'sunlit' replacing 'slender'. It was also in this fifth version that Tolkien introduced 'It sighs among the withered heath', final line 13. The first typescript was made from the final manuscript before revision. Apparently one of its last changes was in line 37, in which 'sloping slowly' became 'slowly sloping'.

'Withered heath' may allude to Whittington Heath, Lichfield, where Tolkien was stationed at the time of writing. The landscape of the heath would not have been literally withered in September or October, unless overrun by troops and vehicles; but Tolkien may have meant 'withered' to reflect his mood, so far from Edith. A 'withered heath' would also come to figure in workings for *The Book of Lost Tales*: 'A great battle between Men at the Heath of the Sky-roof (now the Withered Heath), about a league from Tavrobel' in Tol Eressëa (*Book of Lost Tales, Part Two*, p. 284). Still another, the Withered Heath by name, in *The Hobbit* is said to be the home of the Great Worms or dragons in the Grey Mountains of Middle-earth, marked on maps and mentioned in the dwarves' song 'The wind was on the withered heath, | but in the forest stirred no leaf' (no. 110).

With this poem, Tolkien returned to imagery first conveyed in *Morning* (no. 1), with a blackbird singing at dawn among poplars, and to the swallows singing in the eaves of the later (May 1915) version *Morning-song* and of *Thoughts on Parade*. The slender (or sunlit) boat 'all oared with dreams' is a poetic vision, but the concern with which Tolkien revised this part of the poem suggests that it may refer also to an actual outing, or outings, by boat made by Tolkien with Edith a year or two earlier in Warwick. Among Tolkien's early sketches is one of Warwick Castle as seen from under Castle Bridge (Catherine McIlwaine, *Tolkien: Maker of Middle-earth* (2018), p. 15), clearly made while on the water. The castle is near an ancient weir or low dam (see C8) across the River Avon; an element of the name *Warwick* is Old English *wer* 'weir'. In writing of the 'weir of silver streams', did Tolkien recall David Garrick's ode, 'Thou soft flowing Avon, by the silver stream, | Of things more than mortal thy Shakespeare would dream'?

Tolkien sent *Dark Are the Clouds about the North* with other poems to G.B. Smith in October 1915. Smith replied on 24 October that he had 'never read anything in the least like them, and certainly nothing better than the best. . . . "Dark are the clouds about the North" is very fine indeed. You have all the fluency and delicacy which goes with the perfection of style, and I wait only to see the things published.' On 26 October Tolkien wrote to Edith, referring to the poem as 'the sad one I wrote for you darling', and commenting that he was pleased with Smith's appraisal of it: 'I am always pleased when he is pleased for he is usually rather critical' (Bodleian Library).

A13: Tolkien seems to have considered 'plain' as a substitute for either 'wide' or 'dim'.

A25–6: Immediately before these lines, Tolkien wrote, but struck through, 'and our dream oars cast aside? | Do you watch the sun'.

A27: 'Grey winds' originally read 'autumn winds'.

A28: This line originally read 'and the blackbirds long have flown'. In draft, it was followed by five lines which Tolkien struck through:

> now that days are all gone lonely
> do you watch the red sun fall
> and the stars we watched together leap to flame
> do you hear the old sea calling on the shore we stood of old
> do you hear me calling

Tolkien then restored the line 'now that days are all gone lonely' as he continued the cancelled draft on a second page.

A36: 'Sloping' originally read 'going'.

B7: Next to this line Tolkien wrote 'far off', which was the reading in text A, before he changed it to 'afar'. It seems that he was of two minds about it; but he kept 'afar' in B^1.

B8: Tolkien also considered 'once swiftly sped' rather than 'sped swiftly once'.

B13: Next to this line in text B Tolkien wrote 'warbling us', apparently the first hint of 'Warbling us a madrigal' added to later versions. Immediately before this line, he wrote, but struck through, 'And the weary Earth is dim'. In the third draft (B^1), the line originally read 'For the long night has begun', altered to 'and the Earth is wide and dim'.

B14: In B^1 Tolkien changed 'yet do I hear' to 'but I seem to hear'. But also, on the facing page of his poetry notebook, he played with an extension of this and following lines: 'Yet I seem to hear in [its > breaking] voices [?] | Old laughter and — | of poplars while among leaves'.

B19: In B^1 Tolkien changed 'toward the murmuring poplars tall' to 'warbling us a madrigal'.

B27–8: In B^1 Tolkien wrote next to l. 27 'omit?' and on the facing page of his notebook drafted 'moist winds greyly calling | and the winds of autumn moan'.

B34: This line replaced 'Here the clouds are round the Northern [?heath]'. It is not clear in the manuscript, however, if Tolkien intended it to stand, as it is omitted in the next draft (B^1).

B40: After this line, Tolkien wrote another, 'and moans [?]', as if he were going to continue the poem, but struck it through.

C8: There is a weir (low dam) also across the Withywindle in the poem *Bombadil Goes Boating* (no. 186).

C14: In the final manuscript and the penultimate typescript, Tolkien changed 'Yet in its breath' to 'And in its breath', as in C.

C20: The mention of a madrigal recalls again the early poem *Morning* (*Morning Song*), which at one stage was called *Madrigal*.

C25: In the final manuscript this line read 'Now that [*added:* our] days are all gone empty', continued in text C. Compare 'now that *the* days are all gone empty' (our emphasis) in B.

C37: In the final manuscript and the ribbon copy of the corresponding typescript, 'Orion' reads 'Orion's' (= 'Orion is'), but in the carbon copy typescript Tolkien changed 'Orion's' to 'Orion'. In the final manuscript and the carbon copy, 'sloping slowly' is revised to 'slowly sloping', but not in the ribbon copy.

39

The Lonely Harebell · *Elfalone* (1915–18)

Tolkien wrote the earliest manuscript of this work quickly in one of his poetry notebooks; we have transcribed this as text A. At first it did not have a title, and tailed off after only twenty-seven lines. Further rough workings, with revisions and repetition, are on a facing page.

[A]

O sing me a song of the mighty Earth
my home sing to me. Ease my pain
Tell of the glorious western sun and
the misty autumn skies aflame
Tell of things that move the heart
Recall the spell of a swaying harebell
That the wind has caught on the shaven turf
Of cliffs that lean to the sea
Tell how it echoes the surf below
And the sound of pebbles and foam
Distilled in its delicate bell a strain
Hollow and murmurous strangely sweet
Open and free as the low [?thin] wind
That brushes the springy turf
Glory and loveliness everywhere
Winds and flowers and rain
Hark what I tell of the lonely harebell
That swung on the windy plain.
The last of the summer's magic flowers
It sprung on a slender stem
And all you could see was its delicate bell
Starred at the rim and tenderly slim
like a trumpet from elfinland
Windily swinging and fairily ringing
Chimes too faint to hear
For melody unhummable
a deaf deluded mortal ear

A second, substantially different manuscript text followed, given below as B. Now called *The Lonely Harebell,* Tolkien wrote it beside a column of words rhyming with 'own' (*bone*, *blown*, *cone*, etc.).

[B] I started to sing of the great wide earth
To sing me a song for the ease of pain
The light of the western Sun
Filling the misty skies with flames:
For sorrow was singing in my heart
When her windy voice most sweetly came —
All to herself she was singing a song
For all hearts' ease alone – alone.
Caught by a wind that brushed the turf
On a cliff that leaned to the sea
A music she made that was all her own
A tune from the echoes of long white surf
And the sound of pebbles and foam
Wove such a spell as a swaying harebell
Only can weave and can weave alone
Distilled in her delicate bell a tune
Hollow and murmurous strangely fair
Open and free yet a mystery
From wind on the turf and the seaward air

Glory and loveliness everywhere
Wind and flowers and rain
Were caught in the spell of the lonely harebell
Aswing on the windy plain
Most magic of all is this thoughtful flower
Sprung on so slender a stem
That all you can see is her tremulous bell
Starred at the rim and tenderly slim
Like a trumpet of some blue gem
Windily swinging and fairily ringing
Chimes too faint to hear
Save rarely it be by a lonely sea
When Autumn is creeping near
And sorrow is singing in your heart
And open is your ear.

The latter part of this text too is associated with further workings, which begin:

Glory [*in the margin:* Wonder] and loveliness everywhere
Wind and flowers and rain
Hark what I tell of a lonely harebell

That swings on a windy plain
The last of the summer's magic flowers
O secret and magical fairy flower
Is [or Was] sprung on a slender stem
That all you could see was a delicate bell
Starred at the rim and tenderly slim
Like a trumpet of some blue gem
Windily swinging and fairily ringing
Chimes too faint to hear

Tolkien seems to have struggled to find a consistent rhyme scheme, and to decide when to use internal rhyme (such as *tell/harebell* and *rim/slim*). He continued to work on the poem for the next two or three years, through another four complete drafts. One of these, a fair copy with 'The Lonely Harebell' written with decorative capitals, is given here as text C.

[C] I started to sing to myself alone,
    to make me a song for the ease of pain
Watching the light of the westering Sun
    filling the misty skies with flame:
For sorrow was singing in my heart
    when her windy voice most sweetly came —
— All to herself she was singing a song
    for all hearts' ease — alone, alone.
Caught by a wind that brushed the turf
On a cliff that leaned to the sea below
    a music she made that was all her own
A song from the echoes of long white surf
And the sound of pebbles and foam below;
Wove such a spell as a swaying harebell
    Only can weave and must weave alone;
Distilled in her delicate bell a tune,
A far-away murmur of melody fair
    Open and free yet a mystery
From the wind on the turf and the seaward air.

    Wonder and loveliness everywhere,
        Wind and flowers and rain
    Were caught in the spell of the lonely harebell
        Aswing on the windy plain.
    O secret and magical fairy flower

Sprung on so slender a stem,
That all you can see is her tremulous bell
Starred at the rim and tenderly slim
Like a trumpet of some blue gem,
She is windily swinging and fairily ringing
Chimes too faint to hear
Save rarely it be by a lonely sea
When autumn is creeping near
And sorrow is singing in your heart
And open is your ear.

Inscribed later at the top of this manuscript is '[written in] Hospital Birm[ingham] Nov[ember] 1916 (part f[ounded] on matter wr[itten at] Lichfield Sep[tember] 1915 Insp[ired at] Cromer 1914)'. We cannot explain why Tolkien visited Cromer, a popular Norfolk seaside resort town, presumably in the autumn of 1914 (text A, line 4, has 'misty autumn skies'), nor why during his visit he was inspired to write a poem; the prospect of Cromer, perched on cliffs above golden sands, undeniably suits Tolkien's words. And although he chose to date the work from 1914, we can find no evidence that he began to write *The Lonely Harebell* until the following year at the earliest. He was indeed at Lichfield, in Staffordshire, in September 1915, where he had been posted for army training; and as we comment in our Introduction, it seems to have been a meeting there on 25–6 September 1915 with his TCBS friends Rob Gilson, G.B. Smith, and Christopher Wiseman – their so-called 'Council of Lichfield' – which encouraged him to write, or at least was a factor in advancing his work as a poet. In November 1916 he was in hospital in Birmingham suffering from trench fever, and able to revisit some of his verses in a sort of leisure (see also no. 44).

Having finished manuscript C, he wrote out another version, with rhyming possibilities for 'heart' (*art*, *cart*, *chart*, etc.), 'came' (*aim*, *blame* . . .), and 'pain' (*plain*, *slain* . . .). In this text, partially transcribed below as D, he reversed the order of lines 9 and 10 (to 'On a cliff that leaned to the sea below | Caught by a wind that brushed the turf'), and altered the poem from line 20 to the end, the whole now comprising thirty-five lines:

[D]

Wonder and loveliness everywhere
Essence of dews and winds and rain
Were caught in a spell by the lonely harebell,
And music heard once and never again.

O secret and magical fairy flower
    Few are there hear her tender knell
    Few are there see her sapphire shell.
Diaphanous, slim, with a starry rim,
    A thin little trumpet, a pale blue gem
    Sprung on a slender and elfin stem
Windily swinging and fairily ringing
    Her chimes are too faint to hear
Save rarely it be by a lonely sea
    When autumn is creeping near,
And sorrow is singing in your heart,
    And open is your ear.

Tolkien then substantially revised his new text, further re-ordering lines, omitting five lines from the centre (14–19, from 'Wove such a spell' to 'seaward air'), and adding a new line after 'foam below' (line 13), among other alterations. Additional, apparently later workings on the verso of manuscript D are especially concerned with the last part of the poem; among these, two sections are of particular interest:

Then when the sun is going down
[*deleted:* Maybe [*deleted:* you] her voice will]
Maybe a murmur of melody fair
Will come [*deleted:* to you] or [*deleted:* tossed]
    a delicate threadlike tune
[*deleted:* Brushing the turf]
Maybe her voice on the seaward air
Will [*deleted:* [*illegible*] the rough]
[? Ring through] the turf may be and yet
That secret and magical flower
Clasped with green on thread unseen

Or faraway thread
of delicate tune
will come o'er the turf
down the sea wall
may be her voice you'll hear
Maybe you'll hear and then forget

Yet another manuscript of *The Lonely Harebell*, which we will call D[1] for reference, is similar in its text to manuscript D and is evidently later, as it does not contain the passage 'Wove such a spell . . .' deleted from the initial text D; but in line 10, 'Caught by a wind that brushed the turf' has changed to 'In a whispering wind that brushed the turf', and line 15 (to be compared with line 21 in text D) reads 'Essence of wind, and dews, and rain', not 'Essence of dews and winds and rain'.

The order of revisions on manuscript D, relative to changes in later versions, is not clear: it may be that D[1] was written out before Tolkien made some of his changes to D or workings on the verso of D. The verso of manuscript D[1] likewise is filled with drafting for *The Lonely Harebell*, which led to the final manuscript, and thence to a typescript (E, below) incorporating a few last changes. On this manuscript Tolkien originally wrote the title *The Lonely Harebell*, but revised it to *Elf-alone* and then to *Elfalone*. The typescript has the title *Elf-alone*, likewise amended to *Elfalone*.

[E]

I began to sing to myself alone,
    To make me a song for the ease of pain,
Watching the light of the westering sun
    Filling the misty skies with flame;
For sorrow was singing in my heart
    When her windy voice most sweetly came —

*

All to herself she was singing a song
    For all hearts' ease, alone, alone;
On a cliff that leaned to the sea below
    A music she made that was all her own,
A song from the echoes of long white surf
Caught by the whispering seaward turf.

Of the sound of pebbles and foam below,
    Of wind in the grass and falling rain,
Feet of the fairies that come and go,
    Musics heard once and never again,
Of these did the lonely harebell weave
A song for the ease of hearts at eve.
Hark! when the sun is going down,
    Maybe a murmur of melody fair
Or far-away thread of a delicate tune
    Will come o'er the turf on the listening air —
Maybe her voice you'll hear; and yet
Maybe you'll hear and then forget.

Clasped with green on a thread unseen
She sways in her lonely tower;
From her starry rim comes a ringing dim —
The voice of an elfin flower.
Few are there see her pale blue bell,
Few are there hear her tender knell.

*

Windily swinging and wistfully ringing
Her chimes are too faint to hear,
Save rarely it be by a lonely sea
When Autumn is creeping near,
And sorrow is singing in your heart,
And open is your ear.

With this version, Tolkien divided the poem neatly into sestets, but also into three sections, with the first and last stanzas standing by themselves. Three of the six final stanzas (2, 4, and 5) have the rhyme scheme ABCBDD; the others vary (ABCDED, ABABCC, ABCBDC).

The manuscript of this text includes another later inscription by Tolkien explaining the history of the poem, '[written] 1914–1916, Rewr[itten] 1918 Cromer, Hosp[ital] Birm[ingham and] farmhouse near Easington York[shire]', but also – separated from the inscription – the date '1917'. Still unfit for general service due to his bout with trench fever, in mid-November 1917 Tolkien was transferred to the Royal Defence Corps in Easington, on the Holderness peninsula in Yorkshire, and returned to Thirtle Bridge Camp in late February or early March 1918. The typescript of version E was made using the purple ribbon associated with the early 1920s when he was at Leeds.

Tolkien remarked to his son Christopher that the ancient name *harebell* 'meant the *hyacinth* not the *campanula*. *Bluebell*, not so old a name, was coined for the campanula, and the "bluebells" of Scotland are, of course, not the hyacinths but the campanulas' (24 December 1944, *Letters*, p. 151). In contemporary England *harebell* is sometimes associated with the wild hyacinth (*Scilla nutans*), but usually refers to *Campanula rotundifolia*, which has a slender stem and usually pale blue bell-shaped blooms in late summer. A common wildflower, it may be found colonized in cracks of cliff faces ('On a cliff that leaned to the sea below'). The notion of the harebell ringing or chiming comes naturally from floral 'bells'.

Tolkien's use of *fairy*, *fairily* (in the manner of a fairy), *elfin*, and *elfinland* reflects a folk connection between fairies and the harebell, which among many other names is called 'fairies' thimble'. Diminutive fairies (or 'elves') have long been associated with flowers, most famously and influentially in Shakespeare's *Midsummer Night's Dream*, and interest in them was particularly strong in the Victorian and Edwardian period. (The flower fairies popularized by Cicely Mary Barker were an extension of this interest, but first appeared only in 1923.) In Tolkien's conception, however, the harebell as a 'fairy flower' or 'elfin flower' is not one in which a fairy or elf lives, but is itself a weaver of spells, whose magic can ease a sorrowful heart. Within traditional flower symbolism, the harebell has meanings from eternal love to death; Tolkien seems concerned only with its beauty within the English landscape and the poet's emotional response.

Why, though, is the speaker of the poem sorrowful, in need of 'ease of pain'? If the work is autobiographical, an obvious answer would be that the war in Europe had begun (in August 1914), and Tolkien felt detached from his former life, his future uncertain. When he began to compose *The Lonely Harebell* he was either still working to finish his degree at Oxford while under pressure to enlist, or he had his commission and was in the thick of training if not yet in battle. Towards the end of the period he notes in his inscriptions (1914–18) he was still on medical leave, far from the terror of the trenches in France though still subject to return if and when he regained his health. But he and Edith had had their first child – John, born on 16 November 1917 – and new life is always reason to hope for the better.

The harebell, 'lonely' presumably in the sense of 'solitary', perhaps reflects a solitariness or loneliness in Tolkien too, such as he displayed in poems we examined earlier. But does the curious title *Elf-alone* (or *Elfalone*) refer to the 'elfin' flower or to the speaker? Loneliness, and harebells, appear also in the contemporaneous *Kortirion among the Trees* (no. 40), set in 'the inmost province of the fading isle | Where linger yet the Lonely Companies'; there

> drowsy summer by thy streams
> Already stoops to hear the mystic player
> Pipe out beyond the tangle of her forest dreams
> The long thin tune that still do sing
> The elfin harebells nodding in a jacinth ring
> Upon the castle walls. . . .

B1: The word 'lands' is written above 'earth'.

B11: Below this line is written '(of its far off moan)'.

B12: Below 'tune' is written 'song'.

B24: Next to this line are alternate workings, among which is the phrase 'secret and magical fairy flower'.

E4: In the manuscript of this version, Tolkien wrote 'western' rather than 'misty' before correcting himself.

E6: The final line of the first stanza is indented in the typescript, and in the preceding manuscript. In all other stanzas of this text, the final line is not indented.

E19: In the manuscript, 'Hark!' at the beginning of this sentence was written 'Heark!' before correction.

E28: In the manuscript, 'The voice of an elfin flower' originally read 'O secret fairy flower'.

E31: In the manuscript, 'Wistfully' originally read 'fairily'.

40

Kortirion among the Trees · *The Trees of Kortirion* (1915–?62)

Christopher Tolkien included three versions of this lengthy and textually complex poem in *The Book of Lost Tales, Part One*, noting that its 'very earliest workings (November 1915) . . . are extant, and there are many subsequent texts' (p. 32). The early workings, thirteen manuscript pages in pencil, do not provide a complete text, and are often no more than Tolkien setting down thoughts as they came to him. Parts are illegible, and many words, lines, and sections are struck through. Here, as text A, we have transcribed, as best we can make them out and with Tolkien's revisions indicated, three pages of the rough workings, their most coherent portion. Tolkien inscribed the first of the pages '1' and 'Kortirion', a title perhaps for the poem as a whole; the second '2' with the word 'beech'; and the third simply '3'.

[A] 1

O faded [*above:* saddest] town upon a little hill
Even memory is fading [*above:* dreaming] in your ancient gates
Your castle frowning o'er the gliding water
that winds and falls tween elm trees to the western sea
remembers not itself [?on the] long days
— a sight for the [grey > good] men of new dark towers
a hostel for the cold men from across the sea
whose [?harsh] [?same] tongue and [?quiet] [?] [?beauty]
And yet [*above:* but have] already I do love you more than all the silver towers there are

The fragrance lingering in curious name
of street or lane, the long walls and the
way your streets do suddenly and swift
become open [meadow >] meads as of the [*deleted:* ?shadow] unseen
quit of your vanished walls still sundered
of the [little >] builded homes from the wide [?outer] lands
Sights I see while pacing down your ways
I see elsewhere and often more clothed in joy and radiance

Nowhere more wonderful [does the great bear glitter >] do the seven lampads of the silver bear
[*deleted:* ?hang] appear or the twinkle of a few
stars above dark yews to hang above your walls
[And rooks are >] And great trees [?down] up
behind into the sky [?barely] luminous with [?frosty] autumn
Then [?west] and are still [?only] oershadows
the queen and jewel of the land of elms
Alalminōre as the fairies call it Land of Elms

2

In summer are they full sailed shroud above shroud
[*deleted:* like the clothed masts of great green galleons]
And all through strange sweet sad October [?do they]
The naked winter coming
[*deleted:* But after] [*above, deleted:* Then on] Allhallows whose bright biting days
Then is the wide [*above:* air] full of yellow fluttering like a flock of bird [*sic*]
that fly towards the bosom of the earth
and all their small leaves fall
and soon they stand unclothed
Then have I seen Orion rising slow or the
bright Pleiades above him caught in the tracery of [?their]
filmy boughs or hang above a poplar desolate and bare
[*deleted:* O ?Kortirion ?fairest ?call [*deleted:* you] and Citadel of the World]
[above: Kortirion] Set in a wooded emerald in the heart of that most [?dead] isle
of all the fair earth the isle alone where [?dwell] the elves and [?fairies] [*damaged by fold:* Winter ??? ?inner lands ???]
Spring knows thee sweet for spring is ever fair among the trees
And [*above:* drowsy] summer by the stream doth often stoop [?only] to hear
some long thin half heard tune that still do sing
the elfin harebells nodding in a jacinth ring
upon the castle walls and the mowing of the lush
[*marked to be moved, and deleted:* ???ly here her stars are ?fules of great ?light]
[*deleted:* grasses of thy meads sends up an odour and noise enchanting]

[*deleted:* thy] whose [*deleted:* grand] [?was ?bees] and in the [?magic]
nights of flitting moths and strange pale lights
[*deleted:* A ??? and ??? awaking longer dawns]
But autumn is the season of my heart, befitting thy
[*deleted:* ???] forgetful melancholy
The long stranded mists and
sense of a great pomp departing the trees [?channel]
fading trees with leaves the whispering [?fall]

3

Like vessels floating trim afar down golden seas
leaving forever far behind great crowded [?ports]
wherein her crews awhile held gorgeous festival
but now like ghosts are wafted by slow winds
[out west >] across the ocean of oblivion
Splendid are the dark days and ever [?lighting] [?brights]
[*deleted:* Orion paces up the sky [*above:* until] golden the moon]
and seven lampads of the Silver Bear grew strangely bright
Bare are the trees become and all thy glory gone
Cold are thy humble streets and windy squares
But yet I would I never need see other towns or spires
I need not know the desert and the red palace of the sun
The great seas or the magic isles;
[*deleted:* The cities before where ?all your eyes]
No bells across the [central >] jolly plains need ring
for here I am content
In a small old town upon a little hill
set midmost of the Land of Elms within a [*sic*] the fairies isle
[*margin:* a] Here I am content for [*below*: and] all I love dwells here
Kortirion in Alalminore, land of Elms
(The fading fairies and the lonely elves)

On the first and second of these pages Tolkien also wrote lists of rhyming words: *bill, chill, drill* . . . , *bars, cars, chars* . . . . At the head of the first sheet, in four lines, are the earliest workings for *Narqelion* (poem no. 41), and the inscription 'For the 4 | Warwick | East Caravan | R B S | Grove of Birds'. 'The 4' may be the four key members of the TCBS, Rob Gilson, G.B. Smith, Christopher Wiseman, and Tolkien himself. Edith Bratt lived in Warwick from 1913 to 1916, and the poem is dedicated to that town on one of its copies (as below). Warwick was founded in 914 upon a hill north of the River Avon, which flows through the town to the south-west and is idealized in the poem as the 'Gliding Water'. Warwick's castle 'frowning o'er' the river is a notable landmark which Tolkien drew. Peacocks, which feature in this poem, have long been resident within the castle walls, where their walk can be slow and precise, especially by the males when they spread their long, brilliantly coloured tail-feathers (see the device Tolkien drew for Warwick, labelled 'Cortirion', probably in late 1916 or the first half of 1917, reproduced in McIlwaine, *Tolkien: Maker of Middle-earth*, p. 213).

Although there is more than one desert structure known as the 'Red Palace' (in Kuwait and Saudi Arabia, for example), Tolkien could, perhaps, be referring (in A68, etc.) to Petra in Jordan, dramatically carved into pink sandstone cliffs. At this stage in writing he may have meant 'magic isles' only in a generic sense, but later to indicate (as Christopher Tolkien seems to have thought) the Magic Isles set to guard the Bay of Faëry, or Bay of Eldamar, in Valinor after the destruction of the Two Trees.

Christopher Tolkien describes the first version of the poem printed in *The Book of Lost Tales, Part One* as 'its pre-1937 form, when only slight changes had yet been made', that is, before a major revision took place in 1937. There are in fact among Tolkien's papers five complete manuscripts and two complete typescripts of *Kortirion among the Trees* (as the work came to be called, more briefly *Kortirion*) which precede the typescript (C, below) that was the source of the published 'pre-1937' version; and these eight iterations comprise only the first of three texts in the poem's evolution. In all of its texts, *Kortirion* exists in five manuscripts and ten typescripts, only some of which were known to Christopher when he prepared *The Book of Lost Tales, Part One*. Here, as B, we give the earliest extant complete version, written by Tolkien in ink over partly erased pencil, incorporating changes he made in the course of writing. It includes two interludes, each labelled 'Song', and in the top margin of its second page, above the first 'song', is a separate title, *The Elms of Kortirion*. Three of its five manuscript pages also include lists of trial rhymes.

[B] O fading town upon a little hill
Old memory is waning in your ancient gates;
Your robe gone grey, your old heart almost still;
Your castle only frowning ever waits

And watches how among the elms
The Gliding-water leaves these inland realms
And slips between long meadows to the western sea —
Still bearing downward over murmurous falls
One year and then another to the sea;
And quietly thither have a many gone
Since first the fairies built Kortirion.

O spiry town upon a windy hill
With sudden-winding alleys shady-walled
(Where even now the peacocks pace a stately drill,
Majestic, sapphirine and emerald)
Behold thy girdle of a wide champain,
Sunlit and watered with a silver rain
And richly wooded with a thousand whispering trees
That cast long shades in many bygone noons
And murmured many centuries in the breeze.

You are the city of the Land of Elms
— Alalminōre in the Faery Realms.

Sing of thy trees old old Kortirion
Thy oaks, and maples with their tassels on
Thy singing poplars and the splendid yews
That crown thy aged walls and muse
Of sombre grandeur all the day;
Until the twinkle of the early stars
Entangles palely in their sable bars
Until the seven lampads of the silver bear
Swing slowly in their shrouded hair
And diadem the fallen day.
O towery citadel of the world
When bannered summer is unfurled
Most full of music are thy elms
— A gathered sound that overwhelms
The chanting of all other trees.
Sing then of elms, beloved Kortirion;
When summer crowds their full sails on
Like clothed masts of verdured ships
—A fleet of galleons that proudly slips
Across long emerald seas.

Thou art the inmost province of the fading isle
Where linger yet the Lonely Companies: —
Still undespairing do they sometimes slowly file
Along its paths with plaintive harmonies
The holy fairies and immortal elves
That dance among the trees and sing themselves
A wistful song of things that were and could be yet.
They pass and vanish in a sudden breeze,
A wave of bowing grass — and we forget
Their tender voices like wind-shaken bells
Of flowers; their gleaming hair like golden asphodels.

Spring makes thee happy; spring is ever fair
Among the trees; but drowsy summer by thy streams
Already stoops to hear the mystic player
Pipe out beyond the tangle of her forest dreams
The long thin tune that still do sing
The elfin harebells nodding in a jacinth ring
Upon the castle walls
Already stoops to listen to the clear cold spell
Come up her sunny aisles and perfumed halls
— A sad and haunting magic note
Or strand of silver glass remote.

Song [lines 65–82]

Then all thy trees old township on a windy bent
Do loose a long sad whisper and lament
For going are the gorgeous hours; th'enchanted nights
When flitting ghost-moths dance like satellites
Round tapers in the moveless air:
And doomed already are the radiant dawns;
The fingered sunlights dripping on long lawns;
The odour and the slumbrous noise of meads
When all the sorrel flowers and plumed weeds
Bow down before the scythers share.
Yet all through strange sad sweet October
Still the wide-umbraged elm will not unrobe her:
Then comes All Hallows with bright biting days
And all the moist autumnal ways
Are dappled with her scattered tears

While thy wide air grows full of leafy wings
Her amber fluttering flock of golden things
That fly like birds across the misty meres.

Yet is this season dearest to my heart
Most fitting to the little faded town
With sense of splendid pomps that now depart
In sound of sweet and lonely sadness echoing down
The paths of stranded mists: O gentle time
When the late mornings are bejewelled with rime
And the blue shadows gather on the distant woods
The fairies know thy early crystal dusks
And put in secret on their twilit hoods
Of grey and filmy purple and long bands
Of frosted starlight sewn by silver hands.

They know the season of the brilliant night
The Pleiads tangled with sable lace
Of naked elms; how long-limbed poplars catch the light
Of golden moons with blackbarred face
O fading fairies and most lonely elves
Then sing ye sing ye to yourselves
A woven song of stars and gleaming leaves
Then whirl ye with the sapphire winged winds
Then do ye pipe and call with heart that grieves
To sombre men: Remember what is gone
The magic sun that lit Kortirion.

Song [lines 105–125]

Now are thy trees old old Kortirion
Seen rising up through pallid mists and wan
Like vessels floating vague and long afar
Down opal seas beyond the shadowy bar
Of cloudy ports forlorn
The[y] leave behind for ever havens thronged
Wherein their crews awhile held feasting long
And gorgeous ease who now like windy ghosts
Are wafted by slow airs to empty coasts:
There are they sadly glimmering borne
Across the plumbless ocean of oblivion.
Bare are thy trees become Kortirion

And all their summer glory swiftly gone.
The seven lampads of the silver bear
Are waxen to a wondrous flare
That flames above the fallen year
Though cold thy windy squares and humbled streets:
Though elves dance seldom in thy pale retreats
Save on some rare and moonlit night
A flash a whispering glint of white.
Yet would I never need depart from here.

I would not know the desert or red palaces
Where dwells the sun; the great seas or the magic isles
The forests or the mighty
of great pines on mountain terraces
Or calling plaintive down the windy miles
Touches my heart no distant bell that rings
In golden cities of the Earthly kings.
Here do I find a haunting ever near content
Set midmost of the Land of withered Elms
Alalminore of the Faery realms:
Here circling slowly in a sweet lament
Linger the holy fairies and immortal elves
Singing a song of faded longing to themselves.

Following the first section of the manuscript B (to line 22) are six lines of a rejected 'song', struck through:

Sing of thy trees old old Kortirion
When summer crowds their full sails on
And open to the winds high shroud on shroud
[And >] A green and leafy cloud
About the shapely [masts >] spars of his green galleon
The [?masted] earth

At the head of the fifth manuscript page are four short lines in pencil: 'Save in some | rare and moonlit night | a flash a whispering | ghost of white'.

On 26 November 1915 Tolkien wrote to Edith Bratt from Cannock Chase in Staffordshire, where army camps had been built:

> I have written out a pencil copy of 'Kortirion'. I hope you won't mind my sending it to the T.C.B.S. I want to send them some-

> thing: I owe them all long letters. I will start on a careful ink copy for little you now and send it tomorrow night, as I don't think I shall get more than one copy typed (it is so long). No on second thoughts I am sending you the pencil copy (which is very neat) and shall keep the T.C.B.S. waiting till I can make another. [*Letters*, p. 4]

There are two pencil manuscripts of *Kortirion* among Tolkien's papers, each very similar to the other in regard to text, following on from B. One, however, which for reference we will call B^1, was written with at least moderate speed, with corrections, erasures, and further workings, and is by no means 'very neat'. After the title on its first page Tolkien wrote '(Warwick)', and above the title are the Qenya words 'Narqelion laktu y·aldalin Kortirienwen' ('Autumn among the Trees of Kortirion'). In this manuscript, Tolkien first labelled the parts of the poem as 'First Verses', 'First Song', 'Second Verses', and so forth.

The other instance, which we will call B^2, and which has on its first page the bracketed phrase 'A Song of Autumn in an Inland Town' following the title *Kortirion among the Trees*, is indeed very neatly written, and from its fold marks and wear to the text at those points (later repaired by Tolkien by overwriting in ink) once passed through the post. This could have been the copy sent to Edith, or it may be that that manuscript has been lost, and the copy in hand (now, uniquely among the *Kortirion* manuscripts, preserved among the Tolkien Family Papers in the Bodleian Library) was that which Tolkien sent to his TCBS friends. In any case, B^2 appears to be a fair copy of B^1 before the latter underwent further revision. Remarkably, evidently at some later date, Tolkien vigorously cancelled in ink most of the part labels ('First Verses', etc.). B^2 also includes ironic marginal comments by the poet, noting 'alternate' readings of some words which, in his handwriting, could be misread, such as 'abbeys' for 'alleys'.

These new manuscripts do not differ in their texts appreciably from B, except in two places which Tolkien reworked, and would continue to rework in subsequent versions. One area of concern was a section of eight lines in the 'Second Song' (B75–82):

> Yet all through strange sad sweet October
> Still the wide-umbraged elm will not unrobe her:
> Then comes All Hallows with bright biting days
> And all the moist autumnal ways
> Are dappled with her scattered tears

While thy wide air grows full of leafy wings
Her amber fluttering flock of golden things
That fly like birds across the misty meres.

In B[1] Tolkien altered and expanded these lines to read:

Strange sad October robes her dewy furze
In netted sheen of gold-shot gossamers,
And then the wide-umbraged elm begins to quail;
Her mourning multitude of leaves go pale
Seeing afar the icy shears
Of Winter and his blue-tipped spears
March up behind All-Hallows frosty sun;
Then all the glistening ways of moist autumn
Are dappled with her amber tears,
And thy wide air grows full of leafy wings
Her fluttering flock of yellow things
That rustle sadly to the bosomed Earth
Or fly like birds across the misty meres.

Still not satisfied, Tolkien wrote four alternate lines on the same page of B[1]:

Thy moist autumnal ways Kortirion
Then dapple with her [little >] dripping [amber>] dropping
tears
And thy wide air grows
Her golden flock of fluttering things

And in B[2] he changed the passage further:

Strange sad October robes her dewy furze
In netted sheen of gold-shot gossamers,
And then the wide-umbraged elm begins to fail;
Her mourning multitude of leaves go pale
Seeing afar the icy shears
Of Winter and his blue-tipped spears
March up behind All-Hallows' frosty sun:
Thy moist autumnal ways Kortirion
Then dapple with her amber tears,
And thy wide air grows full of leafy wings,
Her fluttering flock of yellow things

That rustle sadly to the bosomed Earth
Or fly like birds across the misty meres.

An intermediate version of this expanded text among the sheets of Tolkien's early workings is also worth quoting:

Strange [sweet >] sad October robes her dewy furze
In netted sheen of gold shot gossamers
Then the wide-umbraged elm begins to fail;
Her mourning multitude of leaves go pale
(And whispers sadly that the winter nears)
Seeing afar the blue-tipped spears
Of Yelin marching with his icy [*or* wintry] fears
Behind Allhallows bright and biting days
Then all the moist autumnal ways
Are amber dappled with her scattered tears
And thy wide air grows full of leafy wings
Her yellow fluttering golden things
That rustle sadly to the bosomed Earth
Or fly like birds across the misty meres

Yelin is Qenya for 'winter'. In the manuscript 'Yelin' is underlined for replacement by 'winter' written in the margin.

The second area of revision comprised three lines in the 'Third Verses' (B95–97):

The Pleiads tangled with sable lace
Of naked elms; how long-limbed poplars catch the light
Of golden moons with blackbarred face

In B[1] these became:

The Pleiads netted in the sable lace
Of naked elms; how long-limbed poplars bar the light
Of golden moons with orbéd topaz face.

But again, Tolkien wrote a new revision at the foot of the page:

When nakéd Elms entwine the Pleiades
In laced boughs where amber moons alight
Enrondured in the limbs of poplar trees

The original reading in B[1] ('The Pleiads netted', etc.) continued unchanged, however, in B[2].

Tolkien sent a manuscript of *Kortirion* to Rob Gilson probably in late November 1915. Gilson replied on 26 December that, having read it several times, he had forwarded the copy to Christopher Wiseman, and had made another copy to send to G.B. Smith. Gilson liked the work immensely, though he found its vocabulary obtrusive, akin to precious stones, and failed to understand why it was divided into verses and songs. On 12 January 1916 Smith informed Tolkien that he carried his copy of *Kortirion*

> about with me like a treasure. I must beyond measure congratulate you – it is a great and a noble poem, worthy I am sure of the place of which it is reminiscent [Warwick]. I hope Dicky [R.W. Reynolds] has seen it, and anyone else with a good knowledge of what verse – or rather poetry – ought to be. . . . Its effect, coming at a period of depression, has been wonderful. . . . You know as well as I do, my dear John Ronald, that I don't care a damn if the Bosch drops half-a-dozen h.e.s [high-explosive shells] all round and on top of this dug-out I am writing in, so long as people go on making verses about 'Kortirion among the Trees'. . . . [Bodleian Library]

Wiseman wrote to Tolkien on 4 February that he was 'braced' by *Kortirion*, the copy of which he returned with his letter. He had feared, from earlier verses, that Tolkien's poetry would always be 'freakish', however clever and beautiful it may be, but *Kortirion* was a different matter. Tolkien had now, Wiseman felt, at last left his caverns lit by magnesium wire (as Wiseman characterized *Copernicus and Ptolemy*, poem no. 20) – a comment which led to a rebuttal by Tolkien and an argument about his sensibilities and his treatment of his invented world against that of God's creatures.

Edith Bratt, having received her copy of the poem, wrote to Tolkien on 27 January 1916 that she loved it, 'especially as it was written in "our" little house' in Warwick (Bodleian Library). Tolkien's former teacher, R.W. Reynolds, also read a copy and liked it. 'It didn't grip me, it is true,' he admitted, feeling 'somehow that there was more form than content about it, but that may be my own fault. It shows, I think, even more strikingly than anything else I have seen of yours that feeling for the beauty of words and delight in it that struck me so much in the first things you let me see. It is very charming and it marks, I think, a distinct advance in technique!' though it struck him as lacking in interest – perhaps, he thought, a reflection of his mood (Bodleian Library).

Tolkien inscribed the next manuscript in sequence 'Nov[ember] 21–28 [1915]' and '(dedic[ated] to Warwick)'; for reference we will call this B^3. This text also has an added title, *Cor Tirion þǣra bēama on middes*, Old English 'Kortirion among the Trees'. It closely follows B^2, but again, portions were reworked. Where B^2 reads

March up behind All-Hallows' frosty sun:
Thy moist autumnal ways Kortirion
Then dapple with her amber tears,
And thy wide air grows full of leafy wings,
Her fluttering flock of yellow things
That rustle sadly to the bosomed Earth
Or fly like birds across the misty meres.

B^3 became

March up behind All-Hallows frosty sun;
Thy moist autumnal ways Kortirion
Then dapple with her dripping tears
And thy wide air grows full of leafy wings,
Her golden flock of fluttering things
That rustle sadly to the bosomed Earth,
Or fly like birds across the misty meres.

Tolkien struck these lines through and wrote below them:

Marching relentlessly behind the Sun
Of bright All-Hallows, — then their hour is done;
Or slowly dripping like pale amber tears,
Or wanly beating golden leafy wings
They fill the wide air with yellow flutterings:
Sadly they rustle in the bosom'd Earth,
And fly like birds across the misty meres.

This reading arose only after four trials which Tolkien wrote on the facing page of his poetry notebook:

[a] Marching unconquerable behind the Sun
Of bright All-Hallows: then their hour is done;
Then slowly dripping the pale amber tears

Strewing the brown paths they're trodden in the mould,
Or wanly beating wings of leafy gold
They rustle sadly to the enbosomed Earth,
Or fly like birds across the misty meres.

[b] Their wanly beating leafy wings of gold
They sadly rustle to the enbosomed Earth
And fly like birds across the misty meres
Or slowly dripping like pale amber tears
Strewing the brown paths they've trodden in the mould

[c] Marching unconquerable upon the Sun
Of bright All-Hallows: then the brown paths run
With autumn waters 'neath the frosty skies,
And dapple with her amber tears;
The wide air suddenly is filled with leafy wings,
Her fluttering flock of yellow things

[d] Marching relentlessly behind the sun
Of bright All-Hallows: — then their hour is done;
Or slowly dripping, like pale amber tears,
As wanly beating golden leafy wings
They fill the wide air with yellow flutterings:
Sadly they rustle in the bosomed Earth
Or fly like birds across the misty meres.

We have transcribed these in the order they appear on the notebook page, but this was not their order of composition. Trial 'c' appears to have been the first attempt, written opposite the deleted lines of manuscript B^3 across the notebook spread, and preceded by its date and place of working, August 1916 in Thiepval, France. Tolkien was there with his battalion from 24 to 26 August, when he also wrote *The Thatch of Poppies* and *The Forest Walker* (nos. 49, 50). Trial 'd' was written a year later, dated 'Aug[ust] 1917' and inscribed 'Hosp[ital]. Hull'; by then, Tolkien had been invalided home to England with trench fever, and was in the Brooklands Officers' Hospital in Hull, Yorkshire. He struck through trials 'b', 'c', and 'd', but adopted much of 'd' for the later lines written in B^3. Trial 'a', as noted below, is the latest of the four.

The first typescript of the poem, which Tolkien based on B^3, has the title *Kortirion among the Trees*, with the bracketed subtitle *A song of autumn in an inland Town* (capitalized thus) last seen in B^2 but here struck through. Tolkien later inscribed at the top of the first page 'Nov[ember] 1915' and 'Warwick, a weeks leave from camp – written largely in a house in Victoria Street & in one in Northgate St[reet]'. At that earlier date, Edith Bratt was living in a rented house in 15 Victoria Street, Warwick; the latter address may be that of a guest house where Tolkien stayed. The 'Marching' lines given above as trial 'a', labelled by Tolkien 'correct version', appear in the typescript as a manuscript correction, amended yet again and truncated:

Marching unconquerable upon the sun
Of bright All Hallows — then their hour is done,
And wanly borne on wings of amber pale
They beat the wide airs of the fading vale
And fly like birds across the misty meres.

In manuscript B^1, as we have described, three lines in the 'Third Verses' became by revision:

When nakéd Elms entwine the Pleiades
In laced boughs where amber moons alight
Enrondured in the limbs of poplar trees

These carried into B^3, but there Tolkien again amended them, to

When naked elms entwine in cloudy lace
The Pleiades and long-armed poplars bar the light
Of golden-rondured moons with glorious face

In making the first typescript, he altered these lines to

The Pleiads netted in the sable lace
Of naked elms; how long-limbed poplars bar the light
Of golden moons with orbèd topaz face.

Curiously, this is the original reading in B^1 and the sole reading in B^2, though it is clear that the first typescript was based on the intervening manuscript, B^3. It may have been Tolkien's thought to return to the earlier form; in the event, he struck through the old reading in the typescript and substituted the revision from B^3.

In a second typescript, dating probably to around 1924, he incorporated changes added to the first typescript and made a few further, minor revisions. As in the first typescript, the second includes the bracketed subtitle *A song of autumn in an inland Town*, here struck through as well.

There is also in Tolkien's archive another manuscript of *Kortirion*, inscribed 'For England'. It is written on squared paper in a relatively legible hand, and has the appearance of a fair copy. On the basis of certain readings, it seems to fall between the two typescripts met so far; for example, in the 'Second Verses' the new manuscript has 'Already stoops to *hear* the clear cold spell' (emphasis ours), as in the second typescript, whereas the first typescript had 'Already stoops to *listen to* the clear cold spell'. But the further manuscript also contains passages which do not appear in any other version of *Kortirion*. In the 'Second Song':

Strange sad October robes the dewy furze
In netted sheen of gold-shot gossamers —
Then the wide-umbraged Elm begins to fail,
Her mourning multitude of leaves go pale
Seeing afar the icy shears
Of winter midst his blue-tipped spears
That press behind All-Hallows' frosty sun.
Thy moist autumnal ways, Kortirion,
Then dapple with her amber tears
And thy wide air grows full of leafy wings
Her yellow flock of fluttering things
That rustle sadly to the bosomed Earth
Or fly like birds across the misty meres.

Tolkien marked the four lines from 'That press behind . . .' to '. . . leafy wings' to be replaced by five lines:

Marching unconquerable upon the Sun
Of bright All-Hallows: then the brown paths run
With autumn waters neath the frosty skies
And dapple with her amber tears
The wide air suddenly is filled with leafy wings

In the 'Third Verses', in this version labelled 'The third song and last', the first line reads 'Then are thy trees, belov'd Kortirion'. The preceding typescripts have 'Now are thy trees, old old Kortirion'.

We come now, in the evolution of *Kortirion*, to the 'pre-1937' version mentioned earlier; another typescript, it was made by Tolkien on his Hammond typewriter, perhaps as a clean copy before revising the work further. Its first sheet is inscribed, twice, 'To a ruined town in Britain the Blessed', and also 'written 1915–16 revised 1937'. Its text, which follows closely the second of the earlier typescripts, is given here (C) as typed, before subsequent revisions.

[C] *The First Verses*

O fading town upon a little hill,
  Old memory is waning in thine ancient gates,
Thy robe gone grey, thine old heart almost still;
  Thy castle only, frowning, ever waits
And ponders how among the towering elms
The Gliding Water leaves these inland realms
  And slips between long meadows to the western sea —
Still bearing downward over murmurous falls
  One year and then another to the sea;
And slowly thither have a many gone,
Since first the fairies built Kortirion.

O spiry town upon a windy hill
  With sudden-winding alleys shady-walled
(Where even now the peacocks pace a stately drill,
  Majestic, sapphirine, and emerald),
Behold thy girdle of a wide champain
Sunlit, and watered with a silver rain,
  And richly wooded with a thousand whispering trees
That cast long shadows in many a bygone noon,
  And murmured many centuries in the breeze!
Thou art the city of the Land of Elms,
Alalminoré in the Faery realms.

Sing of thy trees, old, old Kortirion!
Thine oaks, and maples with their tassels on,
Thy singing poplars; and the splendid yews
That crown thine aged walls and muse
  Of sombre grandeur all the day —
Until the twinkle of the early stars
Is tangled palely in their sable bars;
Until the seven lampads of the Silver Bear
Swing slowly in their shrouded hair
  And diadem the fallen day.
O tower and citadel of the world!

When bannered summer is unfurled
Most full of music are thine elms —
A gathered sound that overwhelms
    The voices of all other trees.
Sing then of elms, belov'd Kortirion,
How summer crowds their full sails on,
Like clothéd masts of verdurous ships,
A fleet of galleons that proudly slips
    Across long sunlit seas

The Second Verses

Thou art the inmost province of the fading isle
    Where linger yet the Lonely Companies.
Still, undespairing, do they sometimes slowly file
    Along thy paths with plaintive harmonies:
The holy fairies and immortal elves
That dance among the trees and sing themselves
    A wistful song of things that were, and could be yet.
They pass and vanish in a sudden breeze,
    A wave of bowing grass, and we forget
Their tender voices like wind-shaken bells
Of flowers, their gleaming hair like golden asphodels.

Spring still hath joy: thy spring is ever fair
    Among the trees: but drowsy summer by thy streams
Already stoops to hear the secret player
    Pipe out beyond the tangle of her forest dreams
The long thin tune that still do sing
The elvish harebells nodding in a jacinth ring
    Upon the castle walls;
Already stoops to listen to the clear cold spell
    Come up her sunny aisles and perfumed halls:
A sad and haunting magic note,
A strand of silver glass remote.

Then all thy trees, old town upon a windy bent,
Do loose a long sad whisper and lament;
For going are the rich-hued hours, th'enchanted nights
When flitting ghost-moths dance like satellites
    Round tapers in the moveless air;
And doomed already are the radiant dawns,

The fingered sunlight dripping on long lawns;
The odour and the slumbrous noise of meads,
When all the sorrel, flowers, and pluméd weeds
Go down before the scyther's share.
Strange sad October robes her dewy furze
In netted sheen of gold-shot gossamers,
And then the wide-umbraged elm begins to fail;
Her mourning multitudes of leaves go pale
Seeing afar the icy shears
Of Winter, and his blue-tipped spears
Marching unconquerable upon the sun
Of bright All-Hallows. Then their hour is done,
And wanly borne on wings of amber pale
They beat the wide airs of the fading vale,
And fly like birds across the misty meres.

The Third Verses

Yet is this season dearest to my heart,
Most fitting to the little faded town
With sense of splendid pomps that now depart
In mellow sounds of sadness echoing down
The paths of stranded mists. O! gentle time
When the late mornings are bejewelled with rime,
And the blue shadows gather on the distant woods,
The fairies know thy early crystal dusk
And put in secret on their twilit hoods
Of grey and filmy purple, and long bands
Of frosted starlight sewn by silver hands.

They know the season of the brillant night,
When naked elms entwine in cloudy lace
The Pleiades, and long-armed poplars bar the light
Of golden-rondured moons with glorious face.
O fading fairies and most lonely elves,
Then sing ye, sing ye to yourselves
A woven song of stars and gleaming leaves;
Then whirl ye with the sapphire-wingéd winds;
Then do ye pipe and call with heart that grieves
To sombre men: "Remember what is gone —
The magic sun that lit Kortirion!"

Now are thy trees, old, old Kortirion,
Seen rising up through pallid mists and wan,
Like vessels floating vague and long afar
Down opal seas beyond the shadowy bar
    Of cloudy ports forlorn:
They leave behind for ever havens thronged,
Wherein their crews a while held feasting long
And gorgeous ease, who now like windy ghosts
Are wafted by slow airs to empty coasts;
    There are they sadly glimmering borne
        Across the plumbless ocean of oblivion.
Bare are thy trees become, Kortirion,
And all their summer glory swiftly gone.
The seven lampads of the Silver Bear
Are waxen to a wondrous flare
    That flames above the fallen year.
Though cold thy windy squares and empty streets;
Though elves dance seldom in thy pale retreats
(Save on some rare and moonlit night,
A flash, a whispering glint of white),
    Yet would I never need depart from here.

The Last Verse

I need not know the desert or red palaces
    Where dwells the sun, the great seas or the magic isles,
The pinewoods piled on mountain terraces;
    And calling faintly down the windy miles
Touches my heart no distant bell that rings
In populous cities of the Earthly Kings.
    Here do I find a haunting ever-near content
Set midmost of the Land of withered Elms
(Alalminoré of the Faery realms);
    Here circling slowly in a sweet lament
Linger the holy fairies and immortal elves
Singing a song of faded longing to themselves.

Christopher Tolkien includes this text in *The Book of Lost Tales, Part One*, pp. 33–6.

The original two-page typescript of C is almost obscured by revisions in pencil and ink, made by Tolkien in 1937. Few lines escaped amendment, and some were replaced in their entirety. There is no evidence that *Kortirion among the Trees* was part of the 'Silmarillion' material handed by Tolkien to Stanley Unwin to consider for publication following George Allen & Unwin's success with *The Hobbit* (published 21 September 1937), but it seems possible that he picked it up, at least in passing, when assembling items that autumn prior to meeting Unwin in London on 15 November, and took the opportunity to improve it.

Among Tolkien's papers is a fair copy manuscript in ink (D, below), signed 'J.R.R. Tolkien' at the end, which takes up the text of C as revised. The previous division of the poem into 'Verses' and 'Songs' was now abandoned in favour of a simpler arrangement in three numbered parts, though 'sections' are still implied by varying indentation. Tolkien marked a few further (mostly illegible) changes in light pencil, not included in our transcription (some are indicated in notes at the end of this entry), and he inscribed the words 'Autumn among the Elms' beneath the title and 'Envoy' (i.e. a summation) before the final twelve lines.

[D] I

O fading town upon an inland hill,
    Old shadows linger in thine ancient gate,
Thy robe is grey, thine old heart now is still;
    Thy towers silent in the mist await
Their crumbling end, while through the storeyed elms
The Gliding Water leaves these inland realms
    And slips between long meadows to the Sea,
Still bearing downward over murmurous falls
    One year, and then another, to the Sea;
And slowly thither have a many gone,
Since first the Elves here built Kortirion.

O climbing town upon thy windy hill,
    With winding streets, and alleys shady-walled
Where now untamed the peacocks pace in drill
    Majestic, sapphirine and emerald;
Amid the girdle of this sleeping land,
Where silver falls the rain and gleaming stand
    The whispering host of old deep-rooted trees
That cast long shadows in many a bygone noon,
    And murmured many centuries in the breeze;
Thou art the city of the Land of Elms,
    Alalminórë in the Faery Realms!

Sing of thy trees, Kortirion, again!
The beech on hill, the willow in the fen,
The rainy poplars; and the frowning yews
Within thine aged courts that muse
    In sombre splendour all the day;
Until the twinkle of the early stars
Comes glinting through their sable bars,
And the white moon climbing up the sky
Looks on the ghosts of trees that die
    Slowly and silently from day to day.

O Lonely Isle, here was thy citadel,
Ere bannered summer from his fortress fell.
Then full of music were thine elms:
Green was their armour, green their helms,
    The lords and kings of all thy trees.
Sing then of elms, renowned Kortirion,
That under summer crowd their full sails on,
And clothéd stand like masts of verdurous ships,
A fleet of galleons that proudly slips
    Across long sunlit seas.

II

Thou art the inmost province of the fading isle,
    Where linger yet the Lonely Companies;
Still, undespairing, here they sometimes slowly file
    Along thy paths with solemn harmonies:
The holy people of an elder day,
Immortal Elves, that singing fair and fey
    Of vanished things that were, and could be yet,
Pass like a wind among the rustling trees,
    A wave of bowing grass, and we forget
Their tender voices like wind-shaken bells
Of flowers, their gleaming hair like golden asphodels.

Once spring was here with joy and all was fair
    Among the trees; but drowsy summer by the stream
Already stoops to hear the secret player
    Pipe, out beyond the tangle of her forest dreams,
The long-drawn tune that elvish voices made
Foreseeing Winter through the leafy glade;
    The late flowers nodding on the ruined walls

Already stoop to hear that haunting flute
    Beyond the sunny aisles and tree-propped halls;
For thin and clear and cold the note,
As strand of silver glass remote.

Then all thy trees, Kortirion, are bent,
And shake with sudden whispering lament.
For passing are the days, and doomed the nights
When flitting ghost-moths danced as satellites
    Round tapers in the moveless air;
And doomed already are the radiant dawns,
The fingered sunlight drawn across long lawns;
The odour and the slumbrous noise of meads,
Where all the sorrel, flowers, and plumèd weeds
    Go down before the scyther's share.
When cool October robes her dewy furze
In netted sheen of gold-shot gossamers,
Then the wide-umbraged elms begin to fail,
Their mourning multitudes of leaves grow pale
    Seeing afar the icy spears
Of Winter marching blue behind the sun
Of bright All-Hallows. Now their hour is done,
And wanly borne on wings of amber pale
They beat the wide airs of the fading vale,
    And fly like birds across the misty meres.

III

This is the season dearest to my heart,
    The time most fitting to the ancient town,
With waning musics sweet that slow depart,
    Winding with echoed sadness faintly down
The paths of stranded mist. O gentle time,
When the late mornings are begemmed with rime,
    And early shadows fold the distant woods.
The Elves go silent by, their shining hair
    They cloak in twilight under secret hoods
Of grey and filmy purple, and long bands
Of frosted starlight sewn by silver hands.

And oft they dance beneath the roofless sky,
    When naked elms entwine in branching lace
The Seven Stars, and through their boughs the eye

Stares golden-beaming in the moon's round face.
O holy Elves and fair immortal folk,
You sing then ancient songs that once awoke
Under primeval stars, before the Dawn;
You whirl then dancing with the eddying winds,
As once you whirled upon the glimmering lawn
In Elvenhome, before we were, before
You crossed wide seas unto this mortal shore.

Now are thy trees, old grey Kortirion,
Through pallid mists seen rising tall and wan,
Like vessels floating vague, and drifting far
Down opal seas beyond the shadowy bar
Of cloudy ports forlorn
Leaving behind for ever havens loud,
Wherein their crews a while held feasting proud,
And lordly ease, they now like windy ghosts
Are wafted by slow airs to empty coasts,
And glimmering sadly down the tide are borne.

Bare are thy trees become, Kortirion;
The rotted raiment from their bones is gone.
The seven candles of the Silver Wain,
Like lighted tapers in a darkened fane,
Now flare above the fallen year.
Though court and street now cold and windy lie,
And Elves dance seldom neath the barren sky,
Yet under the white moon there is a sound
Of buried music still beneath the ground:
When winter comes, I would meet winter here.

I would not seek the desert or red palaces
Where dwells the sun, the great seas, or the magic isles,
Or pinewoods piled on mountain-terraces;
And tolling faintly over windy miles
To my heart calls no distant bell that rings
In the crowded cities of the earthly Kings.
For here is heartsease still and deep content,
Though sadness haunts the Land of withered Elms
(Alalminórë in the Faery Realms);
And making music still in sweet lament
The Elves here, holy and immortal, dwell
And on the stones and trees there lies a spell.

Another neatly written ink manuscript followed, from its script and design made soon after D, likewise divided into three numbered parts. We give it here as E, transcribed as Tolkien wrote it, with alterations clearly made in the course of writing but without later amendment. A refinement of D, it has differences both small (marks of punctuation) and large.

Tolkien made many textual changes, apparently *ab initio* while writing out the copy – at least, the alterations are not marked on D, and there is no extant intervening draft. Some are substantive: in several readings, for example, Tolkien changed selected verbs from present to past tense, and certain nouns from plural to singular, such as 'crowd their full sails on' to 'crowded full sail on' (E39) and 'eddying winds' to 'eddying wind' (E103). Probably at a later time, he added a few words or phrases in pencil. It was this version of *Kortirion* which Christopher Tolkien included in *The Book of Lost Tales, Part One,* pp. 36–9, as 'the text of the poem as my father rewrote it in 1937, in the later of slightly variant forms' (p. 36). In the process, Christopher took up most of the pencilled jottings as intended revisions, though they are written generally without existing text being struck through or otherwise marked for change.

[E] I

O fading town upon an inland hill,
    Old shadows linger in thine ancient gate,
Thy robe is grey, thine old heart now is still;
    Thy towers silent in the mist await
Their crumbling end, while through the storeyed elms
The Gliding Water leaves these inland realms,
    And slips between long meadows to the Sea,
Still bearing downward over murmurous falls
    One year and then another to the Sea;
And slowly thither have a many gone,
Since first the Elves here built Kortirion.

O climbing town upon thy windy hill
    With winding streets, and alleys shady-walled
Where now untamed the peacocks pace in drill
    Majestic, sapphirine, and emerald;
Amid the girdle of this sleeping land,
Where silver falls the rain and gleaming stand
    The whispering host of old deep-rooted trees
That cast long shadows in many a bygone noon,

    And murmured many centuries in the breeze;
Thou art the city of the Land of Elms,
Alalminórë in the Fairy Realms.

Sing of thy trees, Kortirion, again:
The beech on hill, the willow in the fen,
The rainy poplars, and the frowning yews
Within thine aged courts that muse
    In sombre splendour all the day;
Until the twinkle of the early stars
Comes glinting through their sable bars,
And the white moon climbing up the sky
Looks down upon the ghosts of trees that die
    Slowly and silently from day to day.

O Lonely Isle, here was thy citadel,
Ere bannered summer from his fortress fell.
Then full of music were thine elms:
Green was their armour, green their helms,
    The Lords and Kings of all thy trees.
Sing, then, of elms, renowned Kortirion,
That under summer crowded full sail on,
And stood like clothéd masts of verdurous ships,
A fleet of galleons that proudly slips
    Across long sunlit seas.

II

Thou art the inmost province of the fading isle,
    Where linger yet the Lonely Companies;
Still, undespairing, here they sometimes slowly file
    Along thy paths with solemn harmonies:
The holy people of an elder day,
Immortal Elves, that singing fair and fay [*sic, i.e.* fey]
    Of vanished things that were, and could be yet,
Pass like a wind among the rustling trees,
    A wave of bowing grass, and we forget
Their tender voices like wind-shaken bells,
    Of flowers, their gleaming hair like golden asphodels.

Once Spring was here with joy, and all was fair
    Among the trees; but Summer drowsing by the stream
Heard trembling in her heart the secret player

Pipe, out beyond the tangle of her forest dream,
The long-drawn tune that elvish voices made
Foreseeing Winter through the leafy glade;
The late flowers nodding on the ruined walls
Then stooping heard afar that haunting flute
[Beyond the sunny aisles and tree-propped halls]
For thin and clear and cold the note,
As strand of silver glass remote.

Then all thy trees, Kortirion, were bent,
And shook with sudden whispering lament:
For passing were the days, and doomed the nights
When flitting ghost-moths danced as satellites
Round tapers in the moveless air;
And doomed already were the radiant dawns,
The fingered sunlight drawn across long lawns;
The odour and the slumbrous noise of meads,
Where all the sorrel, flowers, and plumèd weeds,
Go down before the scyther's share.
When cool October robed her dewy furze
In netted sheen of gold-shot gossamers,
Then the wide-umbraged elms began to fail;
Their mourning multitudes of leaves grew pale,
Seeing afar the icy spears
Of Winter marching blue behind the sun
Of bright All-Hallows. Then their hour was done,
And wanly borne on wings of amber pale
They beat the wide airs of the fading vale,
And flew like birds across the misty meres.

III

This is the season dearest to the heart,
And time most fitting to the ancient town,
With waning musics sweet that slow depart
Winding with echoed sadness faintly down
The paths of stranded mist. O gentle time,
When the late mornings are begemmed with rime,
And early shadows fold the distant woods!
The Elves go silent by, their shining hair
They cloak in twilight under secret hoods
Of grey and filmy purple, and long bands
Of frosted starlight sewn by silver hands.

And oft they dance beneath the roofless sky,
When naked elms entwine in branching lace
The Seven Stars, and through the boughs the eye
Stares golden-beaming in the round moon's face.
O holy Elves and fair immortal Folk,
You sing then ancient songs that once awoke
Under primeval stars before the Dawn;
You whirl then dancing with the eddying wind,
As once you danced upon the shimmering lawn
In Elvenhome, before we were, before
You crossed wide seas unto this mortal shore.

Now are thy trees, old grey Kortirion,
Through pallid mists seen rising tall and wan,
Like vessels floating vague, and drifting far
Down opal seas beyond the shadowy bar
Of cloudy ports forlorn.
Leaving behind for ever havens loud,
Wherein their crews a while held feasting proud
And lordly ease, they now like windy ghosts
Are wafted by slow airs to windy coasts,
And glimmering sadly on the tide are borne.

Bare are thy trees become, Kortirion;
The rotted raiment from their bones is gone.
The seven candles of the Silver Wain,
Like lighted tapers in a darkened fane,
Now flare above the fallen year.
Though court and street now cold and windy lie,
And Elves dance seldom neath the barren sky,
Yet under the white moon there is a sound
Of buried music still beneath the ground.
When winter comes, I would meet winter here.

I would not seek the desert, or red palaces
Where dwells the sun, nor cross the seas to the magic isles,
Nor climb the hoary mountains' stony terraces;
And tolling faintly over windy miles
To my heart calls no distant bell that rings
In the crowded cities of the Earthly Kings.
For here is heartsease still, and deep content,
Though sadness haunt the Land of withered Elms

(Alalminórë in the Faery Realms);
And making music still in sweet lament
The Elves here holy and immortal dwell,
And on the stones and trees there lies a spell.

Here we must record a single page of typescript, headed *Kortirion among the Trees: A Lament for the Dying Elms*, which includes the first four stanzas of the poem (through 'Across long sunlit seas'). For the most part, its text follows D and E, but here Tolkien was moving in certain respects towards a substantial revision in late 1961 or early 1962, and it may be that this fragment dates from that time. In lines 3 and 4, for instance, 'Thy robe' and 'Thy towers' read 'Your robe' and 'Your towers' – compare 'Your stones' and 'Your towers' in F, below – and Kortirion is called the 'high city . . . of the Land of Elms' (in F 'of the Inland Realms'). Next to line 14, Tolkien thought to change the 'untamed' peacocks to 'untaught'; neither idea carried into the next version, though there the peacocks still 'pace in drill'. Most notably, line 11 of D and E, 'Since first the Elves here built Kortirion', was replaced by 'Since first the Edain built Kortirion', using the Elvish (Sindarin) word for 'Men', a feature not found in the initial typescript of the final version of the poem, but only added by amendment.

In late 1961 or early 1962 Tolkien considered *Kortirion* for possible inclusion in *The Adventures of Tom Bombadil and Other Verses from the Red Book* (see poem no. 24). It seems certain that he returned to the poem at this time, and had not continued to work on it after the revision of 1937. The new version, which Christopher Tolkien has called 'almost a different poem' (*The Book of Lost Tales, Part One*, p. 32), survives in Tolkien's papers in three complete typescripts (one is a professional copy of no textual interest), as well as an intermediate revised typescript of the second part only. That there are no manuscript workings may be due to Tolkien suffering from arthritis and fibrositis, with which he had already been afflicted for several years by this time, and which made using a typewriter less taxing than writing with a pen. He sent the poem to his publisher, Rayner Unwin, on 5 February 1962, but thought it too long and too elaborate for the *Bombadil* volume. Unwin agreed, and the work was omitted.

Here we give, as F, the first of the new typescripts, entitled *The Trees of Kortirion*. It is divided into four numbered and named sections: *The Trees* (altered in pencil to *Alalminóre*, Quenya 'Land of Elms', here without a final umlaut); *Narquelion* (with a pencilled gloss, 'Lasselanta', Quenya 'leaf-fall, autumn'); *Hríve* (altered in pencil to *Hrívion*); and *Mettië*. According to Appendix D of *The Lord of the*

Rings, the Quenya name of the tenth month was *Narquelië* ('fading'), the word for 'winter' was *hrívë*, and *lasselanta* was 'used for the latter part of autumn and the beginning of winter'. In the final typescript, Tolkien changed *Mettië* to *Mettanyë*, containing Quenya *metta* 'ending'. Here, for the first time, Kortirion is *leaguered*, or besieged, presumably by time as it awaits its 'crumbling end'.

[F] I. *The Trees*

O ancient city on a leaguered hill!
 Old shadows linger in your broken gate,
Your stones are grey, your old halls now are still,
 Your towers silent in the mist await
Their crumbling end, while through the storeyed elms
The Gliding Water leaves these inland realms
 And slips between long meadows to the Sea,
Still bearing down by weir and murmuring fall
 One day and then another to the Sea;
And slowly thither many years have gone
Since first was builded here Kortirion.

Kortirion! Upon your windy hill
 With winding streets, and alleys shadow-walled
Where even now the peacocks pace in drill
 majestic, sapphirine, and emerald,
Once long ago amid this sleeping land
 Of silver rain, where still year-laden stand
 In unforgetful earth the rooted trees
That cast long shadows in the bygone noon,
 And whispered in the swiftly passing breeze,
Once long ago, Queen of the Land of Elms,
High city were you of the Inland Realms.

In summer still of trees your people sing:
The beech on hill, the willow by the spring;
The rainy poplars, and the frowning yews
Within your aged courts that muse
 In sombre splendour all the day;
Until the firstling star comes glimmering
And flittermice go by on silent wing;
Until the white moon slowly climbing sees
In shadow-fields the sleep-enchanted trees
 Night-mantled all in silver-grey.

Alalminor! Here was your citadel,
Ere bannered summer from his fortress fell;
About you stood arrayed your host of elms:
Green was their armour, tall and green their helms,
    High lords and captains of the trees.
But summer wanes. Behold, Kortirion,
The elms their full sail now have crowded on
Ready to the winds, like masts amid the vale
Of mighty ships too soon, too soon, to sail
    To other days beyond these sunlit seas.

II. *Narquelion*

Here is the inmost province of the fading Isle,
    Where linger yet the Faithful Companies;
Still undespairing here they slowly file
    Along the paths with solemn harmonies:
The Fair, the First-born in an elder day,
    Immortal Elves, that singing on their way
Of vanished things that were, though men forget,
    Pass like a wind among the rustling trees,
A wave of bowing grass, and men forget
    Their distant voices like wind-shaken bells
    Across the Sea, their gleaming hair like golden asphodels.

A wave of bowing grass: now wanes the year;
    A shiver in the reeds beside the stream,
A whisper in the trees — afar they hear,
    Piercing the heart of summer's tangled dream,
The music chill that the herald piper plays,
Foreseeing winter and the leafless days.
    The late flowers trembling on the ruined walls
Already stoop to hear that haunting flute
    Through summer's sunny aisles and tree-propped halls
Winding amid the green with clear cold note
Like a thin strand of silver glass remote.

Now all your trees, Kortirion, are bent
The high-tide ebbs, the year will soon be spent;
And all your trees, Kortirion, lament.
For passing are the days, and doomed the nights
When flitting ghostmoths danced as satellites
    Round tapers in the windless air;

And dimmed already is the shining dawn,
On dewy sward the fingered sunlight drawn;
The Scyther has trodden down the fragrant meads,
And flowers, and sorrel red, and pluméd weeds
    Have fallen to his unrelenting share.
Now cool October robes the dewy furze
In netted sheen of glinting gossamers,
And the wide-umbraged elms begin to fail,
Their mourning multitudes of leaves grow pale,
    Seeing afar the icy spears
Of winter march to battle with the sun
When bright All-Hallows fails. Their day is done,
And wanly borne on wings of amber pale
They beat the moist airs of the fading vale,
    And fall like dying birds upon the meres.

III. *Hríve*

Alas! Kortirion, Queen of Elms, alas!
    This season best befits your ancient town,
With echoing voices sad that slowly pass
    Winding with waning music faintly down
The paths of stranded mist. O fading time,
When morning rises late all hoar with rime,
    And early shadows veil the distant woods!
Unseen the Elves go by, their shining hair
    They cloak in twilight under secret hoods
Of grey, their dusk-blue mantles bound with bands
Of frosted starlight sewn by silver hands.

At night they dance beneath the roofless sky,
    When naked elms entwine in branching lace
The Seven Stars, and through the boughs the eye
    Stares down cold-gleaming in the high moon's face.
O Elder Kindred, fair Immortal Folk!
You sing now ancient songs that once awoke
    Under primeval stars before the Dawn,
You dance like shimmering shadows in the wind,
    As once you danced upon the shining lawn
Of Elvenhome, before we were, before
You crossed wide seas unto this mortal shore.

Now are your trees, old grey Kortirion,
Through pallid mists seen rising tall and wan,
Like vessels vague that slowly drift afar,
Out, out to empty seas beyond the bar
Of cloudy ports forlorn;
Leaving behind for ever havens loud,
Wherein their crews a while held feasting proud
In lordly ease, they now like windy ghosts
Are wafted by cold airs to friendless coasts,
And sad and silent down the tide are borne.
Bare has your realm become, Kortirion,
Stripped of its raiment, and its splendour gone.
The seven candles of the Silver Wain
Like lighted tapers in a darkened fane
Now flare above the fallen year.
The winter comes. Beneath the barren sky
The Elves are silent. But they do not die!
They will not die, and where they waiting dwell
Enduring silence, still I too will dwell:
When Winter comes, I will meet winter here.

IV. *Mettië*

I would not seek the burning domes and sands
Where reigns the Sun, nor dare the deadly snows,
Or in mountains old search for the secret lands
Of men long-lost, to whom no pathway goes;
I heed no call of clamant bell that rings
In the dark towers of the iron kings.
Here on the stones and trees there lies a spell
Of unforgotten loss, of memory more blest
Than mortal wealth. Here undefeated dwell
The Folk Immortal under withered elms,
Alalminorë once in ancient realms.

The Trees of Kortirion is more emphatically associated with 'The Silmarillion' than preceding versions of the poem, though it is still an elaborate portrait of Warwick. Both associations in fact were long established. In Tolkien's earliest conception of the mythology (putting it very simply) the island of Tol Eressëa, to which the wandering mariner Eriol (Ottor Wǽfre, later Ælfwine) comes in *The Book of Lost Tales*, would in time become England, while the Land of Elms in Tol

Eressëa would become Warwickshire, and Kortirion, the town at its centre, would become Warwick. In the first part of the *Lost Tales* the elf Lindo tells Eriol that he has

> crossed the borders of that region that is called Alalminórë or the 'Land of Elms', which the Gnomes call Gar Lossion, or the 'Place of Flowers'. Now this region is accounted the centre of the island, and its fairest realm; but above all the towns and villages of Alalminórë is held Koromas, or as some call it, Kortirion, and this city is the one wherein you now find yourself. Both because it stands at the heart of the island, and from the height of its mighty tower, do those that speak of it with love call it the Citadel of the Island, or of the World itself. [*The Book of Lost Tales, Part One*, p. 16]

Christopher Tolkien notes that 'the great tower or *tirion* that Ingol son of Inwe built and the great tower of Warwick Castle are not identified, but at least it is certain that Koromas has a great tower because Warwick has one' (*The Book of Lost Tales, Part One*, p. 25). Warwick was dear to Tolkien because Edith Bratt lived there from 1913 until their marriage, also in Warwick, in 1916.

Opposite the first page of the 'Nov[ember] 21–28' manuscript of *Kortirion among the Trees* (i.e. B^3) in one of his poetry notebooks, Tolkien wrote in pencil a prose prelude. If we judge correctly from its handwriting, it was set down later than the poem proper, though still relatively early: it would not have been inapt for Tolkien to write 'how is the world's estate fallen from the laughter and loveliness of old' during the years of the Great War. The manuscript of the 'prelude' includes two subsequent changes in ink, shown here in square brackets:

> Now on a time the fairies dwell in the Lonely Isle after the great wars with [Melko >] Hell and the ruin of Gondolin. And they builded a fair city amidmost of that island, and it was girt with trees. Now this city they called Kortirion both in memory of their ancient dwelling of Kôr in Valinor and because this city stood also upon a hill and had a great tower tall and grey that Ingil son of [Inwë >] Ing their lord let raise. Very beautiful was Kortirion and the fairies loved it, and it became rich in song and poesy and the light of laughter; but on a time the great Faring Forth was made and the fairies had rekindled once more the magic Sun of Valinor but for the treason and faint hearts

of men. But so it is that the magic sun is dead and the Lonely Isle drawn back unto the confines of the Great Lands and the fairies are scattered through all the wide unfriendly pathways of the world; and now men dwell even on this faded isle and care nought or know nought of its ancient days. Yet still there be some of the Eldar and the Noldoli of old who linger in the island, and their songs are heard faint about the shores of the land that once was the fairest dwelling of the immortal folk. And it seems to the fairies and it seems to me who know that town and have often trodden its disfigured ways that autumn and the falling of the leaf is the season of the year when maybe here or there a heart among men may be open and an eye perceive how is the world's estate fallen from the laughter and loveliness of old. Think on Kortirion and be sad — yet is there not hope.

Melko (Melkor), the evil Vala, has appeared already in our discussion of Tolkien's poems (no. 31, for example), and we have met Gondolin, another city of the Elves, in connection with *Sea Chant of an Elder Day* (no. 13), and also Kôr (poem no. 30). 'Fairies' was Tolkien's name for Elves in his early writings, though (as here) the two terms were sometimes used simultaneously. The 'Faring Forth' is an expedition by the Elves of Tol Eressëa (the Lonely Isle) to seek others of their kind who had never left the Great Lands to go into the West. To do so, the island itself is drawn across the sea, to the position of England (with Wales and Scotland); but Men entered into Tol Eressëa, and the Elves hid and faded. The 'magic Sun of Valinor' refers to Laurelin, one of the Two Trees that gave light (see poem no. 31) before the celestial Sun and Moon were formed. Tolkien used the word *Eldar* variously, but it came to refer to those elves who left the Great Lands and saw the light of Valinor at Kôr. The Noldoli, or Gnomes, the second kindred of the Elves, came to be called *Noldor* as the mythology developed.

The separate typescript of the second part of the poem, *Narquelion*, as mentioned above, is substantially revised from text F, in particular its third stanza. We transcribe this text as G.

[G] II. *Narquelion*

Alalminórë, green heart of this Isle
    Where linger yet the Faithful Companies!
Still undespairing here they slowly file
    Down lonely paths with solemn harmonies:

The Fair, the first-born in an elder day,
Immortal Elves, who singing on their way
    Of bliss of old and grief, though men forget,
Pass like a wind among the rustling trees,
    A wave of bowing grass, and men forget
Their distant voices like wind-shaken bells
            Across the Seas,
Their gleaming hair like golden asphodels.

A wind in bowing grass! Now wanes the year.
    A shiver in the reeds beside the stream,
A whisper in the trees — afar they hear,
    Piercing the heart of summer's tangled dream,
The music chill the herald piper plays
Foreseeing winter and the leafless days.
    The late flowers trembling on the ruined walls
Already stoop to hear that elven-flute,
    Through the wood's sunny aisles and tree-propped halls
Winding amid the green with clear cold note
Like a thin strand of silver glass remote.

The high-tide ebbs, the year will soon be spent;
And all your trees, Kortirion, lament.
At morn the whetstone rang upon the blade,
At eve the grass and golden flowers were laid
    To wither, and the meadows bare.
Now dimmed already comes the tardier dawn,
Paler the sunlight fingers creep across the lawn.
The days wear on. Gone like moths the nights
When white wings fluttering danced like satellites
    Round tapers in the windless air.
Lammas is gone. The Harvest-moon has waned.
Summer is dying that so briefly reigned.
Now the proud elms at last begin to quail,
Their leaves uncounted tremble and grow pale,
    Seeing afar the icy spears
    Of winter march to battle with the sun;
When bright All-Hallows fades, their day is done,
And wanly borne on wings of amber pale
They beat the cool airs of the misty vale,
    And fall like dying birds upon the meres.

The final typescript of *The Trees of Kortirion*, given here as H, takes up a few pencilled notes for revision in text F, and as for F itself a number of alterations enter the new typescript directly. Christopher Tolkien used this copy as the basis of the third version of the poem published in *The Book of Lost Tales, Part One*, pp. 39–43.

[H] I. *Alalminórë*

O ancient city on a leaguered hill!
    Old shadows linger in your broken gate,
Your stones are grey, your old halls now are still,
    Your towers silent in the mist await
Their crumbling end, while through the storeyed elms
The River Gliding leaves these inland realms
    And slips between long meadows to the Sea,
Still bearing down by weir and murmuring fall
    One day and then another to the Sea;
And slowly thither many days have gone
Since first the Edain built Kortirion.

Kortirion! Upon your island hill
    With winding streets, and alleys shadow-walled
Where even now the peacocks pace in drill
    majestic, sapphirine and emerald,
Once long ago amid this sleeping land
Of silver rain, where still year-laden stand
    In unforgetful earth the rooted trees
That cast long shadows in the bygone noon,
    And whispered in the swiftly passing breeze,
Once long ago, Queen of the Land of Elms,
High City were you of the Inland Realms!

Your trees in summer you remember still:
The willow by the spring, the beech on hill;
The rainy poplars, and the frowning yews
Within your aged courts that muse
    In sombre splendour all the day,
Until the white moon slowly climbing sees
In shadow-fields the sleep-enchanted trees
    Night-mantled all in silver-grey.
Alalminor! Here was your citadel,
Ere bannered summer from his fortress fell;
About you stood arrayed your host of elms:

Green was their armour, tall and green their helms,
High lords and captains of the trees.
But summer wanes. Behold, Kortirion!
The elms their full sail now have crowded on
Ready to the winds, like masts amid the vale
Of mighty ships too soon, too soon, to sail
To other days beyond these sunlit seas.

II. *Narquelion*

Alalminórë! Green heart of this Isle
Where linger yet the Faithful Companies!
Still undespairing here they slowly file
Down lonely paths with solemn harmonies:
The Fair, the first-born in an elder day,
Immortal Elves, who singing on their way
Of bliss of old and grief, though men forget,
Pass like a wind among the rustling trees,
A wave of bowing grass, and men forget
Their voices calling from a time we do not know,
Their gleaming hair like sunlight long ago.

A wind in the grass! The turning of the year.
A shiver in the reeds beside the stream,
A whisper in the trees — afar they hear,
Piercing the heart of summer's tangled dream,
The music chill that the herald piper plays,
Foreseeing winter and the leafless days.
The late flowers trembling on the ruined walls
Already stoop to hear that elven-flute,
Through the wood's sunny aisles and tree-propped halls
Winding amid the green with clear cold note
Like a thin strand of silver glass remote.

The high-tide ebbs, the year will soon be spent;
And all your trees, Kortirion, lament.
At morn the whetstone rang upon the blade,
At eve the grass and golden flowers were laid
To wither, and the meadows bare.
Now dimmed already comes the tardier dawn,
Paler the sunlight fingers creep across the lawn.
The days are passing. Gone like moths the nights

When white wings fluttering danced like satellites
Round tapers in the windless air.
Lammas is gone. The Harvest-moon has waned.
Summer is dying that so briefly reigned.
Now the proud elms at last begin to quail,
Their leaves uncounted tremble and grow pale,
Seeing afar the icy spears
Of winter march to battle with the sun
When bright All-Hallows fades, their day is done,
And borne on wings of amber wan they fly
In heedless winds beneath the sullen sky,
And fall like dying birds upon the meres.

III. *Hrívion*

Alas! Kortirion, Queen of Elms, alas!
This season best befits your ancient town
With echoing voices sad that slowly pass,
Winding with waning music faintly down
The paths of stranded mist. O fading time,
When morning rises late all hoar with rime,
And early shadows veil the distant woods!
Unseen the Elves go by, their shining hair
They cloak in twilight under secret hoods
Of grey, their dusk-blue mantles gird with bands
Of frosted starlight sewn by silver hands.

At night they dance beneath the roofless sky,
When naked elms entwine in branching lace
The Seven Stars, and through the boughs the eye
Stares down cold-gleaming in the high moon's face.
O Elder Kindred, fair immortal folk!
You sing now ancient songs that once awoke
Under primeval stars before the Dawn;
You dance like shimmering shadows in the wind,
As once you danced upon the shining lawn
Of Elvenhome, before we were, before
You crossed wide seas unto this mortal shore.

Now are your trees, old grey Kortirion,
Through pallid mists seen rising tall and wan,
Like vessels vague that slowly drift afar

Out, out to empty seas beyond the bar
    Of cloudy ports forlorn;
    Leaving behind for ever havens loud,
Wherein their crews a while held feasting proud
In lordly ease, they now like windy ghosts
Are wafted by cold airs to friendless coasts,
    And silent down the tide are borne.
    Bare has your realm become, Kortirion,
Stripped of its raiment, and its splendour gone.
Like lighted tapers in a darkened fane
The funeral candles of the Silver Wain
    Now flare above the fallen year.
Winter is come. Beneath the barren sky
The Elves are silent. But they do not die!
Here waiting they endure the winter fell
And silence. Here I too will dwell;
    Kortirion, I will meet the winter here.

IV. *Mettanyë*

I would not find the burning domes and sands
    Where reigns the Sun, nor dare the deadly snows,
Nor seek in mountains dark the hidden lands
    Of men long lost to whom no pathway goes;
I heed no call of clamant bell that rings
Iron-tongued in the towers of earthly kings.
    Here on the stones and trees there lies a spell
Of unforgotten loss, of memory more blest
    Than mortal wealth. Here undefeated dwell
The Folk Immortal under withered elms,
Alalminorë once in ancient realms.

Kortirion in all its versions contains elements of abiding interest to Tolkien. We have mentioned his fondness for Warwick. Then there is nature, represented by a variety of plants, such as asphodel and sorrel ('golden asphodels', B53 etc., suggests the yellow 'King's Spear', *Asphodeline lutea*, and 'sorrel red', F74, is presumably *Rumex acetosella*). In this regard, however, trees are foremost: oaks and maples, beeches and willows, poplars and yews, and elms which are 'Lords and Kings of all thy trees' (D, E37). The tall English elm (see also poem no. 34) was once so common in Warwickshire that hedgerow elms were known as the 'Warwickshire Weed'; hence the poem's

Alalminorë is the 'Land of Elms', and Kortirion the 'Queen of Elms'. Only near the end of Tolkien's life did Dutch elm disease nearly eliminate the elms of Warwickshire, which have been replaced by other species, such as ash. The 'long-limbed' or 'long-armed' poplars of the poem may be the Black poplar (*Populus nigra*), a spreading tree, while the 'singing' poplars could be the Quaking or Common aspen (*Populus tremula*), as in poem no. 1, whose leaves make a sound when they move in the wind.

Tolkien both celebrates trees and uses them to illustrate the change of seasons in Kortirion (Warwick). He alludes most clearly to spring in the earlier texts, in which maples have 'their tassels on' prior to leafing, but he is more interested in summer, when trees gloriously appear in leaf like 'verdured' or 'verdurous' ships with all sails set, and autumn, when the leaves 'fail', and winter, when the trees are stripped of their 'raiment' and appear like bare bones. The common gorse, *Ulex europaeus* (furze), flowers in England earlier than October, but Tolkien is concerned with a 'netted sheen of gold-shot gossamers', i.e. cobwebs among the plant's yellow flowers wet with dew, not about the flowering. He also includes more specific calendar references, such as Lammas (1 August), October, and All Hallows (All Saints' Day, 1 November).

The general tone of the poem is autumnal or wintry. Tolkien first wrote it in mid-November, reflecting the mood of seasons and weather, and presumably his own mood at a time of war. He ends with winter and no mention of returning spring. As John Garth has pointed out in *The Worlds of J.R.R. Tolkien*, nature in *Kortirion* is fused with war: autumn is an armed attack by winter with its icy shears or spears, dying leaves are 'mourning multitudes'. The Elves are said to sing *fey*, a word which Christopher Tolkien suggests should be read with the old sense of 'fated, approaching death; presaging death' (*The Book of Lost Tales, Part One*, p. 274). There is a keen feeling of loss, of all things being transitory, of the relentless passing of time, that neither Kortirion and its trees nor the Fairies (Elves) are what they once were. Contributing to this are words which suggest insubstantiality: pallid mists, vaguely floating vessels, a shadowy bar, cloudy ports forlorn, windy ghosts, empty coasts, a plumbless ocean of oblivion. And yet, in other parts of the poem Tolkien is conscious not only of visual changes, but also of sounds and smells, during the year and during night and day.

He describes the year and the turning of the seasons also through astronomical references. In early workings he refers to Orion, a prominent constellation in the Northern Hemisphere during winter nights (see poem no. 38). Throughout the several versions of *Kortirion*, the Pleiades in the constellation Taurus are also bright in the winter sky at night, near Orion; the star cluster is often called the Seven Sisters or (as D98) the Seven Stars, among other names. Tolkien describes seeing it as if through the branches of trees, 'tangled with sable lace | Of naked elms' ('naked' because leafless, in winter), perhaps echoing one of his favourite poets, Alfred, Lord Tennyson, in 'Locksley Hall': 'Many a night I saw the Pleiads, rising thro' the mellow shade, | Glitter like a swarm of fire-flies tangled in a silver braid'.

The 'Silver Bear', momentarily called 'the great bear' in early workings, is the northern circumpolar constellation Ursa Major, and its 'seven lampads' (or 'seven candles') are the seven bright stars which form the Plough (or the Wain, or the Big Dipper). Kristine Larsen has examined these and other aspects of the poem in her essay '"Diadem the Fallen Day": Astronomical and Arboreal Motifs in the Poem "Kortirion among the Trees"' (2018). John Garth has suggested ('Francis Thompson', p. 221) that the 'seven lampads' derive from Francis Thompson's poem 'To My Godchild' ('Pass the crystalline sea, the Lampads seven: — | Look for me in the nurseries of Heaven').

Kortirion also continues, from earlier poems, images of trooping fairies or elves – 'Faithful Companies' who follow 'lonely paths' – with song and dance, but ultimately become silent, shadows: 'Unseen the Elves go by' (F93, H90). The notion of a 'vanishing people' is ancient in English fairy lore, and recurs in Tolkien's writings. We also meet again in *Kortirion* the harebell, an 'elfin' flower, as in poem no. 39, and as noted in discussion of poem no. 30, the harebell grew on the hill of Kôr.

A18: *Lampad* 'lamp' comes from the name of a nymph in Greek mythology who lit the way for the goddess Hekate.

A23: 'Oershadows', without an apostrophe (*o'ershadows*), is correct as written.

B27: 'Of sombre grandeur' originally read 'Of ancient grandeur'.

B38: 'Sing then of elms' originally read 'Sing of thy elms'.

B43: 'Thou art the inmost province' originally read 'This is the inmost province'.

B54: This line originally read 'Spring makes thee sweet for spring is ever fair'.

B73: 'Plumed weeds' originally read 'tasselled weeds'.

B75–82: For a reason we cannot explain, in the manuscript these lines are set off by pencil marks at left and below.

B81: This line originally read 'The yellow fluttering of her flock of golden things'.

B128–129: We have transcribed these lines as Tolkien left them in his manuscript, apparently unfinished.

C3: In *The Book of Lost Tales, Part One*, p. 33, this line is misprinted 'The robe gone gray, thine old heart almost still'.

D54: Tolkien considered whether to change 'joy' to 'hope'.

D63–64: Tolkien's usage of *thin* in 'For thin and clear and cold the note, | As strand of silver glass remote' could mean that the note was weak, or high-pitched – if one follows a definition in the *Oxford English Dictionary*. But in concert with 'clear and cold', this does not seem apt, and is further complicated by changes in phrasing in texts F, G, and H, 'Winding amid the green with clear cold note | Like a thin strand of silver glass remote', in which *thin* no longer modifies *note* but is attached to *strand*. The note remains clear and cold, and the meaning of *thin* must become 'slender' or 'insubstantial'. For D63–64, and again in text E, we are inclined to think that Tolkien used *thin* in a sense meaning 'sharp, able to travel far', as Tennyson did in 'The Splendour Falls': 'O, hark, O, hear! how thin and clear, | And thinner, clearer, farther going!' (see poem no. 34).

D65: At this point in earlier texts, Tolkien used *bent* in the sense 'open, grassy place'. Now he retains *bent*, but in the sense 'curved'.

D69: Tolkien considered whether to change 'moveless' to 'windless'.

D135: Tolkien considered whether to change 'Faery' to 'Elven'.

E3: Tolkien marked this line as if for revision to 'Thy stones are grey, your old hills now are still'. Christopher Tolkien did not take this up in his transcription in *The Book of Lost Tales, Part One* (p. 36), perhaps recognizing that the amendment belonged to the revision of 1962 (see below), or it may be that he could not decipher the handwriting.

E9: Tolkien considered whether to change 'One year' to 'One day'.

E10: Tolkien considered whether to change 'And slowly thither have a many gone' to 'And slowly thither many years have gone'.

E39–40: Tolkien marked these lines as if for revision to 'That under summer crowd their full sail on, | And shrouded stand like masts of verdurous ships'. The reading in *The Book of Lost Tales, Part One* is 'crowds', but the manuscript clearly has 'crowd' (i.e. 'crowded' with '-ed' struck through).

E45: Tolkien circled the word 'sometimes' in 'Still, undespairing, here they sometimes slowly file'. Christopher Tolkien seems to have interpreted this as a deletion, as he omitted the word in transcription.

E48: Tolkien later corrected 'fay' to 'fey'.

E62: Tolkien added this line later in pencil. We have set it in brackets as we suspect its omission in E was inadvertent, merely overlooked when making a new manuscript based largely on D, where the line appears.

E71: Tolkien considered whether to change 'long lawns' to 'the lawns'.

E116: The manuscript reads 'on the tide', but is marked to be changed to 'down the tide'. We suspect that 'on' was an inadvertent error for 'down', as 'down the tide' was the reading already in D.

E128: Tolkien originally wrote, in ink, 'Where dwells the sun, the great Seas, or the magic isles', but altered (in ink) the second line in the course of writing to 'Where dwells the sun, nor cross the seas to the magic isles'. In pencil, he wrote 'reigns' above 'dwells', 'nor sail to magic isles' above l. 127, and 'nor seek the [magic isles]' below l. 128. In *The Book of Lost Tales, Part One* Christopher Tolkien gives the amended line as 'Where reigns the sun, nor sail to magic isles', but a revised reading might also be 'Where reigns the sun, nor cross the seas, nor seek the magic isles'. In any case, this part of the poem was significantly rewritten in text F.

E131: Tolkien wrote in pencil above 'distant' an indistinct word, probably 'clamant' (as in text F). Christopher Tolkien retained 'distant' in his transcription.

E133: Above 'For here is heartsease still, and deep content', Tolkien tried out in pencil an alternate text, which seems to read 'There my heart's home still' and 'is here until the end'. The reading in E is retained in *The Book of Lost Tales, Part One*.

E135: Tolkien considered whether to change 'Faery' to 'ancient'.

E137–138: At the foot of this manuscript page is further drafting in pencil, not entirely legible, apparently considered to replace the two final lines of the poem: 'Here though I [?] the Elves defend | the ancient course where still immortals dwell'. An echo of these workings is found in the final lines of the 1962 version of the poem (F).

F64: As first typed, this line read 'Like a clear strand of silver glass remote'. Tolkien altered it in the course of typing to 'keen strand' and then 'thin strand'.

F65: This line, carried from variant readings in texts D and E, in F is struck through in pencil, and omitted from later texts. Tolkien may have meant to omit it in F as well.

F88–89: As first typed, these lines read 'With waning musics sad that slowly pass | Winding with echoed voices faintly down'. Tolkien amended (or corrected) 'waning musics' and 'echoed voices' to 'echoing voices' and 'waning music' in the course of typing.

F123: As first typed, the beginning of this line read 'Winter is come'. Tolkien altered it in the course of typing.

41

Narqelion (1915–16)

As noted for poem no. 40, where it was used as a section title, *narqelion* (later *narquelion*) is the Qenya word for 'autumn'. A related poem by that title, entirely in Qenya, exists in a manuscript inscribed 'Nov[ember] 1915' and 'March 1916'. Lines 5–9 were first published in Humphrey Carpenter's 1977 biography of Tolkien, with misreadings or misprints. The complete Qenya poem was published, also with small errors, with a linguistic analysis by Paul Nolan Hyde in the journal *Mythlore* for Winter 1988, based on a transcription by Christopher Tolkien. Here, as A, we have made our own transcription from the manuscript, aided by a lengthy discussion of the poem's Qenya vocabulary and structure by Christopher Gilson in the April 1999 number of *Vinyar Tengwar*, which also reproduces Tolkien's manuscript of *Narqelion*. Another manuscript of the poem was transcribed by Dimitra Fimi and Andrew Higgins, including revisions and deletions, in *A Secret Vice: Tolkien on Invented Languages* (2016, corrected 2020).

[A]

N·alalmino lalantila
Ne·súme lasser pinea
Ve sangar voro úmeai
Oïkta rámavoite malinai.

Ai lintuilind(ov)a Lasselanta
Piliningwe súyer nalla qanta
Kuluvai ya karnevalinar
V'ematte sinqi Eldamar.

San rotser simpetalla pinqe,
Súlimarya sidai, hiswa timpe
San sirilla ter i·aldar:
Lilta lie noldorinwa
Ómalingwe lir' amaldar
Sinqitalla laiqaninwa.

N·alalmino hyá lanta lasse
Torwa pior má tarasse:

Tukalla sangar úmeai
Oïkta rámavoite karneambarai.

Ai lindórea Lasselanta
Nierme mintya náre qanta.

We include here, as B, Christopher Gilson's translation of the text into Modern English rhyming couplets, echoing the form of the verse in Qenya.

[B] The elm-tree one by one lets fall
Upon the wind its leaves each small
That ever large as throngs are grown
Whose yellow birds upon their wings have flown.

Oh! Fall, its swallows spring-like trilling
All the airs indeed with feathers filling,
Golden-hued and orange-red, recalls
The gems bestrewn near Elven-halls.

Then pipes sustained their slender whistle,
Columns pearly thin, a fading drizzle
Then meandered through the forest:
Dancing folk of Gnomish-seeming
Raised their voices tender-chorused,
Emeralds and sapphires gleaming.

Here from the elm a leaf is drifted,
Rich-brown haws [hawthorn-berries] are still uplifted:
Fetching the throngs that large are grown
Whose red-breast birds upon their wings have hither flown.

Oh! the Autumn that sings each morrow
Reminds me it is full of sorrow.

Some of this imagery also appears in *Kortirion among the Trees* – elm trees in autumn, a fall of leaves like throngs of yellow birds, elves (gnomes) dancing and singing – perhaps significantly in a part of that poem which Tolkien worked over repeatedly. Both *Kortirion* and *Narqelion* were composed, or began to be composed, in November 1915, according to their inscribed dates. A draft of lines 5–9 of *Narqelion* appears at the head on one of the early sheets for *Kortirion*, 'Y·alalminu lalantila | i-sūmi papti pīnea | se sangar voro ūmeai |

oïkta rāmavoite malinai'. The relatively neat manuscript of *Narqelion*, however, has the appearance of a fair copy, made perhaps in March 1916 (from its second inscribed date), though it is also possible that Tolkien wrote it out later and dated it from memory. The page on which *Narqelion* is written was originally in one of Tolkien's poetry notebooks, and is on the opposite side of a leaf also containing the second text of *The Forest Walker* (poem no. 50), inscribed 'August 25. 26 [1916]'. In March 1916 Tolkien was still in an army training camp in England, but by August had joined the British Expeditionary Force in France.

An unfinished alliterative poem, or fragment of a poem, associated with *Narqelion* has been identified by Carl F. Hostetter in his 'Editing the Tolkienian Manuscript' (2022). This is in Modern English, but with line 4 of *Narqelion* in Qenya, 'oïkta rámavoite malinai' (translated by Hostetter as probably 'of birds having wings of yellow'), appended. Tolkien wrote it on the reverse side of a discarded word-slip for the *Oxford English Dictionary*, on whose staff he worked from the end of 1918 (effectively from 1919) through May 1920, though he made use of such slips for years thereafter. We give here, as C, the poem in its finished form, in our own transcription reflecting Tolkien's minimal punctuation. Hostetter includes notes on Tolkien's revisions in the course of writing, and the manuscript is reproduced in his essay.

[C]

With leaping leaves the lift is filled;
The wind with wings that whispering go
Like fleet winged flocks a wandering
Of birds with plumes of palest gold.
These are the elms children that at chill winters
First bitter breath abandon her arms
Where the beech burns and the bloodred leaves
Of the wallcreepers in weeds of flame
Yet of glowing summer a gleed lingers
& the high housefold & the hoar gables

A8: Tolkien first wrote 'sinqe', apparently a singular form of *sink (q-)* 'gem', before changing it to plural *sinqi* 'gems'.

A14: In the margin opposite this line Tolkien wrote *-álar*, presumably to consider the form *sinqitálar*.

A18: Tolkien first wrote *malinai* 'yellow', as in l. 4, but changed it to *karneambarai* 'redbreasted' (with *oïkta* 'bird' = 'robin').

C10: We agree with Carl F. Hostetter that *housefold* seems to be Tolkien's invention, with its apparent meaning 'roof'.

42

The Pool of the Dead Year · The Pool of Forgetfulness (1915–c. 1920)

Apart from a few stray phrases written on a page with drafting for *Kortirion among the Trees* (no. 40), five complete versions and one partial version of this poem are preserved among Tolkien's papers. The earliest, entitled *The Pool of the Dead Year*, is a manuscript written at speed, with numerous revisions and excisions and only a few marks of punctuation. We have transcribed this as A, incorporating changes Tolkien marked and capitalizing the first word of each line, as he did predominantly but not consistently.

[A]

There is a grey pool in a woodland vale
No sigh of wind nor echo of a sound
Doth ever break its pale crystalline face
Smoother than any fairy glass of dwarfen make
Composed of air thin silver and transparent dews
It lies and dimly dreams in solitude

About it ringed like silent slender ghosts
The white shafts of the birches palely grow
And glimmer through the mists. For ever drip
Entangled in their threadlike sprays enlaced
Uncountably the stilling vaporous tears
Of swathed fogs white moveless mystical
There is no noise save should one lay his ear
To the dank mould and catch the whispering fall
Of ceaseless drops to reach the matted leaves
Unceasingly minute, and moist, and cold grey

On a wan day that wanes through afternoon
Unsunned and the diffuséd light withdrew
Gently and slow to gather in great glooms
And shades then do dim shapes appear
That flee half seen among the birchen stems
Or marched in noiseless phantom file along

Down the hoar hills and cloudy slopes
Of what they are the faintly mirrored forms
Or what vague distant lives they secret live
None know and voices they have none to tell
But all the long year through the pool lies bare
And all the many days the grey shapes come
And dance a shadowy dance reflected clear
Till comes a sudden afternoon nigh eve
And nigh the fading fallen year
When one long single ray of sunset light
Of gold as pale as ever blended yet
Amid the silver scarfing of the moon
Thin filters through and travels haltingly
Along a streaming path. Then comes a music
A long sound from afar borne like a sigh
Among the waiting woods. The one voice of the year
That ever trembles in those misty airs
And after a great pause in which its lamentation
Goes quivering round the pillared ring of birches
There comes a sound of sad and stately feet
That rustle among the brown heaps of the leaves
And plash the silver waters of the ways
And come. Slow sorrowful and sweet they come.

And lo there is a parting of the trees
An arched way of boughs a fenced stair
Terraced in drenchéd moss and filmy fern
Dew hung. The tapered forms of two white trees
Leaning do make a gate-way to the pool
And here the long path ends. And here doth cease
The sound of those sad feet that rustling come
A figure framéd in the arch and sunbeam caught
Stands there. Her long brown hair inaureoled
In a single ray that streams through all her tresses
And her amber robe of elm leaves come to sere
Diapered with the ruddier beech and girt
With berries studded black and burning red
Upon a russet belt is lightly tossed
And shaken by a shadowy wind behind
That blows a little flying whirl of leaves
About her head and sighs like the last breath
Of a great wind blown thin from the world's end

Then turning with a last swift backward glance
She bends her glimmering feet among the trees
And softly they fare across the dripping leaves
And sweetly doth her low voice sing farewell
She passes like a flush of splendid hues
All crusted with the glistening water drops
Among the shadowy trees and like a flush
Of rich notes far away her echoing song
Doth quaver gold in silver silences
Wide are her fair arms spread & splendidly
The wine red gems in twined bracelets flash
And crimson stones amid the carcanet
About her throat and still she sings
Like a quiet voice [?by = but] very great
That sings across the gloom of soundless seas
Of lands beyond the night. And ever more
Doth sorrow enter in, and wondering awe
Until she seems what e'er her words may be
That weave a fearful music of dread stars
That shine in cold about the wintry peaks
And ice is in her voice

Then is she come
To the inviolate margin of the secret mere
Her garments hanging limp and all her hair
Drawn round her and the crystal waters clear
Unruffled mirror her. O glorious the outpour of her voice
In hallows empty weeping solitude
Singing of all the wide things of the golden Earth
And all its majesty and glorious realms
And he who heard would clutch his beating heart
For rapture and regret and all his soul
Grow deep. So pouring on the heavy air
Her splendid hymn mystic & sad & slow
She glides across the gleaming pool and sudden stops
The mist is fired to gold about her by a ray
And at the centre doth she stay and no more sing
But in cavernous silence slowly dips
Into its unplumbed waters and great depths
Of pale oblivious untroubled dreams
Like a rich garnet that a diamond
Engulfs. The year falls dead about the day

And eve grows deep the shadows shapes are thick
The blue hills darker loom and all the ways
Go out and fade in pathless dusk
And as the last echo of her lost voice goes
Faintly in the wildered maze about the mere.
The light is gone and all thy Earth is dead
No sigh of wind nor echo of a sound
Comes more to break the pale crystalline face
Of that grey pool amid the woodland vale
That lies and watches for the frozen stars.

Tolkien made a fair copy manuscript of A as revised, inscribing it 'Nov[ember] 28–Dec[ember] 4 1915', probably when he wrote its text proper and not long after its first composition. To this copy Tolkien made a few small revisions, but also added a new first line, 'Set near the heart of this wide northern isle', set slightly apart from the original first line. In a third manuscript of the poem, he took up the changes indicated on the previous copy, but broke off his new effort after line 42. A fourth (complete) manuscript followed, now entitled more fully *The Pool of the Dead Year (and the Passing of Autumn)*, with the title and subtitle inscribed also in Old English, *Þæt Mere þæs Dēadan Gēares: Hærfestes Forþgang*. Tolkien revised this text further, more extensively than he had earlier versions, then made a fresh copy in typescript. We have transcribed the latter as text B, as it stood before further rewriting.

[B] Set near the heart of this wide northern isle
There is a grey pool in a woodland vale;
No sigh of wind nor echo of a sound
Doth ever break its pale crystalline face.
Smoother than fairy glass of dwarfen make
Composed of air-thin silver and transparent dews
It lies and dimly dreams in loneliness;
While round it ring'd like silent slender ghosts
The white shafts of the birches naked grow
And glimmer through the mist. For ever drip
Uncountably entangled in the threads
Of lacéd sprays the stilling vaporous tears
Of swathing fogs, white, moveless, magical.
There is no noise save should one lay his ear
To the dank mould and catch the whispering fall
Of ceaseless drops that reach the sodden leaves

Unceasingly, minute, and moist, and cold.
    On a wan day that wanes through afternoon
Unsunned, and the diffused light withdraws
Gently and slow to gather in great glooms
And filmy shades, then fleeting shapes appear
That move half seen among the birchen stems
Or troop in noiseless phantom file along
Down the hoar hills and o'er the cloudy slopes.
Of what they are the faintly mirrored forms
Or what vague distant lives they secret live,
None know, and voices they have none to tell:
But all the long year through the pool is bare,
And all the many days the grey shapes come
And dance a shadowy dance reflected clear,
Till comes a sudden afternoon nigh eve
And nigh the grey year's slowing fading end,
When one long sunset light with single ray
Of gold as pale as ever blended yet
Amid the silver scarfing of the moon
Thin filters through and travels haltingly
Along a streaming way. Then comes a music;
A long sound from afar borne like a sigh
Among the waiting woods; the one voice of the year
That ever trembles in those misty airs:
And after a great pause while echoed echoes
Go quivering round the pillared birchen ring
There comes a sound of sad and stately feet.
They rustle among the brown heaps of the leaves,
And plash the silver waters of the ways,
And come — slow sorrowful and sweet they come.
And lo! there is a parting of the trees,
An archèd way of boughs, a fencèd stair,
Terraced in drenchèd moss and filmy fern
Dew-hung. The tapered forms of two white trees
Leaning do make a gateway to the pool,
And there the long path ends; and there doth cease
The sound of those sad feet that halting come.
A figure, framèd in the arch, and sunbeam caught,
Stands there. Her long brown hair is aureoled
In that lone ray that pours through every tress,
And her amber robe of elm leaves come to sere
Is diaper'd with the ruddier beech, and girt

With berries studded black and burning red
Set on a russet belt. 'Tis lightly tossed
And shaken by a shadowy wind behind,
That blows a little flying whirl of leaves
About her head and sighs like the last breath
Of mighty gales blown thin across the world.
Then turning with a last swift backward glance
She bends her glimmering feet among the trees,
And softly they fare across the dripping leaves
And sweetly doth her low voice sing farewell.
She passes like a flush of splendid hues
All crusted with the glistening water-drops
Among the shadowy trees, and like a flush
Of rich notes far away her echoing song
Doth quaver gold in silver silences.
Wide are her fair arms spread and splendidly
The wine-red gems in twinèd bracelets flash,
And crimson stones amid the carcanet
About her throat — and still she sings
Like a quiet voice but very great indeed
That calls across the gloom of soundless seas
Of lands beyond the night. Yet ever more
Doth sorrow enter in, and wondering awe,
Until she seems, whate'er her words may be,
To weave a fearful music of dread stars
That shine in cold about the wintry peaks —
And ice is in her voice. Then is she come
To the inviolate margin of the secret mere,
Her garments hanging limp, her hazel hair
Drawn round her, while the crystal waters clear
About her feet unruffled mirror her.
O! glorious the outpour of her laden voice
Alone in empty weeping solitude
Singing of all the wide things of the golden earth,
And all its majesty and blessed realms —
And he who heard would clutch his beating heart
For rapture and regret, and all his soul
Grow deep. So pouring on the heavy air
Her towering hymn, mystic, and sad, and slow
She glides across the pool — then suddenly
The mist is fired to gold about her by a beam;
There at the centre doth she stay, and no more sing,

But in a cavernous silence slowly dips,
Like a rich garnet that one diamond gulfs,
Into its unplumbed waters and great depths
Of pale, oblivious, untroubled dreams.
The mourning year falls dead about the day,
And eve grows deep; the shadow shapes are thick;
The blue hills shrink to grey, and all the ways
Go out in pathless dusk. Then the last echo
Following her lost voice among the wood
Faints in the wildered maze about the mere:
No sigh of wind nor echo of a sound
Comes more to break the dim crystalline face
Of that grey pool amid the woodland vale
That lies and watches for the frozen stars.

The final version of the poem is a manuscript, extensively revised from the preceding typescript (B, especially lines 54–61 and 74–97); we have transcribed this as C, incorporating a few further changes marked by Tolkien. The work was now entitled *The Pool of Forgetfulness*, after Tolkien considered *The Pool of the Forgetfulness* and *The Pool of the Great Forgetfulness*. Uniquely among the versions, text C omits capitalization at the beginning of lines unless a word begins a new sentence. The manuscript is on examination paper Christopher Tolkien believed his father acquired for use when he was on the English faculty at Leeds in the early 1920s, and has a later inscription, 'Autumn | Rugeley | 1915 | [Nov[ember] | often rewr[itten]'.

[C] Set near the heart of this wide northern isle
there is a grey pool in a woodland vale;
no sigh of wind nor echo of a sound
doth ever break its pale crystalline face.
Smoother than glass by olden dwarves composed
of air-thin silver and transparent dews
it lies and dimly dreams in loneliness.
All round it ring'd like silent slender ghosts
the white shafts of the birches naked grow
and glimmer through the mist. For ever drip
uncountably entangled in the threads
of lacéd sprays the grey tears slow distilled
by swathing mists unmoving, white and blind.
There is no noise save should one lay his ear
to the dank mould and catch the whispering fall

of pattering drops that reach the sodden leaves
unceasingly, minute, and moist, and cold.
    On a wan day that wanes through afternoon
unsunned, and the diffuséd light withdraws
gently and slow to gather in great glooms
and filmy shades, their fleeting shapes appear
that move half-seen among the birchen stems,
or troop in noiseless phantom file along
down the hoar hills and o'er the cloudy slopes.
Of what they are the faintly mirrored forms,
or what vague distant lives they secret live
None know, and voices they have none to tell.
But all the long year through the pool is bare,
and all the many days the grey shapes come
and dance a shadowy dance reflected clear,
till comes a sudden afternoon nigh eve
and nigh the grey year's slow fading end.
Then one long sunset light with single ray
of gold as pale as ever blended yet
amid the silver scarfing of the moon
thin filters through and travels haltingly
along a streaming way. Then comes a music;
a long sound from afar like distant wailing
among the waiting woods; the one voice of the year
that ever trembles in those misty airs.
A great pause follows while the echoed echoes
go quivering round the pillared birchen ring —
then comes a sound of sad and stately feet.
They rustle among the brown heaps of the leaves,
and plash the silver waters of the ways,
and come; slow, sorrowfully slow, they come.
    And, lo!, there is a parting of the trees,
an archéd way of boughs, a fencéd stair
terraced in dew drenchéd moss and filmy fern
dew-hung. The tapered forms of two white trees
in-leaning there make a gateway to the pool,
and there the long road ends; and there the sound
ceases of those sad feet that halting come.
There sunbeam-caught a figure stands alone,
and the thin light tangles in her long brown hair.
Her amber robe is of elm-leaves faded sere
with ruddier beech-leaves broidered, and a belt

of russet clasps it to her girdlestead
studded with berries burning red and black.
There shakes a little shadowy wind behind,
blowing a flying whirl of faded leaves
about her head, sighing as the latest breath
of mighty gales blown thin across the world.
    Then turning with a last swift backward glance
she bends her glimmering feet among the trees;
and softly they pass across the dripping leaves,
and sweetly then her low voice sings farewell.
She passes like a flush of splendid hues
all crusted with the glistening water-drops
among the shadowy trees, and like a flush
of rich notes far away her echoing song
doth quaver gold in silver silences.
Wide are her fair arms spread, where chainéd gold
in bracelets flashes set with wine-red gems;
and crimson stones gleam in the carcanet
about her throat. Still faring on she sings
like a quiet voice but very great indeed
that calls across the gloom of soundless seas
from lands beyond the night; a towering hymn
of all the wide things of the golden earth,
and all its majesty and blessed realms —
a rapture, and regret; for while she sings
doth sorrow enter in and wondering awe,
until she seems, whatever her words may be,
to weave a fearful music of dread stars
that shine in cold about the wintry peaks
— and ice is in her voice.
                                        Then is she come
to the inviolate margin of the secret pool,
her garments hanging limp, her hazel hair
drawn round her, while the crystal waters clear
about her feet unruffled mirror her
alone in empty weeping solitude.
She glides across the mere — and suddenly
the mist is fired to gold about her head,
stayed at the centre where she no more sings,
but in a cavernous silence slowly sinks
like a rich garnet that one diamond gulfs
into the bottomless waters and great depths

of pale, oblivious, untroubled dreams.
The mourning year falls dead about the day,
and eve grows deep; the shadow shapes are thick;
the blue hills shrink to grey, and all the ways
go out in pathless dusk, as the last echo
following her lost voice among the wood
faints in the wildered maze about the mere.
No sigh of wind nor echo of a sound
comes more to break the dim crystalline face
of that grey pool amid the woodland vale,
that lies and watches for the frozen stars.

The Pool of the Dead Year recalls other works Tolkien composed in 1915. Its 'filmy shades' with 'fleeting shapes' are like the fairies or elves of *Kortirion among the Trees* (no. 40) or the shadow people of *A Song of Aryador* (no. 37). The 'grey pool' is at 'the heart of this wide northern isle' as Kortirion is at the centre of the Land of Elms, and as in *Kortirion* trees are featured – birch, beech, elm – if now only as a setting ('a woodland vale') for the secret pool and crystal waters. As in *Goblin Feet* (no. 27) and *The Happy Mariners* (no. 33), an unknown presence is heard, here through music and voice and the rustle of feet. Once more, Tolkien uses 'fairy' imagery, notably the 'fairy glass of dwarfen make' in the earlier versions. (The unusual *dwarfen*, not in the *Oxford English Dictionary*, is abandoned, along with 'fairy', in the final version, which has 'by olden dwarves composed'.) Again as in *Kortirion*, objects entwine, enlace, and entangle, and the insubstantial is suggested by words such as 'grey', 'pale', 'air-thin', 'in swathing mists'.

The oppression Tolkien felt in *Dark Are the Clouds about the North* (no. 38) was still with him when he wrote *The Pool of the Dead Year*. Autumn is traditionally the season in which the year comes to an end, before its death in winter, and poets such as Tennyson and Thomson have written of it in terms of nostalgia and regret. Tolkien follows suit, and yet his mood is lifted by the figure at the pool. If the poem in general seems fantastic and often vague, the singer is vividly rendered, with her long brown hair, amber robe embroidered with leaves, russet belt, flashing bracelets, and jewelled necklace (*carcanet*) – a personification of Autumn, much as Pomona and Flora, say, and all of the seasons, were personified in paintings or tapestries by Edward Burne-Jones. Tolkien's figure, and poem, seem to us much in the vein of the Pre-Raphaelites.

Having received from Tolkien *The Pool of the Dead Year*, Christopher Wiseman replied on 18 January 1917 that he felt uncomfortable reading the poem because of its luxuriant language, and cited Arthur Symons' criticism of George Meredith (from 'George Meredith as a Poet' in *Figures of Several Centuries*, 1916): 'In prose he would have every sentence shine, in verse he would have every line sparkle; like a lady who puts on all her jewellery at once, immediately after breakfast.' Wiseman may have been responding to the unrelenting pace of the poem, unrelieved by rhyme, not unlike James Thomson's treatment of autumn in *The Seasons* (1730, p. 13):

> Then too the pillar'd dome, magnific, heav'd
> His ample roof; and *Luxury* within
> Pour'd out her glittering stores. The canvas smooth,
> With glowing life protuberant, to the view
> Embodied rose. The statue seem'd to breathe,
> And soften into flesh, beneath the touch
> Of forming art, imagination-flushed.

But it is true that Tolkien – hardly for the first time – showed his love of words, using (for example) the relatively familiar *flush* with both 'splendid hues' and 'rich notes', in at least the sense of 'sudden abundance', though the first instance could also have the sense of 'warm glow'. When sending the poem to Wiseman, he suggested that *The Pool of the Dead Year* was in fact 'ludicrously bad', a judgement his friend disputed.

A85: 'Then is she come' is set far to the right in the manuscript.

B32: This line originally read 'And nigh the fading of the fallen year'.

B41: This line originally read 'And after a great pause in which its lament'.

B64: This line originally read 'Of a great wind from the world's [long >] far end [blowing >] thin'.

B111: At this stage Tolkien deleted the preceding line, 'The light is gone and all [thy >] the Earth is dead', which had been present since the first text.

C16: 'Pattering' replaced 'ceaseless' among final revisions to the poem.

C52–53: These lines replaced, in Tolkien's final revisions to the manuscript, 'and there the long road ends; and there doth cease | the sound of those sad feet that halting come'.

C70: 'Shadowy trees' originally read 'pallid trees'.

C83: Written above this line, but struck through, is 'grief grows and sorrow'.

C87: 'Then is she come' is set far to the right in the manuscript. At this point Tolkien also wrote in the left margin, as if considering an addition or change, 'joy fades, grief grows and the cold thought awakes of Death'. Compare our note for C83.

C99: 'Bottomless' originally read 'unplumbed'.

43

Over Old Hills and Far Away (1916–27)

The piper Tinfang Warble (see poem no. 29) reappears in the present work. In *The Book of Lost Tales, Part One*, Christopher Tolkien described five texts of this poem and published the latest. At that time he was not aware of an additional version, which his sister Priscilla found among the Tolkien family papers only in 1991 and is probably the earliest of the six. We have transcribed this manuscript as A. It contains two corrections, made in the course of writing, but otherwise has the appearance of a fair copy, implying an even earlier draft.

[A] 'Twas a very quiet evening once in June —
And I thought the stars had grown bright too soon —
Yet all the trees grew slowly sleepy
In spite of the magic that made me creepy.
I had stolen out with a stealthy tread
Leaving my white and unpressed bed.
Something delightful aloof and queer
Like perfume of flowers by the fairies' mere
Blown through a trellis of starlit rains
Had come as I looked through the lattice panes;
Or was there a sound on the dusky winds?
— I listened and said — 'It begins, it begins:
O! far away there come filtered notes
Enchanting and sweet — 'tis a pipe of oats,
Or of slender stems of the stream-side grass;
Something bewitching is going to pass.
Melodious laughable magical din
'Tis the hoot of a flute with a voice tangled in.[']
Then I left the window and followed the call
Down the creaky stairs and across the hall,
Out through a door that swung tall and grey,
Over the lawn and away, away.

It was Tinfang Warble a-dancing there,
Fluting and tossing his old white hair
Till it sparkled like frost in a winter moon,
Till the stars came out, as it seemed, too soon.

They always come out when he warbles and plays
And they shine bright blue as long as he stays.

My footsteps made just the ghost of a sound
On the tiny white pebbles that ringed him round
In his twilight dance — he leapt in the air
With his conical cap and his glistening hair,
And he cast his long flute behind his back
Where it hung by a ribbon of silver and black.
His slim little body went fine as a shade,
And he slipped through the trees and like smoke up the glade
Over a path barred sable and white
By the moon, and his going was hid by the light.
Out into the wide and the magical world
Went the old leprechaun with his shoe-toe curled.
The glade seemed empty and very bare
Wistfully I stood with a lonely stare —
When suddenly out in the fields beyond
From among the reeds of a gleaming pond,
Or else from a copse where the mosses were thick,
A few little notes came trillaping quick.

I sped down the lawn and out of the glade,
For Tinfang Warble it was that played,
And I followed the hoot of his twilight flute
And the twinkly bells on his blue-grey suit
Over dim fields and through rustling grasses
Over old hills and far away
Where even an old elf seldom passes
Through lands asleep and past stars at play.

Another copy of the poem is inscribed 'Jan[uary]–Feb[ruary] 1916', probably contemporary with the text, and supported by a letter Tolkien wrote to Edith Bratt on 31 January 1916: 'I am starting another poem about Tinfang Warble I believe' (Bodleian Library). He also wrote at the head of the copy its title in Old English, *Ȝeond Fyrne Beorgas ⁊ Heonan Feor*. A relatively clean manuscript written in one of Tolkien's poetry notebooks, it includes only two changes made in the course of writing, but also an alternate reading written on a facing page and annotated (if widely separated from the new lines, and only presumably related to the poem) 'Hospital Nov[ember] 1916'. Tolkien returned to England from the Somme on medical leave on 9 November, and was admitted to the 1st Southern General Hospital in Birmingham.

The text of the second manuscript differs from A in a few respects, especially in its second half. Tolkien carried it over into a typescript, inscribed at some later date 'Brocton Camp Christ[mas]–Jan[uary] 1915–16'. He marked several lines for change, then retyped the text as amended using the purple ribbon associated with his years at Leeds. The second typescript is recorded here as B, with revisions from intervening texts described in our notes.

[B]

'Twas a very quiet evening once in June —
And I thought the stars had grown bright too soon,
When all the trees were drooping sleepy
And magic was under them faint and creepy.
I had stolen out with a stealthy tread
Leaving my white and unpressed bed:
Something alluring, aloof and queer,
Like perfume of flowers by the fairies' mere
Blown through a trellis of starlit rains,
Had come as I peered through the lattice panes —
Or was there a sound on the dusky winds?
I listened, and said — 'It begins, it begins!
O! far away there come filtered notes
Enchanting and sweet: 'tis a pipe of oats,
Or of slender stems of the stream-side grass;
Something bewitching is going to pass.
Bewildering, tremulous, hollow, and thin,
'Tis the hoot of a flute with a voice tangled in!'
Then I left the window and followed the call
Down the creaky stairs and across the hall,
Out through a door that swung tall and grey,
Over the lawn, and away, away.

It was Tinfang Warble a-dancing there
Fluting and tossing his old white hair,
Till it sparkled like frost in a winter moon,
Till the stars came out, as it seemed, too soon.
They always come out when he warbles and plays,
And they shine bright blue as long as he stays.

My footsteps made just the ghost of a sound
On the tiny white pebbles that ringed him round
Where dancing he lifted a long white hand

And his little feet flashed in a dim saraband.
In the wink of a star he had leapt in the air
With his fluttering cap and his glistening hair,
And he cast his long flute behind his back
Where it hung by a ribbon of silver and black.
His slim little body went fine as a shade,
And he slipped through the trees and like smoke up the glade;
And he laughed like thin silver, and piped a thin note,
And the wind as he ran blew his shadowy coat;
The toes of his slippers were twisted and curled,
But he danced like the wind out into the world.

He was gone and the glade seemed empty and bare
As wistful I stood with a lonely stare,
When suddenly out in the fields beyond,
Then down in the reeds of a shimmering pond,
Then again from a copse where the mosses were thick,
A few little notes came trillaping quick.
I sped down the lawn and out of the glade,
For Tinfang Warble it was that played;
And I followed the hoot of his twilight flute
And the twinkling bells on his blue-grey suit
Over dim fields and through rustling grasses,
That murmur and nod as the old elf passes;
Over old hills and far away
Where the harps of the fairies softly play.

Some years later, Tolkien marked the second typescript with further revisions, and incorporated them into a new (untitled) manuscript. Revising this in turn, he made a fresh, final copy, inscribed 'Brocton 1916? Oxford 1927' but with the inscription struck through. On the evidence of his handwriting, a date of 1927 for the manuscript is possible, though not conclusive. We give the final text as C, incorporating Tolkien's last changes to the copy. Christopher Tolkien's transcription in *The Book of Lost Tales, Part One*, pp. 108–10, overlooks two lightly pencilled revisions (in lines 13 and 49).

[C] It was early and still in the night of June,
And few were the stars and far was the moon,
The drowsy trees drooping, and silently creeping
Shadows woke under them while they were sleeping.

I stole to the window with stealthy tread
Leaving my white and unpressed bed;
And something alluring, aloof, and queer,
Like perfume of flowers from the shores of the mere
That in Elvenhome lies, and in starlit rains
Twinkles and flashes, came up to the panes
Of my high lattice-window. Or was it a sound?
I listened and marvelled with eyes on the ground.
For there came from afar a filtering note
Enchanting sweet, now clear, now remote,
As clear as a star in a pool by the reeds,
As faint as the glimmer of dew on the weeds.

Then I left the window and followed the call
Down the creaking stairs and across the hall,
Out through a door that swung tall and grey,
Over the lawn, and away, away!

It was Tinfang Warble that was dancing there,
Fluting and tossing his old white hair,
Till it sparkled like frost in a winter moon;
And the stars were about him, and blinked to his tune
Shimmering blue like sparks in a haze,
As always they shimmer and shake when he plays.

My feet only made there the ghost of a sound
On the shining white pebbles that ringed him round,
Where his little feet flashed on a circle of sand,
And the fingers were white on his flickering hand.
In the wink of a star he had leapt in the air
With his fluttering cap and his glistening hair;
And had cast his long flute right over his back,
Where it hung by a ribbon of silver and black.
His slim little body went fine as a shade,
And he slipped through the reeds like a mist in the glade;
And laughed like thin silver, and piped a thin note,
As he flapped in the shadows his shadowy coat.
O! the toes of his slippers were twisted and curled,
But he danced like a wind out into the world.

He is gone, and the valley is empty and bare
Where lonely I stand and lonely I stare.

Then suddenly out in the meadows beyond,
Then back in the reeds by a shimmering pond,
Then afar from a copse where the mosses are thick
A few little notes came trillaping quick.

I leapt o'er the stream and I sped from the glade,
For Tinfang Warble it was that played;
I must follow the hoot of his trillaping flute
Over reed, over rush, under branch, over root,
And over dim fields, and through rustling grasses
That murmur and nod as the old elf passes,
Over old hills and far away
Where the harps of the Elvenfolk [or Elvendom] softly play.

In the earlier versions of *Over Old Hills and Far Away* Tinfang Warble is described in stereotypical terms, like a fairy or pixie in the popular imagination: he wears a conical cap, slippers with a curled toe ('Persian' slippers), and a suit with bells on. His dress became less eccentric in the final versions, with a 'fluttering' cap and 'shadowy' coat, though the toes of his slippers were still 'twisted and curled'. At the same time, he became an 'the old elf' rather than 'the old leprechaun', echoing his change in *Tinfang Warble* from an 'old mad leprechaun' – a supernatural creature in Irish folklore – to an undefined being. Tolkien also changed 'the fairies' mere' in line 8 to simply 'the mere', as he brought his poem more closely into the world of his mythology. The final text (C) accords with the account of the piper in *The Book of Lost Tales*: 'The Noldoli say that [the stars] come out too soon if Tinfang Warble plays, and they love him, and the children will watch often from the windows lest he tread the shadowy lawns unseen.' Tinfang is 'shier than a fawn – swift to hide and dart away as any vole; a footstep on a twig and he is away, and his fluting will come mocking from afar'. His flute may suddenly 'be heard again at an hour of gentle gloaming, or he will play beneath a goodly moon and the stars go bright and blue' (*The Book of Lost Tales, Part One*, pp. 94–5).

The title *Over Old Hills and Far Away* is a variation on 'over the hills and far away', the title of an English traditional song and a line found in poems such as the anonymous 'Tom, the Piper's Son', *c.* 1795:

Tom, he was a piper's son,
He learnt to play when he was young,

And all the tune that he could play
Was, 'Over the hills and far away';
Over the hills and a great way off,
The wind shall blow my top-knot off.

Similar words are printed with music, and a second stanza, in Moffat's *What the Children Sing*. See also our discussion for poem no. 80.

A13: We cannot be sure what Tolkien meant by 'filtered' in A13 and B13, and especially 'filtering' in C13. One possibility that occurs to us is that the musical notes are *filtered* in the sense of 'pure'. But another sense of the word is 'tangled', from *felter*, and texts A and B do follow on with 'the hoot of a flute with a voice tangled in'. Or Tolkien may have meant something else for *filtering* than he did for *filtered*.

A35: 'Fine as a shade' presumably means 'as insubstantial as a shadow'.

A46: Here and in other lines, in all versions of this poem, Tolkien consistently wrote or typed 'trillaping' though the correct word is *trilluping*, from *trillup* 'a quavering or vibratory sound' (compare *trill*). He used *trillups* correctly in the final (?1927) version of *Tinfang Warble* (poem no. 29).

A50: *Twinkly*, and *twinkling* in B52, are attested alternate spellings for *tinkly* and *tinkling* 'making a bell-like sound'.

B3–4: These lines originally read 'Yet all the trees were grown slowly sleepy | In spite of the magic that made things creepy'.

B7: This line originally read 'Something delightful aloof and queer'.

B34: 'Fluttering cap' originally read 'conical cap'.

B39: As discussed in our note for ll. D63–64 of *Kortirion among the Trees* (no. 40), Tolkien used *thin* in ways that are not always clear. Here, for 'laughed like thin silver, and piped a thin note', we are inclined to think that at least the second instance of *thin* is being used in a poetic sense for 'sharp, able to travel far'. 'Laughed like silver' is a familiar phrase which means a precious laugh, like that of a child, evoking small bells; perhaps the addition of *thin* 'insubstantial' takes the idea further into the delicacy of a 'fairy' realm. 'Air thin silver' occurs in *The Pool of the Dead Year* (no. 42).

B41–42: Opposite these lines in the second manuscript, written in one of his poetry notebooks, Tolkien considered 'Danced the old elf and starrily pearled | I saw his blue slippers with toes that were curled', but retained 'Out into the wide and the magical world | Danced the old elf with his slipper toes curled'. These were replaced in the second typescript by 'O! the toes of his slippers were twisted and curled, | But he danced like a wind out into the world'.

B46: 'Then down in the reeds' was the reading already in the second manuscript. 'Then down' briefly became 'Out' in the first typescript, but reverted to 'Then down' in the revised typescript.

B52: 'Twinkling' originally read 'twinkly' in the first typescript.

B53–56: In the second manuscript, these lines read:

Over dim fields and through rustling grasses
That murmur and nod as the old elf passes;

Over old hills and far away
Where the harps of the fairies softly play.

In the first typescript, these became:

Over dim fields and through rustling grasses
Over old hills and far away,
Where even an old elf seldom passes,
Through lands asleep and past stars at play.

But in the next version (the second typescript, i.e. text B) they reverted to the reading of the second manuscript.

C1: In the preceding manuscript, this line read 'Early and still was [the >] a night [*deleted:* once] in June'.

C4: 'Shadows' originally read 'Magic'.

C9: 'Elvenhome' originally read 'Fairyland'.

C13: This line originally read 'O! far away came a filtered note'.

C21: 'That was dancing' originally read 'a-dancing'.

C41–42: In the penultimate manuscript, Tolkien wrote: 'He [was >] is gone and the [*deleted:* ?river] valley [was >] is empty and bare | Where [sadly I stood >] lonely I [stood >] stand and lonely I stare —'.

C49: 'Trillaping' (*sic*) originally read 'twilight'.

C50: The vocabulary and cadence of 'Over reed, over rush, under branch, over root' recall Shakespeare's 'Over hill, over dale, | Thorough bush, thorough brier' in *A Midsummer Night's Dream*.

C54: The words 'the fairies' are struck through and 'Elvenfolk' and 'Elvendom' written below.

44

The Wanderer's Allegiance · The Sorrowful City · The Town of Dreams and the City of Present Sorrow · Wínsele Wéste, Windge Reste Réte Berofene · The Song of Eriol (1916–?24)

In *The J.R.R. Tolkien Companion and Guide* we discussed these verses under the heading *The Town of Dreams and the City of Present Sorrow*, as this was the overall title of 'the only later copy of the whole poem that is extant', as Christopher Tolkien described it in *The Book of Lost Tales, Part Two* (p. 295). Here 'the whole poem' must mean the work at the point in its history when it had three parts, as there are still later manuscripts related to the whole, though treated as separate entities.

As Christopher wrote, it is not clear that his father conceived the poem originally in three parts, and indeed its first draft has five sections; only in the second and third drafts are there three. The composite title *The Town of Dreams and the City of Present Sorrow* appears twice in one of Tolkien's poetry notebooks, and in both instances is altered: on a page separated from the text of the related manuscripts, but then largely erased, and at the head of the first page of the third draft, but with the later part of the title struck through, leaving only 'The Town of Dreams'.

The earliest manuscript associated with the work, written at speed and with no title, is given below as A. We describe Tolkien's revisions and alternate workings in our notes.

[A] In unknown days the generations of my fathers came
And there from son to son took root
Among the orchards and the river-meads
And the long grasses of the fragrant plain:
And many a summer saw they kindle yellow flame
Of iris in the bowing reeds,
And many a sea of blossom turn to golden fruit
In wallèd gardens of the great champain.
There daffodils in spring nod round the trees
There richly flowed their sap — the inland fields

They loved and sun and flowers and gentle leas
— Yet I perforce in many a town about the lovéd isle
Unsettled wanderer have dwelt awhile.

Long have I watched and waited in this little town
Until the bubble of the Avon's water green,
And rustle of her elms['] rich leaves has been
My constant melody has filled my ears
And love of it has wrapped my heart
And lengthened days in memory to years.
And yet the castle and its mighty tower
More lofty than the tiered elms
More grey than long November rain
Sleep, and nor sunlit moment nor triumphant hour
Nor passage of the seasons or the Sun
Wakes the old lords too long in slumber lain
Or raises more than drowsy echoes in her halls
Or filters far into her splendid dream

The dancing light may flicker on the mossy walls
When radiance is laid upon the murmuring stream
Or be she clad in snow or lashed by windy rains
Or may March whirl the dust along her winding lanes
The elm robe and disrobe her of a million leaves
(Like hours that cluster in a century
And like the hours fall slow to the Earth)
Hears not the present days of misery
Still doth she massive sleep —
Uncomprehending of our fears of death.

O farther to the south a city lies
Amid a vale outcarven in forgotten days
There wider is the grass and lofty elms more rare;
The river-sense is heavy in the lowland air;
There willows make a changéd Earth and different skies
Where feeding brooks wound in by sluggish ways
And down the margin of the sailing Thames
Around his broad old bosom their old stems
Are bowed: and their grey leaves
Do trace more subtle shadows in his streams
Or knit a coverlet to silver pools

Of blue and misty green and filtered gleams.
The dim line of the down rides fast away
So far as men do march a swinging day

O aged city of an all too brief sojourn
I see thy cloistered windows each one burn
With lamps and candles of departed men
The misty stars thy crown the night thy dress:
Most peerless — magical and dost possess
My heart: and old days come to life again
Old mornings dawn and olden evenings bring
The same old twilight noises from the [town]
Thou hast the very core of longing and delight
To thee my spirit dances often in sleep
Along thy great grey streets or down
A little lamplit alley-way at night
Thinking no more of cities it has known
Forgetting for a while the tree-girt keep
Where even if men dwell they do not sing

The thousand pinnacles and fretted spires
Are lit with echoes and are all aflare
With many bells that sweetly ring
Lighting great vistas of majestic days
The windy years have blown on distant ways
But their music tremble[s] in the air
Old voices gust about thy streets, or robed choirs
In darkened chapels faintly sing
Slow dirges and old hymns of praise
Behind great doors or windows inward-lit
Throngs and assemblies and great conclaves sit

Or men carouse while in a lonely roof
Some scholars shaded light shines high aloof
Such grievous magic is here in thy chimes
That when I hear them ring O city of tears
There gleams a mighty mirage of old times
Ere lay in emptiness thy hopeful years
Ere death unlooked for all too early reaped
And though wars all thy prosperous days destroy
And though along thy streets no laughter runs

Thy morn is poignant and thy evening stabs with joy
Compound of every morn and eve and every day
The windy years have strewn;
Have gathered; and have wafted far away

Tolkien made a second manuscript of the work, in ink, then revised it significantly in pencil, dating it probably at the time of revision to 'March 16–17–18 1916'. The new draft includes frequent cancellations and overwriting, and two lists of rhyming words (*bowl, bole, coal . . . , brown, crown, clown . . .*). On its first page Tolkien gave it the title *The Wanderer's Allegiance*, but later changed this to *The Sorrowful City*. In revising, he also gave the work three internal titles: 'Prelude' for the first quarter, 'The Inland Town' for the second, and 'The Sorrowful City' for the final half. Two further pages of workings seem to be contemporary with the second draft, one for the 'Prelude', exceedingly rough and including a list of rhymes for *bow, crow, dough . . .* , and one for 'The Sorrowful City'.

Relative to text A, this draft as first written had few appreciable changes. Perhaps the most notable difference between the two is the length of the first section, which Tolkien expanded from thirteen lines to twenty. We give this part of the second manuscript as B.

[B] In unknown days the generations of my fathers' sires
Came and from son to son took root
Among the orchards and the river-meads
And the long grasses of the fragrant plain:
Many a summer saw they kindle yellow fires
Of iris in the bowing reeds,
And many a sea of blossom turn to golden fruit
In walléd gardens of the great champain.
There daffodils among the ordered trees
Do nod in spring — and men laugh deep and long
Singing as they labour happy lays
And lighting even with a drinking song
There sleep comes easy for the drone of bees
Thronging about cottage-gardens heaped with flowers:
In love of sunlit goodliness of days
There richly flowed their lives in settled hours
But that was long ago
No more they sing nor reap nor sow
And I perforce in many a town about the loved isle
Unsettled wanderer must dwell a while

Tolkien revised the third version of the work more extensively than the second. Some of its changes developed in his earlier draft, but many seem to have appeared *ab initio* as he wrote out a new manuscript in a neat hand. This includes only a few later revisions and excisions, which we document in our notes. Christopher Tolkien published the third draft in *The Book of Lost Tales, Part Two*, pp. 295–7; we give it here as C, incorporating all of Tolkien's revisions. The poem was again divided into three parts, now entitled 'Prelude' (with Old English *Foresang*), 'The Town of Dreams' (Old English *Þaet Slǽpende Tún*), and 'The City of Present Sorrow' (Old English *Seo Wépende Burg*). The overall title *The Town of Dreams and the City of Present Sorrow*, written at the head of the 'Prelude', also has a corresponding version in Old English, *Þaet Slǽpende Tún* ⁊ *Séo Wépende Burg*, and there Tolkien later inscribed 'March 1916 Oxford and Warwick Rewritten B'ham [Birmingham] Nov[ember] 1916'.

[C] *Prelude*

In unknown days my fathers' sires
Came, and from son to son took root
Among the orchards and the river-meads
And the long grasses of the fragrant plain:
Many a summer saw they kindle yellow fires
Of iris in the bowing reeds,
And many a sea of blossom turn to golden fruit
In walléd gardens of the great champain.

*

There daffodils among the ordered trees
Did nod in spring, and men laughed deep and long
Singing as they laboured happy lays
And lighting even with a drinking song.
There sleep came easy for the drone of bees
Thronging about cottage gardens heaped with flowers;
In love of sunlit goodliness of days
There richly flowed their lives in settled hours —
But that was long ago,
And now no more they sing, nor reap, nor sow,
And I perforce in many a town about the isle
Unsettled wanderer have dwelt awhile.

The Town of Dreams

Here many days had gently past me crept
In this dear town of old forgetfulness;
Here all entwined in dreams I long had slept
And heard no echo of the world's distress
Come through the rustle of the elms' rich leaves,
While Avon gurgling over shallows wove
Unending melody, and morns and eves
Slipped down her waters till the Autumn came,
Like the gold leaves that drip and flutter then
Till the dark river gleams with jets of flame
That slowly float far down beyond our ken.

⋆

For here the castle and the mighty tower,
More lofty than the tiered elms,
More grey than long November rain,
Sleep, and nor sunlit moment nor triumphant hour,
Nor passing of the seasons or the Sun
Wake their old lords too long in slumber lain.

⋆

No wakefulness disturbs their splendid dream
Though laughing radiance dance down the stream;
And be they clad in snow or lashed by windy rains,
Or may March whirl the dust about the winding lanes,
The Elm robe, and disrobe her of a million leaves
Like moments clustered in a crowded year,
Still their old heart unmoved nor weeps, nor grieves
Uncomprehending of this evil tide
Today's great sadness or tomorrow's fear:
Faint echoes fade within their drowsy halls
Like ghosts: the daylight creeps across their walls.

The City of Present Sorrow

There is a city that far distant lies
And a vale outcarven in forgotten days —
There wider was the grass, and lofty elms more rare;
The river-sense was heavy in the lowland air.

There many willows changed the aspect of the Earth and skies
Where feeding brooks wound in by sluggish ways,
And down the margin of the sailing Thames
Around his broad old bosom their old stems
Were bowed, and subtle shades lay on his streams
Where their grey leaves adroop o'er silver pools
Did knit a coverlet like shimmering jewels
Of blue and misty green and filtering gleams.

⋆

O agéd city of an all too brief sojourn,
I see thy cloistered windows each one burn
With lamps and candles of departed men.
The misty stars thy crown, the night thy dress,
Most peerless-magical thou dost possess
My heart, and old days come to life again;
Old mornings dawn, or darkened evenings bring
The same old twilight noises from the town.
Thou hast the very core of longing and delight
To thee my spirit dances oft in sleep
Along thy great grey streets or down
A little lamplit alley-way at night —
Thinking no more of other cities it has known,
Forgetting for awhile the tree-girt keep,
And town of dreams, where men no longer sing.

⋆

For thy heart knows, and thou shedst many tears
For all the sorrow of these evil years.
Thy thousand pinnacles and fretted spires
Are lit with echoes and the lambent fires
Of many companies of bells that ring
Rousing pale visions of majestic days
The windy years have strewn down distant ways;
And in thy halls still doth thy Spirit sing
Songs of old memory amid thy present tears,
Or hope of days to come half-sad with many fears;
Lo! though along thy paths no laughter runs
While war untimely takes thy many sons,
No tide of evil can thy glory drown
Robed in sad majesty, the stars thy crown.

In these verses the 'Town of Dreams' is Warwick, on the river Avon 'gurgling over shallows', with its castle and 'mighty tower' and its special place in Tolkien's heart as we have seen in earlier poems; and the 'City of Present Sorrow' is Oxford, with its willows and the river Thames (also mentioned in *From Iffley*, poem no. 10), in which Tolkien had 'an all too brief sojourn' as an undergraduate. Oxford was much changed by the war, already by the end of 1914 while Tolkien was still in residence, and by 1916 fighting had 'untimely [taken its] many sons'. Here the poet looks back to 'unknown days' when his 'fathers' sires came', referring perhaps to Tolkien's forebears who emigrated to England from Germany, or his maternal Suffield ancestors in the West Midlands. He is torn between Warwick and Oxford, but also, at this time, an 'unsettled wanderer' who has 'dwelt awhile' 'in many a town about the isle': a soldier in training, he has been moved from camp to camp, not free to choose where to live while the war lasts. The 'allegiance' of the wanderer is divided: as his 'spirit dances oft in sleep' to the streets and alleys of Oxford, it forgets 'for while the tree-girt keep, | And town of dreams'.

Tolkien describes the war as 'this evil tide | Today's great sadness or tomorrow's fear' (C45–46). In *Tolkien and the Great War* John Garth writes that '"tomorrow" here is not just age . . . but the dreadful prospect of battle that Tolkien and his peers faced. Against this terrible upheaval, the "old lords too long in slumber lain" represent a deceptive continuity, an inertia that rolls unheeding through the changing years.' Oxford, in contrast, in the poem is shown to have 'true continuity, based on academic erudition and the perpetual renewal of its membership' (pp. 131, 132).

Christopher Wiseman criticized the autobiographical elements of the poem, feeling that Tolkien had exhausted this vein in his writing and should, instead, pursue his 'epic' ('The Silmarillion'). John Garth thinks it 'perhaps no coincidence that Tolkien experimented in this more conventional direction' for the poem, the overtly personal rather than the fantastic, 'in the midst of his argument with Wiseman about the "freakishness" of his other poetry' (*Tolkien and the Great War*, p. 130; see poem no. 40).

The dates Tolkien inscribed on the second draft of *The Town of Dreams and the City of Present Sorrow* suggest that he began to compose it when he attended a delayed degree ceremony in Oxford on 16 March 1916. Indeed, on 17 March he wrote to Edith Bratt that 'a poem bubbled up yesterday and came out in snatches in the train and I have worked hard at it today' (Bodleian Library). He and Edith were married in Warwick on 22 March. In November 1916, when (according to later recollection) he rewrote the poem in Birmingham, he was in hospital beginning his recovery from trench fever.

The second section, *The Town of Dreams*, exists also as two separate manuscripts, their texts identical to each other except for a few differences in punctuation; nor was there substantive change relative to text C above, except that the final lines of the first stanza were now within brackets. Tolkien originally entitled each manuscript *The Town of Dreams: An Old Town Revisited*. In one, he changed the title proper to *The Town of Dead Days*, and on the other added a long bracketed extension of the subtitle: this appears to begin 'In Memory of' or 'A Memory of' and ends '(March 1916)', but Tolkien struck through most of its words too heavily to allow them to be read.

For a separate manuscript of part of the third section of the poem, Tolkien returned to the title *The Sorrowful City*, but later replaced it with *1916: Wínsele Wéste, Windge Reste Réte Berofene* (Old English 'The Feasting-hall Empty, the Resting-place Windswept, Bereft of Joy', a near-quotation from *Beowulf*). For this discrete text, given here as D from the typescript, he slightly revised thirteen lines from C above, starting with 'O agéd city of an all too brief sojourn' (line 61), more substantially revised the two lines following (74–75), and appended the final couplet (lines 88–89) with its echoes of the Psalms.

[D] O agéd city of an all too brief sojourn,
I see thy cloistered windows each one burn
With lamps and candles of departed men.
The misty stars thy crown, the night thy dress,
Most peerless-magical thou dost possess
My heart, and old days come to life again;
Old mornings dawn, or darkened evening brings
The same old twilight noises from the town.

Thou hast the very core of longing and delight;
To thee my spirit dances oft in sleep
Along thy great grey streets, or down
A little lamplit alley-way at night.
Thinking no more of other cities it has known,
Forgetting for a while that all men weep
It strays there happy, and to thee it sings
'No tide of evil can thy glory drown,
Robed in sad majesty, the stars thy crown!'

At the foot of this manuscript, struck through, are 'Oxford March 1916' and a list of four of Tolkien's other poems 'in addition' which could not have been written prior to late 1916: 'The Town of Dreams etc., July in England, The Harebell, GBS', i.e. the second section of the present poem; a poem which became part of *Two Eves in Tavrobel*, no. 48; *The Lonely Harebell*, no. 39; and *G.B.S.*, no. 53.

The Old English title *Wínsele Wéste, Windge Reste Réte Berofene* also appears on a typescript copy, made with the purple ribbon associated with Tolkien's years at Leeds (1920–5), with '1916' added in manuscript but struck through. The typescript also has a later scribbled note, 'For Oxford 1916', with the date erroneously altered to '1915'. Tolkien added the title *1916: Wínsele Wéste* in manuscript to a list of poems he considered for a collection, also from the early 1920s. The Leeds text is almost identical to that of D above, apart from a few small differences, such as 'O! aged city' at the start of its first line, indentations, and the two stanzas closed up to form one.

Although there is no evident association between *The Town of Dreams and the City of Present Sorrow* through most of its drafts and Eriol, the wandering mariner of *The Book of Lost Tales* (see poem no. 40), Tolkien recast and extended the 'Prelude' as a third discrete poem, *The Song of Eriol*, tied to the 'Silmarillion' mythology by a prose introduction. The first of the two parts in which it was now presented is a straightforward revision of the 'Prelude', while the second part consists of new verses made for the purpose. The *Song* survives in three manuscripts; each of the later two incorporate changes made to the earlier versions, while the latest, retitled *Song of Eriol* (without the definite article), includes only the second of its two parts (from line 21). Our transcription given below, as E, is taken from the latest texts, the first part from the second manuscript, and the second part from the third manuscript.

[E] 'Eriol made a song in the Room of the Tale-Fire telling
how his feet were set on wandering, so that in the end
he found the Lonely Isle and that fairest town Kortirion.'

I

In unknown days my fathers' sires
Came and from son to son took root
Among the orchards and the river-meads
And the long grasses of the fragrant plain:

Many a summer saw they kindle yellow fires
Of flag-lilies among the bowing reeds,
And many a sea of blossom turn to golden fruit
In walléd gardens of the great champain.

There daffodils among the ordered trees
Did nod in spring, and men laughed deep and long
Singing as they laboured, happy lays
And lighting even with their drinking song.

There sleep came easy for the drone of bees
Thronging about cottage gardens heaped with flowers;
In love of sunlit goodliness of days
There richly flowed their lives in settled hours —
But that was long ago,
And now no more they sing, nor reap, nor sow;
And I, perforce, in many a town about this isle
Unsettled wanderer have dwelt awhile.

2

Wars of great kings and clash of armouries,
Whose swords no man could tell, whose spears
Were numerous as a wheat-field's ears,
Rolled over all the Great Lands, and the Seas

Were loud with navies; their devouring fires
Behind the armies burnt both fields and towns;
And sacked, and crumbled or to flaming pyres
Were cities made, where treasuries and crowns,

Kings and their folk, their wives and tender maids
Were all consumed. Now silent are those courts,
Ruined the towers, whose old shape slowly fades,
And no feet pass beneath their broken ports.

*

There fell my father on a field of blood,
And in a hungry siege my mother died,
And I, a captive, heard the great seas flood
Calling and calling, that my spirit cried

For the dark western shores whence long ago had come
Sires of my mother, and I broke my bands
Faring o'er wasted valleys and dead lands
Until my feet were moistened by the western sea,
Until my ears were deafened by the hum,
The splash, and roaring of the western sea —
— But that was long ago
And now the dark bays and unknown waves I know,
The twilight capes, the misty archipelago,
And all the perilous sounds, and the salt wastes tween this isle
Of magic and the coasts I knew a while.

Christopher Tolkien includes this text in *The Book of Lost Tales, Part Two*, pp. 298–9.

In the first manuscript of text E, lines 29–32 originally read:

Kings and their folk, and maids, and tender things
Were all consumed: now silent are their courts
Ruined their towers; and no voice sings their old [songs]
About their streets and no feet tread beneath their broken ports

Tolkien revised them as:

Kings and their folk, or wives or tender maids
Were all consumed: now silent are those courts
Ruined the towers; their old shape slowly fades,
And no feet pass beneath their broken ports.

In the second manuscript, he wrote out the stanza much as he had done originally in the first manuscript:

Kings and their folk, and maids, and tender things
Were all consumed. Now silent are their courts
Ruined their towers; and no voice sings
About their streets, and no feet [tread >] pass beneath their broken ports.

He then revised this to:

Kings and their folk, e'en wives and tender maids
Were all consumed. Now silent are those courts
Ruined the towers, whose old shape slowly fades
And no feet pass beneath their broken ports.

Tolkien sometimes returned to an earlier draft and marked it with changes he had applied to a later version, but here the revisions are not the same. In l. 29 of the third manuscript, 'their wives' replaced 'e'en wives'.

The second *Song of Eriol* manuscript is inscribed 'Easington 1917–[1]8'. Christopher Tolkien has suggested reasonably that 'the second part of *The Song of Eriol* was written at Easington and added to the first part . . . already in existence' (*The Book of Lost Tales, Part Two*, p. 300). (Tolkien was billeted at Easington, Yorkshire, from mid-November 1917 until late February or early March 1918; see poem no. 39.) If this is so, then Eriol already existed in *The Cottage of Lost Play*, which Tolkien wrote in the winter of 1916–17, and also in linking passages in *The Book of Lost Tales*, notably the 'Link to the Tale of Tinúviel':

> Then Eriol told her [Vëannë, teller of the *Tale of Tinúviel*] of his home that was in an old town of Men girt with a wall now crumbled, and a river ran thereby over which a castle with a great tower hung. . . . 'I lived there but a while, and not after I was grown to be a boy. My father came of a coastward folk, and the love of the sea that I had never seen was in my bones, and my father whetted my desire, for he told me tales that his father had told him before. Now my mother died in a cruel and hungry siege of that old town, and my father was slain in bitter fight about the walls, and in the end I Eriol escaped to the shoreland of the Western Sea, and mostly have lived upon the bosom of the waves or by its side since those far days. [*The Book of Lost Tales, Part Two*, pp. 4–5]

Christopher Tolkien has remarked on 'the fact that the first part of *The Song of Eriol* is also found as the Prelude to a poem of which the subjects are Warwick and Oxford', which

> might make one suspect that the castle with a great tower overhanging a river in the story told by Eriol to Vëannë was once again Warwick. But I do not think that this is so. There remains in any case the objection that it would be difficult to accommodate the attack on it by men out of the Mountains of the East which the duke could see from his tower; but also I think it is plain that the original tripartite poem had been dissevered, and the *Prelude* given a new bearing: my father's 'fathers' sires' became Eriol's 'fathers' sires'. At the same time, certain power-

ful images were at once dominant and fluid, and the great tower of Eriol's home was indeed to become the tower of Kortirion or Warwick, when . . . the structure of the story of the mariner was radically changed. And nothing could show more clearly than does the evolution of this poem the complex root from which the story rose. [*The Book of Lost Tales, Part Two*, p. 300]

A1: Tolkien marked 'ancient sires' as a possible revision of 'fathers'.

A2: Tolkien considered whether to change this line to 'Came and dwelt there from son to son and took deep root'. The word 'came' at the end of l. 1 presumably would have been deleted to accommodate the new text in l. 2.

A4: Tolkien placed this line in brackets.

A5: Tolkien wrote 'fires' as an alternative to 'flame'.

A8: Tolkien wrote 'fragrant plain' as an alternative to 'great champain'.

A12: Tolkien placed 'lovéd' in brackets.

A13: Tolkien wrote 'must dwell' and 'long while' as alternatives to 'have dwelt' and 'awhile'.

A14: Tolkien wrote '(And)' in the margin at the start of this section.

A39: Tolkien considered whether to change 'forgotten' to 'the elder'.

A50–51: Tolkien marked these lines with a query (?). Line 51 is presumably a reference to army maneuvers.

A54: Tolkien considered whether to change 'of departed men' to 'lit by vanished men'.

A55: Tolkien considered whether to change 'misty stars' to 'hazy stars'. In the course of writing, he deleted two lines which originally followed l. 55: 'Or old suns shine at noon and loom again | Thou still alone supremely art'.

A56: Tolkien considered whether to change 'and dost' to 'thou dost'. In the course of writing, he deleted the following line after l. 56: 'The highest throne amid my heart:'.

A57: 'And old days come to life again' originally read 'or old days seem to shine again'.

A58: 'Evenings bring' originally read 'bells ring'.

A59: Tolkien omitted the final word in this line; 'town' seems apt.

A72: 'Music' replaced 'voices', but Tolkien did not change the tense of 'tremble'.

A82: Tolkien considered whether to change 'mighty mirage' to 'happy mirage'.

A84: Words written below this line seem to be ideas to replace it: 'untimely struck thy stalwart thy sons'.

C19: Tolkien considered whether to change 'the isle' to 'this isle'.

C21: Tolkien considered whether to change 'had gently past me crept' to 'did gently past me creep'.

C23: Tolkien considered whether to change 'I long had slept' to 'I long did sleep'.

C36: 'Passing' originally read 'passage'.

C37: Tolkien deleted two lines following this line: 'Or rouses more than echoes in their drowsy halls | As daylight marks its passage on the mossy walls.'

John Garth identifies the 'old lords too long in slumber lain' with the Norman earls lying in the medieval keep in Warwick Castle, 'as if in a blissful reverie, silently rebuked by the passing seasons' (*Tolkien and the Great War*, p. 130).

C38: Tolkien considered whether to change 'wakefulness' to 'watchfulness'. In *The Book of Lost Tales, Part Two*, Christopher Tolkien took this to be a settled revision, though the original reading 'wakefulness' was not struck through.

C39: Tolkien considered whether to change 'dance' to 'dances'.

C45: Tolkien deleted two lines following this line: 'The leaves of Autumn fall like hours to Earth | And they sleep on, nor heed our bitter dearth.'

C47: 'Faint echoes fade within their drowsy halls' originally read 'Faint echoes only are there in the drowsy halls'.

C48: 'Like ghosts:' originally read 'And arches, as'.

C57–9: These lines originally read 'Were bowed, and their grey leaves | Did trace more subtle shadows in his streams | Or knit a coverlet to silver pools'.

C60: Tolkien considered whether to change the start of this line to 'From blue', but ultimately restored 'Of'.

C67: 'Old mornings dawn, or darkened evenings bring' originally read 'Old mornings dawn, or some old evening brings'.

C75: 'And town of dreams, where men no longer sing' originally read 'Where sombre dreams dwell now, and no one sings'.

C86: 'Lo!' originally read 'And,'.

E6: 'Of flaglilies among the bowing reeds' originally read 'Of iris in the bowing reeds' in the second manuscript.

E12: 'Their drinking song' originally read 'a drinking song' in the second manuscript.

E27: In the first manuscript this line read 'Were sacked, and crumbled; [burning >] flaming pyres'. In the second manuscript it became 'All sacked and crumbled, [flaming >] or the flaming pyres'. 'And sacked' replaced 'All sacked' in the third manuscript.

E28: In the first manuscript this line read 'The cities made, where treasuries and crowns'. 'Were cities made' replaced 'Cities were made' in the third manuscript, but Tolkien also marked the change on the second manuscript, where 'Were' replaced 'The'.

E36: 'That' originally read 'for' in the second manuscript.

E41: 'By the hum' replaced 'with the hum' in the second manuscript.

E44: In the first manuscript this line read as written in the third manuscript. In the second manuscript Tolkien expanded it to 'And now the dark bays and misty archipelago | The Evening Islands and the unknown waves I know' before reverting to the earlier text. The 'Evening Islands' seem to be a momentary invention, not found elsewhere in Tolkien's mythology.

45

Habbanan beneath the Stars · *Eruman beneath the Stars* (1916–*c.* 1924)

The poem first entitled *Habbanan beneath the Stars* is found in two manuscripts and a later (*c.* 1924) typescript. The text is the same in each, apart from minor differences of punctuation and capitalization, the presence or absence of ornaments between stanzas, and the notable change of the name *Habbanan* to *Eruman*. 'Eruman' is lightly pencilled on the first manuscript, amended in the title and in two places in the text of the second, and present *ab initio* in the typescript, i.e. of *Eruman beneath the Stars*. Here, as A, we have transcribed the first version, also published by Christopher Tolkien in *The Book of Lost Tales, Part One*, pp. 91–2. If the poem had any preliminary workings – the earliest manuscript has the appearance of a fair copy – they do not seem to have survived.

[A] 'Now Habbanan is that region where one draws nigh to the places that are not of men. There is the air very sweet and the sky very great by reason of the broadness of the Earth. ——'

In Habbanan beneath the stars
Where all roads end however long
There is a sound of faint guitars
And distant echoes of a song,
For there men gather into rings
Round their red fires, while one voice sings —
And all about is night.

⋆

Not night as ours, unhappy folk,
Where nigh the Earth in hazy bars,
A mist about the springing of the stars,
There trails a thin and wandering smoke
Obscuring with its veil half seen
The great abysmal still Serene.

⋆

A globe of dark glass faceted with light
Wherein the splendid winds have dusky flight;
Untrodden spaces of an odorous plain
That watches for the moon, that long has lain
And caught the meteors fiery rain —
Such there is night.

*

There on a sudden did my heart perceive
That they who sang about the Eve,
Who answered the bright-shining stars
With gleaming music of their strange guitars,
These were His wandering happy Sons
Encamped upon those aëry leas
Where God's unsullied garment runs
In glory down His mighty knees.

Text B which follows is the final version, taken from the typescript.

[B] 'Now Eruman is that region where one draws nigh to the places that are not of men. There is the air very sweet and the sky very great by reason of the broadness of the Earth —'

In Eruman beneath the Stars,
Where all roads end however long,
There is a sound of faint guitars
And distant echoes of a song;
For there men gather into rings
Round their red fires, while one voice sings —
And all about is night.

Not night as ours, unhappy folk,
Where nigh the Earth in hazy bars,
A mist about the springing of the stars,
There trails a thin and wandering smoke
Obscuring with its veil half seen
The great abysmal still Serene.

A globe of dark glass faceted with light
Wherein the splendid winds have dusky flight;
Untrodden spaces of an odorous plain

That watches for the moon, that long has lain
And caught the meteors' fiery rain —
Such there is night.

There on a sudden did my heart perceive
That they who sang about the Eve,
Who answered the bright-shining stars
With gleaming music of their strange guitars,
These were His wandering happy sons
Encamped upon those aëry leas
Where God's unsullied garment runs
In glory down His mighty knees.

Tolkien inscribed on the first manuscript 'Written Étaples June 1916' and, possibly later, 'Insp[ired] Brocton Dec[ember] 1915', as well as a title in Old English, *Þā Ʒebletsode Feldá under þām Steorrum* ('The Blessed Fields under the Stars'). 'Brocton 1915' is written on the typescript. Tolkien was posted to Brocton Camp on Cannock Chase from December 1915 to June 1916; on 6 June 1916 he crossed the English Channel to Calais, and from there travelled to Étaples where he was to be trained and 'toughened' before assignment at the front. It is easy to imagine that the poem was inspired by his camp experiences while still in England, with men gathered around fires, none with a life wholly his to control while fighting lasted, or (as John Garth has suggested) by the dusty, rainy, monotonous existence he found in France – both may have played a role.

In the world of Tolkien's mythology as it evolved in *The Book of Lost Tales*, Habbanan was located west of the Great Sea and south of the Mountains of Valinor (see poem no. 31). A land of wide and misty plains, Men are said to come to it after death, judged by Fui Nienna and chosen to wander there 'in the dusk, camping as they may, yet are they not utterly without song, and they can see the stars, and wait in patience till the Great End come', while others remain with their judge, or are sent to Melko to suffer his evil, or to dwell with the Valar (*The Book of Lost Tales, Part One*, p. 77). Those who sojourn in Habbanan may be in a kind of Purgatory, neither in Hell (with Melko) nor in Heaven (with the 'gods'). There is, however, no sense of suffering or expiation in Habbanan or Eruman, indeed the dead are cheerfully close to God.

Habbanan was an early form of the name, with an alternative *Harwalin*, before Tolkien changed them to *Eruman* and *Arvalin*; each indicates that the place was near the Valar but outside the realm of the 'gods'. In his ?1916–17 lexicon of Gnomish, Tolkien says of *Erumàni* (i.e. *Eruman*) that it is 'the dark land outside *Valinor* . . . and to the south of the Bay of Faery . . . beyond the abode of the Mānir' or spirits of the air, and the name includes *-mani* (*-man*) 'good, holy'. Gnomish *manos* means 'a spirit that has gone to the *Valar*, or to *Erumàni*' (*I·Lam na·Ngoldathon*, pp. 31, 56), and in Qenya *manimo* is a 'Holy soul' and **manimuine* is defined as 'Purgatory'.

As Christopher Tolkien has remarked, *Habbanan* (or *Eruman*) *beneath the Stars* offers 'a rare and very suggestive glimpse of [his father's] mythic conception in its earliest phase; for here ideas that are drawn from Christian theology are explicitly present' (*The Book of Lost Tales, Part One*, p. 92). This is especially so in its final lines. John Garth has similarly pointed out that 'there is a spiritual and religious dimension to Tolkien's world, never absent though rarely blatant, that was notably pronounced in his original conceptions' (*Tolkien and the Great War*, p. 112). In Christian thought, an 'unsullied' (clean, white) garment is a symbol of righteous faith; in *The Lord of the Rings* the three Elven-rings were not made or touched by Sauron, and thus themselves 'unsullied', without inherent malice (*The Silmarillion*, p. 288).

In line 13 the (adjectival) word 'abysmal' is present in all three texts. We presume that Tolkien meant to write (the noun) *abyss* or, more archaically, *abysm* 'region of unfathomable depth', here the infinite expanse of a starry sky. Also in all of the texts, 'Serene' is capitalized, which we suppose – along with the adjacency of 'still' – is meant to strengthen the quality of calmness and quietude. The language of the poem, with its 'globe of dark glass', its winds in 'dusky flight' (i.e. at dusk), its 'untrodden spaces of an odorous plain' (i.e. pleasantly fragrant), echoes the work of the Romantics and their love of the sublime, or spiritually transcendent qualities in nature. Wordsworth especially comes to mind, as in *The Excursion* (1814):

> the chasm of sky above my head
> Is heaven's profoundest azure; no domain
> For fickle, short-lived clouds to occupy,
> Or to pass through; but rather an abyss
> In which the everlasting stars abide . . .

And Shelley in 'Stanzas – April, 1814':

> Away! the moor is dark beneath the moon,
> Rapid clouds have drank the last pale beam of even:

Away! the gathering winds will call the darkness soon,
And profoundest midnight shroud the serene lights of heaven.

A1: In *The Book of Lost Tales, Part One*, p. 91, 'stars' at the end of this line is misprinted 'skies'.

A2: Tolkien added this line after the text was written out, probably an oversight if, as we think, he was referring to a draft while making a fair copy.

46

Tol Eressea · *For England: The Lonely Isle* · *The Lonely Isle* (1916–*c*. 1927)

The first manuscript of this poem, transcribed below as A, was linked by Tolkien to his mythology through its title, *Tol Eressea* (*sic*, without a diaeresis), and references in its text to the island, to the Solosimpe, and to the Eldar. We have referred earlier to the 'lonely isle' (Qenya *tol* 'island' + *eressëa* 'lonely'), and to Tolkien's early plans for his mythology, in which Tol Eressëa in time would become England; see especially poem no. 40.

[A]

O Tol Eressea sea-girdled isle alone
— A gleam of white rock through a sunny haze;
O all ye hoary caverns ringing with the moan
Of long green waters in the southern bays;
Ye murmurous never-ceasing voices of a tide;
Ye pluméd foams wherein the Solosimpe ride;
Ye white birds flying from the fading coast
And wailing conclaves of the silver shore,
Sea-voiced, sea-wingéd, lamentable host
Who cry like old things lost for evermore,
Who sadly whistling skim the waters grey
And wheel about my lonely outward way;

Never shall I forget this farewell gaze,
Or cease to hear the sorrow of these seas
To think thee crowned in glory of thy summer days,
Thy shores all full of music and thy lands of ease —
— Old haunts of many children robed in flowers
Until the sun pace down his arch of hours
When 'neath the stars the Eldar with a wistful heart
Dance to soft airs their harps and viols weave
Down bitter wastes and in a gloom apart
I long for thee and thy far citadel
Where echoing through the lighted elms at eve
In a high inland tower there peals a bell —
O Tol Eressea farewell.

The Solosimpe (later Solosimpi, Teleri) are a kindred of the Elves in Tolkien's mythology. In his Qenya lexicon he translated the name as 'shoreland pipers', defined as 'the fairies [who] lived among rocks and shingles of Eldamar, who danced along the beaches of the world – and now they dance and pipe to the waves of the shores of Tol Eressea' (*Qenyaqetsa*, p. 85). *Eldar* at this stage of the mythology was another name for the Solosimpe. It could be that Tolkien connected *Tol Eressea* to his invented world in the first manuscript in response to Christopher Wiseman urging him to write his 'epic' (see poem no. 44); the names *Solosimpe* and *Eldar* were already known to Wiseman by mid-March 1916, when he mentioned them in a letter to Tolkien. But the poem is foremost a lament for the 'lonely outward way' its author followed across the English Channel on 6 June, having been posted at last to France, while the white cliffs of home receded and he heard the plaintive cry of gulls. The 'far citadel', 'lighted elms', and 'inland tower' are nostalgic references, once again, to Warwick.

Harps and viols, or their equivalent, also figure in the musical creation of the world in Tolkien's *Ainulindalë*: 'Then the voices of the Ainur, like unto harps and lutes, and pipes and trumpets, and viols and organs, and like unto countless choirs singing with words, began to fashion the theme of Ilúvatar to a great music' (*The Silmarillion*, p. 15).

In the second manuscript of this poem, made probably not long after the first, Tolkien removed all explicit references to his mythology, and his leave-taking from England became even more affecting, his home now 'crowned in glory through a mist of tears'. We give this revised text as B, as Tolkien wrote it out before making further changes.

[B] O glimmering island set sea-girdled and alone —
— A gleam of white rock through a sunny haze;
O all ye hoary caverns ringing with the moan
Of long green waters in the southern bays;
Ye murmurous never-ceasing voices of the tide
Ye plumèd foams wherein the shoreland spirits ride;
Ye white birds flying from the fading coast
And silver conclaves of a sunlit shore,
Sea-voiced, sea-wingèd, lamentable host
Who cry about unharboured beaches evermore
Who sadly whistling skim these waters grey
And wheel about my lonely outward way;

Never shall I forget how thy white coast appears
Or cease to hear the sound of these seas
To see thee crowned in glory through a mist of tears:
Thy shores all full of music and thy lands of ease —
Old haunts of many children robed in flowers
Until the sun pace down his arch of hours
When neath the stars the fairies with wistful heart
Dance to soft airs their harps and viols weave
Down bitter wastes and in a gloom apart
I long for thee and thy far citadel
Where echoing through the lighted elms at eve
In a high inland tower there peals a bell —
— O lonely sparkling isle farewell.

A few revisions or alternative readings on the second manuscript were carried by Tolkien into a third text, written on squared paper from a notebook, probably of army issue, in which he made still further changes. We give this version, now entitled *For England: The Lonely Isle*, as C.

[C] O glimmering island set sea-girdled and alone —
— A gleam of white rock through a sunny haze;
O all ye hoary caverns ringing with the moan
Of long green waters in the southern bays;
Ye murmurous never-ceasing voices of the tide
Ye pluméd foams wherein the shoreland spirits ride;
Ye white birds flying from the whispering coast
And wailing conclaves of a silver shore,
Sea-voiced, sea-wingèd, lamentable host
Who cry about unharboured beaches evermore
Who sadly whistling skim these waters grey
And wheel about my lonely outward way;

For me for ever thy forbidden marge appears
A gleam of white rock over sundering seas
And thou art crowned in glory through a mist of tears
Thy shores all full of music and thy lands of ease
— Old haunts of many children robed in flowers
Until the sun pace down his arch of hours,
When in the silence fairies with a wistful heart
Dance to soft airs their harps and viols weave
Down awful wastes and in a gloom apart

I long for thee and thy far citadel
Where echoing through the lighted elms at eve
In a high inland tower there peals a bell —
O lonely sparkling isle farewell.

Tolkien also wrote text C in one of his poetry notebooks, inscribing it 'Étaples, Pas de Calais June 1916', and adding a title in Old English, *Seo Unwemmede Ieg* ('The Unstained (or Undefiled) Isle'). In this, he began line 15 'I see thee crowned' before changing it to 'Where thou art', then reverting to 'And thou art', and in line 18 he changed 'his arch' to 'her arch'. Nearly the same text appears also as a further manuscript, inscribed 'Étaples June 1916'; in this Tolkien first wrote 'his arch' in line 18, later changing it to 'her arch', and revised line 21 again by replacing 'awful wastes' with 'the great wastes'.

The Lonely Isle, more simply titled, was further revised in two typescripts, one of which survives in both a ribbon copy and a carbon copy, made probably while Tolkien was at Leeds, the other typed later on Tolkien's Hammond typewriter. Each text was now divided into four, rather than two, stanzas, and many lines end more exuberantly with an exclamation mark. One of the two 'Leeds' copies is inscribed 'Dover 1916', but according to our information, Tolkien sailed for France via Folkestone. We give here, as D, the latest of the typescripts.

[D] O glimmering island set sea-girdled and alone,
A gleam of white rock through a sunny haze!
O all ye hoary caverns ringing with the moan
Of long green waters in the southern bays!
Ye murmurous never-ceasing voices of the tide!
Ye pluméd foams wherein the shoreland spirits ride!

Ye white birds flying from the whispering coast
And silver conclaves of a sunlit shore,
Sea-voiced, sea-wingèd, lamentable host
Who cry about unharboured beaches evermore;
Who sadly whistling skim these waters grey
And wheel about my lonely outward way;

For me for ever thy forbidden marge appears
A gleam of white rock over sundering seas;
And thou art crowned in glory through a mist of tears,
Thy shores all full of music and thy lands of ease,
Old haunts of many children robed in flowers
Until the Sun pace down her arch of hours.

When in the silence fairies with a wistful heart
Dance to soft airs their harps and viols weave,
Over great wastes and to my gloom apart
There echoes through the golden elms at eve
From a high inland tower a pealing bell
Ringing for ever in thy citadel.
O Lonely sparkling isle, farewell!

The Lonely Isle was published in *Leeds University Verse 1914–24* (1924, p. 57), from the text of the final manuscript rather than the later typescript, still with 'his arch' in line 18. As printed, line 22 erroneously reads 'fair citadel' rather than 'far citadel'. John Garth reprinted the *Leeds University Verse* version in *Tolkien and the Great War*.

G.B. Smith was probably referring to *The Lonely Isle* when he wrote to Tolkien on 25 July 1916: 'I have again been reading through your thing about England. Believe me it is one of the best. I copied it out and sent the copy home' (Bodleian Library).

Although we make no claim as to direct inspiration, the earlier versions of Tolkien's poem recall in cadence, in repeated line beginnings, and especially in spirit the most famous speech from Shakespeare's *Richard II*, that frequently quoted paean to England delivered by John of Gaunt in Act II, Scene 2:

This royal throne of kings, this scept'red isle,
This earth of majesty, this seat of Mars,
This other Eden, demi-paradise,
This fortress built by Nature for herself
Against infection and the hand of war,
This happy breed of men, this little world,
This precious stone set in the silver sea,
Which serves it in the office of a wall,
Or as a moat defensive to a house,
Against the envy of less happier lands;
This blessed plot, this earth, this realm, this England. . . .

A13: Tolkien changed 'can' to 'shall', probably in the course of writing.

47

Two-Lieut (1916)

Despite the gravity of the war and his duties as an officer, Tolkien managed to keep a sense of humour. On the reverse side of the sheet on which he wrote the first two manuscripts of *Tol Eressea* (no. 46) – bearing the badge of his regiment, the Lancashire Fusiliers – he composed two similar versions of a short poem, which for lack of a title we have called *Two-Lieut*. We give these as A and B. The first is a limerick which rambles on beyond the five lines standard to the form, while the second is in the form of two limericks joined together.

[A]

There once was a careless Two-Lieut
— Did he know how to drill or to shoot?
  No he got up at nine,
  Spent the day with his wine
In a tavern of evil repute.
He got the eventual boot
For was major C.O.
Or the general too low
For this dissolute Lieut to salute.

[B]

There once was a dashing 'Two-lieut':
Did he know how to drill and to shoot?
  No! he got up at nine,
  Spent the day with his wine
In a tavern of evil repute.
This lordly and lazy 'Two-lieut'
With pale tie and a pale yellow suit
Found both major, C.O.
(Or the general!) too low
For a dissolute Lieut to salute.

'C.O.' is an abbreviation for Commanding Officer. Written above the first version are two unused alternative lines: 'In the end he was given the boot | In spite of his socks and his suit'.

The traditional pronunciation of *lieutenant* in the British Army is '*lef*-tenant', not '*loo*-tenant' as in American English. But in Tolkien's day *loot* was common slang for *lieutenant* and pronounced with *oo*, enabling him to rhyme 'lieut', 'shoot', 'repute', 'boot', 'suit', and 'salute' in the course of only ten lines. A *two-loot* was a second lieutenant, the lowest rank of commissioned officers. Tolkien was himself commissioned a second lieutenant in July 1915, and promoted to full lieutenant two years later.

48

A Dream of Coming Home · A Memory of July in England · July · Two Eves in Tavrobel · An Evening in Tavrobel · Once upon a Time (1916–64)

The related verses discussed here evolved from a poem Tolkien wrote not long after he was sent to the front lines in France. He inscribed the first manuscript of *A Dream of Coming Home*, so titled and given below as A, 'For my wife' and 'A vision of Great Haywood in May', later adding 'Bouzincourt July 4–8 1916' and an Old English title, *Swefen Hāmcymes* ('Dream of Homecoming'). Great Haywood was the Staffordshire village where Edith was then living, near the army camps on Cannock Chase. In May 1916 Tolkien was able to be with her, and G.B. Smith found time to visit them. The Battle of the Somme began on 1 July; two days later, Tolkien marched to Bouzincourt, about three miles to the rear. On 6 July elements of his battalion moved to the trenches, but he himself stayed in Bouzincourt to help with signals, and on that day G.B. Smith arrived for a period of rest. On 6, 7, and 8 July the two friends met as their duties allowed, 'discussing poetry, the war, and the future' (Carpenter, *Biography*, p. 83).

[A] *Prelude*

You know the days when May first looks toward June: —
A time of limpid plenilune
Whereas the tremulous day is done
With golden dancing of the Sun.
The four fair winds have each way strewn
The almond-scented hawthorn bloom,
A rain of shimmering petals on the ways
That skirt her brooks and flowering hays:
And all about the burning stair
She climbs, and round her radiant hair,
The buttercups all filled with yellow light
Had their uncounted goblets bright,
Where all day long the spirits of the sunshine flew

Drinking pure glory, till the sparking dew
Her gentle eve distilled in gems
Among the green blades and slender stems.
Now in the grass lies many a pool
Infinitesimal and cool,
And tiny faces peer therein and laugh
To see the glassy fragments of the stars
About their mirrored faces, or in jars
Of unimagined frailty pour, and quaff,
This essence of the plenilune —
Thirsty, perchance, for dancing all the noon.

Coming Home

'Twas in those days unheated and serene —
No hint of sunburn or of brown was seen
In the new gleaming texture of the leaves;
'Twas in that time of long pellucid eves,
When light is mingled slowly with grey shade,
I wandered down a winding river-glade,
And the long radiance of the westering sun
Ran on the water like pale fire, and spun
Strange patterns 'tween the day and early night
Weaving dim yellow beams with blue dusk-light.
The path I trod became a golden road,
While birds still in the alders sleepy sung —
Low trees that o'er my way enchanted hung
Adrip with flame; and every pebble glowed.
And so I found a gateway in the hays
Beyond whose rugged wood the sky ablaze
Filled with the afterlight the Sun bequeathes
When bowing his great mane he dips, and breathes
The cooler airs beyond the Western deep.
Then sprang a little breeze from early sleep
Just as I entered in this garden rare,
And drank to burst my bosom of the air
Thin and delicious and yet filled with scent
Of flowers — I laughed for perfect merriment.

O! did I not know the secret orchard near
Whose pathway through the apple-boles and pear
Was lined with tufts of golden leopard's-bane,
And those white flowers green-lipped aswing half-seen

Of Solomon's pale lily-seal between.
The murmur-wingéd breeze had passed again
To nestle whispering in the hazel-screen:
A noise of quarrelling robins gone to nest;
A rustle in the leaves — and like a rest
In which a silence grew, and the round moon
Hung silver in the Eve upon the verge of June,
And no fly danced nor late bee hummed a tune
In the warm air beneath the firstling stars.
Then joyfully I pushed aside the bars
And strode all eager through that western gate
Where had we leaned and heard the hollow bell
Strike, as I told you of our long farewell.
There bitterness had swept us like a flame
Until numb sorrow heavy-laden came —
And there I knew that you would all days wait
For this enchanted evening past compare
When all the garden spirits wove their spell
Of scent and half-heard musics and soft air.
You know 'twas just this time of all the year
I found again the orchard, and I found you there.

'When May first looks toward June' suggests a time near the end of the month; this would have been late for hawthorn blossom, however (as we discuss in regard to poem no. 26), unless the petals had not yet dispersed after being strewn by the 'four fair winds'. At least some of the details of landscape in the poem, the 'secret orchard', the 'gateway in the hays [hedges]', are perhaps true (if idealized) reminiscences of Great Haywood. It is hardly to be wondered that, faced with death and destruction, Tolkien's thoughts should turn to a recent memory which, although tinged with sadness, gave him comfort. 'Our long farewell' as 'bitterness . . . swept us like a flame' surely refers to Edith and Tolkien after he was sent a telegram on 2 June 1916, ordering him to embark for France with the British Expeditionary Force three days later; perhaps the striking of a 'hollow bell' announced the arrival of the messenger.

A second manuscript of the poem followed, but is a revision of the second part only, omitting the 'Prelude'; we give this new version below as B. Its title was now preceded by 'Poems of Tavrobel IV', suggesting that *A Dream of Coming Home* was to be one of at least four works connected, at least nominally, with Tavrobel in Tol Eressëa, a village in Tolkien's mythology which in the course of his story (as it then stood) would become Great Haywood. (Regarding Tol Eressëa, see poem no. 40, and further, *The Grey Bridge of Tavrobel*, no. 56.) In any event, he soon abandoned the idea of a series (but see *Two Eves in Tavrobel*, below) and struck through 'Poems of Tavrobel', leaving only the title proper. Later he wrote on the manuscript 'Bouzincourt, during the British barrage July 3 (?) 1914, since rewr[itten]', though according to the battalion's diary he had not arrived in the village before midnight of the 3rd (i.e. early on the 4th).

[B] I dreamt of days unheated and serene —
No brand of sunburn or of brown was seen
In the new texture of the gleaming leaves —
And in that time of long pellucid eves
When light is mingled slowly with grey shade
I wandered down a winding river-glade,
And the long radiance of the westering Sun
Ran on the water like pale fire and spun
Strange patterns 'tween the day and early night
Weaving dim yellow beams with blue dusk-light.
The path I trod there seemed a golden road,
And birds still in the alders sleepy sung —
Low trees that o'er my way enchanted hung
Adrip with flame; and every pebble glowed.
And so I found a gateway in the hays
Beyond whose rugged wood the sky ablaze
Filled with the afterlight the Sun bequeathes
When dipping her great sails she sinks and breathes
The cooler airs beyond the western deep.
Then sprang a little breeze from early sleep,
Just as I entered in this garden rare,
And drank to burst my bosom of the air
Thin and delicious and yet filled with scent
Of flowers — I laughed for perfect merriment.

O! did I not know the secret orchard near
Whose pathway through the apple-boles and pear
Was lined with tufts of golden leopard's-bane
And those white flowers green-lipped aswing half-seen
Of Solomon's pale lily-seal between.
The murmur-wingèd breeze had passed again
To nestle whispering in the hazel-screen:
A noise of quarrelling robins gone to nest;

A rustle in the leaves; and then a rest
In which a silence grew, and the round moon
Hung silver in the eve upon the verge of June;
And no fly danced nor late bee hummed a tune
In the warm air beneath the firstling stars.
Then joyfully I pushed aside the bars
And strode all eager through that Western gate
Where had we leaned and heard the hollow bell
Strike, as I told you of our long farewell.
There bitterness had swept us like a flame
Until numb sorrow heavy-laden came —
And there I knew that you would all days wait
For this enchanted evening past compare
When all the garden spirits wove their spell
Of scent and half-heard musics and soft air.
I dreamed I heard the ringing of a bell;
I dreamed I found the orchard and you there.

Whereas text A is explicitly recollection, in B the poet 'dreamt of days unheated and serene', that he 'heard the ringing of a bell', and that he 'found the orchard and you there'. Enough time passed between the two versions, maybe, that Tolkien's memory of Great Haywood came to seem more like a dream.

On reading *A Dream of Coming Home* Christopher Wiseman had two criticisms, included in his letters to Tolkien. In the first of these, dated 18 January 1917, he thought the poem very good, but that it dealt with ground the poet had already explored. Its nostalgic theme was, indeed, of a piece with other poems Tolkien had then recently composed, such as *The Town of Dreams and the City of Present Sorrow*. Two months later, however, Wiseman declared *A Dream of Coming Home* to be nearly perfect; perhaps he himself was feeling homesick, and the poem now spoke to him more keenly.

Tolkien made, or commissioned to be made, a typescript of *A Dream of Coming Home* probably near the end of his years at Leeds. Based on version B before revision, the poem was now divided into two stanzas at line 25, and included two tentative changes in manuscript, 'well I knew' for 'did I not know' written above line 25, and 'Where we had learned' for 'Where had we learned' in line 40. Ten later lines, beginning with 'Then joyfully', were typed on a second sheet and glued to the bottom margin of the first, and apparently by intention, the two final lines of the poem (in B), after 'soft air', were physically cut off from the sheet, leaving only the tips of two letters in line 48. This typescript was the last iteration of the poem as it was first conceived, before it diverged into separate, and different, parts.

At the end of his time at Bouzincourt Tolkien also wrote a poem entitled *A Memory of July in England*, inscribed 'Bouzincourt July 7–8 1916' and *Sumor on Engalande* (Old English 'Summer in England'). We give this as C, as it stood before further revision. Now Tolkien not only looked back to pleasant memories, but conveyed in the most vivid terms his love of nature, and of the unsullied natural world of England, while living a soldier's life in a landscape of bomb craters and blasted trees.

[C]

O July days! O quintessential times
When the drunk bees beneath the dewy limes
Lie drugged with odour as with heavy wine;
When the wild roses and the horned woodbine
Of prosperous summer clothe the drowsy brakes;
Long dragonflies across your sunny lakes
Go humming with a wingéd flash of green,
Or lightly hover in a sun-blue sheen
Above the island of flat leaves afloat
Where water-lilies moor their shallow boat.
There the low eyots built on muddy reeds
Come to ripe growths of tangled flowers and seeds
— Ragwort, late campion, and melilote,
Rank umbels of the hemlock, and long reeds.

*

O July Eves! A spilling of good gold:
A wealth of many colours that the shadows fold
In sudden veils of twilight crept from lairs
Hidden in hollow tree-roots unawares: —
Then furtive little noises under leaves;
A whisper as of movement in the sheaves
Of flowering grass that border the dim lawns;
A getting ready to come out; a blare of shawms
Minute, low music tremulous and fair —
Till suddenly the moonrise shakes the air
Enchanting the still trees about whose feet,
Moving most silently and moving fleet,
Long strands of secret darkness twist and curl
Lit by a flash of scarlet or a gleaming pearl.

Tolkien carried most of text C into a second manuscript, entitled simply *July*, written on a sheet of ruled notebook paper which may have been army issue. Its words differ from the earlier text only in line 19, which begins 'Come' rather than 'Then', and in line 22, where 'blare of shawms' is replaced with 'sound of shawms'.

Near the end of his years at Leeds, Tolkien once again thought to use Elvish Tavrobel as a link between related poems, and conceived the paired *Two Eves in Tavrobel* in which the second of two verses would be *July* and the first *May*, the latter adapted from the 'Prelude' of *A Dream of Coming Home*. The new *Two Eves in Tavrobel: July*, given below as D, was much reduced from the longer version C and its revision, and had further changes, notably its first lines (equivalent to C15–17); this survives as both a manuscript and a typescript (with identical texts).

[D] Down the red Sun! — and all her phials of gold
Are spilled among the grass; the light grows old,
And sudden veils of twilight creep from lairs
Hidden in hollow tree-roots unawares:

Come furtive little noises under leaves;
A whisper as of movement in the sheaves
Of flowering grass that border the dim lawns;
A getting ready to come out; a sound of shawms
Minute — low music tremulous and fair —
Till, suddenly, the moonrise shakes the air

Enchanting the still trees about whose feet
Moving most silently and moving fleet
Long strands of secret darkness twist and curl
Lit by a flash of scarlet or a gleaming pearl.

A page of manuscript workings for *Two Eves in Tavrobel: May* is rough nearly to the point of illegibility, but there is a *c.* 1924 typescript of the finished work under the 'Two Eves' title (altered in manuscript to *An Evening in Tavrobel*), inscribed by Tolkien as 'excerpted and slightly altered' from *A Dream of Coming Home* – it would be more accurate to say that it was 'freely adapted', since few of the lines drawn from the 'Prelude' went unaltered. We give this text as E, before further revision.

[E] 'Tis the time when May first looks toward June —
Behold the limpid plenilune!
The tremulous day at last has done
With golden dancings of the Sun,
Who brimmed the buttercups with light
Like a clear-wine she spillèd bright —
And gleaming spirits there did dance
To sip those goblets radiance.

Now wane they all; now comes the moon;
Like crystal are the dewdrops strewn
Beneath the Eve, or twinkling gems
Are hung on the leaves and slender stems;
Now in the grass lies many a pool,
Infinitesimal and cool,
Where tiny faces peer, and laugh
At glassy fragments of the stars
About them mirrored, or from jars
Of unimagined frailty quaff
This essence of the plenilune —
Thirsty perchance for dancing all the moon.

While still at Leeds, Tolkien reconceived the poem, as *An Evening in Tavrobel*, in a new typescript. In this he kept the second stanza unchanged from the earlier text, but substantially altered the first (F):

[F] 'Tis the time when May first looks toward June,
With almond-scented hawthorn strewn.
The tremulous day at last has run
Down the golden stairways of the Sun,
Who brimmed the buttercups with light
Like a clear wine she spillèd bright;
And gleaming spirits there did dance,
To sip those goblets radiance.

In this form, with a necessary apostrophe after 'goblets', the poem was published in *Leeds University Verse 1914–24* (1924), p. 56, and reprinted in our extended edition (2014) of *The Adventures of Tom Bombadil and Other Verses from the Red Book*, pp. 284–5.

It remains only to discuss one final poem which evolved from *A Dream of Coming Home*. Three typescripts of *Once upon a Time*, two of them made on Tolkien's Hammond typewriter, were preceded by three manuscript pages with rough workings, one of them shared with the Leeds typescript of *An Evening in Tavrobel*. The most legible of the workings is the start of the poem written on the verso of the typescript leaf, given here as G.

[G]

Once upon a time on the fields of May
the almond-scented petals lay;
the buttercups were filled with light
like yellow wine, and wide and white
there opened in the grassy skies
the earth-stars with their steady eyes
watching the sun climb up and down
Goldberry was there with hawthorn crown
stooping over a lily pool
splashing the water green and cool
the sparkles round her slender arm

The late Rhona Beare proposed in an unpublished paper that *Once upon a Time* was a development of *An Evening in Tavrobel*, and this seemed evident as soon as the two works were laid side by side. The relation is confirmed in Tolkien's papers: added to the final typescript of *An Evening in Tavrobel* is his note, 'eventually became *Once upon a Time*'. From the similarities between the draft text G and *An Evening in Tavrobel* – the setting in May, almond-scented blossom, buttercups brimming with light and compared with clear wine – there can be no doubt that Tolkien initially looked to his earlier poem for inspiration, though *Once upon a Time* soon became twice as long as its predecessor and more sophisticated. We give its latest text as H.

[H]

Once upon a day on the fields of May
there was snow in summer where the blossom lay;
the buttercups tall sent up their light
in a steam of gold, and wide and white
there opened in the green grass-skies
the earth-stars with their steady eyes
watching the Sun climb up and down.
Goldberry was there with a wild-rose crown,
Goldberry was there in a lady-smock
blowing away a dandelion clock,
stooping over a lily-pool
and twiddling the water green and cool

to see it sparkle round her hand:
once upon a time in elvish land.

Once upon a night in the cockshut light
the grass was grey but the dew was white;
the shadows were dark, and the Sun was gone,
the earth-stars shut, but the high stars shone,
one to another winking their eyes
as they waited for the Moon to rise.
Up he came, and on leaf and grass
his white beams turned to twinkling glass,
and silver dripped from stem and stalk
down to where the lintips walk
through the grass-forests gathering dew.
Tom was there without boot or shoe,
with moonshine wetting his big brown toes:
once upon a time, the story goes.

Once upon a moon on the brink of June
a-dewing the lintips went too soon.
Tom stopped and listened, and down he knelt:
'Ha! little lads! So it was you I smelt?
What a mousy smell! Well, the dew is sweet,
So drink it up, but mind my feet!'
The lintips laughed and stole away,
but old Tom said: 'I wish they'd stay!
The only things that won't talk to me,
say what they do or what they be.
I wonder what they have got to hide?
Down from the Moon maybe they slide,
or come in star-winks, I don't know':
Once upon a time and long ago.

In our discussion of *Why the Man in the Moon Came Down Too Soon* (no. 24) we described Tolkien's efforts in 1961 and 1962 to make up a collection of verses with his poem *The Adventures of Tom Bombadil* (no. 121). In the process, he revised the latter work and also wrote a new poem featuring the same character, *Bombadil Goes Boating* (no. 186). But Tom is present as well in *Once upon a Time*: although his surname is never mentioned, readers of the other 'Bombadil' verses, or of *The Lord of the Rings*, could not fail to recognize 'old Tom', especially alongside his wife Goldberry. Tolkien does not seem to have written this poem prior to the 1962 *Bombadil* volume, as there is no mention of it in correspondence as under consideration; instead, he is likely to have composed it after receiving an invitation sometime in 1964 to contribute to the first of a series of anthologies for children called *Winter's Tales for Children*. The poem was complete and in the hands of editor Caroline Hillier by early December 1964, sent to her with *The Dragon's Visit* (no. 107) and *Rosalind Ramage* (no. 187; the latter work was rejected). The anthology was published in October 1965.

Once upon a Time is unlike Tolkien's earlier 'Tom Bombadil' poems. In the others, Tom can communicate with all living creatures, but in *Once upon a Time* the lintips are 'the only things that won't talk to me'. It is also, by comparison, concerned less with Tom and Goldberry than with the natural world: with 'snow in summer' (hawthorn blossom, correctly in the month of May), with buttercups 'in a steam of gold' (in the 'Prelude', 'filled with yellow light'), with 'earth-stars' open 'in the green grass-skies', that is, a green landscape echoing the heavens. 'Earth-stars' may be star-shaped fungi (*Geastrum*) common in the British landscape. Kris Swank has argued, however ('Tom Bombadil's Last Song: Tolkien's "Once upon a Time"', 2013), that Tolkien may have used the name for the common daisy, which opens in the sun and closes again at night, a 'star of earth' as the sun is a star of the sky; and that may be more likely, since *Geastrum* do not respond to light like flowers, though some do open and close according to levels of moisture.

The small, nocturnal, perhaps mouse- or vole-like lintips are descended textually from the 'tiny faces' peering in the grass in *May* and earlier the 'Prelude', and may owe something also to whatever made 'furtive little noises under leaves' in *A Memory of July in England* (C19). They have intrigued readers of *Once upon a Time* since its publication. Some have likened them to pixies, or to other small, supernatural beings in folklore, or have tried to place them within Tolkien's mythology as among the 'lesser spirits' that accompanied the Valar when they descended into the world of which Middle-earth is a part. Like the Mewlips in poem no. 94, however, it may be that they are purely a product of Tolkien's fancy, and have no existence or purpose beyond this poem.

Douglas A. Anderson has suggested that

> the name *lintip/lintips* may be an invented word of Tolkien's like *mewlips*. . . . With the hint in line fourteen of the first stanza, that the poem is set in 'an elvish land', one wonders if *lintip*

might be of elvish construction. The stem *lint/lin* could be interpreted in elvish in a number of ways (the better of several possible stems include Q[uenya] *lint* fluff, down, soft stuff; Q *linte* swift, quickly nimble), but the ending *–ip/–tip* is not of normal elvish construction, and seems to point *lintip* away from being an elvish word. ['The Mystery of Lintips' (2013)]

It would have been like Tolkien, who enjoyed the sounds of words, to call the creatures *lintips* simply because it gave him pleasure. On one of the manuscript pages for *Once upon a Time* he wrote the name twice as *lintits*, and it was given in this form in the second of the three typescripts of the poem, but amended by Tolkien in manuscript to *lintips*. The latter spelling is used in both of the other typescripts.

A9–10: The 'burning stair' and 'radiant hair' presumably refer to the light of the setting sun. Compare 'the long radiance of the westering sun' in A31, the Sun's 'great mane' in A42, as if it were a lion, its 'great sails' in B18, as if it were a ship, and 'the golden stairways of the Sun' in F4.

A11–12: These lines originally read 'The golden goblets filled with yellow light | Of untold buttercups are richly dight' (i.e. arrayed). Tolkien later considered changes to the replacement text: 'The buttercups [all > are] filled with yellow light | [Had > And] their uncounted goblets bright'.

A13: 'Where' originally read 'There'. Tolkien seems to have considered whether to change 'Where' to 'Then'.

A14: 'Drinking' originally read 'And drank'.

A15: Tolkien seems to have considered whether to change 'Her' to 'The'.

A21: Here 'jars' serve as drinking vessels, and a convenient rhyme for 'stars'.

A30: By 'river-glade' Tolkien presumably means an open space through which a river runs.

A32: This line originally read 'Ran on its face like fires, and spun'.

A34: This line originally read 'Palest of pale beams and blue dusk-light'.

A42: Only here among the related poems, with 'bowing his great mane he dips', is the sun is described as male. In all other instances, including l. 10 of this version ('round her radiant hair'), Tolkien gives it female pronouns.

A53: 'Solomon's pale lily-seal' is better known as Solomon's seal (*Polygonatum*).

A55: 'Hazel-screen', i.e. hazel shrubs grown together as a hedge to screen (hide) one property from another.

A62: The 'bars' being pushed are those of the 'western gate'.

B11: 'Seemed' replaced archaic 'meseemed'. Probably at the same time, Tolkien added 'there' before 'seemed', to preserve the rhythm of the earlier reading.

B48–49: Tolkien added the final two lines as given here in pencil, replacing 'You know 'twas just this time of all the year | I found again [this >] the orchard, and I found you there' and writing in the margin '1924'.

C1: Above 'quintessential times' Tolkien wrote 'rich and murmurous' as a possible revision for 'quintessential', but retained 'quintessential' in the next manuscript of *July*.

C2: The 'lime' is here the broad-leafed flowering tree (genus *Tilia*), several species of which grow in Britain; it does not produce citrus fruit. Aphids attracted to its heart-shaped leaves secrete a sweet honeydew which in turn attracts bees.

C4: Woodbine (European honeysuckle, *Lonicera periclymenum*) is 'horned' in the sense that its flowers are trumpet (horn)-shaped.

C5: The brakes (thickets) are 'clothed' by the twining wild roses and woodbine.

C8: The water is 'sun-blue' presumably because it reflects the colour of the sky in sunlight.

C9–10: 'Flat leaves afloat | Where water-lilies moor their shallow boat': the water-lily (*Nymphaeceae*) roots in the soil of pools or ponds, but floats its leaves, shallow pads, and flowers on the surface.

C11: The *eyots* 'small islands' are pads of the water-lilies referred to in l. 10.

D1: 'Down the red Sun!': dramatically, the sun is setting (westering).

H2: Against 'snow in summer', compare 'sweet breathed snow' in *May Day* (no. 26).

H4: *Once upon a Time* was also published in the anthology *The Young Magicians* (1988) edited by Lin Carter, but with '*stream* of gold' for 'steam of gold'. 'Steam' is present in all three typescripts, and more poetically evocative. Compare the buttercups 'all filled with yellow light' in A11.

H8: For the character of Goldberry, see *The Adventures of Tom Bombadil*, poem no. 121. Her 'wild-rose crown' is presumably one of summer flowers (and without thorns); there are many varieties of wild (species) roses in Britain.

H9: 'Lady-smock' originally read 'meadow-smock'. *Smock* in this context (and cf. poems 32, 141) probably means a kind of casual dress worn by women in rural settings, made with gathered (smocked) fabric, sometimes with embroidered patterns. Goldberry is 'in' (i.e. wearing) a 'lady-smock', literally a smock for a lady; Tolkien also may be alluding to the *lady-smock* (or *lady's smock*, or meadow cress, *Cardamine pratensis*), a wildflower.

H10: *Dandelion clock* refers to a children's game of blowing away dandelion seeds and counting the number of puffs, which is supposed to tell the time.

H17: 'Shadows were dark' originally read 'Shadows were falling'. In this latest typescript, l. 17 has a definite article before 'shadows' which is lacking in the other typescripts and in the poem as published in *Winter's Tales for Children 1*.

H19: 'One to another' originally read 'one by one'.

H30: 'A-dewing': the lintips gather, or drink, dew gathered on the grass ('the grass was grey but the dew was white', H16).

H41: We presume that Tolkien used 'star-winks' to mean the twinkling of stars.

49

The Thatch of Poppies (1916–*c.* 1924)

The first of three manuscripts of this poem is inscribed, probably at the time of writing, 'Acheux, Hédauville HQ [headquarters] Thiepval Aug[ust] 24–25' (1916). Tolkien had just completed a course for signalling officers at battalion headquarters at Acheux, where once again he was able to see G.B. Smith. Rob Gilson had been killed in July, on the first day of the Somme, and the surviving friends discussed his greatness and the future of the TCBS. Tolkien rejoined his unit near Thiepval, a German stronghold, on 24 August, travelling by way of Hédauville. On the 24th and 25th, under occasional enemy bombardment, he slept in a dugout and wrote *The Thatch of Poppies* on sheets of squared paper torn from a notebook, yet another of his poems in which he regrets that he is far from home. We give here, as A, its first version, incorporating changes made in the course of composition.

[A] Red falls the sunlight on the broken roof
And still undaunted rings a clock-bell from the tower
Marking the passage of yet one more hour
That I have wandered with my heart aloof
Far far away beyond the distant sea
That I have been so lonely in this multitude
And spoken light words or eaten at their board
With my whole soul and heart bent far abroad
Thinking of other places, other wine and food
Far other voices now beyond the sea.
And for myself in this land one desire
—To find the end of day in some untroubled town,
Pass through the shadowy gateway of a byre
Where darkness falls, and candle-fire
Peeps through the chinks of barns, and lay me down
And sleep, and dream I cross the distant sea.

For there's a magic in the poppies dry and grey
Wherewith this people thatch their courtyard door
That he who passes at an hour of eve leaves war
And weariness almost contented to await the day
He hopes again to find beyond the sea.

Though dead they mingle with their opiate
A feel of winds that fluttered upland crops
Or bore the far-off voices to the gate
Of reapers homing late
Down the white roadways filled with twilight dust.
Down the long avenues whose rustling tops
Could see the moon rise slowly from the dust
Old creaking carts piled high with the pale sheaves
Drew these same poppies nodding their round heads
Down the white roadways spilling faded leaves.

Now at an hour of eve their spirit sheds
A memory of airs and slow sweet rest
On all who pass beneath with weary feet
Piling good slumber with deep dreams most blest
Of hopes delayed or musics incomplete
Fulfilled and happy or played on for evermore
In those sweet gardens on the other shore
That lies beyond the distant sea.

By the time Tolkien wrote this verse Britain and its allies had been at war for more than two years, but despite the devastation the bright red poppy flourished in numbers to match the many thousands killed by fighting and disease. Tolkien and G.B. Smith once, in July 1916, 'walked in a field where poppies still waved in the wind despite the battle that was turning the countryside into a featureless desert of mud' (Humphrey Carpenter, *Biography*, p. 83). In spring 1915, Canadian surgeon John McCrae was inspired by a cluster of poppies to write his poem 'In Flanders Fields':

In Flanders fields the poppies blow
Between the crosses, row on row,
    That mark our place; and in the sky
    The larks, still bravely singing, fly
Scarce heard amid the guns below.

We are the Dead. Short days ago
We lived, felt dawn, saw sunset glow,
    Loved and were loved, and now we lie
        In Flanders fields.

Take up our quarrel with the foe:
To you from failing hands we throw
The torch; be yours to hold it high.
If ye break faith with us who die
We shall not sleep, though poppies grow
In Flanders fields.

The work became widely known, and is still read in memorial services, while the poppy was adopted as a sign of remembrance and perseverance. Tolkien's phrase 'Though dead they mingle with their opiate' was strictly (if perhaps clumsily) true: red poppies, *Papaver rhoeas*, contain an opiate alkaloid, and grew above buried victims of the war, though they are not the source from which heroin and morphine are derived (*Papaver somniferum*).

Associated with the manuscript for A, on the versos of its two leaves, are brief workings for the poem. Some were incorporated into the finished text, but one, 'And still undaunted rings a bell within the tower', replaced line 2 in a second manuscript *ab initio*, and another, 'Strewing the white roadways with their faded leaves', entered the same manuscript as a replacement for line 31 only as a correction to the original reading. The text of the second manuscript, written probably soon after the first, on squared paper from a different notebook in blue pencil reinforced (where faint) in standard pencil, is otherwise identical to the earlier draft. Two workings remained unused: 'That I have been so lonely mid the multitude | Of men though taking meat and drink beside their board', a preliminary or alternative idea for lines 6–7, and 'Beyond the margin of the farthest sea | New shorn and buried'.

Tolkien wrote the text as revised in the second manuscript again in a third, probably also in late August or early September 1916. This has the same inscription of date and places as the first version, as well as the Old English words 'þæt þæc' ('the thatch') followed by queried 'mōna?', and a bracketed phrase which appears to say 'Mesnil'. The latter suggests that Tolkien also stopped at this time in the village of Mesnil-Martinsart. Arden R. Smith has suggested to us that 'mōna?' is an uncertain attempt by Tolkien to reconstruct an Old English cognate of German *Mohn* 'poppy'; if so, *mōna* would be the genitive plural 'of poppies'. In private notes, Christopher Tolkien could not understand why his father did not write Old English *popig*, with its form so close to Modern English *poppy*.

Tolkien considered in the third manuscript whether to delete line 21, 'He hopes again to find beyond the sea', and to revise line 22 as

‘Though dead their spirit mingles with their opiate’. But he left them unchanged, with the rest of the poem, in a typescript made *c.* 1924; we have transcribed this final text as B. Except for lines 2 and 31, versions A and B are nearly identical, differing mainly in punctuation and formatting.

[B]

Red falls the sunlight on the broken roof
And still undaunted rings a bell within the tower
Marking the passage of yet one more hour
That I have wandered with my heart aloof
    Far far away beyond the distant sea;
That I have been so lonely in this multitude
And spoken light words or eaten at their board
With my whole soul and heart bent far abroad
Thinking of other places, other wine and food,
    Far other voices now beyond the sea.
And for myself in this land one desire —
To find the end of day in some untroubled town,
Pass through the shadowy gateway of a byre
Where darkness falls, and candle-fire
Peeps through the chinks of barns, and lay me down
And sleep, and dream I cross the distant sea.

For there’s a magic in the poppies dry and grey
Wherewith this people thatch their court-yard door
That he who passes at an hour of eve leaves war
And weariness almost contented to await the day
He hopes again to find beyond the sea.
Though dead they mingle with their opiate
A feel of winds that fluttered upland crops,
Or bore the far-off voices to the gate
Of reapers homing late
Down the white roadways filled with twilight dust.
Down the long avenues whose rustling tops
Could see the moon rise slowly from the dust
Old creaking carts piled high with the pale sheaves
Drew these same poppies nodding their round heads
Strewing the white roadways with their faded leaves.

Now at an hour of eve their spirit sheds
A memory of airs and slow sweet rest
On all who pass beneath with weary feet,

Piling good slumber with deep dreams most blest
Of hopes delayed or musics incomplete
Fulfilled and happy or played on for evermore
In those sweet gardens on the other shore
That lies beyond the distant sea.

In late August or early September 1916 Tolkien sent a copy of *The Thatch of Poppies* to Edith, who replied on 17 September: 'Your little poem of the poppies was inside [your letter] and O Ron, I do like it, but it seems rather different to most of the others, somehow' (Bodleian Library).

A6: This line originally read 'That I have wandered among multitudes'.

A9: Tolkien considered whether to change 'wine and food' to 'bread more good'. He marked the same tentative change, struck through, also on the second manuscript of the poem.

A18: This line originally read 'That in this land are thatched above the courtyard door'. *Thatch* typically applies to the weaving of plant material, such as straw or reeds, to use as a covering, as for a roof (Old English *þæc* means both 'roof' and 'thatch'). Tolkien seems to be using it to mean 'a cluster or gathering'; there is a difference between poppies 'thatched above [a] door', as in the original reading, and used to 'thatch [a] door' directly, which suggests a group of dried poppies made into a swag or wreath and attached to a door. *Thatch* in the poem proper is used as a verb, but in the title of the work is a noun.

A19: 'That' originally read 'And'.

A28: 'From' originally read 'above'.

A34–37: These lines originally read:

On all who pass there under sorrow wrung
Piling good slumber and deep dreams most blest
Of hopes delayed or musics stopped half-sung
Now filled and happy or played on for evermore

B17: Tolkien considered whether to change 'magic' to 'nature'.

50

The Forest Walker (1916–?24)

Tolkien wrote the earliest complete manuscript of *The Forest Walker*, like that of *The Thatch of Poppies* (no. 49), on squared notebook paper and during a shared span of days in August 1916. This, however, has the appearance of a fair copy. We have transcribed its text as A.

[A]

Have you wandered in a woodland
　When the lights begin to glow
From the tents and noisy lodges;
　Did your wistful footsteps go
Astray from beaten pathways
　Through the bushes and young trees
Till the lights were far behind you
　And men's voices like to bees
That murmur in a clearing
　And their laughter so remote
That it faded in the gloaming
　Where the silent shadows float
Round the tree-boles and tree-hollows.
　For I've often crept alone
Just at moonlight, just at bedtime
　On a journey of my own.
For men's laughter grows so empty
　While the stately woods at eve
Are full of unknown whispers
　For the hearts of those that grieve

And I'm hungry for great forests,
　For great pines that creak and moan
With their bare arms in the moonlight;
　For a wind that has been blown
Over leagues of land untrodden,
　Where the copses and the grass
Where the reedy river borders
　And the pools like pallid glass

Lie dreaming in the starlight
    In a land that knows no men;
Where the laughter's that of wood-fays
    In the moonrise in the glen;
Where the voices but leaf-rustles
    Save it be on magic nights
When uncounted woodland spirits
    Chase the lingering gleaming lights
Through the boughs to die in crannies
    Under ferns, or drown in pools
Dripping among roots of alder
    Whence they fish them up as jewels;

Where the singing is the pine-trees
    Or the leaves of the great beech
Telling tales of the wide ages
    To the saplings — how they reach
Back, back, beyond the legends
    Of the oldest trees that grow
(Save perhaps the gloomy pine-trees
    But they tell not all they know):
Where the people are as shadows
    That awake no noise at all,
Or so very very little
    That, though whiles I think they call
And my heart is touched to longing,
    They are secret and unclear,
Till I yearn to find the forest
    There to wander down the year
Till the dancing in the darkness
    And the voices now unknown
Till the spirit of wide places
    In the gloaming is my own.

Only one page of preliminary workings for the poem is extant, of which the most legible part consists of six lines Tolkien seems to have considered for its conclusion. Although never used, they may help to clarify Tolkien's thoughts and aims:

Or so secret and so hidden
    That though whiles I think they call

I can only guess deep meanings
    And I long with all my heart
To understand the forest
    And to wander there apart.

Tolkien wrote the three pages of the first manuscript in blue pencil, then (at some point, if not immediately) reinforced his writing on the third page in standard pencil, in the process marking the final eight lines of the text with a query. In copying version A into a second manuscript, he replaced 'unknown whispers' with 'untold whispers' in line 19, next to which he jotted an alternative thought, 'whispering unheard ?' Subsequently he marked or numbered more than a dozen lines to be revised and enlarged in the following version, the numbers probably keyed to a now lost page of revisions.

The second manuscript is inscribed 'To Bus-lès-Artois wood, HQ [headquarters] Dugout, Thiepval wood, Aug[ust] 25–26'. This records, after the fact, the date of original composition of the work, while 'To Bus-lès Artois wood' – written in a lighter pencil possibly contemporary with the text proper – is a dedication. Tolkien was at Bus-lès-Artois from 10 to 14 August, and on two of those evenings went into a nearby wood, away from the lights glowing in 'tents and noisy lodges', to think about Rob Gilson's death and its effect on the TCBS. 'I honestly feel that the T.C.B.S. has ended', he had written to G.B. Smith on 12–13 August, that he was 'a mere individual at present', dreading that Gilson would not be the last of his friends to die in the war (*Letters*, p. 6).

Two weeks later, at Thiepval, Smith having sent him consoling words in reply, Tolkien's thoughts cleared enough that he could write *The Thatch of Poppies* and *The Forest Walker*. The latter in particular is an expression of grief ('the stately woods at eve | Are full of unknown whispers | For the hearts of those that grieve'), not yet a direct memorial to Gilson like G.B. Smith's verse 'Let Us Tell Quiet Stories of Kind Eyes' (' . . . he, the fourth, that lies all silently | In some far-distant and untended grave'), but also speaks to the poet's sense of isolation in the army and in a foreign land. 'Gentlemen are non-existent among the superiors,' Tolkien wrote to Edith of his military life, 'and even human beings are rare indeed' (quoted in Carpenter, *Biography*, pp. 77–80). He felt closer to nature, providing in *The Forest Walker* a picture of an almost sentient landscape: the pines 'creak and moan', the great beech tells tales to saplings. The poet longs to understand the forest, shared with wood-fays or nature spirits.

On 12 September Tolkien arrived with his battalion at Franqueville for a long training session, until the 24th, and again had time on his hands. Among other work, he produced a revised text of *The Forest Walker*, given here as B. This third manuscript of the poem is inscribed 'To Bus les Artois wood, Acheux, Thiepval Wood, Aug[ust] 25–26 1916, Franqueville Sep[tember] 1916', with an added title in Old English, *Se Wealdstapa* ('Wood-stepper').

[B]

Have you wandered in a woodland
    When the lights begin to glow
From the tents and noisy lodges?
    Did your wistful footsteps go
Astray from beaten pathways
    Through the bushes and young trees
Till the lights were far behind you
    And men's voices like to bees
That murmur in a clearing,
    And their laughter so remote
That it died into the gloaming
    A faint echo far afloat
Round the tree-boles and tree-hollows?
    — For I've often crept alone
Just at moonrise, just ere bedtime,
    On a journey of my own:
For men's laughter grows so empty,
    While the stately woods at eve
Are full of unknown whispers
    For the hearts of those that grieve;

*

And I'm hungry for great forests
    For great pines that creak and moan
With their bare arms in the moonlight,
    For a wind that has been blown
Over leagues of land untrodden
    Where the copses and the grass,
Where the reedy river-borders
    And the pools like pallid glass,
Lie dreaming in the starlight
    In a land that knows no men,
Nor yet even elfin laughter
    In the moonrise in the glen.

There the voices are leaf-rustles,
    Or vague whispering at night
When the unknown ageless spirits
    At the changing of the light
Troop through the silent spaces
    Of the darkness of the wood,
And the light flees at the coming
    Of this old primeval brood,
Through the boughs to die in crannies
    Under ferns, or some black pool
Dripping among roots of alder
    In a gather'd dark and cool:

⋆

There the singing is the pine-trees,
    Or the leaves of the great beech
Telling tales of the wide ages
    To the saplings — how they reach
Back, back, beyond the legends
    Of the oldest trees that grow
(Save perhaps the gloomy pine-trees
    But they tell not all they know):
There the people are as shadows
    That awake no noise at all
Or so distant and so hidden
    That, though whiles I think they call,
And my heart is touched to longing,
    They are secret and unclear,
Till I yearn to find the forest
    There to wander down the year
Till the dancing in the darkness
    And the voices now unknown,
Till the spirit of wide places
    In the twilight is my own.

Christopher Wiseman read a copy of the poem, probably of this version, and commented in a letter of 18 January 1917 that it did not seem as successful as *The Pool of the Dead Year* (no. 42), and was too long for its metre – clearly a matter of personal taste. Wiseman also asked, quoting two lines of *The Forest Walker*, why all poets and artists were 'hungry for great forests . . . in a land that knows no men'. He himself was too gregarious not to seek out company.

Around 1924 Tolkien made a typescript, or had one made, from the third manuscript of the poem, with the only textual difference in line 43, which now began 'Dripping about'. He marked several lines, and while still at Leeds produced a typescript (using a purple ribbon) incorporating his new changes; and on this, in turn, he marked still further revisions. We give here, as C, the final text of the poem, including Tolkien's late revisions, documented in our notes.

[C]

Have you wandered in a woodland
    When the lights begin to glow
From the tents and noisy lodges;
    Did your halting footsteps go
Astray from beaten pathways
    Through the bushes and young trees,
Till the lights were far behind you.
    And men's voices were like to bees
That murmur in a clearing:
    And their laughter so remote
That it died into the gloaming
    A faint echo far afloat
Round the tree-boles and tree-hollows?
    I have often crept alone
Just at moonrise, just ere bed-time,
    On a journey of my own.

I am hungry for deep forests,
    For great pines that creak and moan
With their bare arms in the moonlight;
    For a wind that has been blown
Over leagues of land untrodden
    Where the copses and the grass,
Where the reedy river-borders
    And the pools like pallid glass
Lie dreaming in the starlight
    In a land that knows no men,
Not even elvish laughter
    In the moon-rise in the glen;
Where the voices are leaf-rustles,
    Or vague whispering at night
When the unknown ageless spirits
    At the changing of the light
Troop through the silent spaces

Of the darkness of the wood,
And the light flees at the coming
Of this old primeval brood
Through the boughs to die in crannies
Under ferns, or some dark pool
Dripping about roots of alder
In a gathered gloom and cool.

There the singing is the pine-trees,
Or the leaves of the great beech
Telling tales of the wide ages
To the saplings, how they reach
Back, back, beyond the legends
Of the oldest trees that grow
(Save perhaps the gloomy pine-trees
But they tell not all they know):
There the people are as shadows
That awake no noise at all,
Or so distant and so hidden
That, though I think they call,
And my heart is touched to longing,
They are secret and unclear,
And I long to find the forest
There to wander down the year,
Till the dancing in the darkness
And the voices now unknown,
Till the spirit of wide places
In the twilight is my own.

B64: Tolkien considered whether to change 'twilight' to 'gloaming'.

C4: 'Halting' replaced 'wistful' as a revision to the final typescript.

C8: Tolkien added 'were' as a revision to the final typescript.

C14: Tolkien marked 'For I've' to be changed to 'I have' on the penultimate typescript.

C16: Four additional lines appeared in the text following l. 16 (i.e. former ll. 17–20) in all copies up to and including the penultimate typescript:

For men's laughter grows so empty,
While the stately woods at eve
Are full of unknown whispers
For the hearts of those that grieve;

Tolkien revised these lines in the professional typescript to read:

From the echo of empty laughter
    To the brooding woods at eve
That are full of unheard whispers
    For the hearts of those that grieve.

and in that form appeared in the final typescript, where, however, Tolkien struck them through.

C17: Tolkien marked 'great' to be changed to 'deep' on the penultimate typescript. As typed, the final text includes a further change, 'And I'm hungry' to 'I am hungry', removing the last contraction Tolkien used in earlier versions.

C27: 'Not even elfin laughter', as in the penultimate typescript, became 'Nor yet elfin laughter' in the final typescript – 'even' probably having been overlooked in typing – and then was revised in manuscript to 'Not even elvish laughter'.

C29: 'Where the voices' became 'There the voices' *ab initio* in the penultimate typescript.

C38: Tolkien marked 'black' to be changed to 'dark' on the penultimate typescript.

C40: Tolkien changed 'gather'd' to 'gathered' in a correction on the penultimate typescript, and marked 'dark' to be changed to 'gloom'.

C57: Tolkien deleted 'whiles' ('though whiles I think they call') on the final typescript.

C60: Tolkien marked 'Till' to be changed to 'And' on the penultimate typescript. There, the line as typed began 'Till I long', a revision from 'Till I yearn' in the preceding manuscript.

51

O Lady Mother Throned amid the Stars · Consolatrix Afflictorum · Stella Vespertina · Mother! O Lady Throned beyond the Stars

(1916–?1950s)

The two earliest drafts of this rhyming prayer are found on one side of a scrap of ruled notebook paper, the reverse of the sheet on which Tolkien wrote brief workings for the third manuscript of *The Forest Walker* (no. 50). Here, as A, is the first version of the prayer before revision.

[A] O Lady Mother throned amid the stars
Whose white feet on the pathways of the moon
Come gently to the darkened Earth at night
Where we poor children at the Great Tribune
Pray our small prayers kneeling without light
Whose tender hands unlock the prison bars
Of sorrow, making tranquil all our fears,
Take thou my little one beside thy knee
And hear her prayers and make her free
From all unhappiness, from all her tears.

Tolkien was brought up in the Roman Catholic faith, after his widowed mother left the Church of England to become a convert, and was especially devoted to the Virgin Mary (upon whom 'all my own small perception of beauty both in majesty and simplicity is founded', letter to Robert Murray, 2 December 1953, *Letters*, p. 257). His prayer to 'Lady Mother', while the Battle of the Somme was still being fought, was made for his wife, whom he often called 'little one', lonely and anxious in England while her husband was at the front; but it was also for himself and his fellow soldiers, 'we poor children', who at any time could be called to judgement before God, the 'Great Tribune'.

The image of Mary 'throned amid the stars' looks ahead to the reverence felt by Tolkien's Elves for Varda (also known as Elbereth), the Vala who kindled the heavens and to whom supplicants turned in times of peril. But it also reflects common Marian titles, the 'Queen of Heaven' and 'the ocean star', and the language of Tolkien's verse echoes part of the Catholic prayer known as the *Salve Regina*:

Hail, holy Queen, Mother of Mercy,
Our life, our sweetness, and our hope,
To thee we cry, poor banished children of Eve,
To thee do we send up our sighs,
Mourning and weeping in this valley of tears.

Tolkien cancelled the first draft of his text and rewrote it on the same page with small differences, notably the addition of 'wistful' before 'prayers' in line 9. Probably before too long, he marked changes to this second manuscript, principally a reordering of lines 4 and 5, and carried them into a third version, given here as B.

[B] O Lady Mother throned amid the stars
  Whose white feet on the pathways of the moon
Come gently to the darkened Earth at night
  Where our small prayers before the Great Tribune
We pray, poor children, kneeling without light;
Whose tender hands unlock the prison bars
  Of sorrow, making tranquil all our fears,
Take thou my little one beside thy knee
  And hear her whispered prayers, and make her free
From all unhappiness, from all her tears.

Tolkien inscribed this manuscript 'Franqueville (Sep[tember])' with a query, but the place and date of composition seem to be correct, coinciding with his revision of *The Forest Walker* similarly marked 'Franqueville Sep[tember] 1916'. Also written on the page is the Old English title *Án Ȝebed tó Ure Hlæfdigan* ('A Prayer to Our Lady').

Much the same text, but with 'O! Lady' for 'O Lady' in line 1, is found in Tolkien's papers as another manuscript, made on notebook paper and contemporary with the earlier iterations, and as a typescript, entitled *O! Lady Mother Throned amid the Stars*, made probably around 1924. Three further typescripts followed, using Tolkien's Hammond machine, from their style and paper possibly from around 1931 (to which we have also dated a version of *A Rhyme Royal upon Easter Morning*, no. 61). The first of these (C, below) is significantly different from B, and was also the first version to be given a title, *Consolatrix Afflictorum* (Latin 'Comforter of the Afflicted', one of the older invocations of the Virgin Mary and in the sixteenth-century Litany of Loreto).

[C]

O! Lady Mother throned above the stars
    Whose white feet on the pathways of the moon
Come gently to the darkened earth at night
    Where our small prayers before the Great Tribune
We pray, poor children kneeling without light;
Whose tender hands unlock the prison bars
    Of sorrow and of wordless shadowy fears,
This night my little one beside thy knee
    From her unhappiness, from many tears,
From all her loneliness, O! make her free,
Seeing the light of Thine who shines in thee!

For the second of the later typescripts, Tolkien changed the title of the work again, to *Stella Vespertina* (Latin 'Evening Star', another name sometimes given to the Virgin). Once again, he revised the prayer (as D), most remarkably changing the final lines from a plea for his 'little one' to a prayer for the poet himself.

[D]

O! Lady Mother throned above the stars,
    Whose white feet on the pathways of the moon
Come gently to the darkened earth at night
    Where our small prayers before the great Tribune
We seek to pray, poor children without light;
Whose tender hands unlock the prison bars
    Of sorrow that here bind each hardened heart,
Hear thou my broken whisper at thy knee,
    Faltering, half-comprehending what thou art!
Heal me my blinded eyes that I may see
The glory of thy Son that shines in thee!

This was followed by another typescript with the same text, below which Tolkien composed a largely different prayer, but abandoned it before completion. He wrote the latter, untitled manuscript (E) very roughly in pencil, then overwrote the pencil text in pen.

[E]

Mother! O lady throned beyond the stars
Who drawn by pity from your blissful seat
At times to this dark earth of grief return,
If I could trembling kneel in dread before your feet
Out of your glory would your voice be stern
As to a fool for folly [*illegible*]
In grief self wrought and self inflicted pain

From Tolkien's handwriting and his use of biro (ballpoint pen), we judge that manuscript E dates from at least the 1950s. It could be that Tolkien was inspired to compose the new prayer when translating Roman Catholic prayers from Latin into Quenya in that decade: the *Pater Noster*, *Ave Maria*, *Gloria Patri*, and *Sub Tuum Praesidium*, and the Litany of Loreto. He frequently used the Latin 'praises' in daily life, as he wrote to his son Christopher (8 January 1944, *Letters*, p. 95):

> the Gloria Patri, the Gloria in Excelsis, the Laudate Dominum; the Laudate Pueri Dominum (of which I am specially fond); one of the Sunday psalms; and the Magnificat; also the Litany of Loretto (with the prayer Sub tuum praesidium). If you have these by heart you never need for words of joy.

52

To Early Morning Tea · An Ode Inspired by Intimations of the Approach of Early Morning Tea (1916–*c.* 1927)

Tolkien's prayer to the Virgin Mary (no. 51) seems to have been the last poem he wrote before falling ill on 27 October 1916 and entering the officers' hospital at Gézaincourt the next day. Diagnosed with trench fever, he was then transferred to No. 1 British Red Cross Hospital at Le Touquet, also known as the Duchess of Westminster's Hospital after its patron. Apparently he was in such good spirits during his stay that he was inspired to write the poem first entitled *To Early Morning Tea*. The text of its first manuscript, written on a sheet of ruled notebook paper, is given here as A.

[A] Most precious distillation of the herbs
Of Ind or of Cathay
And all those sunny lands most far away,
Bearing within your stream the fragrances
And all the subtle odours
Of strange flowers; a thought of bells in old pagodas,
Of unshadowed days of golden warmth,
Deep nights of splendid moons,
Or neath the flaming stars faint mellow tunes
In hidden groves: — do you not know
The Eastern harbours and their crowded quays
Thronging with mariners from many a land
Whose tall ships sail the orient seas;
Or winding caravans that trail through Samarkand
Bearing great store of your sweet leaf
By many roads to reach the Midland Sea.
And had I treasury or held rich lands in fief
You would be shut in cedar gold and porphyry
— Yet pile me deep canisters of scented wood
Fretted in dragons of red and gold;
Lade me high jars, such as the Chinese mould —
Men may have held the grape in praise
But no vine ever sucked a juice

From Southern slopes that has the scent you loose
Upon the morning air
When silver tinkles upon earthenware.

'Orient seas' in line 13 is another way of saying 'Eastern waters'. 'Midland Sea' in line 16 is an old name for the Mediterranean. 'Treasury or . . . rich lands in fief' (line 17) is an elaborate description of wealth, and in this phrase 'lands in fief' refers, under the feudal system in Europe, to income-producing properties held by a vassal under a lord. The modern equivalent would be lands on which tenants pay rents to its owner.

In the final lines of the verse, the comparison is between wine ('the grape') and tea ('sweet leaf'), each of which has its aficionados. 'Silver [tinkling] upon earthenware' (line 26) is the sound of a silver spoon meeting a porcelain teacup.

When writing a second manuscript of this work, now with the simpler title *Morning Tea*, Tolkien left most of his original text unchanged except for lines 11–16, which became:

The winding caravans that slowly go
    Down dusty ways through Samarkand,
Or Eastern havens with their crowded quays
Thronging with mariners of many a land
Whose tall ships sail the orient seas?
    Bearing great store of your sweet leaf
By many roads to reach the Midland Sea.

At the top of the sheet, he inscribed 'Duch[ess] of Westminsters Hospital, Le Touquet, Nov[ember] 8 1916'. This note appears to be contemporary with the text, but if Tolkien in fact wrote the poem in the hospital at Le Touquet, its date of composition cannot be later than the morning of 7 November. Tolkien left Le Touquet for Le Havre that day, and on the 8th boarded the hospital ship *Asturias*. On the final typescript of the poem (see below), he inscribed 'hospital 1916 written in nurses' album'; if indeed he made a fair copy for the nurses, it is not clear which version was the latest before he was invalided home.

Tolkien marked the second manuscript with further revisions, some of which he carried into a third manuscript, again written on notebook paper, but seems to have made other changes on both the second and third manuscripts simultaneously, in the latter overwriting in ink what he had first set down in pencil. We give the later text of *Morning Tea* as B.

[B] Most precious distillation of the herbs
  Of Ind or of Cathay
And all those sunny lands most far away,
Bearing within your stream the fragrances
  And all the subtle odours
Of strange flowers; a thought of bells in old pagodas;
Of unshadowed days of golden warmth,
  Deep nights of splendid moons,
Or neath the flaming stars faint mellow tunes
In hidden groves: — O dost not know
The winding caravans that slowly go
  Down thirsty ways through Samarkand,
Or Eastern havens with their crowded quays
Thronging with mariners of many a land
  Whose tall ships sail the orient seas?
Thence bear they cargoes of thy sweetest leaf
By many ways to reach the Midland Sea;
And had I treasury, or held rich lands in fief
Thou shouldst be shut in onyx or in porphyry: —
Come! lade me canisters of wood ablaze
  With carvéd dragons red and gold;
Deep jars blue-figured that the Chinese mould!
Men may have held the grape in praise
  But no vine ever sucked a juice
From Southern slopes that has the scent you loose
  Upon the morning air
When silver tinkles upon Earthenware.

The final iteration of Tolkien's poem is a typescript (C), made much later in Oxford on his Hammond machine. Now entitled more effusively *An Ode Inspired by Intimations of the Approach of Early Morning Tea*, its text is similar to that of version B, but Tolkien made a few further revisions, and either chose to restore some earlier readings (in lines 10 and 12) or based the typescript on his second rather than the revised third manuscript.

[C] Most precious distillation of the herbs
  Of Ind or of Cathay
And all those sunny lands most far away,
Bearing within your stream the fragrances
  And all the subtle odours

Of strange flowers; a thought of bells in old pagodas;
Unshadowed days of golden warmth,
    Deep nights of splendid moons,
Or neath the flaming stars faint mellow tunes
In hidden groves: — do you now know
The winding caravans that slowly go
    Down dusty ways through Samarkand,
And eastern havens with their crowded quays
Thronging with mariners of many a land
Whose tall ships sail the orient seas?

Thence bear they cargoes of your sweetest leaf
By many ways to reach the Midland Sea;
And had I treasury or held rich lands in fief,
You should be shut in onyx or in porphyry,
Or hid in carven canisters of wood ablaze
    With writhing dragons red and gold,
Or deep blue-figured jars the Chinese mould!

Men may have held the grape in praise,
    But no vine ever sucked a juice
From southern slopes that has the scent you loose
    Upon the morning air
    When silver tinkles upon Earthenware!

Tolkien's reference to Samarkand evokes a romantic image of camel caravans moving along the 'Silk Road' between China and Europe, carrying merchants who among other things traded in tea. Samarkand, an ancient city now in Uzbekistan, was an important stop on the trading route; its name, like 'Ind' (India) and 'Cathay' (China), has long conjured (to Westerners) images of exotic peoples and places. Tolkien mentions both the land and sea routes for the tea traders. We have found no reference in his papers, but wonder if he read the work of his then well known contemporary James Elroy Flecker, who wrote poems with Eastern themes such as 'The Golden Journey to Samarkand' and 'The Gates of Damascus'.

Tolkien's descriptions of red and gold dragons and 'wood ablaze' recall the colours of lacquerware, and 'deep-blue figured jars' the ancient blue and white Chinese porcelain that became much collected and imitated in Europe.

B10: 'O dost not know' replaced 'do you not know' in the third manuscript as overwriting. 'Do you not know' remained, or was restored, in the fourth version (typescript).

B12: 'Thirsty' replaced 'dusty' in the third manuscript as overwriting. The typescript has 'dusty'.

B16: This line replaced 'Bearing great store of your sweet leaf' in the third manuscript as overwriting.

B19: 'Thou shouldst' replaced 'You should' in the third manuscript as overwriting. 'In onyx or in porphyry' is the reading *ab initio* in the third manuscript; in the second manuscript, it replaced 'in cedar, gold, and porphyry'.

B20: 'Come! lade me' replaced 'You pile me deep' in the third manuscript as overwriting; Tolkien considered, and rejected, 'great' as a replacement for 'deep'. 'Canisters of wood ablaze' followed on from the second manuscript, where the phrase replaced 'canisters of scented wood'.

B21: Tolkien originally wrote, but deleted, 'fretted' before 'dragons'. In the second manuscript, 'With carvéd dragons red and gold' replaced 'Fretted in dragons of red and gold'.

B22: 'Deep jars blue-figured that' replaced 'Lade me high jars such as' in the third manuscript by overwriting.

53

G.B.S. (1916–?24)

On 9 November 1916 Tolkien left Le Havre for England and was admitted to hospital in Birmingham. For the next few weeks he was treated for trench fever, until he was well enough (though still weak), between early and mid-December, to join Edith at Great Haywood. It was there he received a letter from Christopher Wiseman informing him that G.B. Smith had died on 3 December, after being wounded by shrapnel. Tolkien's response to the news was surely profound; he had been strongly affected by Rob Gilson's death in July, and now Smith was gone as well, not only a close friend but also a fellow Oxford man and chief critic of his poems.

On 18 January 1917 Wiseman remarked that it was 'ineffably mysterious. To have seen two of God's giants [Gilson and Smith] pass before our eyes, to have lived and laughed with them, to have learnt of them, to have found them something like ourselves, and to see them go back again into the mist whence they came out' (Bodleian Library; quoted in Scull and Hammond, *Chronology*, p. 105). He was concerned that he and Tolkien, the two surviving central members of the TCBS, should have a hand in publishing Smith's poetry, as their friend had wished and his mother wanted also. With the help of their old teacher R.W. Reynolds, they arranged for this to be done as *A Spring Harvest* (1918; see further, our general introduction). But Tolkien was also anxious to remember Smith in a poem, and struggled to do so. On its final version he later wrote 'Great Haywood Chr[istmas] 1916–17', recalling that he began to compose his memorial verses in late December 1916, carrying on into early the next year. (Although on 2 December he was formally attached to the 3rd (Reserve) Battalion of the Lancashire Fusiliers, based on the Holderness Peninsula in Yorkshire, Tolkien continued to be ill, and remained at Great Haywood until late February 1917.)

Many pages of manuscript workings for the poem survive, eight for each of the first two drafts, roughly written with many revisions and excisions, lists of rhyming words, and occasional doodles. We give here, as A, the most coherent part of what is clearly Tolkien's initial draft of his memorial, as best we can decipher it, including revisions made in the course of composition. We have divided the text, which was otherwise not yet broken into sections (compare version D, below), where there is a new page of writing or, on one sheet, where Tolkien wrote on one half of the page, then rotated it and wrote on the other half.

[A] Gramarye and [every >] all [*deleted:* the] most secret runes
Wisdom beyond ages [and veins of >] and the darkest vein
Of unmined lore; whatever [hidden ways >] land or sea
[*deleted:* Or the deep places of the earth]
[*deleted:* deep earth or ?many ?starred firmament]
Or the deep places of the earth contain;
Whatever mystery that the stars [set forth >] unfold
In undeciphered script of blazing light
[*deleted:* Thou knowest now: mounted beyond the stairs]
[*deleted, alternate to 'mounted, etc.':* the ?tales not told and]
You know them now: the great doors key you hold
Mounted beyond the stairway of the [moon >] night
And looking back the narrow passage passed
[*deleted:* Before you crave one only of the]
Before [you go >] the eternal portals shade forever
[*or:* shadow you]
For all our life from us one radiance cast
Of thy grave face now glorious [in mighty >] on me
For some have gone before, and some as [we >] I
Are all among the stones with ??? feet
Or threaded a path confused by noise of waters
[*above:* cliff-walled branched sky]
In a cliff-walled ravine a scanty sun
Or seem deafened with roaring of great waters
Together we [have >] once questioned [all the >] many a rune
Written in the stars or broidered on the land
Or told old tales of gramarye or ?breathed
Only for much lore and loved the land and sea
Discussed of the deep places of the earth and sky
And all that dwell therein and now

That are gone: slipped into the loneliness of the narrow way
Which all must tread alone
Thy voice goes faint across the waste
Thy footfall even now has died upon the stair
And thou art at the final gate
Farewell my brother. I will sing thy songs

Or listen to [thy voice >] the memory of thy voice
Renew them so long as [we who >] I and he who stay
But broad the pathway in the high ravine
Glimpsing the ??? border of the ?sullen sky
Clutching at far off faint whispers of old spells and wonder

Once the enchasmed sides seem low and airs
Come whispering for the edge of things far off
Whispered about the way of many things beyond
And almost all the day the [sunshine >] sun's long course
Was seen, or after dark the moon rode plain
For you and me to see him hunt the stars
Nor had the path nor all the wide world's self
A boundary more than a dark rim of blue
Shrouding still fairer marvels or ?still wider earth[']s ?plain
And round our feet the water spills
Or laughed in many beams that
Now roar in confusion of great wrath and fear

And thou art gone who had especial skill
To see beyond the blue rim o'er the earth,
Who could descry fair visions sweetly fill
The distances, or stoops to catch the mirth
Of far off singers, [tangled ?thou whose ears >] or maybe to hear
The voices of the solemn winds proclaim
Deep matters: down that path our ways [once >] drew near
And many a time together when night came
[*lines 60–65 deleted:* We questioned the great writing of the stars
Or told old tales [of the old world >] of gramarye and lore
In quite forgotten dreaming of the deeps
Or thought of ancient tales and of the old world
Or wondering at new Suns found many a rune
Written upon the land and sky: O]
[We pondered the >] We wondered at the great constellate streams
Or told old tales [of gramarye, new suns, and love >] and raised old questionings
Of lore well nigh forgotten dreaming dreams
[*deleted:* Of the deep places of the Earth and wonderment before]

Of the Earth's deep places and its wondrous things
[*lines 71–73 deleted:* And thou art gone forward now stepped
[all alone >] on beyond
Into the solitude of the narrow way
Which all men must [*deleted:* tread] alone stepped forward all
alone]

Here, as elsewhere among his poems, Tolkien uses *rune* in the sense of 'secret, mystery', or of 'counsel or writing of a secret nature'. 'Secret runes' (line 1) therefore emphasizes a quality already inherent in the noun (in the *Oxford English Dictionary*, see *roun*). *Rune* 'letter in an early Teutonic alphabet' (considered separately in the *OED* under *rune*) also figures in Tolkien's verse, indeed it is not always clear which sense should be considered uppermost; nonetheless, *rune* in this sense also carries with it an aspect of secrecy or mystery, something known only to a select (educated) few.

With the final few lines of this text, Tolkien returned to earlier drafting, from around line 29 (i.e. the second sheet transcribed here). He continued to work at this section on another page, with much repetition and many of the lines struck through in the course of writing, and on another page still, he wrote in unusually large script:

And thou art gone who had the skill
to see so far across the earth and
could descry fair visions far away or
perhaps would stoop to catch the voices
of the solemn winds

For this text, compare lines A52–57 above.

Among the pages of the second draft are two versions of the opening section. Here we have transcribed the first version as B, and the second as C.

[B] All secret runes and ancient gramarye
Wisdom of Eld and every darkest vein
Of unmined lore; whatever land or sea
Or the deep places of the world contain;
What way the scripture of the stars unfold
In secret hieroglyphs of flaming light
Soon will you know, the great doors key who hold
Mounted beyond the stairway of the night
And climbed at last beyond the narrow way

That finds the gateways of eternity.
Thence ere you pass for ever let one ray
Of your grave face fall glorious on me;
Thence let return but one far distant sound
Of your grave voice's deepened melody
Ere yet the eternal shadows wrap you round
Ere yet the silence falls 'tween you and me
Lo you have gone before and yet am I
Still among the stones of fear; my feet
Still thread a weary path far from the sky
In this cliff-walled ravine, this darkened street
Confused with stony voices of the stream
And as its windy waters; shine no gleam

[C] All secret runes and ancient gramarye;
[*deleted:* Old wisdom and every dark profoundest vein]
[*deleted:* Of] Wisdom from old ages; every darkest vein
Of unmined lore; whatever land or sea
Or the deep places of the world contain
Whatever mystery the stars unfold
In undeciphered script of blazing light
Thou [*deleted:* soon] wilt know now the great door's key will hold
Mounted beyond the stairway of the night,
And looking back the narrow passage passed.
Yet ere the eternal portals shadow thee
For all our life from us one radiance cast
Of thy grave face now glorious [in death >] on me.
For some have gone before, and some as I
Are all among the stones of fear with feet
That thread a weary path far from the sky
In this cliff walled ravine a weary street
Of scanty sun confused with roaring water [*above:* noise]
[*deleted:* The water of [our >] my ways before us]
[Of > From >] For many waters shout with a stony voice

It is not clear which of these texts, B or C, was the earliest at this stage; each contains elements found in later versions, though more of these are in C. Nor can we be certain about the order of other scraps of drafting for the poem, some of which is not coherent, and as before shares pages with lists of rhyming words and doodles. Here, however, we have transcribed, for convenience as a continuation of text C, two further pages of workings, with few revisions in the manuscripts. Tolkien wrote the first section below on a page of an abandoned letter to the Secretary of the War Office, as from '2nd L[ieutenant] JRR Tolkien, 11th B[attalio]n Lan[cashire] Fus[iliers]'; he joined the 3rd Battalion in Yorkshire on 19 April 1917, and his promotion to full lieutenant (as of 1 July) was confirmed on 24 November 1917.

Once the forbidding [*above:* enchasmed] sides seemed low;
    wide air
Came whispering from the edge of things afar,
Arched ever golden did the Sun's course flare
Or after dusk the moon's ship left the bar
For you and me to see him clear pursue
The fading stars; not even the wide world
Had boundaries other than a rim of blue
Shrouding wide spaces ceaselessly unfurled
Of fairer marvels, mountains ever new.
Thence round our feet a laughing water spoke
Of distant valleys hills far off to you
Which now roar in confusion and a great smoke,
A torrent that has lost its magic voice
And shakes the grey air with its stony noise.

And thou art gone who had especial skill
To see beyond the blue rim o'er the earth,
Who could descry fair visions sweetly fill
The distances or stoop to catch the mirth
Of far off singers or maybe to hear
The voices of the solemn winds proclaim
Deep matters; here our ways did once draw near
And many a time together when night came
We wondered at the great constellate streams
Or told old histories old questionings
Of lore well nigh forgotten dreaming dreams
Of Earth's deep places and [most >] its deepest things.
And thou art gone, stepped forward all alone
Into the narrow way's dim solitude.
Thy voice across the waste is faintly blown
Dies on the stair thy footfall unpursued
[And >] While thou already near'st the final gate.
Farewell my brother I will sing thy songs

And hoard the memory of thy voice too late
Renewing them — nor I but one that longs
For thy voice singing in the stony road
For thy grave face beside our weariness
And sudden darkness where we gaily strode
Now walled in the ravine of great distress
Confused with many waters roaring noise
That fills our hearts too deep with its sad voice

Tolkien wrote out the first comprehensive manuscript of the poem, now entitled *G.B.S.* and divided into three numbered sections, probably later in 1917, as we conclude from his handwriting and from the apparent level of his engagement with the poem, while his emotions at Smith's death were still fresh. This is a fair copy, on which Tolkien then marked eight lines for replacement. The changes were written on the manuscript after the text proper, following drafting of these revisions, and one other Tolkien chose to abandon, on a separate sheet. We give here (as D) the final text from a typescript copy made around 1924.

[D] I

All secret runes and ancient gramarye,
Wisdom of Eld and every darkest vein
Of unmined lore; whatever land or sea
Or the deep places of the world contain;
Whatever mystery the stars unfold
In undeciphered script of blazing light
Soon will you know, the great door's key who hold
Mounted beyond the stairway of the night.
Thence looking back beyond the narrow way
Ere yet the gateways of eternity
Wrap you in shadow from me, cast one ray
Of your grave face, now glorious, on me.
For some have gone before, and some as I
Are all among the stones of fear, with feet
That thread a weary path far from the sky
In this cliff-walled ravine; a weary street
Of scanty sun confused with roaring noise
Where many waters shout with stony voice.

2

Once the o'erhanging sides seemed low; wide air
Came whispering from the edge of things afar:
Arched over golden did the Sun's course flare,
Or after dusk the moon's ship left its bar
That you and I might see him clear pursue
The fading stars: not even the wide world
Had boundaries other than a rim of blue
Shrouding wide spaces endlessly unfurled
Of fairer marvels, mountains ever new.
Thence round our feet a laughing water spoke
Of distant valleys, hills far-off, to you,
Which now roars in confusion and great smoke
A torrent that has lost its magic voice
And shakes the grey airs with its stony noise.

3

And you are gone who had especial skill
To see beyond the blue rim o'er the earth,
Who could descry fair visions sweetly fill
The distances, or stoop to catch the mirth
Of far-off singers, or maybe to hear
The voices of the solemn winds proclaim
Deep matters. Here our ways did once draw near,
And many a time together, when night came,
We pondered o'er the great constellate streams
Or told old histories, old questionings
Of lore well nigh forgotten, dreaming dreams
Of the Earth's deep places and its deepest things.
But you are gone, stepped forward all alone
Into the narrow way's dim solitude;
Your voice across the waste is faintly blown;
Dies on the stair your footfall unpursued,
While you already near the final gate.
Farewell my brother! I will sing your songs
And hoard the memory of your voice, too late,
Renewing them — nor I but one that longs
For your voice singing in the stony road,
For your grave face beside our weariness
And sudden gloom where once we gaily strode,
Now walled in this ravine of dark distress

Confused with many waters' roaring noise
That fills our hearts too deep with its sad voice.

While setting down Tolkien's workings and decisions for *G.B.S.* we were struck by certain recurring elements. The most obvious of these is a sense of loss, distance from loved ones, not an uncommon theme in Tolkien's works or in English poetry that came out of the First World War. Here Ivor Gurney's 'To His Love' comes to mind:

He's gone, and all our plans
    Are useless indeed.
We'll walk no more on Cotswold
    Where the sheep feed
    Quietly and take no heed.

But *G.B.S.* is more mystical, and is underlaid with the poet's faith, with visions of the afterlife and his reference to 'stones of fear', an obstacle (with stones of doubt, shame, grief) one often finds in Christian literature, rolled back through an embrace of Jesus. There is also a 'stony road', 'stony voice', 'stony noise', rough paths to travel or unsweet to hear. Tolkien's conjunction of 'noise' with 'voice' at the end of each section recalls Robert Graves's memory of the war, that the noise never stopped and could not be communicated to those who did not hear it. Tolkien of course was drawing upon personal experience, as well as private imagery: his picture of 'the moon's ship' leaving the bar to 'pursue the fading stars' is not unlike that of the mariner Éarendel springing up from the ocean 'in the gloom of the mid-world's rim' (poem no. 16).

Tolkien also may have had in mind Smith's early poem 'Rime'. This has a similar mood to *G.B.S.* and shares some of its imagery, as well as the antique word *gramarye*. We give two of its five stanzas for comparison (*A Spring Harvest*, p. 24):

O scholar grey, with quiet eyes,
Reading the charactered pages, bright
With one tall candle's flickering light,
In a turret chamber under the skies;
O scholar, learned in gramarye,
Have you seen the manifold things I see?

. . . . . .

Have you heard the great awakening breath,
Like trump that summons the saints from death,
Of the wild, majestical wind, which blows
Loud and splendid, that each man knows
Far, O far away is the sea,
Breaking, murmuring, stark and free?

Later in 1917, Tolkien wrote a more conventional memorial poem, dedicated to both Gilson and Smith: *Companions of the Rose* (no. 55).

Christopher Tolkien has pointed, in notes on his father's poetry manuscripts, to additional leaves as possible workings for *G.B.S.* If so, they are from sections or themes Tolkien began to develop but abandoned before completion. We have transcribed below the two most substantive pages of these writings, one in a difficult script which has defeated us here and there. Both sets of verses are similar in sentiment to the identified memorial, and appear to be contemporary with it, and the longer group of lines (E) is headed 'Part 4' as if it might carry on from the third part of *G.B.S.*

The twelve lines given below as F, in (mostly) rhyming couplets, are however in a different poetic form than the confirmed texts of *G.B.S.* Tolkien wrote these on the reverse side of a discarded word-slip for the *Oxford English Dictionary*, thus not earlier than 1919, when he began his employment on the *OED* staff.

[E] And even as the great desire of their rich hearts piled up
On golden sails the mighty ships toss free
And every sunrise is a glory unexplored
And every haven is a magic silver pool
Its margin is on the shore of Elfinesse
Where laden winds bear song and perfumed sound
Of infinite delight:
They only know the splendour of a ship
?That comprehend the full song of the sea
None ??? feel the same Earth neath their feet
Or catch the voices of the holy flowers
For they alone have eyes illuminéd
By some chance ray inestimable
Shaken beneath the star white robe of God
Ye track their shining feet o'er land and sea
I follow carrying a small ?unlit lamp with me
Great are y[ou]r hearts and how yet stride anon
Brave ones: ??? do yet overtake

Ah can ye not already see their silver phalanxes
Wind singing down a chasmed mountain gorge
Or up a rocky stair that mounts beyond ?morn
If perchance awhile I yet trample over the ?misty coasts
Ye will have joined that ?burly throng
The holy mariners ?the [*sic*]
Perchance my little lamp will aid ye dark ???
Which love and ye have life in me

[F] For you the heavens are a blazing sign,
For you the outmost dark confine.
Of this unmeasured world leads [*or:* draws] always on
The endless realms, and seas no galleon
Has ever ploughed beyond the isles of night.

O most undaunted in your cleansing fears
O lavish givers of begrudgéd years,
Over the waters and through stony lands
Whose wind was as a sword in cruel hands
Long have ye followed that clear shining light
That is the banner of the leaguéd saints
Th' unconquerable legions

A11: In the manuscript 'great doors' is written without an apostrophe, though the sense is evidently possessive (the great doors' key, the key to the great doors). 'Great doors' is also the reading in B7, but Tolkien included an apostrophe ('great door's') in C8 and D7.

A66: 'Constellate streams', i.e. starry skies.

C24: 'Left the bar', i.e. left the harbour, crossing a sandbar or other obstruction at its mouth, here used figuratively to describe moonrise, as if the moon were a ship pursuing the stars.

D2: This line replaced 'Wisdom from old ages, every darkest vein' in the final manuscript. Tolkien also considered, rather than 'Wisdom of Eld', 'Eld's aged wisdom' and 'Wisdom beyond ages'.

D7: This line replaced 'Thou soon will know, the great door's key will hold' in the final manuscript.

D9–12: These lines replaced in the final manuscript:

> There looking back the narrow [passage >] passed
> Still, ere the eternal portals shadow thee
> For all our life from us, one radiance cast
> Of thy grave face now glorious on me.

Tolkien also considered 'portals of eternity' rather than 'gateways of eternity' in l. 10, and 'darkness' or 'shadow' rather than 'shadows' in l. 11.

D29: Tolkien considered whether to change this line to 'Of distant forests [*or* dwellings] vales, far off to you', but retained the more complementary 'valleys' and 'hills'.

D45: 'But you are gone' replaced 'And thou art gone' in the typescript.

D48: 'Your footfall' replaced 'thy footfall' in the typescript.

D60–61: These lines replaced in the final manuscript:

> And sudden darkness, where we gaily strode,
> Now walled in the ravine of deep distress

Tolkien also considered, in l. 60, 'bravely strode' rather than 'gaily strode'.

54

Ye Laggard Woodlands (?1917)

Eight pages of manuscript are associated with this poem, which we have called *Ye Laggard Woodlands* from the start of its first line in its only (more or less) finished form. These sheets were found in Tolkien's papers with manuscripts for poems from the war years, such as *The Thatch of Poppies* and *The Forest Walker* (nos. 49, 50), suggesting that *Ye Laggard Woodlands* is also of that period. Text referring to 'the second day of spring' and 'echo of the bridal day' almost certainly points to an anniversary of Tolkien's wedding to Edith on 22 March 1916, one day after the vernal equinox (the astronomical beginning of spring). Since the couple were both in Harrogate, Yorkshire in March 1917 (Tolkien in the Furness Auxiliary Hospital), and that month was their first wedding anniversary, we think it likely that *Ye Laggard Woodlands* dates from that occasion, and so have placed it here in the poems' chronological sequence.

At first, composition did not proceed smoothly. Here, as examples, are three selections from the pages of drafts, as amended in the course of writing. Text C in particular recalls the mood and imagery of another very personal work, *You and Me and the Cottage of Lost Play* (no. 28).

[A] let scents of flowers that aroused old memory
be laden on the air, the winds breathe reverie
ye wintry mourning seas
Behold the sun

[B] Amid an endless picture of fair trees
Where countless birds do all together sing
Thus shall it be when that day in itself
comes back again
But now let all the flowers and beasts and birds
Blush and make song and festival
Whenever on the turning of the orbed ?star
That day's remembrance comes to dawn again
It was the second day of spring
let all the multitude of birds most sweetly sing

[C] Methought I woke to find it that great day again
The sun streamed in the golden window
And my white room caught fire
I wandering down the winding ways
And all the shadows were both deep and long
But 'twas not eve
There was a wine and mist upon the air
And at the turning of a well known way
I met you and your eyes were full of light
The dawn of loveliness played round your face and lips
And all the fragrance of laden winds was heaped upon her
Nor ever in the world was in my heart so great a ?joy
And we together went the old and well worn way
Together at the springing of the day
While yet the shadows of the trees were long lean keen bright
And all the Earth cried out to find it was not night
And all our lays sang for the day was come
And then we passed beyond the sight of my dull present self
Into a glorious light were [*sic, for* where] was no ?parting mere [*?for* more] or threat of severance
As one before God who majestic sat serene
Upon a white throne ??? with bright water pure

On yet another page, Tolkien began:

[D] For ever hallowed in deep memory
That aches to see that dearest of all days
Borne ever backward hallowed shall be
That gentle hour that story wandering you and me
Did read together for a while in happier days

Between the hills ye meadow-loving brooks and rills
The rocky shore took on a mellow light
And the spare buds just springing opened more
Beneath the fitful sun Our happy night
Saw all things fair

But as this attempt too petered out, at last he found an approach that suited him. Here, as text E, incorporating Tolkien's marked changes, is the first of three versions of the final form. In this text alone among the three he names the pipers as the Solosimpi, the kindred of Elves from his mythology; in texts F and G they are only the 'shoreland spirits'.

[E] Ye laggard woodlands and ye slumbrous brakes
Must ever on that day of all the year
Put forth your earliest primrose, O ye lakes
That the ungarlanded hills and drear
Adorn your banks with celandines, call daffodils
To dance along your grassy ways
The day is very near. Before that day of memory draws near
Ye wintry mourning seas
Behold the sun give power to the day
Drink ye his fire, that it make golden way
Through all your laughing water and long waves
Of green and purple let your weedy caves
Resound with music and the wistful noise
The Solosimpi's piping voice. The shoreland spirits!
Most fitting to this sweet sad day
Behold the swinging of the changèd year
Has brought the echo of the bridal day
And all the earth is panting at the dawn of spring
And all the countless birds do on a sudden sing
Blest be for ever that gay sloping shore
That looks across the water into Wales
Behold the sea is green set in ivory foam
All dusted is with diamonds in the light
The celandine ?lays thick upon the sward ?thy golden stars
The violets wake to nod a drowsy head
And here I sing

Tolkien next made a new manuscript (F, as amended), revising the text of 'Ye laggard woodlands . . .' as he wrote, while drawing ideas from his abandoned drafts.

[F] Ye laggard woodlands and ye sleeping brakes
Must ever on that day of all the year
Put forth your earliest primrose — O ye lakes
That lie ungarlanded of flowers and drear
Between the hills.
Ye meadow-loving brooks and rills
Adorn your banks with celandine, call daffodils
To dance among your grassy leas
Before that day of memory draws near:
Ye wintry mourning seas
Behold the sun gives honour to the day —

Drink ye his fire that it make golden way
Through all your laughing water and long waves
Of green and purple; let your weedy caves
Resound with music and the wistful noise,
The many shoreland spirits piping voice
That most befitteth this sad happy day.

He attempted to continue this version with a fantasy of coloured jewels, but the idea collapsed within a few lines ('The sea encircleth the awakened lands | As in a many coloured zone | Where the snow white ivory in veinéd hand | Across a floor of blue and emerald stone').

The final version of the poem (G) is a fair copy, though even so Tolkien was undecided whether 'this' in line 2 should be 'that', and whether 'of flowers' in line 4 should not be omitted (as it is in version E).

[G] Ye laggard woodlands and ye slumbrous brakes
For ever on this day in every year
Put forth your earliest primrose — O ye lakes
That lie ungarlanded of flowers and drear
Between the hills:
Ye meadow-loving brooks and rills
Adorn your banks with celandine, call daffodils
To dance along your grassy leas.
Let scent of flowers that wound old memory
Be on the air, the winds breathed reverently
Ye wintry mourning seas
Behold the sun gives glory to the day
Drink of his fire that it make golden way
Though all your laughing water and long waves
Of green and purple; let your weedy caves
Resound with music and the wistful noise —
The many shoreland spirits piping voice —
That most befitteth this most happy day.

E5: By 'celandine' Tolkien probably means the lesser celandine, *Ficaria verna* (formerly *Ranunculus ficaria*), a member of the buttercup family, with heart-shaped leaves and glossy yellow flowers, regarded as a harbinger of spring. The greater celandine, *Chelidonium majum*, does not produce flowers until late spring.

E13–26: The latter part of this text is written on a page below six lines: 'Earendel | Solosimpe | Pansy Eyes | The Chapel | For the Three | The Ship that Sailed at Eve'. At least some of these allude to Tolkien's mythology, or may be ideas for poems he never wrote, or whose conceptions he altered.

E14: For the Solosimpi, see also poem no. 46, *Tol Eressea* (*The Lonely Isle*). There the plural form of the name was *Solosimpe*, also included in Tolkien's Qenya lexicon. By the time of *Ye Laggard Woodlands*, the plural had become *Solosimpi*, attested in Tolkien's Gnomish lexicon of ?1916–17.

E20–21: 'That gay sloping shore | that looks across the water into Wales': after their wedding, Tolkien and Edith spent a week's honeymoon in Clevedon, a town in Somerset on the Severn estuary, on the other side of which is Wales.

F4: 'Of flowers' originally read 'and grey'.

F16: Written below 'piping' (or, above 'happy' in l. 16) is a word which appears to be 'whispering', but 'piping' continued into text G, and the awkward phrase in F, 'sad happy' (compare 'sweet sad' in E15), became in G 'most happy'.

55

Companions of the Rose (1917–?24)

The Battle of Minden, fought in Prussia on 1 August 1759, was an important victory by the Anglo–German army against the French during the Seven Years' War. Among the several British regiments involved that day were the Suffolks, to which Rob Gilson later belonged before his death on the Somme, and the 20th Foot, predecessor to the Lancashire Fusiliers, in which Tolkien and G.B. Smith served as officers in different battalions. According to tradition, the British soldiers of the earlier war wore roses in their hats, plucked en route to the fighting. The turning point of the battle came when the 20th Foot, misunderstanding orders, advanced against the French and, though at high cost, withstood three cavalry charges with musket fire. The event has been celebrated since then every August 1st, as Minden Day. On Minden Day 1917, while attached to the 3rd (Reserve) Battalion of the Lancashire Fusiliers in Yorkshire, Tolkien attended an elaborate celebratory dinner; presumably earlier that day, he wrote the poem *Companions of the Rose* to honour the deaths of those who came long before, but in particular his friends Gilson and Smith who both fell the previous year.

There are two extant manuscripts of *Companions of the Rose*. Tolkien wrote the first on a sheet of ruled notebook paper and with the numeral '1' above lines 1–18 (the remaining text is on the verso of the leaf). The second manuscript is a fair copy in one of Tolkien's poetry notebooks, with lines 1–18 and 19–34 more distinctly numbered as sections 1 and 2; this bears the date 'Aug[ust] 28–29' (1917), when Tolkien was in the Brooklands Officers' Hospital in Hull. Around 1924, a professional typescript of the poem was made, of which ribbon and carbon copies survive. Since all of these texts are almost identical one to another, here we give only the final, typescript version, with differences between the texts mentioned in discussion or notes.

Not those who gathering roses as they came
Fell eager on the foe, and face to face
Slew or were slain; who won them a fair name
Still richly honoured, and undying praise,

While songs be made of red deeds long ago,
When men met men and war was fierce and stark
Yet no inhuman butchery in the dark,
Not wholly sordid 'gainst a sordid foe: —

— Not these, but ye, O thrice immortal dead
Shall wreathe the reddest roses round your head;

For you to-day I drink the silent toast
And pour the wine, and wear my rose, and sing
That yours is now of all the proudest boast
Who, loathing wars and all they mean or bring,
Went forth in horror, charged the Gates of Hell,
And poison-piercèd by a foe unseen
Drenched with your blood the tortured Earth, and fell
Where no rose springs nor any blade of green.

O! God Boisselle and Warlencourt to me
Are names more full of mourning than the sea,
Their poignant glory shines with clearer flame
Than even Minden's ancient valiance
Where Kingsley's Regiment crowned in roses came
Driving the triple cavalry of France:
Yea not to these, but my immortal dead,
To day I drink, have raised my cup, and said
'Hail! whom I love — beyond forgiveness slain
By that most dastard most dishonoured foe
That all the warfare of the world can show.
Yours was the treacherous death, th'envenomed pain;
Yours now be quenchless trumpets of renown,
Undying roses and immortal wine,
Whose crimson chaplets are with odours laden,
Keen deathless fragrance of your love, and mine.'

The intent of 'treacherous' in line 30 is not clear. Did Tolkien mean that the enemy was treacherous when it gunned down Rob Gilson, while he was leading his men over the top at La Boisselle, or was it treachery on the part of Britain and her allies for failing to subdue, as intended, the (unexpectedly well-protected and well-prepared) enemy with explosives before the Battle of the Somme? 'Envenomed' in the same line, i.e. poisonous, presumably refers to the gas gangrene that killed G.B. Smith at Warlencourt, his wounds from a bursting shell having become infected. 'Crimson chaplets' in line 33 refers back to line 10, 'wreathe the reddest roses round your head'.

At the head of the initial manuscript of the poem, below its title, Tolkien wrote the dedication 'For RQG [Robert Quilter Gilson] Suffolk Reg[imen]t, GBS [Geoffrey Bache Smith] Lancashire Fusiliers'. At the head of the second manuscript he expanded this to read: 'For R.Q.G. of the Suffolk Regiment and GBS of the Lancashire Fusiliers who died at La Boisselle and Warlencourt in 1916. Both of these regiments fought at the battle of Minden and still celebrate that victory.' At the foot of each of the two manuscripts Tolkien wrote: 'Roses are worn by all ranks [on Minden Day], and the toast "To those who fell at Minden" is drunk facing the colours and in silence. Kingsley's Regiment was at that time the title of the 20th Foot'.

Tolkien evidently wondered whether to delete lines 28–29, 'By that most dastard most dishonoured foe | That all the warfare of the world can show'. Christopher Wiseman, to whom Tolkien sent a copy of *Companions of the Rose* and who approved of the poem, replied that he saw no reason to remove the comment, since the Germans were indeed dastardly and dishonourable. The lines remained. On 15 October 1917 Edith Tolkien, who was also sent a copy, wrote to her husband that she liked it, 'especially the latter part: I felt sure you had written it on Minden Day, even before I looked!' (Bodleian Library).

15: Here, and at ll. 21, 25, 27, and 31, on one copy of the typescript, Tolkien made marks as if considering whether to add further breaks besides the four he established in the first manuscript.

19: Above this line in the first manuscript, Tolkien wrote as draft text, but struck through:

> God! La Boisselle and Warlencourt to me
> Were cursèd names awhile —but let them be
> Now sacred, robed in undefiled renown
> O'er passing Minden and that

27: In the first manuscript 'Hail! whom' originally read 'To those'.

27–34: In the first manuscript these lines were not within quotation marks.

30–31: In each of these lines in the first manuscript Tolkien changed 'Theirs' to 'Yours'.

24: In the typescript, Tolkien considered whether to change 'Driving' to 'Charging'. Neither verb is precise: the French cavalry did the charging, while the 20th Foot marched forward or stood their ground.

56

The Grey Bridge of Tavrobel (1917–?27)

The Grey Bridge of Tavrobel exists in a single manuscript and two typescripts. Tolkien inscribed the former (A, below) 'Brooklands Red + [Cross] hosp[ital] Cottingham Road, Hull Sept[ember] or Aug[ust] 1917?' The poem undoubtedly reflects his emotion, recollected at a brief remove, on reuniting with Edith after months of separation. Since their farewell in June 1916 she, a 'little damozelle', had 'waited, waited, wearily' for her man to 'come a-homing', while Tolkien lamented their loneliness and lost days never to be regained.

Tavrobel, as we have seen, represents in his early mythology the Staffordshire village of Great Haywood, a place of happy times for the Tolkiens before he was sent to France, and again between December 1916 and February 1917 after he was invalided home. The village stands at the confluence of the rivers Sow and Trent ('two rivers running fleetly'), near which the Trent is crossed by the Essex Bridge, 'an old grey bridge' of stone built in the sixteenth century.

If Tolkien was correct in his guess at a date, he composed the poem while a patient in the Brooklands Officers' Hospital in Hull in August or September 1917. By then, he and his wife had left Great Haywood for Yorkshire, where Tolkien was posted for recuperation and light duties, and then in late August Edith, pregnant with their first son, moved to Cheltenham for greater comfort. Tolkien's ballad inspired by returning home is, then, even more poignant for having been written just as he and Edith were parting once again.

[A]

There's an old grey bridge in Tavrobel,
    And two rivers running fleetly,
And there I saw a damozelle,
    And she was smiling sweetly.

'O! tell me, little damozelle,
    Why smile you in the gloaming
On the old grey bridge of Tavrobel
    As the grey folk come a-homing?'

'I smile because you come to me
O'er the grey bridge in the gloaming:
I have waited, waited, wearily
To see you come a-homing.

In Tavrobel things go but ill,
And my little garden withers
In Tavrobel beneath the hill
When you're across the rivers.'

'Ay, long and long I have been away
O'er sea and land and river
Dreaming always of the day
Of my returning hither.'

And then for joy we kissed, we twain,
And sweetly homeward wandered,
But the lost days who shall give again
That loneliness had squandered.

Both of the typescripts of *The Grey Bridge of Tavrobel*, with identical texts, were made on Tolkien's Hammond typewriter, probably not long before the poem was published, without change, on p. 82 of the *Inter-University Magazine* of the University Catholic Societies' Federation of Great Britain for May 1927. The latter is given here as B. The only important differences from the manuscript are in the poem's final four lines.

[B] There's an old grey bridge in Tavrobel,
And two rivers running fleetly,
And there I saw a damozelle,
And she was smiling sweetly.

'O! tell me, little damozelle,
Why smile you in the gloaming
On the old grey bridge of Tavrobel
As the grey folk come a-homing?'

'I smile because you come to me
O'er the grey bridge in the gloaming:
I have waited, waited, wearily
To see you come a-homing.

In Tavrobel things go but ill,
    And my little garden withers
In Tavrobel beneath the hill,
    When you're across the rivers.'

'Ay, long and long I have been away
    O'er sea and land and river
Dreaming always of the day
    Of my returning hither.'

And there we kissed by evening grey,
    And her arms went soft about me;
But the days of sunlight, where are they
    That she lonely spent without me?

A8: 'Grey folk' is an allusion to elves, either within Tolkien's own mythology or generally in folklore. The folk, the bridge, the evening, and the mood of the poem are all grey.

57

I Stood upon an Empty Shore (?1917)

Workings for this unfinished poem are found on five manuscript pages, with much repetition of words and phrases. There is no fair copy, and none of the drafts obviously precedes or follows another. One page of workings is on the reverse of a draft letter from Tolkien to R.W. Reynolds, in which the writer refers to himself 'on detachment' and unable to get leave; this is undated, but seems likely to have been written while Tolkien was posted to Yorkshire, between April 1917 and early 1918, perhaps at a time immediately before or after Edith gave birth to their first child, on 16 November 1917. (Tolkien was unable to see his wife and son in Cheltenham until nearly a week later.) The text of the poem itself points to this same period, with references to 'the Eastern sea' and 'the estuary' – the North Sea and the Humber tidal estuary, to the east and west of the Holderness peninsula where Tolkien was stationed.

As we remarked in our discussion of *The Grey Bridge of Tavrobel* (no. 56), Edith had moved to Cheltenham in late August 1917, it having proved uncomfortable for her, with advancing pregnancy, to stay in the Holderness area. Tolkien once more was separated from his wife, and again in his new poem there are images of departure, loneliness, and gloom.

Here we have transcribed, as A and B, two of the most legible parts of the work, taken from two drafts, and have given the work a title based on its first line.

[A] I stood upon an empty shore before the sun was born
I stood and listened for the trumpets of the morn
No faintest echo of her music rang
Through all the wide domes of her heavenly halls
No coming whispers of her swift footfalls
Drear spirits of the lonely sands about me sang
Cheerless and cold and grey the Eastern sea
Dark was the west across the estuary
Where low in heaven all alone the light
Twinkled and dipped of one star lost in night
Westward o west I gazed into the gloom
Hearing behind me still the sea's low boom

Where suddenly a sea bird swept across the air
Crying that morn was coming, and most unaware
The little birds awoke their lutelike voices
Seeing that morn indeed was very near
Swelling the long waves changed their solemn noises
Running far far away we hear
The silver trumpets calling at the gates
Of the wide earth that early morn is very near
Woman is coming man no longer waits
Her tremulous feet are set upon the stair

Then a sweet voice went westward on the wind
?By what loneliness was gone and pain and ?might
And the echo of it wavered in the shadows of the west

[B] Loud is the sea and dreary is the land
And grey gulls calling sadly o'er the sand
The wind goes creaking in the faded grass
Dusk gathers on the dunes, and still the sea
Cries out around us that the days do pass
Soon comes the end, and then must we
Fare from the island where our love doth dwell
Go forth into the darkness go and say farewell.

At this time, while in the Royal Defence Corps on the Holderness peninsula, Tolkien was still suffering bouts of illness from trench fever. He was considered by the War Office to be unfit for general service but improving. The final lines of text B may reflect his thoughts on the prospect of being declared fit to return to the front, and leaving England, and Edith, once more ('Fare from the island where our love doth dwell').

A7–8: In a different draft, these lines read 'Grey was the silver East above an angry sea | The dark west slept in night and calling me beyond the estuary'; and in yet another, the estuary goes unmentioned: 'The East was grey above a sea of gloom | The dark west slept in deepest night'.

A11: In other drafts this line begins more simply 'West o west'.

58

Build Me a Grave beside the Sea · The Brothers-in-Arms (1918–*c.* 1920)

With no physical evidence to date the first workings of this poem, we have assumed from its fatalistic mood and personal concern with death that it was written while the war was still in progress and there was still a chance that Tolkien, if recovered sufficiently from illness, could be sent back to the trenches. We suspect that it dates from the first part of 1918, perhaps following the decision of an army medical board on 10 April that Tolkien was able to return to general service. At the end of June that year he was readmitted to hospital, and that September was declared fully disabled: only then could he be assured that a return to fighting was unlikely.

Six pages of manuscript drafts, very rough and miscellaneous in their elements, precede the first completed manuscript of the (as yet untitled) poem. We give the latter as A, incorporating changes made in the course of writing. Tolkien divided the text into stanzas of three lines through line 21, then omitted breaks for the remainder of the draft.

[A]

Build me a grave beside the sea
Heap the brown earth over me
Upon a cliff top above the sea,

Build it broad and high my mound
That ships hereafter homeward bound
May strain to sight my seaward mound

Nor can ye make an end more fit
For an end complete and definite
Sad heavy earth is a symbol fit

Raw at first and torn and red
As though the earth had with me bled
Slowly the green shall hide the red,

And as your tears shall slowly dry,
And as ye one by one shall die
And the spring of the song of my deeds shall dry

Till gently my name new men forget
The rains and dews shall the barrow wet
And greener and smoother it will get,

As Earth by stages slow unseen
Absorbs it, reshapes it to what has been
Till nothing unkindred to the cliffs is seen

No token of the toil and death of men
Scarce a swelling of the grassy earth — what then
What if the world is filled with unknown men
Earth knows; who never man forgot
Who holds them all whose tears dry not
Whose song of sorrow hath forgot
Never the name of one who died
Mourning them in the voices of the tide
Earth will remember when I dyed
With life blood and late forgetful men
Who walk the cliff unwitting then
Shall feel my untold tale again
Of me who lie beneath the grass
Of yesterdays and yesterdays that pass
And fade to faint sounds in the grass
And there shall be who catch as at a dream
Upon the edge of thought — and it will deem
Wrong the loveliness of the sea, their summer dream
The sunlight in the grass, the wind's
Low breath stirring their heart, that binds
Them in a groping wonder of their minds
To that high brow above the mournful sea
Not knowing unforgetting Earth thus speaks of me
With mighty voices of the wind and see [*sic, for* sea].

Almost certainly still before the end of the war, Tolkien made a new manuscript of the poem (transcribed as B), extended and with revisions; a few later changes marked to this copy were taken up in the subsequent version. At the head of the first page Tolkien began to give the poem a title, but wrote only 'The Knight's' before stopping and scribbling across the words. Perhaps he felt that there was nothing chivalric about what he had experienced in France and knew still to be happening – not an uncommon response among soldier-poets who had survived the war long enough to lose any romantic notions about battle they may have held. We have chosen to give the earlier versions of the poem a title based on its first line.

[B]

Build me a grave beside the sea,
Heap the brown earth over me
Upon a cliff above the sea.

Build it broad and high my mound,
That ships hereafter homeward bound
May mark afar my seaward mound:

A cavernous enclosed pit,
Sad heavy earth piled over it —
Of memory a symbol fit,

A fitting and a final end,
For now there's no more tale to spend,
This is the end, this is the end!

Raw at first and torn and red
As though the earth had with me bled,
Slowly the green shall hide the red,

And, as your tears shall slowly dry,
And as you one by one shall die
And your springing songs of me shall dry

Till gently my name new men forget
The rains and dews shall the barrow wet
And greener and smoother it will get,

While Earth by stages slow unseen
Dissolves it, reshapes it to what has been,
Till nothing unkindred to the cliffs is seen,

No token of the toil and death of men,
Scarce a swelling of the grass — what then!
What if the Earth is filled with unknown men!

Earth knows, who never man forgot,
Who holds them all, whose tears dry not.
Whose song of sorrow hath forgot

Never the name of one who died,
Mourning them in the voices of the tide.
Earth will remember, when I dyed

With lifeblood, and forgetful men
Who walk the cliff unwitting then
Shall feel my untold tale again,

Of him that lies beneath the grass
Neath yesterdays and days that pass
And fade to faint sounds in the grass

And there shall be who catch as at dream [*sic*]
Upon the edge of thought, and it will deem
Only the murmur of the sea, a summer dream,

The sunlight in the grass, the wind's
Low breath stirring their heart, that binds
Them in a groping wonder of their minds

To that high brow above the mournful sea,
Nor know that unforgetting Earth doth speak of me
With mighty voices of the wind and sea.

For who shall say where lies the long road's end
The tale is read and we the page must wend —
There is no end, there is no end.

In October 1918, unfit for most of his military duties, Tolkien was authorized to seek sedentary civilian employment in Oxford. The Armistice ending the war was signed on 11 November, but with Britain still in need of troops to intervene in the Russian Civil War, he was not demobilized until 16 July 1919. He set aside *Build Me a Grave beside the Sea* until at least October 1920, after he had joined the English Faculty at Leeds; when writing out a new manuscript on university examination paper, for amusement he used antique orthography, such as the Anglo-Saxon *thorn* (þ) and *eth* (ð) respectively for voiceless and voiced *th-*. The new text had only minor changes from version B, but to this Tolkien made numerous further revisions, then typed the amended text using a purple ribbon. Later he inscribed one of the typescript pages 'Oxford + Leeds 1920–24'. Most notably, in this new version he altered pronouns in several lines: for example, 'Build me' became 'Build him' (line 1), 'my mound' became 'our mound' (line 4), and 'had with me bled' became 'had with us bled' (line 14).

This was the first step in a final transformation of the poem, in which the point of view was turned from the speaker alone, fearing death if not deceased already, to that of a soldier who saw a comrade die then was himself killed and buried in the same grave. Tolkien now gave the work the title *The Brothers-in-Arms*. He marked further revisions to the typescript, repeating some on the final manuscript, and composed twelve new lines to replace those at the start of the existing text. He wrote the first six of the new lines on the manuscript before working out a (barely decipherable) longer text on a separate sheet, then added them to the typescript. At last, he made a fair copy of the passage. The opening lines read as follows before replacement:

Build him a grave beside the sea,
Heap the brown earth over me
    Upon a cliff beside the sea.
Build it broad and high our mound,
That ships hereafter homeward bound
    May mark afar our seaward mound:
A cavernous enclosèd pit,
Sad heavy earth piled over it —
    Of memory a token fit,
A fitting and a final end,
For now there's no more tale to spend,
    This is the end! This is the end!

In line 9, 'token' replaced 'symbol' as a late change made by Tolkien to the typescript.

The ultimate text of the poem is given here as C, consolidating the typescript with its revisions and new opening lines, the latter from the fair copy.

[C]

He fell alone. I heard him cry.
I could not reach him, save to die
    Too late, beside him. Let us lie!
Make him a grave beside the sea,

Heap the same earth over me,
  There together let us be!
Build our barrow broad and high,
That homeward sailors passing by
  May mark the headland where we lie
Silent as long as time shall be,
In narrow house without a key
  That looks upon the shoreless sea.
Raw at first and torn and red,
As though the earth had with us bled,
  Slowly the green shall hide the red,
And when your tears shall slowly dry,
And as you one by one shall die,
  The spring of songs of us runs dry
Till gently our names new men forget,
Then rains and dews shall the barrow wet,
  And greener and smoother it will get,
And Earth by stages slow, unseen,
Dissolve it, reshape it to what has been,
  Till nothing unkindred to the cliffs be seen,
No token of the toil and death of men,
Only a swelling of the grass — what then?
  Though Earth be filled with unknown men,
Earth knows, who never man forgot,
Who holds them all, whose tears dry not,
  Whose song of sorrow has forgot
Never the name of one who died,
Mourning them in the voices of the tide.
  Earth will remember whom we dyed
With lifeblood, and forgetful men
Who walk the cliff unwitting then
  Shall sense a tale untold, of men
Here laid to sleep beneath the grass,
Neath days and yesterdays that pass
  And fade to faint sounds in the grass.
And some shall be who catch as at a dream
Upon the edge of thought, and it will deem
  Only the roaring of the sea, a summer dream,
The sunlight in the grass, the wind's
Low breath stirring their heart, that binds
  Them in a groping wonder of their minds
To that high brow above the mourning sea,

Nor know that Earth doth speak of him and me
    In mighty voices of the wind and sea.
Where lies, a! where, the long road's end? —
The tale is read and we the page must wend.
    Is this the end? Is this the end?

Tolkien seems to have considered still more revisions, to lines 40–43, jotted at the end of the typescript, but took them no further:

There Men may come. There some may dream
they hear a voice, but that will deem
the sighing of the sea, a dream

    of wind across the sunlit grass
a sound of wind on sunlit grass

The poet's request for a barrow, or burial mound, so 'broad and high' that 'homeward sailors passing by | May mark the headland where we lie' (C7–9) recalls the mound in which Beowulf in the eponymous Old English poem is buried, raised upon a cliff, 'high and broad, to voyagers on the waves clear seen afar' (translated by Tolkien, *Beowulf* (2014), p. 105). Immediately following the war, much thought was given to memorials for the dead: on 11 November 1920 the King unveiled the Cenotaph in Whitehall, and the body of an unknown soldier was laid to rest in Westminster Abbey.

In the several drafts of this poem one finds conflicting thoughts about life after death. 'Where lies the long road's end?' he asks in one version, and comes to different conclusions: There is no end (declarative, B). This is the end! (exclamatory, derived from B). Is this the end? (speculative, C). Tolkien had good reason to question and doubt. By the war's end, many of his friends from King Edward's School had been killed, as had many of those with whom he matriculated at Exeter College, Oxford in 1911, and the 11th Lancashire Fusiliers, the battalion in which he had served before falling ill, was nearly annihilated in France in 1918.

C16–20: As initially typed, these lines read:

And while your tears do slowly dry,
And while you one by one shall die
    And the spring of your songs of us shall dry
Till gently our names new men forget
The rain and the dews shall the barrow wet

C27: This line replaced 'What if Earth be filled with unknown men?' in the typescript.

C38: This line replaced 'Neath yesterdays and yesterdays that pass' in the typescript.

C40: This line replaced 'And there shall be who catch as at a dream' in the typescript.

59

A Rime for My Boy (1918)

Tolkien's first son, John Francis Reuel Tolkien, was probably little more than six months old when his father wrote a short poem entitled *A Rime for My Boy*.

> Little John Bobbilinks went to town
> To buy some shoes and a golden crown.
> The shoemaker said I've a beautiful shoe
> And the maker of crowns said here's one that might do;
> It belonged to the King-of-Īverinōr,
> Who suddenly found he'd a hundred in store
> (And pawned ninety-nine to get cash for the war).
> Then little John Bobbilinks popped on the crown —
> And now he is King in his own little town.

The *Rime* (i.e. rhyme) is written and drawn across two pages in three forms, first as a rebus, obviously done for Tolkien's own amusement, or that of his wife, since John was far too young to appreciate its many puns – 'Bobbilinks', for example, is formed by a picture of a bobby (a policeman) followed by a drawing of a golf links. This is followed by the plain text as given above, and then by a simplified transcription from the rebus, beginning 'A rime [from the rhyming 'And/band'] 4 m eye buoy'. The second page is on the reverse side of a leaf with Tolkien's drawing *High Life at Gipsy Green* (Hammond and Scull, *Artist and Illustrator*, fig. 23), which was made around May or June 1918. After he was posted again to Cannock Chase in April or May that year, Edith and John, with Edith's cousin Jennie Grove, found rooms in a cottage nearby at Gipsy Green, and Tolkien was able to stay with them on occasion.

'Little John Bobbilinks' recalls frequent beginnings to nursery rhymes, like 'Little Jack Horner' and 'Little Tommy Tucker'. 'Bobbilinks' seems, by form and sound, to be based on *bobolink*, the name of a noisy songbird with a distinctive call (*bob o'lincoln*) – an American species, but perhaps one that had come to Tolkien's attention. *Īverinōr* is likely a variation on *Íverin*, the name of an island in *The Book of Lost Tales* identified with Ireland (*Ivernia* in Ptolemy's second-century *Geography*); *-nor* is a Qenya element meaning 'land'. Tolkien's Gnomish lexicon notes Gnomish *Aivrin* or *Aîvren* ('an Island off the West coast of *Tol Er[ethrin]*', i.e. Tol Eressëa), with the Qenya forms *Īwerin* and *Iverindor*.

Of course, the recipient of this poem would not have been able to read it, or appreciate its visual aspects, at the time of its writing (though even as a baby he may have enjoyed its spoken rhythms). But Tolkien was inspired to write it at that moment, and the reason was undoubtedly that he was now a father. His *Rime* was a gift he could bestow on his son easily and immediately, and one which might please young John once he learned to read it for himself. It is not too much to say that fatherhood had a profound effect on Tolkien, not only as a man but as a writer: works such as his *Roverandom* and *Farmer Giles of Ham*, and later *The Hobbit*, existed only because he had children to whom he told stories – a quality his three sons and daughter recalled with fondness – and it was only because he wrote *The Hobbit* that we have *The Lord of the Rings*.

A Rime for My Boy is, in its small way, the beginning of a second path in Tolkien's creative thoughts, as he considered the tastes and interests of his young audience in addition to his own, parallel to (if often influenced by) his mythology. The nursery rhyme was an obvious form to use in beginning to write for his children, and one in which he was already experienced (see poem no. 24).

60

Nursery Rhymes Undone, or Their Scandalous Secret Unlocked · The Cat and the Fiddle · They Say There's a Little Crooked Inn · There Is an Inn, a Merry Old Inn · The Man in the Moon Stayed Up Too Late

(?1919–62)

In *The Return of the Shadow* (1988), the first of five books in *The History of Middle-earth* which trace the history of *The Lord of the Rings*, Christopher Tolkien included the text of *The Cat and the Fiddle* (as it is convenient to call this poem in general) 'as it is found in the original manuscript, written on Leeds University paper' (p. 145). Readers of *The Lord of the Rings* will remember the version Frodo sings at *The Prancing Pony* in Bree. In fact, the *Return of the Shadow* text is the second version of the poem, following a manuscript of which Christopher was unaware. Here, as A, we have transcribed the initial draft as it was first written out, including a remarkable series of alternate readings which Tolkien set down in brackets (parentheses), apparently to consider at a later time. At this stage he entitled the poem *Nursery Rhymes Undone, or Their Scandalous Secret Unlocked.*

[A]

They say there's a little crooked inn
    (That's lost among the hills)
    Behind an old grey hill
Where they brew a beer so very brown
The man in the moon himself comes down
    And sometimes drinks his fill

And there the ostler has a cat
    Who plays a five-stringed fiddle,
Mine host has a little dog so clever
He laughs at any joke whatever
    And sometimes in the middle

They also keep a hornéd cow,
    'Tis said, with golden hooves —
But music turns her head like ale
And makes her wave her tufted tail
    And dance upon the rooves

But Oh the rows of silver dishes
    And the store of silver spoons:
For Sunday there's a special pair
And these they polish up with care
    On Saturday afternoons

The man in the moon, he drank too deep;
    The ostler's cat was toty [*sic, for* totty]
A dish made love to a Sunday spoon,
The little dog saw all the jokes too soon
    And the cow was dancing-dotty.

The man in the moon had another mug
    And fell beneath his chair
And there he called for still more ale
Though the stars were getting thin and pale,
    And the dawn was nearly there.

Then the ostler said to his tipsy cat
    'The horses of the Moon
They neigh and champ their silver bits
And the man in the moon has lost his wits
    For the Sun is coming soon.

Come play on your fiddle a hey diddle diddle
    And see what that will do
('Twill make him look alive)
So the cat played a terrible drunken tune
While the landlord shook the man in the moon
    And said it's after two
    (And said it's nearly five)

They rolled him slowly up the hill
    And bundled him in the moon
While the horses galloped up in rear
The cow came capering like a deer
    And the dish embraced the spoon.

The cat then suddenly changed the tune,
    The dog began to roar
The horses stood upon their heads
The guests all bounded from their beds!
    And danced upon the floor.

The cat broke all his fiddle-strings
    The cow jumped over the moon
The little dog howled to see such fun
In the middle the Sunday dish did run
    away with the Sunday spoon.

The round moon rolled off over the hill
    — But only just in time
For the sun looked up with a fiery head
And everybody went back to bed
    Till the ending of the rime.

Ostler (line 7) historically refers to a *hostler* or *hosteler*, with a silent *h*, one who runs a hostelry, but here, as there is specifically and separately a 'host' or 'landlord', Tolkien probably means a stable-man or groom for guests' horses. 'Mine host' (line 9), i.e. 'My host', is phrased here in the archaic fashion in which the consonant *n* is inserted between two words with adjacent vowels (the *y* of 'My' and the *o* of 'host', the *h* being effectively silent) for smoother pronunciation. (The 'host' is the landlord of the inn.) One of many examples in Shakespeare is in *Hamlet*, 'mine uncle is King of Denmark'. A relic of this practice survives in the *n* of phrases such as 'an historical account'.

A *fiddle* is, to all intents and purposes, a violin, though some authorities would distinguish between the two, citing differences of construction, especially of the bridge. By whatever name, this instrument normally has four strings. Sometimes a fifth has been added to a fiddle, a C-string, making it more complicated to play but permitting a wider range of notes and improvisations. As such, it is preferred by some who play jazz, folk, country-western, or Celtic music. The five-stringed fiddle is not a modern invention, but was known in medieval times.

The manuscript of text A unfortunately offers no physical evidence as to its date, but on his second version of the poem Tolkien wrote 'Oxford 1919–20', which we take to be its date of original composition. In 1919–20 he was employed by the *Oxford English*

Dictionary and as a university tutor, and with his family had rooms in Oxford's St John Street. His son John was between one and three years of age, and it is possible that the poem was invented for the boy's amusement (though by no means essential: Tolkien found nursery rhymes amusing on his own account).

The second manuscript of the work can be dated more confidently, between autumn 1920, when Tolkien took up a teaching post at Leeds (his second son, Michael, was born in Oxford that October), and autumn 1923, when a form of the work appeared in *Yorkshire Poetry* for October–November, pp. 1–3. It is written on a sheet of Leeds University examination paper. Now entitled in full *The Cat and the Fiddle, or, A Nursery Rhyme Undone and Its Scandalous Secret Unlocked*, the new manuscript incorporated a few revisions marked on the earlier draft, but none of the alternate readings. Tolkien subsequently marked this version with further changes and, still at Leeds and using a purple ribbon, made a new copy in typescript, changing 'or' in its title to 'being'. We give this text as B.

[B] They say there's a little crooked inn
Behind an old grey hill,
Where they brew a beer so very brown
The Man in the Moon himself comes down,
And sometimes drinks his fill.

And there the ostler has a cat
Who plays a five-stringed fiddle;
Mine host a little dog so clever
He laughs at any joke whatever,
And sometimes in the middle.

They also keep a hornéd cow,
'Tis said, with golden hoofs —
But music turns her head like ale,
And makes her wave her tufted tail,
And dance upon the roofs.

But O! the rows of silver dishes
And the store of silver spoons:
For Sunday there's a special pair,
And these they polish up with care
On Saturday afternoons.

*

The Man in the Moon had drunk too deep,
The ostler's cat was totty,
A dish made love to a Sunday spoon,
The little dog saw all the jokes too soon,
And the cow was dancing-dotty.

The Man in the Moon had another mug
And fell beneath his chair,
And there he called for still more ale,
Though the stars were fading thin and pale,
And the dawn was on the stair.

Then the ostler said to his tipsy cat:
'The white horses of the Moon,
They neigh and champ their silver bits,
For their master's been and drowned his wits,
And the Sun'll be rising soon.

Come play on your fiddle a "hey diddle diddle",
A jig to wake the dead.'
So the cat played a terrible drunken tune,
While the landlord shook the Man in the Moon:
''Tis after three', he said.

They rolled him slowly up the hill
And bundled him in the Moon,
And his horses galloped up in rear,
And the cow came capering like a deer,
And the dish embraced the spoon.

The cat then suddenly changed the tune,
The dog began to roar,
The horses stood upon their heads,
The guests all bounded from their beds,
And danced upon the floor.

The cat broke all his fiddle-strings,
The cow jumped over the moon,
The little dog howled to see such fun,
And the Saturday dish away did run
With the silver Sunday spoon.

The round Moon rolled off down the hill,
But only just in time,
For the Sun looked up with a fiery head,
And ordered everyone back to bed,
And the ending of the rhyme.

It is curious that the form in which *The Cat and the Fiddle* was published in *Yorkshire Poetry* does not exactly match any one of the three versions extant in Tolkien's papers, but is an amalgam of earlier and later readings. This cannot be explained by editorial tinkering alone, unlike, maybe, its hyphenated 'Man-in-the-Moon', omitted accent in 'hornéd' (line 11), and surfeit of semi-colons. Perhaps Tolkien, given the opportunity to publish, could not lay his hands on the latest text and wrote it out again from memory, or else chose to make some changes, or reversions, for the occasion – most remarkably, adopting in line 40 one of his previously unused alternate readings from text A. We reprinted the *Yorkshire Poetry* text in our extended edition of *The Adventures of Tom Bombadil and Other Verses from the Red Book* (2014, pp. 173–6), supposing at the time that it represented Tolkien's latest thoughts (in its earlier stage), and do so again here, as C, for comparison.

[C]

They say there's a little crooked inn
Behind an old grey hill,
Where they brew a beer so very brown
The Man-in-the-Moon himself comes down,
And sometimes drinks his fill.

And there the ostler has a cat
Who plays a five-stringed fiddle;
Mine host a little dog so clever
He laughs at any joke whatever,
And sometimes in the middle.

They also keep a horned cow,
'Tis said, with golden hoofs;
But music turns her head like ale,
And makes her wave her tufted tail
And dance upon the roofs.

But O! the row of silver dishes,
    And the store of silver spoons:
For Sunday there's a special pair,
And these they polish up with care
    On Saturday afternoons.

*

The Man-in-the-Moon had drunk too deep;
    The ostler's cat was totty;
A dish made love to a Sunday spoon;
The little dog saw all the jokes too soon;
    And the cow was dancing-dotty.

The Man-in-the-Moon had another mug
    And fell beneath his chair,
And there he called for still more ale,
Though the stars were getting thin and pale,
    And the Dawn was on the stair.

Then the ostler said to his tipsy cat:
    'The white horses of the Moon,
They neigh and champ their silver bits,
But their master's been and drowned his wits,
    And the Sun will catch him soon.

Come play on your fiddle a hey diddle diddle,
    'Twill make him look alive.'
So the cat played a terrible drunken tune,
While the landlord shook the Man-in-the-Moon,
    And cried ''Tis nearly five!'

They rolled him slowly up the hill
    And bundled him in the Moon:
And his horses galloped up in rear,
And the cow came capering like a deer,
    And the dish embraced the spoon.

The cat then suddenly changed the tune;
    The dog began to roar;
The horses stood upon their heads;
The guests all bounded upon their beds
    And danced upon the floor.

The cat broke all his fiddle-strings;
    The cow jumped over the Moon;
The little dog laughed to see such fun;
In the middle the Sunday dish did run
Away with the Sunday spoon.

The round Moon rolled off over the hill —
    But only just in time,
For the Sun looked up with a fiery head,
And ordered everyone back to bed,
And the ending of the rhyme.

The Cat and the Fiddle is the second of Tolkien's 'Man in the Moon' poems, after *Why the Man in the Moon Came Down Too Soon* (no. 24). This too was inspired by a familiar rhyme, 'probably the best-known nonsense verse in the language':

Hey diddle diddle,
The cat and the fiddle,
The cow jumped over the moon;
The little dog laughed
To see such sport
And the dish ran away with the spoon.

George Burke Johnston has suggested ('The Poetry of J.R.R. Tolkien', 1967) that Tolkien also may have drawn upon 'The True History of the Cat and the Fiddle' by George MacDonald, in *At the Back of the North Wind* (1870), in which 'Hey Diddle Diddle' is combined with the traditional rhyme 'The Man in the Moon Came Down Too Soon' – we have discussed this amalgam already in our comments for poem no. 24. That the Man in the Moon, as a character, appealed to the Tolkien children is indicated by his appearance two other times in the 1920s: in *Roverandom*, the story Tolkien first told to his eldest sons in 1925, and in the letter he wrote to his children as 'Father Christmas' in 1927. In the latter, the Man gets drunk on brandy and has to be rolled out from under a sofa.

Probably in the first half of September 1938, Tolkien wrote the episode in *The Lord of the Rings* in which the hobbit travellers visit the inn at Bree. When their leader, then called Bingo Baggins, attracts unwanted attention, 'in desperation' he sings 'an absurd song, which [his cousin] Bilbo had been fond of' (*The Return of the Shadow*, p. 139). Tolkien intended at first that this should be the poem ultimately called *The Stone Troll* (no. 83), and revised that for the purpose; but then he decided that *The Cat and the Fiddle* would better suit the 'drinking song' Tolkien planned to occur at this point in the story. In his draft text he explained that 'it was about an Inn, and I suppose that is what brought it to Bingo's mind' (*The Return of the Shadow*, p. 142). Here (as D) we present the earliest version of the song in the *Lord of the Rings* archive, as best we can interpret Tolkien's layers of amendment. Parts of the manuscript are heavily worked, and on one page the text is completely struck through.

[D]

They say there stands a merry inn
    beneath a mountain grey,
and there they brew a beer so brown,
that the Man in the Moon at times comes down
    and drinks the night away.

And there the landlord has a cat
    that plays a stringéd fiddle,
and up and down she runs her bow,
now squeaking high, now purring low,
    now sawing in the middle.

The ostler keeps a little dog,
    who's mighty fond of jokes;
when there's good cheer among the guests
he cocks his ear at all the jests,
    and laughs until he chokes.

They also keep a hornéd cow
    as proud as any queen;
but music turns her head like ale,
and makes her wave her tufted tail,
    and dance upon the green.

And O! the rows of silver dishes
    and the store of silver spoons!
For Sunday there's a special pair,
and these they polish up with care
    on Saturday afternoons.

*

The Man in the Moon had drunk too deep;
the cat began to wail;
the dishes and spoons on the table danced,
the cow in the garden madly pranced,
and the little dog chased his tail.

The Man-in-the Moon took another mug
and rolled beneath his chair;
and there he called for yet more ale,
though the stars were growing thin and pale,
and the dawn was in the air.

Then the landlord said to his tipsy cat:
'The white horses of the Moon,
they neigh and champ their silver bits;
but their master has been and drowned his wits,
and the Sun'll be rising soon!'

Then the cat took his fiddle with a hey-diddle-diddle
played a jig to wake the dead;
he squeaked and sawed and tried every tune
while the landlord shook the Man-in-the-Moon:
'Tis after three!' he said.

They rolled the Man slowly up the hill,
and bundled him into the Moon;
and his horses galloped up in rear,
and the cow came leaping like a deer,
and the dish came with the spoon.

So fast the cat played, his fiddle-strings broke;
the cow jumped over the Moon,
and the little dog laughed to see such fun,
and the Sunday dish away did run
with the silver Sunday spoon!

The round Moon rolled behind the hill,
as the Sun raised up her head.
She hardly believed her fiery eyes;
for though it was day, to her surprise
they all went back to bed.

In using it in a new context, Tolkien preserved much of the text of his poem as it had stood alone in earlier manuscripts or in *Yorkshire Poetry*, but also revised it at several points. Gone now was the *hoofs–roofs* rhyme (in the third stanza), in favour of *queen–green*, and the unusual terms *totty* and *dancing-dotty* (in the fifth stanza) gave way to *wail* and *tail*. For some reason known only to Tolkien, the ostler and the landlord have exchanged their pets, cat for dog and dog for cat. Other changes were less permanent, such as the new second line of the poem, 'beneath a mountain grey', and the description of the fiddle as 'stringéd', both of which reverted at last to 'beneath an old grey hill' and 'five-stringed'. Only in this first version of the poem for *The Lord of the Rings* is the cat described as 'she' and 'her', and only here, perhaps overlooked, is there no stanza like the tenth in texts A, B, and C, with actions by the cat, dog, horses, and guests.

In the next iteration of the poem the establishment was 'an old grey inn | beneath an old grey hill'. Tolkien was unsure of the adjective *grey*, trying on 'goodly' in the margin, as in the earlier manuscript he had considered 'good old' instead of 'merry'; but above the first line he wrote, perhaps when returning to the poem later, 'There is an inn, a merry old inn'. Also notably, in the first line of the penultimate stanza Tolkien changed the reading to 'With a twang and a ping the fiddle-strings broke', approaching the final published text, and he restored the missing stanza, now the eleventh in a poem expanded from twelve stanzas to thirteen:

> Quicker and quicker the cat played the fiddle;
>   the dog began to roar,
> the cow and the horses stood on their heads,
> the guests all bounded from their beds,
>   and danced upon the floor.

In the middle of writing this manuscript Tolkien included a version of a stanza from his earlier drafts, before immediately striking it through:

> The Man-in-the Moon once drank too deep,
>   the ostler's cat was totty,
> on the table danced a dish and a spoon,
> the little dog laughed at the jokes too soon,
>   and the cow was prancing dotty.

Between August and autumn 1939, with the central hobbit of the story renamed Frodo Baggins, Tolkien produced a new manuscript of the poem in which it reached nearly its ultimate form, except for a few minor changes in subsequent typescripts. In 1954 the work appeared in print in the first volume of *The Lord of the Rings*, then was selected by Tolkien for his collection *The Adventures of Tom Bombadil and Other Verses from the Red Book* (1962, pp. 31–3, see poem no. 24), where it is entitled *The Man in the Moon Stayed Up Too Late*. The latter text, given here as E, differs from the published *Lord of the Rings* at two points, as described in our notes.

[E] There is an inn, a merry old inn
 beneath an old grey hill,
And there they brew a beer so brown
That the Man in the Moon himself came down
 one night to drink his fill.

The ostler has a tipsy cat
 that plays a five-stringed fiddle;
And up and down he runs his bow,
Now squeaking high, now purring low,
 now sawing in the middle.

The landlord keeps a little dog
 that is mighty fond of jokes;
When there's good cheer among the guests,
He cocks an ear at all the jests
 and laughs until he chokes.

They also keep a hornéd cow
 as proud as any queen;
But music turns her head like ale,
And makes her wave her tufted tail
 and dance upon the green.

And O! the row of silver dishes
 and the store of silver spoons!
For Sunday there's a special pair,
And these they polish up with care
 on Saturday afternoons.

The Man in the Moon was drinking deep,
    and the cat began to wail;
A dish and a spoon on the table danced,
The cow in the garden madly pranced,
    and the little dog chased his tail.

The Man in the Moon took another mug,
    and then rolled beneath his chair;
And there he dozed and dreamed of ale,
Till in the sky the stars were pale,
    and dawn was in the air.

The ostler said to his tipsy cat:
    'The white horses of the Moon,
They neigh and champ their silver bits;
But their master's been and drowned his wits,
    and the Sun'll be rising soon!'

So the cat on his fiddle played hey-diddle-diddle,
    a jig that would wake the dead:
He squeaked and sawed and quickened the tune,
While the landlord shook the Man in the Moon:
    'It's after three!' he said.

They rolled the Man slowly up the hill
    and bundled him into the Moon,
While his horses galloped up in rear,
And the cow came capering like a deer,
    and a dish ran up with a spoon.

Now quicker the fiddle went deedle-dum-diddle;
    the dog began to roar,
The cow and the horses stood on their heads;
The guests all bounded from their beds
    and danced upon the floor.

With a ping and a pong the fiddle-strings broke!
    the cow jumped over the Moon,
And the little dog laughed to see such fun,
And the Saturday dish went off at a run
    with the silver Sunday spoon.

The round Moon rolled behind the hill,
    as the Sun raised up her head.
She hardly believed her fiery eyes;
For though it was day, to her surprise
    they all went back to bed!

In 1952 Tolkien made a private recording of the final version of Frodo’s song at the Prancing Pony, since commercially released.

A19: ‘For’ originally read ‘on’.

A24: ‘Made love’ is used here in the older sense of ‘pay amorous attention to’.

A25: ‘Seeing a joke’ is understanding it and appreciating its humour. The dog ‘saw all the jokes too soon’, i.e. laughed before the teller got to the punchline (‘He laughs at any joke whatever | And sometimes in the middle’).

A33: Tolkien opens a quotation in this line, but nowhere in this version closes it. ‘Horses of the Moon’, later ‘the white horses of the Moon’, may allude to the horses sometimes shown in art drawing the chariot of the moon-goddess Selene (or Luna).

A36: Here ‘Sun’ is capitalized, but not in l. 61. In the second manuscript, and in text B, both instances of the word are capitalized.

A50: Tolkien may have intended *roar* in this context to mean ‘roar with laughter’ – the dog is laughing otherwise – rather than ‘issue a deep cry’. *Howl* presumably is used in the same sense (howl with laughter) in l. 56.

A52: This line originally read ‘And the people all leapt from their beds!’

B12, 15: In the typescript Tolkien chose to replace the plurals ‘hooves’ and ‘rooves’ with ‘hoofs’ and ‘roofs’, which had continued from text A into the second manuscript. *Hooves* is today the more common plural of *hoof*, while *rooves* is considered archaic.

B35: The contraction ‘Sun’ll’ replaced ‘Sun will’ in the typescript. The transcription of the second manuscript text in *The Return of the Shadow* mistakenly has ‘Sun’ll’.

B37: ‘A jig to wake the dead’ originally read ‘And see what that will do’ in the second manuscript.

B40: ‘“’Tis after three”, he said’ originally read ‘And said “it is after two!”’ in the second manuscript.

B52: Here ‘moon’ is not capitalized, though ‘Moon’ is found in ll. 32, 42, and 56, as well as in the proper name ‘Man in the Moon’. Tolkien capitalized the word only once in text A (l. 33) and in the corresponding line of the second manuscript.

B54–55: In the typescript, these lines replaced ‘In the middle the Saturday dish did run | Away with the Sunday spoon’. ‘Saturday dish’ replaced ‘Sunday dish’ in the second manuscript.

C16: This version has ‘row’ as printed.

C53: Only in the *Yorkshire Poetry* version, among the three early texts of the poem, does the dog ‘laugh’ ‘to see such fun’, as in the traditional rhyme, rather than ‘howl’. In later texts he laughs.

D7: ‘Stringéd’ survived until the third *Lord of the Rings* manuscript of the poem, before reverting to the earlier ‘five-stringed’. A fiddle is of course ‘stringed’ by definition.

D31: The hyphenation of 'Man-in-the Moon', thus, occurs only in this line of this text. In the second *Lord of the Rings* manuscript, 'Man-in-the-Moon' has hyphens in all instances, if not always the same number. In later texts, the name consistently has three hyphens.

E36: Here in *The Lord of the Rings* 'The ostler said' reads 'Then the ostler said'. The latter reading appears consistently in the *Lord of the Rings* papers, while the former has appeared in all editions of *The Adventures of Tom Bombadil and Other Verses from the Red Book*.

E50: Here in *The Lord of the Rings* 'a spoon' reads 'the spoon'. The reading 'a spoon' appeared in the final *Lord of the Rings* manuscript of the poem, and continued into the typescript sent to the printer, but became 'the spoon' as set, and was either overlooked or allowed to stand.

61

A Rhyme Royal upon Easter Morning
(?1919–*c.* 1950)

A *rhyme royal* is a stanza of seven lines of ten syllables each, rhyming ABABBCC. The scheme was introduced in the fourteenth century by Geoffrey Chaucer in his *Troilus and Criseyde* and in other poems, and is thought to be called 'royal' because King James I of Scotland adopted it for his *Kingis Quair* (*c.* 1423). Tolkien's example, *A Rhyme Royal upon Easter Morning*, exists in six pages of manuscript trials, with many portions struck through and some lines overwritten, and in a typescript, preserved in both ribbon and carbon copies. Because his bold, flowing handwriting in the manuscript is similar to that in his first draft of *The Cat and the Fiddle* (no. 60, which we have dated to ?1919), one may judge that *Rhyme Royal* is from around the same time. In 1919 Easter was on 20 April.

Here, as A, we have transcribed the more coherent parts of the manuscript draft, incorporating revisions apparently made in the course of writing. The stanzas are given in their apparent order of composition.

[A]

Then as this music every soul doth raise,
Come, echo all our mouths that inward sound
Singing as from a deep unplumbed the praise
Of Him Whose feast it is, Who scourged, and bound
In torment, mocked, with spiny thorns was crowned,
Was pierced with nails and dead and buried
All swathed in white upon the stony bed.

How doth the golden rondure of the Light
All robed in flame leap upward from the dark,
And cast aside sad cerements of Night —
And overthrow the stony hills — an ark
Of glory on th'immortal mountains stark
Until the flowing fire fills all the vale
And the world looks up with wondering faces pale.

The golden moonlit trees bow low, a thousand choirs
Of blossom-wreathéd birds with voice aflame
Sing clear and in the grass the secret fires
Of day are kindled, and a whispered name
Runs trembling o'er the earth and doth proclaim
The risen sun, and men awake and cry
A glory is risen that shall never die.

Ye towns and cities populous, and realms
Of ancient folk, and ye who dwell in toil
On the cornland, on the grassland, neath the elms
Of your wide pastures, on the barren soil
Of fell and hill and mountain; kings most royal
And sons of houses ancient in renown
And children of the townsman, and the clown.

This is the day, and this the radiant feast
When all your joy of life or small or great
With such a sudden inflood is increased
That like a mighty stream in whelming spate
It bursts the barriers of care, the gate
Of the deep soul in flings back wide and lo
Down to wide waters swiftly musics go.

For it is Easter morning and this sun
— A fire too bright for eyes — is but a sign,
A star upon the azure shield of One
By whom all radiances shine.
And the flaming orders of the angels nine
And plumbed the pit where endless shadows dwell
And broke the eternal brazen gates of Hell.

At this point in the manuscript Tolkien's inspiration began to wane, amid false starts and lists of rhyming words (*briar*, *choir*, *crier*, etc.). He began a seventh stanza, but in more than a page of workings delivered just over five finished lines:

And rose a splendour than this Dawn more bright
And rose unlooked for terrible as fire,
Stronger than death; more glorious than light
Or summer on the earth; than all desire
More longed for

The flaming 'ark of glory' (lines 11–12) is a reference to the rising sun, within an extended poetic description of dawn, but also to God's covenant with Man (as in the physical golden Ark of the Covenant) and, metaphorically, to Jesus Christ as the Light of the World. Tolkien continues the Sun–Jesus metaphor in later stanzas. In line 42, 'brazen gates of Hell' are gates made of brass. In Christian belief, Jesus descended into Hell between his crucifixion and resurrection, cast down its doors, and gave salvation to souls held there since Creation. The gates of Hell are often described as made of brass, or of brass and iron (Milton in *Paradise Lost* added a third level, of adamant). Gates of brass are also sometimes used as symbols of life's difficulties which may be overcome by accepting Christ into one's heart.

The 'orders of the angels nine' in line 40 are the ranks in traditional Christian angelology: Seraphim, Cherubim, Thrones, Dominions, Virtues, Powers, Archangels, Principalities, and Angels, from the highest to the lowest (or most ordinary). The name *Seraph* in line 40 of text B, below, refers to the Seraphim, the highest order of angels, who are attendants before the throne of God.

When Tolkien resumed work on this poem roughly a decade later (as we think), in addition to numerous changes of word or phrase he re-ordered stanzas one through four and number six as they appear in text A, omitted entirely the fifth stanza ('This is the day . . . swiftly musics go'), and completed the seventh stanza he had abandoned in mid-sentence. Here, as text B, is the second version of the *Rhyme*, from the single typescript; if there were intermediate workings, they have not been preserved. The markings Tolkien subsequently made on the typescript copies are discussed below.

The typescript of the *Rhyme*, made by Tolkien on his Hammond machine, can be dated to ?1931 because an additional typed page with the title and two lines of the poem is on the back of a sheet with *Earendel at the Helm* (no. 124), a work associated with Tolkien's 1931 lecture *A Secret Vice*. Further thoughts Tolkien wrote on the carbon copy of the typescript, in fountain pen and pencil, are in a style of handwriting which could also date from the 1930s, though equally from decades later; his annotations on the ribbon copy, however, are in biro (ballpoint pen), and thus were made no earlier than the late 1940s (biros were not generally available in Britain until late 1945).

[B] Ye towering cities populous and realms
Of Christendom; all ye who dwell in toil
On cornland, on the grassland, neath the elms
Of your wide pastures, on the barren soil

Of fell and hill and mountain; kings most royal
And sons of houses ancient in renown;
Ye dark-robed weary multitudes of the town!

This is the day when every soul shall raise,
And every mouth shall echo, a great sound,
Singing as from a deep unplumbed the praise
Of Him triumphant, Who was scourged and bound
In torment, mocked, with woven thorns was crowned,
And hung on piercing nails, and dead
Lay swathed in white upon His stony bed.

How doth the golden rondure of the light
All robed in flame leap upward from the dark,
And cast aside the cerements of night,
And overthrow the stony hills, an ark
Of glory on th'immortal mountains stark,
Until the flowing fire fills all the vale
And worlds look up with wondering faces pale!

The burning trees bow down, a thousand choirs
Of blossom-wreathéd birds with voice of flame
Sing clear, and in the grass the secret fires
Of day are kindled, and a whispered name
Runs trembling o'er the earth and doth proclaim
The risen sun, that men awake and cry:
'A glory doth arise shall never die!'

Behold 'tis Easter morn, whose lifted sun,
A fire too bright for eyes, is but a sign,
A star upon the azure shield of One
By whom all radiances shine,
Lord of the Angels' gleaming orders nine,
Who plumbed the pit where endless shadows dwell
And broke the eternal brazen gates of Hell,

And rose, a splendour than this morn more bright,
And rose unlooked-for, glory His attire,
Stronger than Death, inviolate as Light,
Holy, adored, more terrible than Fire —
And 'resurrexit' seraph choir on choir
In ecstasy with golden voices hurled
Beyond the starlit confines of the World.

'Resurrexit' – Latin 'He is risen' – in line B40 refers to the resurrection of Jesus Christ, here announced by heavenly choirs.

As we have said, Tolkien wrote further thoughts on the two typescript copies, clearly at different times as shown by the choice of writing implement, and are not the same on each. As possible revisions, none seems to have been more than tentative, and most are minor. For example, in line 10 Tolkien marked 'Singing' to be replaced with 'Shall sing'; in line 15, 'How doth' would become 'Behold!' or 'See now'; and in line 33, 'gleaming' would change to 'flaming'. Tolkien thought to change line 7 to read 'Ye dark-robed weary workers of the ?mine and town', making more specific the class of people who had been generic 'multitudes', but then drafted a new, more elaborate first stanza. This would have read:

> Ye towering cities populous and realms
> Of Christendom; all ye who dwell in toil
> On cornland, on the grassland, under elms
> In pastures wide, in woods, on barren soil
> Of fell and hill and mountain; kings most royal
> Of moor or stony hill, or by the shore
> The hungry sea hear ever at your door.

We suspect that if he had followed this line of revision further, Tolkien would have seen unnecessary redundancies in his text, such as 'hill' used twice in the amended stanza, and 'stony hills' later in the *Rhyme* despite 'stony hill' earlier, which would have led to still more revision to other parts. That he apparently revisited the work in the 1950s or later – perhaps when reviewing his poetry files in 1961–2 for *The Adventures of Tom Bombadil and Other Verses from the Red Book* – suggests that it held a personal importance for him, although one not strong enough to warrant attempting yet a third version.

A3: 'A deep unplumbed', i.e. a depth (like the sea) too great to be measured.

A8: 'The Light' originally read 'Our Light'.

A30: Following this line, Tolkien wrote and deleted: 'Is filled to a full measure, is increased | Beyond its earthly compass'.

A32: Following this line, Tolkien wrote and deleted: 'It beats the barriers of our dead cares'.

A34: The word 'in' perhaps was meant to be 'it'.

B2: In the fragment of typescript of the poem on the verso of *Earendel at the Helm* (as noted above), this line reads 'Of ancient folk; and ye who dwell in toil'.

B42: On the carbon copy, but not the ribbon copy, this line is followed by a handwritten 'X'. It is not clear if Tolkien meant to replace it.

62

The Ruined Enchanter (?1919–*c.* 1927)

Tolkien composed *The Ruined Enchanter* no earlier than 11 November 1919, writing parts of its first draft on two form letters of that date sent to him by the Ministry of Pensions. His son was now two, and as for *The Cat and the Fiddle* (no. 60), it may be that he wrote this new (if sad and grim) poem for young John's enjoyment, or perhaps Tolkien was merely inspired to create a new story by another familiar nursery rhyme he or Edith read to their child:

> I had a little nut tree, nothing would it bear
>   But a silver nutmeg and a golden pear;
> The King of Spain's daughter came to visit me,
>   And all for the sake of my little nut tree.
> I skipped over water, I danced over sea,
>   And all the birds in the air couldn't catch me.

Tolkien expanded this curious set of images, the seed of which has been dated to the mid-fifteenth century, as *The Ruined Enchanter*, a title which emphasizes the wronged wizard narrator more than the little tree with its remarkable fruit. Although he began with the same five-line stanza he had adopted in *The Cat and the Fiddle*, his initial text was sometimes grouped in lines as few as four and as many as nine. He wrote its first manuscript at speed, in a disjointed manner with rough workings and alternate readings, so that in transcribing the draft (as A) we have had to make some guesses as to what Tolkien intended.

[A]

Long time I dwelt in Belmarye
And fair my garden was to see
For walls of magic ringed it round,
And rooted deep in fairy ground
There grew a slender fairy tree.

And green the grass about its feet
Where gleaming fountains three did meet
But all the fruit it ever bore
Was a pear of gold, a nutmeg sweet
With silver shale, and nothing more.

Many a tall tree there did sing,
Did from enchanted belfries ring
Faint peals of many a shaken flower
Yet sat I rather hour by hour
Beneath my fruit tree wondering.

Its fame passed out beyond my gates:
Lo! with a trump a herald waits
And blows a fanfare proud thereon.
'Bow down ye walls, and ope ye gates
I serve the Queen of Babylon.'

Then looked I up and through the bars
I saw a thousand thronged cars
By lions drawn and round untold
Were dark-haired men with scimitars
And elephants and spears and gold.

Ah me! the Queen of Babylon,
The jewels, the glory she had on
And she came not to speak with me
But came to wonder at my tree

She bid me towers of minted gold
And silver flowing like the sea —
'Ah Lady it may not be sold'
And still she lusted for my tree.

My magic walls her wizards broke
And all my garden fire and smoke
In silent ashes laid — but she
All vainly did command her folk
That they uproot the slender tree

Her wise men sate in circles round
And made of it debate profound
But still unmovéd hung the fruits
And woven to the fairy ground
Still clung its endless fairy roots.

They have haled me far from Belmarye
And charged me with black wizardry.
Where sad my garden was to see

Maybe the magic walls lie low
But none can move the fairy tree
And there it still doth stand and grow
Ah me, I doubt not, as of old
With its silver nut and pear of gold.

Oh mighty Queen of Babylon
Though gold and jewels thou hast on
A captive still has more than thee
Who knows the secret of the tree.

From Belmarye nor land nor sea
Nor hell can long time sunder me
While still there hang the fairy fruits
Upon the tree with fairy roots.

And I shall build me walls anew
Shall flowers golden grow & blue
Among new trees and fountains young
— But all shall seek in vain to view
My tree whereon such fruit is hung.

A wind came out of Belmarye
And brought a leaf from off the tree
I broke their wizards' forged chain
And the birds of air have come to me
And back to Belmarye again
Their wings have borne me o'er the sea.

There came an unknown minstrel there
And sang me a song so elfin fair
I let him in beside my tree
And gave him all he begged of me
The silver nut the golden pear
Lo faded all my garden there
And left me lorn in Belmarye
With naught but echoes of his song
Than mine his magic was more strong

'Bow down ye walls and ope ye gates' in line 19 is a command to lower one's defenses in submission, and allow the Queen and her retinue to enter. 'Charged me with black wizardry' presumably means a charge of using (dark) magic for criminal purposes, while the Queen's wizards are abetting kidnapping and attempted theft.

Tolkien marked his first draft with revisions, and made a fair copy (B) incorporating these and other changes. The title of the poem was now, more expansively but only temporarily, *The Ruined Enchanter: A Fairy Ballad*. One page of three in this manuscript is written in a blank space on a fragment of text for *The Mermaid's Flute* (no. 19) – Tolkien was always frugal, and paper often scarce. Marginal notes in ink on the second draft appear to have been made contemporary with the work proper, but apparently only as passing thoughts: changes such as 'sat' for 'sit' and 'spells' for 'harps' were never taken up. There are also many notes in pencil, which we take to be preparatory to a later version.

[B]

Long time I dwelt in Belmarye
And fair my garden was to see.
There walls of magic ringed it round
And rooted deep in fairy ground
There grew a slender fairy tree

Green the grass about its feet
Where gleaming fountains three did meet,
But all the fruit it ever bore
Was a pear of gold, a nutmeg sweet
With silver shale, and nothing more.

Trees I have both cool and tall
And flowers whose petals never fall
And many silver bells aswing
Yet sit I nigh forgetting all
Beside my fruit-tree wondering

Its fame has passed beyond my gates —
Lo! with a trump a herald waits;
And blows a fanfare proud thereon:
'Bow down ye walls, and ope ye gates!
I serve the Queen of Babylon'.

Then looked I up, and through the bars
I saw a thousand throngéd cars
By lions drawn, and, round, untold

Were dark-haired men with scimitars
And elephants, and spears, and gold.

Ah me! the Queen of Babylon,
The jewels, the glory she had on;
But came she not to speak with me
But came to wonder at my tree.

She bid me towers of minted gold
And silver flowing like the sea —
'Ah, Lady it may not be sold!'
And still she lusted for my tree.

My magic walls her wizards broke,
And all my garden fire and smoke
In silent ashes laid, but she
All vainly did command her folk
That they uproot the slender tree.

Her wizards sat in circles round
And made of it debate profound
They charged me with black wizardry
And bade that I be straitly bound
And sundered far from Belmarye

She haled me far from Belmarye
Where sad my garden was to see
And there the magic walls lie low,
But none can move the fairy tree
And there it still doth stand and grow
Ah me, I doubt not, as of old
With its silver nut, and pear of gold.

'Oh mighty Queen of Babylon
Though gold and jewels thou hast on
A captive still may laugh at thee
Who keeps the secret of the tree.'

'For gold thy toy thou wilt not sell
Nor yet for gems thy secret tell
But harps there are of Fantasye
Whose magic yet may conquer thee.'

'From Belmarye nor land nor sea
Nor hill may long time sunder me
By never a chain may I be bound
While still unmovéd hang those fruits
And woven in the fairy ground
Still cling the endless fairy roots.

Shall magic build me walls anew
And golden flowers grow and blue
Among trees new and fountains young
— But all shall plead in vain to view
The tree whereon such fruit is hung.

A wind came out of Belmarye
And the birds of air have come to me
I broke those wizards' forged chain
And back to Belmarye again
Their wings have borne me o'er the sea.

Then came an unknown minstrel there
And sang me a song so elfin fair
I let him in beside the tree
And gave him all he begged of me
The silver nut, the golden pear —
Lo! faded all my garden there
And left me lorn in Belmarye
Beside an empty withered tree.

The two manuscripts of the poem were followed by two nearly identical typescripts, each made with the purple ribbon associated with Tolkien's years at Leeds. The work was now again simply *The Ruined Enchanter*, with no subtitle. There was likely a gap of time between writing out the second manuscript and making the first typescript in the first half of the 1920s, as Tolkien not only revisited the former to mark possible revisions, but also made a substantial number of changes to the text, probably with intermediate workings now lost. The voice of the enchanter was now predominantly in the present tense, his dialogue with the Queen of Babylon more defined, and the ending, in which the tree is lost to a greater wizard, less hurried. Probably no earlier than 1927, Tolkien again altered his text, marking changes on both existing typescripts almost identically and making a new typescript using his Hammond machine. Here we have transcribed (as C) the final version, with variations and features in the typescripts detailed in our notes.

[C]

Long have I dwelt in Belmarye,
And fair my garden is to see.
    For walls of magic ring it round,
    And rooted deep in enchanted ground
There grows a dark enchanted tree.

Green the grass about its feet
Where gleaming fountains three do meet;
    But fruit nor flower hath ever borne,
Save a pear of gold, a nutmeg sweet
    With silver rind, that silent thorn.

Trees I have both cool and tall,
And flowers that wither not nor fall
    But all day at the sun do stare;
Yet dumb I sit, forgetting all,
    In the shadow of those branches bare.

What voices murmur at my gates?
Behold! with a trump a herald waits,
    And blows a fanfare proud thereon:
'Bow down, ye walls, and ope, ye gates!
    I serve the Queen of Babylon.'

My eyes are dim — but through the bars
I see a thousand throngéd cars
    By lions drawn; a host untold
Of dark-haired men with scimitars
    And elephants and spears and gold.

Ah me! the Queen of Babylon,
The gleaming glory she hath on!
    No magic doth she seek of me,
A wizard wild whose craft is gone;
    She comes to wonder at my tree.

'I bid thee wealth of treasures old,
I bid thee towers of hoarded gold
    And silver flowing like the sea!'

'No lady, it may not be sold.'
    And still she lusteth for my tree.

Her wise men sit in circles round
And make of it debate profound.
    For dark unholy wizardry
They bid that I be straitly bound
    And sundered far from Belmarye —

And sundered far from Belmarye,
Where the leaves are lean upon the tree,
    But where, I doubt not, as of old
    Of silver nut and pear of gold
The shadow lieth dark to see.

'O! mighty Queen of Babylon,
Though glory thee doth wait upon,
    A captive still may laugh at thee,
Not all his wizardry is gone
    Who keeps the secret of the tree.'

'Thy tree for gold thou wilt not sell,
    But harps there be of Fantasye
Whose music moveth like a spell —
    But harps there be of Fantasye
    Whose magic yet may conquer thee.'

From Belmarye nor land nor sea,
Nor fire nor air, may sunder me;
    By never a chain may I be bound,
    While shadowed in enchanted ground
The roots go creeping from that tree.

A wind hath wandered o'er the sea,
A leaf hath fluttered off the tree;
    Great wings shall bear me back once more
    To Belmarye beside the shore,
The birds shall bear me o'er the sea.

Walls have I builded strong and new,
My flowers are springing gold and blue,
    My trees are green, my fountains young;

But all shall plead in vain to view
    The tree whereon that fruit is hung.

What song is that so cold and fair?
    What melody beyond the gate,
A breath of keen and piercing air,
    Doth halt and call, and call and wait?
    Who softly knocketh there so late?

I must let him in beside the tree
And give him all he asks of me.
    'That silver nut, that golden pear —
'Tis only these I ask of thee.'
    And all my garden fadeth bare.

Alone in Belmarye forlorn
Beneath an empty silent thorn,
    Beneath an empty withered tree,
With dust upon my feet I mourn:
    Alas! the harps of Fantasye!
    And still I hear them call to me.

Tolkien would have met the name *Belmarye* in the General Prologue to Chaucer's *Canterbury Tales*, as one of the places the Knight campaigned ('In Gernade at the seege eek hadde he be | Of Algezir, and riden in Belmarye'). Scholars have tended to identify it with Benmarin (Morocco), though some argue it is another name for Almeria, a province of the kingdom of Granada (*Gernade*). There is no reason to associate the original nursery rhyme with Moorish North Africa, or Mesopotamia ('far from Belmarye'), but it is an apt setting for *The Ruined Enchanter*, which has the atmosphere of a tale out of the *Arabian Nights*.

Belmarye reappeared, in passing, in Tolkien's poem *Errantry* (no. 128) from the early 1930s, there with the French spelling *Belmarie* as used by Froissart. *Fantasye* (Fantasy) likewise is mentioned in both *Errantry* (as *Fantasie*) and the present work. On a page of drafting for the poem are the lines 'The songs of Elfinesse were sung | and many silver bells were rung', possibly an alternate idea for the third stanza of text B, where 'many silver bells' are 'aswing'; thus *The Ruined Enchanter* narrowly missed having a connection to Tolkien's mythology.

The Queen of Babylon (Semiramis) is a legendary figure, based on the historical Shammuramat, who has come to exemplify a powerful, strong-willed woman ruler. In less favourable accounts, the Queen is considered lustful and promiscuous. Tolkien presumably felt that she would be more imposing than the 'King of Spain's daughter' when he added the element of a royal person demanding to possess the little tree – and she is, with her lions and elephants and attendant wizards, 'wise men' as they become in the typescripts, evoking the biblical Magi out of the East. Indeed, the name *Babylon* by itself is evocative, bringing to mind a place of mystery and splendour at the centre of ancient empires.

The harps out of Fantasye in the final version of the poem, replacing a compelling voice singing 'elfin fair' in earlier texts, recall the legend of Orpheus and its adaptation in the Middle English poem *Sir Orfeo*, on which Tolkien was an authority (see no. 173). Orpheus, in classical mythology, plays a lyre to regain his deceased wife from the Underworld, while in the English lay Orfeo uses minstrelsy to claim his wife from her abductor, the king of Faërie. Strictly speaking, in neither story does the protagonist use magic in a supernatural sense, only sublime musical skill (Tolkien's translation of *Sir Orfeo*, in *Sir Gawain and the Green Knight, Pearl and Sir Orfeo* (1975), ll. 39–46):

> He played so well, beneath the sun
> a better harper was there none;
> no man hath in this world been born
> who would not, hearing him, have sworn
> that as before him Orfeo played
> to joy of Paradise he had strayed
> and sound of harpers heavenly,
> such joy was there and melody.

Beguiled by his playing, the Faërie king tells Orfeo to 'ask of me whate'er it be, | and rich reward I will thee pay' (ll. 450–451).

A32: Tolkien wrote in the margin two lines he considered whether to insert following l. 32: 'Its fairy roots to fairy ground | By spell unbreakable and bound'.

A38: This line originally read 'That they uproot the slender tree'.

A55: Following this line, at the foot of this portion of the manuscript, Tolkien wrote 'who keeps still may conquer' but never incorporated the phrase in his poem.

A79: Following this line, at the foot of this portion of the manuscript, Tolkien wrote several disconnected phrases, including 'Beside an empty withered tree' and 'Alas the harps of Faery | They have a magic more than mine'.

B4–5: Tolkien marked two alternate readings for this line (if we interpret his directions correctly): 'And deep rooted in the fairy ground | Grew up a slender fairy tree'.

B11–15: Tolkien wrote a draft of these lines on the first manuscript:

Trees I had both cool and tall
And golden flowers and ?vineal [grapevines]
And many silver bells aswing
Yet sat I nigh forgetting all
Beneath my fruit-tree wondering

B43: Tolkien included an alternate reading for this line, 'And sundered far from my fairy tree', but made no choice. The first reading, with 'Belmarye', remained in the next version.

B46: Tolkien struck through 'And there' and wrote 'Maybe' (in ink) in the margin; but later he struck through 'Maybe' and restored (in pencil) 'And there'.

B53: Tolkien considered 'vanquish' and 'conquer' in place of 'laugh'.

B57: Tolkien considered 'spells' in place of 'harps'.

B68: Tolkien considered 'come' in place of 'plead'.

C7–10: On each of the three typescripts Tolkien indicated in light pencil that several words should be either deleted or moved within the stanza, but his circles and arrows are neither consistent nor clear as to his intentions.

C13: Next to this line, Tolkien wrote in the margin of each of the first two typescripts 'but ever sunward daylong stare'. The reading 'But all day at the sun do stare' remained in the final typescript.

C14: As typed, this line began 'Yet sit I dumb'. Tolkien marked these words for revision to 'Yet dumb I sit', but also wrote next to them in the margin (what appears to be) 'in the sun's eye'.

C17: 'Behold!' replaced 'And lo!' in the final typescript.

C21: 'My eyes are dim — but' replaced 'I lift mine eyes, and' in the final typescript.

C51: In the first two typescripts this line was preceded by the following, omitted in the final text: 'I hear a voice like distant bell:'.

C61–65: In the first two typescripts these lines first appeared as:

A wind it is from Belmarye.
A leaf that flutters off the tree!
    Ah! weak their walls and forgéd chain.
The birds of the air have come to me,
    And back to Belmarye again.
Their wings have borne me o'er the sea.

C71: In the first two typescripts this line was preceded by the following, omitted in the final text: 'What hidden minstrel standeth there?' On one of the first typescripts Tolkien altered 'elfin' to 'elvin', and on the other replaced 'elfin fair?' with 'cold and fair?'

C71–75: On one only of the first typescripts Tolkien lightly altered these lines to:

What melody beyond the gates,
A breath of keen and piercing air,
There halts and calls and calls and waits,
Who softly knocketh thereon so late?

C85–86: Written on a separate scrap of paper, an alternate text for these two lines reads: 'Alas the harps of Fantasye | Whose spells fordid [destroyed] me utterly'.

63

The Motor-cyclists (?1919)

Although Tolkien himself had a share in a motorcycle in 1915 and 1916, using it to visit Edith when on leave from his army camp, later he came to dislike the noise of such machines, their polluting emissions, and the behaviour of some of their riders. If this was not so by the time he returned to Oxford at the end of 1918, after experiencing the clank and roar of mechanized war machinery, then he felt it by 1920, before he left Oxford for Leeds. His poem *The Motor-cyclists* speaks to such feelings in alliterative lines, punctuated by verbal reconstructions of sounds not unlike those a two-stroke engine might make if not properly maintained. We have transcribed it here incorporating Tolkien's revisions.

O Filth-spattered fools with your foul fumes
riding on a racket of rackety iron,
dead drunk with dust, driven by desire
of insensate speed you spew your stink
from nowhere to nowhere through nothing worth seeing
— out of hell to hades or to holes more hideous,
din by day and death of night-rest
blasting & battering, banging and blowing
like hooting hobgoblins on harsh horns,
— honk cronk says one crarrack-barrack the other
bap bap you vomit you belch and backfire
you grind and grumble from garage to garage
jolt and jar and jibber and jangle
cutting of [*sic, for* off] corners with the lust to kill
strewing the streets with the innocent dying
dressed the [*sic, for* like] demons in an indigestive dream
goggled like godforsaken ghouls or gorgons,
affecting a pose of impossible ?heathens
crank harrack poof harrack, poof harrack, honk
bap bap harrack crarrack puf bap puf bap
bubber rubber bubber rubber bub — bang bang
by pistons and pumps and petrol substitutes
valve crank control and the whole curséd contrivance
Blast you all for bloody nuisances.

Some of Tolkien's words to suggest the sounds of motorcycles recur again in *The Complaint of Mîm the Dwarf* (poem no. 185), where they actually refer to the labours of a smith.

From one perspective, *The Motor-cyclists* expresses Tolkien's personal views, and with notable venom. The machines produce fumes and stink, and make a racket by day and night. More seriously, in this description, they are a public menace: their riders move with 'insensate speed', cut off pedestrians, kill innocents. 'Bloody nuisances' was strong language for the day, but the only place in the poem where Tolkien minced words, removing 'God' before 'blast' in revision. Similar sentiments, though more temperate, would appear again in the 1925/27 story *Roverandom* ('motor after motor racketed by . . . all making all speed (and all dust and all smell) to somewhere'), and in the ?1928 poem *The Progress of Bimble* (later *Progress in Bimble Town*, no. 103; 'loud garages, where toiling hard | grimy people bang and roar, | and engines buzz, and the lights flare | all night long — a merry noise!'). But *The Motor-cyclists* is also a satire, indeed a satire of a satire, modelled on a particular work.

Tolkien's poem exists in a single manuscript of two leaves, similar in appearance to the first drafts of *The Cat and the Fiddle* and *A Rhyme Royal upon Easter Morning* (nos. 60, 61), which we have dated to ?1919. At the head of the first page, following the title, are the words 'With ack[nowledgement] to the anon[ymous] 14th c[entury] author of Blacksmiths', a Middle English poem sometimes called 'Satire on the Blacksmiths'. Tolkien may have met this as an undergraduate, perhaps in Thomas Wright and James Orchard Halliwell's *Reliquiae Antiquae* (1841), but certainly read it in Kenneth Sisam's collection *Fourteenth Century Verse and Prose* after he was commissioned, probably in mid- to late 1919, to write its glossary. Sisam, one of Tolkien's Oxford tutors, included 'The Blacksmiths' in a section of miscellaneous verse, commenting that 'with onomatopoeic effects it gives a vivid if unfriendly picture of a blacksmith's forge on a busy night' (p. 162). In Middle English the poem begins: 'Swarte smekyd smeþes smateryd wyth smoke | Dryue me to deth wyth den of here dyntes.' This is the work in translation:

> Blackened smiths begrimed with smoke
> Drive me to death with the din of their strokes.
> Such noise on nights men have never heard:
> What knavish clamour and clattering of blows!
> The crooked changelings cry 'coal! coal!'
> And blow their bellows till their brains burst:

'Huff, puff!' says that one; 'haf, paf' the other.
They spit and sprawl and spin many tales;
They gnaw and gnash, they groan together,
And keep themselves hot with their hard hammers.
Of bull's hide are their leather aprons;
Their legs are guarded from fiery sparks;
Heavy hammers they have, and handle them hard,
Sharp blows they strike on a steel block:
Lus, bus! las, das! they beat in turn.
So doleful a noise, may the devil destroy it!
The master lengthens a piece, and strikes a smaller,
Joins them together, and sounds a treble note:
Tik, tak! hic, hac! tiket, taket! tyk, tak!
Lus, bus! lus, das! such a life they lead
These mare-clothers: Christ give them sorrow!
With their water-hissing, no man may have his rest at night!

'Mare-clothers' refers to an insult applied to smiths, that they make armour for horses; 'crooked changelings' is another jibe. 'Water-hissing' alludes to the noise caused by hot metal being doused in water.

1: 'Filth' is capitalized thus.

4: For this line Tolkien also considered 'Of blinding speed insensate you bitch & spew'.

15: Tolkien originally wrote 'You strew the streets with the stricken and dead'. He replaced the first two words with 'Strewing', deleted 'and dead', and added 'innocent' and 'dying', leaving 'stricken'. In private notes, Christopher Tolkien judged that his father probably meant 'stricken' also to be struck (to preserve the metre), though may have meant instead to have 'stricken' rather than 'innocent'. It can be certain only that either word would serve, but not both.

16: In private notes, Christopher Tolkien remarked on *indigestive* by citing Charles Dickens' *Mystery of Edwin Drood*: 'disturbed from an indigestive after-dinner sleep' (Chapter 11). In the manuscript the word has been written quickly and is smudged, but is very likely to be 'indigestive'. Our first thought was 'undigested', recalling Dickens' 'undigested bit of beef' from Scrooge's complaint in *A Christmas Carol* (Stave 1), but the *in-* of Tolkien's word is formed well enough not to be a miswriting of *un-*. In any case, the meaning is 'dyspeptic'.

18: We have assumed that Tolkien intended this line to be part of the final poem, but cannot be certain. It is written in pencil between two lines in ink, and is the only line of the final poem to be in pencil, i.e. other than trial workings. The illegible final word in the line is possibly 'heathens', in the sense of heathen idols or images. In context, the motorcyclists are affecting (striking) a pose in their extraordinary costumes.

The Collected Poems of J.R.R. Tolkien

Edited by

Christina Scull

Wayne G. Hammond

VOLUME TWO

HarperCollins*Publishers*

HarperCollins*Publishers* Ltd
1 London Bridge Street
London SE1 9GF

HarperCollins*Publishers*
Macken House, 39/40 Mayor Street Upper
Dublin 1, D01 C9W8, Ireland

www.tolkien.co.uk · www.tolkienestate.com

Published by HarperCollins*Publishers* 2024

1

Further acknowledgements appear on pp. 1471–2. Every effort has been made to trace all owners of copyright. The editors and publishers apologise for any errors or omissions and would be grateful if notified of any corrections.

A CIP catalogue record for this book is available from the British Library

ISBN 978-0-00-862882-6

Printed and bound in Italy by Rotolito S.p.A.

(B)

The Song of Ælfwine

(on seeing the uprising of Eärendel)

There lingering lights still golden lie
on grass more green than in gardens here,
On trees more tall that touch the sky
with swinging leaves of silver clear.
While world endures they will not die,
nor fade nor fall their timeless year,
As morn unmeasured passes by
o'er mead and mound and shining mere.
When endless eve undimmed is near,
o'er harp and chant in hidden choir
A sudden voice upsoaring sheer
in the wood awakes the Wandering Fire.

The Wandering Fire the woodland fills:
in glades for ever green it glows,
In dells where immortal dews distils
the Flower that in secret fragrance grows.
There murmuring the music spills,
as falling fountain plashing flows,
And water white leaps down the hills
to seek the Sea that no sail knows.
Through gleaming vales it singing goes,
where breathing keen on bent and briar
The wind beyond the world's end blows
to living flame the Wandering Fire

(123)

The Bumpus

The Bumpus sat on an old grey stone
And sang his lonely song: — lay
"O why, o why should I live all alone
In the beautiful land of Bong?" — In the hills of Bimble Bay
The trees are tall & the fields are green, — The grass is green the sky is blue
The sun shines all the day, — on the sea
But never an ogre or giant is seen, — The dragons have crossed the Mountains Blue
No goblins come to stay. — And come no more to me

The dragons have gone, and the gnomes don't call, — No trolls or ogres are left at all
P/ And people slam the door,
Whenever they hear my flat feet fall
Or my tail along the floor."
He stroked his tail and he looked at his feet,
And he said: "they may be long,
Kind is my heart — But I have a kind heart and my smile is sweet;
And sweet and soft my song."

The Bumpus went out, and who did he meet
But old Mrs. Thomas and all
With umbrella and basket walking the street;
And softly he did call:
"Dear Mrs. Thomas, good day to you!
I hope you are quite well?"
But she dropped her brolly and basket too
And yelled a frightful yell.

Policeman Potts was standing near;
When he heard that awful cry,
He turned all purple and pink with fear,
And swiftly turned to fly.
The Bumpus followed surprised and sad.
"Don't go!" he gently said;
But old Mrs. Thomas ran home like mad
And hid beneath her bed.

281

The Collected Poems of J.R.R. Tolkien

Works by J.R.R. Tolkien

THE HOBBIT · LEAF BY NIGGLE · ON FAIRY-STORIES
FARMER GILES OF HAM · THE HOMECOMING OF BEORHTNOTH
THE LORD OF THE RINGS · THE ADVENTURES OF TOM BOMBADIL
THE ROAD GOES EVER ON (WITH DONALD SWANN)
SMITH OF WOOTTON MAJOR

*Works Published Posthumously (*edited by Christopher Tolkien)*

SIR GAWAIN AND THE GREEN KNIGHT, PEARL AND SIR ORFEO*
LETTERS FROM FATHER CHRISTMAS · THE SILMARILLION*
PICTURES BY J.R.R. TOLKIEN* · UNFINISHED TALES*
THE LETTERS OF J.R.R. TOLKIEN*
FINN AND HENGEST · MR. BLISS
THE MONSTERS AND THE CRITICS AND OTHER ESSAYS*
ROVERANDOM · THE CHILDREN OF HÚRIN*
THE LEGEND OF SIGURD AND GUDRÚN* · THE FALL OF ARTHUR*
BEOWULF: A TRANSLATION AND COMMENTARY*
THE STORY OF KULLERVO · THE LAY OF AOTROU AND ITROUN
BEREN AND LÚTHIEN* · THE FALL OF GONDOLIN*
THE NATURE OF MIDDLE-EARTH · THE FALL OF NÚMENOR

The History of Middle-earth – by Christopher Tolkien

I THE BOOK OF LOST TALES, PART ONE
II THE BOOK OF LOST TALES, PART TWO
III THE LAYS OF BELERIAND
IV THE SHAPING OF MIDDLE-EARTH
V THE LOST ROAD AND OTHER WRITINGS
VI THE RETURN OF THE SHADOW
VII THE TREASON OF ISENGARD
VIII THE WAR OF THE RINGS
IX SAURON DEFEATED
X MORGOTH'S RING
XI THE WAR OF THE JEWELS
XII THE PEOPLES OF MIDDLE-EARTH

Also by Christina Scull & Wayne G. Hammond

J.R.R. TOLKIEN: ARTIST AND ILLUSTRATOR
THE LORD OF THE RINGS: A READER'S COMPANION
THE J.R.R. TOLKIEN COMPANION AND GUIDE
THE ART OF THE HOBBIT BY J.R.R. TOLKIEN
THE ART OF THE LORD OF THE RINGS BY J.R.R. TOLKIEN

Contents

VOLUME ONE

VOLUME THREE

Illustrations

64

Light as Leaf on Lind · *As Light as Leaf on Lindentree* · *The Tale of Tinúviel* (?1919–54)

The earliest extant text of this poem is a typescript, given below as A. Each of its two pages, typed with the purple ribbon used by Tolkien during his years at Leeds, bears the added manuscript title *Light as Leaf on Lind*, and above the text proper, also inserted by hand, is an epigraph: 'Light was Tinúviel as leaf on lind | Light as a feather in the laughing wind. | *Tinúviel! Tinúviel!*' *Lind*, from Middle English, is another word for the lime or linden, a broad-leafed tree of the genus *Tilia*. Its name usefully alliterates with 'light', 'leaf', and 'laughing', and it may be that Tolkien knew that the linden, with its heart-shaped leaves, symbolizes (among other things) love and fidelity. But the source of the poem's title was almost certainly (as first pointed out by Joe R. Christopher in 'Tolkien's Lyric Poetry') a proverbial expression in use by at least the fourteenth century, found in *Piers Plowman* ('And whan it [love] hadde of this fold flessh and blood taken, | Was nevere leef upon lynde lighter thereafter') and in Chaucer's 'Clerk's Tale' ('Be ay of chiere as light as leef on lynde'). And yet, the lime or linden tree is mentioned nowhere in the early versions of the poem (beyond the title), only the hemlock and the beech.

Tolkien wrote in a corner of this copy: 'Leeds 1923, retouched 1924, first beginnings Oxford 1919–20 Alfred St[reet]'. Whether or not his memory of 'first beginnings' is correct – we are taking it as such, in placing the poem here in the present book, even if the 'beginnings' were only initial thoughts – it is almost certain that he made draft workings before the first typescript, though none earlier than his years at Leeds survives in his papers.

[A]

The grass was very long and thin,
　　The leaves of many years lay thick,
The old tree-roots wound out and in,
　　And the early moon was glimmering.
There went her white feet lilting quick,
　　And Dairon's flute did bubble thin,

As neath the hemlock umbels thick
    Tinúviel danced ashimmering.

The pale moths lumbered noiselessly,
    And daylight died among the leaves,
As Beren from the wild country
    Came thither wayworn sorrowing.
He peered between the hemlock sheaves,
    And watched in wonder noiselessly
Her dancing through the moonlit leaves
    And the ghostly moths a-following.

There magic took his weary feet,
    And he forgot his loneliness,
And out he danced, unheeding, fleet,
    Where the moonbeams were aglistening.
Through the tangled woods of Elfinesse
    They fled on nimble fairy feet,
And left him to his loneliness
    in the silent forest listening.

Still hearkening for the imagined sound
    Of lissom feet upon the leaves,
For music welling underground
    In the dim lit caves of Doriath.
But withered are the hemlock sheaves,
    And one by one with mournful sound
Whispering fall the beechen leaves
    In the dying woods of Doriath.

He sought her wandering near and far
    Where the leaves of one more year were strewn,
By winter moon and frosty star
    With shaken light ashivering.
He found her neath a misty moon,
    A silver wraith that danced afar,
And the mists beneath her feet were strewn
    In moonlight palely quivering.

She danced upon a hillock green
    Whose grass unfading kissed her feet,

While Dairon's fingers played unseen
    O'er his magic flute aflickering;
And out he danced, unheeding, fleet,
    In the moonlight to the hillock green:
No impress found he of her feet
    That fled him swiftly flickering.

And longing filled his voice that called
    'Tinúviel, Tinúviel',
And longing sped his feet enthralled
    Behind her wayward shimmering.
She heard as echo of a spell
    His lonely voice that longing called
'Tinúviel, Tinúviel';
    One moment paused she glimmering,

And Beren caught the elfin maid
    And kissed her trembling starlit eyes:
The elfin maid that love delayed
    In the days beyond our memory.
Till moon and star, till music dies,
    Shall Beren and the elfin maid
Dance to the starlight of her eyes
    And fill the woods with glamoury.

Wherever grass is long and thin,
    And leaves of countless years lie thick,
And ancient roots wind out and in,
    As once they did in Doriath,
Shall go their white feet lilting quick,
    But never Dairon's music thin
Be heard beneath the hemlocks thick
    Since Beren came to Doriath.

Tolkien had introduced the Elf Tinúviel in his mythology a few years earlier in *The Book of Lost Tales*, as the daughter of Tinwelint and Gwendeling, rulers of the land of Artanor. On a time, she would dance to the music of her brother, Dairon.

> Now the place that they loved the most was a shady spot, and elms grew there, and beech too, but these were not very tall, and some chestnut trees there were with white flowers, but the

> ground was moist and a great misty growth of hemlocks rose beneath the trees. On a time of June they were playing there, and the white umbels of the hemlocks were like a cloud about the boles of the trees, and there Tinúviel danced until the evening faded late, and there were many white moths abroad. [*The Book of Lost Tales, Part Two*, p. 10]

The image of Tinúviel dancing under hemlock umbels was inspired by an event from Tolkien's own life, in early summer 1917, when he and Edith visited a wood near Roos (see our discussion for no. 13) and she herself danced among the flower clusters in a hemlock grove. The tale of Lúthien and Beren therefore had, and continued to have, a special meaning for Tolkien: after Edith's death, he wrote to his son Christopher: 'she was (and knew she was) my Lúthien' (11 July 1972, *Letters*, p. 590).

At this point in the development of the story, Beren was himself an Elf, but 'a Gnome, son of Egnor the forester' and suspicious of 'secret Elves' like Tinúviel and her folk ('secret' in the sense of magically hidden from the evil Melko, as well as physically hidden underground). '[Yet] now did he see Tinúviel dancing in the twilight, and Tinúviel was in a silver-pearly dress, and her bare white feet were twinkling among the hemlock-stems' (*The Book of Lost Tales, Part Two*, p. 11). But she flees in fear, and Beren seeks her, calling her name which he had heard spoken by Dairon. Their romance, and their victory over Melko, are at the heart of the tale which Tolkien considered the chief part of 'The Silmarillion'.

In the second version of *The Children of Húrin*, an alliterative poem on which he worked in the early 1920s (see no. 67), Tolkien wrote (*The Lays of Beleriand*, p. 108):

> Then a song he made them   for sorrow's lightening,
> a sudden sweetness   in the silent wood,
> that is 'Light as Leaf   on Linden' called,
> whose music of mirth   and mourning blended
> yet in hearts does echo.

'He' is a Man, Halog, and the sorrow to be lightened belongs to the young Túrin, son of Húrin, whom Halog is guiding to Doriath. At this point in the manuscript of *The Children of Húrin*, having made reference to a song, Tolkien inserted *Light as Leaf on Lind*, which he had already composed. Its text there is almost identical to version A above, differing only in a few points of punctuation, principally the addition of hyphens, as in *a-shimmering*, *a-glistening*; in line 66, to which a definite article was inserted ('And *the* leaves of countless years lie thick'); and in the penultimate stanza, revised thus:

And Beren caught that elfin maid
    And kissed her trembling starlit eyes,
Tinúviel whom love delayed
    In the woods of evening morrowless.
Till moonlight and till music dies
    Shall Beren by the elfin maid
Dance to the starlight of her eyes
    In the forest singing sorrowless.

By this time, Tolkien had rethought his story and changed certain details. Beren was now a Man, a mortal in love with an immortal Elf named Lúthien, who was also loved by Dairon, a minstrel but not her brother. *Tinúviel* ('nightingale') was only the sobriquet Beren gave to Lúthien when calling her, her parents were now Thingol and Melian, and Artanor was called Doriath (see also poem no. 34).

Associated with this revision are two related pages of manuscript, one of which is headed 'The University, Leeds'. These, then, can have been written no earlier than October 1920, when Tolkien joined the Leeds English faculty, and with the changes marked on the first typescript may be the work to which Tolkien referred by his note 'retouched 1924'. The manuscript on a plain sheet contains a single stanza (B), corresponding to the penultimate stanza of A:

[B] Ere Beren caught the elfin maid,
    And kissed her starlit trembling eyes,
Tinúviel, whom love delayed
    In the woven woods of Nemorie
Till music and till moonlight dies
    Shall Beren by the elfin maid
Dance in the starlight of her eyes
    And fill the woods with glamoury

The letterhead sheet, on the other hand, has two stanzas (given as C), corresponding to the final sixteen lines of A. The first is a development of text B, and preliminary to corrections to the stanza Tolkien made on the typescript of text A.

[C] And Beren caught the elfin maid,
    And kissed her trembling starlit eyes —

Tinúviel, whom love delayed
In the land of laughter sorrowless.
Till moonlight and till music dies
Shall Beren by the elfin maid,
Dance to the starlight of her eyes
In eve unending morrowless

Wherever grass is long and thin,
And leaves of countless years lie thick,
And ancient roots wind out and in,
As once they wound in Doriath,
Shall go their white feet lilting quick,
But never Dairon's music thin
Be heard beneath the hemlocks thick,
with silver sound in Doriath

The first typescript was followed by two others, also typed with a purple ribbon; for reference, and in their evident order of making, we will call them I and II. In regard to the poem proper, their texts are nearly identical, differing only in line 54: in II, the reading follows text A, 'His lonely voice that longing called', but in I, uniquely among the drafts of the poem, it is 'His lonely voice that called and called'. Typescript I, with the title *As Light as Leaf on Lindentree* added by hand, includes an alliterative preface (D):

[D] In the Lay of Leithian, Release from Bondage,
in linkéd words has long been wrought
of Beren Ermabwed, brave, undaunted;
how Lúthien the lissom he loved of yore
in the enchanted forest chained with wonder.
Tinúviel he named her, than nightingale
more sweet her voice, as veiled in soft
and wavering wisps of woven dusk
shot with starlight, with shining eyes
she danced like dreams of drifting sheen,
pale-twinkling pearls in pools of darkness.
And songs were raised for sorrow's lightening,
a sudden sweetness in a silent hour,
that 'Light as Leaf on Linden-tree'
were called — here caught a cadent echo.

As Christopher Tolkien has discussed in *The Lays of Beleriand*, lines 1–2 of D are similar to existing text in the alliterative *Children of Húrin*. In the manuscript of that work, the lines are continued by new text made on a slip pasted in. 'I think (or perhaps rather guess)', Christopher wrote, 'that my father composed an alliterative continuation of 13 lines (beginning *of Beren Ermabwed, | | brave undaunted*) as an introduction to the poem *Light as Leaf on Lindentree*; and then, at the same time as he typed [our typescript I] of this poem, with the alliterative head-piece, he added them to the typescript of the Lay [*Húrin*] already in existence' (p. 121). The text given here as D corresponds to lines 356–366 and 398–402 of *The Children of Húrin*, with a few changes in the latter, most notably 'the boldhearted' substituted for 'brave, undaunted' as an epithet for Beren.

The *Lay of Leithian* mentioned in this prefatory text did not exist, except presumably in concept, until Tolkien began to write it in the summer of 1925; another long poem (no. 92), it tells the greater part of the story of Beren and Lúthien. 'Release from bondage' is a translation of Elvish *leithian*, which Christopher Tolkien in *The Lays of Beleriand* was at a loss to explain conclusively. *Ermabwed* (Gnomish 'one-handed') is a sobriquet of Beren after he has lost a hand, holding a Silmaril taken from the crown of Melko, to the jaws of the wolf Karkaras (later Carcharoth).

Typescript II has a typewritten title, *As Light as Leaf on Lind*, in which Tolkien emended the final word to *Linden-tree*. He also marked this text, possibly at some later date, for minor revision at four points – line 16, 'magic' > 'wonder'; line 22, 'fairy' > 'elvish'; and lines 57 and 61, 'elfin' > 'elvish' – but these changes do not appear in the poem as published in the June 1925 number of the Leeds magazine *The Gryphon*, there (p. 217) entitled *Light as Leaf on Lindentree* (omitting, apparently in error, initial '*As*'). We give this version (E) as the final text of the poem in its first incarnation, incorporating revisions Tolkien marked on a tear-sheet. Its first nine, introductory lines are derived from typescript I with slight revision.

[E] ''Tis of Beren Erchamion bold-hearted,
How Luthien the lissom he loved of yore
In the enchanted forest chained with wonder.
Tinúviel he named her, than nightingale
More sweet her voice, as veiled in soft
And wavering wisps of woven dusk
Shot with starlight, with shining eyes,

She danced like dreams of drifting sheen,
Pale twinkling pearls in pools of darkness.'

The grass was very long and thin,
The leaves of many years lay thick,
The old tree-roots wound out and in,
And the early moon was glimmering.
There went her white feet lilting quick,
And Dairon's flute did bubble thin,
As neath the hemlock umbels thick
Tinúviel danced a-shimmering.

The pale moths lumbered noiselessly,
And daylight died among the leaves,
As Beren from the wild country
Came thither wayworn sorrowing.
He peered between the hemlock sheaves,
And watched in wonder noiselessly
Her dancing through the moonlit leaves
And the ghostly moths a-following.

There magic took his weary feet,
And he forgot his loneliness,
And out he danced, unheeding, fleet,
Where the moonbeams were a-glistening.
Through the tangled woods of Elfinesse
They fled on nimble fairy feet,
And left him to his loneliness
in the silent forest listening.

Still hearkening for the imagined sound
Of lissom feet upon the leaves,
For music welling underground
In the dim-lit caves of Doriath.
But withered are the hemlock sheaves,
And one by one with mournful sound
Whispering fall the beechen leaves
In the dying woods of Doriath.

He sought her wandering near and far
Where the leaves of one more year were strewn,

By winter moon and frosty star
    With shaken light a-shivering.
He found her neath a misty moon,
    A silver wraith that danced afar,
And the mists beneath her feet were strewn
    In moonlight palely quivering.

She danced upon a hillock green
    Whose grass unfading kissed her feet,
While Dairon's fingers played unseen
    O'er his magic flute a-flickering;
And out he danced, unheeding, fleet,
    In the moonlight to the hillock green:
No impress found he of her feet
    That fled him swiftly flickering.

And longing filled his voice that called
    'Tinúviel, Tinúviel,'
And longing sped his feet enthralled
    Behind her wayward shimmering.
She heard as echo of a spell
    His lonely voice that longing called
'Tinúviel, Tinúviel':
    One moment paused she glimmering,

And Beren caught that elfin maid
    And kissed her trembling starlit eyes,
Tinúviel whom love delayed
    In the woods of evening morrowless.
Till moonlight and till music dies
    Shall Beren by the elfin maid
Dance to the starlight of her eyes
    In the forest singing sorrowless.

Wherever grass is long and thin,
    And leaves of countless years lie thick,
And ancient roots wind out and in,
    As once they did in Doriath,
Shall go their white feet lilting quick,
    But never Dairon's music thin
Be heard beneath the hemlocks thick,
    Since Beren came to Doriath.

Readers of *The Lord of the Rings* will recognize *As Light as Leaf on Lindentree* as the precursor to the poem told, or rather chanted, to the four principal hobbits of the story as they shelter under Weathertop, pursued by Black Riders. Their guide, Trotter (as he was first named), who has been telling them histories and legends, chooses 'the tale of Tinúviel' to cheer their hearts. Tolkien undoubtedly recalled that *Light as Leaf* had been sung for that purpose for Túrin in the earlier lay, and again turned to it when he came to the episode in *The Lord of the Rings* (Book I, Chapter 11 as published), evidently in the first half of September 1938. At first he intended simply to insert the existing poem, then decided to compose a fresh text, adopting the structure and tone of the earlier work and borrowing details. This began, 'Lo Beren Gamlost [Noldorin 'empty-handed'] the boldhearted', but Tolkien cancelled these words and wrote out the text given here as F, with revisions detailed in our notes. The same text was published by Christopher Tolkien in *The Return of the Shadow*, pp. 180–2, with initial capital letters regularized.

[F]

The leaves were long, the grass was thin,
  The fall of many years lay thick,
The tree-roots twisted out and in,
  the rising moon was glimmering.
Her feet went lilting light and quick
  to the silver flute of Ilverin:
Beneath the hemlock-umbels thick
  Tinúviel was shimmering.

The noiseless moths their wings did fold,
  the light was lost among the leaves,
As Beren there from mountains cold
  came wandering and sorrowing
He peered between the hemlock leaves,
  and saw in wonder flowers of gold
upon her mantle and her sleeves,
  and her hair like shadow following.

Enchantment took his weary feet,
  that over stone were doomed to roam,
and forth he hastened, strong and fleet,
  and grasped at moonbeams glistening.

Through woven woods of Elvenhome
She fled on swiftly dancing feet,
and left him lonely still to roam,
in the silent forest listening.

He heard at times the flying sound
of feet as light as linden leaves,
or music welling underground
In the hidden halls of Doriath
But withered were the hemlock sheaves
and one by one with sighing sound
whispering fell the beechen leaves
in the wintry woods of Doriath.

He sought her ever, wandering far
where leaves of years were thickly strewn,
by light of moon and ray of star
in frosty heavens shivering.
Her mantle glistened in the moon,
as on a hill-top high and far
she danced, and at her feet was strewn
a mist of silver quivering.

When winter passed she came again,
and her song released the sudden spring,
like rising lark, and falling rain,
and melting water bubbling.
There high and clear he heard her sing,
and from him fell the winter's chain;
No more he feared by her to spring
upon the grass untroubling.

Again she fled, but clear he called:
'Tinúviel, Tinúviel'.
She halted by that name enthralled
and stood before him shimmering.
Her doom at last there on her fell,
as on the hills the echoes called;
Tinúviel, Tinúviel,
In the arms of Beren glimmering.

As Beren looked into her eyes
within the shadows of her hair
the trembling starlight of the skies
he saw there mirrored shimmering.
Tinúviel! O Elven-fair!
immortal maiden elven-wise
About him cast her shadowy hair
and white her arms were glimmering.

Long was the road that fate them bore
O'er stony mountains cold and grey
Through halls of iron and darkling door
and woods of night-shade morrowless.
The Sundering Seas between them lay
and yet at last they met once more
and long ago they passed away
in the forest singing sorrowless

Ilverin, as in F6, is another name for Littleheart, the 'Gong-warden' of Mar Vanwa Tyaliéva (the Cottage of Lost Play, see poem no. 28) in *The Book of Lost Tales*, but Christopher Tolkien points out in *The Return of the Shadow* that 'there seems no basis to seek any kind of connection' (p. 187) between the *Lost Tales* and the present *Tale*. In the margin of the *Lord of the Rings* manuscript is a list of alternate names for Ilverin: *Neldorín*, *Elberin*, *Diorin*, *Dairon*, with the latter (the name of the minstrel in *Light on Leaf as Lindentree*) struck through. In the final text, Tinúviel dances 'to music of a pipe unseen'.

The description of Elvish feet in flight, 'as light as linden leaves', continues the sentiment of the earlier poem's title, in a poem to which we have assigned a title from the accompanying prose text in *The Lord of the Rings*:

> 'I will tell you the tale of Tinúviel . . . , in brief – for it is a long tale of which the end is not known; and there are none now, except Elrond, that remember it aright as it was told of old. It is a fair tale, though it is sad, as are all the tales of Middle-earth, and yet it may lift up your hearts.'

It should be remarked that early in the evolution of *The Lord of the Rings* the speaker (Trotter) was himself a Hobbit, who could have had no familial connection with Beren and Lúthien. But in later phases of writing, when the tale is told by Strider (Aragorn), a Man and the rightful King, it is in fact about his own ancestors.

The pre-*Lord of the Rings* poem is an account only of the wooing of Tinúviel (Lúthien) and her surrender to Beren. Only later did Tolkien include more of their greater story. In earlier texts, Beren comes out of 'wild country'; in the new version he is 'wandering and sorrowing' 'from mountains cold'. Aragorn explains, following his chanting of the poem, that 'Beren escaping [from the Great Enemy, Morgoth] through great peril came over the Mountains of Terror into the hidden Kingdom of Thingol in the forest of Neldoreth' (*The Lord of the Rings*, bk. I, ch. 11). There, in 'Elvenhome' (Doriath), he wanders 'where the Elven-river rolled' – the Esgalduin – and hears 'music welling underground, | In hidden hollows quavering' (in earlier versions, 'dim-lit caves'), the dwellings of Thingol and his court. Seeking the hand of Lúthien, Beren accepts her father's challenge to bring him a Silmaril from Morgoth's crown. Passing through Taur-nu-Fuin, the Forest under Night ('woods of nightshade'), and over 'stony mountains cold and grey', Beren and Lúthien make a daring entry into the Enemy's fortress, Angband, the 'halls of iron' behind a 'darkling door' (i.e. a gate in darkness). They succeed, but Beren dies, and his spirit goes to the halls of Mandos beyond the Western Seas ('the Sundering Seas'). There Lúthien comes in time, having chosen mortality to be with Beren, and 'at last they met once more'.

With the manuscript of text F is a page of rough workings. In this much of Tolkien's writing is illegible, but we are able to extract a few lines of interest:

He sought her ever wandering far
    under bare branches in the moon;
and on a hill he saw a star
    a light that twinkled quivering

by light of moon and ray of star
    in the frosty heavens shivering
as on a hill top high and far
    she danced

her mantle glistened in the moon
    as on a hill-top high and far
she danced and at her feet were strewn
    a mist of silver quivering

On eve of spring she danced again
    upon a hillock green and bare

Later in 1938 Tolkien revisited his 'Tinúviel' poem, filling nearly three pages of manuscript with further trials for its first stanzas, and also marking up the first page of text F. He briefly experimented with the present tense:

> The leaves are long, the grass is green,
> the hemlock-umbels white and tall,
> and in the glade a [glint >] light is seen:
> Tinúviel is shimmering.
> Her feet there lilting lightly fall
> To music of a pipe unseen
> and through the hemlock umbels tall
> the waning moon is glimmering

There is also passing direct mention of 'Neldoreth the forest old', in Tolkien's mythology the beech-forest in the northern part of Doriath.

Apparently between August and autumn 1939, Tolkien made new, revised copies of the poem in pencil and ink. In the latter, the text reached its final form with a few further revisions, most substantively lines 45–47 in the sixth stanza. (Part of the later pencil manuscript, written on a page with a note on stress-conditioned vowel reduction in the development of Quenya, is reproduced in McIlwaine, *Tolkien: Maker of Middle-earth*, p. 54.) We give the ultimate version here (G) as published in the first volume of *The Lord of the Rings* (1954, corrected 2004).

[G]

> The leaves were long, the grass was green,
> The hemlock umbels tall and fair,
> And in the glade a light was seen
> Of stars in shadow shimmering.
> Tinúviel was dancing there
> To music of a pipe unseen,
> And light of stars was in her hair,
> And in her raiment glimmering.
>
> There Beren came from mountains cold,
> And lost he wandered under leaves,
> And where the Elven-river rolled
> He walked alone and sorrowing.
> He peered between the hemlock-leaves
> And saw in wonder flowers of gold
> Upon her mantle and her sleeves,
> And her hair like shadow following.

Enchantment healed his weary feet
    That over hills were doomed to roam;
And forth he hastened, strong and fleet,
    And grasped at moonbeams glistening.
Through woven woods in Elvenhome
    She lightly fled on dancing feet,
And left him lonely still to roam
    In the silent forest listening.

He heard there oft the flying sound
    Of feet as light as linden-leaves,
Or music welling underground,
    In hidden hollows quavering.
Now withered lay the hemlock-sheaves,
    and one by one with sighing sound
Whispering fell the beechen leaves
    In the wintry woodland wavering.

He sought her ever, wandering far
    Where leaves of years were thickly strewn,
By light of moon and ray of star
    In frost heavens shivering.
Her mantle glinted in the moon,
    As on a hill-top high and far
She danced, and at her feet was strewn
    A mist of silver quivering.

When winter passed, she came again
    And her song released the sudden spring,
Like rising lark and falling rain,
    And melted water bubbling.
He saw the elven-flowers spring
    About her feet, and healed again
He longed by her to dance and sing
    Upon the grass untroubling.

Again she fled, but swift he came:
    Tinúviel! Tinúviel!
He called her by her Elvish name;
    and there she halted listening.
One moment stood she, and a spell
    His voice laid on her: Beren came,

And doom fell on Tinúviel
    That in his arms lay glistening.

As Beren looked into her eyes
    Within the shadows of her hair,
The trembling starlight of the skies
    He saw there mirrored shimmering.
Tinúviel the elven-fair,
    Immortal maiden elven-wise,
About him cast her shadowy hair
    And arms like silver glimmering.

Long was the way that fate them bore,
    O'er stony mountains cold and grey,
Through halls of iron and darkling door,
    And woods of nightshade morrowless.
The Sundering Seas between them lay,
    And yet at last they met once more,
And long ago they passed away
    In the forest singing sorrowless.

This, Strider says, 'is a song in the mode that is called *ann-thennath* among the Elves, but is hard to render in our Common Speech, and this is but a rough echo of it'. Thus Tolkien hints at a deep well of poetry in the Elvish tradition, and even of scholarly consideration of such literature, that it should have designated 'modes'. It would have been easy for him to simply toss off such statements, leaving everything else to the reader's imagination, but as Patrick Wynne and Carl F. Hostetter have remarked, Tolkien in fact

> gave much thought to the underlying technical aspects of Elvish prosody, as is amply demonstrated by his detailed notes to *Namárië* [poem no. 162] and *A Elbereth Gilthoniel* [no. 151] in [the 1967 book of the Donald Swann song-cycle] *The Road Goes Ever On*. This attention to technical details included the invention of Elvish names for three modes of Sindarin verse: *ann-thennath*, *Minlamad thent / estent*, and *linnod*. ['Three Elvish Verse Modes' (2000), p. 113]

In 1952 Tolkien made a private recording of Strider's song of Tinúviel, since commercially released.

A6: We imagine that Tolkien intended *bubble* in the same sense one might use *babble* or *burble*, to imitate the sound of water, as in a stream or brook – flute music at its most playful. *Thin* here is probably meant in its sense of 'high-pitched'; compare 'thin hooting fluting voice' in *Outside* (no. 14, B14, B20).

A9: There are many kinds of 'pale' moths, but Tolkien also mentions 'ghostly moths' (A16) and 'white moths' in *The Book of Lost Tales* in connection with Lúthien, and 'ghost-moths' in 'Kortirion' poems (no. 40). There is, in fact, a Ghost Moth (*Hepialus humuli*) common in Europe, of which the males have white or silver wings. The species is named for its hovering (male) display behaviour.

A21: In Tolkien's mythology, *Elfinesse* usually refers to the land of the Elves in the distant West of the world. Here, however, he uses it as another name for Doriath, also an Elvish home. Compare *Elvenhome* in text F.

A32: 'Dying woods' is a reference to autumn and falling leaves. In later versions the phrase is 'wintry woodland'.

A57–63: In the first typescript, Tolkien marked only this stanza for revision:

And Beren caught the elfin maid
    And kissed her trembling starlit eyes:
[The elfin maid that >] Tinúviel whom love delayed
    [In [the days >] years beyond our memory >]
        In the woods of evening morrowless
Till [moon and star >] moonlight and till music dies,
    Shall Beren [and >] by the elfin maid
Dance to the starlight of her eyes
[And fill the woods with glamoury >] In the forest singing sorrowless.

In the alliterative *Children of Húrin* 'the elfin maid' reads 'that elfin maid', as also in the two later typescripts.

B4: Tolkien considered whether to change this line to 'In the tangled trees of Tramarie', or 'In the woven woods of Glamoury', or 'Ere the [days >] birth of mortal memory'. See also our note for B8. In *The Lays of Beleriand* Christopher Tolkien included 'In the tangled trees of Tramarie' in his transcription of the verse as if it were part of the initial writing, but it was clearly added by his father as an alternative.

B8: Tolkien considered whether to change this line to 'Of the silver glades of Amoury'. When discussing ll. 4 and 8 in *The Lays of Beleriand* Christopher Tolkien comments that he could cast no light on the names *Nemorie*, *Tramarie*, *Glamoury*, or *Amoury*. *Nemorie* seems an echo of *memory*, *Glamoury* a name-invention from *glamoury* 'enchantment', and *Amoury* a creation from *amour* 'love'. *Tramerie* may be only an invented name with an *-ry* sound at the end and a 'T' at the beginning to alliterate with 'tangled trees'.

C4: Tolkien considered whether to change 'the land of laughter' to 'spells enchanted'.

C12: Tolkien considered whether to change 'wound' to 'did'.

E title: Tolkien added '*As*' to the printed title *Light as Leaf on Lindentree* on his copy of a cutting from *The Gryphon*.

E1–9: On his copy of the printed poem, Tolkien placed his introductory text in quotation marks.

E1: Tolkien replaced printed 'Ermabwed' with manuscript 'Erchamion', and emended printed 'brokenhearted' (a typo) to 'bold-hearted'.

E2: The name 'Luthien' as printed has no accent.

F1: Among pencilled notes following his initial writing of the manuscript, Tolkien marked 'grass was thin' to become 'stems were green', i.e. the stems of the long leaves. Like other alterations indicated for text F, this did not carry into the next version.

F2: In pencil, Tolkien marked this line to become 'the hemlock umbels white and thick'.

F3: In pencil, Tolkien marked 'out and in' to become 'in between'.

F4: Tolkien considered whether to change 'rising' to 'waning'.

F5: In the margin next to this line Tolkien wrote in ink, then struck through: 'Then lilting quick her feet did fall'.

F6: Tolkien considered whether to change 'silver' to 'bubbly'.

F7: In the margin next to this line Tolkien wrote in ink a phrase which appears to begin 'Bet[ween] the silver of her limbs'.

F9: In pencil, Tolkien marked 'did fold' to become 'unfold'.

F18: In pencil, Tolkien marked 'stone' to become 'hills'.

F21: Here Tolkien uses *Elvenhome* rather than *Elfinesse*: see our note for A21.

F22: In pencil, Tolkien marked 'swiftly' to become 'lightly'

F28: In pencil, Tolkien marked this line to become 'in hidden hollows quavering'. In the next version of the poem, all references to Doriath were removed.

F29: In pencil, Tolkien marked this line to become 'Now withered lay the hemlock sheaves'.

F31: 'Beechen leaves' is an allusion to the beech-forest of Neldoreth.

F32: In pencil, Tolkien marked this line to become 'in the wintry woodland wavering'.

F42: This line originally read 'and her song the sudden spring released'.

F46: 'Winter's chain' is a metaphorical expression, as if one were held captive by cold, wintry weather, but set free by the arrival of spring.

F49–56: Next to this stanza, Tolkien wrote a separate draft:

> Again she fled, but swift he came:
>   Tinúviel, Tinúviel,
> He called her by her elvish name
>   and there she halted listening.
> One moment stood she, and a spell
>   fell on her as he calling came
> Tinúviel Tinúviel
>   in the arms of Beren glistening.

In turn, he revised ll. 5–8 as 'his voice laid on her as he came | then doom fell on her | and looked upon T[inúviel] | that in his arms lay glistening'.

F53: This line originally read 'There doom pursuing on her fell'.

F62: Tolkien considered whether to change 'immortal maiden' to 'O maid immortal'.

F64: In pencil, Tolkien marked this line to become 'and her arms like silver glimmering'.

F65: Tolkien was uncertain about 'road', changing it to 'way' before returning to 'road'. 'Bore' originally read 'led'.

F67: This line originally read 'and through the iron halls of dread'.

F70: This line originally read 'Many ways at last together led'.

G21: 'Through woven woods in Elvenhome' replaced 'Through the woven woods of Elvenhome' in the new ink manuscript.

G25: 'There oft' replaced 'at times' in the new ink manuscript.

G37: 'Glinted' replaced 'glistened' in the new ink manuscript.

G45–47: These lines replaced the following in the new ink manuscript: 'There high and clear he heard her sing, | And from him fell the winter's chain; No more he feared by her to spring'. Tolkien may have intended 'elven-flowers' (G45) to be the white flowers of *niphredil* 'snowdrop' that also greeted Lúthien's birth.

65

Nieninqe · *Nieninque* (?1921–?55)

It is remarkable to find, on reading Tolkien's poems as we have presented them so far, that many feature dancing, usually in a natural setting. In *Wood-Sunshine* (no. 4), the speaker invokes the 'sprites of the wood' to dance for him. In *May Day* (no. 26), the call is 'Come wend to the woodland, come dance ye grey folk!' The goblins in *Goblin Feet* (no. 27) are dancing, as are children in *You and Me and the Cottage of Lost Play* (no. 28). Tinfang Warble in no. 29 is 'dancing all alone in the twilight on the lawn'; Princess Mee (no. 32) is also dancing alone, except for her reflection. In 'forgotten Aryador' (poem no. 37) 'there was dancing and was singing', in the Kortirion poems (no. 40) 'the holy fairies and immortal elves . . . dance among the trees', and Beren comes upon Lúthien (in no. 64) when she is dancing in the woods of Doriath. For the latter, most directly, Tolkien had the inspiration of his wife dancing in the glade near Roos, thus becoming forever 'his' Lúthien – this name, and that of Beren, are on their gravestone. But as some of the relevant poems predate that event, the imagery of dance must have attracted Tolkien in general terms. Indeed, he returned to it again in *Nieninqe*, a brief poem in Qenya with an English translation.

The first manuscript of *Nieninqe* (A) has been dated by consensus to 1921, because it was found among Tolkien's papers in an envelope, which he later labelled 'Elfin Poems', posted to him in Leeds on 5 October 1921 (the year in the postmark is marred, but can be inferred from Tolkien's address). Its (assigned) title word is defined in the Qenya lexicon as 'snowdrop', literally 'white tear' (*nie* 'tear' + *ninqe* 'white'; *Qenyaqetsa*, p. 68).

[A]

Norolinde pirukendea
Elle tande Nielikkilis,
tanya wende nieninqea
yan i vilyar anta miqilis.
Y·oromandi elle tande
ar wingildi wilwarindear,
qant' i lie telerinwa
táli paptalasselindear.

Lightly tripping, whirling lightly
thither came little Nielikki
that maiden like a snow drop
whom the airs give gentle kisses.
The wood-elves too came thither
and the foam-fairies like the butterflies
all the people of Elfin kindred
with feet whose music is that of falling leaves.

This initial version, and the two versions that immediately followed, have been discussed in detail by Christopher Gilson, Bill Welden, and Carl F. Hostetter (Tolkien, *Early Elvish Poetry and Pre-Fëanorian Alphabets*, 2006), especially in regard to their use of Qenya. Gilson, et al. suggest that the name *Nielikkilis* derives from *nie* 'tear' and the root LIQI 'flow, water', with the added element *-lis*, perhaps from Qenya *lis* 'grace, blessing'. In the second version, Tolkien translates the name as 'Niele', the kisses as 'soft' (rather than 'gentle'), and *wingildi* as 'foam-riders' (rather than 'foam-fairies'). For the latter, 'foam' refers to the froth formed on a wave, and another translation of *wingildi* would be 'sea-nymphs'. The comparison of the maiden to a 'snow drop' (in B, 'snowdrop') is presumably to *Galanthus*, which with its small white bell-shaped flowers emerges early in the year, often while snow is on the ground. In the *Lay of Leithian* (poem no. 92), snowdrops spring beneath the feet of Lúthien as she dances near winter's end.

Tolkien included the fourth version of the poem in his lecture *A Secret Vice*, delivered on 29 November 1931 and probably written that autumn (see further, no. 123). In this he discussed the creation of languages for personal enjoyment, and gives *Nieninque* (as he supplies the title) as one of three examples of his use of language-invention in the writing of poetry. *A Secret Vice* was first published by Christopher Tolkien in *The Monsters and the Critics and Other Essays* in 1983, and it is from this book (pp. 215–16) that we have transcribed text B, below. Tolkien provides 'the bare literal meaning' of the verse as continuous prose; we have divided it into shorter lines to correspond with the work in Qenya.

[B]

Norolinde pirukendea
elle tande Nielikkilis,
tanya wende nieninqea
yar i vilya anta miqilis.
I oromandin eller tande

ar wingildin wilwarindeën,
losselie telerinwa,
tálin paptalasselindeën.

Tripping lightly, whirling lightly,
thither came little Niéle,
that maiden like a snowdrop,
to whom the air gives kisses.
The wood-spirits came thither,
and the foam-fays like butterflies,
the white people of the shores of Elfland,
with feet like the music of falling leaves.

'You must remember', Tolkien told his audience,

> that these things were constructed deliberately to be personal, and give private satisfaction – nor for scientific experiment, nor yet in expectation of any audience. A consequent weakness is therefore their tendency, too free as they were from cold exterior criticism, to be 'over-pretty', to be *phonetically and semantically* sentimental – while their bare meaning is probably trivial, not full of red blood or the heat of the world such as critics demand. [*The Monsters and the Critics and Other Essays*, p. 213; italics in the original]

Gilson, et al. reasonably conclude that *Nieninque* (B) and its three preceding versions must date from between 1921 (if the envelope can be taken as good evidence) and (November) 1931, when Tolkien delivered *A Secret Vice*. They also note (*Early Elvish Poetry*, p. 96) that Tolkien wrote a fifth version of his poem, in Qenya only, on the back of a desk calendar leaf for the week of 26 June to 2 July 1955; we give this text below as C.

[C]

Norolinda pirukendëa
lende tanna Nielikkilis,
sana wende nieninquëa
yan i wilyar antar miquelis
I·oromandi tanna lende
ar wingildi wilwarindie
losselie telerinwa:
táli lantalasselingie.

The meanings of these words in English remained the same, but here as elsewhere, Tolkien's invented language evolved. In connection with the second version of *Nieninqe* he wrote:

> This language [Qenya] I may say (though it remains [?perhaps] incomplete – and has often endured grammatical changes especially with verbs) was written of course to the needs of my mythology. I found it necessary to have at least some clear idea of the language spoken by my fairy creatures (the Eldalie) in order to understand them – and of course to invent their names. [*Early Elvish Poetry*, p. 92]

66

The Lay of the Fall of Gondolin (?1921–?25)

Before addressing *The Lay of the Fall of Gondolin*, we must say more about *The Book of Lost Tales*, which we have cited already many times. Christopher Tolkien has called the *Lost Tales* 'the first emergence in narrative' of many features of his father's mythology. It was the first lengthy prose expression of 'The Silmarillion', following on several related poems, beginning with *The Voyage of Éarendel the Evening Star* (1914, no. 16). Tolkien began to write the *Lost Tales* towards the end of 1916 or the beginning of 1917 while convalescing from trench fever, and largely abandoned them after June 1919; as mentioned earlier, he was commissioned to prepare the glossary for Sisam's *Fourteenth Century Verse and Prose*, and then, on 1 October 2020, he took up his post at Leeds with the many labours that occupy an academic's life.

It was in the *Lost Tales* that he first told of Tuor and the fall of Gondolin. At that stage of the story's development, Tuor was a Man of Dor Lómin in the north of Middle-earth. With the aid of the Noldoli (or Gnomes), he reaches the Great Sea. There Ulmo, lord of waters, commands him to find Gondolin, the hidden city of the Gondothlim, and to tell its ruler, Turgon, to prepare for battle with Melko, the evil Vala from whom Turgon's people have escaped death or enslavement. Tuor complies, but the king is unwilling to act. At length, Tuor marries Turgon's daughter, Idril, and they have a son, Eärendel. But Gondolin is attacked by Melko's forces with the aid of the Elf Meglin, who desires Idril and a place by the throne. Although the city falls, Tuor, his family, and others flee along a secret way, Idril having foreseen treachery and that the established Way of Escape would not be safe. The exiles come to the Land of Willows (where Tuor recites to his son the *Sea Chant of an Elder Day*, poem no. 13), and later settle at the mouth of the River Sirion.

Christopher Tolkien considered *The Lay of the Fall of Gondolin* to be his father's first attempt to tell a story from the *Lost Tales* in verse. This is a debatable point, as it depends on whether *Light as Leaf on Lind* (no. 64) was composed as early as 1919, and whether one should count it as telling a story from the *Lost Tales*, as it includes only a small part of the adventures of Beren and Lúthien. We have accepted Christopher's judgement for the sake of placing *Gondolin* chronologically in the present book, and although his father conceivably began to write the poem in 1920, it seems more reasonable to date it to 1921, given how many tasks Tolkien would have had when beginning his teaching at Leeds the previous autumn.

In any case, for our purposes it is particularly interesting that Tolkien should return to a poetic mode for his mythology, and that he experimented with different forms. During his years at Leeds he composed five distinct poems from the mythology. Two of them are extensive: we quote from the alliterative lay *The Children of Húrin* and the *Lay of Leithian* later in this book (nos. 67 and 92). Two of the others, *The Flight of the Noldoli* and a lay of Earendel, both in alliterative verse and both quickly abandoned, are published in full in *The Lays of Beleriand*. The third, *The Lay of the Fall of Gondolin*, is dealt with here. The *Lay*, in rhyming couplets, closely follows the prose tale of Tuor in detail, and to an extent uses similar wording. It was not conceived on as large a scale, however, and indeed the events of the story are heavily compressed as told in verse. Nor did Tolkien ever complete the *Lay*: in its longest version it ends as Meglin is taken by Orcs to the halls of Melko (Morgoth), which in the prose tale occurs less than halfway through.

The *Lay* exists in three versions, apart from a few leaves of workings. None bears a title: we have used the one assigned to the poem by Christopher Tolkien in *The Lays of Beleriand*. The earliest version consists of approximately 93 lines on two leaves, one of which is a sheet of University of Leeds examination paper which Tolkien could not have appropriated before autumn 1920. He did not write the manuscript at a continuous sitting, as shown by variation in his penmanship and by variable use of pencil and ink, and some lines of the poem were replaced and expanded. The text on its first page begins:

> Song[s] have been sung in Elfland since the hills were green & young
> of the deeds of the ancient ages — and some are yet unsung —
> of the days when the Light was made not, and the Gods were in the gloom,
> when the Two Trees were but saplings, and ere the day of doom . . .

By line 23, the poem reaches an account of the names of Gondolin:

> and the Rock of Song they named it, the Burg of Gondolin,
> for the laughter and the music they rekindled therewithin;
> and seven names they gave it as its might and glory grew,
> and their hearts made merry, crying 'Lo Cor is built anew'.

But Tolkien marked these lines for replacement:

And they named that city Gondolin — yet other names they knew.
When laughter again was kindled and their hope and gladness
grew;
when the song about their fountains reawakened echoing far,
then harpers sang the praise of mighty Gondobar,
and Gondothlimbar called it — City Hewn of Stone,
and fortress of the gnome folk who dwell in Halls of Stone,
in Gwarestrin on the hill-top, a Tower of sleepless Ward,
Garthurion the Hidden Dwelling unfound by Melko's horde;
And Loth, the flower, they named it, wherein Cor was born again,
Even [Loth Barodrin >] Loth-a-ladwen, the Lily of the Plain.

And at the foot of the first page are the lines:

But songs have been sung in Elfland since the hills were green &
young
of deeds that were done in Gondolin, and some may not be
sung —

distinct from the opening lines of the page, which have 'deeds of the ancient ages'.

It struck us as curious that the third page of this version should then begin again:

Yea Songs have been sung in Elfland since the hills were green and
young
of deeds that were done in Gondolin — and some are yet
unsung —

with 'Songs' capitalized and 'Yea' written with a gap before 'Songs', and that most of these words ('Songs have been sung in Elfland since the hills were green and young | of deeds that were done i') should be found, broken off, at the end of one of the *c.* 1920–1 typescripts of *The Lay of Earendel* (i.e. *The Bidding of the Minstrel*, poem no. 18). The explanation seems to be that the second leaf of *The Lay of the Fall of Gondolin*, as archived in the Bodleian Library, was composed first in this draft, while the 'first' leaf followed as a new opening to the poem. If this is so, the original opening of the first version read:

Songs have been sung in Elfland since the hills were green and
young
of deeds that were done in Gondolin — and some are yet
unsung —
Gondolin of the Gnome-folk with white and moonlit walls
whose towers were touched by starlight and silver were its halls.
Thither Tuor son of Fengel came out of the dim land
that the Gnomes have called Dor Lomin, with Bronweg at his
hand . . .

The second manuscript of the poem is much longer and more heavily revised, comprising 168 lines. This too was written out over an extended period, with Tolkien's handwriting alternately neat or hurried, partly using the reverse sides of Leeds examination scripts. For its final twenty lines, Tolkien chose regularly to employ the archaic thorn (*þ*) for *th*, which he had not done earlier except in one instance (line 144), and most remarkably, in the final twelve lines, while still employing couplets, he introduced alliteration and caesuras (metrical pauses; see further, our discussion for no. 67). This twenty-line portion is demonstrably later than the rest of the manuscript, as the name previously written 'Melko' is given instead as 'Morgoth', a form which Tolkien seems to have begun to use regularly only late in his years at Leeds, perhaps in 1924 or 1925. 'Morgoth' also appears earlier in the manuscript as subsequent revisions to 'Melko'.

Finally, there is a typescript of only 82 lines, which breaks off near the end of the 'names of Gondolin' sequence. It was made with a purple ribbon like other typescripts of Tolkien's Leeds period, faded or with losses here and there which Tolkien made good by hand while making as well a handful of manuscript revisions. In this version 'Morgoth' is used *ab initio*.

Because all of these texts are so similar, often identical, to one another, we have transcribed in full only the second, longest version, with notes about interesting features of the earliest manuscript and the later typescript. We have used *th* instead of *þ*, and indicate the caesuras in lines 157–168.

Lo! Songs have been sung in Elfland since the hills were green and
young
of the deeds of the ancient ages — and some may not be sung — .
We have heard how the earth lay darkling while the Gods walked
in the gloom,
in the days when light was made not, ere Varda's mighty loom

wove the meshes of the twilight that snared the firstling stars;
how the Gods in Council gathered on the outmost rocky bars
of the Lonely Island westward, and devised a land of ease
beyond the great sea-shadows and the shadowy seas;
how they made the deep gulf of Faërie with long and lonely shore,
and ringed with impenetrable mountains the Land of Valinor.
There Palúrien the Earth-mother set the seed of the Two trees [*sic*],
that from saplings sprang to splendour, & lit the foaming seas
with a light no eye hath imagined or the mountains looked upon
since Laurelin hath faded and withered Silpion.
For the swinging blooms of Silpion were a silvern radiance
with fluttering shadows mingled in its long dark leaves a-dance,
but the golden flowers of Laurelin were a song of glowing flame
that filled the Gods['] wide pastures till the hour of ending came
when Ungoliont and Melko slew the glory of the Gods: —
and songs there be of the Gnome-folk, and their war with hopeless odds —
how those exiles marched from Faërie o'er the bridge of the Fangéd Ice,
and flowers sprang neath their banners till the day of Sacrifice,
and the battle no song dare tell of, and the sea of Tears Untold
that still do fall in Elfland, though countless years have rolled
since men betrayed the Elfkin, and their banners were trod in the dust;
since that great green mound was builded, where the gnomish swords do rust.
And Tales there be of Turgon, who hewed his folk a path
from the slaughter and the ruin that was like the War-god's swath.
In the hills that people vanished, and Melko found them not;
for they made a mountain-fastness, where less evil grew their lot.
In a circle nowhere broken (save but where Thornsir spills
o'er the cliffs his dizzy water) of the still untrodden hills
there with labour never-ceasing they carved Tumladin's plain,
and delved the secret doorway, by which alone might gain
such gnomes as fled from Melko this city that they reared.

Ever its walls waxed valiant, and less was Melko feared;
and the Rock of Song they named it, the Burg of Gondolin
for the laughter and the music they rekindled there within;
and seven names they gave it as its might and glory grew
and their hearts made merry, crying, 'Lo! Côr is built anew.'
Yea songs have been sung in Elfland since the hills were green and young
of the deeds that were done in Gondolin — and many are yet unsung —
Gondolin of the Gnome-folk with white and moonlit walls
whose towers were touched by starlight, and silver were its halls.
Thither Tuor son of Fengel out of the dim land
that the Gnomes have called Dor Lomin, with Bronweg at his hand,
who fled from the Iron Mountains and had broken Melko's chain
and cast his yoke of evil, of torment and bitter pain;
who alone most faithful-hearted had led Tuor by long ways
through empty hills and valleys by dark nights and perilous days
till his blue lamp magic-kindled, where flow the shadowy rills,
beneath enchanted alders, found that gate beneath the hills,
the door in dark Dungorthin that only the Gnome-folk knew.
Thus they came by winding caverns where the black roots darkly grew
of the great Encircling Mountains to a doorway on the vale,
and it looked across Tumladin, and the morning light was pale;
it looked upon Amon Gwareth, the Hill of Watch and Ward,
where the white town in the morning, whose slender turrets soared
rose-stainéd in the sunrise, was gleaming far away —
the seven-naméd city of a fair long-vanished day.
There the guard of the Hidden Gateway in ringing silver mail
closed round them as they gazéd upon that hill amid the vale.
Then Tuor all amazéd in the sweet tongue of the gnomes,
'what folk are ye' he asked 'or what city's towers and domes
of ivory and marble be these where fountains play
high o'er the white walls shimmering in the sunlight far away?'
And it was answered swiftly 'we guard the Hidden Door;
rejoice that ye have found it and rest from endless war —
for the seven-naméd city 'tis stands upon the hill

where all who strive with Melko find hope and valour still.'
'What be those names', said Tuor; 'for I come from long afar?'
''Tis said and 'tis sung', one answered, [']I am calléd *Gondobar*,
and *Gondothlimbar* naméd, the City Hewn of Stone,
the fortress of the Gnome-folk who dwell in Halls of Stone;
and *Gwarestrin* on the hill-top, the Tower of Sleepless Ward;
Gar Thurion, the Hidden Dwelling, where lieth the golden hoard;
and *Loth* the Flower they name me, saying 'Côr is born again,
even in *Loth-a-ladwen*, the Lily of the Plain.'
But *Gondolin* do all songs call me, the songs mine own folk sing,
and for Gondolin tears unquenchéd shall fall and for her king.'
Thence they wander the white pathways o'er Tumladin's grassy plain,
and find the long thin staircase up the hillside, and they gain
the unconquered gates of silver with their bars of forgéd steel,
in rock-hewn marble portals, while white birds whirl and reel
in frightened flocks about them, and the white-robed folk come forth
to meet the gnome forwandered and that mortal of the North.
There, mightiest of death-doomed men that any tale has told,
he spake his word to Turgon, Gnome-king proud & old —
these things and his deathless valour have harps unnumbered stirred,
and of Idril Feet-of-Silver all elves and men have heard,
King's daughter of white Gondolin, the long-haired elfin maid
that he wedded on Amon Gwareth in love that shall not fade.
Thence Earendel sprang in glory, whose eyes held silver flame,
shining seaman of the oceans; and all waves sing his name —
the fairest of all men-folk, who passed the Gates of Dread,
half-mortal & half-elfin, undying and long-dead.
In a house they builded slender on the high walls of the East
he came through the Gates of Summer (the holiest elfin-feast)
to the white town of the Gnome-folk; and laughed he at his birth,
for the ways were flower-laden and the folk all full of mirth.
There seven years of childhood, unshadowed by the fears
that gathered o'er his mother, those seven golden years
he knew of Gondolin's glory, while yet unshaken stood
Turgon's tower of Ivory; ere Meglin's traitorhood
achieved its crown of evil. Lo that prince of Gondobar

was dark Eol's son whom Isfin, in mountain dale afar
in the gloom of Doriath's forest, the white-limbed maiden bare,
the daughter of Fingolfin, Gelmir's mighty heir
'Twas the bent blades of the Glamhoth that drank Fingolfin's life
as he stood alone by Feanor; but his maiden and his wife
were wildered as they sought him in the forests of the night,
in the pathless woods of Doriath, so dark that as a light
of palely mirrored moonsheen were their slender elfin limbs
straying among the black boles where only the dim bat skims
from Thu's dark-delvéd caverns. There Eol saw that sheen
and he caught the white-limbed Isfin, that she ever since hath been
his mate in Doriath's forest, where she weepeth in the gloam;
for the dark elves were his kindred that wander without home.
Meglin she sent to Gondolin, and his honour there was high
as the latest seed of Fingolfin whose glory shall not die;
a Lordship he won of the gnomefolk who quarry deep in the earth,
seeking their ancient jewels; but little was his mirth,
and dark he was and secret and his hair as the strands of night
that are tangled in Taur Fuin the Forest without light.
Often was he in the mountains; for in those days never ceased
the hammer on the anvil, while the hoard of arms increased,
of glaives and shields and hauberks, of arrows and of spears,
till the gnome-folk might not tell them in many tens of years,
and the folk of Meglin's following whose sign was the sable mole
delved ever for ore of metals in the mountains, where on troll
and orc and goblin of Melko at times they wandering fell
and slew them suddenly & swiftly & guarded Gondolin well.
Yet the tale tells how the Glamhoth trapped Meglin in the hills
nigh the Cristhorn Cleft of Eagles whence Thornsir's water spills
high o'er the dark cliffs streaming; and they put him in evil pain
ere they would cruelly kill him, and his white bones should remain
to blanch on the fangéd pinnacles that are set in the abyss.
Then Meglin's heart was melted, and little he hoped to miss
the doom the Glamhoth bade him, and he said in his despair:
'know I am Meglin Eolion, whom Isfin the slender bare,

the king's sister of white Gondolin, for which Melko seeketh still
in the magic circle guarded of the mountains' coronet.
But they laughed 'what is that to the glam-hoth? should they not liever kill
if thou be of the blood of that kingling that thwarts the Strong One's will?
'Elves and all other creatures may your crookéd moon-swords quell,
but, speedy or slow if ye slay me, great tidings there be to tell
of Gondolin the guarded ye will lose, that well may be
w[oul]d rejoice your Master greatly — and would I might him see.
Then they stayed their hands and hearkened, and he spake of the growing power
of the city of secret refuge beneath the king's white tower;
and wroth they dragged him cruelly o'er the rough ways & the long
to the shadows and black dungeons, and the dark & woeful throng
of those red-eyed, redhanded, that stand by Morgoth's throne
& whet their swords with laughter like clash of stone on stone,
With songs like sullen thunder that pent in echoing tombs
Rolls neath the Iron Mountains & shakes their endless glooms.
Cloudhung were the capitals   of the carven columns tall,
twisted and black footed,   that upheld that sable hall,
& serpents wound about them   the long & loathsome spires
of their venom-mottled bellies,   & like lamps the yellow fires
of their lidless eyes there flickered   in the dark and domed abyss
thick with their licking tongues   & ceaseless poisoned hiss.
Wolves of monstrous stature   lay watchful at the feet
of the mighty chair of marble   that was Morgoth's dreadful seat;
black-felled, hungry, evil,   with eyes of tortured flame,
with slavering jaws longfangéd   from the wilderness they came
and filled the house of Morgoth   with shuddering voices bleak —
when the wolves of Bauglir howl   then not even the Balrogs speak.

The first manuscript of the *Lay* began with a much more abbreviated account of Creation and the wars of the Elves, and with an equally brief history of the building of Gondolin. But Tolkien soon expanded the draft, recounting the seven names of the city – following more closely the events of the prose story in the *Lost Tales* – rather than merely stating 'seven names they gave it'. This tendency towards expansion continued with the second manuscript, where Tolkien enlarged the opening lines to include a concise history of the creation of the world and the early travails of the Elves. A summary of this will be useful here, to explain the poem's many references to characters and places in the 'Silmarillion' mythology.

Varda kindled the heavens ('the firstling stars'), bringing light to the 'Gods' – the Ainur, product of the thought of Ilúvatar, the supreme being. 'The Gods in Council' are the Valar and Maiar, those of the Ainur who entered into the world they helped to create and strove to protect, excepting only Melko, who sought power and to spread discord. 'The Lonely Island westward', which afterwards became Tol Eressëa (see our discussion for poem no. 40), here refers to its relocation across the seas into the west, where the 'gods' built Valinor, 'a land of ease'. 'The deep gulf of Faërie' is the Bay of Faëry (Bay of Eldamar). In Valinor, Palúrien (Yavanna) created the Two Trees, Laurelin and Silpion, which gave light to the world. But Melko stole from the Noldoli ('the Gnome-folk') their treasured gems, including the precious Silmarils, and with the gigantic spider Ungoliont destroyed the Trees ('the glory of the Gods'). The Noldoli vowed revenge against Melko, and exiling themselves from their home ('Faërie', i.e. Eldamar) crossed to Middle-earth over the frozen ice-field Helkaraksë ('the Fangéd Ice').

For 'countless years' the Elves and their allies fought Melko and his armies; 'the battle no song dare tell of' is the Battle of Unnumbered Tears, in which Men corrupted by Melko 'betrayed the Elfkin'. The 'great green mound' is that raised after that battle on the barren plain Anfauglith by Melko's Orcs, in which they piled the dead of Men and Elves with their weapons, and it was so high that it could be seen from afar. Turgon, however, and his host were able to cut their way out of the battle and flee to the hills, where they 'made a mountain-fastness', Gondolin on the plain of Tumladin, as if it were the lost city Côr (Kôr) reborn (see poem no. 30). Gondolin in the 'Encircling Mountains' could be entered only by a 'secret doorway', and only by others of the surviving Gnomes (Noldoli). Tuor is able to enter the city because he is accompanied by the faithful Elf Bronweg (or Voronwë).

Christopher Tolkien published only forty-three lines of the *Lay* (edited from the longer manuscript) in *The Lays of Beleriand*, reasoning that it 'does not, so far as the main narrative is concerned, add anything to the Tale [as published in *The Book of Lost Tales, Part Two*]; and my father found, as I think, the metrical form unsuitable to the purpose' (p. 145). We have included the poem to illustrate more fully Tolkien's use of poetry in the development of his mythology and his uncertainty about which verse forms best suited his purposes.

1: Tolkien used 'Elfland' (and 'Elvenland') in several works around this time as a generic name for the lands inhabited by Elves in Middle-earth.

3–19: Tolkien first wrote ll. 3–5 as

of the days when the Light was made not, and the gods were in the gloom,
when the Two Trees were but saplings, and ere the day of doom,
when Ungoliont and Melko slew the glory of the Gods;

He seems next to have written present ll. 3–10 in pencil in the margin above l. 1, before cancelling them and writing them out again in ink on a new sheet, to which he added present ll. 11–19. This text was then indicated for insertion after l. 2.

11: Tolkien later wrote 'Yavanna' above 'Palúrien'. The latter, from Qenya *palurin* 'the wide world', was an early name for the Vala Yavanna, essentially 'Mother Earth'.

24: In the typescript, Tolkien changed 'Elfland' to 'Eressea' (in this line; 'Elfland' remained in ll. 1 and 41).

26: In the typescript, Tolkien changed 'the Gnomish swords do rust' to 'their swords were laid to rest'.

29: Tolkien later wrote in the margin 'Morgoth' as a revision to 'Melko'.

31: Thornsir is a falling stream below Cristhorn (see l. 134).

35: Here as well, Tolkien wrote 'Morgoth' in the margin, referring to 'Melko' in the text.

37: Tolkien later marked 'Burg' to be changed to 'Mount' or 'Tower'. The typescript has 'town of Gondolin'.

40: *Côr* is a later spelling of the name of the Elvish city and hill Kôr; still later, Tolkien called the city *Tûn* (see poem no. 30). In the present manuscript, he later wrote in the margin 'Tun' (i.e. 'Tûn' without a circumflex) as a revision to 'Côr'. In the typescript, the name is 'Cór' (with an acute accent).

45: Tolkien later wrote 'Huor' above 'Fengel', in both this manuscript and the typescript. Christopher Tolkien explains in *The Lays of Beleriand* that Tuor was the son of Peleg in the *Lost Tales*, and in one of the stray workings of *The Lay of the Fall of Gondolin* Tuor is himself called Fengel (Old English 'prince'). In later development of 'The Silmarillion' he is the son of Huor.

46: *Dor Lomin* (*Dor Lómin*, also *Hisilómë*, *Hithlum*, *Aryador*) refers back to 'the dim land' in l. 45; the name is derived from Gnomish *dor* 'land' + *lómin* 'gloom'. See also our discussion for poem no. 37. At the end of l. 46, 'with Bronweg at his hand' originally read 'and his harp was in his hand'.

48: Tolkien later wrote in the margin 'dark' as a revision to 'bitter'; 'bitter', however, appears in the typescript.

50–53: These lines describe the path to the hidden door to Gondolin, which here opens into a valley named 'Dungorthin'. In the first manuscript it is called 'Nan Orwen'; in other works the name is 'Nan Dungortheb', among other forms, and its location varies. In *The Book of Lost Tales* Tuor and Bronweg, seeking for Gondolin, after many days come upon 'a deep dale amid the hills . . . curtained with a heavy growth of alders' (*The Book of Lost Tales, Part Two*, p. 157).

51: In regard to the 'blue lamp magic-kindled', the blue lanterns of the Elves are mentioned here and there in the developing mythology, perhaps most fully in the alliterative *Children of Húrin* (poem no. 67): 'little lanterns of lucent crystal | and silver cold with subtlest cunning | they strangely fashioned, and steadfast a flame | burnt unblinking there blue and pale, | unquenched for ever' (*The Lays of Beleriand*, p. 35).

67: Tolkien later wrote 'him they' above 'it was'. The 'Hidden Door' is the guarded gate into Gondolin and out of the Way of Escape.

78: In *The Book of Lost Tales* the flower is named 'Lothengriol'. In the first manuscript it was first written as 'Loth Barodrin', and later changed to 'Loth-a-ladwen'.

90: 'Feet-of-Silver' is a translation of Gnomish *Talceleb*.

95–96: The phrase 'who passed the Gates of Dread, | half-mortal & half-elfin, undying and long-dead' refers to the fate of Eärendel as set forth in *The Book of Lost Tales*. After many wanderings at sea, he reaches the margin of the world and sets sail in the firmament; chased by the Moon, he dives through the Door of Night (probably the same as 'the Gates of Dread') and is unable to return to the Earth. This story is a further development of the poems in which the mariner appears or to which he is related (nos. 14, 18, 31, 33).

105–124: Christopher Tolkien quotes this passage in *The Lays of Beleriand* in order to discuss 'some puzzling statements' concerning Fingolfin, father of Turgon and grandfather of Meglin. Here Fingolfin is 'Gelmir's mighty heir', whoever Gelmir might be. In l. 108, Tolkien later marked 'Gelmir's mighty heir' to be changed to 'Gnome king proud and fair' (compare a similar epithet for Turgon in l. 88). The story behind Fingolfin's death 'as he stood alone by Fëanor' has vanished. The passage is also the first substantive account in the mythology of Eol (here spelled thus, elsewhere Eöl), Isfin the sister of Turgon, and their son Meglin. In *The Silmarillion* Eöl is 'the Dark Elf', an unpleasant smith who lives in deep shadows.

109: 'Bent blades' presumably refers to scimitars. *Glamhoth* is a Gnomish name for Orcs, soldiers of Melko.

110: 'Feanor' is spelled here in the manuscript without a diaeresis (usually *Fëanor*).

115: Thu (in this manuscript spelled without a circumflex), the precursor of Sauron of *The Lord of the Rings*, is described in the *Lay of Leithian* (poem no. 92) as living within a hill, 'the abode of one most evil'. He is 'Morgoth's mightiest lord', 'the necromancer', master of 'the werewolves of the Wizard's Isle' (*The Lays of Beleriand*, p. 228).

124: 'Forest without light' is a translation of Gnomish *Taur Fuin*. Tolkien later wrote 'na' between the words, changing 'Taur Fuin' to one of its later forms ('Taur-na-Fuin').

129: Meglin's followers represent themselves appropriately with a sable (black) mole because of their skill in digging.

139: 'He said in his despair' originally read 'evil woke in his heart'. In *The Book of Lost Tales* the prose account reads: 'But evil came into the heart of Meglin, and he said to his captors' (*The Book of Lost Tales, Part Two*, p. 168).

141: Tolkien later marked 'still' to be changed to 'yet'.

142: Tolkien wrote this line in the margin for insertion. Since we cannot be sure if he added it in the process of writing rather than later, we have included it as part of the original manuscript. 'The mountains' coronet' presumably refers to the mountains encircling Gondolin like a crown.

143: Here 'glam-hoth' is written thus. At the end of the line, 'should they not liever kill' originally read 'that they should not thee liever kill'.

152: Tolkien wrote 'shadows' as 'schadowes', spelling the word in an archaic manner.

152–153: 'The dark & woeful throng | of those red-eyed, redhanded, that stand by Morgoth's throne' is, perhaps, a description of the Balrogs of Morgoth's halls, mentioned specifically in the prose version of the tale for their 'whips of flame and claws of steel' (*The Book of Lost Tales, Part Two*, p. 169). 'Red-eyed, redhanded' – with fiery eyes and bloody hands – recalls Tennyson's 'red in tooth and claw' (*In Memoriam A.H.H.*), referring to blood and the violence of predation. In l. 153, Tolkien later added 'things' after 'those'.

157: The columns are unusually tall, if their capitals (heads) are 'cloudhung', i.e. high enough to be in the clouds.

158: 'Black footed' originally read 'dark footed'.

168: Tolkien later wrote 'yammer' as a possible revision to 'howl'.

67

The Golden Dragon · Túrin Son of Húrin and Glórund the Dragon · The Children of Húrin · Winter Comes to Nargothrond (?1921–?25)

The tale of Túrin and Nienor, the children of Húrin, varies in its different incarnations, beginning with the account in *The Book of Lost Tales*. Here we summarize its events as Tolkien conceived them in an alliterative lay he wrote during his years at Leeds. Húrin, a man, is captured in the Battle of Unnumbered Tears and appears defiant before Morgoth. The Vala curses him, such that evil and despair will fall upon his family and that he himself will suffer by witnessing the results. Túrin, Húrin's son, is sent by his mother, Morwin (later Morwen), to the court of Thingol in Doriath, where he is raised as the Elf-king's own. Morwin and her infant daughter Nienor meanwhile remain in Dorlómin. In time, Túrin becomes a warrior and fights alongside Beleg the bowman; but after causing the death of the Elf Orgof, he flees into the forest, and a band of outlaws forms around him. Beleg joins Túrin and company in fighting Morgoth's Orcs. Betrayed, Túrin is taken by the enemy. With the aid of the Elf Flinding, Beleg frees him, but is killed by Túrin, who mistakes Beleg for an Orc.

Flinding leads Túrin to Nargothrond, the underground stronghold of the Elf-king Orodreth. There the king's daughter, Finduilas (Failivrin), who had loved Flinding, now gives her love to Túrin – and there, with 'Orcs unnumbered . . . on the realm's borders', the poem (in its longer initial version) abruptly ends. As the tale continued in other texts, Nargothrond falls to a dragon; Nienor loses her memory and is found by Túrin, who, failing to recognize 'Níniel' – she was only a baby when he saw her last – takes her to wife; he slays the dragon, but in dying the creature reveals to Nienor her identity, and realizing that she carries her brother's child, she kills herself. Túrin also commits suicide when he learns that Níniel was his sister.

The lay in question was the earliest major work by Tolkien in alliterative verse, following the few specimens we have presented earlier, and the longest of his poems in alliterative form. The first of its two versions runs to 2,276 lines, but covers only half the story; the second reaches only to 817. Christopher Tolkien is certain that his father abandoned both versions before departing Leeds for Oxford in late 1925, probably when he began to write the *Lay of Leithian* (no. 92) that summer, but it has not been possible to pin down the start of composition. In one source Tolkien wrote that he began the poem '*c.* 1921' before changing the year to '1918'; Christopher was not convinced of the earlier date, and neither are we. A page of the earliest manuscript of the poem is on a discarded word-slip from the *Oxford English Dictionary* date-stamped May 1918, but its content can be shown to be later. If, moreover, Christopher is correct that *The Lay of the Fall of Gondolin* (no. 66) was his father's first attempt at a treatment in verse of one of the prose *Lost Tales*, then it is correct that we place the present work here in our book.

The initial manuscript of the poem is rough, divided among small slips and sheets of University of Leeds examination paper, the latter marked with later revisions; part of one page is reproduced in McIlwaine, *Tolkien: Maker of Middle-earth*, p. 218. On this is based the first typescript, made with a purple ribbon, which introduced new changes and itself was revised, in stages. Its original title was *The Golden Dragon*, but Tolkien changed this to *Túrin Son of Húrin and Glórund the Dragon*. An additional manuscript carried the text further, and there is also an alternate manuscript of some two hundred lines following on the typescript, entitled *Túrin in the House of Fuilin and His Son Flinding*. The second version is a revision and enlargement of the first, but proceeds less far into the story; it ends with Túrin come to manhood and now a mighty warrior, before the introduction of Orgof and Túrin's flight.

Physically the second version survives as rough manuscript notes and a following typescript (also made with a purple ribbon), as well as a further typescript with revisions and another manuscript, the latter written on University of Oxford paper, available to Tolkien from 1924, when he acted at Oxford as an external examiner. The second version was first entitled *Túrin*, but later became *The Children of Húrin*, a title we will apply generally in our discussion (and which should not be confused with the 2007 volume of the same name, which collects Tolkien's various prose narratives of the story of Túrin). Christopher Tolkien thought the second text not 'significantly later than the first', and that his father may have begun it while still working on the earlier draft.

As with Tolkien's other long poems, *The Children of Húrin* cannot be printed here in its entirety. Both versions have been published in full, with Christopher Tolkien's commentary, in *The Lays of Beleriand*, our source for the present entry (pp. 7–8, 100–101). But we have made representative selections, beginning with Húrin's exchange with Morgoth (nicknamed *Bauglir*, Noldorin 'constrainer, tyrant') in his fortress Angband, as the Vala seeks, through Húrin, to find Turgon, who escaped Morgoth in the Battle of Unnumbered Tears and fled to the hidden city of Gondolin. Húrin, also called *Thalion* (Noldorin 'steadfast') and *Erithámrod* ('unbending'), is threatened with torment by Morgoth's fire-demons, the Balrogs, and taken to a peak of Thangorodrim, the forbidding mountains raised by Morgoth above Angband, north of Hithlum, the Land of Shadows, also known as Dorlómin. For comparison, we give this scene as it appears in both versions of the poem.

HÚRIN AND MORGOTH, FIRST VERSION, LINES 51–104

[A] 'Is it dauntless Húrin,' quoth Delu-Morgoth,
'stout steel-handed, who stands before me,
a captive living as a coward might be?
Knowest thou my name, or need'st be told
what hope he has who is haled to Angband —
the bale most bitter, the Balrogs' torment?'

'I know and I hate. For that knowledge I fought thee
by fear unfettered, nor fear I now,'
said Thalion there, and a thane of Morgoth
on the mouth smote him; but Morgoth smiled:
'Fear when thou feelest, and the flames lick thee,
and the whips of the Balrogs thy white flesh brand.
Yet a way canst win, an thou wishest, still
to lessen thy lot of lingering woe.
Go question the captives of the accursed people
I have taken, and tell me where Turgon is hid;
how with fire and death I may find him soon,
where he lurketh lost in lands forgot.
Thou must feign thee a friend faithful in anguish,
and their inmost hearts thus open and search.
Then, if truth thou tellest, thy triple bonds
I will bid men unbind, that abroad thou fare
in my service to search the secret places
following the footsteps of these foes of the Gods.'

'Build not thy hopes so high, O Bauglir —
I am no tool for thy evil treasons;
torment were sweeter than a traitor's stain.'

'If torment be sweet, treasure is liever.
The hoards of a hundred hundred ages,
the gems and jewels of the jealous Gods,
are mine, and a meed shall I mete thee thence,
yea, wealth to glut the Worm of Greed.'

'Canst not learn of thy lore when thou look'st on a foe,
O Bauglir unblest? Bray no longer
of the things thou hast thieved from the Three Kindreds.
In hate I hold thee, and thy hests in scorn.'

'Boldly thou bravest me. Be thy boast rewarded,'
in mirth quod Morgoth, 'to me now the deeds,
and thy aid I ask not; but anger thee nought
if little they like thee. Yea, look thereon
helpless to hinder, or thy hand to raise.'

Then Thalion was thrust to Thangorodrim,
that mountain that meets the misty skies
on high o'er the hills that Hithlum sees
blackly brooding on the borders of the north.
To a stool of stone on its steepest peak
they bound him in bonds, an unbreakable chain,
and the Lord of Woe there laughing stood,
then cursed him for ever and his kin and seed
with a doom of dread, of death and horror.
There the mighty man unmovéd sat;
but unveiled was his vision, that he viewed afar
all earthly things with eyes enchanted
that fell on his folk — a fiend's torment.

HÚRIN AND MORGOTH, SECOND VERSION, LINES 175–247

[B] I will bid men unbind thee [said Morgoth], and thy body comfort!
Go follow their footsteps with fire and steel,
with thy sword go search their secret dwellings;
when in triumph victorious thou returnest hither,

I have hoards unthought of'— but Húrin Thalion
suffered no longer silent wordless;
through clenchéd teeth in clinging pain,
'O accursed king', cried unwavering,
'thy hopes build not so high, Bauglir;
no tool am I for thy treasons vile,
who tryst nor troth ever true holdest —
seek traitors elsewhere.'
Then returned answer
Morgoth amazed his mood hiding:
'Nay, madness holds thee; thy mind wanders;
my measureless hoards are mountains high
my places secret piled uncounted
agelong unopened; Elfin silver
and gold in the gloom there glister pale;
the gems and jewels once jealous-warded
in the mansions of the Gods, who mourn them yet,
are mine, and a meed I will mete thee thence
of wealth to glut the Worm of Greed.'

Then Húrin, hanging, in hate answered:
'Canst not learn of thy lore when thou look'st on a foe,
O Bauglir unblest? Bray no longer
of the things thou hast thieved from the Three Kindreds!
In hate I hold thee. Thou are humbled indeed
and thy might is minished if thy murderous hope
and cruel counsels on a captive sad
must wait, on a weak and weary man.'
To the hosts of Hell his head then he turned:
'Let thy foul banners go forth to battle,
ye Balrogs and Orcs; let your black legions
go seek the sweeping sword of Turgon.
Through the dismal dales you shall be driven wailing
like startled starlings from the stooks of wheat.
Minions miserable of master base,
your doom dread ye, dire disaster!
The tide shall turn; your triumph brief
and victory shall vanish. I view afar
the wrath of the Gods aroused in anger.'

Then tumult awoke, a tempest wild
in rage roaring that rocked the walls;

consuming madness seized on Morgoth,
yet with lowered voice and leering mouth
thus Thalion Erithámrod he threatened darkly:
'Thou has said it! See how my swift purpose
shall march to its mark unmarred of thee,
nor thy aid be asked, overweening
mortal mightless. I command thee gaze
on my deeds of power dreadly proven.
Yet if little they like thee, thou must look thereon
helpless to hinder or thy hand to raise,
and thy lidless eyes lit with anguish
shall not shut for ever, shorn of slumber
like the Gods shall gaze there grim, tearless,
on the might of Morgoth and the meed he deals
to fools who refuse fealty gracious.'

To Thangorodrim was the Thalion borne,
that mountain that meets the misty skies
on high over the hills that Hithlum sees
blackly brooding on the borders of the North.
There stretched on the stone of steepest peak
in bonds unbreakable they bound him living;
there the lord of woe in laughter stood,
and cursed him for ever and his kindred all
that should walk and wander in woe's shadow
to a doom of death and dreadful end.
There the mighty man unmovéd sat
but unveiled was his vision that he viewed afar
with eyes enchanted all earthly things,
and the weird of woe woven darkly
that fell on his folk — a fiend's torment.

In either version, this is a dramatic moment, and offers a rare close view of one of the Valar. Morgoth is mighty, to be sure, but has the self-important manner of an earthly tyrant. The passage also provides a background to the lives of Túrin, Morwin, and Nienor, who are always fated to have bad luck. In fact, they have been genuinely cursed by an evil power, though for Túrin at least, Tolkien leaves open the possibility that the hero's rashness or arrogance might also contribute to his downfall.

In our second selection, from early in the second version of the poem, Morwen (as her name was now spelled), ignorant of her husband's fate when he does not return from battle, has recently given birth to a daughter, Nienor – appropriately, the name means 'lamentation'. Worried that her son Túrin might come to be enslaved, Morwen decides to send him, accompanied by her servants Halog and Mailrond, to be fostered by Thingol in Doriath. This seems a wise choice, but it will lead Túrin to the unwitting relationship with Nienor which will end so tragically for both of them, while mother and son are parted from each other forever. We are left to wonder about the strength of Morgoth's curse versus the vagaries of free will.

MORWEN'S CHOICE, SECOND VERSION, LINES 304–345

[C] Came a day of summer when the dark silence
of the towering trees trembled dimly
to murmurs moving in the milder airs
far and faintly; flecked with dancing
sheen of silver and shadow-filtered
sudden sunbeams were the secret glades
where winds came wayward wavering softly
warm through the woodland's woven branches.
Then Morwen stood, her mourning hidden,
by the gate of her garth in a glade of Hithlum;
at her breast bore she her babe unweaned,
crooning lowly to its careless ears
a song of sweet and sad cadence,
lest she droop for anguish. Then the doors opened,
and Halog hastened neath a heavy burden,
and Mailrond the old to his mistress led
her gallant Túrin, grave and tearless,
with heart heavy as stone hard and lifeless,
uncomprehending his coming torment.
There he cried with courage, comfort seeking:
'Lo! quickly will I come from the courts afar,
I will long ere manhood lead to Morwen
a great tale of treasure and true comrades.'
He wist not the weird woven of Morgoth
nor the sundering sorrow that them swept between,
as farewells they took with faltering lips.
The last kisses and lingering words
are over and ended; and empty is the glen
in the dark forest, where the dwelling faded
in trees entangled. Then in Túrin woke

to woe's knowledge his bewildered heart,
that he wept blindly awakening echoes
sad resounding in sombre hollows,
as he called: 'I cannot, I cannot leave thee.
O! Morwen my mother, why makest me go?
The hills are hateful, where hope is lost;
O! Morwen my mother, I am meshed in tears,
for grim are the hills and my home is gone.'
And there came his cries calling faintly
down the dark alleys of the dreary trees,
that one there weeping weary on the threshold
heard how the hills said 'my home is gone.'

It may be relevant to note that Tolkien had a deep personal experience of the grief of parting. He was not much more than three when he said goodbye to his father, leaving him behind in Bloemfontein when Ronald Tolkien, his mother, and his brother left for England on a visit, with Arthur Tolkien to join them later, and just four when his father died half a world away less than a year later. Tolkien never returned to the land of his birth. Not too many years later, he was not quite thirteen when his mother passed away, and he and his brother were left with a guardian.

Our final selection, from near the end of the first version of the poem, is a description of autumn and winter in the lands around Nargothrond where Túrin lived and for a time was safe and content. Fuilin and his son Flinding are both Gnomes, among the Elves of Nargothrond. *Narog* 'torrent' is the name of the great river above which were built Nargothrond's hidden halls.

TÚRIN IN NARGOTHROND, FIRST VERSION, LINES 2081–2113

[D] Thus Fuilin and Flinding friendship showed him,
and their halls were his home, while high summer
waned to autumn and the western gales
the leaves loosened from the labouring boughs;
the feet of the forest in fading gold
and burnished brown were buried deeply;
a restless rustle down the roofless aisles
sighed and whispered. Lo! the Silver Wherry,
the sailing Moon with slender mast,
was filled with fires as of furnace golden
whose hold had hoarded the heats of summer,

whose shrouds were shaped   of shining flame
uprising ruddy   o'er the rim of Evening
by the misty wharves   on the margin of the world.
Thus the months fleeted   and mightily he fared
in the forest with Flinding,   and his fate waited
slumbering a season,   while he sought for joy
the lore learning   and the league sharing
of the Gnomes renowned   of Nargothrond.

The ways of the woods   he wandered far,
and the land's secrets   he learned swiftly
by winter unhindered   to weathers hardened,
whether snow or sleet   or slanting rain
from glowering heavens   grey and sunless
cold and cruel   was cast to earth,
till the floods were loosed   and the fallow waters
of sweeping Narog,   swollen, angry,
were filled with flotsam   and foaming turbid
passed in tumult;   or twinkling pale
ice-hung evening   was opened wide,
a dome of crystal   o'er the deep silence
of the windless wastes   and the woods standing
like frozen phantoms   under flickering stars.

Tolkien later reworked this passage as an independent idyll. The first of its three manuscripts has no title, but the second is headed *Storm over Narog*, and the third *Winter Comes to Nargothrond*. The second manuscript is developed from the first, with some of its alliteration becoming more taut, while the third, which we give below as E, has only a few changes from the second. Both the first and third texts are published in *The Lays of Beleriand*, pp. 128–9.

[E] The summer slowly   in the sad forest
waned and faded.   In the west arose
winds that wandered   over warring seas.
Leaves were loosened   from labouring boughs:
fallow-gold they fell,   and the feet buried
of trees standing   tall and naked,
rustling restlessly   down roofless aisles,
shifting and drifting.
                    The shining vessel
of the sailing moon   with slender mast,

with shrouds shapen   of shimmering flame,
uprose ruddy   on the rim of Evening
by the misty wharves   on the margin of the world.
With winding horns   winter hunted
in the weeping woods,   wild and ruthless;
sleet came slashing   and slanting hail
from glowering heaven   grey and sunless,
whistling whiplash   whirled by tempest.
The floods were freed   and fallow waters
sweeping seaward,   swollen, angry,
filled with flotsam,   foaming, turbid,
passed in tumult.   The tempest died.
Frost descended   from far mountains
steel-cold and still.   Stony glinting
icehung evening   was opened wide,
a dome of crystal   over deep silence,
over windless wastes   and woods standing
as frozen phantoms   under flickering stars.

In regard to *Winter Comes to Nargothrond*, and to the corresponding portion of *The Children of Húrin*, it is worth noting the similarities of subject (the change of seasons) and language between these verses and the earlier *Kortirion* poems (no. 40), as the leaves fall and fierce winter falls upon the land.

Christopher Tolkien speaks of *The Children of Húrin* as 'the most sustained embodiment' of his father's 'abiding love of the resonance and richness of sound that might be achieved in the ancient English metre' (*The Lays of Beleriand*, p. 1). In alliterative verse each line stands alone, rather than as one of a couplet or in conjunction with other lines in a rhyme scheme. The line is divided into two parts, or half-lines, as we have pointed out for earlier examples, with a pause (caesura) between them, usually marked in typography by an extended space. It is typical for the two stressed syllables in the first half-line (such as 'The *sum*mer *slow*ly' in *Winter Comes to Nargothrond*) and one of the two stressed syllables in the second half-line (such as 'in the *sad for*est') to begin with the same sound (in the first example, an *ess*). This creates a rhythm and aids in recitation. Early English poems, and many poems even of later periods, were meant to be read, in fact sung – indeed, most of Tolkien's writings, of all kinds, were written to please in the first instance the 'mind's ear' of the author.

Tom Shippey has written of alliterative English poetry, an ancient form, that it has changed over time with the language. 'Middle English, and even more Modern English, contain more unstressed syllables, more little filler-words (especially articles and prepositions) than Old English. . . . Since alliterative poetry is based overwhelmingly on stress, this makes its older formats hard to imitate' ('Alliterative Verse by Tolkien', p. 10). Tolkien described five basic patterns of Old English alliterative verse, based on the theories of Eduard Sievers, in his essay on translating *Beowulf* (*Prefatory Remarks on Prose Translation of 'Beowulf'*) made for the 1940 edition of John R. Clark Hall's *Beowulf and the Finnesburg Fragment* (quoted in this book from *The Monsters and the Critics and Other Essays*, published there as *On Translating Beowulf*).

When discussing *The Children of Húrin* in his paper 'Tolkien's Development as a Writer of Alliterative Poetry in Modern English' (2013), Shippey comments that the impression the poem made on him was 'one of strain' as Tolkien struggled to fit Modern English into Old English forms. A sample of only five lines from the poem is 'rhythmically restricted, and rather metrically licentious', following (more or less) several of the antique patterns – which Shippey examines in minute detail – and 'there are certainly other issues, involving word-order, sentence-structure, and focus, and these play their part in preventing Tolkien's verse here from feeling like his Old English models; but the wrestle with metre is perhaps fundamental' (pp. 16, 17). Shippey admits, however, that such criticisms possibly are of no matter to readers who know nothing of Old English verse schemes. Tolkien himself does not seem to have been concerned in his poem as much with mechanical consistency of style as he was to create the right literary atmosphere.

Tolkien also addressed in his essay for the Clark Hall volume the choice of words when translating a work from an earlier era. 'You will misrepresent the first and most salient characteristic of the style and flavour of the author,' he said, 'if . . . you deliberately eschew the traditional literary and poetic diction which we now possess in favour of the current and trivial' (*The Monsters and the Critics and Other Essays*, p. 55). He applied this same concept to his own works like *The Children of Húrin* (and *The Lord of the Rings*), in which characters and events are set in an ancient time relative to our own, and which are full of what Tolkien in his essay on translation called 'high sentence'. In such circumstances, for heroes and kings and divine beings, the modern idiom would simply sound false. When Morgoth says to Húrin, 'Knowest thou my name, or need'st be told what hope he has who is haled to Angband' and Húrin replies, 'I know and I hate. For that knowledge I fought thee by fear unfettered, nor fear I now', the modern alternative – 'Do you know who I am, and what I can do to you?' 'I know, and I'm not afraid' – would be without drama or feeling. On a more practical level, Tolkien's choice of archaic words, and sometimes giving them in an order different from that expected in Modern English – Old English syntax was more flexible – allowed him greater opportunity to achieve his desired effects of sound and rhythm in the alliterative line.

Although Tolkien abandoned work on the alliterative *Children of Húrin* in 1925, in the early 1930s he began to write another version of the story of Túrin in rhyming couplets; see no. 130.

A51: Christopher Tolkien could not give a meaning for the prefix in *Delu-Morgoth*. Arden R. Smith has suggested to us that it may be connected with the initial element in *Deldúwath* 'Deadly Nightshade'.

A65: The 'accursed people' are Morgoth's enemies captured, like Húrin, in the Battle of Unnumbered Tears.

A74: Morgoth refers to Elves, specifically Turgon and his people, as 'foes of the Gods'. Morgoth himself is a 'god', i.e. a Vala, but the Elves are not enemies of the Valar in general, only of Morgoth. In l. A80, Morgoth refers to 'the jealous Gods', i.e. his fellow Valar, but he is jealous of them, not the reverse.

A82: Morgoth's promise of 'wealth to glut the Worm of Greed' could be metaphorical, i.e. as much wealth as can be imagined, or a comment on the avarice of dragons (worms).

A85: Here the term 'Three Kindreds' refers to three kindreds of the Elves. In *The Book of Lost Tales* these were the Teleri, the Noldoli (Gnomes), and the Solosimpi. Later the Teleri became the Vanyar, the Noldoli the Noldor, and the Solosimpi the Teleri. In poem no. 168 the name is applied to Elves, Dwarves, and Men.

A98: 'Lord of Woe', i.e. Morgoth.

B185: *Tryst* 'make an agreement' and *troth* 'pledge one's word' both have a connotation of truth and trust. Húrin rejects Morgoth's offer, vowing ever to be true to his people.

B228: Húrin will have 'lidless eyes' in the sense that he will see everything, unsleeping, so as to witness the tragic fate of his family.

B246: In this line, 'the weird of woe woven darkly', and in C327, 'He wist not the weird woven of Morgoth', *weird* has the sense of 'fate' or 'destiny', a concept in Anglo-Saxon culture, here tied also to the figurative web woven by Morgoth, i.e. his curse on Húrin and his family.

D2088: We have not found an independent representation of the Moon as a wherry, but it is of a piece with other fanciful depictions of heavenly objects, and not unrelated to the 'gleaming galleon' in which Éarendel sailed among the stars. See also poem no. 16, with similar phrasing to present texts D and E, e.g. 'margin of the world'. In E20 the 'Silver Wherry' becomes a 'shining vessel'.

68

The Clerkes Compleinte (?1922–*c.* 1925)

For *The Clerkes Compleinte* we unfortunately have no extant drafts before its publication in the Leeds magazine *The Gryphon* for December 1922, as by 'N.N.' In essays cited below, Tom Shippey has suggested that these initials stand for 'No Name', while Jill Fitzgerald posed that they could be an abbreviation for 'Nomen Nescio', a phrase meant to convey 'I do not know the name' (of the author). The printed title of the poem reads 'The Clerke's Compleinte', with an erroneous apostrophe; this is one of many typographic flaws in the *Gryphon* text, probably due to a compositor or editor misreading (or misunderstanding) the work – it is a pastiche wholly in Middle English. Tolkien marked a copy of the printed poem with at least eleven likely corrections (as far as we can tell without an earlier text), but also several probable alterations. An extant typescript, made with the purple ribbon associated with Tolkien's years at Leeds, postdates publication and shares some of the alterations he marked on the cutting.

The latest text of the poem is a manuscript, which Tolkien wrote using lettering and spelling conventions of the Middle English period, such as the thorn (*þ*). Christopher Tolkien identified its paper as a kind used in Oxford examinations, which his father could have acquired when he served as an external examiner for the English Final Honour School at Oxford in June 1924; it seems more likely, however, that he used it after his return to Oxford in October 1925, as he continued to use the same stock for many years. At some point, he lightly annotated the manuscript, most significantly at the end of the first section where he changed the clerks' (that is, students') destination from Leeds to Oxford.

Since these texts of the poem are largely identical, we have transcribed only the latest, manuscript copy (before revision), but for ease of reading have eschewed its early letterforms, rendered *u* as *v* where appropriate, and spelled out 'and' which Tolkien wrote as Tironian *et* (⁊, an abbreviation for Latin 'and' preserved in Anglo-Saxon writing and in Irish Gaelic). We have, however, retained *y* where later English spelling would have *i* (such as *nygh*; in fact, usage varied), and we have dots above where Tolkien included them to indicate the stressed *e* (*ė*). Errors, alterations, and annotations are described in our notes. The Middle English poem (A) is followed by our translation (B).

[A]

Whanne that Octobre mid his schoures derke
The erthe hath dreint, and wetė windes cherke
and swoghe in naked braunches colde and bare,
and th' oldė sonne is hennes longe yfare;
whan misti cloudes blake ymeind with smoke
her yen blenden and her throtes choke,
and frosty Eurus with his kenė teth
ech man forwelked biteth that him fleth,
and wrecchė cattes youlen umbewhiles,
that slepen nat, bot wandren on the tiles
(so priketh hem nature in her corages) —
than thinken folk to doon her avantages,
and seken hem faire educacioun
in yonge dayes of the sessioun;
and specially from every schires ende
in al the north to Leedės clerkes wende,
and in the derkest toune of Yorkeschire
seken of lore welles depe and schire!

Bifel that in that sesoun dim and mat,
in Leedes alte dores as I sat,
at morne was come in to tho halles hye
wel nygh fyve hondred in my companye
of newė clerkes in an egre presse,
langages olde that wolden lerne, I gesse,
of Fraunce or Engelonde or Spayne or Ruce,
tho tonges harde of Hygh Almayne and Pruce;
or historye, or termes queinte of lawe —
yet nas bot litel Latin in her mawe,
and bolde men, alas, ther were yet lece
that thoghten wrestle with the tonge of Grece,
or doon her hedes aken with etyk
and with philosophye malencolyk.

And yit an heep was ther so huge ythronge,
unnethe mighte I tellen clerkes yonge
that wolde lerne how men in fattes depe
with queynte odoures hydes sethe and stepe,
or weven wolle in webbes softe and fayre,
or brennen col and fylen nat the ayre!
Ther soghte an huge prees matematyk

and fragraunt chymistrie and sleigh physyk,
and mani uncouth sciencė for the nones [thenones]
of floures, fissches, or of oldė stones.

Ther mani vois gan maken swich a din
the hevy ayres schooke, and many a pin
unherd ther fil [fel] upon tho flores wyde,
til that men criden hy myn ere biside
of fees and of examinacioun,
and axede of matriculacioun,
and wher I hadde of Godes faire grace
by aventure ychaunced hit to pace.
Thogh maystres hadde I mo than thryės ten,
and wysdom of an heep of lerned men
that were of lore expert and curious,
yet couthe I nat namore than can a mous
of swich lettrure, ne wiste I what they mente.
Lo! fro the halles swithe men me sente
to dwellen al a yeer withoute yate
and pleynen me of myne unkyndė fate,
withoute yates al ayeer [a yeer] to dwelle
ne durrė drynken of the clerė welle!

[B] When October with his dark showers
has drained the earth, and wet winds crackle
and groan in naked branches cold and bare,
and the old sun is gone far away,
when black clouds mingled with smoke
blind the eyes and choke the throats,
and the frigid East Wind with his sharp teeth
bites every wanderer who flees him,
and wretched cats yowl bewhiles,
that sleep not, but wander on the tiles
(so Nature pricks them in their hearts)
then folk think to do something to their advantage,
and seek a fair education
in the early days of term;
and specially from every shire's end
in all the North to Leeds they wend
and in the darkest town of Yorkshire
seek the well of lore deep and clear!

Befell it in that season dim and drear
in Leeds as I sat by the doors,
at morning there came into those high halls
well nigh five hundred in my company
new clerks in an eager press,
to learn old languages, I guess,
of France or England, or Spain or Russia,
those difficult tongues of High Germany or Prussia,
or history, or quaint terms of law —
yet there was but little Latin in their bellies,
and fewer bold men, alas,
that thought to wrestle with the Greek tongue,
or make their heads ache with ethics
and with melancholy philosophy.
And yet there was so numerous a throng
that it was hard to count the young clerks
that would learn how here in deep vats
with quaint odours men boil and soak hides,
or weave wool in fabrics soft and fair,
or burn coal without fouling the air!
There many sought mathematics
and fragrant chemistry and cunning physic,
and many strange sciences of the moment
of flowers, fishes, or of old stones.
There many voices make such a din
the hot airs shook, and many a pin
unheard there fell upon those wide floors,
till men beside me cried high in my ear
of fees and of examination,
and asked about matriculation,
and whether I had by God's fair grace
by adventure chanced to pass.
Though mastery of skills I had more than thrice ten,
and the wisdom of a heap of learned men
expert in lore and curious,
yet knowledge I had, any more than a mouse
of such letters, nor did I know what they meant.
Lo! from the halls very quickly men sent me
to dwell for a year outside the gates
and complain of my unkind fate,
outside the gates all the year to dwell
not daring to drink of the clear well!

The *Gryphon* text was reprinted in the Tolkien journal *Arda* for 1984, with a commentary and translation by Tom Shippey; *Arda* editor Beregond (Anders Stenström) had discovered the poem while searching volumes of *The Gryphon* for possible contributions by Tolkien. Shippey argues for Tolkien's authorship of the work, and discusses the poet's expert use of Middle English vocabulary and phonetics. He points to one conscious modernism, *pace* in line 50, i.e. to pass an examination in order to matriculate, or enrol in a college or university. '"Matriculation" itself is not recorded in Middle English,' Shippey writes,

> but follows such an obvious route of derivation from Latin that it could easily be imagined as existing in M.E. [Middle English]. 'Pass', however, though very common as a word from an early period, is never recorded in the sense 'pass an examination' till 1600 – and even then the *Oxford English Dictionary* citation is unconvincing. It seems a nineteenth-century phrase, and of course a nineteenth-century idea, dating from the increasing 'mechanisation' of education. The author of 'The Clerkes Compleinte' clearly put it in as a comic *anachronism*, contrasting strongly with his usual careful use of Middle English words like 'cherke', 'ymeind', 'forwelked' (and many more, again not always recognised by the printer . . .). [p. 5]

In the 1986 number of *Arda* there appeared 'The Clerkes Compleinte Revisited', confirming Tolkien's authorship of the poem and reproducing the manuscript copy, with comments by Christopher Tolkien, followed by an extensive account of variations in the texts (supplied by Christopher to *Arda* in photocopy).

The manuscript text was transcribed by Jill Fitzgerald in 'A "Clerkes Compleinte": Tolkien and the Division of Lit. and Lang.' (2009), retaining its early letterforms. Fitzgerald comments that Tolkien replaces in his poem 'the freshness and vitality of springtime' in Chaucer's General Prologue to the *Canterbury Tales* with 'the chill of fall', among other inversions. *The Clerkes Compleinte*, she feels, registers Tolkien's 'private tone on the matter of philology: a deeply personal sense of marginalization and a sense of professional lament . . .' (p. 51). Part of his brief as the relatively new Reader in English Language at Leeds, given him by George S. Gordon as head of the newly remodelled English Department, was to encourage the study of philology, and that this was not a popular pursuit is reflected in his poem. As Fitzgerald writes, 'the clerk-narrator is timid and hesitant about his interest in languages, until he is finally frightened away from pursuing them in his studies. The din of those registering for vocational studies . . . is overwhelming to him and, in the end, the clerk is ushered out of the hall and left to lament his fate for a year' (p. 51). The University of Leeds, formed in 1904 out of the nineteenth-century Leeds School of Medicine and Yorkshire College of Science, was known better in Tolkien's day for its emphasis on scientific and technical subjects than for the study of language or literature.

It is obvious that *The Clerkes Compleinte* is modelled on the General Prologue from its opening line, which echoes Chaucer's 'Whanne that Aprille with his schoures soote' ('When that April with his soothing showers'), wickedly changed to October, and the start of autumn term, with 'schoures derke'. The parenthetical line 11, 'so priketh hem nature in her corages', is line 11 of the General Prologue verbatim. As Shippey points out in *Arda* 1984, the two poems share phrases as well in lines 15 ('from every schires ende') and 19 ('Bifel that in that sesoun'), and 'wysdom of an heep of lerned men' in Tolkien's line 52 is borrowed from line 575 of the General Prologue. Shippey also relates Tolkien's line 28 to the final line of Chaucer's 'Man of Laws Tale' ('Ther is but litel Latyn in my mawe'), to which we would add that 'termes queinte of lawe' in Tolkien's line 27 appears in the penultimate line of Chaucer's tale. Fitzgerald comments that Ruce and Pruce (lines 25, 26) are among the places the Knight is said to have seen (General Prologue, lines 53, 54). One could find more such borrowings, which reflect Tolkien's deep knowledge of Chaucer's works, which he taught at Leeds and much later at Oxford.

In the following notes, for brevity we will refer to the Gryphon *printing of the poem as A, to the typescript as B, and to the manuscript (text A above) as C:*

6: In B Tolkien added a diaeresis over the first letter of 'yen' ('eyes') to indicate its pronunciation as a vowel rather than a consonant, but omitted it in C. (There are no diacritical marks in A.)

14: Tolkien inserted (by hand) over-dots in B which do not appear in C (where the word form is identical): 'yongė' in this line, 'Yorkėschire' in l. 17, 'boldė' in l. 29, 'Unnethė' in l. 34, 'hugė' in l. 39, and 'withoutė' in l. 57. But in C, l. 16, is 'Leedės' which has no over-dot in B.

16: In A and B, 'North' is capitalized, but not in C. In A this line ends 'don they wende' ('down they wend'); on his copy of A Tolkien marked 'don they' to be changed to 'clerkes', and it is the latter reading in B and C. In the margin of C Tolkien lightly wrote, sometime after his move to Oxford in 1925, 'londe to Oxenforde þei wend[e]', to replace 'north to Leedės clerkes wende' if the poem were to be given an Oxford cast.

17: In A and B Leeds is 'the fairest toune' in Yorkshire; in C it has become 'the derkest toune', perhaps in contrast to Tolkien's beloved Oxford, to which he had returned by the time he wrote out the manuscript. Leeds was, in contrast, an industrial city long known for its textile mills and (then) dingy and polluted, a state to which Tolkien probably alludes in ll. 35 and following.

18: In A and B this line reads 'Seken of lore the welle [B: wellė] depe and schire'. Tolkien considered whether to delete 'the' and make 'wellė' plural ('wellės'). In C the line reads 'seken of lore welles depe and clere', but 'clere' seems to have been an error in writing, and Tolkien emended it to 'schire'.

22: In C next to this line Tolkien wrote 'Students are enrolled', to explain what the 'fyve hondred' clerks were doing, i.e. choosing their fields of study.

33: In A and B this line reads 'Bot yonder was an heep so huge ythronge'; Tolkien marked 'Bot yonder' in B to be changed to 'And mid hem' ('And with them'). C has 'And yit an heep was ther so huge ythronge'.

34: In A and B this line ends 'counte tho clerkes yonge'. On his copy of A Tolkien marked 'counte tho' ('count those') to be changed to 'tellen' ('count, tally'), while on B the replacement phrase is 'telle at', with a further change considered in light pencil in the margin, 'hem' ('them') for 'at'. C has 'tellen clerkes yonge'.

35: In A this line is 'That wolden lerne how here in fattes depe'; B is identical except for 'woldė' for 'wolden'. C has 'that woldc lerne how men in fattes depe'.

36: In A and B this line has 'queynte odour'. C has plural 'queynte odoures'.

37: In A and B this line begins 'And', in C 'or'.

39: In A this line reads 'And soghte a grete prees matematyk'; Tolkien marked 'a grete' to be changed to 'an hugė'. In B the line was probably typed as in A, but 'grete' was erased and 'an hugė' written in by hand (adding 'n' to existing 'a'); also, Tolkien wrote faintly in the margin 'Ther' to replace 'And'. C has 'Ther soghte an huge prees matematyk'. Near ll. 39–42 in C Tolkien wrote in the margin by way of explanation, 'large queue for "applied science"', i.e. mathematics, chemistry, etc.

42: Flowers, fishes, and 'old stones' may be taken as further disciplines in the applied sciences – botany, marine biology, geology – though they were also features in medieval herbals, for their (real or supposed) medicinal qualities.

43: In A and B this line reads 'The mani vois ther maden swich a din'. C has 'Ther mani vois gan maken swich a din'.

44: In A this line begins 'The hoote aires schook' ('The hot airs shook'); Tolkien marked the phrase to be changed to 'The hevi aires schoke' (with the same meaning, but *hevi* suggests more than ordinary heat). In B the line as typed probably began 'The hoote aires schook'; Tolkien erased '-oote' of 'hoote' and wrote 'evi' (for 'hevi') by hand, and also emended 'schook' to 'schooke'. C begins 'The hevy ayres schooke'. Next to this line in C Tolkien wrote, 'female students scatter hairpins (now obsolete)', the final comment suggesting that some time had passed between the note and the composition of the poem.

46: In A this line reads 'Till that on cride schille min ere biside'; Tolkien emended 'Till' to 'Til', and marked 'schille' ('shrill') to be changed to 'hy' ('high', i.e. high-pitched). In B the line reads 'Til that on cridė hy myn ere biside', with a lightly pencilled note 'men an don'. C has 'til that men criden hy myn ere biside'.

49: In A and B this line ends 'goddes ful faire grace', in C 'Godes faire grace'.

54: In A and B (A with an error) this line ends 'no more than can a mous', in C 'namore than can a mous'.

55: In A and B this line ends 'he mente'; in B Tolkien marked 'he' to be changed to 'þei' ('they'). C has 'þey mente'.

56: In A this line begins 'And', in B and C 'Lo!' Tolkien marked 'Lo!' as a change or emendation to A.

69

Iúmonna Gold Galdre Bewunden · *The Hoard* (?1922–61)

Tolkien wrote the first version of this poem, entitled *Iúmonna Gold Galdre Bewunden*, probably late in 1922; in January 1923 it was published in the Leeds magazine *The Gryphon*. There are no surviving drafts, for any of its versions. Its earliest texts, each identical to the other except in format, are two finished typescripts made with a purple ribbon. One is divided into five distinct parts, while the other is similarly in five sections, but within each part the lines are in groups of two or four. Since only the former copy includes a revision reflected in the printed poem, it was undoubtedly this which Tolkien supplied to *The Gryphon*, whose editor or compositor introduced errors. In our transcription (A) we have preferred the most compact of these arrangements.

[A]

There were elves olden and strong spells
Under green hills in hollow dells
They sang o'er the gold they wrought with mirth,
In the deeps of time in the young earth,
Ere Hell was digged, ere the dragons' brood
Or the dwarves were spawned in dungeons rude;
And men there were in a few lands
That caught some cunning of their mouths and hands.
Yet their doom came and their songs failed,
And greed that made them not to its holes haled
Their gems and gold and their loveliness,
And the shadows fell on Elfinesse.

There was an old dwarf in a deep grot
That counted the gold things he had got,
That the dwarves had stolen from men and elves
And kept in the dark to their gloomy selves.
His eyes grew dim and his ears dull,
And the skin was yellow on his old skull;
There ran unseen through his bony claw
The faint glimmer of gems without a flaw.

He heard not feet that shook the earth,
Nor the rush of wings, nor the brazen mirth
Of dragons young in their fiery lust;
His hope was in gold and in jewels his trust.
Yet a dragon found his dark cold hole,
And he lost the earth and the things he stole.

There was an old dragon under an old stone
Blinking with red eyes all alone.
The flames of his fiery heart burnt dim;
He was knobbed and wrinkled and bent of limb;
His joy was dead and his cruel youth,
But his lust still smouldered and he had no ruth.
To the slime of his belly the gems stuck thick
And his things of gold he would snuff and lick
As he lay thereon and dreamed of the woe
And grinding anguish thieves should know
That ever set finger on one small ring;
And dreaming uneasy he stirred a wing.
He heard not the step nor the harness clink,
Till the fearless warrior at his cavern's brink
Called him come out and fight for his gold,
Yet iron rent his heart with anguish cold.

There was an old king on a high throne;
His white beard was laid on his knees of bone,
And his mouth savoured nor meat nor drink,
Nor his ears song; he could only think
Of his huge chest with carven lid
Where the gold and jewels unseen lay hid
In a secret treasury in the dark ground,
Whose mighty doors were iron-bound.
The swords of his warriors did dull and rust,
His glory was tarnished and his rule unjust,
His halls hollow and his bowers cold,
But he was king of elfin gold.
He heard not the horns in the mountain pass,
He smelt not the blood on the trodden grass,
Yet his halls were burned and his kingdom lost,
In a grave unhonoured his bones were tossed.

There is an old hoard in a dark rock
Forgotten behind doors none can unlock.
The keys are lost and the path gone,
The mound unheeded that the grass grows on;
The sheep crop it and the larks rise
From its green mantle, and no man's eyes
Shall find its secret, till those return
Who wrought the treasure, till again burn
The lights of Faery, and the woods shake,
And songs long silent once more awake.

Among Tolkien's papers is a cutting of the poem from *The Gryphon* which he emended and revised. He seems then to have set the work aside until at least the late 1920s. Its next iteration is in two typescripts made on Tolkien's Hammond machine, and following these, a fine calligraphic manuscript; we have transcribed the latter as B. All three of these texts are identical except for minor points of capitalization and punctuation.

[B] There were old elves and strong spells
under green hills in hollow dells
they sang o'er gold they wrought with mirth
in the deeps of time on the young earth,
ere Hell was digged, ere the dragons' brood
or the dwarves were spawned in dungeons rude:
there were few men in far lands
that caught the cunning of their mouths and hands.
Their doom came, and their songs failed;
Greed that wrought not to its holes haled
their gems, their pearls, their carved gold;
o'er Elfinesse the shadows rolled.

There was an old dwarf in a deep grot
who counted the golden things he had got,
that the dwarves had stolen from men and elves
and kept in darkness to their gloomy selves.
His eyes grew dim, and his ears dull;
the skin was yellow on his old skull;
there ran unseen through his bony claw
the glimmer of gems without a flaw.
He heard not the feet that shook the earth,
nor the rush of wings, nor the brazen mirth

of dragons young in their fiery lust:
his hope was in gold and in jewels his trust.
Yet a dragon found his dark cold hole,
and he lost the earth and the things he stole.

There was an old dragon under a grey stone
blinking with red eyes all alone.
The flames of his fiery heart burnt dim;
he was knobbed and wrinkled and bent of limb,
his joy was dead and his cruel youth,
but his lust smouldered, and he knew no ruth.
To the slime of his belly the gems stuck thick,
and his things of gold he would snuff and lick
as he lay thereon, or dream of the woe
and grinding anguish thieves should know
that ever set finger on one small ring;
and dreaming uneasy he stirred a wing.
He heard no step, nor the harness clink,
till the fearless warrior at his cavern's brink
him summoned forth to defend his gold.
Iron rent his heart with anguish cold.

There was an old king on a high throne:
his white beard laid on knees of bone;
his mouth savoured nor meat nor drink,
nor his ears song; he could only think
of his huge chest with carven lid
where the gold and jewels unseen lay hid
in a secret treasury in the dark ground
whose mighty doors were iron-bound.
The swords of his warriors were dull with rust,
his glory tarnished, his rule unjust,
his halls hollow, his bowers cold,
but king he was of elvish gold.
He heard not the horns in the mountain pass,
he smelt not the blood on the trodden grass;
yet his halls were burned, his kingdom lost,
in grave unhonoured his bones were tossed.

There is an old hoard in a dark rock,
forgotten behind doors none can unlock;
the keys are lost and the path gone,

the mound unheeded that the grass grows on;
the sheep crop it and the larks rise
from the green mantle, and no man's eyes
shall find its secret, till those return
who wrought the treasure, till again burn
the lights of Faery, and the woods shake,
and songs long silent once more awake.

As with text A, it is not clear why Tolkien should have made multiple copies of B; we can only guess that he was curious to try out different modes of presentation. One of the typescripts is centred on the page, the other flush at the left margin and with the common word *There* italicized at the start of each stanza. In the manuscript, each stanza begins with a decorative initial *T*.

Possibly within a short time, Tolkien substantially revised *Iúmonna Gold Galdre Bewunden*, especially its first three stanzas, again using his Hammond typewriter. The poem, given here as C, was now ten lines longer than before, and in a few places closely approached its final form.

[C]

There were old elves and strong spells
under green hills in hollow dells
they sang o'er gold they wrought with mirth
in the deeps of time on the young earth,
ere Hell was digged, ere its mouth yawned,
ere dwarf was bred or dragon spawned.
there were wise men in far lands
who learned lore of their lips and hands.
The moon was new and the sun young;
silver their voices and gold their tongue:
there were wise men in far lands
who learned lore of their lips and hands.
Yet their doom fell and their songs failed,
by hate hunted and by lust trailed.
Greed that wrought not, nor with mouth smiled,
in dark holes their wealth piled,
engraven silver and carved gold:
o'er Elfinesse the shadows rolled.

There was an old dwarf in a deep grot
fingering the silver and gold he had got,

that his kin stole from elves and men
to keep useless in a dark den.
His eyes grew dim and his ears dull,
the skin was yellow on his old skull;
through his bony claw there flowed unseen
flawless gems with a pale sheen.
He heard not feet that shook the earth,
nor rush of wings, nor the brazen mirth
of fiery dragons in their young lust:
his hope was in gold and in jewels his trust.
Yet a dragon found him in his cold hole,
and he lost the earth and all he stole.

There was an old dragon under grey stone,
blinking with red eyes, dark, alone.
His joy was dead and his youth spent;
he was knobbed and wrinkled, and his limbs bent;
in his heart's furnace the flame waned,
but his lust smouldered and his hate remained.
To his belly's slime the gems stuck thick:
silver and gold he would snuff and lick,
his hard bed where of thieves he dreamed
that caught in his jaws writhed and screamed:
were a finger laid on his least ring
his wrath would wake and his fire spring.
Then his malice slept and his ears drooped —
at his doors darkling a shadow stooped;
he dreamed of wind and cool drink,
he heard not the step nor the mail clink.
Yet a young warrior with long sword
called him forth to defend his hoard.
His fire flickered and his old pride,
but the iron tore him, and his flame died.

There was an old king on a high throne:
his white beard was laid on knees of bone;
his mouth savoured nor meat nor drink,
nor his ears song; he could only think
of his huge chest with carven lid
where gems unseen and gold lay hid
in secret treasury in the dark ground
whose strong doors were iron-bound.

The swords of his warriors were dull with rust,
his glory tarnished, his rule unjust,
his halls hollow, and his bowers cold,
but king he was of elvish gold.
He heard not the horns in the mountain pass,
he smelt not the blood on the trodden grass,
yet his halls were burned, his kingdom lost,
in grave unhonoured his bones were tossed.

There is an old hoard in a dark rock,
forgotten behind doors none can unlock.
The keys are lost and the path gone,
the mound unheeded that the grass grows on;
the sheep crop it and the larks rise
from its green mantle, and no man's eyes
shall find its secret, till those return
who wrought the treasure, till again burn
the lights of Faery, and the woods shake,
and songs long silent once more awake.

Tolkien marked lines 7–8 of the typescript C to follow line 4 (i.e. after 'in the deeps of time on the young earth'), he lightly struck through 'there were' in line 9 and 'who learned' in line 10, and he blocked lines 11–16, for what purpose we cannot divine. But these revisions, or tentative revisions, became moot, as the next version was again considerably changed. This new text is found in two manuscripts; we have transcribed the first of these, as D, illustrating revisions Tolkien made in the course of writing or soon afterward.

[D] When the moon was new and the sun young
of silver and gold the gods sung.
In the green grass [was >] they silver spilled,
and the white waters [were >] they with gold filled.
Ere the pit was dug [and >] or Hell yawned,
ere dwarf was bred or dragon spawned,
there were [old elves >] elves of old, and strong spells
under green hills in hollow dells
they sang as they wrought many fair things,
the bright crowns of the elf-kings.
But their doom fell, and their song waned,
by iron hewn and by steel chained.
Greed that [wrought >] sang not, nor with mouth smiled,

in dark holes their wealth piled,
graven silver and [carved >] carven gold:
[o'er >] over [Elfinesse >] Elvenhome the shadow rolled.

There was an old dwarf in a dark [grot >] cave,
[fingering >] to silver and gold [he had got >] his fingers clave;
with hammer and tongs and anvil-stone
he worked his hands to the hard bone,
and coins he made and strings of rings,
and thought to buy the power of kings.
But his eyes grew dim, and his ears dull,
and the skin yellow on his old skull;
through his bony claw with a pale sheen
the stony jewels slipped unseen.
No feet he heard, though the earth quaked,
when the young dragon his thirst slaked,
and the stream smoked at his dark door,
and flames hissed on the dank floor.
He died alone in the red fire,
and his bones were ash in the hot mire.

There was an old dragon under grey stone;
his red eyes blinked as he lay alone.
His joy was dead and his youth spent,
he was knobbed and wrinkled, and his limbs bent,
[through >] with the long years to his gold chained;
in his heart's furnace the fire waned.
To his belly's slime gems stuck thick,
silver and gold he would snuff and lick —
he knew the place of the least ring
beneath the shadow of his [?worn >] black wing.
Of thieves he thought on his hard bed,
and dreamed that on their flesh he fed,
[and their blood drank, >] their bones crushed and their blood drank:
his ears drooped and his breath sank.
Mail-rings rang. He heard them not.
A voice echoed in his deep grot:
a young warrior with a bright sword
called him forth to defend his hoard.
His teeth were knives, and of horn his hide,
but iron tore him, and his flame died.

There was an old king on a high throne:
his white beard lay on knees of bone;
his mouth savoured neither meat nor drink,
nor his ears song; he could only think
of his huge chest with carven lid
where pale gems and gold lay hid,
in secret treasury in the dark ground
whose strong doors were iron-bound.
    The swords of his thanes were dull with rust,
his glory fallen, his rule unjust,
his halls hollow, his bowers cold,
but king he was of elvish gold.
He heard not the horns in the mountain-pass,
he smelt not the blood on the trodden grass,
[yet >] but his halls were burned, his kingdom lost
in a cold pit his bones were tossed.

There is an old hoard in a dark rock
forgotten behind doors none can unlock;
that grim gate no man can pass.
On the mound grows the green grass;
there sheep feed and the larks soar,
and the wind blows from the sea-shore.
While gods wait and the elves sleep,
its [dark >] old secret shall the earth keep.

Probably in 1937, Tolkien made a fair copy of this text for submission to the *Oxford Magazine*. An editor wrote Tolkien's name and address at the top of the manuscript, as an instruction to send him a proof when the text was set in type. The poem was published in the *Oxford Magazine* for 4 March 1937, as *Iumonna Gold Galdre Bewunden*, i.e. without the accent in the first word, omitted also in the manuscript title.

The phrase 'Iúmonna Gold Galdre Bewunden' is taken from line 3052 of the Old English poem *Beowulf*, a work with which Tolkien was closely concerned as an academic, but which he also knew well from his days as a student. It means, in Tolkien's own translation, 'the gold of bygone men was wound about with spells' (*Beowulf* (2014), p. 102), and refers to a great hoard gathered in ancient days. A dragon watches over it in a 'steep stone-barrow' on a 'high heath'. 'Therein went some nameless man, creeping in nigh to the pagan treasure; his hand seized a goblet deep, bright with gems. This the dragon did not after in silence bear' (*Beowulf*, p. 77). The poet then relates that 'someone . . . among men in days of yore' had concealed in a mound 'jewels of price and mighty heirlooms of a noble race. All of them death had taken in times before, and now he too alone of the proven warriors of his people, who longest walked the earth . . . hoped but for the same fate, that he might only a little space enjoy those longhoarded things.' At last, 'the tide of death touched at his heart', and a dragon came; for 'treasure in the ground it is ever his wont to seize, and there wise with many years he guards the heathen gold – no whit does it profit him' (*Beowulf*, pp.78, 79).

The *Beowulf* dragon features in Tolkien's seminal British Academy paper of 1936, *Beowulf: The Monsters and the Critics*, and prior to that was discussed by Tolkien in a series of lectures he gave at Oxford. Michael D.C. Drout, who published the lectures as *Beowulf and the Critics* (2002, 2nd ed. 2011) – the eventual title of the series – dates them to between August 1932 and October 1935. In these talks, Tolkien recited *Iúmonna Gold Galdre Bewunden* as one of two examples of modern dragon-verse, a playful digression from more serious study. It could be that the revisions that resulted in texts B and C of the poem were inspired by the Oxford lectures, and that Tolkien worked on it further once he was invited, probably in 1934, to speak to the British Academy.

The text of *Iúmonna Gold Galdre Bewunden* does not appear in either of the two manuscripts of the lecture series, but was written out separately, as the manuscript we have transcribed as D; its page numbers fill a gap in the pagination of the first *Beowulf and the Critics* manuscript. (It is nowhere to be found in the more formal British Academy address.) Drout included its text in his transcriptions of the lectures, at the point where Tolkien would have read it. Out of caution, Drout argues that it cannot be proved that text D was the version Tolkien had in mind when he referred to the poem for reading, nor can it be certain that the revisions he marked on its manuscript were made before the lecture series ended. Christopher Tolkien, however, writing in a note preserved in the Bodleian Library, was himself satisfied that this was indeed the pertinent text; and in addition to the evidence of pagination, we would point to a heading, '(1)', written by Tolkien above the title, a number we take to refer to the first of the two poems he chose to recite. (The second was by his friend C.S. Lewis.)

At some later date, Tolkien wrote on a cutting of the poem in the *Oxford Magazine* two lines to replace its final couplet: 'The old hoard shall the Night keep | while earth waits and the Elves sleep'. When the poem appeared in a new, probably professional typescript, the lines read 'The old hoard the Night shall keep, | while earth waits and the Elves sleep', bringing the text at last to its final form. The work was now entitled *The Hoard.* Its new title existed by 30 September 1946, when Tolkien used it to refer to a copy of the text he sent to his publisher George Allen & Unwin, with other poems, to help fill out a volume with his story *Farmer Giles of Ham*, then being considered for publication. This typescript may have been made for that occasion, in the event unnecessarily, as it was decided that the story could be published on its own.

Tolkien returned to *The Hoard* probably in the first half of November 1961, when considering which of his poems to include in *The Adventures of Tom Bombadil and Other Verses from the Red Book.* He sent a copy of the work to his publisher for consideration on 15 November 1961. On 6 December he advised the illustrator of the volume, Pauline Baynes, that she should treat *The Hoard* as a tale of the woes of 'successive (nameless) inheritors' of a treasure and 'a tapestry of antiquity' in which 'individual pity' is not to be deeply engaged. Moreover, having found it interesting that *The Hoard* was Baynes's favourite among the *Bombadil* poems, Tolkien described it as 'the least fluid [of them], being written in [a] mode rather resembling the oldest English verse' – that is, with an (unmarked) pause between each half-line (*Letters*, p. 443).

To complete the sequence of versions, we give here, as E, the final text of the poem, as published in the *Bombadil* volume, pp. 53–4, 56.

[E]

When the moon was new and the sun young
of silver and gold the gods sung.
In the green grass they silver spilled,
and the white waters they with gold filled.
Ere the pit was dug or Hell yawned,
ere dwarf was bred or dragon spawned,
there were elves of old, and strong spells
under green hills in hollow dells
they sang as they wrought many fair things,
the bright crowns of the elf-kings.
But their doom fell, and their song waned,
by iron hewn and by steel chained.
Greed that sang not, nor with mouth smiled,
in dark holes their wealth piled,
graven silver and carven gold:
over Elvenhome the shadow rolled.

There was an old dwarf in a dark cave,
to silver and gold his fingers clave;
with hammer and tongs and anvil-stone
he worked his hands to the hard bone,
and coins he made and strings of rings,
and thought to buy the power of kings.
But his eyes grew dim, and his ears dull,
and the skin yellow on his old skull;
through his bony claw with a pale sheen
the stony jewels slipped unseen.
No feet he heard, though the earth quaked,
when the young dragon his thirst slaked,
and the stream smoked at his dark door,
and flames hissed on the dank floor.
He died alone in the red fire,
and his bones were ash in the hot mire.

There was an old dragon under grey stone;
his red eyes blinked as he lay alone.
His joy was dead and his youth spent,
he was knobbed and wrinkled, and his limbs bent,
with the long years to his gold chained;
in his heart's furnace the fire waned.
To his belly's slime gems stuck thick,
silver and gold he would snuff and lick —
he knew the place of the least ring
beneath the shadow of his black wing.
Of thieves he thought on his hard bed,
and dreamed that on their flesh he fed,
their bones crushed and their blood drank:
his ears drooped and his breath sank.
Mail-rings rang. He heard them not.
A voice echoed in his deep grot:
a young warrior with a bright sword
called him forth to defend his hoard.
His teeth were knives, and of horn his hide,
but iron tore him, and his flame died.

There was an old king on a high throne:
his white beard lay on knees of bone;
his mouth savoured neither meat nor drink,
nor his ears song; he could only think

of his huge chest with carven lid
where pale gems and gold lay hid,
in secret treasury in the dark ground
whose strong doors were iron-bound.
The swords of his thanes were dull with rust,
his glory fallen, his rule unjust,
his halls hollow, his bowers cold,
but king he was of elvish gold.
He heard not the horns in the mountain-pass,
he smelt not the blood on the trodden grass,
but his halls were burned, his kingdom lost
in a cold pit his bones were tossed.

There is an old hoard in a dark rock
forgotten behind doors none can unlock;
that grim gate no man can pass.
On the mound grows the green grass;
there sheep feed and the larks soar,
and the wind blows from the sea-shore.
The old hoard the Night shall keep,
while earth waits and the Elves sleep.

In the fictional frame of the *Bombadil* collection, in which the poems are said to be from the Hobbits' 'Red Book of Westmarch', *The Hoard* is based 'on the lore of Rivendell, Elvish and Númenórean, concerning the heroic days at the end of the First Age [of Middle-earth]; it seems to contain echoes of the Númenorean tale of Túrin and Mim the Dwarf'. Rivendell, in *The Hobbit* and *The Lord of the Rings*, is an Elvish stronghold and said to be an important source of material for Hobbit historians. Númenor was an island kingdom of Men, founded after the fall of Morgoth; at the end of the Second Age, Númenóreans came to Middle-earth and established the realms of Arnor and Gondor.

Túrin Turambar, a Man, was one of the greatest warriors of the First Age (the years after Creation and the casting out of Morgoth); in 'The Silmarillion', as it developed in the 1950s, he spares the life of Mîm the Petty-dwarf. Mîm also figures in the mythology from its earlier tales, in connection with a dragon's hoard in the fortress of Nargothrond, though not at that time with Túrin: in the *Quenta Noldorinwa* (*c.* 1930) Mîm 'sat there in joy fingering the gold and gems, and letting them run ever through his hands; and he bound them to himself with many spells' (*The Shaping of Middle-earth*

(1986), p. 132; see also poem no. 185). The tales of Túrin and Mîm would not become generally known until *The Silmarillion*, edited by Christopher Tolkien from his father's papers, was published in 1977.

After one of his most ardent correspondents, Mrs Eileen Elgar, wrote to him in December 1963 with remarks about *The Hoard*, Tolkien sent a long reply on 5 March 1964, discussing the poem in connection with his mythology.

> 'The Hoard' purports to tell in brief the history of one of the 'hoards' of legend. It begins with the demiurgic making of silver and gold (and other aspects of 'matter'), by the 'gods' (*sc.* not God, but the *Valar*) not at the Creation, but in the carrying out of the idea and vision of the World propounded by the One [God]. It passes to the use made of such things by the Elves, as 'artists' with the original motive only of producing beautiful things. But these things of beauty excited the envy and greed of the evil rebel Vala [Melko, Morgoth] and his servants. . . . They drove away the Elves and plundered them, and hence arose the dark and secret hoards, in some cases possessed and guarded by a dragon. In the heroic age of Men these hoards were sometimes acquired by great warriors, but all dragon-hoards were cursed, and bred in men the dragon-spirit: in possessors an obsession with more ownership, in others a fierce desire to take the treasure for their own by violence or treachery.
>
> Naturally dragon-possession usually preceded acquisition by Men or by Dwarves, but the poet of these verses has arranged the sequence in this order to bring the dragon-slaying into relation with the mortal king, and provide a series of three violent deaths. Evidently not a lover of Dwarves, but one who looked only on their bad side (or knew no other side). He had some justification, for though not servants of the Evil Vala, the Dwarves were by nature and origin specially open to the degeneration of their love and admiration of works of 'craft' into a fierce possessiveness.
>
> The tale of Túrin and Mîm the Dwarf, mentioned in the Preface [to *The Adventures of Tom Bombadil*], is one of the main strands in the 'Silmarillion'. In it a dwarf in fact follows the dragon. The story concerns the great hoard of Nargothrond, which contained much of the treasure and works of Elvish art that had been preserved from the wreckage of the Elven-kingdoms under the assaults of the Dark Lord [Melko/Morgoth] from his unassailable stronghold of Thangorodrim in

> the North. Nargothrond was finally defeated and ravaged and fell into the possession of the first of the Great Dragons. . . . Eventually [Túrin] slew the Dragon, but the Dragon achieved Túrin's death. Mîm the dwarf then took possession of the unguarded hoard in desolate Nargothrond. [*Concerning 'The Hoard'*, Heritage Auctions online, 16 July 2022]

That there was always some connection between the poem and 'The Silmarillion' is suggested by the name 'Elfinesse', later 'Elvenhome', consistently at the end of the first stanza, and by the poem's description of Elves, firstborn of the so-called Children of Ilúvatar, being in existence before 'Hell was digged' – i.e. constructed, if *Hell* can mean Melko's fortress, the 'Hell of Iron' – and before the Dwarves were created. And yet, we wonder if Tolkien's mythology was the foundational inspiration for *Iúmonna Gold Galdre Bewunden*, or if he borrowed for his poem convenient details from 'The Silmarillion' as it developed, taking elements also from *Beowulf*, and fitted the result into the larger context he described to Mrs Elgar only in its final versions – there were no 'gods' in texts earlier than D – and in particular after the poem was published as *The Hoard* and Tolkien began to receive questions about it.

In any case, the work has long stood on its own, its readers unaware (or uninformed) of any deliberate mythological underpinning, as a moral story of peoples and beings possessed by the deadly desire to possess. As Tom Shippey has summarized, the poem traces

> in successive stanzas the transmission of a treasure from elf to dwarf to dragon to hero and ending with the picture of an old and miserly king overthrown by his rivals and leaving his gold to oblivion. All the characters in it are the same: they begin with vitality, mirth and courage, they end in age, wealth and squalor. Their decline is caused by gold. [*The Road to Middle-earth* (1992), p. 80]

The work expresses philosophical ideas about greed and power which one finds also in Tolkien's other works, especially *The Hobbit*, where Thorin is 'bewildered' by the dragon's treasure and lusts for the Arkenstone. (Thorin himself speaks the counter-argument as he dies: 'If more of us valued food and cheer and song above hoarded gold, it would be a merrier world.')

In the earliest texts of *Iúmonna Gold Galdre Bewunden* the treasure held by the 'old dwarf' had been stolen by dwarves (later, 'his kin') 'from men and elves'; and this accords with Tolkien's depiction of Dwarves in *The Book of Lost Tales*, where they are evil, grasping, and treacherous. By version D of the poem, from the early 1930s, Tolkien no longer disparaged the Dwarves as a people, only the 'old dwarf' as an individual. They are no longer 'spawned', like some lower life-form, but 'bred'. One can safely attribute Tolkien's change of heart to his writing of *The Hobbit*, with its generally sympathetic, heroic, even humorous dwarves, beginning in the late 1920s.

Smaug, the dragon in *The Hobbit* with his 'waistcoat of fine diamonds', is a close cousin to the *Hoard* dragon to whose belly 'gems stuck thick' and who 'knew the place of the least ring | beneath the shadow of his black wing'. In Chapter 12 of *The Hobbit* Bilbo enters Smaug's lair and steals a cup, just as an unnamed thief pilfers from the dragon in *Beowulf*; Smaug soon misses the object, though it is only the tiniest part of a vast treasure. 'Dragons', Tolkien explains in *The Hobbit*, 'may not have much real use for all their wealth, but they know it to an ounce as a rule, especially after long possession'. The dragon of the *Hoard* poems is recalled in *The Hobbit* also in Smaug's 'uneasy dream', 'in which a warrior, altogether insignificant in size but provided with a bitter sword and great courage, figured most unpleasantly' – a nightmare, compared with his *Hoard* counterpart's pleasant dream of feasting on the flesh of thieves and crushing their bones.

A close comparison of the different versions of Tolkien's poem is provided by Tom Shippey in his essay 'The Versions of "The Hoard"' (2001), and an analysis of the final version (*The Hoard*) is given by Nancy Martsch in 'Tolkien's Poetic Use of the Old English and Latinate Vocabulary: A Study of Three Poems from *The Adventures of Tom Bombadil*' (2013).

In 1967 Tolkien made a professional recording of *The Hoard* for the album *Poems and Songs of Middle Earth*. It was later reissued.

A7–8: The poet suggests that before the elves perished, some men learned from them both speech and crafts.

A22: *The Gryphon* misprinted 'nor the brazen mirth' as 'not the brazen mirth'. We unknowingly perpetuated this error when we reprinted the *Gryphon* text in the 2014 edition of *The Adventures of Tom Bombadil and Other Verses from the Red Book*, and the same occurred in reprints in *The Annotated Hobbit* by Douglas A. Anderson and *Beowulf and the Critics* by Michael D.C. Drout.

A30: *The Gryphon* misprinted 'He was knobbed' as 'His was knobbed'. There were also punctuation errors in ll. 49 and 56.

A32: The dragon 'had no ruth', i.e. it was ruthless, without pity.

A38: As typed, this line read 'And dreaming he uneasy stirred a wing' in both typescripts. In one copy Tolkien revised 'he uneasy' to 'uneasy he', and the latter form was printed in *The Gryphon*.

A54: In both typescripts, Tolkien marked 'he was king' to be changed to 'king he was'. The unrevised words are in the *Gryphon* printing, but the revision carried into the second version.

B35: In both typescripts, 'or dream' was typed as 'and dreamed', the reading in text A, then revised by hand. 'Or dream' was written *ab initio* in the manuscript.

D1: Tolkien accidentally omitted 'the' after 'When' in the course of writing, but inserted it. In our transcription we have omitted such corrections in progress. They are, however, detailed in Michael D.C. Drout's analysis of the manuscript in *Beowulf and the Critics* (2011), pp. 406–7.

D37: The dragon is 'chained' to his gold figuratively, in his possessiveness. In l. 12, the elves are 'chained' literally, having been conquered by force of arms.

D61: This line, alone, is indented in the original.

70

Sir Gawain and the Green Knight (*c.* 1923–53)

The fourteenth-century alliterative poem *Sir Gawain and the Green Knight* was of particular interest to Tolkien, not only as a work of literature, but because it is one of only a few surviving works written in a West Midlands dialect of Middle English, rather than the dominant London dialect of Geoffrey Chaucer. (Tolkien told W.H. Auden: 'I am a West-midlander by blood [through his Suffield ancestors] (and took to early west-midland Middle English as a known tongue as soon as I set eyes on it)', 7 June 1955, *Letters*, p. 311.) *Sir Gawain* is thought to have been written by the same anonymous poet who composed *Pearl* (see nos. 74, 92).

Set in the time of King Arthur, the work tells of Sir Gawain, who accepts a challenge from a mysterious green knight to give him a stroke with an axe, and to take one in return. Although Gawain decapitates his foe, the latter picks up his severed head and charges his opponent to meet him at the Green Chapel in a year's time. Gawain rides through Wales and beyond until he is welcomed at a castle, whose lord promises to direct him to the Chapel on the appointed date; meanwhile, they agree to exchange whatever fortune they win each day. The lord gives Gawain the results of his hunting, while the man of Camelot gives his host kisses he has received from the lord's wife; but when the lady gives Gawain a magic girdle to make him invulnerable, he keeps it secret. At last Gawain leaves the castle to meet the Green Knight again. He duly takes his opponent's stroke, but it is only a slight wound, and the Knight reveals himself as the lord of the castle, by name Bertilak de Haudesert. Bertilak and his wife have tested Gawain's virtue while enchanted by Arthur's enemy, the sorceress Morgan le Fay. Gawain was able to resist the lady's temptations, but concealed the girdle; ashamed, he confesses his faults and returns home, where in self-rebuke he wears the girdle as a baldric or shoulder-belt.

With his Leeds colleague E.V. Gordon, Tolkien prepared an edition of *Sir Gawain* in Middle English, first published in 1925, which became a standard text; and by mid-November 1923 he translated at least 200 lines of *Gawain* into Modern English. In January 1947 a copy of *Gawain* in his translation was returned to him by his friend Gwyn Jones, to whom it had been lent. In August 1950 Tolkien described his translation as far advanced, and on 11 March 1953 he mentioned in a letter to his friend Norman Davis that he had completed and revised it. In December of that year, the translation was broadcast on BBC Radio. Tolkien later explained his delay in producing a final text in a letter to his grandson Michael George Tolkien: 'In addition to the natural difficulty of rendering verse into verse', he would discover 'many minor points about words, in the course of my work, which lead me off' (6 January 1965, *Letters*, p. 493). He also wished to provide an introduction and commentary, for the sake of students of Middle English, but the first was only tentatively begun, and the second never written, although Tolkien commented on the verse-forms of *Sir Gawain* in drafts for a radio talk.

In the event, his translation was complete only in the sense that it reached the end of the poem, and with one exception (see below) was not published until after the author's death. Edited by his son Christopher, it first appeared in *Sir Gawain and the Green Knight, Pearl and Sir Orfeo* (1975). It is from pp. 42–3 of this printed text that we have drawn the following extract (A), which describes part of Gawain's uncomfortable search for the Green Chapel.

[A] Now he rides thus arrayed through the realm of Logres,
Sir Gawain in God's care, though no game now he found it.
Oft forlorn and alone he lodged of a night
where he found not afforded him such fare as pleased him.
He had no friend but his horse in the forests and hills,
no man on his march to commune with but God,
till anon he drew near unto Northern Wales.
All the isles of Anglesey he held on his left,
and over the fords he fared by the flats near the sea,
and then over by the Holy Head to high land again
in the wilderness of Wirral: there wandered but few
who with good will regarded either God or mortal.
And ever he asked as he went on of all whom he met
if they had heard any news of a knight that was green
in any ground thereabouts, or of the Green Chapel.
And all denied it, saying nay, and that never in their lives
a single man had they seen that of such a colour
could be.
The knight took pathways strange
by many a lonesome lea,
and oft his view did change
that chapel ere he could see.

Many a cliff he climbed o'er in countries unknown,
far fled from his friends without fellowship he rode.
At every wading or water on the way that he passed
he found a foe before him, save at few for a wonder;
and so foul were they and fell that fight he must needs.
So many a marvel in the mountains he met in those lands
that 'twould be tedious the tenth part to tell you thereof.
At whiles with worms he wars, and with wolves also,
at whiles with wood-trolls that wandered in the crags,
and with bulls and with bears and boars, too, at times;
and with ogres that hounded him from the heights of the fells.
Had he not been stalwart and staunch and steadfast in God,
he doubtless would have died and death had met often;
for though war wearied him much, the winter was worse,
when the cold clear water from the clouds spilling
froze ere it had fallen upon the faded earth.
Wellnigh slain by the sleet he slept ironclad
more nights than enow in the naked rocks,
where clattering from the crest the cold brook tumbled,
and hung high o'er his head in hard icicles.
Thus in peril and pain and in passes grievous
till Christmas-eve that country he crossed all alone
in need.
The knight did at that tide
his plaint to Mary plead,
her rider's road to guide
and to some lodging lead.

Verses 30 and 31 in the 1975 volume, these lines correspond to 691–739 in the 1925 edition in Middle English. There the text begins:

Now ridez þis renk þurz þe ryalme of Logres,
Sir Gauan, on Godez halue, þaz hym no gomen þozt.
Oft leudlez alone he lengez on nyztez
Þer he fonde nozt hym byfore þe fare þat he lyked.
Hade he no fere bot his fole bi frythez and dounez,
Ne no gome bot God bi gate wyth to karp,
Til þat he nezed ful neghe into þe Norþe Walez.

'Logres' (line 1) is England south of the Humber, though it is perhaps more a poetic creation than a strictly defined area. According to the medieval historian Geoffrey of Monmouth, *Logres* is derived from

Locrine, the name of the first son of Brutus, the mythical Trojan who led exiles to Britain. In Arthurian romance it is sometimes applied to the British Isles more generally. 'The isles of Anglesey' (line 8) are Anglesey (Ynys Môn) proper, an island off the north-west coast of Wales, and the adjacent Holy Island (Ynys Gybi), where the town and port of Holyhead (Caergybi) is located (see line 10). The critical literature of the poem contains much discussion of Gawain's confusing travels through Logres. The Wirral (line 11) is a small peninsula near Liverpool in north-west England. In the fourteenth century it was largely wild, and the haunt of criminals. The idea that water-crossings are often defended by opponents (lines 25–27) occurs in many Arthurian tales.

One verse of *Sir Gawain* as translated by Tolkien, in fact Verse 32 immediately following those transcribed above, appeared in print in *A Short History of English Poetry 1340–1940* by James Reeves (1961, p. 7), and varies there at a few minor points from the text published in 1975. We give the 1961 version here as B, followed by the later version (C) from pp. 43–4 of *Sir Gawain and the Green Knight, Pearl and Sir Orfeo*. In his preface to that book, Christopher Tolkien cautioned that 'at his death my father had not finally decided on the form of every line in the translations. In choosing between competing versions I have tried throughout to determine his latest intention, and that has in most cases been discoverable with fair certainty' (p. 8).

[B] By a mount in the morning merrily he [Gawain] was riding
into a forest that was deep and fearsomely wild;
high hills at each hand, and hoar wood under them
of aged oaks and huge by the hundred together;
the hazel and hawthorn were huddled and tangled
with rough ragged moss around them trailing,
while many birds bleakly on the bare twigs sat
and piteously piped there for pain of the cold.
The good man on Gringolet [Gawain on his horse] goes now beneath them
through many marshes and mires, a man all alone,
troubled lest a truant at that time he should prove
from the service of the sweet Lord, who on that selfsame night
of a maid became man our mourning to conquer.
And therefore sighing he said: 'I beseech thee, O Lord,
and Mary, who is the mildest of mothers most dear,
for some harbour where with honour I might hear the Mass

and thy Matins tomorrow. This meekly I ask,
and thereto promptly I pray with Pater and Ave
and Creed.'
In prayer he now did ride,
Lamenting his misdeed;
He blest him oft and cried,
'The cross of Christ me speed!'

[C] By a mount in the morning merrily he was riding
into a forest that was deep and fearsomely wild,
with high hills at each hand, and hoar woods beneath
of huge aged oaks by the hundred together;
the hazel and the hawthorn were huddled and tangled
with rough ragged moss around them trailing,
with many birds bleakly on the bare twigs sitting
that piteously piped there for pain of the cold.
The good man on Gringelot goes now beneath them
through many marshes and mires, a man all alone,
troubled lest a truant at that time he should prove
from the service of the sweet Lord, who on that selfsame night
of a maid became man our mourning to conquer.
And therefore sighing he said: 'I beseech thee, O Lord,
and Mary, who is the mildest mother most dear,
for some harbour where with honour I might hear the Mass
and thy Matins tomorrow. This meekly I ask,
and thereto promptly I pray with Pater and Ave
and Creed.'
In prayer he now did ride,
lamenting his misdeed;
he blessed him oft and cried,
'The Cross of Christ me speed!'

Tolkien made his translation of *Sir Gawain*, he said, 'with two objects . . . : to preserve the original metre and alliteration, without which translation is of little value except as a crib; and to preserve, to exhibit in an intelligible modern edition, the nobility and the courtesy of this poem, by a poet to whom "courtesy" meant so much' (*Sir Gawain and the Green Knight*, i.e. Tolkien's W.P. Ker Lecture, 1953, in *The Monsters and the Critics and Other Essays*, p. 74). Following publication of *Sir Gawain and the Green Knight, Pearl and Sir Orfeo*, some critics took a contrary view, complaining of Tolkien's use of archaic vocabulary and diction, and of his choice to retain, as far as possible, the metre and word order of the original work. The result, they feared, is that the poem in translation will feel 'foreign' to readers used to Modern English. Tolkien surely would have replied, as he wrote in his preface to Clark Hall's Modern English *Beowulf*, that a translator should in fact avoid 'colloquialism and false modernity' (quoted in *The Monsters and the Critics and Other Essays*, p. 54; see further, poem no. 67). To this we would add that the 'foreignness' of *Sir Gawain*, a glimpse of another culture and era, is part of the work's appeal.

For another poem, related to Sir Gawain only in Tolkien's thoughts, see no. 91.

A25: 'At every wading or water', i.e. at every ford or stream.

A30: 'Worms', i.e. dragons.

A39: 'Ironclad', i.e. in his armour.

B12: 'That selfsame night', i.e. Christmas Eve (see A44).

B16–17: 'Mass | and thy Matins', i.e. the main liturgical service and central act of worship of the Roman Catholic Church, culminating in the Eucharist, which Gawain wants to hear that evening, followed by Matins, the service of early morning prayer, the following day.

B18–19: 'Pater and Ave | and Creed', i.e. three essential prayers, the Pater Noster (Our Father, the Lord's Prayer), the Ave Maria (Hail Mary), and the Apostle's Creed (or Credo).

71

Enigmata Saxonica Nuper Inventa Duo (?1923)

Two poems by Tolkien appeared under this shared title on p. 20 of *A Northern Venture: Verses by Members of the Leeds University English School Association*, published in Leeds in June 1923. Each is in Old English, and modelled on early English riddles such as are found most famously in the Exeter Book (Exeter Cathedral Library MS 3501). The general title, in Latin, translates as 'Two Saxon Riddles Newly Discovered', a doubly fictitious statement, as neither poem is a genuine early riddle, and neither was discovered by Tolkien, but composed by him. We follow each of the 'new' riddles with a translation.

I

Meolchwitum sind marmanstane
wagas mine wundrum frætwede;
is hrægl ahongen hnesce on-innan,
seolce gelicost; siththan on-middan
is wylla geworht, waeter glaes-hluttor;
Thær glisnath gold-hladen on gytestreamum
æppla scienost. Infær nænig
nah min burg-fæsten: berstath hwæthre
thriste theofas on thrythærn min,
ond thæt sine reafiath — saga hwæt ic hatte!

Milky-white are my marble
walls wondrously adorned;
within is hung a soft garment,
silk-like; afterwards in the middle
a well is made, water clear as glass;
there glistening gold is in a flowing stream
the fairest of apples. There is no door
to my fastness: and yet do break
bold thieves into my palace,
and take that treasure – by what name am I called!

II

Hæfth Hild Hunecan hwite tunecan,
ond swa read rose hæfth rudige nose;
the leng heo bideth, the læss heo wrideth;
hire tearas hate on tan blate
biernende dreosath ond bearhtme freosath;
hwæt heo sie saga, searothancla maga.

Hild Hunic has a white tunic,
and like a red rose is her ruddy nose;
the longer she bides, the less she grows;
her tears are hot on a pale shoot
burning they fall and in a moment freeze;
what is she called, cunning man.

Writing to his publisher in 1947, Tolkien referred to one of Bilbo Baggins' riddles in *The Hobbit*: 'A box without hinges, key, or lid, | Yet golden treasure inside is hid'. This was, he said, a reduction of a longer and older riddle, which is certainly – as Douglas A. Anderson seems to have been the first to identify, in *The Annotated Hobbit* (2002) – the poem frequently reprinted as 'In Marble Halls':

In marble halls as white as milk,
Lined with a skin as soft as silk,
Within a fountain crystal-clear,
A golden apple doth appear.
No doors there are to this stronghold,
Yet thieves break in and steal the gold.

The answer is *an egg*. Anderson also identified a familiar rhyme which seems to have inspired Tolkien's second riddle:

Little Nancy Etticoat,
With a white petticoat,
And a red nose;
She has no feet or hands,
The longer she stands
The shorter she grows.

The answer is *a candle*.

Although today riddles are considered nothing better than 'occasional verse', in earlier times they comprised their own genre, mentioned by Aristotle in his *Rhetoric*. Nearly one hundred riddles survive in Old English. The skill of the early poets who wrote them was in making them sophisticated and enigmatic, and in taking the point of view of the object. Tolkien's aim, in addition to following the ancient poets' mode of expression, was to present verses as if they were 'the lost ancestors of modern riddles surviving only as nursery rhymes' (Tom Shippey, 'Poems by Tolkien in Other Languages' (2006), p. 514). Mark Atherton, providing his own translation of the 'egg' riddle, has said much the same in *There and Back Again: J.R.R. Tolkien and the Origins of* The Hobbit (2012):

> Tolkien's conceit is that the Saxon riddle 'Meolchwitum sind marmanstane' is the putative 'original version' of the later nursery rhyme. The rhyme 'In marble walls as white as milk' certainly might easily give the impression of being very ancient; on the whole its language is modern, but the individual words of the text have a long history, and most of them can be traced back to Old English, such as *walls*, *milk* and *white*, which come from *wagas*, *meolc* and *hwit* . . . notable exceptions being words like *fountain*, *clear*, *appear*, which go back to French, and entered the English language in the medieval period. [p. 225]

72

Úþwita Sceal Ealdgesægenum (1923)

Tolkien worked as an assistant to Henry Bradley, one of the first editors of the *Oxford English Dictionary*, and from 1915 its Senior Editor. Bradley hired Tolkien when the latter returned to Oxford at the end of 1918, and supervised his work on the letter *W*. In June 1922 Tolkien sent him for amusement his original riddles in Old English, published the next year as *Enigmata Saxonica Nuper Inventa Duo* (no. 71). After Bradley died on 23 May 1923, Tolkien wrote his obituary for the October 1923 number of the *Bulletin of the Modern Humanities Research Association*, recalling that to see Bradley 'working in the Dictionary Room at the Old Ashmolean and to work for a time under his wise and kindly hand was a privilege not at that time looked for' (p. 5). Tolkien concluded his praise with a thirteen-line poem in Old English, transcribed here from p. 5 of the *Bulletin*.

úþwita sceal   ealdgesægenum
fród fyrngewritum   féolan georne;
hár ond hygegléaw   hord scéawian
worda ond reorda,   wíde geond eorþan
snyttro sécan,   sméaþoncol mon;
wísdóme þeon,   wunian on áre
rúna rǽdan,   rincas lǽran,
oþþæt scír metod   to gesceap-hwíle
hine ellor aciegþ   eard gesécan.
Þa felaléof féreþ   on fréan wǽre,
werum bewópen   woruldfréondum,
léodwita liþost   ond lárgeornost,
démena gedéfost   ond deophýdgost.

This reads in Modern English:

The scholar to the old sayings
learnéd in ancient writings must apply himself;
grey-haired and wise he is to examine the hoard
of words and languages, widely on earth
sagacity seek, a subtle man;
to flourish in wisdom, live in honour,

read runes, teach others,
until at the fated time the glorious Creator
will call him elsewhere to seek his home.
Then the much-beloved one will go into the Lord's keeping,
mourned by men and friends of his former world,
of men most gentle and eager to teach,
most fitting of judges and deepest in thought.

In his commentary accompanying a reprint of the obituary in *Tolkien Studies* 12 (2015), Tom Shippey writes of the 'cumulative force' of 'hundreds of observations' on words and language by Bradley, to which Tolkien alludes in his poem (p. 145). The *Oxford English Dictionary* alone is a 'hoard' for philologists, but Bradley was widely read, indeed self-made as a scholar. Tolkien once said that he learned more during his time under Bradley than in any other equal period. As Peter Gilliver writes in a second commentary in *Tolkien Studies* 12, 'it was a happy chance that, of the *Dictionary*'s three remaining editors [after the death of *OED* founder James Murray], Tolkien had been assigned to the one who had the greatest interest in the aesthetics of language, and specifically in poetry.' It was, Gilliver says, a characteristic response for Tolkien to pay tribute to his old mentor 'in the forms of Anglo-Saxon funerary panegyric . . . praising Bradley as *úþwita* (distinguished scholar), *hár ond hygegléaw* (experienced and sagacious), and *sméaþoncol mon* (acute thinker)' (pp. 147, 148). Tolkien in fact concludes his poem in words similar to those used at the end of *Beowulf*, when the hero has died in defence of his people:

Swa begnornodon Geata leode
hlafordes hryre, heorðgeneatas,
cwædon þæt he wære wyruldcyninga
manna mildust ond monðwærust,
leodum liðost ond lofgeornost.

In Tolkien's translation, this reads: 'Thus bemourned the Geatish folk their master's fall, comrades of his hearth, crying that he was ever of the kings of earth of men most generous and to men most gracious, to his people most tender and for praise most eager' (*Beowulf*, p. 105).

73

Moonshine (1923–*c.* 1927)

Of the four manuscript leaves associated with this poem, two are clearly earlier than the others, and almost certainly belong to a single text. On one page, Tolkien wrote four stanzas of the poem – as yet untitled – but struck through the fourth. On the other, he wrote two versions of a single stanza, striking through the first, together with a few lines of rough workings. Here, as A, we have transcribed the four stanzas that Tolkien seems to have intended as an initial draft.

[A]

The mounting moon doth whitely shine;
  The curtains wide are open cast;
The trees are trembling, larch and pine,
  And sighing softly in the blast;
The stars are pale, when line on line
  The dancers go a-piping past,
And music with their measures twine,
  And lilt on lawns all greyly grassed.

*

And long they lilt on lawns and meads
  To a hundred harps in hidden hands
And viewless viols in the reeds
  Where waters wander through the lands.
A glint there is of gleaming beads
  That faintly flare on feet and hands.
Of silken robes and silver weeds,
  And moonlit hair in misty strands.

*

With gold is meshed their moonlit hair,
  And, gleaned from pools aglimmering,
The flame of stars is fastened there
  In woodland shades ashimmering.
Their slender limbs are light and bare;
  Their feet like feathers fluttering

With rhythmic beat or breathing air
Or wind in willows whispering.

★

In the willows go the winds awailing
The fading moon is fallen old
The dying starlight dimly paling
In cloudy western havens cold.
Where are fled the flutes awailing
Where are hushed the harps of gold:
The voices of the viols are failing;
The fallen moon is faded old.

The lines deleted after the third stanza read:

From eastward comes a wind awailing;
Slowly sinks the silver moon,
And under cloudy cliffs asailing
Seeks the western havens soon.
The beat of feet afar is failing;
The twinkling fades of shimmering shoon;
The dusk of dawn has dimmed their trailing
Robes and hushed the trembling tune.

And this is the deleted first version of the fourth stanza:

In the willows go the winds awailing
The [falling >] fading moon [hast >] is fallen old
The dying starlight dimly paling
In cloudy western havens cold.
Where are fled the flutes awailing
Where are hushed the harps of gold
The voices of the viols are failing
The fallen moon is faded old.

Tolkien wrote both of these pages of manuscript on the reverse side of long-discarded printed sheets of questions from the 11 June 1908 examination in the Leeds Honours School of English Language and Literature. A third manuscript page was similarly written, together with lines of miscellaneous calligraphy and unrelated writing in Tolkien's invented 'Rúmilian' script, most examples of which date from 1919 to the mid-1920s. This version of the poem includes two stanzas, marked as replacements for the first and fourth of what Tolkien cites as the 'older version' (that is, text A). We give these as B.

[B]

The larches fingers long and fine
 Are trembling in the twilit breeze,
And wavering in the white moonshine;
 From shade to shadow under trees
In dances dim the elves entwine;
 Pale fingers flute and fiddle seize,
And linked in long and rhythmic line
 They lilt on lawns and starlit leas.

The willows in the wind do wail,
 The fading moon is fallen old,
The drooping stars are dim and pale
 In cloudy western havens cold.
Their flying flutes afar do fail,
 And hushed their hidden harps of gold;
No more the viols' voices wail;
 The fallen moon is faded old.

The manuscript drafts were followed by a typescript made by Tolkien with a purple ribbon; it is entitled *Moonshine* and has a handwritten subtitle, *Verses in a Medieval Measure*. Its text is identical to A and B as combined, except that in line 2 'twilit' became 'twilight', and line 19 (in the third stanza), 'The flame of stars is fastened there', was changed to 'The light of stars doth linger there'.

Tolkien subsequently wrote out the revised poem in manuscript, in which the only point of note is again line 19, written as 'The flame of stars doth flutter there' and altered to the reading of the first typescript (with 'linger'). The new manuscript includes a (probably later) note by Tolkien which helps to explain 'Verses in a Medieval Measure': 'Leeds 1923, medieval allit[erative] stanza (as used in Deb[ate] of Body & Soul)'. The 'Debate between the Body and the Soul' is a poem in Middle English which survives in several manuscripts, including three at Oxford. Tolkien did not adopt its subject or motif – *Moonshine* is not a debate, nor does it explore the question of whether the body or the soul is responsible for one's sins – but he employed its form of eight-line stanzas, and its rhyme scheme ABABABAB, together with internal alliteration. Tolkien's poem recalls some of his earlier verses, with dancing elves in a forest setting, perhaps in particular one of his draft workings for *The Trumpet of Faery* (no. 34):

> Like the mighty voice of forests
> When the pines and larches call
> O! the distant song of voices
> And the wail of violins
> And the mellow autumn flutings
> In the branches of the winds

Sometime after he moved to Oxford from Leeds, Tolkien made another typescript of the poem, now entitled only *Moonshine*, using his Hammond machine. The final text, given here as C, was largely unchanged from the intermediate copies, except for a few points of punctuation and two revisions in the fourth stanza. Tolkien's name is typed at the end of the poem, as if he planned to submit it for publication.

[C]

The larches' fingers long and fine
    Are trembling in the twilight breeze
And wavering in the white moonshine;
    From shade to shadow under trees
In dances dim the elves entwine;
    Pale fingers flute and fiddle seize,
And linked in long and rhythmic line
    They lilt on lawns and starlit leas.

And long they lilt on lawns and meads
    To a hundred harps in hidden hands
And viewless viols in the reeds
    Where waters wander through the lands.
A glint there is of gleaming beads
    That faintly flare on feet and hands,
Of silken robes and silver weeds
    And moonlit hair in misty strands.

With gold is meshed their moonlit hair,
    And gleaned from pools a-glimmering,
The light of stars doth linger there
    In woodland shades a-shimmering.
Their slender limbs are light and bare;
    Their feet like feathers fluttering

With rhythmic beat, or breathing air,
Or wind in willows whispering.

The willows in the wind now wail,
The fading moon is fallen old,
The drooping stars are dim and pale
In cloudy western havens cold.
Afar the flutes now faint and fail,
And hushed their hidden harps of gold,
No more the viols' voices wail;
The fallen moon is faded old.

The repetition of elements from the last line of one stanza in the first line of the next is a feature of the Middle English *Pearl*, used also in poem no. 74, *The Nameless Land*, and explained in our discussion.

A4: 'In the blast', presumably as the winds are blowing. In A25 the winds are 'awailing'. In text C, the trees are more reasonably 'trembling in the twilight breeze'.

A29: The fanciful 'flutes awailing' (can flutes *wail*? it seems an odd association) and the 'flying flutes' of B13 (did they 'fly' because they were played quickly?) did not survive into the final text.

74

The Nameless Land · The Song of Ælfwine (1924–*c.* 1955)

The earliest extant version of this poem is a typescript, made with a purple ribbon and inscribed 'Leeds May 1924 & rewr[itten] Darnley Road, 2 verses added Aug[ust] 1924 (insp[ired] [by] reading "Pearl" for exam[ination] purposes)'. Darnley Road was Tolkien's address at the time. The inspiration he refers to, *Pearl*, is an alliterative poem in Middle English attributed to the same anonymous fourteenth-century writer who produced *Sir Gawain and the Green Knight* (see nos. 70, 90). Its subject is the speaker's daughter, his precious 'pearl', who died as a child. Falling asleep at her grave, he dreams of a land of marvels, and his daughter appears to him, now grown to maturity. She upbraids him for excessive grief, as she is now in a blissful state of grace, a bride of Christ in a heavenly city of light. Reassured by the vision, the speaker wakes with his heart at ease.

Tolkien was well acquainted with *Pearl* from his studies, and it was on the curriculum at Leeds when he taught there in the English School, hence his review of the work for examinations. As he explained to his aunt Jane Neave, *Pearl* is

> absurdly complex in technical form. . . . The stanzas have twelve lines, with only three Rhymes: an octet of four couplets rhyming *a b*, and a quartet rhyming *b c*. In addition each line has internal alliteration (it occasionally but rarely fails in the original . . .). And if that is not enough, the poem is divided into fives [i.e. groups of five stanzas, except for one in which there are six]. Within a five-stanza group the chief word of the last line must be echoed in the first line of the following stanza; the last line of the five-group is echoed at the beginning of the next; and the first line of all is to wind up echoed in the last line of all.

Scholars, he added, judged 'that the metrical form [of *Pearl*] was almost impossibly difficult to write in' – though the *Pearl* poet managed 101 stanzas – 'and quite impossible to render in modern English. NO scholars (or, nowadays, poets) have any experience in composing themselves in exacting metres. I made up a few stanzas in the metre to show that composition in it was not at any rate "impossible" (though the result might today be thought bad)' (18 July 1962, *Letters*, p. 448).

In its first incarnation, Tolkien called his work *The Nameless Land*. We give the earliest text of the poem as A, incorporating corrections Tolkien made in manuscript, as well as his replacement for line 29, the original reading of which he obscured beyond recovery.

[A] There lingering lights do golden lie
On grass more green than in gardens here,
On trees more tall that touch the sky
With silver leaves a-swinging clear:
By magic dewed they may not die
Where fades nor falls the endless year,
Where ageless afternoon goes by
O'er mead and mound and silent mere,
Where draws no dusk of evening near,
But birds do sing in blazing choir,
Do shrill with quenchless voices sheer,
And the woods are filled with wandering fire.

With wandering fire the woods do fill,
With sudden gleams that glint and go,
With music sweet but mournful still
That trembling shakes where shadows grow
In rustling green, than gurgling rill
More soft, more faint; that fading slow
In dell and deep like dew doth spill,
Like footfalls dancing to and fro,
Like voices lost that veiled and low
Now sing unseen to muted lyre,
Like winds of yesteryear that blow
And wake to flame a wandering fire —

A wandering fire with tongues of flame
Whose quenchless colours quiver clear
On leaf and land without a name,
No heart may hope to anchor near.
A dreamless dark no stars proclaim,
A moonless night its marches drear,
A water wide no feet may tame,
A sea with shores encircled sheer —
A thousand leagues it lies from here.

And the foam doth flower upon the sea
Neath cliffs of crystal carven clear
On shining beaches blowing free.

There blowing free unbraided hair
Is meshed with light of moon and sun,
And tangled with those tresses fair
A gold and silver sheen is spun;
There feet do beat and white and bare
Do lissom limbs in dances run,
Their robes the wind, their raiment air —
Such loveliness to look upon
Nor Bran nor Brendan ever won,
Who foam beyond the furthest sea
Did dare, and dipped behind the sun
On winds unearthly wafted free.

Than Tír na nÓg more fair and free,
Than Paradise more faint and far,
O! land forlorn where lost things be,
Where my laughter and my longing are!
My dreams an echo o'er the sea
Of solemn surges on the bar
Beyond the world's end waft to me,
In sleep I see a wayward star,
Than beacon-towers in Gondobar
More fair, where faint upon the sky
On hills imagineless and far
The lights of longing flare and die.

The 'wayward star' (line 56) is the planet Venus, the 'morning star' or 'evening star'. It is 'wayward' in the sense of wandering, as all planets appear to do in their celestial paths from an earthly point of view.

Tolkien marked the second stanza of text A (lines 13–24) to be deleted, and in the course of two pages of manuscript workings developed a replacement (B).

[B] With wandering fires the woods do fill,
In glades for ever green they glow;
Those dells immortal dews distill
And fragrance of all flowers that grow.
There melodies of music spill,

And falling fountains plash and flow,
And a water white leaps down the hill
To seek the sea no sail doth know;
Its voices fill the valleys low
Where breathing keen on bent and briar
The winds beyond the world's edge blow
And wake to flame a wandering fire.

Two new typescripts followed, like the first made with a purple ribbon. These present a question of order: for reference, we will call them C^1 and C^2. Most of the text of each follows that of A with the new second stanza B. In C^1, however, lines 9–11 read 'There draws no dusk of darkness near, | And birds do sing in blazing choir | With keen and quenchless voices clear', while in C^2 they are 'Where draws no dusk of evening near, | Where voices move in veilèd choir, | Or shrill in sudden singing sheer'. In C^1, line 23 refers to 'the world's end', but in C^2 is found 'the world's edge'. And in C^1, lines 51–56 read

O! shore beyond the Shadowy Sea
Whose foam more white than nenuphar,
Whose mountaintops no man may see!
The solemn surges on the bar
Beyond the world's edge waft to me;
I dream I see a wayward star,

while in C^2 they are identical to A (with 'world's end' in line 55). (*Nenuphar*, used only in C^1, is the water-lily.)

We are inclined to think that C^1 preceded C^2, since a greater number of readings from C^2 are found in the poem as it was printed on pp. 24–5 of *Realities: An Anthology of Verse*, edited by G.S. Tancred and published in 1927 by the Swan Press, Leeds, for the benefit of the Queen's Hospital for Children in Hackney. But *The Nameless Land* as published draws elements from both typescripts. We give the *Realities* text here as C. Christopher Tolkien included this version in *The Lost Road and Other Writings* (1987), pp. 98–100.

[C] There lingering lights do golden lie
On grass more green than in gardens here,
On trees more tall that touch the sky
With silver leaves a-swinging clear:
By magic dewed they may not die
Where fades nor falls the endless year,

Where ageless afternoon goes by
O'er mead and mound and silent mere.
There draws no dusk of evening near,
Where voices move in veiléd choir,
Or shrill in sudden singing sheer,
And the woods are filled with wandering fire.

The wandering fires the woodlands fill,
In glades for ever green they glow,
In dells that immortal dews distill
And fragrance of all flowers that grow.
There melodies of music spill,
And falling fountains plash and flow,
And a water white leaps down the hill
To seek the sea no sail doth know.
Its voices fill the valleys low,
Where breathing keen on bent and briar
The winds beyond the world's edge blow
And wake to flame a wandering fire.

A wandering fire with tongues of flame
Whose quenchless colours quiver clear
On leaf and land without a name
No heart may hope to anchor near.
A dreamless dark no stars proclaim,
A moonless night its marches drear,
A water wide no feet may tame,
A sea with shores encircled sheer.
A thousand leagues it lies from here,
And the foam doth flower upon the sea
'Neath cliffs of crystal carven clear
On shining beaches blowing free.

There blowing free unbraided hair
Is meshed with light of moon and sún,
And tangled with those tresses fair
A gold and silver sheen is spun.
There feet do beat and white and bare
Do lissom limbs in dances run,
Their robes the wind, their raiment air —
Such loveliness to look upon
Nor Bran nor Brendan ever won,
Who foam beyond the furthest sea

Did dare, and dipped behind the sun
On winds unearthly wafted free.

Than Tir-nan-Og more fair and free,
Than Paradise more faint and far,
O! shore beyond the Shadowy Sea,
O! land forlorn where lost things are,
O! mountains where no man may be!
Of solemn surges on the bar
Beyond the world's edge waft to me;
I dream I see a wayward star,
Than beacon-towers in Gondobar
More fair, where faint upon the sky
On hills imagineless and far
The lights of longing flare and die.

As intended, *The Nameless Land* adopts from *Pearl* its twelve-line stanza, its rhyme scheme ABABABABCDCD, its internal alliteration, its concatenation or repetition of elements between the final line of one stanza and the first line of the next ('wandering fire', 'free'), and a first line ('There lingering lights do golden lie') echoed in the last ('The lights of longing flare and die'). Also like *Pearl*, Tolkien's poem describes a land of wonders. His is 'more fair and free' than Tír na nÓg – the supernatural Land of Youth in Celtic mythology – and 'more faint and far' than Paradise, presumably the biblical Eden. It is explicitly not 'here' (lines 2, 33), but 'a thousand leagues' distant (line 33), beyond reach but keenly to be desired. Its description recalls that of the dream-land in *Pearl* (in Tolkien's own translation, *Sir Gawain and the Green Knight, Pearl and Sir Orfeo*, p. 91):

Wondrous was made each mountain-side
With crystal cliffs so clear of hue;
About them woodlands bright lay wide,
As Indian dye their boles were blue;
The leaves did as burnished silver slide
That thick upon twigs there trembling grew.
When glades let light upon them glide
They shone with a shimmer of dazzling hue.
The gravel on ground that I trod with shoe
Was of precious pearls of the Orient:
Sunbeams are blear and dark to view
Compared with that fair wonderment.

But the 'nameless land' is more grounded, and because it is not presented in the frame of a dream (the word 'dream' in line 56 notwithstanding), it can be thought attainable, if by rare circumstance. 'Nor Bran nor Brendan' (i.e. 'neither Bran nor Brendan') in line 45 refers respectively to an Irish hero and an Irish saint who feature in medieval narratives of voyages to an otherworld: Bran mac Febail sets out with companions to find a Land of Women, and St Brendan to seek the Land of Promise in the West. Tolkien's unnamed land is more lovely than any place Bran or Brendan ever 'won' (reached). It has a 'timeless year', a 'morn unmeasured', an 'endless eve', 'immortal dew', and yet, time does pass there: a flower grows, water flows.

In his letter to Jane Neave, Tolkien wrote of his poem – with only slight exaggeration – that it was 'related inevitably as everything was at one time with my own mythology', and readers of this book may recognize in *The Nameless Land* aspects of other landscapes, in poems such as *Kôr* (no. 30), *The Shores of Faery* (no. 31), and *The Happy Mariners* (no. 33). 'Shadowy seas' have appeared before, for instance in *The Happy Mariners*, and 'Gondobar' is one of the seven names of Gondolin (see poem no. 66). In Tolkien's *Quenta Silmarillion* of the 1930s, it is said that 'to the East [Kôr] looked towards the Bay of Elvenhome, and the Lonely Isle and the Shadowy Seas' (*The Lost Road and Other Writings*, p. 222); and

> In that time, which songs call the hiding of Valinor, the Enchanted Isles were set, and filled with shadows and bewilderment, and all the seas about were filled with shadows; and these isles were strung across the Shadowy Seas, from north to south before Tol Eressëa, the Lonely Isle, is reached sailing west; and hardly might any vessel come between them in the gloom or win through to the Bay of Elvenhome. [*The Lost Road and Other Writings*, p. 243]

Christopher Tolkien guessed, and emphasized that it could be no more than a guess, that his father's next development of *The Nameless Land* belongs to about the time he wrote his unfinished novel *The Lost Road*, probably in 1936 or 1937. There are two extant manuscripts of the poem's intermediate version. The first, entitled *Ælfwine's Song Calling upon Eärendel*, began as neat calligraphy but spun out into illegible workings. The other, called *The Song of Ælfwine (on Seeing the Uprising of Eärendel)*, is written to presentation quality, with decorated initials. These manuscripts were followed by a professional typescript; we give this later text as D (included also in *The Lost Road and Other Writings*, pp. 100–102). There were few changes as the three instances advanced, as detailed in our notes.

[D] There lingering lights still golden lie
on grass more green than gardens here,
On trees more tall that touch the sky
with swinging leaves of silver clear.
While world endures they will not die,
nor fade nor fall their timeless year,
As morn unmeasured passes by
o'er mead and mound and shining mere.
When endless eve undimmed is near,
o'er harp and chant in hidden choir
A sudden voice upsoaring sheer
in the wood awakes the Wandering Fire.

The Wandering Fire the woodland fills:
in glades for ever green it glows,
In dells where immortal dew distils
the Flower that in secret fragrance grows.
There murmuring the music spills,
as falling fountain plashing flows,
And water white leaps down the hills
to seek the Sea that no sail knows.
Through gleaming vales it singing goes,
where breathing keen on bent and briar
The wind beyond the world's end blows
to living flame the Wandering Fire.

The Wandering Fire with tongues of flame
with light there kindles quick and clear
The land of long-forgotten name:
no man may ever anchor near;
No steering star his hope may aim,
for nether Night its marches drear,
And waters wide no sail may tame,
with shores encircled dark and sheer.
Uncounted leagues it lies from here,
And foam there flowers upon the Sea
By cliffs of crystal carven clear
On shining beaches blowing free.

There blowing free unbraided hair
    is meshed with beams of Moon and Sun,
And twined within those tresses fair
    a gold and silver sheen is spun,
As fleet and white the feet go bare,
    and lissom limbs in dances run,
Shimmering in the shining air:
    such loveliness to look upon
No mortal man hath ever won,
    though foam upon the furthest sea
He dared, or sought behind the Sun
    for winds unearthly flowing free.

O! Shore beyond the Shadowy Sea!
    O! Land where still the Edhil are!
O Haven where my heart would be!
    the waves that beat upon thy bar
For ever echo endlessly,
    when longing leads my thought afar,
And rising west of West I see
    beyond the world the wayward Star,
Than beacons bright in Gondobar
    more clear and keen, more fair and high:
O! Star that shadow may not mar,
    nor ever darkness doom to die!

One significant difference in D compared with earlier texts is that there is no longer the repetition of a key word in the final line of the fourth stanza and the first line of the fifth. Tolkien either overlooked this technical point, while focused on the substance of his poem, or consciously abandoned strict adherence to the *Pearl* model. There is also now no mention of Bran and Brendan, of Tír na nÓg or Paradise, as Tolkien aligned the poem more closely with his mythology. The 'land forlorn where lost things are' became the 'Land where still the Edhil are', *Edhil* being another name for the Eldar, the Elves in Tolkien's stories who made a great march from the place of their awakening in Middle-earth to Valinor in Aman, the Undying Lands in the West. The 'Haven where my heart would be' is presumably Tol Eressëa.

Neither Ælfwine nor Eärendel, though named in the titles of this version, appears by name in the body of the poem. Eärendel nearly figured there, but was omitted after revision of the first of the intermediate manuscripts, where the final stanza ended in draft (contrary to the *Pearl* scheme, with a concluding couplet):

> Than beacons bright in Gondobar
>   More clear and keen in darkened sky,
> Mounting above the mists afar
>   Earendel's light is raised on high,
> That another night shall never die.

After revision, it can only be supposed, if one has some knowledge of Tolkien's mythology, that 'the wayward Star' is Eärendel, the mariner who became a 'star' in 'The Silmarillion' (see poem no. 16). Ælfwine does appear, however, in *The Lost Road*, and that is undoubtedly one reason why Christopher Tolkien guessed that *The Song of Ælfwine* was further developed while his father worked on that novel. *The Lost Road* concerns a father and son of the present day, Audoin and Alboin Errol, who travel back in time through historical and legendary periods, in dreams and through the lives of other fathers and sons whose forenames have the same meanings, 'bliss-friend' and 'elf-friend'. As the work was to proceed, Tolkien would introduce elements from his mythology, or which would be joined to it, ending with the father and son in Númenor, an analogue of Atlantis. Among the earlier figures whose episodes Tolkien wrote only in part, or merely outlined, for his book was Ælfwine (Old English 'elf-friend'), a man of tenth-century England who would sail into the West with his son Eadwine and glimpse Tol Eressëa.

A third period of development of the poem occurred much later, Christopher Tolkien judged, 'probably from the years after *The Lord of the Rings*' (*The Lost Road and Other Writings*, p. 100; *The Lord of the Rings* was published 1954–5), or in conjunction with *The Notion Club Papers*, another abandoned work of fiction, in which Tolkien revived elements of *The Lost Road*. He wrote *The Notion Club Papers* probably in late 1945 and the first two-thirds of 1946. There are similarities between *The Song of Ælfwine* in its final version and the poem *The Death of St. Brendan* which forms part of *The Notion Club Papers*, but also with *Imram*, a development of *St. Brendan* published in 1955 (for these works, see poem no. 175). The voyages of Brendan and Ælfwine are much alike in nature if not in detail.

The first text of this third stage of Tolkien's poem, *The Song of Ælfwine on Seeing the Uprising of Earendel*, is a typescript with changes, relative to D, only in the second and fourth stanzas. We give these lines as E.

[E] The Wandering Fire the woodland fills:
in glades for ever green it glows,
In dells where immortal dew distils
the Flower that in secret fragrance grows.
There murmuring the music spills,
as falling fountain plashing flows,
And water white leaps down the hills;
by silver stairs it singing goes
To the field of the unfading Rose,
where breathing on the glowing briar
The wind beyond the world's end blows
to living flame the Wandering Fire.

. . . .

There blowing free unbraided hair
is meshed with beams of Moon and Sun,
And twined within those tresses fair
the stars to silver threads are spun,
As lissom feet in dances fare,
and light as flying leaves they run,
Shimmering in the shining air:
such loveliness to look upon
No mortal man hath ever won,
though foam upon the furthest sea
He dared, or sought behind the Sun
for winds unearthly flowing free.

But now Tolkien filled with revisions the margins of a carbon copy of his new text, as well as the backs of sheets, in pencil with over-writing in red biro (ballpoint pen). Tolkien's use of biro, not generally available in Britain until late 1945, as well as the typewriter he employed, help to date the later texts of the poem, probably to the 1950s. Most of his workings are illegible, but some appear to be existing text written out again, as if Tolkien needed to be convinced of its worth. In the next typescript (F) he refined the three central stanzas of the poem and introduced another element specific to his mythology, 'the dreaming niphredil', a specific variety replacing the undefined 'Flower that in secret fragrance grows'. Tolkien introduced *Niphredil* 'snowdrop' in his *Lord of the Rings* manuscript towards the end of 1941 or the beginning of 1942, as a white flower which grew on the hill Cerin Amroth in Lothlórien. In the published *Silmarillion* it is said that when Lúthien Tinúviel was born, 'the white flowers of *niphredil* came forth to greet her as stars from the earth' (p. 91).

[F] There lingering lights still golden lie
On grass more green than gardens here,
On trees more tall that touch the sky
With swinging leaves of silver clear.
While world endures they will not die,
Nor fade nor fall their timeless year,
As morn unmeasured passes by
O'er mead and mound and shining mere.
When endless eve undimmed is near,
O'er harp and chant in hidden choir
A sudden voice upsoaring sheer
In the wood awakes the Wandering Fire.

With Wandering Fire the woodlands fill:
In glades for ever green it glows,
In dells where the dreaming niphredil
As star awakened gleaming grows.
There ever murmuring musics spill,
And ever the fount immortal flows;
Its water white leaps down the hill,
By silver stairs it singing goes
To the field of the unfading Rose,
Where breathing on the glowing briar
The wind beyond the world's end blows
To living flame the Wandering Fire.

The Wandering Fire with quickening flame
Of living light illumines clear
The land unknown by mortal name.
No man may ever anchor near,
No steering star his hope may aim;
For nether Night its marches drear,
And waters wide no sail may tame,
With shores encircled dark and sheer.
Uncounted leagues it lies from here,
And foam there flowers upon the Sea
By cliffs of crystal carven clear
On shining beaches blowing free.

There blowing free unbraided hair
    Is meshed with beams of Moon and Sun,
And twined within those tresses fair
    The stars to silver threads are spun,
As lissom feet in dances fare,
    And light as flying leaves they run,
Shimmering in the shining air:
    Such loveliness to look upon
    No mortal man hath ever won,
Though foam upon the furthest sea
    He dared, or sought behind the Sun
For winds unearthly flowing free.

O Shore beyond the Shadowy Sea!
    O Land where still the Edhil are!
O Haven where my heart would be!
    The waves that beat upon thy bar
For ever echo endlessly,
    When longing leads my thought afar,
And rising west of West I see
    Beyond the world the wayward Star,
    Than beacons bright in Gondobar
More clear and keen, more fair and high.
    O Star that shadow may not mar,
Nor ever darkness doom to die!

Tolkien further revised his poem by marking up a carbon copy of the typescript F and filling a page with workings for the third stanza, then made a fair copy of the whole in manuscript, which itself was lightly revised. Thus the final text was reached. We give it here as G, from a professional typescript. The 'lingering lights' of line 1 are now specifically 'elven-lights', the land now 'beyond the Shadow dark and drear | And waters wild' rather than 'wide', though still 'uncounted leagues it lies from here'. With the final manuscript, Tolkien returned to the uncapitalized form 'wandering fire', and the name of the mariner in the poem title had come to be spelled 'Eärendil'. Remarkably, in these two final instances Tolkien reduced the poem from five stanzas to four, in the process restoring concatenation (with 'Sea') between the penultimate and final sections; and at the same time, he added a long prose appendix concerning Ælfwine and extended the poem's title with the cry 'Eressëa! Eressëa!' making the name of the 'nameless land' explicit.

[G] Eressëa! Eressëa!

There elven-lights still gleaming lie
  On grass more green than in gardens here,
On trees more tall that touch the sky
  With swinging leaves of silver clear.
While world endures they will not die,
  Nor fade nor fall their timeless year,
As morn unmeasured passes by
  O'er mead and mound and shining mere.
When endless eve undimmed is near,
  O'er harp and chant in hidden choir
A sudden voice up-soaring sheer
  In the wood awakes the wandering fire.

With wandering fire the woodlands fill:
  In glades for ever green it glows;
In a dell there dreaming niphredil
  As star awakened gleaming grows.
And ever-murmuring musics spill,
  For there the fount immortal flows:
Its water white leaps down the hill,
  By silver stairs it singing goes
To the field of the unfading rose,
  Where breathing on the glowing briar
The wind beyond the world's end blows
  To living flame the wandering fire.

The wandering fire with quickening flame
  Of living light illumines clear
That land unknown by mortal name
  Beyond the Shadow dark and drear
And waters wild no ship may tame.
  No man may ever anchor near,
To haven none his hope may aim
  Through starless night his way to steer.
Uncounted leagues it lies from here:
  In wind on beaches blowing free
Neath cliffs of carven crystal sheet
  The foam there flowers upon the Sea.

O Shore beyond the Shadowy Sea!
  O Land where still the Edhil are!

O Haven where my heart would be!
    The waves still beat upon thy bar,
The white birds wheel; there flowers the Tree!
    Again I glimpse them long afar
When rising west of West I see
    Beyond the world the wayward Star,
Than beacons bright in Gondobar
    More fair and keen, more clear and high.
O Star that shadow may not mar,
    Nor ever darkness doom to die.

Ælfwine (Elf-friend) was a seaman of England of old who, being driven out to sea from the coast of Erin, passed into the deep waters of the West, and according to legend, by some strange chance or grace found the 'straight road' of the Elven-folk and came at last to the isle of Eressëa in Elvenhome. Or maybe, as some say, alone in the waters, hungry and athirst, he fell into a trance and was granted a vision of that isle as it once had been, ere a West-wind arose and drove him back to Middle-earth. Of no other man is it reported that he ever beheld Eressëa the fair. Ælfwine was never again able to rest for long on land, and sailed the western seas until his death. Some say that his ship was wrecked upon the west shores of Erin and there his body lies; others say that at the end of his life he went forth alone into the deeps again and never returned.

It is reported that before he set out on his last voyage he spoke these verses:

Fela bið on Westwegum werum uncúðra
wundra and wihta, wlitescýne lond,
eardgeard Ylfa and Ésa bliss.
Lýt ænig wát hwylc his longað sý
þám þe eftsíðes yldu getwǽfeð.

'Many things there be in the West-regions unknown to Men, many wonders and many creatures: a land lovely to behold, the homeland of the Elves and the bliss of the Valar. Little doth any man understand what the yearning may be of one whom old age cutteth off from returning thither.'

Christopher Tolkien included this text also in *The Lost Road and Other Writings*, pp. 102–4.

Here 'Erin' is Ireland (Éire). The Old English text is also, in *The Lost Road*, quoted and translated, with several differences, by Alboin Errol to his father, after the lines come to him in a dream as from 'Ælfwine the far-travelled' (from *The Lost Road and Other Writings*, p. 44).

> Fela bith on Westwegum werum uncúthra
> wundra and wihta, wlitescéne land,
> eardgeard elfa, and ésa bliss.
> Lýt ǽnig wát hwylc his longath síe
> thám the eftsíthes eldo getwǽfeth.

> 'There is many a thing in the West-regions unknown to men, marvels and strange beings, a land fair and lovely, the homeland of the Elves, and the bliss of the Gods. Little doth any man know what longing is his whom old age cutteth off from return.'

And in *The Notion Club Papers* similar words are reported by Alwin Arundel (Arry) Lowdham, who 'picks up echoes' of curious languages:

> Fela bið on Westwegum werum uncúðra,
> wundra and wihta, wlitescýne land,
> eardgeard ælfa and ésa bliss.
> Lýt ænig wát hwylc his langoð síe
> þám þe eftsíðes eldo getwǽfeð.

> There is many a thing in the west of the world unknown to men; marvels and strange beings, [a land lovely to look on,] the dwelling place of the Elves and the bliss of the Gods. Little doth any man know what longing is his whom old age cutteth off from return. [*Sauron Defeated*, p. 244, brackets in the original]

Tolkien wrote varying accounts of the mariner Ælfwine (earlier Eriol) as he developed his mythology. A man of northern Europe, he was originally to visit Tol Eressëa and hear the 'lost tales' of the Elves. In one version, he and his companions reach 'the never-dying shore' and, hearing music coming gently over the waters, weep 'softly each for his heart's half-remembered hurts, and memory of fair things long lost, and each for the thirst that is in every child of Men for the flawless loveliness they seek and do not find' (*The Book of Lost Tales, Part*

Two, p. 321). Ælfwine suddenly springs into the sea, but a great wind blows his friends back into the East, 'hearts all broken with regret and longing' (p. 322). Tolkien outlined a variation of this account for *The Lost Road*, in which Ælfwine and his crew sail the Straight Road into the True West, following a path made for the Elves when the Undying Lands were sundered from the Earth. 'Ælfwine falls insensible when he smells a marvellous fragrance as of land and flowers' (*The Lost Road and Other Writings*, p. 78), and awakes to find that he has come to Eressëa. But in other workings for *The Lost Road*, Ælfwine and his son sail with ten neighbours into the West and either (it is left ambiguous) see Eressëa and hear its voices, or have a vision of that land in delirium, before a wind blows the travellers back to Ireland from whence they came.

When Tolkien wrote this outline, he had only recently conceived of the destruction of Númenor, its people punished when ambitious men invade Valinor, and of the concomitant reshaping of the world and creation of the Straight Road: 'For the Plain of the Gods being straight, whereas the surface of the world was bent, and the seas that lay upon it, and the heavy airs that lay above, cut through the air of breath and flight . . .' (*The Fall of Númenor*, in *The Lost Road and Other Writings*, p. 17). This is the sea-path Frodo experiences at the end of *The Lord of the Rings* when, passing by divine grace into the West, he smells 'a sweet fragrance on the air' and hears 'the sound of singing that came over the water', before a curtain of rain rolls back and he sees 'white shores and beyond them a far green country under a swift sunrise' (2005 edn., p. 1030).

It may be that Tolkien removed the fourth stanza from *The Song of Ælfwine* because it gave too vivid an account of the speaker reaching 'that land unknown' and seeing its people, once he added a prose text which leaves it open to question whether Ælfwine truly reached Eressëa or merely hallucinated its wonders.

In *Fantasies of Time and Death: Dunsany, Eddison, Tolkien* (2020), Anna Vaninskaya explores the tradition of the 'final departure over sea' in literature in general and Tolkien's work in particular. The idea of a land of wonder reached by ship, a place unattainable but eminently to be desired, is at least as old as the Fortunate Isles or Isles of the Blessed in Greek mythology, the Elysian Fields, the Garden of the Hesperides. *The Nameless Land* and its later versions, Vaninskaya argues, embody 'the essence of this desire' (p. 200). They are not, though, the first examples of this tradition in Tolkien's poetry – *The Happy Mariners* (no. 33) is certainly of a kind with *The Song of Ælfwine* – and one could legitimately point as well to the wartime verses in which Tolkien treats England as if it were a Paradise to be desired, but which circumstances bar to the poet.

It remains only to question, but we fear not answer definitively, the nature of the 'Wandering Fire' (or 'fires'), and whether the term is meant to gain in importance, as if personified, with capital letters. Stefan Ekman, in his 'Echoes of *Pearl* in Arda's Landscape' (2009), identifies it with 'the mariner Eärendel who sails across the sky with a silmaril on his brow and his ship filled with divine flame' (pp. 62–3). Massimiliano Izzo rightly calls this argument problematic, for the fire fills woodlands and is 'on leaf and land', hardly a celestial body; 'though', Izzo says, 'one could still surmise that the first is the light of Eärendel, rather than the star itself' ('In Search of the Wandering Fire: Otherworldly Imagery in "The Song of Ælfwine"' (2018), p. 16).

There are also possible sources in literature, such as Milton's *Paradise Lost*, in which Satan is compared to a 'wandering fire', that is, a will-o'-the-wisp, a phenomenon of burning gas sometimes seen over bogs or marshes and thought to trick the unwary traveller. Tennyson uses the phrase and concept in his *Idylls of the King*, where King Arthur is concerned that his questing knights will 'follow wandering fires' and become 'lost in the quagmire'. This is the import as well of the lights Frodo, Sam, and Gollum find in the Dead Marshes in *The Lord of the Rings*. Izzo rejects this interpretation in regard to *The Nameless Land*, however, instead identifying the 'fire' with 'the quickening of a human soul from the breath of life, the creative Spirit of God' (p. 25). If so, it would bear comparison with the 'Secret Fire' the God of *The Book of Lost Tales*, Ilúvatar, placed at the heart of the world to give it Life and Reality, and which informed the further fashioning of nature by the Ainur, the divine spirits, including Eressëa as a refuge for the Elves and a place of beauty.

This is a convenient place to mention a fragment – perhaps all that ever existed – of a different poem by Tolkien entitled *Nameless Land* which appears in the manuscript (Bodleian Library) of his introduction to the 1940 edition of Clark Hall's *Beowulf*, as an example of alliterative verse. It is not in the published essay, where Tolkien used *Beowulf* itself to illustrate his explanation of the poetic form.

> Over Water West — woe filled my breast
> I wandered lost. [The waves me tossed >] On the waves
> I tossed
> [*deleted:* long-rolling grim land]
> Dim land faded dark night shaded;

no cry there came none calling my name
To the marge I sailed middle earth there failed;
Waters thundered the world foundered.
From chaos cold cruel winds uprolled
my sails bending my soul rending.
East I wended old and bended
wildered wandering witless pondering
land loomed ahead: the lights were dead

Below this is a single line, 'there were mounds by the waves of men in graves'.

A46–7: 'Foam beyond the furthest sea | Did dare', i.e. dared to sail into unknown seas rough with foam.

B15: 'Those dells' originally read 'Where dells'. Here, and in text C, Tolkien spelled 'distill' with double letters, but later as 'distil'.

B18: 'Falling' originally read 'plumèd'.

B21–22: These lines originally read 'There the voices are in the valleys low | Singing unseen the muted lyre'. On one manuscript page, Tolkien wrote 'there' above 'are' – perhaps to indicate 'there are' – and 'steep' above 'valleys', and 'whose' tentatively to replace 'Its'. But the line remained unchanged when Tolkien wrote it on a second page; there he struck through the two lines 21 and 22 and indicated replacements. Line 22 read before further revision 'and the ?shaws are shaken with desire' or 'and the ?shaws are swept with sweet' (a *shaw* is a thicket or small wood). The first manuscript page also includes a column of words rhyming with 'fire'.

B23: This line originally began 'And the winds'.

C13–15: In C^2 these lines were typed and revised:

[With >] The wandering [fire >] fires the [woods do >] woodland fill,
In glades for ever green they glow,
[Those >] In dells [*added:* that] immortal dews distill

C49: 'Tir-nan-Og' is spelled thus as published.

C51–53: Next to these lines as typed in C^1 Tolkien wrote:

O mountains where no man may be,
O land forlorn where lost things are
O shore beyond the Shadowy Sea

In *Realities* these were incorporated but reversed in order, preserving 'O! shore beyond the Shadowy Sea' as l. 51, as in C^1, and taking 'O! land forlorn where lost things be' from C^2 (and A).

D30: By 'nether Night' Tolkien is presumably referring to a darkness or gloom as deep as may be found in the Underworld.

D39: In the second intermediate manuscript, this line began 'And tangled with' (as in the first intermediate manuscript), but was marked by Tolkien to become 'And twined within', the reading in the intermediate typescript.

D40: Tolkien marked 'a gold and silver sheen' in the second intermediate manuscript to be changed to 'a net of stars by night', but retained the first reading in the typescript

D41: 'As fleet' originally read 'There fleet'. In the first intermediate manuscript, Tolkien began to write this stanza with '[There >] As fleet and white their feet go bare' and continued to 'for winds unearthly flowing free', then wrote the present ll. 37–40 (from 'There blowing free . . .') as a new beginning for the stanza.

D49: Next to the final stanza in the first manuscript Tolkien wrote but abandoned: 'more fair and keen it cleaves the sky | mounting above all mists the star | of Earendel raised on high'.

D59–60: 'O! Star that shadow may not mar, | nor ever darkness doom to die!' refers to Eärendel as a beacon of hope to the peoples of the world under the darkness of evil.

E21: 'The unfading Rose' is presumably the wild rose earlier, and in the next line, referred to as *briar*.

F41–2: The inhabitants' 'lissom feet' dancing, and running 'light as flying leaves', recall Lúthien's 'lissom feet on leaves' and the 'flying sound of [her] feet as light as linden leaves', in versions of poem no. 64.

G28: 'The Shadow', i.e. the Shadowy Sea.

G41: The Tree that flowers is presumably Celeborn, the White Tree of Tol Eressëa, derived from Galathilion, the Tree of Tirion made for the Elves by Yavanna in the image of Telperion.

75

Ave atque Vale · Lines Composed on an Evening · Lines Composed in a Village Inn (1924–?*c.* 1950)

The earliest complete version of this poem, written in ink on what appears to be a stray leaf of examination paper, is entitled *Ave atque Vale: Farewell to the Rural Pleasures of Vacation.* (*Ave atque Vale* is Latin for 'Hail and Farewell'.) Added in pencil, however, are the date 'Aug[ust] 1924' and two draft titles, *Ode: Intimations of the Hospitality in a Village Inn from Recollections at the End of the Long Vacation* and *Composed upon an Evening of Extraordinary Liquid Beauty (in a Village Inn at the End of an Annual Holiday)*. We give this text as A, and include in notes alternate readings from a partly illegible page of manuscript workings.

[A]

The dark was falling down like dough,
    The moon was rising like a flower,
The stars in threes went to and fro —
    Alas! the passing of the hour!
And 'O! for goodness sake' said he,
[']Don't let the morning break for me!'

The morning broke in smithereens,
    The cocks were gurgling in their throats,
The dew was on the kidney-beans,
    And o! the bleating of the goats.
'I love those billy-goats', said he,
'I love their tender tones of glee.'

The slimy slug with wary eye,
    The sneaking snail, I love them all,
The bad old beetle, and the fly —
    They're gone, they're gone beyond recall:
The dainty duckling in the mire,
The loud effluvium of the byre,

Ah me! the bulging bantam's eggs,
The mournful mooing of the cow,
The daddy's long and dancing legs
That nimbly skipt from bough to bough,
The playful biting of the flea —
All, all is over now for me.

The cauliflower must bloom alone,
The onion weep with none to hear,
The vegetable marrows moan —
Ah! cabbage-patch of yesteryear
'I loved, alas, and lost', said he,
'And never never more shall see,
That cabbage-patch now closed to me. [']

A new manuscript version, now *Lines Composed on an Evening of Extraordinary Liquid Beauty in a Village Inn (at End of a Summer Holiday)*, closely followed text A in content and perhaps also in date: for the latter, it is impossible to say, Tolkien's handwriting having become fairly consistent by the end of his years at Leeds. The first of two pages is inscribed 'Intimations of Intoxication in ?ford' – the final word does not appear to be 'Oxford'. Tolkien made a few changes to this version, which he carried into a typescript almost certainly made after he left Leeds for Oxford. As typed, this version was called *Lines Composed on the Morning After an Evening of Extraordinary Liquid Beauty in a Village Inn*, but Tolkien changed his mind and restored the title to that of the preceding manuscript, without the bracketed extension. He also marked this text for revision, almost identically on ribbon and carbon copies, and it was here that a majority of changes entered the poem, notably in the first and second stanzas, as well as a four-line 'envoy'.

Finally, Tolkien wrote out a new manuscript (B), with a slightly rearranged title, *Lines Composed in a Village Inn on an Evening of Extraordinary Liquid Beauty*. Again, we cannot be sure of its date; it is possibly as late as the 1950s.

[B]

The dark is falling down like dough,
The moon is rising like a flower,
The stars in pairs go to and fro —
Alas! the passing of the hour!
'Alas! I would not have', said he,
[']Another morning break for me!'
When last I woke amongst the greens,
The cocks were gurgling in their throats,

The dew was on the might-have-beans,
  And O! the bleating of the goats.
[']Farewell, you billy-goats', said he,
  'I loved your tones of sneering glee!'

'The slimy slug with wary eye,
  The sneaking snail, I loved them all,
The bad old beetle and the fly —
  But they are gone beyond recall,
The dainty duckling in the mire,
  The loud effluvium of the byre!'

'Ah me! the bony bantam's eggs,
  The mournful mooing of the cow,
The daddy's long and dancing legs
  That nimbly skipped from bough to bough,
The playful biting of the flea —
  All, all, are over now for me!'

The cauliflower must bloom alone,
  The onion weep with none to hear,
The vegetable marrows moan —
  Ah! cabbage-patch of yesteryear
[']I loved, alas, and lost', said he,
  [']And never, nevermore, shall see.'

Envoy

Yet no doubt soon 'twill pass from mind,
When better beer I elsewhere find.
Farewell, you inn, with a tinker's curse.
Better beer? It could not be worse!

Lines, as we might now call this work for the sake of brevity – an otherwise blank sheet among Tolkien's papers has the much simpler title *Lines in an Inn* – unfortunately leaves us with questions unanswered. The 'long vacation' referred to in one of its titles is the summer break at university; in 1924, the long vacation at Leeds began at the end of spring term on 5 July and ended at the start of autumn term on 1 October. We have no record of Tolkien on holiday that summer, though he is known to have been in Oxford *c.* 20 July, at times in the company of his former Leeds colleague George S. Gordon, and otherwise had free time to develop some of his poems.

On 16 July the University of Leeds promoted Tolkien from a readership to the new post of Professor of English Language, perhaps something to be celebrated at the 'village inn'.

If Tolkien found inspiration for his poem in August 1924, at the end of a holiday, and Leeds autumn term did not begin until 1 October, there was still a month of the long vacation yet to run. Did he cut his holiday short because of added duties in his new professorship, or did he allow time before the beginning of term to prepare his lectures? Also, does his poem refer only to an evening of heavy drinking ('liquid beauty') – and the morning after – or had he been staying for a period with friends? Was his family with him, though Edith was then six months pregnant with their third son? If Tolkien was staying at or near a farm, as his remarks about domesticated animals and vegetable patches suggest, might it have been in Evesham, Worcestershire, where his brother had an orchard and market garden?

His sorrow in ending his holiday is of course feigned, neither bad-tempered billy-goats nor the 'loud' (powerful) effluvium (stink) of the byre (cowshed) genuinely to be missed. The poem is not truly an ode, as one of its early titles has it, that is, not a lyric work praising the inn or its rural setting, but ironic nonsense, overplaying everything. That it was inspired also by the poems of Lewis Carroll is hardly to be doubted. *Lines* is in a distinctly Carrollian style, calling easily to mind 'The Walrus and the Carpenter' in *Through the Looking-glass*,

> The sun was shining on the sea,
>   Shining with all his might:
> He did his very best to make
>   The billows smooth and bright —
> And this was very odd, because it was
>   The middle of the night.

or from *Sylvie and Bruno*:

> There was a pig that sat alone,
>   Beside a ruined Pump.
> By day and night he made his moan:
> It would have stirred a heart of stone
> To see him ring his hoofs and groan,
>   Because he could not jump.

Tolkien would later attempt, but reject, a brief Carrollian poem as the song with which Marmaduke (later Merry) surprises his friends in a 1938 draft of *The Lord of the Rings* (*The Return of the Shadow*, p. 98):

As I was sitting by the way,
    I saw three hobbits walking:
One was dumb with naught to say,
    The others were not talking.

'Good night!' I said. 'Good night to you!'
    They heeded not my greeting:
One was deaf like the other two.
    It was a merry meeting!

Although the ABABCC rhyme scheme (a sestain) of *Lines* was not often used by Carroll (see, though, his prefatory poem to *Through the Looking-glass and What Alice Found There*), it is not uncommon in English poetry in general.

A1: 'Falling down like dough', i.e. like a yeast dough that has risen, then deflated.

A3: In draft, this line read 'The stars were playing peep and bo', i.e. the children's game in which the face is hidden and suddenly revealed with the cry 'peep-bo!' (or 'peekaboo'). Tolkien may have meant that clouds were intermittently obscuring or revealing the stars, or that they were rising and setting while time passed. The new reading in A3, 'The stars in threes went to and fro', and that in B3, where the stars are 'in pairs', may be meant to suggest that the poet, in his cups, was seeing treble or double.

A6: The 'morning break' not to be desired could suggest that the poet is hung over and hopes to avoid the light and commotion of dawn.

A8: Tolkien considered 'gargling' instead of 'gurgling', but the latter remained in all versions of the poem. The cocks (roosters) are crowing at dawn. In draft, this line read 'The cocks all gurgled in their throats'.

A12: The voices of billy-goats (male goats) are by no means tender (soft).

A13: Tolkien played in draft with additional lines for the slug: 'The slug then cleared his slender throat | And on he slipped his slimy coat'.

A21: 'Daddy's long and dancing legs' is a play on *daddy-long-legs*, a name which in Britain means the crane-fly.

A22: 'Skipt', i.e. skipped.

A24: In draft, this line read 'But all is over now for me'.

A26: Onions do not themselves weep, but may cause weeping in someone slicing them.

A29: 'I loved, alas, and lost' is indebted to Tennyson in *In Memoriam A.H.H.*: ''Tis better to have loved and lost | Than never to have loved at all'.

B7: Whereas in A the dawn 'broke in smithereens' (into small pieces), now the poet wakes 'amongst the greens', presumably having slept in the vegetable patch where he passed out from drinking.

B9: 'Might-have-beans' (replacing 'kidney-beans') is a play on *might-have-beens*, things which might have happened, or persons who might have been greater or more eminent, under different circumstances.

B33: To give a 'tinker's curse' is not to care in the least.

76

From One to Five (*c.* 1924)

During his years at the University of Leeds in the first half of the 1920s, Tolkien wrote occasional verses for the amusement of English language students. So, too, did his colleague E.V. Gordon, who came to Leeds in 1922 as an Assistant Lecturer and succeeded to Tolkien's professorship there in 1926. Gordon compiled their original poems, written in Old, Middle, and Modern English, Gothic, Old Norse, and Latin, as well as traditional pieces from Icelandic student songbooks, and had them mimeographed for student use. In 1935 or 1936 A.H. Smith, who had read English at Leeds, gave copies of some of these 'Leeds Songs' to a group of University College London students to print as an exercise on a handpress. The result was a booklet of thirty poems, *Songs for the Philologists* (1936), or *Songs* as we will call it sometimes for brevity. Not all of the known Leeds verses were included – the editors omitted several not by Tolkien, and one which he did write, *Smakkabagms* (Gothic 'fig tree'), which we have not seen. Moreover, the poems were generally altered or truncated, either by design or in error in the process of typesetting. At length, A.H. Smith realized that he had never asked permission of Tolkien and Gordon to publish their original work, and restricted the number of printed copies of the collection. Most of the stock of *Songs* that had not yet been distributed perished in a fire.

We do not know how many 'songs' Tolkien wrote altogether, precisely when he wrote each of them, or if he began to write them before Gordon arrived at Leeds. The dates bibliographers have given to the individual poems have been guesswork, lacking physical or documentary evidence; the Leeds archivists, for example, date manuscript copies of Tolkien's poems printed in *Songs for the Philologists* to the 1920s or to *c.* 1924, in the first instance acknowledging (more broadly than necessary) Tolkien's Leeds years, and in the second (perhaps) assuming composition when Tolkien was more established, rising to the new English Language professorship in 1924, but not yet in his final year at Leeds when he prepared to take up the Anglo-Saxon chair at Oxford. We have used the later date (*c.* 1924) arbitrarily for ten of Tolkien's poems in *Songs*, not including three written after he moved to Oxford in 1925: we have dated these to ?1928, as Tolkien sent their manuscripts to Gordon with a letter dated 2 January 1929.

Tolkien himself dated a set of the 'Leeds Songs' to '*c.* 1925–6', and Dr Cyril Jackson, said to have studied at Leeds soon after Tolkien left for Oxford, recalled singing songs set to nursery rhymes on 'boozy evenings', and referred to parties at which Tolkien was a visitor (from a letter sold with a copy of *Songs* by Bloomsbury Auctions, 6 November 2003). But Tolkien and Gordon had formed a club somewhat earlier, probably not long after Gordon came to Leeds, at which students interested in Old Norse read sagas, drank beer, and sang comic songs – presumably including those by their hosts.

Thirteen poems by Tolkien are in *Songs for the Philologists*. Of these, we will deal with ten beginning with the present work, in their order of appearance in the booklet; the remaining three, those from ?1928, are in the later sequence 97–99. None of the verses in *Songs* is credited in print, but in a personal copy of the booklet Tolkien wrote his initials next to his poems in the table of contents, as well as alterations to many of the poems themselves – it is not always possible to know which mark is a correction, and which was intended as an improvement. Tolkien also added numerous accents, if inconsistently, and he identified the traditional tunes to which his verses were to be sung when this information was not provided in print. He owned at least two copies of *Songs* and annotated each of them, sometimes marking one different from the other: in the course of our discussions, we will refer to these as 'copy 1' and 'copy 2'. Christopher Tolkien allowed 'copy 1' to be photocopied after fans of his father's work learned of the existence of the exceedingly rare *Songs for the Philologists* and asked to see it; we have a reproduction in our files and have referred to it for this book. We have also referred to an original printing from 1936.

In dealing with this group of Tolkien's poems we have been fortunate to have access to several of them in manuscripts he gave to E.V. Gordon, now held in the Library of the University of Leeds and referred to here in brief as the Gordon archive. These differ in many respects compared with the printed works in *Songs*, sometimes notably so, and in such instances it is interesting to wonder if the manuscripts are, as we have supposed, the original texts which led ultimately to the printed *Songs*, and how much the physical capabilities of the day, skill in reading Tolkien's handwriting, and scholarly preference played roles in creating the booklet of 1936. The printed poems lack many of the diacritical marks Tolkien used in his manuscripts, and sometimes have different punctuation and indentation. It may be that the student printers at University College London lacked a good supply of accented characters in the metal type available to them, though it is also possible that the students were merely following, as a copy-text, exactly what they saw in the mimeographed 'Leeds Songs' – we have not seen any of the poems in that form. The printed texts also often use the character eth (ð) where Tolkien wrote a thorn (þ), again suggesting a lack of special characters, or else an editorial preference. For our transcriptions, we have used Tolkien's manuscripts where they were available; where they were not, we have transcribed the printed *Songs*, incorporating or noting revisions Tolkien marked in his personal copy 1.

The first of Tolkien's poems in *Songs for the Philologists* is entitled *From One to Five*. We give its text (A) as printed on p. 6 of the booklet.

[A]

One old man of Durham
Wrote a perished play;
Had he not lost the play, sir,
The royalties would pay, sir! — Poor he!

Three wise men of Yorkshire
Tried to train a boy;
Had the boy been brighter
Their task had been lighter — O yea!

Two poor loons of London
Tried to talk in Norse;
Had their tongues been stronger
Their talk had been longer — Ah me!

Four young nameless noodles
Took the English School —
Nearly failed in winter —
They ploughed 'em in the Inter — Wela wa!

Five fat Middlesex maidens
Tried to print a book;
They used as ink-ball, sir,
The roundest of all, sir! — Hee hee!

In his copy 1 of *Songs* Tolkien noted that his text in print was 'altered to fit UCL [University College London] conditions'. Using his annotations as a guide, we have attempted (in B) to reconstruct the poem as Tolkien wrote it in relation to the University of Leeds.

[B] One Old man of Yorkshire
Wrote in dialect;
Had his verse been sounder, sir,
't'royalties had been rounder, sir! — Poor he!

Two wise men of Oxford
Tried to train a bee;
Had the bee been brighter
Their task had been lighter — O yea!

Two poor loons of Loidis
Tried to talk in Norse;
Had their tongues been stronger
Their talk had been longer — Ah me!

Four young nameless noodles
Took the English School —
Nearly failed in winter —
They ploughed 'em in the Inter — waylaway!

Five fat maids of Roundhay
Tried to play at fives;
They used one as the ball, sir,
The roundest of all, sir! — Hee hee!

According to a printed caption in *Songs for the Philologists*, Tolkien's poem was to be sung to the tune of 'Three Wise Men of Gotham'. The shape of each stanza is indebted to that of the nursery rhyme famous for its brevity:

Three wise men of Gotham
Went to sea in a bowl;
And if the bowl had been stronger
My song would have been longer.

From One to Five also nods to counting-out rhymes, though as printed in *Songs for the Philologists* its stanzas are out of order (One old man, Three wise men, Two poor loons, Four young noodles, Five fat maidens). It seems as if the second and third stanzas should be reversed, or that the 'three wise men' should number two and the 'two poor loons' number three, but Tolkien marked no change to this end.

The music and lyrics for 'Three Wise Men of Gotham', and for other songs on which Tolkien based rhymes published in *Songs for the Philologists*, are included in Moffat's *What the Children Sing* (see our discussion for poem no. 24).

Next to line 1, in his original version 'One old man of Yorkshire', Tolkien wrote 'G.H.C.' These are presumably the initials of his Leeds colleague, the Chaucer scholar George Herbert Cowling, who joined the English faculty in 1919 as a Lecturer and in 1925 became Reader in English Language and Literature. He was an amateur poet who wrote in dialect ('A's gotten t'bliss o' moonten-tops ti-neet' in *Leeds University Verse 1914–24*) as well as conventional English.

B9: *Loon* is used here perhaps in the old sense of 'stupid person'; compare *noodle* in l. 13. *Loidis* is an ancient name for Leeds, mentioned by the Venerable Bede around 730 in his *Historia Ecclesiastica*.

B13: *Noodle*, like *loon* in l. 9, in this context means 'simpleton'.

B16: 'Ploughed 'em in the Inter', i.e. failed the students in their Intermediate Examination. *Waylaway*, from Middle English *weilawei*, perhaps more frequently seen as *wellaway*, is an archaic expression of sadness or regret. In the margin of his copy of *Songs* Tolkien wrote 'Scheme A!': if this refers to Leeds, Scheme A was a course of study in English which focused on Literature, as opposed to Scheme B which emphasized Language. At Oxford this order was reversed, with the English School course of study 'A' focused on Language.

B17: Roundhay is a suburb in north-east Leeds.

B18: To 'play at fives' is to play a game with a ball hit against a wall. The uncomfortable joke in ll. 19–20 is that one of the 'fat maids', 'the roundest of all', was used as the ball in Fives. In the altered version in *Songs*, the 'roundest' maid is used as an ink-ball, traditionally a leather ball-like tool for transferring ink onto metal type for printing.

77

Ruddoc Hana (*c.* 1924)

Ruddoc Hana (literally 'robin cock', i.e. the male robin) is Tolkien's inventive translation into Old English of the nursery rhyme 'Who Killed Cock Robin?' Here we have transcribed the work from the manuscript in the Gordon archive at Leeds, with selected differences in the printed *Songs for the Philologists* (1936) described in notes. *Ruddoc Hana* is the third of Tolkien's poems to appear in *Songs* (pp. 8–9), after *Syx Mynet* (no. 97).

According to a note by Tolkien, in his personal copy of *Songs* (copy 1) as well as on the manuscript, the work is to be sung to the tune 'Cock Robin', which we take to mean some traditional setting to music of the nursery lyrics. Latin *bis* is a direction to repeat the line, and is meant to apply to the first line of each stanza.

Hí grornodon (3), gnornodon (3),
  sworetton þá sáre;
ne æfter wine déadum næs
  nǽfre wóp mára.

1.

'Hwá felde Ruddoc?' (*bis*)
'Ic,' cwæþ se spearewa,
'mid bogan and arewan,
wiþ felda buttoc.'

2.

'Hwá geseah þæt morþ?'
'Ic,' cwæþ seo péo,
'ongan hit geséon,
fléogende forþ.'

3.

'Hwá nóm his blód?'
'Ic,' cwæþ se fisc,
'on mínne disc,
þá ic þider wód.'

4.

'Hwá wyrcþ his hrægl?'
'Ic,' cwæþ se fína,
'mid nǽdle and líne
wyrce hit swa segl.'

5.

'Hwá bringeþ tapor?'
'Ic, línetwige,
bere hine' on swíge,
gif ic neom slápor.'

6.

'Hwá biþ cantére?'
'Ic,' cwæþ se stær,
'beo ræpsa wær;
þider ic fére.'

7.

'Hwá weorþeþ préost?'
'Ic,' cwæþ se hróc,
'Ic bringe mine bóc;
Sár is mín bréost.'

8.

'Hwa singeþ "dirige"?'
'Wit,' cwæþ se þrosle;
'húru wit ósle
singað unmyrge.'

9.

'Hwá gnornaþ hine?'
'Ic,' cwæþ séo dúfe,
'Ic mid þam úfe,
þurh módes myne.'

10.

'Hwá bereþ þrúh?'
'Ic,' cwæþ se glida,
'þurh sýferne sido,
þéah hío béo rúh.'

II.

'Hwá cnylleþ bellan?'
'Ic' cwæþ þæt hríþer,
'Oþrum swiþor;
Hlude sceal scellan!'

For comparison, we give here the text of 'Who Killed Cock Robin?' (as 'The Death and Burial of Cock Robin') from the 1871 *National Nursery Rhymes and Nursery Songs*, there set to music by J.W. Elliott.

Who killed Cock Robin?
'I,' said the Sparrow,
'With my bow and arrow,
I killed Cock Robin.'

Who saw him die?
'I,' said the Fly,
'With my little eye,
And I saw him die.'

Who caught his blood?
'I,' said the Fish,
'With my little dish,
And I caught his blood.'

Who'll make his shroud?
'I,' said the Beetle,
'With my thread and needle,
I'll make his shroud.'

Who'll bear the torch?
'I, the Linnet,
Will come in a minute,
I'll bear the torch.'

Who'll be the clerk?
'I,' said the Lark,
'I'll say Amen in the dark,
I'll be the clerk.'

Who'll dig his grave?
'I,' said the Owl,
'With my spade and shovel,
I'll dig his grave.'

Who'll be the parson?
'I,' said the Rook,
'With my little book,
I'll be the parson.'

Who'll be chief mourner?
'I,' said the Dove,
'I mourn for my love,
I'll be chief mourner.'

Who'll sing his dirge?
'I,' said the Thrush,
'As I sing in a bush,
I'll sing his dirge.'

Who'll carry his coffin?
'I,' said the Kite,
'If it be in the night,
I'll carry the coffin.'

Who'll toll the bell?
'I,' said the Bull,
'Because I can pull,
I'll toll the bell.'

All the birds of the air
Fell sighing and sobbing,
When they heard the bell toll
For poor Cock Robin.

The earliest known printing of the rhyme, *c.* 1744, had only the first four stanzas; its longer, more familiar versions began to be recorded in the late eighteenth century, though some elements suggest a greater antiquity. Variants abound: the text in Iona and Peter Opie's *Oxford Dictionary of Nursery Rhymes*, for example, in addition to differences of phrasing has the Thrush agree to sing a psalm rather than a dirge, and includes a stanza in which 'the Wren, | Both the cock and the hen' (i.e. male and female), agree to bear the pall. In still another version, this task is taken by the Crow.

In his version, Tolkien omitted the owl, lark, and wren (or crow), and wrote new text to rhyme more creatively with the Old English vocabulary, rather than follow the stanza scheme of the traditional poem in which the first and fourth lines end with the same word. Thus the sparrow (*spearewa*) admits to killing Cock Robin (*Ruddoc*) with his bow and arrow ('mid bogan and arewan'), near the rear of the field ('wiþ felda buttoc'). The fly (*péo* 'parasite, insect') saw the deed ('hit geséon') while flying forth ('fléogende forþ'). The fish (*fisc*) caught the robin's blood in his dish ('on mínre disc'), where he thither went ('þa ic þider wód'). Instead of a beetle to make a shroud (*hrægl* 'garment, robe'), Tolkien has a woodpecker (*fína*), who with needle and thread ('mid nǽdle and líne') works it like a sail ('wyrce hit swa segl'), i.e. as if he were a sailmaker. A linnet offers a torch to light the way, here a *tapor* 'taper, candle' which he will bring in silence ('on swíge') if he is not sleepy ('gif ic neom slápor'). A starling (*stær*), not a thrush, agrees to sing a psalm ('cantére') because he knows the responses in the church service ('béo ræpsa wær'). A rook, as traditionally, agrees to officiate, here as a worthy priest ('weorþeþ préost'); he will bring his (holy) book ('Ic bringe mine bóc'), feeling sorrow in his breast ('Sár is min bréost'). A throstle (*þrostle*), i.e. the song thrush, offers to sing a dirge (*dirige*) for the robin, though he warns that it will be a duet with a blackbird (*ósle*), and their singing is not pleasant ('singað unmyrige'). A (mourning) dove (*dúfe*) appropriately agrees to mourn the robin ('gnornaþ hine'), and a kite (*glida*) to bear the coffin, though the latter would be rough ('þeah hio béo rúh'). The bull (*hriðer*) volunteers to toll the bell ('cnylleð bellan'), promising because of its strength that it will be rung loudly ('hlude sceal scellan'). (It has been reasonably argued that the 'bull' of the traditional rhyme is a bullfinch, not a quadruped, though the creature is clearly stronger than a bullfinch. If the 'bull' is indeed a bird, there is still one participant without wings, the fish; in medieval natural history, winged insects such as the fly and beetle were classed with birds as things of the air.)

The chorus of four lines roughly translates as 'Oh, we mourned, we mourned, we sighed in grief; in memory of our deceased friend we weep no more'. The emotions are reflected in the final stanza, as in the familiar rhyme.

1–4: In the Leeds manuscript Tolkien wrote out the chorus after the rest of the text. We have it at the beginning, where it is printed in *Songs for the Philologists*.

2: In the printed booklet, and in the Leeds manuscript, 'sworetton' is given as 'sworelton'. In his personal copy of *Songs* (copy 1), Tolkien marked 'sworelton' to be emended to 'sworetton', and we have followed suit here.

11: In the printed booklet 'ongan' is given as 'ongann'.

15: In the printed booklet 'mínne' is misprinted 'minre'.

33: In the printed booklet 'dirige' is misprinted 'dinge'.

34: In the printed booklet 'þrosle' is misprinted 'þrostle'.

35: In the printed booklet 'ósle' is misprinted 'ostle'.

47: In the printed booklet 'oþrum' is misprinted 'oðerum'.

78

Ides Ælfscýne (*c.* 1924)

The fourth of Tolkien's poems in *Songs for the Philologists* (1936, pp. 10–11) is *Ides Ælfscýne* (there lacking the accent). The Old English title means 'elf-fair lady', that is, a woman as beautiful as an elf (or fairy). Here, as A, we have transcribed Tolkien's manuscript of the poem in the Gordon archive at Leeds.

[A]

Þa ǽr ic wæs cniht, þa cóm ic on pliht;
þá métte me mægden and mǽlde:
'Lá! léofa wes hál! Sceal uncer gedál
nú nǽfre má weorþan on eorþan!'
Nó má weorþan on eorþan! (*bis*)
Wá! ides ælfscýne, and wá! wine míne!
Sceal nǽfre má weorþan on eorþan.

Héo cyste má sóna, þǽr líxte se móna;
on clammum me clypte ond sǽlde;
on ofste mé nóm mid hire' under glóm,
þǽr sceadugang ǽfre wæs wǽfre,
wælmist ǽfre wæs wǽfre. (*bis*)
Wá! ides ælfscýne, and wá! wine míne!
Þǽr sceadugong ǽfre wæs wǽfre.

Hwǽr wǽre' hit ic nát: wé stigon on bát,
þǽr murcnede mere on mealme.
Ofer lagu ic láþ, and módes ic máþ,
ac ǽfre me strangode langoþ,
áwá strangode langoþ. (*bis*)
Wá! ides ælfscýne, and wá! wine míne!
Þǽr ǽfre mé strangode langoþ.

Þǽr gréne wæs grund, and hwít hire hund,
and gylden wæs hwǽte on healme,
on fyrlenum lande, on silfrenum sande,
þǽr brante' ymbe þrunton þá muntas,
þéostre þrunton þá muntas. (*bis*)

Wá! ides ælfscýne, and wá! wine míne!
Þǽr brante' ymbe þrunton þá muntas.

Tó Gode' ic gebæd, elþéodunga sæd
be dimmum and dréorigum wǽgum.
Þǽr sunne ne scán, ac micel gimstán
on lyfte þǽr gléow mid his léomum,
léohte gléow mid his léomum. (*bis*)
Wá! ides ælfscýne, and wá! wine míne!
On lyfte þær gléow mid his léomum.

Ofer missera hund ic wǽdla and wund
eft cyrde tó mennisce' and mǽgum:
on moldan wæs nú se þe cúþe mé iú,
and hár ic nú wánige ána,
sáre wánige ána. (*bis*)
Wá! ides ælfscýne, and wá! wine míne!
And hár ic nú wánige ána.

Following is a translation of the poem into Modern English:

[B] Before I was a boy, I came into danger;
a maiden met me and said:
'Oh, love, be well! Now we shall never separate,
never be apart on Earth!'
No more be apart on Earth.
Woe! elf-fair lady, and woe, my friend!
Never shall we be apart on Earth.

Soon she kissed me, there shone the moon;
in her grasp she embraced and bound me;
quickly she took me under the gloom,
where the shadow-passage was ever wavering,
the mist of death was ever wavering.
Woe! elf-fair lady, and woe, my friend!
Where the shadow-passage was ever wavering.

Where we were I knew not: we climbed into a boat,
where the sea murmured on the sand.
Over the sea I went, my moods I hid,
but ever my longing grew stronger,
always stronger longing.

Woe! elf-fair lady, and woe, my friend!
Ever my longing grew stronger.

Where green was the ground, and white was her hound,
and golden was the wheat on the stalk,
in a distant land, on silver sand,
where nearby rose the high mountains,
darkly rose the mountains.
Woe! elf-fair lady, and woe, my friend!
Where nearby rose the high mountains.

To God I prayed, a weary traveller
by the dim and dreary waves.
There the sun did not shine, but a great gem
glowed with light in the sky,
radiantly glowed with light.
Woe! elf-fair lady, and woe, my friend!
Glowed with light in the sky.

After fifty years poor and wounded
I returned to men and kin:
one who once had known me was in the earth,
and now I diminish, grey and alone,
diminish in pain and alone.
Woe! elf-fair lady, and woe, my friend!
And now I diminish, grey and alone.

In his personal copy (copy 1) of *Songs for the Philologists* Tolkien marked next to line 2 'Sum maegden mé métte' ('A certain maiden met me'), apparently as a revision to 'þá métte mé mægden'. Next to lines 25 and 28, he wrote 'darode dweorg under beorgum' ('the dwarf lurked under the mountain'), apparently as a revision to 'brante' ymbe þrunton þá muntas' ('nearby rose the high mountains').

In *The Road to Middle-earth*, pp. 306–7, Tom Shippey gives a transcription from *Songs* and provides his own Modern English translation of the poem, both with Tolkien's alterations just mentioned. He includes *Ides Ælfscýne* as an 'asterisk-poem', that is, intended by Tolkien as the (invented) 'original' from which a later, more familiar poem was ultimately derived (see also *Syx Mynet*, no. 97). Here it is an 'ancestor' of ballads such as 'Tam Lin' and 'The Queen of Elfan's Nourice' (i.e. nurse), in which a mortal is trapped by a supernatural being. This is certainly the mode in which Tolkien set his work, regardless of whether he intended it as a 'reconstruction'.

In *A Question of Time: J.R.R. Tolkien's Road to* Faërie (1997) Verlyn Flieger finds 'the seeds of "Looney" [poem no. 134] . . . plain to see' in *Ides Ælfscýne*, 'not just in the theme of the poem, but in the details – the sudden journey by boat, the far-off land, the silver strand, the dim and dreary waves' (p. 217). In her later essay 'Fays, Corrigans, Elves, and More: Tolkien's Dark Ladies', Flieger writes of Tolkien

> using the fairy-tale motif . . . of the mortal, trapped in a faërian time-warp where years pass like minutes, who returns to a world that has passed him by. But behind this motif is the less familiar but equally ominous notion of the seduction/abduction of a mortal by a fairy lover. Tolkien's Ælfscyne, his Corrigan [see no. 116], and his Guinever [in *The Fall of Arthur*, see no. 139] are sisters under the skin. [*There Would Always Be a Fairy Tale* (2017), p. 174]

According to a printed caption in *Songs for the Philologists*, *Ides Ælfscýne* is to be sung to the tune of 'Daddy Neptune', an eighteenth-century ballad, the lyrics of which are unrelated to Tolkien's poem: 'Daddy Neptune one day to Freedom did say, | if ever I liv'd upon dry-land, | the spot I should hit on wou'd be little Britain', etc. As in *Ruddoc Hana* (no. 77), Latin *bis* in Tolkien's poem is a direction to repeat the line: this increases the stanza length to eight lines, which matches that of 'Daddy Neptune'.

A2: In the printed text, here and in all other instances, 'and' is given as 'ond'. Both are legitimate spellings in Old English of the conjunction 'and', but Tolkien in fact wrote 'and'. One might guess that the typesetter misread Tolkien's *a* as an *o*, which would not be hard to do – we also find printed 'strongode' for manuscript 'strangode' in ll. 19 and 21, and 'bronte' for 'brante' in ll. 25 and 28 – and yet there can be no question of the correct letter in l. 42, where it is capitalized. We suspect that there was a preference for 'ond' among the student printers, or else one was applied when the poem was typed and mimeographed at Leeds, and thus was in the printers' copy-text. As noted earlier, we have been unable to see any of the 'Leeds Songs' as they were originally distributed.

A24: In the printed text 'sande' ('sand') is given as 'stronde' ('strand'). The word is clearly written in the Leeds manuscript. Tolkien made no change to 'stronde' in his personal copy of *Songs*, presumably because the meaning was little different.

79

Bagmē Blōma (*c.* 1924)

Bagmē Blōma ('The Flower of Trees') is the fifth of Tolkien's works in *Songs for the Philologists* (1936), and the only poem he is known to have composed in Gothic. The macrons above the *e* and *o* in the title were added by him in the table of contents of his personal copy (copy 1) of *Songs*. Here, as A, we give the Gothic text as printed on p. 12 of the booklet, followed by a translation (B). For the latter, in which we have aimed to effect a 'Tolkienian' style, we have drawn from the translations by Tom Shippey in *The Road to Middle-earth* (after one by the late Rhona Beare) and Lucas Annear in *Tolkien Studies* 8 (2011), and are indebted also to Arden R. Smith's analysis of the poem in his essay 'Tolkienian Gothic' (2006).

[A]

Brunaim bairiþ Bairka bogum
laubans liubans liudandei,
gilwagroni, glitmunjandei,
bagme bloma, blauandei,
fagrafahsa, liþulinþi,
fraujinondei fairguni.

Wopjand windos, wagjand lindos
lutiþ limam laikandei;
slaihta, raihta, hweitarinda [ƕeitarinda]
razda rodeiþ reirandi,
bandwa bairhta, runa goda,
þiuda meina þiuþjandei.

Andanahti milhmam neipiþ,
liuhteiþ liuhmam lauhmuni;
laubos liubai fliugand lausai,
tulgus, triggwa, standandei
Bairka baza beidiþ blaika
fraujinondei fairguni.

[B]

The Birch brings forth on shining boughs
beloved leaves springing,
yellow-green, glittering,

flower of trees, blossoming,
fair-haired, lithe-limbed,
ruling over the mountain.

Winds cry, branches shake,
bending limbs leaping;
smooth, straight, white of bark,
it speaks a trembling speech,
a bright sign, a good mystery,
blessing my people.

Evening grows dark with clouds,
flashes bright with lightning;
beloved leaves fly free,
firm, true, standing
the Birch bides pale and bare
ruling over the mountain.

Tolkien discovered Gothic, the earliest recorded Germanic language, while still at school. It was

> the first [language] to take me by storm, to move my heart. . . . I have since mourned the loss of Gothic literature. . . . The contemplation of the vocabulary in *A Primer of the Gothic Language* [1899, by his Oxford mentor Joseph Wright] was enough: a sensation at least as full of delight as first looking into Chapman's *Homer*. Though I did not write a sonnet about it. I tried to invent Gothic words. [*English and Welsh* (1955), in *The Monsters and the Critics and Other Essays*, pp. 191–2].

(The allusion here is to 'On First Looking into Chapman's Homer' by John Keats, which refers to the poet's delight in reading the vigorous English translation of Homer's works by George Chapman.) Tolkien is said to have taken part in a Latin debate at King Edward's School in the character of a barbarian envoy, in which he broke into fluent Gothic – no mean feat, given the complexity of the language and the limits of its vocabulary, much of it surviving in Bible translations.

In 'Tolkienian Gothic' Arden R. Smith counts fifty-five discrete words in *Bagmē Blōma*, of which 'only thirty-eight (including two repetitions) are attested in the historical corpus of Gothic. In fact, many of these thirty-eight are not attested in the inflected forms in which they appear in Tolkien's poem.' The remaining seventeen words (including one repetition) are reconstructions by Tolkien, made by a comparative method from cognates in other Germanic languages, such as Old English and Old Norse. Smith supplies in his essay a complete list of the reconstructed words, with their etymologies. Lucas Annear similarly analyses Tolkien's reconstruction process in 'Language in Tolkien's "Bagme Bloma"' (2011).

Tom Shippey observes that *Bagmē Blōma* is one of two poems Tolkien wrote about birches, 'defier of wind and lightning' (*The Road to Middle-earth*, p. 245); the other is *Éadig Béo Þu* (no. 80), also in *Songs for the Philologists*. For Tolkien, Shippey argues, the birch 'represents learning, severe learning, even discipline', in fact his own field, philology, 'but those who subject themselves to serious study are under its protection' (p. 245). Tolkien wrote a runic 'B' above *Bagmē Blōma* in copy 1 of *Songs*, symbolizing both the birch – the Anglo-Saxon rune *B* is called *beorc* 'birch-tree' – and scheme (course) B, which emphasized language (philology) rather than literature (scheme A), in the English School at Leeds.

Birches appear frequently in Tolkien's writings and art, and seem to have been among his favourite trees, apart from any deeper meaning he may have intended in *Bagmē Blōma*. Among his poetry, it is striking to find in *The Pool of the Dead Year* (no. 42) the lines

About it ringed like silent slender ghosts
The white shafts of the birches palely grow
And glimmer through the mists.

In *The Road to Middle-earth* Tom Shippey notes parallels for *Bagmē Blōma* also with Tolkien's 1967 story *Smith of Wootton Major*, which he sees as an allegory of philological scholarship. More specifically, he quotes a passage in which the titular smith, exploring Faery, is saved from a fierce wind by clinging to a birch: 'the birch was bent down to the ground by the blast and enclosed him in its branches. When at last the Wind passed on he rose and saw that the birch was naked. It was stripped of every leaf, and it wept, and tears fell from its branches like rain' (1967 edn., pp. 29–30).

A caption following the title of *Bagmē Blōma* in *Songs for the Philologists* instructs that the poem is to be sung to the tune of 'O Lazy Sheep!', presumably a setting of the nursery rhyme 'The Sheep' by Ann and Jane Taylor:

Lazy sheep, pray tell me why
In the pleasant fields you lie,
Eating grass, and daisies white,
From the morning till the night?

7: Arden R. Smith glosses the reconstructed **lindōs* (plural of **linda*) in connection with Old Norse *lind*, Old English *lind(e)*, Old High German *linta* 'linden-tree'. This would suggest 'wagjand lindos' = 'lindens shake', but it seems odd to introduce another tree species in the midst of a poem about the Birch, a word Tolkien took care to capitalize (*Bairka*). Lucas Annear translates l. 7 as 'Winds cry out, branches shake', while Shippey has 'The winds call, they shake gently'.

80

Éadig Béo Þu (*c.* 1924)

Éadig Béo Þu ('Good Luck Be with You', or 'Good Luck to You') is the sixth of Tolkien's works in *Songs for the Philologists* (1936), and the second of his 'Birch' poems, as Tom Shippey has called them. Like *Bagmē Blōma* (no. 79), this too was marked by the author in his personal copy (copy 1) of *Songs* with a runic *B* (*beorc* 'birch-tree') above the title. We give first, as version A, the printed Old English text (p. 13), with Tolkien's supplied accents and one clear correction ('lang' for 'long' in line 16). This is followed by our translation (B).

[A]

Éadig béo þu, góda mann!
Éadig béo þu, léofe wif!
Langre lisse ic þe ann —
hafa lof and líþe lif!
Hé þe hér swa sáre swanc,
rúna reord and fyrngewrit,
hál béo hé, on sálum wlanc,
halde láre' and wís gewit!

Éadge béo we eft swa nú!
Dréam ne dréose, dryne genóg
flówe' on fullum síþ swa iu —
fyllaþ wǽge, fyllaþ crog!
Byrla! byrla! medu briht —
Dóm is feor þeah dóm síe strang.
Swinc tomorgen, drinc toniht!
Lust is lýtel, earfoþ lang.

Uton singan scirne sang,
herian Beorc und byrcen cynn,
láre' and láreow, leornungmann —
sie us sǽl and hǽl and wynn!
Ác sceal feallan on þǽt fýr
lustes, leafes, lífes wan!
Beorc sceal ágan langne tir,
bréme glǽme glengan wang!

[B]

Good luck to you, good man!
Good luck to you, dear wife!
Lasting joy I give thee —
Have praise and a pleasant life!
He who worked you here so hard,
discoursing on runes and ancient writings,
may he be healthy, and proudly happy,
keep up learning and good sense!

May we be happy later as we are now!
May joy not fail, drink in cups enough
flow in times to come as of old —
fill the cups, fill the pitchers!
Waiter! waiter! bring mead —
Doom is far though doom is strong.
Work tomorrow, drink tonight!
Pleasure is little, labour long.

Let us sing a splendid song,
praise the Birch and birchen kind,
the subject and the teacher, the student —
may we be happy and healthy and joyous!
The Oak shall fall into the fire
joys, leaves, life gone!
The Birch shall keep glory long,
its splendour gleaming on the bright plain!

In his copy 1 of *Songs for the Philologists* Tolkien underscored 'reord' in line 6 and wrote in the margin as an alternative *rǽdde* 'explaining'. In line 13 he struck through 'briht' and substituted 'scene' ('bright'), noting that '*briht* is not an OE [Old English] form' (it is Middle English); and in line 15 he struck through 'tomorgen, drinc toniht!' after 'Swinc' and substituted 'forlǽt and géot [*or:* gif] ús drene', i.e. 'abandon work and pour [give] us drink'. We do not know if the rhyming (if erroneous) *briht* and *toniht* appeared in the original 'Leeds song', but it seems likely that this was so, rather than an invention of the London students. In *The Road to Middle-earth* Tom Shippey records a different change to line 15, presumably in Tolkien's other copy of *Songs* (see our discussion for no. 76): there the line became 'Scenc nu his and scenc nu mín' ('Now give him his and give me mine').

In *Éadig Béo Þu* Tolkien addresses his students, praising them and also himself, who has enlighted them about ancient writing and texts. The drinking described in the second stanza may not be exaggerated: Tolkien's Leeds language students aimed to drink beer as well as read sagas. That they sang 'splendid' songs (Shippey prefers 'cheerful' in his translation in *The Road to Middle-earth*) is attested by the surviving 'Leeds Songs' sheets, as well as Tolkien and Gordon's poems in *Songs for the Philologists*. The third stanza emphasizes their allegiance to the Birch, i.e. language and comparative linguistics, in course B at Leeds, opposed to course A, literature and literary criticism, represented by the Oak – the Anglo-Saxon *A*-rune is called *ac* 'oak' – which falls into the fire while the Birch long keeps its glory. This rivalry is also the subject of the poem *Lit' and Lang'* (no. 85).

According to a printed caption in *Songs for the Philologists*, *Éadig Béo Þu* is to be sung to the tune of 'Twinkle, Twinkle, Little Star', the familiar rhyme which, like 'The Sheep' (for poem no. 79), was written by Ann and Jane Taylor:

Twinkle, twinkle, little star,
How I wonder what you are!
Up above the world so high,
Like a diamond in the sky.

This is a convenient place to mention two manuscripts and two typescripts among Tolkien's papers containing versions of 'Twinkle, Twinkle, Little Star' he wrote in Middle English and Latin. We believe these to have been made no earlier than the late 1920s, potentially as late as the 1950s. Here we refer to the manuscripts, in the order we think they were written, as A and B, and to the typescripts (made on Tolkien's Hammond machine) in order as C and D. Typescript D has:

Twincle, twincle lutle storre!
Wu ich wndri wuch þu bo
On houene heiȝe, urom worlde uorre,
So cristal brun and briȝt o blo.

Manuscript A has a variation, 'an briȝt of blo', completing line 4. Manuscript B has 'and briȝt of bleo', and typescript C 'an briȝt of bleo'. In typescript D the Latin version reads:

Dic quid sis que pererras
cælum super humiles terras,

O bella coruscula stellula,
crystallina gemma tenellula!

But in manuscript A it is written as:

Qualis tu, dic, quae pererras
caelum super humiles terras,
pulchella coruscula stellula,
gemma crystallina bellula?

A Latin version does not appear in the other manuscript and typescript.

Typescript C also includes a rendering by Tolkien in Middle English of the first four lines of the song often called 'So Early in the Morning':

Whanne ȝong I was, ne nadde wit,
I bouȝte a crouþ for tweie pens;
on elpy note pleide hit:
'ouer þe hulles and longe hens'.

This is also included in manuscript A, with line 1 beginning 'Whan'. The lyrics in Modern English read:

When I was young, I had no sense,
I bought a fiddle for two pence;
the only tune that I could play
was 'over the hills and far away'.

'Over the Hills and Far Away' is a traditional English song, dating to at least the late seventeenth century (see also poem no. 43). In performances of 'So Early in the Morning' the price of a fiddle tends to be much higher than tuppence (eighteen, fifty), if only for the sake of rhythm in line 2.

All of the aforementioned manuscripts include as well a version of the nursery rhyme 'Humpty Dumpty' in Middle English:

Sir Homfrey Brotelhyde him sat apon a walle,
Sir Homfrey Brotelhyde swiþe gan aualle.
Þer erl ne barun ne kynges þein
Ne mihte rihte beten him aȝein.

In manuscript A Tolkien considered whether to change 'aualle' (i.e. *avalle* 'fell') to 'afalle'. The familiar Modern English text reads:

> Humpty Dumpty sat on a wall,
> Humpty Dumpty had a great fall.
> All of the horses and all the king's men
> Couldn't put Humpty together again.

The final lines have varied in the history of the rhyme: an early version has 'Three score men and three score more | Could not put Humpty Dumpty as he was before'. Tolkien playfully renames the character *Brotelhyde* 'Fragileskin', and declares that 'neither the earl nor the baron nor the king's men (thanes) with might or right could beat him again', the verse being a riddle about an egg.

81

Ofer Wídne Gársecg (*c.* 1924)

In *The Road to Middle-earth* Tom Shippey states that 'the corrected version' of *Ofer Wídne Gársecg*, the seventh poem by Tolkien in *Songs for the Philologists* (1936) 'includes the note, in Tolkien's hand, "An OE [Old English] version of 'Twas in the broad Atlantic in the equinoctial gales That a young fellow fell overboard among the sharks and whales'" (1992 edn., p. 303). There is no such note in Tolkien's other personal copy of *Songs* (copy 1), and judging by the transcription of the poem Shippey includes in his book, Tolkien made different changes to the text in each of his copies.

Here, as A, we have transcribed the poem as printed in *Songs*, pp. 14–15, but with Tolkien's supplied accents (in his copy 1) and two clear corrections ('meremenna' for 'meremanna' in lines 11 and 19), with variations detailed in notes.

[A] Þa ofer wídne gársecg wéow unwidre ceald,
Sum hagusteald on lagu féoll on nicera geweald.
He legde lást swa fýres gnást, and snúde' on sunde fléah,
Oþþæt he métte meremenn déopan grunde néah.

La! hwæt, ic Gardena on géardagum geseah,
Þéodcyninga-ninga-ninga þrym and —
brýdealoþ under brimfaroþ déopan grunde néah!

Þæt merewif hine greteþ, and úplang heo gestent;
Mid fágum fintan fægniende: fægre finnas þenþ.
And smearciende smǽre' hie wendeþ, tæceþ hire hand;
'Nú, wilcuma, lá, hlaford min, on meremenna land!'

'Hér leng ne mót ic bídan, gedǽle' nu wiþ þé!'
Heo cwæþ: 'Ná, ná! ne biþ hit swá! þu gewífest nú on me.
Nú eft þu gá, and cweþ: "Nó má fare ic on sunde héah;
Gemæcca min is meremenn déopan grunde néah."'

On nacan his genéatas hine sóhton wíde ymb sund;
Hi wéopon and hi hréopon and hi sméadon þone grund.
Þa úp he sprang and hlúde sang and hearde helman hrand;
'Gáþ eft ongén! me béodeþ cwén on meremenna land!'

'Todǽleþ nú mín ágen, pannan, páde, préon!
  Gifaþ hrægelciste mínre nifte, méder míne méon!'
Se stéorman stód on stefne wód, and he to brime béah;
  Cwæþ: 'Far nú wel! þe habbe Hel, déopan grunde néah!'

Rather than reconstruct the version in *Songs* as Tolkien seems to have wanted it revised, we have transcribed, as B, a manuscript of the poem Tolkien gave to E.V. Gordon, now in the Gordon archive at Leeds. For our present purpose, we have assumed that this was the original reading, provided to English students while Tolkien taught at Leeds, and thence to the publisher of *Songs*, though against this, there are some substantive differences between the manuscript and the text in *Songs*, notably in the second stanza.

[B] 1.

Þá ofer wídne Gársecg wéow unwidre ceald,
Sum hagusteald on lagu féoll on nicera geweald.
Hé legde lást swa fýres gnást, and snúde' on sunde fléah,
Oþþæt he métte meremenn déopan grunde néah.

  La! hwæt, ic Gárdena on géardagum geseah,
  Þéodcyninga-ninga-ninga þrym and —
    brýdealoþ under brimfaroþ déopan grunde néah!

2.

Þæt merewíf hine gréteþ, and úplang héo gestent;
Mid fágum fintan fægniende fægre finnas þeuþ,
and smearciende smǽre' hie wendeþ, tǽceþ hire hand:
'Nú, wilcuma, lá, hlaford min, on meremenna land!'

  La! hwæt, ic Gardena on géardagum onfand
  Þéodcyninga-ninga-ninga þrym and —
    brýdealoþ under brimfaroþ geond meremenna land!

3.

'Hér leng ne mót ic bídan, ic gedǽle' nu wiþ þé!'
Heo cwæþ: 'Ná, ná! ne biþ hit swá! þu gewífest nú on me.
Nú eft þu gá, and cweþ: "Nó má fare' ic on sunde héah;
Gemæcca min is meremenn déopan grunde néah."'

  La! hwæt . . . (&c. as in 1)

4.

On nacan his genéatas hine sóhton wíde' ymb sund;
Hí wéopon and hí hréopon, and hí sméadon þone grund.
Þá úp he sprang and hlúde sang, and hearde helman hrand:
'Gáþ eft ongén! me béodeþ cwén on meremenna land!'

La! hwæt . . . (&c. as in 2)

5.

'Tó-dǽlaþ nú mín ágen, pannan, páde, préon!
Gifaþ hrægel ciste mínre nifte, méder míne méon!'
Se stéorman stód on stefne wód, and he to brime béah;
Cwæþ: 'Far nú wel! þé habbe Hel, déopan grunde néah!'

La! hwæt . . . (&c. as in 1)

Finally, as C, we give a translation (of B) into Modern English. In *The Road to Middle-earth* Tom Shippey translates the title of the poem as 'Across the Broad Ocean'; 'Over the Wide Ocean' would do as well.

[C] When over the wide ocean cold gales blew,
A young man fell into the sea, under the nickers' spell.
He went down like sparking fires, and speedily through the water flew,
Until he met the mermen near the bottom of the deep.

Oh! listen, I have seen the glory of the clan-kings
Of the Spear-Danes in days of yore and —
the marriage-feast under the sea near the bottom of the deep!

The mermaid now greeted him, and up she stood,
With spotted tail she fawned, beautiful fins of her people,
and smiling with her lips as she went, reached out her hand:
'Now, welcome, oh, my lord, to the mermen's land!'

Oh! listen, I have discovered the glory of the clan-kings
Of the Spear-Danes in days of yore and —
the marriage-feast under the sea in the mermen's land!

'Here no longer may I stay, I will separate now from thee!'
She said: 'No, no! it will not be so! you are now married to me.
Now again go, and say: "No more will I journey on the sea;
my wife is from the mermen near the bottom of the deep."'

Oh! listen, I have seen the glory of the clan-kings
Of the Spear-Danes in days of yore and —
the marriage-feast under the sea near the bottom of the deep!

On the ship his companions searched for him widely on the sea;
They wept and wailed and looked on the sea-bottom.
Then up he sprang and loudly sang, and pushed the rudder hard:
'Go back again! the queen has commanded me in the mermen's land!'

Oh! listen, I have discovered the glory of the clan-kings
Of the Spear-Danes in days of yore and —
the marriage-feast under the sea in the mermen's land!

'Divide now my belongings, pans, coats, brooches!
Give my chest to my niece, my shoes to my mother!'
The steersman stood raging on the prow, and turned to the sea,
Saying: 'Fare well now! Hell have you, near the bottom of the deep!'

Oh! listen, I have seen the glory of the clan-kings
Of the Spear-Danes in days of yore and —
the marriage-feast under the sea near the bottom of the deep!

Shippey observes in *The Road to Middle-earth* that the first words of Tolkien's refrain (lines 5–6, etc.) are derived from the first words of *Beowulf*, 'Hwaet! We Gardena in geardagum, | þeodcyninga, þrym gefrunon' ('Listen! We have known of the glory of the clan-kings of the Spear-Danes in days of yore'). The greater part of the poem, however, was inspired by the song 'The Mermaid', to the tune of which Tolkien's work is to be sung. He acknowledged this in a note on the reverse of the manuscript sheet at Leeds, and it is indicated in the printed *Songs*. Written by 'A.J.C.' (possibly, in fact, William Makepeace Thackeray), 'The Mermaid', also known by other titles, incorporates words from the patriotic song 'Rule, Britannia'. Tolkien had its music and lyrics at hand in his wife's copy of *The Scottish Students' Song Book*, first published in 1891, also acknowledged by him on his manuscript if with a query. The same lyrics appeared also in the *Oxford Song Book* of 1921 (p. 145):

Oh, 'twas in the broad Atlantic,
'Mid the equinoctial gales,
That a young fellow fell overboard
Among the sharks and whales.
And down he went like a streak of light,
So quickly down went he,
Until he came to a mer-ma-id
At the bottom of the deep blue sea.

Chorus

Singing, Rule Britannia, Britannia, rule the waves!
Britons never, never, never shall be
Mar-ri-ed to a mer-ma-id at the bottom of the deep blue sea.

She raised herself on her beautiful tail,
And gave him her soft, wet hand,
'I've long been waiting for you, my dear,
Now welcome safe to land.
Go back to your mess-mates for the last time
And tell them all from me,
That you're mar-ri-ed to a mer-ma-id
At the bottom of the deep blue sea.
Singing . . . .

We sent a boat to look for him,
Expecting to find his corpse,
When up he came with a bang and a shout,
And a voice sepulchrally hoarse.
'My comrades and my messmates,
O do not look for me,
For I'm mar-ri-ed to a mer-ma-id
At the bottom of the deep blue sea.'
Singing . . . .

'In my chest you'll find my half-year's wage,
    Likewise a lock of hair,
This locket from my neck you'll take,
    And bear to my young wife dear.
My carte-de-visite to my grandmother take,
    Tell her not to weep for me,
For I'm mar-ri-ed to a mer-ma-id
    At the bottom of the deep blue sea.'
        Singing . . . .

The anchor was weighed, and the sails unfurled,
    And the ship was sailing free,
When we went up to our cap-i-taine,
    And our tale we told to he.
The captain went to the old ship's side,
    And out loud bellowed he,
'Be as happy as you can with your wife, my man,
    At the bottom of the deep blue sea.'
        Singing . . . .

From this it will be seen that the curious 'Þéodcyninga-ninga-ninga' in Tolkien's chorus is meant to echo rhythmically 'Britons never, never, never' in the chorus of 'The Mermaid', and that 'brýdealoþ under brimfaroþ' is the multisyllabic equivalent of 'mar-ri-ed to a mer-ma-id' (sung thus).

In private correspondence, Jessica Yates has convincingly argued that aspects of Tolkien's 1925/27 story *Roverandom* were also inspired by 'The Mermaid', notably repeated instances of the phrase 'the bottom of the Deep Blue Sea'.

A3: In Tolkien's copy 1 he marked 'and' to be changed to 'he'. Shippey gives the latter reading, and does not include an acute accent in 'snúde" as in copy 1. In the Leeds manuscript (B) 'and' is here, and elsewhere, indicated by a Tironian *et* (⁊).

A5: In copy 1 Tolkien marked 'geseah' and added a note: 'In alt[ernate] verses *onfand*'. This alternation is followed in the Leeds manuscript. Shippey's transcription omits the final comma, and includes an acute accent ('Gárdena') not present in copy 1; both the comma and the accent are present in the Leeds manuscript.

A7: In copy 1 Tolkien marked 'déopan grunde néah' and added a note: 'In alternate verses substitute *meremenna land*'. In his transcription Shippey includes the second refrain in full, i.e. after l. 11, with directions to indicate 'First refrain' (i.e. ll. 5–7) or 'Second refrain' (i.e. ll. 5–7 with the substituted words); Tolkien treats the refrains similarly in the Leeds manuscript.

A8: In copy 1 Tolkien marked this line to be changed to 'Þæt merewif hine grétte, and úplang heo gestód', with the final semi-colon struck through in whole or in part. In Shippey's transcription, presumably from Tolkien's other personal copy (copy 2), the line reads 'Þæt merewif þá of stóle úplang héo gestód', with a final comma. Except for some of the accents, the Leeds manuscript (B) agrees with the text printed in *Songs* (A).

A9: In copy 1 Tolkien marked an insertion, 'wæs hire', before 'fægre', but also made a note that the final words of the line should read 'wæs hire hǽlsung-gód'. In Shippey's transcription the line ends 'wæs hire grétung gód'. The Leeds manuscript agrees with the printed text in *Songs*.

A10: In copy 1 Tolkien wrote 'Héo' before the start of this line, evidently as a replacement for 'And'; Shippey's transcription of the line begins 'Héo'. Tolkien also marked 'wendeþ, tæceþ' to be replaced with 'wende, tæhte'; Shippey's transcription has 'wende, tǽhte'. The Leeds manuscript agrees with the printed text in *Songs*.

A11, 19: In copy 1 Tolkien emended 'meremanna' to 'meremenna'. Shippey's transcription has 'meremenna', as does the Leeds manuscript.

A12: In copy 1 Tolkien marked an insertion, 'ic', after 'gedæle'. Shippey's transcription includes the insertion. The Leeds manuscript has 'ic' *before* 'gedǽle'.

A13: In Shippey's transcription 'Heo' reads 'Héo', and 'me' reads 'mé', presumably both with supplied accents in Tolkien's copy 2 (absent in copy 1). This agrees with the Leeds manuscript.

A14: In Shippey's transcription, and in the Leeds manuscript, 'fare' is given as 'fare'', with an added apostrophe.

A15: In Shippey's transcription, and in the Leeds manuscript, 'min' reads 'mín', with an added acute accent.

A16: In Shippey's transcription 'sohton' has no acute accent (present in copy 1) and 'wíde'' has an added acute accent and apostrophe; in copy 1 the latter has no added apostrophe. The accents and apostrophe are present in the Leeds manuscript.

A18: In copy 1 Tolkien marked for insertion a comma after 'sang', and to replace the semi-colon with a colon. Shippey's transcription reflects these changes, and the Leeds manuscript agrees.

A19: In copy 1 Tolkien added an acute accent to 'ongén' (thus); the accent is also present in the Leeds manuscript. In Shippey's transcription, which has 'ongen' (thus), and in the Leeds manuscript, this line ends with a full stop, the printed text with an exclamation mark.

A20: In copy 1 Tolkien marked 'Todǽleþ' to be changed to 'Todǽlaþ'. Shippey's transcription has the altered reading. In the Leeds manuscript the reading is 'To-dǽlaþ'.

A23: In copy 1 Tolkien marked 'Far' to be changed to 'Fær'. Shippey's transcription retains printed 'Far', and has 'nu' without the acute accent Tolkien added to copy 1. The Leeds manuscript has 'Fær nú'.

82

I Sat upon a Bench (*c.* 1924)

In *Songs for the Philologists* (1936) the ninth of Tolkien's poems is printed (p. 17) in an abbreviated form, with only the first, six-line verse given in full. Each subsequent verse repeats original lines *b* and *f*, with new lines *a*, *c* (repeating *a*), *d*, and *e* as given. Here, for clarity, we have transcribed the work as it would be set out in its entirety, from the manuscript in the Gordon archive at Leeds. The jocular mood of the song reminds us of *The Cat and the Fiddle* (poem no. 60), also composed during Tolkien's Leeds period.

1.

I sat upon a bench and I up and I sang:
'Fol de rol de rol de rol de rol de ri—do!'
I sat upon a bench and I up and I sang:
'The beer's a-going round, let the world go hang!
Ha! Ho! Flow, beer, flow!
Fol de rol de rol de rol de rol de ri—do!'

2.

The bench began to heave, the table did a dance,
Fol de rol de rol de rol de rol de ri—do!
The bench began to heave, the table did a dance,
The barrels and the bottles all about began to prance.
Ha! Ho! Woa, lads, woa!
Fol de rol de rol de rol de rol de ri—do!

3.

The bench went over bang, the table stood on end,
Fol de rol de rol de rol de rol de ri—do!
The bench went over bang, the table stood on end,
The barrels they were bust, the roof began to bend!
Ha! Ho! Beer did flow.
Fol de rol de rol de rol de rol de ri—do!

4.

A-lying on the floor I gave a mighty roar:
'Fol de rol de rol de rol de rol de ri—do!'
A-lying on the floor I gave a mighty roar:
'The tide's a-coming in, there's beer upon the shore!
        Ha! Ho! Swimming I'll go.
    Fol de rol de rol de rol de rol de ri—do!'

5.

'The tide's a-flowing in, there's froth upon the sea.
Fol de rol de rol de rol de rol de ri—do!
The tide's a-flowing in, there's froth upon the sea.
O blow all yet winds! O blow the froth for me!
        Ha! Ho! A good strong blow!
    Fol de rol de rol de rol de rol de ri—do!'

6.

'Adown a-derry-down in a sea so very brown
Fol de rol de rol de rol de rol de ri—do!
Adown a-derry-down in a sea so very brown
A merry merry death 'twill be for me to drown.
        Ha! Ho! To the bottom I'll go!
    Fol de rol de rol de rol de rol de ri—do! [']

A printed caption in *Songs for the Philologists* directs that *I Sat upon a Bench* should be sung to the tune of 'The Carrion Crow', a song included in Moffat's *What the Children Sing*. Its first verse reads (p. 28):

A carrion crow he sat upon an oak,
    Fol de rol, de rol, de rol, de rido!
A carrion crow he sat upon an oak,
    Watching a tailor a-shaping of his cloak,
        Hi, Ho, poor old crow!
    Fol de rol, de rol, de rol, de rido!

2, 6: In *Songs for the Philologists* 'de ri—do' is given as 'de-rido'.

83

Pēro & Pōdex · The Root of the Boot · Sam's Song · The Stone Troll (*c.* 1924–62)

Tolkien originally gave this poem the Latin title *Pēro & Pōdex*, which is usually translated 'boot and bottom' to keep the alliteration. A *pero* is a peasant's heavy shoe or boot, and *podex* is the rump. As we have not been able to see its earliest version, the pencilled manuscript of this poem identified by Christopher Tolkien in *The Return of the Shadow*, we give here (as A) its text as printed in *The History of* The Hobbit by John D. Rateliff (2007), pp. 101–2. The abbreviation '&c.' (et cetera) at the end of each of the later stanzas indicates that the third and fourth lines should be repeated when sung, on the example of lines 7–8.

[A]

1.

A troll sat alone on his seat of stone
And munched and mumbled a bare old bone,
And long and long he had sat there lone
    And seen nor man nor mortal
        Ortal!
        portal!
And long and long he had sat there lone
    And seen nor man nor mortal.

2.

Up came Tom with his big boots on;
'Hullo!' says he 'pray, what is yon?
It looks like the leg of me uncle John,
    As should be a-lyin' in churchyard'.
        Searchyard
        birchyard &c.

3.

'Young man' says the troll, 'that bone I stole;
But what be bones, when mayhap the soul
In heaven on high hath an aureole
    As big and as bright as a bonfire?'
        On fire
        Yon fire &c.

4.

Says Tom 'Oddsteeth! 'tis my belief,
If bonfire there be 'tis underneath;
For old man John was as proper a thief
    As ever wore black on a Sunday,
        Grundy
        Monday &c.

5.

But still thou old swine 'tis no matter o' thine
A-trying thy teeth on an uncle o' mine,
So get to Hell before thou dine
    And ask thee leave of me nuncle
        uncle
        buncle &c.

6.

In the proper place upon the base
Tom boots him right — but alas that race
Hath as stony a seat as it is in face
    And Pero was punished by Podex
        Odex!
        Codex! &c.

7.

Now Tom goes lame since home he came,
And his bootless foot is grievous game;
But troll will not gnaw that bone for shame
    To think it was boned of a boner
        owner!
        donor! &c.

Rateliff comments that the poem 'underwent a great deal of revision and substitution even as it was being written', and describes changes made by Tolkien, most of which were reflected in the next extant version. An exception is the final stanza, whose lines, Rateliff writes, 'seem to have given Tolkien special trouble: first he changed them to "But troll's old seat is much the same | And the bone he boned from its owner | Donor | Boner" – the reading he adopted in *Songs for the Philologists*'. (The revised reading appeared first in text B, below.) 'But on the manuscript', Rateliff continues, Tolkien 'follows this at once with "That it was once in the boot of a burglar | Jurgler | <burgler>", taking quite literally Tom's earlier description of his Uncle John as "a thief".' This did not survive into later texts. 'Burgler', i.e. *burglar*, is Rateliff's uncertain reading of the final word.

Some of the exclaimed 'words' in version A – 'ortal', 'searchyard', and so forth –exist merely for the sake of rhyme or near-rhyme. The most meaningful of these are 'Grundy' and 'Monday' (lines 25, 26), which refer to the nursery rhyme 'Solomon Grundy, | born on a Monday'. *Codex* in line 38 means 'a manuscript with sequential pages in book form', as opposed to a scroll; but its definition is unrelated to the poem. In the final stanza, Tolkien plays with *bone* in three senses: as the skeletal remnant of John's body, as a slang word for 'steal', and presumably by extension (*boner*), though we have not found it attested, as a word for 'thief'.

Two manuscripts contain the revision Rateliff describes, now entitled *The Root of the Boot*. *Root* in this context is slang for 'kick', a sense Tolkien recalled from his youth, and *boot* is the backside. We give here, as B, the earliest of the two texts, from the Gordon archive at Leeds.

[B] 1.

A troll sat alone on his seat of stone,
And munched and mumbled a bare old bone;
& long and long he had sat there lone
    And seen nor man nor mortal
        Ortal! Portal!
& long & long he had sat there lone
    And seen nor man nor mortal.

2.

Up came Tom with his big boots on:
'Hullo!' says he, 'pray, what is yon?

It looks like the leg of me nuncle John
    As should be a-lyin' in churchyard.
        Searchyard, birchyard! &c.'

3.

'Young man', says the troll, 'that bone I stole;
But what be bones, when mayhap the soul
In heaven on high hath an aureole
    As big and as bright as a bonfire?
        On fire, yon fire, &c.'

4.

Says Tom: 'Oddsteeth! 'tis my belief,
If bonfire there be, 'tis underneath;
For old man John was as proper a thief
    As ever wore black on a Sunday —
        Grundy, Monday! &c.

5.

But still I doan't see what is that to thee,
With me kith and me kin a-makin' free:
So get to Hell and ax leave o' he,
    Afore thou gnaws me nuncle!
        Uncle, Buncle, &c.'

6.

In the proper place upon the base
Tom boots him right — but, alas! that race
Hath a stonier seat than its stony face;
    So he rued that root on the rump-o,
        Lumpo, bumpo, &c.

7.

Now Tom goes lame since home he came,
And his bootless foot is grievous game;
But troll's old seat is much the same,
    And the bone he boned from its owner,
        Donor, Boner! &c.

Tolkien had already in version A clearly distinguished both of his poem's characters by their respective manners of speaking. The troll, against expected type, is like a polite scholar, addressing Tom as 'young man', philosophizing about the difference between the body and the soul, and using the less common *aureole* rather than *halo*. Tom, on the other hand, and increasingly so in version B, is brash and colloquial, clipping his speech ('a-lyin'', 'a-makin''), using 'ax' instead of 'ask' – 'ax leave o' he' in B25, i.e. 'ask leave of him' – and coarsely swearing ('Oddsteeth!'). He also differs from the troll by his accent, marked especially in B by 'doan't' (line 23, i.e. 'don't') with its broad vowel sound often associated with speech from the north of England, in contrast to the troll's received pronunciation.

The later manuscript of this version, in one of Tolkien's poetry notebooks, differs from the first only in a few minor points. But in this the author considered whether to add 'Then' at the start of line 8 ('Then up came Tom'), and whether to replace line 15 with 'hath a halo in heaven upon its poll', omitting one uncommon word (*aureole*) while including another (*poll*, the human head). Also, in line 20 Tolkien indicated that 'proper' should be replaced with dialectal 'prapper', again with a broad vowel.

The Root of the Boot first appeared in print in *Songs for the Philologists* (1936, pp. 20–1)). It is the eleventh poem by Tolkien in that booklet, and set apart from his other twelve works in *Songs* in that it is not an adaptation, or a translation, or a *jeu d'esprit* about language or drinking, but a story with a fairy-tale setting. We suspect that Tolkien wrote it for his personal pleasure, not originally for the entertainment of students, though it could be used for the latter as well. If we accept that the source of the *Songs for the Philologists* printing was one of the mimeographed sheets of 'Leeds Songs' (see poem no. 75), we may suppose that the source of the sheet was the first manuscript for version B. Even allowing for changes by the University College London students in typesetting *Songs*, and there are several – for example, in line 11 'a-lyin' in churchyard' was editorially smoothed out as 'lying in the churchyard' – the *Songs* text of the poem is closer in detail to that of the first manuscript than to the second. In his personal copy of *Songs* (copy 1) Tolkien corrected the text to make it agree with what he had written, and again altered lines 8, 15, and 20 as in the second manuscript, confirming his intentions.

In *The Return of the Shadow* Christopher Tolkien printed the poem as it appears in *Songs*, with his father's corrections but without the alterations (the first, only, is mentioned in discussion). He comments that his father was 'extremely fond of' *The Root of the Boot*, 'and my delight in the line *If bonfire there be, 'tis underneath* is among my very early recollections' (p. 142). Christopher was born in Leeds in November 1924.

Probably in the first half of September 1938, while in the early stages of writing *The Lord of the Rings*, Tolkien needed a song for Bingo (later Frodo) Baggins to sing at Bree, ultimately in Book I, Chapter 9. At first he chose his 'Troll-song', and wrote out a text in pencil; this seems to have been changed from the Leeds version, but it is possible to make out only part of the original writing beneath revisions in ink. Tolkien wrote this at speed, with many insertions and marginal notes, not all of which are legible. Here, as C, is our reconstruction of much of the poem at this stage, which will illustrate Tolkien's struggle with the text for his new purpose.

[C] A troll sat alone on [his >] a seat of stone,
and munched and mumbled a bare old bone:
[and longer than long he had munched alone
    and seen no man nor mortal >]
for many a year he had gnawed it near,
    and sat there hard and hungry

Then up came John [*above:* Tom] with his big boots on;
said he to the Troll: 'Pray, what is yon?
For it looks like the shin [*above:* leg] of my nuncle Jim
        [*above:* John]
    as used to walk [*above:* went to climb] in the Mountains
        countin fountains

'Young man!' said the troll, '[that >] this bone I stole,
[but what be bones if they lie in a hole >]
and the rest be lying in a deep dark hole
I can get no sleep, and this one I keep
    To stop my gums [*above:* teeth] from aching
        making waking

Said John [*above:* Tom]: 'I doan't see why that should be
I'll have no troll a-making free
with my kith and my kin; so I'll have that shin
    or else I learn [*above:* know] the reason
        season peason

'[Now >] For [*above:* but] two pins' says the troll and grins
'[I'll >] I'd eat thee too, and gnaw *thy* shins;
For I've a fancy for bones and skins,
And mayhap thee'll join thy nuncle.'
uncle buncle

But just when he thought that [John >] Tom was caught
he found that his hands had hold of naught;
for Tom skipped behind and quickly brought
the boot to bear where needed!
he did he did

The Troll fell [*above:* tumbled] down & cracked his crown
But Tom went bootless back to town
For that stony seat was hard to meet [*margin:* was too hard for feet]
and he was lame for

For a seat of stone [?when] boot and bone
and he rued that root and his broken boot
found that seat was stony

and his boot and toe were broken
token spoken

There the Troll lies no more to rise
With his face beneath and his seat to the skies
[?Down] under the stone is a bare old bone
for it was stole by the troll from its owner
boner donor

It was evidently an oversight by Tolkien that the first stanza of C has no 'chorus' of exclamations, as he provided one in later versions. For the first few stanzas, he was unsure if the 'young man' was named John or Tom, and if the uncle was Jim or John. But he was deliberate in omitting from C, compared with earlier versions, all allusions to Christianity, such as a churchyard, an aureole in heaven, God's teeth, wearing black on a Sunday, and Hell. ('I am in any case myself a Christian', he wrote in a biographical statement (*Letters*, p. 319); 'but the "Third Age" [in which *The Lord of the Rings* is set] was not a Christian world.') Nor did Tolkien retain a reference to the Solomon Grundy rhyme, which likewise lies outside of the matter of Middle-earth.

Soon after this attempt, he decided that *The Cat and the Fiddle* (no. 24) should be Bingo's (Frodo's) song at Bree, and that *The Root of the Boot* should serve instead in Book I, Chapter 12 as the 'bit of nonsense' Sam Gamgee sings for his friends after they come upon the three trolls turned to stone. The poem as it later developed in *The Lord of the Rings* as Sam's song is found in three careful manuscripts, following three pages of workings so rough, scribbled in pencil and pen with overwriting and inverting of sheets, that we can decipher little of it. All of these versions appear to date from between August and autumn 1939. We give the first of them as D. Christopher Tolkien also transcribed this manuscript in *The Treason of Isengard* (1989), pp. 59–61.

[D] A troll sat alone on his seat of stone,
And munched and mumbled a bare old bone;
For many a year he had gnawed it near,
And sat there hard and hungry[.]
Tongue dry! Wrung dry!
For many a year he had gnawed it near,
And sat there hard and hungry.

Then up came John with his big boots on[.]
Said he to the troll: 'Pray, what is yon?
For it looks like the shin o' my nuncle Jim,
As went to walk on the mountain.
Huntin'! Countin'!
It looks like the shin o' my nuncle Jim,
As went to walk on the mountain.'

'My lad,' said the troll, 'this bone I stole,
But what be bones that lie in a hole?
Thy nuncle were dead as a lump o' lead,
Afore I found his carkis[.]
Hark'ee! Mark'ee!
Thy nuncle were dead as a lump o' lead,
Before I found his carkis.'

Said John: 'I don't see why the likes o' thee
Without axin' leave should go makin' free
With the leg or the shin o' my kith and my kin
So hand the old bone over!
Rover! Trover!

So give me the shin o' my kith and my kin,
And hand the old bone over! [']

'For a couple o' pins,' says the troll, and grins,
'I'll eat thee too, and gnaw thy shins.
A bit o' fresh meat will go down sweet!
And thee shall join thy nuncle!
Sunk well! Drunk well!
A bit o' fresh meat will go down sweet,
And thee shall join thy nuncle.'

But just as he thought his dinner was caught,
He found his hands had hold of naught;
But he caught a kick both hard and quick,
For John had slipped behind him [.]
Mind him! Blind him!
He caught a kick both hard and quick,
For John had slipped behind him.

The troll tumbled down, and he cracked his crown,
But John went hobbling back to town,
For that stony seat was too hard for feet,
And boot and toe were broken.
Token! Spoken!
That stony seat was too hard for feet,
And boot and toe were broken.

There the troll lies, no more to rise,
With his nose to earth and his seat to the skies;
But under the stone is a bare old bone
That was stole by a troll from its owner.
Donor! Boner!
Under the stone lies a broken bone
That was stole by a troll from its owner.

With version D, the troll is presented not as polite and (in its stony form) passively dangerous, but more in keeping with its cousins Tolkien described in *The Hobbit*, hungry, threatening, and with a manner of speech 'which was not drawing-room fashion at all, at all' (*The Hobbit*, ch. 2). Indeed, there was now much less of a distinction between the troll and John (or Tom). Each character has a degree of bloodthirstiness, and each justifies his actions, by hunger or revenge.

Tolkien made numerous revisions to this manuscript, some of which he abandoned, and drafted readings which he adopted in the next version, an abbreviated copy in which only the first stanza was written out in full. (For reference in our notes, we will call this D^1.) Here Tolkien worked out new text and confirmed existing readings, brought together in version E, entitled *Sam's Song*. The anonymous troll ('the troll') of the earlier texts is now 'Troll', personified.

[E] Troll sat alone on his seat of stone,
And munched and mumbled a bare old bone;
For many a year he had gnawed it near,
For meat was hard to come by
Some by! Gum by!
In a cave in the hills he dwelt alone,
And meat was hard to come by[.]

Up came John with his big boots on[.]
Said he to Troll: 'Pray, what is yon?
For it looks like the shin o' my nuncle Jim,
As should be a-lyin' in graveyard.
Caveyard! Paveyard!
This many a year has Jim been gone,
And I thought he were lyin' in graveyard.'

'My lad,' said Troll, 'this bone I stole.
But what be bones that lie in a hole?
Thy nuncle was dead as a lump o' lead,
Afore I found his carkis[.]
Hark'ee! Mark'ee!
He can spare a bone for a poor old troll:
He's got no use for his carkis[.]'

Said John: 'I don't see why the likes o' thee
Without axin' leave should go makin' free
With the leg or the shin o' my father's kin;
So hand the old bone over!
Rover! Trover!
Though dead he be, it belongs to he,
So hand the old bone over!'

'For a couple o' pins,' says Troll, and grins,
'I'll eat thee too, and gnaw thy shins.
A bit o' fresh meat will go down sweet!
Thee'll be a nice change from thy nuncle.
Sunkle! Drunkle!
I'm tired o' gnawing old bones and skins;
Thee'll be a nice change from thy nuncle.'

But just as he thought his dinner was caught,
He found his hands had hold of naught[.]
Before he could mind, John slipped behind
And gave him the boot to larn him[.]
Warn him! Darn him!
A bump o' the boot on the seat, John thought,
Would be the way to larn him[.]

But harder than stone is the flesh and bone
Of a troll that sits in the hills alone
As well set your boot to the mountain's root;
For the seat of a troll don't feel it[.]
Deal it! Peel it!
Old Troll laughed, but John did groan,
For his poor toes did feel it.

John's leg is game, since home he came,
And his bootless foot is lasting lame,
But Troll don't care, and he's still there
With the bone he boned from its owner[.]
Donor! Boner!
Troll's old seat is still the same,
And the bone he boned from its owner!

In 1952 Tolkien made a private recording of this version, since commercially released, singing 'Sam's song' from the manuscript of *The Lord of the Rings* as it then stood, including the introductory words 'Standing up, with his hands behind his back, as if he was at school, he [Sam] began to sing to an old tune'.

Tolkien made still further revisions to the song in the printer's typescript of *The Lord of the Rings*, and the same retrospectively on his initial typescript of the chapter. Notably, 'John' now reverted to 'Tom' as in the early versions of the work, and 'Jim' was renamed 'Tim'. We give the final text of the poem as F; with one minor change of punctuation, it was reprinted in Tolkien's 1962 collection *The Adventures of Tom Bombadil and Other Verses from the Red Book* as *The Stone Troll.*

[F] Troll sat alone on his seat of stone,
And munched and mumbled a bare old bone;
For many a year he had gnawed it near,
For meat was hard to come by
Done by! Gum by!
In a cave in the hills he dwelt alone,
And meat was hard to come by.

Up came Tom with his big boots on.
Said he to Troll: 'Pray, what is yon?
For it looks like the shin o' my nuncle Tim,
As should be a-lyin' in graveyard.
Caveyard! Paveyard!
This many a year has Tim been gone,
And I thought he were lyin' in graveyard.'

'My lad,' said Troll, 'this bone I stole.
But what be bones that lie in a hole?
Thy nuncle was dead as a lump o' lead,
Afore I found his shinbone.
Tinbone! Thinbone!
He can spare a share for a poor old troll.
For he don't need his shinbone.'

Said Tom: 'I don't see why the likes o' thee
Without axin' leave should go makin' free
With the shank or the shin o' my father's kin;
So hand the old bone over!
Rover! Trover!
Though dead he be, it belongs to he;
So hand the old bone over!'

'For a couple o' pins,' says Troll, and grins,
'I'll eat thee too, and gnaw thy shins.
A bit o' fresh meat will go down sweet!
I'll try my teeth on thee now.
Hee now! See now!
I'm tired o' gnawing old bones and skins;
I've a mind to dine on thee now.'

But just as he thought his dinner was caught,
He found his hands had hold of naught.
    Before he could mind, Tom slipped behind
        And gave him the boot to larn him.
            Warn him! Darn him!
    A bump o' the boot on the seat, Tom thought,
        Would be the way to larn him.

But harder than stone is the flesh and bone
Of a troll that sits in the hills alone
    As well set your boot to the mountain's root,
        For the seat of a troll don't feel it.
            Peel it! Heal it!
    Old Troll laughed, when he heard Tom groan,
        And knew his toes could feel it.

Tom's leg is game, since home he came,
And his bootless foot is lasting lame,
    But Troll don't care, and he's still there
        With the bone he boned from its owner.
            Donor! Boner!
    Troll's old seat is still the same,
        And the bone he boned from its owner!

When illustrating the *Bombadil* volume, artist Pauline Baynes identified 'Tom' in *The Stone Troll* with the character Tom Bombadil in *The Lord of the Rings* (and earlier in a poem, see no. 83). Tolkien does not seem to have had this in mind when giving Sam the work to sing.

At the head of the second manuscript of version B, Tolkien noted that *The Root of the Boot* was to be sung to the tune of 'The Fox Came Out on a Winter's Night', a familiar English song of which there are many variations. (In his personal copy of *Songs* Tolkien referred to it as 'The Fox Went Out'.) Its most common lyrics begin:

The fox went out on a chilly night,
He prayed to the Moon to give him light,
For he'd many a mile to go that night
Before he reached the town-o, town-o, town-o,
He had many a mile to go that night
Before he reached the town-o.

In the course of the song, the fox enters the town, steals a fat goose, and runs home before farmer John can pursue him. At last, in the typical version,

> the fox and his wife without any strife
> Cut up the goose with a fork and knife.
> They never had such a supper in their life
> And the little ones chewed on the bones-o, bones-o, bones-o,
> They never had such a supper in their life
> And the little ones chewed on the bones-o.

In Moffat's *What the Children Sing* the song begins (p. 3):

> A fox went out in a hungry plight,
> And he begged of the moon to give him light,
> For he'd many miles to trot that night,
> Before he could reach his den, O!
> den, O! den, O!
> For he'd many miles to trot that night,
> Before he could reach his den, O!

In this more violent version, the fox never returns home with his prize, the farmer having shot him dead.

A17–22: Tolkien contrasts the notion of John in Heaven, with an enormous halo or heavenly crown (*aureole*), with the likelihood (in l. 22) of John's soul being in Hell ('If bonfire there be 'tis underneath').

A21: *Oddsteeth* is an abbreviation of the Elizabethan oath 'God's teeth'.

A24: Although John was a thief, he piously wore black on Sunday.

A30: 'Me nuncle' is a dialectal version of 'my uncle' (or, in l. 11, 'me uncle'), the added *n* allowing easier elision between two words which, respectively, end and begin with a vowel.

A33–8: In *The Return of the Shadow* Christopher Tolkien transcribes these lines with added punctuation, possibly editorial:

> In the proper place upon the base
> Tom boots him right — but, alas! that race
> Hath as stony a seat as it is in face,
> And Pero was punished by Podex.
> Odex! Codex!

B10: The second manuscript has 'o' me nuncle' rather than 'of me nuncle'.

B14: In the second manuscript Tolkien included a comma before and after 'mayhap'.

B22: The first manuscript of B includes a closing quotation mark at the end of this line, which we have editorially omitted. Tom's dialogue continues into the next stanza – which correctly has no opening quotation mark – and ends after 'Buncle, &c.'

B24: The second manuscript has 'Wi' my kith and my kin' rather than 'With me kith and me kin'.

B31: 'Rued that root', i.e. regretted giving the kick.

B36: 'Owner' now takes the place of 'boner'. Tolkien may have felt that 'boner' did not clearly convey the meaning of 'thief' in reference to uncle John. In the second manuscript 'owner' is followed by an exclamation mark.

C23: A *pin* in this context is something of little or no value, as in the saying 'not worth a pin'.

C33: The Troll falling down and cracking his crown was perhaps too close to the language of the nursery rhyme of Jack and Jill. It survived into version D, but no further.

D4–5: D^1 has 'And sat there hard and hungry. | Hungry! Hungry!'

D18: 'Carkis' is an alternate, dialectal spelling of *carcase* (body), pronounced car-kiss (as by Tolkien in his recording of the poem) despite the long *-e* endings in l. 19.

D19: 'Hark'ee', 'mark'ee', i.e. 'hark ye [you]', 'mark ye [you]'.

D24: The reading of E, 'With the leg or the shin o' my father's kin', enters in D^1, following a pencilled change in D.

D26: Whether intended by Tolkien or not, *Trover* is apt in the context of John demanding that his uncle's bone be handed over, as this is a legal term which means 'to compel the payment of damages by someone who has made improper use of one's property'.

D31: In the margin Tolkien wrote in pencil 'I'm tired of gnawing old bones & skins'. Compare E34.

D32, 35: Tolkien marked 'thee shall' to be changed to 'thou shalt', but the reading was abandoned. In the margin by D35 Tolkien wrote: 'And will be thy graveyard'.

D33: In D^1 Tolkien drafted 'Drunkle! Munkle' before settling on 'Sunkle! Drunkle!' The latter seems to be the 'Sunk well! Drunk well!' of D in abbreviated, or perhaps dialectal, form.

E4–5: These lines read, before revision, 'And seen no man nor mortal. | Ortal! Portal!' – a reversion to texts A and B.

E7: This line read, before revision, 'And saw no man nor mortal'.

E10: In his 1952 recording of the song, Tolkien pronounced 'my' in ll. 10 and 24 as 'me', and 'thy' in l. 35 as 'thee'.

E39: 'Larn' is a dialectal spelling of *learn*, in the now archaic or slang sense 'to teach'. (The Badger uses the verb similarly in *The Wind in the Willows* by Kenneth Grahame.)

F45: Here Tolkien cleverly uses *root* in a wholly different sense (the base of a mountain) than the one he used earlier ('kick'). – In the first edition of *The Lord of the Rings*, and in the printer's typescript and proofs of that book, this line ends in a colon; in E45, it has a final semi-colon. In *The Adventures of Tom Bombadil and Other Verses from the Red Book* (1962 and later editions), and in *The Lord of the Rings* since its second edition (1965), the line ends in a comma.

84

Frenchmen Froth (*c.* 1924)

The sentiments of *Frenchmen Froth*, the twelfth poem by Tolkien in *Songs for the Philologists* (1936), stem from his personal antipathy towards the French language which, as he saw it, had had adverse effects on the English language as a result of the Norman Conquest. 'English', he is said to have remarked, is 'a language that could move easily in abstract concepts when French was still a vulgar Norman patois', but had become 'adulterated' with 'a large Franco-Latin ingredient largely floating about like oil' (quoted, from two sources, in *Reader's Guide*, p. 343). In his essay *English and Welsh* he wrote that 'French and Latin together were my first experience of second-learned language. Latin' – which he encountered every day in the Catholic liturgy – '. . . seemed so *normal* that pleasure or distaste was equally inapplicable. French has given to me less of this pleasure than any other language with which I have sufficient acquaintance for this judgement' (*The Monsters and the Critics and Other Essays*, p. 191).

Nonetheless, it is important to understand that *Frenchmen Froth* is a deliberate *exaggeration* of prejudice against French – and, as it proceeds apace, of mathematics, and the classical languages, and literary critics, and the forces of education in general – and should be read in that spirit of parody, as no doubt it was sung by the Leeds English School students. (We might also remark that whatever he thought of the French language, Tolkien enjoyed, from time to time, French wine and French cuisine.)

The text of *Frenchmen Froth* is given here as printed on pp. 24–5 of *Songs for the Philologists*.

Though Frenchmen froth with furious sound
And fill our frousty mansions,
And gurgling uvulas are ground,
And tremblers pay 'attention';
Though History roll in dreary round
Colonial expansion,
And king and parliamentary hound,
And constitutional sanction,
This is my faith, I do maintain, until the stars
shall fall, sir!

Let other lands be what they claim, is England
best of all, sir.

In mathematics' mouldering shed
Though tangled runes be written
By faces grave of men long dead
That worms have sorely bitten;
Though Greek and Latin in one bed
With sleeping-sickness ridden
Do dream of days when classics bled
A weary world unchidden,
This is my faith, I do maintain, until the stars
shall fall, sir!
Of all the arts this hath my heart — the English
tongue fore all, sir!

Though Education quack, quack, quack
And force upon our weasands
The nostrums from its nonsense pack
In endless silly seasons
Though tyrant force behind our back
Shall thrust us without reason
To halls that light and learning lack
Where teachers talk of treason,
This is my faith, I do maintain, until the stars
shall fall, sir!
That fear and false report shall not make English
fall, sir!

Though some may strip their stupid souls
(At least to the pyjamas),
Though sages green with puny polls
Write dismal little dramas;
Though critics jibber in their holes
Of style and form and metre,
Yet literature (the little moles!)
They miss her when they meet her,
This is my faith, I do maintain, while songs by
men are sung, sir!
They only earn the English name who learn the
English tongue, sir!

A printed caption at the head of the poem directs that it should be sung to the tune of 'The Vicar of Bray'. That eighteenth-century song tells of a vicar in Bray, a village in the county of Berkshire, who lived under several kings and queens of England, and changed his faith and his politics to suit the ruling monarch. As printed in *The Scottish Students' Song Book*, which Tolkien had at hand, its lyrics begin:

In good King Charles's golden days,
When loyalty no harm meant,
A zealous High Church man was I,
And so I got preferment;
To teach my flock I never missed.
Kings were by God appointed,
And damn'd are those who do resist,
Or touch the Lord's anointed.

And this is law, that I'll maintain,
Until my dying day, sir,
That whatsoever King shall reign,
I'll be the Vicar of Bray, sir.

'King Charles' is Charles II, 'by God appointed', that is, king by divine right. *Preferment* is appointment to an ecclesiastical office. The vicar later alters his principles – Catholic or Protestant, Tory or Whig – to accommodate James II, William III, Anne, and Georges I and II.

1: 'Froth', i.e. frothing at the mouth, is a much exaggerated description of animated speech in French.

2: We interpret 'frousty' not as the slang word meaning 'unpleasant-smelling' – although one could perhaps relate that unkindly to the reputed French love of garlic – but rather as another spelling of *frowsty* 'stuffy'.

3–4: 'Gurgling uvulas' and 'tremblers' are references to the making of sounds particular to French speech.

13: In his personal copy of *Songs for the Philologists* (copy 1) Tolkien wrote next to this line in the margin, by way of explanation of 'mathematics' mouldering shed': 'Maths was in Leeds 1920–26 taught under [an] old army hut'.

14: The 'tangled runes' are the symbols of mathematical discourse. Mathematics is itself a language, in which symbolic description is more efficient to achieve its ends than common words.

17–20: The classics were once the unchallenged ('unchidden') centre of all education. Tolkien himself read Greats (the Greek and Latin classics) as an undergraduate at Oxford before he followed his heart and took up study in the English School. Even there, however, it was essential (as indeed it is still essential) to understand the influence of Greek and Latin on the development of the English language.

25: 'Quack, quack, quack' is perhaps a rendering of academic blather, as Tolkien saw it, in disciplines other than his own. But it also implies that there were unqualified practitioners delivering the educational equivalent of 'quack' medicine, the *nostrums* of l. 27.

26: 'Force upon our weasands [gullets]', i.e. 'shove down our throats'.

35: In his personal copy of *Songs* (copy 1) Tolkien added the words 'force and' before 'false'.

37, etc.: The rivalry of English language (philology) and English literature (criticism) continued in *Lit' and Lang'*, poem no. 85.

39: 'Puny polls', i.e. small heads, with (implied) small brains to match.

44: In his personal copy of *Songs* (copy 1) Tolkien inserted 'they' before 'meet', omitted in printing. We have included this evident correction in our transcribed text.

85

Lit' and Lang' (*c.* 1924)

The thirteenth and final poem by Tolkien in *Songs for the Philologists* (1936) is *Lit' and Lang'*. We give its text as printed in the booklet, p. 27.

Once there were two little groups,
Once there were two little groups,
Once there were two little groups,
    Called Lit' and Lang'.
Lit' was lazy till she died,
Lit' was lazy till she died,
Lit' was lazy till she died,
    Of homophemes.
'I don't like philology,'
    Poor Lit' said.
Psychotherapeutics failed,
    And now she's dead.

Doctors cut up all the corpse,
Doctors cut up all the corpse,
Doctors cut up all the corpse,
    But searched in vain;
They couldn't find it anywhere,
They couldn't find it anywhere,
They couldn't find it anywhere,
    They couldn't find the brain.
Did Lang' go into mourning-weeds?
    I don't think!
He quickly wiped a tear away
    And had another drink.

As discussed earlier, the English School at the University of Leeds had two schemes or courses: A, which emphasized literature, and B, which focused on the structure and development of the English language (philology). These are the subject of the present poem. In his personal copy of *Songs for the Philologists* (copy 1) Tolkien wrote on the page 'Leeds Version schemes', and 'A and B' next to line 4. According to Tom Shippey in *The Road to Middle-earth*, Tolkien also entitled the work *The Two Schemes*, which we take to be an addition to his second copy of *Songs*. Shippey thinks that the poem is the worst Tolkien ever wrote, 'so bad indeed that it makes me think (or hope) that something must have gone wrong with it *en route* between poet and printer' (p. 5). Granted that it is not as clever as other of his poems, and much of its imagery is unpleasant, even insulting – however much it was meant to be tongue-in-cheek – still, in writing it, Tolkien never meant to rival Tennyson or Keats.

While at both Leeds and Oxford, he raised high the banner of Language; he was in fact named to the faculty at Leeds specifically to help develop Language study in the English School. In his Oxford valedictory address of 5 June 1959, before he left his last professorial chair, he spoke of 'the bogeys *Lang* and *Lit*', Language and Literature, and of the popular myths 'that *Lang* came from a cuckoo-egg laid in the nest, in which he takes up too much room and usurps the worms of the *Lit* chicken', or 'that *Lit* was the cuckoo, bent on extruding her nest-fellow or sitting on him' (*Valedictory Address to the University of Oxford*, in *The Monsters and the Critics and Other Essays*, p. 230). Such thinking led to 'sides' being taken, with a divide between their respective enthusiasts. There was no need for this, Tolkien knew and said. Neither 'side' was 'normally exclusive, neither the sole property of this or that scholar, nor the sole object of any one course of study' (p. 231).

Nonetheless, the divisions in the Leeds and Oxford English schools were real, intentionally so, with different schemes designed to appeal to different student interests. So too was the rivalry between 'Lang' and 'Lit', and this had a practical effect. As Shippey puts it in *The Road to Middle-earth*, 'for most of his active life Tolkien taught Old English, Middle English, the history of the English language; in doing so he was competing with teachers of English literature for time, funds and students, on the whole a thankless task since for all that Tolkien could do the current was setting firmly away from him and from his subjects' (p. 5). At least two of his poems in *Songs for the Philologists*, Shippey suggests, show him holding a partisan grudge: *Frenchmen Froth* (no. 84) and *Lit' and Lang'*.

The nursery rhyme 'Polly Put the Kettle On', set to music, is printed in Moffat's *What the Children Sing* (p. 17), but would have been widely known to the Leeds students. Tolkien identified this as the tune for *Lit' and Lang'* in a note added to his copy 1 of *Songs*. There are many variations on its lyrics, but these are typical:

Polly put the kettle on,
Polly put the kettle on,
Polly put the kettle on,
We'll all have tea.

Sukey take it off again,
Sukey take it off again,
Sukey take it off again,
They've gone all away.

(*Polly* and *Sukey* were once common nicknames for *Mary* and *Susan*.) We have not found a version of the song with additions such as those in lines 9–12 and 21–24 of *Lit' and Lang'*.

8: *Homophemes* (or *homophenes*) are different words or phrases which when pronounced are made with the same apparent lip movements. An example is 'elephant juice' and 'I love you'. – In his copy 1 of *Songs* Tolkien noted that 'Of homophemes' 'breaks the rhyme scheme', that is, 'homophemes' does not rhyme with 'Lang" in l. 4 (compare 'vain' and 'brain' in the second stanza). This may have led him to write 'Lang' and Lit" next to l. 4, and 'In a fainting fit ?' next to l. 8, presumably as suggested replacements. He also wrote next to this line 'And left Scheme B'.

9: Next to this line in his copy 1 of *Songs*, and also next to ll. 11, 21, and 23, Tolkien wrote '(ber)'. We have no good explanation of what he meant by this.

10: Next to this line in his copy 1 of *Songs* Tolkien wrote 'A', as a reference to 'Lit". Similarly, next to l. 21 he wrote 'B', referring to 'Lang".

21: 'Mourning-weeds', i.e. mourning clothes.

86

All Hail! (*c.* 1924)

Tolkien probably wrote *All Hail!* as one of the 'Leeds Songs', but it was not included in *Songs for the Philologists*. Its fair copy manuscript is preserved in the Gordon archive at Leeds. Lacking other evidence, we have grouped it with other poems of its kind, from Tolkien's last years at Leeds, though it could belong instead with songs sent to Gordon after Tolkien had moved to Oxford.

1. *Unus.* All hail! Come up to heaven, do!
You too, come up to heaven, too!
O do, come up to heaven, do!
    I will be up there before.
I promise I'll send you your harp and your halo
(I don't promise, mind you, 'twon't be a bit pale-o);
I know a good place, too, where wings are on sale-o —
    O how you will sing as you soar!

★

2. *Alii.* Bless me! Heaven we're flying to!
Gee, yes! We are just dying to!
I guess we are just trying to;
    We've never been there before.
He promised to purchase us haloes from Moses,
And lilies and lyres and garlands of roses;
He promised to powder our naughty red noses —
    But someone has bolted the door!

★

3. *Unus.* O Hell! Go to the devil, you!
And you, go to the devil, too!
O do, go to the devil, do!
    Should I go thither before,
I promise to stoke up the furnace for you, lads;
The fires I will poke up, and see that you stew, lads;

I promise to see that the oven's hot too, lads —
    Could any friend ever do more?

★

4. *Alii.* Hell's bells! What are we waiting for?
Good lor! What are we waiting for?
What more can we be waiting for,
    Knocking and banging the gate?

Diaboli. Ah welcome! ah, welcome to all at the door-o!
Such sinners come seldom. The furnaces roar-o.
We'll frizzle you, fry you, we'll sizzle you sore-o!

Alii. Ah no, we don't think we can wait!

5. *Alii omnes.* Back, back! we must go back again;
No crown, put on our black again;
Done brown, given the sack again —
    Doesn't seem really quite fair:
In heaven no welcome, in hell a too warm one —
It's almost enough to convert and reform one.
Let's stop upon earth then, and jerk off a jorum,
    If drink's still in fashion up there.

The four parts indicated by Latin labels are to be sung by one (*unus*) person, by others (*alii*) present, by some representing devils (*diaboli*), and by all together (*alii omnes*).

Tolkien indicated on the manuscript that the work is to be sung to 'Oh, Dear! What Can the Matter Be?' The lyrics to that tune differ among song books, but the most traditional include:

Oh, dear! What can the matter be?
Dear, dear, what can the matter be?
Oh, dear! What can the matter be?
Johnny's so [*or* too] long at the fair.

He promised he'd buy me a fairing should please me,
And then for a kiss, oh, he vowed he would tease me,
He promised he'd bring me a bunch of blue ribbons,
To tie up my bonny brown hair.

In line 39, *jerk* has the meaning 'dispense', as in 'to jerk beer', from the action of moving the handle on a tap to fill a glass or pitcher. A *jorum* is a drinking-vessel, from a cup to a large jug or bowl; the phrase 'push about (or around) the jorum' appears in traditional comic songs, meaning 'pass around the container of drink'. One example is in the late eighteenth-century burletta *The Golden Pippin*:

When bickerings hot
To high words got,
Break out at Gamiorum;
The flame to cool,
My golden rule
Is — push about the jorum!

87

The Lion Is Loud and Proud (*c.* 1924)

Tolkien wrote this curious short poem quickly on a scrap of University of Leeds examination paper. There are apparently two voices, one in fear of the Lion – or whatever the Lion is meant to represent – the other who makes light of it. Tolkien seems to have given its single manuscript to his friend and colleague E.V. Gordon, as it is in the Gordon archive at Leeds.

The Lion is loud and proud, and Strong —
    is loud and proud, I said —
His mane is shaggy, fierce, and long —
    but hides an empty head, I said —
'Tis sometimes seen in Devonshire —
    And that's a lot too near, I said —
And fills all Yorkshire full of fear —
    Ah! that's the catlike tread, I said!

Devonshire is in the south-west of England, far from Yorkshire in the north-east.

2: This line read, before revision (possibly altered in the course of writing), 'is loud and proud, is what I said'.

88

The Song of Beewolf Son of Echgethew (*c.* 1925–?40)

Beowulf, the longest and most important surviving poem in Old English, tells – to give it the barest of summaries – of a hero of the Geats (a tribe of southern Sweden) who sails to Denmark where a monster, Grendel, is killing the warriors of the king, Hrothgar. Endowed by God with superhuman strength, Beowulf slays Grendel in terrible combat, and also Grendel's mother when she seeks revenge. Returning home, in time he becomes king of his people, and his fame in battle keeps them free from invasion. After fifty years, when a dragon wreaks havoc, Beowulf once again takes up his sword, and with only one faithful retainer, he kills the dragon but loses his own life.

Tolkien lectured on *Beowulf* at Leeds and Oxford, and in 1936 delivered his landmark British Academy paper, *Beowulf: The Monsters and the Critics*, emphasizing the work as poetry rather than as a mine for historical nuggets. He also translated the poem twice into Modern English, as a companion rather than a 'crib', to help *Beowulf* students grasp the work before they themselves engaged with the Old English text. His Modern English *Beowulf* in prose was complete by April 1926, but despite later efforts, Tolkien never revised it to his satisfaction; it was published only in 2014, as *Beowulf: A Translation and Commentary*, edited by his son Christopher.

Even earlier, probably no later than 1925, he began a translation in alliterative verse. In our *J.R.R. Tolkien Companion and Guide* (2017) we wrote that he abandoned this after 594 lines. We do not now recall where we learned this figure; it was not from personal examination of the file in the Bodleian Library, which we saw many years ago but did not record the length of the translation relative to the original poem. In fact, Tolkien's work is longer than we stated, and more fragmentary than we knew. Many of its surviving pages are rough workings, written on any scrap of paper that came to hand, including Leeds examination scripts and discarded word-slips (for *wan*) from Tolkien's months on the staff of the *Oxford English Dictionary*.

The most finished text of the verse translation began as a careful manuscript, entitled *The Song of Beewolf Son of Echgethew* (with 'Tale' later pencilled above 'Song'), but after a few pages became a typescript; this text, to its end as typed, is indeed the equivalent of the first 594 lines of the Old English poem. On its final page, however, Tolkien added in manuscript twelve more lines, extending the work to line 606 in the original ('sunne swegl-wered sūþan scīneð'). There are also in his archive several more manuscript sheets, written at different times while he was at Leeds, perhaps for lectures, on which he translated part of Hrothgar's report of sightings of Grendel and his mother (lines 1345–1372 of the original), and other pages with his translation of the end of the poem, beginning with line 3137.

Only a few lines from Tolkien's verse translation of *Beowulf* have been published before the present book. Some appeared in his preface to the 1940 edition of John R. Clark Hall's *Beowulf* in prose (revised by C.L. Wrenn), formally *Prefatory Remarks on Prose Translation of 'Beowulf'* (see our discussion for poem no. 67). While planning this collection we felt that more of the alliterative version deserved to be read than that tantalizing sample, considering the importance of *Beowulf* to Tolkien's scholarship and the influence of the work on his fiction. Space has allowed us to include four extracts and some alternate readings; the work, if published whole and properly explicated, would need a volume to itself. In general, from its various texts we have transcribed the most finished, giving Tolkien's words as he wrote them out, including corrections made in the course of writing but with subsequent revisions or alternate workings described in our commentary or notes. The line numbers indicated in extracts A through F refer to the translation as a whole; extract G is an outlier.

Our first passage (A) is from the start of the poem, which in the original begins:

Hwæt wē Gār-Dena   in geār-dagum
þēod-cyninga   þrym gefrūnon
hū ðā æþelingas   ellen fremedon.

Tolkien rendered these lines in prose as 'Lo! the glory of the kings of the people of the Spear-Danes in days of old we have heard tell, how those princes did deeds of valour'.

[A]

Hark! of the Danes   in the days agone
what of their folk-kings   fame then tell
of their princes' prowess   proven in deeds.
Oft Shield of the Sheaf   did shend the hosts
and marred the meadhalls'   mirth of his foemen,
and fear was fallen   on folk unnumbered

sith first men found him   faring helpless.
Easement he knew   of his need thereafter —
yea! waxed in the world   and in worship throve,
till neighbour princes   must name him lord;
over the waves   where the whale rideth
all must hearken   his hests and yield
tithe and tribute   — in truth a king!
In the afterdays   an heir he got him,
a child in his house,   yet chosen of God
to the folk's comfort;   for the fell anguish
wherein long while lordless   they laboured erst
full well He wist;   and world-glory
the Lord and Life-giver   lent him after —
— to Beewolf the bold   that blazéd widely
the name in Shedland   of Shield's offspring.
So becomes a king's son   in the courts of his father
with his brave bounty   to breed him love
and constant comrades   to cleave to his eld
steadfast in service   when strife waketh,
and leal to their lord: in all lands of men
shall praiséd deeds   the doer prosper.
Doughty was Shield,   but doom's hour cometh,
and he got him gone   to God's keeping.
His belovéd lieges   to the loud sea-margin
then bare him forth   as he bade himself,
while his word was law   in the land of the Shieldings,
and love held he long,   and lordship wielded.
There rode at the hythe   — and her ringéd stern
in the ice-cold water   waded eager —
the prince's bark;   in her bosom laid they
their lord belovéd,   laid in glory
the giver of gold   by the galleon's mast
great tale of treasure   and trappings costly
fet from far-off   folk about him.
No ship, 'tis sung,   was more seemly ever
with warrior's weeds   and wargear dight,
with glaives and hauberks;   they heaped his bosom
with many a jewel   to journey nigh him
far on the sea-flood's   fastness wending.
In nowise more niggard   they now enriched him
with wealth of king's   than once of yore
did those who forth   afaring cast him

a waif on the waves a wandering infant.
Yea! high o[']er his head they hung his token
a gonfanon golden and gave him to sea
for the flood to bear far from their weeping
and hearts' sadness — ah! who can say,
or what tales of truth men tell in their halls
o'er the wide world wot, who welcomed him home?

The fifty-five lines of extract A are the equivalent of lines 1–52 in the Old English *Beowulf*. Because Modern English relies on word order, compared with Old English, an inflected language which conveys much of its information by word endings, and because Tolkien chose to keep the expansive alliterative form of the original, his translated text is necessarily longer, and could not consistently follow his source line by line. A prologue to *Beowulf*, text A provides a background to the poet's tale, with the lineage of Hrothgar back to the supposed ancestor of his royal house: *Scyld* 'shield', a given name deduced from the family name *Scyldingas*, further called *Scéfing* 'of the Sheaf' from the figure's legendary arrival in a boat accompanied by a handful of corn (i.e. wheat). The passage tells of Scyld's prowess, of his departure from his people in old age, and how he was succeeded by Beowulf, here 'Beewolf' – the son of Scyld, not the hero of the poem (see our note for line 20). For Tolkien's original poem concerning Scyld, *King Sheave*, see no. 146.

Extract B is a translation of the Old English lines 86–125. It is disappointing that Tolkien did not in this text reach as far as Beowulf's battle with Grendel in Hrothgar's hall, but we have at least a vigorous description of the monster's gruesome handiwork before the hero appears on the scene.

[B] Lo! a ghoul was there grim and grievous him seemed,
as his weary hours he wore in darkness,
day after day the din to hearken
and the loud hall's laughter when lilted the harp
to the minstrel clear-singing, or such as had lore
to recall the far days of the coming of men
told of th'Almighty's making of Earth,
whose bright-hued vale He belted with waters,
with majesty stationed the Sun and Moon,
radiant lamps to enlighten earth's folk,
and the lands' wide bosom with bough and leaf
He beauteous made, and brought to life

all kinds on mould that move and live.
Thus the king's men in mirth abode —
good hap them seemed till the hell-fiend gan
to work his deeds of direst woe.
That grimmest guest men Grendel calléd,
haunter of march and moor ill-famed,
and of fens untrodden. The trollkind's lair,
accursed wight he kept long while
an outlaw doomed to dwell by God
with the kindred of Cain (that killer of Abel
whose murder the Lord Immortal avenged.
Ill hap he found in his feud with heaven,
for cast for his crime from the kinship of men
he was sire of all the seed inhuman.
of ogres and goblins and ghoulish hosts,
of the giants who warred a weary age
with God, Who gave them a guerdon sure.)
Now drew he near, when night was come,
to spy how that high roofed hall for rest,
their drinking done, the Danes had ordered.
There found he a press of princely folk
that sated slept of sorrow unmindful
or mortal woes. Then the monstrous wight
grim in his greed soon got him in
in ravening wrath; from their resting places
seized thirty thanes and thence to his lair
gloating was gone in his gruesome spoil
to seek his dwellings with slaughter drunk.
At the grey of dawn as daylight grew
was Grendel's murderous might revealéd.
Where revel was now weeping rose,
a mighty cry at morn that came
to that praiséd prince, their peerless king.
Grieving his thanes on his throne in gloom
that stout-heart sat and sorrow knew
for the loathsome slot had his lieges seen
of the curséd ghoul: — too grim his care,
too lasting bitter; nor longer space
than a night he gave or he new vale wrought,
murder yet more, and mourned it not,
not his devilry dread, too deep in sin.
Not far were to seek who then sought their rest

on other beds   in bowers remote.
When the hall's haunter   his hate proclaimed
with token clean   and true they dwelt
far from scathe   who the foe escaped.
Thus he wrongful reigned   and wrought with war
alone 'gainst all   till empty lay
that house most lovely   — ah! long that time;
Twelve winter's [*sic*] tide that teen he bore,
the Lord of the Shieldings, and lived in woe;
knew deepest dole that all death doomed men
in songs of sadness his secret heard,
how Grendel wagéd war on Hrothgar,
and felly fought in feud awhile;
wrong and ruin he wrought long years
in strife unceasing and stayed for none
of the Danish host his deadly hand;
for truce he would not and treasure scorned.

With line 150 of his translation, Tolkien abandoned the use of visual pauses, and we have followed this in our transcription. It is also at this point that the manuscript text ends and a typescript begins, made on a machine with a purple ribbon, as often in Tolkien's years on the faculty at Leeds; and with this change as well, he no longer marked textual breaks with indentation. We suspect that there was a gap of time between his writing the manuscript and beginning the typescript, as the final three lines of the former, breaking off in mid-phrase in line 152, are repeated and revised in the latter. Before revision, they read:

twelve winters' tide   that teen was borne
by the Shieldings' lord,   each shape of woe
and deepest dole

It is evident also that Tolkien paid close attention to this part of the poem, as a stray sheet of manuscript in his papers contains workings for lines 150–159. This text is identical to that in the typescript, except that line 152 reads 'knew deepest sorrow || that all sons of men' – words he also wrote on the typescript.

Extract C is a translation of the Old English lines 194–257, omitting, however, after translation line 205, the three original lines 202–204 ('Þone sīð-fæt him || snotere ceorlas | lȳt-hwōn lōgon, || þēah hē him lēof wǣre; | hwetton hige-rōfne, || hǣl scēawedon'). This was in error, as Tolkien realized when he came to review his typescript; he marked the omission, but did not make good the text. In his prose version he translated the missing lines as: 'With that voyage little fault did wise men find, dear though he were to them; they encouraged his valiant heart, and they observed the omens' (*Beowulf: A Translation and Commentary*, pp. 18–19).

[C] Then heard in his homeland Hygelac's thane [Beowulf],
the goodly Geat, Grendel's prowess.
In that day was he deemed of the days of men
among mankind mightiest of body
of birth and valour. He let build a ship
on the waves sea-worthy, said 'the warrior-king
will I seek o'er the sea where the swan rideth;
for that lord renowned has need of men'.
Him chose then the Geat that chieftain goodly
a band of warriors, boldest of those
that were to find, and fifteen in all
they sought their ship — sea-lore knew he
and landmarks all who led them there.
Time fared forward: afloat on the waves
neath the cliff was their craft. Then clomb her stem
those brave men blithely, and the breakers pounding
ground the shingle as their shining harness
to the bark's bosom they bore, their armour
forgéd-cunning; then forth cast her
to voyage triumphant, valiant-timbered.
O'er the waves she wended by the wind hasted,
foamnecked fleeting as flies a bird,
till a time was told of twelve hours thrice,
when her bended beak had beaten far,
and labouring a-sea the land they saw,
the shore-wall shining and the sheer headlands
and vasty capes — that vessel had come
to her sea-way's ending. Thence swiftly up
to the beach waded the Weder-chieftains;
there moored their craft while their mail clattered
and their battle-raiment; and blessed they God
that plain had made them the paths o'er the ocean.
From the shore-wall saw the Shieldings guard;
who the dunes by the sea of duty kept,
their gleaming targes o'er the gangways borne

and harness valiant, that his heart was pierced
by wonderment who such warriors be.
To the strand he got him astride his horse,
even Hrothgar's thane, whose hands mightily
his spear did shake as he speaking asked
'Who be ye then in battle-raiment
and corslets clad that are come thus far
on the watery ways and waves steering
your towering ship? Long time have I
these confines kept, and coast-ward held,
that no foemen fell might fall with war
in their longships raiding the land of the Danes;
but less secret have none here sought to bear
their shields ashore, who surely knew not
or countersign or kinsmen's leave
to warfain men. Than one among you
a mightier on earth ne'er met mine eyes
of mailclad men. No menial he
in brave weapon-show, if his bearing lie not
and peerless mien. Now prithee must I
your lineage know ere longer way,
as spies maybe, ye speed from hence
on the Danish land. Lo! dwellers afar,
o'er the waters wending, my words hear ye
from heart outspoken: with haste were best
plain to reveal me whence your paths have led.'

Tolkien seems have found special difficulty with, or particular interest in, roughly twenty lines beginning with line 211 ('Time fared forward', etc.): there are four manuscript drafts of this portion in the Bodleian Library's file. Two of these texts are similar to the typescript, with only minor differences; of the others, the earliest (as we judge) was written quickly, perhaps as Tolkien made his translation, while the later text was more carefully written, then marked to indicate stresses. We have transcribed these as D and E respectively.

[D] The hour onward fared   on ocean afloat
neath the cliff was their craft.   Then clomb her stem
those brave men blithely   breakers pounding
ground the shingle   gleaming harness
to the bark's bosom   they bore, their arms
with cunning forgéd,   then cast her forth

to voyage triumphant valiant-timbered.
O'er the waves she wended by the wind hasted
foamnecked fleeting as flies a bird
till at selfsame hour of the second morning
her bended beak had beaten afar
that labouring sea the land they saw
shere walls shining and sheer headlands
and vasty capes — that vessel was come
to her seaways end. Thence swiftly up
there waded to the beach the Weder chieftains;
there moored their craft while the mail clattered
their battle raiment and blessed they God
that their paths on ocean plain had made them.

[E] The hour onward fared: on ocean afloat
neath the cliff was their craft; then clomb her stem
those brave men blithely; breakers pounding
ground the shingle; gleaming harness
they bore to the bosom of the bark, armour
with cunning forgéd then cast her forth
to voyage in triumph valiant-timbered.
O'er the waves she wended by the wind hasted
foam-necked fleeting as flies a bird
till at the same [hour >] season on the second morning
her bended beak had beaten far
so that labouring a-sea the land they saw,
the shere wall shining with sheer headlands
and vasty capes — had that vessel journeyed
to her seaways end. Thence swiftly up
there waded to the beach the Weder-chieftains;
there moored their craft while their mail clattered
and their battle-raiment. Then blessed they God
who plain had made them the paths of the sea.

Michael D.C. Drout remarks on this passage on p. 152 of his review of the 2014 prose *Beowulf* in *Tolkien Studies* (2015), suggesting that Tolkien selected it to include in his *Prefatory Remarks on Prose Translation of 'Beowulf'* as an illustration of the metre of the poem, because he believed it to be 'the most successful and finished section of the translation'; this more polished version is transcribed below (F) from the printed text. Tolkien wrote his preface, or at least completed it, at the beginning of 1940. Drout also notes that Tolkien included 'an apparently antecedent version' of the same passage in his lectures collected as *Beowulf and the Critics*, written in the mid-1930s and printed in Drout's edition of that work (2nd edn., 2011).

[F] Time passed away. On the tide floated
under bank their boat. In her bows mounted
brave men blithely. Breakers turning
spurned the shingle. Splendid armour
they bore aboard, in her bosom piling
well-forged weapons, then away thrust her
to voyage gladly valiant timbered.
She went then over wave-tops, wind pursued her,
fleet, foam-throated like a flying bird;
and her curving prow on its course waded,
till in due season on the day after
those seafarers saw before them
shore-cliffs shimmering and sheer mountains,
wide capes by the waves: to water's end
the ship had journeyed. Then ashore swiftly
they leaped to land, lords of Gothland,
bound fast their boat. Their byrnies rattled,
grim gear of war. God thanked they then
that their sea-passage safe had proven.

In his preface Tolkien also included, for comparison, the Old English text as in the *Beowulf* manuscript, and a literal translation of that text into Modern English, word by word and in the order of the manuscript, which illustrates well the confusion such an approach would result for a modern reader, compared with the more poetic translation Tolkien attempted.

In his commentary to *Beowulf* associated with his prose translation (2014), Tolkien called this

> a good passage of description. The long march to the sea is compressed to *fyrst forð gewát* ('Time passed on' . . .). For a moment the vision is of a cliff-top, the boat is seen below half drawn up prow foremost on the sand; we see the men busy lading it, then pushing it with oars or poles out into the water. The wind fills the sails, and it is off swiftly, as marked by the foam at the prow, like a white gull, which gives an impression of increasing distance, catching the gleam of far off cliffs and mountains in a strange land. [p. 192]

Finally we give, as G, from its manuscript prior to further revision, the most advanced of three translations by Tolkien of the end of *Beowulf*, depicting the hero's funeral.

[G]

For him then fashioned the folk of the Goths
a pyre on the earth proudly raiséd,
o'erhung with helms and hauberks bright,
with warrior's shields as his will had been.
Then laid they amidmost the mighty chieftain,
their lord belovéd those lieges sighing.
Of funeral fires on the fell the mightiest
then war-men woke: —the wood-reek rose
black o'er the burning, and the blaze a-roaring
was with weeping ringed: the wind's tumult
was stayed till the corse was crumbled wholly
in the heart fire-hot. Unhappy men,
they bemoaned their misery and their master's fall;
and a lamentable lay his lady aged
with braided tresses for Beowulf made,
sorrowfully singing and saying ever,
how days of evil she dreaded sore,
thronging murders, & thraldom and shame,
and the foeman's fear to find her yet—
the fume of the burning faded in heaven.
A mound they made, the men of the Storm
on the hill by the sea; it was high and broad,
that who fared on the waves saw far and wide
the battle chief's beacon they buildéd there
in ten day's toil: what the flame took not
they closed in a wall on such comely wise
the most tried in skill could contrive for him.
In that tomb then laid they the torques and gems
such trinketry all as had taken forth
high-hearted men from the hoard erewhile.
The treasury of princes they entrusted to earth,
gave the gold to the ground where it glimmers yet
as profitless to men as it proved of old.
Then about that mound rode men most bold,
children of chieftains, a chosen twelve
who their care would mourn and their king lament
a song upraising & their sire praising;
remembering his manhood and his mighty works

with ungrudging glory as good it is
that a man's dear master should be meted praise,
and held in heart's love when he hence must go,
set free from his garb of flesh at last.
Such lamentation in the land of the Goths
made his hearth-comrades for their high lord's fall,
crying that he was ever of the kings of earth
of men the mildest and of mercy fullest,
to his people fairest and of praise fainest.

Christopher Tolkien has suggested that his father left this verse translation for a prose version after finding that the alliterative form did not allow him to come close enough to the exact meaning of the poem. Its surviving leaves of manuscript and typescript – almost certainly there were once other pages of workings – also reveal the task to have been laborious, with false starts and second thoughts. As he moved his career and home from Leeds to Oxford in 1925–6, Tolkien had less time to devote to either project, if no less interest.

Readers of this poem may take note of its number of unfamiliar words, and recall our discussion of the vocabulary and diction of *Sir Gawain and the Green Knight* (poem no. 70) in connection with Tolkien's philosophy of translating early literature. He wrote in the preface to the Clark Hall *Beowulf*:

> Personally you may not like an archaic vocabulary, and word-order, artificially maintained as an elevated and literary language. You may prefer the brand new, the lively and the snappy. But whatever may be the case with other poets of past ages (with Homer, for instance) the author of *Beowulf* did not share this preference. If you wish to translate, not re-write, *Beowulf*, your language must be literary and traditional: not because it is now a long while since the poem was made, or because it speaks of things that have since become ancient; but because the diction of *Beowulf* was poetical, archaic, artificial (if you will), in the day that the poem was made. Many words used by the ancient English poets had, even in the eighth century, already passed out of colloquial use for anything from a lifetime to hundreds of years. [*The Monsters and the Critics and Other Essays*, p. 54]

Some years later, the American scholar Burton Raffel produced a slim volume, *Poems from the Old English* (1960), and sent a copy to

Tolkien; in 1963 he would publish his own translation of *Beowulf*. For these, Raffel chose to approximate the Old English alliterative verse form while writing unapologetically in Modern English and at times omitting metaphors which an Anglo-Saxon audience would have understood but not (he supposed) a modern reader. His approach, hailed as rescuing Old English from the academics, was not unpopular. Tolkien, however, privately took issue in a largely unpublished essay about Raffel's translations in particular and the translation of poetry in general. Its first paragraphs are worth quoting in full, in conjunction with Tolkien's views in the Clark Hall volume given above, and more widely in relation to the several instances of translation by Tolkien in the present book.

> The making of translations should be primarily for private amusement, and profit. The profit, at any rate, will be found in the increased and sharpened understanding of the language of the original which the translator will acquire in the process, and can acquire in no other way; though his gain may not be evident in his version. He may not possess the skill, and in any case the increase in understanding will only increase the natural difficulty of equating two different idioms. But that will not matter as long as the affair remains private, a labour of devotion (as it should be), the most attentive possible mode of reading the work of another writer. But publication of the result needs some defence.
>
> The most obvious one is that the work translated is worth reading, intrinsically or for some other reason of history or scholarship, and worth reading by those who do not know and cannot be expected to learn the language of the original author. This, I suppose, is the defence usually put forward. But there are many degrees between total ignorance and complete mastery of an alien idiom. The latter is seldom acquired by any one, not even by translators, certainly not by me. And even if a certain mastery is assumed, it is I think a fact that in the case of texts that have become the objects of study, that have been trampled in the Schools by lecturers, editors, and students, the actual *hearing* of the original work is less and less often attended to. *Hearing* not *reading*; for reading suggests close and silent study, the pondering of words, the solution of a series of puzzles, but hearing should mean receiving, with the speed of a familiar tongue, the immediate impact of sound and sense together. In all real language these are wedded; separated, even

by the necessity of study, they wither. A translator may hope (or rashly aspire) to heal the divorce, as far as is possible. And if he is in any degree successful, then he may serve even those whose knowledge is greater than his own. The immediacy of a native language can seldom be matched or even approached by an acquired language. And when, as with *Pearl* and *Sir Gawain* and the modern English reader, the language to be translated is English, but of a kind that the passage of time and the changes in literary English have rendered unintelligible without study, there are few even of those who have endured the study that have in fact ever 'heard' either of these poems. That is who have received them with the same immediacy as a man would who belonged to the time and circumstances of the author. To do that would, of course, require a time-machine, allowing one first to acquire the dialect and literary idiom familiar to the author, and then to listen to his work. For such a machine translation is the only practical substitute, however imperfect.

How can a translation be made to operate in this way, however imperfectly? First of all by absolute allegiance to the thing translated: to its meaning, its style, technique, and form. The language used in translation is, for this pupose, merely an instrument, that must be handled so as to reproduce, to make audible again, as nearly as possible, the antique work. Fortunately modern (modern literary, not present-day colloquial) English is an instrument of very great capacity and resources, it has long experience not yet forgotten, and deep roots in the past not yet all pulled up. It can, if asked, still play in modes no longer favoured and remember airs not now popular; it is not limited to the fashionable cacophonies. I have little sympathy with contemporary theories of translation, and no liking for their results. In these the allegiance is changed. Too often it seems given primarily to 'contemporary English', the present-day colloquial idiom as if being 'contemporary', that most evanescent of qualities, by itself guaranteed its superiority. In many the primary allegiance of the 'translator' is to himself, to his own whims and notions, and the original author is evidently considered fortunate to have aroused the interest of a superior writer. This attitude is often a mask for incompetence, and for ignorance of the original idiom; in any case it does not encourage close study of the text and its language, the laborious but only sure way of acquiring a sensitive understanding and appreciation, even for those of poetic temperament, who might have acquired them, if they had started with a more humble and loyal allegiance. [Bodleian Library]

A further quotation from this essay is given in our discussion for poem no. 166. Further on the subject of *Beowulf*, see *The Lay of Beowulf*, poem no. 117.

A1: Tolkien changed 'Hark' to 'Heark' in his ink manuscript, and wrote above the line in pencil 'Hark! of the Danish spears | | in days that are sped [i.e. concluded, in the past]'.

A2: At the end of this line Tolkien wrote in pencil 'us' and 'have told', evidently considering 'have told us' rather than 'then tell'.

A9: 'Easement he knew', i.e. comfort.

A16: Tolkien considered whether to change 'anguish' to 'distress'.

A20: Tolkien speculated that the name rendered 'Beowulf' in the Old English manuscript, here 'Beewolf', should have been *Beow* 'barley'. 'Beowulf' may have been a scribal error; another explanation may be that the scribe anticipated the name of the hero of the poem before he appeared. In his own manuscript, where Shield's son is mentioned in ll. 20 and 56, Tolkien underlined 'Beewolf' and wrote above it 'Bew' and in the margin, 'Béaw', presumably to indicate alternate readings 'Bewolf' or 'Béawolf'. 'Beewolf' is a literal translation of the name *Beowulf*, from Old English *bēo* 'bee' + *wulf* 'wolf'. It has been suggested by scholars such as R.W. Chambers that 'bee-wolf' is a kenning, or metaphorical expression, for 'bear' (the bear is a foe of the bee because it attacks the hīve for honey), thus *Beowulf* is a warrior with bear-like strength and ferocity.

A21: 'Shedland' is Tolkien's translation in verse ('Scedeland' in his prose version) of Old English *Scede-landum*. The 1940 Clark Hall–Wrenn translation has 'North-lands'; other translators prefer 'Swedish lands'. In his commentary attached to his prose *Beowulf* (2014), Tolkien notes that '*Scedeland* contains the Old English form of the very ancient name seen now in the name *Scandinavia*. . . . The Old English form was *Scedenig*' (p. 148), with the *sc*- pronounced *sh*-.

A28: 'Doom's hour cometh': Shield (Scyld, Sheaf) chose to return whence he came when the shadow of old age fell upon him. Tolkien and other scholars interpret Scyld's departure to be a ship-burial.

A30: Tolkien considered whether to change 'sea-margin' to 'ocean'.

A32: Tolkien considered whether to change 'his word was law' to 'as law his word was'.

A34: 'Ringéd stern' is Tolkien's translation of *hringed-stefna*. Bosworth and Toller's dictionary of Old English refers to a 'stern [rear part of a ship] adorned with spiral or ring-shaped ornaments (?), or furnished with a ring or hook; or having a curved stern'.

A35: Tolkien considered whether to change 'waded eager' to 'eager waded'.

A41: At the end of this line Tolkien wrote in pencil 'shapéd'.

A43: Tolkien considered whether to change 'glaives and hauberks' to 'hauberks and glaives'.

A49: Next to this line Tolkien wrote in pencil: 'a waif unnamed on the waves alone'.

A50: Tolkien considered whether to change 'Yea' to 'Now'.

B97: Tolkien seems to have considered (his markings are not clear) whether to change this line to read 'of the Sun and the Moon with majesty stationed'.

B98: Tolkien seems to have considered whether to change this line to read 'the radiant lamps that enlighten earth's folk'.

B101: *Mould* is used here in the sense of 'fashion, make'. In his prose translation (2014) Tolkien renders this part 'life too he devised for every kind that moves and lives' (p. 16).

B105: Tolkien seems to have considered whether to change 'grimmest' to 'gruesome'.

B117: Tolkien seems to have considered whether to change 'Who gave' to 'and got'.

B132: In this line, since the manuscript does not clearly indicate where Tolkien wished to place the caesura, we have made an educated guess.

B137: Tolkien seems to have considered whether to change 'curséd ghoul' to 'ghoul accursed', and 'his care' to 'that war', 'that woe', or 'that strife'. He also marked in pencil next to the line: 'of below'.

B139: Tolkien seems to have considered whether to change 'gave' to 'knew' and 'he' to 'one'. – *Vale* is used here in the sense of 'a place of sorrow or misery' – a vale of tears.

B146: Tolkien seems to have considered whether to change 'the foe escaped' to 'escaped the foe'.

B148: Tolkien seems to have considered whether to change 'empty lay' to 'lay empty'.

B150: 'Twelve winter's [*sic*] tide that teen he bore', i.e. Hrothgar suffered the harm (*teen*) caused by Grendel for the length (*tide*) of twelve winters.

C198: Tolkien seems to have considered whether to change this line to read 'Then Hygelac's thane in his homeland learnt'.

C199: Tolkien inserted in pencil 'of' before 'Grendel's'.

C205: Tolkien seems to have considered whether to change 'lord renowned' to 'renownéd lord'.

C206: Tolkien seems to have considered whether to change 'chieftain goodly' to 'goodly chieftain'.

C207: Tolkien inserted in pencil 'the' before 'boldest'.

C208: Tolkien struck through 'and' in pencil.

C211: At the end of this line Tolkien wrote in pencil 'On went the hours', presumably as a replacement for 'Time fared forward', and 'The hours onward fared on ocean afloat', presumably as a replacement for the line.

C212: In one manuscript draft, Tolkien wrote 'prow' rather than 'stem'.

C213: Tolkien circled 'and the' in pencil.

C214: Tolkien seems to have considered whether to change this line to read 'ground the shingle; shining harness', while also considering, then rejecting, 'gleaming' to replace 'shining'.

C217: *Valiant* in 'valiant-timbered' (and in 'harness valiant', C233) means 'fine, of quality'. 'Valiant-timbered' is Tolkien's translation of *wudu bundenne*, in his prose version 'well-joined timbers', in the Clark Hall–Wrenn translation (1940) 'braced timbers'. In his edition of *Beowulf* (1973, revised by W.F. Bolton), C.L. Wrenn says of *wudu bundenne*: 'This may refer to the use of iron bands and of nails in constructing the ship, or may be merely an expression meaning "well-braced", "well-built"' (p. 106).

C218: *Haste* is used here ('the wind hasted') in the archaic sense of 'hasten'.

C221: Compare 'bended beak' (also D221, E221) with 'curving prow', F220.

C226: The 'Weder-chieftains' are the men of the ship. *Weder*, an archaic spelling of *weather* in Modern English, is also the Old English word for 'weather', also for 'storm, tempest'. Compare 'men of the Storm', G21. The Geats, Beowulf's people, are called in the poem, among other names, *Wederas*, *Weder-Gēatas*, which Wrenn has noted possibly once referred to the position of the Geats on the coast of their land and their seafaring habits. In his prose translation (2014), Tolkien preferred 'the men of the Windloving folk' (p. 19). The Clark Hall–Wrenn translation has, more simply, 'the people of the Geats'.

C229: 'That plain had made them the paths o'er the ocean', i.e. God smoothed the waves for their passage. In his later translation (F229), Tolkien makes this 'that their sea-passage | | safe had pròven', and in his prose translation (2014): 'They gave thanks to God that the passage of the waves had been made easy for them' (p. 19).

C230: A manuscript draft survives of ll. 230 and following, ending abruptly in the midst of the coast-ward's conversation with Beowulf.

C236: In the typescript, Tolkien included an alternate reading for this line: 'that thane of Hrothgar whose thewn [muscular] hands'.

C238: Tolkien considered, but rejected, 'gear' to replace 'raiment'. In his surviving manuscript draft the reading is 'battle-gear'.

C244: Tolkien considered whether to change this line to read 'in longships to raid the land of the Danes'. A *longship* is a type of Scandinavian war vessel (a 'Viking' ship) propelled by sails and oars.

C250: In the typescript, Tolkien typed '(?minion)' after 'menial'.

D229: This line originally read 'that he plain had made | | the paths of the sea'.

E211: Tolkien considered whether to change 'The hour onward fared' to 'On went the hours'.

F226: 'Gothland', i.e. Götaland in southern Sweden, the land of the Geats.

G2: Tolkien considered whether to change this line to 'a pyre upraised | | proudest on earth'.

G4: Tolkien considered whether to change this line to 'with the blazons of battle | | as he begged of them'.

G6: 'Sighing' originally read 'weeping'; Tolkien then considered whether to change 'weeping' to 'mourning'.

G10–11: Tolkien considered whether to add 'stilled' at the end of l. 10, and to change l. 11 variously to 'till the body's dwelling | | and bones were ?untroubled' or 'till the body's dwelling | | was burst asunder'. He also considered whether to change 'corse' to 'body', presumably before he thought to revise the lines more substantially.

G12: Tolkien considered whether to change 'in the heart fire-hot' to 'in the hot fire[']s heart'.

G16: Tolkien considered whether to change 'ever' to 'always'.

G28: Tolkien considered whether to change this line to read 'In that barrow then laid they | | bracelet and torque'.

G32: Tolkien circled 'gave' in pencil, as if unsure of the word, and marked 'it glimmers' to be changed to 'is guarded'.

G34: Tolkien marked 'bold' to be changed to 'brave'.

G44: 'Hearth-comrades', i.e. close companions, those who share a hearth.

89

The Owl and the Nightingale (*c.* 1925–*c.* 1953)

The Owl and the Nightingale, written in the late twelfth century, was the first poem composed in English in the *débat*, or debate, form already common in the Middle Ages in Latin and French. A narrator introduces the work:

> Ich was in one sumere dale;
> In one suþe diȝele hale
> Iherde ich holde grete tale
> An Hule and one Niȝtingale.
> Þat plait was stif & starc & strong,
> Sum wile softe & lud among.
> An aiþer aȝen oþer sval
> & let þat vvole mod ut al;
> & eiþer seide of oþeres custe
> Þat alre worste þat hi wuste.
> & hure & hure of oþere[s] song
> Hi holde plaiding suþe stronge.

Here the dispute is between two birds, each of which is depicted according to its traditional character. In the words of Eric Gerald Stanley (a student of Tolkien and C.S. Lewis at Oxford), 'the Nightingale delights; and the crab-faced Owl disapproves of our delight, of our frivolity, and of the Nightingale's lascivious promptings. We are allowed to listen to the debate of the two birds, not asked to judge between them' (*The Owl and the Nightingale*, ed. Stanley (1960), p. 3). To begin with, the birds insult each other's songs and habits, but go on to argue topics such as marriage, love, and religion.

Mentioned in the text as the person to whom the birds defer judgement is a Master Nicholas of Guildford, perhaps the author of the poem, perhaps only someone the author wished to bring to the notice of his superiors for the sake of promotion. (Not by coincidence, Tolkien chose the name 'Nicholas Guildford' for one of the characters in his abandoned story *The Notion Club Papers*.) The poem's verse form is the octosyllabic couplet, or rhyming pair of eight-syllable lines, derived from the French. Its language shows two influences: its author's dialect of Middle English appears to have been south-eastern, but its scribe seems to have come from the West Midlands, the part of England Tolkien felt to be his ancestral home.

The poem was required reading for English students when Tolkien was an Oxford undergraduate. It was probably on the curriculum at Leeds when he taught there, and he lectured on it at Oxford in 1953–6 as Merton Professor of English Language and Literature. In one of his lectures he said that the work 'probably deserves to be read by students of "English Literature" more than some of the things that are presented to them in snippets. It is not very long (1794 short lines); it has great interest (linguistic & historical), considerable literary merit, and belongs to a period from which little of like merit and good form has been preserved' (Bodleian Library).

As he had done for other works (such as *Sir Gawain and the Green Knight*, no. 70), Tolkien made a Modern English translation of *The Owl and the Nightingale*, but never finished it to his satisfaction. Elsewhere we have inferred from a mention of the work by C.S. Lewis, in a letter written on 8 April 1932, that it was complete by that date, but now we wonder if Tolkien managed to translate only about half of the poem. The longest of two drafts of the translation in his papers is numbered only to line 900. He worked on it only now and then, using several typewriters or writing variously in ink or pencil; his handwriting suggests that some manuscript pages could be separated by years. In the earlier draft, the ink on the typewritten pages is purple, dating them to Tolkien's years at Leeds, and by this token we have dated the work to *c.* 1925, at the end of Tolkien's Leeds employment and around the same time that he was working on his *Beowulf* translation in alliterative verse, though he could have begun the *Owl and the Nightingale* effort earlier in the 1920s. There are some purple typewritten pages in the later draft too, but also one made instead on the Hammond machine, no earlier than around 1927. And then there are revisions to the second draft, especially on its heavily marked first page, made by Tolkien in a clearly later hand and partly with black and red biros (ballpoint pens), which were unavailable in Britain until the late forties.

On 28 April 1967 Tolkien informed John Leyerle, a former student, now a professor in Toronto, that he had given up his translation of *The Owl and the Nightingale* 'at present'. 'It comes off well enough in certain passages,' he wrote, 'but in general octo-syllabic couplets are defeating for a translator; there is no room to move' (Bodleian Library). Leyerle had asked to include the work in an anthology, a request which presupposes that he knew of the translation, probably through attending Tolkien's Oxford lectures. It would not be unreasonable to think that when Tolkien delivered those talks in the 1950s he revisited his work begun in the 1920s, and found readings he wanted to change.

For the present book, we have chosen the first 158 lines of the translation to represent the whole. These are necessarily from the earlier draft, not only because it presents fewer questions of transcription, but also because the later draft is incomplete as preserved, wanting lines 49–258. Here we give Tolkien's text as he revised it in the first draft, with previous or alternate readings described in notes.

I once was in a certain vale,
in a secret corner of the dale,
and there I heard their long converse
an owl and nightingale rehearse.
Their strife was strong and stern and proud,
from time to time both soft and loud;
and each with other burns with wrath,
and lets the evil rancour forth;
and each against the other's ways
the foulest charge she knows of lays;
but most and most of the other's song
they make their plaint exceeding strong.

The nightingale began the address
within a spinney's deep recess,
and sat upon a goodly bough —
about it were there flowers enow —
within a dense and thickset hedge
entwined with grasses green and sedge.
The gladder was she for that spray,
and sang in many a diverse way:
the merry music seemed, to me,
rather of harp and flute to be,
and uttered rather seemed the note
of harp and flute than any throat.
There stood an old stump there–beside,
where the owl her hours of office cried;
it was with ivy all o'ergrown —
the owl had there her dwelling lone.
The nightingale her did espy,
did look her up and down, and eye;

and evil thought she of the owl,
for loathly is she held and foul.
'Ill creature', said she, 'hence do flee!
worse is my lot that I thee see.
Indeed thine evil looks do make
me oft my singing to forsake;
my tongue it fails, and flies my heart,
when nigh to me too close thou art.
Me liever were to spit than sing
because of thy foul hallooing.'
That owl till it was eve did wait,
no longer might she leave debate,
for so indignant swelled her heart,
almost away her breath did start.
Thus spake she after silence long:
'What thinkest thou then of my song?
Dost fancy that I cannot sing,
though nought I know of chirruping?
Full oft thou bringest me to shame
with taunting words and evil name;
if in my claws I held thee tight
(would fortune send that so I might),
and thou wert ventured from thy spray,
then shouldst thou sing another lay.'

The nightingale gave answer there:
'If of the open I beware,
and take of bitter weather heed,
to fear thy threat I nothing need;
if in my hedge I safely rest,
then care I never what thou saist.
I wot thou show'st them no mercy
that cannot them defend from thee,
and dost most cruel and pitiless,
where'er thou canst, small birds oppress.
So to all bird-kind an offence
thou art, who all do hunt thee hence,
shrieking and screaming out on thee,
and do pursue thee narrowly;
so too the titmouse would delight
herself to rend thee if she might.
For thou are loathsome to behold —

thy loathsomeness is manifold:
the body is short, thy neck is small,
thy head the greatest part of all;
thine eyes are black as coal and broad
as though they painted were with woad;
thou starest as if to eat wouldst like
all those that thou with claws canst strike:
thy beak is hard and sharp and crookéd
just like a rending prong all hookéd;
therewith thou clackest oft and long,
and that is what thou callest song.
Against my flesh thou makest threat
crushed in thy claws wouldst have me set.
More natural food for thee were frogs
that sit beneath the mill-wheel's cogs;
snails and mice and unclean beasts
are right and natural for thy feasts.
Thou sittest by day and fliest by night,
and show'st thyself an evil wight;
and thou art loathsome and unclean —
this of that nest of thine I mean;
and also of thy filthy brood,
in whom thou rearest offspring lewd.
Well knowst thou what they do therein:
they foul the nest up to their chin,
and there they sit as they were blind.
For this a proverb men do find
'May curses have that bird unblest
that ever fouleth its own nest'.
Did on a time a falcon breed;
but he his nest not well did heed,
and there thou stolest one fine day
and thy foul egg therein didst lay.
When came the eggs to hatch at last,
and out the chicks alive had passed,
then did he bring his nestlings meat,
and watched his nest and saw them eat;
and saw he too that at one side
his nest was all defiled outside.
Wroth was the falcon with his young,
and still and stern his chiding rung:
'Now tell me who 'twas this did do —

a thing unnatural quite in you
someone has vilely servéd you;
tell me if ought of this ye knew'.
Then said first one and then another:
'Indeed it was our very brother,
who, yonder, has that great big head
(would it were off and he were dead!)
Throw him out without more ado,
and break his neck for him in two!'
The falcon then believes his chicks,
by the middle up the foul bird picks,
and from the wild-wood bough it throws
to be devoured by pies and crows.
In this a parable men see,
though incomplete the story be:
just so with one of little worth
it is, who, come of vicious birth,
may mix with men of noble kin,
but ever shows his origin;
from addle-egg he came 'tis plain,
though he in noble nest have lain;
though the apple roll far from the tree,
where once it grew in company,
and though from there it now be gone,
it shows what tree it grew upon.'
These words thus spake the nightingale,
and, after this her lengthy tale,
she sang as loudly and as sharp
as though one plucked a thrilling harp.

The owl did harken to that sound,
and cast her eyes upon the ground,
and sitting blown with wrath she swelled
as though a bolted frog she held;
for well aware she knew clearly
the other sang in mockery.
But nonetheless she made reply:
'Why wilt not to the open fly,
and plainly show which of us two
has fairer form and brighter hue?'
'No, no! for thou hast claws most keen,

to be clawed by thee I do not mean;
talons exceeding strong thou hast
wherewith like tongs thou nippest fast.
Thou thoughtest, as do all thy kind,
with speeches fair to make me blind. . . .

B.S. Benedikz recalled with pleasure Tolkien's Oxford lectures on *The Owl and the Nightingale*. These, he said,

> took us in a wide sweep through the whole gamut of flyting (exchanges of abusive and insulting language) and medieval vulgarity, as well as through some very pertinent textual questions caused by the two variant forms available and concerning why the [two extant manuscripts] differed. We were, I am sure, vastly informed by them – even when the Professor spent a highly contentious hour inducing us to believe that *The Owl and the Nightingale* was one of the great humorous poems of European literature. It says much for his persuasiveness that as we left the lecture room quite a few of us were convinced by the argument – until the cold winter winds in the High Street blew common sense back into our minds. ['Some Family Connections with J.R.R. Tolkien', *Amon Hen* 209 (January 2008), p. 12]

5: 'Strong and stern' originally read 'stern and strong'.

12: 'Make' originally read 'made'. Tolkien reversed the change in his later draft.

21: 'To me' originally read 'pardee', from French *pardieu* 'by God', i.e. 'certainly, indeed'.

26: 'Hours of office' refers to psalms and prayers to be said at particular hours of the day, according to church canon.

28: 'Had there' originally read 'it made'.

32: 'Is she' originally read 'she is'.

40: 'Hallooing', cf. *hallow* 'shout', probably refers to the owl's hooting cries.

60: Tolkien considered whether to change 'saist' to 'sayst' (i.e. say).

77 etc.: For the most part, the nightingale speaks truth. An owl is a predator, mostly nocturnal, and will eat small animals, frogs, snails, etc., as well as other birds if chance allows, rending with beak and talons. In the process, it makes a mess of its nest. But the charge of laying its egg for a falcon to raise is a slander.

80: 'Rending [i.e. tearing] prong' originally read 'fork with prong'.

86: For centuries owls have been welcome in mill buildings because they control vermin. A 'mill-wheel's cogs' are projections on a piece of water-driven machinery, which transfers power to grindstones.

94: Here *lewd* means 'base, vile, ill-bred'. Tolkien is translating Middle English *ful* 'foul' while needing to rhyme with 'brood' (Middle English *brode*).

109: Tolkien considered other readings of this line, not all of which can be deciphered, but including 'he too spied'.

115–116: These lines originally were reversed in order.

126: *Pie* is an archaic name for the magpie (e.g. the Eurasian magpie, *Pica pica*), an intelligent bird with black and white plumage.

137: Tolkien considered whether to change 'there' to 'thence'.

138: This line originally began 'it shows from what tree'.

147–148: Tolkien first typed these lines with a different reading, 'for well she knew and was aware | the other sang in mock of her', before having second thoughts and typing the words given above, then marking the original lines for deletion. Next to these, he wrote as a possible alteration, 'well knew & well aware was she'.

152: 'Has' originally read 'hath'.

154: Tolkien considered whether to change this line to 'not to be clawed by thee I mean'.

90

Pearl (?1925–?42)

As we explained as necessary background to *The Nameless Land* (no. 74), *Pearl* is an alliterative poem from the fourteenth century, attributed to the author of *Sir Gawain and the Green Knight* (no. 70) – both works are contained in the same manuscript in the British Library – and like *Sir Gawain*, it is written in the West Midlands dialect of Middle English, which Tolkien found of special interest. Concerned, as we have said earlier, with the speaker's daughter, his 'pearl', who died as a child and who appears to him in a dream-vision, now in a state of divine grace in a city of light, the work has been debated extensively as allegory and elegy.

Tolkien first read *Pearl* as an undergraduate, as a required text in the Oxford English School, and later taught it at Leeds and Oxford. His professional interest led him in 1925 to begin an edition in Middle English with his colleague E.V. Gordon, with whom he had edited *Sir Gawain*; but he made little or no contribution for many years, and when the *Pearl* edition was published at last in 1953, it was based mostly on Gordon's work alone, and completed by Gordon's widow, Ida, herself a competent scholar. In spare moments during ?1925–6 Tolkien was, however, able to translate the poem into Modern English.

In April 1926 he sent a copy of this text to Kenneth Sisam at Oxford University Press, and by summer 1936 offered it to the publisher J.M. Dent, without success. According to Christopher Tolkien, by then it was much revised from its early form. In August 1936 the BBC thought well enough of it to have it read (not by Tolkien himself) on radio in the London region. By August 1942 Tolkien lent the translation to the Oxford publisher Basil Blackwell, who had it in hand long enough for the work to be set in type, but Tolkien never completed an introduction, and Blackwell eventually relinquished his rights. Ultimately George Allen & Unwin agreed to publish the translation, together with Tolkien's Modern English *Sir Gawain*.

In the event, he only tentatively began its introduction, and failed to write the desired commentary. His *Pearl* did not appear in print until after his death, edited by his son Christopher from competing versions. It is from this edition (*Sir Gawain and the Green Knight, Pearl and Sir Orfeo*, 1975, pp. 92–3) that we have drawn the following extract, the third of twenty sections, or five of 101 stanzas altogether. Here the speaker sees his child, grown to maturity, in a fair land across a stream.

The wondrous wealth of down and dales,
Of wood and water and lordly plain,
My mirth makes mount: my mourning fails,
My care is quelled and cured my pain.
Then down a stream that strongly sails
I blissful turn with teeming brain;
The further I follow those flowing vales
The more strength of joy my heart doth strain.
As fortune fares where she doth deign,
Whether gladness she gives or grieving sore,
So he who may her graces gain,
His hap is to have ever more and more.

There more was of such marvels thrice
Than I could tell, though I long delayed;
For earthly heart could not suffice
For a tithe of the joyful joys displayed.
Therefore I thought that Paradise
Across those banks was yonder laid;
I weened that the water by device
As bounds between pleasances was made;
Beyond that stream by steep or slade
That city's walls I weened must soar;
But the water was deep, I dared not wade,
And ever I longed to, more and more.

More and more, and yet still more,
I fain beyond the stream had scanned,
For fair as was this hither shore,
Far lovelier was the further land.
To find a ford I did then explore,
And round about did stare and stand;
But perils pressed in sooth more sore
The further I strode along the strand.
I should not, I thought, by fear be banned
From delights so lovely that lay in store;
But a happening new then came to hand
That moved my mind ever more and more.

A marvel more did my mind amaze:
I saw beyond that border bright
From a crystal cliff the lucent rays
And beams in splendour lift their light.
A child abode there at its base:
She wore a gown of glistening white,
A gentle maid of courtly grace;
Erewhile I had known her well by sight.
As shredded gold that glistered bright
She shone in beauty upon the shore;
Long did my glance on her alight,
And the longer I looked I knew her more.

The more I that face so fair surveyed,
When upon her gracious form I gazed,
Such gladdening glory upon me played
As my wont was seldom to see upraised.
Desire to call her then me swayed,
But dumb surprise my mind amazed;
In place so strange I saw that maid,
The blow might well my wits have crazed.
Her forehead fair then up she raised
That hue of polished ivory wore.
It smote my heart distraught and dazed,
And ever the longer, the more and more.

For comparison, the first of these stanzas reads in the original:

The dubbement dere of doun and dalez,
Of wod and water and wlonk playnez,
Bylde in me blys, abated my balez,
Fordidden my stresse, dystryed my paynez.
Doun after a strem þat dryzly halez
I bowed in blys, bred-ful my braynez;
Þe fyrre I folzed those floty valez,
Þe more strenghþe of joye myn herte straynez.
As fortune fares þer as ho fraynez,
Wheþer solace ho sende oþer ellez sore,
Þe wyz to wham her wylle ho waynez
Hyttez to haue ay more and more.

All of the stanzas in *Pearl* are of twelve lines, and have a complex verse form, as Tolkien explained to his aunt Jane Neave, quoted in our discussion for *The Nameless Land*. *Pearl* is in fact one of the most metrically complex poems in English. Writing to his grandson in January 1965, Tolkien called it 'about as difficult a task as any translator could be set. It is impossible to make a version in the same metre close enough to serve as a "crib". But I think anyone who reads my version, however learned a Middle English scholar, will get a more direct impression of the poem's impact (on one who knew the language)' (letter to Michael George Tolkien, *Letters*, p. 493). To this end, as in his Modern English *Sir Gawain* and *Beowulf* (no. 88), Tolkien again incorporated archaic vocabulary and diction.

Tolkien scholars have seen parallels with *Pearl* in Tolkien's fiction, especially the dreamlike land of Lothlórien in *The Lord of the Rings*:

> It seemed to him [Frodo, on the hill Cerin Amroth] that he had stepped through a high window that looked on a vanished world. A light was upon it for which his language had no name. All that he saw was shapely, but the shapes seemed at once clear cut, as if they had been first conceived and drawn at the uncovering of his eyes, and ancient as if they had endured for ever. He saw no colour but those he knew, gold and white and blue and green, but they were fresh and poignant, as if he had at that moment first perceived them and made for them names new and wonderful. [*The Lord of the Rings* (2004), p. 350]

In this regard, the essay 'Echoes of *Pearl* in Arda's Landscape' (2009) by Stephan Ekman is most instructive.

91

Gawain's Leave-Taking (?1925)

The poem misleadingly called, by Tolkien, *Gawain's Leave-Taking* is his translation of the first three stanzas, and the last, of the medieval poem generally known (in translation) as 'Against My Will I Take My Leave', after a recurring line.

Now Lords and Ladies blithe and bold,
To bless you here now am I bound:
I thank you all a thousand-fold,
And pray God save you whole and sound;
Wherever you go on grass or ground,
May He you guide that nought you grieve,
For friendship that I here have found
Against my will I take my leave.

For friendship and for favours good,
For meat and drink you heaped on me,
The Lord that raised was on the Rood
Now keep you comely company.
On sea or land where'er you be,
May He you guide that nought you grieve.
Such fair delight you laid on me
Against my will I take my leave.

Against my will although I wend,
I may not always tarry here;
For everything must have an end,
And even friends must part, I fear;
Be we beloved however dear
Out of this world death will us reave,
And when we brought are to our bier
Against our will we take our leave.

Now good day to you, goodmen all,
And good day to you, young and old,
And good day to you, great and small,
And grammercy a thousand-fold!

If ought there were that dear ye hold,
    Full fain I would the deed achieve —
Now Christ you keep from sorrows cold
    For now at last I take my leave.

As contained in MS. Vernon in the Bodleian Library, Oxford, the original Middle English text of the poem begins:

Nou Bernes, Buirdus, bolde and blyþe,
    To blessen ow her nou am I bounde;
I þonke ȝou alle a þousend siþe,
    And prei god saue ȝou hol and sounde;
Wher-euer ȝe go, on gras or grounde,
    He ow gouerne with-outen greue.
For frendschipe þat I here haue founde;
    A-ȝeyn mi wille I take mi leue.

In its complete form, the work enlarges upon the theme of the inevitability of death. When we die, we go to endless bliss or to hellfire, and when we depart this life we must leave our friends behind and take only our good works.

Christopher Tolkien included *Gawain's Leave-Taking* at the end of *Sir Gawain and the Green Knight, Pearl and Sir Orfeo* (1975), p. 149, as a coda to the chief poems. In his introduction, he notes that in choosing its title his father must have had in his thoughts the passage in *Sir Gawain and the Green Knight* (no. 70) in which Gawain leaves Bertilak's castle for the Green Chapel (*Sir Gawain and the Green Knight, Pearl and Sir Orfeo*, p. 76):

'Now solemnly myself I [Gawain] swear on my troth
there is a company in this castle that is careful of honour!
Their lord that them leads, may his lot be joyful!
Their beloved lady in life may delight befall her!
If they out of charity thus cherish a guest,
upholding their house in honour, may He them reward
that upholds heaven on high, and all of you too!
And if life a little longer I might lead upon earth,
I would give you some guerdon [reward] gladly, were I able.'

Gawain's Leave-Taking reads very differently with the knight and his impending fate in mind, rather than the extended farewell of a guest after a happy stay with friends or family.

Our transcription of the poem is made from a manuscript reproduced in the later, de luxe edition of *Sir Gawain and the Green Knight, Pearl and Sir Orfeo* (2020), in which the indentation of the lines differs from the (less regular) arrangement of its several printings. On the second page of the manuscript is also part of an early draft of the opening canto of the *Lay of Leithian* (no. 92), and since Tolkien is known to have begun that work no later than 23 August 1925, *Gawain's Leave-Taking* must also have been composed by that date. (This point was first observed by Ugo Truffelli, in online discussion. The Tolkien–Gordon edition of *Sir Gawain and the Green Knight* was published on 23 April 1925.) It is possible that earlier manuscripts of *Gawain's Leave-Taking* once existed, as the one reproduced in the de luxe volume appears to be a fair copy, without significant revision except that 'God' and (twice) 'He' are capitalized, overwriting 'god' and 'he'.

28: 'Grammercy', *sic* for *gramercy* 'thank you', from French *grand merci.*

92

Lay of Leithian (1925–*c.* 1949 or 50)

This work, expressed in octosyllabic couplets, is a development of Tolkien's tale of Beren and Lúthien, encountered in the present book already in *Light as Leaf on Lind* and its successors (poem no. 64). The relationship of the characters in the *Lay* is much elaborated, and more deeply felt, than in either the earlier poems or the prose account in *The Book of Lost Tales*. The manuscript of its first version has no title, but at the head of its typescript is *The Gest of Beren Son of Barahir and Lúthien the Fay Called Tinúviel the Nightingale, or the Lay of Leithian, Release from Bondage*. Tolkien sometimes referred to it as *Tinúviel*; here we will shorten the title to *Lay of Leithian*.

Tolkien began to write the first incarnation of the *Lay* during the summer of 1925 – it may not be a coincidence that *Light as Leaf on Lindentree* was published in *The Gryphon* that June – and left it unfinished in September 1931, with the wolf Carcharoth devouring Beren's hand and the Silmaril it holds. At several points in the work's progress, he recorded dates of composition, for Tolkien an uncommon practice. He wrote in stages, beginning with rough drafts, then adding text to a fair copy, and finally making a typescript with further changes. At intervals, he made synopses or outlines for parts of the poem yet to be written, some of which were overtaken as he had further thoughts: these are included, along with the poem proper, by Christopher Tolkien in *The Lays of Beleriand*.

During the six years of initial writing, Tolkien also had many new ideas for his 'Silmarillion' mythology, which influenced the *Lay*. In late November or early December 1929, he lent his typescript of the poem, as it then stood, to C.S. Lewis, and at the end of the year or in early 1930 Lewis produced detailed criticism. Tolkien seems to have altered some of the first version of the *Lay* in response to his friend's comments.

Abandoning the poem after fourteen cantos and 4223 lines, except for some draft workings which looked ahead, Tolkien turned to other writings, and as always was busy with academic work. Then around 1949 or 1950 he revisited, or recommenced, the *Lay of Leithian*, intending at first, as Christopher Tolkien has said, probably not much more 'than a revision, an improvement of individual lines and short passages, but all on the original plan and structure. This, at least, is what he did with Canto I', carrying out his work on his old typescript.

> But with Canto II he was quickly carried into a far more radical reconstruction, and was virtually writing a new poem on the same subject and in the same metre as the old . . . a new impulse had entered, seeking a new rather than a merely altered expression. The old typescript was still used as at least a physical basis for the new writing, but for a long stretch the typed verses were simply struck through and the new written on inserted pages and slips. [*The Lays of Beleriand*, p. 330]

Out of a now chaotic text Tolkien made a fine manuscript, with additional changes. Later, an amanuensis typescript was produced, apparently under Tolkien's supervision. Part of the first page of Canto I is reproduced in McIlwaine, *Tolkien: Maker of Middle-earth*, p. 222, and the first page of Canto II at the start of *The Lays of Beleriand*.

Here, as A, to represent the first version of the *Lay of Leithian* we have chosen from Canto IV a long extract which describes the splendours of Menegroth, the Thousand Caves, the hidden halls of Doriath, and the dramatic confrontation between its Elven ruler, Thingol, and the Man Beren. Thingol has promised his daughter Lúthien that he will not harm her beloved if she brings Beren to him, but manages to both keep and break his promise, giving Beren what seems a suicidal task. Line numbers are given here as in the original text, as transcribed from *The Lays of Beleriand*, pp. 188–94.

[A] . . . for Lúthien that night
led Beren by the golden light
of mounting moon unto the shore
and bridge before her father's door;
and the white light silent looked within
the waiting portals yawning dim.

Downward with gentle hand she led
through corridors of carven dread
whose turns were lit by lanterns hung
or flames from torches that were flung
on dragons hewn in the cold stone
with jewelled eyes and teeth of bone.
Then sudden, deep beneath the earth
the silences with silver mirth

were shaken and the rocks were ringing,
the birds of Melian were singing;
and wide the ways of shadow spread
as into archéd halls she led
Beren in wonder. There a light
like day immortal and like night
of stars unclouded, shone and gleamed.
A vault of topless trees it seemed,
whose trunks of carven stone there stood
like towers of an enchanted wood
in magic fast for ever bound,
bearing a roof whose branches wound
in endless tracery of green
lit by some leaf-emprisoned sheen
of moon and sun, and wrought of gems,
and each leaf hung on golden stems.
    Lo! there amid immortal flowers
the nightingales in shining bowers
sang o'er the head of Melian,
while water for ever dripped and ran
from fountains in the rocky floor.
There Thingol sat. His crown he wore
of green and silver, and round his chair
a host in gleaming armour fair.
Then Beren looked upon the king
and stood amazed; and swift a ring
of elvish weapons hemmed him round.
Then Beren looked upon the ground,
for Melian's gaze had sought his face
and dazed there drooped he in that place,
and when the king spake deep and slow:
'Who art thou stumblest hither? Know
that none unbidden seek this throne
and ever leave these halls of stone!'
no word he answered, filled with dread.
But Lúthien answered in his stead:
'Behold, my father, one who came
pursued by hatred like a flame!
Lo! Beren son of Barahir!
What need hath he thy wrath to fear,
foe of our foes, without a friend,
whose knees to Morgoth do not bend?'

'Let Beren answer!' Thingol said.
'What wouldst thou here? What hither led
thy wandering feet, O mortal wild?
How hast thou Lúthien beguiled
or darest thus to walk this wood
unasked, in secret? Reason good
'twere best declare now if thou may,
or never again see light of day!'
Then Beren looked in Lúthien's eyes
and saw a light of starry skies,
and thence was slowly drawn his gaze
to Melian's face. As from a maze
of wonder dumb he woke; his heart
the bonds of awe there burst apart
and filled with the fearless pride of old;
in his glance now gleamed an anger cold.
'My feet hath fate, O king,' he said,
'here over the mountains bleeding led,
and what I sought not I have found,
and love it is hath here me bound.
Thy dearest treasure I desire;
nor rocks nor steel nor Morgoth's fire
nor all the power of Elfinesse
shall keep that gem I would possess.
For fairer than are born to Men
a daughter hast thou, Lúthien.'

Silence then fell upon the hall;
like graven stone then stood they all,
save one who cast her eyes aground,
and one who laughed with bitter sound.
Dairon the piper leant there pale
against a pillar. His fingers frail
there touched a flute that whispered not;
his eyes were dark; his heart was hot.
'Death is the guerdon thou hast earned,
O baseborn mortal, who has learned
in Morgoth's realm to spy and lurk
like Orcs that do his evil work!'
'Death!' echoed Dairon, fierce and low,
but Lúthien trembling gasped in woe.
'And death,' said Thingol, 'thou shouldst taste,

had I not sworn an oath in haste
that blade nor chain thy flesh should mar.
Yet captive bound by never a bar,
unchained, unfettered, shalt thou be
in lightless labyrinth endlessly
that coils about my halls profound
by magic bewildered and enwound;
there wandering in hopelessness
thou shalt learn the power of Elfinesse!'
'That may not be!' Lo! Beren spake,
and through the king's words coldly brake.
'What are thy mazes but a chain
wherein the captive blind is slain?
Twist not thy oaths, O elvish king,
like faithless Morgoth! By this ring —
the token of a lasting bond
that Felagund of Nargothrond
once swore in love to Barahir,
who sheltered him with shield and spear
and saved him from pursuing foe
on Northern battlefields long ago —
death thou canst give unearned to me,
but names I will not take from thee
of baseborn, spy, or Morgoth's thrall!
Are these the ways of Thingol's hall?'
Proud are the words, and all there turned
to see the jewels green that burned
in Beren's ring. These Gnomes had set
as eyes of serpents twined that met
beneath a golden crown of flowers,
that one upholds and one devours:
the badge that Finrod made of yore
and Felagund his son now bore.
    His anger was chilled, but little less,
and dark thoughts Thingol did possess,
though Melian the pale leant to his side
and whispered: 'O king, forgo thy pride!
Such is my counsel. Not by thee
shall Beren be slain, for far and free
from these deep halls his fate doth lead,
yet wound with thine. O king, take heed!'
But Thingol looked on Lúthien.

'Fairest of Elves! Unhappy Men,
children of little lords and kings
mortal and frail, these fading things,
shall they then look with love on thee?'
his heart within him thought. 'I see
thy ring,' he said, 'O mighty man!
But to win the child of Melian
a father's deeds shall not avail,
nor thy proud words at which I quail.
A treasure dear I too desire,
but rocks and steel and Morgoth's fire
from all the powers of Elfinesse
do keep the jewel I would possess.
Yet bonds like these I hear thee say
affright thee not. Now go thy way!
Bring me one shining Silmaril
from Morgoth's crown, then if she will,
may Lúthien set her hand in thine;
then shalt thou have this jewel of mine.'

Then Thingol's warriors loud and long
they laughed; for wide renown in song
had Fëanor's gems o'er land and sea,
the peerless Silmarils; and three
alone he made and kindled slow
in the land of the Valar long ago,
and there in Tûn of their own light
they shone like marvellous stars at night,
in the great Gnomish hoards of Tûn,
while Glingal flowered and Belthil's bloom
yet lit the land beyond the shore
where the Shadowy Seas' last surges roar,
ere Morgoth stole them and the Gnomes
seeking their glory left their homes,
ere sorrows fell on Elves and Men,
ere Beren was or Lúthien,
ere Fëanor's sons in madness swore
their dreadful oath. But now no more
their beauty was seen, save shining clear
in Morgoth's dungeons vast and drear.
His iron crown they must adorn,
and gleam above Orcs and slaves forlorn,

treasured in Hell above all wealth,
more than his eyes; and might nor stealth
could touch them, or even gaze too long
upon their magic. Throng on throng
of Orcs with reddened scimitars
encircled him and mighty bars
and everlasting gates and walls,
who wore them now amidst his thralls.
    Then Beren laughed more loud than they
in bitterness, and thus did say:
'For little price do elven-kings
their daughters sell — for gems and rings
and things of gold! If such thy will,
thy bidding I will now fulfill.
On Beren son of Barahir
thou hast not looked the last, I fear.
Farewell, Tinúviel, starlit maiden!
Ere the pale winter pass snowladen,
I will return, not thee to buy
with any jewel in Elfinesse,
but to find my love in loveliness,
a flower that grows beneath the sky.'
Bowing before Melian and the king
he turned, and thrust aside the ring
of guards about him, and was gone,
and his footsteps faded one by one
in the dark corridors. 'A guileful oath
thou sworest, father! Thou hast both
to blade and chain his flesh now doomed
in Morgoth's dungeons deep entombed,'
said Lúthien, and welling tears
sprang in her eyes, and hideous fears
clutched at her heart. All looked away,
and later remembered the sad day
whereafter Lúthien no more sang.
Then clear in the silence the cold words rang
of Melian: 'Counsel cunning-wise,
O king!' she said. 'Yet if mine eyes
lose not their power, 'twere well for thee
that Beren failed his errantry.
Well for thee, but for thy child
a dark doom and a wandering wild.'

'I sell not to Men those whom I love'
said Thingol, 'whom all things above
I cherish; and if hope there were
that Beren should ever living fare
to the Thousand Caves once more, I swear
he should not ever have seen the air
or light of heaven's stars again.'
But Melian smiled, and there was pain
as of far knowledge in her eyes;
for such is the sorrow of the wise.

From the second version of the *Lay of Leithian* we have extracted, as B, the fourth part of the text published in *The Lays of Beleriand* (pp. 346–8), an account of the first meeting of Melian and Thingol. Here Tolkien revised part of Canto III of the first version of the *Lay*, in which Thingol touches Melian's hair 'and his mind | was drowned in the forgetful deep, | and dark the years rolled o'er his sleep', but is still attracted to the garden by Melian's voice and the singing of a nightingale. The later text, below, contains a closer parallel to the first encounter of Lúthien and Beren in Doriath. In each case, the female is of higher status than the male: Melian, a Maia, one of the lesser gods, weds a noble Elf, while her daughter, equally of the immortal Maiar and Elf-kind, weds a mortal Man. Thingol, one feels, in the circumstances should have had more sympathy for his daughter and Beren, but he is a protective father, and at any rate desires a Silmaril.

[B] There long ago in Elder-days
ere voice was heard or trod were ways
the haunt of silent shadows stood
in starlit dusk Nan Elmoth wood.
In Elder-days that long are gone
a light amid the shadows shone,
a voice was in the silence heard:
the sudden singing of a bird.
There Melian came, the Lady grey,
and dark and long her tresses lay
beneath her silver girdle-seat
and down unto her silver feet.
The nightingales with her she brought,
to whom their song herself she taught,
who sweet upon her gleaming hands
had sung in the immortal lands.

Thence wayward wandering on a time
from Lórien she dared to climb
the everlasting mountain-wall
of Valinor, at whose feet fall
the surges of the Shadowy Sea.
Out away she went then free,
to gardens of the Gods no more
returning, but on mortal shore,
a glimmer ere the dawn she strayed,
singing her spells from glade to glade.
A bird in dim Nan Elmoth wood
trilled, and to listen Thingol stood
amazed; then faraway he heard
a voice more fair than fairest bird,
a voice as crystal clear of note
as thread of silver glass remote.

Of folk and kin no more he thought;
of errand that the Eldar brought
from Cuiviénen far away,
of lands that beyond the Seas that lay
no more he recked, forgetting all
drawn only by that distant call
till deep in dim Nan Elmoth wood
lost and beyond recall he stood.
And there he saw her, fair and fay:
Ar-Melian, the Lady grey,
as silent as the windless trees,
standing with mist about her knees,
and in her face remote the light
of Lórien glimmered in the night.
No word she spoke; but pace by pace,
a halting shadow, towards her face
forth walked the silver-mantled king,
tall Elu Thingol. In the ring
of waiting trees he took her hand.
One moment face to face they stand
alone, beneath the wheeling sky,
while starlit years on earth go by
and in Nan Elmoth wood the trees
grow dark and tall. The murmuring seas

rising and falling on the shore
and Ulmo's horn he heeds no more.

But long his people sought in vain
their lord, till Ulmo called again,
and then in grief they marched away,
leaving the woods. To havens grey
upon the western shore, the last
long shore of mortal lands, they passed,
and thence were borne beyond the Sea
in Aman, the Blessed Realm, to be
in evergreen Ezellohar
in Valinor, in Eldamar.

Of the verse-form of the *Lay*, Richard C. West wrote that

> Tolkien chose to use octosyllabic couplets . . . associated with medieval romance and thus more appropriate than the alliterative metre to a tale of love overcoming great obstacles. The form has an inherent danger of monotony, which he avoids to a large degree (if not entirely) by such means as ending a sentence within a line (and sometimes then beginning a new paragraph) so that the rhymes are not stressed and rhyming English with Elvish words so that the rhymes are not overly familiar. ['*The Lays of Beleriand*' (2006), p. 349]

Other critics of the poem have pointed to the tetrameter form as a weakness, disliking a rhythm they consider sing-song and constructions (especially involving word-inversion) they find forced.

In October 1937 Tolkien submitted the *Lay* to George Allen & Unwin for consideration, the publisher having asked for more of his writing after *The Hobbit* proved successful. The publisher's reader, Edward Crankshaw, taking the *Lay* to be a version of a genuine Celtic *geste*, thought its verse 'of a very thin, if not always downright bad, quality' (Tolkien–George Allen & Unwin archive, HarperCollins). Tolkien replied that he did 'not mind about the verse-form, which in spite of certain virtuous passages has grave defects, for it is only for me the rough material' (letter to Stanley Unwin, 16 December 1937, *Letters*, p. 35). This seems to us humility born of diplomacy. Octosyllabic couplets are the form typically used in lays – lyrical narrative poems dealing with romance and adventure – and were adopted by earlier poets of no little note, such as Chaucer in *The Book of the*

Duchess and Milton in *Il Penseroso*. How one 'hears' such a metre is personal, of course, and in our time we have been conditioned to think of it as more appropriate for children's verse than for poems with serious aims.

An unidentified critic, but someone who knew and admired Tolkien's poetry, sent him 'a detailed, and remarkably unconstrained, criticism' of the *Lay of Leithian* sometime around 1950. Christopher Tolkien comments in his preface to *The Lays of Beleriand*:

> In choosing 'the staple octosyllabic couplet of romance,' [the critic] wrote, my father had chosen one of the most difficult of forms 'if one wishes to avoid monotony and sing-song in a very long poem. I am often astonished by your success, but it is by no means consistently maintained.' [Tolkien's] strictures on the diction of the Lay included archaisms so archaic that they needed annotation, distorted order, use of emphatic *doth* or *did* where there is no emphasis, and language sometimes flat and conventional (in contrast to passages of 'gorgeous description'). There is no record of what my father thought of this criticism . . . but it must be associated in some way with the fact that in 1949 or 1950 he returned to the *Lay of Leithian* and began a revision that soon became virtually a new poem; and relatively little though he wrote of it, its advance on the old version in all those respects in which that had been censured is so great as to give it a sad prominence in the long list of his works that might have been. [pp. 1–2]

A still later critic, A.N. Wilson, has said that although at times the *Lay* 'is technically imperfect, it is full of passages of quite stunning beauty; and the overall conception must make it, though unfinished, one of the most remarkable poems written in English in the twentieth century' (*C.S. Lewis: A Biography* (1990), p. 117).

In his expansive thesis *The 'Romantic Faëry': Keats, Tolkien, and the Perilous Realm* (2019), William Sherwood finds (p. 28) a 'strong Keatsian aesthetic' in the *Lay of Leithian* and suggests that Tolkien critically reworked Keats's poems for his own work, in particular 'Hyperion', 'La Belle Dame sans Merci', and 'The Eve of St Agnes'.

The composer Donald Swann made a musical setting of twelve lines from the *Lay* as they appeared in *The Silmarillion* (p. 178), where they are part of Beren's 'Song of Parting, in praise of Lúthien and the lights of heaven; for he believed that he must now say farewell to both love and light' as he continued his quest for a Silmaril.

Farewell sweet earth and northern sky,
for ever blest, since here did lie
and here with lissom limbs did run
beneath the Moon, beneath the Sun,
Lúthien Tinúviel
more fair than mortal tongue can tell.
Though all to ruin fell the world
and were dissolved and backward hurled
unmade into the old abyss,
yet were its making good, for this —
the dusk, the dawn, the earth, the sea —
that Lúthien for a time should be.

These lines were drawn from Canto XI of the *Lay of Leithian* (3322–3333), in which – as given in *The Lays of Beleriand* – there are a few differences, notably in the penultimate line, which begins 'the dawn, the dusk'. Swann's setting appears in the 2002 third edition of *The Road Goes Ever On: A Song Cycle*, where it was issued with a recording of the work by Swann on piano with the singer Clive McCrombie.

A1060: For Dairon, see poem no. 64.

A1087–1088: In the Dagor Bragollach, one of the great battles of the Wars of Beleriand, Barahir and his men rescued the Elven-king Finrod Felagund, who was cut off from his people. Returning to his fortress of Nargothrond, Finrod 'swore an oath of abiding friendship and aid in every need to Barahir and all his kin, and in token of his vow he gave to Barahir his ring' (*The Silmarillion*, p. 152).

A1132–1161: These lines summarize the story of the Silmarils: how in the distant past the Gnome (Noldo) Fëanor fashioned the three great Elvish jewels in Tûn (a later name of Kôr, see poem no. 30) in Eldamar, and caught in them the light of the Two Trees, Glingal and Belthil (i.e. Laurelin and Telperion, see poem no. 31) which gave radiance to Valinor; how Morgoth stole the Silmarils, taking them to his fortress and mounting them in his crown; and how Fëanor and his sons swore to regain them, defying the Valar and cursing anyone who would take these treasures for themselves (see also poem no. 176). Thingol covets a Silmaril nonetheless.

B603: *Girdle-seat* is presumably the *girdlestead*, or waist.

B610: *Lórien* here refers to the gardens and dwelling-place of the Vala Irmo (Lórien) in Aman.

B634: The prefix *ar-* (Sindarin 'high') in 'Ar-Melian' is an Elvish honorific.

B642: *Elu* is the Sindarin form of *Elwe*, a name of Thingol in Quenya.

B645: A starry sky 'wheels' when, with the passing of hours, it appears to turn overhead like a wheel.

B650: 'Ulmo's horn', i.e. the horn of the Vala who is lord of waters, and the mention of Ulmo 'calling again' in B652, refer to his summoning the Elves of Middle-earth who awoke at Cuiviénen (B627) to go with him to Aman in the West.

93

Shadowland (?1926–*c.* 1955)

Shadowland exists in two preliminary manuscripts and a final typescript. We give its earliest text as A, including revisions Tolkien seems to have made at or near the time of writing. He apparently added its title to the page after writing out the poem proper, as the ink differs between title and text.

[A]

O Kelimar! Thy shingle grey,
thy shores that faded East and West;
the cold and silent seas that lay
for ever stretched before thy breast;
thy dunes that all the winds possessed,
thy bent and twisted trees and grass,
by sunless breezes long distressed,
I see them and the clouds that pass
and rain that patters on thy grass!

The mists come up from mournful seas
o'er shingle long, and endless shore,
and dusty dunes; the dreary trees
they lonely lean for evermore;
since once a ship without an oar
without a sail without a crew
there came and thence me swiftly bore
to lands where light and laughter grew —
but not for those that once thee knew.

Who once has known thy loneliness,
thy spaces wide and boundless sky,
the freedom that thou dost possess,
he longs for ever till he die
for silence and a sweeping sky,
for pondering no voices break,
for air that keenly passes by
unbreathed of men, for thoughts that wake
amid the shapes thy shadows make.

Although quickly written on the page, manuscript A has the appearance of a fair copy, suggesting that there was an earlier draft, now lost. The text has only a few alterations marked, notably that 'Kelimar' in line 1 should be replaced with 'Shadowland'. The second manuscript of the poem, entitled *Shadowland* at the time of writing, certainly began as a fair copy, taking up the revisions of the first text and, as always with Tolkien, changing or inserting a few marks of punctuation, before it was itself altered. Here Tolkien replaced 'Shadowland' with 'Eruman' in line 1, and removed all instances of archaic 'thy', 'thee', 'o'er', and 'dost', as part of a significant makeover. In one corner of the page, he wrote a column of rhyming words – *ache*, *bake*, *cake*, etc. – as he revised the final two lines (which rhyme with *break*). At some later time, he wrote '1926' on the page, but it is impossible to know if he meant this as the date of original composition or of the fair copy – either would be possible.

Apart from differences due to speed, Tolkien's handwriting is alike in both manuscripts, as far as the primary text is concerned. His revisions to the second are in a distinctly later hand, not earlier than the late 1940s, as some of his markings are in red biro (ballpoint pen; as we have said, the biro was not generally available in Britain until late 1945). If he revised the poem around the time he typed its final, untitled text (given as B below), for which he used a typewriter he is known to have in the later part of his life, then one could reasonably date it to the 1950s or even the 1960s, when Tolkien was considering which of his poems to include in his *Tom Bombadil* collection of 1962 – *circa* 1955 seems a good compromise date, for want of conclusive evidence.

[B] O Araval! your shingle grey,
your shores I see beyond the West,
the cold and silent seas that lay
for ever stretched before your breast,
your dunes by writhen weeds possessed,
your mournful meres, your twisted trees
by shrill and sunless winds distressed,
the clouds about your mountains' knees,
the driving rain upon the screes.

There mists still blow from wintry seas
across your lost and endless shore,
the stones endure, the dreary trees
now lonely lean for evermore,

since once a ship with muffled oar
with ragged a sail and hungry crew
forsook your coast and far me bore
to lands where light and laughter grew:
but not for one who thinks of you!

Who once has known your loneliness,
your spaces wide and boundless sky,
the houseless freedom you possess,
he longs for ever till he die
for wastes untilled, untrod, that lie,
for silence that no voices break,
for air that keenly passes by
unbreathed by men, for barren lake
unstained by shadows that they make.

Among Tolkien's writings, we can find no other instance of *Kelimar*, as in text A. The second element of the name, *-mar*, means 'home' in the Elvish languages Qenya (Quenya) and Sindarin (compare *Eldamar*, *Valimar*); its first element, *Keli-*, might refer to running water (from Qenya KELE, KELU 'flow, run, ooze, trickle'), but it is also possible that it did not have a definite meaning before Tolkien replaced *Kelimar* with *Shadowland* in the second manuscript. We have met *Eruman* before in this book, in the later title of poem no. 45, *Eruman beneath the Stars*, the name having replaced *Habbanan*. In *The Book of Lost Tales* Tolkien describes Eruman, also called Arvalin, as the land south of the Mountains of Valinor and east and south of the Shadowy Seas; later, *Arvalin* alone was the name of this area, while *Eruman* (changed to *Araman*) was a wasteland between the mountains and the sea north of the great peak Taniquetil (see poem no. 31). *Araval*, as in text B, is recorded in Tolkien's writings only as the name of one of the Kings of Arthedain, a kingdom in the north of Middle-earth; in *Shadowland* it could be, perhaps, a conflation of *Araman* and *Arvalin*, or a development from *Arvalin*.

We have returned in this poem, as may be, to the land of *Eruman beneath the Stars*, in Aman in the West of Tolkien's invented world, with greater fidelity to the 'Silmarillion' landscape and no longer containing elements of Christianity. We have dated *Eruman beneath the Stars*, the final version of its sequence of poems, to ?1924, not long before the 1926 date Tolkien applied to *Shadowland*. But who is the speaker of the latter poem, who was borne away by ship and wishes to return? The place he describes sounds inhospitable next to the 'lands where light and laughter grew', to which he was taken, and yet – he seems to say – it is home.

Should we consider *Shadowland* wholly an offshoot of Tolkien's mythology, or is there a connection with his personal life? There is indeed a parallel between the sentiments of the poem and the nostalgia he expressed for the land of his birth in a letter he wrote to his son Christopher on 12 August 1944: 'All you say about the dryness, dustiness, and smell of the satan-licked land' – South Africa, where Christopher was stationed with the RAF and where Tolkien was born in 1892 (in the Orange Free State) – 'reminds me of my mother; she hated it (as a land) and was alarmed to see symptoms of my father growing to like it. . . . Oddly enough all that you say, even to its detriment, only increases the longing I have always felt to see it again.' Tolkien had left Africa at the age of three and never returned. 'Much though I love and admire little lanes and hedges and rustling trees and the soft rolling contours of a rich champain,' he continued,

> the thing that stirs me most and comes nearest to heart's satisfaction for me is space, and I would be willing to barter barrenness for it; indeed I like barrenness itself, whenever I have seen it. My heart still lingers among the high stony wastes among the morains and mountain-wreckage, silent in spite of the sound of thin chill water. Intellectually and aesthetically, of course; man cannot live on stone and sand, but I at any rate cannot live on bread alone; and if there was not bare rock and pathless sand and the unharvested sea, I should grow to hate all green things as a fungoid growth. [*Letters*, pp. 129–30]

It is probably no coincidence that we meet the same sort of mysterious land and eerie introspection found in *Shadowland* again in Tolkien's poem *Looney* (*The Sea-Bell*, no. 134), published in 1934:

'I come from a land, where cold was the strand,
    Where no men were me to greet.

I came on a boat empty afloat.
    I sat me thereon; swift did it swim;
Sail-less it fled, oar-less it sped;
    The stony beaches faded dim.

A11: Tolkien changed the first 'the' to 'o'er' and the second 'the' to 'and' in the course of writing.

A12: Tolkien changed the first 'the' to 'and'.

94

Knocking at the Door · The Mewlips

(?1927–61 or 62)

The earliest version of this poem is a manuscript which in its first four stanzas may be based on workings no longer extant, as Tolkien wrote these out in a fairly confident hand. The rest of the work, however, becomes progressively hard to read. The title *Knocking at the Door* was added to the first sheet only after Tolkien finished the poem proper. We give this text, such as we can decipher it, as A, while incorporating a few revisions.

[A]

The places where the Mewlips dwell
  Are dark as deepest ink,
And soft and softly rings the bell
  As in the bogs you sink,

As in the bogs you sink, who dare
  To knock upon their door,
While fireworks flicker in the air
  And shine upon the shore;

And shine upon the floors of sand
  All wet with weeping fountains,
Where little larrilances dance
  Beneath the Mingol mountains.

Over the Mingol mountains far and far away
The Sun climbs never high enough this side the day;
The Moon goes never near them but the silent stars
Look down on them and dream on them through cloudy bars.

The caverns where the Mewlips sit
  Are cool as cellars old,
With single sickly candle lit;
  And wet the walls of gold.

There wet the walls, the ceilings drip;
    Their feet upon the floor
Go splashing with a squish-flap-flip
    As they sidle in the door.

They sidle to the door to fish,
    And pipe like pepperdilloes;
And bones they gather in a dish
    Beneath the weeping willows.

Beyond the Mingol mountains a long and lonely way
Tunnelling under night and climbing over day
And through the Trees of Tormalone and the gallows weed
You go to find the Mewlips — and the Mewlips feed

As first written, the final couplet appears to read 'And through the Trees of Tormalone and the thick gallows ?thorn | Those go who find the Mewlips — and the Mewlips ?feed ?find at ?morn'. The three words at the end of line 31 are heavily struck through; under them seems to be written 'gallow's thorn', but we cannot be sure of the final word. Tolkien's final revision, to 'the gallows weed', accommodates in rhyme his new, more macabre ending, 'the Mewlips feed'.

Below the close of the poem on the second page of the manuscript are a few lines of rough workings, including the trials 'and the gallows-grass | and the Mewlips feed alas!' and 'The Mewlips [hear >] see you coming with their eyes like glass'. The bottom half of the page contains workings for the final version of *The Ruined Enchanter* (no. 62), which we date to *c.* 1927.

The first manuscript was followed by a typescript of A as revised, made on Tolkien's Hammond machine with 'miniature' fonts. At the head of this sheet he wrote (in a later hand) 'Ox[ford] 1927?' and 'rev[ised] 1937'. After the title is an introductory note, 'Lines induced by sensations on waiting for an answer at the Door of a Reverend and Academic Person', which puts the weirdness of the poem in a new light. By 1927 Tolkien was established in Oxford as the Rawlinson and Bosworth Professor of Anglo-Saxon: was he the 'Reverend and Academic Person' at whose door a student waited with apprehension, or was he recalling his own experience as a student? The situation is exaggerated in either case, and Tolkien was unsure of the joke: he struck through the lines, then restored them.

Tolkien subsequently marked the typescript heavily. We give the revised text as B.

[B]

The places where the Mewlips dwell
Are dark as deepest ink,
And slow and softly rings the bell
As in the bog you sink,

You sink into the bog, who dare
To knock upon their door,
While fireworks flicker in the air
And shine upon the shore.

The sparks hiss on the floors of sand
All wet with weeping fountains,
Where grey the glooming gargoyles stand
Beneath the Morlock mountains.

Over the Morlock mountains, a long and weary way,
Down in mouldy valleys where trees are wet and grey,
By the dark pool's borders without wind or tide,
Moonless and sunless, there the Mewlips hide.

The caverns where the Mewlips sit
Are cool as cellars old
With single sickly candle lit;
And wet the walls of gold.

Their walls are wet, their ceilings drip;
Their feet upon the floor
Go splashing with a squish-flap-flip
As they sidle to the door.

They peep out slyly through a crack,
All cased like armadilloes;
And your bones they gather in a sack
Beneath the weeping willows.

Beyond the Morlock mountains a long and lonely road,
Through the spider-shadows and the marsh of Toad,
And through the wood of hanging trees and the
gallows-weed,
You go to find the Mewlips — and the Mewlips feed.

Among many other changes, the 'Mingol mountains' have given way to the 'Morlock mountains'. *Mingol* in text A seems to have been Tolkien's invention, with no meaning other than a name to alliterate with *mountains*. In text B *Morlock* serves the same purpose, but rings a bell as the name of one of the future peoples in H.G. Wells' novel *The Time Machine* (1895) – so familiar, maybe, that Tolkien changed it to *Merlock* in the next version of the poem to avoid the association.

Here, too, entered the combination in line 31 of 'hanging trees and the gallows-weed'. *Gallows-weed* is presumably *gallows-grass* (*gallow-grass*) – that is, hemp – but with 'weed' to rhyme with 'feed'. Its name stems from its use in making rope for hanging at gallows. In their *Flora of Middle-earth* (2017) Walter S. Judd and Graham A. Judd suggest that the combination of 'hanging trees' and 'gallows-weed' in the poem is no coincidence, 'the two essential components of execution by hanging being a tree and a rope' (p. 188). Tolkien is ambiguous on this point, however, as 'hanging trees' comes after a mention of weeping willows, whose branches are famously pendulous. In B, only three lines separate willows from 'hanging trees'; in the final version 'drooping willows' are much earlier in the poem, though still present.

Knocking at the Door was published in the *Oxford Magazine* for 18 February 1937. This text is identical to B, except that in the two instances of 'Morlock Mountains' the second word is capitalized, giving it the appearance of a place-name, and the note following the title reads: 'Lines induced by sensations when waiting for an answer at the door of an Exalted Academic Person'. As printed, it does not bear Tolkien's name, only the pseudonym 'Oxymore', from *oxymoron* 'a joining of contradictory ideas'.

In 1961 or 1962 Tolkien returned to the poem when considering which of his works to include in the collection *The Adventures of Tom Bombadil and Other Verses from the Red Book*. Two typescripts of his final revision, retitled *The Mewlips*, are among his papers (in our notes we refer to these as B^1 and B^2). In the earlier of them, Tolkien eliminated the incongruous mention of armadilloes in the penultimate stanza, and in the later made most of his final changes (variously in ribbon and carbon copies), making the poem still more atmospheric and macabre. In the process, he also deleted his note about waiting at an academic's door, removing any notion that the work was meant to be satirical. Here, as C, we give the ultimate text, as published in the *Bombadil* volume, pp. 45–6.

[C] The shadows where the Mewlips dwell
    Are dark and wet as ink,
And slow and softly rings their bell,
    As in the slime you sink.

You sink into the slime, who dare
    To knock upon their door,
While down the grinning gargoyles stare
    And noisome waters pour.

Beside the rotting river-strand
    The drooping willows weep,
And gloomily the gorcrows stand
    Croaking in their sleep.

Over the Merlock mountains a long and weary way,
    In a mouldy valley where the trees are grey,
By a dark pool's borders without wind or tide,
    Moonless and sunless, the Mewlips hide.

The cellars where the Mewlips sit
    Are deep and dank and cold
With single sickly candle lit;
    And there they count their gold.

Their walls are wet, their ceilings drip;
    Their feet upon the floor
Go softly with a squish-flap-flip,
    As they sidle to the door.

They peep out slyly; through a crack
    Their feeling fingers creep,
And when they've finished, in a sack
    Your bones they take to keep.

Beyond the Merlock mountains, a long and lonely road,
    Through the spider-shadows and the marsh of Tode,
And through the wood of hanging trees and the gallows-weed,
    You go to find the Mewlips — and the Mewlips feed.

As Tolkien wrote in his preface to *The Adventures of Tom Bombadil and Other Verses from the Red Book*, the poems contained in the volume were 'concerned with legends and jests of the Shire at the end of the Third Age, that appear to have been made by Hobbits, especially by Bilbo and his friends, or their immediate descendants' (p. 7). All of its contents are 'explained' in the preface in some fashion, except for *The Mewlips*, which is not even among those verses said to be 'often unintelligible even when legible' (p. 7). It was one of the last of the poems Tolkien sent to his publisher for the book, and one he felt would need 'thorough re-handling' (letter to Rayner Unwin, 5 February 1962, Tolkien–George Allen & Unwin archive, HarperCollins). In a letter to a Miss Allen, written on 13 February 1963, he replied to questions about *The Mewlips* by explaining (no doubt inventing on the spot) that Mewlips were merely legend to Hobbits, and that Hobbit minds would not dwell only on comfort, implying that on occasion they would turn to thoughts of the grotesque.

The Mewlips was, and remains, the most difficult of the *Bombadil* poems to imagine being collected, let alone written, by a Hobbit, and to place within the matter of Middle-earth. In 're-handling' the work Tolkien discarded obvious anachronisms, such as the gargoyles of the third stanzas (replacing them with *gorcrows*, a name for carrion-crows) and the armadilloes of the seventh, a New World mammal. The 'Trees of Tormalone' and 'The marsh of Tode' (or 'Toad') are foreign to the Middle-earth established in Tolkien's writings as much as the 'Mingol' ('Morlock', 'Merlock') mountains, or the Mewlips themselves, whatever they may be. But 'the spider-shadows', at least, echo the forest of Mirkwood in *The Hobbit*, whose spiders are defeated by Bilbo Baggins, or the darkness surrounding the spider-like Ungoliant in 'The Silmarillion', while the 'rotting river-strand' and 'drooping willows' of the final text recall the Old Forest in *The Lord of the Rings*.

In *The Worlds of J.R.R. Tolkien* (2020) John Garth describes the 'mouldy valleys where trees are wet and grey' of the *Oxford Magazine* text as a precursor of the Dead Marshes in *The Lord of the Rings*, and argues that the general landscape of the poem 'is like nowhere on earth except the Western Front at night [in the First World War], with its drowning mud, its bursts of artillery fire and flares. There are also those "spider shadows" that Tolkien seems to have linked with war terrors.' The name of the marsh of Toad, he suggests, may be a pun on *Tod*, the German word for 'death'. He describes the Mewlips as 'Gollum-like', and 'reminiscent of a trench rumour' during the war that No Man's Land – the blasted area between opposing armies –

was peopled with wild men who came out at night to plunder and kill. And he thinks the description of the Mewlips 'cased like armadilloes' to be like 'a surreal fusion between man and tank' (p. 170).

In 1967 Tolkien made a professional recording of *The Mewlips* for the album *Poems and Songs of Middle Earth*. It was later reissued.

A11: The word *larrilances* seems to be Tolkien's invention, to alliterate with 'little' and partially rhyme with 'dance'.

A15: 'Silent' originally read 'silver'.

A18: 'Cellars' originally read 'caverns'.

A26: The word *pepperdilloes* was probably Tolkien's invention, to alliterate with 'pipe' and rhyme with 'willows'. Christopher Tolkien could not find it attested, nor can we. Its construction would suggest a kind of pickled pepper, but it need not have a definition.

C1: In B^2, Tolkien changed 'places' (B1) first to 'caverns' and then to 'shadows'.

C7: In B^2 this line first read 'Where on you grinning gargoyles stare', and was changed to 'While down grinning gargoyles stare'. The definite article was added in C.

C25–28: These lines reached their final text in B^2. On sheets of stationery from the Hotel Miramar in Bournemouth, Dorset, where he and his wife took holidays in later years, Tolkien wrote trials for this stanza, preferring almost to the last 'their slimy feelers creep' in l. 26, though he also considered 'their fingers crawl like feelers' and tested rhymes for 'crawl', 'heap', and 'drink'. (On fhe reverse sides of these sheets is rough drafting for *The Complaint of Mîm the Dwarf*, no. 185.)

95

Fastitocalon (?1927–1961 or 62)

Some of Tolkien's poems concerning animals were inspired by a work known as *Physiologus* ('Naturalist'), one of the most popular books of the Middle Ages, in which the natural history of a creature (*natura*) is followed by a Christian moral or spiritual meaning (*significacio*). Its author's science is questionable, to say the least, but his main concern was the use to which natural history could be put in the service of a Christian life. Originally written in Greek, the book was widely translated into Latin and then into the vernacular.

Tolkien is said to have written four poems drawn from this tradition. *Reginhardus, the Fox* and *Monoceros, the Unicorn* unfortunately are known only by their titles; their texts have not been located. The other two poems, *Iumbo, or Ye Kinde of ye Oliphaunt* (no. 96) and the present work, were published in the *Stapeldon Magazine* for June 1927 as by 'Fisiologus', with the shared title *Adventures in Unnatural History and Medieval Metres, Being the Freaks of Fisiologus*. For neither of these, too, have we traced an extant manuscript. The 1927 *Fastitocalon* is transcribed here (A) from its *Stapeldon Magazine* printing, pp. 123–5.

[A] *Natura fastitocalonis.* [The Nature of Fastitocalon]

Old Fastitocalon is fat:
His grease the most stupendous vat,
    If He perchance were boiled,
Or tank or reservoir would fill,
Or make of margarine a hill,
    Or keep the wheels well oiled
                                that squeak
On all the carts beneath the sun,
Or brew emulsion in a tun
    For those whose chests are weak!

He wallows on a bed of slime
In the Ocean's deep and weedy clime;
    As merry organs roll,
So snores He solemn sweet and loud,
And thither tumble in a crowd

The sardine, and the sole
so flat,
And all the little foolish fry
Who pry about with goggle eye,
The skipper and the sprat
in glee
Approach the portals of His jaws;
What feast or frolic be the cause
They enter in to see.

Alas! they come not ever thence;
The joke is all at their expense,
As is the dinner too.
Yet are there times of storm and strife,
When equinoctial gales are rife,
And there is much ado
down there.
He finds the depths devoid of rest,
Then up He comes and on His chest
Floats in the upper air.

His ribs are tender, and his eye
Is small and wicked, wondrous sly;
His heart is black and fickle.
Beware his vast and blubbery back;
His slumbrous sides do not attack,
Nor ever seek to tickle.
Beware!
His dreams are not profound or deep,
He only plays at being asleep;
His snoring is a snare.

He, floating on the inky sea,
A sunny island seems to be,
Although a trifle bare.
Conniving gulls there strut and prink,
Their job it is to tip the wink,
If any one lands there
with kettle
To make a picnic tea, or get
Relief from sickness or the wet,
Or some, perhaps, to settle.

Ah! foolish folk, who land on HIM,
And patent stoves proceed to trim,
Or make incautious fires
To dry your clothes or warm a limb,
Who dance or prance about the glim —
'Tis just what He desires.
He grins.
And when He feels the heat He dives
Down to the deeps: you lose your lives
Cut off amid your sins.

Significacio sequitur. [Meaning follows]

This mighty monster teaches us
That trespassing is dangerous,
And perils lurk in wait
For curious folk who peep in doors
Of other folk, or dance on floors
Too early or too late
with jazz;
That too much grease is worse than none,
To spare the margarine on bun
Content with what one has
on hand;
That many noises loud and strong
Are neither music nor a song
But only just a band.

Many among Tolkien's intended audience for this work in 1927 – the learned community at Oxford – would have been familiar with bestiaries, and probably also with the tale of St Brendan, a monk of the sixth century who is said to have sailed with his companions west from Ireland and landed on a vast island, where the men lit a fire and celebrated Mass. The 'island', however, proved to be a huge beast of the sea floating on the surface, who was awakened when it felt the heat of the campfire on its back and dove beneath the waves. The monks barely escaped with their lives. (See also *The Death of St. Brendan*, poem no. 175.)

In *Fastitocalon* the creature is explicitly a whale, whose fat (blubber) was avidly sought for making oil. It attracts fish to eat, including small ones ('small fry'), by the sound of its snoring, which is like 'merry organs' – in the bestiary tradition the attraction is the whale's breath, sweet as flowers. During equinoctial gales (stormy winds in spring and autumn) it is said to rise from turmoil in the deeps, but its 'slumber' is a ruse, and gulls, vainly strutting and primping, give warning to the whale ('tip the wink') should men come and land.

As the whale attracts fish and drags them down into the deep, says the bestiary, so Satan attracts men weak in their faith and carries them to Hell. In Tolkien's modernized version of this cautionary tale, with its margarine and squeaky wheels, the moral is directed rather to 'curious folk who peep in doors | Of other folk, or dance on floors . . . with jazz'. Years later, Tolkien would write to his son Christopher that '[postwar] music will give place to jiving: which as far as I can make out means holding a "jam session" round a piano (an instrument properly intended to produce the sounds devised by, say, Chopin) and hitting it so hard that it breaks' (31 July 1944, *Letters*, p. 127).

In 1961 or 1962 Tolkien revised *Fastitocalon* for his collection *The Adventures of Tom Bombadil and Other Verses from the Red Book*; we give this text below as B, from pp. 49, 51. Tolkien shortened and simplified his earlier poem, but retained its title, as well as the notion of a false island, with birds deceptively sitting on it, and a crafty beast, now a giant 'Turtle-fish' with a horny shell. 'Middle-earth' is mentioned almost at the end, to place the poem within the context of *The Lord of the Rings* – the conceit of the *Bombadil* collection (see no. 24) – while its new 'moral', 'Set foot on no uncharted shore!' better suits an unadventurous Hobbit author. Tolkien says in his preface to the book that *Fastitocalon* was composed by the Hobbit Sam Gamgee.

[B]

Look, there is Fastitocalon!
An island good to land upon,
    Although 'tis rather bare.
Come, leave the sea! And let us run,
Or dance, or lie down in the sun!
    See, gulls are sitting there!
            Beware!
        Gulls do not sink.
There they may sit, or strut and prink:
Their part it is to tip the wink,
    If anyone should dare
    Upon that isle to settle,
Or only for a while to get
Relief from sickness or the wet,
    Or maybe boil a kettle.

Ah! foolish folk, who land on HIM,
And little fires proceed to trim
And hope perhaps for tea!
It may be that His shell is thick,
He seems to sleep; but He is quick,
And floats now in the sea
With guile;
And when He hears their tapping feet,
Or faintly feels the sudden heat,
With smile
HE dives,
And promptly turning upside-down
He tips them off, and deep they drown,
And lose their silly lives
To their surprise.
Be wise!
There are many monsters in the Sea,
But none so perilous as HE,
Old horny Fastitocalon,
Whose mighty kindred all have gone,
The last of the old Turtle-fish.
So if to save your life you wish
Then I advise:
Pay heed to sailors' ancient lore,
Set foot on no uncharted shore!
Or better still,
Your days at peace on Middle-earth
In mirth
Fulfil!

Two years after this new version was published, Tolkien wrote to Eileen Elgar that he had taken the name *Fastitocalon* 'from a fragment of an Anglo-Saxon bestiary that has survived, thinking that it sounded comic and absurd enough to serve as a hobbit alteration of something more learned and elvish' (5 March 1964, *Letters*, pp. 483). Of course, the need to relate the poem to Hobbits was true only for its 1962 revision, not for the original work of 1927; but 'fragment of an Anglo-Saxon bestiary' is necessarily the three poems, among them 'The Whale', included in the tenth-century Exeter Book in Exeter Cathedral Library, the only *Physiologus* to survive in Old English. In his 2014 essay 'Inside Literature', John D. Rateliff acknowledged this source, but argued that Tolkien also consulted the sole Middle

English manuscript of *Physiologus* (MS Arundel 292 in the British Library), in which the creature's habits of enticing fish into its jaws and pretending to be an island are described in the same order that Tolkien used in his 1927 poem, whereas the Exeter Book version has the mock-island before the fish-lure. This is undoubtedly correct. Tolkien would have known the Middle English version already from required reading he had as an Oxford English School student, in *An Old English Miscellany* (1872) edited by Richard Morris ('old' in this title means 'early').

Tolkien further wrote in his letter to Mrs Elgar (*Letters*, p. 483) that

> the learned name [*Fastitocalon*] . . . seems to have been [originally, in Greek] *Aspido-chelōne* 'turtle with a round shield (of hide)'. Of that *astitocalon* is a corruption no worse than many of the time; but I am afraid the F was put on by the versifier simply to make the name alliterate, as was compulsory for poets in his day, with the other words in his line. Shocking, or charming freedom, according to taste.
>
> He [the bestiary author] says: *þam is noma cenned | fyrnstreama geflotan Fastitocalon*, 'to him is a name appointed, to the floater in the ancient tides, Fastitocalon'. The notion of the treacherous island that is really a monster seems to derive from the East: the marine turtles enlarged by myth-making fancy; and I left it at that. But in Europe the monster becomes mixed up with whales, and already in the Anglo-Saxon version he is given whale characteristics, such as feeding by trawling with an open mouth. In moralized bestiaries he is, of course, an allegory of the devil, and is so used by Milton [as Leviathan in *Paradise Lost*].

In regard to its metre, Rateliff points out that the 1927 *Fastitocalon* resembles neither its progenitors [Old or Middle English bestiary poems about the Whale] nor indeed its companion piece [*Iumbo*], instead using a complex stanza (typically rhymed AABCCB.D.EED, but occasionally AABCCB.D.EED.F.GGF) ending in a variant of the bob-and-wheel typically associated with Middle English tail-rhyme romances' ('Inside Literature: Tolkien's Explorations of Medieval Genres' (2014), p. 136). He suggests that the poem in its form follows most closely Chaucer's 'Tale of Sir Thopas' from the *Canterbury Tales*, and indeed there is a resemblance to parts of that work.

96

Iumbo, or Ye Kinde of ye Oliphaunt (?1927)

Iumbo is the second of Tolkien's two 'bestiary' poems published in the *Stapeldon Magazine* for June 1927 as *Adventures in Unnatural History and Medieval Metres, being the Freaks of Fisiologus*; see our discussion for *Fastitocalon* (no. 95) for their historical background.

Like its companion work, *Iumbo* proceeds from the *Physiologus* but departs almost at once from the medieval tradition into a modern world of flannel (cloth), rubber hoses, and vacuum cleaners. Its subject is the Elephant, a word earlier spelled 'Oliphaunt', as here, or 'Olifaunt'. Its title is 'Jumbo', spelled in the Roman alphabet which lacked *J*, after the name of the famous zoo and circus elephant of the later nineteenth century, from which we have the word *jumbo* 'large in size'. In Chaucer's 'Tale of Sir Thopas' the hero meets a giant named Sir Olifaunt.

As for *Fastitocalon*, lacking a manuscript of *Iumbo* we have transcribed it from its original printing (pp. 125–7), signed 'Fisiologus'.

Natura iumbonis. [The Nature of Jumbo]

The Indic oliphaunt's a burly lump,
A moving mountain, a majestic mammal
(But those that fancy that he wears a hump
Confuse him incorrectly with the camel).
His pendulous ears they flap about like flannel;
He trails a supple elongated nose
That twixt his tusks of pearly-white enamel
Performs the functions of a rubber hose
Or vacuum cleaner as his needs impose,

Or on occasion serves in trumpet's stead,
Whose fearful fanfares utterly surpass
In mighty music from his monstrous head
The hollow boom of bells or bands of brass.
Nor do these creatures quarrel (as alas!
Do neighbours musical in Western lands);
In congregations do they tramp the grass,

And munch the juicy shoots in friendly bands,
Till not a leaf unmasticated stands.

This social soul one unconvivial flaw
Has nonetheless: he's poor in repartee,
His jests are heavy, for Mohammed's law
He loves, and though he has the thirst of three,
His vast interior he fills with tea.
Not thus do water-drinkers vice escape,
And weighty authors state that privily
He takes a drug, more deadly than the grape,
Compared with which cocaine's a harmless jape.

The dark mandragora's unwholesome root
He chews with relish secret and unholy,
Despising other pharmaceutic loot
(As terebinth, athanasie, or moly).
Those diabolic juices coursing slowly
Do fill his sluggish veins with sudden madness,
Changing his grave and simple nature wholly
To a lamb titanic capering in gladness,
A brobdingnagian basilisk in badness.

The vacuous spaces of his empty head
Are filled with fires of fell intoxication;
His legs endure no longer to be led,
But wander free in strange emancipation.
Then frightful fear amid his exaltation
Awakes within him lest he tumble flat,
For apparatus none for levitation
Has he, who falling down must feebly bat
The air with legs inadequate and fat.

Then does he haste, if he can coax his limbs,
To some deep silent water or dark pool
(Where no reptilian mugger lurks or swims)
And there he stands — no! not his brow to cool,
But thinking that he cannot fall, the fool,
Buoyed by his belly adipose and round.
Yet if he find no water, as a rule,
He blindly blunders thumping o'er the ground,
And villages invades with thunderous sound.

If any house oppose his brutish bump,
Then woe betide — it crumples in a heap,
Its inmates jumbled in a jellied lump
Pulped unexpecting in imprudent sleep.
When tired at last, as tame as any sheep
Or jaded nag, he longs for sweet repose,
In Ind a tree, whose roots like serpents creep,
Of girth gigantic opportunely grows,
Whereon to lean his weary bulk and doze.

Thus will his dreams not end in sudden jerk,
He thinks. What hopes! For hunters all too well
Acquainted with his little habits lurk
Beneath the Upus' shade; a nasty sell
For Oliphas they plan, his funeral knell.
With saws they wellnigh sever all the bole,
Then cunning prop it, that he may not tell,
Until thereto he trusts his weight, poor soul —
It all gives way and lands him in a hole.

Significacio. [Meaning]

The doctrine that these mournful facts propound
Needs scarcely pointing, yet we cannot blink
The fact that some still follow base Mahound,
Though Christian people universally think
That water neat is hardly fit to drink.
Not music nor fat feeding make a feast
But wine, and plenty of it. Good men wink
At fun and frolic (though too well policed)
When mildly canned or innocently greased;
But those whose frenzy's root is drugs not drink
Should promptly be suppressed and popped in clink.

In line 31, the *terebinth* is a tree which yields turpentine, *athanasie* the medicinal plant tansy, and *moly* is the herb in Homer's *Odyssey* given by Hermes to Odysseus as a charm against Circe (Kirkê). In the Middle Ages moly (also called molü) tended to be identified as a kind of wild garlic ('Sorcerers Garlic', *Allium*), while modern biologists associate it with the snowdrop (*Galanthus*). The 'reptilian mugger' of line 48 is presumably the *mugger*, or broad-nosed Indian crocodile. In line 61, the 'tree, whose roots like serpents creep' is the *Upas* (Tolkien spells it 'Upus'), *Antiaris toxicaria*, which appears in travellers' tales, and most notably in Erasmus Darwin's *Botanic Garden* (1789–91) where it is 'the Hydra tree of death'. The true Upas is indeed a large tree, but in height rather than 'girth gigantic', and it grows not in India but in Java.

'Oliphas' in line 68 refers to the scientific name of the Asiatic elephant, *Oliphas maximus* (*Elephas maximus*). In line 75, *Mahound* is a corrupt form of the name of the prophet Muhammad, recorded from medieval times.

Unlike 'The Whale', which inspired *Fastitocalon*, 'The Elephant' is not among the Exeter Book's bestiary poems, only three of many in the *Physiologus* tradition. John D. Rateliff has pointed instead to the Middle English *Physiologus* as Tolkien's source, and M.H. Porck, in 'Medieval Animals in Middle-earth: J.R.R. Tolkien and the Old English and Middle English *Physiologus*' (2022), also concludes that Tolkien drew from this, because of the similarity of his phrases 'burly lump' and 'moving mountain' to the second line of the source, 'on bodi borlic berges ilike' ('in a burly body like a mountain').

As noted for *Fastitocalon*, the sole Middle English text was familiar to Tolkien in Richard Morris's *Old English Miscellany* (1872). Tolkien followed the traditional description of the Elephant closely, but made from it his own work, modernizing and occasionally alliterating with vigour. Rateliff has commented that Tolkien chose for this work 'a deliberately elaborate polysyllabic vocabulary', such as *pendulous*, *unmasticated*, and *repartee* ('Inside Literature: Tolkien's Explorations of Medieval Genres', p. 147). In this, *Iumbo* stands in contrast to the much simpler language of Tolkien's later, distinctly different 'elephant' poem, *Oliphaunt* (no. 167).

The elephant in *Iumbo*, as in *Physiologus*, is Indian (*Indic*) rather than African. There appears to be no description in medieval literature – there could hardly be one – of the creature abstaining from alcohol ('Mohammed's law', a prohibition in Islam) or drinking tea, but it is said to be so chaste that when it wants to conceive it must eat mandragora, or mandrake, a reputed fertility drug and aphrodisiac. Tolkien compares this to cocaine, and to three items from the medieval pharmacopeia. Under the 'diabolic' influence of mandrake, 'more dangerous than the grape' (wine), the gentle Elephant becomes like a basilisk, the most terrible of all mythological beasts, with a lethal gaze or breath.

Its 'badness' is then *brobdingnagian*, after Brobdingnag in *Gulliver's Travels* by Jonathan Swift (1726), a land where everything is enormous relative to its hero. According to the bestiaries, the Elephant lives in fear of falling down – its legs were thought to have no joints. To prevent this it often stands in water, buoyed by its belly fat. The ancients note as well that because the Elephant has a (reputed) habit of sleeping while leaning against a tree, hunters would set a trap by cutting a favoured tree in half, to collapse under the creature's weight and leave it defenceless.

Tolkien's satire concludes with moral conflict between drugs and drink. His exaggerated picture of 'wine, and plenty of it', the notion of Christians 'universally' embracing excess (Britain is a nation traditionally of tea-drinkers), and the pursuit of 'fun and frolic' are contrasted with Muslim abstinence.

97

Syx Mynet (?1928)

As explained in our discussion of *From One to Five* (no. 76), on 2 January 1929 Tolkien sent to E.V. Gordon three poems to join those he had composed in the early 1920s while teaching at Leeds, and which the two friends had copied as 'Leeds Songs' for the amusement and education of students in the English School. Like most of those other verses, the new poems were included, with editorial changes, in the 1936 booklet *Songs for the Philologists*; the present work was published there as the second of thirteen poems by Tolkien.

Syx Mynet ('Six Coins') is to be sung to the tune of 'I Love Sixpence', and indeed is a version in Old English of that familiar counting-down rhyme, sometimes entitled 'The Jolly Tester'. We give here, as A, the text as printed in *Songs*, p. 7, with accents inserted by Tolkien in his personal copy (copy 1; see poem no. 76).

[A]

Verses 2 and 3

*Syx** mynet lufige' ic, * *Feower*; *twa.*
Maðum mynelic,
*Syx** mynet lufige ic * *Feower*; *twa.*
ofer selfe lif.
Heora ánes ic ann,
Óþer sceal óþer mann
And *féower** habban fréolic‡ wif.

**twá sceal*; *náwiht*. ‡tornmod; nahtlic.

Náwiht lufige ic,
Maðum mynelic,
Náwiht lufige ic
bet þanne ic mín wíf.
Þu nimest naht æt mé,
naht nimeð swilce hé —
Lá! næfde ic náwiht þurh min líf.

The words printed at upper right instruct the singer to substitute 'Feower' ('four') for 'Syx' ('six') in the second verse, repeating the rest, and 'Twa' ('two') for 'Syx' in the third. 'Náwiht lufige ic', etc., constitutes the fourth and final verse. Similarly, the words printed below the first verse instruct the singer to substitute 'twá sceal' ('two shall') and 'náwiht' ('nothing, naught') for 'féower', and 'tornmod' ('angry') and 'nahtlic' ('good for nothing') for 'fréolic' ('comely, goodly'), in the second and third verses respectively.

In copy 1 of *Songs* Tolkien marked in line 2 'Maðum' ('precious or valuable thing', compare *mathom* in *The Lord of the Rings*) to read 'Syx* mynet' ('six coins'), but also suggested: 'or, use invariable *mín mynet* ["my coins"] in 2nd line'. In line 5 he inserted 'þé' before 'ann', thus 'one of them [the coins] I give to thee', and in line 9 he replaced 'Maðum' with 'Náwiht' ('nothing'). Here, as B, we have transcribed the manuscript of *Syx Mynet* in the Gordon archive at Leeds, with the stanzas and refrains (abbreviated by Tolkien) filled out for clarity.

[B]

1.

Syx mynet lufige' ic,
Máþum mynelic,
Syx mynet lufige' ic
ofer selfe lif!

Heora ánes ic þé ann,
Óþer sceal óþer mann
And féower (sceal) habban fréolic wíf.

2.

Féower mynet lufige' ic,
Máþum mynelic,
Féower mynet lufige' ic
ofer selfe lif!

Heora ánes ic þé ann,
Óþer sceal óþer mann
And twá sceal habban tornmód wíf.

3.

Twa mynet lufige' ic,
Máþum mynelic,
Twa mynet lufige' ic
ofer selfe lif!

Heora ánes ic þé ann,
Óþer sceal óþer mann
And náwiht habban náhtlic wíf.

4.

Náwiht lufige' ic,
Máþum mynelic,
Náwiht lufige' ic
bet þonne' ic mín wíf!

Þú nimest náht æt mé,
náht nimeþ swilce hé —
Lá! næfde' ic náwiht þurh mín líf.

Finally, as C, we provide a rough translation of text B into Modern English:

[C]

1.

I love six coins,
Pleasing treasure,
I love six coins
better than my life.

One of them I give to thee,
Another I give to another man
And four I (shall) have for my good wife.

2.

I love four coins,
Pleasing treasure,
I love four coins
better than my life.

One of them I give to thee,
Another I give to another man
And two I shall have for my angry wife.

3.

I love two coins,
Pleasing treasure,
I love two coins
better than my life.

One of them I give to thee,
The other I give to another man
And nothing I have for my worthless wife.

4.

I love nothing,
Pleasing treasure,
I love nothing
better than my wife.

You get nothing from me,
And naught can he take —
Oh! I had nothing throughout my life.

The earliest known version of the poem on which Tolkien based *Syx Mynet* is recorded in the collection *Gammer Gurton's Garland* (1810). His most immediate inspiration was, perhaps, the version ('O, Dear Sixpence') printed in Moffat's *What the Children Sing* (p. 8). There the lyrics read:

O, dear sixpence! I love sixpence!
I love sixpence as I love my life;
I'll spend a penny on't, I'll lend another on't,
And I'll carry fourpence home to my wife.

O, dear fourpence! I love fourpence!
I love fourpence as I love my life;
I'll spend a penny on't, I'll lend a penny on't,
I'll carry twopence home to my wife.

O, dear twopence! I love twopence!
I love twopence as I love my life;
I'll spend a penny on't, I'll lend a penny on't,
I'll carry nothing home to my wife.

O, dear nothing! I've got nothing!
I love nothing better than my wife;
I'll spend nothing, I'll lend nothing,
For I've earned nothing all through my life.

In *The Road to Middle-earth* Tom Shippey writes of *Syx Mynet* (and *Ruddoc Hana*, no. 77, among others) as another 'asterisk-poem' (see no. 78). In this context it is a 'reconstruction' of something which might have been in different circumstances, in line with what Shippey describes (1992 edn., p. 18) as 'the characteristic activity' of philologists like Tolkien, who reconstructed earlier languages (such as Indo-

European) from clues surviving in descendant languages (such as Sanskrit, Latin, and Greek). *Syx Mynet* is not, however, a straightforward translation of the nursery rhyme into Old English, taking its variant texts into account, but offers creative twists. Tolkien's version is unusual in adding progressively harsh adjectives for the speaker's wife, when the point of the work is that the speaker accepts his poverty because he needs no more than his wife's love.

B7: The word 'sceal' is in brackets in the original.

98

Lá, Húru (?1928)

The eighth of Tolkien's poems published in *Songs for the Philologists* (1936) is a celebration of drink and drinking, and appears to be an original composition in Old English rather than an adaptation. Here, as A, we have transcribed the manuscript of the poem Tolkien sent to E.V. Gordon on 2 January 1929, now in the Gordon archive at Leeds. The printed text in *Songs* (p. 16) is almost identical, except in regard to diacritical and punctuation marks.

[A] Éalá hú is wynsum þéos woruld to-niht,
And módġu and myrġu þéos déore gedryht!
Hér is blǽd, hér is bliss, hér is hróþor and hyht;
Nis hér nǽnig pǽca, ne prattas, ne pliht.
Lá húru, lá húru, lá léofa, lá hú! (*4 times*)

Hér is medu and béorþegu, ealu and wín,
And hunig and hǽlu and héahlufu mín.
Ic drince, ic drenċe, is scenċe þe þín;
We hebbaþ úp hornas nú týn síþum týn.
Lá húru, &c.

Ic wlaffige', ic woffige', ic wéde swá þú.
Þú druncnast, þú drýmest, þú dysigast nú,
Þú spréawlast, þú spellast swa snottrast, swa snellast —
La! hwá wisse' ǽr swelcne gebéor swá bistú!
Lá húru, &c.

Following, as B, is a translation into Modern English.

[B] Oh, how joyful is this world tonight,
Pride and pleasure, this dear gathering;
Here is splendour, here is bliss, here is solace and hope;
Here are no deceits, tricks, or risks.
Oh truly, oh truly, oh beloved, oh how! (*4 times*)

Here is mead and beer-drinking, ale and wine,
Honey and health and my great love.

I drink, I give drink, I pour out a cup for you;
We raise up drinking-horns ten times ten.
Oh truly, etc.

I stammer, I rave, I am mad like you.
You drank, you made merry, you are a fool now,
You sprawl, you speak so cleverly, so keenly.
Oh! who has known a drinking-friend like you?
Oh truly, etc.

A printed caption in *Songs* directs that *Lá, Húru* is to be sung to the tune of 'O'Reilly'. This song, more fully known as 'Are You the O'Reilly', was composed by vaudevillian Pat Cooney in 1883, and revived in a new version in 1915 by P. Emmett. Although it is distinctly American in content, the work somehow reached northern France in the early years of the First World War, before the United States' entry into the war, and rivalled 'It's a Long Way to Tipperary' in popularity among soldiers. Its chorus seems to have been better known than the rest of its lyrics, if not consistently recalled; here are its words as it was sung by Billy Murray on a 1915 Edison recording:

Are you the O'Reilly that keeps this hotel?
Are you the O'Reilly they speak of so well?
Are you the O'Reilly they speak of so highly?
Gor blime me O'Reilly, you are looking well.

It is evident that the students who read the Leeds verses, as we have discussed, knew 'O'Reilly' well, as three of the poems in *Songs for the Philologists*, including two by Tolkien (see also *Natura Apis*, no. 99), were set to its tune. In *Lá, Húru* the instruction to repeat the fifth line of each stanza four times creates three further four-line groups, each with the same rhythm of the 'O'Reilly' chorus.

In a letter to E.V. Gordon dated 2 January 1929, accompanying manuscripts of *Lá, Húru, Syx Mynet* (no. 97), and *Natura Apis*, Tolkien referred to the present work as 'the "O'Reilly" one in Old English [which] makes a good noise. Also I think [it] is in fair A[nglo]-Saxon (& introduces a word or two such as [in line 11] *wlaffian* ['stammer'] & *woffian* ['shout, rave'] which deserve to be better known)' (Gordon archive, Leeds).

A1: In Tolkien's copy 1 of *Songs for the Philologists* (see poem no. 76) he inserted an exclamation mark after 'Éala'.

A2: In the printed *Songs* the second word of this line is given as 'medu' ('mead') and the final word as 'gedricht'.

A3: As printed, the word 'is' was omitted before 'hroþor'.

A13: As printed, the word 'spellast' was given as 'spellest'.

A14: As printed, there was no mark of punctuation at the end of this line. Tolkien inserted a question mark, but in the Leeds manuscript he used an exclamation mark.

99

Natura Apis: Morali Ricardi Eremite (?1928)

Natura Apis is the tenth poem by Tolkien in *Songs for the Philologists* (1936), and the third of the three works he sent to E.V. Gordon at Leeds with a letter dated 2 January 1929, as an additional song to entertain students in the English School. Like *Lá, Húru* (no. 98), it is to be sung to the tune of 'O'Reilly'. Here we have transcribed the poem from the manuscript held in the Gordon archive at Leeds, and note significant differences with the 1936 printed text (p. 18).

Tolkien omitted reference to the chorus after the third stanza, though it is to be understood by a singer; in the printed *Songs* the chorus is given only after the first stanza. The acute accents above certain instances of *z* in the chorus indicate stress or emphasis in singing.

1.

The night is still young and our drinks are yet long,
The fire's burning bright and here brave is the throng,
So now I will sing you a sooth little song
Of the busy brown Bee — with a ding and a dong,
With a fal-lal-lal-la and a ź, z, z, ź
a ź, z, z ź z z ź z z ź (*thrice*)

2.

Three virtuous habits hath ev'ry brown Bee:
Ah no never, no never, idle is she;
If drone will not labour, then out bundles he
And the hive and the honey no more will he see!
With a fal-lal &c.

3.

No wind from her pathway the bee ever bore,
For ballast she beareth, and (yea, what is more)
There's good mother earth on her feet, though she soar;
She's no fool of a fly nor a dull dumbledore.
With &c.

4.

Yet gleaming she cleaneth her well-polished wings
That lift her aloft over lowlier things,
(But note also this that the Bees have their stings,
And leave oft a mark on those lowlier things).

5.

For Aristotle saith (in his quaint sort of Greek)
That Bees will give battle to robbers that seek
To harry their hives or their honey to sneak;
Their own will they hold, for the Bees are not meek!

6.

Let A, C, D, E F on broke-winded Gee
Go weary their ways to a long purgatoree!
Over all other letters the flower beareth B,
Yea, B is the best, for the B's you and me!

The final stanza of the manuscript text was not included in *Songs for the Philologists*; probably it was too esoteric for the University College London students printing the booklet. Tolkien himself felt, as he wrote on the verso of the Leeds manuscript, that 'the last verse is not very good'. In his personal copy (copy 1) of *Songs*, however, and also on the manuscript verso, he added by hand a new concluding quatrain:

O B bears the flower of the A B C D
As Birch bears the palm from each bush and each tree,
Or Bee doth her plunder from blossoms — so we
Will buzz with the buzz of the busy brown Bee.

On the significance of the birch (runic B) and its relation to the teaching of philology, 'scheme B', at the University of Leeds, see our discussion for poem no. 80.

The Latin title of this poem means 'The Nature of the Bee, a Moral Interpretation by Richard the Hermit'. (In his personal copy (copy 1) of *Songs* Tolkien altered the adjectival *Morali* to the noun *Moralitas*.) 'Richard the Hermit' is Richard Rolle, a fourteenth-century mystic and religious writer who abandoned his studies at Oxford to live a solitary life. Tolkien read his brief work, 'Moralia Richardi

Heremite de Natura Apis', in Kenneth Sisam's *Fourteenth Century Verse and Prose* when writing the glossary for that book if not before. Here *Natura Apis* adapts four of Richard's comments (Sisam, p. 41):

> 'The bee has thre kyndis. Ane es þat sho es neuer ydill, and scho es noghte with thaym þat will noghte wyrke, bot castys thaym owte, and puttes thaym awaye' ('The bee has three characteristics. One is that she is never idle, and does not associate with those that will not work, but casts them out, and drives them away').
>
> 'Anothire es þat when scho flyes scho takes erthe in hyr fette, þat scho be noghte lyghtly ouerheghede in the ayere of wynde' ('Another is that when she flyes she takes earth on her feet, that she not easily be blown too high in the windy air').
>
> 'The thyrde es þat scho kepes clene and bryghte hir wyngeȝ' ('The third is that she keeps her wings clean and bright').
>
> 'Arestotill sais þat þe bees are feghtande agaynes hym þat will drawe þaire hony fra thayme' ('Aristotle says that the bees fight against one who takes their honey from them').

Richard's aim was to draw from bee behaviour – and in part, Aristotle's description of bees in his history of animals – examples of moral life, such as that righteous people who love God are never idle, and that good people acknowledge themselves to be 'vile and erthely' so as not to be blown by the winds of vanity and pride. In medieval times, the bee exemplified the qualities of hard work and (spiritual) persistence; so too, says Tolkien, is it a model for diligent students of language.

Unlike Richard, Tolkien does not attempt to moralize, but effects a jocularity, and vocabulary, he would also apply in later works such as the Elves' songs in *The Hobbit* ('tra-la-la-lally', see poem no. 113) and in *Errantry* (poem no. 128). The repetition of *z z z z* or *z z z z z* thirty-five times in the course of the song must have been a challenge if the singers were in their cups. In his January 1929 letter to Gordon, Tolkien wrote of his 'mock-moral' poem that it 'goes well with a chorus buzzed entirely in *z* – it is approved by the family' (Gordon archive, Leeds).

Title: In his copy 1 of *Songs for the Philologists* Tolkien placed the subtitle of the poem in brackets, and changed 'Morali' to 'Moralitas'.

4: Here and throughout the poem as printed in *Songs*, 'bee' and 'bees' are not capitalized except for 'Bees' in l. 23.

5–6: As printed in *Songs*, 'fal-lal' etc. is 'fal-lal-lal là', none of the *z*'s is given an accent, and they are separated by only one comma, after the fifth *z* in l. 6.

8: As printed in *Songs*, this line reads 'Ah, no, never, no, never idle is she'.

25: 'Broke-winded', i.e. 'broken-winded', refers to a debilitating respiratory condition in horses.

26: 'Purgatoree', i.e. purgatory.

100

The Hills Are Old (?1928–?61 or ?62)

The Hills Are Old exists in a single manuscript, later inscribed by Tolkien 'Taunton 1928'. Taunton, Somerset, was the home of Christopher Wiseman, and it is possible that Tolkien visited his boyhood friend in 1928, though we have no independent evidence of him doing so. The inscription may reflect Tolkien's memory of writing the poem; we cannot be sure that the manuscript was written in 1928, but cannot date it any better. Revisions he marked in its text are, however, certainly later. It is not inconceivable that he revisited *The Hills Are Old* in 1961 or 1962 when choosing poems to include in *The Adventures of Tom Bombadil and Other Verses from the Red Book.*

We transcribe here, as A, the manuscript as it was first written, and as B the text incorporating Tolkien's revisions.

[A]

The hills are old, but older are the seas,
and older still the earth, more old the sun
and the illimitable stars that shine
upon the confines of the timeless deep
and everlasting nothingness of dark.
And we are young, like shivering babes new-born,
yet tired as blunted men with ancient toil,
wearier than hills, more restless than the seas,
lowly as stars on the confines of the dark,
we drag from shade to shadow under clouds,
looking like startled things beneath the trees,
like children play with pebbles on the shore,
desiring and unable to endure the world,
clasping the green earth with our naked arms,
and building in frail air a place of dreams —
places of dreams, lands and shores unmade,
seas, stars, and a darkness all our own,
our own, our own beautiful Unreal;
while the old hills and older Earth and Sun,
and stars untouched by us, go on,
on, on into the everlasting that must end
the timeless darkness that doth wait for all.

[B]

The hills are old, but older are the seas,
and older still the earth, more old the sun
and the illimitable stars that shine
upon the confines of the timeless deep
and everlasting nothingness of dark.
And we are young, like shivering babes new-born,
yet tired as blunted men with ancient toil,
wearier than hills, more restless than the seas,
lowly as stars on the confines of the dark,
we drag from shade to shadow under clouds,
looking like startled things beneath the trees,
like children play with pebbles on the shore,
desiring and unable to endure the world,
half clasping the green earth with naked arms,
half building in frail air a place of dreams —
places of dreams, lands and shores unmade,
seas, stars, and a darkness all our own,
our own, our own beautiful Unreal;
while the old hills and old Earth and old Sun,
and stars untouched by us, go on,
on, on into the never ending that must end
in timeless darkness that awaits them all.

The poem's theme of timelessness and the insignificance of Men beside the vastness of nature reminds one of earlier works by Tolkien, such as *The Grimness of the Sea* and its successors (no. 13) and *Dark* (no. 20).

A16: Above 'places of dreams' Tolkien wrote what appears to be 'forebears', but did not strike through the original text.

A21: Tolkien circled the first 'on' but did not delete it.

A22: Above 'doth wait' Tolkien wrote 'ever waits', before striking through 'that doth wait for all' and inserting 'that awaits them all'.

101

Natura Formice (et Significacio Simul) (?1928)

The beginnings of this poem are in two rough manuscripts, each written quickly and with not a few illegible words. Neither version has a title. One of the drafts, struck through, is clearly the earliest: its lines are fragmentary and in no certain order on the page. The other, less heavily worked, may or may not be complete at the point it ends. We give the latter text below as A, as best we can make it out, incorporating revisions Tolkien made in the course of writing.

[A]

There is no cant
about the ant
it does not rant
or agitate
for better pay
or shorter day,
but does obey
the Sovereign State.
It needs no joy
nor any toy,
but does employ
its time entire
in busy toil,
to till the soil
with service loyal
for minim hire
to guard the brood,
to gather food
for the multitude
(O not for self!),
to seek out seed
for workers' need
from grassy weed,
from pantry shelf,
barn or bin
or house or inn
it wealth doth win[.]
And wood & field

doth richly yield
all which concealed
in earthen halls[.]
It marches out
in warlike rout
And fights a bout,
or gladly falls
before the fire[.]
Bewails no woe
& says why so
or what's the use
only should I
consent to die
or herd green fly
or fuss with eggs
for common good
for all his brood
this would be done
with willing legs
I want a drink
and time to think
I will not sink

In the first manuscript, but omitted in the second, are the lines 'for three times eight' (i.e. twenty-four hours) and 'its every hour', replaced in the later text with 'its time entire'; 'six hour day'; 'and double pay'; and 'Bourgeois'. By *cant* we assume that Tolkien meant 'hypocritical or sanctimonious talk', as opposed to straightforward honesty. 'Minim hire' in line 16 is short for 'minimum hire'.

Probably with intervening workings now lost, the poem developed into a fair copy manuscript headed *Natura Formice (et Significacio Simul)*, given here as B from the Walter Hooper archive in the Bodleian Library.

[B]

There is no cant
    about the ant:
    it does not rant,
        or agitate
    for better pay
    or shorter day,
    but does obey
        the Sovereign State.

It needs no joy,
nor any toy,
but does employ
its time entire
in busy toil
to till the soil
with service loyal
for minim hire,

To guard the Brood,
to gather Food
for the Multitude
(O, not for self!),
to seek out seed
for winter's need
from grassy weed,
from pantry shelf.

From barn and bin,
from house and inn,
it wealth does win;
and underground
the fruitful yield
of wood and field
is then concealed
in grassy mound —

That fort and mart
with wondrous art
that it builds apart
with earthen walls
Thence it marches out
in warlike rout,
and fights a bout,
or gladly falls

Before the foe;
bewails no woe,
or says *Why so*?
or *What's the use*?

or *Why should I*
consent to die,
or herd green-fly;
and why the deuce

Do I tug and tustle,
and haste and hustle,
in busy bustle?
Why fuss with eggs
for the common good
of all this brood,
this multitude
with silly legs?

I want a drink!
and time to think!
I will not sink
my Ego thus!
The trodden track
ever there and back
does something lack —
I want to cuss!

Such a wicked word
is never heard;
no thoughts absurd
do vex its soul.
Its soul! Indeed
it does not heed
(it has no need)
such fancies droll.

O! emmet wise,
to organize,
to do what lies
before thy nose!
O! noble ant
to rail nor rant
to cast off cant,
and likewise clothes!

O perfect form
and city's norm
thus free from storm!
O government
of general will
plus perfect drill!
O holy hill!
O monument

That morals deep
doth endless keep
for helpless sheep
or mithered men.
The socialist
your turf has kissed,
Capitalist
your labourers' den

With envy fills.
And torn with ills
of wayward wills
can we debate
that words profane
(that we did feign
above) are vain
in antly state,

And yet are fine,
an outward sign
of soul divine
in foolish us?
Why would we drink?
Why would we think?
Why would not sink
our Egoes thus?

The later of the two drafts mentioned above (text A) is found on the back of the first manuscript of *Shadowland* (no. 93), which dates possibly to 1926, while the earlier is on the verso of the sheet containing *The Hills Are Old* (no. 100), dated to ?1928. We are inclined to assign the present work to the later end of this span: its content, with references to employment, service, 'the common good', 'general will', and so forth, seems to evoke the agitated state of labour relations in Britain following the General Strike of 1926, but before the country sank into deep depression in 1930. The fair copy manuscript from which we took version B appears to have been sent by Tolkien to, if not made for, C.S. Lewis, whom he first met as an Oxford English faculty colleague in May 1926. Lewis was a fast friend by the end of 1929, when Tolkien lent him the typescript of the *Lay of Leithian* (no. 92).

Also during this period in the late 1920s, as we have seen, Tolkien looked to medieval bestiary texts for inspiration, to the *Physiologus* and to Richard Rolle. From these, in ?1927 he produced *Fastitocalon* and *Iumbo* (nos. 95, 96), and in ?1928 *Natura Apis* (no. 99); *Natura Formice* ('The Nature of Ants') is of the same ilk. (See also Tolkien's later 'bestiary' verses, *The Merryman*, no. 137; *Grey as a Mouse*, i.e. *Oliphaunt*, no. 167; and *Cat*, no. 179.) *Fastitocalon* and *Iumbo* follow the bestiary division of *natura* (description) and *significacio* (meaning), but for *Natura Formice (et Significacio Simul)* Tolkien only nods to this in his title.

It seems clear, however, that he had the *Physiologus* explanation of the ant in mind when he wrote of its dutiful behaviour, acting in concert with its fellows for the common Brood, 'seek[ing] out seed | for winter's need | from grassy weed'. 'Ðe mire is magti' ('the ant is mighty'), the Old English poet says.

> In ðe heruest
> hardilike gangeð,
> and renneð rapelike,
> and resteð hire seldum,
> and fecheð hire fode
> ðer ge it mai finden,
> gaddreð ilkines sed
> boðen of wude and of wed,
> of corn and of gres . . .

At harvest time the ant rests little, but fetches food where it may be found, in wood or field, gathering seeds. It seeks out wheat in preference to barley, and each ant carries a grain in its mouth, taking it to the nest where it is kept for the winter. Its industry and efficiency, pursued peacefully, without complaint, were to be a lesson to readers. So it is for a few stanzas in Tolkien's verse, until the violence of his age intrudes: the ant gathers food, but also 'marches out in warlike rout' and 'gladly falls before the foe'. Nor were those of Tolkien's time willing to obey without question. 'Why so?' they ask, and 'What's the use?' Much had changed in the minds and hearts of Men since they marched willingly by the thousands onto the killing fields of the Great War.

A29: Next to this line is an alternate reading: 'The fruitful yield'.

A42: 'Green fly' (in B48 'green-fly') may refer to the common green bottle fly (*Lucilia sericata*) or to the insect also known as the aphid.

B34–41: In the manuscript these lines are not indented as clearly as in other stanzas – there is even a hint of a break between ll. 37 and 38 – but we have assumed that Tolkien meant them to have the same format and transcribed them accordingly.

B34: *Mart* here presumably has a broad meaning, more or less indicating a 'gathering place', at any rate another construction by the ants, like 'fort'.

B74: *Emmet* is another word for 'ant'. Old English *ǣmete* became *āmete* and *ēmete* in Middle English; the former became Modern English *ant* and the latter its synonym *emmet*.

B113: 'Egoes' is Tolkien's spelling of the plural.

102

A Song of Bimble Bay (?1928)

Around 1928 Tolkien wrote six poems centred on an imaginary English coastal town and harbour, collectively the Tales and Songs of Bimble Bay. In some of these, 'Bimble Bay' is not much more than a name for the barest sketch of a setting; in others, the place is fleshed out, so that one could almost draw a map. Lacking evidence for precisely when Tolkien wrote each of the 'Bimble Bay' poems – or, alternatively, how he thought to arrange them (excepting *The Dragon's Visit*, no. 107) – we have chosen to present them in the order they appear in one of the four groups of his preserved poetry ('Verse File I'). The first is *A Song of Bimble Bay*, a light fantasy with the playfulness of Lewis Carroll or Edward Lear.

Three manuscripts of this poem are extant. Tolkien wrote the earliest (A) quickly, and at first without a title: he added this later, in red (fountain) ink, while also marking a few alterations. His second manuscript was based on the first before revision, and itself has a few changes or potential changes lightly indicated. Presumably as a lark, Tolkien wrote it out in a medieval insular script, complete with archaic characters such as the thorn (*þ*) and decorated initials, the whole in black and red inks. At the end of each stanza, as we illustrate in the first stanza below, the 'chorus' is to be read (or sung) twice, followed by a repetition of the third and fourth lines of the verse.

[A] There was an old man by Bimble Bay,
He slid down hill on an old tin tray.
When he came to the bottom he bumped his nose,
And tore a big hole in his beautiful clothes
    In Bimble Bay
    In Bimble Bay
When he came to the bottom he bumped his nose,
And tore a hole in his beautiful clothes.

He washed in the waves and sang 'hooray!
There are lovely stones in Bimble Bay.
I will build a house on the long seashore
And never slide back up the hill no more.
    Hooray, hooray! [' etc.]

The tide came in over Bimble Bay
And washed the man and his tray away.
He sang as he floated out to sea:
'I'll never get home in time for tea!'
        In Bimble Bay &c.

He came to the land on the other side
And he lay in the sun till his trousers dried;
And the people said 'what a funny fish
Has washed ashore on an old tin dish!'
        On the other side &c.

They tried to cook him; but out of the pot
He jumped as soon as the water was hot,
And off he ran and took his tray,
And the people chased him far away
        Far away &c.

At last he came to the Mountains Blue,
And climbed to where the fir trees grew,
And he looked and looked and far away
He could see the hills of Bimble Bay
        Far away &c.

And he sang and said: 'You can eat your tea,
You can eat your dinner. Don't wait for me;
For I am going to cross the Mountains Blue,
And never come back no more to you.'
        Don't wait for me &c.

And over the Mountains Blue he went.
He slid down hill, till the tray was bent;
And he lost his hat and lost his shoes,
And both his knees had a big black bruise.
        Down he went &c.

They picked him up and gave him tea
And jelly and jam, and rubbed his knee
With oil and treacle and cream and soap,
And tied his trousers up with rope
        With jelly & jam &c.

They polished his tray till it shone as bright
As the sun by day and the moon by night;
They gave him slippers and a shady hat,
And he laughed and laughed till he grew fat
A shady hat &c.

And so he lives right far away
And never comes back to Bimble Bay.
Though the tide comes in as the tea bell rings
Beyond the Mountains Blue he sings:
Eat your dinner
Eat your tea
Here I am, here I'll stay
And never come back to Bimble Bay.

The third manuscript of the poem, transcribed below as B, is a fair copy, with 'Tales & Songs of Bimble Bay' written at the top of the first page in red. Later Tolkien also added to the page the words 'Air The Fox Went Out', indicating that *A Song of Bimble Bay* is to be sung to the same traditional, and variously titled, air or tune as *The Root of the Boot* (no. 83).

[B] There was an old man of Bimble Bay;
He slid down hill on an old tin tray.
When he came to the bottom he bumped his nose,
And burst his buttons and tore his clothes.
In Bimble Bay
In Bimble Bay
When he came to the bottom he bumped his nose,
And burst his buttons and tore his clothes.

He washed in the waves, and sang: 'Hooray!
There are lovely stones in Bimble Bay.
I will build a house on the long sea-shore,
And never slide back up hill no more'.
Hooray, hooray! &c.

The tide came in over Bimble Bay,
And washed the man and his tray away,
And he sang as he floated out to sea:
'I'll never get home in time for tea!'
He was washed away! &c.

He came to the land on the Other Side,
And he lay in the sun, till his trousers dried.
The People said: 'What a very funny fish
Has washed ashore on an old tin dish!'
    On the Other Side &c.

They tried to cook him, but out of the pot
He jumped as soon as the water was hot;
And off he ran, and took his tray,
And the People chased him far away.
    Far away &c.

At last he came to the Mountains Blue,
And climbed to where the fir-trees grew;
He looked and looked, and far away
He could see the hills of Bimble Bay.
    Far away &c.

And he sang and said: 'You can eat your tea,
You can eat your dinner! Don't wait for me,
For I am going to cross the Mountains Blue
And never come back no more to you.'
    Don't wait for me &c.

And over the Mountains Blue he went;
He slid down hill, and the tray was bent,
And he lost his hat, and he lost his shoes,
And both his knees had a big black bruise:
    Down he went &c.

They picked him up and gave him tea
With jelly and jam, and rubbed each knee
With oil and treacle, cream and soap,
And tied his trousers up with rope.
    With jelly and jam &c.

They polished his tray, till it shone as bright
As the sun by day and the moon by night;
They gave him slippers and a shady hat,
And he laughed and laughed, till he grew fat.
    A shady hat &c.

And so he lives right far away
And never comes back to Bimble Bay.
Though the tide comes in and the tea-bell rings,
Beyond the Mountains Blue he sings:
'Eat your dinner
Eat your tea
Here I am and here I'll stay,
And never come back to Bimble Bay.'

A1: *Bimble* in the sense 'short, meandering walk' appears to have been coined long after Tolkien composed his 'Bimble Bay' poems. In the nineteenth century, however, *bimble* was in use as a nonsense word, as in the nursery rhyme which begins (in one version):

There was an old woman, who rode on a broom,
With a high gee ho! gee humble;
And she took her Tom Cat behind for a groom
With a bimble, bamble, bumble.

A4: Here, as elsewhere in the poem, Tolkien revised the first manuscript with the reading of the third.

A11: In the second manuscript this line begins 'I'll build', but returned in B to 'I will build'.

A13: This line originally read 'Hooray Hooray', was changed apparently in the course of composition to 'In Bimble Bay &c.', then again to 'Hooray hooray'. In the second manuscript the chorus reads 'Hurray, hurray!'

A19: The 'other side' (capitalized in the third manuscript) is presumably the other side of the sea, into which the old man was swept.

A21: In the second manuscript Tolkien considered whether to change 'funny' to 'curious'.

A29: The 'Mountains Blue', or Blue Mountains, of the poem are not to be confused with the Ered Luin, the Blue Mountains of Middle-earth west of the Shire.

A30: In the second manuscript Tolkien wrote in the margin what appears to be 'fog-trees', presumably as a possible replacement for 'fir-trees'.

A32: In the second manuscript Tolkien considered whether to change 'hills' to 'cliffs'.

A34: 'Eat your tea': By *tea* Tolkien is referring to a traditional British afternoon meal.

A54: In the second manuscript Tolkien considered whether to change 'right' to 'now'.

103

The Progress of Bimble · *Progress in Bimble Town* (?1928)

In the second of his 'Bimble Bay' poems Tolkien expressed his feelings about quiet seaside towns transformed by tourists, who brought crowds, noise, litter, and petrol fumes, but also by the accommodations made to entice visitors, such as postcard racks, cinemas, and esplanades. He and his family were themselves no strangers to the English coast. For example, Humphrey Carpenter records in his *Biography* that the Tolkiens visited Filey, in Yorkshire, for some weeks in 1922. 'Tolkien did not like the place', Carpenter says; 'he called it "a very nasty little suburban seaside resort"' (p. 105). On that occasion, Tolkien had to take time from his holiday to mark School Certificate examination papers, 'but he also wrote several poems'. Carpenter implies that the 'Tales and Songs of Bimble Bay' date from this earlier time, but he was mistaken.

The Tolkiens' eventful second visit to Filey, in 1925, coincided with a great storm, which led to the story *Roverandom*. Originally (as we have said) an oral tale told in 1925 to the eldest Tolkien boys, this was written down probably in 1927 and partly illustrated that summer while the family holidayed at another popular destination, the charming Lyme Regis in Dorset. In private correspondence, Christopher Tolkien has denied that Lyme Regis, which his father visited many times, was the inspiration for Bimble Town or Bimble Bay; it seemed largely unspoiled when we ourselves visited there in the 1990s. Filey seems a good 'Bimble' candidate, to judge by photographs of the town and beach from the 1920s, but in truth we do not need to look for one place alone as Tolkien's model.

The earliest version of this poem, entitled *The Progress of Bimble*, runs to 131 lines and exists in a single manuscript, probably a fair copy. We give this text below as A.

[A]

Bimble town has a steep street,
it runs down with many houses,
tall ones, short ones; shops with meat;
shops with cabbages; shops with blouses,

jumpers, jerseys, and umbrellas;
a post office (new and squalid);
a library filled with best-sellers
in yellow jackets; an old solid
many-windowed inn where motors
make strong smells, and no horse goes
in cobbled yard; a place where bloaters
from wooden boxes lie in rows
(brought by train for sea-side air);
a pharmacy with sunburn-lotion
and picture-cards (of Godknowswhere
and fat women dipped in ocean);
a toy-bazaar with things of tin,
bits of crock, and all the news;
windows, windows with chocolates in,
cigarettes, and gum one chews
(wrapped in paper, cased in card,
for folk to strew on grass and shore);
loud garages where working hard
grimy people bang and roar,
and engines buzz, and the lights flare
all night long — a merry noise!
Sometimes through it (this is rare)
one can hear the shouts of boys;
sometimes late, when motor-bikes
are not passing with a screech,
one hears faintly (if one likes)
the sea still at it on the beach.

At what? At churning orange-rind,
piling up banana-skins,
gnawing paper, trying to grind
a broth of bottles, packets, tins,
before a new day comes with more;
before next morning's charabangs,
stopping at the old inn-door,
with reek and rumble, hoots and clangs,
bring more folk to Godknowswhere,
to Theydontmind, to Bimble town,
where the steep street (that once was fair)
with many houses staggers down.

There once at night a quiet lay
on shuttered window, cottage dark,
and slow moonlight far away;
to wind in trees then one could hark
and shingle rolled in Bimble Bay.
But seldom strangers came at all,
and Bimble had its work by day;
the mill went by the waterfall,
ships were laden, handlooms went,
wrights were busy — for their play
with wind and sea must rest content
the fools that came to Bimble Bay[.]

Wherefore none can doubt at all
that Bimble daily now improves,
with bright advertisements on wall
and corrugated-iron rooves;
in the summer full of touts,
in the winter, workless, cold —
The mayor at least, he has no doubts
(he is bald), he makes so bold
as he affirms 'this Bimble Bay
a coming place, a tourist centre'.
That means he hopes to see the Bay
so jammed with cars you cannot enter;
little half-baked villas raising
on slope and cliff their useless poles;
and cinemas, and most amazing
'palaces of fun'; and holes
where men drink standing; ragged shanties;
radio-bands and gramophones;
minstrel-songs where once were chanties;
esplanades where once were stones.
He's glad the days are past when fish
were caught in Bimble Bay by Bimble men
(straight from hook and net to dish),
when his land-agent's ugly den
was not yet built and not yet paying
were stores of distant companies
doing a margarine-purveying
jam-adulterating bizz
throughout the sea board counties fair;

those unprogressive days, ere Ben
(who now keeps tents for the same mayor)
was ever born. But still Ben minds
when boats from Bimble went with sail
to other lands, when ale was ale,
when sunshine dried the nets and lines
where Bimble men now stand and spit
in the brown sea or tout for trips
(three bob an hour), or dully sit
staring at scum from oily ships.
And Ben (like me) is not quite sure
what is the purpose of this noise,
why one rushes to sea and moor,
hearing them fair, and then destroys
and leaves them filthy where one stood.
But Ben remembers that as a lad
many things were in wild and wood,
(remember Ben's considered mad!),
in sea and field and by the road,
in old towns, villages, and lanes,
that motor-headlights have never showed,
that can't be got in aeroplanes.
But Ben thinks apples from a yard,
or herrings fresh from Bimble Bay,
better than 'pine-chunks' (devilish hard)
or 'pilchards' packed in U.S.A.

I myself would rather walk
once in a life to some small town
with old walls as white as chalk
to the deep sea going down,
where men wear beards and women hair,
and sing at work until they die,
where horses step, and ringing fair
are bells in towers beneath the sky,
where night is night and day is day,
and holy Mass is still in town,
and men to Mary still may pray
to the deep sea going down —
men rush six times a blessed year
with other herds in rattling car
to place where Light and Progress are

(i.e. the same fish, and same small beer,
same talk and racket, same tinned food,
same stores (same names), same clothes and gear,
same fags, same rags, same pictures lewd,
same 'fun', same scum, as we have here.

Probably in 1931, Tolkien reduced his poem to only its first forty-four lines, copying them into a second manuscript. Still called *The Progress of Bimble*, its surviving text was identical to that of the first manuscript except that in line 1 Tolkien changed 'Bimble town' to 'Bimble-Bay' ('Bimble town' remained in line 42), and he removed the brackets in line 43. Two typescripts of the shorter version followed, made by Tolkien on his Hammond machine. Both of these are entitled *Progress in Bimble Town*. The earliest of the two follows the second manuscript, except that Tolkien added by hand a longer title, *Bimble Town or Progress by the Sea*, not taken up in later versions, and a new final line, 'See Britain First!' New line 45 is included *ab initio* in the later typescript, as are two lines added below the title, which read '(dedicated to the Mayor and Corporation)'. In this text Tolkien also made a few minor changes, mainly of punctuation.

The later typescript seems to have been the copy Tolkien sent to the *Oxford Magazine*, who published the poem in their number for 15 October 1931, p. 22. We transcribe the final, printed version below as B. In the magazine the poem is credited to 'K. Bagpuize', a pseudonym for Tolkien which plays on the name of Kingston Bagpuize, a village west of Oxford.

[B]

Bimble-Bay has a steep street:
it runs down with many houses,
tall ones, short ones; shops with meat,
shops with cabbages, shops with blouses,
jersies, jumpers and umbrellas;
a post-office (new and squalid);
a library filled with best-sellers
in yellow jackets; an old, solid,
manywindowed inn where motors
make strong smells, and no horse goes
in cobbled yard; a place where bloaters
from wooden boxes lie in rows
(brought by train for sea-side air);
a pharmacy with sunburn-lotion
and picture-cards (of Godknowswhere

and fat women dipped in ocean);
a toy bazaar with things of tin,
and bits of crock, and all the news;
windows, windows with chocolates in,
cigarettes, and gum one chews
(wrapped in paper, cased in card,
for folk to strew on grass and shore);
loud garages, where toiling hard
grimy people bang and roar,
and engines buzz, and the lights flare
all night long — a merry noise!
    Sometimes through it (this is rare)
one can hear the shouts of boys;
sometimes late, when motor-bikes
are not passing with a screech,
one hears faintly (if one likes)
the sea still at it on the beach.
At what? At churning orange-rind,
piling up banana-skins,
gnawing paper, trying to grind
a broth of bottles, packets, tins,
before a new day comes with more,
before next morning's charabangs,
stopping at the old inn-door
with reek and rumble, hoots and clangs,
bring more folk to Godknowswhere,
to Theydontcare, to Bimble Town,
where the steep street, that once was fair,
with many houses staggers down.

See Britain First!

Throughout the several texts of this work Tolkien seems to have found it hard to make up his mind as to the forms of 'Bimble Town' and 'Bimble Bay' (to give these two variants only as examples). In the first manuscript, the name in the first line (A1) seems to have an internal space, i.e. 'Bimble town', with no second capital, but could be continuous 'Bimbletown', while in line 42 (A42) it appears to be 'Bimbletown' but could be 'Bimble town' written without care for the space. We are inclined to think that 'Bimble town' is correct, to indicate the town called simply 'Bimble' in lines 51, 58, and 89, and to distinguish it from the bay by the same name, written 'Bimble

Bay' in five lines of text A. In the first line of the second manuscript, Tolkien refers to the bay, as hyphenated 'Bimble-Bay', rather than to the town, which however is named in line 42, probably as 'Bimble town' though again 'Bimbletown' is also possible. But then in the first typescript one finds 'Bimble Bay', thus, in line 1, and 'Bimble-town' in line 41, with 'Bimble Town' in the added title, and in the second manuscript there is 'Bimble Bay' again (line 1), but 'Bimble Town' (line 42). Perhaps as an editorial choice, the published text has the hyphenated 'Bimble-Bay' once more in line 1.

In its longer form, Tolkien's poem falls conceptually into three parts. The first is mainly descriptive of the current state of affairs in a popular, commercialized seaside resort, concentrating on what the poet dislikes, especially pollution by noise and rubbish. There is also an occasional note of loss: horses replaced by motor-cars overwhelming the sound of the sea. The brief middle part of the work, lines 45–56, describes the town as it once was, with its people earning honest livings as fishermen, weavers, workers at a water-driven mill. Finally, Tolkien considers 'improvements' that have been introduced by the mayor which have turned the town into 'a coming place, a tourist centre', providing jobs of different kinds but less rewarding. Instead of fishing, the boatmen conduct tours. Instead of local apples and fresh fish from the bay, one eats hard 'pine-chunks' (tinned pineapple) and sardines ('pilchards') imported from abroad. Tolkien also nods to earlier days when one could visit a small town and find a Catholic Mass and men praying to the Virgin Mary. His sad complaint about the 'same talk and racket, same tinned food, | same stores (same names)' everywhere one goes, where 'men rush . . . with other herds in rattling car' was remarkably prescient for the late twenties; today, chains and franchises are very much the rule. As we have noticed in relation to *The Motor-cyclists* (no. 63), Tolkien expressed similar thoughts in *Roverandom*, where 'motor after motor racketed by, filled (Rover thought) with the same people, all making all speed (and all dust and all smell) to somewhere', half of them not knowing where they are going, or why (p. 87).

Although the later version of the poem is dedicated 'to the Mayor and Corporation', no town official is named in the published lines, and the mayor's ambitions are described only in the text omitted from the *Oxford Magazine* printing. Perhaps Tolkien added the dedication to let his readers know succinctly whom to blame. Douglas A. Anderson is probably right to suggest, in *The Annotated Hobbit*, that 'the Mayor and Corporation' owe their inspiration to the officials of Hamelin in Robert Browning's 'Pied Piper' (1842), which despite

Tolkien's known antipathy towards the work also seems to have inspired the corrupt mayor and councillors of Lake-town in *The Hobbit.*

In her doctoral thesis *An Exploration of Changing Visions of Faërie through His Non-Middle-earth Poetry* (2021), Penelope Anne Holdaway draws parallels between *Progress in Bimble Town* and *England and the Octopus* by the architect Clough Williams-Ellis, the latter first published in 1928 by the Council for the Preservation of Rural England. Williams-Ellis did not speak out against the widespread changes occurring to the rural English environment so much as against the lack of thought, and of beauty, that went into them. He was by no means the first to do so, following the nineteenth-century preservation efforts of John Ruskin and William Morris, and the sentiments of poets like Tom Taylor (in Myles Birket Foster's 1863 *Pictures of English Landscape*) when country inns on quiet roads began to give way to the press of railway tourists:

> But now we are ruled by the iron-ways,
> Where no Red Lion [inn sign] swings from its tree;
> At the Station Hotel the traveller stays,
> And few are the pence and scanty the praise
> That come to the landlord of other days. . . .

But Williams-Ellis's book was pioneering for the twentieth century, and influential. We do not know if Tolkien read *England and the Octopus*, and he could speak well from personal observation; still, his sentiments and those of Williams-Ellis, about noise, and fouled air, and litter, are very much of a piece.

A5: In the U.S.A. a *jumper* is a *pullover sweater*.

A7–8: Douglas A. Anderson suggests in *The Annotated Hobbit* that the mention of 'best-sellers | in yellow jackets' 'probably refers to the publications of the firm Victor Gollancz Limited, founded in 1927, whose books for many years sported bright yellow dust jackets' (2nd edn., p. 254). This may be so, though Gollancz would not have been in operation very long to have filled a library with its books – which included many works by distinguished authors – by *c.* 1928. The London publisher Hodder & Stoughton, however, had issued mysteries, thrillers, and westerns in its 'H&S Yellow Jacket' line since 1917, following on the Victorian 'yellowbacks'.

A11: A 'cobbled yard' was typical of a coaching inn, where horses could be stabled (like the Prancing Pony at Bree in *The Lord of the Rings*). A *bloater* is technically a herring cured by bloating, i.e. salting and smoking lightly, but Tolkien is using it as slang to mean an overweight, unattractive person.

A12: The 'wooden boxes' are small huts which served as changing-rooms for bathers, who 'lie in rows' on the beach.

A15–16: 'Picture-cards', i.e. picture postcards. It was, and to an extent still is, the custom for vacationers to send postcards to friends or relatives with a photograph of their destination on one side. In earlier days, the card might have had instead a picture of a comic figure, sometimes notably fat or thin, or sexually suggestive (compare l. 130, 'pictures lewd').

A17: A 'toy-bazaar' may be a shop or arcade of shops with fancy goods, including cheap toys ('things of tin', as opposed to wood).

A18: 'Crock', i.e. crockery – perhaps with the legend 'Souvenir of Bimble Bay'. 'All the news', i.e. newspapers and magazines.

A29–30: In regard to screeching motor-bikes, compare poem no. 63, *The Motor-cyclists*.

A38: A *charabanc*, pronounced *charabang* ('sharra-bang') in colloquial British English, is a coach, here probably a motor-coach, usually open-topped, popular for transporting sight-seers.

A72–73: 'Holes | where men drink standing' are drinking-dens compared with reputable bars with tables and chairs. 'Ragged shanties' is a redundancy, *shanties* being crudely-built shacks by definition (in this context; compare *chanties*, l. 75, often spelled *shanties* 'sea-songs, originally sung by sailors while doing manual labour').

A83–84: Tolkien's point about 'a margarine-purveying | jam-adulterating bizz', i.e. business, is that neither margarine, a manufactured substitute for butter, nor jam made with ingredients other than are found in 'pure' recipes, is the genuine (traditional) article.

A88: 'Ben minds', i.e. Ben remembers.

A94: 'Three bob', i.e. three shillings in pre-decimal British currency.

A126: 'Light and Progress' is one of a number of phrases used to promote the (usually) scientific development of civilization or, more generally and whether warranted or not, whatever change to society the user wishes to support.

A130: By 'rags' Tolkien probably means (cheap) newspapers or magazines.

B5: Tolkien changed 'jumpers, jerseys' in A to 'jumpers, jersies' in the second manuscript; the latter carried into the first typescript, but was changed to 'jersies, jumpers' in the second typescript.

B7: In the second typescript the word 'filled' was omitted, presumably by accident as it appears in the printed poem.

B42: In the first typescript, Tolkien changed by hand 'Theydontmind' to 'Theydontcare', but retained 'Theydontmind' in the second typescript. If, as we think, the second typescript was the copy-text for the *Oxford Magazine* printer, Tolkien presumably changed the 'name' in proof.

B45: 'See Britain First!' possibly alludes to the advertising campaign 'See Britain First on Shell' launched by Shell Oil in 1925, to promote tourism by car – fuelled and lubricated by Shell products. The slogan was to be seen everywhere on posters still in the early 1930s.

104

Glip (?1928)

There are two manuscripts of the poem *Glip* in Tolkien's papers. Both appear to be fair copies; no draft workings are extant. Each manuscript, unusually, is written in green ink, and each is almost identical to the other, except for a few marks of punctuation and line 17: there one version reads 'He slinks through weeds at highwater mark', and the other 'He slinks through the weeds at water mark'. Here we have transcribed the former copy, on which Tolkien wrote a decorative title and the words 'Tales and Songs of Bimble Bay'.

Under the cliffs of Bimble Bay
    Is a little cave of stone
With wet walls of shining grey;
    And on the floor a bone,
A white bone that is gnawed quite clean
    With sharp white teeth.
But inside nobody can be seen —
    He lives far underneath,
Under the floor, down a long hole
    Where the sea gurgles and sighs.
Glip is his name, as blind as a mole
    In his two round eyes
While daylight lasts; but when night falls
    With a pale gleam they shine
Like green jelly, and out he crawls
    All long and wet with slime.
He slinks through weeds at highwater mark
    To where the mermaid sings,
The wicked mermaid singing in the dark
    And threading golden rings
On wet hair; for many ships
    She draws to the rock to die.
And Glip listens, and quietly slips
    And lies in shadow by.
It is there that Glip steals his bones.
    He is a slimy little thing

Sneaking and crawling under fishy stones,
    And slinking home to sing
A gurgling song in his damp hole;
    But after the last light
There are darker and wickeder things that prowl
    On Bimble rocks at night.

In his *Biography* Humphrey Carpenter describes Glip, 'a strange slimy creature who lives beneath the floor of a cave and has pale luminous eyes', as a glimpse 'of important things to come' (p. 106). His inference is clearly to Gollum in *The Hobbit*, a similar being with similar gruesome habits, in a different context:

> There are strange things living in the pools and lakes in the hearts of mountains: fish whose fathers swam in . . . and never swam out again . . . ; also there are other things more slimy than fish. . . . Deep down here by the dark water lived old Gollum. I don't know where he came from, nor who or what he was. He was Gollum – as dark as darkness, except for two big round pale eyes. . . . Goblin he thought good, when he could get it; but he took care they never found him out. He just throttled them from behind, if they ever came down alone anywhere near the edge of the water, while he was prowling about. [*The Hobbit*, ch. 5]

In *The Annotated Hobbit* Douglas A. Anderson calls Glip Gollum's 'antecedent', not mincing words (2nd edn., p. 119), and indeed, the similarity is too great to discount. The connection is especially likely if Tolkien wrote *Glip* around the same time that he began to work on *The Hobbit* (see our discussion for poem no. 108).

The name *Glip* is nowhere explained by Tolkien, and it seems pointless to speculate on what it means, if in fact it is more than a random sound, like the gurgling described twice in the poem. It may be like *Mewlips*, pure invention by the author. The poem *Glip* in fact recalls the eerieness of *The Mewlips* (*Knocking at the Door*, no. 94), with its bones and slime, and in this it stands in contrast to the other, lighter verses in the 'Bimble Bay' series.

105

The Bumpus · *William and the Bumpus* · *Perry-the-Winkle* (?1928–61)

The 'Bumpus' has a tail long enough to 'thump', flat, flapping feet, a lap to sit in, and a sweet disposition to belie his startling appearance – this much we can glean from the poem in its earliest versions. Also, that he is not an ogre, a giant, or a goblin, or a dragon or a gnome, let alone an ordinary person, as he is set apart from all of these. What is he, then? Something unique, and we are fortunate that Tolkien illustrated him at the top of the first manuscript of this poem: plump and lizard-like, with an apron tied around his middle. Probably his smile is meant to appear friendly, but as drawn his face is not unlike that of the sinister dragon in Tolkien's 'Silmarillion' illustration *Glórund Sets Forth to Seek Túrin*, painted in September 1927 (Hammond and Scull, *J.R.R. Tolkien: Artist and Illustrator*, fig. 47).

The curious Bumpus is the subject of the work we are treating as the fourth of Tolkien's 'Bimble Bay' poems, though the earliest of its texts, a fair copy manuscript, originally had nothing to do with that setting. We give its first version, entitled *The Bumpus*, here as A.

[A]

The Bumpus sat on an old grey stone
And sang his lonely song:
'O why, o why should I live all alone
In this beautiful land of Bong?
The trees are tall & the fields are green,
The sun shines all the day,
But never an ogre or giant is seen,
No goblins come to stay.

The dragons have gone, and the gnomes don't call,
And people slam the door,
Whenever they hear my flat feet fall
Or my tail along the floor.'
He stroked his tail and he looked at his feet,
And he said: 'they may be long,
But I have a kind heart and my smile is sweet;
And sweet and soft my song.'

The Bumpus went out, and who did he meet
But old Mrs. Thomas and all
With umbrella and basket walking the street;
And softly he did call:
'Dear Mrs. Thomas, good day to you!
I hope you are quite well?'
But she dropped her brolly and basket too
And yelled a frightful yell.

Policeman Pott was a-standing near;
When he heard that awful cry,
He turned all purple and pink with fear,
And swiftly turned to fly.
The Bumpus followed surprised and sad.
'Don't go!' he gently said;
But old Mrs. Thomas ran home like mad
And hid beneath her bed.

The Bumpus then came to the market-place
And looked up over the walls.
The sheep went wild when they saw his face,
The cows jumped from their stalls.
Old Farmer Hogg he spilled his beer,
And the butcher threw his knives,
And Harry and his father howled with fear
And ran to save their lives.

The Bumpus sat and sadly wept
Outside the cottage door;
And William Winkle out he crept
And sat down on the floor:
'Why do you weep, you great big lump,
And wash the step like rain?'
The Bumpus gave his tail a thump
And smiled a smile again:

'O William Winkle, my lad,' he said;
'Come, you're the boy for me,
And though you ought to be in bed
I'll take you home to tea.

Jump on my back and hold on tight!'
    And off they went flop, flap;
And William had a feast that night,
    And sat on the Bumpus' lap.

There was toast, and buttered pikelets too,
    And jam and cream and cake;
And the Bumpus made a scrumptious Gloo,
    And showed him how to bake,
To bake the beautiful Bumpus-bread
    And bannocks light and brown;
And then he tucked him up in a bed
    Of feathers and thistle-down.

'Bill Winkle, where have you been?' they said.
    'I have been to a Bumpus tea,
And I feel so fat, for I have fed
    On Bumpus bread' said he.
The people all knocked at the Bumpus' door:
    'O bake, O bake, O bake,
O bake for us, please', they all now roar
    [']A beautiful Bumpus cake!'

Policeman Pott came puffing fast;
    And made them form a queue.
And old Mrs. Thomas was late and last;
    And her bonnet was all askew.
'Go home! go home!' the Bumpus said.
    'Too many there are of you!
Only on Thursdays I bake my bread,
    And then but for one or two.

Go home! go home, for goodness sake!
    I did not expect a call,
I have no pikelets, toast, or cake,
    For William has eaten all.
Old Mrs. Thomas and Mr Pott
    I wish no more to see.
Good bye! Don't argue, it's much too hot —
    Bill Winkle's the boy for me!'

Now William Winkle he grew so fat
A-eating of Bumpus-bread,
His waistcoat bust, and never a hat
Would sit upon his head.
And Every Thursday he went to tea
And sat on the kitchen mat
And smaller the Bumpus seemed to be
As he grew fat and fat.

And Bill a Baker great became:
Right through the land of Bong
From sea to sea there went his fame
Of his bread both short and long.
But it war'nt so good as Bumpus bread;
No jam was like the Gloo
That every Thursday the Bumpus spread
And William used to chew!

Tolkien marked this text for revision, then made a fresh copy. The second manuscript of the poem is identical to its first except for five changes we have described in notes, and more substantial alterations to its first two stanzas, given here as B. It was at this stage that Tolkien brought the poem explicitly into the 'Bimble Bay' series.

[B]

The Bumpus sat on an old grey stone
And sang his lonely lay:
'O why, o why should I live all alone
In the hills of Bimble Bay?
The grass is green, the sky is blue,
The sun shines on the sea,
But the Dragons have crossed the Mountains Blue
And come no more to me.

No Trolls or Ogres are left at all,
And People slam the door
Whenever they hear my flat feet fall
Or my tail along the floor.'
He stroked his tail and he looked at his feet,
And he said: 'They may be long,
But my heart is kind, and my smile is sweet,
And sweet and soft my song.'

Unusually among Tolkien's poems, we can date the second manuscript of *The Bumpus* moderately well, as a draft of its first ten lines is written on the back of a sheet of workings for the *Lay of Leithian* (no. 92), specifically a part whose finished text – made probably not much later than the draft – Tolkien dated to 29 March 1928. We suspect that it was the revised version of *The Bumpus*, which Tolkien copied in a fine hand, that he sent to his publisher George Allen & Unwin on 30 September 1946, with other poems, to fill out a volume with his story *Farmer Giles of Ham*, then being considered for publication.

With its third version, now a typescript made on the Hammond machine, Tolkien changed the poem significantly and expanded it to 111 lines. We give this text, now entitled *William and the Bumpus*, below as C. Tolkien included only a single ornament, following line 72.

[C]

The Bumpus sat on an old grey stone
    and sang his lonely lay:
'O! why, O! why should I live all alone
    in the hills of Bimble Bay?
The grass is green, the sky is blue,
    the sun shines on the sea,
But Dragons now are far and few,
    and never come to me.

No Trolls or Ogres are left at all,
    and People slam the door,
Whenever they hear my flat feet fall
    or my tail along the floor.'
He stroked his tail, he looked at his feet,
    and he said: 'They may be rough;
But my heart is soft, my smile is sweet,
    and my cooking good enough!'

The Bumpus went out, and who did he meet
    but old Mrs. Thomas and all
With umbrella and basket walking the street;
    and he smiled and stopped to call:
'Dear Mrs. Thomas, good day to you!
    I hope you are quite well?'
But she dropped her brolly and basket too,
    and yelled a frightful yell.

Policeman Pott was standing near;
    when he heard that awful cry,
He turned all purple and pink with fear,
    and swiftly turned to fly.
The Bumpus followed surprised and sad:
    'Don't go!', he gently said;
But old Mrs. Thomas ran home like mad
    and hid beneath the bed.

The Bumpus came to the market-place
    and peeped above the walls:
The sheep went wild when they saw his face;
    and the cows jumped from their stalls.
Old Farmer Hogg, he spilled his beer;
    and the butcher threw his knives;
And Harry and his father howled with fear,
    and ran to save their lives.

The Bumpus sadly sat and wept
    outside a cottage door;
And William Winkle, out he crept
    and sat down on the floor:
'O! why do you weep, you great big lump,
    and wash the step like rain?'
The Bumpus gave his tail a thump,
    and smiled a smile again.

'O! William Winkle, my lad,' he said,
    [']come; you're the boy for me;
And though you ought to be in bed,
    I'll take you home to tea.
Jump on my back, and hold on tight!'
    Then off they went, flop flap;
And William had a feast that night,
    and sat on the Bumpus' lap.

There were pikelets, there was buttered toast,
    and jam, and cream, and cake;
And William strove to eat the most,
    though his buttons all should break.

The kettle sang, the fire was hot,
    the pot was large and brown;
And William strove to drink the lot,
    in tea though he should drown.

When full and tight was coat and skin,
    they rested without speech,
Till the Bumpus said: 'I'll now begin
    the baker's art to teach,
The making of beautiful Bumpus-bread,
    of bannocks light and brown,
Before I tuck you up in a bed
    of feathers and thistle-down.

*

'Bill Winkle! Where have you been?' they said.
    'I've been to a Bumpus-tea,
And I feel so fat, for I have fed
    on Bumpus-bread,' said he.
The People all knocked on the Bumpus' door:
    'A beautiful Bumpus-cake
O bake for us, please!' they all now roar,
    'O bake, O bake, O bake!'

Policeman Pott came puffing fast
    and made them form a queue,
and old Mrs. Thomas was late and last,
    and her bonnet was all askew.
'Go home! Go home!' the Bumpus said,
    'there's such a crowd of you!
Only on Thursdays I bake my bread,
    and only for a few.

Go home! Go home, for goodness' sake!
    I did not expect a call.
I have no pikelets, toast, or cake,
    for William has eaten all.
Old Mrs. Thomas and Mr. Pott
    I wish no more to see.
Be off! Be off now all the lot —
    Bill Winkle's the boy for me!'

Now William Winkle he grew so fat
    through eating of Bumpus-bread,
His weskit bust, and never a hat
    would sit upon his head.
And Every Thursday he went to tea,
    and sat on the kitchen floor;
And smaller the Bumpus seemed to be,
    as he grew more and more.

And Bill a Baker great became:
    from Bimble Bay to Bong,
From sea to sea there went the fame
    of his bread both short and long.
But it weren't so good as the Bumpus-bread;
    no butter so rich and free,
    As Every Thursday the Bumpus spread
    for William Winkle's tea!

Probably in the first half of November 1961, when considering which of his poems to include in *The Adventures of Tom Bombadil and Other Verses from the Red Book*, Tolkien marked tentative changes to text C, then made a new typescript substantially revised to suit the fiction that the *Bombadil* poems were composed or gathered by Hobbits. He removed the names 'Bimble Bay' and 'Mountains Blue', and inserted locations in Middle-earth mentioned in *The Lord of the Rings* – Weathertop, the Shire, (Michel) Delving, Bree – while the Bumpus became a troll (remarkably, vegetarian and teetotal) without the exaggerated features of a tail and flapping feet.

The new, enlarged typescript (D), which does not have a title, was evidently a working copy: Tolkien made it at speed and with little regard for errors of spelling or spacing. (Here we have silently corrected obvious errors, and inserted missing marks of punctuation, mainly in the latter half of the draft.) Tolkien wrote further workings in an illegible scrawl across the typed text on the second page.

[D] The Lonely Troll he sat on a stone
    and sang his mournful lay:
'O why, O why should I live on my own
    in the hills of Faraway?

My folk are gone beyond recall
    and take no thought of me;
alone I'm left, the last of all
    from Weathertop to the Sea.'

'I steal no gold, I drink no beer,
    I eat nor bone nor meat;
but People slam their doors in fear,
    whenever they hear my feet.'
He looked at his hands and he looked at his feet,
    and he said: 'They may be rough,
but my heart is soft, my smile is sweet,
    and my cooking good enough!'

'Come, come!' he thought, 'this will not do!
    I must go and find a friend.
From North to South I'll wander through
    the Shire from end to end.'
Down he came, and he walked all night
    with his feet in boots of fur;
to Delving he came in the morning light,
    when folk were just astir.

He looked around, and who did he meet
    but old Mrs. Bunce and all
with umbrella and basket walking the street;
    and he smiled and stopped to call:
'Good morning, ma'am! Good day to you!
    I hope I find you well?'
But she dropped umbrella and basket too,
    and yelled a frightful yell.

Old Pott the Mayor was strolling near;
    when he heard that awful sound,
he turned all purple and pink with fear,
    and dived down underground.
The Lonely Troll was hurt and sad:
    'Don't go!' he gently said,
but old Mrs. Bunce ran home like mad
    and hid beneath her bed.

The Troll went on to the marketplace
    and peeped above the walls:
the sheep went wild when they saw his face,
    and the cows jumped from their stalls.
Old Farmer Hogg he spilled his ale,
    Bill butcher threw a knife,
and Grip his dog, he turned his tail
    and ran to save his life.

The Old Troll sadly sat and wept
    outside the Lockholes gate,
and Tiddly Winkle up he crept
    and patted him on the pate.
'O why do you weep, you great big lump?
    You're better outside than in!'
He gave the Troll a friendly thump,
    and laughed to see him grin.

'O Tiddly Winkle boy,' he cried,
    'come; you're the boy for me!
and if you're willing to take a ride
    I'll take you home to tea.
Jump on my back, and hold on tight!'
    Then off they went in glee;
and the Winkle had a feast that night
    and sat on the old Troll's knee.

There were pikelets, there was buttered toast,
    and jam, and cream, and cake
and the Winkle strove to eat the most
    though his buttons all should break.
The kettle sang, the fire was hot,
    the pot was large and brown;
and Winkle strove to drink the lot
    in tea though he should drown.

When tight and full was coat and skin,
    they rested without speech,
till the Old Troll said: 'I'll now begin
    the baker's art to teach,

the making of beautiful cramsome bread,
    of bannocks light and brown,
and then you can sleep on a heather bed
    with pillows of owlets' down.'

'Young Winkle, where have you been,' they said.
    'I have been to a fulsome tea,
and I feel so fat for I have fed
    on cramsome bread,' said he.
'And where, my boy, in the Shire was that?
    Or out in Bree?' said they.
But Winkle he up and answered flat:
    'I ain't a-going to say!'

'But I know where,' said Peeping Jack,
    'I watched him go away;
he went upon the Old Troll's back
    to the hills of Faraway.'
Then all the People went with a will
    by pony, cart, or moke
until they came to a house in the hill
    and saw a chimney smoke.

They hammered on the Old Troll's door;
    'A beautiful cramsome cake
O bake for us, please, or two or more,
    O bake,' they cried, 'O bake!'
'Go home, go home!' the troll he said,
    'I never invited you.
Only on Thursdays I bake my bread,
    and only for a few.'

'Go home, go home! there's some mistake.
    My house is far too small;
and I've no pikelets toast or cake,
    for Winkle has eaten all!
Jack and Hogg, old Bunce and Pott
    I wish no more to see.
Be off! Be off now all the lot!
    The Winkle's the boy for me!'

Now Tiddly Winkle grew so fat
through eating of cramsome bread,
his weskit bust, and never a hat
would sit upon his head;
for Every Thursday he came to tea,
and sat on the kitchen floor
and smaller the Old Troll seemed to be,
as he grew more and more.

The Winkle a Baker great became
from Faraway to Tong,
from the Sea to Bree there went the fame
of his bread both short and long.
But it weren't so good as the cramsome bread;
no butter so rich and free
as Every Thursday the Old Troll spread
for Tiddly Winkle's tea!

On version D Tolkien made a few notes for revision, which he carried into a new, more careful typescript. He now called the work *Perry-the-Winkle*, and gave it a secondary title, *A Nursery Rhyme in the House of Master Samwise* – in the preface to the *Bombadil* collection, he identifies the poet as the Hobbit Sam Gamgee. Further changes followed, marked on ribbon and carbon copies of the new typescript, bringing the text nearly to its published form. A final typescript in Tolkien's papers has the alternate, subsequently abandoned title *A Children's Song in the Shire (Attributed to Master Samwise)*. Tolkien sent a copy of the poem to his publisher on 15 November 1961, as a candidate for the *Bombadil* volume. Here, as E, we give *Perry-the-Winkle* as it was printed in the 1962 collection, pp. 41–4.

[E] The Lonely Troll he sat on a stone
and sang his mournful lay:
'O why, O why should I live on my own
in the hills of Faraway?
My folk are gone beyond recall
and take no thought of me;
alone I'm left, the last of all
from Weathertop to the Sea.'

'I steal no gold, I drink no beer,
I eat no kind of meat;

but People slam their doors in fear,
 whenever they hear my feet.
O how I wish that they were neat,
 and my hands were not so rough!
Yet my heart is soft, my smile is sweet,
 and my cooking good enough.'

'Come, come!' he thought, 'this will not do!
 I must go and find a friend;
a-walking soft I'll wander through
 the Shire from end to end.'
Down he came, and he walked all night
 with his feet in boots of fur;
to Delving he came in the morning light,
 when folk were just astir.

He looked around, and who did he meet
 but old Mrs. Bunce and all
with umbrella and basket walking the street;
 and he smiled and stopped to call:
'Good morning, ma'am! Good day to you!
 I hope I find you well?'
But she dropped umbrella and basket too,
 and yelled a frightful yell.

Old Pott the Mayor was strolling near;
 when he heard that awful sound,
he turned all purple and pink with fear,
 and dived down underground.
The Lonely Troll was hurt and sad:
 'Don't go!' he gently said,
but old Mrs. Bunce ran home like mad
 and hid beneath her bed.

The Troll went on to the market-place
 and peeped above the stalls:
the sheep went wild when they saw his face,
 and the geese flew over the walls.
Old Farmer Hogg he spilled his ale,
 Bill butcher threw a knife,
and Grip his dog, he turned his tail
 and ran to save his life.

The old Troll sadly sat and wept
    outside the Lockholes gate,
and Perry-the-Winkle up he crept
    and patted him on the pate.
'O why do you weep, you great big lump?
    You're better outside than in!'
He gave the Troll a friendly thump,
    and laughed to see him grin.

'O Perry-the-Winkle boy,' he cried,
    'come; you're the lad for me!
Now if you're willing to take a ride,
    I'll take you home to tea.'
He jumped on his back and held on tight,
    and 'Off you go!' said he;
and the Winkle had a feast that night,
    and sat on the old Troll's knee.

There were pikelets, there was buttered toast,
    and jam, and cream, and cake,
and the Winkle strove to eat the most,
    though his buttons all should break.
The kettle sang, the fire was hot,
    the pot was large and brown;
and Winkle tried to drink the lot,
    in tea though he should drown.

When full and tight were coat and skin,
    they rested without speech,
till the old Troll said: 'I'll now begin
    the baker's art to teach,
the making of beautiful cramsome bread,
    of bannocks light and brown;
and then you can sleep on a heather-bed
    with pillows of owlets' down.'

'Young Winkle, where've you been?' they said.
    'I have been to a fulsome tea,
and I feel so fat, for I have fed
    on cramsome bread,' said he.

'And where, my lad, in the Shire was that?
Or out in Bree?' said they.
But Winkle he up and answered flat:
'I ain't a-going to say!'

'But I know where,' said Peeping Jack,
'I watched him go away:
he went upon the old Troll's back
to the hills of Faraway.'
Then all the People went with a will
by pony, cart, or moke
until they came to a house in a hill
and saw a chimney smoke.

They hammered upon the old Troll's door.
'A beautiful cramsome cake
O bake for us, please, or two, or more;
O bake,' they cried, 'O bake!'
'Go home, go home!' the old troll said.
'I never invited you.
Only on Thursdays I bake my bread,
and only for a few.'

'Go home! Go home! There's some mistake.
My house is far too small;
and I've no pikelets, cream, or cake:
the Winkle has eaten all!
You Jack, and Hogg, old Bunce and Pott
I wish no more to see.
Be off! Be off now all the lot!
The Winkle's the boy for me!'

Now Perry-the-Winkle grew so fat
through eating of cramsome bread,
his weskit bust, and never a hat
would sit upon his head;
for Every Thursday he went to tea,
and sat on the kitchen floor,
and smaller the old Troll seemed to be,
as he grew more and more.

The Winkle a Baker great became,
    as still is said in song;
from the Sea to Bree there went the fame
    of his bread both short and long.
But it weren't so good as the cramsome bread;
    no butter so rich and free,
as Every Thursday the old Troll spread
    for Perry-the-Winkle's tea.

In 1967 Tolkien made a professional recording of *Perry-the-Winkle* for the album *Poems and Songs of Middle Earth*. It was later reissued.

A1: Christopher Tolkien could not tell us if the name 'Bumpus' had any special significance for his father, other than being shared by a well known London bookseller of the day. It seems possible that it was a private joke, an echo of a sound, or a word to suggest something that goes bump in the night. Tolkien abandoned 'Bumpus' in version D, but the place-name 'Bumpus Head' remained in *The Dragon's Visit* (no. 107).

A4: *Bong* seems to have no more meaning than as a convenient rhyme for 'song' (and in l. 98 for 'long'), in the manner of Edward Lear.

A16: Tolkien marked this line to read 'And soft and sweet my song'. The original reading, however, continued into the second manuscript, where Tolkien marked the same revision. The change was moot in the substantially rewritten third version (C).

A25: Here and in l. 73, 'Pott' originally read 'Potts'.

A36: In the second manuscript Tolkien changed 'jumped from' to 'jumped out of', but 'jumped from' returned in the first typescript (C).

A41: In the second manuscript Tolkien changed this line to read 'The Bumpus sadly sat and wept'.

A46: Tolkien considered whether to change this line to read 'We don't want no more rain'.

A52: *Tea* for the Bumpus is afternoon tea, with breads and cakes, butter and jam; there is no mention of the traditional tea sandwiches.

A57: In the second manuscript Tolkien changed this line to read 'There was buttered toast, and pikelets too'.

A59: 'Gloo' originally read 'stew'. We are at a loss to know what *Gloo* (deliberately capitalized) may be.

A68: 'Bumpus bread' probably could be defined as whatever scrumptious baked treat the reader may call to mind. Compare 'cramsome bread' in later versions.

A74: The policeman dutifully puts things in order. Waiting patiently in a *queue*, or line, to be served or to proceed is a quintessentially British thing to do.

A93: Both words in 'Every Thursday' are capitalized in the original, but not in l. 103. Compare 'Every Thursday' in C100 and C110, and in texts D and E.

A98: In the second manuscript Tolkien changed this line to read 'From Bimble Bay to Bong'.

A99: In the second manuscript Tolkien changed 'his fame' to 'the fame'.

A101: 'War'nt', i.e. 'were not'.

C1: Above 'The Bumpus' Tolkien wrote 'Lonely' and what appears to be 'Worm'. This revision, like others Tolkien scrawled in pencil on version C, is nearly illegible. Those changes which can be read are clearly the poet's thoughts for a new text to appear in *The Adventures of Tom Bombadil and Other Verses from the Red Book*.

C62: For the 'large and brown' teapot Tolkien undoubtedly had in mind a plain style popular in Britain for centuries (and still today), familiarly known as 'Brown Betty'. Made from Staffordshire red clay and distinctly round in shape, it is usually finished with a brown glaze which does not show tea stains over time.

C98: *Weskit*, pronounced thus, is a variation of *waistcoat* (as in A91).

C105: Tolkien marked 'Bong' to be changed to 'Tong'. See D122.

D4: 'Faraway' is either far away – if the Troll must walk all night to reach Delving, and most of the day to return (with the Winkle on his back) – or not far away at all, if the Winkle can visit weekly for tea, and people can make their way to the Troll's home to clamour for cakes.

D19–20: If the Troll were to wander 'end to end' through the Shire from north to south, it would be a relatively short walk. The Shire is an elongated area running primarily west to east.

D36: 'Dived down underground': most Hobbits live below ground.

D47: 'Grip' is one of Farmer Maggot's dogs in *The Lord of the Rings*. Presumably this is another dog of the same name.

D50: The *Lockholes* are the Hobbit jail in Michel Delving, thus the Winkle's jest that the Troll was 'better outside than in'.

D51: *Tiddlywinks*, or *Tiddly-winks*, is a game in which small, hard counters are flicked into a central cup using a larger counter. It was invented in England in the Victorian period, and became widely popular. By the time Tolkien used the name 'Tiddly Winkle' in his poem, the game was played on a competitive level – at Oxford there was a formal Tiddlywinks Society. Tolkien abandoned the name in his final version of the poem (with the next typescript) in favour of 'Perry-the-Winkle'.

D77: We find no source for *cramsome*, and suppose that it was coined by Tolkien from the verb *cram* 'overfeed, stuff, fill to satiety', or the noun meaning 'dough or paste used in fattening poultry' or more generally any food used to fatten animals. Any of these would fit the purpose, and explain the Winkle's eventual girth.

D94: In this line Tolkien first typed 'and tramped for many a mile', then after a space, 'by pony, cart, or moke' (the reading in text E) without marking the first words for deletion.

D95: The Troll's 'house in the hill' seems similar to the comfortable holes dug into hillsides occupied by Hobbits.

E13–15: This reading entered as a revision in the second *Perry-the-Winkle* typescript, changed from 'He looked at a foot, and he looked at a hand, | and he said: 'They may be rough, | But my heart is soft, my smile is bland'.

E42–44: This reading entered after revisions to the second *Perry-the-Winkle* typescript; before, l. 42 ended with 'walls', and l. 44 read 'and the cows jumped out of their stalls'.

E51: 'Perry-the-Winkle' is presumably a play on *periwinkle*, which is both an edible mollusc and the trailing plant *Vinca*.

106

Poor Old Grabbler · Old Grabbler (?1928)

In his penultimate 'Bimble Bay' poem, Tolkien returned to social commentary, with perhaps even greater bite. As in *The Progress of Bimble* (*Progress in Bimble Town*, no. 103), he addressed the evils of noise and litter, but now with a focus on two older residents who recall when the lands were clean and wild, while 'all these places are now defiled'. Grabbler, one of the locals, seems to have lost his wits, roaming in the night, putting things in his great bag; in fact, he is picking up discarded paper, and banana-skins, and cigarette butts, quietly doing his part. He and Mrs Day have their homes on the outskirts, 'above the cliffs over Bimble Bay', unable to afford town amenities but closer to nature and preferring it that way. It may be no coincidence that the Tolkien family, at least on their 1925 holiday at Filey, stayed in a cottage on a cliff overlooking the sea.

The first of two manuscripts of the poem (A) is entitled *Poor Old Grabbler*. Written out quickly, it appears to represent Tolkien's thoughts as they came to him in a rush.

[A] Above the cliffs over Bimble Bay,
Where little white-tailed rabbits play,
There is close turf, and the thyme blows,
And the cloud's long shadow goes.
But at twilight the grass lies grey
Right up to the doors of Mrs. Day.
Old Mrs. Day still lives up there,
And her garden is fluttered by sea-air,
And sea-winds in her chimney roar
In winter, and cry beneath her door.
But in the white moon under summer
Her dark windows shine and glimmer,
While the soft sea rustles far below,
And night things scurry to and fro
And scuffle in the bushes. That's Grabbler's time;
And puffing and panting from his long climb
He plods with soft feet in the gloom
Down narrow paths, where hedges loom
Like great caverns with climbing weeds

All hung and draped. His pathway leads
Under bryony, ivy, and clematis,
Wide seas of pale wild clematis.
Where is he going with his great bag?
Nobody cares. His slow feet lag,
And he rests on a rabbit-shaven mound,
And sees the sea, and hears its sound;
And he mutters and mumbles: 'Grabbler's old.
In Grabbler's cottage the fire is cold,
The walls are wankle and windows blank.
In Grabbler's garden the weeds are rank,
But Grabbler remembers a merry time
When pretty things once used to climb
On to the cliff-tops under the gloaming
And sing and dance, and then go roaming
With sound of music and of laughter;
And Grabbler was young and followed after
And wandered in lands all free and wild.'
But all these places are now defiled:
Everywhere, everywhere, paper-bags
And banana-skins and yellowing rags
Of picture papers and stumps of fags;
And over dark hills the hoot of horn.
Dragons — the loathliest worm would scorn
To trouble quiet villages with such braying
All about nothing. There is no saying,
But one can guess what Grabbler's at,
What he puts in his bag. He's as mad as his hat,
For 'banana-skins have come to stay',
And so have papers, papers say.
And one can guess why it is of late
So many things Bimble folk all hate
Have wandered & walked, crept or flown
From Bimble Bay, or left alone
Look over the sea to the distant view
Of the far peaks of the Mountains Blue.

Tolkien soon reworked this manuscript, inserting eight lines near the beginning. He then made an attractive fair copy with a decorative initial letter at the start of each stanza, entitled more simply *Old Grabbler*. We give the second version, with a few final alterations included, as B.

[B] Above the cliffs over Bimble Bay,
Where little white-tailed rabbits play,
There is close turf, and the thyme blows,
And the cloud's long shadow goes.
But at twilight the grass lies grey
Right up to the doors of Mrs. Day.

Old Mrs. Day still lives up there,
And her garden is fluttered by sea-air,
And sea-winds in her chimney roar
In winter, and cry beneath her door.
Unsanitary and inconvenient!
But in Bimble Bay there is high rent,
And not much air, and a short view.
There are several chemists, it is true,
Tap-water and gas, if you care to pay,
And a noise like hell all the dull day.

But the old woman listens to the birds' voices
And things growing, and the night-noises;
And in the white moon under summer
Her dark windows shine and glimmer,
While the soft sea rustles far below,
And night-things scurry to and fro
And scuffle in the bushes. That's Grabbler's time —
Puffing and panting from his long climb
He plods with soft feet in the gloom
Down narrow paths, where hedges loom
Like great caverns with climbing weeds
All hung and draped. His pathway leads
Under bryony, ivy and clematis,
Wide seas of pale wild clematis.
Where is he going with his great bag?
Nobody cares. His slow feet lag,
And he rests on a rabbit-shaven mound,
And sees the sea, and hears its sound.

And he mumbles and mutters: 'Grabbler's old.
In Grabbler's cottage the fire is cold,
The walls are wankle, the windows blank.
In Grabbler's garden the weeds are rank;
But Grabbler remembers a merry time

When pretty things did use to climb
On to the cliff tops under the gloaming
And sing and dance, and then go roaming
With sound of music and of laughter;
And Grabbler was young and followed after
And wandered in lands all clean and wild.'

But all these places are now defiled:
Everywhere, everywhere paper-bags,
And banana-skins, and yellowing rags
Of picture-papers, and stumps of fags;
And over dark hills the honk of horn.
Dragons — the loathliest worm would scorn
To trouble quiet villages with such braying
All about nothing. There is no saying,
But one can guess what Grabbler's at,
What he puts in his bag. He's as mad as his hat,
For banana-skins have come to stay.
And so have papers, papers say.
And one can guess why it is of late
So many things Bimble-folk all hate
Have wandered or walked, crept or flown
From Bimble Bay; or left alone
Look over the sea to the distant view
Of the far peaks of the Mountains Blue.

In text A Tolkien placed the phrase 'banana-skins have come to stay' (line 56) between quotation marks, as if it were a slogan issued by banana-growers or marketers to excuse eaters of the fruit carelessly tossing its skin (peel) on the ground. He expressed similar feelings in *On Fairy-Stories*: writing of mass-produced electric street-lamps as an element in a story, he suggested that

> it may, almost certainly does, proceed from a considered disgust for so typical a product of the Robot Age, that combines elaboration and ingenuity of means with ugliness, and (often) with inferiority of result. These lamps may be excluded from the tale simply because they are bad lamps; and it is possible that one of the lessons to be learnt from the story is the realization of this fact. But out comes the big stick: 'Electric lamps have come to stay', they say. Long ago Chesterton remarked that, as soon as he heard that anything 'had come to stay', he

knew that it would be very soon replaced – indeed regarded as pitiably obsolete and shabby. [*Tree and Leaf* (2001), p. 61]

A15: *Grabble*, as in the name 'Grabbler', means 'to feel or search with the hand, grope'.

A25: 'Rabbit-shaven', i.e. grass closely cropped by foraging rabbits.

A47: 'Mad as his hat': the usual phrase is 'mad as a hatter', from the nineteenth century, of uncertain origin.

B13–16: Among revisions added to the first manuscript, these lines read:

And not much air and very short view
There are several chemists it is true
Water and gas, if you care to pay
And a noise like hell all the day.

Assuming that Tolkien is referring by *chemist* (l. 14) to the shop and not profession, in the U.S.A. this would be called a *pharmacy* or *drugstore* (compare Tolkien's use of *pharmacy* in no. 103). *Gas* (l. 15) is natural gas, for cooking or heating, i.e. not petrol (gasoline).

B17–18: Among revisions added to the first manuscript, these lines originally read 'But old Mrs Day listens to the sea | and watches things grow alone is she'. Tolkien then tried 'But old Mrs Day listens to birds' voices | And things growing & night noises'; this is the first reading of the lines in the second manuscript. Still dissatisfied, Tolkien returned to his first text, struck through the previously revised lines, and altered them again, then marked the new revisions on the second manuscript.

B26: Tolkien seems to have considered whether to change 'Down narrow paths' to 'Along deep alleys'.

B50: 'Honk of horn': the change from 'hoot' in text A to 'honk' in B is curious, in that in the 1920s *hoot* was typically used in England for the sound of a car horn, whereas *honk* is a much later usage in terms of popularity. Tolkien used *hoot*, *hooting* in connection with the sound of a flute in his early poems, as in *Tinfang Warble* (no. 29).

B59: Tolkien considered whether to change 'Bimble-folk' to 'that Bimble Bay'.

107

The Dragon's Visit (?1928–64)

Ten iterations of the sixth of Tolkien's 'Bimble Bay' poems survive, composed or revised in three phases, and with three different conclusions. Its earliest text, a manuscript entitled *The Dragon's Visit*, is a fair copy; we have transcribed this below as A. At some later date, Tolkien extended its title to *The Dragon's Visit to Upper Bimble*, but this was no more than a passing thought. On all other copies, where a title is given, he continued to call the poem simply *The Dragon's Visit*.

[A]

The Dragon sat in the Cherry Tree
  and whistled all the morning.
Green was he, and the blossom white;
  it was a shining morning.

He came from the land of Further Bong
  from over the Blue Mountains
Where dragons live, and the sun shines
  on high white fountains.

'Please, Mister Higgins, do you know
  what's waiting in your garden?
There's a dragon in your cherry-tree!'
  'Eh? what? I beg your pardon!'

Mister Higgins fetched the garden hose,
  and the dragon stopped his whistling;
He stopped and cocked his long green ears,
  when he heard the water fizzling.

'How cool' he said, 'delightfully cool
  is Mister Higgins['] fountain!
I'll sit and sing a golden song,
  till the moon above the mountain

Like cherry-blossom rises bright.
  I'll sing for Mister Higgins,
And Mister Box, his friend next door,
  and dear old Mrs. Biggins.'

Mister Higgins sent for the fire-brigade
with a long red ladder,
And men with golden helmets on.
The dragon's heart grew sadder:

'It reminds one of the bad old days,
when men without kind feeling
Used to hunt dragons to their caves,
their bright gold stealing.'

Captain George he up the ladder came.
The dragon said: 'Good people,
Why all this fuss? Please go away,
or your church-steeple

I shall throw down, and blast your trees
and kill and eat for supper
You, Captain George, and Higgins, Box,
and Biggins and old Tupper!'

'Turn on the hose!' said Captain George,
and scrambled down the ladder.
The dragon's eyes from green went red,
his heart grew bad and badder.

He steamed, he smoked, he threshed his tail,
and down the blossom fluttered;
Like snow upon the lawn it lay;
and the dragon growled and muttered.

A rusty spear behind a door
they found, and jabbed from under;
The dragon gave a dreadful cry
and rose like thunder.

He knocked the village all to bits,
and over the Bay of Bimble
Sailors could see the burning red
from Bumpus Head to Trimble.

Mister Higgins was tough, and as for Box —
that's just like what he tasted.
The dragon munching supper said:
'So all my trouble's wasted.'

So he buried Tupper and Captain George,
and the remains of Mrs. Biggins
On a cliff above the long white shore;
he sang a dirge for Higgins —

A sad song, while the moon rose,
with the sea below sighing
On the grey rocks of Bimble Bay,
and the red blaze dying.

Long over the sea he saw the peaks
round his own land ranging,
And he mused on the folk of Bimble Bay
and the old order changing.

'These folk,' he thought, 'haven't got the wit
to like a dragon's colour,
Or song, or even to kill him quick —
the world is getting duller';

And the moon shone through his great green wings
the night winds beating,
As he flew back over the crinkled sea
to a green dragons' meeting.

Tolkien marked a few revisions to this text, which he included in a second manuscript (B) made probably not long after he completed the first. But these were only a fraction of the changes he conceived while writing it out, or (as undoubtedly occurred for A) after first drafting on separate sheets now lost. Very little was left untouched. Tolkien also changed the structure of the poem, which was now made up of stanzas comprising eight lines rather than four.

[B] The Dragon lay on the cherry tree
a-simmering and a-dreaming.
Green was he, and the blossom white,
and the yellow sun gleaming.

He came from the land of Further Bong,
 from over the Blue Mountains,
Where dragons live, and the sun shines
 on high white fountains.

'Please, Mister Higgins, do you know
 what's a-sitting in your garden?
There's a dragon in your cherry-trees!'
 'Eh, what? I beg your pardon?'
Mister Higgins fetched the garden hose,
 and the dragon woke from dreaming;
He blinked, and cocked his long green ears,
 when he heard the water teeming.

'How cool' he said, 'delightfully cool
 is Mister Higgins['] fountain!
I'll sit and sing a golden song,
 till the moon above the mountain
Like cherry-blossom rises bright;
 I'll sing for Mister Higgins,
And Mister Box, his friend next door,
 and dear old Missis Biggins.'

Mister Higgins sent for the fire-brigade
 with a long red ladder,
And men with golden helmets on.
 The dragon's heart grew sadder:
'It reminds one of the bad old days,
 when warriors unfeeling
Used to hunt dragons to their dens,
 their bright gold stealing.'

Captain George up the ladder came.
 The dragon said: 'Good people,
Why all this fuss? Please go away!
 Or your church-steeple
I shall throw down, and blast your trees,
 and kill and eat for supper
You, Cap'n George, and Higgins, Box
 and Biggins, and old Tupper!'

'Turn on the hose!' said Captain George,
    and down the ladder tumbled.
The dragon's eyes from green went red,
    and his belly rumbled.
He steamed, he smoked, he threshed his tail,
    and down the blossom fluttered;
Like snow upon the lawn it lay,
    and the dragon growled and muttered.

A rusty spear behind a door
    they found, and jabbed from under:
The dragon gave a dreadful cry
    and rose like thunder.
He knocked the village all to bits,
    and over the Bay of Bimble
Sailors could see the burning red
    from Bumpus Head to Trimble.

Mister Higgins was tough; and as for Box,
    'twas just like box he tasted.
The dragon munching supper said:
    'So all my trouble's wasted!'
And he buried Tupper and Captain George,
    and the remains of Missis Biggins,
On a cliff above the long white shore;
    and he sang a dirge for Higgins —

A sad song, while the moon rose,
    with the sea below sighing
On the grey rocks of Bimble Bay,
    and the red blaze dying.
Far over the sea he saw the peaks
    round his own land ranging;
And he mused on the folk of Bimble Bay
    and the old order changing.

'They haven't got the wit to admire
    a dragon's song or colour,
Nor heart to kill him brave and quick —
    the world is getting duller!'

And the moon shone through his green wings
    the night winds beating,
As he flew back over the dappled sea
    to a green dragons' meeting.

From text B, without further change, Tolkien made a typescript using his Hammond machine. This is notable for having a series title, Tales of Bimble Bay, and a numeral '4' in front of its title *The Dragon's Visit,* perhaps to indicate that – at least at that moment – Tolkien thought to place this 'tale' fourth in his sequence of six. No copy of any of the other 'Bimble Bay' poems, however, is similarly numbered. Also on the typescript, Tolkien later added the inscription 'Oxford 1928? rev[ised] 1937'. The second date can be reasonably certain (though 1936 would also be possible), since *The Dragon's Visit* was published in the *Oxford Magazine* for 4 February 1937, p. 342. There the text included still more revisions – the third stanza was almost entirely replaced – which Tolkien had marked on his typescript. (Given the confused state of some of his alterations, surely a new, clean typescript would have been made for the printer; but none is extant.) We give the *Oxford Magazine* text as C.

[C]

The dragon lay on the cherry trees
    a-simmering and a-dreaming:
Green was he, and the blossom white,
    and the yellow sun gleaming.
He came from the land of Finis-Terre,
    from over the Blue Mountains,
Where dragons live, and the moon shines
    on high white fountains.

'Please, Mister Higgins, do you know
    what's a-laying in your garden?
There's a dragon in your cherry-trees!'
    'Eh, what? I beg your pardon?'
Mister Higgins fetched the garden hose,
    and the dragon woke from dreaming;
He blinked, and cocked his long green ears
    when he heard the water streaming.

'How cool' he said, 'delightfully cool
    is Mister Higgins' fountains!

I'll sit and sing till the moon comes,
as they sing beyond the mountains;
And Higgins, and his neighbours, Box,
Miss Biggins, and old Tupper,
Will be enchanted by my voice:
they will enjoy their supper!'

Mister Higgins sent for the fire brigade
with a long red ladder,
And men with golden helmets on.
The dragon's heart grew sadder:
'It reminds one of the bad old days
when warriors unfeeling
Used to hunt dragons to their dens,
their bright gold stealing.'

Captain George, he up the ladder came.
The dragon said: 'Good people,
Why all this fuss? Please go away!
Or your church-steeple
I shall throw down, and blast your trees,
and kill and eat for supper
You, Cap'n George, and Higgins, Box,
and Biggins and old Tupper!'

'Turn on the hose!' said Captain George,
and down the ladder tumbled.
The dragon's eyes from green went red,
and his belly rumbled.
He steamed, he smoked, he threshed his tail,
and down the blossom fluttered;
Like snow upon the lawn it lay,
and the dragon growled and muttered.

They poked with poles from underneath
(where he was rather tender):
The dragon gave a dreadful cry
and rose like thunder.
He smashed the town to smithereens,
and over the Bay of Bimble
Sailors could see the burning red
from Bumpus Head to Trimble.

Mister Higgins was tough; and as for Box
just like his name he tasted.
The dragon munching supper said:
'So all my trouble's wasted!'
And he buried Tupper and Captain George,
and the remains of Miss Biggins,
On a cliff above the long white shore;
and he sang a dirge for Higgins:

A sad song, while the moon rose,
with the sea below sighing
On the grey rocks of Bimble Bay,
and the red blaze dying.
Far over the sea he saw the peaks
round his own land ranging;
And he mused on the folk of Bimble Bay
and the old order changing.

'They haven't got the wit to admire
a dragon's song or colour,
Nor heart to kill him brave and quick —
the world is getting duller!'
And the moon shone through his green wings
the night winds beating,
As he flew back over the dappled sea
to a green dragons' meeting.

The second phase in the evolution of the poem dates probably to the first half of November 1961, when Tolkien considered which of his past writings to include in *The Adventures of Tom Bombadil and Other Verses from the Red Book*. He sent a copy to his publisher on 15 November. *The Dragon's Visit* must have seemed a good candidate, as dragons were an established feature of Middle-earth and known to Hobbits, in history if not in person.

Tolkien seems to have begun by faintly writing a few tentative revisions on a copy of the printed poem from the *Oxford Magazine*. Then in succession he made, or caused to be made, three typescripts, each with ribbon and carbon copies. (Christopher Tolkien felt that the third of these was typed by his father's secretary, but if so Tolkien would have had to guide the work closely, as it merged text from different sources.) These show him struggling both to improve the work after it had been set aside for a quarter-century, and to turn it to his new purpose. The first typescript in particular includes many textual changes relative to the version of 1937.

In a letter to Caroline Hillier dated 10 December 1964, Tolkien noted that the version from this phase 'was rejected from "The Adventures of Tom Bombadil" for its deficiencies' – he does not enumerate them – 'and also it was impossible to remodel to bring it into the Hobbit world', the *Bombadil* collection (as we have said) being based on the fiction that its poems were written or collected by Hobbits. *The Dragon's Visit* 'belongs actually to a different group, relating to an imaginary seaside town called Bimble Bay, mostly satirical, and few successful enough to print' (Bodleian Library). Indeed, in this phase references to Bimble Bay, Bumpus Head, and so forth remained in all of the texts.

Between the first and second typescripts of this phase, there are only a few differences. Tolkien marked the first (in our notes, we will refer to this as D^1) in more than one stage, with different revisions on its ribbon and carbon copies, and in layers of black ink, pencil, and red biro (ballpoint pen); some words are illegible, others obscured. The earliest changes (as they seem to us) were carried into the second typescript (D^2), but others did not enter until the third (D^3). Since most of the text is identical across all three, we will transcribe the latest copy as D, and with one notable exception, will describe variants in our notes.

[D]

The dragon lay on the cherry-trees
 a-simmering and a-dreaming:
The blossom was white, but he was green
 with hard scales gleaming.
He came overseas from Noman's Land
 where dragons were long untroubled
But now they were short of room and food,
 for their numbers had more than doubled.

'Please, Mister Higgins, ave you seen
 what's a-come into your garden?
There's a dragon in your cherry-trees!'
 'A what? I beg your pardon!'
Mister Higgins fetched the garden-hose,
 and the dragon woke from dreaming;
He blinked and snortled in his nose,
 when he felt the water streaming.

'How cool,' he said, 'delightfully cool!
    I did not expect a fountain!
I'll sit and sing till daylight fails
    and the full moon's mounting.'
But Higgins called his neighbours: Box,
    Miss Biggins, and old Tupper;
'If you don't help me quick,' he said,
    'he'll eat us all for supper.'

Miss Biggins sent for the Fire Brigade
    with a long red ladder,
And men with golden helmets on.
    The dragon's heart grew sadder:
'It reminds me of the bad old days
    when warriors unfeeling
Used to hunt dragons to their dens,
    their bright gold stealing.'

The Captain up with his hatchet went:
    'Now what d'you think you're doing?'
He said, 'You'd best be moving on!'
    But the dragon laughed: 'I'm stewing.
I like to stew. So go away
    or your church-steeple
I'll batter down, and blast your trees,
    and you, and eat these people.'

'Turn on the ydrant!' said Captain George,
    and down the ladder tumbled.
The dragon's eyes from green went red,
    and his belly rumbled.
He steamed, he smoked, he threshed his tail,
    and down the blossom fluttered;
Like snow upon the lawn it lay,
    and the dragon growled and muttered.

They poked him with poles from underneath
    (where he was rather tender):
The dragon gave a dreadful cry
    and rose in splendour.
He smashed the town to smithereens,
    and over the Bay of Bimble

Sailors could see the burning red
   from Bumpus Head to Trimble.

The Higgins was tough, and as for Box
   just like his name he tasted.
The dragon trying Tupper said:
   'No, all this munching's wasted.'
So he buried the hatchet and Captain George,
   and he sang a dirge for Higgins
On a cliff above the long white shore —
   somehow he'd missed Miss Biggins.

Sadly he sang, while the moon rose,
   with the sea below sighing
On the grey rocks of Bimble Bay,
   and the red blaze dying.
Far over the sea he saw the peaks
   round his own land ranging;
And he mused on the folk of Bimble Bay
   and the old order changing.

'None of them's got the wit to admire
   a dragon's song or colour,
Nor the heart to kill him brave and quick —
   the world is getting duller!'
The moon shone through his opened wings,
   but just as he was rising,
Miss Biggins stabbed him in a vital spot;
   and that he found surprising.

'I regret this very much,' she said;
   'You're a very splendid creature,
And your voice is quite remarkable
   for one who's had no teacher.
But wanton damage I will not have,
   I really had to end it.'
The dragon sighed before he died:
   'At least she called me splendid!'

As we have seen, the first version of *The Dragon's Visit* concludes with the death of the inhabitants of Bimble Bay (at least, those in immediate reach of the dragon) and the destruction of their village.

Some twenty-five years later, Tolkien decided that the dragon himself should die, at the unlikely hands of Miss Biggins, though the beast is consoled by her praise: this is the conclusion of text D (typescript D^3), and of the ultimate version of the work. But in an addition to D^1 and in text integral to D^2, the dragon recovers, his wound a surprise but not mortal, or even debilitating for more than a moment.

In D^1 as originally typed, the final lines of the poem read:

'I regret this very much,' she said;
   'You're a rather splendid creature,
And your voice is quite remarkable
   for one who's had no teacher;
But you make such a mess of things
   I really had to end it.'
The dragon sighed as he expired:
   'At least she called me splendid!'

The formatting of the then single page of the typescript, with '"I regret this very much,"' etc. centred by itself below the rest of the text in two columns, leaves no doubt that Tolkien intended this to be the end. Then, after some undetermined space of time, he typed a new stanza on a separate sheet:

The dragon sighed to himself: 'How kind!
   Did she say "*rather* splendid"?'
With a tail-flick over the cliff she went,
   and on the rocks she ended.
He licked the prick, then with green wings
   the night winds beating,
He flew back over the dappled sea
   to a Green Dragons' Meeting.

With this Tolkien began to move away from his previous conclusion. He marked no revisions to the original closing lines of D^1, in which the dragon 'expired', but at the foot of the new sheet he typed 'The dragon groaned to himself; "How kind! | At least she called me splendid!"': this text was evidently meant to replace lines 87–88, and it does so in D^2. Also with this new stanza, Tolkien returned to the first conclusion of the poem, as in texts A through C, with a flight home across the sea 'to a Green Dragons' Meeting', the event now capitalized as if it were a scheduled conference.

Having removed any reference to the dragon's death, Tolkien typed a second version of his new final stanza:

Then he snorted: [']No! I won't take that.
    What she said was "*rather* splendid!"'
With a tail-flick over the cliff she went,
    and on the rocks she ended.
He licked the prick, and with his green wings
    the night-winds beating
He flew back over the dappled sea
    to a Green Dragons' Meeting.

To this Tolkien made two manuscript revisions, changing 'prick' to 'puncture' and 'his green' to 'great'. In the context of the poem, *prick* means 'puncture', but Tolkien may have realized that its sexual connotation, current in his day as now, would be too easily read as innuendo in conjunction with 'licked' (a semi-rhyme with 'flick' two lines earlier).

Following the additions and changes to D^1, the final stanzas of the new typescript D^2 read:

'I regret this very much,' she said;
    [']you're rather a splendid creature,
And your voice is quite remarkable,
    for one who's had no teacher;
But wanton damage I will not have.
    I really had to end it.'
The dragon groaned to himself; 'How kind!
    At least she called me splendid.'

Then he snorted: 'No! I won't take that!
    What she said was "*rather* splendid"!'
With a tail-flick over the cliff she went,
    and on the rocks she ended.
He licked the puncture, and with great wings
    the night-winds beating
He flew back over the dappled sea
    to a Green Dragons' Meeting.

The only further revision Tolkien marked on D^2 was to lines 93–94, which would have become 'He licked the puncture, and spread his wings, | and the night-winds beating'. But the new final stanza was not seen again, as he returned in D3 to Miss Biggins' remarkable victory. It may be that, on second thought, he found the sudden reversal of the dragon's (and Miss Biggins') fortunes too much of an anti-climax.

In subsequently shaping text D, however, Tolkien used both the ribbon and carbon copies of D1 as working drafts, changing in line 82, for example (see also our notes below), 'a rather splendid creature' to the earlier reading, 'a very splendid creature'. (D2 has 'rather a splendid creature'.) He had been struggling to wring humour out of the dragon's objection to *rather*, interpreted as an adverb of degree ('slightly, somewhat'), as opposed to an emphatic *very* – there could be no question of his splendour, or Miss Biggins would suffer the consequences. In the end it was probably too subtle a point.

On 15 November 1961 he sent D3 to George Allen & Unwin for possible, if doubtful, inclusion in the *Bombadil* volume; it was rejected for that purpose by author and publisher early in 1962. Then sometime in 1964 Tolkien was invited to submit works for consideration by editor Caroline Hillier in a new anthology, *Winter's Tales for Children* (see our discussion for *Once upon a Time*, no. 48). By early December that year he turned yet again to *The Dragon's Visit*, producing two further manuscripts and two additional typescripts; in our notes we will refer to these as E1, E2, E3, and E4. The first of the new manuscripts is rough, and became increasingly haphazard as it progressed, to the point of general illegibility; initial writing in pencil was mostly overwritten in ink. Enough can be read, however, to see that Tolkien was not yet departing from the form or substance of previous versions of the poem, except to question some of his choices. He tested, for instance, whether he should restore 'Finis-Terre' in place of 'Noman's Land' in line 5. But with his second manuscript, he made another substantial change to the work by abandoning the ABCB scheme of his earlier versions in favour of ABAB. Naturally this required not a little rewriting. *Once upon a Time* (no. 48) and *Rosalind Ramage* (no. 187), both in rhyming couplets, were considered along with *The Dragon's Visit* for *Winter's Tales for Children*, and it may be that Tolkien felt that he should make the latter less complex in its rhyme scheme for the sake of younger readers.

The first typescript of this new text, extant in both ribbon and carbon copies, was probably made by a secretary or other professional typist, not by Tolkien himself: this was Christopher Tolkien's conclusion, based on the number of errors made in typing (such as 'Trindor' for 'Trimble' and 'Higgins' for 'Biggins') which he felt was due to misreading his father's handwriting. Apart from corrections, Tolkien made no changes to the typescript other than the replacement of lines 5–8. He entered a small number of further revisions on a final typescript, which appears to have been made on his Hammond machine, before *The Dragon's Visit* in its final version (given here as E, from the final typescript as revised) was published in *Winter's Tales for Children 1* in October 1965.

[E]

On the cherry trees the dragon lay
    a-simmering and a-dreaming.
The blossom was white in the early day,
    but green his scales were gleaming.
Over the seas he had flown by night,
    for his land was dragon-haunted,
Stuffed with gold and jewels bright,
    but food and sport he wanted.

'Excuse me, Mr. Higgins, please!
    Ave you seen what's in your garden?
There's a dragon on your cherry-trees!'
    'A what? I beg your pardon!'
Mr. Higgins fetched the garden-hose,
    and the dragon woke from dreaming.
He blinked and snortled in his nose.
    when he felt the water streaming.

'How cool! he said. 'So good for scales!
    I did not expect a fountain!
I'll sit and sing here, till daylight fails
    and the full moon's mounting.'
But Higgins runs, on the doors he knocks
    of Miss Biggins and old Tupper.
'Come help me quick! Come, Mr. Box,
    or he'll eat us all for supper!'

Miss Biggins sent for the Fire Brigade
    with a long red ladder;
And a brave show their helmets made;
    but the dragon's heart grew sadder:
'It reminds me of the wicked ways
    of warriors unfeeling,
Hunting us in the bad old days
    and our bright gold stealing.'

The Captain up with his hatchet came:
'Now what d'you think you're doing?'
The dragon laughed: 'Cap'n What's-your-name,
I'm sitting here and stewing.
I like to stew. So let me be!
Or your church-steeple
I'll batter down, blast every tree,
and you, and eat these people.'

'Turn on the ydrant!' said Captain George
and down the ladder tumbled.
The dragon's eyes like coals in a forge
glowed, and his belly rumbled.
He began to steam, he threshed his tail,
and away the blossom fluttered.
But the Brigade were not the men to quail,
although he growled and muttered.

With poles they jabbed him from below,
where he was rather tender:
Havoc! the dragon cried, *Haró!*
and rose in splendour.
He smashed the town to a rubbish-heap,
and over the Bay of Bimble
Sailors could see the red flames leap
from Bumpus Head to Trimble.

The Higgins was tough, and as for Box:
just like his name he tasted:
The dragon threw Tupper on the rocks,
and said 'This munching's wasted.'
So he buried the hatchet and Captain George,
and he sang a dirge for Higgins
On a cliff above the long white shores —
and he did not miss Miss Biggins.

Sadly he sang, till the moon went down,
with the surf below sighing
On the grey rocks, and in Bimbletown
the red blaze dying.

He saw the peaks far over the sea
    round his own land ranging;
And he mused on Men, and how strange they be,
    and the old order changing.

'None of them now have the wit to admire
    a dragon's song or colour,
Nor the nerve with steel to meet his fire —
    the world is getting duller!'
He spread his wide wings to depart;
    but just as he was rising
Miss Biggins stabbed him to the heart,
    and that he found surprising.

'I regret this very much,' she said.
    'You're a very splendid creature,
And your voice is quite remarkable
    for one who has had no teacher;
But wanton damage I will not have,
    I really had to end it.'
The dragon sighed before he died:
    'At least she called me splendid.'

Tolkien's final typescript of *The Dragon's Visit* is found in his archives only in a carbon copy, the ribbon copy presumably having been sent for publication and not returned. In his letter of 10 December 1964 to *Winter's Tales for Children* editor Caroline Hillier he apologized for sending her the earlier version prepared for the *Tom Bombadil* collection, and asked to substitute 'a slightly different version', which he enclosed. 'The revision is (I think) both technically better and in places funnier' (Bodleian Library).

It may have occurred to the author – the parallel occurs to us – that the dragon of his final version, who flies away from his home in search of 'food and sport', is not unlike Chrysophylax Dives in Tolkien's story *Farmer Giles of Ham*, 'cunning, inquisitive, greedy, well-armoured, but not over bold', and 'mortally hungry' (1949, p. 25) – though the Bimble Bay dragon seems more interested in a lark, lounging in cherry-trees, than in a meal (until provoked). Tolkien recalled in *On Fairy-Stories* that as a boy he 'desired dragons with a profound desire. Of course, I in my timid body did not wish to have them in the neighbourhood . . .' (*Tree and Leaf* (2001), p. 41).

A32: 'Bright gold stealing'. This is cheeky, as the dragons of legend typically came by their gold through violence.

A50: 'Jabbed from under'. The dragon Fáfnir, of Norse mythology, was killed by Sigurd who stabbed him from underneath while hiding in a trench. Tolkien followed this model in 'The Silmarillion' with the killing of Glórund (Glaurung, etc.) by Túrin, who pierces the dragon's belly while in a ravine, and with the death of Smaug in *The Hobbit* by the archer Bard, whose arrow reaches the dragon's one unprotected spot.

A56: 'Bumpus Head' recalls the name of the creature in *The Bumpus* (poem no. 105). 'Trimble' seems to have no meaning other than as a rhyme for 'Bimble'.

A57–58: Tolkien jokes about Mr Box tasting like his name, i.e. like cardboard. *Box* is an actual English surname.

A79: 'Crinkled sea', presumably a sea with a rippling surface.

B24: 'Missis', i.e. Mrs. (as pronounced).

B39: 'Cap'n', i.e. Captain.

C5: By *Finis-Terre*, altered in the typescript from the comparatively silly 'Further Bong', Tolkien undoubtedly did not mean the headland on the west coast of Spain (Cabo Finisterre), or Finistère in Britanny, but an imaginary place home of dragons with a similarly evocative name derived from Latin *finis terrae* 'end of the earth', 'lands' end'.

C33: 'He up the ladder came': thus Tolkien restored the reading in text A.

C49–50: The text as typed read (as in B) 'A rusty spear behind a door | they found and jabbed from under'. In the typescript Tolkien first changed these to read 'A blunderbuss behind a door | they found, and shot from under', then wrote the published lines in the margin as an alternative. (A *blunderbuss* is a short, large-bored gun. It appears again early in Tolkien's story *Farmer Giles of Ham*.)

D3–4: As typed, D^1 and D^2 have 'Green was he, and the blossom white | and the yellow sun gleaming'. Lines 3–8 of the ribbon copy of D^1 are heavily marked, as part of a general revision of the first stanza, with a circled numeral '1' probably indicating a draft on a separate sheet (not extant). Tolkien marked l. 4 of D^2 to be changed to 'gleaming with hard scales'.

D5–6: As typed, D^1 and D^2 have 'He came from the land of Finis-Terre | beyond the Blue Mountains'. On the carbon copy of D^1 Tolkien wrote new text for these lines, 'He came from overseas from Noman's Land [i.e. a land where no man lives] | where the dragons had lived untroubled'.

D7–8: As typed, D^1 has 'Where dragons live, and the moon shines | on high white fountains' (as in C). On the carbon copy of D1 Tolkien wrote new text for these lines, 'But now were short of food & room, | for their numbers had more than doubled'. D^2 as typed has 'Where dragons lie in rivers of gold | and bathe in silver fountains', a revision faintly written on D^1. Tolkien also wrote on D^1 a trial revision for these lines, 'Where dragons lie in rivers of gold | & bathe in silver'.

D9: 'Ave', without an *h*, is intentional, as is 'ydrant' in D41, indicating clipped speech. These were originally typed ''ave' and ''ydrant', but Tolkien deleted the apostrophes.

D15: As typed, D^1 and D^2 have 'cocked his long green ears' (as in C). Tolkien changed this to 'snortled in his nose' on the ribbon copy of D^1.

D19: As typed, D^1 and D^2 have 'till evening comes' (compare C19, 'till the moon comes'). Tolkien changed this to 'till daylight fails' on the ribbon copy of D^1.

D33–37: As typed, D^1 and D^2 have:

The Captain up with his hatchet went,
and said: 'You'd best be moving!'
The dragon laughed: 'Pray, what's your name?
Well, Cap'n George, stop fooling!
I like it here. So go away,

Tolkien marked these lines for revision heavily on the ribbon copy of D^1, with a circled numeral '2' probably indicating a separate draft (see also our note for line D5). He also wrote on the copy a trial revision,

The Captain up with his hatchet went,
Now what be you a-doing
He said you'd best be moving on
[the dragon] said I'm stewing
I like to stew

D46: As typed, D^1 has 'and away the blossom fluttered'. As typed, D^2 has 'and down the blossom fluttered', incorporating a revision faintly marked on D^1.

D52: As typed, D^1 and D^2 have 'rose like thunder'. Tolkien changed this to 'rose in splendour' on the ribbon copy of D^1.

D57: As typed, D^1 has 'Old Higgins'. Tolkien changed this to 'The Higgins' on the ribbon copy of D^1, and typed 'Old Higgins' in D^2.

D79: As typed, D^1 has 'stabbed him hard and deep'. Tolkien changed 'hard and deep' to 'hard and sharp', and then to 'in a vital spot', on the ribbon copy of D^1. D^2 as typed has 'hard and sharp'.

E5–8: This text entered as a revision to the first typescript of this phase (E^3), and carried into the second (E^4). In the second new manuscript (E^2) and in E^3, the lines read:

He came from the land of Finis Terre,
where dragons were untroubled
(For no man ever ventured there),
until their numbers doubled.

In the first new manuscript (E^1), as we have said, 'Finis Terre' was still 'Noman's Land'.

E9: Here, and in line E23, the printed poem in *Winter's Tales for Children 1* has 'Mr', omitting the full stop, presumably an editorial decision.

E10: The printed poem has 'Have'. All manuscripts and typescripts of this version have 'Ave'.

E20: In E^1 and E^2 this line reads 'and the full moon is mounting'. The contraction 'moon's', as in D, returned in E^3.

E43–44: In E^2 these lines originally read 'The dragon's eyes glowed like a forge, | and his belly rumbled'. Tolkien changed them in the manuscript to the final reading. (In E^1 there is no decipherable text after l. 32.)

E51: In E^2 this line originally read 'The dragon cried *havoc*! *haró*!' Tolkien changed it in the manuscript to the final reading. In the printed poem, the two cries are placed within quotation marks. *Havoc* 'destruction, disorder' is an archaic military command permitting men to pillage, plunder, etc. (compare 'cry "Havoc!" and let slip the dogs of war' in Shakespeare's *Julius Caesar*). *Haró* is an old exclamation of distress ('alas').

E61: 'Bury the hatchet' is an Americanism meaning 'cease hostilities, make peace', used here (we presume) ironically. The dragon's method of doing so is extreme, burying Captain George's firefighting tool and Captain George himself.

E64: In E^2 this line originally read 'Somehow he'd missed Miss Biggins' (as in D). Tolkien changed it in E^2 to the final reading, 'and he did not miss Miss Biggins'. Presumably *miss* here is meant to mean 'regret her loss', as the dragon did *miss* her in the sense of 'overlook', or he would not have been surprised. The reader is surprised, too, without the warning 'somehow he'd missed' in earlier texts.

E65: In E^2 Tolkien changed 'while' to 'till'.

E67: In E^2 and E^3 the place is named 'Bimble-town'. In E^4 it is given as 'Bimbletown', without a hyphen.

E73: In E^2, E^3, and E^4 this line read 'None of them's got the wit to admire' (as in D). Tolkien changed it in the second typescript to the final reading.

E75: E^2 has 'Nor the nerve to stab him and risk the fire'. E^3 has the same, revised as 'Nor the nerve to stick steel into his fire'. E4 originally had the revised reading of E3, before Tolkien changed it to 'Nor the nerve with steel to meet his fire', as in the printed poem.

E77–80: Tolkien marked up these lines heavily in E^2, unfortunately only the earlier reading of 77–78, as in D, and the final reading of the four lines are legible among his workings.

108

Chip the Glasses and Crack the Plates! (*c.* 1929–37)

The poems we have considered thus far have been independent creations, even those in the shared setting of 'Bimble Bay' or connected with 'The Silmarillion'. Now we begin a selection of poems from *The Hobbit*, which are of a different kind, each of them conceived as integral to one larger, prose tale. In the world of that story it is natural for characters to sing or recite. This concept was not original to Tolkien: one finds it in Carroll's *Alice* stories, Grahame's *Wind in the Willows*, MacDonald's *At the Back of the North Wind*, Morris's *Roots of the Mountains*. It reflects a time, in fact, when poetry was a more common part of shared culture than it is today (except perhaps in respect to song lyrics). The *Hobbit* verses also serve important functions: they help to distinguish different races and reveal their history, they clarify the thoughts and feelings of individuals, and they advance the plot. They are not mere adornments or interludes.

All of them are brief, some very brief indeed – we do not discount the several riddles in Chapter 5, one of which runs to only two lines, no less poetry for their lack of length. And like the narrative of the book as a whole, the *Hobbit* poems vary in mood. Some are serious or evocative, others light-hearted, even silly. *The Hobbit* was originally an oral tale, told by Tolkien to his three young sons in instalments during their winter 'reads'; and because the children were known to respond to humour in his storytelling, and their father enjoyed it very much himself, he was happy to provide it. The darker aspects of *The Hobbit* also impressed them, indeed the duality of the work – scenes of comedy alternating with moments of tension – is one reason why it has appealed to so many readers.

For the present book, we have selected from *The Hobbit* eight poems or songs, only a fraction of those included in its story, but in our judgement representative of the work and among the most interesting or effective. For each we have assigned a title based on its first line. We also mention other poems in passing. We assume that those who would read the present book are familiar with the story of *The Hobbit*, and do not need us to explain fully its characters and events.

Information on the development of poems we have not included here may be found in John D. Rateliff's invaluable *History of* The Hobbit.

As we have discussed at length in *The J.R.R. Tolkien Companion and Guide*, one cannot be sure when Tolkien began to write *The Hobbit*, or when he completed it. Evidence for its dating is contradictory. But we know that he told at least part of the story to his sons on New Year's Day 1930, because it is mentioned in young John Tolkien's diary. We do not know how far it had progressed to that point, but Tolkien must have begun it no later than the end of 1929, perhaps as early as 1928 or even late 1927. John D. Rateliff argues in *The History of* The Hobbit that the story was complete – to its end as published – by January 1933, when Tolkien lent it to C.S. Lewis; against this, however, is the account in Humphrey Carpenter's authorized biography that Tolkien wrote *The Hobbit* in full only to the death of the dragon, providing an impromptu conclusion for the benefit of his sons, and that the final chapters were written in full only in 1936, when a finished text was wanted by George Allen & Unwin for publication. Other scholars, including Christopher Tolkien, have accepted Carpenter's argument, pointing to a greater maturity of Tolkien's writing in the final chapters of *The Hobbit* and to relevant physical evidence in the story's manuscripts and typescripts.

It is not our aim here to settle this dispute, but it must be mentioned, along with a lack of evidence for the dating of individual chapters of *The Hobbit*, in order to explain why we have grouped most of our selected *Hobbit* poems within the same convenient period, bounded at one end by *circa* 1929 when writing began (that is, no later than 1929) and at the other by early 1937, when Tolkien read proof, having sent George Allen & Unwin copy for typesetting in October 1936. If Carpenter is correct, and the final chapters of *The Hobbit* date from 1936, the poems presented here as nos. 112–115 were composed then rather than (by Rateliff's argument) by the start of 1933. Tolkien revised only one of our selection of poems (no. 111) in proof, in February 1937. Manuscripts, typescripts, and proofs of *The Hobbit* for its first edition are held at Marquette University, Milwaukee, Wisconsin.

The first *Hobbit* poem, *Chip the Glasses*, is pure humour, if alarming to those, like the titular hobbit Bilbo Baggins, inclined to polite behaviour. The dwarves who have come unexpectedly to Bilbo's home imply as they are washing up that they are mistreating his crockery and serving ware, and generally making a shambles of his usually well-ordered hobbit-hole. 'Of course', the narrator assures his audience once the song is complete, 'they did none of those dreadful things' – it was all a tease.

Unfortunately, this poem does not appear in the earliest manuscript of *The Hobbit*, which comprises only six pages of writing from the end of the first chapter; John D. Rateliff calls this the 'Pryftan fragment' after Tolkien's original name for the dragon of the story. The earliest extant text of the poem, given below as A, is found in the first typescript of the first chapter, twelve pages which do not reach quite to the end, typed by Tolkien on his Hammond machine. Considering how closely the dwarves' song is interwoven with the narrative, however, it is hard to imagine that it was not present from the inception of the story. In *The History of* The Hobbit Rateliff argues that the typescript was 'clearly preceded by drafting that does not survive' (p. 42), though it cannot be certain that *Chip the Glasses* was included in missing parts of the 'Pryftan' manuscript.

[A]

Chip the glasses and crack the plates!
    Blunt the knives and bend the forks!
That's what Bilbo Baggins hates —
    Smash the bottles and burn the corks!

Cut the cloth and tread on the fat!
    Pour the milk on the pantry floor!
Leave the bones on the bedroom mat!
    Splash the wine on the cellar door!

Put the things in a boiling bowl,
    Pound them up with a thumping pole,
And when you've finished, if any are whole,
    Send them down the hall to roll.

That's what Bilbo Baggins hates —
So careful, carefully with the plates!!

By this stage, the text was already well advanced, and notably complex considering its brevity: in its first two stanzas the rhyme scheme is ABAB, but in the third it becomes AAAA, and it concludes with a couplet. It reached its final form (B), with only a few differences from A (chiefly in lines 8, 9, and 14), in the first full typescript of *The Hobbit*, also made on the Hammond typewriter.

[B]

Chip the glasses and crack the plates!
    Blunt the knives and bend the forks!
That's what Bilbo Baggins hates —
    Smash the bottles and burn the corks!

Cut the cloth and tread on the fat!
    Pour the milk on the pantry floor!
Leave the bones on the bedroom mat!
    Splash the wine on every door!

Dump the crocks in a boiling bowl;
    Pound them up with a thumping pole:
And when you've finished, if any are whole,
    Send them down the hall to roll!

That's what Bilbo Baggins hates!
So, carefully! carefully with the plates!

This is a vigorous work, with a strong rhythm and many hard consonants. It defines the bold, sharp nature of Dwarves at least as well as any prose exposition. Tolkien also uses a similar effect in Chapter 4, for the song the Goblins sing while 'keeping time with the flap of their flat feet on the stone, and shaking their prisoners as well'; this begins:

Clap! Snap! the black crack!
Grip, grab! Pinch, nab!
And down down to Goblin-town
    You go, my lad!

The Goblins' unpleasant personality is shown again in Chapter 6, in yet another 'horrible song':

Fifteen birds in five firtrees!
their feathers were fastened in a fiery breeze!
But, funny little birds, they had no wings!
O what shall we do with the funny little things?
Roast 'em alive, or stew them in a pot;
fry them, boil them and eat them hot?

Tolkien made a private recording of his own exuberant performance of *Chip the Glasses*. To date, this has been issued only as part of an enhanced e-book of *The Hobbit*.

109

Far over the Misty Mountains Cold (*c.* 1929–37)

In the course of only two pages in Chapter 1 of *The Hobbit*, from almost the moment the dwarves have finished their song and put away the last of Bilbo's dishes, the heretofore humorous mood of *The Hobbit* turns serious. The prose narrative leaves us no doubt that the atmosphere is becoming dark: the hobbit, who has been beside himself with an 'unexpected party', is suddenly 'swept away' by music the dwarves play 'into dark lands under strange moons. . . . The dark came into the room. . . . The dark filled all the room. . . . And suddenly first one and then another began to sing as they played, deep-throated singing of the dwarves in the deep places of their ancient homes. . . .' Their song now is *Far over the Misty Mountains Cold*, and it could not be more of a contrast with the jolly *Chip the Glasses* (no. 108). We give its earliest version as A, from the first (partial) typescript of the book.

[A] Far over the misty mountains cold
To dungeons deep and caverns old
We must away, ere break of day,
To seek the pale enchanted gold.

The dwarves of yore made mighty spells,
While hammers fell like ringing bells
In places deep, where dark things sleep,
In hollow halls beneath the fells.

For ancient king and elvish lord
There many a gleaming golden hoard
They shaped and wrought; and light they caught
To hide in gems on hilt of sword.

On silver necklaces they strung
The flowering stars, on crowns they hung
The dragon-fire, in twisted wire
They meshed the light of moon and sun.

Far over the misty mountains cold
To dungeons deep and caverns old
We must away, ere break of day,
To claim our pale enchanted gold.

And cups they carved there for themselves
And harps of gold; where no man delves
There lay they long, and many a song
Was sung, unheard of men or elves.

The pines were roaring on the height,
The winds were moaning in the night.
The fire was red, it flaming spread;
The trees like torches blazed with light.

The bells were ringing in the vale
And men looked up with faces pale;
The dragon's ire more fierce than fire
Laid low their towers and houses frail.

The mountain smoked beneath the moon;
The dwarves, they heard the tramp of doom.
They fled their hall to dying fall
Beneath his feet, beneath the moon.

Far over the misty mountains grim
To dungeons deep and caverns dim
We must away, ere break of day,
To take our harps and gold from him!

John D. Rateliff observes in *The History of* The Hobbit that this poem, at least, was already part of the story in the 'Pryftan fragment', which begins with a reference to the dwarves' song. 'A single line of this song ("To claim our long forgotten gold")', he remarks (p. 14), survives by chance, written on one side of the first surviving sheet of the fragment, then struck through. This form of the line, however, does not appear in text A.

Tolkien marked a few revisions to this text, most notably changing the repeated 'pale enchanted' to 'long-forgotten' in line 20, and 'take' to 'win' in the final line. These, with some changes of punctuation, entered in the first complete typescript (B), where the final form of the text was reached.

[B]

Far over the misty mountains cold
To dungeons deep and caverns old
We must away ere break of day
To seek the pale enchanted gold.

The dwarves of yore made mighty spells,
While hammers fell like ringing bells
In places deep, where dark things sleep,
In hollow halls beneath the fells.

For ancient king and elvish lord
There many a gleaming golden hoard
They shaped and wrought, and light they caught
to hide in gems on hilt of sword.

On silver necklaces they strung
The flowering stars, on crowns they hung
The dragon-fire, in twisted wire
They meshed the light of moon and sun.

Far over the misty mountains cold
To dungeons deep and caverns old
We must away, ere break of day.
To claim our long-forgotten gold.

Goblets they carved there for themselves
And harps of gold; where no man delves
There lay they long, and many a song
was sung unheard by men or elves.

The pines were roaring on the height,
The winds were moaning in the night.
The fire was red, it flaming spread;
The trees like torches blazed with light.

The bells were ringing in the dale
And men looked up with faces pale;
The dragon's ire more fierce than fire
laid low their towers and houses frail.

The mountain smoked beneath the moon;
The dwarves, they heard the tramp of doom.
They fled their hall to dying fall
Beneath his feet, beneath the moon.

Far over the misty mountains grim
To dungeons deep and caverns dim
We must away, ere break of day,
To win our harps and gold from him!

In the context of the story, this song wakens Bilbo's desire to do what no respectable Hobbit should ever want to do: leave his comfortable home and go with the dwarves, to 'see the great mountains, and hear the pine-trees and the waterfalls, and explore the caves, and wear a sword instead of a walking-stick'. He does not yet know that his guests are telling their own history in song, of the time when a dragon – originally named Pryftan, later Smaug – attacked their home in and around the Lonely Mountain far to the east of Hobbit lands, killed or dispersed their people, and took their wealth as his own. Nor does Bilbo know yet that the dwarves are stating their literal intent to leave the next morning, or that they intend to hire him to help them regain their treasure and kingdom. For their leader – Thorin, in the final text – this quest is an obsession, shown at the end of Chapter I where he is 'still humming to himself' a variation on the song's initial verse of the song:

Far over the misty mountains cold
To dungeons deep and caverns old
We must away, ere break of day,
To find our long-forgotten gold.

The dwarves' song helps to define for the reader what a Dwarf is: one who delves deep into mountains and crafts objects of beauty and value, with 'ringing hammers' in 'hollow halls', for Men and Elves necklaces and swords, 'many a gleaming golden hoard', and for themselves carved goblets and golden harps, singing in secret. In 'The Silmarillion' by this time Tolkien had depicted Dwarves as a grasping and possessive, sometimes evil, race. Something of this nature follows in *The Hobbit*, but in the course of the book is ameliorated.

In his essay 'The Poems of *The Hobbit*' Josh Brown points out that *Far over the Misty Mountains Cold* follows the *ruba'i* quatrain form, with an AABA rhyme scheme, well known in Tolkien's day from

Edward FitzGerald's translation of *The Rubáiyát of Omar Khayyám* (1859):

> Wake! For the Sun, who scatter'd into flight
> The Stars before him from the Field of Night,
> Drives Night along with them from Heav'n, and strikes
> The Sultan's Turret with a Shaft of Light.

Tolkien, however, included an extra feature, an internal rhyme in the third line of every stanza ('We must *away*, ere break of *day*').

Julian Eilmann, who discusses this poem at length in his *J.R.R. Tolkien: Romanticist and Poet*, suggests that it has the shape 'of a typical folk song. In its most frequent form, this kind of stanza has four lines, alternating with three or four feet, i.e. in a regular change between arsis and thesis (iambus). Especially German and English folk songs are often based on iambic tetrameter, which thus creates an easily memorable, rhythmical pattern which favours joint speaking and singing' (p. 414). Eilmann also points out that in *The Lord of the Rings* Tolkien explicitly calls back to *Far over the Misty Mountains Cold* in the song *Farewell We Call to Hearth and Hall!* (no. 153).

A1: In the song, the words 'misty mountains' are not capitalized, though in the course of the story Bilbo and company will cross a range called the Misty Mountains.

A3: 'We must away, ere break of day': only in version A is there a comma after 'away' in l. 3. By version B it is absent, and has remained so. Where the phrase recurs in ll. 19 and 39, the comma is present in both A and B, in the second typescript, and in printings of *The Hobbit* up to the fourth edition (1978), where due to a typesetting error (as it must be) commas were omitted in all three lines, thus 'We must away ere break of day'. Douglas A. Anderson restored the commas in his *Annotated Hobbit* (1988, 2002).

A31: In some printings of *The Hobbit* the first word of this line is misprinted 'Then'.

A34: 'Tramp of doom' refers to the imaginary heavy footsteps of approaching (personified) doom or danger.

110

The Wind Was on the Withered Heath (*c.* 1929–37)

Our third selection from *The Hobbit* has a remarkable affinity with *Far over the Misty Mountains Cold* (no. 109). Indeed, Julian Eilmann has argued that if one were to read their first stanzas one after the other, without knowing they are from different songs – *The Wind Was on the Withered Heath* is in Chapter 7 – one could take them to be from the same, much longer poem, 'so similar are the stanzas in their metrical structure and poetic sound' (*J.R.R. Tolkien: Romanticist and Poet*, p. 414).

Before the dwarves sing these verses, their host – named Beorn in the final text – has been telling 'tales of the wild lands on this side of the mountains [i.e. the eastern side of the Misty Mountains], and especially of the dark and dangerous wood, that lay outstretched far to North and South a day's ride before them, barring their way to the East, the terrible forest of Mirkwood'. The dwarves know 'that they must soon venture into that forest and that after the mountains it was the worst of the perils they had to pass before they came to the dragon's stronghold'. They talk of 'gold and silver and jewels', things to lift a Dwarf's spirits, but in the end it does not lighten their mood. Darkness again enters explicitly: 'The dark night came on outside', the pillars of Beorn's house (on a Norse model) are 'dark at the top like trees of the forest'. Thus the song comes upon them – and it is another song:

> The great door had creaked and slammed. Beorn was gone. The dwarves were sitting cross-legged on the floor round the fire, and presently they began to sing. Some of the verses were like this, but there were many more, and their singing went on for a long while.

Its earliest version, given here as A, is from the first (manuscript) text of Chapter 7.

[A]

The wind was on the withered heath,
But in the forest stirred no leaf:
There shadows lay by night and day,
And dark things silent crept beneath.

The wind came down from mountains cold,
And like a tide it roared and rolled;
The branches groaned, the forest moaned,
and leaves were laid upon the mould.

The wind went on from West to East —
all movement in the Forest ceased,
But shrill and harsh across the marsh
Its whistling voices were released.

The grasses hissed[,] their plumes were bent,
The reeds were rattling — on it went
O'er shaken pool neath heavens cool
Where racing clouds were torn & rent.

It passed the lonely Mountain bare
And swept above the Dragon[']s lair.
There black and dark lay boulders stark —
No light but of the moon was there.

John D. Rateliff has suggested in *The History of* The Hobbit, from the 'fluency' of text A, that it 'was probably drafted on loose sheets that have not survived' (p. 249), and indeed this seems likely.

The poem reached its final form (B) in the first complete typescript of *The Hobbit*. In its earliest version, the song ended at line 20; now Tolkien replaced that line and added a new final stanza, in addition to a small number of other changes.

[B]

The wind was on the withered heath,
but in the forest stirred no leaf:
there shadows lay by night and day,
and dark things silent crept beneath.

The wind came down from mountains cold,
and like a tide it roared and rolled;
the branches groaned, the forest moaned,
and leaves were laid upon the mould.

The wind went on from West to East,
all movement in the forest ceased,
but shrill and harsh across the marsh
its whistling voices were released.

The grasses hissed, their tassels bent,
the reeds were rattling — on it went
o'er shaken pool under heavens cool
where racing clouds were torn and rent.

It passed the lonely Mountain bare
and swept above the dragon's lair:
there black and dark lay boulders stark
and flying smoke was in the air.

It left the world and took its flight
over the wide seas of the night.
The moon set sail upon the gale,
and stars were fanned to leaping light.

Unlike the earlier Dwarf-song, *The Wind Was on the Withered Heath* does not excite Bilbo's nascent sense of adventure, but puts him to sleep. It went on, Tolkien says, for 'a long while', and spares us the lyrics in full (which he never wrote beyond those published). Also in contrast to *Far over the Misty Mountains Cold*, this poem does not tell us much about the dwarves, but it does say something about the landscape the company must travel through, a long way yet, before reaching their destination, 'the lonely Mountain bare' and 'the dragon's lair'. Since the wind of the poem came from the west, the 'mountains cold' are surely the Misty Mountains, west of Beorn's house. The forest which 'stirred no leaf', in which 'shadows lay by night and day, | and dark things silent crept beneath', is clearly Mirkwood, looming in the east. On both of the maps published in *The Hobbit* a 'Withered Heath' is marked north of the Lonely Mountain; on *Thror's Map* it is captioned 'whence came the Great Worms', i.e. dragons. Notably on the *Wilderland* map, marshes (line 11 and following) are indicated near the Long Lake, south of the Desolation of Smaug.

Beyond these mentions of landmarks, foreshadowing the direction of the story for the reader and increasing narrative tension, it is not clear what the song means, or if it is meant to have any deeper meaning. Is this an historical account of a great wind, from the dwarves' cultural memory, perhaps part of a long tale of the Dwarves, as Julian Eilmann wonders? Or is it an allegory of what Thorin and company mean to do in taking revenge on Smaug? In *Exploring J.R.R. Tolkien's* The Hobbit (2012), Corey Olsen suggests that it is 'a kind of heroic, fantasy version of the dwarves' quest', depicting 'the path of Thorin and Company down the Misty Mountains, through Mirkwood, and to the Mountain . . . as a howling gale that sweeps away irresistably all obstacles and dangers' and 'finally sweeps over Smaug's lurking-place, driving him before it like smoke before the wind' (pp. 144–5). If so, it seems remarkable that these words came to all of the dwarves spontaneously and at this moment.

A7: 'The branches' originally read 'Till branches'.
A16: 'Where' originally read 'Neath'.

III

Down the Swift Dark Stream You Go (*c.* 1928–37)

In Chapter 9 of *The Hobbit* Bilbo and the dwarves, walking through Mirkwood, are captured by Wood-elves and taken to the underground halls of their king. There the hobbit, made invisible by a magic ring, frees his friends from imprisonment and concocts a plan to escape in empty wine-barrels the elves will push into the Forest River flowing under the halls. By this, they will be carried south-east to Lake-town, from whence wine had been delivered to the king, and perhaps further south from there: 'the Wood-elves, and especially their king, were very fond of wine, though no vines grew in those parts. The wine, and other goods, were brought from far away, from their kinsfolk in the South, or from the vineyards of Men in distant lands.'

The Elf-workers sing as they go about their tasks. Tolkien first gives a brief rhyme 'as first one barrel and then another rumbled to the dark opening and was pushed over into the cold water some feet below':

Roll — roll — roll — roll,
roll-roll-rolling down the hole!
Heave ho! Splash plump!
Down they go, down they bump!

Then, as some of the elves 'haul on the ropes which pulled up the portcullis at the water-gate so as to let out the barrels as soon as they were all afloat below', they sing a further song, which is our next selected poem.

It seems most instructive to present, from the manuscript, the earliest version of this song (A), scribbled with some plot notes, with Tolkien's changing thoughts shown as they occurred in the act of writing. John D. Rateliff includes this draft in *The History of* The Hobbit (pp. 364–6), rendered in his own system and with some different readings. Tolkien crowded the text onto a manuscript page in four segments, the three shortest added in the margins after the first, longer part, here transcribed from top to bottom.

[A] Down the swift dark stream you go
Back to woods you once did know.
[*deleted:* Leave the northern forest deep]
Leave the halls and caverns deep
Leave the northern mountains steep
Where the forest [dark >] wide and dim
Stoops in shadow grey and grim.
[Pass >] Float beyond the world of trees
[pass the >] out into the whispering breeze
past the rushes past the reeds
[where >] past the marsh's waving weeds
through the mist that rises [pale >] white
[*deleted:* from > where the land of lake and mere]
up from mere and pools and night
[*deleted:* Then > find the lake of many isles]
[*deleted:* Gather at the town]
Find [the town of ??? >] the bridges and the piles
[*deleted:* Where the town is]

[*deleted:* Seek > find the garden and the fields]
Back to pasture, back to mead
[back to >] where the [herds are fat >] kine & oxen feed
Back to gardens on the hills
where the berry swells and fills

Under sunlight under day
South away and south away
Down the swift dark stream you [go]
Back to woods you once did know

Follow [follow >] the high leaping stars
[*deleted:* Spring from the mist,]
[*deleted:* Spring > ?Ring from the]
Up the heavens high & steep
[So >] Through the mist above the land
Over rapid over sand
South away and south away
Seek the sunlight and the day
[*deleted:* Seek the gardens and the field]

Tolkien reached nearly the final form of the song in the next manuscript, and carried it forward through two typescripts. Here, as B, is the text from the published *Hobbit*. In the first (February 1937) proof of the book, Tolkien altered 'woods' in lines 2 and 27 to 'lands', in concert with other changes and additions at this point. The barrels will return to Lake-town, built away from the shore in Esgaroth, the Long Lake, thus not to 'woods', though the Forest River passes through the wooded Elf-realm.

[B]

Down the swift dark stream you go
Back to lands you once did know!
Leave the halls and caverns deep,
Leave the northern mountains steep,
Where the forest wide and dim
Stoops in shadow grey and grim!
Float beyond the world of trees
Out into the whispering breeze,
Past the rushes, past the reeds,
Past the marsh's waving weeds,
Through the mist that riseth white
Up from mere and pool at night!
Follow, follow stars that leap
Up the heavens cold and steep;
Turn when dawn comes over land,
Over rapid, over sand.
South away! and South away!
Seek the sunlight and the day,
Back to pasture, back to mead,
Where the kine and oxen feed!
Back to gardens on the hills
Where the berry swells and fills
Under sunlight, under day!
South away! and South away!
Down the swift dark stream you go
Back to lands you once did know!

Beyond its immediate interest as a description of the landscape through which the barrels, and thus the escaping dwarves and hobbit, will be passing, the song also says much about the Elves who composed it. It is an ode to the natural world that is the Elves' home and their delight: caverns and hills, forest and marsh, mere and pool, all under the sun and stars which they hold sacred. Corey Olsen (*Explor-*

ing J.R.R. Tolkien's The Hobbit) writes of it as if it were a benediction and a prophecy, as the dwarves, no less than the barrels, are returning home. Josh Brown ('The Poems of *The Hobbit*') emphasizes its regular beat, consistent with the elves' repetitive work, and remarks on its anthropomorphic language – 'whispering breeze', 'waving reeds', 'leaping stars' – which suggest that the elves see the natural world as a living thing in itself.

A1: John D. Rateliff reads a mark preceding 'Down', hanging at left beyond the line of text, as 'O'. We see this as an indeterminate mark which may have been an 'S' or an 'O', or one or the other obliterated by Tolkien, in any case not present in any later manuscript or typescript.

A26: Rateliff reads the final word as 'go'.

A28: Stars 'leap' when they rise higher in the sky.

112

Under the Mountain Dark and Tall (*c.* 1929–37)

By Chapter 15 of *The Hobbit*, Bilbo and company have arrived at Lake-town, and then at last have reached the Lonely Mountain. The dragon, rising in anger, is killed over Lake-town by the archer Bard. Thorin is now free to claim the Dwarves' ancient treasure, but Elves and Men are gathering to do the same. As the dwarves wait for aid from their people, they make music to soften their king's mood; 'but their song was not an elvish song, and was much like the song they had sung long before in Bilbo's little hobbit-hole'. Indeed, it has the same structure as *Far over the Misty Mountains Cold* (no. 109), and even includes an entire stanza and other lines and phrases from the earlier work.

The earliest manuscript of the new poem is a rough draft made on a loose sheet. It can hardly be called a version, but rather, thoughts and trial phrases. John D. Rateliff attempts a full reading in *The History of* The Hobbit (p. 647); here, as A, we give only the first few lines as a sample.

[A]

Under the Mountain dark and tall
The King [is ?returned to his h >] is come unto his hall
The [?throne] worm of dread
The foe is dead the Worm of Dread ???
And [so shall >] ever so his foes shall fall

The poem reached its full and final form (B) in the first complete typescript of *The Hobbit*.

[B]

Under the mountain dark and tall
The King has come unto his hall
His foe is dead, the Worm of Dread,
And ever so his foes shall fall.

The sword is sharp, the spear is long,
The arrow swift, the Gate is strong;
The heart is bold that looks on gold;
The dwarves no more shall suffer wrong.

The dwarves of yore made mighty spells,
While hammers fell like ringing bells
In places deep, where dark things sleep,
In hollow halls beneath the fells.

On silver necklaces they strung
The light of stars, on crowns they hung
The dragon-fire, from twisted wire
The melody of harps they wrung.

The mountain throne once more is freed!
O! wandering folk, the summons heed!
Come haste! Come haste! across the waste!
The king of friend and kin hath need.

Now call we over mountains cold,
'Come back unto the caverns old'!
Here at the gates the king awaits,
His hands are rich with gems and gold.

The king has come unto his hall
Under the Mountain dark and tall,
The Worm of Dread is slain and dead,
And ever so our foes shall fall!

Rateliff comments that *Under the Mountain Dark and Tall* and *Far over the Misty Mountains Cold* 'are clearly meant to be companion pieces, depicting the hoped-for goal at the onset of the quest and its apparent achievement at what Bilbo had optimistically hoped would be its end' (pp. 646–7). The present poem continues the history of the Dwarves begun in the earlier work and continued in *The Wind Was on the Withered Heath* (no. 110), but it is a case of history as written by the victors. It was not Thorin and company who slew the 'Worm of Dread', in fact it was their actions which led to Smaug's attack on Lake-town.

The song is overblown – a challenge to the gathering armies of Men and Elves – and Thorin will have to face rightful claims to the treasure by those who also have suffered loss due to the dragon. His, though, is the bold heart that has looked on gold (line 7). Rateliff relates this to an underlying idea in *The Hobbit*, that a heart may be kindled to ferocity by 'dragon-sickness', or the desire to possess gold or jewels. In Chapter 18 Bilbo remarks to a wounded Thorin that their adventure is bitter if it must end with his death, 'and not a mountain of gold can amend it'. To this the king replies sagely: 'If more of us valued food and cheer and song above hoarded gold, it would be a merrier world.'

B2: Only in this line is 'King' capitalized. In the first and second typescripts of *The Hobbit* it is not, but has had a capital since the first typesetting, as it does in the rough draft.

B3: 'His foe', i.e. the dragon.

B6: In fact, the lesser gates were broken or blocked by Smaug, and the Front Gate is open, a gate in name only.

B9–12: This stanza is identical to the second of *Far over the Misty Mountains Cold.*

B13–16: Compare in *Far over the Misty Mountains Cold*:

> On silver necklaces they strung
> The flowering stars, on crowns they hung
> The dragon-fire, in twisted wire
> They meshed the light of moon and sun.

'Wrung' is an archaic spelling of *ring* 'cause to make a clear sound'.

B18: The 'wandering folk' are the dwarves' kin, to whom Thorin has sent messages requesting aid.

B23–26: A similar thought is expressed in a song sung in Chapter 10 by men of Lake-town, 'concerning the return of the King under the Mountain; that it was Thror's grandson not Thror himself that had come back did not bother them at all.' Among their lyrics is the promise that the King's 'wealth shall flow in fountains | And the rivers golden run.'

113

O Where Are You Going · *The Dragon Is Withered* (*c*. 1929–37)

There are twenty-four poems in *The Hobbit* by our count, all but four in the first ten of the book's nineteen chapters. As Bilbo and the dwarves reach the Lonely Mountain, in Chapter 11, the narrative becomes increasingly serious, and for the space of four chapters is wholly in prose; it may be that Tolkien felt that poetry would distract from the tension. *Under the Mountain Dark and Tall* (no. 112) appears in Chapter 15, but that is the only poem until three appear in quick succession in Chapter 19: Bilbo is returning home, and the mood is right for a flurry of verse.

The earliest text of the first of these final *Hobbit* poems is a manuscript which appears to be a fair copy, though for all that was set down quickly, with inconsistent capitalization. It has minor revisions, made probably in the course of writing, which we have included in our transcription (A).

[A]

O where are you going,
    so late in returning?
The river is flowing,
    the stars are all burning!
O whither so laden
    so sad and so dreary?
Here elf and elf-maiden
    Now welcome the weary

    Come, tra-la-la lally,
    Come back to the valley

The stars are far brighter
    than gems without measure,
The moon is far whiter
    than silver in treasure;
The fire is more shining
    on hearth in the gloaming
Than gold won in mining,
So cease from your roaming!

Come tra-la-lalley
come back to the valley!

The dragon is withered
His bones are now crumbled,
His armour is shivered,
his splendour is humbled.
Though sword shall be rusted,
and crown and throne perish,
with strength that men trusted
and wealth that they cherish.
Here grass is [yet >] still growing
And leaves are yet swinging,
the white water flowing
and elves [are all >] are yet [*or* at their] singing

Come tra la lally
come back to the valley!

In the version that followed A, in addition to revisions of text and a thorough change of capitalization, punctuation, and formatting, Tolkien reversed in order the first and last stanzas. We give the published version of the poem as B, established in the first complete typescript.

[B]

The dragon is withered,
His bones are now crumbled;
His armour is shivered,
His splendour is humbled!
Though sword shall be rusted,
And throne and crown perish,
With strength that men trusted
And wealth that they cherish,
Here grass is still growing,
And leaves are yet swinging,
The white water flowing,
And elves are yet singing
Come! Tra-la-la-lally!
Come back to the valley!

The stars are far brighter
Than gems without measure,
The moon is far whiter

Than silver in treasure;
The fire is more shining
On hearth in the gloaming
Than gold won by mining,
So why go a-roaming?
O! Tra-la-la-lally
Come back to the Valley.

O! Where are you going,
So late in returning?
The river is flowing,
The stars are all burning!
O! Whither so laden,
So sad and so dreary?
Here elf and elf-maiden
Now welcome the weary
With Tra-la-la-lally
Come back to the Valley,
Tra-la-la-lally
Fa-la-la-lally
Fa-la!

This is a song of the Elves in the valley of Rivendell, following on one they sing in Chapter 3. There, under stars 'burning bright and blue' Bilbo hears 'a burst of song like laughter in the trees'. It begins:

O! What are you doing,
And where are you going?
Your ponies need shoeing!
The river is flowing!
O! tra-la-la-lally
here down in the valley!

'So they laughed and sang in the trees', says the narrator, 'and pretty fair nonsense I daresay you think it.' In Chapter 19, Bilbo returns to Rivendell and hears the elves 'still singing in the trees, as if they had not stopped since he left; and as soon as the riders came down into the lower glades of the wood they burst into a song of much the same kind as before.' And so it is. These are not the dignified, noble Elves of 'The Silmarillion' or *The Lord of the Rings*, but of fairy-stories. In Rivendell, as described in *The Lord of the Rings*, the elves make music, but nothing of the 'tra-la-la-lally' variety – Tolkien would not revisit that mode of writing. Instead, Frodo is enchanted by 'the beauty of the melodies and of the interwoven words in elven-tongues' (Book II, Chapter 1), all of it left to the imagination.

And yet, the later *Hobbit* song of the elves has an element of seriousness lacking in the first. This is partly because it refers back to the story Tolkien has just told. Bilbo and the wizard Gandalf are riding west, laden with baggage and treasure. The dragon has been defeated and the Dwarf-kingdom under the Mountain restored, but from the elves' point of view 'throne and crown' will perish in time, regardless of strength or wealth – we have returned to the theme of *The Hoard* (poem no. 69). But there will still be grass growing and rivers flowing (at least in Rivendell), and stars, moon, and a hearth fire are more valuable than jewels, silver, or gold. Again, Tolkien comments on the dangers of possessiveness.

Verlyn Flieger has commented that 'the striking change in mood wrought by difference in subject matter and diction' in this poem, relative to *O! What Are You Doing* in Chapter 3 of *The Hobbit*, 'suggests an alteration in the Elves' sensibilities as well as their poetic gifts. Whether intended as such or not, the later poem comments on the frivolity of the earlier version' ('Poems by J.R.R. Tolkien: *The Hobbit*' (2006), p. 522).

A29: In writing this line, Tolkien inserted the word 'grass' after he had accidentally left it out. John D. Rateliff suggests in *The History of* The Hobbit that Tolkien overlooked it when making a fair copy from a lost draft.

B14: The word 'valley' is not capitalized in this line, but 'Valley' in ll. 24 and 34.

114

Sing All Ye Joyful, Now Sing All Together · *Elvish Song in Rivendell* (*c.* 1929–37)

Soon after the elves of Rivendell sing *The Dragon Is Withered* (no. 113) in Chapter 19 of *The Hobbit*, Bilbo falls asleep. He wakes near dawn to find himself in bed, and below his window 'many elves [are] singing loud and clear on the banks of the stream'. Their song – they say – is a lullaby, and yet is sung so loudly that Bilbo tells the singers it 'would waken a drunken goblin!' Tolkien surely meant this to be ironic; and if so, the joke was on the elves, as their guest promptly goes back to sleep.

The earliest text of the song is a fair copy manuscript (A):

[A] Sing all ye joyful, now sing all together!
The wind's in the tree-top the wind's in the heather;
The stars are in blossom, the moon is in flower,
Bright are the windows of night in her tower!

Dance all ye joyful, now dance all together!
Soft is the grass, and let foot be like feather!
The river is silver, the shadows are fleeting,
Merry is May time and merry our meeting.

Sing we now softly, and dreams let us weave him,
Wind him in slumber and there let us leave him!
The wanderer sleepeth, now soft be his pillow!
Lullaby, lullaby, alder and willow!
    Hush, hush, oak ash and thorn,
    Sigh no more pine till the wind of the morn;
    Fall Moon, dark be the land,
    Hushed be all water, till dawn is at hand!

The same text remained in the first and second complete typescripts of *The Hobbit*, if with variations in format, capitalization, and punctuation. With the first printed proof, however, presumably with the author's permission, lines 13–16 were re-ordered, and the published version (B) was reached.

[B] Sing all ye joyful, now sing all together!
The wind's in the tree-top, the wind's in the heather;
The stars are in blossom, the moon is in flower,
And bright are the windows of Night in her tower.

Dance all ye joyful, now dance all together!
Soft is the grass, and let foot be like feather!
The river is silver, the shadows are fleeting;
Merry is May-time, and merry our meeting.

Sing we now softly, and dreams let us weave him!
Wind him in slumber and there let us leave him!
The wanderer sleepeth. Now soft be his pillow!
Lullaby! Lullaby! Alder and Willow!
Sigh no more Pine, till the wind of the morn!
    Fall Moon! Dark be the land!
    Hush! Hush! Oak, Ash, and Thorn!
Hushed be all water, till dawn is at hand!

'By oak and ash and thorn' is an ancient oath, referring to three trees commonly found in England and related by some to mysticism. They also figure in a familiar poem by Rudyard Kipling, 'A Tree Song', published in *Puck of Pook's Hill* (1906); this begins:

Of all the trees that grow so fair,
    Old England to adorn,
Greater are none beneath the Sun,
    Than Oak, and Ash, and Thorn.
Sing Oak, and Ash, and Thorn, good sirs,
    (All of a Midsummer morn!)
Surely we sing no little thing,
    In Oak, and Ash, and Thorn!

On the flowering of the oak, ash, and thorn (hawthorn) in May, see our discussion for *May-Day* (poem no. 26).

Here it is convenient also to discuss another poem, *Elvish Song in Rivendell*, which may be related to *Sing All Ye Joyful* and evidently was written around the same time. Both poems speak of home, and nature, and the beauty of night. There is no direct evidence that *Elvish Song* was written for *The Hobbit*; the manuscript of the book calls for a 'song' in Chapter 19 where *Sing All Ye Joyful* ultimately appeared, with the work in question to be composed separate from the primary text. It may be that *Elvish Song* was an alternate candidate, but it is also possible that it was originally unrelated to *The Hobbit*, and connected with the elves of Rivendell only later through its title.

Elvish Song in Rivendell exists in two manuscripts. In the first, it has no title, and occupies half of a page shared with a manuscript of Tolkien's (here untitled) poem *The Shadow Man* (no. 147). Since the latter was published in 1936, *Elvish Song* must have been composed by that date. We have transcribed its first text as C.

[C]

Come home, come home, ye merry folk!
The sun is sinking and the oak
    Has wrapped his feet in gloom.
Come home! The evening shadows loom
Beneath the hills and palely bloom
    White flowers in the dark.

The birds are twittering sleepy — hark!
And in the sky a silver spark
    The earliest star has lit.
Come home! The bats begin to flit,
And by the hearth 'tis time to sit.
    Come home! Come home, and sing:

Sing merrily, sing merrily, sing all together,
    Let the song go! Let the sound ring!
The moon with his light, the bird with his feather:
    Let the moon sail, let the bird wing!
The flower with her honey, the tree with his weather:
    Let the flower blow, let the tree swing!
Sing merrily, sing merrily, sing all together!

The second manuscript of the poem is on a page to itself. In this (D) Tolkien made revisions, and at some later time added a title (hastily, compared with the careful script of the work proper). We describe one textual revision in our notes.

[D]

Come home, come home, ye merry folk!
The sun is sinking, and the oak
    In gloom has wrapped his feet.
Come home! The shades of evening loom
Beneath the hills, and palely bloom
    Night-flowers white and sweet.

Come home! The birds have fled the dark,
And in the sky with silver spark
    The early stars now spring.
Come home! The bats begin to flit,
And by the hearth 'tis time to sit.
    Come home, come home and sing!

Sing merrily, sing merrily, sing all together!
    Let the song go! Let the sound ring!
The moon with his light, the bird with his feather:
    Let the moon sail, let the bird wing!
The flower with her honey, the tree with his weather:
    Let the flower blow, let the tree swing!
Sing merrily, sing merrily, sing all together!

A8: 'May time': the chapter begins 'It was on May the First that the two [Bilbo and Gandalf] came back at last to the brink of the valley of Rivendell. . . .'

A12–14: In Chapter 3 Tolkien mentions pine, beech, and oak in the elves' valley.

D9: This line originally read 'The earliest star doth swing'. Compare, in text C, 'The earliest star has lit'.

115

Roads Go Ever Ever On · *The Road Goes Ever On and On* (*c.* 1928–48)

The final poem in *The Hobbit* is spoken by Bilbo in Chapter 19 as he comes in sight of his own country, 'the shapes of the land and of the trees were as well known to him as his hands and toes', in particular the hill where he lives. He reflects on his journey through *The Hobbit*, and on the nature of roads to lead one there and back again.

The earliest version of the work is a hastily written manuscript, which we have transcribed (as A) with Tolkien's revisions included.

[A] Roads go ever ever on
[under >] over rock and under tree
by caves where never sun has shone
by streams that never find the sea.

[*deleted:* ?R, *probably for* Roads] over grass and over stone
and under mountains in the moon
over snow by winter sown
and through the merry flowers of June

Roads go ever ever on
under cloud and under [sun >] star
[*deleted:* But [never >] foot hath never never gone]
[*deleted:* Beyond the seas to Gondobar]
yet feet that wandering have gone
turn at last to home afar

Eyes that [have >] fire and sword have seen
[and terror walking in the wild [*or possibly* world] >]
    And [terror >] horror in the halls of stone.
Look at last on meadows green
and the trees and hill they long have known.

At the head of this manuscript Tolkien wrote the words 'Bilbo['s] First Poem'. It was, however, neither the first poem by Bilbo to appear in *The Hobbit*, nor the first that Bilbo composed. One of the riddles Bilbo asked Gollum in Chapter 5 was made up on the spot ('An eye in a blue face'), and so were both of the songs he invented 'on the spur of a very awkward moment' to mock the spiders in Chapter 8.

Tolkien reached the final text of *Roads Go Ever Ever On* in the first complete typescript of *The Hobbit*, though he did not indent its alternate lines until it was set in type for the first proof. We give the published version as B.

[B]

Roads go ever ever on,
  Over rock and under tree,
By caves where never sun has shone,
  By streams that never find the sea;
Over snow by winter sown,
  And through the merry flowers of June,
Over grass and over stone,
  And under mountains in the moon.

Roads go ever ever on,
  Under cloud and under star,
Yet feet that wandering have gone
  Turn at last to home afar.
Eyes that fire and sword have seen
  And horror in the halls of stone
Look at last on meadows green
  And trees and hills they long have known.

The Hobbit was issued in September 1937, and was so successful that its publisher asked for a sequel. Although he would have preferred to continue to work on 'The Silmarillion', Tolkien began that December to write a new story about Hobbits, which became *The Lord of the Rings*. This too would involve a journey; it was not immediately clear to Tolkien whose journey it was, or to what purpose. At first its central character was again Bilbo Baggins, then it was Bilbo's son Bingo, and then Bilbo's adopted cousin Bingo Bolger-Baggins. Somehow the magic ring Bilbo found in *The Hobbit* would be involved. As drafts progressed, Bingo and his friends Odo Took (later Bolger), Frodo Took, and Vigo Took (later Marmaduke Brandybuck) set out for Rivendell, and probably between late February and 4 March 1938 Tolkien introduced another poem about a road, echoing his final *Hobbit* verse.

Its trials occupy most of two manuscript pages, in pencil, ink, and ink overwriting pencil, and include two columns of words which rhyme with 'road'. Here, as C, we have transcribed the most substantive of these very rough workings, as best we can make them out.

[C]

Ever onward runs the road
Till it joins some larger way
For it bears no weary load
and makes no count of night or day,
up hill down hill over stones
white with dust or brown with leaves

Ever onward runs the road
from your door where it begins

we follow it as best we can
until it joins some larger way

It has no errand but to stay
down from the door where it began
until it joins some larger way

pursuing it with weary feet
until it joins some larger way
and whither then we cannot say

These thoughts coalesced in a text of which a few lines are clear:

Ever onward runs the Road
down from the door where it began.

The Road runs ever on and on
down from the door where it began,
[*deleted:* and ever so the Road has go]
Before us far the Road has gone
and we come after it who can.

In the draft story, the hobbits have been walking through their country when Odo begins 'to lag behind. At last he stopped, and gave a big yawn. "I am so sleepy" he said ["]that soon I shall fall down on the road! What about a place for the night, or are you fellows going to sleep on your legs." "The road goes on forever, but we can't until we rest" [Frodo >] Bingo said.' This dialogue is followed by the poem

(D), after which Odo comments 'How Bilboish', that is, like something Bilbo would write.

[D]

[*deleted:* Roads go ever ever on]
The Road goes ever on and on
down from the Door where it began:
before us far the Road has gone,
and we come after it who can;
pursuing it with weary feet,
until it joins some larger way,
where many paths and errands meet,
and whither then? — we cannot say!

In *The Return of the Shadow* Christopher Tolkien notes that 'there is no indication, in the manuscript as written, who spoke the verse' (p. 47), but it would seem to follow that the speaker is Bingo, as the poem immediately follows his prose remark about the road.

With only minor revision to this text, and still early in writing *The Lord of the Rings*, Tolkien reached the final form of the poem (E) in its first typescript. In Book I, Chapter 3 of the published story the lines are spoken by Frodo (Bilbo's adopted nephew, formerly Bingo), 'aloud but as if to himself'.

[E]

The Road goes ever on and on
    Down from the door where it began.
Now far ahead the Road has gone,
    And I must follow, if I can,
Pursuing it with weary feet,
    Until it joins some larger way,
Where many paths and errands meet.
    And whither then? I cannot say.

Frodo's cousin Pippin remarks – enlarging on Odo's comment in the previous version – that the poem 'sounds like a bit of old Bilbo's rhyming. Or is it one of your imitations? It does not sound altogether encouraging.' 'I don't know,' replies Frodo. 'It came to me then, as if I was making it up; but I may have heard it long ago. Certainly it reminds me very much of Bilbo in the last years, before he went away. He used often to say there was only one Road; that it was like a great river: its springs were at every doorstep, and every path was its tributary.' Thus Bilbo's *Hobbit* poem celebrating a return home from his journey to the Lonely Mountain was adapted to suit other hobbits' adventures in a much wider world.

In the completed *Lord of the Rings*, when Frodo is uncertain about Bilbo's authorship of the poem, we the readers are not, for Bilbo has already recited it at the end of Chapter 1. This version of that chapter, however, belongs to a later phase of composition, in late September or early October 1938, when Tolkien returned to the beginning of his narrative and made significant revisions. At first he inserted the existing text of the poem (E), with 'weary feet' in line 5, but changed those words in manuscript [F] to 'eager feet'.

[F]

The Road goes ever on and on
    Down from the Door where it began.
Now far ahead the Road has gone,
    And I must follow, if I can,
Pursuing it with eager feet,
    Until it joins some larger way,
Where many paths and errands meet.
    And whither then? I cannot say.

Bilbo is happy to leave his comfortable home once more, but Bingo (Frodo) is not, and therefore the latter's feet are 'weary' (that is, reluctant) rather than 'eager'.

In his last stage of writing *The Lord of the Rings*, probably in 1948 after delays and distractions during the war years, Tolkien included a third version of *The Road Goes Ever On and On* in Book VI, Chapter 6, written between 14 August and 14 September 1948. The Ring has been destroyed, and Frodo has returned to Rivendell, where Bilbo has been a guest of the elves since he left Hobbiton. Bilbo laments having seen little of the world during the events of *The Hobbit*, compared with Frodo's experiences in the War of the Ring, but declares it 'too late now' for him to have another adventure; 'and really I think it's much more comfortable to sit here and hear about it'. He reprises his verse appropriately, transcribed here (as G) from the printed text with details of its initial form in our notes. The final text of this final version of the poem was fixed in the second manuscript of the chapter.

[G]

The Road goes ever on and on
    Out from the door where it began.
Now far ahead the Road has gone,
    Let others follow it who can!
Let them a journey new begin,
    But I at last with weary feet

Will turn towards the lighted inn,
    My evening-rest and sleep to meet.

John D. Rateliff has remarked that *Roads Go Ever Ever On* in *The Hobbit* is 'a celebration of both the allure of possibilities of unending travel and the joy of homecoming by someone whose journeys are now ending' (*The History of* The Hobbit, p. 724), while Verlyn Flieger has called *The Road Goes Ever On and On* a poem which 'most fully epitomizes' *The Lord of the Rings*. The latter, she writes, 'reprises the circular structure of *The Hobbit* and foreshadows that of *The Lord of the Rings*, sets the stage for Frodo's greater journey, and brings him and the story There and bittersweetly Back Again' ('Poems by Tolkien: *The Lord of the Rings*' (2006), p. 523). Using the title 'Old Walking Song' to encompass both poems, Julian Eilmann has said that they possess 'the quality of a *leitmotif*', reflecting 'the motif of wandering, which is constitutive of the Middle-earth novels, in poetic form' (*J.R.R. Tolkien: Romanticist and Poet*, p. 361).

In *The History of* The Hobbit Rateliff wonders if Tolkien was inspired to write his *Hobbit* poem by a work his friend G.B. Smith composed, 'Songs on the Downs', which appeared with *Goblin Feet* (no. 27) in *Oxford Poetry 1915* (p. 60). Its first part reads:

This is the road the Romans made,
    This track half lost in the green hills,
Or fading in a forest-glade
    ''Mid violets and daffodils.

The years have fallen like dead leaves,
    Unwept, uncounted, and unstayed
(Such as the autumn tempest thieves),
    Since first this road the Romans made.

Rateliff also considers the 'Romance' of E.F.A. Geach, printed immediately after *Goblin Feet* in the anthology *Fifty New Poems for Children* (1922), issued by Basil Blackwell in Oxford, publisher of the *Oxford Poetry* series. Geach's poem reads (p. 28):

Round the next corner and in the next street
Adventure lies in wait for you.
Oh, who can tell what you may meet
Round the next corner and in the next street!

Could life be anything but sweet
When all is hazardous and new
Round the next corner and in the next street?
Adventure lies in wait for you.

Martin Simonson, meanwhile, has suggested in The Lord of the Rings *and the Western Narrative Tradition* (2008) a possible influence in 'Roads', composed in 1916 by the Georgian poet Edward Thomas. This poem begins:

I love roads:
The goddesses that dwell
Far along invisible
Are my favourite gods.

Roads go on
While we forget, and are
Forgotten like a star
That shoots and its gone.

Although any of these is possible, Tolkien would not have needed a specific inspiration for either of the poems in question. The image of the open road was common in poetry and story when he was young. Consider also, for example, the chapter 'The Open Road' in *The Wind in the Willows* by Kenneth Grahame (1908), or the work of W.H. Davies (1871–1940), the Welsh poet who lived part of his life as a tramp. The idea of the Road was literally attractive to some of Tolkien's contemporaries, with its promise of freedom and adventure, as it was for Bilbo, setting out again for Rivendell, if balanced against risk and uncertainty, as it was for Frodo and his companions.

In 1952 Tolkien made a private recording of version F of *The Road Goes Ever On and On*, since commercially released. A musical setting of the poem by Donald Swann appeared in *The Road Goes Ever On: A Song Cycle* (1967), and was performed by pianist Swann and baritone William Elvin on the recording *Poems and Songs of Middle Earth* (1967).

A5–8: Tolkien marked these lines for rearrangement as follows: 3, 4, 1, 2. The revised order is seen in the final text.

A6: The construction 'in the moon', i.e. *in* rather than, but meaning, *on* or *of*, reflects an old, once-common usage, as in the name 'Man in the Moon', or the question 'where in the world'. Bilbo has walked under the lunar mountains in the sense that the moon has been in the sky as he travelled.

A12: In *The History of* The Hobbit John D. Rateliff by preference reads the final word of this line as 'Gondobar'. He suggests that 'find the bar' is also a possible reading, perhaps an allusion to Tennyson's 'Crossing the Bar'; to our eyes this is unlikely, as the letters in question are clearly joined up. *Gondobar*, as we have seen (poem nos. 33, 66, 74), is one of the seven names of Gondolin, and Gondolin is mentioned in Chapter 3 of *The Hobbit*. It is not certain, however, if Bilbo's use of 'Gondobar' was to be a reference to Gondolin, lost ages before the events of *The Hobbit*, or merely an invention to suggest a place fantastic and far distant; and at any rate, Tolkien deleted it in the act of writing.

A13: This line is written in ink over what appears to be the same text in pencil.

A14: This line is written in ink over a partial line in pencil, possibly 'Come at last'.

A15: This line is written in ink over a line in pencil, 'Turn at last to home afar'.

D1: It seems clear that Tolkien intended at first to reprise Bilbo's poem from Chapter 19 of *The Hobbit*, beginning 'Roads go ever ever on'.

D3: 'Door' is not capitalized in C, gains a capital in D, loses it again in the first typescript (possibly in error), regains it in the next (manuscript) text, and keeps it through subsequent typescripts and proofs in Marquette University's Tolkien papers, but 'door' is the reading in the first printing and in later editions (as E). In the version that Bilbo speaks (ultimately Book I, Chapter 1), 'Door' is capitalized in the first manuscript (F), and also in subsequent manuscripts, but becomes 'door' in the first typescript and remains without a capital. In the final version (G) the word is rendered 'door' from the first manuscript. We presume that Tolkien, or a copy-editor, noticed the variation in the first version (i.e. the second in order of appearance in *The Lord of the Rings*) and regularized 'Door' to 'door'. The word *door*, without a capital, is generic – one may begin a journey from any door – but the *Road* to be travelled is the Road of Life, capitalized consistently in all three versions of the poem to indicate its iconic importance.

D4: Tolkien considered whether to change 'far' to 'long'.

G4: In its first manuscript appearance, this line ends with a full stop.

G5: This line originally read 'Let others journeys new begin'.

G8: This line originally read 'There sleep and rest at last to meet'.

116

The Corrigan · The Lay of Aotrou and Itroun (?1929–41)

It seems likely that Tolkien wrote the three poems discussed here, all of them inspired by Breton lays, between November 1929 and summer 1930, during a hiatus from writing the *Lay of Leithian* (no. 92). Two of these are a pair, each entitled *The Corrigan*, and the third is *The Lay of Aotrou and Itroun*. In her 2016 edition of these works (*The Lay of Aotrou and Itroun together with the Corrigan Poems*), Verlyn Flieger describes the two 'Corrigan' poems as 'a kind of diptych, adjoining works hinged by a shared title', while Christopher Tolkien calls them 'a composite poem' in two parts (pp. 29, xii). Each is a pastiche of a Breton original, its source identified by Tolkien in notes on a fair copy manuscript. The first was suggested by 'Ar bugel Laec'hiet' ('The Changeling'), and the second by 'Aotrou Nann Hag ar Gorrigan' ('Lord Nann and the Corrigan'); these are lays of Cornuoaille and Léon respectively, two feudal states of Brittany in north-western France, an area settled by Celtic emigrants from the island of Britain in the 5th century. Christopher notes that there is no evidence with which to date the 'Corrigan' verses, but felt it unlikely that there was a long interval between the writing of those and the composition of *Aotrou and Itroun*.

The first 'Corrigan' poem comprises seventy-six lines in nineteen stanzas of four lines, rhyming AAAA, with the fourth line of each quatrain shorter than the other three. Flieger reproduces (p. 34) the first page of the fair copy manuscript of the work, and discusses differences between that and rough drafts. The words of the poem are spoken variously by the Virgin Mary, by a mother whose child has been stolen by a corrigan (here the word means simply a fay or witch) and replaced with a changeling (a human-like, often ill-featured fairy creature), by a hermit whom the Virgin instructs the mother to consult, by the changeling itself, and finally by the child returned to his cradle. The hermit advises the mother:

> 'Bid them grind an acorn, bid them feign
> In a shell to cook it for master and men

At midday hour. If he [the changeling] sees that then,
He will speak again.

And if he speaks, there hangs on thy wall
A cross-hilt sword old and tall —
Raise it to strike and he will call,
And the spell will fall.'

Similar stories of changelings and ways to recover a real child, such as cooking a meal in an eggshell to trick the fairy creature into speaking (because what it sees is so remarkable), are common in folk and fairy tales all over Europe. Here an iron sword, whose hilt forms the Christian sign of the cross, is also used, as an object of power against the supernatural.

The second 'Corrigan' poem is a longer work, in 104 lines, also arranged in quatrains but rhyming AAAB, except for two stanzas in five lines (AABBC) and one in six (AABCCB). In addition, except for the concluding stanza, the final lines in each pair of stanzas rhyme with each other. For this, too, Flieger reproduces (p. 48) the first page of its fair copy, noting that the final manuscript was preceded by two shorter drafts with many deletions and revisions. We give the fair copy text complete as A, as printed by Flieger, pp. 47, 49–52.

[A]

See how high in their joy they ride,
The young earl and his young bride!
May nought ever their joy divide,
Though the world be full of wonder.

There is a song from windows high.
Why do they sing? Light may she lie!
Yestreve there came two babes' cry
As I stood thereunder.

A manchild and a fair maid
Were as lilies fair in cradle laid,
And the earl to his young wife said:
'For what doth thy heart hunger?

A son thou hast given me,
And that will I find for thee,
Though I should ride o'er land and lea,
And suffer thirst and hunger.

For fowl that swim the shallow mere?
From greenwood the fallow deer?'
'I would fain have the fallow deer.
    But I would not have thee wander.'

His lance of ash he caught in hand,
His black horse bore him o'er the land.
Under green boughs of Broceliand
    His horn winds faintly yonder.

A white doe startled beneath the leaves,
He hunted her from the forest-eaves;
Into twilight under the leaves
    He rode on ever after.

The earth shook beneath the hoof;
The boughs were bent into a roof,
And the sun was woven in that woof,
    And afar there was a laughter.

The sun was fallen, evening grey.
There twinkled the fountain of the fay
Before the cavern where she lay,
    A corrigan of Brittany.

Green was the grass, clear the pool;
He laved his face in water cool,
And then he saw her on silver stool
    Singing a secret litany.

The moon through leaves clear and cold
Her long hair lit; through comb of gold
Each tress she drew, and down it rolled
    Beside her falling fountain.

He heard her voice and it was cold;
Her words were of the world of old,
When walked no men upon the mould,
    And young was moon and mountain.

'How darest thou my water wan
To trouble thus, or look me on?

Now shalt thou wed me, or grey and wan
    Ever stand as stone and wither!'

'I will not wed thee! I am wed;
My young wife lieth in childbed,
And I curse the beast that long me led
    To thy dark cavern hither.

I will not stand here turned to stone,
But I will leave thee cold alone,
And I will ride to mine own home
    And the white waters of Christendom.'

'In three days then thou shalt die,
In three days on thy bier lie!'
'In three days I shall live at ease,
And die but when God doth please
    In the brave wars of Christendom.

But rather would I die this hour
Than lie with thee in thy cold bower,
O! Corrigan, though strange thy power
    In the old moon singing.'

*

'A! mother mine, if thou love me well,
Make me my bed! My heart doth swell,
And in my limbs is poison fell,
    And in my ears a singing.

Grieve her not yet, do not tell!
Sweet may she keep our children well;
But a corrigan hath cast on me a spell,
    And I die on the third morning.'

On the third day my lady spake:
'Good mother, what is the noise they make?
In the towers slow bells shake,
    And there is sound of mourning.

Why are the white priests chanting low?'
'An unhappy man in the grave doth go.
He lodged here at night, and at cock-crow
    He died at grey of morning.'

'Good mother, say, where is my lord?'
'My child, he hath fared abroad.
Ere the candles are set upon the board,
    Thou wilt hear his feet returning.'

'Good mother, shall I wear robe of blue
Or robe of red?' 'Nay, 'tis custom new
To walk to church in sable hue
    And black weeds wearing.'

I saw them pass the churchyard gate.
'Who of our kin hath died of late?
Good mother, why is the earth so red?'
'A dear one is buried. We mourn him dead
    Our black weeds wearing.'

They laid him in the night.
I heard bells ring. There was taper light.
    Priests were chanting a litany.
Darkness lay upon the land,
But afar, in pale Broceliand
    There sang a fay in Brittany.

The corrigan of this poem, unlike the mere mention in its predecessor, is fully formed and of the type common in Breton folklore, a female fairy or witch who desires sexual contact with humans. *Korr* is Breton for 'dwarf', but the *korrigan* (*corrigan*) is not a diminutive being. Here, as often in the literature, she is found near a fountain and in the forest of Broceliand (Broceliande), a place of particular enchantment.

The second 'Corrigan' poem was then the basis of *The Lay of Aotrou and Itroun*, a work of 506 lines in rhyming couplets. In style as well as its time of composition, as Christopher Tolkien has said, *Aotrou and Itroun* is closely related to the *Lay of Leithian*, and such alliteration as it has 'is decorative, not in any way structural, though here and there it becomes very marked' (Flieger edition, p. xii). Flieger reproduces (p. 60) and transcribes the manuscript of a fragment of twenty-nine alliterative lines which, she writes, 'marks Tolkien's transition, first from the two ballad-like "Corrigan" poems to the much longer and more psychologically complex *Aotrou and Itroun*, and second from reworking existing material to producing a newly created poem' (p. 59). Tolkien followed this with a fair copy manuscript incorporating the fragment, now in rhymed couplets, which breaks off roughly halfway relative to the finished work; and then by a complete fair copy manuscript, its first page reproduced (p. 66, and as a plate preceding the initial half-title) and the whole transcribed in the Flieger edition. Tolkien dated the final page of the later manuscript to 23 September 1930.

From this he made a typescript on his Hammond machine, with the title *Aotrou and Itroun ('Lord and Lady'), a Breton Lay*, then set it aside for perhaps a decade. He returned to it, probably in late 1941 (some new rough workings are on the reverse side of a synopsis for the end of Book I of *The Lord of the Rings*), and revised it heavily. In June 1945 he lent the revised text to his friend Gwyn Jones, editor of the *Welsh Review*, who published it in December that same year as *The Lay of Aotrou and Itroun*. In her edition, Flieger reproduces (p. 86) the first page of the typescript and comments on Tolkien's revisions, and Christopher Tolkien notes a few textual differences between the typescript and the *Welsh Review* printing, nearly all of them 'insignificant points of punctuation and spacing' (p. xii). Using the *Welsh Review* printing (pp. 254–6, 260–2, 265–6) as our copy-text, with reference to the Flieger edition, we present here three extracts as B, C, and D.

The poem concerns a lord, Aotrou (Breton 'lord'), who has had no heir by his wife, Itroun (Breton 'lady'). Knowing of a corrigan, he obtains from her a fertility potion. He offers a fee in return, but ominously she delays claiming her 'rich reward'. Tolkien's description of the ruined state of the lord's hall creates an atmosphere of melancholy, which he enhances by repeating, at intervals and with variation, the moody four-line stanza beginning 'In Britain's land': 'In Britain's land beyond the seas', etc. 'Britain's land' in fact is Brittany (see lines 493, 495).

[B] In Britain's land beyond the seas
the wind blows ever through the trees;
in Britain's land beyond the waves
are stony shores and stony caves.

There stands a ruined toft now green
where lords and ladies once were seen,
where towers were piled above the trees
and watchmen scanned the sailing seas.
Of old a lord in archéd hall
with standing stones yet grey and tall
there dwelt, till dark his doom befell,
as still the Briton harpers tell.

No child he had his house to cheer,
to fill his courts with laughter clear;
though wife he wooed and wed with ring,
who love to board and bed did bring,
his pride was empty, vain his hoard,
without an heir to land and sword.
Thus pondering oft at night awake
his darkened mind would visions make
of lonely age and death; his tomb
unkept, while strangers in his room
with other names and other shields
were masters of his halls and fields.
Thus counsel cold he took at last;
his hope from light to darkness passed.

A witch there was, who webs could weave
to snare the heart and wits to reave,
who span dark spells with spider-craft,
and as she span she softly laughed;
a drink she brewed of strength and dread
to bind the quick and stir the dead.
In cave she housed where winging bats
their harbour sought, and owls and cats
from hunting came with mournful cries,
night-stalking near with needle-eyes.
In the homeless hills was her hollow dale,
black was its bowl, its brink was pale;
there silent on a seat of stone
before her cave she sat alone.
Dark was her door, and few there came,
whether man, or beast that man doth tame.

In Britain's land beyond the waves
are stony hills and stony caves;
the wind blows ever over hills
and hollow caves with wailing fills.

The sun was fallen low and red,
behind the hills the day was dead,
and in the valley formless lay
the misty shadows long and grey.
Alone between the dark and light
there rode into the mouth of night
the Briton lord, and creeping fear
about him closed. Dismounting near
he slowly then with lagging feet
went halting to the stony seat.
His words came faltering on the wind,
while silent sat the crone and grinned.
Few words he needed; for her eyes
were dark and piercing, filled with lies,
yet needle-keen all lies to probe.
He shuddered in his sable robe.
His name she knew, his need, his thought,
the hunger that thither him had brought;
while yet he spoke she laughed aloud,
and rose and nodded; head she bowed,
and stooped into her darkening cave,
like ghost returning to the grave.
Thence swift she came. In his hand she laid
a phial of glass so fairly made
'twas wonder in that houseless place
to see its cold and gleaming grace;
and therewithin a philter lay
as pale as water thin and grey
that spills from stony fountains frore
in hollow pools in caverns hoar.

He thanked her, trembling, offering gold
to withered fingers shrunk and old.
The thanks she took not, nor the fee,
but laughing croaked: '*Nay, we shall see!*
Let thanks abide till thanks be earned!

Such potions oft, men say, have burned
the heart and brain, or else are nought,
only cold water dearly bought.
Such lies you shall not tell of me;
Till it is earned I'll have no fee.
But we shall speak again one day,
and *rich reward then you shall pay,*
whate'er I ask: it may be gold,
it may be other wealth you hold.'

Aotrou secretly gives his wife the potion, 'pale as water thin and frore | in hollow pools of caverns hoar', and at length she gives birth to a son and daughter, 'fair as flowers [who] danced and played | on lawns of sunlight without hedge | save a dark shadow at their edge'. As in the second 'Corrigan' poem, Aotrou offers to bring his wife venison, and going forth to hunt he is led astray by a white doe.

[C] He hunted her from the forest-eaves
into the twilight under leaves;
the earth was shaken under hoof,
till the boughs were bent into a roof,
and the sun was woven in a snare;
and laughter still was on the air.

The sun was falling. In the dell
deep in the forest silence fell.
No sight nor slot of doe he found
but roots of trees upon the ground,
and trees like shadows waiting stood
for night to come upon the wood.

The sun was lost, all green was grey.
There twinkled the fountain of the fay,
before a cave on silver sand,
under the dark boughs in Broceliande.
Soft was the grass and clear the pool;
he laved his face in water cool.
He saw her then, on silver chair,
before her cavern, pale her hair,
slow was her smile, and white her hand
beckoning in Broceliande.

The moonlight falling clear and cold
her long hair lit; through comb of gold
she drew each lock, and down it fell
like the fountain falling in the dell.
He heard her voice, and it was cold
as echo from the world of old,
ere fire was found or iron hewn,
when young was mountain under moon.
He heard her voice like water falling
or wind upon the long shore calling,
yet sweet the words: *'We meet again*
here after waiting, after pain!
Aotrou! Lo! thou hast returned —
perchance some kindness I have earned?
What hast thou, lord, to give to me
whom thou hast come thus far to see?'

'I know thee not, I know thee not,
nor ever saw thy darkling grot.
O Corrigan! 'twas not for thee
I hither came a-hunting free!'

'How darest, then, my water wan
to trouble thus, or look me on?
For this at least I claim my fee,
if ever thou wouldst wander free.
With love thou shalt me here requite,
for here is long and sweet the night;
in druery dear thou here shalt deal,
in bliss more deep than mortals feel.'

'I gave no love. My love is wed;
my wife now lieth in child-bed,
and I cursed the beast that cheated me
and drew me to this dell to thee.'

Her smiling ceased. and slow she said:
'Forget thy wife; for thou shalt wed
anew with me, or stand as stone
and wither lifeless and alone,
as stone beside the fountain stand
forgotten in Broceliande.'

'I will not stand here turned to stone;
but I will leave thee cold, alone,
and I will ride to mine own home
and the waters blest of Christendome.'

'But three days then and thou shalt die;
in three days on thy bier lie!'

Aotrou makes his way home, but lies in a fever and begs his servants not to tell his wife of his condition:

'My death is near — but do not tell,
though I am wounded with a spell!
But two days more, and then I die —
and I would have had her sweetly lie
and sweet arise; and live yet long,
and see our children hale and strong.'

Itroun waits in vain for her husband to return to her. At last, learning of his death, she mourns for him in church, then dies of grief.

[D] In robe of black and walking bent
the lady to her churching went,
in hand a candle small and white,
her face so pale, her hair so bright.
They passed beneath the western door;
there dark within on stony floor
a bier was covered with a pall,
and by it yellow candles tall.
The watchful tapers still and bright
upon his blazon cast their light:
the arms and banner of her lord;
his pride was ended, vain his hoard.

To bed they brought her, swift to sleep
for ever cold, though there might weep
her women by her dark bedside,
or babes in cradle waked and cried.

There was singing slow at dead of night,
and many feet, and taper-light.
At morn they rang the sacring knell;

and far men heard a single bell
toll, while the sun lay on the land;
while deep in dim Broceliande
a silver fountain flowed and fell
within a darkly woven dell,
and in the homeless hills a dale
was filled with laughter cold and pale.

Beside her lord at last she lay
in their long home beneath the clay;
and if their children lived yet long,
or played in garden hale and strong,
they saw it not, nor found it sweet
their heart's desire at last to meet.

In Brittany beyond the waves
are sounding shores and hollow caves;
In Brittany beyond the seas
the wind blows ever through the trees.

In the stanza beginning with line 487, it is left open to wonder if the lord and lady's children lived long lives, 'hale and strong' as their father prayed. The tragedy, as the poem ends, is that they may have done, but if so their parents did not live to see it. In the fair copy manuscript their fate is less uncertain, as the word in line 489 is not tentative *if* but positive *though*.

More than one scholar has remarked that the lord in *Aotrou and Itroun* brought his fate on himself, by seeking out the corrigan for the potion. He may be especially naïve for not asking its price before accepting it, though his thoughts were clouded even before he left his home. In the second 'Corrigan' poem the young earl comes upon the witch by chance, or at least – allowing for the supernatural attraction of the white doe – through no fault of his own. To their credit, both the earl and Aotrou remain faithful to their wives, despite the corrigan's power of seduction in Breton lore. Neither is successful with his appeal to Christendom. In Tolkien's depictions, the corrigan is more dominatrix than seducer. In *Aotrou and Itroun* she appears beautiful when first seen, combing her long pale hair, smiling in the moonlight, beckoning with a white hand, but when demanding her 'fee' from Aotrou she is 'shrunk and old, 'in her claw | a comb of bony teeth he saw, | with which she raked her tresses grey'.

Jessica Yates, one of the earliest critics to seek for Tolkien's sources for *Aotrou and Itroun*, has argued in 'The Source of "The Lay of Aotrou and Itroun"' (1991) that he came to his ultimate inspiration, Théodore Claude Henri Hersart de la Villemarqué's *Barzaz-Breiz: Chants populaire de la Bretagne* (first published 1838), through reading *The English and Scottish Popular Ballads* edited by Francis James Child (1882). That may be so, although Carl Phelpstead, who devotes a sizeable part of his *Tolkien and Wales: Language, Literature and Identity* (2011) to Tolkien and Breton lays, has shown that by 1922 Tolkien owned a copy of *Barzaz-Breiz* in its fourth edition (1846). As Verlyn Flieger points out, both Child and Villemarqué were part of a movement in nineteenth-century Europe to preserve indigenous folk literature and regional dialects, along with the Grimms in Germany and Lönnrot in Finland, and Tolkien had an interest in all of these.

A40: The corrigan's 'secret litany' will be a recitation of dark magic, in contrast with the priests' Christian litany in A101.

A71: Flieger glosses 'make me my bed' as 'a traditional ballad line signifying the Lord's awareness of his fatal illness' (p. 54), citing the ballad 'Lord Randall' with its repeated line 'Mother mak my bed soon' as possibly a conscious influence on Tolkien. One might also mention a familiar prayer designed to be said by those with bodily suffering, which includes the plea 'Blessed Lord, do Thou make my bed in my sickness'.

B12: 'Briton', i.e. Breton. In the fair copy manuscript 'still' read 'yet'.

B13–26: In the fair copy manuscript these lines read:

No children he had his house to cheer,
his gardens lacked their laughter clear;
though wife he wooed and wed with ring,
who long her love to bed did bring,
his bowers were empty, vain his hoard,
without an heir [*marked for deletion:* did] to land and sword.
His hungry heart did lonely eld,
his house's end, his banners felled,
his tomb unheeded, long forbode,
till brooding black his mind did goad
a mad and monstrous rede to take,
pondering oft at night awake.

In the subsequent typescript before revision, l. 16 read 'who love to board and bed did bring', and l. 20 'his house's end, his banner felled'. Flieger discusses Tolkien's revision process in this section of the typescript. For l. 17, 'his bowers were empty, vain his hoard', compare 'His halls hollow and his bowers cold' in *Iúmonna Gold Galdre Bewunden* (poem no. 69).

B22: 'Unkept', i.e. not kept up, let go to ruin. Aotrou worries that his family will end, with no one left to fulfil obligations such as keeping up an ancestral tomb or grave.

B23: 'Shield' refers to heraldry, i.e. another family will have the lord's property.

B27–42: In the fair copy manuscript these lines read:

A witch there was, who webs did weave
to snare the heart and wits to reave,
who span dark spells with spider-craft,
and, spinning, soundless shook and laughed,
and draughts she brewed of strength and dread
to bind the live and stir the dead.
In a cave she housed where winging bats
their harbour sought, and owls and cats
from hunting came with mournful cries
night-stalking near with needle-eyes.
In the homeless hills was that hollow dale,
black was its bowl, its brink was pale;
there silent sat she on seat of stone
at cavern's mouth in the hills alone;
there silent waited. Few there came,
or man, or beast that man doth tame.

The same text appeared in the typescript before revision, at least to the end of the page (li.35) reproduced in the Flieger edition.

B36: 'Needle-eyes', perhaps sharp-eyed, sharp as a needle (compare 'needle-keen', B61).

B61: 'Needle-keen', i.e. sharp, like the pointed end of a needle.

C275: 'The sun was woven in a snare', i.e. could be seen only through closely woven branches.

117

The Lay of Beowulf (*c.* 1930)

In *Beowulf: A Translation and Commentary* (2014), in which this work was first published, Christopher Tolkien describes *The Lay of Beowulf* as 'two poems, or two versions of a poem' (p. 415). Numbered I and II, they are entitled respectively *Beowulf and Grendel* and *Beowulf and the Monsters*. These exist only as typescripts, made by Tolkien on his Hammond machine. Christopher recalls his father singing the 'Lay' to him, very probably the shorter 'part' I only, and that it was his 'first acquaintance with Beowulf and the golden hall of Heorot' (p. xiii). This was in the early 1930s, 'but of course [the "Lay"] may have been in existence years before that' (p. 416).

We have transcribed its two 'parts' from their typescripts, including revisions Tolkien made in manuscript, and present them as A and B. The latter was first called simply *Beowulf*, with '& the Monsters' inserted later by hand, as were the Roman numerals, as if the poems were two parts of a larger work. It is clear that the second 'part' is a development from the first.

Preserved with the typescripts is a cover page on which Tolkien wrote 'States in the accretion of new matter to The Lay of *Beowulf*', hence the title of these two parts together. The words 'accretion' and 'new matter' could suggest a development of the 'Lay' over time, but could also mean that Tolkien had created new elements for the *Beowulf* story, retelling in *Beowulf and Grendel* the battle between those opponents, and in the expanded *Beowulf and the Monsters* the hero's fights with both Grendel and Grendel's mother. Christopher Tolkien called his father's inscription 'a satiric suggestion of the importance of these poems expressed in the academic vocabulary of this branch of *Beowulf* studies' (*Beowulf: A Translation and Commentary*, p. 416).

[A] I

Grendel came forth in the dead of night;
the moon in his eyes shone glassy bright,
as over the moors he strode in might,
    until he came to Heorot.

Dark lay the dale, the windows shone;
by the wall he lurked and listened long,
and he cursed their laughter and cursed their song
and the twanging harps of Heorot.

King Hrothgar mourns upon his throne
for his lieges slain, he mourns alone,
but Grendel gnaws the flesh and bone
of the thirty thanes of Heorot.
A ship there sails like a wingéd swan,
and the foam is white on the waters wan,
and one there stands with bright helm on
that the winds have brought to Heorot.

On his pillow soft there Beowulf slept,
and Grendel the cruel to the dark hall crept,
the doors sprang back, and in he leapt
and grasped the guard of Heorot.
As bear aroused from his mountain lair
Beowulf wrestled with Grendel there,
and his arm and claw away did tear,
and his black blood spilled in Heorot.

'O! Ecgtheow's son' he then dying said,
'Forbear to hew my vanquished head,
or hard and stony be thy death-bed,
and a red fate fall on Heorot!'
'Then hard and stony must be the bed
where at the last I lay me dead':
and Beowulf hewed the demon's head
and hung it high in Heorot.

Merry the mead men quaffed at the board,
and Hrothgar dealt his golden hoard,
and many a jewel and horse and sword
to Beowulf gave in Heorot.
The moon gleamed in through the windows wan;
as Beowulf drank he looked thereon,
and a light in the demon's eyes there shone
amid the blaze of Heorot.

On the sails of a ship the sunlight smiled,
its bosom with gleaming gold was piled,
and the wind blew loud and free and wild
    as it left the land of Heorot.
Voices followed from the sounding shore
that blessed the lord those timbers bore,
but that sail returned thither never more,
    and his fate was far from Heorot.

The demon's head in the hall did hang
and grinned from the wall while minstrels sang,
till flames leapt forth and red swords rang,
    and hushed were the harps of Heorot.
And latest and last one hoar of head,
as he lay on a hard and stony bed,
and venom burned him and he bled,
    remembered the light of Heorot.

[B] II

Grendel came forth in the dead of night;
the moon in his eyes shone glassy bright,
as over the moors he strode in might,
    until he came to Heorot.
Dark lay the dale, the windows shone,
by the wall he lurked and listened long,
and he cursed their laughter and cursed their song
    and the twanging harps of Heorot.

The lights were quenched and laughter still;
then Grendel entered and ate his fill,
and the blood was red that he did spill
    on the shining floor of Heorot.
No Dane ever dared that monster meet,
or abide the tramp of those dread feet;
in the hall alone he held his seat,
    the demon lord of Heorot.

At morn King Hrothgar on his throne
for his lieges slain there mourned alone,
but Grendel gnawed the flesh and bone
    of the thirty thanes of Denmark.
A ship there sailed like a wingéd swan,

and the foam was white on the waters wan,
and one there stood with bright helm on
    that fate had brought to Denmark.

Beowulf soft on his pillow slept,
and Grendel in lust to the dark hall crept,
the door sprang back and in he leapt
    and grasped the guard of Heorot.
As bear aroused from his mountain lair
Beowulf grappled with Grendel there,
and his arm and claw away did tear,
    and black blood spilled in Heorot.

Merry the mead goes round the board,
and merry are men, and glad their lord,
and many a jewel and horse and sword
    he gives in gift to Beowulf.
The Danes in slumber all careless lie,
nor dream of a fiend that draweth nigh
to avenge the death her son did die
    and his blood spilled there by Beowulf.

The laughter was still and the lights were low;
the mother of trolls there wrought them woe.
with a Danish corpse she turned to go
    and shrieking fled from Heorot.
Like a shadow cast on the mountain mist,
where the winds were bleak and the heather hissed,
she fled, but none could keep her tryst
    since her son found death in Heorot.

There was one who dared over mountain road
to follow her fleeing with dreadful load
to the foaming fall where she abode,
    while men made moan in Heorot,
far over the misty moorlands cold
where the wild wolf howled upon the wold,
passed dragon's lair and nicor's hold,
    and far from the lights of Heorot.

There sheer was the shore over waters frore
and withered and bent the trees it bore;

those waters black were blent with gore
 of the noblest knights of Denmark.
The flaming force there in thunder fell,
that cauldron smoked with the fires of hell,
and there the demons dark did dwell
 amid the bones of Denmark.

Quoth Beowulf 'Farewell, comrades free!
this journey none may share with me',
and his shining helm plunged in the sea
 to avenge the woes of Heorot.
The nicors gnashed his ringéd mail;
he saw their white fangs gleaming pale;
a green light burned in the deep sea-dale
 in halls more high than Heorot.

The demon lurked at her cave's dark door;
her fangs and fingers were red with gore,
and skulls of men lay on the floor
 beneath the feet of Beowulf.
At his corslet tore her claws accursed,
her teeth at his throat for blood did thirst,
and the sword there failed and asunder burst
 that Unferth gave to Beowulf.

There nigh was his death in the shadowy deep,
where a corpse lay low on bony heap,
where Grendel slept on his long sleep
 and strode no more to Heorot.
A sword hung huge on the cavern's wall,
once forged by ancient giants tall;
Beowulf seized it — as lightnings fall
 it fell on the foe of Heorot.

'O Ecgtheow's son' she then dying said
'forbear to hew my vanquished head,
or hard and stony be thy death-bed
 and a red fate fall on Denmark!'
'Then hard and stony must be the bed
where at the last I lay me dead':
and Beowulf hewed the demon's head
 and haled it back to Denmark.

Merrily mead men quaffed at the board,
and Hrothgar dealt his golden hoard,
but Beowulf wore no more the sword
    that Unferth gave in Heorot.
The moon gleamed in through the windows wan;
as Beowulf drank he looked thereon,
and the light in the eyes of the demon shone
    amid the blaze of Heorot.

On the sails of a ship the sunlight smiled,
its bosom with gleaming gold was piled,
and the wind blew loud and free and wild
    as it left the land of Denmark.
Voices followed from the sounding shore
    that blessed the lord those timbers bore,
but that sail returned there never more
    and his fate was far from Denmark.

The demon's head in the hall did hang
and grinned from the wall while minstrels sang,
    till flames leapt forth and red swords rang
    and hushed were the harps of Heorot.
Latest and last one hoar of head,
as he lay on a hard and stony bed
and venom burned him, and he bled,
    remembered the light of Heorot.

In these verses Tolkien generally follows the actions of the Old English *Beowulf* (see poem no. 88) concerned with the attacks by monsters in Heorot, the hall of the Danish king Hrothgar, Beowulf's arrival at that place, his defeat of Grendel, and the slaying of Grendel's mother after diving to her cave through a pool of water-demons (nicors). Tolkien introduces new elements, however. In the first version, as in the original story, Beowulf tears off Grendel's arm, but here the monster does not flee to die in his mother's home. Grendel warns his foe not to remove his head or both Beowulf and Heorot would suffer a cruel fate; Beowulf hews Grendel's head regardless and hangs it in the hall. In the second version, he is given the same warning by Grendel's mother, and it is her head he takes back to Heorot, after killing her in the lair where Grendel lay dead; in the Old English original, they battle without conversing, and once the mother is dead Beowulf takes Grendel's head from his corpse.

The final stanza of each version is similar to the other: a head hangs on the wall in Heorot until the hall is attacked by enemies and destroyed, while Beowulf in old age ('one hoar of head') lies on a hard and stony bed, bleeding and burned by venom, due to his fight with a dragon at the end of the Old English poem. Thus, apparently, in this alternate history, the demon's death-curse comes to pass.

Christopher Tolkien's recollection of hearing his father sing the 'Lay' in the early 1930s suggests a *terminus ad quem* for composition of the work. Another clue to its date may lie in line 53 of the second version, 'far over the misty moorlands cold', a clear echo of 'far over the Misty Mountains cold' from the dwarves' song (poem no. 109) in chapter 1 of *The Hobbit*, begun by the end of 1929. It seems safe to date *The Lay of Beowulf* to *c.* 1930.

Tolkien's cover sheet for the work also includes a note that it is to be sung to the tune of 'Old King Cole'. But its rhymes and rhythm, generally following AAABCCCB, are hardly suited to the music for the familiar nursery rhyme in Moffat's *What the Children Sing* (p. 21):

> Old King Cole was a merry old soul,
> And a merry old soul was he:
> And he called for his pipe,
> And he called for his bowl,
> And he called for his fiddlers three. [etc.]

Rather, as Dimitra Fimi first observed ('Tolkien and Folklore: *Sellic Spell* and *The Lay of Beowulf*', 2014), it fits perfectly well 'The Fox Went Out on a Winter's Night', clearly a favourite tune of Tolkien: see also *The Root of the Boot* (no. 83) and *A Song of Bimble Bay* (no. 102).

A21: 'As bear aroused' is a reference to Beowulf's name, supposed by scholars to derive from 'bee wolf', meaning 'bear'. See our discussion for poem no. 88.

A41: This line originally read 'A ship there sailed on pinions wild'.

A49: Tolkien considered whether to change this line to read 'In the hall the head of the demon hung', with 'sang' and 'rang' in the following lines changed to 'sung' and 'rung'.

B9–11: Tolkien considered whether to change these lines to read:

> The lights were quenched and laughter stilled;
> then Grendel fed till he was filled,
> and the blood was red that he [?then ?there] spilled

B14: This line originally read 'when darkness fell they fled him fleet'.

B80: In the Old English poem, Unferth (Unferð), a thane of King Hrothgar, lends Beowulf a sword for his fight with Grendel's mother. It fails in battle, however, and the hero defeats her instead with another sword he finds in her cave.

118

Hengest (*c.* 1930)

The Old English 'Fight at Finnesburg' is told in part in the so-called 'Finnesburg episode' in *Beowulf*, and partly in what remains of an Old English lay (the 'Finnesburg fragment'). In brief, Finn, the ruler of the Frisians, has married Hildeburh, a woman from a tribe connected with the Danes. But when Hildeburh's brother Hnæf and sixty men pay a winter visit to Finn's hall (i.e. Finn's *burg* or *burh*), they are attacked by the Frisians. Hnæf is killed, as are many others on both sides of the conflict, including a son of Finn and Hildeburh. With neither side able to end the battle through force of arms, Finn and the chief surviving Dane, Hengest, agree to a truce. The Frisians give the Danes shelter for the winter – they cannot sail home in frozen seas – while the Danes on their part act as peaceful followers of Finn. At last, with the coming of spring and despite their oath of peace, desire for vengeance rises in the Danes. They kill Finn and his warriors, sack his hall, and take Hildeburh back to her homeland.

Tolkien's poem *Hengest* reveals, as it were, the thoughts of that Danish leader as he sits impatient for winter's end, and to avenge the death of his prince (Hnæf). The work exists only in a single manuscript, a fair copy though written out very quickly. It contains no clue to its date (other than that Tolkien's handwriting is from neither his earlier nor his later years), but as he gave the first of his Oxford lectures on 'Finn and Hengest' in April 1930, it seems appropriate to place *Hengest* at this point in our book – also, aptly, following *The Lay of Beowulf* (no. 117).

O mighty sun, who hath thee now in thrall?
The wind is keen and snow is over all,
the sea is frozen and the waves stand still,
and ships are idle, and my heart is chill.

O mighty sun, from under winter's caves,
Leap back and loosen all the frozen waves!
Drive far the mists and turn the snow to rain,
And call my ship to journeying again!

O mighty sword why sleep thou in thy sheath,
Keeping too long from blood & bone thy teeth?
Why is the arm so slow, the heart so weak
My prince's fall and many friends to wreak?

O mighty sword, leap forth beneath the sun
and flame in anger! Let the red blood run
of Finn and all his folk, and let the gold
be spilled that he hath garnered long in hold!

O may swords that wait within the sheath
where fearless men walk free the windy heath
in Denmark far away, when spring returns
Remember then the grief that in us burns.

One may set against this a portion of *Beowulf* in Tolkien's prose translation:

> Still Hengest abode with Finn that bloodstained winter, keeping fully to his word [his oath of truce]. He thought of his own land, even though he could not speed upon the sea his ship with curving beak. The deep was tossed in storm and battled with the wind; winter locked the waves in icy bond, until another year came to the dwellings of men. . . . Now past was winter, and fair the bosom of the earth. The exile, the guest of Finn [i.e. Hengest], was eager to be gone from those courts. Therein more thought did he give to vengeance for his sorrow than to the passage of the sea, pondering if he might again achieve a clash of wrath, wherein he would in his heart remember the children of the Jutes. [*Beowulf*, p. 45]

Tolkien studied the 'Finnesburg matter' deeply, in particular the question of whether Jutes – a Germanic people from an area in parts of present-day Denmark and Germany – were on both sides of the 'Finnesburg' conflict: Hengest, for one, among Hnæf's men, and Jutish exiles in the Frisian court whom Hnæf had dispossessed. Tolkien's lectures on the subject were published as *Finn and Hengest: The Fragment and the Episode* (1982), edited by Alan Bliss.

119

The Derelicts (*c.* 1930)

Of the two extant manuscripts of this poem, the earliest is a fair copy, to which Tolkien made a few alterations. In one corner is a list of words which alliterate with the letter *el*, to guide a revision to line 11 which Tolkien evidently found difficult. Additional workings for the purpose fill the reverse of the sheet, written in pencil and ink and in two directions; these include, among the more coherent phrases, 'laid their ship dark shrouded', 'their bark forlorn', 'forlorn their bark', 'their luckless bark ship', 'their laden ship', and 'luckless ship'.

Tolkien incorporated his revisions to the first text in the second manuscript, transcribed below with marks separating the stanzas as in the original.

Long-gazing they lingered
lonely beside the stony
beaches dark, where breakers
boomed resounding gloomy.
Pools lay gleaming palely
pricked by stars there flick'ring,
in winds wanly bending
winter's candles glinting.

⋆

Winter's winds had hunted,
waves as dark as ravens,
their lordly ship laden,
lightless, sea-benighted.
Forth now fared they mirthless
far from mortal laughter,
in caves coldly-builded
kindled fires that dwindled.

⋆

Songs by the fires they sang not,
silent loomed the island
washed by shouting waters,
waves as dark as ravens.
The moon the cloud mantled;
mist the starlight twisted;
in wind's vainly bending
winter's candles glinted.

Christopher Tolkien recorded that he found the earlier text and workings laid into a volume of the William Morris–Eiríkr Magnússon translation of the Old Norse *Heimskringla*, published in the Saga Library, which Tolkien purchased probably in 1922. *The Derelicts* is certainly not as old as that, however. Its subject, mariners prevented from sailing by the ferocity of a winter sea, echoes the plight of the surviving Danes in *Hengest* (no. 118), and for that reason we have placed *The Derelicts* here in our chronological sequence.

At the top of its later manuscript Tolkien wrote 'Lines in "Dróttkvætt" metre'. *Dróttkvætt*, or 'court metre', was popular among the *skalds*, or poets, writing in Old Norse. It is a complex and remarkably strict form, requiring stanzas of eight lines, with a syntactic break after the fourth; six syllables in each line, the final two in a stressed–unstressed pattern; two alliterating staves in each odd-numbered line which also alliterate with the first syllable of the following line (such as '*Long*-gazing they *lingered* | *lonely*'); and internal rhyme – using the same vowel or consonant sound – according to a set of sub-rules. For the latter, in odd lines the poet uses either half-rhymes (in which the consonant sound is the same, but the vowel sound is different) or full rhymes (also called true or exact rhymes, in which the stressed vowel and following sounds in two words are identical but preceding consonants differ, as in *sky* and *high*); and in even lines only full rhymes are to be used, but for each, the first half of the rhyme can be anywhere in the line, while the second half is in the fifth (penultimate) syllable. And yet – perhaps we should not be surprised – not all skalds held to the rules of *dróttkvætt* in every instance, and it is even harder to do so when writing in Modern English, which relies on word order rather than word-endings.

In her essay 'Dróttkvætt' in *New Literary History* (2019), Roberta Frank quotes the second stanza of *The Derelicts* in its entirety, from a copy given her more than forty years earlier by the late Eric Christiansen of New College, Oxford, who had himself discovered the draft sheet in Tolkien's *Heimskringla*. Frank altered the third line from 'their shrouded ship laden' to 'their leaden ship laden' and the sixth from 'far from mortal laughter' to 'far from mortal portals', according to her preference, 'to procure a correct half- and full rhyme respectively' (p. 398). Of the quoted stanza, she comments that although Tolkien includes 'the rhyme-scheme, alliteration, and syllable count of dróttkvætt', he missed 'its poetry: the hypnotic sound and memory links, the jagged wit and suggestiveness, the sudden glory of rounded perception' (p. 393).

Writing in the Tolkien Society's Facebook forum (26 April 2020), Nelson Goering disagreed, finding Tolkien's verse in fact 'visually effective as well as sonically' and 'syntactically very straightforward'. In response to Frank's alterations to the poem, Goering suggested that in line 11 the '-oud-' and '-ad-' of the original reading was a sufficient half-rhyme, while in line 14 'far' and 'mor-' could have seemed close to a full rhyme for Tolkien in British pronunciation, without the change of 'laughter' to 'portals'. Frank had seen only the draft text, and was unaware that Tolkien revised 'shrouded' to 'lordly' in his revised version.

The title of this poem presumably refers not to the ship mentioned in line 11, which is not described as damaged or decrepit, but to its crew, as if they had been abandoned in their 'caves coldly-builded', unable to act while winter lasts.

11: As noted also in our discussion, in the first manuscript this line read 'their shrouded ship laden'. The *shrouds* of a ship are its rope-lines forming part of its rigging, though as we have noted earlier (see poem no. 16, 'with bellying clouds as his vessel's shrouds'), Tolkien seems to have been capable of confusing *shroud* with *sail*. Here, however, it is also possible that by 'shrouded' Tolkien meant 'concealed from view', hidden perhaps by the waves 'dark as ravens' (l. 10), and 'lightless' (l. 12).

18: In the first manuscript this line read 'silent lurked the island' and closed with a comma.

120

Brydleoþ (1930)

On 30 July 1930, Eric Valentine Gordon married Ida Lilian Pickles. In honour of the occasion, Tolkien composed a poem in Old English, *Brydleoþ* ('Bridal Song'), to celebrate the wedding and to praise Gordon as a scholar and friend, and presented it to the couple as a decorated manuscript in black and red, using Anglo-Saxon letter-forms. We give its text here as A, from the Leeds Gordon archive. We have spelled out occasional words abbreviated in the medieval manner, such as 'burgū' for 'burgum' in line 9, and have substituted 'and' where Tolkien wrote the Tironian *et* (7).

[A]

Forþ namcúþes norþan
nẏwan word ætẏwde,
wuldres wóma gelóme
wíshẏcgendes hlísa.

Ic ǽr gefrægn féran
féþecempan of éþle,
Scotta land forlǽtan,
líðan earfoðsíþas.
Unearg eafora' on burgum
æfter wóc him cræftig —
blǽd sprang beornes wíde
Bretlanda on Westsetlum.

Forþ þa westan furþor
fór word hider on óran,
bréme wuldres wóma,
wíshẏcgendes hlísa.
Rídan to beorgum brádum
brimhengest com Engla,
bær ofer bæþweg feorran
beorn módigne georne.

Béor he æt blíþum dẏre
borda Oxnaforda —
dómas hẏrde déman —

dranc mid rincum wlancum;
salwigpáda sméade
sóþword monig wóþa,
bóca láre brúcan
beald ongan and healdan.

Forþ cóm nýwe norþor
namcúþes word súþan,
wuldres wóma on moldan,
wíshýcgendes hlísa.
Norþerne nóm mǽrne
níwne burg þa híwan;
rófne léode léofne
láreow héoldon árum.

Dóm arǽrde rúmne:
rǽde þegnas lǽdde,
rýmde and ýcte ríce.
reorda lærde cneordum.
Hláford liþost léofum,
láðgeníðlum wráþost,
dwæse cwelmde dwolmenn
dolgwordum — wæs bolgen.

Forþ namcúþes furþor
fóron word geond óran,
wuldres wóma of foldan,
wíshýcgendes hlísa.
Eorl sohte' éþel feorlen
Islendinga wísra:
blicon heahmuntas brante
brimstréam ofer dimne.

Feorrancundum fíras
fand he holde' on lande —
healdréamas menn héoldon,
hlýnsode reced wýnsum — ;
weorðmýndum þáh wundrum
wíde þǽr — sceal bídan
folcum fæst under wolcnum
fréod mid úrum þéodum.

Word ða wide' on earde
wóc namcúþes bóca,
wuldres woma mid ẏldum,
wíshẏcgendes hlísa.
Þone Ingwina þengel
þegn heht healsgeregne
glengan gódne mid Englum —
guðhafoces menn úþe.

Brẏd he on lífes blǽde
bundenheorde funde,
mægden modgehẏgde
mǽre, bócgelǽred.
Swá nu bám ætsomne
sæle bliss and hælo;
brẏdguman, nu brẏde,
brẏdsang scopes hlẏde!

Forþ namcúþra norþan
nẏwe tír ætẏweþ,
wuldres wóma gesómra
wíshẏcgendra hlísa.

Fréond óþerne sceal on feorhdagum
ferhþe fréogan on friðusibbe.
Sume gold gifaþ gearwum hondum;
sume ræd witon, rúna healdaþ
léofum geseldan; sum æt lindplegan
ealgað unforht eaxlgesteallan
wiþ lað werod; sume lẏt magon
nefne wẏnsum word, wóða mætost,
léoþ asingan to luftácne,
dóm fore duguðe dẏrne arǽran,
lof gewẏrcan léofes mannan.

For þam þritigoðan dæge æfterran liðan
þæs geares MCMXXX æfter úres hæl[-]
endes acennednesse geworht.
. IRRT .

We follow the original text with a translation into Modern English (B) made for this book by Arden R. Smith, to whom we are also indebted for transcribing Tolkien's Old English manuscript.

[B]

Forth newly from the north
came word of a renowned one,
a frequent sound of glory,
the fame of a wise man.

I heard that champions earlier
had fared from their homeland,
left the land of the Scots,
made difficult journeys.
A fearless son in the cities,
a learned one afterward was born to them —
the spirit of the warrior spread far and wide
in the Western Settlements of Britain.

Forth then further from the west
word came onto the shores hither,
a famous sound of glory,
the fame of a wise man.
Sailing to the broad mountains
a sea-horse of the Angles came,
carried over the bath-way from afar
many a brave warrior.

Beer he drank at the friendly gate
of the board of Oxford —
he heard judgements decreed —
in the company of proud warriors;
the dark-coated one thought out
many a word of poetry,
he boldly endeavoured to enjoy
the lore of books and to retain it.

Forth came newly further northward
word of a renowned one from the south,
a sound of glory in the land,
the fame of a wise man.
A northern city received the famous

newcomer [and] members of his household;
the people held the renowned,
beloved teacher in honour.

He established a great reputation:
he led ready vassals,
widened and enlarged his authority.
He taught languages zealously.
A lord kindest to friends,
most hostile to foes,
he destroyed foolish heretics
with wounding words — when provoked.

Forth the words of a renowned one
went beyond the borders,
a sound of glory out of the country,
the fame of a wise man.
The brave man sought the far-off country
of the learned Icelanders:
steep mountains appeared
over the dark current.

Foreign men
he found friendly in the land —
men celebrated in the hall,
the joyful house resounded — ;
he thrived in honours wonderfully,
widely there — peace must endure
among peoples under the heavens,
firm among our peoples.

Word of the renowned one's books
awoke far and wide on earth,
a sound of glory among men,
the fame of a wise man.
A vassal bade the prince of the Ingwines
adorn with a neck ornament
a good man among the Angles —
he granted the man a war-hawk.

A bride in the riches of life
he found, with bound tresses,
a maiden of great
intelligence, educated.
So now for both together
may happiness and prosperity come to pass;
to the bridegroom, now to the bride,
may the poet's wedding song resound!

Forth newly from the north
came word of the renowned ones,
a sound of the glory of the friendly ones,
the fame of wise people.

A friend shall embrace another in days of life
with peace-keeping in mind.
Some give gold with ready hands;
some know counsel, keep secrets
for beloved retainers; some at shield-play
fearlessly protect their comrades
from a hostile army; some are little able,
except for a pleasant word, the poorest of sounds,
to compose a song as a love-token,
to spread honour before a noble host,
to sing the praises of a beloved man.

Composed for the thirtieth day of July
in the year 1930 after our
Saviour's birth.

.JRRT.

The second stanza refers to E.V. Gordon's ancestors, the Gordon and McQueen families, who emigrated from Scotland to Canada and spread across the country. Gordon's father, James, was born in Ontario, and Eric in British Columbia. The third stanza alludes to Gordon's journey to Oxford as a Rhodes Scholar in 1915; his studies were interrupted by the war, but he returned to continue them under Tolkien's tutelage. He took his Bachelor of Arts degree in 1920 – the subject of the fourth stanza. He began work towards a B.Litt., but abandoned it when he was hired, at Tolkien's recommendation, to teach in the English School at the University of Leeds, the 'northern city' of line 33. Tolkien goes on to refer to Gordon's industry while at Leeds, where he introduced to the curriculum Old Norse and Modern Icelandic. 'The renowned one's books' included *Sir Gawain and the Green Knight* (1925), edited with Tolkien (see poem no. 70), and *An Introduction to Old Norse* (1927). For the latter, in 1930 the King of Iceland and Denmark made Gordon a Knight of the Royal Icelandic Order of the Falcon – the 'war-hawk' of line 68. The king is the 'prince of the Ingwines' (line 65); in *Beowulf*, *Ingwine* 'friends of Ing' refers to the Danes (in 1930 Iceland was united with Denmark under a common monarch). Ida Pickles was Gordon's 'bride in the riches of life . . . a maiden of great intelligence' (lines 69–72), one of his students at Leeds and herself an accomplished scholar.

A2: Tolkien marked 'word' with underdots, and wrote the alternative *tír* in the margin.

A4: Throughout the poem Tolkien chose to write the letter *y* with a dot above it (as sometimes in medieval script), except in this line. Here we have added the dot to 'wíshẏcgendes' for consistency.

A38: Tolkien emended 'rǽdde' to 'rǽde'.

A43: Tolkien emended 'dwese' to 'dwæse' by adding a hook to the left of the first *e*.

B18: 'Sea-horse', i.e. ship.

B19: 'Bath-way', i.e. sea.

B85: 'Shield-play', i.e. battle.

121

The History of Tom Bombadil · *The Adventures of Tom Bombadil* (*c.* 1931–62)

The original 'Tom Bombadil' was a flamboyantly dressed Dutch doll, i.e. a toy made of jointed wooden pegs. According to Humphrey Carpenter in *Biography*, it belonged to Tolkien's second child, Michael. In the decade following Michael's birth in 1920, Tolkien told his children stories about a character named, and dressed, after the doll; out of an unknown number of these, most of them probably never written down, only one fragment of three paragraphs survives in his papers. Its narrative is set 'in the days of King Bonhedig' (Welsh 'noble'), and concerns one of the oldest inhabitants of the realm, one 'Tombombadil' (a spelling also found in an early draft of *The Lord of the Rings*). A 'hale and hearty' fellow, Tom was 'four foot high in his boots . . . and three foot broad; his beard went below his knees; his eyes were keen and bright, and his voice deep and melodious. He wore a tall hat with a blue feather[;] his jacket was blue, and his boots were yellow'. We give this prose text in its entirety in our 2014 edition of *The Adventures of Tom Bombadil and Other Verses from the Red Book*.

Tolkien would come to write three poems featuring the character of Tom Bombadil, in addition to the portion of *The Lord of the Rings* in which he appears. The first was *The Adventures of Tom Bombadil*, composed evidently around 1931 – Tolkien wrote out excerpts from it no fewer than five times in an 'Elvish' script which has been dated to 1931 or thereabouts (see Arden R. Smith, ed., *The Qenya Alphabet*, i.e. *Parma Eldalamberon* 20 (2012), pp. 122–36). Three years later, the poem appeared in print in the *Oxford Magazine* for 15 February 1934. It seems clear from its opening lines that it was inspired at least in its first instance by the physical appearance of Tom the Dutch doll and from the story of 'Tombombadil', perhaps from other 'Bombadil' stories as well.

Here we must also mention a short poem quoted in *The Return of the Shadow*. This begins: '(Said I) | "Ho! Tom Bombadil | Whither are you going | With John Pompador | Down the River rowing?"' Christopher Tolkien concluded, presumably from his father's handwriting, that its manuscript 'is certainly quite late' – we would say, possibly as late as the 1960s – but 'there is no trace of the text from which it was copied' (p. 115). Tolkien labelled the extant sheet 'Date unknown – germ of Tom Bombadil so evidently in mid 1930s', a note Christopher took to mean that this was the work from which *The Adventures of Tom Bombadil* grew, and indeed, there are similarities between the two poems in their rhythms and imagery. Even so, there is no physical evidence of the 'germ' developing into the *Adventures*, while it is demonstrable that Tolkien used it as the foundation of a wholly different poem, *Bombadil Goes Boating*, composed in 1962. We will continue our comments on the 'germ' when we discuss that work, poem no. 186.

Discounting the 'germ', the earliest identifiable version of *The Adventures of Tom Bombadil* is an untitled manuscript with many revisions made in the course of writing. Tolkien appears to have had it in mind to present the work in divided half-lines, as in Anglo-Saxon poetry, but as he was neither consistent nor always clear in doing so, we have not reproduced this device in our transcription (A), which does, however, illustrate the alterations Tolkien made as he wrote.

[A] Old Tom Bombadil [*added:* he] was a merry fellow
His house was Underhill; his boots [*added:* they] were yellow,
[*at right*: Green his jacket was and his boots were yellow]
[Green >] Bright blue his jacket [*added:* was] and a peacock's feather
[*at right:* He lived under Hill, and a peacock's feather]
Nodded in his [*added:* old] hat, tossing in the weather.

Old Tom Bombadil walked [?by >] about the meadows
Gathering buttercups, a-chasing of the shadows,
Tickling Bumblebees a-buzzing in the flowers,
Sitting by [*added:* the] water for hours upon hours.

His beard [was dangling >] dangled long down into the water:
There came Goldberry, the river-woman's daughter,
Pulled old Tommy's hair, and in he went [wallowing >] a-wallowing
Under the water lilies, bubbling and swallowing.

'Ho! Tom Bombadil! Whither are you going?'
Said fair Goldberry in this river flowing;
'Frightening the fishes [*at left*: the fish] and the brown water-rat

[And dabchicks diving >] and the diving dabchicks, drowning
your feather-hat?'

'Just fish it out again, there's a pretty maiden!'
Said Tom Bombadil, 'I do not care for wading.'
Back to her mother's house in the [deep >] deepest hollow
Went fair Goldberry — Tom [did not >] he did not follow!

Old Tom Bombadil sat on the willow-roots
His green coat drying and his [*bracketed:* old] yellow boots.
[*at left:* Drying his green jacket > Drying his jacket green]
Up woke Willow-man, began [on >] upon his singing,
Sang [him >] Tom to slumbering under branches swinging,
[*at left:* Singing Tom to sleep]

Caught him in an old crack which he closed together,
Trapped Tom Bombadil, coat and hair [*above:* head; *below:* hat]
and feather.
'Ho, Tom Bombadil, what be you a-thinking,
Peeping right in my tree, watching me a-drinking,
Looking in my wooden house tickling me with feathers,
Dripping wet on my nose like the rainy weathers [?']

'Just you let me out again, Old Man Willow
I am stiff lying here 'tis no sort o' pillow
On your [*added:* hard] crooked roots. Drink river-water
Go back to sleep again like river-woman's daughter!'
Willow unfastened him went back in his tree,
Locked his wooden house so Tom could not see.

Old Tom went away; rain began to shiver
Round rings pattering in the running river.
[*originally l. 43:*] Hail came slanting down falling helter-skelter,
[*originally l. 42:*] Old Tom Bombadil crept into a [?door way >]
shelter
[*deleted:* Wind driven showers]

Out popped [*deleted:* the] Badger-man [*deleted:* Brock] with his
[white >] snowy forehead
Old Brock [snuffling >] a-snuffling looking very worried;
Called to his wife and sons; by the jacket caught him,
Pulled him inside the hole, down the tunnels brought him

Into a secret house. There they sat a-mumbling:
'Now! Tom Bombadil, where have you come tumbling
Bursting in our front door? Badger-folk have caught you;
You'll never find it out, the way that we have brought you!'

'Now, old Brock and all — do you hear me talking! —
You show me [to your back >] out at once, I must be a-walking.
Show me to your back door under briar-roses,
Then clean your white paws, and wipe your sharp noses,
Go back to sleep again on your straw pillow,
Like young Goldberry and the old man Willow!'

Then all the Badger-folk said 'I beg your pardon.'
Showed him straight out again to their thorny garden;
Went back and hid themselves a-shivering and a-shaking.
Block up all their doors, briars together raking.
Old Tom Bombadil hurried home to supper,
Popped in his house again, opened up the shutter,
Let in the setting sun in the kitchen shining;
Watch stars peering out and the moon a-climbing.

Dark came under Hill; Tom he lit a candle,
Upstairs creaking went, turned the door handle.
'Boo! Tom Bombadil, I am waiting for you
Just here behind the door. I came here before you.
I am the old Barrowwight dwelling in the green mound
Up there atop the hill where broken stones lean round
I've got loose tonight. Ho! my merry fellow,
I come for Bombadil coat and boots so yellow.'

'Go out and shut the door, & don't you slam it after!
I don't like your shining eyes, nor your hollow laughter
Go back to grassy mound! On your stony pillow
Lay your old bony head — like the Old Man Willow,
Like fair Goldberry, and Badgerman in burrow
Go back & count your gold and weep your old sorrow. [']

Out went Barrow-wight through the window flying,
[Stumbling in the dark > Stumbling >] Stumbled in the wood pile, up the hill a-crying
Past white drowsy sheep, past the leaning stones
Rushed back to grassy mound rattling [?all] his bones

Old Tom Bombadil lay upon his pillow
Like young Goldberry, like the Old man Willow.
Like the dark Badger-folk, like the barrow-dwellers;
Slept like a humming-top, snored like a bellows;
Woke up in morning-time, whistled like a starling,
Sang, 'Come! derry-down, merry-down, my darling!'
Put on his battered hat boots and coat and feather;
Opened the windows wide to the sunny weather.

Old Tom Bombadil he was a merry fellow,
Bright [green >] blue his jacket was and his boots were yellow
No one caught old Tom walking in the meadows,
Winter and summer time in the lights and shadows,
Down dale over hill jumping over water.
But one day Tom he went and caught the River's daughter,
In green gown, flowing hair, sitting in the rushes
An old song singing fair to birds upon the bushes.

[*two lines added from foot of page:*]
[*added:* He] caught her held her fast water rats went scuttering
Reeds hissed herons flew, how her heart was fluttering
Said Tom Bombadil 'There's a pretty maiden!
You are coming home with me, the table is all laden:
Yellow cream, honey comb, white bread and butter.
Roses at window pane peeping through the shutter.
You come along with me never mind your mother
In her deep pool below. I will have no other!'

Old Tom Bombadil had a merry wedding
Crowned all in buttercups, his old feather shedding,
his bride with forgetmenots & flaglilies for garland
Robed all [in silver >] silver-green. He sang like a starling
Hummed like a honeybee to the squeaky fiddle
    [*at right:* danced to the squeaky fiddle]
Clasping his river-maid round her slender middle.
Lamps gleamed in his house, white was the bedding.
In the bright honey moon Badger folk came treading
Danced down to under Hill, and old man Willow
Tapped tapped at window pane as they slept on the pillow
On the bank in the reeds River-woman sighing
Heard old Barrow wight in his mound crying.
But [*deleted:* old] Tom Bombadil heeded not their voices,

Taps, knocks, dancing feet, nor the nightly noises.
Old Tom Bombadil lived in merry laughter
With his wife under hill there forever after.

This first manuscript was followed – probably in quick succession – by a second, now with a title, *The History of Tom Bombadil*. We give its text as B, already changed at a number of points relative to A, retaining his inconsistent capitalization at line beginnings, and illustrating revisions added to the original manuscript, some of which Tolkien abandoned before writing out the next manuscript in the sequence.

[B] Old Tom Bombadil, [*circled for deletion:* he] was a merry fellow,
bright blue his jacket was, and his boots were yellow.
He lived [*added:* down] under Hill; and a peacock's feather
nodded in his old hat, tossing in the weather.

Old Tom Bombadil walked about the meadows
gathering the buttercups, a-chasing of the shadows,
tickling bumble-bees a-buzzing in the flowers,
sitting by the water-side for hours upon hours.

[*added:* There] his beard [was dangling >] dangled long down into the water:
up came Goldberry, the River-woman's daughter,
pulled [Tom by his hair >] Tom's hanging hair; and in he went a-wallowing
under the water-lilies, bubbling and a-swallowing.

'Ho! Tom Bombadil! Whither are you going?'
said fair Goldberry, [in the river flowing >] (what) bubbles you are blowing,
frightening the dabchicks and the brown water-rat,
startling the finny fish, drowning your feather-hat?'

'[Just pick it out again > Just fetch it out again >] You pick it out again, there's a pretty maiden!'
said Tom Bombadil; 'I do not care for wading!'
Back to her mother's house in the deepest hollow
swam fair Goldberry — [and Tom he did not follow >] but Tom he would not follow.

Old Tom Bombadil sat on [*added:* the] willow-roots
drying his jacket blue and [*added:* both] his yellow boots:
up woke [*circled for deletion:* the] Willowman, began upon his singing,
[singing Tom to slumber > sang Tom to slumber deep >] sang Tom into sleep under branches swinging.

[He caught him [*added:* in] an old crack >] In old crack caught him tight: [snap >] quiet it closed together,
trapped Tom Bombadil, coat and hair and feather.
'Ha! Tom Bombadil, what be you a-thinking,
peeping inside my tree, watching me a-drinking,
looking in my wooden house, tickling me with feathers,
dripping wet down my nose like the rainy weathers?'

'You let me out again [*added:* you] Old Man [*added:* of] Willow!
I am stiff lying here — ['tis >] they're no sort o' pillow,
[*deleted:* On] your hard crooked roots. Drink the river-water,
Go back to sleep again like [River-woman's daughter >] the River-woman's daughter!'
Old Grey Willowman let him loose, and creaking
Locked fast his wooden house, to himself a-speaking,
whispering inside the tree. Tom he sat a-listening.

Tom [called >] cried to merry birds, piping, [chirping >] ?chirruping, whistling;
Tom hailed butterflies, [flutter-quiver-winking >] quivering and winking;
Tom called coneys out, till the sun was sinking.

Then Tom went away. Rain began to shiver,
Round rings pattering in the running river;
hail came slanting down falling helter-skelter.
Old Tom Bombadil crept into a shelter.

[Out >] Up came [Badger-man >] Badger-brock with his snowy forehead;
Old Brock snuffling [*added:* out], looking very flurried,
called to his wife and sons; [they >] and by his [jacket >] coat they caught him,
pulled him inside the hole, down their tunnels brought him

into [a >] their secret house. There they sat a-mumbling:
'Now! Tom Bombadil, where have you come tumbling,
[bursting our front door >] our front door bursting in?
Badger-folk have caught you!
You'll never find it out, the way [*added:* that] we have brought you!'

'Now, old badger Brock, do you hear me talking!
You show me out at once! I must be a-walking.
Show me to your back door under briar-roses,
then clean your grimy paws and wipe your [sharp >] earthy noses!
Go back to sleep again on your straw pillow
Like young Goldberry, and the old man Willow!'

Then all the Badger-folk said 'We beg your pardon!'
Showed him out again, to their thorny garden;
went back and hid themselves a-shivering and a-shaking.
Blocked up all their doors, earth together raking.

Old Tom Bombadil hurried home to supper,
unlocked his house again, opened up the shutter,
let in the setting sun in the kitchen shining,
watched stars peering out and the moon a-climbing.

Dark came under Hill. Tom, he lit a candle,
upstairs creaking went, turned the door handle.
'[You! >] Hoo! Tom Bombadil. I am waiting for you
just here behind the door. I came here before you:
I am [old >] grey Barrow-wight, dwelling in the [green >] old mound
up there atop the hill [where broken stones lean >] with the ring of stones round.
I've got loose tonight! [Ho! my merry fellow > under ground I'll take you >] under earth I'll take you
[I am come for Bombadil, coat and boots so yellow >] poor Tom Bombadil, pale and cold I'll make you.'

'Go out! Shut the door, and don't you slam it after!
[I don't like >] Take away [shining >] gleaming eyes, [nor >] take your hollow laughter.

Go back to grassy mound, on your stony pillow
[Lay your old >] Lay down your bony head, like the old man Willow,
Like fair Goldberry, and Badger-folk in burrow;
Go back! [count your gold, and weep [*added:* for] your [*deleted:* old] >] to buried gold and forgotten sorrow!'

Out fled Barrowwight, through the window flying.
[Setting hens >] Through yard over wall, up the hill a-crying,
past white drowsy sheep over leaning stone [ring >] rings
back under grassy mound rattling his bone rings.

Old Tom Bombadil lay upon his pillow
Sweeter than Goldberry. Quieter than old Willow,
[warmer >] safer than Badger-folk [or >] warmer than the barrow-dwellers;
slept like a humming-top, snored like a bellows;
Woke up in morning-time, whistled like a starling,
Sang: 'Come derry-dol, merry-dol, my darling!'
[He put >] clapped on his battered hat, boots and coat and feather,
opened the windows wide to the sunny weather.

Old Tom Bombadil, [*circled for deletion:* he] was a clever fellow,
Bright blue his jacket was and his boots were yellow.
[No one >] None ever caught old Tom, walking in the meadows,
winter and summer-time, in the lights and shadows,
Down dale, over hill, jumping over water.
But one day Tom he went and caught the River's daughter.
In green gown, flowing hair, sitting in the rushes,
an old song singing fair to birds upon the bushes.

He caught her, held her fast — water rats went scuttering,
reeds hissed, herons cried, how her heart was fluttering.
Said Tom Bombadil: 'There's a pretty maiden!
You shall come home with me! the table is all laden:
yellow cream, honey-comb, white bread and butter;
Roses at window pane, peeping through the shutter.
You come under hill —never mind your mother
In her deep weedy pool; there you'll find no lover.'

Old Tom Bombadil had a merry wedding
crowned all in buttercups, his old feather shedding;
his bride with forgetmenots and flaglilies for garland,
Robed all in silver-green. He sang like a starling,
Hummed like a honey-bee, lilted to the fiddle
clasping his river-maid round her slender middle.

Lamps gleamed inside his house, and white was the bedding.
In the bright honey-moon, badger folk came treading,
Danced down under Hill, and the old man Willow
Tapped, tapped at window as they slept on the pillow.
On the bank in the reeds River-woman sighing
Heard old Barrowwight in his mound crying
But Tom Bombadil heeded not their voices,
taps, knocks, dancing feet, nor the nightly noises.

Old Tom Bombadil lived in merry laughter
with his wife under hill there for ever after.

The existence of Tom Bombadil the Dutch doll may have been Tolkien's central inspiration for his poem, but he also drew upon other influences. In pulling 'old Tommy's' beard, Goldberry acts like a traditional water-sprite or nixie, who in folklore is said to pull humans into a river or lake to drown. Goldberry, however, is playful rather than malicious; in *The Lord of the Rings*, she is depicted more like a nature-spirit, related to seasonal change. According to Humphrey Carpenter in *Biography*, Tolkien once suggested that the idea of Old Man Willow shutting someone in a crack may have been inspired by pictures of gnarled trees drawn by renowned illustrator Arthur Rackham. But Michael Tolkien recalled that his family used to have riverside picnics with willows nearby – the Cherwell in Oxford is very like the river of the poem – and on one occasion he tripped over willow roots and fell in the water, nearly drowning before his father rescued him.

A *barrow-wight* (or *barrowwight*) is an unearthly being inhabiting a *barrow* or burial mound. In Europe there is a long tradition of ancient mounds and stone circles ('where broken stones lean round'), in some of which the dead were interred with gold and other precious things. According to folklore, wights guard such treasure, thus Tom's reference in B80 to 'buried gold'. There are many burial mounds not far from Oxford on the Berkshire Downs, though grave-spirits are indebted largely to Norse mythology rather than to English lore.

In *The Lord of the Rings* Tolkien transferred the Barrow-wight of *The Adventures of Tom Bombadil* to the spirit who traps the four hobbits on the Barrow-downs; there, it is said to be an evil spirit who came to the barrows some two hundred years earlier, as an agent of the Witch-king of Angmar.

Closely following manuscript B, if we may judge by a similarity of layout and script, Tolkien made a fair copy of his poem, again with the title *The History of Tom Bombadil*; for reference, we will call this B^{1}. In this he incorporated the changes marked on the earlier text, and made still more alterations in the course of writing it out. He indicated a few further revisions, but these, we suspect, were not picked up in another copy until closer to the time that the poem was to appear in the *Oxford Magazine*, thus perhaps not for another two or three years.

The next text in this line, which we will call B^{2}, is a typescript based on B^{1}, made on the Hammond machine and with manuscript corrections; Tolkien sent this to the *Oxford Magazine* in 1934. But he also wrote out the text of B^{2}, in a blank examination booklet, as an attractive calligraphic manuscript, now with the title *The Adventures of Tom Bombadil*; we will refer to this as B^{3}. Here, as C, we have transcribed the work from its magazine appearance (pp. 464–5), with significant differences between this and B^{1}, B^{2}, and B^{3} described in our notes.

[C] Old Tom Bombadil was a merry fellow:
bright blue his jacket was, and his boots were yellow.
He lived down under Hill; and a peacock's feather
nodded in his old hat, tossing in the weather.

Old Tom Bombadil walked about the meadows
gathering the buttercups, a-chasing of the shadows,
tickling the bumblebees a-buzzing in the flowers,
sitting by the waterside for hours upon hours.

There his beard dangled long down into the water:
up came Goldberry, the Riverwoman's daughter,
pulled Tom's hanging hair. In he went a-wallowing
under the waterlilies, bubbling and a-swallowing.

'Hey! Tom Bombadil, whither are you going?'
said fair Goldberry. 'Bubbles you are blowing,
frightening the finny fish and the brown water-rat,
startling the dabchicks, drowning your feather-hat!'

'You bring it back again, there's a pretty maiden!'
said Tom Bombadil; 'I do not care for wading!
Go down! Sleep again, where the pools are shady
far below willow-roots, little water-lady!'

Back to her mother's house in the deepest hollow
swam fair Goldberry; but Tom, he would not follow.
On knotted willow-roots he sat in sunny weather
drying his yellow boots and his draggled feather.

Up woke Willow-man, began upon his singing,
sang Tom fast asleep under branches swinging;
in a crack caught him tight: quiet it closed together,
trapped Tom Bombadil, coat and hat and feather.

'Ha! Tom Bombadil, what be you a-thinking,
peeping inside my tree, watching me a-drinking
deep in my wooden house, tickling me with feather,
dripping wet down my face like a rainy weather?'

'You let me out again, Old Man Willow!
I am stiff lying here; they're no sort of pillow,
your hard crooked roots. Drink your river water!
Go back to sleep again, like the River-daughter!'

Willow-man let him loose, when he heard him speaking;
locked fast his wooden house, muttering and creaking,
whispering inside the tree. Tom, he sat a-listening.
On the boughs piping birds were chirruping and whistling.
Tom saw butterflies quivering and winking;
Tom called the conies out, till the sun was sinking.

Then Tom went away. Rain began to shiver,
round rings pattering in the running river.
Clouds passed, hurrying drops were falling helter-skelter;
old Tom Bombadil crept into a shelter.

Out came Badger-brock with his snowy forehead
and his dark blinking eyes. In the hill he quarried
with his wife and many sons. By the coat they caught him,
pulled him inside the hole, down their tunnels brought him.

Inside their secret house, there they sat a-mumbling:
'Ho! Tom Bombadil, where have you come tumbling,
bursting in the front-door? Badgerfolk have caught you:
you'll never find it out, the way that we have brought you!'

'Now, old Badger-brock, do you hear me talking?
You show me out at once! I must be a-walking.
Show me to your backdoor under briar-roses;
then clean grimy paws, wipe your earthy noses!
Go back to sleep again on your straw pillow
like fair Goldberry and Old Man Willow!'

Then all the Badgerfolk said 'We beg your pardon!'
showed Tom out again to their thorny garden,
went back and hid themselves a-shivering and a-shaking,
blocked up all their doors, earth together raking.

Old Tom Bombadil hurried home to supper,
unlocked his house again, opened up the shutter,
let in the setting sun in the kitchen shining,
watched stars peering out and the moon climbing.

Dark came under Hill. Tom, he lit a candle,
up-stairs creaking went, turned the door-handle.
'Hoo! Tom Bombadil, I am waiting for you
just here behind the door! I came up before you.
You've forgotten Barrow-wight dwelling in the old mound
up there a-top the hill with the ring of stones round.
He's got loose to-night: under the earth he'll take you!
Poor Tom Bombadil, pale and cold he'll make you!'

'Go out! Shut the door, and don't slam it after!
Take away gleaming eyes, take your hollow laughter!
Go back to grassy mound, on your stony pillow
lay down your bony head, like Old Man Willow,
like young Goldberry, and Badgerfolk in burrow!
Go back to buried gold and forgotten sorrow!'

Out fled Barrow-wight, through the window flying,
through yard, over wall, up the hill a-crying,
past white drowsing sheep, over leaning stone-rings,
back under lonely mound, rattling his bone-rings.

Old Tom Bombadil lay upon his pillow
sweeter than Goldberry, quieter than the Willow,
snugger than Badgerfolk, or the barrow-dwellers;
slept like a hummingtop, snored like a bellows.

He woke up in morning-light, whistled like a starling,
sang 'come, derry-dol, merry-dol, my darling!';
clapped on his battered hat, boots and coat and feather,
opened the window wide to the sunny weather.

Old Tom Bombadil was a clever fellow;
bright blue his jacket was, and his boots were yellow.
None ever caught old Tom, walking in the meadows
winter and summer-time, in the lights and shadows,
down dale, over hill, jumping over water —
but one day Tom he went and caught the River-daughter,
in green gown, flowing hair, sitting in the rushes,
an old song singing fair to birds upon the bushes.

He caught her, held her fast! Water-rats went scuttering,
reeds hissed, herons cried; and her heart was fluttering.
Said Tom Bombadil: 'Here's my pretty maiden!
You shall come home with me! The table is all laden:
yellow cream, honeycomb, white bread and butter;
roses at window-pane, peeping through the shutter.
You shall come under Hill —never mind your mother
in her deep weedy pool: there you'll find no lover!'

Old Tom Bombadil had a merry wedding
crowned all in buttercups, his old feather shedding;
his bride with forgetmenots and flaglilies for garland,
robed all in silver-green. He sang like a starling,
hummed like a honeybee, lilted to the fiddle,
clasping his river-maid round her slender middle.

Lamps gleamed within his house, and white was the bedding;
in the bright honey-moon, Badgerfolk came treading,
danced down under Hill, and Old Man Willow
tapped, tapped at window-pane, as they slept on the pillow;
on the bank in the reeds Riverwoman sighing
heard old Barrow-wight in his mound crying.

Old Tom Bombadil heeded not the voices,
taps, knocks, dancing feet, all the nightly noises;
slept till the sun arose, then sang like a starling:
'Hey! come, derry-dol, merry-dol, my darling!'
sitting on the doorstep chopping sticks of willow,
while fair Goldberry combed her tresses yellow.

As we have said, towards the end of 1937 Tolkien was asked by his publisher for a sequel to *The Hobbit*. Unable to think of what else he might write on Hobbits, he suggested instead a story about 'Tom Bombadil, the spirit of the (vanishing) Oxford and Berkshire countryside' (letter to Stanley Unwin, 16 December 1937, *Letters*, p. 36), whom he had put into a poem. Instead, only three days later, he began to write what became *The Lord of the Rings*, and in doing so he did not forget Tom, Goldberry, Old Man Willow, and Barrow-wight, all conveniently at hand for an 'adventure' as his story developed. Indeed, Tolkien thoroughly mined his poem for details in writing early chapters of his new work. In the final text of *The Lord of the Rings* Tom enters near the end of Book I, Chapter 6, in 'a blue coat' and 'great yellow boots', 'singing carelessly and happily' in 'a deep glad voice':

'Hey dol! merry dol! ring a dong dillo!
Ring a dong! hop along! fal lal the willow!
Tom Bom, jolly Tom, Tom Bombadillo!'

The four hobbits are lulled by Willow-man in the same manner that Tom is sung 'fast asleep under branches swinging'. Also like Tom, Pippin and Merry are caught in a crack, but freed by Tom's more powerful singing: 'You let them out again, Old Man Willow! What be you a-thinking of? You should not be waking. Eat earth! Dig deep! Drink water! Go to sleep!' Goldberry, dressed in 'green, green as young reeds, shot with silver like beads of dew; and her belt was of gold, shaped like a chain of flag-lilies set with the pale-blue eyes of forget-me-nots', tells Frodo that 'no one has ever caught old Tom walking in the forest, wading in the water, leaping on the hill-tops under light and shadow'. On entering his house, Tom asks: 'Is the table laden? I see yellow cream and honeycomb, and white bread, and butter; milk, cheese, and green herbs and ripe berries gathered.' And – to say no more in this regard – both he and Goldberry advise the hobbits to 'heed no nightly noises', such as willows tapping on the window-pane.

In our discussion for poem no. 24 we remarked that Tolkien's aunt Jane Neave was fond of Tom Bombadil in *The Lord of the Rings*, and in late 1961 asked her nephew if he would write a small book with Tom at its heart. From this emerged *The Adventures of Tom Bombadil and Other Verses from the Red Book* (1962). Tolkien now, in late 1961 or early 1962, returned to his poem of 1934, making a new typescript of the *Oxford Magazine* text (in our notes, C^1) except for a few revisions, notably with 'don't slam it after' changed to 'never come back after' in line C77, and 'an old song singing fair' revised to 'singing old river-songs to birds upon the bushes' in line C102. Curiously, Tolkien made another typescript around this time (C^2), also with further additions and changes, but in places this text reverted to earlier readings, including those in lines 77 and 102. The final text of the poem was reached only in a third typescript (C^3), itself marked with corrections and changes. Below, as D, we have transcribed the poem as it appeared in the first printing of *The Adventures of Tom Bombadil and Other Verses from the Red Book*, pp. 11–13, 15–16.

[D] Old Tom Bombadil was a merry fellow:
bright blue his jacket was, and his boots were yellow,
green were his girdle and his breeches all of leather;
he wore in his tall hat a swan-wing feather.
He lived up under Hill, where the Withywindle
ran from a grassy well down into the dingle.

Old Tom in summertime walked about the meadows
gathering the buttercups, running after shadows,
tickling the bumblebees that buzzed among the flowers,
sitting by the waterside for hours upon hours.

There his beard dangled long down into the water:
up came Goldberry, the River-woman's daughter;
pulled Tom's hanging hair. In he went a-wallowing
under the water-lilies, bubbling and a-swallowing.

'Hey, Tom Bombadil! Whither are you going?'
said fair Goldberry. 'Bubbles you are blowing,
frightening the finny fish and the brown water-rat,
startling the dabchicks, and drowning your feather-hat!'

'You bring it back again, there's a pretty maiden!'
said Tom Bombadil. 'I do not care for wading.

Go down! Sleep again, where the pools are shady
far below willow-roots, little water-lady!'

Back to her mother's house in the deepest hollow
swam fair Goldberry. But Tom, he would not follow;
On knotted willow-roots he sat in sunny weather
drying his yellow boots and his draggled feather.

Up woke Willow-man, began upon his singing,
sang Tom fast asleep under branches swinging;
in a crack caught him tight: snick! it closed together,
trapped Tom Bombadil, coat and hat and feather.

'Ha! Tom Bombadil, what be you a-thinking,
peeping inside my tree, watching me a-drinking
deep in my wooden house, tickling me with feather,
dripping wet down my face like a rainy weather?'

'You let me out again, Old Man Willow!
I am stiff lying here; they're no sort of pillow,
your hard crooked roots. Drink your river-water!
Go back to sleep again like the River-daughter!'

Willow-man let him loose when he heard him speaking;
locked fast his wooden house, muttering and creaking,
whispering inside the tree. Out from willow-dingle
Tom went walking on up the Withywindle.
Under the forest-eaves he sat a while a-listening:
on the boughs piping birds were chirruping and whistling.
Butterflies about his head went quivering and winking,
until grey clouds came up, as the sun was sinking.

Then Tom hurried on. Rain began to shiver,
round rings spattering in the running river;
a wind blew, shaken leaves chilly drops were dripping;
into a sheltering hole Old Tom went skipping.

Out came Badger-brock with his snowy forehead
and his dark blinking eyes. In the hill he quarried
with his wife and many sons. By the coat they caught him,
pulled him inside their earth, down their tunnels brought him.

Inside their secret house, there they sat a-mumbling:
'Ho, Tom Bombadil! Where have you come tumbling,
bursting in the front-door? Badger-folk have caught you.
You'll never find it out, the way that we have brought you!'

'Now, old Badger-brock, do you hear me talking?
You show me out at once! I must be a-walking.
Show me to your backdoor under briar-roses;
then clean grimy paws, wipe your earthy noses!
Go back to sleep again on your straw pillow,
like fair Goldberry and Old Man Willow!'

Then all the Badger-folk said: 'We beg your pardon!'
They showed Tom out again to their thorny garden,
went back and hid themselves, a-shivering and a-shaking,
blocked up all their doors, earth together raking.

Rain had passed. The sky was clear, and in the
    summer-gloaming
Old Tom Bombadil laughed as he came homing,
unlocked his door again, and opened up a shutter.
In the kitchen round the lamp moths began to flutter;
Tom through the window saw waking stars come winking,
and the new slender moon early westward sinking.

Dark came under Hill. Tom, he lit a candle;
upstairs creaking went, turned the door-handle.
'Hoo, Tom Bombadil! Look what night has brought you!
I'm here behind the door. Now at last I've caught you!
You'd forgotten Barrow-wight dwelling in the old mound
up there on hill-top with the ring of stones round.
He's got loose again. Under earth he'll take you.
Poor Tom Bombadil, pale and cold he'll make you!'

'Go out! Shut the door, and never come back after!
Take away gleaming eyes, take your hollow laughter!
Go back to grassy mound, on your stony pillow
lay down your bony head, like Old Man Willow,
like young Goldberry, and Badger-folk in burrow!
Go back to buried gold and forgotten sorrow!'

Out fled Barrow-wight through the window leaping,
through the yard, over wall like a shadow sweeping,
up hill wailing went back to leaning stone-rings,
back under lonely mound, rattling his bone-rings.

Old Tom Bombadil lay upon his pillow
sweeter than Goldberry, quieter than the Willow,
snugger than the Badger-folk or the Barrow-dwellers;
slept like a humming-top, snored like a bellows.

He woke in morning-light, whistled like a starling,
sang, 'Come, derry-dol, merry-dol, my darling!'
He clapped on his battered hat, boots, and coat and feather;
opened the window wide to the sunny weather.

Wise old Bombadil, he was a wary fellow;
bright blue his jacket was, and his boots were yellow.
None ever caught old Tom in upland or in dingle,
walking the forest-paths, or by the Withywindle,
or out on the lily-pools in boat upon the water.
But one day Tom, he went and caught the River-daughter,
in green gown, flowing hair, sitting in the rushes,
singing old water-songs to birds upon the bushes.

He caught her, held her fast! Water-rats went scuttering,
reeds hissed, herons cried, and her heart was fluttering.
Said Tom Bombadil: 'Here's my pretty maiden!
You shall come home with me! The table is all laden:
yellow cream, honeycomb, white bread and butter;
roses at the window-sill and peeping round the shutter.
You shall come under Hill! Never mind your mother
in her deep weedy pool: there you'll find no lover!'

Old Tom Bombadil had a merry wedding,
crowned all in buttercups, hat and feather shedding;
his bride with forgetmenots and flag-lilies for garland
was robed all in silver-green. He sang like a starling,
hummed like a honey-bee, lilted to the fiddle,
clasping his river-maid round her slender middle.

Lamps gleamed within his house, and white was the bedding;
in the bright honey-moon Badger-folk came treading,

danced down under Hill, and Old Man Willow
tapped, tapped at window-pane, as they slept on the pillow,
on the bank in the reeds River-woman sighing
heard old Barrow-wight in his mound crying.

Old Tom Bombadil heeded not the voices,
taps, knocks, dancing feet, all the nightly noises;
slept till the sun arose, then sang like a starling:
'Hey! Come derry-dol, merry-dol, my darling!'
sitting on the door-step chopping sticks of willow,
while fair Goldberry combed her tresses yellow.

In his preface to the *Bombadil* collection Tolkien wrote that *The Adventures of Tom Bombadil* and *Bombadil Goes Boating* (no. 186) 'evidently come from the Buckland', on the eastern border of the Hobbits' Shire.

> They show more knowledge of that country, and of the Dingle, the wooded valley of the [River] Withywindle, than any Hobbits west of the Marish [adjoining Buckland] were likely to possess. They also show that the Bucklanders knew Bombadil, though, no doubt, they had as little understanding of his powers as the Shire-folk had of Gandalf's: both were regarded as benevolent persons, mysterious maybe and unpredictable but nonetheless comic. No. 1 [*The Adventures of Tom Bombadil*] is the earlier piece, and is made up of various hobbit-versions of legends concerning Bombadil. [pp. 8–9]

Just as he had drawn from his 1934 poem in writing *The Lord of the Rings*, now the later work informed the verses of 1962, notably in the establishment of Bombadil's country along the Withywindle, giving a name to what in earlier versions of the poem is only the water, or the river. *Withywindle* is mentioned three times in the revised poem, a name based on *withywind* 'convolvulus, bindweed'; *withy* is another word for 'willow', and the river is winding. Tolkien also realized that, in the landscape of the Shire and the Old Forest, a peacock's feather would not be appropriate for Tom's tall hat, thus he changed it to 'a swan-wing feather' in the final text.

Tom does not speak in verse solely because *The Adventures of Tom Bombadil* is a poem, with rhyme. It is his natural manner, as Tom Shippey has observed, and as seen in *The Lord of the Rings*; see further, our discussion for poem no. 154.

In 1967 Tolkien made a professional recording of *The Adventures of Tom Bombadil* for the album *Poems and Songs of Middle Earth*. It was later reissued.

A19: 'Fish it out': here Tolkien compares *fish* as a verb ('retrieve') versus *fish(es)* as a noun in A17, but chose to abandon the wordplay in version B.

A46: 'Brock' is an old word for *badger*, from Old English *broc(c)*; the compound *badger-brock* (e.g. B45) is therefore a doubled word. A badger typically has a white mark on its head, thus '[white >] snowy forehead'.

A89: Tom sleeps 'like a humming-top', a variation on the adage 'slept like a top', i.e. very soundly, like a spinning, humming top at its steadiest.

A118: *Honey moon* is an old European name given to the full moon of June (the last full moon in spring), possibly because June was the month honey was ready to be harvested from beehives. Tolkien is probably also playing on *honeymoon* in the sense of the first period of married life, a word which may be related to a widespread custom of marrying in June.

B39: 'Winking', i.e. a butterfly closing and opening its wings is likened to the winking of an eye, and butterflies often have wing markings which resemble eyes (eyespots); compare 'lantern eyes' in no. 35.

B72: In the margin next to this line Tolkien wrote an alternate reading, 'stony ring round'.

B84: The wight's 'bone rings' may be rings made from bone, of the sort sometimes found in burials. In *The Lord of the Rings* Tom Bombadil speaks of barrow-wights who 'walked in the hollow places with a clink of rings on cold fingers' (Book I, Chapter 7).

C10: The mark of punctuation at the end of this line varies throughout the manuscripts and typescripts of the poem, either a comma (as in the earliest versions and the printed *Oxford Magazine* text) or a semi-colon (as in the *Bombadil* collection, text D). Tolkien's calligraphic copy B^3 follows the magazine version, but in a second calligraphic manuscript probably of about the same time, which Tolkien gave to C.S. Lewis, this line ends with a semi-colon.

C15: In B^1 this line reads 'frightening finny fish and little water-rat', with 'little' changed to 'brown' in the margin.

C18: In B^1 Tom says 'I do not care for wading', full stop; in B^3 he says 'I do not care for wadin'!' with the final word changed to 'wading' in the margin.

C22: In B^1 this line reads 'swam fair Goldberry. But Tom he would not follow', with 'fair' changed to 'young' in the margin.

C27: In B^1 this line begins 'In old crack'.

C32: In B^1 this line ends 'like the rainy weather'.

C33: In B^1 this line reads 'You let me out again, you Old Man Willow!'

C34: In B^3 Tolkien first wrote 'lyin'', changed to 'lying' in the margin.

C35: In B^1, B^2, and B^3 this line ends 'river-water', with a hyphen.

C36: In B^1 this line ends 'river-daughter', without a capital R.

C37–38: In B^1 these lines read 'Old grey Willow-man let him loose, and creaking | locked fast his wooden house, to himself a-speaking'. The same lines are in B^2 as typed, changed there to the form in B^3 and C. Tom refers to 'old grey Willow-man' in *The Lord of the Rings*.

C41: In B^3 this line begins 'Tom saw the butterflies'.

C42: In B^1 'conies' is spelled 'coneys'.

C45: In B^1 this line begins 'Clouds went by'.

C48: In B^1 this line begins 'and dark blinking eyes', changed to 'and his dark blinking eyes'.

C53: In B^1 this line begins 'the front door bursting in', and ends with an exclamation mark.

C58: In B^1 this line ends with a comma. The sentence continues on l. 59.

C60: In B^1 this line reads 'like young Goldberry, and the Old Man Willow', with 'young' changed to 'fair' in the margin.

C72: In B^1 this line ends 'I came here before you'.

C73: In B^1 this line begins 'I'm the grey Barrow-wight'.

C75–76: In B^1 these lines read 'I have got loose tonight; under earth I'll take you. | Poor Tom Bombadil! pale and cold I'll make you!' The wight speaks in the first person consistently in B^1. The same lines are in B^2 as typed, changed there to the form in B^3 and C, where the wight speaks of itself initially in the first person ('I am waiting for you'), then changes to the third ('He's got loose tonight'). The *Oxford Magazine* text hyphenates 'to-night' in l. 75.

C80: In B^1 this line ends 'like the Old Man Willow'.

C86: In B^1 this line begins 'back under grassy mound', with 'grassy' changed to 'lonely' in the margin.

C88: In B^1 this line ends 'quieter than Old Willow'.

C89: In B^1 this line ends 'more warm than barrow-dwellers'.

C90: In B^1 'humming-top' is spelled with a hyphen, in B^2 as two words, 'humming top', in C as one word.

C94: In B^1 Tom opens 'windows', plural.

C104: In B^1 this line ends 'how her heart was fluttering!' Tolkien changed 'how' to 'and' in B^2.

C119: In B^1 this line ends 'and the Old Man Willow'.

C120: In B^1 'window pane' is spelled as two words.

C122: In B^1 'Barrowwight' is spelled as one word, though it is hyphenated 'Barrow-wight' earlier in the poem.

C126: The *Oxford Magazine* printed 'derry-dol' as 'derry-rol', almost certainly an error, which we have corrected here.

C128: Manuscript B^1 includes two additional lines (129–130), carried forward from A and B: 'Old Tom Bombadil lived in merry laughter | with his wife under Hill there for ever after.' The same lines are in B^2 as typed, but struck through. They are omitted from the *Oxford Magazine* text, and from B^3.

D3–4: In C^2 Tolkien wrote above the first stanza, apparently as alternate lines 3–4, 'of silver was his buckle broad, his girdle was of leather; | he wore in his tall hat a swan's white feather'. This is the first indication of the peacock's feather being changed to that of a swan.

D5–6: Tolkien added these lines in C^2, with l. 6 beginning 'ran from its stony well'. Tolkien changed 'its stony well' to 'a grassy well' in C^3.

D7: Tolkien changed 'Old Tom Bombadil walked' to 'Old Tom in Summer-time walked' in C^2.

D8: Tolkien changed 'a-chasing of the' to 'running after' in C^2.

D9: Tolkien changed 'a-buzzing in' to 'that buzzed among' in C^2.

D26–27: In C^3 Tolkien wrote in the space between these lines '[3-line space]', apparently desiring a visual pause between the 'episodes' of Goldberry and Willow-man. In the published *Bombadil* collection the space between stanzas is equal throughout the poem.

D29: In C^3 as typed, this line ended 'it slowly closed together'. Tolkien changed 'it slowly closed' in manuscript to 'snick! it closed'.

D34–35: In C^3 Tolkien wrote in the space between these lines '[1-line space]'.

D41: In C^3 as typed, this line began 'Down by the wood's end'. Tolkien changed the words in manuscript to 'Under the forest-eaves'.

D44: In C^3 as typed, this line began 'till dark clouds'. Tolkien changed the words in manuscript to 'until grey clouds'.

D48–49: In C^3 Tolkien wrote in the space between these lines '[3-line space]'.

D52: *Earth* in this sense is another word for *sett* (or *set*), a badger's underground home, typically lined with straw, hay, or grass, and with multiple tunnels and exits, hence references in the poem to the 'front-door', 'backdoor', and 'all their doors'. In *The Lord of the Rings* (Book I, Chapter 7) Tom tells the hobbits 'an absurd story about badgers and their queer ways'.

D66–67: In C^3 Tolkien wrote in the space between these lines '[3-line space]'.

D73: In C^3 as typed, this line began 'Night came under Hill'. Tolkien changed the words in manuscript to 'Dark came under Hill'. It could be that 'Night' was an error in typing, since 'Dark' was the reading in all previous texts.

D75: In C^1, as earlier, this line ends 'I am waiting for you'. In C^2 Tolkien changed the words to 'I've been waiting for you'. In C^3 as typed, they read 'Long time I've sought you', changed in manuscript to 'Look what night has brought you'.

D75–76: In marginal notes on C^2 Tolkien wrote alternate readings for these lines (to follow 'Hoo! Tom Bombadil'):

> Why are you belated?
> Here I am behind the door; long for you I've waited!
>
> Long here I've sought you
> Here behind the door
> Now at last I've caught you
>
> Long here I've [delayed >] sought you
> I'm here behind the door.
> Now at last I've caught you!

D79: In C^3 as typed, this line began 'He's got loose tonight'. Tolkien changed the words in manuscript to 'He's got loose again'.

D81: In C^2 as typed, this line ended 'don't slam it after!' Tolkien changed the words to 'never come back after!' as in C^1.

D99: In C^2 as typed, this line reads 'Old Tom Bombadil was a clever fellow'; Tolkien marked 'was a clever fellow' for revision to 'he was wise, and a wary fellow'. In C^3 this line originally read 'Old Tom, he was wise and a wary fellow'; Tolkien revised it in manuscript to the final text.

D101: In C^1 this line ends 'walking in the meadows'. In C^2 Tolkien wrote 'in upland or in dingle' above, and without striking through, 'walking in the meadows'.

D102–103: Tolkien added these lines in C^2.

D106: In C^1 this line reads 'singing old river-songs to birds upon the bushes'. In C^2 the earlier reading is still present ('an old song singing fair to birds upon the bushes'), but Tolkien marked it with different possibilities for revision. Here 'river-songs' eventually gave way to 'water-songs'.

122

Monday Morning (*c.* 1931–4)

Monday Morning exists in a single, fair copy manuscript, with a few changes made after the fact, most notably to the names 'Chris' and 'Michael', which became 'James' and 'William'. In private notes, Christopher Tolkien remarked that these were 'obviously' himself and his elder brother Michael, and since both are shown to leave for school from home, and their brother John is not present, the time must be in the early 1930s. In September 1931 John went away to the Oratory School near Reading (south-east of Oxford), and Michael followed him there in September 1934.

We have transcribed the poem with revisions indicated in the text.

On Monday morning all agree
that most annoying things can be.
Now I will tell you in this song
of one when everything went wrong.
The sun was early shining bright,
but not, of course, for my delight:
it woke the birds who woke mama,
who woke the boys, who woke papa;
it came and hit me in the eye,
though still I wished in bed to lie.
I rolled upon the other side,
and tried with sheets my head to hide;
but someone said: ''Tis nearly eight!
Get up! Get up, or you'll be late!'
I filled the bath and took the sponge —
and then I took a sudden plunge:
some soap was lying on the floor,
I don't know what the dickens for.
I slipped and fell in with a splash,
and gave my knee a nasty bash,
and [half the water out did > out I saw the water] pour
to join the soap upon the floor.
Of course my clothes were all upset
and lying in a pool of wet.
The breakfast bell I heard them ring,

but still I could not find the thing:
my stupid stud had rolled away
at hide-and-seek with me to play.
I trod on it and squashed it flat.
It served it right, a thing like that
to play such tricks. But what a bother!
I simply could not find another!
And still I had to scrape and shave —
O lucky chaps that in a cave
lived long ago and grew their hair
and did not wash or collars wear.
Though you may laugh, I did not grin
when off I sliced a piece of chin;
though you may snigger, I was hurt,
and spoiled my temper, towel and shirt.
    At last I started to come down,
but someone else, some silly clown
(no doubt by purest accident,
these nasty turns are seldom meant)
had left the carpet on the stair
all ruckled up, and unaware
I tripped, and gave a startled yell
as down a dozen stairs I fell.
I landed on a sliding mat,
and in the hall went sprawling flat.
    Just as I spoke an angry word,
the postman at the door I heard.
A pile of letters rattled in,
but still he rang and made a din;
and when I went and asked him why,
he held his hand out in reply:
a stampless letter sent to me
required a wretched double fee.
I opened it, and stood amazed,
for on a lengthy bill I gazed
demanding payment by return:
the sort of thing that ought to burn.
The rest, the ones that had their stamps
were just advertisements for lamps,
for motors, wine, cigars and books,
or begging-letters sent by crooks.

So feeling faint and hardly able
to look at food I came to table.
The boys all shouted in a chorus:
'You never can get down before us!
You're last again, and we must go,
It's time for school. Your watch is slow!'
Then promptly [Chris > James] upset his tea,
and most of it went over me!
When mess and [Chris > James] were cleared away,
I took a sip without delay;
but only one, when through the door
he popped again and gave a roar;
the hair was wild upon his head,
'I've left my pen behind!' he said.
Then out he went, and never shut
the wretched door. I turned to cut
a piece of bread, when back he jumped
and cried: 'I shall be late! I've pumped,
and pumped, and still my tyres are flat!
And also where, O where's my hat?'
His hat was in the rack for boots,
his pen in another of his suits;
his tyres required that I should go
and give to each a hefty blow.
He mounted on his bike at last,
but started off a bit too fast:
he hit the kerb, and off he crashed.
Though nothing but his bell was smashed,
his books were tumbled in the dust,
and so was he. And so we must
return to have a wash and brush.
At last he went! There fell a hush.
The tea was cold, my face was hot.
Then in came [Michael > William] at a trot.
It seemed his trousers were all split,
and what did mother think of it!
She thought a lot, and said some more,
but not being father never swore.
When they were gone repairs to make,
I thought another bite I'd take.
I bit a [bit > piece] of buttered crust,
and crack! an ancient tooth I bust.

I sprang up with a yowl of pain,
and spilled a cup of tea again;
then rang the bell to clear away
and gave up breakfast for the day.
    I sat and groaned. I stamped the ground,
and thus I heard a ghastly sound:
a jingling, crashing, banging bump
that made my startled heart go thump.
The maid had dropped the tray of crocks,
and all was cracked upon the rocks:
[every > the] cups and saucers, plates, and pot
in smithereens, the whole bang lot!
    Then mother in dismay came tearing
to view the damage — never caring,
around a corner quick she slid
where some infernal nail was hid.
A rip — and half her frock was torn!
O joyous day! O happy morn!
But if you think that that's the end
of all the fuss, you're wrong, my friend.
    While in the kitchen all was bother,
folk tumbling over one another,
two birds got out and left their cages.
We chased and hunted them for ages
with duster and with fishing-net,
and all the pictures were upset.
The steps we brought, and all in vain:
we only broke a window-pane.
Though one was caught, he lost a wing;
the other had the cheek to sing,
and through the broken window flew,
and vanished swiftly in the blue.
    And still my tooth would not forget
the only crust that day I ate.
It nagged, until I gave a groan,
and said: 'I will! I'll telephone!
I'll ring the dentist up and say:
Pull out what's left of it to-day!'
    But just as to the 'phone I went,
it rang itself. My ear I lent,
and heard an angry voice and loud
that said my name. My head I bowed.

'O are you there?' I heard it say
'Have you forgotten! What's to-day?
You said you'd meet me here at nine!
It's ten o'clock, and still no sign!'
I answered sweetly: 'No I'm not!
It's Monday, and I've not forgot,
and never shall. But I'm *not* here.
I'm ill in bed and feeling queer.
Just go to blazes right away,
and ring me up from there some day!'
    I slammed the thing upon the hook,
and back to bed my way I took —
no! not to bed! For it was Monday,
the jolly holiday, the fun-day,
the laundry day, the washing morn,
the day it's pleasant to be born!
The bed was stripped, the mattress bare;
the room was filled with chilly air.
    And so I sat upon the floor,
wondering what anything was for.
A stump of pencil then I found,
and squatting there upon the ground
upon a bill (they have clean backs,
unless they ask for income-tax)
I wrote this tale of fate unkind.
O laugh away! Don't think I mind!

We do not for a moment believe that all of these events actually happened to the Tolkiens in a single morning. It is certainly possible that they occurred each at some time to the family, though – charitably – we hope that Tolkien exaggerated while having this bit of fun. There is no mention of his daughter Priscilla, though she must have been present if our assumption as to the date of the poem is correct, as she was born in 1929. If we did not already know from Humphrey Carpenter's biography, *Monday Morning* would suggest that the family had servants to help in the house, and Edith had an aviary. Christopher and Michael both attended the Dragon School in Bardwell Road, Oxford, not far from their home in Northmoor Road; cycling there would have been quicker than walking, flat tyres notwithstanding.

18: 'What the dickens' is a polite oath, substituted for 'what the devil' (or the like).

27: Men's dress shirts at this time featured a separate starched collar (see l. 36) which fastened to the rest of the shirt with two studs, or fasteners.

42: *Clown* in this sense means 'an unthinking, stupid person'.

93: In the U.S.A. *kerb* is spelled *curb*.

133: By 'duster' Tolkien presumably means feathers attached to the end of a rod, an implement for dusting furniture, etc. A fishing-net, i.e. a net with an attached handle, would seem a more practical tool for catching an errant bird.

159: 'Go to blazes' is another polite oath, with 'blazes' standing in for 'Hell'.

161: 'Slammed the thing upon the hook', i.e. replaced the telephone handset forcefully.

123

Oilima Markirya · *The Last Ship* · *The Last Ark* (*c.* 1931–?61 or ?62)

Tolkien delivered his lecture *A Secret Vice*, which we have mentioned already in connection with other poems, to the Johnson Society of Pembroke College, Oxford on 29 November 1931. His subject was invented languages – 'artificial' languages such as Esperanto, and those created solely for personal amusement. Linguistic invention, he said, gave him 'incipient pleasure'. It was 'more personal and fresh, more open to experiment of trial and error' than learning a language that already existed, 'and it is capable of developing into an art' (*A Secret Vice*, in *The Monsters and the Critics and Other Essays*, p. 206). In the course of his lecture, Tolkien included examples of languages he himself had created, most importantly his 'Elvish' language Qenya, 'expressly designed to give play to my own most normal phonetic taste' (p. 212); and he read to his audience three poems in Qenya, showing that his language invention was not just in the abstract. One of these works we have quoted already, *Nieninque* (no. 65); another was *Earendel at the Helm* (no. 124); and the third, but the first to be presented in the lecture, was *Oilima Markirya* ('The Last Ark').

There are twelve extant versions of this poem in its Qenya form. These are discussed in detail in *Early Elvish Poetry and Pre-Fëanorian Alphabets* by Tolkien (*Parma Eldalamberon* 16, 2006). The earliest (p. 56) is a mere couplet, each line of which contains six sets of syllables:

[A] kildo kirya ninqe lutilya lúne veasse
ar tanda kiryaiko lunte kiryinqen tinweninqen.

From this, as shown in *Early Elvish Poetry* (p. 57), Tolkien expanded the work to three stanzas (B) and introduced rhyme, between the first or second line and the last, in each trimetric quatrain – that is, each line has three sets of syllables.

[B] kildo kirya ninqe
lutsilya lúne veasse
ar tanda kiryaiko lunte

kirilde tinwelinqe
vean falastanére
falmain lótanéren
kulukalmalínen
kiryan kalliére.

surussin surdon lausto
falma funduváre
ondoisen andalissen
kiryan lantumáre.

In the third draft, the poem stood at sixteen lines (four quatrains), and in the fourth it reached thirty-four lines in stanzas of varying length. At this point – with the fourth text – Tolkien began to write versions of the work in English. We give here, as C, the first of these, from *Early Elvish Poetry*, p. 68, where details of Tolkien's development of the text are provided as notes by editors Christopher Gilson, Bill Welden, and Carl F. Hostetter.

[C]

The sea was surging
with foamcrests like flowers.
The boat was shining
with (or in) golden lights.

He saw a white ship
sailing like a butterfly
in the flowing blue sea
upon wings like stars.

The wind was roaring
like leaves of a forest[.]
The dark rocks were white
and gleamed in the moon.

The moon went down
like a corpse into a grave.
The clouds of hell came out of the East.
Heaven leaned upon the hills.

A ship lay upon the green rocks
when the sky was red.
The sun gazed through a haze of tears
upon the last shore of all lands.
It was the morning before the last night.

In all, Tolkien produced six versions in English, in the process creating a longer and more complex work, following a separate line of development which diverged from that of the poem in Qenya. With the second English text, the opening became an interrogative – 'Who shall see a white ship' – rather than an indefinite statement ('He saw a white ship'), and with the fourth Tolkien moved mention of the enigmatic 'last shore' from the end of the poem to its beginning.

Gilson, et al. point out that the fourth English version is on the same sheet as the fifth Qenya text, and that in the latter Tolkien changed the spelling so that it was closer to that of Finnish, for example, with long vowels represented by doubled letters. 'If read out loud', the editors remark, 'according to the spelling conventions of Finnish it would sound like Qenya with a "Finnish accent".' This characteristic may relate to a heading on the fourth English text: 'The Last Ark (from the Finnish)'. 'Given the divergence in literal meaning between the English and Qenya,' Gilson, et al. speculate, 'we might take this to indicate that the English is supposed to be the rendering of a Finnish version, perhaps traditionally associated with the Qenya version, though only indirectly related to it. In that case the Qenya text itself might be conceived of as having been preserved in a Finnish source, where it has undergone a certain amount of influence from its context' (*Early Elvish Poetry*, p. 54). Qenya was strongly influenced by Finnish, by way of Tolkien's enthusiasm for the *Kalevala* and his study as an undergraduate of C.N.E. Eliot's *Finnish Grammar*.

The fifth Qenya version, at twenty-nine lines, is shorter than the fourth, and the sixth one line shorter still. A similar text, of twenty-seven lines, was published by Christopher Tolkien in an appendix to *A Secret Vice* in *The Monsters and the Critics and Other Essays*, presented here from that source (pp. 220–1) as D.

[D]

Kildo kirya ninqe
pinilya wilwarindon
veasse lúnelinqe
talainen tinwelindon.

Vean falastanéro
lótefalmarínen,
kirya kalliére
kulukalmalínen.

Súru laustanéro
taurelasselindon;

ondolin ninqanéron
Silmeráno tindon.

Kaivo i sapsanta
Rána númetar,
mandulómi anta
móri Ambalar;
telumen tollanta
naiko lunganar.

Kaire laiqa'ondoisen
kirya; karnevaite
úri kilde hísen
níe nienaite,
ailissen oilimaisen
ala fuin oilimaite,
alkarissen oilimain;
ala fuin oilimaite
ailinisse alkarain.

Once again, Tolkien added to the poem, and now wrote in tetrameter as well as trimeter. He labelled this 'first version', though that can be correct only in the sense that the text belongs to the first sequence of the work's (Qenya) development. In their expanded edition of *A Secret Vice* (*A Secret Vice: Tolkien on Invented Languages*, 2016, corrected 2020), transcribed from the original manuscript, Dimitra Fimi and Andrew Higgins give the second word of line 5 of this text as 'falastanére'. In their *Parma Eldalamberon* analysis, Gilson, et al. comment that this version of the poem ('OM1')

> was based on OM1f [the sixth draft] with mostly minor changes in some of the grammatical suffixes and particles used. For example *falastanére* was revised to *falastanéro* in line 4, a slight change in meaning from 'she was surging' to 'he was surging', apparently reflecting a change in how *vean* 'the sea' is personified, rather than a change in the grammar. [p. 55]

Tolkien also translated this version into English, given here as E from *The Monsters and the Critics and Other Essays*, p. 221.

[E] A white ship one saw, small like a butterfly
upon the blue streams of the sea with
wings like stars.

The sea was loud with surf, with waves
crowned with flowers. The ship shone with
golden lights.

The wind rushed with noise like leaves of forests,
the rocks lay white shining in the silver moon.

As a corpse into the grave the moon went down
in the West; the East raised black shadows out of
Hell. The vault of heaven sagged upon the
tops of the hills.

The white ship lay upon the rocks; amid red
skies the Sun with wet eyes dropped tears of
mist, upon the last beaches after the last night
in the last rays of light — after the last night
upon the shining shore.

Gilson, et al. include one further draft Qenya text in the first line of development, in which Tolkien expanded formerly trimetric lines into tetrameter. 'This was accomplished' they write, 'by numerous small changes in each line, adding a word or a compound element, or using a longer inflected form, so that the overall sense of the poem was not altered very much. The result is verse that is quite similar in rhythm to the Finnish *Kalevala*' (p. 54). The new text begins:

maano kiluvando ninkve
lutya kirya wilwarindon
laivarisse luunelinkve
talaliinen tinwelindon?

It was on this, Gilson, et al. remark, that Tolkien based the version of *Oilima Markirya* he read in *A Secret Vice*. Paul Strack has argued, however, on his website *Eldamo: An Elvish Lexicon* (*eldamo.org*), that the draft 'does not match either the first or second versions of the poem, or any of the English translations, and seems to be an experimental bridge between the first and second versions'. He prefers to describe it as an intermediate text, separately considered.

Be that as it may, Tolkien seems to have reached the form of *Oilima Markirya* read in his lecture, via a draft with a very similar text, by translating his more developed English poem back into Qenya. Gilson, et al. observe that 'in the course of three reworkings the

English . . . had diverged from the Elvish in both rhythm and style, and Tolkien may have felt that this would obscure the differences in the phonetic patterning of the words, which was a primary point to be illustrated by reciting parallel verses in Qenya and English' in *A Secret Vice* (*Early Elvish Poetry*, p. 55). It was in the draft of the second text that the title *Oilima Markirya* first appeared, above which Tolkien wrote 'prose'. 'This term', Gilson, et al. say, 'is perhaps meant only to describe the style of the poem, for while parts of it are rhythmical, nevertheless it differs from [the first version] in having no rhyme-scheme or regular metre, using the looser rhythms of prose instead' (p. 55). Gilson, et al. note variant readings between the draft and its text as revised; Fimi and Higgins include a transcription of the draft manuscript in their edition of *A Secret Vice*.

The English text Tolkien read with his lecture differs only in a few respects from the version 'from the Finnish' described above. Fimi and Higgins include a separate transcription from its typescript, on which Tolkien altered its original title, *The Last Ship*, to that of the 'Finnish' text, *The Last Ark*. Here, as F, we give 'another text of this English version', as Christopher Tolkien described it in *The Monsters and the Critics and Other Essays* (p. 220, n. 8), that is, in addition to the version published with the lecture text. This is taken from a typescript made on the Hammond machine, still with the title *The Last Ship*, and includes two changes in manuscript. We have described differences between this and the published English text in our notes.

[F]

Who shall see a white ship
Leave the last shore,
The pale phantoms
In her cold bosom
Like gulls wailing?

Who shall heed a white ship,
Vague as a butterfly,
In the flowing sea
On wings like stars,
The sea surging,
The foam blowing,
The wings shining;
The light fading?

Who shall hear the wind roaring
Like leaves of forests;

The white rocks snarling
In the moon gleaming,
In the moon waning,
In the moon falling
As a corpse-candle;
The storm mumbling,
The abyss moving?

Who shall see the clouds gather,
The heavens bending
Upon crumbling hills,
The sea heaving,
The abyss yawning,
The old darkness
Beyond the stars falling
Upon fallen towers?

Who shall heed a broken ship
On the dark rocks
Under ruined skies,
A bleared sun blinking
On bones gleaming
In the last morning?
Who shall see the last evening?

Here, as G, is the Qenya poem as delivered in the lecture, from *The Monsters and the Critics and Other Essays*, pp. 213–14.

[G] Man kiluva kirya ninqe
oilima ailinello lúte,
níve qímari ringa ambar
ve maiwin qaine?

Man tiruva kirya ninqe
valkane wilwarindon
lúnelinqe vear
tinwelindon talalínen,
vea falastane,
falma pustane,
rámali tíne,
kalma histane?

Man tenuva súru laustane
taurelasselindon,
ondoli losse karkane
silda-ránar,
minga-ránar,
lanta-ránar,
ve kaivo-kalma;
húro ulmula,
mandu túma?

Man kiluva lómi sangane.
telume lungane
tollalinta ruste,
vea qalume,
mandu yáme
aira móre ala tinwi
lante no lanta-mindon?

Man tiruva rusta kirya
laiqa ondolissen
nu karne vaiya,
úri nienaite híse
píke assari silde
óresse oilima?

Hui oilima man kiluva,
hui oilmaíte?

It remains only to discuss one further Elvish text of *Oilima Markirya*, created long after the *Secret Vice* lecture. This exists in two typescripts, made on one of Tolkien's later machines. The earlier is on a single page, crowded with workings and glosses for the Elvish words, the second a fair copy, incorporating changes made to the first; the latter survives in both ribbon and carbon copies, each of which Tolkien revised, though not identically. Christopher Tolkien included the later text, and the glosses accompanying the earlier, in an appendix to *A Secret Vice* in *The Monsters and the Critics and Other Essays*: there the second text is given as it stood before Tolkien revised it, with notes on variant readings in the draft and changes made to the second text. Here, as H, we give the final version, taken from the second typescript and incorporating Tolkien's revisions, with variations described in notes.

[H]

Man kenuva fáne kirya
métima hrestallo kíra,
i fairi néke
ringa súmaryasse
ve maiwi yaimië?

Man tiruva fáne kirya,
wilwarin wilwa,
ëar-kelumessen
rámainen elvië,
éar falastala,
winga hlápula,
rámar sisílala,
kále fifírula?

Man hlaruva rávëa súre
ve tauri lillassië,
ninqui karkar yarra
isilme ilkalasse,
isilme píkalasse,
isilme lantalasse
ve loikolíkuma;
raumo nurrua,
undume rúma?

Man kenuva lumbor [ahosta, nahosta]
Menel akúna
ruxal' ambonnar,
ëar amortala,
undume hákala,
enwina lúme
elenillor pella
talta-taltala
atalantea mindonnar?

Man tiruva rákina kirya
ondolisse morne
nu fanyare rúkina,
anar púrëa tihta
axor ilkalannar
métim' auresse?
Man kenuva métim' andúne?

Fortunately for the sake of dating this version, Tolkien typed the draft on the reverse side of a sheet he had earlier used for a late version of his poem *Firiel* (no. 141). The *Firiel* page, a carbon typescript rejected due to a mistyped stanza, was made in 1961 or early 1962, when Tolkien revisited the poem for inclusion in *The Adventures of Tom Bombadil and Other Verses from the Red Book*; he submitted a revised *Firiel* to his publisher on 5 February 1962. We have no reason to think that Tolkien considered *The Last Ark* for the *Bombadil* collection, but revising *Firiel* may have put him in mind of the earlier work, which also features a white ship, and he chose at that time to revisit it, at least in its Elvish form.

We cannot know what Tolkien's audience for *A Secret Vice* thought of his Elvish verses, or of their translations. Today it is impossible to read *Oilima Markirya* or *The Last Ark* without considering their relationship to Tolkien's mythology. Is the 'white ship' like Círdan's white ship which bore Bilbo and Frodo, with their friends, away from the Havens at the end of *The Lord of the Rings*? Is the 'last shore' (or 'ultimate shore', or 'final shore', as Tolkien had it in different drafts) the 'white shores' Frodo sees at the end of his journey into the West? In the early versions of *The Last Ark*, the ship reaches the 'last shore', but in the later texts the 'last shore' is what it leaves. In either case, neither the destination of the white ship, where it lies (in different texts) 'drowned', or 'dead', or 'broken' on rocks, nor its journey, through roaring winds and heaving seas, does not seem particularly inviting. The poem suggests the End Times – 'the last morning', 'the last evening' – rather than Paradise. At least, it is a sentimental reflection on things past, or passing, and in this sense, as well as in its form ('Who shall see', 'Who shall heed', 'Who shall hear'), it recalls the *ubi sunt* motif of Old English poems such as *The Wanderer* (see poem nos. 133 and 166).

Patricia Reynolds has suggested that the first stanza of *The Last Ark* (of text E) is indebted to the Old English *Seafarer*, in which the poet speaks of lost kinsmen – Tolkien's 'pale phantoms' – and of the cries of gulls. In her 1990 essay 'Green Rocks: White Ship: *Oilima Markirya* (*The Last Ark*)' Reynolds also argues that Tolkien's poem is 'an apocalyptic vision' which 'owes some of its imagery to the Icelandic version of Ragnarök [in Norse mythology, the last battle and death of the gods] used by Snorri Sturluson [in the Prose Edda] – where "mountains will crash down" and "the sky will be rent asunder". A ship, made from dead-men's nails, will be launched upon a tempestuous sea' (p. 34).

C2: 'Foamcrest', i.e. the foam at the crest of a wave. E4–5, 'waves | crowned with flowers', evokes the same image.

D11: Fimi and Higgins note that in the manuscript, the final three letters of the word 'ondolin' ('rocks') are circled. In OM1f (*Parma Eldalamberon* 16) Tolkien used the earlier form *ondoin*.

F1: Throughout this typescript Tolkien preferred to capitalize the beginning of each line.

F12: In the texts published in *The Monsters and the Critics and Other Essays* and Fimi and Higgins' edition of *A Secret Vice*, this line ends with a comma.

F20: In *The Monsters and the Critics and Other Essays* and the Fimi–Higgins edition, this line reads 'a corpse-candle', without 'as'. A *corpse-candle* is a lighted candle placed beside a corpse before burial; in earlier versions of the poem the moon sets in the west like a corpse being lowered into a grave. Both are unsettling images.

F32–33: In *The Monsters and the Critics and Other Essays* and the Fimi–Higgins edition, these lines read 'on the green rocks | under red skies'.

F35: In *The Monsters and the Critics and Other Essays* and the Fimi–Higgins edition, this line is separated from the preceding text.

H1: In *The Monsters and the Critics and Other Essays*, this line begins 'Men'.

H3: In the draft typescript of this version, this line reads 'i néka fairi'.

H16: In the draft typescript of this version, this line reads 'ninqui ondor yarra'.

H21: On the ribbon copy of this typescript, Tolkien marked 'nurrula' to be changed to 'nurrua'.

H22: On the ribbon copy of this typescript, Tolkien marked 'rúmala' to be changed to 'rúma'.

H23: On the ribbon copy of this typescript, Tolkien marked 'na-hosta' to be changed to 'ahosta', but on the carbon copy to be changed to 'nahosta'; hence we have included both readings in our transcription.

H24: On the ribbon copy of this typescript, Tolkien marked 'na-kúna' to be changed to 'akúna'.

H25: On the ribbon copy of this typescript, Tolkien lightly circled 'ruxal" and wrote 'del[ete]' next to it. This seemed too tentative to apply to our transcription.

H31: In the carbon copy of this typescript, this line reads 'atalantië mindoninnar?' On the ribbon copy, Tolkien marked the line to be changed to 'atalantea mindonnar?' In his notes in *The Monsters and the Critics and Other Essays*, Christopher Tolkien recorded the first word as changed from 'atalantië' to 'atalantëa', but his father clearly wrote 'ea' at the end, without an umlaut.

H35: In the draft typescript of this version, this line reads 'anar púrea tihtala'.

H37: In the draft typescript of this version, this line reads 'métima amaurëasse?' In the margin of the ribbon copy of the final typescript next to this line Tolkien wrote 'orróne ?'

H38: In the draft typescript of this version, the final word of this line originally read 'andúnie'. Tolkien altered it to 'andúne'.

124

Earendel · Earendel at the Helm (?1931)

As mentioned in our previous entry, Tolkien read three poems composed in Qenya within his 1931 lecture *A Secret Vice*. Of these *Earendel* was the last, following *Oilima Markirya* (poem no. 123) and *Nieninqe* (no. 65). We give here, as A, its final Qenya text, taken from *A Secret Vice* as published in *The Monsters and the Critics and Other Essays*, p. 216. Earendel, or Earendil, is the mariner we have met in earlier poems, who in Tolkien's mythology sailed into the West and was transformed into a bright star of hope in the heavens.

[A]

San ninqeruvisse lútier
kiryasse Earendil or vea,
ar laiqali linqi falmari
langon veakiryo kírier;
wingildin o silqelosseën
alkantaméren úrio
kalmainen; i lunte linganer,
tyulmin talalínen aiqalin
kautáron, i súru laustaner.

Two drafts of this poem, written on the reverse sides of the manuscripts of two of the English versions of *Oilima Markirya* (*The Last Ark*), are transcribed and discussed by Christopher Gilson, Bill Welden, and Carl F. Hostetter in *Early Elvish Poetry and Pre-Fëanorian Alphabets* (*Parma Eldalamberon* 16). In the first, the Qenya text is identical to that printed in *The Monsters and the Critics and Other Essays* and in the edition of *A Secret Vice* edited by Fimi and Higgins (see poem no. 123), and has a glossarial commentary; in the second, the poem has the spelling conventions of Finnish (discussed in conjunction with no. 123). Tolkien says in his lecture that the Qenya *Earendel* is in 'a strict and quantitative metre', and he labelled the first of its drafts a 'specimen of quantitative metre' – that is, a metre based on the quantity, or length, of syllables rather than on stresses. Quantitative metre is common in Greek and Latin poetry, both languages in which long vowels take significantly more time to pronounce than short ones, but it is uncommon in English, where the difference in vowel length is less pronounced.

Tolkien accompanied each of his Qenya texts of *Earendel* with an English translation, or version. The first is described by Gilson, et al. as 'a line-by-line and largely word-for-word rendering in prose that seems to closely anticipate the prose translation given in the essay' (p. 98), immediately following the Qenya text. We quote it here (B) as presented in *Early Elvish Poetry*, p. 100.

[B] Then upon a white horse sailed
Earendel, upon a ship over the sea,
and green wet waves
the neck of the sea-ship clove
the foam maidens with flower white hair
made (it) shine of the sun
in the lights; the boat hummed like a harp string
the masts tall bent to the sails
the wind rushed.

In *The Monsters and the Critics and Other Essays*, p. 216, Christopher Tolkien printed the English version accompanying the lecture as continuous prose. Here as C we give it with the line breaks followed by Fimi and Higgins:

[C] Then upon a white horse sailed Earendel,
upon a ship upon the sea,
and the green wet waves the throat of the sea-ship
clove. The foam-maidens with blossom-white
hair made it shine in the lights of the sun; this boat
hummed like a harp-string; the tall masts bent with the
sails; the wind 'lausted' (not 'roared' or 'rushed' but made
a windy noise).

To accompany the second draft text in Qenya, Tolkien wrote a longer version of the poem in English. Gilson, et al. describe a manuscript with false starts and 'many revisions in wording and the expansion of the final tag', that is, the final four lines, 'into a sort of coda' (p. 98). We give this text as D, from *Early Elvish Poetry*, p. 104, with selected notes on Tolkien's revisions (described more fully by Gilson, et al.).

[D]

A white horse in the sun shining
a white ship in the sea gliding
    Earendel at the helm
Green waves in the sea moving
white foam at the prow spuming
    The sun upon the sails
Foam riders with hair like blossom
Leaping upon the sea's bosom
    They sing and call
The ropes like harps ringing
The sea spirits like echoes singing
    The masts against the sky
The deep sails billowing
The wild wind bellowing
    The road going on forever.

A revised version of this text exists in a fair copy manuscript and a typescript made on the Hammond machine; on the reverse of the typed sheet is a fragment of *A Rhyme Royal for Easter Morning* (no. 61). We give the manuscript text here (as E), with notes concerning the related typescript and differences in the poem as published in *A Secret Vice*. The manuscript is entitled *Éarendel at the Helm*, with the name given an accent, but the typescript has *Earendel at the Helm*.

[E]

A white horse in the sun shining,
A white ship in the sea gliding,
    Éarendel at the helm;
Green waves in the sea moving,
White froth at the prow spuming
    Glistening in the sun;
Foam-riders with hair like blossom
And pale hands on the sea's bosom
    Chanting wild songs;
Taut ropes like harps tingling,
From far shores a faint singing
    On islands in the deep;
The bent sails in the wind billowing,
The loud wind in the sails bellowing,
    The road going on for ever,
    Éarendel at the helm,
    His eyes shining, the sea gliding,
        To havens in the West!

B2: The mariner's name is given as 'Earendil' in the Qenya text, but 'Earendel' in the English text.

B5: 'Foam maidens' (in text D, 'foam riders'), i.e. foam on cresting waves. Compare 'foamcrests like flowers' in *The Last Ark* (no. 123).

C4: Fimi and Higgins note that 'blossom-white' was changed by Tolkien from 'flower-white' (compare B5).

C5: Fimi and Higgins have 'this boat'. *The Monsters and the Critics and Other Essays* has 'the boat', and this is also the reading in text B.

D1: Gilson, et al. note that the text originally began 'Then sailed on his gleaming galleon | Earendel', but Tolkien struck this through.

D7: This line originally read 'Foam riders with hair like flowers'.

D10: 'Ringing' originally read 'singing'.

D11: 'Sea spirits' originally read 'seagull'.

E3: The name *Éarendel* is written thus in ll. 3 and 16, in the manuscript but not in the related Hammond typescript. The indentations shown here, in this line and later, reflect those in both the manuscript and typescript in hand, and with the exception of ll. 16 and 18 were also followed in *The Monsters and the Critics and Other Essays*. As given by Fimi and Higgins, the text has no indentations; we have not seen the typescript of the poem preserved with the *Secret Vice* lecture proper.

E8: Both the manuscript and the Hammond typescript have 'pale hands'. The typescript from which Christopher Tolkien drew for *The Monsters and the Critics and Other Essays*, and which Fimi and Higgins transcribed, has 'pale arms'.

E9: On the Hammond typescript ('another text of the poem' as described in *The Monsters and the Critics and Other Essays*, p. 220, n. 10), Tolkien marked this line to be changed to 'Speeding the ship'.

E14: On the Hammond typescript, Tolkien marked 'loud' to be changed to 'east'.

E18: The final exclamation mark is present in both the manuscript and related typescript. In the published text, the poem ends with a full stop.

125

Dir Avosaith a Gwaew Hinar (?1931)

In addition to three poems in Qenya (nos. 65, 123, 124), Tolkien also recited to the audience of his lecture *A Secret Vice*, as another example of his Elvish language invention, a few lines of verse which begin 'Dir avosaith a gwaew hinar'. We give this text, as A, as it appears in *The Monsters and the Critics and Other Essays*, p. 217.

[A]

Dir avosaith a gwaew hinar
engluid eryd argenaid,
dir Tumledin hin Nebrachar
Yrch methail maethon magradhaid.
Damrod dir hanach dalath benn
ven Sirion gar meilien,
gail Luithien heb Eglavar
dir avosaith han Nebrachar.

A draft version also exists, given here as B (as emended by Tolkien), which was transcribed and analyzed by Dimitra Fimi and Andrew Higgins in their edition of *A Secret Vice*, p. 101.

[B]

Dir avosaith a gwaew hinar
éngluid eryd argenaid
Dir tûmledin hui Nebrachar
yrch melhail maethon magradhaid
Damrod dir hanach dalath benn
ven Sirion gar meilien
Gail Lúthien heb Eglavar
Dir avosaith han Nebrachar

In his lecture Tolkien also read a version of the poem in English, presented in *The Monsters and the Critics and Other Essays* (p. 217) as prose. Here, as C, we have divided its lines to accord with the Elvish text, and with reference to a draft transcribed by Fimi and Higgins.

[C] Like a wind, dark through gloomy places
the Stonefaces searched the mountains,
over Tumledin (the Smooth Valley) from Nebrachar,

orcs snuffling smelt out footsteps.
Damrod (a hunter) through the vale,
down mountain slopes, towards (the river)
Sirion went laughing. Lúthien he saw, as a star from Elfland
shining over the gloomy places, above Nebrachar.

The draft English text in Fimi and Higgins (D, as emended by Tolkien), p. 101 of *A Secret Vice*, differs from the lecture version (C) in several respects.

[D] Like a wind dark through gloomy places
the 'Stonefaces' (Orcs) searched the mountains
over Tumlad, from Nebrachar (a place of goblins)
Orcs snuffling scented footsteps. Damrod (the
hunter) through the vale down the mountain slopes
to awaited Sirion went smiling. Luthien he
saw as a Fay from Fayland shining over the places above
Nebrachar

Tolkien introduced this poem as 'a fragment from the same mythology [in which the preceding poem in the lecture, *Earendel at the Helm*, figures], but a totally different if related language' (*The Monsters and the Critics and Other Essays*, p. 217). The language is Noldorin, which as we have mentioned (in discussion for poem no. 13) shares a thread of evolution with Gnomish. Unlike Qenya, which was influenced by Finnish, Noldorin and others of its linguistic line – ultimately Sindarin, as in *The Lord of the Rings* – were influenced by Welsh. These languages were (or came to be) conceived by Tolkien 'to have a relation to High-elven [Qenya, or Quenya] similar to that existing between British (properly so-called, *sc.* the Celtic languages spoken in this island at the time of the Roman Invasion) and Latin' (statement for the Houghton Mifflin Company, 1955, *Letters*, p. 318).

'Eglavar' (A7), in other works 'Eldamar', became 'Elfland' (C7) and 'Fayland' (D7), i.e. land of the fays, or fairies. *Tumledin* (C3), later *Tumlad* (D3), is a variant of *Tumladin* 'Valley of Smoothness', the plain of Gondolin (see poem no. 66). In *The Monsters and the Critics and Other Essays* Christopher Tolkien states that 'the name *Nebrachar* occurs nowhere else [in Tolkien's papers], and whatever story may be glimpsed in this poem cannot be identified in any form of the mythology that is extant' (p. 220, n. 11). Fimi and Higgins, however, in their edition of *A Secret Vice* note that Tolkien established two Noldorin roots, NEB 'near' and RHACH 'carnage, slaughter', 'so Nebrachar may mean "near a place of slaughter"' (p. 57). Tolkien notably identifies it in D as 'a place of goblins', i.e. Orcs.

A4, 8: In Fimi and Higgins' edition there is no punctuation at the end of these lines of Noldorin text, though full stops are present in the English text.

A5: Fimi and Higgins identify Damrod as the son of the Noldorin Elf Fëanor, maker of the Silmarils.

C4: As fully transcribed by Fimi and Higgins, this line reads '[*deleted:* orcs snuffling [*illegible*] foul creatures scented] snuffling goblins smelt out footsteps'.

126

The Last of the Old Gods (?1931)

This poem survives only in a fair copy typescript, made by Tolkien on his Hammond machine. From its appearance and paper, it seems to date from around the time of his lecture *A Secret Vice* (see poem no. 123). It contains a few handwritten marks, variably on ribbon and carbon copies, detailed in our notes; most notably, Tolkien amended, or corrected, the original typewritten title *The Last of the Gods* to *The Last of the Old Gods*.

Twixt Earth and Heaven towers tall
are mounted above wall on wall,
their windy peaks are fierce and free,
their feet are founded in the sea;
and to those towers of light and snow
faint comes the murmur far below
of the green waves and the white seas
and little tempests like a breeze.

One sits there gazing long afar
beyond the realm of things that are,
with old eyes and grey cheek,
and those eyes find not what they seek:
a light upon the margins dun
of this deep world beneath the sun,
an echo of a glimmer dim
beyond the sea-infested rim
of this grey island of sad earth,
an echo of an ancient mirth.

Beyond the awful mountains white,
the pale hills built above the night,
the deserts cold, the chasms wide,
the seas that have no shore nor tide,
the dark and stormless waters steep
where stars swim silently and deep,
even to Old Darkness and the gloom,
the nothingness that was the womb

of things, of time, of gods, of light,
the old eyes wander beyond sight —
and see no hope, but only dead
cold ruin in the pale rays shed
by weary suns, shadow and sad cloud
above the battlements once proud
upon the confines of the world;
the halls of gods in ruin hurled,
the dykes against the outer seas
crumbling, crumbling into screes.

2.

'Tis all they see; and ears that knew
A timeless time when musics grew
to harmonies that wrought the world,
unfolding slow, as slow uncurled
this flower of crystal now destroyed,
a lily in the dark and void
of chaos, this new world now old,
beauty and wonder fading cold —
these ears now hear the mortal hum
of little men that go and come,
and go and come and make their toys
and cluster in a pygmy noise,
while ever outside the silent Dark
eyeless it watches them, the Dark,
the old darkness and the gloom,
the nothingness that is their doom
and end of things, of men, of light,
watches awaiting the last night.

But down below, whence faint and far
that throne is, twixt sea and star,
a blur upon the sky, we crawl
and look not thitherward at all,
or think of darkness lying in wait
or gods that would have walled out fate;
or if we think, we shrug and turn,
snap our small fingers, and make burn
another tiny candle-spark,
a twinkle in the gathering dark.

Yet we have songs, brief songs and frail —
perchance they mount not from this vale,
dim is our singing in those ears;
the eyes, whose wisdom looks on fears
so vast, in knowledge and despair,
see not our puny courage flare
beneath the everlasting sky,
the doomed to death who will not die.
The walls the gods no more will build;
can we like ants with fury filled
the beacons pile against the dark,
and rear again the ramparts stark,
the wall delaying what must be,
the dykes against the outer sea?

This does not have any overt connection with Tolkien's mythology, though it is possible to find (or imagine) elements in common – for example, the notion of 'a timeless time when musics grew | to harmonies that wrought the world', compared with the creation of the world from music in the *Ainulindalë* or creation story in 'The Silmarillion', and the 'One [who] sits', presumably the titular old god himself, watching for 'a light upon the margins dun | of this deep world beneath the sun' as the Valar waited for the coming of Elves and Men. It should also be noted, however, that in a list of his poems prepared probably in the 1930s as a plan of publication, Tolkien included *The Last of the Old Gods* in a sequence with *Éalá! Éarendel Engla Beorhtast!* (*The Voyage of Éarendel the Evening Star*, no. 16), *The City of the Gods* (*Kôr: In a City Lost and Dead*, no. 30), and *The Shores of Faery* (no. 31), all of which are explicitly related to the 'Silmarillion' mythology.

And yet, it is also easy to read this poem as a comment on the state of the world in the early 1930s, when trouble was again stirring on the Continent and fears of another war loomed. Most of the work is told from the point of view of the 'old god', who sees 'dead cold ruin' and the (metaphorical) crumbling of dykes which have held back 'the outer seas'; but towards its end the emphasis shifts to Men, who no longer look to the old gods, who 'shrug and turn', yet retain a spark of defiance. Are they to be considered 'new gods' in contrast to the 'old'? The poet expresses a hope that beacons and ramparts can be erected again against the dark, though it is a weak, indeed fatalist view: a wall or dyke will only delay 'what must be' – the 'end of things'.

In this respect, Tolkien's Latin poem *Quare Fremunt Omnes Gentes* (no. 135), written slightly later (as we think), has a similar outlook.

Tolkien's repetition of 'dark', 'darkness', 'gloom' in the fourth stanza in fact echoes his emphasis on darkness in some of his poems of the First World War years. Much of this stanza also recalls his comments, in his 1936 British Academy lecture *Beowulf: The Monsters and the Critics*, on the Anglo-Saxon view of the 'long defeat' of Man: 'the exaltation of undefeated will', as in the words of Byrhtwold in *The Battle of Maldon* ('Will shall be the sterner, heart the bolder, spirit the greater as our strength lessens'; see poem no. 129), against a 'paradox of defeat inevitable yet unacknowledged, . . . man at war with the hostile world, and his inevitable overthrow in Time' (*The Monsters and the Critics and Other Essays*, p. 18).

At the end of the first section of the poem, Tolkien wrote 'end?' as if considering whether to discard lines 37 and following, perhaps if and when the work was published. On the ribbon copy of its typescript he also marked separately for possible deletion the final two stanzas (from line 55), but restored (with 'stet') all except lines 73 to the end.

1: Tolkien did not number the first part of the poem, as he did the second (from l. 37).

12: Tolkien seems to have considered whether to change 'those' to 'his'.

13–18: Tolkien bracketed these lines in the margin, as if considering whether to change or delete them.

34: As typed, 'ruin' read 'ruins'.

35: In the U.S.A. *dyke* is spelled *dike*.

44: As typed, 'fading' read 'faded'.

45: As typed, the word 'hear' was omitted, presumably overlooked from a (lost) draft.

47: Tolkien tentatively marked 'go and come' to be changed to 'come and go'.

48: 'Pygmy noise', i.e. insignificant sounds.

59: Tolkien seems to have considered whether to change 'or' to 'nor'.

73: As typed, 'will' read 'can'.

127

Vestr um Haf · *Bilbo's Last Song (at the Grey Havens)* (?1931–*c.* 1960)

The poem *Vestr um Haf* (Old Norse 'West over Sea') is found in Tolkien's papers only in a fair copy typescript (A), made on his Hammond machine.

[A]

Long the road and wild the way,
The sea is roaring in the bay.
Farewell, friend! I hear the call;
The ship's beside the stony wall.
Foam is white and waves are grey;
Beyond the sunset leads our way.
Foam is salt, the wind is frore,
The sea is crying on the shore.

Farewell, friend! the sails are set,
The wind is East, the moorings fret.
Islands lie behind the sun
That we shall raise ere all is done;
Lands there are to West of West
Where night is quiet and sleep is rest,
Islands faint beyond the deep
Where sands are white and soft is sleep.

Twilight filled with streaming stars
Behind the sunset's rocky bars
Looks upon a foaming sea
And shores for ever fair and free.
Ship, my ship, we seek the West
And fields and mountains ever blest,
Farewell calling o'er the sea
That lies before us fair and free.

We have placed this poem in sequence here for two reasons. One is that its physical appearance and the paper on which it is typed are similar to those of *The Last Ship* (no. 123) and *Earendel at the Helm* (no. 124), which as we have seen are associated with Tolkien's 1931 lecture *A Secret Vice*. But *Vestr um Haf* is also thematically related to these works. *The Last Ship* tells of another voyage, of a white ship leaving 'the last shore', and in *Earendel at the Helm* a white ship sails 'to havens in the West'. In *Vestr um Haf* a ship likewise sails west, seeking islands lying 'behind the [setting] sun': no one with a knowledge of Tolkien's mythology could mistake this place for anything other than Aman, the Undying Lands.

Looking forward, it seems possible that Tolkien had the imagery of these poems in mind when he wrote (in a late revision) almost the final words of *The Lord of the Rings* (Book VI, Chapter 9), in which Frodo and Bilbo Baggins take their leave of Middle-earth:

> Then Frodo kissed Merry and Pippin, and last of all Sam, and went aboard [a white ship at the quay of the Grey Havens]; and the sails were drawn up, and the wind blew, and slowly the ship slipped away down the long grey firth; and the light of the glass of Galadriel that Frodo bore glimmered and was lost. And the ship went out into the High Sea and passed on into the West, until at last on a night of rain Frodo smelled a sweet fragrance on the air and heard the sound of singing that came over the water. And then it seemed to him that as in his dream in the house of Bombadil, the grey rain-curtain turned all to silver glass and was rolled back, and he beheld white shores and beyond them a far green country under a swift sunrise.

In 1931 *Vestr um Haf* could not of course have had any connection with *The Lord of the Rings*, as Tolkien did not begin to write the latter until the end of 1937, and he did not conceive of its end, with a passage over sea, until late 1944. But the idea of lands 'West of West' and of a sea journey there were well established in 'The Silmarillion'.

Tolkien later filled the margins of the *Vestr um Haf* typescript with revisions, copiously so. From variations in his handwriting, it seems that he worked at these on three or four occasions. Many of them, in pencil and biro (ballpoint pen), are illegible, erased, struck through, or overwritten; but among the readable text is a new title, *Bilbo's Last Song*. It may be – we have no direct evidence – that Tolkien revisited *Vestr um Haf* in 1961 or 1962, when he was reviewing old work to include in *The Adventures of Tom Bombadil and Other Verses from the Red Book*. It would have been reasonable to make the poem over into a composition by Bilbo as he waited for his ship to sail from the Grey Havens. Several of the works in the *Bombadil* collection are said, in Tolkien's preface, to have been written by Bilbo. But in the end, the poem was not included in the volume, and Tolkien did not mention it in surviving correspondence as being sent to his publisher for consideration.

The marked typescript was followed by a fair copy manuscript, entitled more fully *Bilbo's Last Song (at the Grey Havens)*. We give this text as B, as Tolkien first wrote it.

[B]

The Sun is fallen, daylight dies,
but journey long before me lies.
Farewell, friends! I hear the call.
The ship's beside the stony wall.
Foam is white and waves are grey;
beyond the sunset leads my way.
Foam is salt, the wind is free;
I hear the rising of the Sea.

Farewell, friends! The sails are set,
the wind is east, the moorings fret.
Islands lie behind the Sun
that we shall raise ere all is done;
lands there are to west of West,
where night is quiet and sleep is rest

Guided by the Lonely Star,
beyond the final harbour-bar
we'll find the beaches fair and free
the foaming of the Outer Sea.
Ship, my ship! I seek the West,
and fields and mountains ever blest.
Farewell to middle-earth at last,
I see the Star above your mast!

Tolkien marked revisions also to this manuscript, replacing a few words, including the whole of lines 1 and 18, and he added two lines, 11 and 12 as below. These were carried into the final text of the poem, a fair copy (and probably amanuensis) typescript, given here as C.

[C]

Day is ended, dim my eyes,
but journey long before me lies.
Farewell, friends! I hear the call.
The ship's beside the stony wall.

Foam is white and waves are grey;
beyond the sunset leads my way.
Foam is salt, the wind is free;
I hear the rising of the Sea.

Farewell, friends! The sails are set,
the wind is east, the moorings fret.
Shadows long before me lie,
beneath the ever-bending sky,
but islands lie behind the Sun
that I shall raise ere all is done;
lands there are to west of West,
where night is quiet and sleep is rest.

Guided by the Lonely Star,
beyond the utmost harbour-bar
we'll find the havens fair and free,
and beaches of the Starlit Sea.
Ship, my ship! I seek the West,
and fields and mountains ever blest.
Farewell to middle-earth at last,
I see the Star above your mast!

The content and mood (if not the form) of *Bilbo's Last Song* inevitably call to mind Tennyson's 'Crossing the Bar' (1889), generally seen to represent the passage from life to death:

> Sunset and evening star,
>   And one clear call for me!
> And may there be no moaning of the bar,
>   When I put out to sea. . . .

In *Bilbo's Last Song* the spelling 'middle-earth' in the penultimate line, without a capital letter, suggests that although Bilbo is in fact sailing away from Middle-earth, the Great Lands east of the sea, he is also saying good-bye, ultimately after a time in the West, to the 'middle-earth' of early cosmology, the world of mortal life. (Also compare 'middle-earth' in text D of *Firiel*, poem no. 141.) In drafts of *The Happy Mariners* (no. 33, first composed 1915), Tolkien briefly used the term 'midworld' with the same meaning. *Bilbo's Last Song* also looks back to that earlier poem in reference to a 'Lonely Star', undoubtedly Eärendil; in *The Happy Mariners* Tolkien refers to the 'shining mariner' as 'the lonely star the silver watcher of the west', whom the sailors follow 'to Islands blest'.

If our theory of Tolkien revising *Bilbo's Last Song* for the *Bombadil* volume is correct, then both the manuscript and later typescript may belong to that time at the beginning of the 1960s. The poem was in its final form by October 1968, when Tolkien's assistant, Joy Hill, discovered its typescript while helping to arrange the author's books after he moved from Oxford to Poole in Dorset. On 3 September 1970, in gratitude for years of friendship and service, Tolkien gave her a copy of the typescript and copyright in the work. She arranged for its publication as a poster in 1974, one year after Tolkien's death, and again in book form in 1990. The British poster issue and the book version include illustrations by Pauline Baynes which tie the poem firmly to events at the end of *The Lord of the Rings*.

Although it is not an integral part of *The Lord of the Rings*, *Bilbo's Last Song* was incorporated into the 1981 BBC radio production of that work adapted by Brian Sibley and Michael Bakewell. Earlier, in 1978, Donald Swann included a musical setting of the poem in the second edition of *The Road Goes Ever On: A Song Cycle*, based on a song from the Isle of Man and reminiscent of a Cephallonian Greek melody. Several recordings of this exist, most notably that by Swann himself (piano and vocals) on a disc included with the 2002 third edition of *The Road Goes Ever On: A Song Cycle*.

A4: 'Stony wall', i.e. the quay where the ship is moored.

A10: 'The wind is East', i.e. from the east, blowing west. The mooring ropes are strained, rubbing (*fret*), the ship pulling at them.

A23: Tolkien considered whether to place 'Farewell' in quotation marks.

C22: Here we have corrected, as Tolkien did on his retained copy, the typist's 'over blest' for 'ever blest'.

C24: The British poster issue of the poem misprinted 'my mast' for 'your mast'.

128

Errantry · Eärendil Was a Mariner · The Short Lay of Earendel: Earendillinwë (*c.* 1931–62)

In a letter of 14 October 1966 to the composer Donald Swann, Tolkien remarked that he conceived this poem, which he came to call *Errantry*, 'very many years ago, in an attempt to go on with the model that came unbidden into my mind: the first six lines, in which, I guess, *D'ye ken the rhyme to porringer* had a part' (quoted in *The Treason of Isengard*, p. 85). His reference is to a Jacobite song about the Revolution of 1688, in which the Catholic King James II of England (James VII of Scotland) was deposed by his Protestant son-in-law, William of Orange:

O what's the rhyme to porringer?
Ken ye the rhyme to porringer?
King James the Seventh had ae dochter [a daughter],
And he ga'e [gave] her to an Oranger.

The song also inspired a nursery rhyme:

What is the rhyme for porringer?
What is the rhyme for porringer?
The king he had a daughter fair
And gave the Prince of Orange her.

The initial texts of *Errantry* have not been available to us, but in *The Treason of Isengard* (pp. 85–6) Christopher Tolkien transcribed its earliest retained version, as his father first set it down. We give this here as text A. Christopher describes it (p. 85) as 'a rough pencilled manuscript without title: there were certainly preliminary workings behind it, now lost, since this text was set down without hesitations or corrections'. 'It seems very probable', however, 'that it was in fact the first complete text of the poem'.

[A]

There was a merry passenger,
a messenger, an errander,
he took a tiny porringer
and oranges for provender;
he took a little grasshopper
and harnessed her to carry him;
he chased a little butterfly
that fluttered by, to marry him.
He made him wings of taffeta
to laugh at her and catch her with;
he made her shoes of beetle-skin
with needles in to latch them with.
They fell to bitter quarrelling,
and sorrowing he fled away;
and long he studied sorcery
in Ossory a many day.
He made a shield and morion
of coral and of ivory;
he made a spear of emerald
and glimmered all in bravery;
a sword he made of malachite
and stalactite, and brandished it,
he went and fought the dragon-fly
called wag-on-high and vanquished it.
He battled with the Dumbledores,
and bumbles all, and honeybees,
and won the golden honey-comb,
and running home on sunny seas,
in ship of leaves and gossamer
with blossom for a canopy,
he polished up and burnished up
and furbished up his panoply.
He tarried for a little while
in little isles, and plundered them;
and webs of all the attercops
he shattered, cut, and sundered them.
And coming home with honey-comb
and money none — remembered it,
his message and his errand too!
His derring-do had hindered it.

The manuscript, Christopher Tolkien writes, 'has many alterations and suggestions leading to the second version'. Tolkien also wrote on it new concluding lines, presumably to follow A40 (quoted here from *The Treason of Isengard*, p. 107), which he did not take up into the next draft:

So now he must depart again
and start again his gondola,
a silly merry passenger,
a messenger, an errander,
a jolly, merry featherbrain,
a weathervane, a mariner.

Passenger in line A1 means 'traveller, wayfarer' rather than 'one carried in a vessel' (such as a ship or plane). This sense was already unusual when it was published, as the first definition of *passenger*, in 1904 in the *Oxford English Dictionary*. An interesting point in its etymology is that in late Middle English *n* was added phonetically before *-ger* in words such as *passager* (adopted from the French), creating *passenger*, *messenger*, and *porringer* among others.

Tolkien also told Donald Swann that he had read *Errantry* 'to an undergraduate club that used to hear its members read unpublished poems or short tales, and voted some of them into the minute book' (*The Treason of Isengard*, p. 85; his text may have been A, above). The club in question was the original 'Inklings', founded by an undergraduate at University College, Oxford, Edward Tangye-Lean; this group did not stay together long, probably not beyond Tangye-Lean's graduation in summer 1933. At some stage its name was transferred to another group of friends, who met regularly with Tolkien and C.S. Lewis at their centre. Tolkien's reading of *Errantry* to the first 'Inklings' places its origin therefore in the early 1930s. We have dated it to *c.* 1931, also on the evidence of manuscripts of the poem, in whole or in part, written out by Tolkien in his Elvish script *tengwar*, in a mode Arden R. Smith has dated to *c.* 1931. The latter are reproduced and transcribed in *The Qenya Alphabet* (*Parma Eldalamberon* 20, 2012).

Christopher Tolkien notes in *The Treason of Isengard* that there are five further texts of the poem among his father's papers, each entitled *Errantry*, culminating in its publication in the *Oxford Magazine* for 9 November 1933. The second version (B) begins and ends thus (from *The Treason of Isengard*, p. 89):

[B]

There was a merry messenger,
a passenger, an errander;
he gathered yellow oranges
in porringer for provender;
he built a gilded gondola
a-wandering to carry him
across the rivers seventeen
that lay between to tarry him.

He landed there in loneliness
in stoniness on shingle steep,
and ventured into meadow-land
and shadow-land and dingle deep.

. . . . .

for ever still a-tarrying,
a mariner, a messenger,
a-roving as a feather does,
a weather-driven passenger.

Notable in text B are the lines 'he wrought her raiment marvellous | and garments all a-glimmering' (compare C39–40) and 'He made a sword and morion | of coral and of ivory, | a spear he made of emerald' (compare C57–59); see *The Treason of Isengard*, p. 107.

The third version, Christopher reports (*The Treason of Isengard*, p. 89), begins 'There was a merry messenger, a passenger, a mariner', and has in its second stanza the lines

He landed all in loneliness
in stoniness on shingle steep,
and wandered off to meadowland,
to shadowland, to dingle deep.

The fourth version reached the *Oxford Magazine* form except in the third stanza (*The Treason of Isengard*, p. 89):

He landed all in loneliness
where stonily on shingle go
the running rivers Lerion
and Derion in dingle low.
He wandered over meadow-land
to shadow-land and dreariness, etc.

Here, as C, we give the *Oxford Magazine* text, also found in *The Treason of Isengard*, pp. 86–9, and in our extended edition (2014) of *The Adventures of Tom Bombadil and Other Verses from the Red Book*, pp. 155–9.

[C]

There was a merry passenger
a messenger, a mariner:
he built a gilded gondola
to wander in, and had in her
a load of yellow oranges
and porridge for his provender;
he perfumed her with marjoram
and cardamom and lavender.

He called the winds of argosies
with cargoes in to carry him
across the rivers seventeen
that lay between to tarry him.

He landed all in loneliness
where stonily the pebbles on
the running river Derrilyn
goes merrily for ever on.
He wandered over meadow-land
to shadow-land and dreariness,
and under hill and over hill,
a rover still to weariness.

He sat and sang a melody
his errantry a-tarrying;
he begged a pretty butterfly
that fluttered by to marry him.
She laughed at him, deluded him,
eluded him unpitying;
so long he studied wizardry
and sigaldry and smithying.

He wove a tissue airy-thin
to snare her in; to follow in
he made him beetle-leather wing
and feather wing and swallow-wing.
He caught her in bewilderment

in filament of spider-thread;
he built a little bower-house,
a flower house, to hide her head;
he made her shoes of diamond
on fire and a-shimmering;
a boat he built her marvellous,
a carvel all a-glimmering;
he threaded gems in necklaces —
and recklessly she squandered them,
as fluttering, and wavering,
and quavering, they wandered on.

They fell to bitter quarrelling;
and sorrowing he sped away,
on windy weather wearily
and drearily he fled away.

He passed the archipelagoes
where yellow grows the marigold,
where countless silver fountains are,
and mountains are of fairy-gold.
He took to war and foraying
a-harrying beyond the sea,
a-roaming over Belmarie
and Thellamie and Fantasie.

He made a shield and morion
of coral and of ivory,
a sword he made of emerald,
and terrible his rivalry
with all the knights of Aerie
and Faërie and Thellamie.
Of crystal was his habergeon,
his scabbard of chalcedony,
his javelins were of malachite
and stalactite — he brandished them,
and went and fought the dragon-flies
of Paradise, and vanquished them.

He battled with the Dumbledores,
the Bumbles, and the Honeybees,
and won the Golden Honeycomb;

and running home on sunny seas
in ship of leaves and gossamer
with blossom for a canopy,
he polished up, and furbished up,
and burnished up his panoply.

He tarried for a little while
in little isles, and plundered them;
and webs of all the Attercops
he shattered them and sundered them —
Then, coming home with honeycomb
and money none, to memory
his message came and errand too!
In derring-do and glamoury
he had forgot them, journeying,
and tourneying, a wanderer.

So now he must depart again
and start again his gondola,
for ever still a messenger,
a passenger, a tarrier,
a-roving as a feather does,
a weather-driven mariner.

A presumably earlier version of this text is given in *The Qenya Alphabet*. We have described differences between this *tengwar* version and text C in our notes.

As illustrated by Pauline Baynes in the *Bombadil* collection of 1962, the mariner's 'gondola' – merely a ship's boat, or small war-vessel – became a fantastic ('gilded') elaboration of the typical Venetian canal boat, with a unicorn figurehead. Two barrels beneath its canopy, or awning, are probably meant to be the mariner's *provender* (food, supplies). Marjoram, cardamom, and lavender are aromatics used in perfumes as well as cooking. 'Winds of argosies' are those favourable to *argosies* or large merchant sailing ships. *Derrilyn* (or *Lerion*, or *Derion*), *shadow-land* (later *Shadow-land*, *Shadowland*), *Belmarie*, *Thellamie*, *Fantasie*, *Aerie*, and *Faërie* (in 1962, *Faerie*), as well as the 'rivers seventeen', *Paradise*, and 'the archipelagoes | where yellow grows the marigold' are not particular places except in the poet's fancy, but their names provide convenient rhymes and spark the reader's imagination. In his preface to *The Adventures of Tom Bombadil and Other Verses from the Red Book* Tolkien states that 'the names used [in the poem] (*Derrilyn, Thellamie, Belmarie, Aerie*) are mere inventions in the Elvish style, and are not in fact Elvish at all' (p. 8).

Hummerhorn seems also to be a Tolkien invention. In context with bumblebees and honeybees, it is probably meant to suggest another 'humming' insect, such as a hornet. The prize of a 'Golden Honey-comb', meanwhile, recalls the Golden Fleece from the Greek myth of Jason and the Argonauts, or the golden apples of the Garden of the Hesperides.

In 1952 Tolkien received a letter from a woman asking if he could explain the origin of some verses she had received from a friend, who in turn had had them from his son-in-law, who had learned them in Washington, D.C., and knew only that they were connected with English universities. By remarkable chance, they were a version of *Errantry*, and Tolkien was intrigued that a work of his had entered into an oral tradition, as if it were folklore. This, he said in a letter to his publisher Rayner Unwin, 'bore out my views on oral tradition (at any rate in early stages): [namely] that the "hard words" are well preserved, and the more common words altered, but the metre is often disturbed' (22 June 1952, *Letters*, pp. 234–5). One such 'hard word' was *sigaldry* ('enchantment, sorcery'), which Tolkien had taken from a thirteenth-century text and which was 'last recorded in the [fourteenth-century] Chester Play of the Crucifixion' (letter to Donald Swann, 14 October 1966, *Letters*, p. 518). He felt that *Errantry* had escaped into the wild, as it were, after he read it to the early Inklings and it was put into their minutes book, but we have never seen this book and do not know if it survives. It seems more likely that the source of the 'oral' *Errantry* was the *Oxford Magazine* printing of 1933.

When Tolkien revisited his existing poems in 1961, to make a selection for *The Adventures of Tom Bombadil and Other Verses from the Red Book* (see no. 24), *Errantry* seems to have been one of the first that came to mind: on 14 December 1961 he told Rayner Unwin of his experience 'looking out, furbishing up, or re-writing of further items to go with *Tom Bombadil* and *Errantry*' (Tolkien–George Allen & Unwin archive, HarperCollins). It appears third in the collection, revised in many places and slightly enlarged from the *Oxford Magazine* version. We give the final text as D, from the first printing of the *Bombadil* volume, pp. 24–5, 27.

[D]

There was a merry passenger,
a messenger, a mariner:
he built a gilded gondola
to wander in, and had in her

a load of yellow oranges
and porridge for his provender;
he perfumed her with marjoram
and cardamom and lavender.

He called the winds of argosies
with cargoes in to carry him
across the rivers seventeen
that lay between to tarry him.
He landed all in loneliness
where stonily the pebbles on
the running river Derrilyn
goes merrily for ever on.
He journeyed then through meadow-lands
to Shadow-land that dreary lay,
and under hill and over hill
went roving still a weary way.

He sat and sang a melody,
his errantry a-tarrying;
he begged a pretty butterfly
that fluttered by to marry him.
She scorned him and she scoffed at him,
she laughed at him unpitying;
so long he studied wizardry
and sigaldry and smithying.

He wove a tissue airy-thin
to snare her in; to follow her
he made him beetle-leather wing
and feather wing of swallow-hair.
He caught her in bewilderment
with filament of spider-thread;
he made her soft pavilions
of lilies, and a bridal bed
of flowers and of thistle-down
to nestle down and rest her in;
and silken webs of filmy white
and silver light he dressed her in.

He threaded gems in necklaces,
but recklessly she squandered them

and fell to bitter quarrelling;
then sorrowing he wandered on,
and there he left her withering,
as shivering he fled away;
with windy weather following
on swallow-wing he sped away.

He passed the archipelagoes
where yellow grows the marigold,
where countless silver fountains are,
and mountains are of fairy-gold.
He took to war and foraying,
a-harrying beyond the sea,
and roaming over Belmarie
and Thellamie and Fantasie.

He made a shield and morion
of coral and of ivory,
a sword he made of emerald,
and terrible his rivalry
with elven-knights of Aerie
and Faerie, with paladins
that golden-haired and shining-eyed
came riding by and challenged him.

Of crystal was his habergeon,
his scabbard of chalcedony;
with silver tipped at plenilune
his spear was hewn of ebony.
His javelins were of malachite
and stalactite — he brandished them,
and went and fought the dragon-flies
of Paradise, and vanquished them.

He battled with the Dumbledors,
the Hummerhorns, and Honeybees,
and won the Golden Honeycomb;
and running home on sunny seas
in ship of leaves and gossamer
with blossom for a canopy,
he sat and sang, and furbished up
and burnished up his panoply.

He tarried for a little while
in little isles that lonely lay,
and found there naught but blowing grass;
and so at last the only way
he took, and turned, and coming home with
honeycomb, to memory
his message came, and errand too!
In derring-do and glamoury
he had forgot them, journeying
and tourneying, a wanderer.
So now he must depart again
and start again his gondola,
for ever still a messenger,
a passenger, a tarrier,
a-roving as a feather does,
a weather-driven mariner.

As we have said, the poems of the *Tom Bombadil* collection are represented as written or collected by Hobbits, a conceit Tolkien explains in his 'editorial' preface. There *Errantry* is said to be an example of a kind of poem 'which seems to have amused Hobbits: a rhyme or story which returns to its own beginning, and so may be recited until the hearers revolt. Several specimens are found in the [Hobbits'] Red Book [of Westmarch], but the others are simple and crude'; in the reality of our world, they appear not to exist. *Errantry*, Tolkien continues,

> is much the longest and most elaborate. It was evidently made by Bilbo [Baggins], as his own composition, in the house of Elrond [in Book II, Chapter 1 of *The Lord of the Rings*]. In origin a 'nonsense rhyme', it is in the Rivendell version found transformed and applied, somewhat incongruously, to the High-elvish and Númenórean legends of Eärendil [see the third phase of the poem described below]. Probably because Bilbo invented its metrical devices and was proud of them. They do not appear in other pieces in the Red Book. The older form, here given [i.e. the pre-*Lord of the Rings* poem *Errantry*, though its form in the 1962 *Tom Bombadil* collection post-dates *The Lord of the Rings*], must belong to the early days after Bilbo's return from his journey [to the Lonely Mountain in *The Hobbit*]. [*The Adventures of Tom Bombadil and Other Verses from the Red Book* (1962), pp. 7–8]

In his 14 October 1966 letter to Donald Swann, Tolkien described *Errantry* as

> a piece of verbal acrobatics and metrical high-jinks; and was intended for recitation with great variations of speed. It needs a reciter or chanter capable of producing the words with great clarity, but in places with great rapidity. The 'stanzas' as printed indicate the speed-groups. In general these were meant to begin at speed and slow down. Except the last group, which was to begin slowly, and pick up at *errand too!* and end at high speed to match the beginning. Also of course the reciter was supposed at once to begin repeating (at even higher speed) the beginning, unless somebody cried 'Once is enough'. [*The Treason of Isengard*, p. 85]

Writing to Rayner Unwin on 22 June 1952, Tolkien described *Errantry* as a poem he found particularly attractive among his work. 'It is for one thing in a metre I invented (depending on trisyllabic assonances or near-assonances, which is so difficult that except in this one example I have never been able to use it again – it just blew out in a single impulse)' (*Letters*, p. 235). *Assonance* is the repetition of consonants and vowels, and the work does indeed flow from beginning to end on the strength of groups of three-syllable words: *passenger, messenger, mariner; marjoram, cardamom, lavender; wizardry, sigaldry* (enchantment, sorcery), *smithying*. In his notes to *Letters*, Humphrey Carpenter comments on Tolkien's statement that he had used the *Errantry* metre only once: 'It may appear at a first glance that Tolkien did write another poem in this metre, "Eärendil was a mariner" [see below]. . . . But this poem is arguably a development of "Errantry" rather than a separate composition' (*Letters*, p. 621).

Verlyn Flieger has challenged Tolkien's claim to have invented the *Errantry* metre, when 'it is in fact octosyllabic rhymed couplets with feminine endings on the model of the rapidly moving patter-songs in Gilbert and Sullivan' ('Poems by Tolkien: *The Lord of the Rings*', p. 525). In '"A Metre I Invented": Tolkien's Clues to Tempo in "Errantry"' (2013), the most extensive criticism of the poem, John Holmes comments that 'three-syllable rhymes are so rare that in English poetry they cease to be ornamental or structural as other rhymes can be, and begin to draw the listener's attention to the complexity of rhyme for its own sake. For this reason three-syllable rhymes in English tend to be limited, when they appear at all, to comic verse, and part of the comic effect is the rapid delivery.' Gilbert and Sullivan, he points out, did not invent rapid delivery, which is found earlier in Rossini's *Barber of Seville* with its 'Largo al factotum' aria for baritone, an example of *sdruccioli* or triple-assonance; and this device itself has a still earlier origin.

Holmes defends Tolkien's claim of invention (for himself, or for Bilbo) by pointing to his exceedingly complex use of rhyme interval. Tolkien mentions 'speed-groups' in his letter to Swann, which are indicated by the poem's printed 'stanzas'. Holmes suggests that Tolkien placed that term in quotation marks because the divisions in *Errantry* 'are not structural units, and not of uniform length . . . eight lines or twelve lines, alternating at first (8, 12, 8, 12), then five groups in a row of 8 lines each, closing with the final speed-group of 12. . . . [These start] at a tempo normal for recitation, and gradually [slow] down', though 'other factors affect the speed of recitation' (p. 31). Against this, though, it must be remarked that the 'stanzas' of *Errantry* are not divided the same in both the *Oxford Magazine* printing – where changes may have been made by editorial fiat – and the printing of 1962, that Tolkien's recording of the poem in 1967 (see below) varies in pace more (as it seems) according to the need to enunciate complex words than by printed 'stanzas', and that Swann's setting and its recording for Caedmon Records (also see below) are fairly regular in speed, marked 'with easy motion', except for a few bars in which the words are spoken rather than sung ('and so at last the only way he took . . . journeying and tourneying, a wanderer').

Holmes also comments (p. 37) on Tolkien's use of 'mosaic rhyme . . . the use of multiple words to rhyme a single polysyllabic word', such as William Gilbert used in *H.M.S. Pinafore* (the 'Major General' song), and earlier by Samuel Butler in *Hudibras* and Lord Byron in *Don Juan*. Two examples are 'rest her in' with 'dressed her in' (lines D38, 40) and 'marigold' with 'fairy gold' (D50, 52). Corey Olsen ('Poetry', 2022) refers to this feature as 'internal rhyme or near rhyme', and notes that 'the basic structural unit of the poem is a quatrain' (p. 158).

John D. Rateliff ('J.R.R. Tolkien: "Sir Topas" Revisited' (1982), p. 348) has suggested that an obvious inspiration for *Errantry* was Chaucer's 'Tale of Sir Thopas' (mentioned in connection with other poems in this book), from the *Canterbury Tales*. There, Rateliff notes, 'the hero rides off in search of adventures, arming himself in the following remarkable manner':

His jambeux were of quyrboilly,
His swerdes shethe of yvory,
His helm of latoun bright;
His sadel was of rewel boon,
His brydel as the sonne shoon,
Or as the moone light.

('His leg armour [greaves] were of hardened leather, his sword's sheath of ivory, his helm of bright brass [*latten*], his saddle of ruel-bone [marine ivory], his bridle shone like the sun, or like moonlight.') Rateliff compares the passage – and there are others like it in 'Sir Thopas' – to Tolkien's

He made a shield and morion
of coral and of ivory,
a sword he made of emerald . . .

and concludes that in *Errantry* Tolkien took Chaucer's descriptions and exaggerated them 'to even greater absurdity'. In addition, Rateliff finds it apt that Tolkien produced a poem which 'may be recited until the hearers revolt' based on a work which, in the frame of the *Canterbury Tales*, is halted by the host before its teller can finish ('Namoore of this, for Goddes dignitee').

Jason Fisher ('The Origins of Tolkien's "Errantry"', 2008) has suggested that in writing *Errantry* Tolkien drew upon Michael Drayton's mock-epic *Nimphidia, the Court of Fayrie*, first published in 1627. Despite Tolkien's later criticism of that work in *On Fairy-Stories* as 'one ancestor of that long line of flower-fairies and fluttering sprites with antennae that I so disliked as a child, and which my children in their turn detested' (2001 edn., p. 6), Fisher is right to point out similarities of expression (if much less so of form) between Drayton's poem about a fairy knight errant, Pigwiggen, and Tolkien's mariner: 'A little Cockle-shell his shield', 'His Speare a Bent [a stalk of grass] both stiffe and strong', 'His Rapier was a Hornets sting', 'His Helmet was a Beetles head'. Fisher also remarks on the common use in both poems of words such as *thistledown* and *gossamer*, and an emphasis on memory.

That Tolkien's errant mariner is, in fact, as diminutive as Drayton's fairies is evident by his environment and the creatures he encounters. In *Errantry*, Corey Olsen comments, 'the little mariner . . . slays dragonflies, woos a butterfly, battles bumblebees, and cuts his way through spider-webs with a sword made from an emerald.

For all of Tolkien's oft-cited rejection of "flower-fairies and fluttering sprites with antennae," he is plainly describing a figure of a very similar sort in this poem, with little trace of self-consciousness' ('Poetry', p. 159).

In 1967 Tolkien made a professional recording of the final version of *Errantry* for Caedmon Records, much of it at speed and, once he had finished, returning to the start of the poem to read it again; after a few lines of the second reading, the track fades out. This recording, withheld from the album *Poems and Songs of Middle Earth* (1967), was issued in 2001 as part of *The J.R.R. Tolkien Audio Collection* (Harper Audio/Caedmon). A musical setting of the poem by Donald Swann appears in *The Road Goes Ever On: A Song Cycle* (1967), and was performed by pianist Swann and baritone William Elvin on *Poems and Songs of Middle Earth*. Swann had long been fascinated by *Errantry*, after a friend gave him a copy from the 'oral tradition' in 1949, with many variations from the published work. For his song cycle, he considered whether to rework the poem as a duet, with changes to the text, but in the event made no alterations (at least, not in the published or recorded music; elements of the song cycle have been performed separately on various occasions).

The first manuscript of the portion of *The Lord of the Rings* that became Book II, Chapter 1 tells of Frodo waking at Rivendell 'to the sound of ringing laughter. There was no longer any music, but on the edge of his waking sense was the echo of a voice that had just stopped singing. He looked, and saw that Bilbo was seated on his stool, set now near to the middle fire, in the centre of a circle of listeners' (*The Return of the Shadow*, p. 393). Christopher Tolkien comments:

> When my father wrote this passage he evidently had in mind, at least as one possibility, a comic song, received with the 'ringing laughter' that wakened Frodo; for at the top of the page he wrote 'Troll Song' – a passing idea before it [*The Stone Troll*, no. 83] was given far more appositely to Sam in the Trollshaws. But he also wrote 'Let B[ilbo] sing *Tinúviel*' [presumably *The Tale of Tinúviel*, no. 64, though this could hardly be called a comic song], and the word '?Messenger'. [*The Return of the Shadow*, p. 412]

'?Messenger' refers to *Errantry*, which Tolkien proceeded to adapt for the purpose.

In *The Treason of Isengard* Christopher identifies 'no less than fifteen manuscript and typescript texts of the "Rivendell version"' in two groups. The earlier group of texts begins (with one exception) 'There was a merry messenger'; in the later group the first line is 'Earendel was a mariner' (by the final text, 'Eärendil'). The earliest manuscript of this 'merry messenger' phase consists of rough workings in ink and pencil, with some parts overwritten. Its text begins with the third line of the poem and quickly becomes illegible. We have transcribed (as E) as much of this as we can, as it was first written.

[E] he built a boat and gilded her,
and silver oars he fashioned her,
he perfumed her with marjoram
and cardamom and lavender
& laded her with oranges
& porridge for his provender
He floated from a haven fair
of maidenhair and lady-fern;
the waterfalls he proudly rode
where loudly flowed the Merry-burn,
and dancing on the foam he went
on roving bent for ever on
beyond the morning journeying;
and murmuring the river [?ran >] down
to Gloaming [in the >] valleys gleaming [? >] ran,
    [*deleted:* and dreaming then;]
[*deleted:* to twilight valleys gleaming ???]
and dreaming then

he laid his head and fast asleep
he passed [through >] the Weeping-willow pools,
and reeds at evening whispering
where misty lay the meadowland:
and down the river carried him
and hurried him to Shadowland
The sea beside a stony shore
there lonely roared and under moon
a path was laid that led beyond

a wind arose and wafted him
a castaway beyond the moon

This is not 'the earliest text of all' that Christopher describes in *The Treason of Isengard* (p. 91), but rather workings for the manuscript

(F, below) from which he transcribed eight lines 'so close to the first verse of *Errantry* as to be scarcely more than a variant'. (He does not mention the incomplete draft, perhaps because he did not discover it until April 1988.) Later in this text, however, Tolkien moved away from the original poem dramatically. Manuscript F, too, is written in both ink and pencil, with overwriting. Most of its pencil text is drafting for this version, except for one note which looks ahead to an addition (in G) in which the Elves the mariner visits 'enchant his boat & give it wings'. Here we have transcribed as much of text F as we can decipher of the writing in ink (before revision), and present it in the order we think that Tolkien intended: more than half of the manuscript consists of disconnected stanzas.

[F]

There was a merry messenger
a passenger a mariner:
he built a boat and gilded her,
and silver oars he fashioned her;
he perfumed her with marjoram
and cardamom and lavender,
and laded her with oranges
and porridge for her provender

[*Tolkien seems immediately to have replaced lines 5–8:*]
her sails he wove of gossamer
and blossoms of the cherry-tree,
and lightly as a feather in
the weather went she merrily.

He floated from a haven fair
of maidenhair and lady-fern;
the waterfalls he proudly rode,
where loudly flowed the Merry-burn;
and dancing on the foam he went
on roving bent for ever on
beyond the morning journeying,
while murmuring the river down
to gloaming valleys gleaming ran,
and dreaming then on pillow cool
he laid his head, and fast asleep
he passed the Weepingwillow Pools.

The reeds of Evening whispered low,
and misty lay the meadowland;
and down the River carried him
and hurried him to Shadowland

The sea beside a stony shore
there lonely roared, and under moon
a wind arose and wafted him
and cast away beyond the Moon.

He woke at last forlorn afar
by shores that are without a name,
and by the Shrouded Island o'er
the silent water floating came.

He passed the archipelagoes
where yellow grows the marigold,
and landed on the Elven-strands
of silver sand and fallow gold,
beneath the Hill of Ilmarin
where glimmer in a valley sheer
the lights of elven Tirion
the city on the Shadow-mere,

He tarried there his errantry,
and melodies they taught to him,
and lays of old and marvels told,
and harps of gold they brought to him.

Of glamoury he tidings heard
and binding words of sigaldry;
of wars they spoke with Enemies
that venom used and wizardry.

He vowed he would to errantry
and derring-do now turn again
to battle with enchanted foes
undaunted go a-journeying

In panoply of Elvenkings
in silver rings they armoured him;

his shield they writ with Elven-runes
that never wound did harm to him

His bow was made of dragon-horn,
his arrows hewn of ebony;
of woven steel his habergeon,
his scabbard of chalcedony;
his sword was wrought of adamant,
and valiant the might of it;
his helm a shining emerald,
and terrible the light of it.

Ungoliant abiding there
in Spider-lair her thread entwined,
for countless years a gloom had spun
the moon and sun in web to wind.
She caught him in her strangle-hold
entangled all in ebon thread
and seven times with sting she smote
his ringéd coat with venom dread.

[*alternate lines 75–76:*]
with venom of her sting she strove
through ringed coat his breast to bite/smite.

His sword was like a flash of light
as slashing white he smote with it;
and shove away her poisoned neb,
and noisome webs he broke with it.
Then shining as a risen star
from prison bars he sped away
and borne upon a blowing wind
on flowing wings he fled away

From Evereven's lofty hills
where softly silver fountains fall
he passed away, a wandering light,
beyond the mighty Mountain-wall,
and unto Ever-night he came
and like a flaming star he fell:
his javelins of diamond
as fire into the darkness fell.

To Evernoon at last he came
and passed the flame-encircled hill,
where wells of gold for Melineth
her never-resting workers build

Here the manuscript proper ends, with its curious description of 'Evernoon', 'the flame-encircled hill', 'wells of gold', and 'never-resting workers'. Arden R. Smith has suggested to us in correspondence, and is almost certainly correct, that

> Melineth in Evernoon is the antithesis of Ungoliant in Evernight, and where Ungoliant is a spider, Melineth is a queen bee, continuing the bee imagery from *Errantry*. The 'wells of gold' (honey in honeycomb) and 'never-resting workers' [worker bees] support this interpretation, as does her name. The Indo-European root for 'honey' is **melit*, seen for example in Greek *méli* and Latin *mel*, both meaning 'honey'.

(The element *mel* is also found in *caramel*, *marmalade*, and *molasses*.) Melineth, and Ungoliant, remained in the poem through version H below.

Tolkien marked text F with deletions and changes, and took them up in a new manuscript (G), the first complete text of the 'merry messenger' phase. Christopher Tolkien included this version in *The Treason of Isengard*, pp. 91–4, with the caveat that in transcribing he ignored all variants 'though a few, as *merry* written above *gallant* in line 1, *ladyfern* above *everfern* (the oak fern or ditch fern) in line 10, may belong to the time of writing', that 'a few inconsistencies of hyphenation are preserved', and that 'in the latter part of the poem the stanza-divisions are not perfectly clear' (p. 108). Here we have made our own transcription of the text as (it seems to us) Tolkien first wrote it, before further revision, with comments in our notes.

[G] There was a gallant passenger
a messenger, a mariner:
he built a boat and gilded her
and silver oars he fashioned her;
her sails he wove of gossamer
and blossoms of the cherry-tree,
and lightly as a feather in
the weather went she merrily.

He floated from a haven fair
of maiden-hair and everfern;
the waterfalls he proudly rode
where loudly flowed the Merryburn;
and dancing on the foam he went
on roving bent for ever on,
from Evermorning journeying,
while murmuring the River on
to valleys in the gloaming ran;
and slowly then on pillow cool
he laid his head, and fast asleep
he passed the Weepingwillow Pool.

The windy reeds were whispering,
and mists were in the meadow-land,
and down the River hurried him
and carried him to Shadowland.

The Sea beside a stony shore
there lonely roared, and under Moon
a wind arose and wafted him
a castaway beyond the Moon.

He woke again forlorn afar
by shores that are without a name,
and by the Shrouded Island o'er
the Silent Water floating came.

He passed the archipelagoes
where yellow grows the marigold,
and landed on the Elven-strands
of silver sand and fallow gold,
beneath the Hill of Ilmarin
where glimmer in a valley sheer
the light of Elven Tirion,
the city on the Shadowmere.

He tarried there his errantry,
and melodies they taught to him,
and lays of old, and marvels told,
and harps of gold they brought to him,

Of glamoury he tidings heard,
and binding words of sigaldry;
of wars they spoke with Enemies
that venom used and wizardry.

In panoply of Elvenkings,
in silver rings they armoured him;
his shield they writ with elven-runes,
that never wound did harm to him.
His bow was made of dragon-horn,
his arrows shorn of ebony,
of woven steel his habergeon,
his scabbard of chalcedony.
His sword was hewn of adamant,
and valiant the might of it;
his helm a shining emerald,
and terrible the light of it.

His boat anew for him they built
of timber felled in Elvenhome;
upon the mast a star was set,
its spars were wet with silver foam;
and wings of swans they made for it,
and laid on it a mighty doom
to sail the seas of wind and come
where glimmering runs the gliding moon.

From Evereven's lofty hills,
where softly spill the fountains tall,
he passed away, a wandering light
beyond the mighty Mountain-wall;
and unto Evernight he came,
and like a flaming star he fell:
his javelins of diamond
as fire into the darkness fell.
Ungoliant abiding there
in Spider-lair her thread entwined;
for endless years in gloom she spun
the Sun and Moon in web to wind.

She caught him in her stranglehold
entangled all in ebon thread,

and seven times with sting she smote
his ringéd coat with venom dread.

His sword was like a flashing light
as flashing bright he smote with it;
he shore away her poisoned neb,
her noisome webs he broke with it.
Then shining as a risen star
from prison bars he sped away,
and borne upon a blowing wind
on flaming wings he fled away

To Evernoon at last he came,
and passed the flame-encircled hill,
where wells of gold for Melineth
her never-resting workers build.

His eyes with fire ablaze were set,
his face was lit with levin-light;
and turning to his home afar
a roaming star at even-light
on high above the mists he came,
a distant flame, a marineer
on winds unearthly swiftly borne,
uplifted o'er the Shadowmere.
He passed o'er Carakilian,
where Tirion the Hallowed stands;
the sea far under loudly roared
on cloudy shores in Shadowland.

And over Evermorn he passed,
and saw at last the haven fair,
far under by the Merry-burn
in everfern and maidenhair.
But on him mighty doom was laid,
till moon should fade, and all the stars
to pass, and tarry never more
on hither shore where mortals are,
for ever still a passenger,
a messenger, to never rest,
to bear his burning lamp afar,
the Flammifer of Westernesse.

Evermorning and *Evermorn* here possibly mean no more than 'the East', where morning begins, or simply Middle-earth, east of Aman.

The variants Christopher Tolkien mentions – alternate words written at the same place in the manuscript without deletion of the other, such as 'merry' above 'gallant' in line 1, 'lady' (= 'ladyfern') above 'everfern' in line 10, 'from' above 'his' in line 41, and 'wrought' above 'shorn' in line 54 – could be from the time of writing, but as most of them are in a comparatively lighter ink, we are inclined to think them revisions Tolkien marked after laying down the initial text. Some, indeed, indicate changes made in the next manuscript, while others appear there also as the same variants, suggesting that Tolkien was still of two minds about them.

The 'changes introduced on this manuscript' that Christopher describes on p. 94 of *The Treason of Isengard* are subsequent revisions to G, that is, not changes made in the course of initial writing. The thirteen lines he quotes on the same page, beginning 'The seven-branchéd Levin-tree', were also a later revision, inserted while also cancelling lines 97–100 ('His eyes with fire ablaze were set,' etc.); these next appeared in version H. Christopher's note that 'the *seven-branchéd Levin-tree* was first *everbranching*, and it bore a *living fruit of light*' refers to extensive workings written on the same page and firmly struck through.

On p. 108 of *The Treason of Isengard* Christopher notes 'a four-line stanza . . . struck out, apparently at once, since the line-numbering does not take account of it'. These are lines 81–84 above, which we have chosen to include in the main body of version G for two reasons. First, because Tolkien struck through, and circled, the lines in pencil, like most of the many revisions he made to G; and second, because the line-numbers in the manuscript appear (again, on the evidence of ink) to have been added only after he chose to delete 'She caught him . . . venom dread'.

When Christopher wrote *The Treason of Isengard* the manuscript immediately following text G was missing from the Tolkien archive at Marquette University; for his analysis of the poem, he had to rely on a transcription supplied by independent researcher Taum Santoski. The manuscript is now in hand, however, and we are able to make use of it here. This text is the first in which Tolkien placed the poem within the continuous text of *The Lord of the Rings*, following a brief introduction already in its published form except for differences of punctuation: '[Frodo >] there he wandered long in a dream of music that turned into running water and then suddenly into a voice: it seemed to be the voice of Bilbo chanting verses. Faint at first and then clearer ran the words.' We give here, as H, Bilbo's poem as it then stood, before Tolkien revised it still further, and have described changes marked on the manuscript in our notes.

[H]

There was a merry messenger,
a passenger, a mariner:
he built a boat, and gilded her,
and silver oars he fashioned her;
her sails he wove of gossamer
and blossom of the cherry-tree,
and lightly as a feather in
the weather she went merrily.

He floated from a haven fair
of maidenhair and everfern;
the waterfalls he proudly rode,
where loudly flowed the Merryburn;
and dancing on the foam he went
on roving bent for ever on,
from Evermorning journeying,
while murmuring the River on
to valleys in the gloaming ran;
and slowly then on pillow cool
he laid his head, and fast asleep
he passed the Weepingwillow Pools.
The windy reeds were whispering,
and mists were in the meadowland,
and down the River hurried him,
and carried him to Shadowland.

The Sea beside a stony shore
there lonely roared, and under Moon
a wind arose and wafted him
a castaway beyond the Moon.

He woke again forlorn afar
by shores that are without a name,
and by the Shrouded Island o'er
the Silent Water floating came.
He passed the archipelagoes
where yellow grows the marigold,
and landed on the Elven-strands

of silver sand and fallow gold,
beneath the Hill of Ilmarin,
where glimmer in a valley sheer
the lights of Elven Tirion,
the city on the Shadowmere.

He tarried there from errantry,
and melodies they taught to him,
and lays of old and marvels told,
and harps of gold they brought to him.
Of glamoury he tidings heard
and binding words of sigaldry;
of wars they spoke with Enemies
that venom used and wizardry.
In panoply of Elven-kings,
in silver rings they armoured him;
his shield they writ with elven-runes,
that never wound did harm to him.
His bow was made of dragon-horn,
his arrows shorn of ebony,
of woven steel his habergeon,
his scabbard of chalcedony.
His sword was wrought of adamant,
and valiant the might of it;
his helm a shining emerald,
and terrible the light of it.

His boat anew for him they built
of timber felled in Elvenhome;
upon the mast a star was set,
her spars were wet with driven foam;
and wings of swans they made for her,
and laid on him a mighty doom,
to sail the seas of wind and come
where glimmering runs the gliding Moon.

From Evereven's lofty hills,
where softly spill the fountains tall,
he passed away, a wandering light,
beyond the mighty Mountain Wall,
and unto Evernight he came,
and like a flaming star he fell:

his javelins of diamond
as fire into the darkness fell.
Ungoliant abiding there
in Spider lair her web entwined;
for endless years a gloom she spun,
the Moon and Sun in web to wind.

His sword was like a searing light,
as shearing bright he smote with it;
he clave away her ghastly head,
her darkling thread he broke with it.
Then shining as a risen star
from prison-bars he sped away,
and borne upon a blowing wind
on flowing wings he fled away.

To Evernoon at last he came,
and passed the flame-encircled hill,
where wells of gold for Melineth
her never-resting workers build.
The seven branchéd Levin-tree
on Heavenfield he shining saw
upflowering from its writhen root:
a living fruit of fire it bore.

The lightning in his face was lit,
ablaze were set his tresses long,
his eyes with levin-beams were bright,
and gleaming-white his vessel shone.

From World's-end then he turned away,
and yearned again to seek afar
his land beneath the morning-light,
and burning like a beacon-star
then high above the mists he came,
a distant flame, a marineer,
on winds unearthly swiftly borne,
uplifted o'er the Shadowmere.

He passed o'er Carakilian,
where Tirion the hallowed stands:
the Sea below him loudly roared

on cloudy shores in Shadowland.
And over Evermorn he passed,
and saw at the last the haven fair,
far under by the Merryburn
in everfern and maidenhair.

But on him mighty doom was laid,
till moon should fade, an orbéd star
to pass, and tarry never more
on hither shore where mortals are;
for ever still a passenger,
a messenger, to never rest;
to bear his burning lamp afar,
the Flammifer of Westernesse.

By now in the poem, as Christopher Tolkien remarked, the mariner had emerged

> as the figure of Eärendel (though he is not named). At the beginning *he dances on the foam* in his boat with *sails of gossamer and blossom of the cherry-tree* and he still *passed the archipelagoes where yellow grows the marigold* [as in *Errantry*], but he is drawn into the gravity of the myth [of Eärendel in 'The Silmarillion'] and *mighty doom* is laid on him; the dance dies out of the verse and he ends as the *Flammifer of Westernesse*. There is no question now of returning to the beginning, even though the fate of Eärendel remains that of the merry Messenger: *for ever still a passenger, a messenger* to never rest. [*The Treason of Isengard*, p. 95]

We have met Eärendel, his name variously spelled, several times in this book, beginning with poem no. 16, *The Voyage of Éarendel the Evening Star*. To quote again Tolkien's August 1967 draft letter to Mr Rang: 'Before 1914 [*sic*] I wrote a "poem" upon Earendel who launched his ship like a bright spark from the havens of the Sun. I adopted him into my mythology – in which he became a prime figure as a mariner, and eventually as a herald star, and a sign of hope to men' (*Letters*, pp. 542–3). The 'herald star', in the present work 'a beacon-star', is Venus, the morning star and evening star, as we explain in our discussion for no. 16. We have also seen that Tolkien conceived of earthly adventures for his mariner, described in connection with *The Minstrel Renounces the Song* (no. 18): his voyage to a 'land of strange men [and] of magic', his escape 'from the meshes of Night' and 'the Spider', how he 'has a new boat builded' and sails west 'just as the sun is diving into the sea. He set sail upon the sky and returns no more to Earth.' Tolkien developed his story further in *The Shores of Faery* (no. 31) and *The Happy Mariners* (no. 33).

In the prose 'Silmarillion' Eärendel is born to the Elf Idril, daughter of Turgon, King of Gondolin, and the man Tuor, to whom it has been foretold that 'a child shall come of thee than no man shall know more of the uttermost deeps, be it of the sea or of the firmament of heaven' (*The Book of Lost Tales, Part Two*, p. 155). Escaping the fall of Gondolin, Eärendel becomes a seafarer and marries Elwing, granddaughter of Beren and Lúthien; one of their sons is Elrond, master of Rivendell, and the other Elros, a distant ancestor of Aragorn, the king Elessar as he developed in *The Lord of the Rings*. In the version of his story published in *The Silmarillion*, Eärendil (spelled thus), a descendant of both Men and Elves, with the aid of a Silmaril brought to him by Elwing sails to Valinor on behalf of his peoples to ask the help of the Valar against Morgoth. They grant his plea, hallow his ship, and set it to sail through the heavens with Eärendil at its helm, the Silmaril on his brow and glistening with the dust of elven-gems. 'Far he journeyed in that ship, even into the starless voids; but most often was he seen at morning or at evening, glimmering in sunrise or sunset, as he came back to Valinor from voyages beyond the confines of the world' (*The Silmarillion*, p. 250). Then Elwing, who remained in Valinor in a tower by the sea and had the power of flight, would rise to meet her husband like a bird.

In *Errantry* the mariner roves 'as a feather does', driven by weather and chance more than by intent. The 'merry messenger' of the second phase of the poem travels similarly in the first stanzas, floating from his 'haven fair', riding waterfalls and rivers; soon, however, he finds himself in places which, although 'not by any means entirely identifiable in terms of *The Silmarillion*', as Christopher Tolkien comments, nonetheless suggest elements of the mythology:

> Was [Eärendel's] journey to the Sea a journey down [the river] Sirion? Are *the Weepingwillow Pools* Nan-tathren, the Land of Willows? Or are they still 'mere inventions in the *Silmarillion* style? And what of *the seven-branchéd Levin-tree on Heavenfield*, and *the wells of gold for Melineth* that *her never-resting workers build*? These certainly do not suggest 'mere invention' like *Thellamie* or *Derrilyn*. [*The Treason of Isengard*, p. 95]

Whether the 'Levin-tree' is an actual tree, made of lightning, or a bolt of branched (jagged) lightning in the sky ('heavenfield') and a tree only in the abstract, is open to debate. The 'Shrouded Island' is presumably the Lonely Isle, Tol Eressëa; in the last text of the 'merry messenger' phase Tolkien marked 'Shrouded Island' to be changed to 'Lonely Island'.

The mariner's encounter with Ungoliant, which enters in text F but disappears in the next phase of the poem, hearkens back to notes Tolkien made for his unwritten *Tale of Eärendel*, where the great spider is called *Ungweliantë* and *Wirilómë* 'Gloomweaver'. In his *Sketch of the Mythology* (*c.* 1926–30) he tells how Eärendel 'builds [the ship] Wingelot and wishes to sail in search of his father. Ylmir [Ulmo] bids him to sail to Valinor. Here follow the marvellous adventures of Wingelot in the seas and isles, and of how Eärendel slew Ungoliant in the South' (*The Shaping of Middle-earth*, pp. 37–8). Tolkien alludes to this incident in the earliest text of *Errantry*, 'and webs of all the attercops [spiders] | he shattered, cut, and sundered them'.

And yet, Christopher Tolkien remarked, 'the legend of Eärendel as found in the existing sources is not present here. Indeed, it seems as if he arose unbidden and unlooked for as my father wrote this new version of the poem: for how could Eärendel be called *a merry messenger*?' In the poem's next phase, the mariner becomes explicitly Eärendel, the change Tolkien in his preface to the *Tom Bombadil* collection (and in his role as 'editor') called incongruous. 'Yet there was a "congruity"', Christopher continued,

> that made this original transformation possible, and even natural. Behind both figures lay the sustaining idea of the wanderer, a restless spirit who seeks back to the places of his origin, but cannot escape the necessity of passing on. At this stage [as the poem evolved] therefore we should not, I believe, try to determine where was Evernoon, or to give any other name to
>
> the haven fair,
> far under by the Merry-burn
> in everfern and maidenhair.
>
> They belong to the same geography as *the archipelagoes where yellow grows the marigold*. [*The Treason of Isengard*, p. 96]

With text F, Tolkien introduced the idea of the mariner being cast away, and subsequently exploring 'the Elven-strands | . . . beneath the Hill of Ilmarin'. There he is taught by the Elves melodies and lays and hears their history, not unlike the experience of another mariner of Tolkien's creation, Eriol (Ælfwine), in *The Book of Lost Tales*:

> Now it happened on a certain time that a traveller from far countries, a man of great curiosity, was by desire of strange lands and the ways and dwellings of unaccustomed folk brought in a ship as far west even as the Lonely Island, Tol Eressëa in the fairy [Elvish] speech. . . .' [*The Book of Lost Tales, Part One*, p. 13]

Unlike the story of *Errantry* in which the mariner fends for himself, in the recast poem it is the Elves who armour him 'in panoply of Elven-kings | in silver rings' and craft his weapons, as well as build a new ship for him.

Following H, Tolkien made six more texts of the poem in its 'merry messenger' phase. The 'beautiful small manuscript' Christopher Tolkien describes, 'written on four slips of paper the last of which is the back of a letter addressed to my father and dated 13 December 1944' (soliciting a donation for St Andrews Hospital, London, operated by the Catholic Sisters of Mercy), proceeds from H, as does one of the five remaining 'merry messenger' typescripts; for reference, we will call this typescript H[1] and the manuscript H[2]. The manuscript is reproduced in full in William M. Fliss and Sarah C. Schaefer, *J.R.R. Tolkien: The Art of the Manuscript* (2022), figs. 35–8, where it is called 'Version A', according to Christopher Tolkien's designation when he gave the papers to Marquette University in 1990. In *The Treason of Isengard* (p. 96) Christopher guessed that the manuscript 'most likely . . . preceded the first typescript', and 'thus there was an interval of several years between the first three and the next six texts'. Later, in a note included with H[2] when he gave it to Marquette University, Christopher decided that the typescript in fact preceded the manuscript; this is also our conclusion.

H[1] is a fair copy, taking up most of the revisions indicated on H, such as 'gloaming-fields' in line 17 (changed from 'gloaming ran'). H[2] also takes up revisions, but uniquely among the versions has 'to valleys under Gloaming-bree' (*bree* 'hill') in line 17, 'ghastly head' changed to 'poisoned neb' (nose) in line 83, and 'darkling thread' changed to 'noisome web' in line 84. H[1] is not marked for further change, but on H[2] Tolkien altered 'Carakilian' to 'Calakirian' (line 109) and 'to never rest' to 'that never rests' (line 122), and revised and enlarged lines 25–28 (before 'He woke again'):

The Sea beside a stony shore
there lonely roared; and wrathful rose
a wind on high in Tarmenel,
by paths that seldom mortal goes
on flying wings it passed away
and wafted him beyond the grey
and long forsaken seas distressed
from East to West that sombre lay.

Tarmenel is Quenya 'high heaven'.

The reading of line 123 of text H, 'to bear his burning lamp afar', survived in H², but in H¹ this changed to 'to bear the burning lamp' (*his* > *the*) and remained thus in all later 'merry messenger' versions. But '*his* burning lamp' was restored in the third, 'Eärendil' phase of the poem, and in *The Lord of the Rings*.

The next typescript, which we will call H³, continued the spelling 'Carakilian', but Tolkien amended it there to 'Caracilian'. 'To never rest' remained the reading throughout the rest of the 'merry messenger' phase. As typed in H³, lines 25–28 also continued unchanged from H, but Tolkien revised and enlarged them as he had marked on H². This illustrates well Christopher Tolkien's comment that 'the textual history of the first group [i.e. the 'merry messenger' versions] is very complex in detail, and difficult to unravel with certainty owing to the fact that my father hesitated back and forth between competing readings in successive texts' (*The Treason of Isengard*, pp. 90–1). On H³ Tolkien wrote, among other (largely illegible) workings, an alternate text to the eight lines given above ('The Sea beside', etc.), in the event abandoned:

He heard there moan in stony caves
the lonely waves of Orfalas;
the winds he heard of Tarmenel:
by paths that seldom mortals pass
they wafted him on flying wings
a dying thing across the grey
and long-forsaken seas distressed
from East to West he passed away.

Orfalas in Noldorin may mean 'high shore' or 'above shore'; as a place-name it does not appear elsewhere in Tolkien's writings, as far as we can tell.

A marginal note here mentions *mithril*; in *The Lord of the Rings* it is said that mithril, or 'true-silver', 'could be beaten like copper, and polished like glass; and the Dwarves could make of it a metal, light and yet harder than tempered steel' (Book II, Chapter 4). In the penultimate 'merry messenger' typescript, the mariner's habergeon is made of this substance rather than of 'woven steel' (see version I, line 59). In the next phase his habergeon is of 'silver', but his boat 'of mithril and of elven-glass', and finally (text N) of 'triple steel'.

A few minor revisions to H^3 were taken up into a new typescript, a fair copy except that 'World's-end' in line 101 was changed to 'World's End' (and remained in that form). Yet another typescript followed, in which Tolkien marked the fourth stanza thus:

Through Evernight then borne afar
by waters dark beyond the Day
he saw the Shrouded Islands rise
where twilight lies upon the Bay [*deleted full stop*]
[*deleted:* He passed the archipelagoes
where yellow grows the marigold]
of Valinor, of Elvenhome,
and ever-foaming billows roll,
[and >] he landed on the elven-strands
of silver sand and [fallow >] yellow gold
beneath the Hill of Ilmarin,
where glimmer in a valley sheer
the lights of [Elven >] towering Tirion,
the city on the Shadowmere.

The 'Shrouded Islands', plural, are evidently the Enchanted Isles (Shadowy Isles, Twilit Isles) mentioned further below. Written below the final two lines of this passage is an alternate text: 'the lamplit towers of Tirion | were mirrored in the Shadowmere'. In this version also, Tolkien rewrote his description of the mariner's armour and weaponry (almost identical with the sixth stanza of text I below), and he removed the violent passages concerned with the mariner's battles and the death of Ungoliant, from 'and unto Evernight he came' to 'and gleaming white his vessel shone' (H73–100).

One further, final typescript of the 'merry messenger' phase remained, given here as I, also printed in *The Treason of Isengard*, pp. 96–102.

[I]

There was a merry messenger,
a passenger, a mariner:
he built a boat, and gilded her,
and silver oars he fashioned her;
her sails he wove of gossamer
and blossom of the cherry-tree,
and lightly as a feather in
the weather she went merrily.

He floated from a haven fair
of maidenhair and ladyfern;
the waterfalls he proudly rode
where loudly flowed the Merryburn;
and dancing on the foam he went
on roving bent from Hitherland
through Evermorning journeying,
while murmuring the River ran
to valleys in the Gloaming-fields;
and slowly he on pillow cool
let fall his head, and fast asleep
he passed the Weeping-willow Pools.

The windy reeds were whispering,
and mists were in the meadowland,
and down the River hurried him,
and carried him to Shadowland.
He heard there moan in stony caves
the lonely waves; there roaring blows
the mighty wind of Tarmenel.
By paths that seldom mortal goes
his boat it wafted pitiless
with bitter breath across the grey
and long-forsaken seas distressed;
from East to West he passed away.

Through Evernight then borne afar
by waters dark beyond the Day
he saw the Shrouded Islands rise
where twilight lies upon the Bay
of Valinor, of Elvenhome,
and ever-foaming billows roll;
he landed on the elven-strands

of silver sand and yellow gold
beneath the Hill of Ilmarin,
where glimmer in a valley sheer
the lights of towering Tirion,
the city on the Shadowmere.

He tarried there from errantry,
and melodies they taught to him,
and lays of old and marvels told,
and harps of gold they brought to him.
Of glamoury he tidings heard
and binding words of wizardry;
they spoke of wars with Enemies
that venom used and sigaldry.

In panoply of Elven-kings,
in silver rings they armoured him;
his shield they writ with elven-runes
that never wound did harm to him.
His bow was made of dragon-horn,
his arrows shorn of ebony,
of mithril was his habergeon,
his scabbard of chalcedony.
His sword of steel was valiant;
of adamant his helm was wrought,
an argent wing of swan his crest,
upon his breast an emerald.

His boat anew they built for him
of timber felled in Elvenhome;
upon the mast a star was set,
her spars were wet with driven foam;
and eagle-wings they made for her,
and laid on her a mighty doom,
to sail the windy skies and come
behind the Sun and light of Moon.

From Evereven's lofty hills,
where softly silver fountains fall,
he passed away a wandering light
beyond the mighty Mountain Wall.
From World's End then he turned away,

and yearned again to seek afar
his land beneath the morning-light,
and burning like a beacon-star
on high above the mists he came,
a distant flame, a marineer,
on winds unearthly swiftly borne,
uplifted o'er the Shadowmere.

He passed o'er Calacirian,
where Tirion the Hallowed stands:
the Sea below him loudly roared
on cloudy shores in Shadowland;
and over Evermorn he passed
and saw at last the haven fair
far under by the Merryburn
in ladyfern and maidenhair.

But on him mighty doom was laid,
till Moon should fade, an orbed star
to pass, and tarry never more
on Hither Shores where mortals are;
for ever still a passenger,
a messenger, to never rest,
to bear the burning lamp afar,
the Flammifer of Westernesse.

Christopher Tolkien found 'a strong presumption that there was a further long interval between the "Merry Messenger" versions' of the poem and the later texts in which the mariner is named Earendel or Eärendil. Our judgement is that this final period of revision and composition belongs to the end of August and the beginning of September 1952, when Tolkien stayed at his son Michael's cottage at the Oratory School, Woodcote, to read through and correct *The Lord of the Rings*. It seems possible that he returned to Bilbo's song at Rivendell because it was on his mind after his discussions about *Errantry* earlier in the year; at any rate, he now made significant changes to the poem, beginning a new line of development. Here, as J, we give the first extant text in this concluding phase, a fine manuscript to which Tolkien later added the title *The Short Lay of Eärendil* and the note 'earliest preserved version', suggesting that it was preceded by workings now lost. This manuscript is reproduced in full in Fliss and Schaefer, *J.R.R. Tolkien: The Art of the Manuscript*, figs. 39–41, where it is called 'Version G' according to Christopher Tolkien's designation in 1990. (See also *The Treason of Isengard*, pp. 99–102.)

[J]

Earendel was a mariner
that tarried in Arvernien;
he built a boat of timber felled
in Nimbrethil to journey in;
her sails he wove of silver fair,
of silver were her lanterns made,
her prow he fashioned like a swan,
and light upon her banners laid.

Beneath the moon and under star
he wandered far from northern strands,
bewildered on enchanted ways
beyond the days of mortal lands.
From gnashing of the Narrow Ice
where shadow lies on frozen hills,
from nether heat and burning waste
he turned in haste, and roving still
on starless waters far astray
at last he came to night of Naught,
and passed, and never sight he saw
of shining shore nor light he sought.
The winds of wrath came driving him,
and blindly in the foam he fled
from West to East, and errandless,
unheralded he homeward sped.

As bird then Elwing came to him,
and flame was in her carcanet,
more bright than light of diamond
was fire that on her heart was set.
The Silmaril she bound on him
and crowned him with a living light,
and dauntless then with burning brow
he turned his prow, and in the night
from otherworld beyond the Sea
there strong and free a storm arose,
a wind of power in Tarmenel;
by paths that seldom mortal goes
his boat it bore with mighty breath

as driving death across the grey
and long-forsaken seas distressed,
from East to West he passed away.

Through Evernight then borne afar
by waters dark beyond the Day,
he saw the Lonely Island rise,
where twilight lies upon the Bay
of Valinor, of Elvenhome,
and ever-foaming billows roll[.]
He landed on forbidden strands
of silver sand and yellow gold,
beneath the Hill of Ilmarin
a-glimmer in a valley sheer
the lamps of towering Tirion
were mirrored on the Shadowmere[.]

He tarried there from errantry
and melodies they taught to him,
and lays of old and marvels told,
and harps of gold they brought to him.
In panoply of Elven-kings,
in serried rings they armoured him;
his shield they writ with elven-runes
that never wound did harm to him;
his bow was made of dragon-horn,
his arrows shorn of ebony,
of silver was his habergeon,
his scabbard of chalcedony;
his sword of steel was valiant,
of adamant his helmet tall,
an argent flame upon his crest,
upon his breast an emerald.

His boat anew they built for him
of mithril and of elven-glass;
the Silmaril was hanging bright
as lantern light on slender mast,
and eagle-wings they made for her,
and laid on her a mighty doom,
to sail the shoreless skies and come
behind the Sun and light of Moon.

From Evereven's lofty hills,
where softly silver fountains fall,
he rose on high, a wandering light
beyond the mighty Mountain Wall[.]
From World's End then he turned away,
and yearned again to seek afar
his land beneath the morning-light,
and burning like a beacon-star
on high above the mists he came,
a distant flame, a marineer,
on winds unearthly swiftly borne,
uplifted o'er the Shadowmere.

He passed o'er Calacirian
where Tirion the hallowed stands;
the sea below him loudly roared
on cloudy shores in Shadowland;
and over Middle-earth he passed,
and heard at last the weeping sore
of women and of Elven-maids
in Elder Days, in years of yore.

But on him mighty doom was laid,
till Moon should fade, an orbéd star,
to pass, and tarry never more
on Hither Shores where mortals are;
for ever still on errand, as
a herald that should never rest,
to bear his shining lamp afar,
the Flammifer of Westernesse.

From this manuscript Tolkien made a typescript copy with only a few textual differences (described in our notes). He marked the typescript heavily, relocating sections, revising lines, and substantially adding to the text. These changes are reflected in yet another typescript, given here as K before further revision.

[K] Earendel was a mariner
that tarried in Arvernien;
he built a boat of timber felled
in Nimbrethil to journey in;
her sails he wove of silver fair,

of silver were her lanterns made,
her prow he fashioned like a swan,
and light upon her banners laid.

In panoply of ancient kings,
in chainéd rings he armoured him;
his shining shield was scored with runes
to ward all wounds and harm from him;
his bow was made of dragon-horn,
his arrows shorn of ebony,
of silver was his habergeon,
his scabbard of chalcedony;
his sword of steel was valiant,
of adamant his helmet tall,
an argent flame upon his crest,
upon his breast an emerald.

Beneath the moon and under star
he wandered far from northern strands,
bewildered on enchanted ways
beyond the days of mortal lands.
From gnashing of the Narrow Ice
where shadow lies on frozen hills,
from nether heats and burning waste
he turned in haste, and roving still
on starless waters far astray
at last he came to night of Naught,
and passed, and never sight he saw
of shining shore nor light he sought.
Then winds of wrath came driving him,
and blindly in the foam he fled
from West to East, and errandless,
unheralded he homeward sped.

As bird there Elwing came to him,
and flame was in her carcanet,
more bright than light of diamond
was fire that on her heart was set.
The Silmaril she bound on him
and crowned him with the living light,
and dauntless then with burning brow
he turned his prow; and in the night

from otherworld beyond the Sea
there strong and free a storm arose,
a wind of power in Tarmenel;
by paths that seldom mortal goes
his boat it bore with biting breath
as might of death across the grey
and long-forsaken seas distressed;
from East to West he passed away.

Through Evernight he back was borne
on black and roaring waves that ran
o'er leagues unlit and foundered shores
that drowned before the Days began;
until he heard on strands of pearl
where ends the world the music long,
where ever-foaming billows roll
the yellow gold and jewels wan.
He saw the Mountain silent rise
where twilight lies upon the knees
of Valinor, and Eldamar
beheld afar beyond the seas.
As lonely star escaped from night
to haven white he came at last,
to Elvenhome the green and fair,
where keen the air, where pale as glass
beneath the Hill of Ilmarin
a-glimmer in a valley sheer
the lamplit towers of Tirion
are mirrored on the Shadowmere.

He tarried there from errantry,
and melodies they taught to him,
and sages old him marvels told,
and harps of gold they brought to him.
They clothed him then in elven-white,
and seven lights before him sent,
as through the Calacirian
to hidden land forlorn he went.
He came unto the timeless hall
where shining fall uncounted years,
and endless reigns the Elder King,
for ever king on Mountain sheer;

and words unheard were spoken then
of folk of Men and Elven-kin,
beyond the earth were visions showed
forbid to those that dwell therein.

A ship then new they built for him
of mithril and of elven-glass
with shining prow; but shaven oar
nor sail she bore, on silver mast;
the Silmaril as lantern light
and banner bright with living flame
to gleam thereon by Elbereth
herself was set, who thither came
and wings of wind she made for him,
and laid on him undying doom,
to sail the shoreless skies and come
behind the Sun and light of Moon.

From Evereven's lofty hills,
where softly silver fountains fall,
his wings him bore, a wandering light
above the mighty Mountain Wall.
From World's End then he turned away,
and yearned again to seek afar
his home through shadows journeying,
and burning like an island-star
on high above the mists he came,
a distant flame before the Sun,
a wonder ere the waking dawn,
where grey the Norland waters run.

And over Middle-earth he passed
and heard at last the weeping sore
of women and of Elven-maids
in Elder Days, in years of yore.
But on him mighty doom was laid,
till Moon should fade, an orbéd star
to pass, and tarry never more
on Hither Shores where mortals are;
for ever still a herald on
an errand that should never rest
to bear his shining lamp afar,
the Flammifer of Westernesse.

With the passage now beginning 'In panoply of ancient kings' (revised from 'In panoply of Elven-kings') moved earlier in the poem relative to text J, before the mariner arrives in Valinor, Earendel's armour and weapons are gathered according to his own agency.

Typescript K is marked with a few corrections and further revisions. These were then taken up into a typescript for the printer of *The Lord of the Rings*, on which Tolkien indicated a few corrections while also correcting galley proofs of the poem. The final published text of Bilbo's song is given here (L) from Book II, Chapter I of the current edition of *The Lord of the Rings*. The mariner's name at last was in its final form, *Eärendil.*

[L]

Eärendil was a mariner
that tarried in Arvernien;
he built a boat of timber felled
in Nimbrethil to journey in;
her sails he wove of silver fair,
of silver were her lanterns made,
her prow he fashioned like a swan,
and light upon her banners laid.

In panoply of ancient kings,
in chainéd rings he armoured him;
his shining shield was scored with runes
to ward all wounds and harm from him;
his bow was made of dragon-horn,
his arrows shorn of ebony,
of silver was his habergeon,
his scabbard of chalcedony;
his sword of steel was valiant,
of adamant his helmet tall,
an eagle-plume upon his crest,
upon his breast an emerald.

Beneath the Moon and under star
he wandered far from northern strands,
bewildered on enchanted ways
beyond the days of mortal lands.
From gnashing of the Narrow Ice
where shadow lies on frozen hills,
from nether heats and burning waste
he turned in haste, and roving still

on starless waters far astray
at last he came to Night of Naught,
and passed, and never sight he saw
of shining shore nor light he sought.
The winds of wrath came driving him,
and blindly in the foam he fled
from west to east, and errandless,
unheralded he homeward sped.

There flying Elwing came to him,
and flame was in the darkness lit;
more bright than light of diamond
the fire upon her carcanet.
The Silmaril she bound on him
and crowned him with the living light,
and dauntless then with burning brow
he turned his prow; and in the night
from Otherworld beyond the Sea
there strong and free a storm arose,
a wind of power in Tarmenel;
by paths that seldom mortal goes
his boat it bore with biting breath
as might of death across the grey
and long-forsaken seas distressed:
from east to west he passed away.

Through Evernight he back was borne
on black and roaring waves that ran
o'er leagues unlit and foundered shores
that drowned before the Days began,
until he heard on strands of pearl
where ends the world the music long,
where ever-foaming billows roll
the yellow gold and jewels wan.
He saw the Mountain silent rise
where twilight lies upon the knees
of Valinor, and Eldamar
beheld afar beyond the seas.
A wanderer escaped from night
to haven white he came at last,
to Elvenhome the green and fair
where keen the air, where pale as glass

beneath the Hill of Ilmarin
a-glimmer in a valley sheer
the lamplit towers of Tirion
were mirrored on the Shadowmere.

He tarried there from errantry,
and melodies they taught to him,
and sages old him marvels told,
and harps of gold they brought to him.
They clothed him then in elven-white,
and seven lights before him sent,
as through the Calacirian
to hidden land forlorn he went.
He came unto the timeless halls
where shining fall the countless years,
and endless reigns the Elder King
in Ilmarin on Mountain sheer;
and words unheard were spoken then
of folk of Men and Elven-kin,
beyond the world were visions showed
forbid to those that dwell therein.

A ship then new they built for him
of mithril and of elven-glass
with shining prow; no shaven oar
nor sail she bore on silver mast:
the Silmaril as lantern light
and banner bright with living flame
to gleam thereon by Elbereth
herself was set, who thither came
and wings immortal made for him,
and laid on him undying doom,
to sail the shoreless skies and come
behind the Sun and light of Moon.

From Evereven's lofty hills
where softly silver fountains fall
his wings him bore, a wandering light,
beyond the mighty Mountain Wall.
From World's End then he turned away,
and yearned again to find afar
his home through shadows journeying,

and burning as an island star
on high above the mists he came,
a distant flame before the Sun,
a wonder ere the waking dawn
where grey the Norland waters run.

And over Middle-earth he passed
and heard at last the weeping sore
of women and of elven-maids
in Elder Days, in years of yore.
But on him mighty doom was laid,
till Moon should fade, an orbéd star
to pass, and tarry never more
on Hither Shores where mortals are;
for ever still a herald on
an errand that should never rest
to bear his shining lamp afar,
the Flammifer of Westernesse.

Early in the development of Book II, Chapter 1 of *The Lord of the Rings*, 'quite a lot' of Bilbo's song was composed by 'Tarkil', a name for Trotter in 'the old tongue' (as Aragorn ultimately is called 'the Dúnedan', or man of the West, Númenórean). By the time Tolkien finished his book, the song was entirely by Bilbo except for the words 'Upon his breast an emerald': 'Aragorn insisted on my putting in a green stone', Bilbo says, presumably meant to refer to the Elessar, a brooch associated with Aragorn's ancestry (see Book II, Chapter 8). The completed song is a curious work, and was even more curious to early readers of *The Lord of the Rings* (the present authors among them) before the release of *The Silmarillion* in 1977. It is a glimpse into the distant history underlying *The Lord of the Rings*, in fact the story of the father of Elrond, master of Rivendell, as interpreted by a Hobbit.

Eärendil begins his journey in *Arvernien*, a southern region of Beleriand at the time of *The Lord of the Rings* long ago destroyed (see also our discussion for poem no. 164). *Nimbrethil* (Sindarin 'silver birches') was a wooded part of Arvernien; in *The Silmarillion* it is said that there Eärendil built his ship of birch, with sails 'as the argent [silver] moon' (p. 246; compare the poem's 'sails . . . of silver fair'). He journeys 'far from northern strands', passing the *Narrow Ice*, the Helcaraxë, an ice-bound strait in the remote North between Middle-earth and the 'Otherworld beyond the Sea', Aman, the lands in the far West of the world. But he is 'bewildered on enchanted ways', presumably a reference to the Enchanted Isles which were 'strung in a net in the Shadowy Seas from the north to the south' and prevented mariners from reaching Valinor; indeed, 'of the many messengers that in after days sailed into the West none came ever to Valinor – save . . . the mightiest mariner of song [Eärendil]' (*The Silmarillion*, p. 102; see also our discussion for poem no. 74).

At last Eärendil comes to *Night of Naught*, or *Evernight*, a dark region south of Valinor, passing by the 'shining shore' without catching sight of it. He is driven away by 'winds of wrath', from 'west to east' – back the way he came. But given a precious Silmaril by Elwing – that recovered from Morgoth by Beren and Lúthien, with the 'living light' of the lost Two Trees of Valinor – he is guided again 'east to west' by a 'wind of power', by implication sent by Manwë, lord of the winds. He comes to Valinor, home of the Valar, and sees 'the Mountain', Taniquetil (Oiolossë, Mount Everwhite). There too is Eldamar, the land of the Eldar or High Elves, Elvenhome, on the shores of Valinor, with 'strands of pearl | . . . where ever-foaming billows roll | the yellow gold and jewels wan'. In *The Silmarillion* it is told that many jewels were given to the Teleri, the seafaring Elves of Aman, 'opals and diamonds and pale crystals, which they strewed upon the shores and scattered in the pools' (p. 61). In text J, these are 'forbidden strands' – mortals are forbidden to set foot in Aman – but in K Tolkien omits the words: in the circumstances, they are not forbidden to Eärendil.

The mariner now sees the towers of *Tirion* (Quenya 'watchtower', the later name of Kôr) mirrored in the *Shadowmere*, also called Luvailin, a mere in the shadow of Taniquetil. He passes through the *Calacirian* (earlier *Carakilian*, *Caracilian*), a region of Eldamar, near the Calacirya or ravine of light in the Pelóri, mountains which guard the eastern shore of Aman. The 'foundered shores | that drowned before the Days began' are, perhaps, a reference to Melkor (Morgoth) casting down and destroying the two Lamps that lit Middle-earth 'before the Days began', that is, before the raising of the Sun at the beginning of the First Age, and the resulting floods and change in the shape of the lands when they foundered (were submerged).

At last Eärendil comes to *Ilmarin*, the 'mansion of the high airs', the home of Manwë the 'Elder King', chief of the Valar, and his wife Varda (Elbereth), on the *Hill of Ilmarin* – the great mountain Taniquetil, also referred to simply as 'the Mountain'. ('Hill of Ilmarin' also appears in an early version of Galadriel's song, no. 161.) 'Words unheard were spoken then | of folk of Men and Elven-kin': Eärendil pleads with Manwë on behalf of Men and Elves in seeking the aid of the Valar against Morgoth's oppression in Middle-earth.

The Valar build him a new, wondrous ship, without oar or sail, and set it in the sky like a star. From *Evereven* (another name for Eldamar) he rises beyond the *Mountain Wall* (the Pelóri), turns from the *World's End* (the remote side of Valinor), and journeys in the sky like the Sun and Moon. He sees and hears at last his home in Middle-earth, but can never return in body: it is his doom, or fate, to be a beacon-star, a *flammifer* or fire-bearer, 'to sail the shoreless skies and come | behind the Sun and light of Moon'. When, before the Third Age, men of Middle-earth set sail for Númenor (*Westernesse*) they are guided by the light of Eärendil in the heavens, the 'Flammifer of Westernesse'.

Tolkien published version L in *The Lord of the Rings* after making one final alteration in proof (in line 84) as well as corrections to four instances of 'elven' which the printer had chosen to set as 'elfin'. But this was not the latest text of the poem. A typescript, a partial manuscript, and a complete manuscript followed, in which significant changes were made. Christopher Tolkien believed that his father mislaid these when *The Lord of the Rings* was needed by the printer, and that they 'did not turn up again until many years had passed, by which time my father no longer remembered the history' (*The Treason of Isengard*, p. 103).

In the typescript 'Earendel' is still spelled thus at the start of the text, but an added title reads *The Short Lay of Ëarendel*. Tolkien also later added a note: 'Revised version nearly identical with final version in LR [*The Lord of the Rings*] But ?centre is still the reference to the sons of Fëanor'. In this the fourth stanza reads, before further revision:

[M] In wrath the Fëanorians
that swore the unforgotten oath
brought war into Arvernien
with burning and with broken troth;
and Elwing from her fastness dim
then cast her in the roaring seas
but like a bird was swiftly borne,
uplifted o'er the roaring waves.
Through hopeless night she came to him,
and flame was in the darkness lit,
more bright than light of diamond
the fire upon her carcanet.
The Silmaril she bound on him,
and crowned him with the living light,
and dauntless then with burning brow

he turned his prow at middle-night.
From otherworld beyond the Sea
then strong and free a storm arose,
a wind of power in Tarmenel;
by paths that seldom mortal goes
his boat it bore with mighty breath
through night and death across the grey
and long-forsaken seas distressed
from East to West he passed away.

Tolkien also made one other change to the text, in the seventh stanza (the equivalent of line L91), 'crystal keel' (of the mariner's new ship) rather than 'shining prow'. There are no extant workings between the typescript for *The Lord of the Rings* (L) and typescript M with the new changes *ab initio*, though one could speculate that Tolkien made at least one manuscript trial. Typescript M is reproduced in full in Fliss and Schaefer, *J.R.R. Tolkien: The Art of the Manuscript*, figs. 42–4, where it is called 'Version J' according to Christopher Tolkien's designation in 1990.

The 'unforgotten oath' is that sworn by the Noldorin Elf Fëanor and his seven sons in regard to the Silmarils, the three great jewels fashioned by Fëanor which captured the radiance of the Two Trees that gave light to Valinor. After Morgoth destroyed the Trees and stole the jewels, the Fëanorians, cursing the Valar, vowed vengeance against anyone who would keep a Silmaril from their possession (see also poem no. 176). At the time of Eärendil's voyage to Aman, the surviving sons of Fëanor learned that Elwing held the Silmaril Lúthien and Beren had wrested from Morgoth's crown, and came upon her people at the Havens of Sirion. Elwing cast herself into the sea with the Silmaril; but the Vala Ulmo, lord of waters, bore her up out of the waves and transformed her into a great white bird. In that manner, bearing the Silmaril on her breast, she flew to Eärendil and was restored to her own form.

Tolkien marked typescript M on at least two occasions. At some later date, he compared it to the published poem in *The Lord of the Rings*, noting differences and omissions, and summarized these on two quickly written pages ending with the note 'N.B. [*nota bene*] L.R. [*The Lord of the Rings*] uses form Eärendil', with the final *i* emphasized. Christopher Tolkien comments that his father was evidently puzzled in finding the later versions: 'his analysis at that time contains demonstrably incorrect conclusions – because he assumed, as I did, that all these texts must have *preceded* the "final form" in FR

[*The Fellowship of the Ring*, the first volume of *The Lord of the Rings*]' (*The Treason of Isengard*, p. 103). Tolkien also made a number of corrections and revisions to the typescript, notably to the second half of the first stanza, then took these up in a new, calligraphic manuscript decorated in red and blue, entitled *The Short Lay of Earendel: Earendillínwë* (for reference, M[1]). This, however, reached only the end of its first page before Tolkien abandoned it, having filled most of its margins with further changes and rough workings, partly restoring the earlier reading of the second half of the first stanza and rewriting the first half of the second. It is reproduced in Fliss and Schaefer, *J.R.R. Tolkien: The Art of the Manuscript*, fig. 45, where it is called 'Version K' according to Christopher Tolkien's designation in 1990.

The final text of the poem, incorporating Tolkien's last revisions, is another calligraphic manuscript, entitled *The Short Lay of Earendel: Earendillinwe* without accents, on which he marked no additional changes. This is reproduced in full in Fliss and Schaefer, *J.R.R. Tolkien: The Art of the Manuscript*, figs. 46–9, where it is called 'Version L' according to Christopher Tolkien's designation in 1990. Christopher includes the final text of the poem in *The Treason of Isengard*, pp. 103–5, in relation to the published text; here, as N, we give the text in full, with textual changes in the final typescript and manuscripts described in notes.

[N]

Earendel was a mariner
that tarried in Arvernien:
he built a boat of timber felled
in Nimbrethil to journey in.
Her sails he wove of silver fair,
with silver were her banners sewn;
her prow he fashioned like the swans
that white upon the Falas roam.

His coat that came from ancient kings
of chainéd rings was forged of old;
his shining shield all wounds defied,
with runes entwined of dwarven gold.
His bow was made of dragon-horn,
his arrows shorn of ebony,
of triple steel his habergeon,
his scabbard of chalcedony;
his sword was like a flame in sheath,
with gems was wreathed his helmet tall,

an eagle-plume upon his crest,
upon his breast an emerald.

Beneath the Moon and under star
he wandered far from northern strands,
bewildered on enchanted ways
beyond the days of mortal lands.
From gnashing of the Narrow Ice
where shadow lies on frozen hills,
from nether heats and burning waste
he turned in haste, and roving still
on starless waters far astray
at last he came to Night of Naught,
and passed, and never sight he saw
of shining shore nor light he sought.
The winds of fear came driving him,
and blindly in the foam he fled
from west to east, and errandless,
unheralded he homeward sped.

In might the Fëanorians
that swore the unforgotten oath
brought war into Arvernien
with burning and with broken troth;
and Elwing from her fastness dim
then cast her in the waters wide,
but like a mew was swiftly borne,
uplifted o'er the roaring tide.
Through hopeless night she came to him,
and flame was in the darkness lit,
more bright than light of diamond
the fire upon her carcanet.
The Silmaril she bound on him,
and crowned him with the living light,
and dauntless then with burning brow
he turned his prow at middle-night.
Beyond the world, beyond the Sea,
then strong and free a storm arose,
a wind of power in Tarmenel;
by paths that seldom mortal goes
from Middle-earth on mighty breath

as flying wraith across the grey
and long-forsaken seas distressed
from East to West he passed away.

Through Evernight he back was borne
on black and roaring waves that ran
o'er leagues unlit and foundered shores
that drowned before the Days began,
until he heard on strands of pearl
where ends the world the music long,
where ever-foaming billows roll
the yellow gold and jewels wan.
He saw the Mountain silent rise
where twilight lies upon the knees
of Valinor, and Eldamar
beheld afar beyond the seas.
A wanderer escaped from night
to haven white he came at last,
to Elvenhome the green and fair
where keen the air, where pale as glass
beneath the Hill of Ilmarin
a-glimmer in a valley sheer
the lamplit towers of Tirion
are mirrored on the Shadowmere.

He tarried there from errantry,
and melodies they taught to him,
and sages old him marvels told,
and harps of gold they brought to him.
They clothed him then in elven-white,
and seven lights before him sent,
as through the Calacirian
to hidden land forlorn he went.
He came unto the timeless halls
where shining fall the countless years,
and endless reigns the Elder King
for ever king on mountain sheer;
and words unheard were spoken then
of folk of Men and Elven-kin,
beyond the world were visions showed
forbid to those that dwell therein.

A ship then new they built for him
of mithril and of elvenglass
with crystal keel; no shaven oar
nor sail she bore, on silver mast
the Silmaril as lantern light
and banner bright with living flame
of fire unstained by Elbereth
herself was set, who thither came
and wings immortal made for him,
and laid on him undying doom,
to sail the shoreless skies and come
behind the Sun and light of Moon.

From Evereven's lofty hills
where softly silver fountains fall
his wings him bore, a wandering light,
beyond the mighty Mountain Wall.
From World's End then he turned away,
and yearned again to find afar
his home through shadows journeying,
and burning as an island star
on high above the mists he came,
a distant flame before the Sun,
a wonder ere the waking dawn
where grey the Norland waters run.

And over Middle-earth he passed
and heard at last the weeping sore
of women and of Elven-maids
in Elder Days, in years of yore.
But on him mighty doom was laid,
till Moon should fade, an orbéd star
to pass, and tarry never more
on Hither Shores where mortals are;
till end of Days on errand high,
a herald bright that never rests,
to bear his burning lamp afar,
the Flammifer of Westernesse.

Christopher Tolkien notes that by this final text, only one line survived from the *Errantry* of 1933, 'his scabbard of chalcedony'.

'It could be argued of course', Christopher wrote, 'that my father actually *rejected* all the subsequent development after the text [that was published, i.e. L], deciding that that was the version desirable at all points; but this would seem to me to be wholly improbable and far-fetched' (*The Treason of Isengard*, pp. 108–9). Although text N was the form in which the poem 'should have been published', in Christopher's judgement, when we came to consider it for the fiftieth anniversary edition of *The Lord of the Rings* in 2004 we hesitated to replace large portions of the established version of *Eärendil Was a Mariner*, even with lines likely to have been preferred by its author. Nor did we ignore the fact that Tolkien had not taken the opportunity to replace Bilbo's song with its ultimate version in the second edition of *The Lord of the Rings* in 1965, or later. In the event, we thought it prudent to let the published text stand and to print the later version, in its entirety, in our *Lord of the Rings: A Reader's Companion* (pp. 210–13).

Comparing *Errantry* and *Eärendil Was a Mariner*, Verlyn Flieger comments that 'as the subject matter' of the poem 'altered from adventuring for its own sake to Eärendil's purposeful journey to Valinor . . . the [verbal] acrobatics [found in *Errantry*] were subdued, the interior and end-rhymes reduced, and the diction elevated, resulting in . . . a more serious poem with commensurate slowing of pace' ('Poems by Tolkien: *The Lord of the Rings*', p. 525).

Comparing *Errantry* and the intermediate 'merry messenger' version of the song at Rivendell, Corey Olsen remarks on tone as the chief difference between the two. 'The later version', he writes,

> has almost none of the mere silliness of 'Errantry'. . . . Gone are the overtly forced and comical pairings in which Tolkien invents a nonsense name such as 'Derrilyn' in order for it to stand as a rhyming pair with 'merrily'. . . . Tolkien retains some of the strong pairings he used in 'Errantry', such as 'meadow-land' and 'shadow-land' or 'sigaldry' and 'wizardry', but he shifts them from internal rhyme pairings to the end-rhyme position. Instead of jangling internal repetition of sound (which is often very funny in 'Errantry'), he uses the close long rhymes to give a stately finality to the ends of the quatrains. ['Poetry', p. 160]

Whereas the narrative of *Errantry* is 'fundamentally episodic', the Rivendell poem 'is a story with a very definite plot' (p. 160). These shifts of tone and story were not, says Olsen, 'merely the reflection of a shift in literary taste on Tolkien's part', but the result of a need to make the poem, for the sake of *The Lord of the Rings*, 'appropriate to a Hobbit [Bilbo] who is now on permanent holiday among Elves [i.e. resident in Rivendell], a story of a mortal inalterably changed by contact with immortals, a story glimpsing high things but cognizant of their distance from mortal experience and of the dangers inherent in crossing that divide'. When the 'merry messenger' texts evolved at last into *Eärendil Was a Mariner*, Tolkien took yet another step away from *Errantry*, with its 'trisyllabic near-rhymes . . . now less near even at the alternate line-ending positions, and the echoes in the internal pairings . . . still perceptible but generally even more distant' ('Poetry', pp. 161–2).

Tom Shippey devotes several long paragraphs of *The Road to Middle-earth* to Bilbo's song (in its final published form), observing that the poet makes use of five devices: 'one is rhyme, which everyone recognises, but the others are less familiar – internal half-rhyme, alliteration (i.e. beginning words with the same sound or letter), alliterative assonance (the *Macbeth* device [combinations such as *life–leaf* and *fear–fair*]), and a frequent if irregular variation of syntax. All appear in the first eight lines . . .' (p. 173). 'Describing the technique is difficult,' Shippey admits,

> but its result is obvious: rich and continuous uncertainty, a pattern forever being glimpsed but never quite grasped. In this way sound very clearly echoes or perhaps rather gives the lead to sense. Just as the rhymes, assonances and phrasal structures hover at the edge of identification, so the poem as a whole offers romantic glimpses of 'old unhappy far-off things' (to cite Wordsworth), or 'magic casements opening on the foam | Of perilous seas in *faery lands forlorn*' (to remember Keats). [p. 174]

A3: A *porringer* is a small bowl or vessel for eating soup, porridge, or the like. The word gradually disappeared from the poem, and was gone by the *Oxford Magazine* appearance.

A16: There is an Ossory in Ireland (Osraighe), but it seems likely that Tolkien chose the name (or invented it) for the sake of a rhyme with 'sorcery' rather than for any connection with the occult.

A23–24: 'The dragon-fly | called wag-on-high': the 'name' *wag-on-high* may be an invention. It suggests the flitting of a dragonfly, able to move in any direction (*wag* 'move, shake').

A35: Tolkien also used *attercop* 'spider' in *The Hobbit*, written contemporary with *Errantry*.

C16: In the longest *tengwar* version of *Errantry* in *Parma Eldalamberon* 20 (referred to there as Q35, and hereafter as 'the *Parma* version'), 'goes' is rendered 'runs'.

C17–18: In the *Parma* version 'over meadow-land | to shadow-land' is rendered 'then to meadowland and shadowland'.

C27–28: In the *Parma* version 'wizardry | and sigaldry' is rendered 'sigaldry and wizardry'. In his 14 October 1966 letter to Donald Swann, Tolkien mentioned that he found *sigaldry* in 'a 13th century text (and [it] is last recorded in the Chester Play of the Crucifixion' (*The Treason of Isengard*, p. 108). *Smithying*, forging or working with metal, accords with sigaldry and wizardry in its mythical connection with knowledge and magical powers, for example in the persons of Hephaestus (Vulcan) and Wayland (or Weyland); the errant mariner seems to have learned the skill so that he could make jewellery for the 'pretty butterfly'.

C35: In the *Parma* version 'built' is rendered 'made'.

C37: In the *Parma* version 'made' is rendered 'gave'.

C46: In the *Parma* version 'sped' is rendered 'fled'.

C51: In the *Parma* version 'where' is rendered 'and'.

C53–54: In the *Parma* version 'war and foraying | a-harrying' is rendered 'wars and harrying a-foraying'.

C63: In the *Parma* version 'crystal' is rendered 'silver'.

C75–76: In the *Parma* version 'furbished up, | and burnished up' is rendered 'burnished up and furbished up'.

C85: In the *Parma* version 'he had forgot' is rendered 'he forgot'.

C90: 'Tarrier', i.e. one who tarries or lingers.

D32: 'Feather wing of swallow-hair': birds do not have hair, but parts of their feathers are sometimes as fine as hairs. In text B this read 'feather wing and swallow-wing', which Tolkien may have thought redundant. Presumably the mariner made wings from the smaller parts of swallow feathers.

D73: In printings of *Errantry* since 1962, *Dumbledors* is spelled thus. In earlier texts, including the *Oxford Magazine* printing, it is spelled *Dumbledores*. The *Oxford English Dictionary* gives *dumbledore* as the primary spelling, though records *dumbledor* among historical examples.

E12: 'Merry-burn' (later 'Merryburn') is not found elsewhere in Tolkien's Middle-earth stories. A *burn* is a large stream or small river.

F6: In regard to this line, Christopher Tolkien states in *The Treason of Isengard*, p. 108, that '*cardamon* is so spelt, but *cardamom* in preliminary rough workings, as in the *Oxford Magazine* version of *Errantry*'. The word in the manuscript does appear at first to read *cardamon*, but we judge that Tolkien wrote final *m* such that the second shoulder of the letter is nearly flat.

F58: 'Rings', i.e. mail armour made of rings.

F59: 'Writ with Elven-runes': the magical power of runic inscriptions on weapons or other objects, is well established in Northern legend.

G3: Tolkien wrote 'gilder her'; we have silently corrected this to 'gilded her', as Christopher Tolkien did also in *The Treason of Isengard*.

G7: In *The Treason of Isengard* 'in' is given incorrectly on l. 8.

G102: 'Marineer' is one of many old spellings of *mariner*, used here to rhyme with *Shadowmere*.

H1: Tolkien again marked 'gallant' as an alternative to 'merry', but struck it through.

H10: Tolkien marked, in the margin, 'lady' (for 'ladyfern') as an alternative to 'everfern', but struck it through; however, he wrote 'lady' above 'everfern' in the text as well, without then deleting it. 'Everfern' remained in H^2 but in all other later texts in this phase became 'ladyfern'. See also l. 116.

H14: Tolkien marked 'bent for ever on' to be changed to '[went >] bent from Hitherland'. Both H^1 and H^2 have the revision.

H15: Tolkien marked 'from' to be changed to 'through'. Both H^1 and H^2 have the revision.

H16: Tolkien marked 'River on' to be changed to 'River ran'. Both H^1 and H^2 have the revision.

H17: Tolkien marked 'gloaming ran' to be changed to 'gloaming-fields', written above the initial text; but he also wrote in the margin, twice, 'under Gloaming-bree'. H^1 has 'gloaming-fields', H^2 'Gloaming-bree'. Despite capitalization of 'Gloaming', it seems likely that none of these combinations indicates a specific place, rather than an area of gloaming (shadows).

H18: Tolkien marked 'and slowly then' to be changed to 'till slowly he'. H^1 has 'and slowly he', H^2 'till slowly he' but with 'and' in the margin as a correction to 'till'.

H19: Tolkien marked 'he laid' to be changed to 'then laid'. Both H^1 and H^2 have the revision.

H47: Tolkien circled 'they spoke' and indicated that they were to precede 'of wars', but we cannot be sure if he did so in the course of writing or subsequently. In any case, both H^1 and H^2 have the revision.

H67–68: Tolkien marked these lines to be changed to 'to sail the windy skies and come | behind the Sun & light of Moon'. Both H^1 and H^2 have the revision.

H70: Tolkien marked this line to be changed to 'when softly silver fountains fall'. Both H^1 and H^2 have the revision.

H83: Tolkien marked 'ghastly head' to be changed to 'poisoned neb' (nose). H^1 has 'ghastly head', H^2 'poisoned neb'.

H84: Tolkien marked 'darkling thread' to be changed to 'noisome web'. H^1 has 'darkling thread', H^2 'noisome web'.

H105: Tolkien marked 'then high' to be changed to 'on high'. Both H^1 and H^2 have the revision.

H116: Tolkien marked 'lady' (for 'ladyfern') next to l. 116, as a revision to 'everfern'. 'Everfern' remained in H^2 but H^1 and all other later texts in this phase have 'ladyfern'.

H120: Tolkien marked 'hither shore' to be changed to 'Hither Shores'. H^1 has 'Hither Shores', but H^2 'hither shore'. *Hither Shores* is a name for Middle-earth.

I14: 'Hitherland' probably means no more than the place from which the mariner journeyed.

I50, 52: In earlier versions, the first of these lines ended 'sigaldry', and the second 'wizardry'. Tolkien reversed their order – 'binding words of wizardry', etc. – in the penultimate typescript.

I69: Tolkien gave the mariner's ship 'eagle-wings' in the penultimate typescript, altered from earlier 'wings of swans', presumably so as not to repeat the bird-image after giving the mariner 'an argent wing of swan his crest' in l. 63.

J7: 'Her prow he fashioned like a swan' recalls the ships of the Teleri, made in the likeness of swans, and the swan-ship in which Celeborn and Galadriel arrive in Book II, Chapter 8 of *The Lord of the Rings*.

J15: In the following typescript, Tolkien changed 'nether heat' to 'nether heats'.

J25: In the following typescript this line reads 'Bird-Elwing thither came to him', with the text as in J written beside it, and 'Then flying Elwing' written above 'Bird-Elwing thither'.

J37–38: In the following typescript, these lines became 'his boat it bore with biting breath | as might of death across the grey'.

J51: In the following typescript, this line reads 'the lamplit towers of Tirion', an alternate text from the previous phase.

J96–97: In the following typescript, there is no stanza break between 'in Elder Days, in years of yore' and 'But on him mighty doom was laid'.

K72: Tolkien marked 'in' as typed ('in the Shadowmere') to be corrected to 'on', and we have done so here.

K112: 'Norland', i.e. the North-west of the world of the Elder Days, especially Beleriand and adjacent regions.

L1: In the printer's typescript Tolkien changed 'Earendel' to 'Eärendil'.

L7: The reading 'he fashioned' is correct, but was long misprinted 'was fashioned'. We repaired the error in the 2004 edition of *The Lord of the Rings*. Also repaired at that time were commas in ll. 42 and 52 which were either omitted in the unauthorized second printing of *The Fellowship of the Ring* or disappeared as printing plates wore down. It is curious to note that typescript M has 'he fashioned', which Tolkien changed to 'was fashioned' in M[1], then back to 'he fashioned' in N.

L32–33: Tolkien changed these lines from 'of shining shore nor light he sought, | and winds of wrath came driving him' in K only in galley proof.

L35: In this line 'west to east', and in l. 52 'east to west', 'West' and 'East' were capitalized in drafts and the printer's typescript, but in all lower case in proof. Tolkien either overlooked the changes or chose not to object to them; without clear direction, and with the concurrence of Christopher Tolkien, 'east' and 'west' were allowed to stand in the 2004 *Lord of the Rings*. 'From west to east, and errandless' was the reading of this line in the first (Allen & Unwin) printing of *The Lord of the Rings*, with a comma after 'east', so intended by Tolkien; in the second printing, the comma dropped out when the printer, having failed to keep the original type standing as instructed, reset the text, and in the process introduced a large number of errors. This was done without the authorization of either publisher or author, and remained unknown for many years: there were still errors from this source to be made right when we edited *The Lord of the Rings* for its fiftieth anniversary.

L37–40: Tolkien revised these lines in the printer's typescript from their reading in K.

L65: In the printer's typescript Tolkien changed 'As lonely star' to 'A wanderer'.

L82: In the printer's typescript Tolkien changed 'uncounted' to 'the countless'.

L84: Tolkien changed 'for ever king' (as in K) to 'In Ilmarin' only in galley proof. In *The Treason of Isengard* (p. 109) Christopher Tolkien notes that 'for ever king, etc.' remained in the later versions of the poem: 'This must have been a final emendation in the "first line" of development, and might of course have been made to the "second line" as well if that had been available.'

L87: In the printer's typescript Tolkien changed 'earth' to 'world'.

L91: In the printer's typescript Tolkien changed this line to the present reading from 'with shining prow, but shaven oar'.

L97: In the printer's typescript Tolkien changed 'wings of wind she made' to 'wings immortal made', while considering 'unearthly' rather than 'immortal'.

N1: 'Earendel' is the form in the manuscript. When including this text in *The Lord of the Rings: A Reader's Companion* we spelled the name 'Eärendil', probably inadvertently, though we suspect that if Tolkien had included text N in *The Lord of the Rings* he would have altered the spelling as he did at the eleventh hour for the earlier version.

N5–8: In L these lines read:

her sails he wove of silver fair,
of silver were her lanterns made,
her prow he fashioned like a swan,
and light upon her banners laid.

In M[1] Tolkien changed them to:

Her woven sails were white as snow,
as flying foam her banner flowed;
her prow was fashioned like a swan
that white upon the Falas goes

Falas (Sindarin 'beach, shore') refers to shorelands on the west coast of Beleriand. In the mythology it is also called *Harfalas*. Alternate drafting on M1 suggests:

Her sails of woven silver shone
as glimmer of the fallen snow;
her prow was fashioned like a swan
that white upon the shoreland go

Finally text N has, in l. 5 returning to L, and despite only near-rhyme for *sewn* and *roam*:

Her sails he wove of silver fair,
with silver were her banners sewn;
her prow he fashioned like the swans
that white upon the Falas roam.

N9–12: On M[1] Tolkien marked these lines to be changed to:

His coat that came from ancient kings
of chainéd rings was forged of old;
his shining shield all wounds defied,
entwined with runes of dwarven gold.

The same text is in N except that l. 12 reads 'with runes entwined of dwarven gold'.

N15: In N Tolkien changed 'silver' to 'triple steel', as marked on M[1].

N17–18: In N Tolkien changed these lines to read 'his sword was like a flame in sheath, | with gems was wreathed his helmet tall', as marked on M[1].

N33: In M[1] Tolkien changed 'winds of wrath' to 'winds of fear', as marked on M.

N37: In M[1] Tolkien changed 'wrath' (as in M) to 'might'.

N41–2: In typescript M Tolkien marked 'and Elwing from her fastness dim | then cast her in the roaring seas' to be changed to 'and Elwing from her fastness grey | was cast away to stormy grave', and alternatively, 'and Elwing from her fastness dim | then cast her in the waters wide'. The latter text is in N.

N43: In N Tolkien changed 'bird' (as in M) to 'mew'.

N44: In N Tolkien changed 'waves' (as in M) to 'tide', to rhyme with altered 'wide' in l. 42.

N57–58: In N Tolkien changed 'his boat it bore with mighty breath | through night and death across the grey' to 'from Middle-earth on mighty breath | as flying wraith across the grey', as marked on M.

N98: In this manuscript 'elvenglass' is spelled thus, without a hyphen.

NOTE ON THE TEXTS Given the particularly confusing history of manuscripts and typescripts in this entry, we offer here an account of the different versions we have described, mentions of them in *The Treason of Isengard* by page, and the texts preserved at Marquette University by catalog number.

A, *Treason* 85–6, 107; first *Errantry* version
B, *Treason* 89, 107
Third version, *Treason* 89
Fourth version, *Treason* 89
C, *Treason* 86–9; printed text in the *Oxford Magazine*
D, *Treason* 90; printed text in the *Tom Bombadil* collection
E, Marquette MSS-3/1/9/1; first 'merry messenger' version
F, *Treason* 91, 108, Marquette MSS-3/1/9/2
G, *Treason* 91–4, Marquette MSS-3/1/9/3
H, *Treason* 94–6, Marquette 3/3/1
H[1], Marquette MSS-3/1/11/13–15
H[2], Marquette MSS-3/1/10/1–4
H[3], *Treason* 108, Marquette 3/3/8/8, MSS-3/1/12/4–6
Typescript, Marquette MSS-3/1/13/1–3
Typescript, Marquette MSS-3/1/14/1–2
I, *Treason* 96–102, Marquette MSS-3/1/15/1–2
J, *Treason* 99–102, Marquette MSS-3/1/16/1–3; first *Earendel* version
Typescript, Marquette MSS-3/1/17/1–2
K, Marquette 3/3/18/15–17
Printer's typescript, Marquette 3/4/1/14–16
Galley proofs, Marquette 3/4/16/16–19, 3/4/18/11–13
L, printed text in *The Lord of the Rings*
M, *Treason* 102, Marquette MSS-3/1/18/1–3; first *Earendillinwë* version
M[1], *Treason* 102–3, Marquette MSS-3/1/19/1
N, *Treason* 103–5, Marquette MSS-3/1/20/2–5

129

The Homecoming of Beorhtnoth Beorhthelm's Son (?1931–53)

The Homecoming of Beorhtnoth Beorhthelm's Son (hereafter *Beorhtnoth*) is a verse drama set immediately after the Battle of Maldon, which was fought in Essex in August 991. In this conflict a local force commanded by Beorhtnoth (Byrhtnoð), *ealdorman* or chief officer of the region (in Latin *dux*, or duke), opposed a host of Northmen (Tolkien's preferred term for the *wicinga* or Vikings) who had camped on an island in the Pante, or Blackwater. Since the mainland could be reached from the island only by means of a causeway at low tide, so narrow a path conceivably could have been held by a small group of determined men. But Beorhtnoth, challenged to a formal fight and 'for his *ofermode*' – 'pride', 'overconfidence', 'excess of courage'; the meaning is disputed – allowed the enemy to cross unhindered. It was a fatal choice: his men were routed and many of them killed, as was Beorhtnoth himself. After the battle his remains were taken to the cathedral at Ely in Cambridgeshire, then an island in the Fens.

These events are recalled in an Old English poem, *The Battle of Maldon*, only part of which survives. It was a set text for students of English when Tolkien was an Oxford undergraduate, and he himself lectured on it there as the Rawlinson and Bosworth Professor of Anglo-Saxon. It may also have been part of his teaching curriculum at Leeds. Its most famous lines are spoken by an old retainer, Beorhtwold, while exhorting his men: 'Hige sceal þe heardra, heorte þe cenre, | mod sceal þe mare, þe ure mægen lytlað' – 'Will shall be the sterner, heart the bolder, spirit the greater as our strength lessens'. As Tolkien remarked, this has been held 'the finest expression of the northern heroic spirit, Norse or English; the clearest statement of the doctrine of uttermost endurance in the service of indomitable will' (*Beorhtnoth*, in *Essays and Studies 1953*, p. 13).

Building upon his interest in *The Battle of Maldon* – he also made his own translation in prose – Tolkien wrote a sequel, or epilogue, in which two servants of the slain Beorhtnoth converse while they recover his body. He described its circumstances in a preface to its first publication:

> According to the late, and largely unhistorical account in the twelfth-century *Liber Eliensis* the Abbot of Ely went himself with some of his monks to the battlefield. But in the following poem it is supposed that the abbot and his monks came only as far as Maldon, and that they there remained, sending two men, servants of the duke, to the battlefield some distance away, late in the day after the battle. They took a waggon, and were to bring back Beorhtnoth's body. They left the waggon near the end of the causeway and began to search among the slain: very many had fallen on both sides. Torhthelm (colloquially Totta) is a youth, son of a minstrel; his head is full of old lays concerning the heroes of northern antiquity. . . . Tídwald (in short Tída) was an old *ceorl*, a farmer who had seen much fighting in the English defence-levies. Neither of these men were actually in the battle. After leaving the waggon they become separated in the gathering dusk. Night falls, dark and clouded. Torhthelm is found alone in a part of the field where the dead lie thick. [*Essays and Studies 1953*, p. 2]

Christopher Tolkien has noted that his father wrote part of a version of *Beorhtnoth* on the back of a sheet containing the earliest text of *Errantry* (poem no. 128), 'with every appearance of having been written at the same time' (p. 106). We have not seen this in the original (for reference, we will call it A^2), but its lines are printed in *The Treason of Isengard*, pp. 106–7. 'This text is extremely rough,' Christopher comments,

> one would say in the first stage of composition, were there not another text still rougher, but in very much the same words (though with no ascription of the speeches to speakers), in the Bodleian Library, where it is preserved (I believe) with my father's pictures. This begins at *In the shadows yonder* and continues a few lines further. On it my father wrote: 'early version in rhyme of Beorhtnoth'. [p. 107]

The latter manuscript (A^1), which we have seen, certainly precedes the text on the reverse of *Errantry*, as it is comparatively further from the earliest complete versions of *Beorhtnoth* among Tolkien's papers. This less developed fragment, from around the midpoint of the poem, comprises twenty-six lines arranged as half-lines, and begins more fully:

In the shadows yonder. He won't wait
Such sort don't fight early or late
But creep when all's over. Up again
Ready once more. Tibba, where's the wain
I wish we were there. By the bridge you say
Well we are nigh the bank.

For comparison, the equivalent lines in A² read:

Tibba There goes a third
In the shadows yonder. He will not wait,
That sort fight no odds, early or late,
But sneak in when all's over. Up again!
Steady once more.

Pudda Say, Tibba, where's the wain?
I wish we were at it! By the bridge you say —
Well, we're nearer the bank.

The name *Tibba* appears in both A¹ and A², and in A² there is also the name *Pudda*. In the earliest complete manuscript of *Beorhtnoth* the dialogue is between *Totta* and *Tudda*, and remained so until late in the history of the work.

A¹ shares a leaf with a pencil drawing by Tolkien, an imaginary landscape with a winding river and storybook castle, which in style is not unlike some of the art he drew for *The Hobbit* while he was inventing that story in the late 1920s and early 1930s. It was also in this period that he lectured at Oxford on the 'Old English Minor Poems', including *The Battle of Maldon* (he had dealt with the poem also in earlier Oxford lectures, on verse in Henry Sweet's *Anglo-Saxon Reader*). As for A², if the manuscript of *Errantry* mentioned above dates from ?1931, as we argue in the previous entry, then so too must the accompanying portion of *Beorhtnoth*. We have chosen to call ?1931 the start of the history of *Beorhtnoth* largely on the strength of our dating of A² and our supposition that Tolkien worked on A¹ and A² closely together in time; in any case, it seems safe to say that *Beorhtnoth* was conceived *c.* 1930.

The text of *Beorhtnoth* underwent many changes in the course of at least twelve manuscripts and at least one typescript, until it was published in the annual of the English Association, *Essays and Studies*, for 1953. There Tolkien augmented his verse drama with a scholarly preface, 'Beorhtnoth's Death', and an afterword, 'Ofermod'. We do not have space here to examine every version of *Beorhtnoth*, nor for any version can we include its text complete. Instead, we have made a selection of extracts which illustrate what we judge to be the most important variations among the texts.

Before discussing these, however, it is important to mention the analysis of most of the *Beorhtnoth* papers by Thomas Honegger in '*The Homecoming of Beorhtnoth*: Philology and the Literary Muse' (2007). Honegger identifies eleven manuscripts and typescripts held in the Bodleian Library as (his designations) A through K, and a brief related text published in *The Treason of Isengard* as Greek alpha (α). In doing so, he takes it as given that the papers are arranged in the Bodleian in their correct chronological order, and Peter Grybauskas in his edition of *Beorhtnoth* (*The Battle of Maldon, together with The Homecoming of Beorhtnoth Beorhthelm's Son and 'The Tradition of Versification in Old English'*, 2023) follows suit, accepting Honegger's lettering scheme while also noting an additional complete manuscript held at Leeds (see below). Through our own comparison of all extant versions of *Beorhtnoth*, we have come to a partly different conclusion as to their order, in which Honegger's texts A and B are instead the second and first in sequence, and F and G the eighth and seventh respectively, with the Leeds version falling before Honegger's manuscript C. The letter designations given below refer only to our analysis, not to the work of Honegger or Grybauskas, to whose writings we referred only after making an independent study. See also our note on the texts at the end of this entry.

The first two extant complete manuscripts of *Beorhtnoth* are brief, each only four pages, and at a glance their texts appear to be nearly identical. One, however, can be distinguished as the earlier by close examination of Tolkien's punctuation choices and other textual points, relative to the third manuscript in the series, while the other can be shown to be later, despite Tolkien's inscription 'earlier copy', by correlation of changes marked on it which Tolkien took up in the third of his longer texts (see below). Here, as extract A, we have transcribed a portion from the start of the poem, drawn from the first of the complete manuscripts, as Tolkien wrote it prior to revision. At this stage, he preferred to hyphenate the title of the work, as *The Homecoming of Beorhtnoth Beorhthelm's Son*.

[A]

Totta: Hist! Who is there? You, Tudda! I had thought
that, God! 'twas one of them. An hour I have sought,
as I waited for you, groping among the slain
alone.

Tudda: Nigh here is where he should have lain.
But the moon is sunk.

Totta: No! no! cover the light!
Hish! what was that?

Tudda: Come, come, lad! what's your fright?
Help me to lift them, and spare breath. Less talk!
What do you think? That their ghosts so soon should walk?
That wolves of the old songs feed on battles still
in Essex here? That twolegged wolves that kill
are likely to come back tonight and prowl
round corpses stripped nigh naked? 'Twas an owl!

Totta: Come on, then! Glad I am you're here. But 'fright'!
I am not afraid, though I little love the night
with all these dead unburied. Where do you lie,
my dear lord, naked, staring at the sky?

Tudda: Look where they're thickest, lad! Here. God! see,
This is Wulfmær. Then not far will his master be.

Totta: Which one is that?

Tudda: Which of them? Both are here,
With limbs all jumbled. One he held most dear —
not far will the uncle be from sister's son.
Yes! Wulfstan's boy, too.

Totta: He that used to run
So swift, and swim! It seems an hour ago.
And Ælfnoth by him, too; and rightly so —
they were never far apart.

Tudda: Nor far from their lord!
I'll warrant we find him near with reddened sword.

Totta: Poor lads! While men with beards and tried blades ran,
the young boys died like men. God curse the man
who left them to it! Young Ælfwine, look!

Tudda: He was a stout one! *His* knees never shook.
Proud heart, proud tongue, like Offa.

Totta: There were some
As took him ill, and would have had him dumb;
his words have proved too true, and he — dear God!
here is my lord, and the ground about all trod
to a bloody mire.
Tudda: His sword is over here.
You know it, with the gold hilts. Nay, I fear
'tis well the moon's gone! Little have they left
of him we knew.
Totta: Woe! Tudda, they have reft
the head, and with cruel axes mangled him.
And the body — a! 'tis a foul sight and grim.
Tudda: Yes, yes! War! But we must make a shift
To bear what there is. You hold here. Now, come, lift!
Totta: None the less dear should be this flesh and bone,
though foes have ruined it. And him alone
we've strength to carry. But may God them heal
who lie here after him! May others feel
pity and remember them!

We cannot guess why Tolkien should have made two very similar copies of *Beorhtnoth* at this point, unless he planned to give one to a friend, as he ultimately did with the next (third) manuscript, now in the E.V. and Ida Gordon papers at Leeds. In any case, having two copies, he felt free to mark some of the same revisions on each, but also different additions and changes. He also played (by addition) with stage directions in the first copy, such as '(Tudda uncovers lantern)' following line 6, and '(Tudda recovers light)' after line 8, and in both manuscripts he divided the whole into four numbered sections. The last of these parts consisted only of the final couplet, 'Sadly they sing, the monks in Ely isle. | Row lads, row! Let us listen still a while!' but Tolkien added selections from the Latin Office of the Dead, beginning 'Dirige Domine in conspectu tuo viam meam' ('Guide my path, Lord, in Thy sight'), and the result was more atmospheric. Most of his revisions to the early text which carried into the third manuscript are marked on the copy we have judged the second, such as 'little I love' for 'I little love' in line 17, though some are on both the second and the first, and it is evident that Tolkien referred to both copies when he made a thorough revision of the whole.

At six pages, the third manuscript of the poem is slightly longer than the earlier texts, in part due to the addition of expository passages. After 'with the gold hilts' (A44), for example, Tolkien wrote:

'He [Tudda] comes over to Totta, and looks down on B[eorhtnoth]. He drops the sword he has picked up with a clatter.' And slightly later, when a corpse-stripper is spotted and Tudda commands Totta to draw his sword, or to pick one up as 'there are many left about', Tolkien added:

> Totta picks up B[eorhtnoth]'s sword (previously dropped by Tudda). A man comes on him [Totta] in the act [of picking up the sword]; he [Totta] catches his [the thief's] leg and throws him, and then stabs him. At some time Tudda has crossed swords with a second — who turns to run as soon as he sees his companion is down. Tudda stabs him from behind.

None of these passages would appear again, and we are left to wonder if Tolkien wrote them for E.V. Gordon's benefit, never intending them to be permanent. (This is indicated, maybe, in the Leeds manuscript where the passages in question are in pencil, but were written concurrent with the rest of the text, which is in ink.) In the final text of the poem, the skirmish between Beorhtnoth's men and those scavenging the battlefield is depicted solely through the two characters' dialogue and sound effects.

In the next (fourth) manuscript of the poem, which occupies seven pages, Tolkien greatly expanded Tudda and Totta's conversation, and added a brief prose passage to set the scene:

> Complete darkness. Throughout two voices are heard, those of *Totta*, a young stable-lad, and *Tudda* an old servant of Beorhtnoth, sent by the Abbot of Ely to the battle-field. The Abbot and some monks are waiting at Maldon to convey Beorhtnoth's body back to Ely. At the end the voices of the monks are heard singing the *Dirige*. Nothing is seen save the occasional light of Tudda's dark-lantern.

Tolkien wrote out the early pages of this copy with relative care, its later part more roughly. Since he did not mark it with many revisions, he seems to have created a fresh, fifth copy for the sake of a more legible text; but by then new ideas, readings, and directions had come to mind. This version begins with a more abbreviated preface:

> The scene throughout is in darkness. Two voices are heard: those of *Totta* the gleeman's son, a young man, and *Tudda* an old servant of the duke *Beorhtnoth*, who have been sent by the

Abbot of Ely to the battlefield not far from Maldon. There the abbot and some monks are waiting to bear Beorhtnoth's body to Ely.

Gleeman is an old word for a professional entertainer at social gatherings. Tolkien eventually discarded it in favour of *minstrel*, as in his 1953 introduction quoted above.

Here, as B, is the equivalent of our selection A as found in the fifth complete manuscript.

[B]

Darkness. Noise of a man moving about & breathing heavily.

Totta A! Who is there? You, Tudda! I had thought
that, God!, 'twas one of them. An hour I've sought
here, waiting for you, groping among the slain,
alone.
Tudda Nigh here is where he should have lain;
but the moon is sunk. [*He lets a light shine from a dark-lantern*
Totta No, no! cover that light! [*An owl hoots*
Hish! What was that?
Tudda Come, come, lad! What's your fright?
[*He covers the light*
Help me to lift 'em, and spare breath! Less talk!
What do you think? That their ghosts so soon would walk?
Or wolves wander out of lays of Goths and Huns
in Essex here? Nay! Not two-leggéd ones
neither — they'll not come here to-night, to prowl
round corpses stripped near naked! 'Twas an owl!
Totta Curse owls! I'm glad you're here at last. But 'fright'!
I'm not afraid — though I don't like the night,
with all these dead unburied. 'Tis like the shade
of heathen hell. Where has our master laid
his mighty head, so proud and old, to-night —
so cold and strange, when soul has taken flight?
Tudda Look where they're thickest lad! As here. Come, see!
[*Opens the light*
Here Wulfmaer lies! And close to his lord *he*'ll be.
Totta Which one is that?
Tudda Which? Why, they both are here,
tumbled together: the man he held most dear —

not far from kin will lie his sister-son —
and Wulfstan's boy, too.

Totta He that used to run
So swift, and swim? It seems an hour ago.

Tudda And Ælfnoth by him too.

Totta And rightly so,
They were never far apart.

Tudda Nor far from him!
A plague on this lamplight, and my eyes are dim.
But if 'twas here they made their last stout stand,
I'll warrant we'll find the old man near at hand.

Totta Poor lads! While men with beards and tried blades ran,
the young boys died, God's pity! Curse the man
who left them to it. Young Ælfwine, look!

Tudda *He* was a stout one. *His* knees never shook.
Proud heart, proud tongue, like Offa.

Totta There were some
took Offa's words with scowls, and wished him dumb —
they cut too nigh — or so I'm told, that day
at council of the lords. As old songs say:
''Tis shame to take the ring and drink the mead,
and leave the giver of the gift at need.'
But days are worsened. I wish that I'd been here,
not left with the baggage like a thrall in rear.
I loved him as much as they. A plain churl
may prove more tough when tested than an earl
that traces kin to Woden and old Kings!

Tudda You talk! Your time'll come my lad. Then things
will look less easy. Iron has a bitter taste
and swords are cruel. If you'd ever faced
the yell of spears, now thanking God you'd be
you're neither dead nor shamed. Come stand by me!

[*A pause in which they struggle with bodies. The lamp is stood open on the ground*]

Now! Heave him off! 'Tis only a cursed Dane,
great hulking heathen.

Totta Shutter that light again!
I can't abide his eyes. They glare so grim —
like Grendel's in the moon. Look! There's a limb
like three men's legs!

Tudda Peace! It's the master! Yes,
that's him — the longest in this land, I guess.
Totta His head was o'er the crowns of heathen Kings!
Here lies he now at last, who dealt the rings
like princes in old songs. He's gone to God,
Beorhtnoth our lord.
Tudda And the ground about is trod
to bloody mire.
Totta His sword is over here!
You know it, Tudda; with the golden hilts.
Tudda I fear
'tis well the moon's gone. Little have they left
Of what we knew.
Totta Woe! Tudda, they have reft
his head, and with their axes mangled him!
And the body — a! is battle then so grim?
Tudda Yes, yes — 'tis war. But we must make a shift
to bear what's left. Hold here! Now come! You lift!
Totta None the less dear shall be this flesh and bone,
though foes have marred it. Now for ever moan

The Saxon and the English men
From Mercian wood to eastern fen.
The wall is fallen. Women weep.
Build high the mound his bones to keep!
And there shall lie his helm and sword,
And golden rings be laid in hoard.
For of the friends of men was he
The first and best from sea to sea;
To folk most fair, to kin most kind,
And ever shall be held in mind
While from the sea there riseth sun;
Glory he loved and glory won!

On 24 October 1952 Tolkien mentioned in a letter to Rayner Unwin that he was 'producing a contribution to "Essays and Studies" by December 2nd' in addition to academic and scholarly work. This was *Beorhtnoth*, and it was probably in February or March 1953 that he handed it over to the journal with its editorial additions. This may have been the period when he decided that the form in which he had written the poem years earlier was not appropriate, or at any rate not satisfying, and as a consequence he drafted a new version, at times rapidly but over a period of time, to judge by his varying penmanship and changing use of ink and pencil. Instead of rhyming couplets, which he may have come to feel did not convey the gravity of his themes, now he structured his work in the typical Anglo-Saxon alliterative mode. In his preface to it in *Essays and Studies 1953* he notes that 'the old poem' on which *Beorhtnoth* is based 'is composed in a free form of the alliterative line, the last surviving fragment of ancient English heroic minstrelsy. In that measure, little if at all freer (though used for dialogue) than the verse of *The Battle of Maldon*, the present modern poem is written' (p. 3).

His initial alliterative version, the sixth complete manuscript altogether, was followed by a fresh copy, also of sixteen pages, with the (non-hyphenated) title *The Homecoming of Beorhtnoth Beorhthelm's Son*. The text was now substantially longer than in the rhyming version. Tudda and Totta have much more to say, their speech and opinions drawn out and of greater complexity. The result makes for a decidedly fuller drama, whereas the previous version of the work was barely a vignette. But Tolkien continued to refine *Beorhtnoth* in the course of three additional manuscripts. The first of these, the eighth by our count, is largely a fair copy. In the ninth, Tolkien changed the name *Tudda* to *Tída*, and in the final (tenth complete) manuscript he named his characters more fully *Torhthelm* and *Tídwald*, among other changes in both versions. He also made revisions at the eleventh hour in the typescript he sent to *Essays and Studies*. At least four sheets of typescript survive which Tolkien revised and retyped for submission, and some of the changes he recorded in the final manuscript were evidently made first in the typescript and copied over.

In his first alliterative manuscript, Tolkien wrote his text in half-lines with remarkably wide medial gaps. In the seventh and eighth versions, his mid-line spacing is inconsistent – some divisions are obvious, others less so, or not at all – and with the ninth manuscript he abandoned this approach but left unnecessarily wide spaces between sentences. The latter practice was repeated in the printer's typescript and reflected in *Essays and Studies 1953*, though it seems to have been part of the journal's house style. This introduces a visual pause where even a silent reader would pause naturally, but does not necessarily distinguish half-lines (as it would not, for example, in the first line of C, below). Wide post-sentence spacing is also found in the setting of *Beorhtnoth* when it was added to Tolkien's *Tree and Leaf* and *Mythopoeia* (no. 136) in a HarperCollins edition of 2001, perhaps following the model of *Essays and Studies*. Standard spacing was used, however, when *Beorhtnoth* was published by Unwin Paperbacks in

1975 with *Tree and Leaf* and *Smith of Wootton Major*, and with other short works by Tolkien in *Poems and Stories* in 1980 (there illustrated by Pauline Baynes).

Here we have chosen to use normal spacing also, a mid-line pause being detectable in Tolkien's composition even without a typographic gap. Related to this, it is amusing to note that in the earliest printings of *The Tolkien Reader* (Ballantine Books, 1966), in which *Beorhtnoth* also appeared (as it still does), the typesetters broke the text with abandon to accommodate the paperback's short line length, and in doing so affected Tolkien's careful rhythm and alliteration. When he saw this, Tolkien marked a copy 'This is verse!' a fact overlooked possibly because of the lack of rhyme. Instructions were given to Ballantine for correction, which was accomplished in a later printing. On the printer's typescript for *Essays and Studies* was prudently written (by an editor): 'division into lines as here must be preserved'.

Below, as C, is the first part of *Beorhtnoth* once more, through Totta's (Torhthelm's) lament, from the printed text in *Essays and Studies 1953* (pp. 3–7). We have described in notes selected differences and late revisions in its later manuscripts and typescript.

[C]

The sound is heard of a man moving uncertainly and breathing noisily in the darkness. Suddenly a voice speaks, loudly and sharply.

Torhthelm. Halt! What do you want? Hell take you! Speak!
Tídwald. Totta! I know you by your teeth rattling.
Torhthelm. Why, Tída, you! The time seemed long
alone among the lost. They lie so queer.
I've watched and waited, till the wind sighing
was like words whispered by walking ghosts
that in my ears muttered.
Tídwald. And your eyes fancied
barrow-wights and bogies. It's a black darkness
since the moon foundered; but mark my words:
not far from here we'll find the master,
by all accounts.

Tídwald lets out a faint beam from a dark-lantern. An owl hoots. A dark shape flits through the beam of light. Torhthelm starts back and overturns the lantern, which Tída had set on the ground.

What ails you now?

Torhthelm. Lord save us! Listen!
Tídwald. My lad, you're crazed.
Your fancies and your fears make foes of nothing.
Help me to heave 'em! It's heavy labour
to lug them alone: long ones and short ones,
the thick and the thin. Think less, and talk less
of ghosts. Forget your gleeman's stuff!
Their ghosts are under ground, or else God has them;
and wolves don't walk as in Woden's days,
not here in Essex. If any there be,
they'll be two-leggéd. There, turn him over!

An owl hoots again.

It's only an owl.
Torhthelm. An ill boding.
Owls and omens. But I'm not afraid,
not of fancied fears. A fool call me,
but more men than I find the mirk gruesome
among the dead unshrouded. It's like the dim shadow
of heathen hell, in the hopeless kingdom
where search is vain. We might seek for ever
and yet miss the master in this mirk, Tída.
O lord beloved, where do you lie tonight,
your head so hoar upon a hard pillow,
and your limbs lying in long slumber?

Tídwald lets out again the light of the dark-lantern.

Tídwald. Look here, my lad, where they lie thickest!
Here! lend a hand! This head we know!
Wulfmær it is. I'll wager aught
not far did he fall from friend and master.
Torhthelm. His sister-son! The songs tell us,
ever near shall be at need nephew to uncle.
Tídwald. Nay, he's not here — or he's hewn out of ken.
It was the other I meant, th' Eastsaxon lad,
Wulfstan's youngster. It's a wicked business
to gather them ungrown. A gallant boy, too,
and the makings of a man.
Torhthelm. Have mercy on us!
He was younger than I, by a year or more.

Tídwald. Here's Ælfnoth, too, by his arm lying.
Torhthelm. As he would have wished it. In work or play
they were fast fellows, and faithful to their lord,
as close to him as kin.
Tídwald. Curse this lamplight,
and my eyes' dimness! My oath I'll take
they fell in his defence, and not far away
now master lies. Move them gently!
Torhthelm. Brave lads! But it's bad when bearded men
put shield at back and shun battle,
running like roe-deer, while the red heathen
beat down their boys. May the blast of Heaven
light on the dastards that to death left them
to England's shame! And here's Ælfwine:
barely bearded, and his battle's over.
Tídwald. That's bad, Totta. He was a brave lordling,
and we need his like: a new weapon
of the old metal. As eager as fire,
and as staunch as steel. Stern-tongued at times,
and outspoken after Offa's sort.
Torhthelm. Offa! he's silenced. Not all liked him;
and many would have muzzled him, had master let
them.
'There are cravens at council that crow proudly
with the hearts of hens': so I hear he said
at the lords' meeting. As lays remind us:
'What at the mead man vows, when morning comes
let him with deeds answer, or his drink vomit
and a sot be shown.' But the songs wither,
and the world worsens. I wish I'd been here,
not left with the luggage and the lazy thralls,
cooks and sutlers! By the cross, Tída,
I loved him no less than any lord with him;
and a poor freeman may prove in the end
more tough when tested than titled earls
who count back their kin to kings ere Woden.
Tídwald. You can talk, Totta! Your time'll come,
and it'll look less easy than lays make it.
Bitter taste has iron, and the bite of swords
is cruel and cold, when you come to it.
Then God guard you, if your glees falter!
When your shield is shivered, between shame and death

is hard choosing. Help me with this one!
There, heave him over — the hound's carcase,
hulking heathen!

Torhthelm. Hide it, Tída!
Put the lantern out! He's looking at me.
I can't abide his eyes, bleak and evil
as Grendel's in the moon.

Tídwald. Ay, he's a grim fellow,
but he's dead and done-for. Danes don't trouble me
save with swords and axes. They can smile or glare,
once hell has them. Come, haul the next!

Torhthelm. Look! Here's a limb! A long yard, and thick
as three men's thighs.

Tídwald. I thought as much.
Now bow your head, and hold your babble
for a moment Totta! It's the master at last.

There is silence for a short while.

Well, here he is — or what Heaven's left us:
the longest legs in the land, I guess.

Torhthelm. (*His voice rises to a chant.*)
His head was higher than the helms of kings
with heathen crowns, his heart keener
and his soul clearer than swords of heroes
polished and proven; than plated gold
his worth was greater. From the world has passed
a prince peerless in peace and war,
just in judgement, generous-handed
as the golden lords of long-ago.
He has gone to God glory seeking,
Beorhtnoth beloved.

Tídwald. Brave words, my lad!
The woven staves have yet worth in them
for woeful hearts. But there's work to do,
ere the funeral begins.

Torhthelm. I've found it, Tída!
Here's his sword lying! I could swear to it
by the golden hilts.

Tídwald. I'm glad to hear it.
How it was missed is a marvel. He is marred cruelly.

Few tokens else shall we find on him;
they've left us little of the Lord we knew.

Torhthelm. Ah, woe and worse! The wolvish heathens
have hewn off his head, and the hulk left us
mangled with axes. What a murder it is,
this bloody fighting!

Tídwald. Aye, that's battle for you.
And no worse today than wars you sing of,
when Fróda fell, and Finn was slain.
The world wept then, as it weeps today
you can hear the tears through the harps twanging.
Come, bend your back! We must bear away
the cold leavings. Catch hold of the legs!
Now lift — gently! Now lift again!

They shuffle along slowly.

Torhthelm. Dear still shall be this dead body,
though men have marred it.

Torhthelm's voice rises again to a chant.

Now mourn for ever
Saxon and English, from the sea's margin
to the western forest! The wall is fallen,
women are weeping; the wood is blazing
and the fire flaming as a far beacon.
Build high the barrow his bones to keep!
For here shall be hid both helm and sword;
and to the ground be given golden corslet,
and rich raiment and rings gleaming,
wealth unbegrudged for the well-beloved;
of the friends of men first and noblest,
to his hearth-comrades help unfailing,
to his folk the fairest father of peoples.
Glory loved he; now glory earning
his grave shall be green, while ground or sea,
while word or woe in the world lasteth.

Critics of *The Homecoming of Beorhtnoth Beorhthelm's Son* have often focused on two issues explored in the poem and its afterword: the consequences of heroic excess, and the nature of war. That the historical Beorhtnoth disastrously allowed the Northmen to cross the ford is attested in *The Battle of Maldon*. That work was composed soon after the event, when, as E.V. Gordon has said, 'memory of all that happened was still fresh, and the heroism of individual deeds and speeches still seemed of primary importance, their glory undimmed by the defeat' (*The Battle of Maldon* (1937), p. 21). The poem would become an admired statement on heroic ideals, loyalty, and duty. In his 1953 preface to *Beorhtnoth*, Tolkien notes that the duke was 'played' by his foe: 'the vikings knew, or so it would seem, what manner of a man they had to deal with', one susceptible to 'pride and misplaced chivalry' (*Essays and Studies 1953*, p. 1) – in *The Battle of Maldon*, the Northmen are explicitly said to practise deceit. In his afterword ('Ofermod') Tolkien argues that Beorhtnoth was not strictly heroic. 'Honour was in itself a motive, and he sought it at the risk of placing his *heorðwerod* [hearth-warriors, or personal guard], all the men most dear to him, in a truly heroic situation, which they could redeem only by death. Magnificent perhaps, but certainly wrong. Too foolish to be heroic' (p. 15). 'It was a noble error', Tolkien continues, 'or the error of a noble' (p. 16). His men, loyal to their lord as a measure of honour, probably would not have blamed him, though it was by his act that they suffered death.

Two parts of Tolkien's poem speak most directly to these points. In the final text of the rhyming version, Tudda (in earlier manuscripts, Totta) wonders:

> How came they thus to win
> across the causeway, think you? There's little sign
> here of hard fight, and yet just here the brine [sea-water]
> should have been choked with them. But by the bank
> there's only one there lying.

Totta replies:

> They've him [Beorhtnoth] to thank,
> alas! Or so men say now in the town.
> Too bold, too proud! But he is fallen down,
> made fool of by great heart. So we'll not chide.
> He let them cross to taste his sword — and died:
> the last of the true sons of men of old. . . .

In the alliterative version, it is the younger Totta (Torhthelm) who asks the question, and the seasoned Tídwald who replies. This passage (D) is transcribed from *Essays and Studies 1953* (p. 10):

[D]

Torhthelm. It's strange to me
how they came across this causeway here,
or forced a passage without fierce battle;
but there are few tokens to tell of fighting.
A hill of heathens one would hope to find,
but none lie near.

Tídwald. No, more's the pity.
Alas, my friend, our lord was at fault,
or so in Maldon this morning men were saying.
Too proud, too princely! But his pride's cheated,
and his princedom has passed, so we'll praise his valour.
He let them cross the causeway, so keen was he
to give minstrels matter for mighty songs.
Needlessly noble. It should never have been:
bidding bows be still, and the bridge opening,
matching more with few in mad handstrokes!
Well, doom he dared, and died for it.

Torhthelm. So the last is fallen of the line of earls,
from Saxon lords long-descended
who sailed the seas, as songs tell us,
from Angel in the East, with eager swords
upon war's anvil the Welsh smiting.
Realms here they won and royal kingdoms,
and in olden days this isle conquered.
And now from the North need comes again:
wild blows the wind of war to Britain!

Tídwald. And in the neck we catch it, and are nipped as chill
as poor men were then. Let the poets babble,
but perish all pirates! When the poor are robbed
and lose the land they loved and toiled on,
They must die and dung it. No dirge for them,
and their wives and children work in serfdom.

Tídwald's comment is at the heart of the matter, or of Tolkien's view of it: 'Needlessly noble. It should never have been.' In 'Ofermod' Tolkien argues that Beorhtnoth was not a free agent, like Beowulf choosing to face a foe alone, but

> responsible for all the men under him, not to throw away their lives except with one object, the defence of the realm from an

> implacable foe. . . . It was heroic for him and his men to fight, to annihilation if necessary, in the attempt to destroy or hold off the invaders. It was wholly unfitting that he should treat a desperate battle with this sole real object as a sporting match, to the ruin of his purpose and duty. [*Essays and Studies 1953*, p. 15]

Beorhtnoth's actions, Tolkien says, were 'not only formed by nature, but moulded also by "aristocratic tradition", enshrined in tales and verse of poets now lost save for echoes' (p. 15). And they were influenced by pride, by hubris: 'Too proud, too princely!' Tídwald says. 'But his pride's cheated'. The question runs through the development of *Beorhtnoth*, as Thomas Honegger shows in his 2007 essay, and so does the parallel matter of heroism, which is examined by Mary R. Bowman in 'Refining the Gold: Tolkien, *The Battle of Maldon*, and the Northern Theory of Courage' (2010).

These issues are tied also to a reverie spoken by the younger servant, half-asleep near the end of the poem. In the final manuscript of the rhyming version, this reads (E):

[E]

Ay! candles and singing, and the holy Mass
in Ely, ere he's buried. And days will pass,
and men — and women weep in Angelcynn —
and new days follow . . . . . . and his tomb begin
to fade, and all his kith pass out of ken.
The candles gutter in the wind. Like men.
They soon go out, the candles in the dark.
Come smite the flint, and strike a spark!
A flame — a light — a fire that won't go out!
A yes, I hear them. Good words thou, and stout!

[*A solemn voice says slowly:*

hige sceal þe heardra, heorte þe cenre,
mod sceal þe mare, þe ure mægen lytlað.

Well said the scop! That will not be forgot
for many an age . . . an age . . . an age . . . [*sleeps*]

A *scop* is a bard or poet.

Tolkien reworked this for the alliterative version, now with a pointed reply by Tídwald (F, from *Essays and Studies 1953*, p. 12):

[F] *The lights disappear as he speaks. Torhthelm's voice becomes louder, but it is still the voice of one speaking in a dream.*

It's dark! It's dark, and doom coming!
Is no light left us? A light kindle,
and fan the flame! Lo! Fire now wakens,
hearth is burning, house is lighted,
men there gather. Out of the mists they come
through darkling doors whereat doom waiteth.
Hark! I hear them in the hall chanting:
stern words they sing with strong voices.
(*He chants*) Heart shall be bolder, harder be purpose,
more proud the spirit as our power lessens!
Mind shall not falter nor mood waver,
though doom shall come and dark conquer.

There is a great bump and jolt of the cart.

Hey! what a bump, Tída! My bones are shaken,
and my dream shattered. It's dark and cold.
Tídwald. Aye, a bump on the bone is bad for dreams,
and it's cold waking. But your words were queer,
Torhthelm my lad, with your talk of wind
and doom conquering and a dark ending.
It sounded fey and fell-hearted,
and heathenish, too: I don't hold with that.
It's night right enough; but there's no firelight:
dark is over all, and dead is master.
When morning comes, it'll be much like others:
more labour and loss till the land's ruined;
ever work and war till the world passes.

It is clear that by the end of the poem Torhthelm (Totta) is still enamoured of what Tídwald (Tída) calls 'gleeman's stuff', old tales of heroes and wonders and acts of valour, despite mutilated corpses lying cold on the field before him – the fruits of 'valour' – and despite Tída's warning that Totta's time will come, and then 'it'll look less easy than lays make it'. 'What a murder it is, | this bloody fighting!' Torhthelm says, without having yet seen it himself; 'Aye, that's battle for you', Tídwald replies, perhaps with a sigh of weariness, 'and no worse today than wars you sing of, | when Fróda fell, and Finn was slain', referring to the stories of Finn, king of Frisia, and Fróda of the Hathobards, both of whom figure in the Old English *Widsith* and *Beowulf*. Earlier, in text D above, Tídwald suggested that it was the influence of these same tales, the 'babble' of poets, which led Beorhtnoth to his folly.

Totta (in E and F) is drawn to Beorhtwold's famous exhortation in *The Battle of Maldon*, which Tolkien thought was older than the poem, 'an ancient and honoured expression of heroic will' (*Essays and Studies 1953*, p. 3). In some of his drafts for 'Beorhtnoth's Death', Tolkien considered a fictional history in which Totta, following the events of *Beorhtnoth*, would become the author of *The Battle of Maldon*; in one, he wrote: 'It is here supposed that Totta afterwards becomes the author of the poem the fragment of which survives. It is based (on this theory) partly on survivors' reports, partly on imagination and epic tradition.' In the event, Tolkien chose to omit explicit mention of Totta (Torhthelm) as the *Maldon* poet, else *Beorhtnoth* would have had a faux-scholarly background not unlike that found in, say, Tolkien's *Farmer Giles of Ham*. Peter Grybauskas has examined this point in 'A Portrait of the Poet as a Young Man: Noteworthy Omission in *The Homecoming of Beorhtnoth Beorhthelm's Son*' (2020), suggesting that Tolkien may have omitted mention of Totta as the supposed *Maldon* author out of concern that it would be inappropriate in a distinguished academic journal.

In several of his books and essays – we will list them in our bibliography – Tom Shippey strongly disagrees with Tolkien's views on heroic excess in *The Battle of Maldon*, and his application of these in *Beorhtnoth*. He objects, for example, to what he sees as a systematic blackening of the character of Torhthelm, who 'in a sense represents the tradition of Old English poetry'. 'Tolkien's suggestion', Shippey continues,

> is that Beorhtnoth made his mistake out of diabolical pride; but that that diabolical pride was actually created by heroic tradition as expressed in Old English poetry. Beorhtnoth wanted to be a hero. He was prepared to sacrifice his own life for that. But he was also prepared to sacrifice the lives of the Essex levy. Tolkien's view was that he had no right to expend the lives of his men as well as his own. But since piety prevents one from criticising the dead in Beorhtnoth, Tolkien has created a character to represent the bad qualities of Old English poetry in Torhthelm: and the criticism which might be directed at Beorhtnoth is directed at Torhthelm instead. ['Tolkien and "The Homecoming of Beorhtnoth"' (2007), pp. 329, 331–2]

As Paul H. Kocher writes in *Master of Middle-earth: The Fiction of J.R.R. Tolkien* (1972), the reader of *Beorhtnoth* is placed 'right among the corpses on the battlefield after nightfall', thus driving home 'with utter immediacy the horror of a carnage that need never have taken place' (p. 187). It is hard to imagine that this imagery was not influenced by recent memories. Tolkien saw the bodies of men, some of whom he had known, lying in the trenches and the fields of France in 1916, and the First World War had ended barely more than a decade before (as we think) Tolkien began to compose his poem. There they were, men of all sorts, 'long ones and short ones, | the thick and the thin', as Tolkien writes in text C, or as a popular British war song put it, 'the long and the short and the tall'. Then came the second war, with Hitler being defeated only a few years before the publication of the revised *Beorhtnoth* in *Essays and Studies*. Tolkien had plenty of time to reflect on the cost of such conflicts. In both wars, many thousands lost their lives, some of them as much through foolish choices made by their superiors as through enemy action – and most of these were young. Nearly half the men with whom Tolkien matriculated at Exeter College, Oxford, did not survive the war of 1914–18. In *Beorhtnoth* Tídwald and Torhthelm lament 'on the youth and worth of the slain men' (p. 188); 'it's a wicked business', Tídwald says, 'to gather them ungrown'.

Kocher identifies as a sub-theme of *Beorhtnoth* 'Torhthelm's gradual and by no means uninterrupted discovery that the heroic grandeur he sees in his sagas is not compatible with the unheroic reality he is finding on the Essex battlefield' (p. 190). It seems to us that by the end of the poem, Torhthelm still clings to some degree to the old tales, which someone of a romantic nature finds difficult to discard.

Not long after the appearance of *Beorhtnoth* in *Essays and Studies*, by 3 May 1954, Tolkien made a private tape-recording of the drama, speaking all of the voices and ingeniously making sound effects – the sound of waggon wheels, for example, by moving furniture in his study. This was issued, with a brief introduction and readings of 'Beorhtnoth's Death' and 'Ofermod' by Christopher Tolkien, as an audio tape given to those attending the Tolkien Centenary Conference in 1992, and was later released commercially on compact disc.

In December 1954, repeated in June 1955, a small cast recording of *Beorhtnoth* was broadcast on BBC Radio's Third Programme. Tolkien found it 'incompetent' (letter to Philip Unwin, 29 January 1955, Tolkien–George Allen & Unwin archive, HarperCollins). During development of the work for reading, Tolkien advised that the difference between the voices for Torhthelm and Tídwald should be

> rather one of temper, and matter, than 'class'. The young minstrel bursts into formal verse, and so uses an archaic style – as anyone would capable of verse at the time, and as Tídwald himself does when he mocks Torhthelm.
>
> It is not indicated what part of the country either came from. Torhthelm is in fact much more likely to have come from the West Midlands, as did many who fell at Maldon. But in a period when 'dialect' merely marked place and not rank or function, and at any rate details of grammar and vowels had no social implications, it would be best to avoid any modern rusticity. [letter to Rayner Heppenstall, 23 September 1954, *Letters*, p. 281]

On 22 November 1954 Tolkien informed Miss F.L. Perry, a *Lord of the Rings* enthusiast, that

> on Dec. 3rd you can hear (if you wish) a dramatic dialogue in alliterative verse concerning the '*Battle of Maldon*' (fought A.D. 991), broadcast by the B.B.C. It might interest you since it concerns one of the most heroic events in Anglo-Saxon history, and in the history of Essex: the death of the great Duke Byrhtnoth of Essex in battle with the Vikings of Aulof (Olaf Tryggvason) of Norway. And also because it is really on the theme which has always engrossed me and in the foundation of 'The Lord of the Rings': the noble and the ignoble. For hobbitry you have the plain farmer–soldier; for the chivalry, a young minstrel or poet. [Bonhams, New York sale of 22 June 2023, lot 152]

On 11 August 1991 Tolkien's drama was performed in the open air, at Maldon, as part of a festival to mark the millennium of the battle. Also that year, Anglo-Saxon Books published *Beorhtnoth*, with its scholarly appendages, as a separate booklet, though with numerous deviations from the text in *Essays and Studies 1953*.

In 2023 Peter Grybauskas included the final text of *Beorhtnoth* with Tolkien's prose translation of *The Battle of Maldon* and related papers. In appendices to his book are also the complete text from which we took extract B, a discussion of 'noteworthy developments in the drafts' of *Beorhtnoth*, and a brief essay suggesting that the verse-drama is a prelude of sorts to *The Lord of the Rings*.

A2: 'One of them', i.e., a Northman.

A13: Essex had been an Anglo-Saxon kingdom, but from 825 it was controlled by the kingdom of Wessex. In 878 it had been acquired, by treaty, by the Danish king Guthrum, but early in the tenth century it was won back by the Wessex dynasty and then under the authority of ealdormen like Beorhtnoth.

A21: Wulfmær was Beorhtnoth's 'sister's son' (A25), i.e. his nephew, and son of Wulfstan (A26). He is praised for his bravery three times in *The Battle of Maldon*.

A26: Wulfstan is named in *The Battle of Maldon* as one of three warriors who initially held the causeway, until the Northmen deceived Beorhtnoth into allowing them to cross.

A29: Ælfnoth is named in *The Battle of Maldon* as one of two men, with Wulfmær, who stood fast beside Beorhtnoth.

A33: 'Men with beards and tried blades', i.e. older men, experienced in fighting with swords. Several are named in *The Battle of Maldon* as having fled the battle despite their allegiance to Beorhtnoth; see also our note for B46–51.

A35: Ælfwine, son of Ælfric and one of the young warriors.

A37: 'Proud heart, proud tongue, like Offa.' The reference is to Ælfwine's speech in *The Battle of Maldon*, in which he reminds his fellow warriors of the boasts about their prowess they made in the mead-hall. 'Now he who is brave may show it in the test' (R.K. Gordon translation, 1967 printing, p. 333). Offa is another, older retainer; see also our note for B46–51.

A44: 'Gold hilts': in *The Battle of Maldon* Beorhtnoth's sword is described as 'golden-hilted' (*fealohilte*).

A47–48: 'They have reft | the head', i.e. cut off Beorhtnoth's head. According to the *Liber Eliensis*, the invaders decapitated Beorhtnoth and took his head back to their home. His body was interred at Ely with a ball of wax in place of its head.

B14: 'Lays of Goths and Huns': an allusion, maybe, to the Old Norse *Hlöðskviða*, or *Battle of the Goths and Huns*.

B24, 26: This reading was changed in the third manuscript from that of A.

B28–31: This reading was changed in the third manuscript from that of A, except that Tolkien made l. 30 a parenthetical comment in the second and third manuscripts, removing its brackets only in the fourth.

B30: 'Sister-son', i.e. nephew; compare 'sister's son', A25.

B35–36: Until the fourth manuscript, these words were spoken by Tudda, as in A.

B44: Tolkien was of two minds whether to emphasize *He* and *His* in this line. *His* is emphasized (underlined) in the first, second, and third manuscripts, not in the fourth (possibly overlooked), and again emphasized in the fifth, which also emphasizes *He*. Similar instances are found in the later (alliterative) text, before being wholly omitted.

B46–51: Offa speaks, or is reported to have spoken, three times in *The Battle of Maldon*. Here 'Offa's words . . . that day at council of the lords' refers to a mention in a paragraph excoriating those who fled the battle and did not honour their duty to their lord, rather than remember the rewards Beorhtnoth had given them. 'Thus erstwhile Offa once said to him [Beorhtnoth] in the meeting-place, when he held assembly, that many spoke bravely there who would not endure in stress' (R.K. Gordon translation, p. 332). Later in the poem, Offa names Godric, son of Odda, who fled on Beorhtnoth's own horse, leading others to believe that their lord was leaving the field and thus dividing their forces.

B47: Tolkien changed this line in the third manuscript to 'as took that ill, and would have Offa dumb'. In the fourth manuscript, he changed it to 'took Offa's words with scowls, I'm told, that day'. In the fifth manuscript, he changed 'I'm told, that day' to 'and wished him dumb', and added a new line following ('they cut too nigh — or so I'm told, that day').

B56: Woden, or Odin, chief of the gods in Northern mythology.

B63: 'Dane' is used generically, for a Northman or Viking.

B65–68: These lines are an example of Tolkien's enlargement of his text in the fourth manuscript. There they read:

> Dowse that light again!
> I can't abide his eyes. They glare so grim,
> like a fen-dweller[']s in the moon. Look! there's a limb,
> like three men's legs.

Tolkien changed 'fen-dweller's' to 'Grendel's' in the fifth manuscript (after marking the revision on the fourth), introducing a reference to the *Beowulf* monster; compare ll. 1–2 of Tolkien's *Lay of Beowulf* (*c.* 1930, no. 117), 'Grendel came forth in the dead of night; | the moon in his eyes shone glassy bright'. 'Three men's legs' is the first reference in *Beorhtnoth* to the lord's reputed size: 'his white head towered high above other men, for he was exceedingly tall', as Tolkien writes in his 1953 preface.

B70: In the fourth manuscript this line read 'the longest man in all this isle, I guess'. Tolkien marked these words to change to 'that's he[,] the longest in this isle, I guess', but revised the line again in writing out the fifth manuscript, as above.

B72: 'Dealt the rings': in the Anglo-Saxon period, kings (lords, rulers) were often referred to as 'ring-givers' because they gave out wealth as rewards for service, as to a warrior for his courage. Such gifts were sometimes actual rings (arm-rings, neck-rings), but *ring* could be used metaphorically in referring to the practice.

B90: 'Mercian', i.e. from the English Midlands. Mercia had been a large Anglo-Saxon kingdom; at the time of the Battle of Maldon, it was controlled by Wessex.

C1: In the seventh complete manuscript, i.e. the first coherent text of the alliterative version, the first direction reads '*Darkness. There is noise of a man moving about and breathing heavily*'. Tolkien altered this in the eighth manuscript, again in the ninth, and for the last time in the tenth and final manuscript.

C9: In the typescript Tolkien changed 'in my ears muttering' to 'that in my ears muttered'.

C11: A barrow-wight features in *The Adventures of Tom Bombadil* (*c.* 1931, poem no. 121), and was part of Tolkien's plan for *The Lord of the Rings* by 1938. A *bogey* (plural *bogies*) is an evil or mischievous spirit. The realist Tída is sceptical about the existence of either creature, while Totta, influenced by stories, has an active imagination.

C12: 'The moon foundered' is present in the sixth manuscript (initial alliterative text), and in the seventh. In the eighth manuscript the reading was briefly 'the moon went down', but returned to 'foundered' in the ninth. (Compare 'sunk' in B7.)

C15–17: In the seventh manuscript, this direction read '*Tudda lets out a faint beam from a dark-lantern. There is a flap of wings. Totta starts back and knocks the lantern over. An owl hoots.*'

C21: In the typescript this line read, before revision, 'Your fancies and your words make fears of nothing'.

C28: In the typescript Tolkien changed 'not in Essex here' to 'not here in Essex'.

C33: In the seventh and eighth manuscripts Tolkien emphasized Totta's statement: 'But *I'm* not afraid'. He removed the emphasis with the ninth manuscript.

C36: In the tenth manuscript Tolkien changed 'the dead unburied' to 'the dead unshrouded'.

C46: In the typescript Tolkien changed 'And Wulfmaer it is' to 'Wulfmaer it is'. *Essays and Studies* set all 'ae' combinations as *æ*, as a matter of style. Tolkien wrote (for example) 'Wulfmær' consistently in his manuscripts, but evidently lacked special characters (and accents) on the typewriter used for this work.

C48: In the ninth manuscript Tolkien changed 'His sister's son' to 'His sister-son'.

C50–54: In the eighth manuscript, these lines read:

> Ay, *he's* here too.   But it wasn't *him* I meant,
> but Wulfstan's youngster.   It's a wicked business
> to gather them ungrown: a gallant boy too,
> and the makings of a man.

Tolkien carried this text into the ninth manuscript, where he marked it for revision, and in the tenth manuscript reached the final text except for one final change there, replacing 'the Essex lad' with 'th' Eastsaxon lad'.

C62: In the eighth manuscript Tolkien changed 'An oath' to 'My oath'.

C77: In the typescript Tolkien changed 'he's gone too' to 'he's silenced'.

C78: In the seventh manuscript, this line was followed by 'he saw through them and said what he thought', changed to 'he said what he thought, and saw through them' in the eighth. This persisted in the ninth manuscript, until Tolkien omitted it (by design or oversight) in the final manuscript and in the typescript.

C88: In the typescript Tolkien changed 'lord among them' to 'lord with him'.

C94: 'Bite of swords', i.e. swords piercing flesh.

C96: In the typescript Tolkien changed 'glees fail you' to 'glees falter'.

C102: In the typescript Tolkien changed 'He looks at me' to 'He's looking at me'.

C113: In the typescript this line originally read 'for a moment's space! It's the master, Totta'.

C159: 'Flaming' originally read 'blazing'.

D15: 'Bows', i.e. archers ready to shoot arrows.

D16: 'Matching more with few': there is no evidence that the English defenders were outnumbered by the enemy, at least initially before men fled the battle.

D21: 'Angel', i.e. Anglia, a peninsula on the east coast of Jutland.

D31: 'Die and dung it', presumably, die and return to the earth.

E3: 'Angelcynn', i.e. the English people (Angles' kin).

E8: 'Come smite the flint, and strike a spark!' Striking a piece of flint (a form of quartz) with steel creates a spark, with which one can light a fire.

F5–7: In the typescript these lines read, before revision:

and fan the flame! Lo! fire wakens,
the hearth is burning. The house is lit,
and there men gather, out of the mists coming

F11–12: In the typescript these lines read, before revision, 'Let heart be prouder, harder be purpose, | more stern the will, as our strength weakens'.

NOTE ON THE TEXTS Here, for comparison with Thomas Honegger's description of the *Beorhtnoth* papers, we give the order we believe to be correct, with references to our transcriptions (by boldfaced letter); to papers in the Bodleian Library, Oxford (MS. Tolkien and MS. Tolkien Drawings); to a file in the Gordon archive in the University of Leeds Library; to the printed *Essays and Studies* for 1953; and to *The Treason of Isengard*. Honegger does not state in his essay the folio ranges of his versions F and G; for these, we have interpolated from the Bodleian papers.

Draft, not seen by Honegger: MS. Tolkien Drawings 88, fol. 24 verso
Draft, Honegger α: *The Treason of Isengard*, pp. 106–7
Text 1, Honegger B, our **A**: MS. Tolkien 5, fols. 5–8
Text 2, Honegger A: MS. Tolkien 5, fols. 1–4
Text 3, not seen by Honegger but acknowledged by Grybauskas: Leeds MS. 1952/2/1
Text 4, Honegger C, our **B**, **E**: MS. Tolkien 5, fols. 9–12
Text 5, Honegger D: MS. Tolkien 5, fols. 14–22 (Honegger includes in D, on fol. 13, part of what became the prose 'Beorhtnoth's Death')
Text 6, Honegger E: MS. Tolkien 5, fols. 23–30
Text 7, Honegger G: MS. Tolkien 5, fols. 46–61
Text 8, Honegger F: MS. Tolkien 5, fols. 31–45
Text 9, Honegger H: MS. Tolkien 5, fols. 65–71 (Honegger includes in H fols. 62–4 and 72–3, drafts for 'Beorhtnoth's Death')
Text 10, Honegger I: MS. Tolkien 5, fols. 76–88 (Honegger includes in I fols. 74–5, draft for 'Beorhtnoth's Death')
Text 11 (or 11 and 12), typescript for *Essays and Studies*, Honegger J, K: MS. Tolkien 5, fols. 94–7, 103–12 (Honegger assigns 'J' to fols. 94–7, and includes in K fols. 100–102, draft for 'Beorhtnoth's Death', and 113–17, draft for 'Ofermod')
Printed text in *Essays and Studies 1953*, our **C**, **D**, **F**

THE SEA-BELL

I walked by the Sea, and there ~~was borne~~ [came] to me,
[as a star-beam on] ~~a star fallen in~~ the wet sand,
~~it was~~ a white shell like a sea-bell,
trembling it lay in my wet hand.
In my fingers shaken I heard waken
~~the bell~~ [a ding] within, by a harbour bar
~~in~~ a buoy swinging, a call ringing
over endless seas, faint now and far.

I saw then a boat ~~to the shingle~~ [silently] float
on the night-tide, empty and grey.
"It is later than late! Why do we wait?"
I leapt in and cried: "Bear me away!"

It bore me away, wetted with spray,
wrapped in a mist, wound in a sleep,
to a forgotten strand in a strange land.
In the twilight beyond the deep
I heard a sea-bell swing in the swell,
[dinging, dinging, and] ~~a beacon shone on a ruined quay,~~ [the breakers roar]
~~a shore lay wide in a slow tide,~~ [on the hidden teeth of a perilous reef;]
~~and there I landed, lonely and free.~~ [and at last I came to a long shore.]
White it glimmered, and the sea simmered
with star-mirrors in a silver net;
cliffs of stone pale as ruel-bone
in the moon-foam were gleaming wet.
Glittering sand slid through my hand,
dust of pearl and jewel-grist,
trumpets of opal, roses of coral,
flutes of green and amethyst.

But under cliff-eaves there were ~~hidden~~ [glooming] caves,
weed-curtained, darkling grey;
[a cold air stirred in my hair, and the light waned, as I hurried away.]
Down from ~~far~~ [a] hill~~s~~ ran [a] green rill~~s~~;
[its] ~~their~~ water I drank ~~and went on my way,~~ [for my heart's ease.]
climbing into meadows ~~of~~ of fluttering shadows:
flowers lay there like ~~golden~~ [fallen] stars,
and on a blue pool, glassy and cool,
like floating moons the nenuphars.
[Up its fountain-stair to a country fair of ever-eve I came, far from the sea.]

(177)

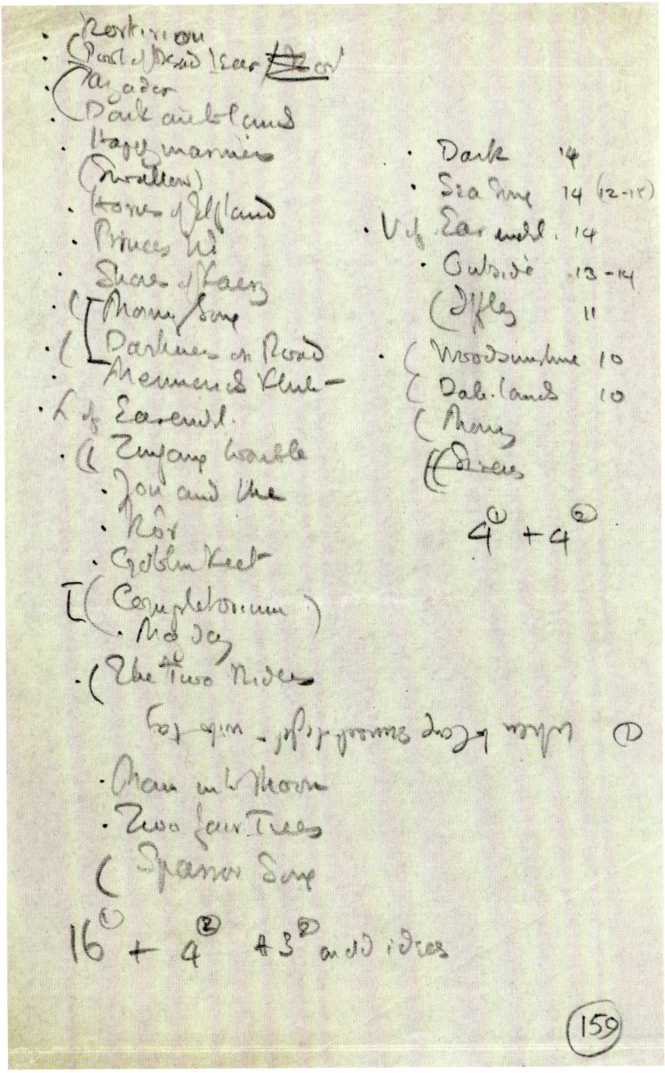
· Kortirion
· (Pool of Dead Year ~~[illegible]~~
· ([illegible]
· (Dark are the lands
· Happy mariners
(Swallows)
· Horns of Elfland
· Princess Ni
· Shores of Faery
· ([Mary Song
· ([Darkness on Road
· Mermaids Flute —
· L of Earendel.
· ((Tinfang Warble
· You and the
· Kôr
· Goblin Feet
[(Completorium)
· [illegible]
· (The Two Riders
① When the day smeared light – with ..., written upside down
· Man in the Moon
· Two fair Trees
(Sparrow Song
16① + 4② + 3② and ideas

· Dark 14
· Sea Song 14 (12-15)
· V of Earendel. 14
· Outside 13-14
(Ofley 11
· { Woodsunshine 10
{ Dale-lands 10
(Mary
((Sirens
4① + 4②

(159)

The Collected Poems of J. R. R. Tolkien

Works by J.R.R. Tolkien

The Hobbit · Leaf by Niggle · On Fairy-Stories
Farmer Giles of Ham · The Homecoming of Beorhtnoth
The Lord of the Rings · The Adventures of Tom Bombadil
The Road Goes Ever On (with Donald Swann)
Smith of Wootton Major

*Works Published Posthumously (*edited by Christopher Tolkien)*

Sir Gawain and the Green Knight, Pearl and Sir Orfeo*
Letters from Father Christmas · The Silmarillion*
Pictures by J.R.R. Tolkien* · Unfinished Tales*
The Letters of J.R.R. Tolkien*
Finn and Hengest · Mr. Bliss
The Monsters and the Critics and Other Essays*
Roverandom · The Children of Húrin*
The Legend of Sigurd and Gudrún* · The Fall of Arthur*
Beowulf: A Translation and Commentary*
The Story of Kullervo · The Lay of Aotrou and Itroun
Beren and Lúthien* · The Fall of Gondolin*
The Nature of Middle-earth · The Fall of Númenor

The History of Middle-earth – by Christopher Tolkien

I The Book of Lost Tales, Part One
II The Book of Lost Tales, Part Two
III The Lays of Beleriand
IV The Shaping of Middle-earth
V The Lost Road and Other Writings
VI The Return of the Shadow
VII The Treason of Isengard
VIII The War of the Rings
IX Sauron Defeated
X Morgoth's Ring
XI The War of the Jewels
XII The Peoples of Middle-earth

Also by Christina Scull & Wayne G. Hammond

J.R.R. Tolkien: Artist and Illustrator
The Lord of the Rings: A Reader's Companion
The J.R.R. Tolkien Companion and Guide
The Art of The Hobbit by J.R.R. Tolkien
The Art of The Lord of the Rings by J.R.R. Tolkien

The Collected Poems of J.R.R. Tolkien

Edited by

Christina Scull
Wayne G. Hammond

VOLUME THREE

HarperCollins*Publishers*

HarperCollins*Publishers* Ltd
1 London Bridge Street
London SE1 9GF

HarperCollins*Publishers*
Macken House, 39/40 Mayor Street Upper
Dublin 1, D01 C9W8, Ireland

www.tolkien.co.uk · www.tolkienestate.com

Published by HarperCollins*Publishers* 2024

1

Further acknowledgements appear on pp. 1471–2. Every effort has been made to trace all owners of copyright. The editors and publishers apologise for any errors or omissions and would be grateful if notified of any corrections.

A CIP catalogue record for this book is available from the British Library

ISBN 978-0-00-862882-6

Printed and bound in Italy by Rotolito S.p.A.

Contents

VOLUME ONE

VOLUME THREE

Illustrations

130

The Children of Húrin (?1931 or ?32)

Earlier in this book we presented selections from the lay *The Children of Húrin* (no. 67), written in alliterative verse in the early 1920s. Abandoning that work around 1925, Tolkien began the *Lay of Leithian* (no. 92), composed in octosyllabic couplets, but set it aside in turn around 1930. Then, in the early 1930s, he returned to the tale of Húrin and his children but now told it in rhyming couplets, following his practice for the *Lay of Leithian*. This too unfortunately was never completed, ending abruptly after only 171 lines. As Christopher Tolkien describes it in *The Lays of Beleriand*, his father's second *Children of Húrin* consists of 'a short prologue based on the opening of the later version of the alliterative Lay and an incomplete second section titled "The Battle of Unnumbered Tears and Morgoth's Curse"' (p. 130).

Here we give the work in its entirety, from a fair copy ink manuscript entitled *The Children of Húrin* on the first of its six pages. There do not seem to be any extant drafts. We have transcribed the text as Tolkien first set it down, but have incorporated his changes made at the time of writing. Tentative revisions he marked later in faint pencil are described in our notes.

Give me a harp and I will sing!
Ye Gods of whom is Manwë King,
who girt your guarded realm of old
with pathless mountains crowned with gold
beyond the isles that westward lie,
with pinnacles that pierced the sky
uprising sheer above the shores
whereon the outer ocean roars!
Ye men, who came too late to Earth
to know its springtime or its mirth,
and now forget the ancient woes,
the mighty wars with demon foes
when first your fathers trod the mould,
of Morgoth's power then slowly rolled
like thunder and lightning from the North
remembering naught — now stand I forth,
and now in English tongue will sing

the tale whereto yet sadly ring
the silver harps of elves forlorn
who still forgotten sorrows mourn,
and lingering yet in lonely lands
their music make with slender hands
in forest pathways sounding clear,
or on the foaming beaches sheer
or shadowy isles by shadowy seas,
to mingle with the surf and breeze.

Of Húrin and his son they tell,
and speak the name of Níniel,
the child of sorrow, and their doom
darkly entwined on Morgoth's loom.

I

THE BATTLE OF UNNUMBERED TEARS AND MORGOTH'S CURSE

Behold! before the gates of Hell
Fingolfin, son of Finwë, fell,
and Morgoth's might, unleashed at last,
the Gnomish leaguer broke and passed
to work on earth his grievous will.
But yet there gathered under hill,
and under darkling forest-eaves
where whispers ran among the leaves,
the scattered might of Elven-lords;
the moon still glinted on their swords.
For Maidros, son of Fëanor,
bade elves and men prepare for war,
and many hearkened to his call
resolved on one last field to fall,
or else o'erthrow the Northern throne
and vanquish Morgoth's towers of stone.

Fingolfin's son both spear and blade
in Hithlum in the West arrayed
for Fingon fierce and fair and tall
burned to avenge his father's fall,
his towering helm was burnished bright
and blue his banners were and white
unfurled upon the mountains height

and marched beneath the helm of night.
There with him strode the fair of face,
the noblest men of mortal race —
their eyes were bright, their cheeks were pale.
their breasts were clad in sable mail —
the house of Hador strong and proud,
whose lord was Húrin. Long and loud
their trumpets brayed at dawn of day,
the reckless laughter of the fey.
Thus rose the sun upon the plain
with slanting red the sands to stain
where little later blood more red
the sands insatiable fed.
By Dor-na-Fauglith's dreary edge
they halted in the woods, a hedge
of hidden steel, and waited long
in the East to hear the rising song,
the marching music proud and fair
of Maidros' host upon the air.

The sun turned west and no sound came;
then Fingon's patience burst to flame,
and forth the host of Hithlum sprang;
their banners streamed, their trumpets rang.

That battle there was fought of old
whereof in full no song hath told,
for tears the singer's voice that choke,
whose memory is like a smoke,
a cloud above a dreadful flame
wherein all hope is put to shame.

Now hearken! for I will not tell
the death and evil there befell,
how plundering orcs there piled the slain
heaped in a hill upon the plain;
nor speak of the ill-woven fate
that brought King Maidros' host too late,
of treason and the dastard deed
the accurséd men of Uldor's seed
there wrought, nor of the withering flame
that with the golden dragon came,

when Fingon fell in flame of swords
beside his standard and his lords,
and as his helmet burst and rang
a fire like flame of lightning sprang.
But even as the elves I sing
of axe that rushed like eagle's wing
as livid lightning shearing fell
and rove the champions of Hell,
like blasted trees in thunderstorm.
Not Maidros nor proud Celegorm,
nor any of the Elven-lords,
that day of doom with desperate swords
such deeds of hopeless valour wrought.
Thus Húrin lord of Hithlum fought.
His brother Huor pierced to heart
there fell before a venomed dart
his men were reaped like ripened wheat
and trampled under ruthless feet;
but none gave way, till alone he stood
between the desert and the wood,
and cast his broken shield away.
His thirty thanes about him lay,
his banner sewn with leaves of trees
was torn from shaft, and to his knees
he seven times was beaten low,
and seven times against the foe
he rose renewed, and clove a path
two-handed like a scyther's swath
through thronging ranks of bending grass:
not yet could Morgoth's servants pass.
Behind him was a narrow way
between the hills that southward lay,
and thither Turgon made retreat
to the vales of Sirion the fleet,
and saved the last of Finwë's folk.
In the green shadows of the oak,
and up beneath the pinewoods dim,
and over mountain passes grim
he vanished from the darkened land
and passed into Beleriand,
and never after search nor tale,
nor any spy by hill or dale,

found ever echo of their feet.
Thus Húrin guarded their retreat,
and ever songs of elves him praise,
his name has sounded down the days
uncounted; for he kept his troth,
for death nor torment broke his oath
and death in the mouth of hell defied
and saved a remnant of the pride
and glory of the elves, that yet
a hope of vengeance, and a threat
lurked in the shadows unexplored,
a dream unquiet, a hanging sword.

So Morgoth thought, and the defeat
of all his foes, though passing sweet,
held still a bitter, and he cursed
his captains on the Plains of Thirst.
He bade them bring him living bound
and cast him chained upon the ground
before his feet to cringe and cry.
Though a thousand orcs should shriek and die
neath Húrin's axe, they now must go
and drag him down to their own woe.
Now swarmed they round him like a tide
of waters black by rock defied
that rears its rugged head on high,
till down it founders with a sigh
and the ever beaten waves return
and o'er its sinking swirl and churn.
Their hideous arms his feet enmesh,
and cling there, though through bone and flesh
he clears them from the trunk. They pressed
the corpses heaped against his breast.
To his shoulders with their teeth they clung,
and round his neck like leeches hung;
and thus at last that prince most proud
was overwhelmed, his might was bowed,
and marred with wounds, and

Here the text ends, in mid-sentence and with only a single line (171) on the final manuscript page.

At the head of the first page of the work, Tolkien scribbled 'For first part ??? O.E. version see A-S verse'. We cannot explain this, other than to note that 'O.E.' (Old English) and 'A-S' (Anglo-Saxon) are synonymous. The words may refer to the opening lines of *The Children of Húrin* compared with those of Anglo-Saxon verse, such as in *Beowulf*: 'Lo! the glory of the kings of the people of the Spear-Danes in the days of old we have heard tell. . . .'

The Battle of Unnumbered Tears, or Nirnaeth Arnoediad, was the fifth and most disastrous of the battles in the Wars of Beleriand, fought against Morgoth by Elves (or Gnomes, as Tolkien still called them), Dwarves, and Men. These forces were brought together by Maidros (later Maedhros), the eldest son of Fëanor. In the battle, Maidros commanded one host, while the other was under Fingon, son of Fingolfin, the deceased High King. Húrin and his men followed Fingon. 'The accursèd men of Uldor's seed' were Easterlings under Maidros who turned on the king, being secretly in league with Morgoth. The 'golden dragon' is Glaurung (Glórund).

5: 'Beyond the isles that westward lie', i.e. the Enchanted Isles and Tol Eressëa, lying between Valinor in the East and Middle-earth in the West.

8: The 'outer ocean' is the Encircling Sea, the ocean surrounding Arda (the Earth). Compare the 'outer seas' of poem no. 33.

14, 16: Tolkien marked 'of Morgoth's power' in l. 14 to be changed to 'who Morgoth's power', in concert with 'remembering naught' changed to 'remember not' in l. 16.

22: Tolkien considered whether to change 'slender' to 'skilful?' (queried) or 'trembling'.

24: Tolkien considered whether to change 'or' to 'and'.

30: This line originally began 'entwined darkly'. Next to the following part-title, Tolkien faintly wrote 'The Fall of Húrin'.

31–32: Fingolfin, High King of the Noldor, was killed at the gates Angband ('Hell'), where he had challenged Morgoth to single combat.

45: 'Northern throne', i.e. the power of Morgoth in the North of Middle-earth.

47–53: These lines originally read:

> Fingolfin's sons both spear and blade
> in Hithlum in the West arrayed,
> for Fingon fierce and Turgon tall
> burned to avenge their father's fall,
> and now unfurled their banners white
> and marched beneath the helm of night.
> There with them strode the fair of face

49: Tolkien considered whether to change 'for' to 'thus', and 'fierce' to 'proud'.

51: Tolkien considered whether to change 'helm' to 'shade'.

53: Tolkien presumably meant the singular or plural possessive *mountain's* or *mountains'* but did not write an apostrophe in the manuscript.

58: Tolkien considered whether to change 'sable' to 'silver'.

63: Tolkien considered whether to change 'Thus' to 'There'.

65–66: Tolkien considered whether to change these lines to 'that soon were drenched with blood more red | the sands insatiable fed and strewn with corpses of the dead'.

67: Tolkien considered whether to change 'dreary' to 'barren'. 'Dor-na-Fauglith', also called *Anfauglith*, is the 'Land of Thirst' (compare 'Plains of Thirst', l. 150), a charred desert north of Beleriand, devastated by Morgoth.

78: 'No song' originally read 'no tale'.

82: Tolkien considered whether to change 'is' to 'was'.

85: Tolkien considered whether to change 'plundering' to 'slavering'.

93: Tolkien considered whether to change 'when' to 'how'.

109: Tolkien considered whether to change 'reaped' to 'laid'.

111: Tolkien considered whether to change 'alone' to 'last'.

113: Tolkien considered whether to change 'and' to 'he'.

121: 'Thronging' originally read 'bending'.

127: Tolkien considered whether to change 'Finwë's' to 'Fingon's'.

131: Next to this line, Tolkien wrote '?they', evidently as a possible change to 'he'.

132: Below this line, in the bottom margin of the page, are workings in pencil, most of them struck through: 'and takes a course into', 'and how the ?twice enchanted vale', 'enchanted ?gates', 'to Gondolin's ??? vale', 'had been already ??? pale', 'and where ever sleepless wardens ?went'.

140: Tolkien considered whether to change 'death' to 'fear'.

149: 'Held still a bitter': *bitter* is a noun, i.e. bitterness.

151: Tolkien considered whether to change 'him' to 'Húrin'. Next to this and the following line, Tolkien wrote workings in pencil:

> Húrin he bade them bring him bound
> Húrin alive he bade them bring
> in chains and on the ground him fling

On the point of Morgoth wanting Húrin captured alive (to learn secrets of the Elves, in particular the location of Turgon), see poem no. 67.

157: Tolkien considered whether to change 'Now swarmed they round him ' to 'They swarmed about him'.

131

The New Lay of the Völsungs · *The New Lay of Gudrún* (?1931 or ?32–*c.* 1950)

Writing to W.H. Auden in 1967, Tolkien described an attempt he made years earlier 'to unify the lays about the Völsungs from the Elder Edda' (29 March 1967, *Letters*, p. 533). The Elder (or Poetic) Edda, a collection of anonymous Old Norse poems, is preserved most notably in the thirteenth-century Codex Regius. This is the chief source for the complex tale of the Völsungs and the Niflungs (Nibelungs), but lacks one gathering which would have told the central part of the legend of Sigurd; for that, one must refer to other works, especially the prose *Völsunga Saga*, another work in Old Norse from the same period as the Codex. In fact, it is misleading to say 'the legend of Sigurd' when there are contradictory accounts even in the Edda, whose poems were not composed by one person or at one time. Therefore the author of any retelling must pick and choose from sources. It is the *Völsunga Saga*, for example, which establishes Sigurd's descent from Ódin, chief of the Norse Gods.

Tolkien's 'unification' of the old poems took the form of two closely associated works, *Völsungakviða en nýja*, or *The New Lay of the Völsungs*, and *Guðrúnarkviða en nýja*, *The New Lay of Gudrún*, of 339 and 166 stanzas respectively. They 'stand in a complex relation to their ancient sources', Christopher Tolkien states; 'they are in no sense translations. Those sources themselves, various in their nature, present obscurities, contradictions, and enigmas, and the existence of these problems underlay my father's avowed purpose in writing the "New Lays"' (*The Legend of Sigurd and Gudrún* (2009), p. 5).

Tolkien's poems exist in a single fair copy manuscript, with few revisions made at the time of writing. Christopher Tolkien was inclined to date them to the earlier 1930s, after his father abandoned the *Lay of Leithian* (poem no. 92) near the end of 1931. 'The final manuscript of the poems', he writes,

> did however itself undergo correction at some later time. By a rough count there are some eighty to ninety emendations scattered through the two texts, from changes of a single word to (but rarely) the substitution of several half-lines; some lines are marked for alteration but without any replacement provided.

> The corrections are written rapidly and often indistinctly in pencil, and all are concerned with vocabulary and metre, not with the substance of the narrative. I have the impression that my father read through the text many years later (the fact that a couple of the corrections are in red ball-point pen [biro] points to a late date) and quickly emended points that struck him as he went – perhaps with a view to possible publication, though I know of no evidence that he ever actually proposed it. [*The Legend of Sigurd and Gudrún*, p. 40]

It will be useful to summarize the 'New Lays' briefly. An apocalypse (Ragnarök) has been foretold in which the old Gods will die and the Earth itself will perish. Against this, Ódin has been gathering to him those slain in battle to fight alongside the Gods at the end of days, and has also been striving to produce a mortal descendant, a prophesied 'serpent-slayer' who would defy the coming forces of darkness and save the world. At length, his efforts produce Sigurd, a descendant of the Völsung clan, who kills the serpent (dragon) Fáfnir, takes its cursed hoard of gold, and frees the sleeping Valkyrie Brynhild. At the courts of the Niflungs, through magic and deceit Sigurd is made to fall in love with the Niflung princess Gudrún, and Brynhild to marry the Niflung king Gunnar. Sigurd is murdered, and Brynhild joins him on his funeral pyre. Fáfnir's hoard is now desired by King Atli of the Huns; the Niflungs give him the widowed Gudrún as his wife. Invited to Hunland for a feast, the Niflungs fall into a trap. Atli demands Fáfnir's gold, but the Niflungs had thrown it into the Rhine after Sigurd's death. Despite Gudrún's pleas, Atli kills her brothers, the Niflung leaders Gunnar and Högni. In revenge, she kills Atli as well as their sons.

Christopher Tolkien published the 'New Lays' in 2009 as *The Legend of Sigurd and Gudrún*. He describes both the introduction to the first lay and the entirety of the second as having been written in stanzas of eight short lines (half-lines), and the rest of *Völsungakviða en nýja* in long lines, without a metrical space between halves; but since his father declared in a note that the whole of both poems should be written 'in short line form, which looks better', Christopher followed this direction for all of the published text. In addition to the two lays, the book includes as appendices the related *Prophecy of the Sibyl* (poem no. 132) and fragments of an alliterative heroic poem of Attila in Old English, with translations by Christopher (not included in our collection).

For the present book, we have made four selections from the published lays. Two are from *Völsungakviða en nýja*: all twenty stanzas of the introduction (*Upphaf* 'Beginning', based in part on the first Eddaic poem, *Völuspá*), concerning the creation of the world, the war between the Gods and giants, and Odin's plan (A), pp. 59–65 of *Sigurd and Gudrún*; and the final seven stanzas of the ninth and final part (*Deild* 'Strife'), in which Sigurd and Brynhild die and Sigurd enters into Valhöll (B), pp. 178–80. The remaining two selections, twenty stanzas altogether, are from *Guðrúnarkviða en nýja*, concerned with the battle between the Huns on one side and the Niflungs (Burgundians), led by the brothers Gunnar and Högni, with their Goth allies on the other (C, D), pp. 279–81 and 283–7. In *The Legend of Sigurd and Gudrún* stanza numbers are given in separate sequences for the introduction and each of the nine parts of *Sigurd*, but in a single sequence for *Gudrún*.

VÖLSUNGKAVIÐA EN NÝJA OR THE NEW LAY OF THE VÖLSUNGS

[A]

1

Of old was an age
when was emptiness,
there was sand nor sea
nor surging waves;
unwrought was Earth,
unroofed was Heaven —
an abyss yawning,
and no blade of grass.

2

The Great Gods then
began their toil,
the wondrous world
they well builded.
From the South the Sun
from seas rising
gleamed down on grass
green at morning.

3

They hall and hallow
high uptowering,
gleaming-gabled,

golden-posted,
rock-hewn ramparts
reared in splendour,
forge and fortress
framed immortal.

4

Unmarred their mirth
in many a court,
where men they made
of their minds' cunning;
under hills of Heaven
on high builded
they lived in laughter
long years ago.

5

Dread shapes arose
from the dim spaces
over sheer mountains
by the Shoreless Sea,
friends of darkness,
foes immoral,
old, unbegotten,
out of ancient void.

6

To the world came war:
the walls of Gods
giants beleaguered;
joy was ended.
The mountains were moved,
mighty Ocean
surged and thundered,
the Sun trembled.

7

The Gods gathered
on golden thrones,
of doom and death

deeply pondered,
how fate should be fended,
their foes vanquished,
their labour healed,
light rekindled.

8

In forge's fire
of flaming wrath
was heaviest hammer
hewn and wielded.
Thunder and lightning
Thór the mighty
flung among them,
felled and sundered.

9

In fear then fled they,
foes immortal,
from the walls beaten
watched unceasing;
ringed Earth around
with roaring sea
and mountains of ice
on the margin of the world.

*

10

A seer long silent
her song upraised —
the halls hearkened —
on high she stood.
Of doom and death
dark words she spake,
of the last battle
of the leaguered Gods.

11

'The horn of Heimdal
I hear ringing;
the Blazing Bridge
bends neath horsemen;
the Ash is groaning,
his arms trembling,
the Wolf waking,
warriors riding.

12

The sword of Surt
smoketh redly;
the slumbering Serpent
in the sea moveth;
a shadowy ship
from the shores of Hell
legions bringeth
to the last battle.

13

The wolf Fenrir
waits for Ódin,
for Frey the fair
the flames of Surt;
the deep Dragon
shall be doom of Thór —
shall all be ended,
shall Earth perish?

14

If in day of Doom
one deathless stands,
who death hath tasted
and dies no more,
the serpent-slayer,
seed of Ódin,
then all shall not end,
nor Earth perish.

15

On his head shall be helm,
in his hand lightning,
afire his spirit,
in his face splendour.
The Serpent shall shiver
and Surt waver,
the Wolf be vanquished
and the world rescued.'

*

16

The Gods were gathered
on guarded heights,
of doom and death
deep they pondered.
Sun they rekindled,
and the silver Moon
they set to sail
on seas of stars.

17

Frey and Freyia
fair things planted,
trees and flowers,
trembling grasses;
Thór in chariot
thundered o'er them
through Heaven's gateways
to the hills of stone.

18

Ever would Ódin
on earth wander
weighed with wisdom
woe foreknowing,
the Lord of lords
and leaguered Gods,
his seed sowing,
sire of heroes.

19

Valhöll he built
vast and shining;
shields the tiles were,
shafts the rafters.
Ravens flew thence
over realms of Earth;
at the doors an eagle
darkly waited.

20

The guests were many:
grim their singing,
boar's-flesh eating,
beakers draining;
mighty ones of Earth
mailclad sitting
for one they waited,
the World's chosen.

Here we meet some of the Norse Gods. Thór wields thunder and lightning. His father, Ódin, the Allfather in Norse mythology, is accompanied by ravens who act as his eyes and ears. Heimdal (Heimdallr), sentinel of the Gods, stands on Bifröst, a blazing rainbow bridge between Midgard (Earth, the world of Men) and Ásgard (the land of the Gods, or Æsir); but at Ragnarök, the day of Doom, the bridge will break beneath fire-giants riding across from their land of Múspell, and Heimdal and the treacherous God Loki will die by each other's hand. Frey (Freyr) and his twin sister Freyia (Freya) are associated with fertility, among other attributes. Valhöll (Valhalla) is a majestic hall in Asgard presided over by Ódin, in which warriors killed in battle reside until the day of Ragnarök ('the guests were many'); its roof is made of shields, its rafters are spear-shafts, and above the doors is an eagle.

The 'Ash' is Yggdrasil, the World Tree, the centre of Creation, with branches stretching over Earth and Heaven. Fenrir, the 'Wolf waking', was chained by the Gods, but at Ragnarök will break free and slay Ódin. Surt (Surtr, Surtur), a demon of fire with a flaming sword, will kill Frey in the last battle. The 'slumbering Serpent' or 'deep Dragon' is the Miðgarðsormr, the Midgard Serpent or World Serpent, an enormous creature coiled within the seas surrounding the

Earth; at Ragnarök Thór will die in battle with it. The 'shadowy ship' is Naglfar, made of dead men's finger- and toenails. Hell (Hel) is a physical place in Norse mythology, in some accounts an underworld beneath one of the three roots of Yggdrasil.

In *The Legend of Sigurd and Gudrún* Christopher Tolkien comments that the introduction to *Völsungakviða en nýja* is similar to the *Völuspá*, the most famous poem in the Elder Edda, in which a wise woman or sibyl tells of the creation of the world, of the Gods, and of the prophecies surrounding their Doom. But Tolkien inserts 'an entirely original theme: for the sibyl declares . . . that the fate of the world and the outcome of the Last Battle will depend on the presence of "one deathless who death hath tasted and dies no more"; and this is Sigurd, "the serpent-slayer, seed of Ódin", who is "the World's chosen" for whom the mailclad warriors wait in Valhöll'. Tolkien makes it explicit in a note that 'it is Ódin's hope that Sigurd will on the Last Day become the slayer of the greatest serpent of all, *Miðgarðsormr* . . . , and that through Sigurd "a new world will be made possible"' (p. 184). Christopher finds it 'extremely probable' that this 'special function' of Sigurd is associated in his father's own mythology with 'Túrin Turambar, slayer of the great dragon Glaurung, [who] was also reserved for a special destiny, for at the Last Battle he would himself strike down Morgoth, the Dark Lord' (p. 184).

[B]

76

Flames were kindled,
fume was swirling,
a roaring fire
ringed with weeping.
Thus Sigurd passed,
seed of Völsung,
there Brynhild burned:
bliss was ended.

77

On the hell-way hastened
the helméd queen,
never born again
from bleak regions.
In Valhöllu
Völsungs feasted.

'Son's son welcome,
seed of Ódin!'

78

Thus soon came Sigurd
the sword bearing
in glad Valhöll
greeting Ódin.
There feasts he long
at his father's side,
for War waiting,
the World's chosen.

79

When Heimdall's horn
is heard ringing
and the Blazing Bridge
bends neath horsemen,
Brynhild shall arm him
with belt and sword,
a beaker bear him
brimmed with glory.

80

In the day of Doom
he shall deathless stand
who death tasted
and dies no more,
the serpent-slayer,
seed of Ódin:
not all shall end,
nor Earth perish.

81

On his head the Helm,
in his hand lightning,
afire his spirit,
in his face splendour.

When war passeth
in world rebuilt,
bliss shall they drink
who the bitter tasted.

82

Thus passed Sigurd,
seed of Völsung,
hero mightiest,
hope of Ódin.
But woe of Gudrún
through this world lasteth,
to the end of days all shall hear her.

GUÐRÚNARKVIÐA EN NÝJA OR THE NEW LAY OF GUDRÚN

[C] 79

In hall sat Gudrún
at heart weary,
from mood to mood
her mind wavered.
The din she hearkened,
deadly crying,
as back were beaten
the Borgund-lords.

80

Gudrún ‘Little I love them,
long I hated!
A wolf they gave me
for woe’s comfort.
Yet the wolf rends them,
and woe is me!
Woe worth the hour
that of womb I came!’

81

Her hands she wrung
on high standing,
loud called she clear
to lieges there:
Gudrún 'If any honour me
in these evil halls,
let them hold their hands
from this hell-labour!

82

Who would love requite,
who would lies disown,
who remember misery
by these masters wrought,
arm now! arm now!
aid the fearless
betrayed and trapped
by this troll-people!'

83

Atli sat there,
anger burned him;
yet murmurs mounted,
men were rising.
Goths were there many:
griefs they remembered,
wars in Mirkwood
and wars of old.

84

From the hall striding
high they shouted,
foes turned to friends
fiercely greeted:
'Goths and Niflungs
our gods helping
will hew the Huns
to hell's shadow!'

85

The few and fearless
fiercely answered
(their backs were driven
to the builded walls):
Niflungs 'Friends, come welcome!
The feast is high.
Now songs let us sing
of our sires of yore.'

86

Of the Goths' glory
Gunnar sang there;
of Iormunrek
earth-shadowing king;
of Angantýr
and old battles,
of Dylgja, Dúnheið,
and Danpar's walls.

In *The Legend of Sigurd and Gudrún* Christopher Tolkien examines the sources of this lay, calling it 'essentially a complex interweaving of the Eddaic poems *Atlakviða* and *Atlamál*, together with some wholly independent developments' (p. 311). In our selection above, the presence of Goth warriors at Atli's court, on whom Gudrún calls for aid, is a new element introduced by the author. The Niflung leaders are the 'Borgund-lords' (Burgundian lords). *Iormunrek* (*Jörmunrekkr*) is the Norse form of the name of Ermanaric, king of the Ostrogoths in the fourth century, who faced the Huns on the South Russian plains; Christopher Tolkien interprets 'earth-shadowing' to refer to the vastness of the king's realm. The other names in stanza 86 are from *The Battle of the Goths and the Huns*, a Norse poem (*Hlöðskviða*) within *Heiðreks Saga* (*Hervarar Saga*): Angantýr was a Gothic king, Dylgja and Dúnheið (Dúnheiðr) sites of great battles. 'Danpar's walls' derives from the Gothic name of the river Dnieper (Norse *Danparstaðir*). The Goths and Huns also fought in Mirkwood, Norse *Mirkviðr*, identified by scholars as a wooded region in Ukraine.

Later in the lay, the Niflung and Goth warriors led by Gunnar and Högni sweep through Atli's halls. They spare Atli's life only at Gudrún's plea.

[D]

91

Gudrún 'If for wrongs ye wrought
ruth now moves you,
doom forestall not!
This deed forego!'
Gunnar & Högni 'At our sister's prayer
let him slink away!
Woman's robes ward him,
not warrior's mail!'

92

Forth went Atli,
anguish gnawed him;
to Gudrún Högni
said grim farewell:
Högni 'Thy price is paid,
thy prayer granted!
At life's forfeit
we have loosed our foe.'

*

93

Forth sent Atli
his errand-riders;
Hunland hearkened,
hosts were arming.
Gallowsfowl to gladden
Goths and Niflungs
from the hall they hurled
the Hunnish corpses.

94

Daylight drew dim,
dark shadows walked
in echoing halls
that Atli loved.
In need most dire
the Niflung lords
doom awaited;
the doors were shut.

95

Night lapped the world
and noiseless town;
under ashen moonlight
the owls hooted.
At guarded doorways
Gunnar and Högni
silent sat they
sleepless waiting.

96

First spoke Högni:
Hogni 'Are these halls afire?
Of day untimely
doth the dawn smoulder?
Do dragons in Hunland
deadly flaming
wind here their way?
Wake, O heroes!'

97

Gunnar answered:
Gunnar 'Guard the doorways!
Here dawn nor dragon
dreadly burneth;
the gabled houses
are gloom-shrouded,
under ailing moon
the earth is shadowed.

98

There is tramp of men
torches bearing,
clink of corslet,
clank of armour.
There is crying of ravens,
cold howls the wolf,
shields are shimmering,
shafts uplifted.'

99

Gunnar & Högni

'Wake now, wake now!
War is kindled.
Now helm to head,
to hand the sword.
Wake now, warriors,
wielding glory!
To wide Valhöll
ways lie open.'

*

100

At the dark doorways
they dinned and hammered;
there was clang of swords
and crash of axes.
The smiths of battle
smote the anvils;
sparked and splintered
spears and helmets.

101

In they hacked them,
out they hurled them,
bears assailing,
boars defending.
Stones and stairways
streamed and darkened;
day came dimly —
the doors were held.

102

Five days they fought
few and dauntless;
the doors were riven,
dashed asunder.
They barred them with bodies,
bulwarks piling
of Huns and Niflungs
hewn and cloven.

'This part of the narrative', Christopher Tolkien comments,

> is entirely independent of the Norse sources. Atli, being released, now sent for reinforcements ([stanza] 93), while the Niflungs held the doors of the hall (95) – and in this the German tradition of the legend appears, but strongly influenced by the Old English poetic fragment known as *The Fight at Finnsburg* (which is not in itself in any way connected with the Niflung legend). [*The Legend of Sigurd and Gudrún*, p. 324]

Tolkien's composition of his 'New Lays' was an opportunity to use a particular metrical form known as *fornyrðislag*. This is one of three metres found in the Elder Edda; its name may mean 'old story metre' or 'old lore metre'. Tolkien himself explained that 'the norm of the strophe [stanza] for *fornyrðislag* is four lines (eight half-lines) with a complete pause at the end, and also a pause (not necessarily so marked) at the end of the fourth half-line' (quoted in *The Legend of Sigurd and Gudrún*, p. 48). The Eddaic texts do not follow this plan regularly, but Tolkien does in the 'New Lays'. He also follows the principles of alliteration found in Old English poetry. See further, '*The Fall of Arthur* and *The Legend of Sigurd and Gudrún*: A Metrical Review of Three Modern English Alliterative Poems' by Nelson Goering in *Journal of Inklings Studies* (October 2015).

A17–24: 'Hall and hallow | high uptowering': these are the courts and temples of the Gods (Æsir), towering high. To give an example of an equivalent stanza in the *Völuspá* (*The Elder or Poetic Edda*, edited and translated by Olive Bray (1908), pp. 278–9):

> Hittusk ǽsir   á Iþavelli
> þeirs hörg ok hof   háimbruþu;
> afla lögþu,   auþ smíþuþu,
> tangir skópu   ok tól görþu.
>
> Gathered the gods   on the Fields of Labour;
> they set on high   their courts and temples;
> they founded forges,   wrought rich treasures,
> tongs they hammered   and fashioned tools.

B9: The 'hell-way' (Helvergr) is the road to Hel.

B10: 'Helméd queen': in the *Helreið Brynhildr* ('The Hel-ride of Brynhildr'), one of the poems in the Elder Edda, which describes Brynhild's journey to the afterlife, it is said that she was once called Hildr the helmed, from her headgear.

B13: 'Valhöllu' is a dative form, used here for metrical reasons.

B25: 'Heimdall' is printed thus in *The Legend of Sigurd and Gudrún*, but 'Heimdal' in A81.

C8: 'Borgund-lords', i.e. Burgundian (Niflung) leaders, Gunnar and Högni.

C11–12: 'A wolf they gave me | for woe's comfort': Gudrún refers to Atli, whom she married after the death of her beloved Sigurd.

D15–16: 'At life's forfeit | we have loosed our foe', i.e. we have ensured our death by releasing Atli. Högni speaks unsentimental truth.

D21: A *gallowsfowl*, or *gallows fowl*, more commonly *gallows bird*, is a person who deserves to be hanged (on a gallows), by extension a scoundrel or villain. Compare German *Galgenvogel*.

D83–84: 'Bears assailing, | boars defending', i.e. the Huns attack with the strength of bears, the Niflungs and Goths defend with the ferocity of boars.

132

The Prophecy of the Sibyl (?1931 or ?32)

These twelve stanzas in rhyming couplets are an adaptation, a simplification, and in some respects an imaginative expansion of the later part of the *Völuspá* or 'Prophecy of the Sibyl', the first of the poems in the Elder Edda. In the *Völuspa* Ódin, chief of the Gods, consults a *völva*, an oracle or seeress, who recounts the creation of the nine worlds, the World Tree Yggdrasil, the Earth and the heavens, Dwarves, Gods, and Men. She tells Ódin some of his own secrets, and foretells events of the day of Doom, when dark forces will battle with the old Gods and defeat them. The sun will fail, the Earth founder, and the stars fall, and evil men will be punished, but the Earth will rise again from the Ocean and the younger Gods will build anew.

The Prophecy of the Sibyl exists as a single, decorated manuscript, with no drafts extant. Christopher Tolkien included it in *The Legend of Sigurd and Gudrún*, pp. 364–7, from which we have taken its text, as a companion to the first section (*Upphaf*) of *Völsungakviða en nýja* (poem no. 131).

From the East shall come the Giant of old
and shield of stone before him hold;
the Serpent that the world doth bind
in towering wrath shall him unwind
and move the Outer Sea profound,
till all is loosed that once was bound.

Unloosed at last shall then set forth
the ship of shadow from the North;
the host of Hel shall cross the sea
and Loki shall from chain be free,
and with the wolf shall monsters all
upon the world then ravening fall.

Then Surtur from the South shall fare
and tree-devouring fire shall bear
that bright as sun on swords shall shine
in battle of the hosts divine;

the hills of stone shall bend their head;
all men the paths of death shall tread.

Then darkened shall the sunlight be,
and Earth shall founder under sea,
and from the cloven heavens all
the gleaming stars shall flee and fall;
the steam shall rise in roaring spires
and heaven's roof be licked with fires.

*

A house there is that sees no sun,
dark-builded on the beaches dun
where cold waves wash the Deadly Shore,
and northward looks its shadowy door;
the louver poisoned rain lets fall,
of woven serpents in the wall.

Laden in heavy streams there wade
men perjured, men who have betrayed
the trust of friend; and there the coward
and wolvish murderer is devoured:
the dragon who yet Yggdrasil
gnaws at the roots there takes his fill.

Dim-flying shall that dragon haste
over the beaches dark and waste,
up from the Nether-fells shall spring
bearing those corpses under wing,
then plunge, and sea close o'er his head
for ever, o'er the doomed and dead.

*

At last once more uprising slow
the Earth from Ocean green shall grow,
and falls of water shimmering pour
from her high shoulders to the shore;
the eagle there with lonely cry
shall hunt the fish on mountains high.

The younger gods again shall meet
in Idavellir's pastures sweet,
and tales shall tell of ancient doom,
the Serpent and the fire and gloom,
and that old king of Gods recall
his might and wisdom ere the fall.

There marvellous shall again be found
cast in the grass upon the ground
the golden chess wherewith they played
when Ásgard long ago was made,
when all their courts were filled with gold
in the first merriment of old.

A house I see that standeth there
bright-builded, than the sun more fair:
o'er Gimlé shine its tiles of gold,
its halls no grief nor evil hold,
and there shall worthy men and true
in living days delight pursue.

Unsown shall fields of wheat grow white
when Baldur cometh after night;
the ruined halls of Ódin's host,
the windy towers on heaven's coast,
shall golden be rebuilt again,
all ills be healed in Baldur's reign.

On the day of Doom, the old Gods' enemies will come for battle, such as the giants who live in other lands far beyond the Gods' home in Ásgard. 'The Serpent that the world doth bind' is the Miðgarðsormr, a creature coiled within the Ocean surrounding the Earth. The 'ship of shadow' is Naglfar, made of dead men's finger- and toenails, which will carry the host of Hel, the Norse underworld. The treacherous Loki, who had been chained by the Gods, will be freed also to attack, as will the wolf Fenrir. Surtur (Surt), a great demon from Múspell, will wield his fiery sword. Lines 25 to 30 describe Náströnd (the 'Deadly Shore'), a place in Hel where the dragon Niðhoggr lives, chewing on corpses and gnawing at the roots of Yggdrasil; a hall built there is made of serpents. Náströnd is where the dead are sent who have committed the crimes mentioned in lines 31 to 36. Idavellir, the meeting-place of the Gods, is sometimes rendered as *Iðavöllr*.

The ‘old king of Gods’ is Ódin. Gimlé (or Gimli) is the most beautiful place in Ásgard yet to be, where worthy survivors of Ragnarök are foretold to live. Baldur the Beautiful, a son of Ódin, had been slain but is to return from the dead when the world is reborn.

9: ‘Hel’ is spelled thus here, but ‘Hell’ in no. 131.

13: The fire-demon is named ‘Surtur’ here, ‘Surt’ in no. 131.

29: Here *louver* (not *louvre*) is probably a slatted window or other opening of this sort, meant to admit air but not rain. It is simpler to define it as ‘aperture’.

133

Bleak Heave the Billows (*c.* 1932)

Bleak Heave the Billows is another short poem by Tolkien found in the Gordon archive at Leeds.

Bleak heave the Billows
under black mountains,
a wilderness of waves;
Sheer stand the shores
by shouting seas
in lands where dwell the lost.

★

There are masts in the mist,
moonsilvered souls,
a light of lanterns dim;
On a gleaming gunwale
a glint of shields,
a white foaming furrow.

★

There are harps humming,
a hail fading;
a silent night of seas.
The winds have waned,
a wanderer has passed
to seas unsoiled by men.

This work may be simply an exercise in alliterative verse. And yet, its imagery and vocabulary, and especially its elegiac mood, call to mind two other alliterative poems, the Old English *Wanderer* and *Seafarer*, preserved in the tenth-century Exeter Book manuscript, a combined edition of which Tolkien and Gordon planned to make for the series Methuen's Old English Library. In the first poem, a solitary wanderer is far from his own land, lordless, bereft of friends and fellow warriors. He recalls his kinsmen, but as he greets them they fade, and he sees only waves and sea-birds; his world is desolate, and he contemplates the swiftness of death. In the second, the speaker recalls his life at sea, the crashing waves, cold, storm, sorrow, and loneliness; a seafarer faces the dangers and discomforts of life as one prepares oneself for death. Tolkien and Gordon began to prepare their edition around 1932, and it was listed by Methuen as forthcoming from 1933 until at least 1937. In the event, most of the work was done by Gordon, and it was left unfinished when he died in 1938. His widow, herself a talented scholar, published an edition of *The Seafarer* alone in 1960, while Tolkien's students T.P. Dunning and A.J. (Alan) Bliss edited *The Wanderer* in 1969.

The single manuscript of *Bleak Heave the Billows* bears no date or other evidence for dating; the Leeds archivists assign it arbitrarily to *c.* 1924, when both men were on the Leeds English School faculty. But it seems possible – and we can only suppose – that Tolkien and Gordon's joint project, concerned with two poems Tolkien knew well since he was an undergraduate (they were set texts), inspired him to compose some alliterative lines of his own in a similar mood, hence our placement of the work at this point in our book.

13: This line read, before revision (possibly altered in the course of writing), 'Harps are humming'.

134

Looney · *The Sea-Bell* (*c.* 1932 or 33–1961)

The earliest version of this intriguing poem is a manuscript written quickly on two pages and entitled *Looney*. That it was set down with little hesitation may suggest that there were still earlier workings, no longer extant. We give this text as A, including revisions Tolkien made in the course of writing.

[A] Where have you been? What have you seen,
walking in rags down the street?
I've been to a land, and cold was the strand
where no men were, me to greet.
I walked in a wood that silent stood
and no leaf bore; bare were the boughs.
There did I sit wandering in wit,
owls went by to their hollow house.
I [wandered >] journeyed away a year and a day
(shadows were on me, stones beneath)
under the hills, over the hills:
wind whistled [low >] cold through the heath,
Birds there were flying, ceaselessly crying;
voices I heard in the grey caves
Down by the shore. Waters were frore,
mist was there lying on the long waves.
There lay a boat, empty afloat,
I sat me therein; swift did it swim,
Sailless it fled, oarless it sped
and the stony beaches faded dim.
It bore me away wetted with spray,
wrapped in the mist to another land.
Stars were there glimmering, the shore was shining,
moon on the foam, silver the sand.
I gathered me stones whiter than bones,
pearls and crystals and glittering shells;
I climbed into meadows fluttered with shadows;
culling there flowers with shivering bells,
Garnering the leaves and grasses in sheaves
I clad me in raiment jewel green;

Purple and gold did my body enfold;
stars were in my eyes and the moon sheen.
There [??? >] many a song all the night long
passed in the valley. There [were >] went many things
Running to and fro: hares white as snow
voles out of holes, moths on their wings
with lantern eyes; in sudden surprise
badgers were staring from their dark doors;
There was dancing there, wings in the air,
feet going quick on the green floors.
But I was alone, far from my home.
Laden with riches, robbed of the sun
I sought for the boat, still did it float
Tossed in the water. Swift did it run
[Away >] Carrying me over perilous sea
passing great ships laden with light,
Coming to haven, dark as a raven
silent as an owl, deep in the night.
Houses were shuttered, wind muttered,
Roads were empty; I sat on a stair
In pattering rain counting my gain:
only withering leaves and pebbles were there
[*deleted:* But far out
[*deleted:* ?still in a shell I heard]
I keep still a shell and hear there the spell
Echoing far, as down the street
Ragged I walk to myself I talk
seldom they speak, men that I meet.

Tolkien wrote new rough workings for the poem at the top of the first page of manuscript A and at the foot of its second page. These include references to a dark cloud, a hurrying wind, and a boat spinning in the tide, among other elements which appear in the second version of the work (B), here incorporating Tolkien's concurrent revisions.

[B] 'Where have you been, what have you seen,
walking in rags down the street?'
'I have been to a land where cold was the strand,
where no men were me to greet.
I came on a boat empty afloat
I sat me therein; swift did it swim,

Sailless it fled, oarless it sped;
  the stony beaches faded dim.
It bore me away wetted with spray,
  wrapped in mist to another land.
Stars were glimmering, the shore was shimmering,
  moon on the foam, silver the sand.
I gathered me stones whiter than bones,
  pearls and crystals, glittering shells.
I climbed into meadows fluttered with shadows;
  culling there flowers with shivering bells,
Garnering leaves and grasses in sheaves
  I clad me in raiment jewel green.
My body enfolding in purple and gold;
  stars were in my eyes, and the moon sheen.
There went a song all the night long
  down in the valley; and many a thing
Running to and fro: hares white as snow,
  voles out of holes, moths on the wing
With lantern eyes; in sudden surprise
  badgers were staring out of dark doors;
There was dancing there, wings in the air,
  feet going quick on the green floors.
There came a dark cloud. I shouted aloud;
  there was no answer, as onward I went.
In my ears dinned a hurrying wind;
  my hair was a-blowing my back was bent,
I walked in a wood that silent stood
  and no leaf bore; bare were the boughs.
There did I sit wandering in wit;
  owls went by to their hollow house.
I journeyed away for a year and a day —
  shadows were on me, stones beneath —
under the hills, over the hills,
  and wind a-whistling through the heath.
Birds there were flying, ceaselessly crying,
  voices I heard in the grey caves
Down by the shore. The water was frore,
  mist was there lying on the long waves.
There stood the boat, still did it float
  in the tide spinning, on the water tossing.

I sat me therein. Swift did it swim
the waves climbing, the seas crossing
Passing old hulls clustered with gulls
as the great ships laden with light,
Coming to haven dark as a raven,
silent as (an) owl, deep in the night.
Houses were shuttered, wind (round them) muttered,
roads were (all) empty. I sat on a stair
In pattering rain, counting my gain:
only withering leaves and pebbles were there.
I keep still a shell and hear there the spell
echoing far, as down the street
Ragged I walk. To myself I (must) talk
for seldom they speak, men that I meet.

In version A, the protagonist tells of lonely wandering before he finds the boat, then he describes his journey to the other land and the land itself, before his return. His experience in the silent wood, and hearing voices by the shore, seem to have occurred before he goes upon the water. In contrast, version B makes it clear that all of the speaker's solitary travels occur in the otherworld. The new text also introduces elements such as a dark cloud and the protagonist shouting, and there is a stronger suggestion of unseen beings among the emptiness.

Readers of *Smith of Wootton Major* will find similarities between that late work by Tolkien and both *Looney* and *The Sea-Bell*, especially in the exploration of the otherworld and the traveller's encounter with a wind. But Smith made no sea journey – Faery was next to his village of Wootton Major – and except by the hunting Wind, he was welcomed, for he had swallowed a Faery star as a boy. Eventually Smith must give the star back, so that it might pass to another worthy child; he never returns to Faery, but devotes himself to family and forge.

Tolkien marked manuscript B of *Looney* with revisions, carrying most of these into a third manuscript and making further changes as he wrote. That copy in turn received minimal revision, and was followed by a typescript made by Tolkien on his Hammond machine, also with revisions, including stanza breaks, the capitalization of every line, and many changes to punctuation. In our notes we will refer to these copies as B^1 and B^2. Tolkien sent the typescript to the *Oxford Magazine*, who published *Looney* in its number for 18 January 1934, p. 340. We give the *Oxford Magazine* text as C.

[C] 'Where have you been: what have you seen,
Walking in rags down the street?'

'I come from a land where cold was the strand,
Where no men were me to greet.

I came on a boat empty afloat.
I sat me thereon; swift did it swim;
Sail-less it fled, oar-less it sped;
The stony beaches faded dim.

It bore me away, wetted with spray,
Wrapped in the mist, to another land:
Stars were glimmering; the shore was shimmering.
Moon on the foam, silver the sand.
I gathered me stones whiter than bones,
Pearls and crystals and glittering shells;
I climbed into meadows fluttered with shadows,
Culling there flowers with shivering bells,
Garnering leaves and grasses in sheaves.
I clad me in raiment jewel-green,
My body enfolding in purple and gold;
Stars were in my eyes, and the moonsheen.

There was many a song all the night long
Down in the valley, many a thing
Running to and fro: hares white as snow,
Voles out of holes, moths on the wing
With lantern eyes. In quiet surprise
Badgers were staring out of dark doors.
There was dancing there, wings in the air,
Feet going quick on the green floors.

There came a dark cloud. I shouted aloud;
Answer was none, as onward I went.
In my ears dinned a hurrying wind;
My hair was a-blowing, my back was bent.
I walked in a wood; silent it stood
And no leaf bore; bare were the boughs.
There did I sit wandering in wit;
Owls went by to their hollow house.

I journeyed away for a year and a day —
    Shadows were on me, stones beneath —
Under the hills, over the hills,
    And the wind a-whistling through the heath.
Birds there were flying, ceaselessly crying;
    Voices I heard in the grey caves
Down by the shore. The water was frore,
    Mist was there lying on the long waves.
There stood the boat, still did it float
    In the tide spinning, on the water tossing.
I sat me therein; swift did it swim
    The waves climbing, the seas crossing,
Passing old hulls clustered with gulls,
    And the great ships laden with light,
Coming to haven, dark as a raven,
    Silent as owl, deep in the night.

Houses were shuttered, wind round them muttered:
    Roads were all empty. I sat by a door
In pattering rain, counting my gain:
    Only withering leaves and pebbles I bore,
And a single shell, where I hear still the spell
    Echoing far, as down the street
Ragged I walk. To myself I must talk,
    For seldom they speak, men that I meet.'

Elsewhere we have described *The Sea-Bell*, first published in *The Adventures of Tom Bombadil and Other Verses from the Red Book* in 1962, as a revision and expansion of *Looney*. While this is strictly true, it does not do justice (as we now see from its drafts) to the remarkable amount of labour Tolkien put into crafting the later poem around the central concept and selected parts of its predecessor, and at twice its length. It is evident that he returned to *Looney* in 1961, while reviewing his existing poems as candidates for the *Bombadil* collection. In a late hand, he marked up a copy of the *Oxford Magazine* printing, apparently intending at first to make only a few minor changes to the poem. Then his ambition, or inspiration, grew, and he addressed the work with vigour. If he made any manuscript drafts, they have not survived; instead, he developed the poem through five typescripts, even in the final typescript he sent to his publisher. (He had been suffering from arthritis, and came to find using a typewriter more comfortable than writing with a pen.) For three of these drafts, only the first page is extant, probably of three for each version, and another has only its first two pages. The fifth draft alone is complete. Each copy was then revised, in the typewriter or in manuscript, and some of the changes are extensive.

Here, as D, we give all that survives of the first draft, entitled *Sea-Bell* (without the definite article), as it stood before revision.

[D] I walked by the Sea, and it seemed to me
that a star was mirrored in the wet sand:
It was a white shell like a sea-bell;
trembling it lay in my wet hand.
In my fingers shaken I heard waken
the bell within, by some harbour bar
In a buoy swinging, a call ringing
over endless seas, faint now and far.

I saw then a boat to the shingle float
on the night-tide, empty and grey.
'It is later than late! Why do we wait?'
I leapt in and cried: 'Bear me away!'

It bore me away, wetted with spray,
wrapped in a mist, to a strange land:
Stars were glimmering, the short shimmering,
moon on the foam
White it glimmered, and the sea simmered
as with stars uncounted in a silver net;
Builded of stone pale as ruel-bone
the cliffs gleamed with moonfoam wet

To the hidden haven of Ever-even
past beacons dim and sea-bells
The boat bore me to a long shore
There roses of coral and opal shells
and the glittering sand slid through my hands
Down from the hills ran green rills;
water I drank in mossy wells

In the final stanza above, Tolkien abandoned regular indentation and became uncertain of his text. At the foot of the page, he typed these lines freely:

By a slow river trailing long weeks
I heard a sea-bell swing in the swell
saw beacon dim oan [i.e. on an] empty quay
the shore lay wide in the ebb(ing) tide
and there I wandered lonely and free.
The glittering sand slid through my ha[n]d,
dust of pearl and jewel-grist
[*deleted:* many a triton-flute under my fott [*i.e.* foot]
    many a triton flute]
trumpets   shells of opa[l], roses of coral
            flutes of green and amethyst
under the cliff-eaves there were hidden caves
weedcurtained, darkling grey.
Down from the hills, ran green rills;
their water I drank, and went on my way,
climbing into meadows
under evening-shadows; there flowers lay like golden stars

A *triton flute* (or *triton's trumpet*), named after the Greek god of the sea, is a kind of large shell, or conch, which can be blown into like a horn.

In the next typescript, the first fifteen lines are identical to those in text D, but the remainder departs from D in several respects. We give this new version as E, as it read before revision. From line 19 Tolkien again became unclear of his direction.

[E] I walked by the Sea, and it seemed to me
    that a star was mirrored in the wet sand:
It was a white shell like a sea-bell;
    trembling it lay in my wet hand.
In my fingers shaken I heard waken
    the bell within, by some harbour bar
In a buoy swinging, a call ringing
    over endless seas, faint now and far.

I saw then a boat to the shingle float
    on the night-tide, empty and grey.
'It is later than late! Why do we wait?'
    I leapt in and cried: 'Bear me away!'

It bore me away, wetted with spray,
    wrapped in a mist, to a strange land:

Stars were glimmering, the shore shimmering,
moon on the foam, silver the sand.
And many a stone white as ruel-bone,
roses of coral, and opal shells.
I climbed into meadows
I climbed into hills, drinking from rills
of sweet waters, and passed ever on,
The sea leaving into the fields of evening

I climbed into meadows in the evening shadows,
drinking the waters of secret wells

Down from the hills ran green rills;
water I drank in mossy wells.
I climbed into meadows in the evening shadows
flowers there were like golden stars,
And in a blue pool glassy and cool
like floating moons the nenuphars
Trees I saw sleeping, and the willows weeping
by slow rivers of long weeds
the green spears guarding the meres
gladdon swords and arrow-reeds.

gladdon-swords guarding the fords,
and green spears and arrow-reeds
I gathered the leaves and grasses in sheaves
and made me a mantle of jewel-green
a tall wand to hold and a flag of gold.
My eyes were as stars and the moonsheen

When making his third draft, Tolkien incorporated most of the revisions he had added to E and also made many other changes as he typed. We have transcribed this new text as F, as it stood before revision; its title was now *The Sea-Bell*. Compared with later, complete texts, F is lacking its final two stanzas.

[F] I walked by the Sea, and there was borne to me
a star fallen in the wet sand:
It was a white shell like a sea-bell,
trembling it lay in my wet hand.
In my fingers shaken I heard waken
the bell within, as in harbour bar

In a buoy swinging, a call ringing
over endless seas, faint now and far.

I saw then a boat to the shingle float
on the night-tide, empty and grey.
'It is later than late! Why do we wait?'
I leapt in and cried: 'Bear me away!'

It bore me away, wetted with spray,
wrapped in a mist, wound in a sleep
To a forgotten strand in a strange land
in the twilight beyond the deep.
White it glimmered, and the sea simmered
with stars flickering in a silver net;
reared of stone pale as ruel-bone
the cliffs gleamed with moon-foam wet.
I heard a sea-bell swing in the swell
saw a dim beacon on an empty quay
A shore lay wide in the ebb-tide,
and there I wandered, lonely and free.
The glittering sand slid through my hand,
dust of pearl and jewel-grist,
Trumpets of opal, roses of coral,
flutes of green and amethyst.
But under cliff-eaves there were hidden caves,
weed-curtained, darkling grey.

Down from far hills ran green rills;
their water I drank, and went on my way,
Climbing into meadows of fluttering shadows;
there flowers lay like golden stars,
And on a pool glassy and cool
like floating moons the nenuphars.
Alders were sleeping, and the willows weeping
by a slow river of silver weeds;
Gladdon-swords guarded the fords,
and green spears and arrow-reeds.

There was many a song all the evening long
down in the valley; many a thing
Running to and fro: hares white as snow,
voles out of holes, moths on the wing

With lantern eyes. In quiet surprise
brocks were staring out of dark doors.
I heard dancing there, music in the air;
feet going quick on the green floors.
Then I gathered leaves and great rush-sheaves,
made me a mantle of jewel-green,
A tall wand to hold with a flag of gold;
and my eyes shone like the star-sheen.
I strode to a mound in the dancing ground,
and shrill as a call at cock-crow
Proudly I cried: 'Why do you hide?
Why do none speak, wherever I go?
Here now I stand, king of this land,
with gladdon-sword and reed-mace.
Come forth all, hear now my call!
Bring me a voice, show me a face!'

Night fell like a cloud. I shouted aloud,
but no answer heard, as flying I went.
In my ears dinned a withering wind;
my hair was blowing, my back was bent.
I came to a wood: silent it stood
in its dead leaves; bare were its boughs.
There must I sit, wandering in wit,
while owls snored in their hollow house.
For a year and a day there must I stay,
beetles were tapping in the rotten trees,
Spiders were weaving, and in the mould heaving
puffballs loomed about my knees.
At last there was light in my long night,
and I saw my hair hanging grey.
'Bent though I be, I would find the sea;
I have lost myself, and know not the way.
But let me be gone!' Then I stumbled on,
like a blackbat shadow was over me
stones beneath; on the whistling heath
and the ragged briars I tried to cover me
My back was torn and my knees worn
my burden heavy upon my back
When the rain in my face took a salt taste
and I smelled the smell of sea-wrack

We will pass over the surviving part of the fourth, further revised typescript of *The Sea-Bell*, again so titled, as its text is nearly identical to that of the final draft (differences are described in our notes, in which the fourth typescript is called F[1]). Remarkably, Tolkien marked identical changes to both initial pages, which he carried into the published text. The fifth typescript contains the penultimate version of the complete poem, incorporating revisions Tolkien wrote or typed on F; we have transcribed this as G, as it appeared before revision.

[G] I walked by the Sea, and there was borne to me
a star fallen in the wet sand:
It was a white shell like a sea-bell,
trembling it lay in my wet hand.
In my fingers shaken I heard waken
the bell within, as in harbour bar
in a buoy swinging, a call ringing
over endless seas, faint now and far.

I saw then a boat to the shingle float
on the night-tide, empty and grey.
'It is later than late! Why do we wait?'
I leapt in and cried: 'Bear me away!'

It bore me away, wetted with spray,
wrapped in a mist, wound in a sleep,
to a forgotten strand in a strange land
in the twilight beyond the deep.
I heard a sea-bell swing in the swell
a beacon shone on a ruined quay,
a shore lay wide in a slow tide,
and there I wandered, lonely and free.
White it glimmered, and the sea simmered
with star-mirrors flickering in a silver net;
cliffs of stone pale as ruel-bone
in the moon-foam were gleaming wet.
Glittering sand slid through my hand,
dust of pearl and jewel-grist,
trumpets of opal, roses of coral,
flutes of green and amethyst.

But under cliff-eaves there were hidden caves,
weed-curtained, darkling grey.
Down from far hills ran green rills;
their water I drank, and went on my way,
climbing into meadows of fluttering shadows;
there flowers lay there like golden stars,
and on a pool glassy and cool
like floating moons the nenuphars.
Alders were sleeping, and the willows weeping
by a slow river of rippling weeds;
gladdon-swords guarded the fords,
and green spears, and arrow-reeds.

I heard the echo of song all the evening long
down in the valley; there was many a thing
running to and fro: hares white as snow,
voles out of holes; moths on the wing
With lantern-eyes; in quiet surprise
brocks were staring out of dark doors.
I heard dancing there, music in the air,
feet going quick on the green floors.
But wherever I came 'twas ever the same:
the feet fled, and all was still.
Never a greeting, only the fleeting
pipes, voices, horns on the hill.

Of river-leaves and the rush-sheaves
I made me a mantle of jewel-green,
a tall wand to hold, with a flag of gold;
my eyes shone like the star-sheen.
With flowers crowned I stood on a mound,
and shrill as a call at cock-crow
proudly I cried: 'Why do you hide?
Why do none speak wherever I go?
Here now I stand, king of this land,
with gladdon-sword and reed-mace.
Answer my call! Come forth all!
Speak to me words! Show me a face!'

Black came a cloud as a night-shroud.
Like a dark mole groping I went,

to the ground falling, on my hands crawling
    with eyes blind and my back bent.
I crept to a wood: silent it stood
    in its dead leaves; bare were its boughs.
There must I sit, wandering in wit,
    while owls snored in a hollow house.
For a year and a day there must I stay:
    beetles were tapping in the rotten trees,
spiders were weaving, and in the mould heaving
    puffballs loomed about my knees.

At last there was light in my long night,
    and I saw my hair hanging grey.
'Bent though I be, I would find the Sea!
    I have lost myself, and know not the way,
but let me be gone!' Then I stumbled on.
    Like a hunting bat shadow was over me;
in my ears dinned a withering wind,
    and with ragged briars I tried to cover me.
My hands were torn and my knees worn,
    the years heavy upon my back,
when the rain in my face took a salt taste,
    and I smelled the smell of sea-wrack.

Birds came sailing, mewing, wailing;
    I heard voices in hollow caves,
seals barking, and rocks snarling,
    and spout-holes the gulping of waves.
Dusk came fast; into a mist I passed,
    to land's end my years I bore;
snow was in the air, ice in my hair,
    darkness was lying on the last shore.

There was the boat waiting afloat,
    in the tide lifting, its prow tossing.
Weary I lay as it bore me away,
    the waves climbing, the seas crossing,
passing old hulls clustered with gulls,
    and great ships laden with light,
coming to haven, dark as a raven,
    silent as owl, deep in the night.

Houses were shuttered, wind round them muttered,
roads were empty. I sat by a door
in pattering rain counting my gain;
but in clutched hand all that I bore
was a dull stone, a broken bone,
and a sea-shell silent and dead.
Never will my ear that bell hear,
never my feet that shore tread,
never again, as in sad lane,
in blind alley and in long street
ragged I walk. To myself I talk;
for still they speak not, men that I meet.

Tolkien marked text G more heavily than any of the earlier versions. With these changes, and a small number of others to words or punctuation, he reached the final form of the poem. We give that text (H) as printed in *The Adventures of Tom Bombadil and Other Verses from the Red Book*, pp. 57–60.

[H] I walked by the sea, and there came to me,
as a star-beam on the wet sand,
a white shell like a sea-bell;
trembling it lay in my wet hand.
In my fingers shaken I heard waken
a ding within, by a harbour bar
a buoy swinging, a call ringing
over endless seas, faint now and far.

Then I saw a boat silently float
on the night-tide, empty and grey.
'It is later than late! Why do we wait?'
I leapt in and cried: 'Bear me away!'

It bore me away, wetted with spray,
wrapped in a mist, wound in a sleep,
to a forgotten strand in a strange land.
In the twilight beyond the deep
I heard a sea-bell swing in the swell,
dinging, dinging, and the breakers roar
on the hidden teeth of a perilous reef;
and at last I came to a long shore.

White it glimmered, and the sea simmered
with star-mirrors in a silver net;
cliffs of stone pale as ruel-bone
in the moon-foam were gleaming wet.
Glittering sand slid through my hand,
dust of pearl and jewel-grist,
trumpets of opal, roses of coral,
flutes of green and amethyst.
But under cliff-eaves there were glooming caves,
weed-curtained, dark and grey;
a cold air stirred in my hair,
and the light waned, as I hurried away.

Down from a hill ran a green rill;
its water I drank to my heart's ease.
Up its fountain-stair to a country fair
of ever-eve I came, far from the seas,
climbing into meadows of fluttering shadows:
flowers lay there like fallen stars,
and on a blue pool, glassy and cool,
like floating moons the nenuphars.
Alders were sleeping, and willows weeping
by a slow river of rippling weeds;
gladdon-swords guarded the fords,
and green spears, and arrow-reeds.

There was echo of song all the evening long
down in the valley; many a thing
running to and fro: hares white as snow,
voles out of holes; moths on the wing
with lantern-eyes; in quiet surprise
brocks were staring out of dark doors.
I heard dancing there, music in the air,
feet going quick on the green floors.
But wherever I came it was ever the same:
the feet fled, and all was still;
never a greeting, only the fleeting
pipes, voices, horns on the hill.

Of river-leaves and the rush-sheaves
I made me a mantle of jewel-green,

a tall wand to hold, and a flag of gold;
    my eyes shone like the star-sheen.
With flowers crowned I stood on a mound,
    and shrill as a call at cock-crow
proudly I cried: 'Why do you hide?
    Why do none speak, wherever I go?
Here now I stand, king of this land,
    with gladdon-sword and reed-mace.
Answer my call! Come forth all!
    Speak to me words! Show me a face!'

Black came a cloud as a night-shroud.
    Like a dark mole groping I went,
to the ground falling, on my hands crawling
    with eyes blind and my back bent.
I crept to a wood: silent it stood
    in its dead leaves; bare were its boughs.
There must I sit, wandering in wit,
    while owls snored in their hollow house.
For a year and a day there must I stay:
    beetles were tapping in the rotten trees,
spiders were weaving, in the mould heaving
    puffballs loomed about my knees.

At last there came light in my long night,
    and I saw my hair hanging grey.
'Bent though I be, I must find the sea!
    I have lost myself, and I know not the way,
but let me be gone!' Then I stumbled on;
    like a hunting bat shadow was over me;
in my ears dinned a withering wind,
    and with ragged briars I tried to cover me.
My hands were torn and my knees worn,
    and years were heavy upon my back,
when the rain in my face took a salt taste,
    and I smelled the smell of sea-wrack.

Birds came sailing, mewing, wailing;
    I heard voices in cold caves,
seals barking, and rocks snarling,
    and in spout-holes the gulping of waves.

Winter came fast; into a mist I passed,
to land's end my years I bore;
snow was in the air, ice in my hair,
darkness was lying on the last shore.

There still afloat waited the boat,
in the tide lifting, its prow tossing.
Weary I lay, as it bore me away,
the waves climbing, the seas crossing,
passing old hulls clustered with gulls
and great ships laden with light,
coming to haven, dark as a raven,
silent as snow, deep in the night.

Houses were shuttered, wind round them muttered,
roads were empty. I sat by a door,
and where drizzling rain poured down a drain
I cast away all that I bore:
in my clutching hand some grains of sand,
and a sea-shell silent and dead.
Never will my ear that bell hear,
never my feet that shore tread,
never again, as in sad lane,
in blind alley and in long street
ragged I walk. To myself I talk;
for still they speak not, men that I meet.

In his preface to the *Adventures of Tom Bombadil* collection, Tolkien describes *The Sea-Bell* as 'certainly of hobbit origin', but 'an exception' to the generally 'lighthearted or frivolous' poems Hobbits tended to write or prefer. 'It is the latest piece' in the collection,

> and belongs to the Fourth Age [of Middle-earth, after the destruction of the Ring], but it is included here, because a hand has scrawled at its head *Frodos Dreme*. That is remarkable, and though the piece is most unlikely to have been written by Frodo himself, the title shows that it was associated with the dark and despairing dreams which visited him in March and October during his last three years. But there were certainly other traditions concerning Hobbits that were taken by the 'wandering-madness', and if they ever returned, were afterwards queer and uncommunicable. The thought of the Sea was

> ever-present in the background of hobbit imagination; but fear of it and distrust of all Elvish lore, was the prevailing mood in the Shire at the end of the Third Age. . . . [p. 9]

('March and October' are the anniversaries of Frodo's poisoning by Shelob and his wounding on Weathertop.) This is a clever, if laboured, way to integrate *The Sea-Bell* with the other works in the collection, with some support from *The Lord of the Rings*. As Verlyn Flieger has pointed out, *The Sea-Bell* is 'the dark brother' of Frodo's 'dream or vision in the house of Tom Bombadil of the end of his voyage to the Undying Lands' (*A Question of Time: J.R.R. Tolkien's Road to* Faërie, p. 213). Even earlier in *The Lord of the Rings*, while sleeping at Crickhollow Frodo 'fell into a vague dream' with 'tangled trees' and the sound (but not sight) 'of creatures crawling and snuffling', and 'the sound of the Sea far-off; a sound he had never heard in waking life, though it had often troubled his dreams' (Book I, Chapter 5). In the revised edition of her *Splintered Light: Logos and Language in Tolkien's World* (2002) Flieger associates *The Sea-Bell*

> with the medieval literary convention of the dream vision, the function of which is to imply that truth beyond observable reality is being revealed to the dreaming-voice, and through that voice to the reader. As a scholar and teacher of medieval literature, Tolkien, of course, knew this perfectly well. He was familiar with the dream framework of Langland's *Piers Plowman* and Chaucer's *Book of the Duchess* as well as the mad logic and modern surreality of Lewis Carroll's *Alice* books. He knew that dream is powerfully effective both as real experience and as literary device, for in each case it serves to bypass the rational intellect, speaking directly from the unconscious to the waking mind. [p. 164]

Despite Tolkien's pleading, one cannot quite get away from the feeling that *The Sea-Bell* is very un-Hobbitish, because it is not 'light-hearted or frivilous', though the same could be said about *The Last Ship* (no. 141), or about any one of the darkest of the *Bombadil* poems, probably not by coincidence grouped together at the end of the book (in a class Tolkien termed 'Dubious', rather than 'Bilboish' and 'Sam-like'); and also, in spite of any statement, post- *Lord of the Rings*, that 'the thought of the Sea was ever-present' among Hobbits in general rather than with Frodo in particular. Tolkien himself feared that the poem did not fit well with the rest of his *Bombadil* selection.

On 6 December 1961, only weeks after he sent *The Sea-Bell* to George Allen & Unwin with his first group of poems for the volume, he told the illustrator Pauline Baynes that he considered *The Sea-Bell* the poorest of the several works he had prepared to that date (about half of the whole), and now would not wish to include it – she prepared drawings for it anyway. Then, on 8 December Tolkien suggested to Rayner Unwin that perhaps *The Sea-Bell* ought to be removed as it was 'the vaguer, more subjective and least successful piece' he had submitted. That it was included after all is almost certainly due to a lack of time for Tolkien to prepare a better candidate: he was hard pressed by other business. Since two of the poems he sent to his publisher were ultimately rejected (*The Trees of Kortirion*, no. 40, and *The Dragon's Visit*, no. 107), he just barely managed to satisfy requirements. Six years later, however, W.H. Auden said that he found *The Sea-Bell* 'wonderful', praise indeed from a poet of no small renown, which made Tolkien 'really . . . wag my tail' (letter to Auden, 29 March 1967, *Letters*, p. 533).

We wonder if Tolkien would have been surprised that of all of the *Bombadil* poems, *The Sea-Bell* has received the most attention from critics. It is an emotionally moving work, but also mysterious – and mysteries invite interpretation. What does it mean? If it is a dream, it need not mean anything, though it seems as if it should be more than simply another example of the motif common in fairy-stories, that of a traveller to an otherworld who returns transformed, perhaps after an extraordinary length of time. Within the editorial fiction of his preface that the poems in the *Bombadil* collection were written or collected by Hobbits, and thus connected to *The Lord of the Rings*, Tolkien suggests that *The Sea-Bell* is a manifestation of Frodo's post-traumatic stress following his return from the quest of the Ring. But this was not Tolkien's purpose in writing *Looney*, which predates even the thought of *The Lord of the Rings*, and it was not necessarily his purpose in crafting *The Sea-Bell* out of *Looney*.

In *The Road to Middle-earth* Tom Shippey says that these 'are poems of "disenchantment" (as "The Last Ship" was not), and in both, the speaker, who has been in a magic boat to a far land, finds himself hunted out of it by a "dark cloud", and returned to lonely and ragged craziness, scorned by others' (p. 249).

> In 'The Sea-Bell', though, a whole series of significant changes has been made. For one thing the boat is much more like the boat of Fíriel, the *last* boat; when he sees it the voyager calls out 'It is later than late!', and leaps into it with a new haste. [In

> *Looney* he sits in it simply and without remark.] For another the menacing elements in the far country have been much expanded, with 'glooming caves' seen beneath the cliffs as soon as the speaker lands; in 'Looney' the impression of paradise lasted for a couple of stanzas. The 'Sea-Bell' landscape also includes 'gladdon-swords' (i.e. of wild iris) and 'puffballs' in the mould. [p. 250]

It could also be said that the two poems are cautionary tales, illustrating ideas Tolkien expressed in his 1939 lecture *On Fairy-Stories*, most strongly in a draft text:

> The Land of Fairy Story is wide and deep and high, and is filled with many kings and all manner of men, and beasts, and birds; its seas are shoreless and its stars uncounted, its beauty an enchantment and its peril ever-present; both its joy and sorrow are poignant as a sword. In that land a man may (perhaps) count himself fortunate to have wandered, but its very mystery and wealth make dumb the traveller who would report. And while he is there it is dangerous for him to ask too many questions, lest the gates shut and the keys be lost. The fairy gold (too often) turns to withered leaves when it is brought away. [*Tolkien On Fairy-Stories* (2008), p. 207]

In *An Exploration of Changing Visions of Faërie through His Non-Middle-earth Poetry* Penelope Anne Holdaway points out that the protagonists in the poems behave in ways traditionally taboo in fairy-lands, such as speaking aloud. The hubristic traveller in *The Sea-Bell* is especially guilty, by declaring himself king of the land and demanding that the inhabitants show themselves – which they never do. His immediate punishment is loneliness, and the sentence is extended. At the end of *Looney* the speaker's 'gain' from his visit is 'withering leaves and pebbles' and 'a single shell', while in *The Sea-Bell* the returned traveller has only 'grains of sand, | and a sea-bell silent and dead' – fairy gold, or fairy gems, cannot be taken out of the fairy world. The protagonist of *Looney*, who has been comparatively courteous, at least is left with a shell in which 'the spell' of the distant land can still be heard 'echoing far'; in *The Sea-Bell* the speaker is cut off: 'Never will my ear that bell hear, | never my feet that shore tread, | never again'.

The 'dream' of *The Sea-Bell* may seem to a reader like a nightmare, but to the one who experiences it at first hand 'waking' is a loss. Tom Shippey argues in *The Road to Middle-earth* that *Looney* and *The*

Sea-Bell differ in the results of the protagonists' actions. In the latter, the traveller 'seems in a way guilty, as "Looney" [i.e. the speaker in *Looney*] did not. In both poems the "black cloud" comes, but in the earlier it is for no reason, while in the later it appears to be called, or provoked, by the speaker presumptuously naming himself "king". It casts him down, turns him into a kind of Orfeo-in-the-wilderness [see poem no. 173], till eventually he realises he must find the sea . . .' (p. 250). Shippey also points out that in *The Sea-Bell* the possibility of a return to the otherworld is banned 'even in memory'. He relates this to *Smith of Wootton Major* (published 1967), and to a suggestion that in these works of the 1960s Tolkien had become uncertain about 'the legitimacy of his own mental wanderings' (pp. 250–1). Verlyn Flieger considers this an overstatement, as do we, though she is persuaded by Shippey's association of the voice of *The Sea-Bell* with Tolkien's own.

On her part, Flieger devotes an entire chapter to *The Sea-Bell* in *A Question of Time: J.R.R. Tolkien's Road to* Faërie, and finds the 'bereavement' expressed in *Looney* and *The Sea-Bell* – the loss of connection to Faërie and its wonders – to be 'a dark and bitter counterpart . . . to the feelings of loss and estrangement' Tolkien would have known from his experience in the First World War. 'The lost world is not Faërie but a curious mixture of the world [combatants] left to go to war and the world of mud and death and destruction they found at the front' (pp. 218–19). In *Tolkien and the Great War* John Garth makes the related points that in Tolkien's mythology from its earliest days, Faërie is shown as indifferent to humanity, and in Tolkien's plans for the unfinished *Book of Lost Tales* the mariner Eriol, having visited the otherworld, was to 'eventually become alienated from his kind' (p. 297).

Flieger suggests that the seeds of *Looney* are in Tolkien's *Ides Ælfscýne* (no. 78), 'not just in the theme of the poem, but in the details – the sudden journey by boat, the far-off land, the silver strand, the dim and dreary waves', and 'the motif of exile from Faërie' (*A Question of Time*, p. 217). In that work too the protagonist returns home to 'diminish, grey and alone', though in his case he was away for fifty years, and unlike the travellers in *Looney* and *The Sea-Bell* he did not go over the sea willingly.

'The thought of the Sea' was often in Tolkien's own imagination, as we have seen in other poems in the present book, and as one finds generally in his mythology. The 'glittering sand' and 'dust of pearl and jewel-grist' of *The Sea-Bell*, for example, recall a description of Valinor in *The Silmarillion* (Chapter 5): 'Many jewels the Noldor gave [the Teleri], opals and diamonds and pale crystals, which they strewed upon the shores and scattered in the pools; marvellous were the beaches of Elendë in those days.' We may also compare 'Evereven's lofty hills | where softly silver fountains fall' in the song of Eärendil in *The Lord of the Rings* (see no. 128), again referring to Valinor, with the 'fountain-stair to a country fair of ever-eve' in text H above, as well as 'the hidden haven of Ever-even' in A.

More than one critic has remarked that the dialogue in *Looney* recalls that of Coleridge's *Rime of the Ancient Mariner*, an account told by a 'grey-beard loon'. (The title of the earlier poem, *Looney*, is a judgement on its protagonist, unspoken in the work proper. Some have taken it to be his name, though there is no evidence that this was Tolkien's intent.) Coleridge's Wedding-Guest, however, is compelled to hear the mariner's story, while the speaker in *Looney* tells his tale only after being asked to do so: 'Where have you been: what have you seen, | walking in rags down the street?' In *The Sea-Bell* there is no opening exchange; the traveller is alone, telling his story to himself, and the men he meets 'speak not' to him. By what agency does the boat in *Looney* take the traveller to and from the distant land? He does not seem surprised or upset at his journey, it simply happens. In *The Sea-Bell* he seems to be invited, or enticed, by finding the shell which in the published version 'came' to him, earlier 'was borne' to him, the latter phrase suggesting intent. Traditionally it is said that if one holds a (large) seashell to one's ear one can hear the sound of the sea – some imagination is involved – but the traveller's find trembles in his hand and then rings 'like a sea-bell', that is, like a ship's (brass) bell, or a bell in a navigation buoy.

Christine Davidson observes in '*The Sea-Bell*: A Voyage of Exploration' (1999) that the intriguing image of an 'empty, inviting boat' which allows the traveller to follow his longing 'goes back a long way in fantasy and romance' (p. 12). She cites Sir Thomas Malory's *Morte d'Arthur*, in which Sir Bors hears a voice instructing him to take his way to the sea, to seek Sir Percival. There, 'on the strand he found a ship covered all with white samite [a rich silk], and he alit, and betook him to Jesu Christ. And as soon as he entered into the ship, the ship departed into the sea, and went so fast that him seemed the ship went flying . . .' (Book XVI, Chapter 17).

In her essay 'What Is It but a Dream?: Tolkien's "The Sea-Bell" and Yeats' "The Man Who Dreamed of Faeryland"' (2013) Sue Bridgwater observes that *The Sea-Bell* is filled with the 'imagery of motion – *walked*, *leapt*, *hurried*, *climbing*, *crept*, *stumbled*, and finally *walk* again', and that Tolkien also 'uses many positive images of nature. . . . Hares, voles, moths and badgers people a near-romantic picture of nature and its effect on the beholder; here Tolkien sets up a fall for protagonist and reader, since the tone of the poem is shortly to darken into fear' (p. 127).

In 1967 Tolkien made a professional recording of *The Sea-Bell* for the album *Poems and Songs of Middle Earth*. It was later reissued.

A9: 'A year and a day': in law, a common period of time in which a right or liability is determined. In *Looney* the duration of the traveller's stay in the Otherworld has no physical consequences, but in *The Sea-Bell* he returns with grey hair and a bent back.

A17: Tolkien considered whether to change 'There lay a boat' to 'I came upon a boat'.

A37: 'Lantern eyes': some moths have in their wing patterns spots which resemble eyes, a device thought to have evolved to frighten away predators.

A43: Tolkien considered whether to change 'I sought for the boat' to 'There stood the boat'.

B19: This line originally read 'Purple and gold did my body enfold'.

B48: Tolkien considered whether to change 'climbing' to 'a-climbing' and 'tossing' to 'a-tossing'.

B52–54, 59: The bracketed words in these lines seem to have been so marked in the course of writing, not subsequently.

C3: Tolkien changed 'I have been to a land' to 'I come from a land' in B^2.

C6: 'I sat me thereon' is the reading in B^1, B^2, and C; in A and B it is 'I sat me therein'. On a tearsheet of his poem from the *Oxford Magazine*, Tolkien marked 'thereon' to be changed to 'therein'. Line 47 has 'therein' in versions B and later of *Looney*; Tolkien avoids the issue in *The Sea-Bell*.

C7: 'Sail-less' and 'oar-less' were first hyphenated in B^2.

C21: Tolkien changed this line to 'There was many a song all the night long' in B^1.

C22: Tolkien changed this line to read 'Down in the valley, many a thing' in B^1.

C25: Tolkien changed 'sudden surprise' to 'quiet surprise' in B^2.

C30: Tolkien changed 'there was no answer' (B) to 'But answer was none' in B^1. As typed, B^2 has 'But no answer came', altered in manuscript to 'Answer was none' (as C).

C50: Tolkien changed 'As the great ships' to 'And the great ships' in B^1.

C54: Tolkien changed 'sat on a stair' to 'sat by a door' in B^1.

C56: Tolkien changed 'pebbles were there' to 'pebbles I bore' in B^1. As written, B^1 begins 'But withering leaves', altered in manuscript to 'Only withering leaves' (as C).

C57–58: Tolkien changed these lines to 'And a single shell, where I hear still the spell | Echoing far, as down the street' in B^1.

D15: As typed, 'Stars were' read 'Stars where'. This is one of many typographical errors in the *Sea-Bell* drafts – Tolkien seems to have typed rapidly or carelessly – we have silently corrected.

D16: This line ends abruptly. In A, B, and C, and again in E, 'moon on the foam' is followed by 'silver the sand'. Tolkien abandoned the phrases altogether in F.

D19: 'Ruel-bone', i.e. ivory. In *The Ring of Words: Tolkien and the Oxford English Dictionary* (2006) Peter Gilliver, et al. note that Tolkien would have found a reference to *ruel*, an obsolete word meaning 'ivory (possibly that of the narwhal)', in the etymology for *walrus*, a word on which he worked for a long time while employed by the *Oxford English Dictionary* after the First World War.

D20: 'Moonfoam' (later 'moon-foam'): since the cliffs are wet with this, we suppose it to be spray from the sea. G and H have 'cliffs of stone pale as ruel-bone | in the moon-foam were gleaming wet'. It seems a stretch to associate this element of the 'atmosphere' of *The Sea-Bell* with the *virus lunare* 'moon foam' described by the ancient poet Lucan as foam dropped by the moon (in *Macbeth* a 'vaporous drop'), which was said to have occult uses.

D21: 'Ever-even': here, probably, eternal twilight, with no connection to the Blessed Realm of Tolkien's mythology. Compare 'an ever-eve of gloaming light' in *You and Me and the Cottage of Lost Play*, no. 28; 'Ever-eve' and 'Evereven' associated with Eldamar in Bilbo's song at Rivendell, no. 128; and 'Evereve [or Ever-eve] in Eldamar' in Galadriel's song, no. 161, possibly referring to the eternal twilight of Valinor after the destruction of the Two Trees.

D23–26: Tolkien marked these in the typewriter to be rearranged as:

The boat bore me to a long shore
past beacons dim and sea-bells
and glittering sand slid through my hands
The roses of coral and open bells

E19–22: Next to these lines, Tolkien typed:

I climbed into hills,
    drinking from rills
of gurgling water,
    gathering pebbles

E34: 'Gladdon-sword', i.e. a gladiolus, a type of iris, also known as *flag*, or 'sword-lily' because its leaves are shaped like swords.

E39: 'A tall wand to hold and a flag of gold': the 'wand' is presumably a reed, and the 'flag of gold' a yellow iris (*flag*), representing symbols of royalty.

F22: As typed, this line begins 'pas a dim beacon'. We have assumed that Tolkien meant the first word to be 'saw', as in draft text D, and not 'past'.

F26: 'Jewel-grist', i.e. gems crushed into *grist*, like ground meal.

F27–28: 'Trumpets of opal, roses of coral, | flutes of green and amethyst', i.e. pieces of irridescent opal in the shape of flower-trumpets (like the tubular corona of a daffodil), coral red like roses, 'green' (emerald?) and amethyst (i.e. purple, like the variety of quartz) in fluted shapes, like a tall, slender wine glass. But see also our comment preceding text E concerning the *triton flute* or *trumpet*.

F78: 'Blackbat shadow' is typed thus, but was probably intended as 'black bat shadow', i.e. the black shadow of a bat flying overhead. Compare 'hunting bat shadow' in G and H, i.e. the shadow of a flying bat, hunting.

G6: In F^1 this line begins 'a ding'. G and F begin 'a bell', but in G Tolkien marked 'a bell' to be changed to 'a ding' (as in H).

G18: In F^1 this line ends 'a dim quay', changed from 'an empty quay' in F. In G the line ends 'a ruined quay'; in H Tolkien changed the text of ll. 18–20 significantly.

G29: In F^1 this line ends 'glooming caves'. In F and G it ends 'hidden caves', but in G Tolkien marked 'hidden' to be changed to 'glooming' (as in H).

G34: In F1 this line ends 'fallen stars'. In F and G it ends 'golden stars', but in G Tolkien marked 'golden' to be changed to 'fallen' (as in H).

G94: 'Land's end': the furthest extent of land before reaching the sea, here used figuratively.

G120: In the first Allen & Unwin printing, 'men that I meet' is misprinted 'men that meet'.

H34: 'Heart's ease', i.e. to put one's heart at rest, to ease one's worries, not to be confused with *heartsease* 'pansy'.

H35: 'Up its fountain-stair to a country fair', i.e. climb the slope of the rill running down the hill (the stream from which the speaker drinks, as from a fountain) to a fair country, a pleasant part of the land the traveller is in.

135

Quare Fremunt Omnes Gentes (1932)

There are two manuscripts of this brief Latin poem, with only minor differences of punctuation and probably no appreciable gap between their writing. Below, as A, we have transcribed what seems to be the earlier of the two, which has a less formal calligraphic presentation.

[A]

Quare fremunt omnes gentes
furiosae et dementes,
queribundae, inconstantes,
infideles, titubantes,
sævæ simul et trementes,
alieni appetentes,
sui sordidi tenaces;
nunc audaces, nunc fugaces;
gratam consectatae sortem
mortem fugiunt in mortem.
Omnem terram, omne mare,
foedat vulgus sæculare;
spes æternæ vitae vana,
spurca vita fit humana.

This may be roughly translated as (B):

[B]

Why do all the peoples howl
furious and insane,
complaining, inconstant,
faithless, faltering,
at once fierce and trembling,
strange things craving,
sordidly holding tight to them,
now audacious, now timid;
eager for a pleasant fate
driving death to death.
Every land, every sea,
Common folk of the world corrupted;
hope for eternal life in vain,
a foul life made for Men.

The text of the second manuscript differs only in that Tolkien spelled out all instances of 'ae', without use of a joined character, 'tenaces' in line 7 is followed by a comma, and 'mortem' in line 10 is followed by a question mark.

To the (possibly) earlier manuscript Tolkien added: 'Thoughts on 1932 aroused by looking at any daily paper in January'. It is not possible to know exactly which part of the news most upset him, but we suspect that, as for *The Last of the Old Gods* (no. 126), it was the continued rise of the Nazis in Germany. He would have been closely concerned as well, though, with news from Spain, where Roman Catholic churches and convents had been burned since an anti-clerical government was elected in 1931.

Tolkien's poem recalls Psalm 2, which begins 'Quare turbabuntur gentes et tribus meditabuntur inania' ('Why do the heathen rage, and the people imagine a vain thing?').

136

Mythopoeia (?1932 or ?33–?35)

On the night of 19–20 September 1931, Tolkien met with his friends C.S. Lewis and H.V.D. 'Hugo' Dyson in Magdalen College, Oxford, where Lewis was a fellow. They strolled in the College grounds, following the footpath known as Addison's Walk, talking of metaphor and myth, then continued in Lewis's rooms. Lewis delighted in certain myths, such as that of the dying Norse god Baldur (see our discussion for poem no. 132), but nonetheless considered them 'lies and therefore worthless, even though breathed through silver' (quoted in Humphrey Carpenter, *The Inklings*, p. 43). Tolkien disagreed. Man, he said, does not lie by nature, and myths are not lies since, in making a myth – in practising 'mythopoeia', from the Greek *mythos* 'myth' and *poeisis* 'to make' – Man exercises an imaginative invention which must originate with God, and therefore must reflect eternal truth. This argument is credited with helping Lewis embrace Christianity, by concluding that the story of Christ is a 'true myth'. The essence of the discussion, perhaps even specific arguments Tolkien made that September night, stayed with him to resurface in a poem ultimately called *Mythopoeia*.

According to Christopher Tolkien, there are seven extant versions of this work. None of these, except for the final text, has been available for us to consult; therefore, we have relied upon Christopher's description of the manuscripts in his preface to *Tree and Leaf* first published in 1988. On the fifth and sixth drafts of *Mythopoeia* Tolkien inscribed 'J.R.R.T. for C.S.L. [C.S. Lewis]'. On the seventh, he added two notes which Christopher has dated to November 1935 or later, in one of which Tolkien commented that he referred to trees in the opening lines of the poem ('You look at trees') 'because they are at once easily classifiable and innumerably individual; but as this may be said of other things, then I will say, because I notice them more than most other things (far more than people). In any case the mental scenic background of these lines is the Grove and Walks of Magdalen at night' (quoted in *Tree and Leaf* (2001), p. viii). Also on the seventh version is the inscription 'Written mainly in the Examination Schools during Invigilation', which suggests a date between June 1932 and June 1933, the years between 1931 and 1935 when Tolkien acted as an examiner in the Oxford English School.

In his 1939 lecture *On Fairy-Stories*, as eventually published, Tolkien quoted fourteen lines from the poem (compare lines 55–70 below), edited and adapted to suggest that he had written them in a letter. There he discussed the concept of Fantasy as a 'sub-creative art', observing that some found this 'suspect, if not illegitimate' (*Tree and Leaf* (2001), pp. 54–5).

> To some it has seemed at least a childish folly, a thing only for peoples or for persons in their youth. As for its legitimacy I will say no more than to quote a brief passage from a letter I once wrote to a man who described myth and fairy-story as 'lies'; though to do him justice he was kind enough and confused enough to call fairy-story making 'Breathing a lie through silver'.
>
> 'Dear Sir,' I said — 'Although now long estranged,
> Man is not wholly lost nor wholly changed.
> Dis-graced he may be, yet is not de-throned,
> and keeps the rags of lordship once he owned:
> Man, Sub-creator, the refracted Light
> through whom is splintered from a single White
> to many hues, and endlessly combined
> in living shapes that move from mind to mind.
> Though all the crannies of the world we filled
> with Elves and Goblins, though we dared to build
> Gods and their houses out of dark and light,
> and sowed the seed of dragons — 'twas our right
> (used or misused). That right has not decayed:
> we make still by the law in which we're made.

Christopher Tolkien could find no trace among his father's papers of any such letter. In a preface to *Tree and Leaf* he commented that of the seven extant versions of the poem,

> none has any form of personal address – indeed, the first four texts begin 'He looks at trees' not 'You look at trees' (and the title of the earliest was '*Nisomythos*: a long answer to short nonsense'). Since the words *Although now long estranged* depend on and require the preceding lines
>
> The heart of man is not composed of lies.
> but draws some wisdom from the only Wise,
> and still recalls Him

and since all this passage goes back with little change to the earliest version, it is clear that the 'letter' was a device. [*Tree and Leaf* (2001), p. vii]

There is also no 'device' in manuscript A of *On Fairy-Stories*, published in the 2008 extended edition of that work edited by Verlyn Flieger and Douglas A. Anderson (*Tolkien On Fairy-Stories*), where the extract from *Mythopoeia* (beginning 'Though now long estranged') appears without 'Dear Sir'.

Here we give *Mythopoeia* in full from its final version, first published with *Tree and Leaf* in 1988 and corrected in 2001 (pp. 85–90). It is dedicated 'To one who said that myths were lies and therefore worthless even though "breathed through silver"', from 'Philomythus' ('Myth-lover') to 'Misomythus' ('Myth-hater').

You look at trees and label them just so,
(for trees are 'trees', and growing is 'to grow');
you walk the earth and tread with solemn pace
one of the many minor globes of Space:
a star's a star, some matter in a ball
compelled to courses mathematical
amid the regimented, cold, Inane,
where destined atoms are each moment slain.

At the bidding of a Will, to which we bend
(and must), but only dimly apprehend,
great processes march on, as Time unrolls
from dark beginnings to uncertain goals;
and as on page o'erwritten without clue,
with script and limning packed of various hue,
an endless multitude of forms appear,
some grim, some frail, some beautiful, some queer,
each alien, except as kin from one
remote Origo, gnat, man, stone, and sun.
God made the petreous rocks, the arboreal trees,
tellurian earth, and stellar stars, and these
homuncular men, who walk upon the ground
with nerves that tingle touched by light and sound.
The movements of the sea, the wind in boughs,
green grass, the large slow oddity of cows,
thunder and lightning, birds that wheel and cry,
slime crawling up from mud to live and die,

these each are duly registered and print
the brain's contortions with a separate dint.

Yet trees are not 'trees', until so named and seen —
and never were so named, till those had been
who speech's involuted breath unfurled,
faint echo and dim picture of the world,
but neither record nor a photograph,
being divination, judgement, and a laugh,
response of those that felt astir within
by deep monition movements that were kin
to life and death of trees, of beasts, of stars:
free captives undermining shadowy bars,
digging the foreknown from experience
and panning the vein of spirit out of sense.
Great powers they slowly brought out of themselves,
and looking backward they beheld the elves
that wrought on cunning forges in the mind,
the light and dark on secret looms entwined.

He sees no stars who does not see them first
of living silver made that sudden burst
to flame like flowers beneath an ancient song,
whose very echo after-music long
has since pursued. There is no firmament,
only a void, unless a jewelled tent
myth-woven and elf-patterned; and no earth,
unless the mother's womb whence all have birth.

The heart of man is not composed of lies,
but draws some wisdom from the only Wise,
and still recalls him. Though now long estranged,
man is not wholly lost nor wholly changed.
Dis-graced he may be, yet is not dethroned,
and keeps the rags of lordship once he owned
his world-dominion by creative act:
not his to worship the great Artefact,
man, sub-creator, the refracted light
through whom is splintered from a single White
to many hues, and endlessly combined
to living shapes that move from mind to mind.
Though all the crannies of the world we filled

with elves and goblins, though we dared to build
gods and their houses out of dark and light,
and sow the seed of dragons, 'twas our right
(used or misused). The right has not decayed.
We make still by the law in which we're made.

Yes! 'wish-fulfilment dreams' we spin to cheat
our timid heart and ugly Fact defeat!
Whence came the wish, and whence the power to dream,
or some things fair and others ugly deem?
All wishes are not idle, not in vain
fulfilment we devise – for pain is pain,
not for itself to be desired, but ill,
or else to strive or to subdue the will
alike were graceless; and of Evil this
alone is dreadly certain: Evil is.

Blessed are the timid hearts that evil hate,
that quail in its shadow, and yet shut the gate;
that seek no parley, and in guarded room,
though small and bare, upon a clumsy loom
weave tissues gilded by the far-off day
hoped and believed in under Shadow's sway.

Blessed are the men of Noah's race that build
their little arks, though frail and poorly filled,
and steer through winds contrary towards a wraith,
a rumour of a harbour guessed by faith.

Blessed are the legend-makers with their rhyme
of things not found within recorded time.
It is not they who have forgot the Night,
or bid us flee to organized delight,
in lotus-isles of economic bliss
forswearing souls to gain a Circe-kiss
(and counterfeit at that, machine-produced,
bogus-seduction of the twice-seduced).

Such tales they saw afar, and ones more fair,
and those that hear them yet may yet beware.
They have seen Death and ultimate defeat,
and yet they would not in despair retreat,

but oft to victory have tuned the lyre
and kindled hearts with legendary fire,
illuminating Now and dark Hath-been
with lights of suns as yet by no man seen.

I would that I might with the minstrels sing
and stir the unseen with a throbbing string.
I would be with the mariners of the deep
that cut their slender planks on mountains steep
and voyage upon a vague and wandering quest,
for some have passed beyond the fabled West.
I would with the beleaguered fools be told,
that keep an inner fastness where their gold,
impure and scanty, yet they loyally bring
to mint in image blurred of distant king,
or in fantastic banners weave the sheen
heraldic emblems of a lord unseen.

I will not walk with your progressive apes,
erect and sapient. Before them gapes
the dark abyss to which their progress tends —
if by God's mercy progress ever ends,
and does not ceaselessly revolve the same
unfruitful course with changing of a name.
I will not tread your dusty path and flat,
denoting this and that by this and that,
your world immutable wherein no part
the little maker has with maker's art.
I bow not yet before the Iron Crown,
nor cast my own small golden sceptre down.

*

In Paradise perchance the eye may stray
from gazing on everlasting Day
to see the day-illumined, and renew
from mirrored truth the likeness of the True.
Then looking on the Blessed Land 'twill see
that all is as it is, and yet made free:
Salvation changes not, nor yet destroys,
garden nor gardener, children nor their toys.
Evil it will not see, for evil lies

not in God's picture but in crooked eyes,
not in the source but in malicious choice,
and not in sound but in the tuneless voice.
In Paradise they look no more awry;
and though they make anew, they make no lie.
Be sure they still will make, not being dead,
and poets shall have flames upon their head,
and harps whereon their faultless fingers fall:
there each shall choose for ever from the All.

The earliest critic of *Mythopoeia* to point out that it is written in heroic couplets (rhyming pairs in iambic pentameter) was, we believe, Clive Tolley in 'Tolkien's "Essay on Man": A Look at *Mythopoeia*' (1992). As Tolley observes, this was not an approach Tolkien tended to favour, and he seems to have adopted it for *Mythopoeia* through the influence of Alexander Pope's *Essay on Criticism* (1711) and *Essay on Man* (1733). Tolley points first to similarities of content and style with Tolkien's poem in the *Essay on Criticism*:

First follow NATURE, and your judgment frame
By her just standard, which is still the same:
Unerring Nature, still divinely bright,
One clear, unchang'd, and universal light,
Life, force and beauty, must to all impart,
At once the source, and end, and test of Art.

'Pope is talking here about the critical faculty,' Tolley writes, whereas Tolkien in his fifth stanza (beginning 'The heart of man is not composed of lies'), to which Tolley compares quotations from Pope, is concerned with 'the more essential quality of man as subcreator, but the resemblance is clear. Both emphasise that while man's mind or nature is faulty, it still possesses the original correctness of vision as given by God or Nature' (pp. 222–3).

One of the themes of *Mythopoeia* is creation by God (the 'maker's art') and the part Man plays in creation as 'the little maker' or 'subcreator'. The second stanza in particular describes the 'bidding of a Will, to which we bend', and 'great processes' which go 'from dark beginnings to uncertain goals', though we may 'only dimly apprehend' them. This has resulted in 'an endless multitude of forms', all 'kin from one | remote Origo', that is, a single point of origin, which is God. To Alexander Pope in his *Essay on Man*, 'the proper study of Mankind is Man'; Tolkien's view, Clive Tolley argues, is that 'since man is in the image of God, it is proper for him to study everything' (p. 224). For Pope, Man is a 'wondrous creature' who shall 'mount where Science guides'; for Tolkien, 'man is not essentially a scientific beast, but a creative one' (p. 224). In *Mythopoeia* Tolkien rejects the definition of Man in Pope's essay, saying 'I will not walk with your progressive apes, | erect and sapient. Before them gapes | the dark abyss to which their progress tends'. Where the *Essay on Man* is 'ostensibly a rationalist's poem', *Mythopoeia*

> is explicitly theist, and implicitly Christian: God is declared to be Creator of all, man derives his creative powers from him, the reality of evil is stated, those with faith in heaven are called blessed. The picture of the men of Noah's race building little arks to weather the storm on the way to the hoped for harbour relies for much of its strength on the recognition that Noah's ark is an ecclesiastical symbol for the Church, a vessel of security in a storm-tossed world that will lead its passengers to safe haven. [Tolley, pp. 225–6]

Tolley also argues that Tolkien drew upon Sir Philip Sidney's *Apologie for Poetrie* (or *Defence of Poesie*, 1595): both authors are concerned with 'world-dominion by creative act', as Tolkien puts it in *Mythopoeia*. 'Like Sidney,' Tolley writes, 'Tolkien stresses that man is above nature, does not worship it. Tolkien's talk of man's right to fill the world with elves and dragons echoes Sidney's point that by imagination man can create new worlds. Tolkien does not say specifically that man's will is corrupt, simply that he is "dis-graced", i.e. deprived of grace . . .' (p. 228).

Tolkien's image of 'the refracted light' of Creation 'splintered from a single White | to many hues' through Man's 'sub-creation' has been frequently remarked and analyzed, most extensively by Verlyn Flieger (in *Splintered Light: Logos and Language in Tolkien's World* and elsewhere), who builds upon Owen Barfield's theory of the fragmentation of meaning in language. Sources and effects of light figure throughout Tolkien's works, and sometimes can be interpreted as the embodiment of the Creator. The picture Tolkien gives of 'refracted light' is of course that of the prism, through which visible light is broken into its components – white light not being the absence of colour, but containing all colours of the spectrum in nearly equal proportions.

Another theme in *Mythopoeia* is the place of imagination in Man's understanding of the natural world, and related to that, the tension between Science and Art. 'A star's a star, some matter in a ball | compelled to courses mathematical', Tolkien says, reflecting the view of an individual who sees nature in purely scientific terms; but 'he sees no stars who does not see them first | of living silver made that sudden burst | to flame like flowers beneath an ancient song'. Before science there must be imagination, the desire to dream and think and explain; before science there was poetry. Tolkien himself was not ignorant of science, far from it: see, for example, poem no. 20, initially *Dark*, in which the poet sees the heavens on successive nights from the Ptolemaic (earth-centred) and Copernican (sun-centred) points of view. Nor, by any means, did he oppose science on principle (its application could be another matter). His position, rather, was that one should not denigrate products of the imagination while declaring truth to be defined only by measurement and observation.

The definition of truth depends in the first instance on language. 'Trees are not "trees", until so named and seen — | and never were so named, till those had been | who speech's involuted breath unfurled, | faint echo and dim picture of the world'. In the Old Testament, all things were named by Adam, and their names became points of reference to nature. Since Eden, humans have enlarged the vocabulary, a point Tolkien makes in three lines which combine synonymous adjectives and nouns: 'God made the petreous rocks, the arboreal trees, | tellurian earth, and stellar stars, and these | homuncular men, who walk upon the ground | with nerves that tingle touched by light and sound.' (*Petreous* means 'rock-like', *arboreal* 'pertaining to trees', and so forth.) Moreover, the growth of language relative to the natural world is a continuing process:

> The movements of the sea, the wind in boughs,
> green grass, the large slow oddity of cows,
> thunder and lightning, birds that wheel and cry,
> slime crawling up from mud to live and die,
> these each are duly registered and print
> the brain's contortions with a separate dint.

To make a further point, language and myth are not distinct, but interrelated. In the 1928 book *Poetic Diction: A Study in Meaning*, which had a profound influence on Tolkien's thinking about language, his friend Owen Barfield argued that

> the historical separation of literal and metaphorical meanings of words divided what had been an original semantic unity: words had originally themselves been mini-myths, embodying

> a view of reality in which experienced phenomena were at one and the same time physical and spiritual. . . .
>
> Barfield's conception of the primordial unity of physical and spiritual, concrete and abstract, is evident in Tolkien's 'Mythopoeia' in the claim that phenomena are named only by humans 'digging the foreknown from experience | and panning the vein of spirit out of sense' . . . [Carl Phelpstead, 'Myth-making, Sub-creation, and World-building' (2022), p. 71]

In '"The Language Learned of Elves": Owen Barfield, *The Hobbit* and *The Lord of the Rings*' (1999) Stephen Medcalf describes the start of *Mythopoeia* as a direct address to C.S. Lewis and to positivism, which holds that truth is solely a matter of labelling ('You look at trees and label them just so'; compare later in the poem, 'denoting this and that by this and that'). 'But this is not how perception happens even now,' Medcalf says, 'much less how it happened when language was beginning. . . . Naming and seeing were originally an act of participation in what was named and seen ("response of those that felt astir within | by deep monition movements that were kin | to life and death of trees, of beasts, of stars")' (p. 37). 'Great powers' these inventors of language 'slowly brought out of themselves', Tolkien writes, 'and looking backward they beheld the elves | that wrought on cunning forges in the mind, | the light and dark on secret looms entwined'.

Contrary to Medcalf's argument, Frank Weinreich suggests that it is more likely that Tolkien did not address his poem to Lewis (as 'Misomythus'), 'but instead thought of the materialists, people who believe in (natural) sciences and empirical knowledge only. . . . The materialist and the empirical sciences recognise phenomena in the perceptible world and classify them according to an explanatory system which attaches labels like "tree", "earth", "globe" and so on' ('Metaphysics of Myth: The Platonic Ontology of "Mythopoeia"' (2008), pp. 329–30).

In lines 7–8 of *Mythopoeia*, 'amid the regimented, cold, Inane | where destined atoms are each moment slain', *Inane* does not mean 'silly, stupid', but 'the void of infinite space'. The idea that an infinite number of atoms exist in infinite space is most famously expressed in *De Rerum Natura* ('On the Nature of Things') by the Roman philosopher Lucretius, though it was not original to him. In ancient thought, an atom could not be divided (Greek *atomos* means 'indivisible'), let alone 'slain'; in later atomic theory, an atom can be divided into smaller parts (such as electrons) and converted to another state (mass to energy), but still not destroyed. Frank Weinreich ('Metaphysics of Myth') suggests that Tolkien's phrase 'destined atoms' 'stands for atoms as the basis of all matter and all material things' and also for the 'planetary' model of atomic structure described by Niels Bohr, which 'allows a view that describes atoms as "fated"' (pp. 330–1). If we take Weinreich's meaning correctly, Tolkien's 'atoms' are 'destined' in the sense of divinely designed, 'fated' only in that their structure and ultimate disposition are determined by God.

Lines 93–98 evoke Homer's *Odyssey* in the context of a materialistic society. Tolkien compares fleeing to 'organized delight' and 'economic bliss' to 'lotus-isles', that is, like the island of the Lotus-eaters where the inhabitants, and some of Odysseus's sailors, forget their life and loved ones through eating a narcotic plant. 'Circe kiss' refers to the enchantress who turns some of Odysseus's crew into swine through magic and uses her beauty against Odysseus himself, who becomes her lover for a year. Tolkien himself explained the phrase 'bogus-seduction of the twice-seduced' in a note to his final text of *Mythopoeia*: '*Twice-seduced*, since to return to earthly well-being as a *sole* end is one seduction, but even this end is mis-sought and depraved.'

Related to these thoughts is Tolkien's phrase 'I will not walk with your progressive apes, | erect and sapient. Before them gapes | the dark abyss to which their progress tends — | if by God's mercy progress ever ends'. Some critics have taken 'progressive apes' to mean positivists, or modernists, or a criticism of Darwinian evolution. But since Tolkien suggests that their actions will tend to lead to a 'dark abyss', he is presumably referring again to materialists, whose desire for possessions and diversions is more important to them than spiritual values. 'Progress' here is presumably meant ironically – progress for the sake of progress, rather than for a meaningful end, whatever *progress* may mean, though probably technological progress in particular. Tolkien makes his position clear in the tenth stanza: he would rather be with the minstrels who 'stir the unseen', or with 'the mariners of the deep | that cut their slender planks on mountains steep' – the honest labour of harvesting wood for ships – 'and voyage upon a vague and wandering quest', or with 'beleaguered fools' whose gold may be 'impure and scanty', yet they keep in mind their 'distant king' and 'lord unseen', surely images of their faith.

In its earlier drafts, *Mythopoeia* was shorter, without the three stanzas beginning 'Blessed are' (81–98), and the whole ended with present line 130, 'nor cast my own small golden sceptre down'. The ornament following line 130, included in our source, marks the text added later. Carl Phelpstead has described this final stanza as 'a Platonic conception of the relationship between perceived and ultimate reality again [coming] to the fore with the hope that Paradise may "renew | from mirrored truth the likeness of the True" . . . : this world is derivative from the ultimate reality to be experienced in heaven'. He relates the poets with 'flames upon their head' to 'the biblical figure of the Holy Spirit descending on the apostles in the form of flames at Pentecost (Acts 2:1–4)' and the 'harps whereon their faultless fingers fall' to 'the celestial choirs of musical angels', linked with the image of a minstrel with his lyre from earlier in the poem ('Mythmaking, Sub-creation, and World-building', p. 72).

Clive Tolley considers *On Fairy-Stories* to be 'an expanded version of *Mythopoeia*' which borrows the arguments and 'much of the imagery of the poem', and explains many of its 'obscurer passages' (p. 235). Phelpstead prefers to say more simply that 'the essay expands on and clarifies the ideas expressed in the poem' ('Myth-making, Sub-creation, and World-building', p. 70). We would say, rather, that *On Fairy-Stories* makes some of the same points as *Mythopoeia* in different words (apart from the semi-quotation from the poem itself): for example, 'Fantasy remains a human right: we make in our measure and in our derivative mode, because we are made: and not only made, but made in the image and likeness of a Maker' (2001 edn., p. 56). But one should not expect to find in it glosses on specific readings in the poem, which among Tolkien's works is one of the most open to interpretation. We have included further comments in our notes.

In *Tolkien's Faith: A Spiritual Biography* (2023) Holly Ordway suggests that in writing *Mythopoeia* Tolkien drew upon 'the circularity of Addison's Walk' – the path circumnavigates a water meadow – 'in order to symbolize Lewis's pre-Christian and un-mythic tendency to "ceaselessly revolve the same | unfruitful course"' (p. 180). Ordway also argues that *Mythopoeia* is itself an argument, 'to address the objection that Christianity is nothing more than a wish-fulfillment story' (p. 181), its idea of the Christian faith as a 'true myth' probably influenced by G.K. Chesterton in *The Everlasting Man* (1925).

40: 'Panning the vein of spirit out of sense': Tolkien's analogy is to the panning of gold, i.e. using a shallow pan to separate gold from soil in the bed of a stream.

54: 'The only Wise', i.e. God.

58: In the 1988 *Tree and Leaf* 'once' was misprinted 'one'. This was corrected in the reset HarperCollins edition of 2001.

105: 'Hath-been', i.e. what has been.

112: 'Fabled West', i.e. the mythological paradise found, or at least sought, far across the seas to the west. In Tolkien's private mythology this was Aman, the land of the Valar.

125: In the 1988 *Tree and Leaf* 'tread' was misprinted 'treat'.

129: In Tolkien's mythology, the 'Iron Crown' was that of the dark lord Morgoth.

130: 'Nor cast my own small golden sceptre down', i.e. not relinquish his gift of creativity.

139–141: 'Evil lies | not in God's picture but in crooked eyes, | not in the source but in malicious choice': Tolkien uses 'crooked' figuratively (as opposed to 'straight') as a reference to moral character, shown by 'malicious choice' (disposed to evil).

137

The Merryman (*c.* 1933)

Tolkien later inscribed the single, fair copy manuscript of this poem 'written for | The Mermaid Club'. That undergraduate society, founded at Oxford in 1902, was devoted to the reading and study of Elizabethan and post-Elizabethan drama. Tolkien attended its annual dinners in at least 1933 (25 February) and 1938 (5 March), and in a list for 1936–7 was recorded as an Honorary Member. The club was a more recent incarnation of a Mermaid Club supposed to have numbered Shakespeare, Ben Jonson, and other writers of the sixteenth and seventeenth centuries among its members, who are said to have met at the Mermaid Tavern in London (there were at least three taverns of that name in Shakespeare's day). In his poem, Tolkien plays on the notion of a drinking establishment named for a mermaid, and on the attributes of mermaids in general.

The manuscript is on a sheet shared with a draft for *A Cherry with No Stone* (no. 138). We have dated both to *c.* 1933, from Tolkien's first recorded attendance at a Mermaid Club dinner.

The Merryman is maiden fair,
At least she has a maiden's hair
Above her middle, and her face
Has woman's beauty, woman's grace;
But if to other points we pass,
We search in vain, and find, alas!
The merrymaiden's promise fail
And end up in a lying tail.

*

Great store of drink she keeps at hand,
A very sea upon the land,
And in her mansion men may drink
Until they drown themselves and sink.
Yet music loves she even more,
That turns the very ships to shore;
Her words are clear and honey-sweet,
As on her harp her fingers beat.

Thus wine and verse her art doth blend,
That, though the feast in death may end,
For men the land is no more dry,
And almost sweet it is to die.

Merryman in this context echoes the word for 'merman' once used by fishermen and sailors of Cornwall, as *merrymaid* (here *merrymaiden*) is their dialect word for 'mermaid'. (Compare Middle English *mereman* 'merman', from Old English **meremann*, and Old English *meremenn* 'mermaid, siren', and see also poem nos. 5 and 81.) Tolkien uses *merryman* in a non-gendered sense, applying 'merrymaiden' only once her female attributes are established – from the waist up, 'woman's beauty, woman's grace', below only 'a lying tail'. In doing so, he follows the Old English *Physiologus*:

In ðe se senden
selcuðes manie;
ðe mereman is
a meiden ilike
on brest and on bodi,
oc al ðus e is bunden;
fro ðe noule niðerward
ne is ge no man like,
oc fis to fuliwis
mid finnes waxen.

As noted in our discussion of poem no. 5, the legend of the siren, who lured sailors and their ships onto rocks and their doom but was not a creature of the sea, later evolved so that sirens and mermaids were alike in action and form. In the bestiary, the mermaid's music puts a sailor to sleep, so that his ship sinks and 'ne cumen he nummor up'; in the poem, he is drawn to drink, and drowns himself.

19: 'No more dry' originally read 'almost dry'.

138

A Cherry with No Stone (*c.* 1933)

A Cherry with No Stone is found in two manuscripts. One is a draft, written on a leaf shared with *The Merryman* (no. 137), which we have dated to *c.* 1933, and the other, transcribed here, is a fair copy.

A cherry with no stone, a goose without a bone,
A living coat, a leafy boat,
A flowing sword, a flowering cord,
Beer none can drink — what will ye think
Of these things seven that to me were given?

The blossom is bright, the egg is white;
And a sheep I see, and a tall oak-tree,
And molten metal, and the blue petal
of flax blowing, and the barley growing.

The draft, an ink manuscript written over a largely erased pencil text, differs from the later manuscript only in line 6, which read before revision: 'The blossom bright, and goose-egg white'.

A Cherry with No Stone is Tolkien's version of the venerable riddle which asks how there can be a cherry without a stone, how there can be a bird without a bone, and so forth. 'Blossom' refers to the flowering of the cherry tree, before the setting of any fruit, and therefore without any stone. A goose still in the egg has no bone, a sheep has a living coat of wool, oak is the tree whose timber was commonly used in shipbuilding (in the days of the wooden ship), a sword 'flows' when it is still molten metal, cord (twine) is traditionally made from flax (*Linum usitatissimum*), which bears blue flowers, and barley in its natural state – not yet used to brew beer – cannot be drunk.

Tolkien's verse ultimately derives from a poem or song at least five centuries old, though no doubt he encountered at least one of its more recent incarnations. The traditional ballad 'Captain Wedderburn's Courtship', for example, includes a challenge by the woman the captain wishes to wed (or bed); she refuses, unless he can solve a series of riddles. One of these is to bring her three dishes for her supper: a chicken without a bone, a cherry without a stone, and a bird without a gall. To this the answers are: a chicken still in the egg, a cherry still in blossom, and a dove, which is such a gentle bird that it has no gall (that is, expresses no rancour).

On the same page as the draft text, with no connection with the cherry riddle (as far as we can see), Tolkien wrote out six lines of verse in Middle English:

> Hit was an olde mon fro Pimbilmere
> þat hadde a grete cou, and lees hir þere,
> þan seide men: 'ne seestou nat, perdee,
> Sche is iclomben in a hiȝe tre!
> Þat men her kyn to eten leves sende
> a wnder is þat neuer can amende. [']

These lines appear, in whole or in part and with variations, also on the two typescripts we describe as C and D in our discussion for poem no. 80, on which Tolkien also wrote Middle English and Latin versions of 'Twinkle, Twinkle, Little Star', 'So Early in the Morning', and 'Humpty Dumpty'. Typescript C has the text:

> Hit was an olde mon fro Pimbilmere
> þat hadde a grete cou, and lees hir þere
> þan seide þai 'ne sestou nat, perdee!
> sche is iclomben in a hiȝe tre!
> Þat folk here kyn to eten leves sende
> a wnder is þat neuer can amende.'

And typescript D:

> Hit was an olde mon of Pimbilmere
> þet hedde a grete cou, and lees hir þere.
> Þan seide þei: 'Ne sistu nat perdee!
> Ho is iclomben in a hiȝe tre!
> Þet mon his kun to eten leues sende
> A wnder is þet neuer con amende!'

Roughly translated, the poem reads:

> There was an old man from Pimbilmere,
> who had a great cow, and sheltered her there.
> Then men said: 'By God! do you not see,
> she has climbed into a high tree!
> That men send their kine here to eat leaves
> is a wonder that never can be surpassed.'

Pimbilmere is another name for Llyn Tegid, or Bala Lake, in Wales, fed by the River Dee.

Given the nature of most of the poems (save for two Latin quotations) sharing space on typescripts with the 'old man from Pimbilmere', one would expect the latter to be likewise a version of a nursery rhyme or familiar song; but we cannot trace anything like it.

139

Doworst · *Visio de Doworst* (?1933–53)

Doworst, to use its shortest title, is a humorous 'report' of errors committed by a nervous Oxford English School student in his oral examinations, and more generally of the process with its four dons and attendants. Although in Modern English, it has the style and metre of the alliterative Middle English poem *Piers Plowman*. That enduring work from the fourteenth century, written by (or ascribed to) a man called William Langland, is about sin and penance and the difficulty of living life as a good Christian. Largely allegorical, it concerns a pilgrim named Will who has a series of dream visions, in some of which he is in the company of a ploughman, Piers (Pierce, or Peter), who acts as a guide to a group of pilgrims. In some of its manuscripts – there are many – the poem is divided into two parts, 'Visio Willelmi de Petrus Plowman' ('William's Vision of Peter the Plowman'), and 'Vita de Dowel, Dobet, et Dobest' ('Life of Do-well, Do-better, and Do-best'); in the latter, Will seeks to learn what it means to 'do well', 'do better', and 'do best' on his journey towards salvation, aided by personifications of these virtues. In Tolkien's poem, the hapless student is named 'Doworst' because he does very badly ('does worst') in his examination, indeed he is hopeless.

Tolkien's original calligraphic manuscript of *Doworst,* apart from any preliminary workings now lost, was elaborately written and decorated, with coloured inks, in a medieval style, and was entitled both *Doworst* and *Visio Petri Aratoris de Doworst* ('The Vision of Peter the Plowman of Doworst', the narrator of the work being the said Peter). On 21 December 1933 Tolkien gave it to his friend R.W. Chambers with a covering note: 'I send you – it may possibly amuse you – a report on last year's Examinations in Oxford: held by myself, [C.L.] Wrenn, [H.F.B.] Brett-Smith, & C.S. Lewis (whose *Pilgrim's Regress* you may have read). The howlers are genuine except the nonsense about Percy S.' (reproduced in 'Fantasy That! – A Tolkien Original', *Monash Review,* July 1975; on 'Percy S.', see our comments following text B).

In addition to his other accomplishments, Chambers was a leading expert on *Piers Plowman,* working towards, but not completing, a definitive edition. He died in 1942, leaving the manuscript of *Doworst* to his secretary, Winifred Husbands, also a senior lecturer at University College London. She, in turn, on her retirement in 1957, presented it to Arthur Brown, then Reader in English at the same institution, later Professor of English at Monash University in Australia. Brown died in 1979, and the manuscript of *Doworst* he possessed is nowhere to be found. Part of its first page, however, was reproduced in 1975 in the *Monash Review*, with an article about the poem and its history, quoting an additional dozen lines. A greater part of the same page, with its titles and nineteen lines, was included in the ?Summer 1978 number of *A Elbereth Gilthoniel!* the newsletter of the Monash University Tolkien fan group, the Fellowship of Middle Earth; text A, below, was transcribed from this image. According to Professor Brown, Tolkien had the manuscript specially bound for Chambers, with the binder's title *Do Worst*, but Tolkien recorded (see below) that the work was commissioned by Chambers himself.

[A] In a summer season when sultry was the sun
with lourdains & lubbers I lounged in a hall,
& wood in his wits was each wight as meseemed:
on his [head] was a hat as hard as a board,
on his neck was there knotted a noose all of white
with bow big & broad like a butterfly's wings.
Most of that meiny had on mantles of stuff,
shrouds short as shrift & shapeless as sacks
that never covered their tails nor their touts either.
The clamour of that company was like the cackle of hens,
till a bell rang brazenly — that abated their noise.
They were summoned it seemed to an assize to be held
by four clerks very fell whom few could appease
that would judge them ungently with jesting unkind.
Then I went in their wake walking slowly,
as they passed down a passage paved all with marble
to a double doorway in a dim corner.
An usher it opened, & we entered in fear,
filing in like footmen or folk of the street

The first few lines of Tolkien's poem closely echo the opening of *Piers Plowman* (here from the designated B-text):

In a somer season   whan soft was the sonne,
I shope me in shroudes   as I a shepe were,
In habite as an heremite   vnholy of workes,
Went wyde in þis world   wondres to here.

On a summer season when soft [gentle] was the sun,
I clothed me in [woolen] garments as if I were a sheep,
In dress like a hermit, unholy of works [i.e. not doing
good Christian works]
Went wide in this world, wonders to hear.

The speaker of *Doworst* is similarly 'in a summer season', at the end of Oxford's Trinity Term, which runs to around the end of June, though the sun is *sultry* (hot, oppressive), not 'soft'. Queuing at the door are *lourdains* (idlers) and *lubbers* (clumsy folk), each with 'wood in his wits' (without sense), 'each wight as meseemed' (each person as seemed to me). The 'hat as hard as a board' is the student's hard cap or mortarboard, the 'noose all of white' the white, butterfly-style bow tie traditionally worn by a student at examinations, and the 'shrouds short as shrift' the so-called 'commoner's gowns' which are so short they do not cover one's 'tail' or 'tout' (rump). An *assize* is a law court, which an examination may resemble to a student under scrutiny; the *four clerks* are the examining dons.

By good fortune, another manuscript of *Doworst*, headed *Incipit Visio Petri Aratoris de Doworst* ('Here Begins the Vision of Peter the Plowman of Doworst') and with a simpler *explicit* or concluding title, *Visio de Doworst*, has come to the Bodleian Library from the archive of Walter Hooper. Written in a fine hand without decoration, its early lines are almost identical to those in text A above. We give this version of the poem here as B. In writing out some lines of the manuscript, Tolkien included a noticeably wider space to mark a caesura, but in most he omitted it, as we have chosen to do throughout this transcription.

[B] In a summer season when sultry was the sun
with lourdains and lubbers I lounged in a hall,
and wood in his wits was each wight as meseemed:
on his head was a hat as hard as a board,
on his neck there was knotted a noose all of white
with big bow and broad like a butterfly's wings.
Most of that meiny had on mantles of stuff,
shrouds short as shrift and shapeless as sacks
that never covered their tails nor their touts either.
The clamour of that company was the cackle of hens,
till a bell rang brazenly — that abated their noise!

They were summoned, it seemed, to an assize to be held
by four clerks very fell whom few could appease,
that should judge them ungently with jesting unkind.
I went in their wake, walking slowly,
as they passed down a passage pave all with marble
to a double doorway in a dim corner.
An usher it opened, and we entered in fear,
filing in like footmen, or folk off the street
that lacking labour are like lambs herded.
In a long line forlorn we looked at our boots,
till a ferret-faced freke (half famished he seemed,
with a nose like a nark, and narrow in the chest)
doffed his hat donnishly, and dourly beheld us,
mumbled us good morning with mouthing unclear,
asking each after each to answer his name.

'That is Grim the Grammar-man', the gomes whispered,
as I crept to a corner and cowered in the shadows,
and held me there hid, and hoped to escape.
Then most of those men he dismissed for the nonce;
but four full of fright sat fainting in chairs,
till the starveling stood up and sternly exclaimed
'Atkins!' as if in anger. Then up jumped a boy —
his cheeks were chopfallen, no chin could be seen —
and he trotted to the table with tottering feet.
There he sat down sideways, as if sore in his seat,
and they eyed him an instant, as earwig on leaf,
ere one wipes it away with a wave of the hand.

Then a clerk at the corner that crouched at his book
looked up with a leer, and louted full low
in mirth or in mockery. As a mask was his face;
one eye only opened, ill-omened he looked.
'That is Regulus the ruthless, a render of youth[,]
a Goth full of gall, a grinder of tears',
the unhappy behind then hissed through their teeth;
and I marked in amaze how his mouth hardened,
as with sibilant sound he softly began.
'I see, sir," he said, 'you have signed here your name
to many reams of rubbish. You write like a crab,
so maybe what you meant is less monstrous folly
than appears in your papers, as I puzzle them out.

Come! tell me now truly — your time is your own,
there is no haste here or hurry, you are wholly at ease —
when the *Wanderer* was written. I'll wait while you think!'

Then all of them eyed him like an eel on a fork;
but no word for a while could he work with his tongue,
and a still stony silence stole in the chamber,
while he licked on his lips; and at last stuttered:
'John–johnson' he jibbered, 'I judge it was he!'
'John Johnson you judge', jeered then in echo
that courteous clerk, and coldly he stared.
'He is printer at the Press and no poem-maker;
but I guess that you gabble and garble your words.
Sam Johnson it seems, the sage doctor,
you would name in your nonsense. Is there nothing you know,
mixing in your madness many matters distinct?
Ramblers and wanderers in the roaming of your wits
are all one to your wisdom! I wish you good-day!'

Not so lightly was he loosed — as he leaped to his feet,
Sir Grim with a grin and a glint in his eye:
'Sit down for a second', he said, 'my good sir!
There is much I would mention; a moment I crave!
You jest here of Julius that jousted of old
and slew many Saxons, and Cæsar you deem
on a time them did tame and taught them the Latin.
I would learn, by your leave, of this land's story:
give dates, if you dare, that your doom be the lighter!'
Then Atkins uneasy half opened his mouth,
and gazed on Sir Grim with piteous glance,
as a hare that men hunt till its heart is nigh burst.
'Your pardon' he pleaded, 'I pray you to show!
In ten sixty six, or so I have read,
to this land sailed the lords of Latin and Greek;
and christendom and courtesy then came to these shores,
where savages had settled — on swine they feasted,
and beer out of buckets they bouzed at their will.
William Cæsar it was that won all this land,
and Julius was his jester and jangled a harp,
and emboldened to battle the brave legions;
and Gregory the great, that Augustine is called,

was their bishop, and books he brought in a boat.'
'Who taught you this tale, it were tiresome to ask',
Sir Grim him gainsaid with a glare in his eye.
'I will pass from such piffle, and pose you once more:
When a name in the nominative (if you know what I mean)
is set in a sentence, what serves it to show?'
Then the boy looked up brighter and boldly replied:
'No noun can be such, for the nominative voice
is a privilege purely appointed for verbs,
when the person is passive and plural in number.'

Sir Grim was aghast, as a ghost he had seen,
and wordless he waggled a wavering hand,
and beckoned to the booby to budge to the left.
There suddenly, meseemed, from slumber awoke
a clerk with a countenance comely to see
(red as ripe apples, or roses in June,
as he blushed on the boy with a beam on his face),
but hoar was his hair, and his hat crumpled,
for long had he laboured to learn and to teach.
''Tis Sir Britoner', they burbled, the boys at the back;
'his blushes are but blinds, he is bawdy of jest,
and knoweth more naughtiness than nine men besides.
Look out when he laughs! As like then as not
some horrible howler has hopped to his mind.'

Then I marked how with mirth his maw was a-quake,
and he shook all in silence with some secret delight.
At length he looked up and laughingly cried:
'Ah! Mister Atkins! your answers are good,
though a little them lacks of learning, 'tis true;
and your wit runneth wild and wayward at times.
One Percy you praise, yet it puzzles me somewhat
to make out whom you mean among men of that name'.
The prisoner was pleased, and plucking up heart
as pert as a pie he replied without fear:
'Sir Percy, I opine, was a peer of the realm;
duke Douglas the Jew he dinged once to death,
and he pottered with poetry for profit of his age;
a fellowship they found him when failing in years,
and bribed him with a bishopric, for Ben Jonson's sake,
to bring his book to an end; but he babbled as a child,

and the marshal Montgomery mortally smote him,
and his reliques now rot among rubbish on the shelves
in some charnel or church vault — so champions end.'

Sir Britoner as a bull then burst in a roar,
he rocked like a rowing boat, and his ribs he embraced.
Then beating his breast like a babewin of the woods,
''Tis sweet sooth that you say!" he sobbed at the last.
'It is long since such lore I learned in this place!
You must pass to my companion — no power is me left,
by the ears of king Midas, to ask you aught else.'
Then the lede on the left uplifted his face
(he had bowed o'er the board, as if beads he would say;
or pencil on paper some picture, maybe,
or make for his merriment a morsel of verse).
He was black-haired and broad, and balled a little,
as a tonsure he had taken some terms now ago;
''Tis Sir Plato the pilgrim — he hath a pitiless wit;
he passes no pleasantry, nor any pert reason,
till he hath proof on each point, and double-proven at that':
so they sighed who still sat on seats there unsoft,
and long it them thought ere they were loosed from their
woe.

Then I marvelled how that master then mightily spake,
with right ringing rerd his reasons he uttered,
each cutting and clear, and some cruel at the end,
that the boy at the board there blenched at the thrust.
Thus Sir Plato him posed (and pleasantly smiled):
'Is prosody but prose, as your paper declares,
enlarged by the learned for delight in long words?
A letter more or less but little imports,
if I read you not awry — am I wrong, sir, in this?[']
Then Atkins full humbly him answered in haste:
'So I wrote as seemed right, pray rue on me sir!
As a pup in a prep-school this patter I learned,
and repeated it on paper, perplexed by the heat;
I know it is nonsense, and acknowledge my fault.'
'That is enough then for now. 'Tis nonsense in sooth,
but you are liable for libel — you lie on your school
that they taught you such trash. I turn now from that.

Other matters of metre I would mention a while:
what is verse that is blank, I beg you reveal.
Who wrote it and wrought it, can you reckon their names?'

Then blankly the boy, rebuffed with that blow,
stared like a stuck pig, and startled he seemed;
but a light seemed to dawn at length on his darkness,
as though a riddle he had read and was right in the end.
'Such verses, I would venture, in advertisements stand;
they are writ in the rough with the rhymes missing,
often in papers they appear for the people to finish
who compete for some prize in praise of a cheese;
but what man ever makes them is a mystery of God,
and publicity agents that blear all our eyes.'
Sir Plato turned pale as with pang at the heart,
cast his hood o'er his head and hid up his face;
Sir Britoner bawled forth 'the bastard is mad',
and Sir Regulus retched and wrinkled his nose;
Sir Grim rent his gown and gulped in his throat,
then spinfoot he sprang and sprinted to the bell.

An usher then entered and asked what he wished,
and the clerks with a clamour all cried out together:
'Hale forth this harlot, and hew him with staves!
Kick him from these cloisters to Carfax and further,
then plough him in pieces with ploughshares keen,
as red hot as wrath — no ruth he deserves!'
Catchpolls came crowding, and caught him by the arms,
and drove him to the door with dint of their boots.
He shrieked as it shut, and I shivered in my shoes.
and swallowed in a swoon I slipped to the ground.

When I looked up at length, alone there I lay;
all had fled from the fury of the fearful assize —
what became of the clerks, I dared not ask!
But a voice out of view from some veiled corner
then said, as meseemed, all soft in my ear:
'Now Doworst is doomed! Do not deem it a jape;
for many such assemble in this city by the ford,
and Falsehood and Folly are the friends that they make.
No right have they to rest here, to rot in their youth

and waste here their while, working no profit.
Were such served at assize as their deserts merit,
they would end all as Atkins with iron or with rope.'

So I passed from that place and pondered in heart,
and I privily prayed, though pupils perchance
be somewhat of the sort that I saw in my dream,
that clerks of such kind may be counted a fable,
that dons have dignity and their dooms mercy.
Then summer grew sere, and the sun faded;
wind woke in the west and warred with the trees,
and the world withered away, as winter approached.
Then seed-time ensued, season of labour,
and I passed to my plough that is appointed a symbol
of the wounds that yet work our weal in the end;
and fair through the fold my furrow I drew,
and I sowed many seeds in the sweat of my brow,
hoping for the harvest in hunger and cold.
Yet though high be the hope oft the heart is cheated;
neither countryman nor clerk hath all corn for his swink.

Explicit Visio de Doworst

The speaker's dismissive comments on the students he finds are of a piece with those of the ploughman in the sixth book of the medieval poem, where Piers invites those he would guide on their pilgrimage first to help him plant his crops. He will provide food for all men who work, he says, but there will be none for Jack the juggler, or Janet from the stews (brothels), or Daniel the dice-player, or others who are idlers or whose labour is of ill repute. Near the end of *Doworst*, the poet concludes that 'many such assemble' in Oxford who take 'Falsehood and Folly' as friends, 'and waste here their while'.

If, as seems likely, the 'clerks' of *Doworst* are versions of the four dons who administered the Oxford English School examinations in 1932, one could hazard a guess at their identities. We need not speculate about one: 'Regulus the ruthless' is identified by Tolkien in the margin of text B as the 'hedge-king or wrenne', thus C.L. Wrenn. (The wren is sometimes called 'the hedge-king', in German *Zaunkönig*.) Also one might note that *Regulus* and *Wren* begin with the same *R*- sound. 'Sir Brittoner' may be H.F.B. Brett-Smith, whose surname begins *Br*- and who is said to have enjoyed a good joke. We suppose 'Sir Plato the pilgrim' to be C.S. Lewis, author of *The*

Pilgrim's Regress, himself broad and balding and a terror to students who were not rigorous in their thinking. This leaves Tolkien to be 'Grim the Grammarman'; 'Grim' is presumably a nod to Jakob Grimm, philologist and folklorist, of 'Grimm's Law' fame. Of course, one could argue otherwise, with different criteria. Indeed, before we saw the manuscript of B, on the basis only of the typescript text given below, we would have thought 'Regulus the ruthless' was Tolkien, as he too has a name with *R* (Ronald) and was of German ('Goth') ancestry; and here he asks about the Old English poem *The Wanderer* (see our discussion for no. 133), an edition of which he and E.V. Gordon were preparing when *Doworst* was composed. In any case, the four 'clerks' were intended by Tolkien to be exaggerations, with his prayer that such of their kind 'may be counted a fable, | that dons may have dignity and their dooms mercy'.

Atkins' first words (line B59) are truly nonsense. They do not answer the question asked (when was *The Wanderer* written), and appear to confuse the medieval poem with *The Rambler*, an eighteenth-century periodical by Dr. Samuel Johnson ('the sage doctor'). With good reason does Sir Regulus say that 'Ramblers and wanderers in the roaming of your wits | are all one to your wisdom!' And since Atkins stutters his reply 'Johnson', the don thinks first of John Johnson, 'printer at the Press', the John Johnson who was Printer to the University (director of the Oxford University Press) from 1925 to 1956. Neither, though, is his answer to Sir Grim less muddled. He remembers the important date 1066, known to every pupil whether or not their knowledge of British history goes much further; but he seems to confuse the invasion of England that year, by William of Normandy (the Conqueror), with the Roman incursion under Julius Caesar begun in 55 B.C. Since the Anglo-Saxons did not enter Britain until the mid-fifth century, Julius (Caesar) could not have 'jousted of old | and slew many Saxons' (the Romans encountered native Celts). The 'Julius' said by Atkins to be William's jester and harpist seems to be a clouded reference to Taillefer, the Conqueror's minstrel, who is said to have slain English soldiers at the Battle of Hastings (1066) while juggling and singing. The Normans were Christian, indeed they entered England under a papal banner, but Christianity was introduced to Britain much earlier, in 597 by Augustine, a prior of Rome (later St Augustine of Canterbury), sent on his mission by Pope Gregory the Great. Augustine is traditionally said to have brought with him at least the manuscript known as the St Augustine Gospels, now at Corpus Christi College, Cambridge ('books he brought in a boat').

Sir Grim rightly dismisses Atkins' attempt at history 'piffle', and gives him a simple question: what does a name in the nominative, used in a sentence, serve to show? The answer is that it is the subject of a verb. When the verb is active, the name (proper noun) indicates the person doing the action; when the verb is passive, it is the person receiving the action. But here too, Atkins is out of his depth, and Sir Grim is rightly 'aghast' at the further nonsense.

Sir Brittoner next raises the question of the 'Percy' mentioned in the candidate's written paper. Tolkien refers to Atkins' reply (B125–133) in his note to R.W. Chambers: 'The howlers are genuine except the nonsense about Percy S.' That is, this part of the poem is wholly Tolkien's invention rather than a memory of examinations. 'Percy S.' is almost certainly Percy Simpson (1865–1962), who at the time Tolkien devised his poem was a fellow of Oriel College, Oxford (since 1921), Goldsmith's Reader in English Literature (since 1930), and librarian of the English Faculty Library (since 1914). He had been a schoolmaster until, at age forty-eight, he was brought to Oxford to work for the Clarendon Press, and was also made a Lecturer in English. For many years he taught research methods to B.Litt. students, and served with Tolkien on the English Faculty Board and as an examiner. By the time he came to Oxford, he was already a leading figure in the study of Elizabethan literature, especially the writings of Shakespeare; but his chief claim to fame is his work on a critical edition of the works of Ben Jonson, initially with C.H. Herford. The series was to be completed in five years, but took more than fifty, with Simpson blamed for the delay because of the endless pains he took with the smallest points – hardly the only Oxford scholar with this trait. A roly-poly sort to judge by his portrait, Simpson seems also to have been a figure of fun to others, at least behind his back; C.S. Lewis called him 'Percy Tweedlepippin'.

Simpson was neither a knight nor a peer, but many with the surname *Percy* were nobles, such as Henry Percy (1341–1408), the Earl of Northumberland, and Thomas Percy (1343–1403), the Earl of Worcester. Henry's brash son, Harry, known as 'Hotspur' (1364–1403), fought against James, the Earl of Douglas, in the Battle of Otterburn in 1388, in which Douglas was killed – though there is no record that he was 'dinged [beaten] once to death' by a Percy. We cannot explain Tolkien's (as the addled Atkins) mention of a Jew – surely not Douglas – unless he was thinking of the account by Shakespeare, in *Henry IV, Part One*, of the Percys' revolt against their king. There Falstaff, boasting of a fight against many foes, remarks: 'You rogue, they were bound, every man of them, or I am a Jew else, an Ebrew

Jew' – a tenuous notion, admittedly, though related to one of Simpson's subjects. The 'fellowship' could be that given Simpson by Oriel, though in 1921 he was not yet 'failing in years'.

'[Bribing] him with a bishopric, for Ben Jonson's sake, | to bring his book to an end' could refer to the long years when the Clarendon Press allowed Simpson to work on (and on) preparing the Jonson edition; but he was a leading expert, and had other duties also. The reference to 'marshal Montgomery' escapes us. It may be that in 1932 Tolkien thought of Simpson's Jonson research lying dormant ('rot[ting] among rubbish on the shelves'), C.H. Herford having died in 1931, but this was not its fate.

The word 'reliques' surely suggests that Doworst confused Percy Simpson with another Thomas Percy (1729–1811), the antiquarian famous for his *Reliques of Ancient English Poetry* (1765), the first of the great ballad collections and the work most responsible for the ballad revival in English poetry that was a significant part of the Romantic movement. That Percy was also not a knight or a peer, but did become Bishop of Dromore, County Down, Ireland.

In B192 Tolkien uses *plough* as a verb in two senses, 'to fail at exams' and 'to break ground' (metaphorically, the flesh of the offending student). Then, nodding more seriously to *Piers Plowman*, in the final lines of *Doworst* he names the plough as 'a symbol | of the wounds that yet work or weal in the land', making the argument that although one may work hard and have high hopes for the result, 'oft the heart is cheated', for a scholar as for a farmer.

In summer 1953 Tolkien gave a copy of *Doworst* to his Oxford colleague Kathleen Lea. Lea, Vice Principal of Lady Margaret Hall, Oxford, was an official in the English Final Honours School examinations that year, under Tolkien as chairman, with David Cecil, E.J. Dobson, E.C. Horwood, J.I.M. Stewart, and Dorothy Whitelock. Miss Lea sent him a letter of thanks for the poem on 5 August that year, referring to a 'copy' which must have taken Tolkien some time to make. We have assumed that this was the typescript of which a copy is in Tolkien's papers, and from which we have made the transcription below (C), incorporating changes in manuscript. The work was now entitled *Visio de Doworst* ('Vision of Doworst'), with an *explicit* or concluding statement, *The Visio de Doworst of Johon Plowman* ('The Vision of Doworst of John Plowman'), using Tolkien's given name instead of 'Peter'.

[C] In a summer season when sultry was the sun
with lourdains and lubbers, I lounged in a hall,
and there wood in his wit was each wight as meseemed:
on his head was a hat as hard as a board,
on his neck was there knotted a noose all of white
with bow big and broad like a butterfly's wings.
The most of that meiny had on mantles of stuff,
shrouds short as shrift and shapeless as sacks
that never covered their tails nor their touts either.
The clamour of that company was like the cackle of hens,
till a bell rang brazenly — that abated their noise!
They were summoned, it seemed, to an assize to be held
by four clerks very fell whom few could appease,
justices ungentle in the judgement of fools.

I went in their wake, as they walked slowly
and passed down a passage paved all with marble
to a double doorway in a dim corner.
An usher it opened, and we entered in fear,
filing in like footmen, or folk of the street
that lacking labour are like lambs herded.
In long line forlorn we looked at our boots,
till a ferret-faced freak (half-famished he seemed,
with a nose like a nark, and narrow in the chest)
doffed his hat donnishly, and dourly beheld us,
mumbled us good-morning with mouthing unclear,
asking each after each to answer his name.
'That is Grim the Grammarman', the gomes whispered;
so I crept to a corner and hoped to escape.

Then most of the men he dismissed for the nonce;
but four full of fright sat fainting in chairs,
till the starveling stood up and sternly exclaimed
as in dudgeon: 'Doworst come to doom!' Up darted a boy —
his cheeks were all chop-fallen, no chin could be seen —
and trotted to the table with tottering feet.
There he sat him sideways as if sore in his seat,
and they eyed him an instant, as earwig on leaf,
ere one wipes it away with a wave of the hand.
Then a clerk at the corner that crouched at his book
looked up with a leer, and louted full low,
in mirth or in mockery: as a mask was his face;

one eye only opened, ill-omened he looked.
'That is Regulus the Ruthless, a render of youth,
a Goth full of gall, and a grinder of tears':
the unhappy men behind then hissed through their teeth;
and I marked in amaze how his mouth hardened
as with sibilant sound he softly began:
'I see, sir,' he said, 'you have signed here your name
to many reams of rubbish. You write like a crab,
so maybe what you meant is less monstrous folly
than appears in your papers as I puzzle them out. [']

Sir Grim was aghast as a ghost he had seen;
without a word then he waggled a wavering hand,
and beckoned the booby to budge to the left.
There suddenly, meseemed, from slumber awoke
a clerk with a countenance comely to see,
red as ripe apples or roses in June,
as he blushed on the boy with a beam in his eye;
but hoar was his hair, and his hat crumpled,
for long had he laboured in learning and teaching.
''Tis Sir Brittoner!' the boys burbled behind him.
'His blushes are but blinds; he is bawdy of jest,
and knoweth more naughtiness than nine men besides.
Look out when he laugheth! As like then as not
some horrible howler has hopped to his mind.'

Then I marked how with mirth his maw was aquake,
and he shook all in silence with secret delight.
At length he looked up and laughingly cried:
'Sir Loon, I love you, and like well your answers,
though a little they lack in learning, 'tis true,
and your wit runneth wild and wayward at times.
One Percy you praise, yet it puzzles me somewhat
to make out whom you mean among men of that name.'
Then the prisoner was pleased, and plucking up heart
as pert as a pie he replied without pause:
'Sir Percy, I opine, was a peer of the realm:
Duke Douglas the Jew he dinged once to death,
and then pottered with poetry for the profit of his age.
They found him a fellowship when failing in years.
and bribed him with a bishopric, for Ben Jonson's sake,
to bring his book to an end; but he babbled as a child,

till the Marshal Montgomery mortally smote him,
and his reliques now rot among rubbish on the shelves
in some charnel or church-vault — so champions end.'

Sir Brittoner as bull then bellowed aloud,
he rocked like a rowing-boat, and his ribs he embraced,
and beating on his breast like a babewin of the woods,
''tis sweet sooth you say!' he sobbed at the last.
'It is long since such lore I learned in this place!
You must pass to my companion. No power is me left,
by the ears of King Midas, to ask you aught else!'
Then the lede on the left uplifted his face.
He had bowed o'er the board as if beads he would say
(or pencil on paper some picture maybe,
or make for his merriment some morsel of verse).
He was blackhaired and broad, and balled was a little,
as a tonsure he had taken some terms now ago;
his jowl was ungentle and his jaw weighty.
''Tis Sir Plato the Pelegrim! He hath a pitiless wit;
he passes no pleasantry nor any pert reason,
till he hath proof on each point by page and by line':
so they sighed who still sat on seats there unsoft
and long it them thought ere they were loosed from their woe.
But I marvelled how that master then mightily spoke,
and with right ringing rerd his reasons he uttered,
each cutting and clear, and some cruel at the point,
till the boy at the board blanched at the thrust.
At last he relented (as to the loon it appeared),
and this Sir Plato him posed, and pleasantly smiled:
'Is *prosody* but *prose*, as your paper declares,
enlarged by the lewd for delight in long words?
A letter more or less but little imports,
if I read you not awry. Am I wrong, sir, in this?'
Then the urchin full humbly him answered in haste:
'So I wrote as seemed right. Pray, rue on me, sir!
As a pup in a prep-school this patter I learned
and repeated on paper perplexed by the heat.
I know it is nonsense, and acknowledge my fault.'
'That is enough then for now. 'Tis nonsense, in sooth;
but you are liable for libel, you lie on your school
that they taught you such trash. I turn now from that.

Other matters of metre I would mention a while:
what is verse that is *blank*, I beg you reveal.
Who wrote it and wrought it, can you reckon their names?'

Then blankly the boy, rebuffed at that blow,
stared like a stuck pig, and startled he seemed;
but a light seemed to dawn at length on his darkness,
as though a riddle he had read and was right in the end.
'Such verses, I would venture, in advertisements stand;
they are writ in the rough with the rhymes missing,
often in the papers they appear for the people to finish
who compete for some prize in praise of a cheese.
But what man ever makes them is a mystery of God,
and the publicity agents that blear all our eyes.'

Sir Plato turned pale as with pang at the heart,
cast his hood o'er his head and hid up his face;
Sir Brittoner bawled forth 'the bastard is mad!',
and Sir Regulus retched and wrinkled his nose;
Sir Grim rent his gown and gulped in his throat,
then spin-foot he sprang and sprinted to the bell.
An usher then entered and asked what he wished;
and the clerks with a clamour all cried out together:
'Hale forth this harlot and hew him with staves!
Kick him from these cloisters to Carfax and further,
then plough him in pieces with ploughshares keen,
as red-hot as wrath — no ruth he deserves!'

Catchpolls came crowding and caught him by the arms,
and drove him to the doors with dint of their boots;
and he shrieked as they shut, that I shivered in my shoes,
and swallowed in a swoon I slipped to the ground.
When I looked up at length alone there I lay;
all had fled from the fury of that assize.
What became of the clerks I cared not to ask.
But a voice out of view from some veiled corner
then said, as meseemed, all soft in my ear:
'Now Doworst is doomed. Do not deem it a jape!
For many such assemble in this city by the ford,
and Falsehood and Folly are the friends that they take.
No right have they to rest here, to rot in their youth
and waste here their while, working no profit.

Were such served at assize as their deserts merit,
they would all end as this urchin, with iron or with rope.'

So I passed from that place, and pondered in heart,
and I privily prayed, though pupils perchance
be somewhat of the sort that I saw in my dream,
that clerks of such kind may be counted a fable,
that dons may have dignity and their dooms mercy.

Now summer grew sere, and the sun faded;
wind woke in the west and warred with the trees:
the world withered away as winter approached.
So I passed to my plough that is appointed a symbol
of the wounds that yet work or weal in the land;
and fair through the fold my furrow I drew,
and I sowed many seeds in the sweat of my brow.
Yet though high be the hope, yet oft the heart is cheated;
neither countryman nor clerk hath all corn for his swink.

EXPLICIT: THE VISIO DE DOWORST
OF IOHON PLOWMAN

Preserved with the typescript copy is a note by Tolkien:

> The original copy (in calligraphic script) was sent to RWC [R.W. Chambers] – the recipient of many such squibs, I believe, from H.C. Wyld [another distinguished scholar of English] & others. RWC had *Doworst* bound by [Douglas] Cockerell; but I do not know what became of it, when he died (in exile from U.C.L.) in Aberystwyth, I think. [University College London had relocated to Wales at the outbreak of war; Chambers was 'in exile' from London if not from the College.] This copy was revised before going to Miss K. Lea. *Atkins* does not appear in it. Doworst was substituted.

This version, in which the clerks become 'justices ungentle in the judgement of fools', is fifty lines shorter than text B, largely due to Tolkien removing the exchanges between Sir Regulus and Sir Grim with the candidate, now nameless except for 'Doworst'. Perhaps he felt that the references were too obscure, some twenty years after the 1932 examinations, or that they would be less amusing to Miss Lea than to Professor Chambers. It was a significant loss, not least because although Sir Grim is still 'aghast', the student replies that made him so are no longer evident. The lines about 'Percy' remained, however: by 1953, Percy Simpson was long retired, but was still known in Oxford.

Musing in the final stanza about scars on the land, or (as may be) on the soil as a site of renewal, would have had added poignancy after the hardships of the Second World War, still not much abated in the early 1950s. On the other hand, imagery of digging – 'fair through the fold my furrow I drew', surely an echo of the best-known line in *Piers Plowman*, 'a fair field full of folk found I there between' – and of sowing ('I sowed many seeds in the sweat of my brow') would apply to an academic life of research and thought as well as to the life of a ploughman.

In the same vein as *Doworst*, see *The Clerkes Compleinte*, poem no. 68.

A4: Tolkien forgot to include 'head'.

A8: 'Short as shrift' is a play on 'short shrift', i.e. curt treatment. A *shrift* is a confession to a priest.

A15: 'Went in their wake', i.e. followed behind.

B19–20: 'Folk off the street | that lacking labour are like lambs herded': presumably like men loitering without employment, told by an authority to move along.

B22–23: If our identification of Sir Grim is correct, 'a ferret-faced freke (half famished he seemed, | with a nose like a nark, and narrow in the chest)' must be meant as a description of the poet himself. If so, 'ferret-faced' is unfair, but 'half famished' and 'narrow in the chest' accord with Tolkien's slight build. In a 1967 interview, he said that for most of his life he had been thin and underweight. *Freke*, from Middle English, means 'bold man', or simply 'man'. The phrase 'a nose like a nark' is curious: *nark* is slang for a police informer, derived from the Romany word for 'nose'. Perhaps Tolkien was thinking of his love of ferreting or nosing out new things to learn. Of course, his choice of words here was partly to serve alliteration.

B33: We cannot explain the name *Atkins*, unless Tolkien had in mind *Tommy Atkins*, common slang for an ordinary British soldier (the American equivalent is *G.I. Joe*); or perhaps there was an actual student by that name in the 1932 examinations.

B34: 'Cheeks were chop-fallen', i.e. his jaw was hanging open.

B49: 'You write like a crab': 'crabbed' handwriting is poorly formed and hard to read. Tolkien himself was criticized for poor penmanship when he was an undergraduate.

B55: 'Like an eel on a fork', i.e. like a piece of jellied eel, a traditional British food.

B101: 'Aghast, as a ghost he had seen': both *aghast* 'frightened' and *ghost* are related to Old English *gāst* 'ghost, spirit, demon'.

B124: 'Pert as a pie', i.e. as bold or impudent as a magpie. In his 'Reeve's Tale' Chaucer calls the miller's wife 'peert as a pye'.

B136: 'Babewin of the woods': *babewin* means 'baboon', and is also a medieval term for a grotesque animal figure, such as a gargoyle. Here Tolkien plays on the phrase 'babe in the woods', meaning an innocent or naïve person.

B140: 'Ears of King Midas': in Greek legend, it is said that when Midas (he who, in another story, turned all he touched to gold) was appointed judge of a musical competition between Apollo and Pan, he favoured the latter, whereupon Apollo gave the king asses' ears.

B142: 'Bowed o'er [over] the board as if beads he would say', i.e. bowed his head over the table at which the examiners are seated, as if he were praying with rosary beads.

B148: 'Pert reason': here *pert* (from *apert*) means 'evident'.

B150: 'Seats there unsoft', i.e. on hard chairs or benches, without cushions.

B157: *Prosody* is the study of rhythm and versification, *prose* is language not intended as poetry. Sir Plato seems to be saying that Doworst has argued that verse is merely fancy prose. Later in this line, 'paper' originally read 'papers', probably in error.

B159: 'A letter more or less but little imports': presumably, Doworst has suggested that small details are of little matter. But a difference of a letter would have a great bearing on, say, alliterative verse.

B162: 'Rue on me', i.e. have pity.

B163: 'Pup in a prep-school', i.e. a schoolboy.

B176–181: Doworst confuses *blank verse* (verse with regular metre, usually iambic pentameter, but unrhymed) with advertisements in magazines for competitions in which the applicant fills in a blank to complete a phrase.

B183: In academic costume, a *hood* does not cover the head, but is draped over the shoulders.

B187: 'Spinfoot he sprang': presumably, turning around while rising. C139 has 'spin-foot'.

B190: *Harlot* here means a vagabond or beggar, not the familiar 'prostitute'.

B191: Carfax (from Latin *quadrifurcus* 'four-forked') is the ancient heart of Oxford, where four roads meet from the city's four gates.

B204: 'City by the ford', i.e. Oxford.

B212: 'Be' originally read 'were'.

B213: 'May' originally read 'might'.

B214: 'Their' originally read 'the'.

B218: 'Season' originally read 'the season'.

C19: 'Folk of the street' was 'Folk off the street' in B19. Since either 'of' or 'off' makes sense, one cannot be sure whether 'of' in C is an error.

C68: 'I love you' originally read 'I love thee', and 'your answers' read 'thy answers'.

C70: 'Your wit' originally read 'thy wit'.

C71: 'You praise' originally read 'thou praisest', and 'puzzles' read 'puzzleth'.

C99: *Pelegrim* is Middle English 'pilgrim'; cf. 'pilgrim' in B147.

C100: 'By page and by line': two methods of citing specific locations in a text.

C177: 'Plowman' is the spelling preferred by most scholars of *Piers Plowman*. The usual (British) spelling of the word when not in the poem title is 'ploughman'.

140

The Fall of Arthur (?1933–2013)

The Fall of Arthur was the last of the longer poems Tolkien composed in imitation of Old English alliterative verse. He seems to have begun to write it in the early 1930s, after he finished work on his 'New Lays' (no. 131); making an educated guess, we have assigned their completion, and the origin of *The Fall of Arthur*, to ?1933. The poem was still incomplete towards the end of 1934, when Tolkien lent it to R.W. Chambers, the prominent *Beowulf* scholar of University College London. On 9 December Chambers informed his friend that the work was 'very great indeed . . . really heroic, quite apart from its value in showing how the *Beowulf* metre can be used in modern English', and urged him to finish it (quoted in *The Fall of Arthur* (2013), p. 10). In the event, Tolkien left it incomplete, even after working on it apparently as late as August 1937, a date he wrote on a related page of notes. Christopher Tolkien believed that his father abandoned *The Fall of Arthur* at that time due to his turning to work on *The Lost Road* and, after publication of *The Hobbit*, to *The Lord of the Rings*.

In the published *Fall of Arthur* Christopher describes the prodigious series of manuscripts through which his father developed the poem, including 120 pages of drafts. The completed work, of 954 lines, is presented in five cantos, but Tolkien did not write them in their final order of arrangement; he conceived Canto I, for example, only while composing Canto III. He spent a great deal of time and thought on the poem, searching 'unceasingly for a better rhythm, or a better word or phrase within the alliterative constraints' (pp. 171–2). 'The movement from the earliest workings (often only partly legible)', Christopher states, 'can be largely followed through succeeding manuscripts that underwent abundant emendation. In some parts of the poem confusing elements are the parallel development of different versions, and the movement of blocks of text to stand in different contexts' (p. 171). The first manuscript page of Canto II is reproduced in McIlwaine, *Tolkien: Maker of Middle-earth*, p. 248.

For the present book, we have first made a selection from *The Fall of Arthur* of sixty-seven lines from the start of Canto III (pp. 35–8); we give these as A. Tolkien begins with an evocative description of storm and sea, then segues to the equally stormy emotions of Lancelot, Guinever, and Mordred, each of them driven by love or lust.

[A] In the South from sleep to swift fury
a storm was stirred, striding northward
over leagues of water loud with thunder
and roaring rain it rushed onward.
Their hoary heads hills and mountains
tossed in tumult on the towering seas.
On Benwick's beaches breakers pounding
ground gigantic grumbling boulders
with ogre anger. The air was salt
with spume and spindrift splashed to vapour.

There Lancelot over leagues of sea
in heaving welter from a high window
looked and wondered alone musing.
Dark slowly fell. Deep his anguish.
He his lord betrayed to love yielding,
and love forsaking lord regained not;
faith was refused him who had faith broken,
by leagues of sea from love sundered.

Sir Lancelot, Lord of Benwick
of old was the noblest knight of Arthur,
among sons of kings kingly seeming,
deemed most daring, in deeds of arms
all surpassing, eager-hearted;
among folk whose beauty as a flower blossomed
in face the fairest, formed in manhood
strong and gracious steel well-tempered.
White his hue was; his hair raven,
dark and splendid; dark his eyes were.
Gold was Gawain, gold as sunlight,
but grey his eyes were gleaming keenly;
his mood sterner. By men holden
almost equal envy he knew not,
peer and peerless praising justly,
but to his lord alone his love giving;
no man nor woman in his mind holding
dearer than Arthur. Daily watchful
the Queen he doubted, ere the cold shadow
on her great glory grey had fallen.

To Lancelot her love gave she,
in his great glory gladness finding.
To his lady only was his love given;
no man nor woman in his mind held he
than Guinever dearer: glory only,
knighthood's honour, near his lady
in his heart holding. High his purpose;
he long was loyal to his lord Arthur,
among the Round Table's royal order
prince and peerless, proudly serving
Queen and lady. But cold silver
or glowing gold greedy-hearted
in her fingers taken fairer thought she,
more lovely deeming what she alone treasured
darkly hoarded. Dear she loved him
with love unyielding, lady ruthless,
fair as fay-woman and fell-minded
in the world walking for the woe of men.
Fate sent her forth. Fair she deemed him
beyond gold and silver to her grasp lying.
Silver and golden, as the sun at morning
her smile dazzled, and her sudden weeping
with tears softened, tender poison,
steel well-tempered. Strong oaths they broke.

Mordred in secret mirthless watched them
betwixt hate and envy, hope and torment.
Thus was bred the evil, and the black shadow
o'er the courts of Arthur as a cloud growing
dimmed the daylight darkling slowly.

As the title of his poem implies, Tolkien was concerned with the end of an era, the passing of something which had once been glorious. King Arthur's Round Table has been rent by the adultery of Lancelot, his 'noblest knight', with Arthur's queen, Guinever (Guinevere), and by the death of the three brothers of Sir Gawain at Lancelot's hand while rescuing Guinever from a pyre. Although Arthur gave the Queen his pardon, there was none for Lancelot ('faith was refused him || who had faith broken'). The latter has gone to his castle of Benwick in France, the scene at the opening of Canto III; and Arthur having led an army against heathen Saxons on the Continent, Mordred has moved to seize the crown. Lusting after Guinever ('mirthless watched them | | betwixt hate and envy'), he offers to share the kingdom with her, but she flees to her childhood home. The Queen wonders if Lancelot will hear of her fate and come to her aid; Lancelot wonders if she will summon him, or if Arthur will ask his aid in recovering Britain, half hoping that the King will call upon him, half wishing he will not. On hearing of Mordred's treachery, Arthur returns from the Continent, on Gawain's advice choosing not to seek help from Lancelot. He destroys the ships of Mordred's allies, but doubts his strength to take the walled city of Romeril, and decides to land further west.

There the finished text of the poem ends. Notes for its conclusion and scraps of verse, however, give hints of unexpected developments after the battle in which Arthur and Mordred slay each other, and the dying Arthur is borne away on a ship. The most intriguing of these is that Lancelot comes to Britain seeking news of Arthur, and does not turn aside even when he meets Guinever. A note reads: 'The hermit by the sea shore tells him of Arthur's departure. Lancelot gets a boat and sails west and never returns. – Eärendel passage' (p. 136). The latter appears to refer to an eighteen-line account in alliterative verse of the voyage of Eärendel – the figure in Tolkien's private mythology – as an analogy for Lancelot's voyage, a fragment Tolkien later considered for separate publication (see Appendix III, list H). We give this text (*The Fall of Arthur*, pp. 137–8) as B, as Tolkien wrote it before revision.

[B] The moon mounted the mists of the sea,
and quivering in the cold the keen starlight
that wavered wan in the waiting East
failed and faded; the foam upon the shore
was glimmering ghostly upon grey shingle,
and the roaring sea rose in darkness
to the watchers on the wall.
O! wondrous night
when shining like the moon, with shrouds of pearl,
with sails of samite, and the silver stars
in her blue banner embroidered white
in glittering gems, that galleon was thrust
on the shadowy seas under shades of night!
Eärendel goeth on eager quest
to magic islands beyond the miles of the sea,
past the hills of Avalon and the halls of the moon,
the dragon's portals and the dark mountains
of the Bay of Faery on the borders of the world.

Christopher Tolkien comments (p. 138) that the first seven lines of this passage 'were later hastily altered by my father thus, largely for metrical improvement':

> The moon was fallen into misty caves,
> and quivering cold the keen starlight
> wavered wanly in the waiting East
> failed and faded; the foam upon the shore
> was glimmering ghostly upon grey shingle,
> and the roaring sea rising and falling
> under walls of stone.

In the published *Fall of Arthur* Christopher examines at length the connections between his father's later workings of the poem and the 'Silmarillion' mythology. The mariner Eärendel and his voyage into the West, as above, is only one of these, with its references to 'magic islands' and 'the Bay of Faery'. Another is the presence in the 'Eärendel passage' of the name *Avalon*. In the context of Arthurian legend, Avalon is the Fortunate Isle, *Insula Pomorum* (the Isle of Apples), dominion of Morgan la Fée, an earthly paradise to which the wounded Arthur is taken after the Battle of Camlan. In *The Fall of Arthur* Tolkien associates *Avalon* with his own invented earthly paradise, Tol Eressëa. *Avallon*, so spelled, entered Tolkien's writings, Christopher observes, 'at the time when the Fall of Númenor and the Change of the World [see poem no. 74] entered also, with the conception of the Straight Path out of the Round World that still led to Tol Eressëa and Valinor, a road that was denied to mortals, and yet found, in a mystery, by Ælfwine of England' (p. 162). The resemblance between Arthurian *Avalon* and Tolkien's *Avallon* was surely deliberate.

In a letter of ?late 1951 to the publisher Milton Waldman, concerning 'The Silmarillion', Tolkien explained that he did not adopt Arthurian legend as a basis for his mythology – originally to have linked his 'Lost Tales' with historical England (see poem no. 40) – because it was 'associated with the soil of Britain but not with English', 'its "faerie" is too lavish, and fantastical, incoherent and repetitive', and it 'explicitly contains the Christian religion' (*Letters*, p. 203). John D. Rateliff has commented that in *The Fall of Arthur* Tolkien instead 'made a place within his legendarium into which the Arthurian tales could be fitted. So the whole Matter of Britain becomes, conceptually, through the Lost Road, a subordinate element to the legendarium, another contributory stream to the great river that is the Matter of Middle-earth' ('"That Seems to Me Fatal": Pagan and Christian in *The Fall of Arthur*' (2016), p. 46).

Tolkien was well aware of the long development of the Arthurian legends, the 'Matter of Britain', from Geoffrey of Monmouth's mid-twelfth-century *Historia Regum Britanniae* (*History of the Kings of Britain*) to Alfred, Lord Tennyson's *Idylls of the King*. In the published *Fall of Arthur* Christopher Tolkien points especially to the medieval 'Alliterative Morte Arthure', a Middle English poem composed around 1400, and the Arthurian tales of Sir Thomas Malory. Nelson Goering has pointed out that although Tolkien drew for *The Fall of Arthur* from narrative sources in Middle English, he did not use Middle English verse forms, but turned instead to the Old English tradition – and yet, Arthurian legend is not known in Anglo-Saxon literature. See further, Goering's '*The Fall of Arthur* and *The Legend of Sigurd and Gudrún*: A Metrical Review of Three Modern English Alliterative Poems' (2015). T.S. Sudell, meanwhile, has written a detailed study of the scansion of the poem, in 'The Alliterative Verse of *The Fall of Arthur*' (2016).

In a review of *The Fall of Arthur* in *Tolkien Studies* (2014), Verlyn Flieger observes that Tolkien gives us 'no jousts, no tournaments, no knights and ladies playing games of love, no glittering, enclosed world of Camelot. There is no Merlin, no Morgan le Fay, no magic or Otherworld. There is no Grail, no Quest for a spiritual vision to expose the frailty of the earthly kingdom. There is no hint of a return.' He does, however, give us 'a somber story whose overriding image is the tide, embodying the ebb and flow of events on which the human actors are carried' (p. 215). And among this is a point Flieger thinks unique to Tolkien,

> the fact that three of the four principals – Arthur, Lancelot, and Guinevere – are waiting for word that never comes. Lancelot hopes in vain for a summons from Arthur; Arthur waits and hopes Lancelot will come to his aid voluntarily; Guinevere, fleeing Mordred, wonders if Lancelot will come to her rescue, while Lancelot waits for her to summon him. All these hesitations are balanced one against another, with the result that nobody reaches out to anybody. [p. 216]

141

Firiel · The Last Ship (?1933–62)

We have dated this poem to ?1933 because that is when Tolkien submitted a version of it for publication in the *Chronicle of the Convents of the Sacred Heart* (no. 4, for 1934). He was in touch with the Society of the Sacred Heart, an order of Roman Catholic nuns, who since 1929 had operated a hostel in Oxford for female students; from 1932, their convent was in Norham Gardens, not far from the Tolkien home in Northmoor Road. Tolkien's daughter Priscilla attended children's parties with the nuns in summer, and at Christmas while her father provided entertainment. We suppose that he was asked to contribute to the order's journal, and chose to send them *Firiel*; he received a letter of praise for it on 2 November 1933. It is possible that he composed the work around that time, though it equally may be that it belongs to an earlier date.

The fair copy manuscript we have transcribed below as A, for which no drafts are extant, is written on good paper of the kind used for examinations at Oxford, and thus is likely no earlier than the late 1920s, after Tolkien returned to Oxford from Leeds. A subsequent typescript, made on Tolkien's Hammond machine, is of the same vintage: its text is almost identical to that of the manuscript, with only a few changes to punctuation and the start of every other line capitalized.

[A]

Fíriel looked out at three o'clock:
    the grey night was going,
far away a golden cock
    clear and shrill was crowing.
The trees were dark, the light was pale;
    waking birds were cheeping;
a wind moved, cool and frail
    through dim leaves creeping.

She watched the gleam at window grow,
    till the long light was shimmering
on land and leaf; on grass below
    the grey dew was glimmering.

Over the floor her white feet crept,
    down the stairs they twinkled,
through the grass they dancing stepped
    all with dew besprinkled.

Her gown had jewels upon its hem,
    as she ran down to the river,
and leaned upon a willow-stem,
    and watched the water quiver.
A kingfisher plunged down like a stone
        in a blue flash falling,
bending reeds were softly blown,
    lily-leaves were sprawling.

A sudden music to her came,
    as she stood there gleaming
with free hair in the morning's flame
    on her shoulders streaming.
Flutes there were, and harps were wrung,
    and there was sound of singing
like wind-voices keen and young
    in green leaves swinging.

A boat with golden beak and oar
    and timbers white came gliding;
swans went sailing on before
    her swift course guiding.
Fair folk out of Elvenland
    robed in white were rowing,
and three with crowns she saw there stand
    with bright hair flowing.

They sang their song, while minstrels played
    on harp and flute slowly
like sea heard in a green glade
    under mountains holy.
The beak was turned, the boat drew nigh
    with elven-treasure laden.
'Fíriel! Come aboard!' they cry,
    'O fair earth-maiden!'

‘O whither go ye Elvenfolk
    down the waters gliding?
Under willow, elm, and oak
    to a far forest-hiding?
To foam that falls upon the shore
    and the white gulls crying?
To Northern isles grey and frore
    on strong swans flying?’

‘Beyond that, and beyond, away
    past oak and elm and willow,
Leaving western havens grey,
    cleaving the green billow;
tarrying not for Northern isles,
    nor further coasts and stranger;
wearying not for unmeasured miles,
    ensnared by dread nor danger.

We go back to Elvenhome
    beyond the last mountains,
whose feet are in the outer foam
    of the world’s deep fountains.
There things are as they seem to be
    in a fair song’s making;
there Light is clear as melody
    to one in music waking.

In Elvenhome the sweet bells
    are in white towers shaking,
and thither longing us compels
    thy land and stream forsaking.
Come, Fíriel! No longer stay!
    Now is the hour of waking.
Farewell to wood and water say,
    the long road taking!

Here grass fades and leaves fall,
    and sun and moon wither;
and never comes again the call
    to thou once bidden thither.’

Fíriel looked from the river-bank,
    one step daring;
and then her heart misgave, and shrank,
    and she halted, staring.

She held forth her white hand,
    and dim tears were starting
for the white ship of Elvenland
    passing and departing.
Higher climbed the round sun,
    and the dew was drying;
faint faded one by one
    their far voices crying.

No jewels bright her gown bore,
    as she walked back from the water,
under roof and dark door,
    earth's fair daughter.
At eight o'clock in green and white,
    with long hair braided,
She tripped down leaving night
    and a vision faded.

Breakfast was on table laid;
    there were voices loud and merry;
there was jam, honey, marmalade,
    milk, and fruit, and berry.
Of this and that people spoke,
    jest, work, and money,
shooting bird, and felling oak,
    and, 'please pass the honey'.

Up climbed the round Sun,
    and the world was busy,
in and out, walk and run,
    like an anthill dizzy.
Inside the house were feet
    going pitter-patter;
brooms, dusters, mats to beat;
    pails and dishes' clatter.

Fíriel looked out in the noon-hour:
the sunlight was glaring.
At tree, grass, and summer-flower
her wide eyes were staring.
She looked and she saw them not
half-seen too often:
no music came, or voice forgot,
heart again to soften.

Firiel is linked to Tolkien's mythology from its first word, which is Elvish for 'mortal woman'. The name occurs in his writings several times, attached to different persons; for example, in his preface to *The Adventures of Tom Bombadil and Other Verses from the Red Book* he states that it is a Gondorian name 'of High-elvish form', 'borne by a princess of Gondor, through whom Aragorn claimed descent from the Southern line. It was also the name of a daughter of Elanor, daughter of Sam, but her name, if connected with the rhyme [*The Last Ship*], must be derived from it; it could not have arisen in West-march [west of the Hobbits' Shire, and ultimately a part of it]' (p. 8). See, as well, the song of yet another Firiel in poem no. 145.

To someone unfamiliar with Tolkien's mythology – and this would have been true of almost any reader of his works in the 1930s – the name *Firiel* would have sounded merely strange and melodious. But the notion that human involvement with otherworldly folk may be fraught with danger was widely familiar from centuries of fairy lore. Tolkien makes a clear distinction between the Elven mariners, singing in their ship of white and gold, and the 'fair earth-maiden' born into a nature where, inevitably, grass must fade and leaves must fall.

Tolkien used the Hammond typescript twice as a working copy. Probably in 1933, beginning with the seventh stanza, he deleted large portions of the text, rewriting most of the omitted passages except for the final stanza ('Fíriel looked out in the noon-hour') which was excised without replacement, and adjusting stanza breaks to preserve his ABABCDCD rhyme scheme. Finally, he moved the original penultimate stanza ('Up climbed the round sun') to come before that which had preceded it ('Breakfast was on table laid'). Thus *Firiel* appeared in the *Chronicle*, on pp. 30–2, in a revised and shortened form, given below as text B.

[B]

Firiel looked out at three o'clock:
the grey night was going,
Far away a golden cock
clear and shrill was crowing.
The trees were dark, the light was pale;
waking birds were cheeping;
A wind moved cool and frail
through dim leaves creeping.

She watched the gleam at window grow,
till the long light was shimmering
On land and leaf; on grass below
grey dew was glimmering.
Over the floor her white feet crept,
down the stairs they twinkled,
Through the grass they dancing stepped
all with dew besprinkled.

Her gown had jewels upon its hem,
as she ran down to the river,
And leaned upon a willow-stem,
and watched the water quiver.
A kingfisher plunged down like a stone
in a blue flash falling,
Bending reeds were softly blown,
lily-leaves were sprawling.

A sudden music to her came,
as she stood there gleaming
With free hair in the morning's flame
on her shoulders streaming.
Flutes there were, and harps were wrung,
and there was sound of singing
Like wind-voices keen and young
in green leaves swinging.

A boat with golden beak and oar
and timbers white came gliding;
Swans went sailing on before,
her swift course guiding.

Fair folk out of Elvenland
    robed in white were rowing,
And three with crowns she saw there stand
    with bright hair flowing.

They sang their song, while minstrels played
    on harp and flute slowly
Like sea heard in a green glade
    under mountains holy.
The beak was turned, the boat drew nigh
    with elven-treasure laden.
'Firiel! Come aboard!' they cry,
    'O fair earth-maiden!'

'O whither go ye, Elvenfolk,
    down the waters gliding?
To the twilight under beech and oak
    in the green forest hiding?
To foam that falls upon the shore
    and the white gulls crying?
To Northern isles grey and frore
    on strong swans flying?'

'Nay! Out and onward, far away
    past oak and elm and willow,
Leaving western havens grey,
    cleaving the green billow,
We go back to Elvenhome
    beyond the last mountains,
Whose feet are in the outer foam
    of the world's deep fountains.

In Elvenhome a clear bell
    is in white tower shaking!
To wood and water say farewell,
    the long road taking!
Here grass fades and leaves fall
    and sun and moon wither;
And to few comes the far call
    that bids them journey thither.'

Firiel looked from the river-bank,
    one step daring;
And then her heart misgave and shrank,
    and she halted staring.
Higher climbed the round sun,
    and the dew was drying;
Faint faded, one by one,
    their far voices crying.

No jewels bright her gown bore,
    as she walked back from the water,
Under roof and dark door,
    earth's fair daughter.
At eight o'clock in green and white,
    with long hair braided,
She tripped down, leaving night
    and a vision faded.

Up climbed the round sun,
    and the world was busy,
In and out, walk and run,
    like an anthill dizzy.
Inside the house were feet
    going pitter-patter;
Brooms, dusters, mats to beat,
    pails, and dishes clatter.

Breakfast was on table laid;
    there were voices loud and merry;
There were jam, honey, marmalade,
    milk and fruit, and berry,
Of this and that people spoke,
    jest, work, and money,
Shooting bird, and felling oak,
    and 'please pass the honey!'

As printed, this version was accompanied by two illustrations by a talented but inattentive artist, who chose to draw Firiel as a young, short-haired girl in a summer dress and shoes despite the poet's explicit description of long hair, a gown, and bare feet, and an elven ship with only three occupants and no oars. In private notes Christopher Tolkien wondered what his father thought of the drawings.

After its *Chronicle* appearance, Tolkien seems to have set *Firiel* aside until he reviewed his existing poems for the *Tom Bombadil* collection, beginning in 1961. Returning to the Hammond typescript, he made further revisions, in pencil, which (with one exception) can be distinguished from those for the *Chronicle* text, made in ink. He also marked changes on the final page of the printed poem, removed from a copy of the Sacred Heart *Chronicle*. Finally, he scribbled workings for the new version on the back of a leaf of manuscript of *Iúmonna Gold Galdre Bewunden* (no. 69) from the early 1930s, another example of Tolkien using any blank paper that came to hand. We have transcribed, as C, as much of this largely illegible draft as we can decipher.

[C]

Firiel looked from the river-bank
One step daring
Then deep in clay her feet sank
and she halted staring
Slowly the Elvenship went by
whispering through the water:
'I cannot come!' they heard her cry
I was made Earth's daughter
Earth ?can? hold her daughter

No jewels bright her gown bore
as she walked back from the meadows
under roof and dark door
and the house ?in shadows

At eight o'clock brown & white
with her hair braided
she stepped down leaving night
and a vision faded

F. looked out in the noon hour
her grey eyes were staring
Tired and dull ?too she saw them grow

To hear the call and not to go

The next full text of *Firiel*, a typescript, is unusual in that after typing two pages Tolkien marked stanzas six through nine for deletion, and replaced them with five stanzas typed on an additional page, to be followed by the original tenth stanza and then another three on a final page. (We are grateful to Christopher Tolkien for making this analysis in private notes.) The first few, and last few, stanzas are largely the same as in text B. Tolkien now returned to his original scheme for the poem throughout, in which only the first word of a complete sentence is capitalized. Here, as D, we have transcribed the whole of this version, with original stanzas six through nine in place, followed by the new stanzas so indicated, and finally the concluding stanzas.

[D] Firiel looked out at three o'clock:
the grey night was going;
far away a golden cock
clear and shrill was crowing.
The trees were dark, the light was pale,
waking birds were cheeping;
a wind moved cool and frail
through dim leaves creeping.

She watched the gleam at window grow,
till the long light was shimmering
on land and leaf; on grass below
grey dew was glimmering.
Over the floor her white feet crept,
down the stairs they twinkled,
through the grass they dancing stepped
all with dew besprinkled.

Her gown had jewels upon its hem,
as she ran down to the river,
and leaned upon a willow-stem,
and watched the water quiver.
A kingfisher plunged down like a stone
in a blue flash falling,
bending reeds were softly blown,
lily-leaves were sprawling.

A sudden music to her came,
as she stood there gleaming
with free hair in the morning's flame
on her shoulders streaming.
flutes there were, and harps were wrung,
and there was sound of singing
like wind-voices keen and young
in green leaves swinging.

A boat with golden beak and oar
and timbers white came gliding;
swans went sailing on before,
her swift course guiding.
Fair folk out of Elvenland
robed in white were rowing,
and three with crowns she saw there stand
with bright hair flowing.

Tolkien marked lines 41–72 for replacement:

They sang their song, while minstrels played
on harp and flute slowly
like sea heard in a green dale
under mountains holy.
The beak was turned, the boat drew nigh
with elven-treasure laden:
'Fíriel! Come aboard!' they cry,
'O fair earth-maiden!'

'O whither go ye, Elvenfolk,
down the waters gliding?
To the twilight under beech and oak
in the green forest hiding?
To foam that falls upon the shore
and the white gulls crying?
To Northern isles grey and frore
on strong swans flying?'

'Nay! Out and onward far away
past oak and elm and willow,
leaving western havens grey,
cleaving the green billow,
we go back to Elvenhome
beyond the last mountains,
Whose feet are in the outer foam
of the world's deep fountains.

'In Elvenhome a clear bell
is in white tower shaking!
To wood and water say farewell,
the long road taking!

Here grass fades and leaves fall
    and sun and moon wither;
And to few comes the far call
    that bids them journey thither.'

Here begin the five stanzas (lines 73–112) written to replace the previous four; for purposes of reference, we have continued the line numbering as above:

With harps in hand they sang their song
    to the slow oars swinging:
'Green is the land, the leaves are long,
    and the birds are singing.
Many a day with dawn of gold
    this earth will lighten;
Many a flower will yet unfold,
    ere the cornfields whiten. [']

'Then whither go yet, boatmen fair,
    down the river gliding?
To twilight and to secret lair
    in the great forest hiding?
To Northern isles and shores of stone
    on strong swans flying,
by cold waves to dwell alone
    with the white gulls crying?'

'Nay!' they answered. 'Far away
    on the last road faring,
leaving western havens grey,
    the seas of shadow daring,
we go back to Elvenhome,
    where the White Tree is growing,
and the Star shines upon the foam
    on the last shore flowing.

'To mortal fields say farewell,
    middle-earth forsaking!
In Elvenhome a clear bell
    in the high tower is shaking!

Here grass fades and leaves fall,
    and sun and moon wither,
and we have heard the far call
    that bids us journey thither!'

The oars were stayed. They turned aside:
    'Do you hear the call, Earth-maiden?
Firiel! Firiel!' they cried.
    'Our boat is not full-laden.
One more only we may bear.
    Come! For your days are speeding.
Come! Earth-maiden elven-fair,
    our last call heeding!'

Now follow the original tenth stanza (as first typed), here lines 113–120, and the remaining stanzas to the end of the poem, line 121 and following.

Fíriel looked from the river-bank,
    one step daring;
then deep in clay her feet sank,
    and she halted staring.
Higher climbed the round sun,
    and the dew was drying;
Faint faded, one by one,
    their far voices crying.

No jewels bright her gown bore,
    as she walked back from the meadows,
under roof and dark door,
    under the house-shadows.
At eight o'clock in brown and white,
    with long hair braided,
she stepped down, leaving night
    and a vision faded.

Up climbed the round sun,
    and the world was busy,
in and out, walk and run,
    like an anthill dizzy.

Inside the house were feet
going pitter-patter;
brooms, dusters, mats to beat,
pails and dishes' clatter.

Breakfast was on table spread;
there were voices loud and merry;
yellow butter, white bread,
milk and fruit and berry.
Of this and that people spoke,
of jest, work, and money,
shooting bird, and felling oak,
and 'please, pass the honey!'

In most respects, this version nearly reached the final form of the poem, as it was published in *The Adventures of Tom Bombadil and Other Verses from the Red Book* in 1962, there retitled *The Last Ship*. After making further changes, Tolkien sent the work, still called *Firiel*, to his publisher on 5 February 1962. We give this ultimate text below as E, from pp. 61–4 of the collection. It has a few minor differences in its earlier stanzas relative to version D, but most notably, at its end Tolkien omitted any mention of the busy activities of a household, a feature of the poem in every previous version, and he wrote a new final stanza which brought the poem to a more solemn conclusion – or perhaps we should say, brought it again to such a result, recalling the final lines of text A.

[E] Fíriel looked out at three o'clock:
the grey night was going;
far away a golden cock
clear and shrill was crowing.
The trees were dark, and the dawn pale,
waking birds were cheeping,
a wind moved cool and frail
through dim leaves creeping.

She watched the gleam at window grow,
till the long light was shimmering
on land and leaf; on grass below
grey dew was glimmering.

Over the floor her white feet crept,
down the stair they twinkled,
through the grass they dancing stepped
all with dew besprinkled.

Her gown had jewels upon its hem,
as she ran down to the river,
and leaned upon a willow-stem,
and watched the water quiver.
A kingfisher plunged down like a stone
in a blue flash falling,
bending reeds were softly blown,
lily-leaves were sprawling.

A sudden music to her came,
as she stood there gleaming
with free hair in the morning's flame
on her shoulders streaming.
Flutes there were, and harps were wrung,
and there was sound of singing,
like wind-voices keen and young
and far bells ringing.

A ship with golden beak and oar
and timbers white came gliding;
swans went sailing on before,
her tall prow guiding.
Fair folk out of Elvenland
in silver-grey were rowing,
and three with crowns she saw there stand
with bright hair flowing.

With harp in hand they sang their song
to the slow oars swinging:
'Green is the land, the leaves are long,
and the birds are singing.
Many a day with dawn of gold
this earth will lighten,
many a flower will yet unfold,
ere the cornfields whiten.'

'Then whither go ye, boatmen fair,
    down the river gliding?
To twilight and to secret lair
    in the great forest hiding?
To Northern isles and shores of stone
    on strong swans flying,
by cold waves to dwell alone
    with the white gulls crying?'

'Nay!' they answered. 'Far away
    on the last road faring,
leaving western havens grey,
    the seas of shadow daring,
we go back to Elvenhome,
    where the White Tree is growing,
and the Star shines upon the foam
    on the last shore flowing.

'To mortal fields say farewell,
    Middle-earth forsaking!
In Elvenhome a clear bell
    in the high tower is shaking.
Here grass fades and leaves fall,
    and sun and moon wither,
and we have heard the far call
    that bids us journey thither.'

The oars were stayed. They turned aside:
    'Do you hear the call, Earth-maiden?
Fíriel! Fíriel!' they cried.
    'Our ship is not full-laden.
One more only we may bear.
    Come! For your days are speeding.
Come! Earth-maiden elven-fair,
    our last call heeding.'

Fíriel looked from the river-bank,
    one step daring;
then deep in clay her feet sank,
    and she halted staring.

Slowly the elven-ship went by
    whispering through the water:
'I cannot come!' they heard her cry.
    'I was born Earth's daughter!'

No jewels bright her gown bore,
    as she walked back from the meadow
under roof and dark door,
    under the house-shadow.
She donned her smock of russet brown,
    her long hair braided,
and to her work came stepping down.
    Soon the sunlight faded.

Year still after year flows
    down the Seven Rivers;
cloud passes, sunlight glows,
    reed and willow quivers
as morn and eve, but never more
    westward ships have waded
in mortal waters as before,
    and their song has faded.

In the first version of the poem, Firiel returns to her everyday life, to the pitter-patter of feet and the clatter of pails and dishes. But in the work's final lines she is melancholy, evidently thinking of what might have been had she gone with the elves into the West – freedom, perhaps, from responsibilities to which she seems to be tied. She stares 'at tree, grass, and summer-flower', but 'no music came'. Her hair that had been free and streaming is now braided; that morning she had crept from the house and danced towards the river, but 'walked back from the water'.

There seems to have been nothing to prevent her boarding the ship except her own misgivings, and she knows it: 'She held forth her white hand, | and dim tears were starting | for the white ship of Elvenland | passing and departing'. She has been offered paradise, or what sounds like paradise, and hesitated. Now the chance is lost: 'never comes again the call | to thou once bidden thither'. And yet, it was the elves who heard a call, not Firiel; she merely had an invitation, of a kind generations of cautionary tales have told us not to accept. In texts B and, before it was revised, D, the elves remark that only to a few 'comes the far call | that bids them journey', suggesting that their offer to take Firiel with them as a last passenger amounts to a 'call'. But with the revision in D it is explicitly the elves who have 'heard the far call', and they wish to know if Firiel has heard it too. The poem raises the question whether mortals have any place in a land like that the elves describe. Firiel supposes that the Elvenfolk are going to a hidden place in the forest, to a bleak ocean shore, or 'to Northern isles grey and frore' – the stuff of Northern myth and legend. No, she is told, their destination is more rarified.

Did Firiel make the right choice to stay true to herself as 'earth's fair daughter' by not going with the elves? Or is there another part of her nature, 'elven-fair', which calls to her in a different voice? In version A, Tolkien shows that she feels regret; in B, with the original final stanza omitted, the poem ends on a more positive note, or at least one which is less introspective. With version D as revised, whatever Firiel may want to do in her heart, she is bound to a mortal life, to 'speeding' days, as the elves put it; she 'cannot come'. This is most tellingly shown by the words Tolkien added to text D, 'deep in clay her feet sank' – a stunning image, made stronger by its suggestion of 'feet of clay', meaning an inherent weakness.

In E, Fíriel dares a step, but at once understands that she cannot leave: 'I was born Earth's daughter!' It is not clear if Tolkien meant this to be a cry of anguish; it can easily be taken as such. Fíriel returns to a 'dark door' and a 'house-shadow', and to a mundanity implied by her homely brown clothing (formerly green), but not necessarily to lasting sorrow. That is now the province of the poet himself, who laments that 'never more | westward ships have waded | in mortal waters . . . | and their song has faded'. In *J.R.R. Tolkien: Author of the Century* (2000), Tom Shippey comments that 'the sense of loss, and of death, is very much stronger' in *The Last Ship* than in *Firiel* (that is, the version in the Sacred Heart *Chronicle*), 'and is presented as an inevitable loss. Firiel is made of "clay", like all children of Adam, she is "Earth's daughter", and this is the fate she has to accept. . . . Hers is an "anti-fairy story", about the "Escape from Death" rejected' (pp. 280–1).

Unlike some other poems in the *Bombadil* volume, *Firiel* was well suited to become, in the fictional frame of the book and recognizably to readers of *The Lord of the Rings*, a work composed or collected by Hobbits; nonetheless, Tolkien added (in D and E) other elements to support the conceit. Already, the work was set in a world where Elves and Men co-exist, and where Elves, at least, could hear a call to sail into the West. With the latter we bring to mind Legolas late in *The Lord of the Rings*, mesmerized by the sight and sound of gulls – 'deep in the hearts of all my kindred [the Elves]', he says, 'lies the sea-longing, which it is perilous to stir' (Book VI, Chapter 9) – and Tolkien's statement early in that work that 'at times elven-ships set sail' from the Grey Havens, beyond the western borders of the Shire, 'never to return' (Book I, Chapter 2). In his preface to the *Bombadil* collection Tolkien states that 'in the Langstrand and Dol Amroth [both in the southern part of Gondor] there were many traditions of the ancient Elvish dwellings, and of the haven at the mouth of the Morthond from which "westward ships" had sailed as far back as the fall of Eregion in the Second Age' (p. 8). 'Elvenland' is so named in the poem as the current home of the elves Firiel meets in Middle-earth, in contrast to 'Elvenhome', which in Tolkien's mythology is Aman in the far West of the world. (We first met the name *Elvenhome* in the 'Kortirion' poems, no. 40.) The elves' destination in *Firiel* is said to be 'beyond the last mountains, | whose feet are in the outer foam | of the world's deep fountains', which sounds very much like Valinor behind the walls of the Pelóri, the Mountains of Aman.

In revised text D and in E, the elves dare 'the seas of shadow' on 'the last road', a sea-path 'filled with shadows and bewilderment' as it is said in *The Silmarillion* (p. 102; see also the Shadowy Seas in poem nos. 33 and 66). There a white tree is growing, presumably Galathilion, the White Tree of Tirion. The Star that 'shines upon the foam | on the last shore flowing' is surely Eärendil, the celestial mariner. We cannot place the 'clear bell' ringing in a high tower which bids the elves journey west, but there are several towers in 'The Silmarillion' which might suit, such as the Tower of Ingwë with a silver lamp, and the white tower of Elwing on the edge of the Sundering Seas.

Tolkien identifies the 'Seven Rivers' of the final stanza of text E in his *Bombadil* preface as those which 'flowed into the Sea in the South Kingdom' (Gondor), namely the Lefnui, Morthond–Kiril–Ringló, Gilrain–Serni, and Anduin (the dashed names indicate rivers which join before they reach the sea).

A1: The name 'Fíriel' appears in the manuscript with an acute accent over the first *i*, but is without an accent in later texts until *The Last Ship* in the *Bombadil* collection. Tolkien also omitted the accent when he wrote the title *Firiel* in pencil at the head of the manuscript.

A17: 'Her gown had jewels upon its hem', i.e. drops of dew, like those 'besprinkled' on her feet. Tolkien uses the image of dew to show the passing of time. As 'the round sun' climbs higher (l. 93), 'the dew was drying', and finally (l. 97) 'no jewels bright her gown bore'. Dew is also, perhaps, symbolic of the fresh morning when Firiel sets out, compared with her return later 'under roof and dark door'.

A27: 'Morning's flame', i.e. sunlight.

A35: The swans that go 'sailing on before' recall those in Tolkien's mythology which guide the ships of the seafaring elves, the Teleri.

A37: 'Fair folk' is a traditional term for elves or fairies.

A116: 'Like an anthill dizzy': Tolkien evokes the busy chaos of a colony of ants.

D98: Here 'middle-earth' is spelled thus, without a capital, and has the sense of 'mortal lands', the ancient Midgard (*middangeard*), the world of Men between Heaven and Hell. In E66, when the poem was revised to suit Tolkien's invented world, the name became 'Middle-earth', capitalized, referring to the continent in which the action of *The Lord of the Rings* takes place.

142

The Wanderers (*c.* 1935)

In private notes, Christopher Tolkien dated this poem possibly to the 1930s, based on the paper his father used to write its four manuscripts. Its first version, before it gained its title, is a rough and incomplete draft on a single page, the connections between its parts uncertain and Tolkien's handwriting progressively harder to read. We give this as A, as far as we can decipher it, illustrating Tolkien's revisions.

[A] Three children [lived >] once upon a time
lived in a cottage white
[*deleted:* The garden]
Behind the hills

Three children once upon a time [built >] found
a little house of stone
[with >] its walls [all >] were painted white with lime
and there it stood alone
The hills behind it rolled and climbed
The forest stalked it near
No bell of church there ever chimed
and yet they loved it dear.

The garden clung about its [walls >] feet
with flowers gold and red
[*deleted:* And scent of honeysuckle ?flowed]
They smell [*deleted:* the] honeysuckle sweet
[*deleted:* as each ?lay in]
at evenings in their bed.
The wind came through the windows [fresh >] keen
when high above the trees
The stars [*deleted:* were opened sharp and pale small and keen] [were hushed >] who nod their silver sheen
were opened
The wind [*deleted:* came through round upon garden pale]
[*deleted:* came from the mountains]

When [high above the trees   down from >] through the leaves of trees
when high [up >] above the hills.
The stars

When wind was stirring in the leaves
and high above the wood [*or* hills]
The stars look in beneath eaves
with distant ghostly eyes

and they saw slowly rise

and there dwelled till spring grew ripe
and summer turned to gold
[and >] till autumn [ghostly played its theme >] played its pipes
??? time of

And there they dwelt as light as bird
till summer turned to gold

And there they dwelt [as >] till summer grew
and turned from green to gold
till autumn played its pipe
and far away the pipes were heard
with music faint but cold
that autumn played upon the hill
and stirred until ???

the ?ghosts that rose in mounds of ?? [*above:* climbed and rolled]
?on evening air to float
[*illegible*]

[*deleted:* and beside a silent mere]
[*deleted:* beside a hidden mere]

In the next manuscript of the poem, now entitled *The Wanderers*, Tolkien consolidated and enlarged upon his thoughts in A, arranging the work in three stanzas of eight lines and one of twelve. In our transcription (B) we give the text as it stood before revision. Only after line 4 did Tolkien begin to indent every other line.

[B]

Three children found upon a time
A little house of stone:
Its walls were painted white with lime,
and there it stood alone.
The hills behind it climbed and rolled,
the forest stalked it near;
No bell of church there ever chimed
across the silent mere.

A garden clung about its feet
with flowers gold and red;
they smelled the honeysuckle sweet
at evening in their bed,
when wind was stirring in the leaves
and they saw slowly rise
the stars, that looked beneath the eaves
with distant glinting eyes.

And there they dwelt as light as bird
till brown was in the green,
and far away the pipe was heard
with music faint but keen,
that autumn played upon the hill
and stirred with piercing note
the misty ghosts that white and still
upon the evening float.

Then when the waters in the wood
were flecked with yellow leaves
and swallow-houses empty stood
beneath the dripping eaves,
and far off neath a silver sun
a cloak of snow lay white
about the mountain's shoulders dun
one morning cold and bright,
they took the downhill path that wound
between the stones and fern
until the long white road they found
awaiting their return[.]

Marking changes to several lines in B, Tolkien carried most of them into a fresh manuscript (C). Now he called the work *The Wanderers: A Moral Lay*, and the 'three children' of texts A and B were now 'two wanderers'. Tolkien also made other changes to the poem he had not marked, and more than trebled its length. It seems certain that he would have needed one or more draft manuscripts before making C, a fair copy, but none has survived.

[C]

Two wanderers found upon their way
  a house of whitened stone,
shining at the turning of the day
  among the hills alone.
The lands behind it climbed and rolled,
  the forest stalked it near,
but round it all was green and gold
  and the waters of a mere.

A garden clung about its feet
  with flowers pale and red;
they smelled the honeysuckle sweet
  at evening in their bed,
when wind was stirring in the leaves,
  and slow the moon would rise,
and stars look in beneath the eaves
  with distant glinting eyes.

And there they dwelt as light as bird,
  till brown was in the green,
and far away the pipes were heard,
  with music faint but keen,
playing in the hollows of the hill
  and stirring with far note
the misty ghosts that white and still
  upon the evening float.

Then when the waters in the wood
  were flecked with yellow leaves,
and swallow-houses empty stood
  beneath the dripping eaves,
and far off under a silver sun
  a cloak of snow lay white
about the mountain's shoulder dun
  one morning cold and bright,

They took the down-hill path that wound
between the stones and fern,
until the long white road they found
awaiting their return.
They put behind them wood and hill,
and rivers swift they crossed,
flying from that music chill
and deadly breath of frost.

They reached at last the leaguered town
where water ran like blood;
its heart was fire, and smoke its crown,
there snow was turned to mud;
and all the winter they held them warm
with death beyond the walls;
the roar of voices for the storm
they took in crowded halls.

For pipes that stir with music keen
the silence on the hill,
for the slow beating of the life unseen
beneath the winter's chill,
they took the tunes of drum and horn
repeated endlessly,
knowing no bounds of night and morn,
but beating sleeplessly.

From windows shut they looked one day
and saw with weary eyes
Spring walking-up the valley grey
under the doubtful skies.
They saw her footprints green and fair,
as she slowly climbed the hill,
but the wind that stirred her yellow hair
still wavered keen and chill.

When Summer wide the windows thrust,
they thought of woodland air;
for in their throats were smoke and dust
and in their eyes a glare.

The sun unfriendly faded paint
    and leered through grimy glass;
the fires were a torment to the faint,
    and the wheels that ever pass.

And the streets that go on turning round
    all seasons out and in,
engines above and under ground,
    bruised their brains with din.

They said: 'We'll go back to the hills,
    we'll take the climbing way,
and where the mountain-water spills
    into the lake, we'll stay!
In the garden flowers will be blowing,
    and many birds be calling,
and tall the grasses will be growing
    and cool the dews be falling.'

They took the hot and thirsty road,
    and wore their feet to bone,
and at last they laid their weary load
    before the house of stone.
One said: 'The weeds are waxen rank,
    and it is lonesome here!'
The other said: 'These walls are dank,
    and the forest stalks too near.'

'The birds sing not with rhyme or tune!
    No merry neighbours come;
and dim 'tis under star and moon
    to sit at evening dumb.
The mountains stand with threat behind,
    and friends are far away;
and silence weighs upon the mind
    all through the empty day.'

They said: 'Now whither shall we turn,
    and what then shall we seek?
We are weary both of stone and fern,
    of plain and mountain-peak!'

They lifted up their little load,
    and cursing crooked fate
they went back to the dusty road,
    bent as with great weight.

And whither afterward they came
    no man knows but God,
whether drowned they were or burned with flame
    or cast beneath the sod,
at the bitter ending of their quest
    for song that never tires,
for weary islands curstly blest
    with neither frost nor fires.

Perchance at the end of wandering
    when waters deep were crossed
in wonderness they welcomed spring
    when they had breathed the frost.

Tolkien marked this version too with changes, though it is not certain in all cases if he did so before or after he wrote yet another manuscript of the poem, in small lettering and two columns to save paper. That text, once more entitled simply *The Wanderers*, is problematic for several reasons. When Tolkien reached again 'bent as with great weight' (C108), he stopped, as if uncertain how to proceed – though he was only twelve lines away from the end of the work in the previous version. Now he wrote new text, filling much of the remaining blank space on the page, but this is disconnected, and without clear direction what the author intended to be done with it. One group of lines even has three different readings.

In lieu of an authoritative finished version of *The Wanderers*, we have transcribed its latest manuscript and in D have created editorially a final text as it might have been, had Tolkien been able to wrestle his work into a satisfactory form and give it a definite conclusion. For much of the poem, his intentions are unambiguous; where they are not, we have made editorial decisions we think reasonable, as documented in our notes. The division of the poem into two numbered sections follows the original.

[D] I.

Two wanderers found upon their way
a house of whitened stone,
shining at the turning of the day
among the hills alone.
The lands behind it climbed and rolled,
the forest stalked it near,
beside it lay all green and gold
the waters of a mere.

A garden clung about its feet
with flowers pale and red;
they smelled the honeysuckle sweet
at evening in their bed,
when wind was moving in the leaves,
and slow the moon would rise,
or stars look in beneath the eaves
with distant glinting eyes.

They lived as light as bird on spray,
till brown was in the green,
and pipes they heard from far away,
with music faint but keen,
playing in the hollows of the hill
and stirring with cold note
the misty ghosts that white and chill
upon the evening float.

When on the waters cold were flowing
the homeless yellow leaves,
and swallow-houses empty hung
beneath the darkling eaves;
when far off under silver sun
one morning cold and bright,
about the mountain's shoulder dun
a cloak of snow lay white,

They took the down-hill path that wound
between the stones and fern,
until the long white road they found
awaiting their return.

They put behind them wood and hill,
and waters deep they crossed,
ever flying from that music chill
and deadly breath of frost.

They reached at last the leaguered town,
where water ran like blood,
where heart was fire and smoke its crown;
where snow was turned to mud.
And there they held them safe and warm
with death beyond the walls,
and took for the crying of the storm
the roar of crowded halls.

For pipes that stir with music keen
the silence on the hill,
For slow beating of the life unseen,
beneath the winter's chill,
They took the tunes of drum and horn
repeated endlessly,
knowing no bounds of night and morn,
but beating sleeplessly.

II.

From windows shut they looked one day,
and saw with weary eyes
Spring walking up the valley grey
under the doubtful skies.
They saw her footprints green and fair,
as she slowly climbed the hill;
but the wind that stirred her blowing hair
still shivered keen and chill.

When Summer wide their windows thrust,
they thought of woodland air;
for in their throats were smoke and dust,
and in their eyes a glare.
and the wheels that go on turning round
all seasons out and in
engines above and under ground
now bruised their brains into din.

They said: 'We'll go back to the hills,
we'll take the climbing way,
and where the mountain-water spills
into the lake we'll stay.
In the garden flowers will be blowing,
and merry birds be calling,
and tall the grasses will be growing.
and cool the dews be falling.'

They took the hot and thirsty road,
and wore their feet to bone;
at last they laid their weary load
before the house of stone.
One said: 'The weeds are waxen rank,
and it is lonesome here!'
The other said: 'These walls are dank,
and the forest stalks too near!'

'The birds sing not with rhyme or tune!
No merry neighbours come;
and dim 'tis under star and moon
to sit at evening dumb.
The mountains stand with threat behind,
and friends are far away;
and silence weighs upon the mind
all through the empty day.'

They lifted up their little load,
and cursing crooked fate
they went back to the dusty road
bent as with great weight.
And one in hopeless wandering passed
unto a houseless shore
where deadly winter caught him fast,
when he could fly no more.

The other turned back in his way
and alone he climbed the height,
and faced the searing wind by day
and grinding frost by night.
And even in that frozen place
as one risen from cold stone

he saw a Spring with shining face
    more fair than he had known.

And whither afterward they came
    no man knows but God,
Whether drowned they were, or burned with flame
    or cast beneath the sod,
At the bitter ending of their quest
    for songs that never tire,
for phantom countries curstly blest
    with neither frost nor fire.
Maybe, at the end of wandering,
    when walking cold and lost
at a sudden turn they came on Spring
    when they had faced the frost.

It is not clear if Tolkien knew what direction his poem would take when he began its first manuscript 'Three children lived upon a time'. He would be able to use these words some years later (see no. 188), but they must have come to seem inappropriate as *The Wanderers* became long and dark. Its underlying thought, or moral – its third version is a 'moral lay' – may be that one should try to be content with what one has. The work is like an extended fable, or a religious lesson: the Apostle Paul learned always to be content, since he always had his faith. Here we have a parable of two friends who, becoming content with neither city nor country, found that they had no home at all. One was caught on 'a houseless shore' in 'deadly winter'; the other suffered the elements but 'saw a Spring with shining face | more fair than he had known', which seems a good analogue for the Christian Saviour. And then the poem also serves to comment on industrialization and urban living, a companion to works such as *The Motor-cyclists* (no. 63) and *Progress in Bimble Town* (no. 103).

A7: 'Painted with lime', i.e. with limewash, made from slaked lime (calcium hydroxide), traditional and inexpensive, generally chalk-white.

C92: 'Stalks too near', i.e. approaches close in a threatening manner.

C115: 'Curstly blest', i.e. cursed. A land is unnatural if it has 'neither frost nor fires', that is, if it is without seasons.

D7–8: These lines replaced, according to Tolkien's direction, 'but round it all was green and gold | by the waters of a mere'.

D9–16: Tolkien bracketed this stanza, then deleted the brackets.

D13: 'Moving' replaced 'stirring' by Tolkien's direction. He had marked this change already, or did so retroactively, in manuscript C.

D17: This line replaced 'And there they dwelt as gay as bird', taking up an alternate reading Tolkien wrote next to the original.

D19: This line replaced 'and far away the pipes were heard', taking up an alternate reading Tolkien next to the original.

D20: Tolkien marked 'but' to replace 'and', though without striking through the latter.

D38: Tolkien marked 'waters deep' to replace 'rivers swift', though without striking through the latter.

D63: Above 'yellow' Tolkien wrote 'blowing'. We adopted his suggestion.

D68: Tolkien bracketed and struck through the eight lines originally written to follow l. 68. He seems to have meant to delete original ll. 69–72, perhaps because he came to dislike them, or simply to maintain a stanza of no more than eight lines (i.e. 65–72):

> The sunlight frowned on jaded paint
> and leered through grimy glass;
> the fires were a torment to the faint,
> and the wheels that ever pass,

D69–72: As written, these lines read:

> The wheels that go on turning round,
> all seasons out and in,
> engines above and under ground,
> now bruised their brains with din.

Tolkien struck these through, and wrote a very similar replacement text next to them in pencil. We have used the later reading in the body of our transcription D.

D101–104: Tolkien first wrote in the manuscript:

> In bitter wandering they passed
> unto a houseless shore,
> where deadly winter caught them fast,
> when they could fly no more.

There they were immediately followed by four lines beginning 'Yet sudden in that frozen place': see our note for ll. 109–112. Tolkien wrote the lines we have adopted as part of a longer passage of twelve lines (present 101–112).

D103: Tolkien seems to have considered an alternate text for this line, 'and in the deadly sea was cast'. We have retained 'where deadly winter caught him fast', to maintain Tolkien's emphasis on seasons.

D108: This line read, as written, 'and the grinding frost by night'. Tolkien circled 'the', an indication in many of his other manuscripts that he meant the word to be deleted.

D109–112: Tolkien first wrote in the manuscript:

> Yet sudden at that frozen place,
> as had she sprung of stone,
> they saw Spring walking face to face,
> more fair than they had known.

To replace these, he first wrote:

And even in that frozen place
    as one risen from cold stone
he saw Spring come with shining face
    as a queen that mounts her throne.

Then, dissatisfied, he bracketed the final three lines and wrote the text we have used above.

D117–120: Tolkien first wrote in the manuscript:

pursuing still their weary quest
    for songs that never tire,
for [weary islands >] phantom countries curstly blest
    with neither frost nor fire.

Beneath this, following the word 'or', he wrote ll. 117–120 as we have transcribed them, in the process replacing 'pursuing still their weary quest' etc.

D122: This line read, as written, 'when walking wild and lost'. Tolkien wrote 'cold' above 'wild', which we took as direction to replace the word.

143

When Little Louis Came To Stay (1935)

E.V. Gordon left Leeds in 1931, when he was made Smith Professor of English Language and Germanic Philology at the University of Manchester. Tolkien remained in touch with his friend, and often stayed with Gordon and his family (wife Ida and four children) in Manchester once a year – 'the annual nuisance and intruder' – when acting as an external examiner for the university. His thank-you note in verse after his visit of 26 June 1935 (the manuscript is dated, and preserved in the Gordon archive at Leeds) is based largely on the route of his return journey to Oxford, through Shropshire and the industrial 'Black Country' of the Midlands (Crewe, Wellington, Wrekin), then to Birmingham (Brum) and points south-east until reaching the willows along the Thames, recalling 'the many-willow'd meadows' and travel narrative of *Lemminkainen Goeth to the Ford of Oxen* (poem no. 9).

When little Louis came to stay
his thanks in verse he used to say,
and turn a graceful compliment,
which by return of post he sent.*
This custom all should imitate
on whom a lively muse doth wait.
But if on scripts you feed your muse,
too soon to sing she will refuse,
and mine had gone all stiff and hoarse
(rusty her Latin, worse her Norse),
a dull old beta-minus gammer,
beating bad lines out with a hammer
in croaked English lame and creaking
from Crewe to Wellington and Wrekin,
from Shropshire down into the black,
bleak, blasted country made of slack,
cinders, old iron, and poisoned water.
And there a sudden frenzy caught her,

* *At least I hope that this was so – the verses you forgot to show!*

till by the time we came to Brum
she beat like a savage on a drum,
blaspheming the bright sun on high
proud and pitiless in clean sky
disdainful of the human blight
writhing in unaccustomed light.
O jubilee of the reign of dirt,
hang out stained sheet and tattered shirt!
Let noisome curtains, nameless rags,
at each foul window flap like flags!

Most foolish muse! Her curse was heard!
A dark wind in the East was stirred,
and as to Wessex we drew nigh
(a line of willows near the sky
denoting Thames and waters slow
that southward with their tribute flow),
the sun from gold was changed to brass
above the ghastly green of grass;
from brass it sickened into lead,
corroded, blackened, and was dead,
and cast into a pit of gloom.
The thunder rolled up slow as doom —
and cracked. And so we're back again
bent under the white blades of rain;
beneath the ever-hanging cloud
our muse is damped. But not quite cowed —
for though your weather may have changed,
and marauding thunder northward ranged,
I have brought hither in my mind
a glimpse of country bright and kind,
green curtains flapped by hill-side air,
and children climbing on the stair.
To belong a moment, as a guest,
to your dear house is greater rest
than many drowsy days to be
on idle beaches by the sea;
to see you both, good wife and man,
is more refreshment than I can
in bashful words, while I am there,
the grace discover to declare.
And so I jog my poor old muse

back in her stable here to choose
some rhyming words, to do her best
to beg your pardon for your guest,
the annual nuisance and intruder.
Than wagging tongue what could be ruder,
that talks of much it little knows.
and yet the chance, before it goes,
can never find to bless you all,
to wish that grace of God may fall
on door and roof and board and bed,
on feasting and on daily bread,
your toil, your rest, your hope of heart.
And may your children each have part
in this quintuple wish I send,
from A, B, C unto the end.
That's perhaps enough — although well meant,
it falls much short of my intent.

'Little Louis' was evidently C.S. Lewis, who sent the Gordons a twelve-line poem of thanks after he had been their guest in Manchester. This too survives in the Leeds archive; see Andoni Cossio, 'The Unpublished "Mód Þrýþe Ne Wæg" by C.S. Lewis: A Critical Edition' (2024). 'Little Louis' is also likely an allusion to Chaucer's 'Treatise on the Astrolabe', which is addressed to 'lyte Lowys my sone' ('little Lewis my son'). Tolkien planned to include an extract from the 'Treatise' in the book of selected works by Chaucer he and George S. Gordon were assembling (but did not complete) for Oxford University Press.

'Scripts' in line 7 refers to examination scripts, or written examinations. Tolkien and Gordon (and Lewis) were sometimes joint examiners in the Oxford English School, in addition to Tolkien at the University of Manchester. In line 11, 'beta-minus' (B-minus) is a comparatively poor examination mark, and *gammer* is an archaic word for 'old woman', as in the name of the widow in *Gammer Gurton's Needle* (?1533; the male equivalent is *gaffer*).

144

Monað Modes Lust mid Mereflode (?1936 or ?37–?1946)

In our discussion of *The Nameless Land* and its development (poem no. 74), we spoke of Tolkien's invention of the character Ælfwine for his novel *The Lost Road*, written probably in 1936 or 1937. A man of North Somerset in the days of Edward the Elder, king of Wessex (reigned 899–924), Ælfwine would have featured in an early chapter; in the event, he appeared only briefly in narrative before Tolkien abandoned the work, though he would later figure in *The Notion Club Papers*. In *The Lost Road* narrative Ælfwine is in a hall with King Edward and a crowd of other men, at a time of crisis: the Danes have attacked England, their ships are 'still at large on the Welsh coast; and the men of Somerset and Devon were on guard'. As in a dream, Ælfwine thinks of seas he has sailed, and the sound of blowing wind brings back 'old longings':

> He heard the crash of waves on the black cliffs and the sea-birds diving and crying; and snow and hail fell. Then the seas opened pale and wide; the sun shone on the land and the sound and smell of it fell far behind. He was alone towards the setting sun [that is, towards the west] with fear and longing in his heart, drawn against his will. [*The Lost Road and Other Writings*, pp. 83–4]

In plot-notes, Ælfwine's son Eadwine is said to be sick of conflict with the Danes, and wants to sail west to a new land. But Ælfwine's thoughts are broken when the king calls on him to sing, and he does so, chanting an Old English verse (given here as A, from *The Lost Road* as published, p. 84).

[A]

Monað modes lust mid mereflode
forð to feran, þæt ic feor heonan
ofer hean holmas, ofer hwæles eðel
elþeodigra eard gesece.
Nis me to hearpan hyge ne to hringþege
ne to wife wyn ne to worulde hyht
ne ymb owiht elles nefne ymb yða gewealc.

The narrative also includes an adjacent prose translation of the poem into Modern English, which (as B) we have divided according to the Old English lines.

[B] The desire of my spirit urges me
to journey forth over the flowing sea,
that far hence across the hills of water and the whale's country
I may seek the land of strangers.
No mind have I for harp, nor gift of ring,
nor delight in women, nor joy in the world,
nor concern with aught else save the rolling of the waves.

The 'hills of water' are waves, and the 'whale's country' the open sea.

Ælfwine's song is met with 'some laughter, and a few jeers', but mainly silence. The words were 'old and familiar', 'words of the old poets whom most men had heard often'. Those who spoke in reply were not of a like mind with Ælfwine: they 'have had enough of the sea'. But one old man comes to his defence: 'Let him say what his mood bids' (p. 84).

Ælfwine's poem is not wholly original to Tolkien, but adapted in part from lines 36–47 of the Old English *Seafarer*:

[M]onað modes lust mæla gehwylce
ferð to feran, þæt ic feor heonan
elþeodigra eard gesece —
forþon nis þæs modwlonc mon ofer eorþan,
ne his gifena þæs god, ne in geoguþe to þæs hwæt,
ne in his dædum to þæs deor, ne him his dryhten to þæs hold,
þæt he a his sæfore sorge næbbe,
to hwon hine Dryhten gedon wille.
Ne biþ him to hearpan hyge ne to hringþege
ne to wife wyn ne to worulde hyht
ne ymbe owiht elles nefne ymb yða gewealc;
ac a hafað longunge se þe on lagu fundað.

As Christopher Tolkien notes in *The Lost Road and Other Writings*, in composing Ælfwine's poem his father omitted five lines of *The Seafarer* after line 4 of text A, and changed some of the wording. Also, 'the third line [of Tolkien's text] is an addition (and is enclosed, both in the Old English and in the translation, in square brackets in the manuscript)' (p. 85).

Probably in 1946, Tolkien included a revision of Ælfwine's poem in the second part of *The Notion Club Papers* (see no. 74). There it is recited by Arry Lowdham, as lines which came to him 'when I was only sixteen, before I had read any of the old verse', and on 'a windy evening: I remember it howling round the house, and the distant sound of the sea'. Here, as C, we have transcribed the 'Lowdham' text from the published *Notion Club Papers* in *Sauron Defeated* (p. 243).

[C]

Monath módaes lust mith meriflóda
forth ti foeran thaet ic feorr hionan
obaer gaarseggaes grimmae holmas
aelbuuina eard uut gisoecae.
Nis me ti hearpun hygi ni ti hringthegi
ni ti wíbae wyn ni ti weoruldi hyct
ni ymb oowict ellaes nebnae ymb ýtha giwalc.

'It sounds to me now', Lowdham says, 'almost like my own father speaking across grey seas of world and time' (p. 244). He gives a translation (D) similar to B in meaning but different in execution:

[D]

My soul's desire over the sea-torrents
forth bids me fare, that I afar should seek
over the ancient water's awful mountains
Elf-friends' island in the Outer-world.
For no harp have I heart, no hand for gold,
in no wife delight, in the world no hope:
one wish only, for the waves' tumult.

In the context of the story, both the Old English and Modern English words are 'translated' through Lowdham, which itself would account for different texts. Nonetheless, there is a vivacity to Lowdham's translation lacking in that of the literal readings in *The Lost Road*, notably in 'the ancient water's awful mountains' versus 'the hills of water and the whale's country', and in 'Elf-friends' island' rather than 'the land of strangers'.

In *The Road to Middle-earth* Tom Shippey comments on the two versions of the Old English passage, in *The Lost Road* and *The Notion Club Papers*, noting that the first is in the Old West Saxon dialect and the second in Old Mercian. He also argues that Ælfwine's chant 'is highly inappropriate' in the circumstances. 'He is in a king's hall, full of Dane-hunters and experienced warriors. Their view is that if Ælfwine would rather go to sea than receive gifts in the hall, let him get on with it. His yearning leaves him socially isolated, a "raver", a "looney"' (p. 264).

145

Ilu Ilúvatar en Káre Eldain a Firimoin (?1936 or ?37)

As described in our discussion of poem no. 74, Tolkien's intention in his unfinished novel *The Lost Road* was to tell the story of Audoin and Alboin Errol, who would travel through time and in the lives of other fathers and sons, ending in Númenor. There, among other wonders, Elendil and Herendil, the father and son of this era, hear a voice 'from a high window . . . falling down like silver into the pool of twilight'. It is that of Fíriel, 'a maiden of [Elendil's] household, daughter of Orontor', singing 'an even-song in the Eressëan tongue, but made by men, long ago'. We give its Elvish (Qenya) text as A, followed by the song in English (B), both from Christopher Tolkien's transcription in *The Lost Road and Other Writings* (p. 72). For the latter, we have divided Tolkien's prose rendering to accord with the lines of the poem.

[A]

Ilu Ilúvatar en kárẹ eldain a firimoin
ar antaróta mannar Valion: númessier.
Toi aina, mána, meldielto — enga morion:
talantie. Mardello Melko lende: márie.
Eldain en kárier Isil, nan hildin Úr-anar.
Toi írimar. Ilqainen antar annar lestanen
Ilúvatáren. Ilu vanya, fanya, eari.
i-mar, ar ilqa ímen. Írima ye Númenor.
Nan úye sére indo-ninya símen, ullume;
ten sí ye tyelma, yéva tyel ar i-narqelion,
írẹ ilqa yéva nótina, hostainiéva, yallume:
ananta úva táre fárea, ufárea!
Man táre antáva nin Ilúvatar, Ilúvatar
enyárẹ tar i tyel, irẹ Anarinya qeluva?

[B]

The Father made the World for Elves and Mortals,
and he gave it into the hands of the Lords. They are in the West.
They are holy, blessed, and beloved: save the dark one.
He is fallen. Melko has gone from the Earth: it is good.
For Elves they made the Moon, but for Men the red Sun;

> which are beautiful. To all they gave in measure the gifts
> of Ilúvatar. The World is fair, the sky, the seas,
> the earth, and all that is in them. Lovely is Númenor.
> But my heart resteth not here for ever;
> for here is ending, and there will be an end and the Fading,
> when all is counted, and all numbered at last,
> but yet it will not be enough, not enough.
> What will the Father, O Father, give me
> in that day beyond the end when my Sun faileth?

In revising *The Lost Road*, however, Tolkien chose to omit from his narrative all but the first two lines of the Qenya text and, slightly altered, the first two lines of the translation.

Fíriel's song gives in short an account of the beliefs of the descendants of the Edain, or fathers of Men, who had fought with the Elves against the evil Vala Morgoth in the First Age and been rewarded with a dwelling place set in the ocean to the west: Andor, the Land of Gift, also called Númenor, part of neither Middle-earth nor Valinor, but closer to the latter. At the time of the story in *The Lost Road*, the rulers of Númenor had become envious of Elvish immortality, and further corrupted by Sauron, once a servant of Morgoth; now they were plotting to attack Valinor. Herendil comments that it not safe for Fíriel to sing her song from a window: 'They sing it otherwise now. Melko cometh back, they say, and the king shall give us the Sun forever.' But his father believes that the shadow of Morgoth has already come: 'it lieth upon the hearts and minds of men. . . . The open is insecure; walls are dangerous. Even by the heart of the house spies may sit. . . . The old songs are forgotten or altered; twisted into other meanings' (*The Lost Road and Other Writings*, pp. 63, 68). Of this, Christopher Tolkien commented that when his father 'reached back to the world [of Númenor in *The Lost Road*] he found there an image of what he most condemned and feared in his own' (p. 77) – notably, in the late 1930s, the civil war in Spain and the growing threat of Nazi Germany, both of which would soon lead to a new world war.

In regard to the Moon and Sun, it is convenient to quote from *The Silmarillion*:

> Isil the Sheen the Vanyar of old named the Moon, flower of Telperion in Valinor; and Anar the Fire-golden, fruit of Laurelin, they named the Sun. But the Noldor named them also Rána, the Wayward, and Vása, the Heart of Fire, that awakens

and consumes; for the Sun was set as a sign for the awakening of Men and the waning of the Elves, but the Moon cherishes their memory. [p. 99]

As noted in discussion for poem no. 141, the name *Fíriel* means, in Elvish, 'mortal woman'.

A2: 'Valion: númessier' originally read 'Valion númenyaron' ('of the Lords of the West', i.e. the Valar).

A4: Tolkien subsequently changed 'Mardello Melko' to 'Melko Mardello'. Still later, he revised, in the Qenya and English texts, 'Melko' to 'Alkar'.

A5–6: Tolkien subsequently changed these lines to read 'En kárielto eldain Isil, hildin Úr-anar. | Toi írimar. Ilyain antalto annar lestanen'.

A9: 'Indo-ninya' originally read 'hondo-ninya'.

146
King Sheave (?1936 or ?37–?46)

The figure of Sheave (Sheaf, Sceaf, Scef) appears in many chronicles and stories. Come to a far land as a child, carried in a boat out of the unknown, often with a sheaf or handful of corn (wheat), sometimes with weapons, he is fostered by the inhabitants and grows to lead them; but the details of his story vary in different accounts. He most notably appears in *Beowulf* (poem no. 88), in the person of Scyld Scéfing (Shield Sheafing), the progenitor of the dynasty in which the Danish king Hrothgar is descended. *Scyld* 'shield' is his given name, while *Scéfing* means 'son of Sheaf' or 'with a sheaf'. Tolkien called the matter of Shield Sheafing a tangle, and that is putting it mildly. In *Beowulf*, two myths or traditions are conflated: Scyld, the founder of the Scyldings (Danes) who brings peace (a 'shield' against invaders), and a corn-god (symbolized by a sheaf of grain) who brings abundance. In a list of kings in the Old English poem *Widsith*, one Sceaf, Sceafa Longbeardum, is mentioned as a ruler of the Lombards, a people who originated in northern Europe and later dominated medieval Italy. (See *The Lost Road and Other Writings*, pp. 93–4.)

Probably in 1936 or 1937, Tolkien incorporated the Sheaf legend in his abandoned novel, *The Lost Road*. The larger story, which as we have seen (poem no. 74) is concerned with a father and son in various historical episodes, among much else deals with 'the traditions of the North Sea concerning the coming of corn and culture heroes, ancestors of kingly lines, in boats (and their departure in funeral ships). One such Sheaf, or Shield Sheafing, can actually be made out as one of the remote ancestors of the present Queen [Elizabeth II]' (letter to Christopher Bretherton, 16 July 1964, *Letters*, p. 487). The legend of Sheaf, called by Tolkien *King Sheave*, would have entered in a chapter set in Anglo-Saxon times, when the father and son were named Ælfwine and Eadwine (Elf-friend and Bliss-friend).

In *The Lost Road and Other Writings* Christopher Tolkien notes that *King Sheave* exists in both prose and verse forms. At the time he prepared that book (Volume 5 of *The History of Middle-earth*, published 1987), he believed that these were contemporary with each other, and in printing only the verse manuscript he introduced section breaks according to the paragraphing of the prose text. But when preparing *Sauron Defeated* (published 1992, volume 9 of the *History*), he saw that the prose *King Sheave* was in fact part of *The Notion Club Papers*, another abandoned story by Tolkien, written years after *The Lost Road* (the part with the recounted tale probably dates to 1946). Here we have transcribed the verse text without section breaks, and with caesuras, as it appears in the original manuscript.

In days of yore   out of deep Ocean
to the Langobards,   in the land dwelling
that of old they held   amid the isles of the North,
a ship came sailing   shining-timbered
without oar or mast,   eastward floating.
The sun behind it   sinking westward
with flame kindled   the fallow water.
Wind was wakened.   Over the world's margin
clouds greyhelméd   climbed slowly up
wings unfolding   wide and looming,
as mighty eagles   moving onward
to eastern Earth   omen bearing.
Men there marvelled,   in the mist standing
of the dark islands   in the deeps of time;
Laughter they knew not,   light nor wisdom;
shadow was upon them,   and sheer mountains
stalked behind them   stern and lifeless,
evilhaunted.   The East was dark.
The ship came shining   to the shore driven,
and strode upon the strand,   till its stern rested
on sand and shingle.   The sun went down.
The clouds overcame   the cold heavens.
In fear and wonder   to the fallow water
sadhearted men   swiftly hastened
to the broken beaches   the boat seeking,
gleaming-timbered   in the grey twilight.
They looked within,   and there laid sleeping
a boy they saw   breathing softly:
his face was fair,   his form lovely,
his limbs were white,   his locks raven
golden-braided.   Gilt and carven
with wondrous work   was the wood about him.
In golden vessel   gleaming water
stood beside him;   strung with silver
a harp of gold   neath his hand rested;
his sleeping head   was soft pillowed

on a sheaf of corn shimmering palely
as the fallow gold doth from far countries
west of Angol. Wonder filled them.
The boat they hauled and on the beach moored it
high above the breakers; then with hands lifted
from the bosom its burden. The boy slumbered.
On his bed they bore him to their bleak dwellings
dark walled and drear in a dim region
between waste and sea. There of wood builded
high above the houses was a hall standing
forlorn and empty. Long had it stood so,
no noise knowing, night or morning,
no light seeing. They laid him there,
under lock left him lonely sleeping
in the hollow darkness. They held the doors.
Night wore away. New awakened
as ever on earth early morning;
days came dimly. Doors were opened.
Men strode within, then amazed halted;
fear and wonder filled the watchmen.
The house was bare, hall deserted;
no form found they on the floor lying,
but by bed forsaken the bright vessel
dry and empty in the dust standing.
The guest was gone. Grief o'ercame them.
In sorrow they sought him, till the Sun rising
over the hills of heaven to the homes of men
light came bearing. They looked upward
and high upon a hill hoar and treeless
the guest beheld they: gold was shining
in his hair, in hands the harp he bore
at his feet they saw the fallow-golden
cornsheaf lying. Then clear his voice
a song began sweet unearthly,
words in music woven strangely,
in tongue unknown. Trees stood silent
and men unmoving marvelling hearkened.
Middle-earth had known for many ages
neither song nor singer; no sight so fair
had eyes of mortal, since the world was young,
seen when waking, in that sad country
long forsaken. Nor lord they had,

no king nor counsel among them,   but the cold terror
that dwells in the desert,   the dark shadow
that haunted the hills   and the hoar forest.
Dread was their master.   Dark and silent,
long years forlorn   lonely waited
the hall of kings,   house forsaken,
without fire or food.   Forth men hastened
from their dim houses.   Doors were opened,
and gates unbarred.   Gladness wakened.
To the hill they hastened,   and their heads lifting
on the guest they gazed.   Grey bearded men
bowed before him   and blessed his coming
their years to heal;   youths and maidens,
wives and children   welcome gave him.
His song was ended.   Silent standing
he looked upon them.   Lord they called him:
king they made him,   crowned with golden
wheaten garland,   white his raiment,
his harp his sceptre.   In his house was fire
food and wisdom: there fear came not.
To manhood he grew   might and wisdom.
Sheave they called him   whom the ship brought them,
a name renowned   in the North countries
ever since in song.   For a secret hidden
his true name was,   in tongue unknown
of far countries   where the falling seas
wash western shores   beyond the ways of men
since the world worsened.   The word is forgotten
and the name perished.   Their need he healed,
and laws renewed   long forsaken.
Words he taught them   wise and lovely —
their tongue blossomed   in the time of Sheave —
to song and music.   Secrets he opened
runes revealing.   Runes he gave them
reward of labour,   wealth and comfort
from the earth calling,   acres ploughing,
sowing in season   seed of plenty,
hoarding in garner   golden harvest
for the help of men.   The hoar forests
in the days drew back   to the dark mountains;
the shadow receded,   and shining corn,

white ears of wheat, whispered in the breezes
where waste had been. The woods trembled.
Halls and houses hewn of timber,
strong towers of stone, steep and lofty,
golden-gabled, in his guarded city
they raised and roofed. In his royal dwelling
of wood well-carven the walls were wrought;
fair-hued figures, filled with silver,
gold and scarlet, gleaming hung there,
stories boding of strange countries,
were one wise in wit the woven legends
to thread with thought. At his throne men found
counsel and comfort and care's healing,
justice in judgement. Generous-handed
his gifts he gave. Glory was uplifted.
Far sprang his fame over fallow water,
through Northern lands the renown echoed
of the shining king Sheave the mighty.

Following the text proper in *The Lost Road and Other Writings* (pp. 87–90), Christopher Tolkien included a further sixteen lines of verse at the end of the poem, which his father had written in pencil after the ink text of the prose *King Sheave* but struck through. The verse manuscript, in contrast, includes only the first eight of these lines, themselves apparently as a later addition, following line 137, but earlier than the addition to the prose text. Here we give the final lines of the poem from the later (prose) manuscript.

Seven sons he begat, sire of princes,
men great in mind, mighty handed,
and highhearted. From his house cometh
the seed of kings as songs tell us,
fathers of the fathers who before the change
in the elder years the earth governed,
northern kingdoms named & founded,
Shields of their people: Sheave begat them:
Seadanes and Goths, Swedes and Northmen,
Franks and Frisians, folk of the islands
Swordmen and Saxons, Swabes and English
and the Langobards who long ago
beyond Myrcwudu a mighty realm

and wealth won them   in the Welsh countries
where Ælfwine   Eadwine's heir
in Italy was king.   All that has passed.

'Langobards', or longbeards, is another form of the (Anglicized) name 'Lombards'. *Angol* (Old English *Angel*) is the ancestral home of the Angles before their migration to Britain. The *Seadanes* (Christopher Tolkien adds a hyphen in the printed text; there is none in the manuscript) are Danes living on the coast of the North Sea on its eastern side, in *Widsith* foes of the Frisians to the south. The *Goths* are the Geats, the tribe of southern Sweden to which Beowulf belonged. Tolkien may have meant *Northmen* to mean something more specific, such as men from Norway; more generically, it refers to people who speak a North Germanic language. The *Franks* are, presumably, tribes specific to Germany. *Frisians* were a Germanic people indigenous to the coast of what is now the Netherlands and northern Germany. 'Folk of the islands' perhaps refers to people living on the Frisian Islands (Wadden Islands) off the coast of mainland Frisia.

Christopher Tolkien could not conclusively explain 'Swordmen', but speculated that his father was thinking of the Brondingas, or Brondings, one of the Germanic tribes of Sweden, whose name is interpreted to contain *brond* (*brand*) 'sword'. *Saxons* were peoples from northern Germany who, like the Angles, emigrated to Britain. Christopher relates the *Swabes*, or Swabians, to Germanic peoples dwelling in the North next to the Angles.

Found with the verse and prose versions of *King Sheave* in Tolkien's papers is a page with nine lines of verse, whose text is written out also in prose. These seem not to have been part of the poem transcribed above, but may comprise an alternate approach to an account of Sheave which went only so far before Tolkien abandoned it, maybe a second thought after the larger work was already complete. We have transcribed the fragment with Tolkien's revisions made in the course of composition.

Lo! we in olden days   ancient stories
heard of how the houses   of the high princes
were built and founded.   Bright was their glory:
after need plenty,   after night morning. [*at left*: in the land was light]
[To >] In the lands of shadow   [*deleted:* where] the Langobards
amid the northern isles   [their >] in a narrow country
lived long ago,   lordless unguided [*deleted:* peoples]

beside the grey [water >] ocean — grimhearted men
out of the deeps of the sea in the dark places [*at right:* in the
dark ages]

One of the most striking features of *King Sheave* is the amount of detail Tolkien brings to the tale of Sheaf, which is traditionally very brief. He expands its drama, and emphasizes the emotional experience of the Langobards in finding a beautiful child, mysteriously arrived in a boat by himself: they bless him, learn from him, and take him as their leader and the father of a line of leaders. Anna Smol has commented on Tolkien's additions to the story, 'such as the harp that comes with the child, and how Sceaf reveals his extraordinary powers through song. In most legends, Sheaf is meant to bring agricultural fertility; in Tolkien's version, he also brings linguistic and artistic ripeness to the people' ('Tolkien's King Sheave Story', in *A Single Leaf* (blog), 27 May 2016).

Tom Shippey analyzes the poetic structure of *King Sheave* in his essay 'Tolkien's Development as a Writer of Alliterative Poetry in Modern English' (2013), noting that Tolkien frequently used words ending in *-ing* ('wings unfolding || wide and looming', line 10) for the sake of metre, that in order to vary the rhythm of his sentences in the Old English manner he often used parataxis, that is, successive clauses without linking conjunctions ('They held the doors. | Night wore away', lines 51–52), and that he used one line to echo another, giving as examples line 47, 'forlorn and empty. || Long had it stood so', and line 83, 'long years forlorn || lonely waited'.

In a later essay, '"King Sheave" and "The Lost Road"' (2022), Shippey finds a number of links between Tolkien's poem, the related prose story in *The Lost Road*, and Christian mythology. For example, the final text of *King Sheave* has 153 lines, the biblical 'Number of Salvation' expressed in John 21. He also points to an Anglo-Saxon poem, 'The Descent into Hell', with which *King Sheave* has

> a clear thematic connection . . . in that both describe the liberation from doom and despair of groups of pre-Christians, respectively the Patriarchs and Prophets, and the heathen Langobards. Furthermore, and curiously, if perhaps coincidentally, the Anglo-Saxon poem is 137 lines long – the same length as 'King Sheave', before Tolkien added the sixteen-line coda which brought it up to 153. There must be at least a possibility that Tolkien had the Anglo-Saxon poem in mind as a model, a mythological parallel. [p. 176]

2: In *The Lost Road and Other Writings*, Christopher Tolkien reads 'Langobards' as 'Longobards'.

34: In a draft manuscript, Tolkien wrote several trials for this line: 'at his side was set || with silver strings'; 'at his left was set; || and laid at his right'; 'his hand rested || on a harp of gold', changed to 'on a harp of gold || his hand rested'; 'around him at his side || strung with silver'.

40: In draft, 'hauled' first read 'drew'.

45: In draft, this line began 'between the sea & cold waste'.

46: In draft, this line read 'a house stood high || amid the homes of men'.

59: In draft, this line read 'but the bright vessel || by the bed forsaken'.

62: In draft, this line read 'They sought in vain. || Sun was rising.'

65: Tolkien added this line after most or all of the poem was in draft.

67: Tolkien seems to have considered whether to change 'he bore' to 'bore he'.

69: 'Clear' originally read 'clear and low'.

74: 'Middle-earth', i.e. the Earth, the world of mortal Men between Heaven and Hell.

79: In draft, this line began 'no king among them'.

82: In draft, 'Dread' was originally 'Fear'.

84: In draft, Tolkien struggled with this line, trying in sometimes disconnected fragments: 'dark and empty the hall had stood', 'forlorn and empty || hollow and dim', 'empty and useless || in that dim region', etc.

85: 'Fire or food' originally read 'food or fire'.

88: Tolkien seems to have considered whether to change 'hastened' to 'thronged'. The printed text in *The Lost Road and Other Writings* has 'thronged'.

91: Tolkien seems to have considered whether to change 'heal' to 'lighten', and 'youths and maidens' to 'young men and maids'. The printed text in *The Lost Road and Other Writings* has 'youths and maidens', the prose version (see above) has 'young men & maids'. All texts have 'heal'.

110: The printed text in *The Lost Road and Other Writings* has 'ripened'. The reading of the verse manuscript is 'blossomed'; in the prose manuscript Tolkien first wrote 'blossomed', then changed the word to 'ripened'.

113: 'Comfort' originally read 'plenty'.

128: Tolkien wrote next to this line 'green and gold', apparently considering a replacement for 'gold and scarlet'.

143: In the lines added to the prose text, the words 'elder years' are capitalized, and thus appear as such printed in *The Lost Road and Other Writings*; in the lines added to the verse manuscript, they are not capitalized. Christopher Tolkien could not explain the meaning of 'before the change in the Elder Years' in ll. 142–143.

145: In the addition to the verse manuscript, 'Shields of their peoples' originally read 'strong men of old'. The addition to the prose manuscript has 'Shields of their peoples' *ab initio*.

150: Immediately before this line, Tolkien deleted 'wide realms won them || beyond the Welsh Mountains'. *Myrcwudu* is Old English 'Mirkwood', in general a dark boundary forest, here in the Eastern Alps (the Welsh Mountains).

151: *Welsh* is used here in the ancient sense 'foreign'. Christopher Tolkien notes the relationship with Old English *Walas* (from which, modern *Wales*), i.e. the Celts of Britain.

147

The Shadow Man · Shadow-Bride (?1936–62)

The first version of this poem was published as *The Shadow Man* on p. 9 of the *'Annual' of Our Lady's School, Abingdon* for 1936, in which *Noel* (no. 148) also appeared. For the sake of dating, we have supposed that Tolkien was asked to write a contribution for the *Annual*, and composed both poems in response. It is possible, however, that he had at least the present work already in hand as early as 1933 or 1934: see Appendix III, list H. Our Lady's School, now Our Lady's Abingdon, was founded in 1860 as a convent school by the Roman Catholic Sisters of Mercy. Tolkien met members of this order of nuns while in hospital during the First World War, and Abingdon (Abingdon-on-Thames) was not far from his home in Oxford.

We have transcribed the earliest text of *The Shadow Man*, as A, from an untitled manuscript shared with the earliest version of *Elvish Song in Rivendell* (no. 114).

[A]

There was a man who dwelt alone
  Beneath the moon in shadow.
He sat as long as lasting stone,
  And yet he had no shadow!
The owls, they perched upon his head
  Beneath the moon of summer.
They wiped their beaks and thought him dead
  Who sat there dumb all summer.

There came a lady clad in grey
  Beneath the moon a-shining.
One moment did she stand and stay,
  Her hair with flowers entwining.
He woke, as had he sprung of stone,
  Beneath the moon in shadow,
And clasped her fast, both flesh and bone,
  And they were clad in shadow.

And never more she walked in light,
  Or over moonlit mountain,

But dwelt within the hill, where night
    Is lit but with a fountain —
Save once a year when caverns yawn,
    And hills are clad in shadow:
They dance together then till dawn
    And cast a single shadow.

'Where night | Is lit but with a fountain' in lines 19–20 recalls Psalm 36:9, 'For with thee [God] is the fountain of life; in thy light shall we see light.'

The poem as printed in the Abingdon *Annual* follows this form except for a few changes of punctuation. The same text is found among Tolkien's papers also in a discrete manuscript and a typescript, in both of which it is called *Shadow-Bride*; we suspect that these were made in late 1961 or early 1962, when Tolkien was considering which of his earlier poems to include in his *Tom Bombadil* collection. Subsequently he made numerous changes, most notably reducing the repetition of 'shadow' and making it explicit that the 'man who dwelt alone' was under a spell. One version went to his publisher on 5 February 1962. We give the final, printed text of *Shadow-Bride* as B, from *The Adventures of Tom Bombadil and Other Verses from the Red Book*, p. 52.

[B] There was a man who dwelt alone,
    as day and night went past
he sat as still as carven stone,
    and yet no shadow cast.
The white owls perched upon his head
    beneath the winter moon;
they wiped their beaks and thought him dead
    under the stars of June.

There came a lady clad in grey
    in the twilight shining:
one moment she would stand and stay,
    her hair with flowers entwining.
He woke, as had he sprung of stone,
    and broke the spell that bound him;
he clasped her fast, both flesh and bone,
    and wrapped her shadow round him.

There never more she walks her ways
by sun or moon or star;
she dwells below where neither days
nor any nights there are.
But once a year when caverns yawn
and hidden things awake,
they dance together then till dawn
and a single shadow make.

Shadow-Bride raises many questions. Why does the 'man who dwelt alone' have no shadow? Why is the lady clad in grey? How far should one associate being 'wrapped in shadow' with death? And especially, did Tolkien intend the poem (in either version) to have a particular meaning, or is it only an exercise in creating an eerie atmosphere? Of course it is possible to suggest analogues. *Shadow-Bride* brings to mind the ballad of Tam Lin, a mortal captured by the Queen of Fairies, as well as other works of that kind, including Tolkien's own *Ides Ælfscýne* (no. 78), in which an unfortunate man is taken into a 'shadow-passage', and his *Lay of Aotrou and Itroun* (no. 116), with the Corrigan's threat that Aotrou would 'stand as stone | and wither lifeless and alone' if he did not forget Itroun and take the witch for his wife. In *Shadow-Bride*, though, and in *The Shadow Man*, it is a woman who is captured by a man.

In *Master of Middle-earth: The Fiction of J.R.R. Tolkien* Paul H. Kocher compared the events of the poem with the myth of Hades, lord of the Underworld, who takes the maiden Persephone (Proserpine) as his wife. This leads her distraught mother, the goddess of the harvest, to fail in her duties, and the earth becomes desolate. In some versions of the tale, Persephone returns to her mother each spring, but lives beneath the earth in winter, thus explaining the cycle of the seasons. Tolkien's poem refers to 'once a year when caverns yawn' and the time of the year when 'hidden things awake', like the return of spring after a long winter.

148

Noel (?1936)

Noel is known only from its publication on pp. 4–5 of the *'Annual' of Our Lady's School, Abingdon* for 1936, where *The Shadow Man* (poem no. 147) also appeared. In the absence of any manuscript or typescript, we have transcribed its printed text.

Grim was the world and grey last night;
  The moon and stars were fled,
The hall was dark without song or light.
  The fires were fallen dead.
The wind in the trees was like to the sea,
  And over the mountains' teeth
It whispered bitter cold and free,
  As a sword leapt from its sheath.

The lord of snows upreared his head;
  His mantle long and pale
Upon the bitter blast was spread
  And hung o'er hill and dale.
The world was blind, the boughs were bent,
  All ways and paths were wild:
Then the veil of cloud apart was rent,
  And here was born a Child.

The ancient dome of heaven sheer
  Was pricked with distant light;
A star came shining white and clear
  Alone above the night.
In that dale of dark in that hour of birth
  One voice on a sudden sang:
Then all the bells in Heaven and Earth
  Together at midnight rang.

Mary sang in the world below:
  They heard her song arise
O'er mist and over mountain snow
  To the walls of Paradise,

And the tongue of many bells was stirred
    In Heaven's towers to ring
When the voice of mortal maid was heard,
    That was mother of Heaven's King.

Glad is the world and fair this night
    With stars about its head,
And the hall is filled with laughter and light,
    And fires are burning red.
The bells of Paradise now ring
    With bells of Christendom,
And *Gloria*, *Gloria* we will sing
    That God on earth is come.

For all the laughter and light in the final stanza, celebrating the birth of Jesus Christ, the mood of the greater part of the poem is cold, like an English winter, recalling 'A Christmas Carol' by Christina Rossetti (1872):

In the bleak mid-winter,
    Frosty wind made moan,
Earth stood hard as iron,
    Water like a stone;
Snow had fallen, snow on snow,
    Snow on snow,
In the bleak mid-winter
    Long ago.

17: Here 'heaven' is not capitalized, denoting the night sky, rather than the capitalized Heaven, the transcendent Paradise.

149

Three Rings for the Elven-kings under the Sky (1938–54)

Here we begin a series of twenty-three entries for poems Tolkien wrote, or adapted, for *The Lord of the Rings*, grouped together in the period when the poems were written and revised (1938–54), but presented in the order they appear in the published book, not necessarily the order in which they were written. There are seventy-three poems in *The Lord of the Rings*, according to our count – an inflated number, maybe, which includes individually all of Tom Bombadil's pieces of verse-dialogue (see no. 154) and even separate couplets or alliterative lines. (In '"With Chunks of Poetry in Between": *The Lord of the Rings* and Saga Poetics' Carl Phelpstead counts more than eighty, but without certainty of which should be considered poems. It is inevitably a subjective number.) Our selection documents a variety of subjects and metres, purposes the poems serve in the larger work, and characters who recite them. Like his poems for *The Hobbit* (as discussed for no. 108), those for *The Lord of the Rings* are, in Tolkien's own words,

> an integral part of the narrative (and of the delineation of the characters) and not a separable 'decoration' like pictures by another artist. . . .
>
> I myself am pleased by metrical devices and verbal skill (now out of fashion), and am amused by representing my imaginary historical period as one in which these arts were delightful to poets and singers, and their audiences. But otherwise the verses are all impersonal; they are as I say dramatic, and fitted with care in style and content to the characters and the situations in the story of the actors who speak or sing. [letter to the German translator of *The Lord of the Rings*, Margaret Carroux, 29 September 1968, Tolkien–George Allen & Unwin archive, HarperCollins]

Five additional poems in *The Lord of the Rings* appear earlier in our book, because Tolkien revised them from earlier writings: Frodo's song at the Prancing Pony (originally *The Cat and the Fiddle*, no. 60), Aragorn's tale of Tinúviel (originally *Light as Leaf on Lind*, no. 64), Sam's song of the troll (originally *Pēro & Pōdex*, no. 83), Bilbo and

Frodo's walking song (derived from *Roads Go Ever Ever On*, no. 115, which we have counted as a single poem in *The Lord of the Rings* despite three appearances with variations), and Bilbo's song at Rivendell (*Earendil Was a Mariner*, no. 128). Also as for *The Hobbit*, we have assumed that readers of the present book know the characters and events of *The Lord of the Rings* well enough that we do not need to explain them at length.

Evidence for dating the poems of *The Lord of the Rings* is limited and confusing, except for a period in 1944 when Tolkien documented his writing in letters to his son Christopher. At times, the work moved forward with remarkable speed as inspiration took hold, but often it was interrupted by weeks or months, according to the demands of academic duties and conditions during the Second World War. Also, more than once Tolkien returned to text he had already completed, and revised, rewrote, or expanded, leaving a complicated puzzle of drafts, fair copies, and typescripts, now largely at Marquette University. Some *Lord of the Rings* manuscript pages, however, are found on the blank sides or covers of examination scripts Tolkien is known to have acquired no earlier than August 1940, which gives them at least a *terminus a quo* (the supply was exhausted by the end of 1941). We have commented on this writing process extensively in *The J.R.R. Tolkien Companion and Guide*, and more briefly in *The Lord of the Rings: A Reader's Companion*, building upon Christopher Tolkien's work on *The Lord of the Rings*, and his own attempts to date its elements, in *The History of Middle-earth*. Readers are advised to consult those works in relation to the dates we give below.

❦

To repeat part of our discussion for no. 115, the popularity of *The Hobbit* after its publication in September 1937 led George Allen & Unwin to ask Tolkien for a sequel. He began to write his 'new Hobbit' that December, and for some time was unclear of its direction. At the start, he effected a semi-comical style like that of the earlier parts of *The Hobbit*, and also in the manner of that book he included poetry. Eventually he began to focus on the ring Bilbo found in *The Hobbit*, where it was no more than a convenient fairy-tale device to turn the wearer invisible. Now Tolkien wondered about its origin, and its dangers.

In draft, with the appearance of the Black Riders and Bingo's (i.e. Frodo's) meeting with elves in the Woody End, we hear of a dark lord who gives out rings. 'Elf' (not yet named Gildor) explains that

> in the very ancient days the Ring-lord made many of these Rings: and sent them out through the world to snare people. He sent them to all sorts of folk – the Elves had many, and there are now many elfwraiths in the world [having been overcome by their rings], but the Ring-lord cannot rule them; the goblins got many, and the invisible goblins are very evil and wholly under the Lord; dwarves I don't believe had any; some say the rings don't work on them: they are too solid. Men had few, but they were most quickly overcome. . . . [*The Return of the Shadow*, p. 75]

Tolkien followed this account with another, in which the Elves had 'many' rings and the Goblins 'some'. The Dwarves 'it is said had seven' which kindled in them 'the fire of greed, and the foundation of each of the seven hoards of the Dwarves of old was a golden ring'. And Men had three, but 'others they found in secret places cast away by the elf-wraiths'. Bilbo's ring had fallen from the hand of an elf as he swam across a river and came at last to Gollum.

Tolkien began to conceive the idea that Bilbo's ring was not just a useful trinket, but the One Ring to rule over the other rings of power. Between ?late September and ?early October 1938 he wrote a new chapter, 'Ancient History' (later 'The Shadow of the Past'), in which Gandalf explains to Bingo the number and nature of the rings, and there introduced the short poem that has come to be known as the Ring Verse. In an interview Tolkien recalled that he invented the verse while in the bath, but the rhyme as published emerged only after three drafts. The first of these is a page of rough manuscript workings, which we have transcribed as A as far as we can make out the writing, illustrating Tolkien's revisions. Next to the workings proper is a list of words to rhyme with *stone*, *bone*, *throne*: *own*, *blown*, *lone*, *cone*, etc.

[A] Seven for the dwarf Lords [*above:* Kings] in their halls of stone;
Three for [*deleted:* the] Mortal Men, born of flesh and bone;
One for the Dark lord [*above:* Master] on his dark throne
    In the Land of Mordor

        [*deleted:* ?In] One to rule them all

Nine for the [Elf- >] Elves he made
Nine for the Elf-kings [*deleted:* in his realm]
[*deleted:* Nine for the Elven [kings >] lords]

Nine for the Elven-kings
[*deleted:* Seven for Mortal Men born of flesh & bone,]
[*deleted:* Three for the dwarf-kings in their]
[*deleted:* Two for the Elven King]
[*deleted:* 7, 2, 3, 1]

[Three >] Nine for the Elven-kings [*deleted:* ?neath] on his
    [*deleted:* On the hills] under [sun & moon >] moon &
    [sun >] star
Seven for the dwarf-lords in [the >] their halls of stone
Three for Mortal Men that wander far
One for the Dark Lord on his dark throne
In the Land of Mordor, [one to gather them >] where the
    shadows are.

One Ring to rule them all One ring to [bind >] find them
One to bring them all and in the darkness bind them
[*deleted:* One ring was lost ?beyond ?all ?]
[*deleted:* was lost] But ?to the Land of Mordor where the
    shadows are

Following text A, Tolkien made a fair copy in ink of lines 14–23, then revised that draft as well, roughly adding a few alternate lines in pencil. We have transcribed this version as B, again with changes Tolkien made in the course of writing.

[B] Nine for the Elven-kings [under moon & star >] under the sky,
Seven for the Dwarf-lords in their halls of stone,
Three for Mortal Men [that wander far >] who fear to die,
        [*or* on earth that die *or* doomed to die]
        [*or* Mighty Men who yet shall die]
    One for the Dark Lord on his dark throne
    In the land of Mor-dor, where the shadows [are >] lie.
One Ring to rule them all, One Ring to find them,
One Ring to bring them all and in the darkness bind them
    In the Land of Mor-dor where the shadows [are >] lie.

[Twelve >] 9 for Mortal Men doomed to die,
[Nine >] 7 for the dwarf-lords in their halls of stone
Three for the Elven Kings of earth, sea, and sky
One for the Dark Lord on his dark throne

In *The Return of the Shadow* Christopher Tolkien calls lines 1–10 of this version 'the first complete form' of the poem (p. 269). He also reproduces (p. 259) and transcribes the first appearance of the Ring Verse within the prose text of *The Lord of the Rings*. Here, as C, is our own transcription from Tolkien's manuscript, before further revision. Bilbo's ring having been thrown into the fire at Bag-End, Gandalf declares that the 'fiery letters' engraved on it are 'part of a verse that I know now in full' (as published, 'a verse long known in Elven-lore').

[C] Nine rings for the Elven-kings under the sky,
Seven for the Dwarf-lords in their halls of stone,
Three for Mortal Men doomed to die
One for the Dark Lord on his dark throne
In the Land of Mor-dor where the shadows lie.
One Ring to rule them all, One Ring to find them,
One Ring to bring them all, and in the darkness bind them.
In the Land of Mor-dor where the shadows lie.

Tolkien subsequently made two changes to text C, replacing 'Nine' in line 1 with 'Three', and 'Three' in line 3 with 'Nine'. Thus he reached the published text of the Ring Verse, except for hyphenated *Mor-dor* which he abandoned for *Mordor* in the next draft manuscript. For completeness, we give as D the poem in its final version, as it appears in published Book I, Chapter 2. Slight changes of capitalization and punctuation occurred in drafts of this chapter subsequent to manuscript text C (such as 'Elven-kings' for, briefly, 'Elven-Kings'), with the final form of the verse settled in the third typescript of *The Lord of the Rings*.

[D] Three rings for the Elven-kings under the sky,
Seven for the Dwarf-lords in their halls of stone,
Nine for Mortal Men doomed to die,
One for the Dark Lord on his dark throne
In the Land of Mordor where the Shadows lie.
One Ring to rule them all, One Ring to find them,
One Ring to bring them all and in the darkness bind them
In the Land of Mordor where the shadows lie.

Reproductions of manuscript and typescript versions of the Ring Verse may be found in our *Art of The Lord of the Rings* (2015), fig. 1, in McIlwaine, *Tolkien: Maker of Middle-earth*, p. 332, and in Fliss and Schaefer, *J.R.R. Tolkien: The Art of the Manuscript*, figs. 87–91.

In 1952 Tolkien made a private recording of the final version of the Ring Verse, since commercially released.

When in Book I, Chapter 2 the fiery letters appear on the Ring, Gandalf remarks that 'the language is that of Mordor, which I will not utter here', then proceeds to read the text 'in the Common Tongue' (English):

> One Ring to rule them all, One Ring to find them,
> One Ring to bring them all and in the darkness bind them.

But at the Council of Elrond in Book II, Chapter 2, he does speak the lines in the Black Speech:

> Ash nazg durbatulûk, ash nazg gimbatul,
> ash nazg thrakatulûk agh burzum-ishi krimpatul.

150

Upon the Hearth the Fire Is Red (1938–54)

In *The Lord of the Rings* as for *The Hobbit*, the greatest concentration of poetry within its prose narrative is in the earlier part of the work. Indeed, more than half of the poems in *The Lord of the Rings* are found in its first two books (of six), comprising the first of its three parts, *The Fellowship of the Ring*. The greatest number of poems, twenty-nine by our count, are in the first book (which takes Frodo and company to the Ford of Rivendell, followed by eleven and fourteen in Books II and III respectively, but the numbers of poems in the final three books are single digits. The first to appear in the published *Lord of the Rings*, in Book I, Chapter 1, is appropriately the walking-song *The Road Goes Ever On and On* (no. 115), carrying over the theme of the Road from *The Hobbit* as Bilbo says farewell to his home. The same poem appears again, with variation, in Chapter 3, when Frodo also leaves the Shire. Between these, in Chapter 2, is the Ring Verse, which lays out the background of the present circumstances of the story in eight memorable lines. (The Ring Verse is typically included as well as a kind of epigram preceding the table of contents.)

Also in Chapter 3 is yet another walking-song, which in the published narrative Frodo, Sam, and Pippin 'hum softly, as hobbits have a way of doing as they walk along', as they move quietly through the Shire. 'Bilbo Baggins had made the words, to a tune that was as old as the hills, and taught it to Frodo as they walked in the lanes of the Water-valley and talked about Adventure.' The earliest version of *Upon the Hearth the Fire Is Red* is a manuscript in pencil, partly overwritten in ink, made probably between late February and 4 March 1938; there the words are given to earlier versions of the three hobbits, Bingo Baggins, Frodo Took, and Odo Took. Tolkien's handwriting is rough, but we can make out the following (A) from the ink portion. Legible trial lines are described in our notes.

[A]

Upon the hearth the fire is red
beneath the roof there is a bed
And there at last we hope to lie
And sleep while darkness passes by.

But not yet weary are our feet
Still round the corner we may meet
Some sudden tree or standing stone
That none has seen but we alone.

And round the corner there may wait
A new road or a secret gate,
and even if we pass them by,
we still shall know which way they lie,
and whether hidden pathways run
towards the moon or to the sun.

May be shall return one day
And set our feet upon a way
that leads behind the sun & moon
past standing stones no hand has hewn
through gates that ever open lie

At this point the manuscript unfortunately becomes too chaotic to decipher.

Tolkien next began to make a fair copy of the poem in pencil, but the new manuscript soon became another sheet of workings, eventually filling most of the page, with sweeping arrows indicating (by no means clearly) that parts of the text were to be relocated within the poem. Here, as B, we give the text as it appears from top to bottom, not necessarily in the order it was written down.

[B] Mist and [shade >] twilight cloud and star
[*deleted:* Say good night, Say good] night a glimpse of

Home is behind, the world ahead
And there are many paths to tread
[*deleted:* under water under bough > leaf]
[over >] through the grass and over stone

Upon the hearth the fire is red
[and >] beneath the roof there is a bed,
but not yet weary are our feet
still round the corner we may meet
some sudden tree or standing stone
that none [has >] have seen, but we alone

[*deleted:* Down hill up hill let us go]
And round the corner there may wait
a new road or a secret gate;
and even if we pass them by
we still shall know which way they lie,
[*at right, largely illegible:*] [*deleted:* ?when] the hidden ?? ?green ??
and whether hidden pathways run
towards the moon or to the sun.

Down hill up hill [?runs the >] walks the [?road >] way
From sunrise to the falling day
[*at right:*] [?so on >] lets walk on to the edge of
[*deleted:* and ?we'll walk on till the stars]
[*at right:*] and we will walk on until night
[and we will walk on >] we ?walk until the
[*at right:*] until the stars are all alight

Tree and [stone >] flower and leaf and grass
    Let them pass, let them pass
[Cloud and >] Hill and water under sky
    pass them by pass them by

and ?we will put the world behind
and ?drive ahead and hope to find
[*at right:*] the world behind & home ahead
?again the [fire >] hearth & the fire still red
[*at right:*] we'll ?hark back to fire & bed
beneath the roof
[*deleted:* we will]
[*deleted:* we will]

Apple ?berry and nut and sloe
    Let ?them go let them go
Sand and stone and pool and [well >] dell
    fare you well fare you well

In the first typescript of *Upon the Hearth the Fire Is Red* – part of a replacement section of *The Lord of the Rings* in which its story was substantially altered and expanded – the poem became much more coherent. We give the new text as C, with further details in our notes.

[C] Upon the hearth the fire is red,
Beneath the roof there is a bed;
But not yet weary are our feet,
Still round the corner we may meet
A sudden tree or standing stone
That none have seen, but we alone.
  Tree and flower and leaf and grass
    Let them pass! Let them pass!
  Hill and water under sky,
    Pass them by! Pass them by!

Home is behind, the world ahead,
And there are many paths to tread;
And round the corner there may wait
A new road or a secret gate,
And hidden pathways there may run
Towards the Moon or to the Sun.
  Apple, thorn, and nut, and sloe,
    Let them go! Let them go!
    Sand and stone and pool and dell,
    Fare you well! Fare you well!

Down hill, up hill walks the way
From sunrise to the falling day,
Through shadow to the edge of night,
Until the stars are all alight;
Then world behind and home ahead,
We'll wander back to fire and bed.
  Mist and twilight, cloud and shade,
    Away shall fade! Away shall fade!
  Fire and lamp and meat and bread,
    And then to bed! And then to bed!

It is interesting to mention that on this typescript Tolkien expanded his prose introduction to the verse, adding in manuscript that Bilbo and Bingo's walks in the Water-valley were 'not of course without any mention of bed and supper': this is not only natural behaviour for Hobbits, but pertinent to the poem, with its references to sleep and food. But Tolkien never included it in any later text, possibly because the homeliness of 'bed and supper' might diminish the reader's thrill in the original end to the paragraph, in which the two hobbits talk of Adventure – a word capitalized for effect. As the story proceeds, the hobbits will have far more adventure than they could expect, and fewer of the comforts in Bilbo's song.

As Tolkien continued to refine this part of *The Lord of the Rings*, in a new typescript he included yet another revised text of *Upon the Hearth*, given here as D.

[D] Upon the hearth the fire is red,
Beneath the roof there is a bed;
But not yet weary are our feet,
Still round the corner we may meet
A sudden tree or standing stone
That none have seen, but we alone.
Tree and flower and leaf and grass,
Let them pass! Let them pass!
Hill and water under sky,
Pass them by! Pass them by!

Still round the corner there may wait
A new road or a secret gate,
And even if we pass them by,
We still shall know which way they lie,
And whether hidden pathways run
Towards the Moon or to the Sun.
Apple, thorn, and nut and sloe,
Let them go! Let them go!
Sand and stone and pool and dell,
Fare you well! Fare you well!

Home is behind, the world ahead,
And there are many paths to tread
Through shadow to the edge of night,
Until the stars are all alight.
Then world behind and home ahead,
We'll wander back to fire and bed.
Mist and twilight, cloud and shade,
Away shall fade! Away shall fade!
Fire and lamp and meat and bread,
And then to bed! And then to bed!

To the left of line 13 Tolkien wrote 'though today', and to the right, 'And though we pass them by to-day | Tomorrow we may come this way | And take the hidden paths', both of which point to his last major change to the poem. In the next version of the chapter, a manuscript, he replaced singular 'shadow' with plural 'shadows' in line 23, and 'fire' with 'home' in line 26, and with some slight changes to punctuation and indentation at last reached the published form of the poem. We give its final text (E) as printed.

[E]

Upon the hearth the fire is red,
Beneath the roof there is a bed;
But not yet weary are our feet,
Still round the corner we may meet
A sudden tree or standing stone
That none have seen but we alone.
    Tree and flower and leaf and grass,
        Let them pass! Let them pass!
    Hill and water under sky,
        Pass them by! Pass them by!

Still round the corner there may wait
A new road or a secret gate,
And though we pass them by to-day,
Tomorrow we may come this way
And take the hidden paths that run
Towards the Moon or to the Sun.
    Apple, thorn, and nut and sloe,
        Let them go! Let them go!
    Sand and stone and pool and dell,
        Fare you well! Fare you well!

Home is behind, the world ahead,
And there are many paths to tread
Through shadows to the edge of night,
Until the stars are all alight.
Then world behind and home ahead,
We'll wander back to home and bed.
    Mist and twilight, cloud and shade,
        Away shall fade! Away shall fade!
    Fire and lamp and meat and bread,
        And then to bed! And then to bed!

This, however, was not the last iteration of *Upon the Hearth* in *The Lord of the Rings*. In the story's final chapter (Book VI, Chapter 9), six lines of the poem appear again, with variation, as Frodo is leaving not only the Shire but also Middle-earth, wounded by war and the loss of the Ring. In the published text he is 'singing softly to himself, singing the old walking-song, but the words were not quite the same'. In draft the lines read, before revision (F):

[F]

Still round the corner there may wait
A new road or a secret gate;
and though we often pass them by
A day will come when we
[and >] shall take the hidden paths that run
[at >] towards the moon beyond the sun

To the right of lines 3 and 4, Tolkien wrote 'I oft [*or* ever] have passed them by' and 'at last when I', and below line 6, 'west of the moon & east of [the sun]'. These led to the final form of the words, in the next manuscript of the chapter and as published (G):

[G]

Still round the corner there may wait
  A new road or a secret gate;
And though I oft have passed them by,
  A day will come at last when I
Shall take the hidden paths that run
  West of the Moon, East of the Sun.

For Frodo, the day in question is not hypothetical: it will come a week later, when he sets sail from the Grey Havens on the Straight Road into the True West. 'West of the Moon, East of the Sun' is also the opening of text A of *The Shores of Faery* (poem no. 31), which refers to Aman, the Undying Lands where Frodo will be healed and, at last, die.

Upon the Hearth the Fire Is Red is thematically related to *The Road Goes Ever On and On*, with its images of road, gate, and travel. John D. Rateliff's suggestion that Tolkien may have been influenced to write his 'road' verses for *The Hobbit* and *The Lord of the Rings* by E.F.A. Geach's 'Romance' (see our discussion for no. 115) would seem to apply equally, if not more so, to *Upon the Hearth*.

In 1952 Tolkien made a private recording of the final version of the poem (text E), since commercially released. A musical setting of the poem by Donald Swann appeared in *The Road Goes Ever On: A Song Cycle* (1967), and was performed by pianist Swann and baritone William Elvin on the recording *Poems and Songs of Middle Earth* (1967).

A1: In the margin, next to the first lines of the draft, are (mostly illegible) trials, such as 'the gates that open only out', 'upon a wild and ?pathless way'

A2–3: Between these lines, Tolkien wrote and deleted 'Upon the table stands the bread | Butter beer and cheese'.

A4: Following this line, we can make out two lines in pencil from the earlier text, 'But alongside the road the air | Is sweet'.

A7: A *standing stone*, or menhir, is a large stone stood upright by human intent, often for a ceremonial purpose, and a remnant of megalithic culture. Standing stones are found individually and in groups, such as the Rollright Stones near Oxford.

A10: Beneath this line, we can make out 'down hill, up hill walks the way'.

A15: 'May be shall return' is the reading of the manuscript, not 'May be we shall return'. Preceding this line, Tolkien wrote, but struck through, 'One day maybe shall come back'. In the margin nearby, he also struck through another trial, '[And >] For one day we may yet return'.

B28–31: Next to these lines Tolkien wrote 'bis', as if he wished them to be repeated. There is no sign of this idea in later versions.

B40: 'Nut', presumably a nut-bearing bush or tree.

C11–12: Next to these lines Tolkien wrote 'trs to 3rd v.', i.e. transfer to third verse (stanza); compare text D.

C13: Next to 'And' Tolkien wrote 'Still', a replacement made in the next version.

C15: Tolkien wrote 'whether' as an addition before 'hidden', and in the margin, two lines to be inserted before C15: 'And even if we pass them by | We still shall know which way they lie'; compare A11–12.

C17: 'Thorn', i.e. a thorny bush or tree, such as the hawthorn.

C21–22: Next to these lines Tolkien wrote 'or substitute complete at head of 2nd verse'. Instead, he omitted them in later versions.

G6: In the manuscript in which the final form of this text appears, 'moon' is not capitalized. This was corrected in the following typescript.

151

Snow-White! Snow-White! O Lady Clear! (1938–54)

In Book I, Chapter 3 of *The Lord of the Rings* the three hobbits, continuing their walk, reach the Woody End where they meet elves singing 'in the fair elven-tongue, of which Frodo knew only a little, and the others knew nothing. Yet the sound blending with the melody seemed to shape itself in their thought into words which they only partly understood.' The words of the song as published did not come easily to Tolkien, however, nor can they be deciphered easily in their earliest manuscripts, which date probably between late February and 4 March 1938. Here, as A, is our attempt to read the first few lines of the initial version.

[A] [*deleted:* The stars are far ?brighter]
O sky of
[*deleted:* Hail daughter of stars]
[*deleted:* Hail light   and light sl???]
[*deleted:* Hail night and moon   and ?northern ?sky]
[*deleted:* Hail tree and ?centre   and ?tree ?wonder]

O stars of twilight long gone by
[For >] O Elbereth Elbereth
O Queen beyond the western sea.
Thy stars [*deleted:* of the white]
[*deleted:* the white] the silver [light >] flame
O cold and ??? is thy breath
The ??? ?you the ?fields
O light to those that wander
amid the world of woven trees

At the foot of this page, Tolkien then wrote a revised text (B), but it fell into repetition within a few lines.

[B] O Elberil O Elberil
O queen beyond the Western Seas
We see thy silver flowers still

amid the world of woven trees.
O stars that in the Sunless Year
were [strewn >] sown by her with shining hand
Now [*deleted:* flowering] in the heavens clear
Your flower now in the heavens clear
We see your flowers with a
We see your flowers now flowering [white >] clear

In a third attempt (C), Tolkien was still uncertain if the song was to be addressed to *Elbereth* (as in the published *Lord of the Rings*) or to *Elberil*, an issue which continued as the drafts progressed.

[C] O Elbereth [*or* Elberil] O Elbereth [*or* Elberil]
O queen beyond the western seas
O light to those that wandereth
amid the world of woven trees
O stars that in the Sunless Year
were kindled by [her >] thy silver hand
that under night the shade of fear
should fly like shadow from the land
O Elbereth O Elbereth
clear are thy eyes and cold thy breath
and we are in a world of fear

Here again, Tolkien struggled with the poem, writing and deleting or altering trial lines and fragments of lines. And again, as for B, he began a new version (D) on the same page.

[D] O Elberil! O Elberil!
O Queen beyond the Western Seas
[We see thy silver flowers still >] O light to us that wander still
Amid the world of woven trees.

O stars that in the Sunless Year
Were kindled by her shining hand
[*deleted:* and under night]
[*deleted:* whose silver flowers ??? clear]

The drafting process continued in two more scribbled manuscripts, one of them begun in pencil and overwritten in ink. This page begins with still further variations (E), one of which, as we will see, is of particular interest.

[E] O Elberil! O Elberil!
O Queen beyond the Western Seas!
O Light to us that wander still
Amid the world of woven trees.
O stars that in the Flowering Years
were kindled by her silver hand [*or* in her shining ?halls]
and hung as flame.
Snow-white, Snow-white thy eyes are clear
[*deleted:* Thy hands are shining]
and with thy shining hands
you kindled

Eventually, in the first typescript to contain the poem, Tolkien settled on five four-line stanzas (F).

[F] O Elbereth! O Elbereth!
O Queen beyond the Western Seas!
O Light to him that wandereth
Amid the world of woven trees!

O Stars that in the Sunless Year
Were kindled by her silver hand,
That under Night the shade of Fear
Should fly like shadow from the land!

O Elbereth! Gilthonieth!
Clear are thy eyes, and cold thy breath!
Snow-white! Snow-white! We sing to thee
In a far land beyond the Sea!

O Stars that in the Sunless Year
With shining hand by her were sown,
In windy fields now bright and clear
We see your silver blossom blown.

O Elbereth! Gilthoniel!
We still remember, we who dwell
In this far land beneath the trees,
Thy starlight on the Western Seas.

Immediately, though, Tolkien made changes to the first and third stanzas, and deleted the second. His corrected text carried into the next typescript (G), where he made one further manuscript revision ('cold' to 'bright' in line 6, reflected here) and at last reached the published form.

[G] Snow-white! Snow-white! O Lady clear!
O Queen beyond the Western Seas!
O Light to us that wander here
Amid the world of woven trees!

Gilthoniel! O Elbereth!
Clear are thy eyes and bright thy breath!
Snow-white! Snow-white! We sing to thee
In a far land beyond the Sea.

O Stars that in the Sunless Year
With shining hand by her were sown,
In windy fields now bright and clear
We see your silver blossom blown!

O Elbereth! Gilthoniel!
We still remember, we who dwell
In this far land beneath the trees,
Thy starlight on the Western Seas.

In his appendix to *The Road Goes Ever On: A Song Cycle* Tolkien explains that '*Elbereth* was the usual name in S[indarin] of the *Vala*, called in Q[uenya] *Varda*, "the Exalted". It is more or less the equivalent of Q[uenya] *Elentári*, "Star-queen" . . . ; but *bereth* actually meant "spouse", and was used of one who is "queen" as spouse of a king. *Varda* was spouse of Manwe [i.e. Manwë], "the Elder King", chief of the Valar' (p. 66). She lives in Aman, 'a far land' which as we have seen in earlier poems is 'beyond the Western Seas'. 'Snow-white' is a title of Elbereth, translated from Sindarin *Fanuilos*. 'The world of woven trees' is Middle-earth; compare *galadhremmin ennorath* 'tree-tangled middle-lands', below.

The Tolkien encyclopaedists Robert Foster (*The Complete Guide to Middle-earth*) and J.E.A. Tyler (*The Complete Tolkien Companion*) associate 'Sunless Year' with the time of darkness between the destruction of the Two Trees and the creation of the Sun and Moon, a period Tolkien came to call the 'Long Night'. Christopher Tolkien seems to have interpreted the term differently, stating that 'extensive rough workings' of the poem – our text E above – explain the meaning of the phrase, 'since my father first wrote *the Flowering Years* (with reference to the Two Trees . . .)' (*The Return of the Shadow*, p. 68). Here Christopher must mean that *in this particular draft* his father first used the words 'Flowering Years', referring to the long period in which the Two Trees flowered and gave light to Valinor (see poem no. 31), then changed his mind in favour of 'Sunless Year'. 'Flowering Years' is written in ink at the top of the manuscript, and in pencil, abbreviated, later on the page, where it is overwritten in ink 'Sunless Year'; but Tolkien used the former term only in this manuscript, while 'Sunless Year' appears several times in earlier drafts.

Christopher points in his comment to the *Quenta Silmarillion*, his father's account of the mythology as it stood around the end of 1937 and the beginning of 1938, when he was beginning to write *The Lord of the Rings*. There one reads that Varda 'looked out upon the darkness, and was moved'. Mighty lamps the Valar had made to illuminate the world had been overthrown by Morgoth, and the Two Trees later created by the Valar gave light only to their home in Valinor. Elsewhere all was dark, and evil things multiplied. 'Therefore [Varda] took the silver dew that dripped from Silpion and was hoarded in Valinor, and therewith she made the stars. And for this reason she is called Tintallë, the Star-kindler, and Elentári, Queen of Stars. She strewed the unlit skies with these bright vessels, filled with silver flame . . .' (*The Lost Road and Other Writings*, p. 212). Thus, as in the deleted stanza in text F, stars were made by Varda (Elbereth) 'That under Night the shade of Fear | Should fly like shadow from the land!' From this it seems that Christopher read *Sunless Year* to mean a period – not necessarily a (solar) year as mortals perceive it – *in which there was no sun* to light the world, only the stars made by Varda.

In the *Quenta Silmarillion* it is said that the Elves awoke in Middle-earth at the opening of the first stars. The Elves therefore loved the stars and venerated their maker, whom they also called *Gilthoniel*, Sindarin 'star-kindler' (with the element *gil* 'bright spark'). The 'windy fields' mentioned in texts F and G are the sky, and stars are the 'silver blossom'. Tolkien's poem also refers to the Elves 'wandering' in Middle-earth, and that those who dwell there remember Varda's 'starlight on the Western Seas': this too is a glimpse of the larger mythology, in which the Valar, 'filled with love of [the Elves'] beauty', 'feared for them in the dangerous world amid the deceits of the starlit dusk' and therefore arranged to bring them into the West (*The Lost Road and Other Writings*, p. 213). Those who obeyed the summons of the Valar to journey west therefore saw the light of the stars while in Aman; but after the theft of the Silmarils (see poem no. 66), many of the Elves returned to Middle-earth to wage war against Morgoth.

The amount of labour Tolkien put into the Elves' hymn to Elbereth – it is correct to call it that (we are hardly the first to do so), for it is a song of praise and devotion – is remarkable but not inexplicable. In *The Hobbit* the Elves had, in the person of Elrond, a certain *gravitas*, but otherwise, in their songs, were playful, to say the least. In *The Lord of the Rings* they are of a different sort, demonstrably old, wise, and noble (as they are in 'The Silmarillion'), and Tolkien had to tailor their poetry and speech to suit. *Snow-White!* includes its several words of Sindarin, but is presented as a 'translation' of the song heard by the hobbits. A version wholly in Sindarin, written between late August 1940 and ?autumn 1941, appears in Book II, Chapter 1, chanted by the elves in Rivendell:

A Elbereth Gilthoniel,
silivren penna míriel
o menel aglar elenath!
Na-chaered palan-díriel
o galadhremmin ennorath,
Fanuilos, le linnathon
nef aear, sí nef aearon!

In *The Road Goes Ever On: A Song Cycle* (p. 64) Tolkien translates these words literally as:

O Elbereth Star-kindler,
(white) glittering slants-down sparkling like jewels
from firmament glory [of] the star-host
to-remote distance after-having-gazed
from tree-tangled middle-lands,
Fanuilos, to thee I will chant
on this side of ocean here on this side of the Great Ocean.

Three further translations appear in Tolkien's unfinished commentary, *Words, Phrases and Passages in The Lord of the Rings* (*Parma Eldalamberon* 17, 2007). There the last of them reads (p. 21):

O Elbereth who lit the Stars,
from heaven on high now slanting falls
like light from jewels of crystal clear

the glory of the starry host.
To lands remote I have looked afar
and now to thee, Fanuilos
bright spirit clothed in ever-white,
I here will sing beyond the Sea,
beyond the wide and Sundering Sea.

Of *A Elbereth Gilthoniel*, Bilbo tells Frodo (in the final narrative) that the elves 'will sing that, and other songs of the Blessed Realm, many times tonight'. An earlier, somewhat different Elvish text of the chant, written probably between mid-October and December 1938, is printed in *The Return of the Shadow* (p. 394):

Elbereth Gilthoniel sir evrin pennar oriel
dir avos-eithen miriel
bel daurion sel aurinon
pennáros evrin ériol.

And in Book VI, Chapter 9 of *The Lord of the Rings*, written between 14 August and 14 September 1948, Tolkien looks back to both versions of the hymn as the elves sing:

A! Elbereth Gilthoniel!
silivren penna míriel
o menel aglar elenath,
Gilthoniel, A! Elbereth!
We still remember, we who dwell
In this far land beneath the trees
The starlight on the Western Seas.

In *The Power of the Ring: The Spiritual Vision behind* The Hobbit *and*The Lord of the Rings (2012, p. 79), Stratford Caldecott suggests, as others have done also (see poem no. 51), that Elbereth, Queen of the Stars, represents the Virgin Mary, Queen of Heaven, and that Tolkien's poem is 'markedly close' in 'tone and mood' to the Roman Catholic hymn by Father John Lingard:

Hail, Queen of Heaven, the ocean star,
Guide of the wand'rer here below,
Thrown on life's surge, we claim thy care,
Save us from peril and from woe.
Mother of Christ, star of the sea,
Pray for the wanderer, pray for me.

In 1952 Tolkien made a private recording of the final version of *Snow-white!* and also of *A Elbereth Gilthoniel* within an extract from Book II, Chapter 1 of *The Lord of the Rings*, and in 1967 he made a professional recording of *A Elbereth Gilthoniel* for the album *Poems and Songs of Middle Earth*. These were later reissued. A musical setting of *A Elbereth Gilthoniel* by Donald Swann appears in *The Road Goes Ever On: A Song Cycle* (1967) incorporated with *I Sit beside the Fire and Think* (no. 158), and was performed by pianist Swann and baritone William Elvin on *Poems and Songs of Middle Earth*.

152

Sing Hey! for the Bath at Close of Day (1938–54)

In an early draft of published Book I, Chapter 5 of *The Lord of the Rings*, made probably between late February and 4 March 1938, as Bingo Baggins, Frodo Took, and Odo Took approach Bucklebury Odo stumbles into a muddy puddle, exclaims 'Do you think there is any chance of a bath to-night?' and 'without waiting for an answer he suddenly began a hobbit bathroom song' (*The Return of the Shadow*, p. 98).

O Water warm and water hot!
O Water boiled in pan and pot!
O Water blue and water green,
O Water silver-clear and clean,
    Of bath I sing my song!
O praise the steam expectant nose!
O bless the tub my weary toes!
O happy fingers come and play!
O arms and legs, you here may stay,
    And wallow warm and long!
Put mire away! Forget the clay!
Shut out the night! Wash off the day!
In water lapping chin and knees,
In water kind now lie at ease,
    Until the dinner gong!

This is hardly more than doggerel, but Tolkien aimed to be playful, as he had been with his poems or songs in *The Hobbit*, and the rhyme suits the character of Odo, just as a wholly different verse is fitted to Pippin. That other song (A, before revision) first appears in a manuscript from late September or early October 1938, there sung by Frodo Took whose voice is 'suddenly lifted up in one of the favourite hobbit bath-songs'.

[A]

Sing hey! For the bath at close of day
that washes the weary mud away.
A loon is he that will not sing —
O water hot is a noble thing!

O sweet is the sound of falling rain,
and the brook that leaps from hill to plain;
but better than rain or rippling streams
is water hot that smokes and steams.

O water cold we may pour at need
down a thirsty throat and be glad indeed,
but beer is better if drink you lack,
and water hot poured down the back.

O! water is fair that leaps on high
in a fountain white beneath the sky,
but never a fountain sounds so sweet
as splashing hot water with my feet!

In a subsequent manuscript, towards the end of 1938, Tolkien altered 'beer is better' to 'better is beer' in line 11 and began to capitalize 'water', 'water hot' (or 'hot water'), and 'water cold'. He soon achieved the final text of the song in typescript. We give this here, as B, from the published book, where it is sung by Pippin.

[B]

Sing hey! for the bath at close of day
that washes the weary mud away!
A loon is he that will not sing:
O! Water Hot is a noble thing!

O! Sweet is the sound of falling rain,
and the brook that leaps from hill to plain;
but better than rain or rippling streams
is Water Hot that smokes and steams.

O! Water Cold we may pour at need
down a thirsty throat and be glad indeed;
but better is Beer, if drink we lack,
and Water Hot poured down the back.

O! Water is fair that leaps on high
in a fountain white beneath the sky;
but never did fountain sound so sweet
as splashing Hot Water with my feet!

In 1952 Tolkien made a private recording of the final version of the song, since commercially released.

A11: Tolkien began to write 'but better [is beer], then struck through 'better' and wrote 'beer is better'. In subsequent texts he decided that he preferred his first thought.

153

Farewell We Call to Hearth and Hall (1938–54)

Tolkien wrote the earliest extant manuscript of this song between ?late September and ?early October 1938. We present it here as A, before revision. This seems to have been originally a fair copy made after a draft now lost.

[A]

Farewell! farewell, now hearth and hall!
Though wind may blow and rain may fall,
We must away ere break of day
Far over wood and mountain tall.

The hunt is up! Across the land
The Shadow stretches forth its hand
We must away ere break of day
To where the Towers of Darkness stand.

With foes behind and foes ahead,
Beneath the sky shall be our bed,
Until at last the Ring is cast
In Fire beneath the Mountain Red.

We must away, we must away,
We ride before the break of day

As first written, when the central hobbit was still named Bingo, these words were sung by Merry Brandybuck and Frodo Took. Tolkien struck through his references to 'Merry and Frodo', however, and added in the margin of the page: 'Merry, Frodo, and Odo began a song which they had apparently got ready for the occasion. It was of course made on the model of the dwarf-song that started Bilbo on his adventure long before [in *The Hobbit*]; and it went to the same tune.' The 'dwarf-song' was *Far over the Misty Mountains Cold* (poem no. 109), the first lines of which we repeat here:

Far over the misty mountains cold
To dungeons deep and caverns old
We must away, ere break of day,
To seek the pale enchanted gold.

In the *Lord of the Rings* manuscript Tolkien briefly considered whether to call back to his *Hobbit* poem more explicitly by writing, above his new lines already on the page, 'Far over wood and mountains cold'; but he struck these words through, probably at once.

The same text, marks of punctuation notwithstanding, appears in the next manuscript of the chapter, from late 1938, but is struck through; and it is present still in its first typescript, but there Tolkien revised it heavily, replacing the second stanza whole. These latter changes, however, appear to follow a separate manuscript page, on which Tolkien first wrote quickly his revised text, omitting only the final couplet, then struck this through and made a more legible copy, including the final two lines. The only substantive difference between the two versions is in line 7: in the first, Tolkien wrote 'Though wild and wide the Road we ride', but in the second 'Through moor and waste we ride in haste'. Thus the song reached its ultimate form, which we give here, as B, from Book I, Chapter 5 of the published book.

[B]

Farewell we call to hearth and hall!
Though wind may blow and rain may fall,
We must away ere break of day
Far over wood and mountain tall.

To Rivendell, where Elves yet dwell
In glades beneath the misty fell,
Through moor and waste we ride in haste,
And whither then we cannot tell.

With foes ahead, behind us dread,
Beneath the sky shall be our bed,
Until at last our toil be passed,
Our journey done, our errand sped.

We must away! We must away!
We ride before the break of day!

The original text of this song (A) differs most strikingly from its final version in referring to the hobbits journeying to the 'Towers of Darkness' – that is, to Mordor – where they intend to cast the Ring into the 'Mountain Red' – Mount Doom. Tolkien removed these lines, perhaps having realized that although Bingo (as later Frodo Baggins) knows of the need to destroy the Ring, and of the means of doing so, there is no thought at this point in the story that he himself will go to the fire-mountain, let alone that his Hobbit friends would go with him.

Tolkien seems to have been too closely focused on echoing *Far over the Misty Mountains Cold* to see at once that too similar a poem would be out of character for sheltered Hobbits with no experience of conflict, in contrast (in *The Hobbit*) to a seasoned company of Dwarves bent on revenge. The revised song sung by Merry and Pippin tells correctly that the hobbits are to go to Rivendell, beyond which they have no plan. Also its words are more believably of the sort that two younger hobbits might prepare, when they were eager for adventure but not yet aware of the dangers in store. Their vision of crossing wood, mountain, fell, moor, and waste is romantic rather than realistic. *Farewell We Call to Hearth and Hall!* in fact recalls painfully the naïveté of so many of Tolkien's contemporaries at the start of the First World War, when battle seemed only another sport to be played and won.

In 1952 Tolkien made a private recording of the final poem, since commercially released.

A10: Tolkien briefly considered whether to change 'Beneath' to 'Under'.
B12: *Sped* is used here in the sense 'concluded'.

154

Hey! Come Merry Dol! · *Hop Along, My Little Friends* (1938–54)

We have met Tom Bombadil already in this book, in the 1934 poem Tolkien published in the *Oxford Magazine* and its later incarnation in the 1962 *Adventures of Tom Bombadil* collection (poem no. 121). From around the end of August 1938, Tolkien included Tom in *The Lord of the Rings* as the centre of an 'adventure' for the hobbits, and in this carried over Tom's curious manner of expression: 'Come, derry-dol, merry-dol, my darling!' In *The Road to Middle-earth* Tom Shippey remarks that it is the language Tom Bombadil uses which seems to give him his mastery, over creatures such as the Barrow-wight and generally over 'wood, water and hill'.

> He is the great singer; indeed he does not yet seem to have discovered, or sunk into, prose. Much of what he says is printed by Tolkien as verse, but almost all of what he says can be *read* as verse, falling into strongly-marked two-stress phrases, with or without rhyme and alliteration, usually with feminine or unstressed endings. . . . [p. 97]

For our purposes, we too have read Tom's dialogue as verse, and have selected two examples, from published Book I, Chapter 6, to represent the whole.

The first is heard as Tom is responding to a cry for help in the Old Forest, two of the journeying hobbits having been caught by Old Man Willow. A song emerges from 'a long string of nonsense-words (or so they seemed)'. Its earliest draft in the *Lord of the Rings* papers is jotted lightly in pencil, to the point of illegibility (or incoherence), but by its second manuscript, in ink over an initial pencil version and from a later phase of writing (in the surrounding prose text, the chief hobbit is 'Frodo' and Sam Gamgee is present), the lines were already close to their final form. We give this latter text as A, illustrating revisions Tolkien made in the course of writing.

[A] Hey! come merry dol, derry dol, my darling!
Light [of >] goes the weather-wind and the feathered starling.

[Up, down >] Down along under Hill, shining in the sunlight
Waiting on the doorstep for the [hidden moonlight >] cold starlight
[There's >] There my pretty lady [*added:* is] the River-woman's daughter
Slender as a willow wand, clearer than the water,
Old Tom Bombadil waterlilies bringing
Comes hopping home again. [Can't >] Can you hear him singing?
Hey come merry dol, derry dol and merry-o
Goldberry, Goldberry, merry yellow berry-o!
Poor old Willowman [*deleted:* just] you tuck your roots away
Tom's in a hurry now. Evening will follow day
Tom's going home again waterlilies bringing
Hey come merry dol Can't you hear me singing!

The published form of the song (B) was achieved in the next manuscript of the chapter, written probably between late September and early October 1938.

[B] Hey! Come merry dol! derry dol! My darling!
Light goes the weather-wind and the feathered starling.
Down along under Hill, shining in the sunlight,
Waiting on the doorstep for the cold starlight,
There my pretty lady is, River-woman's daughter,
Slender as a willow-wand, clearer than the water.
Old Tom Bombadil water-lilies bringing
Comes hopping home again. Can you hear him singing?
Hey! Come merry dol! derry dol! and merry-o,
Goldberry, Goldberry, merry yellow berry-o!
Poor old Willow-man, you tuck your roots away!
Tom's in a hurry now. Evening will follow day.
Tom's going home again water-lilies bringing.
Hey! Come merry dol! Can you hear me singing?

Having rescued the hobbits, Tom tells them: 'You shall come home with me! The table is all laden with yellow cream, honeycomb, and white bread and butter. . . . You follow after me as quick as you are able!' Frodo, Sam, Merry, and Pippin follow Tom 'as fast as they could. But that was not fast enough.' Tom disappears from view, then 'his voice came floating back to them in a loud halloo!' In Tolkien's first draft of this song (C), Tom's words are laid out in half-lines.

[C] Hop along my little [men >] friends up the Withywindle!
Tom's going on ahead candles for to kindle
[*deleted:* Sun's going westward quick]
Down west sinks the sun [Then > But you'll see a twinkle >]
Soon you will be groping
[*deleted:* Shine out of]
[*deleted:* Shine out of window pane]
When mist and shadows rise but the door'll be open
and out of window panes light will twinkle [golden >] yellow
[*deleted:* Hold fast to the path]
?Heed not the alder black fear [not >] no grey willow
Hold fast to the path Tom goes on before you.
Hey now merry dol we'll be waiting for you.

Tolkien marked this text heavily, and carried his revisions into the next manuscript of the chapter (D).

[D] Hop along, my little friends, up the Withywindle!
Tom's going on ahead candles for to kindle
Down west sinks the sun: soon you will be groping,
When mist and shadow rise, but the door will be open;
Out of window-panes light will twinkle yellow
Heed not the alder black! Fear no grey willow!
Hold fast to my path! Tom goes on before you.
Hey now! merry dol! We'll be waiting for you!

This too was revised in the manuscript. The text reached its final form (E) in the next, typescript draft of the chapter.

[E] Hop along, my little friends, up the Withywindle!
Tom's going on ahead candles for to kindle.
Down west sinks the Sun: soon you will be groping.
When the night-shadows fall, then the door will open,
Out of the window-panes light will twinkle yellow.
Fear no alder black! Heed no hoary willow!
Fear neither root nor bough! Tom goes on before you.
Hey now! merry dol! We'll be waiting for you!

In *J.R.R. Tolkien: Romanticist and Poet* Julian Eilmann observes that Tolkien characterizes Tom Bombadil directly 'as a poetic being. His songs themselves show the traits of a pronounced playful joy of being. . . . For him, singing and existential joy are inextricably linked to each other.' Tom's 'frolicking jumping together with his singing suggest he lives in harmony with the poetic structure of the cosmos'. For him, 'singing is more natural than speaking. Poetry is superior to profane, mundane communication – a truly Romantic insight' (pp. 374–6).

More than one critic has made the obvious comparison between Tom Bombadil and the wizard Väinämöinen in the *Kalevala*; see, for example, David Elton Gay's comments in 'J.R.R. Tolkien and the *Kalevala*: Some Thoughts on the Finnish Origins of Tom Bombadil and Treebeard' (2002). As Elias Lönnrot tells in Runo III of the *Kalevala* (ll. 1–6):

Väinämöinen, old and steadfast
Passed the days of his existence
Where lie Väinölä's sweet meadows,
Kalevala's extended heathlands:
There he sang his songs of sweetness
Sang his songs and proved his wisdom.

But he also sings songs of power, mighty songs against which Tom's exhortations, as to Old Man Willow or the Badger-folk, are mild in comparison. Contending with 'the youthful Joukahainen', for example, who challenges Väinämöinen to 'measure swords together', the latter sings so powerfully that

Lakes swelled up, and earth was shaken,
And the coppery mountains trembled,
And the mighty rocks resounded,
And the mountains clove asunder;
On the shore the stones were shivered.

Joukahainen sinks into a quicksand, and knows that 'in singing he was beaten' (ll. 296–300, 335).

In 1952 Tolkien made a private recording of texts B and E, since commercially released.

A2: 'Weather-wind' seems to be Tom's way of referring to the weather and the wind as one. At any rate, they are presently 'light' and favourable.

A6: *Wand* in 'willow wand' has the sense 'slender, straight stick'.

D4: Tolkien's use of 'open' as a rhyme for 'groping' suggests that Tom clipped his speech, with 'groping' pronounced 'gropin''.

155

Cold Be Hand and Heart and Bone (1938–54)

The Barrow-wight's chant in Book I, Chapter 8 of *The Lord of the Rings* could not be more different in tone than the playful nonsense of Tom Bombadil featured in Chapters 6 and 7. In the narrative, a song begins, an 'incantation', 'a cold murmur, rising and falling. . . . Out of the formless stream of sad but horrible sounds, strings of words would now and again shape themselves: grim, hard, cold words, heartless and miserable.' They describe the death of everything, even the Sun, Moon, and stars, and over all is the threat of a dark lord. Frodo is 'chilled to the marrow'.

As first written in the chapter around the end of August 1938, the Barrow-wight's words were somewhat different from those published. We give some of them here as A, extracted from two manuscript pages filled with trials written up and down in the margins as well as across.

[A] The moon has waned and all fire dies.
The moon has fallen under the bottomless sea.
The wind has blown out all the stars.
Cold cold cold it is under the stone.
Cold is the ?eye, cold the heart and cold the bone

And the dark lord sits in the tower and looks over the dark seas
and the dark world, and

Dark sits in the dark tower and his hand
stretches over the cold sea and dead world

The sun shall wane and the moon fail
The sea be stilled and the earth cold
The wind out of nowhere shall blow the stars out

Cold cold cold. Who shall waken the old days
and make ?mournful

It is cold cold under stone
where we dwell cold alone

who shall waken the old days
or ?call back the vanished shadows

In the black wind stars shall die
and still here under gold they'll lie
Till the King of the Dark Tower stretch his hand

In the first coherent manuscript, 'the burden of the song, which at first had few formed words, seemed like "*cold and alone, cold and alone, strong as iron, hard as stone*"', and the incantation read as in B.

[B] Cold is hand and heart and bone
and cold is sleep under the stone:
never more to wake on their stony bed
never till the sun fails and the moon is dead.
In the black wind the stars shall die
and still on the gold [they'll lie >] here they'll lie
till the king of the dark tower lifts his hand
over the dead sea and the withered land

Tolkien struck this through, however, and in the next manuscript of the chapter reached almost the final text, most notably changing 'cold is' to the more archaic 'cold be' in the first two lines, and compressing the Barrow-wight's speech by removing instances of 'the' and 'their'. The published chant, still with a few differences of capitalization and punctuation relative to B as revised (such as *Sun* for *sun*), is given here as C.

[C] Cold be hand and heart and bone
and cold be sleep under the stone:
never more to wake on stony bed,
never, till the Sun fails and the Moon is dead.
In the black wind the stars shall die,
and still on gold here let them lie,
till the dark lord lifts his hand
over dead sea and withered land.

As he does also in *The Adventures of Tom Bombadil* (no. 121), Tom expels the Barrow-wight with the mastery of his own song, though in *The Lord of the Rings* his action has a comparatively cold fierceness and finality:

Get out, you old Wight! Vanish in the sunlight!
Shrivel like the cold mist, like the winds go wailing,
Out into the barren lands far beyond the mountains!
Come never here again! Leave your barrow empty!
Lost and forgotten be, darker than the darkness,
Where gates stand for ever shut, till the world is mended.

A6: As Christopher Tolkien comments in *The Return of the Shadow*, the dark tower of the dark lord (the Necromancer, Sauron) is referred to by Gandalf in an early draft of *The Lord of the Rings*, and even earlier in *The Hobbit*, where the tower in question is in the south of Mirkwood. By the time he wrote of the incident on the Barrow-downs, Tolkien had conceived of Mordor, the Black Land or Black Country.

B3: Tolkien considered whether to change 'to wake' to 'shall they wake'.

156

All That Is Gold Does Not Glitter (1938–54)

Tolkien developed the brief alliterative poem in *The Lord of the Rings* which begins 'All that is gold does not glitter' in the period between August and autumn 1939, in a series of drafts for the text that became Book I, Chapter 10. In every version, the rhyme is part of a letter written by Gandalf to Frodo at the 'Prancing Pony' in Bree, warning him of dangers and advising him to seek a friend and ally, initially named 'Trotter'. Tolkien had been uncertain, as his story evolved, whether Trotter was a Hobbit, 'Peregrin Boffin that Bilbo took away with him or who ran off with Bilbo' (*The Treason of Isengard*, p. 7), or perhaps a disguised Elf from Elrond's household pretending to be a 'ranger'. In the end, he decided that Trotter was a Man, a hunter and wanderer, and in the earliest manuscript of the rhyme (A, see also *The Treason of Isengard*, p. 49) Gandalf reveals that Trotter is 'Aragorn son of Celegorn, of the line of Isildur Elendil's son, known in Bree as Trotter; enemy of the Nine, and friend of Gandalf'. Gandalf further advises Frodo that 'the real Trotter' will 'have a sealed letter from me' containing these words:

[A] All that is gold does not glitter; all that is long does not last.
All that is old does not wither; not all that is over is past.

On the next page of this manuscript, the same lines are said to be written on 'a small paper in Gandalf's hand' enclosed with Trotter's letter. As may be seen, from this and other early versions, Tolkien initially wrote the poem in long lines, with their halves separated by semicolons or commas. Only later, and in transcriptions in *The Treason of Isengard*, are they broken for easier reading.

Tolkien heavily revised, and finally struck through, both of these initial pages with the rhyme. Of text A, he deleted all of the words except 'All that is gold does not glitter', with no replacement; but he paid more attention to the same lines when they were repeated for Trotter's letter. Here, as B, is that second text, illustrating Tolkien's (subsequent) revisions.

[B] All that is gold does not glitter; [all that is long does not last >] not all those who wander are lost;
All that is old does not wither; [not all that is over is past > and winter may come without frost >] not every leaf falls in the frost.
[*two lines added:*] Not all that have fallen are vanquished; a king may yet be without crown,
[A >] Let [?sword >] blade that was broken be brandished; and towers that were strong may fall down.

On the same page, Tolkien quickly wrote the following, as well as other words we cannot decipher:

all that is bowed does not bend
not all that is past is at end
and fire may burn bright in a frost

He seems to have intended the rhyme, as first written, to mean: Do not judge someone by appearance. But with the revelation of Trotter's ancestry, it also expressed a hope in the restoration of the King, though he 'may yet be without crown'.

After making further, very rough trials on a separate sheet, Tolkien wrote out a fresh copy of the initial two pages. In this he carried forward some of his revisions to the earlier manuscript, but also changed parts of his text in the act of writing. The rhyme in Gandalf's letter to Frodo now read (C):

[C] All that is gold does not glitter, not all those that wander are lost;
All that is old does not wither, and fire may burn bright in the frost;
Not all that have fallen are vanquished, not only the crowned is a king.
Let blade that was broken be brandished, and Fire be the Doom of the Ring!

The same words are given one manuscript page later, in the account of Trotter's letter. The defiant words '[let] Fire be the Doom of the Ring' recall the hobbits' vow in the first version of *Farewell We Call to Hearth and Hall!* (no. 153), 'Until at last the Ring is cast | In Fire beneath the Mountain Red', and were just as short-lived as the present rhyme evolved.

New revisions, chiefly to the first instance of the rhyme, now followed as Tolkien struck through the second of the new pages, probably when simplifying the chapter by eliminating the letter to Trotter and having Strider – as he now became by revision – quote part of the rhyme by chance, confirming him as a friend. In the first typescript of the chapter, the poem read (D, before further revision):

[D] All that is gold does not glitter, not all those that wander are lost;
All that is old does not wither, and bright may be fire in the frost.
The flame that was low may be woken, and sharp in the sheath is the sting;
Forged may be blade that was broken; the crownless again may be king!

Tolkien subsequently marked changes to this text as well, replacing the third line with 'The smouldering flame may be woken, and sharp from the sheath come the sting'; this reading, however, did not survive into later versions. The idea of a 'blade that was broken' existed in the rhyme from its first version, as something to be 'brandished'; now it was suggested that the sword may be reforged, though already 'sharp in the sheath'.

Tolkien seems to have made the next developments of the rhyme on two small pieces of paper. On the first (E) he wrote, now using short lines:

[E]

All that is gold does not glitter,
  not all those that wander are lost;
The old that is strong does not wither
  and roots may run deep in the frost.
From the ashes a fire may be woken,
  a light in the darkness may spring;
Renewed may be blade that was broken;
  the crownless again may be king.

Here, and afterward, the blade is to be 'renewed' rather than 'forged' (anew). In the margin of this slip Tolkien wrote a queried alternate reading for line 6, 'a voice in the silence may sing'. On the second slip, he wrote the same text as E but marked revisions to four of its lines. These brought the poem to its final form, which we have transcribed as F:

[F]

All that is gold does not glitter,
  Not all those who wander are lost;
The old that is strong does not wither,
  Deep roots are not reached by the frost.
From the ashes a fire shall be woken,
  A light from the shadows shall spring;
Renewed shall be blade that was broken,
  The crownless again shall be king.

'Who wander' now became the final reading in line 2, and in the final four lines Tolkien replaced 'may' with 'shall', making the outcome described in *All That Is Gold* emphatic certainty rather than mere possibility.

In *The Lord of the Rings* the poem is used twice to advance the plot. Its first purpose is to characterize Trotter/Strider/Aragorn as a hero, and to hint at his history – only a hero, or at any rate someone of exceeding importance, has his own poem or song. But it also does duty as a second confirmation of Aragorn's bona fides, in Book II, Chapter 2, when Bilbo declaims it before the Council of Elrond and to Boromir in particular. 'I made that up myself', he tells Frodo, 'for the Dúnadan [Aragorn], a long time ago when he first told me about himself.'

The lines come close on the heels of Frodo revealing the Ring, and before that, Aragorn casting his broken sword on a table, which in turn was a response to the verse Boromir recounts from a dream:

Seek for the Sword that was broken:
  In Imladris it dwells;
There shall be counsels taken
  Stronger than Morgul-spells.
There shall be shown a token
  That Doom is near at hand,
For Isildur's Bane shall waken,
  And the Halfling forth shall stand.

The reader never learns who sent these words to Boromir; some have suggested that it was Gandalf, or Manwë, chief of the Valar. But there can hardly be any doubt that Tolkien meant them to be a pendant to Bilbo's rhyme, which they resemble in structure. They constitute a prophecy: Boromir is to seek a broken sword (Narsil, whose shards were kept at Imladris, that is, Rivendell), and he will be shown a deadly token (the One Ring, 'Isildur's Bane'), and a 'Halfling'

(Frodo, a Hobbit) who will step forward (as Frodo does, to take the Ring to Mordor) – all veiled behind vague but impressive words. On the face of it, *All That Is Gold Does Not Glitter* also seems prophetic, in that it looks ahead to Aragorn ('the crownless') gaining the throne of Gondor and Arnor; and yet, it is not strictly a prophecy, if it was composed by the Hobbit Bilbo Baggins who knows of the sword and of Aragorn's history and hopes. Again at the Council of Elrond, the poem reinforces the thought that one should not judge a person, or an object, solely by appearance, whether it is Aragorn, the weather-beaten ranger who is heir to a kingdom, or an unadorned ring with the power to dominate and corrupt.

As Judith J. Kollmann has remarked, Tolkien's adage 'all that is gold does not glitter' 'remains stubbornly evocative of Shakespeare's "All that glisters is not gold" (*The Merchant of Venice* 2.7.65)' ('How "All That Glisters Is Not Gold" Became "All That Is Gold Does Not Glitter": Aragorn's Debt to Shakespeare' (2007), p. 110). Kollmann's greater argument, however, relates Aragorn to Henry V (Prince Hal) in Shakespeare's history plays. Each is part of 'a sweeping history of kings embedded within a matrix of dynasty and destiny, and above all, a fascination with the qualities of kings that lead to monarchic greatness or to failure' (p. 111). Both 'assume disguises that make them seem less and other than what they truly are' (p. 119). For each, there are questions of authenticity. Kollmann suggests that *All That Is Gold Does Not Glitter* is an analogue to part of Hal's speech in *Henry IV, Part One*, Act I, Scene 2:

> So, when this loose behavior I throw off
> And pay the debt I never promised,
> By how much better than my word I am,
> By so much shall I falsify men's hopes;
> And like bright metal on a sullen ground,
> My reformation, glitt'ring o'er my fault,
> Shall show more goodly and attract more eyes
> Than that which hath no foil to set it off.

B1: The reading 'those who wander' now temporarily replaced 'those that wander'. 'That wander' would return, then give way to final 'who wander'.

D2: On the second revised manuscript page, Tolkien marked an alternate reading for the latter half of this line, 'and brighter is fire in the frost'.

D3: On the first revised manuscript page, Tolkien wrote the first half of this line as 'The flame that was low may be woken', i.e. 'was', not 'is'.

157

Gil-galad Was an Elven-king (1938–54)

In Book I, Chapter 11 of *The Lord of the Rings*, Strider speaks of his ancestor Elendil standing in the Tower of Amon Sûl on Weathertop 'watching for the coming of Gil-galad out of the West, in the days of the Last Alliance', the armies of Men and Elves who fought against the Dark Lord, Sauron. Merry asks, 'Who was Gil-galad?' but before Strider can answer, Sam murmurs twelve lines of poetry in 'a low voice' on that very subject.

The earliest version of the words Sam recites is found on a page of rough workings; we have transcribed the more legible of its lines below as A. Written in two layers of pencil and ink on one side of an order form issued by the Oxford bookseller Blackwell's, the manuscript also includes part of a draft for Book I, Chapter 10, in which Sam is named, a feature which dates it to no earlier than the later part of 1939. In *The Treason of Isengard* Christopher Tolkien places the poem within the 'fourth phase' of writing for *The Lord of the Rings*, between August and autumn 1939.

[A]

Gilgalad was an Elvenking;
of him the harpers sadly sing:
the last whose realm was fair and free
between the Mountains and the Sea.

The argent moon upon his argent shield
Of silver like the moon was ???
his shining shield and on this blue

upon his shield the moon

The moonlight on his silver shield
his helm was crowned with silver stars
upon his helm a silver star

of silver were his shield and crown

the sky's stars were set therein

His banner blue with stars was sown
and on his helm a gem was

The seven stars gleaming in

The [stars >] countless stars of heaven's field
were mirrored in his [starry >] silver shield

His blazons blue with [*deleted:* stars] were seen
upon his helm a star

His sword was long his blade was keen
His shining helm afar was seen
The countless stars of heaven's field
were mirrored in his silver shield

But [*deleted:* long ago he rode away
to Mordor where the night is day]

Although Tolkien initially struggled to advance past the first stanza, he soon rallied with a more coherent manuscript text (B).

[B]

Gilgalad was an Elven king;
of him the harpers sadly sing:
the last whose realm was fair and free
Between the Mountains and the Sea.
His sword was long his blade was keen
His shining helm afar was seen
The countless stars of heaven's field
were mirrored in his silver shield
But long ago he rode away
and where he lieth none can say
For under shadow came his star
in Mordor where the shadows are

In line 10 Tolkien struck through 'lieth' and wrote 'dwelleth' (dwells), and in line 11 he wrote 'into darkness fell' above 'under shadow came'; both revisions carried into the next manuscript. He also considered whether to change 'rode' to 'went' in line 9, but retained 'rode'.

With the next (third) manuscript, Tolkien introduced further changes, and reached the published form of the poem with only a few small differences of capitalization and punctuation. *Gilgalad*, Sindarin for 'starlight', would gain a hyphen (*Gil-galad*) in the first typescript of the work, as a manuscript revision. We give here, as C, the final text as printed.

[C]

Gil-galad was an Elven-king.
Of him the harpers sadly sing:
the last whose realm was fair and free
between the Mountains and the Sea.

His sword was long, his lance was keen,
his shining helm afar was seen;
the countless stars of heaven's field
were mirrored in his silver shield.

But long ago he rode away,
and where he dwelleth none can say;
for into darkness fell his star
in Mordor where the shadows are.

The lines 'the countless stars of heaven's field | were mirrored in his silver shield' are probably a poetic way of saying that his shield was emblazoned with stars – not an actual reflection of stars as in a mirror, although it is possible for a shield to be highly polished. In the early 1960s Tolkien designed two heraldic devices for Gil-galad, each showing a pattern of stars on a blue ground.

In the published *Lord of the Rings* Sam explains that he had learned the poem from Bilbo, 'as taught me my letters. He was mighty book-learned was dear old Mr. Bilbo. And he wrote *poetry*. He wrote what I have just said.' But Strider corrects him: Bilbo did not himself compose the lines. Rather, they are 'part of the lay that is called *The Fall of Gil-galad*, which is in an ancient tongue. Bilbo must have translated it.' Here again – as remarked for poem no. 64 – Tolkien refers to a tradition of poetry in Middle-earth which the reader can barely glimpse.

In 1952 Tolkien made a private recording of the final version of the poem, since commercially released.

A16: 'Seven stars', i.e. the Pleiades. See our discussion for poem no. 40.

158

I Sit beside the Fire and Think (1938–54)

As the hobbits meet to discuss their future in published Book II, Chapter 3 of *The Lord of the Rings*, Bilbo warns that if the Ring is to be taken from Rivendell it must leave soon, considering the time of year:

> When winter first begins to bite
>   and stones crack in the frosty night,
> when pools are black and trees are bare,
>   'tis evil in the Wild to fare.

In his preface to *The Adventures of Tom Bombadil and Other Verses from the Red Book*, Tolkien implies that this is Bilbo's composition; it seems as if it should be a Hobbit adage, from a people who saw bleak winters. An analogue in English culture would be

> When icicles hang by the wall,
>   And Dick the shepherd blows his nail,
>   [i.e. blows on his hands to warm them]
> And Tom bears logs into the hall,
>   And milk comes frozen home in pail,
> When blood is nipped [cold], and ways be foul,
> Then nightly sings the staring owl . . .

These words, from Shakespeare's *Love's Labours Lost*, are (or used to be) generally well known, and moreover are from a set play for Tolkien's final examinations at Oxford in 1915. Tom Shippey makes this connection with the Shakespeare coda also in *The Road to Middle-earth*, commenting that 'every single word' in both rhymes

> is ordinary if colloquial English; every single word is also (with the doubtful exceptions of 'logs' and 'nipped') rooted in Old English. Both poems would require little change to make sense at any time between AD 600 and now. Yet they are representatives of a tradition Tolkien thought, if not too short, very much too scanty. [p. 166]

By this point in *The Lord of the Rings* Bilbo has spent sixteen years at Rivendell, resting, studying, and working on his memoirs. He has learned to reflect, and as Frodo is preparing to head south with the Company of the Ring, Bilbo sings quiet words of things that he has seen in his long life and others he will never see – a song of nostalgia and longing, and of mortality. In two pages of manuscript workings, Tolkien devised nearly all of the final elements of *I Sit beside the Fire and Think*, as well as a few phrases he chose to abandon: 'of shallow waters cool', 'of islands', 'of shadows on the sea' – one wonders when Bilbo would have had a sea journey at this stage of his life, though he ultimately does, sailing from the Grey Havens into the West. At the end of the workings, Tolkien added: 'He [Bilbo] ends [his reverie] that all the while he will think of *Frodo*'; but this too was not included in the published text.

Tolkien consolidated his thoughts in a new manuscript of the poem, producing the text given here as A.

[A]

I sit beside the fire and think
    of all that I have seen;
of meadow-flowers and butterflies
    in summers that have been;

Of yellow leaves and gossamer
    in autumns that there were,
with morning mist and silver sun
    and wind upon my hair.

I sit beside the fire and think
    of how the world will be
when winter comes without a spring
    that I shall ever see;

For still there are so many things
    that I have never seen:
in every wood in every spring
    there is a different green.

But all the while I sit and think
    I listen for the door
and hope to hear the voices come
    I used to hear before.

I sit beside the fire and think
of people long ago,
and people who will see a world
that I shall never know.

Next to the opening lines, Tolkien wrote 'or in *future* I'll sit etc.', that is, he considered in passing whether to have the poem in the future tense ('I'll sit beside the fire and think'). Next to lines 19 and 20, he wrote and struck through trial changes, 'your voice return' for 'the voices come', and 'your hand upon the door' for 'I used to hear before'; and at the foot of the page, he drafted another version of lines 18–20, 'of times there were before | I'll listen for your voice [*or* feet] to come | your hand upon the door'. He marked lines 21–24 to be moved before line 17, and in this form included the poem in the first typescript of the chapter. There he revised the final three lines in manuscript and achieved the published version of the poem, given here as B from the printed *Lord of the Rings*.

[B]

I sit beside the fire and think
of all that I have seen,
of meadow-flowers and butterflies
in summers that have been;

Of yellow leaves and gossamer
in autumns that there were,
with morning mist and silver sun
and wind upon my hair.

I sit beside the fire and think
of how the world will be
when winter comes without a spring
that I shall ever see.

For still there are so many things
that I have never seen:
in every wood in every spring
there is a different green.

I sit beside the fire and think
of people long ago,
and people who will see a world
that I shall never know.

But all the while I sit and think
    of times there were before,
I listen for returning feet
    and voices at the door.

The beginnings of *I Sit beside the Fire and Think* (as well as *When Winter First Begins to Bite*) can be dated to the period between late August 1940 and ?autumn 1941, and it seems possible that it contains Tolkien's personal reflections as well as Bilbo's. He would have been nearing his fiftieth birthday (3 January 1942), with memories of the 1914–18 conflict and of times of normality made more precious during a new war. His second son, Michael, then in the Army, had been injured in December 1940, and his youngest son, Christopher, aged seventeen, would be called up before long. Tolkien also would have been aware of former students then in service, and of colleagues in occupied territory such as the Belgian Simonne d'Ardenne.

A musical setting of *I Sit beside the Fire and Think* by Donald Swann appeared in *The Road Goes Ever On: A Song Cycle* (1967), and was performed by pianist Swann and baritone William Elvin on the recording *Poems and Songs of Middle Earth* (1967). In this setting, it incorporates *A Elbereth Gilthoniel* (see poem no. 151).

159

The World Was Young, the Mountains Green (1938–54)

Gimli's song in Book II, Chapter 4 of *The Lord of the Rings*, written between late August 1940 and ?autumn 1941, recounts the history of the Dwarves from the waking of their progenitor, Durin, to the time when the Company of the Ring stands in Durin's halls, 'in Moria, in Khazad-dûm' beneath the Misty Mountains. 'This is the great realm and city of the Dwarrowdelf', Gimli tells his companions. 'And of old it was not darksome, but full of light and splendour, as is still remembered in our songs.' Four pages of drafting for the poem are among Tolkien's papers, but the lines they contain are miscellaneous, and do not account for the whole of the text. Here, as A, we have transcribed the most substantive, and legible, parts of these early pages.

[A] He climbed and named the nameless hill,
he drank from yet untasted rill
He [*deleted:* [looked >] stooped and looked in Mirrormere
and saw there first a face appear]
He looked for ages in Mirrormere
and saw the smaller stars appear [about his face >] about his head

The world was young, the mountains green,
No mark [upon >] yet on the moon was seen,
When Durin came and gave [their >] them name
To [lands >] hills where [none before >] nameless lands had been.

The world was fair, the mountains tall,
[When >] With gold and silver gleamed his hall,
When Durin's throne of carven stone
Yet stood behind the guarded wall.

The world is dark, the mountains [cold >] old,
[The >] In shadow lies the [heapéd >] fallen gold;
In Durin's halls no hammer falls.
The forges' fires are grey and cold

When Durin woke and gave to gold
its first and secret name of old

When Durin [first >] came to Azanûl
And found and named the nameless pool

When Durin woke the fire of gold
and found the golden ore

When Durin first in dwarvish tongue and speech??? the name of gold
and silver in his ??? cold
to gold he gave   gave the gold ??? ?flame
and struck from   struck with a steel a flame

The world was young the mountains green,
No mark yet on the moon was seen,
When Durin [first Khazad-dûm to >] in the dawn of days
first [found the nameless > found >] climbed and named the nameless hills

The world was green when on his
When Durin [still >] yet was on his throne
in carven halls of vaulted stone

Christopher Tolkien included some of these workings, 'no doubt the earliest', in a slightly different manner than we have followed, in *The Treason of Isengard*, pp. 183–4. There he notes their 'form in four-line stanzas with a rhyme scheme *aaba* and internal rhyme in the third line', rather than the rhyming couplets of the published song (B, below). It seems likely that Tolkien composed these quatrains with some of his Dwarf-centred *Hobbit* poems in mind, such as *Far over the Misty Mountains Cold* (no. 109), as they have the same structure.

Following the pages of rough workings, Tolkien made a new manuscript of the poem complete and, except for a few small differences and two of the final lines, in its final form. This is obviously a fair copy, which must have been written after further drafting, but no other workings are extant. We give here, as B, the text as published in *The Lord of the Rings*, with differences in intermediate copies described in our notes.

[B]

The world was young, the mountains green,
No stain yet on the Moon was seen,
No words were laid on stream or stone,
When Durin woke and walked alone.
He named the nameless hills and dells;
He drank from yet untasted wells;
He stooped and looked in Mirrormere,
And saw a crown of stars appear,
As gems upon a silver thread,
Above the shadow of his head.

The world was fair, the mountains tall,
In Elder Days before the fall
Of mighty kings in Nargothrond
And Gondolin, who now beyond
The Western Seas have passed away:
The world was fair in Durin's Day.

A king he was on carven throne
In many-pillared halls of stone
With golden roof and silver floor,
And runes of power upon the door.
The light of sun and star and moon
In shining lamps of crystal hewn
Undimmed by cloud or shade of night
There shone for ever fair and bright.

There hammer on the anvil smote,
There chisel clove and graver wrote;
There forged was blade, and bound was hilt;
The delver mined, the mason built.
There beryl, pearl, and opal pale,
And metal wrought like fishes' mail,
Buckler and corslet, axe and sword,
And shining spears were laid in hoard.

Unwearied then were Durin's folk;
Beneath the mountains music woke;
The harpers harped, the minstrels sang,
And at the gates the trumpets rang.

The world is grey, the mountains old,
The forge's fire is ashen-cold;
No harp is wrung, no hammer falls:
The darkness dwells in Durin's halls;
The shadow lies upon his tomb
In Moria, in Khazad-dûm.
But still the sunken stars appear
In dark and windless Mirrormere;
There lies his crown in water deep,
Till Durin wakes again from sleep.

Durin was the eldest of the Seven Fathers of the Dwarves, created by the Vala Aulë. He slept for ages, until the Firstborn (the Elves) waked under the stars. 'No stain yet on the Moon was seen' because the Moon had not yet been created. This was in the Elder Days, the First Age of the world; we have mentioned Nargothrond and Gondolin already in our book. The 'mighty kings' who 'beyond the Western Seas have passed away' are Finrod, Orodreth, and Turgon, all killed in Beleriand. 'Durin's Day' must mean the time in which Durin lived, not the specific day 'when the last moon of Autumn and the sun are in the sky together' (*The Hobbit*, ch. 3).

From the beginning, Tolkien depicted Durin as a kind of Adam who named the hills, streams, and other aspects of the land, if not the living creatures (who are not mentioned). Most remarkably, it was also Durin in draft who gave gold and silver their names in the secret language of the Dwarves, and he was the first to 'wake the fire of gold', that is (if we interpret Tolkien correctly), to shape gold in a forge. In 'The Silmarillion', and in *The Hobbit*, the Dwarves are shown to lust for metals and gems, and to be expert in working them; and in *The Lord of the Rings* it is revealed that in mining for 'Moria-silver', the precious *mithril*, they delved too deep and awoke a Balrog, 'Durin's Bane'. Still, in Gimli's song as published, although gold and silver, gems, and crystal are mentioned, the impression given to the reader is not one of greed but of fineness of craft. In Appendix F of *The Lord of the Rings* it is said that Dwarves are 'lovers of stone, of gems, of things that take shape under the hands of the craftsman rather than things that live by their own life'.

In 1952 Tolkien made a private recording of the final version of Gimli's song, since commercially released.

A8: Next to this line, Tolkien wrote 'and on the moon was yet no stain'.

A10: Next to this line, Tolkien wrote in ink: 'to gold that nameless long had [lain >] been'. In the opposite margin, he wrote in pencil: 'to gold where none before ?was'. And below the line, he wrote in pencil: 'to gold where never gold before was shaped'.

A11–14: Tolkien marked revisions to these lines which are apparently incomplete, but would have replaced ll. 12–14:

> The world was fair, the mountains tall,
> In Elder Days before the fall
> of
> amid his gold & silver hall

It seems that Tolkien was unclear at this point what it was that fell: space was left blank after 'of'. In the published text the fall is 'Of mighty kings in Nargothrond | and Gondolin'.

A21: 'Azanûl', i.e. Azanulbizar, the Dimrill Dale, the valley below the east-gate of Moria, with its lake Kheled-zâram, the Mirrormere.

B7: 'Mirror-mere' was spelled thus, with a hyphen, in draft, but changed to 'Mirrormere' in proof.

B22: 'Shining lamps' replaced 'countless lamps' in the first typescript of the chapter.

B29: 'Beryl, pearl' replaced 'ruby, beryl' in the first typescript.

B43–46: In the first complete manuscript of the poem, these lines read:

> And dark and still is Mirror-mere;
> Wherein the sunken stars appear:
> There lies his crown in water deep,
> Till Durin wakes again from sleep.

Tolkien changed ll. 43–44 in the manuscript to the reading of the published text.

160

The Song of Legolas · An Elven-maid There Was of Old (1938–54)

'Do you hear the voice of Nimrodel?' Legolas asks his friends in Book II, Chapter 6 of *The Lord of the Rings*. 'I will sing you a song of the maiden Nimrodel, who bore the same name as the stream beside which she lived long ago. It is a fair song in our woodland tongue; but this is how it runs in the Westron [Common] Speech, as some in Rivendell now sing it.' The finished song, in thirteen quatrains of ballad metre (see p. li), is indeed fair in the result, but it gave Tolkien a great deal of trouble in the composing. Beginning in the period between late August 1940 and ?autumn 1941, he wrote out multiple trials for the song and lists of rhyming words, working rapidly and, more often than not, illegibly, starting anew several times. Among these drafts is a group of seven stanzas (A), next to which Tolkien marked alternate readings as described in our notes.

[A]

There was an elven maid of old
    Before the birth of men
When first the trees bore flowers of gold
    in fair Lothlórien

Her beauty elven songs have told
    a shining star by day;
Her mantle white was hemmed with gold,
    her shoes were silver grey

A silver star upon her brows
    a light upon her hair
as sun upon the golden boughs
    of Lórien the fair.

Her arms were white
    and fair she was and free,
and in the wind she went as light
    as leaf on linden-tree.

An elven maid there was of old:
a shining star by day
her mantle sewn with flowers of gold
her shoes of silver grey.

An elven maid there was of yore
a silver voice at night [*or* a shadow in the night]
a harp of many strings she bore
and played with fingers white

As falls the foaming Linglorel
with water clear and cool
The notes as falling silver fell
Into the starlit pool.

Tolkien numbered stanzas three, four, and five of this text to be reordered as two, three, and one, and he placed a mark as well, but not a number, also next to stanza seven. With revision, these correspond to the four stanzas he wrote on another of his working sheets, transcribed here as B.

[B] An elven-maid there was of old:
a shining star by day;
Her mantle white was hemmed with gold,
her shoes were silver grey.

A star was bound upon her brows,
A light upon her hair
As sun upon the golden boughs
in Lórien the fair.

Her hair was long her limbs were white,
and fair she was and free
and in the wind she went as light
as leaf on linden-tree.

Beside the falls of Linglorel
with water clear and cool
her voice as falling silver fell
into the shining [*or* foaming] pool.

The first three of the quatrains of B are written in ink on the initial manuscript, the fourth added in pencil at the top of the same page but fourth in order (by default) according to manuscript A, or if we use the published poem as a guide. Except for the name *Linglorel*, this draft text is not too far from its finished form.

To text B, Tolkien added a short prose passage: 'So they sang of Linglorel and they gave her name to the mountain River. For there she used to sing playing on a harp beside the water falls. There in springtime when wind is in the new leaves the echo of her voice may still be heard of. For long ago she went away.' The song then continued in draft, written first in pencil, then overwritten in ink. Unfortunately, we can decipher little of Tolkien's hurried script for the remainder, except for the discrete lines 'In spring when wind is in the leaves' and 'The wind from off the winter shore', and the pair 'But where now she wanders none can tell | in shadow or in sun in moonlight or in shade', followed later by 'For long ago fair Linglorel'.

Seven further leaves of mostly rough workings followed, as Tolkien wrote with speed and, we would guess from the heaviness of some of his script and strikethroughs, frustration. In the process, the name of the elven-maid changed from *Linglorel* variously to *Nimladel*, *Nimlothel*, and *Nimlorel*, as well as *Inglorel* in passing. The name of her lover, for long *Ammalas*, evolved more briefly to *Amaldor* and finally *Amroth*. The song tells his story too, with his impulsive but romantic act of diving from the ship bearing him away from his love. In one draft, 'He leaped into the flying sea | as fishing bird he leaped | as fowl that dives for fish', before Tolkien reached nearly the final reading:

Then in the sea they saw him leap
  as arrow from the string
and dive into the waters deep
  as mew upon the wing

Linglorel's 'harp of many strings' soon disappeared from the drafts.

At last, Tolkien felt ready to attempt a more settled manuscript, which he headed *The Song of Legolas*. We give its text as C, before further revision.

[C] An elven maid there was of old:
  a shining star by day:
her mantle white was hemmed with gold
  her shoes of silver grey.

A star was bound upon her brows
    A light was on her hair
As sun upon the golden boughs
    in Lórien the fair.

Her eyes were bright, her arms were white,
    and fair she was and free;
and in the wind she went as light
    as leaf of linden-tree.

Beside the falls of Nimlothel,
    by water clear and cool,
Her voice as falling silver fell
    into the shining pool.

Where now she wanders none can tell,
    In sunlight or in shade.
For lost of yore was Nimlothel,
    and in the mountains strayed.

The elven-ship in haven grey
    beneath the mountain-lee
Awaited her for many a day
    beside the roaring sea.

A wind awoke in Northern lands
    and loud it blew and free,
And bore the ship from Elven-strands
    across the streaming sea.

Beyond the waves the shores were grey,
    the mountains sinking low;
as salt as tears the driving spray,
    the wind a cry of woe.

When Amroth saw the fading shore
    beyond the heaving swell
He cursed the faithless ship that bore
    him far from Nimlothel.

An Elven lord he was of old
    before the birth of men

when first the boughs were hung with gold
in fair Lothlorien

From helm to sea they saw him leap
as arrow from the string,
and dive into the waters deep
as mew upon the wing

The foam was in his flowing hair,
A light about him shone;
Afar they saw the waves him bear,
as floats the northern swan.

But from the West has come no word,
And on the Hither Shore
No tidings Elven folk have heard
of Amroth evermore.

Although the most coherent version of the poem to this point, manuscript C was nonetheless another transitional copy. Its most remarkable feature is a space Tolkien deliberately left blank in line 9, 'Her [*blank*] her arms were white', evidently because he could not at once make up his mind what to write. After the manuscript was complete, written in ink, he returned to line 9 and added 'eyes were bright' in pencil. But he also considered 'eyes were grey', pencilled in the right margin, and 'Her hair was long', pencilled at left, 'clear' pencilled above 'bright', and 'limbs' pencilled above 'arms'. Other alternate readings are written here and there on the two pages of the manuscript, as we describe in our notes.

Tolkien followed manuscript C with a fair copy, carefully written in two columns and again entitled *The Song of Legolas*; for reference in notes, we will call this C[1]. This he marked with only a few revisions before making the first typescript of the chapter, where the text of the poem continued to change. For D below, we have transcribed the poem as published, and describe in our notes changes to the text made in its final manuscript and typescripts.

[D]

An Elven-maid there was of old,
A shining star by day:
Her mantle white was hemmed with gold,
Her shoes of silver-grey.

A star was bound about her brows,
    A light was on her hair,
As sun upon the golden boughs
    In Lórien the fair.

Her hair was long, her limbs were white,
    And fair she was and free;
And in the wind she went as light
    As leaf of linden-tree.

Beside the falls of Nimrodel,
    By water clear and cool,
Her voice as falling silver fell
    Into the shining pool.

Where now she wanders none can tell,
    In sunlight or in shade;
For lost of yore was Nimrodel
    And in the mountains strayed.

The elven-ship in haven grey
    Beneath the mountain-lee
Awaited her for many a day
    Beside the roaring sea.

A wind by night in Northern lands
    Arose, and loud it cried,
And drove the ship from elven-strands
    Across the streaming tide.

When dawn came dim the land was lost,
    The mountains sinking grey
Beyond the heaving waves that tossed
    Their plumes of blinding spray.

Amroth beheld the fading shore
    Now low beyond the swell,
And cursed the faithless ship that bore
    Him far from Nimrodel.

Of old he was an Elven-king,
   A lord of tree and glen,
When golden were the boughs in spring
   In fair Lothlórien.

From helm to sea they saw him leap,
   As arrow from the string,
And dive into the water deep,
   As mew upon the wing.

The foam was in his flowing hair,
   As light about him shone;
Afar they saw him strong and fair,
   Go riding like a swan.

But from the West has come no word,
   And on the Hither Shore
No tidings Elven-folk have heard
   Of Amroth evermore.

Here, in the published book, Legolas ceases to sing. 'That is but a part' of the song, he explains, 'for I have forgotten much. It is long and sad, for it tells how sorrow came upon Lothlórien', the refuge of the Elves east of the Misty Mountains. Fearing the Balrog dwarves had roused in Moria,

> many of the Elves of Nimrodel's kindred left their dwellings and departed, and she was lost far in the South, in the passes of the White Mountains; and she came not to the ship where Amroth her lover waited for her. But in the spring when the wind is in the new leaves the echo of her voice may still be heard by the falls that bear her name. And when the wind is in the South the voice of Amroth comes up from the sea. . . . But neither Nimrodel nor Amroth came ever back.

The song, or the larger work from which Legolas supposedly drew, is mentioned later in *The Lord of the Rings* (Book VI, Chapter 4), when 'one [from the principality of Dol Amroth, 'Hill of Amroth', named after the lost king] would sing amid the gloom some staves of the Lay of Nimrodel, or other songs of the Vale of [the river] Anduin out of vanished years'. Tolkien later wrote a short tale concerning Nimrodel and Amroth, published in *Unfinished Tales* (1980) but with no addition to the 'lay'.

The songs of Legolas and Gimli (poem no. 159) in *The Lord of the Rings* reveal some of the history and customs of their races, and contribute to our appreciation of their characters, Elf and Dwarf, as they heal ancient prejudices. They are also two further examples of a series of poems Tolkien wrote, or adapted, for *The Lord of the Rings* which celebrate peoples and events of the past: to this point, Eärendil, Beren and Lúthien, Gil-galad, Durin, Amroth and Nimrodel. Each helps to develop a sense that the work is based not on an author's imagination but on a foundation of history, or at least of lore.

In 1952 Tolkien made a private recording of the final version of the song, since commercially released.

A1: Next to 'of old' Tolkien wrote 'of yore'. The latter reading appears again on the page in l. 21, but Tolkien chose to prefer 'of old'.

A2: 'Before the birth of Men', i.e. before the race of Men was born into the world, after the Elves.

A2, 4: Tolkien indicated with arrows that these lines were to change place. In the event, he abandoned this description for Linglorel (Nimrodel) and gave it to Amroth; see manuscript C.

A3: 'Flowers of gold', i.e. the blossoms of the mallorn tree.

A15–16: These lines recall Strider's 'tale of Tinúviel' in Book I, Chapter 11, with its phrase 'feet as light as linden leaves'.

A25–28: This quatrain, alone of those in manuscript A, is written in ink rather than in pencil, suggesting that Tolkien wrote it after a gap of time, perhaps before he began to write manuscript B, in which his handwriting (in ink) is similar in appearance to these lines.

C2: Tolkien considered whether to change this line to 'as flower upon the spray'.

C5: Tolkien considered whether to change 'bound' to 'set'. He also wrote 'a shining star was on' next to the line, evidently as a possible replacement for 'a star was bound upon'.

C11: Tolkien considered whether to change 'wind' to 'woods'.

C13: The elven-maid's name was first written *Nimlothel*, then changed in pencil to *Nimlorel*. At right, Tolkien pencilled *ladel* and *lorel* as possible endings (with the latter adopted), and above the name is *rodel*.

C19, 36: Tolkien marked 'Nimlothel' in pencil to be changed to 'Nimlorel'.

C22: 'Mountain-lee', i.e. the side of a mountain sheltered from the wind.

C24: Tolkien considered whether to change 'roaring' to 'flowing'.

C26: At left, Tolkien wrote 'came blowing cold & free', evidently as a possible replacement for this line. At right, he wrote 'At night a wind [arose and [loud >] wild it blew >] awoke and wild it blew'.

C27: Tolkien considered whether to change 'bore' to 'drove'.

C29: 'Shores were' originally read 'shore was'. To the right of this line, Tolkien wrote 'lands' as a possible revision for 'shores'.

C33: Tolkien considered whether to change 'saw' to 'beheld'. The name of the elven-maid's lover was now *Amroth*.

C37–40: Tolkien considered whether to change 'lord' to 'king', but also more extensive revisions to this stanza, as written around the ink manuscript and at the top of the sheet. One version would have read:

> An Elven king he was of old
>   a lord of tree and glen
> when first the boughs bore flowers of gold
>   in fair Lothlorien

A second would have read:

> An Elven king he was of old
>   when all the woods were young
> and in Lothlorien with gold
>   the boughs of trees were hung

And a third:

> Of old he was an elven-king
>   a lord of tree and glen
> when golden were the [boughs >] flowers in spring
>   in fair Lothlorien.

An alternate text for the third and fourth lines of the last version reads: 'when boughs were golden in the spring | of fair Lothlorien'.

C45: Tolkien considered whether to change 'in' to 'on'.

C49: 'From the West', i.e. from Valinor or Tol Eressëa.

C50: 'Hither Shore', i.e. Middle-earth, across the sea from Aman.

D9: This line reached its final form in C^1.

D26, 28: In C^1 this line continued to read 'And loud it blew and free'. In the first typescript it was changed (in the typing) to 'Came blowing cold and free'; Tolkien first changed 'cold' to 'wild', then replaced the line entirely with 'Arose, and loud it cried'. This required a change of rhyme in l. 28, where Tolkien changed 'sea' to 'tide'.

D29–32: In C^1 these lines continued the reading of C, except that in l. 29 Tolkien changed 'shores were grey' to 'land was grey'. In making the first typescript, Tolkien followed C^1, then revised the stanza in manuscript to the form of the published text.

D30: 'Mountains sinking grey', i.e. as the ship moves away, the distant land appears to sink below the horizon and becomes grey in appearance.

D33–36: In C^1 these lines continued the reading of C. In making the first typescript, Tolkien followed C^1, then revised the stanza in manuscript to the form of the published text.

D45–48: In l. 45 of C^1 Tolkien changed 'in' to 'on'; otherwise, he continued the reading of C. In making the first typescript, he followed C^1, then revised the stanza in manuscript to the form of the published text. In his typescript for the printer Tolkien changed this stanza, in the act of typing (or in an interim draft, not extant), to:

The foam before his breast was white,
    His limbs were young and strong;
Until he floated far from sight
    They wept and watched him long.

To the left of these lines, Tolkien wrote workings in pencil, beginning 'The foam was wreathed about his hair', before striking them through. To the right, he wrote 'or' followed by the text of the stanza as he had amended it in the previous typescript. The typed words themselves he largely struck through and made a new text:

The foam was white before his breast,
    a light about him shone
Afar they saw from crest to crest
    Him riding like a swan

In the end, he returned to his previous version ('The wind was in his flowing hair'), but because he had made such a mess of the page, he retyped it for the printer's sake.

D49: In the rejected page of printer's typescript (see our note above), Tolkien considered whether to change 'West' to 'Sea', but immediately noted in the margin that 'West' would remain.

161

I Sang of Leaves · Galadriel's Song (1938–54)

As the Company of the Ring prepare to leave the refuge of Lothlórien in Book II, Chapter 8 of *The Lord of the Rings*, they are in their boats on the Silverlode. Sunlight is 'glittering on the water', and 'here and there golden leaves' toss and float 'on the rippling stream. The air was very bright and still, and there was a silence, except for the high distant song of larks.' Then from around a bend in the river appears a ship, 'wrought and carved with elven-skill' in the likeness of a swan; and in it Galadriel, the lady of Lothlórien, plays a harp and sings 'sad and sweet'.

The first draft of Galadriel's song, like no. 160 composed late in 1941, is a fragmentary and largely illegible manuscript. We find in it, however, these lines (A) which suggest that Tolkien's initial thoughts were to comment on the passage of time through the change of seasons:

[A] O Lorien the winter comes, [*added:* and] the river flows away
The leaves are falling in the stream, dead leaves are borne away
O Lorien ??? of [and >] the bare & leafless Day
The leaves are falling in the stream   the river flowing

Another draft page is not much better in terms of legibility, but has more of substance. We give here, as B, as much of its text as we can decipher.

[B] I sang of leaves and leaves of gold and leaves of gold there grew
[*deleted:* I sang   I sang of]
[and wind >] Of wind I sang [and >] a wind there came and in my branches grew
Beyond the seas beyond the seas the foam was on the sea
And by the mere of Tirion there grew a golden tree
Beneath the Hill of Ilmarin [the >] beside the [*added:* lies Aelinuial]
The Pool of
The leaves of gold are falling are falling over ?years

??? are sailing in the river
??? the mere of Tirion in Eldamar
And in the light of ?Caranel in Eldamar ???

For the Elvish city of Tirion in Eldamar, see also poem no. 30. Its 'mere' is presumably Luvailin, the Shadowmere. Elements of this draft recall Bilbo's song in Rivendell (no. 128). Since the 'golden tree' is described as growing in Eldamar, it cannot be Laurelin the golden, one of the Two Trees which grew in Valinor (see also poem no. 31). In *The Lord of the Rings: A Reader's Companion* we speculate that 'golden tree' may be symbolic of the life of the Elves in the Blessed Realm, compared with the Winter of their life in mortal lands. A simpler explanation could be that the tree in question is a mallorn, whose 'leaves fall not, but turn to gold' in autumn, and fall only when 'the new green opens' and 'the boughs are laden with yellow flowers' (Book II, Chapter 6) – hence Lothlórien is called 'the Golden Wood'.

The 'Hill of Ilmarin' (B6) is Taniquetil, *Ilmarin* proper the mansion of Manwë and Varda (see poem no. 128). *Aelinuial* (line 6) 'Lakes of Twilight' is 'the name of the region of great pools at the confluence of the rivers Aros and Sirion in Beleriand' (Christopher Tolkien, *The Treason of Isengard*, p. 292). 'The light of ?Caranel in Eldamar' (B11) suggests that this should be the light of the Two Trees passing through the Calacirya, the gap in the Pelori, or defensive mountain-wall around Valinor. But the word in question is almost certainly not *Calacirya* ('Pass of Light') or any of the familiar variations of the name (compare no. 128).

Tolkien further developed Galadriel's song in another draft (C), written in pencil with overwriting in ink and likewise hard to make out.

[C] I sang of leaves and leaves of gold, and leaves of gold there grew;
Of wind I sang, a wind there came and in [my >] the branches blew.
Beyond the [Seas >] Sun, beyond the [Seas >] Moon the foam was on the Sea,
And by the mere of Tirion there grew the golden tree
[*deleted:* and by the light of Evermorn]
Beneath the stars of Evereve in Eldamar it shone
In Eldamar beside the walls of Elven Tirion
Now far away [now >] o far away across the Shoreless Sea
Now far away and far away beyond

Now long the golden leaves have grown upon the branching years
[and gold >] and flowing ever far away [upon the sea >] beyond the Shadow meres
[*added:* now long] the golden leaves have grown upon the branching years

[A ship >] I sang ?of ships with silver sails and I ?shall ever ?bear
and sing of swan and winds   and ???
I sing a swan with silver wings and wings shall come to me
a wind amid the stars shall blow   shall bear me over the Sea

Now far away far away beyond the Shadow meres

In line C5 Tolkien may have meant 'Evermorn' to refer to the continuous light of the Two Trees which emanated from Valinor and fell on one side of Tirion through the Calacirya. 'Evereve' (C6; later 'Ever-eve' in E5) could refer to the eternal twilight of Valinor after the destruction of the Two Trees, or to the darkness of Aman beyond the light of the Trees; compare 'Evernight' in no. 128. In a manuscript index of place-names, Tolkien associated *Ever-eve* and *Evereven* with Eldamar, as used in Bilbo's song at Rivendell (no. 128), but the meaning here must be different. The 'Shoreless Sea' (C8) is the great ocean between Aman and Middle-earth, the Sundering Seas. 'Shadow meres' (C11) is probably equivalent to the 'Lakes of Twilight' or Aelinuial.

Following another page of rough workings, Tolkien at last wrote the first settled text of his poem, entitled *Galadriel's Song*. We give it here (D) before he revised the text further.

[D] I sang of leaves, of leaves of gold, and leaves of gold there grew;
Of wind I sang, a wind there came and in the branches blew.
Beyond the Sun, beyond the Moon, the foam was on the Sea,
And by the strand of Tirion there grew a golden Tree.
Beneath the stars of Evereve in Eldamar it shone,
In Eldamar beside the walls of Elven Tirion.
But far away and far away beyond the Shadow-meres
Now long the golden leaves have grown upon the branching years.
And Lórien, O Lórien! the river flows away

And leaves are falling in the stream, and leaves are born [*sic*] away;
O Lórien too long I dwell upon this Hither Shore
And in a fading crown I twine the golden elanor
But if a ship I now should sing, what ship would come to me,
What ship would bear me ever back across so wide a sea?

The 'Hither Shore' (D11) is Middle-earth, across the sea from Aman. The flower *elanor* is first encountered in *The Lord of the Rings* in Book II, Chapter 6, when the Company arrive at Cerin Amroth in the heart of Lothlórien: 'small golden flowers shaped like stars'.

Tolkien marked text D with numerous changes, and thus achieved the published form of the poem except for minor points of punctuation. We give this final text (E) as it is printed in *The Lord of the Rings*.

[E] I sang of leaves, of leaves of gold, and leaves of gold there grew;
Of wind I sang, a wind there came and in the branches blew.
Beyond the Sun, beyond the Moon, the foam was on the Sea,
And by the strand of Ilmarin there grew a golden Tree.
Beneath the stars of Ever-eve in Eldamar it shone,
In Eldamar beside the walls of Elven Tirion.
There long the golden leaves have grown upon the branching years,
While here beyond the Sundering Seas now fall the Elven-tears.
O Lórien! too long I have dwelt upon this Hither Shore
And in a fading crown have twined the golden elanor.
But if of ships I now should sing, what ship would come to me,
What ship would bear me ever back across so wide a Sea?

Galadriel had not appeared in Tolkien's writings before *The Lord of the Rings*. In later additions to 'The Silmarillion', he wrote of her having been among the Noldorin Elves who went with Fëanor to Middle-earth in the First Age to recover the Silmarils stolen by Morgoth. In doing so, the group defied the will of the Valar and slew many of the sea-going Elves, the Teleri, who would not give up their ships. For these acts, Fëanor and his followers, among whom Galadriel was a leader, received the 'Doom of the Noldor': 'Tears unnumbered ye shall shed; and the Valar will fence Valinor against you, and shut you out' (*The Silmarillion*, p. 88). It is for this reason, one may suppose, that Galadriel, fondly recalling her former home 'in Eldamar beside the walls of Elven Tirion' but subject to the Doom, asks 'what ship would bear me ever back across so wide a Sea?' And yet, at the point in *The Lord of the Rings* when Frodo offers her the Ring and she declines, she says, 'I pass the test. I will diminish, and go into the West, and remain Galadriel' (Book II, Chapter 7), suggesting that she believes she already has the option to return. In *Unfinished Tales* Christopher Tolkien stated his belief that when his father wrote the Lothlórien chapters he had in mind no idea of a ban on Galadriel's return; if so, there must be a different reason for her question at the end of *I Sang of Leaves*.

In her essay 'Lyrics on Lost Lands: Constructing Lost Places through Poetry in J.R.R. Tolkien's *The Lord of the Rings*' (2019) Michaela Hausmann remarks that Galadriel's reference to 'Elven-tears' conveys

> the sadness, the pains of exile and nostalgia of the Elves for the Undying Lands, sentiments which Tolkien had defined as [their] central characteristics. . . . All these emotions govern the presentation of Lothlórien as an imperfect place that is no longer immune to change because the destruction of the One Ring would also destroy the preserving power of Galadriel's ring Nenya. [p. 272]

Galadriel says as much herself, to Frodo in Book II, Chapter 7: if he succeeds in his charge and destroys the Ring, 'then [the Elves'] power is diminished, and Lothlórien will fade, and the tides of Time will sweep it away. We must depart into the West, or dwindle to a rustic folk of dell and cave, slowly to forget and to be forgotten.' But by this point in his story, Tolkien has already established a general theme of loss, which Galadriel's song serves to confirm. As Gildor says in Book I, Chapter 3, absent any consideration of the Ring, 'most of our kindred have long ago departed and we too are now only tarrying here a while, ere we return over the Great Sea'. In the end this is shown by Tolkien to be a natural if profoundly sad progression, the old world of Elves giving way to the Dominion of Men.

In 'Could Gollum Be Singing a Sonnet?: The Poetic Project of *The Lord of the Rings*' (2017), Kathy Cawsey describes this poem as in the form of 'stately, elegant iambic heptametric couplets . . . [in which] the stress pattern mimics idiomatic English speech patterns. The only deviation from the very regular rhythm is "O Lórien! Too long I have dwelt upon this Hither Shore". "I have" becomes awkward; it must either be elided to "I've", an informal contraction at odds with the formality of the song,' or the rhythm is affected. Either way, the word 'I' 'disrupts the regular heptametric rhythm. This could be simply a common poetic deviation from an overly-regular rhythm, but in a song about Galadriel's exile from her homeland [Aman] because of her prideful rebellion (a story told in the *Silmarillion*), her stumble upon the word "I" is suggestive' (p. 55).

E8: Tolkien introduced the hyphen in 'Elven-tears' in the first typescript, though it appears in his revision to the line in manuscript B.

162

Ai! Laurië Lantar Lassi Súrinen · *Namárië* (1938–54)

At the same time that Tolkien was composing *I Sang of Leaves* (no. 161), late in 1941, he was also writing the other poem sung by Galadriel in Book II, Chapter 8 of *The Lord of the Rings*; drafts of both share a leaf of manuscript. The Company of the Ring are again on the river, moving swiftly away from Lothlórien, but they hear Galadriel's voice, 'far but piercing-clear', singing 'in the ancient tongue of the Elves beyond the Sea' (Quenya). Frodo 'did not understand the words: fair was the music, but it did not comfort him'. A pendant to Galadriel's earlier song, it is another lament of falling leaves and passing years, and of the starlit lands in the West now seemingly lost to Elves in Middle-earth.

We give here, as A, some of Tolkien's workings for the second lament. The first six lines are in ink, the rest in pencil, apparently added at a different time.

[A]

Ai! laurie lantar lassi sūrinen
inyalemīne rāmar aldaron
inyali ettulielle turme mārien
anduniesse la mīruvōrion
Varda telūmen falmar kīrien
laurealassion ōmar mailinon.

Elentārin Vardan Oiolossëan
Tintallen māli rāmar ortelūmenen
arkandavā-le qantamalle tūlier
e falmalillon morne sindanōrie
no mīrinoite kallasilya Valimar

Christopher Tolkien includes these lines in *The Treason of Isengard* (pp. 284–5), but with 'Elentāri' for clearly written 'Elentārin'. Only the first line of text A survived unchanged (barring vowel marks) into the published version (B):

[B]

Ai! lauriё lantar lassi súrinen,
yéni únótimё ve rámar aldaron!
Yéni ve lintё yuldar avánier
mi oromardi lisse-miruvóreva
Andúnё pella, Vardo tellumar
nu luini yassen tintilar i eleni
ómaryo airetári-lírinen.

Sí man i yulma nin enquantuva?

An sí Tintallё Varda Oiolossёo
ve fanyar máryat Elentári ortanё,
ar ilyё tier undulávё lumbulё;
ar sindanóriello caita morniё
i falmalinnar imbё met, ar hísiё
untúpa Calaciryo míri oialё.
Sí vanwa ná, Rómello vanwa, Valimar!

Namárie! Nai hiruvalyё Valimar.
Nai elyё hiruva. Namáriё!

Following the Elvish text in *The Lord of the Rings*, Tolkien gives a version in English prose:

> Ah! like gold fall the leaves in the wind, long years numberless as the wings of trees! The years have passed like swift draughts of the sweet mead in lofty halls beyond the West, beneath the blue vaults of Varda wherein the stars tremble in the song of her voice, holy and queenly. Who now shall refill the cup for me? For now the Kindler, Varda, the Queen of the Stars, from Mount Everwhite has uplifted her hands like clouds, and all paths are drowned deep in shadow; and out of a grey country darkness lies on the foaming waves between us, and mist covers the jewels of Calacirya for ever. Now lost, lost to those from the East is Valimar! Farewell! Maybe thou shalt find Valimar. Maybe even thou shalt find it. Farewell!

For Varda (Elbereth), see earlier in the present book, especially our discussion for poem no. 151. 'Mount Everwhite' is Taniquetil; see poem no. 31. As noted for the previous poem, the Calacirya was the gap in the mountains around Valinor in which the Elvish city Tirion (Kôr) was built. *Valimar*, as Tolkien explains in *The Road Goes Ever*

On: A Song Cycle (p. 62), is 'properly the city of the Valar, near the mound upon which the Two Trees stood, but it is here used (it means dwellings of the Valar) to stand for the land of the Valar as a whole', that is, Valinor. In regard to the 'paths drowned deep in shadow', Tolkien writes in the *Song Cycle*:

> After the destruction of the Two Trees, and the flight from *Valinor* of the revolting *Eldar* [who went east to Middle-earth], *Varda* lifted up her hands, in obedience to the decree of *Manwë* [the Doom of the Noldor], and summoned up the dark shadows which engulfed the shores and the mountains and last of all the *fana* (figure) of Varda with her hands turned eastward in rejection, standing white upon *Oiolosse*. [p. 60, italics in the original]

As for 'Maybe thou shalt find Valimar', Tolkien comments in the *Song Cycle* that this was Galadriel's wish, that although she herself could not go into the West, Frodo might be allowed to do so, as he does at the end of *The Lord of the Rings* by special dispensation. This seems to be yet another indication that Galadriel considered herself under a ban from returning to Eldamar, as discussed in our previous entry.

Also in *The Road Goes Ever On: A Song Cycle*, Tolkien provides a word by word translation of the poem, comments on pronunciation and stress, a rendering in his Elvish script *tengwar*, and a manuscript Quenya text showing verbal construction and accentuation. There it is entitled *Namárië*, by which title the verse is best known, and also *Altariello Nainië Lóriendesse* (*Galadriel's Lament in Lórien*).

In 1952 Tolkien made private recordings of the Elvish text, both sung and read, varying from the published text in lines 2–3: 'inyar únótinar ve rámar aldaron! | Inyar ve linte yulmar vánier'. These have since been commercially released. Tolkien's musical setting of the poem appeared in *The Road Goes Ever On: A Song Cycle* by Donald Swann (1967), with accompanying music by Swann, and was first professionally recorded by pianist Swann and baritone William Elvin for *Poems and Songs of Middle Earth* (1967).

B3: In the first edition of *The Lord of the Rings*, this line read 'yéni ve linte yuldar vánier'. Tolkien emended 'vánier' to the perfect form, 'avánier'.

163

Lament of Denethor for Boromir · *Through Rohan over Fen and Field* (1938–54)

Following the death of Boromir at the end of Book II of *The Lord of the Rings*, Aragorn, Legolas, and Gimli place him in a boat and give him to the river Anduin and the falls of Rauros. Aragorn and Legolas then sing a lament for their companion. In *The Treason of Isengard* Christopher Tolkien describes 'the earliest extant text' of this poem as 'finely written' and with the title [*Song* >] *Lament of Denethor for Boromir*. By this he meant the earliest complete version, for he also mentions rough workings with 'the most primitive sketching of phrases for the lament (including the East Wind, that blows "past the Tower of the Moon"), and another . . . for the North Wind (which seems to have been swiftly achieved)' (p. 384). In the initial draft for this part of the story, there is no lament, but Tolkien changed his mind, probably around early December 1941 or mid-January 1942, based on contemporary jottings on the draft manuscript of the chapter which refer to events in Thailand and Malaya.

The first page of rough workings described by Christopher is not present among the *Lord of the Rings* papers at Marquette University. The second, quickly scribbled in pencil and partly overwritten in ink, begins with a series of notes ('Aragorn sings West Wind | Legolas the South Wind | Aragorn the North Wind') and thoughts for the prose introduction to the lament in Book II, Chapter 1: 'They shall look out from the white tower and look to the sea' sang Trotter in a low voice', 'They shall look out from the Tower of Guard and hear the sea [*or* roaring sea] far off', 'And north they shall look and hear far off the roaring of the falls', 'And at the rising of the sun, and its going down'. The lament proper then begins, transcribed here (as A) with Tolkien's revisions illustrated.

[A] Let the South Wind blow to Belfalas and from the Sea
The seagulls come flying wailing
[*deleted:* O have you seen him and]
We saw him pass
The North wind blows from the [*deleted:* Calen-Bel]
The North wind blew ??? from the Gate of Kings

From the Gate of Kings the North wind Rides [above >] past the roaring falls
And clear and cold about the Tower its loud horn calls

'What news from the North O mighty wind do you bring to us today?
Where now is Boromir the bold? For he is long away. [']
'Beneath Amon-Hen I heard his horn. There many foes he fought.
His cloven horn, his broken sword they to the water brought
[*deleted:* He long hair they his hair so long his]
His head so proud, his face so fair, his limbs they laid to rest,
and Rauros, Golden Rauros-falls received him [at her >] on its breast'
[*added:* then took him to its > bore him on its breast]
'O Boromir, the Tower of Guard shall ever northward [look > stare >] gaze
To Rauros, Golden Rauros-falls than [*sic*] on her breast you took'
[*added:* until the end of days]
upon whose breast you lay
that you on breast did bear
that bore you [to the sleep >] to the ?deep

From this Tolkien developed the (comparatively) fine manuscript of the *Lament of Denethor for Boromir*. It is, however, a lament by Denethor, Boromir's father and the Steward of Gondor, only in the sense that its speakers put themselves in his place, in the couplet at the end of each stanza ('O Boromir!'). Tolkien added these couplets, and the title of the draft, to the manuscript after most of the rest of the text was set down, but probably without an appreciable gap of time. Here we give this text, as B, as it stood after the couplets were added and the first line was altered, but before later revisions.

[B] Through Rohan over fen and field where the long grass grows,
The West Wind comes walking, and about the walls it goes.
'What news from the West, O wandering wind, do you bring to me tonight?
Have you seen Boromir the tall, by moon or by starlight?'
'I saw him ride over seven streams, over waters wide and grey;
I saw him walk in empty lands, until he passed away

Into the shadows of the North. I saw him then no more.
The North Wind may have heard the horn of the son of Denethor.'
[']O Boromir! from the high walls westward I looked afar;
But you came not from the empty lands where no men are. [']

From the mouths of the sea the South Wind flies, from the sandhills and the stones;
The wailing of the gulls it bears, and at the gate it moans.
'What news from the South O sighing wind, do you bring to me at eve?
Where now is Boromir the fair? He tarries and I grieve.'
'Ask not of me where he doth dwell — so many bones there lie
Upon the white shores and the dark shores under the stormy sky.
So many have passed down Anduin to find the flowing sea —
Ask of the North Wind news of them that the North Wind sends to me!'
[']O Boromir! beyond the gate the seaward road runs south,
But you came not with the wailing gulls from the grey sea's mouth. [']

From the Gate of Kings the North Wind rides, and past the roaring falls;
And clear and cold about the Tower its loud horn calls
'What news from the North, O mighty wind, do you bring to me today?
What news of Boromir the bold? For he is long away.'
'Beneath Amon-Hen I heard his cry. There many foes he fought.
His cloven shield, his broken sword, they to the water brought
His head so proud, his face so fair, his limbs they laid to rest;
And Rauros, golden Rauros-falls bore him upon its breast.'
'O Boromir! the Tower of Guard shall ever northward gaze
To Rauros, golden Rauros-falls, until the end of days[.]'

Following text B, Tolkien wrote out a fair copy of the poem within the prose frame of its chapter. There he reached its final words except in minor respects, though not its final arrangement. The poetry is divided, such that each long line (as in B) is written as two (half) lines, sometimes with added punctuation, and the stanzas are grouped in four or eight lines; but the couplets at the end of each stanza, beginning 'O Boromir!' are written separately, and not made over into half-lines. For example:

From the mouths of the Sea the South Wind flies,
    From the sandhills and the stones;
The wailing of the gulls it bears,
    And at the gate it moans.

'What news from the South, O sighing wind,
    Do you bring to me at eve?
Where now is Boromir the fair?
    He tarries, and I grieve.'

. . . .

'O Boromir! beyond the gate the seaward road runs south,
But you came not with the wailing gulls from the grey sea's
    mouth.'

Tolkien abandoned this approach, however, in the next version of the chapter, a typescript, where no lines are indented but the stanzas are divided into groups of two or four lines. A typescript made for the printer follows this alternate arrangement, but in proof, apparently by decision of the typesetter as there are no authorial or editorial directions, the poem was again divided into ten-line stanzas, as in B. Pencil marks next to lines 9 and 10 on the galley proof of the section, almost certainly by Tolkien, suggest that he considered whether to separate the couplet from the rest of the stanza (presumably as a guide for the other two stanzas as well), but the setting remained as published.

We give here, as C, the lament in the printed *Lord of the Rings*. The reference to the White Tower in the introductory paragraph is to the chief tower in the Citadel of Minas Tirith (the Tower of Guard) in Gondor, the seat of Denethor.

[C] For a while the three companions remained silent gazing, after him [Aragorn]; then Aragorn spoke. 'They will look for him from the White Tower,' he said, 'but he will not return from mountain or from sea.' Then slowly he began to sing:

Through Rohan over fen and field where the long grass grows
The West Wind comes walking, and about the walls it goes.

'What news from the West, O wandering wind, do you bring to me tonight?
Have you seen Boromir the Tall by moon or by starlight?'
'I saw him ride over seven streams, over waters wide and grey;
I saw him walk in empty lands, until he passed away
Into the shadows of the North. I saw him then no more.
The North Wind may have heard the horn of the son of Denethor.'
'O Boromir! From the high walls westward I looked afar,
But you came not from the empty lands where no men are.'

Then Legolas sang:

From the mouths of the Sea the South Wind flies, from the sandhills and the stones;
The wailing of the gulls it bears, and at the gate it moans.
'What news from the South, O sighing wind, do you bring to me at eve?
Where now is Boromir the Fair? He tarries and I grieve.'
'Ask not of me where he doth dwell — so many bones there lie
On the white shores and the dark shores under the stormy sky;
So many have passed down Anduin to find the flowing Sea.
Ask of the North Wind news of them the North Wind sends to me!'
'O Boromir! Beyond the gate the seaward road runs south,
But you came not with the wailing gulls from the grey sea's mouth.'

Then Aragorn sang again:

From the Gate of Kings the North Wind rides, and past the roaring falls;
And clear and cold about the tower its loud horn calls.
'What news from the North, O mighty wind, do you bring to me today?
What news of Boromir the Bold? For he is long away.'
'Beneath Amon Hen I heard his cry. There many foes he fought.
His cloven shield, his broken sword, they to the water brought.
His head so proud, his face so fair, his limbs they laid to rest;
And Rauros, golden Rauros-falls, bore him upon its breast.'
'O Boromir! The Tower of Guard shall ever northward gaze
To Rauros, golden Rauros-falls, until the end of days.'

As published, the lament includes the West, South, and North Winds, but not the East. Gimli remarks: 'You left the East Wind to me, but I will say naught of it.' In the context of the story, this is because Mordor, the domain of Sauron, is in the East; 'in Minas Tirith they endure the East Wind, but they do not ask it for tidings'. One wonders, though, if there would have been an additional stanza if Tolkien had succeeded with his rough workings for it. The work is sufficient as it is. It praises Boromir as tall, fair, and bold, and it involves different features of Minas Tirith: the West Wind goes about its walls, the South moans at its gate, the North loudly calls at its tower.

Tolkien's poem has an obvious analogue in Rudyard Kipling's well known national ode of 1891, 'The English Flag': 'Winds of the World, give answer! They are whimpering to and fro — | And what should they know of England who only England know?' In this the North Wind blows ('From Bergen my steel-shod vanguards go'), the South Wind sighs ('From the Virgins [Virgin Islands] my mid-sea course was ta'en'), the East Wind roars ('From the Kuriles, the Bitter Seas, I come'), and the West Wind calls ('In squadrons the thoughtless galleons fly'), celebrating Britain's far-flung empire in the four corners of the world. The purpose of Tolkien's poem is far different, but its structure similar. Since ancient days the winds have been personified in myth and legend; particularly important to seafarers folk in the age of sail, they appeared on more elaborate medieval maps, puffing and blowing. Four were most prominent, representing the four cardinal points of the compass, and varied according to culture – in the Classical world, the principal winds (Venti) were Boreas (North), Notus (South), Eurus (East), and Zephyrus (West), ruled by Aeolus.

Of the several laments in *The Lord of the Rings* this is perhaps the most moving, coming as it does after Boromir's tragic death and the abduction of Merry and Pippin by Orcs. Aragorn recalls Boromir's lonely and difficult journey to Rivendell to learn the meaning of a prophetic dream, and his final fight in defence of the hobbits, and he gives voice to those in Minas Tirith who will look for Boromir's return in vain. Aragorn appropriately sings of lands in which he himself has walked, and of the city where he would hope to be crowned king. Legolas, on his part, sings of the sea and the wailing of gulls, reflecting the 'sea-longing' of his people.

A song Frodo composes in Lothlórien puts 'something of his sorrow' at Gandalf's fall in Moria 'into halting words'. It is simple and naïve, though Frodo is relatively sophisticated for a Hobbit. We will quote here only its first two stanzas, written between late August 1940 and ?autumn 1941, from published Book II, Chapter 7.

When evening in the Shire was grey
his footsteps on the hill were heard;
before the dawn he went away
on journey long without a word.

From Wilderland to Western shore
from northern waste to southern hill,
through dragon-lair and hidden door
and darkling woods he walked at will.

Frodo is said to be 'seldom moved to make song or rhyme; even in Rivendell he had listened and had not sung himself, though his memory was stored with many things that others had made before him. But now as he sat beside the fountain in Lórien and heard about him the voices of the Elves' making songs of lamentation for Gandalf, 'his thought took shape in a song that seemed fair to him; yet when he tried to repeat it to Sam only snatches remained, faded as a handful of withered leaves.' Sam's added verse, on Gandalf's skill with fireworks ('The finest rockets ever seen'), is even more typically Hobbitish.

When reading the several laments in *The Lord of the Rings* one should remember that Tolkien had not only suffered the early losses of his father and mother, but had lived through the Great War with its many thousands dead, and at the moment of writing his verses he was living through yet another worldwide conflict. The Britain of the first half of the twentieth century was a land of memorial tablets and requiems.

In 1952 Tolkien made private recordings of the final version of the lament for Boromir and of Frodo's lament for Gandalf. These have since been commercially released.

B1: This line originally read 'Through the mountain-pass, through Rohan where the long grass grows'. Tolkien marked 'Through the mountain-pass' to be changed to 'Over mountains tall', then struck through the latter and revised the line to its (final) form in B.

B2: 'Walls', i.e. the walls of Minas Tirith.

B3: Tolkien considered whether to change 'tonight' to 'this morn'.

B4: Tolkien considered whether to change 'tall' to 'fair', and 'by moon or by starlight' to 'or heard his blowing horn'.

B5: 'Seven' originally read 'many'. 'Seven streams' seems to be a shadow of an idea Tolkien did not fully develop; the suggestion is that Boromir needed to cross seven streams or rivers on his journey from Minas Tirith to Rivendell (for the Council of Elrond in Book II, Chapter 2). In a draft text for Book II, Chapter 4, Boromir mentions 'the Country of Seven Streams' (*The Treason of Isengard*, p. 311).

B9–10, 19–20: Tolkien supplied these lines after completing the rest of the text, which concludes with a similar couplet (29–30). Next to the latter, Tolkien wrote a note to himself: 'Correct? or put extra couplet on to the other stanzas, or under?'

B12: 'Bears' originally read 'brings'. 'Gate', i.e. one of the gates of Minas Tirith.

B13: Tolkien considered whether to change 'at eve' to 'tonight'.

B14: 'Where now is' originally read 'Where tarries', and 'He tarries and' originally read 'For Boromir'. Tolkien considered whether to change this line to 'Where tarries Boromir the tall by moon or by starlight'.

B24: 'What news of' originally read 'Where now is'.

B25: 'Cry' originally read 'horn'.

C11, 17: With the first typescript, Tolkien chose to capitalize 'Sea' in these lines, but not in l. 20.

C25: Tolkien removed the hyphen in 'Amon-Hen', in favour of 'Amon Hen', with the first typescript.

164

In the Willow-Meads of Tasarinan I Walked in the Spring (1938–54)

In Book III, Chapter 4 of *The Lord of the Rings*, Merry and Pippin having entered Fangorn Forest, they meet the great Ent, Treebeard. He explains to them the nature of Ents, the guardians of trees who are themselves like trees in appearance, and tells of days when 'there was all one wood once upon a time from here to the Mountains of Lune': he 'could walk and sing all day and hear no more than the echo of my own voice in the hollow hills'. Then, passing 'into a murmuring chant', his words continue Tolkien's theme of loss and the passage of time, as in Galadriel's lament (no. 161) marked by the change of seasons and the fall of leaves.

Tolkien first set down Treebeard's song in late 1941 or the start of 1942, apparently with little pause for thought, and at first in the form of prose (within the prose frame of the narrative) though the words have the rhythm of poetry. We give this text as A, illustrating Tolkien's marked revisions.

[A] In the willowmeads of Tasarinan I walked in the spring[.]
Ah the sight and the smell of the spring in Nantasarinan
[*added:* and I said it was good]. In the elm woods of Ossiriand
I wandered in the summer[,] ah the light and the music in
the summer by the seven rivers of Ossir [*added:* and I saw
it was best]. In the beechwood of Neldoreth I laughed in
the autumn, ah the gold and the red leaves of autumn in
the Taur na Neldor[.] To the pine trees of Dorthonion
I climbed in the winter[,] ah the wind and the whiteness
and black ?gales in the winter upon [Thonod > Orod Thon >]
Orod Thun [*added:* and that I saw was good ?as well] and all
those lands lie now under the wave and I walk in Ambaróna
in Tauremorna, [in the old wood > in the ?time] in
?Hiselum[orn >]alda in my own land in the country of
Fangorn where the roots are [deep > long] and the years
[are numberless >] lie deeper than the leaves.

In *The Treason of Isengard* Christopher Tolkien read the name in the third line from the end of text A as 'His . . eluinalda'. Our best reading is '?Hiselum[orn >]alda', presumably a conglomeration of Elvish words in the Entish fashion, like 'Taurelilómëa-tumbalemorna' in this chapter (translated by Tolkien in Appendix F as 'Forestmanyshadowed-deepvalleyblack'). If our reading is correct, more or less, the name would have the Quenya elements *híse* 'dusk', *lóme* 'gloom, darkness', and *alda* 'tree' (*orn* is also 'tree', but in Sindarin); compare *Hisilómë* 'Shadowy Twilights' as discussed for poem no. 37. In any case, Tolkien seems to have meant this as another name for the forest of Fangorn, evoking the idea of darkness among trees as in his ultimate choice of *Aldalómë*.

In the next manuscript of the chapter, Tolkien wrote Treebeard's song more carefully, now broken into lines as poetry. With a few further changes, most notably to place names, in the first typescript of the chapter Tolkien achieved the final text of the song. We give this (B) as it appears in the printed book, with the revisions made in the intervening manuscript described in notes.

[B] In the willow-meads of Tasarinan I walked in the Spring.
Ah! the sight and the smell of the Spring in Nan-tasarion!
And I said that was good.
I wandered in Summer in the elm-woods of Ossiriand.
Ah! the light and the music in the Summer by the Seven Rivers
of Ossir!
And I thought that was best.
To the beeches of Neldoreth I came in the Autumn.
Ah! the gold and the red and the sighing of leaves in the
Autumn in Taur-na-neldor!
It was more than my desire.
To the pine-trees upon the highland of Dorthonion I climbed
in the Winter.
Ah! the wind and the whiteness and the black branches of
Winter upon Orod-na-Thôn!
My voice went up and sang in the sky.
And now all those lands lie under the wave,
And I walk in Ambaróna, in Tauremorna, in Aldalómë,
In my own land, in the country of Fangorn,
Where the roots are long,
And the years lie thicker than the leaves
In Tauremornalómë.

In speaking with the hobbits, Treebeard uses the Common Speech of Middle-earth (Westron, represented as English), but in Entish fashion includes words in Elvish, both Quenya and Sindarin. He recalls places he once knew, especially the woods of Beleriand where he roamed in the First Age, but which were drowned by the sea ('lie under the wave') in the tumults of the battle in which Morgoth was overthrown. Aptly for a 'tree-herd', he identifies these lands with predominant tree-species: willow, elm, beech, and pine. *Tasarinan* 'Willow-vale' and *Nan-tasarion* (*tasar* 'willow', *nan* '(wide) vale, valley') are Quenya names for the same region. *Ossiriand*, Sindarin 'land of Seven Rivers' (*-ian(d)* 'land'), also known as *Ossir* ('seven rivers'), was an area of Beleriand under the west sides of the Ered Luin or Blue Mountains; part of it survived the floods and became Lindon. *Neldoreth* and *Taur-na-neldor* both mean 'Beech-forest' in Sindarin (*neldor* 'beech', *taur* 'forest'); see also our discussion for poem no. 64. *Dorthonion* was a land (Sindarin *dor*) of pines (*thôn*) on the northern borders of Beleriand, *Orod-na-Thôn* a mountain (Sindarin *orod*) in that region. The Quenya names *Ambaróna* 'uprising, sunrise' (from *ambaróne* 'dawn', *róna* 'east'), *Tauremorna* 'black forest' (*morna* 'black, dark'), *Aldalóme* 'tree-twilight' (*alda* 'tree' *lómë* 'dimness, twilight'), and *Tauremornalómë* 'forest-dark-twilight' all refer to Fangorn Forest, described in this chapter as old, dark, and tangled.

In 1952 Tolkien made a private recording of the final version of the poem, since commercially released. A musical setting by Donald Swann appeared in *The Road Goes Ever On: A Song Cycle* (1967), and was performed by pianist Swann and baritone William Elvin on the recording *Poems and Songs of Middle Earth* (1967).

B2: In the intervening manuscript the name at the end of this line read 'Nan-Tasarien'.

B7: In the intervening manuscript Tolkien wrote '?stirred' before changing it to 'came'.

B11: In the intervening manuscript this line began '[And >] My [joy >] voice'.

165

When Spring Unfolds the Beechen Leaf (1938–54)

It is remarkable that five poems punctuate the conversation between Treebeard and the hobbits in Book III, Chapter 4 of *The Lord of the Rings*. The longest of these concludes the 'strange and sad story' Treebeard tells Merry and Pippin, of the Ents and their female counterparts, the Entwives, who once walked and lived together but whose hearts grew apart. While the Ents loved 'the great trees, and the wild woods, and the slopes of the high hills', and to wander in nature, the Entwives preferred the lesser growing things, fruits and herbs and grasses, neatly ordered and plentiful. 'Then when the Darkness came in the North' – millennia before, when Morgoth spread his power over Middle-earth – to expand their gardens and tilled fields the Entwives crossed the Anduin. These 'blossomed richly'; but in time they were laid waste by Sauron, and the Entwives have not been seen again. 'There was an Elvish song that spoke of this,' says Treebeard, 'or at least so I understand it. It used to be sung up and down the Great River. It was never an Entish song, mark you: it would have been a very long song in Entish! But we know it by heart, and hum it now and again.'

Tolkien worked on the 'Song of the Ent and the Entwife', as it is often called, in late 1941 or the start of 1942. There are four pages of manuscript rough workings, for the most part with text not far from the poem's final form, but not yet continuous. The most interesting of these trials is a preliminary version of the closing couplet, rendered as prose: 'I'll come back to thee and look for thee again. I'll come to thee and comfort thee, and find thee in the rain. We'll walk the land together and gather seed and set and journey to an island where both can live again.' On a fifth page (A), Tolkien consolidated his thoughts, with trials and alternate readings in groups of two or four lines.

[A] When Spring unfolds the beechen leaf and sap is in the bough,
When sun is on the wildwood stream, and wind is on the brow;
When stride is long, and breath is deep, and sweet the
 mountain-air,
Come back to me! Come back to me! and say my land is fair.

When Spring is in the sprouting corn and flames of green arise,
When blossom like a living snow upon the orchard lies,
When earth is warm, and wet with rain, and the smell is in the
air,
I'll linger here, and will not come, because my land is fair.

When Summer lies upon the world, and in a noon of gold
beneath the roof of sleeping leaves the dreams of trees unfold
When woodland halls are green and cool, and wind is in the
West
Come back to me, come back to me! and say my land is best!

When Summer warms the hanging fruit and burns the berry
brown,
When straw is long and ear is white and harvest comes to town,
When honey spills and apple swells and days are wealthiest
I'll linger here and will not come, because my land is best.

and

I'll stay when blows the southern wind and care not for the
west
When blows the winter wind I stay and say my land is best

and

When winter comes and boughs are bare and all the grass is
grey
When [*blank*] and starless night o'ertakes the sunless day,
When storm is wild and trees are felled then in the bitter rain
I'll look for thee, and call to thee, I'll come to thee again.

When winter comes, when winter comes, when darkness falls
at last,
When broken is the barren bough and light and labour past,
I'll look for thee, and wait for thee, until we meet again
Together we will take the road beneath the bitter rain

Together will we take the roads that lead into the west
and far away we'll find a land where both our hearts may rest

Tolkien continued to develop the poem in a further manuscript (B), now with the speakers identified.

[B]

ENT. When Spring unfolds the beechen leaf, and sap is in the bough;
When sun is on the wild-wood stream, and wind is on the brow;
When stride is long, and breath is deep, and keen the mountain-air,
Come back to me! Come back to me, and say my land is fair!

ENTWIFE. When Spring is in the sprouting-corn, and corn is in the blade;
When blossom like a living snow is on the orchard laid;
When scent of earth by shower and sun is drawn into the air
I'll linger here, and will not come, because my land is fair.

ENT. When Summer lies upon the world, and in a noon of gold
Beneath the roof of sleeping leaves the dreams of trees unfold;
When woodland halls are green and cool, and wind is in the West,
Come back to me! Come back to me, and say my land is best!

ENTWIFE. When Summer warms the hanging fruit and burns the berry brown;
When straw is long, and ear is white, and harvest comes to town;
When honey spills, and apple swells, though wind be in the West,
I'll linger here beneath the Sun, because my land is best!

ENT. When winter comes, and boughs are bare, and all the grass is grey;
When trees shall fall and starless night o'ertake the sunless day;
When storm is wild and trees are felled, then in the bitter rain
I'll look for thee, and call to thee; I'll come to thee again!

ENTWIFE. When winter comes, when winter comes and darkness falls at last;
When broken is the barren bough, and light and labour past,
I'll look for thee, and wait for thee, until we meet again:
Together we will take the road beneath the bitter rain!

BOTH. Together we will take the road that leads into the West,
And far away may find a land where both our hearts may rest.

After marking this manuscript with many revisions, notably in the second and fifth stanzas, Tolkien achieved the final text of the poem at last in the first typescript of the chapter. We give the published poem as C.

[C]

ENT. When Spring unfolds the beechen leaf, and sap is in the bough;
When light is on the wild-wood stream, and wind is on the brow;
When stride is long, and breath is deep, and keen the mountain-air,
Come back to me! Come back to me, and say my land is fair!

ENTWIFE. When Spring is come to garth and field, and corn is in the blade;
When blossom like a shining snow is on the orchard laid;
When shower and Sun upon the Earth with fragrance fill the air,
I'll linger here, and will not come, because my land is fair.

ENT. When Summer lies upon the world, and in a noon of gold
Beneath the roof of sleeping leaves the dreams of trees unfold;
When woodland halls are green and cool, and wind is in the West,
Come back to me! Come back to me, and say my land is best!

ENTWIFE. When Summer warms the hanging fruit and burns the berry brown;
When straw is gold, and ear is white, and harvest comes to town;
When honey spills, and apple swells, though wind be in the West,
I'll linger here beneath the Sun, because my land is best!

ENT. When winter comes, the winter wild that hill and wood shall slay;
When trees shall fall and starless night devour the sunless day;
When wind is in the deadly East, then in the bitter rain
I'll look for thee, and call to thee; I'll come to thee again!

ENTWIFE. When winter comes, and singing ends; when darkness falls at last;
When broken is the barren bough, and light and labour past,
I'll look for thee, and wait for thee, until we meet again:
Together we will take the road beneath the bitter rain!

BOTH. Together we will take the road that leads into the West,
And far away will find a land where both our hearts may rest.

At the conclusion of his song, Treebeard says: 'That is how it goes. It is Elvish, of course: lighthearted, quickworded, and soon over. I daresay it is fair enough. But the Ents could say more on their side, if they had time!' After so long, he is still not ready to concede the point. The Ents believe that they 'may meet' the Entwives 'again in a time to come, and perhaps we shall find somewhere a land where we can live together and both be content'. In the final line of the final version of the song, Tolkien changed 'may find' to 'will find', a more optimistic view; but still Treebeard says that 'it is foreboded that this will only be when we have both lost all that we now have. And it may well be that that time is drawing near at last. For if Sauron of old destroyed the gardens, the Enemy today seems likely to wither the woods.'

Later in the chapter, written contemporaneous with the Treebeard poems, the love the Ents feel for their trees is shown more eloquently by Bregalad's elegy, as he tells of Saruman's Orcs cutting down his rowan trees (also called mountain ash). 'I came and called them by their long names, but they did not quiver, they did not hear or answer: they lay dead.

O Orofarnë, Lassemista, Carnimírië!
O rowan fair, upon your hair how white the blossom lay!
O rowan mine, I saw you shine upon a summer's day,
Your rind so bright, your leaves so light, you voice so cool and soft:
Upon your head how golden-red the crown you bore aloft!
O rowan dead, upon your head your hair is dry and grey;
Your crown is spilled, your voice is stilled for ever and a day.
O Orofarnë, Lassemista, Carnimírië!

The Quenya names of the rowans mean 'mountain-dwelling, leaf-grey, with adornment of red jewels' (Tolkien, letter to Richard Jeffery, 7 September 1955, *Letters*, p. 326).

Writing to W.H. Auden on 7 June 1955, Tolkien commented on his invention of Ents – from his desire to have trees actually march to war, unlike the coming of 'Great Birnam wood to high Dunsinane hill' in Shakespeare's *Macbeth* with its soldiers disguised as trees – and how into this 'crept a mere piece of experience, the difference of the "male" and "female" attitude to wild things, the difference between unpossessive love and gardening' (*Letters*, p. 310).

In his essay 'The Myth of the Ent and the Entwife' (2008), Corey Olsen holds that the Elvish poet who composed the song Treebeard sings shared the agenda of neither side; we ourselves would suggest that Tolkien, a lover of trees as well as a keen gardener, understood both. Through the layering of the two voices, however, 'Tolkien is able to convey several different meanings,' Olsen says, 'praising the beauties of nature while simultaneously showing the dangers inherent in loving anything in this world, even nature itself, too much and too blindly'. His association of the masculine with the wild, striding through woods in the mountain air, seeing but not possessing, and the feminine with cloistered domesticity and a desire to domesticate, is a generalization whose accuracy 'might be questioned', though 'not merely a blind appeal to stereotypes'. His 'depiction of the Entish and Entwifely perspectives runs exactly counter to the traditional gender concepts that characterize the feminine as the passive principle and the masculine as the active'. The Entwife's life, Olsen argues, is one of energy and industry, while the Ent's is comparatively 'rather indolent by contrast', focused on observing but not doing. 'In truth', Olsen says, 'there need be no competition between the active and contemplative perspectives. They are two different but valuable ways of celebrating natural beauty.' Both 'may have something constructive to teach the Children of Ilúvatar about the appreciation of growing things. They would also, of course, have a great deal to teach each other' with their 'perfectly complementary perspectives' (pp. 41–4).

In 1952 Tolkien made private recordings of the final version of the song of the Ents and the Entwives and of Bregalad's song. These have since been commercially released.

A1: In his trials Tolkien was uncertain whether to write 'unfolds the beechen leaf' or 'unfolds [*or* unlocks] the living leaf'.

A2: Tolkien considered whether to change 'wildwood' to 'falling'.

A3: Tolkien considered whether to change 'sweet' to 'keen'.

A5: The line evokes the sight of sprouts beginning to emerge from the soil like green flames.

A7: 'The smell' originally read 'its smell'.

A8: 'My land' originally read 'this land'.

A14: *Ear* refers to the seed-bearing head of a cereal plant (corn).

A15: Tolkien considered whether to change 'days are wealthiest' to 'wealth is in the breast'.

A17, 20: The intervening conjunctions are in the original.

B5: Tolkien abandons the image of sprouting grain as green flames, in favour of a more botanical description of its blades, i.e. flat leaves.

B11: Tolkien considered whether to change 'halls' to 'aisles'.

B24: 'Bitter rain' suggests a bitterly cold rain of winter, but also, poetically, the griefs and tragedies of life.

166

Where Now the Horse and the Rider? (1938–54)

Riding over the grass-lands in Book III, Chapter 6 of *The Lord of the Rings*, Aragorn, Legolas, Gimli, and Gandalf pass the burial mounds of the Kings of Rohan. Aragorn remarks that these represent 'many long lives of men', which Legolas equates to the fall of leaves in Mirkwood five hundred times, 'and but a little while does that seem' to the Elves. It is, though, a very long time to the Rohirrim, and the thought inspires Aragorn to 'chant softly in a slow tongue unknown to the Elf and Dwarf; yet they listened, for there was a strong music in it'. The language of Roham in Tolkien's scheme for *The Lord of the Rings* is Old English, to all intents and purposes, 'rich and rolling in part, and else hard and stern as the mountains'. But Aragorn translates for his friends into the Common Speech (Modern English) the eight lines composed by 'a forgotten poet long ago in Rohan, recalling how tall and fair was Eorl the Young', the progenitor of the Rohirrim, 'who rode down out of the North; and there were wings upon the feet of his steed, Felaróf, father of horses. So men still sing in the evening.'

Until two lines added in the margin, the earliest draft of this brief poem seems to be concerned with Eorl's ride from the North rather than the days that have passed like the rain and wind, as in the published text – yet another contribution of poetry in support of this theme of *The Lord of the Rings*, as we have seen now several times. Although this first discrete manuscript of the poem, written probably between February and midsummer 1942, is rough and halting, we can extract from it (as A) a few lines of interest:

[A]

Silver was the crown upon his golden hair
Bright were his eyes, his voice was clear and fair,
Swift was his steed and long his spear and sword

As the northern wind he rode

In the forgotten years over rivers swift & grey

The years are gone like smoke of dead wood burning
Like water that runs to Sea

In a subsequent draft manuscript, Tolkien adopted for his verse the style of the Old English poem *The Wanderer* and its convention known as *ubi sunt* (Latin 'where are'), in which the poet comments on the passing of time (compare no. 123). 'Hwær cwom mearg? Hwær cwom mago?' 'Where has the horse gone? Where the young warrior?' Tolkien filled most of a page with new workings, writing quickly in pencil, overwriting just as rapidly in ink. The draft contains many fragments of undeveloped thoughts: 'Where is the horse and bow', 'Where is the horse with braided mane', 'Where is the helm and the golden horn', 'Where is the rider proud and fair', 'Where is the helm and the laughter'. But in the centre of the sheet, six lines (B) can be made out (more or less) which show Tolkien settling on a structure.

[B] Where now the horse and the rider? Where is the horn that was blowing?
Where is the helm and the hauberk, and the bright hair flowing?
Where is the hand on the harpstring, and the hearth-flame glowing?
Where is the spring and the harvest and the tall corn growing?
They have passed like a wind in the grass like rain on the mountains
Their day has gone down in the west behind the hills into shadow

Only in its third manuscript was Tolkien able to write the entire poem coherently, within the prose narrative of the chapter, though the page is heavily worked and marked for a supplemental manuscript, or rider (not present among the *Lord of the Rings* papers), just before the poem begins. Its final two lines appear, with revisions, after a series of false starts. Here Tolkien nearly reached the published version of the text. Only minor changes remained, and would be made in the first typescript. We give the text here (C) as published, and describe Tolkien's final revisions in our notes.

[C] Where now the horse and the rider? Where is the horn that was blowing?
Where is the helm and the hauberk, and the bright hair flowing?
Where is the hand on the harpstring and the red fire glowing?
Where is the spring and the harvest and the tall corn growing?

They have passed like rain on the mountain, like a wind in the
    meadow;
The days have gone down in the West behind the hills into
    shadow.
Who shall gather the smoke of the dead wood burning,
Or behold the flowing years from the Sea returning?

In 1952 Tolkien made a private recording of the final version of the poem, later commercially released.

In 'J.R.R. Tolkien and *The Wanderer*: From Edition to Application' (2009), Stuart D. Lee remarks on Tolkien's use (in the published version) of end-rhyme – *blowing, flowing, glowing*, a feature not found in Old English poetry – nor does Tolkien always attempt to retain the alliteration of the earlier work. He establishes 'a rhythm with lines 1–4, changing this with lines 5–6 (and thus the end rhyme), and finishing with a mixture of both (6 and 5 stress lines for 7–8). The reader, however, is brought along because the rhythm, reinforced by verbal repetition and parallelism, is not lost' (p. 203). Lee finds it appropriate that a poem inspired by *The Wanderer* is recited by Aragorn, a Ranger, one of the 'wandering folk'.

In his criticism of Burton Raffel's *Poems from the Old English*, mentioned in our discussion for poem no. 88, Tolkien remarked on the words Raffel inscribed in the copy he sent him, describing the translated poems as 're-creations' and Tolkien, writer of Hobbit-lore, as himself a 're-creator'. 'I must protest', wrote Tolkien:

> I have never attempted to 're-create' anything. My aim has been the basically more modest, and certainly the more laborious one of trying to make something new. (I do not say 'create' and usurp a sole prerogative; I might say 'sub-create', indicating that if successful the result may be new (in art), though all its material is given.) No one would learn anything valid about the 'Anglo-Saxons' from any of my lore, not even that concerning the Rohirrim; I never intended that they should. Even the lines beginning 'Where now the horse and the rider', though they echo a line in 'The Wanderer', and are indeed not much further removed from it verbally, metrically, or in sentiment than are parts of Raffel's 'translation', are certainly *not* a translation, re-creative or other wise. They are integrated (I hope) in something wholly different, the only excuse for the borrowing: they are particular in reference, to a great hero and his renowned horse, and they are supposed

to be part of the song of a minstrel of a proud and undefeated people in a hall still populous with men. Even the sentiment is different: it laments the ineluctable ending and passing back into oblivion of the fortunate, the full-lived, the unblemished and beautiful. To me that is more poignant than any particular disaster, from the cruelty of men or the hostility of the world. But if I were to venture to *translate* 'The Wanderer' – the lament of the lonely man withering away in regret, and the poet's reflexions upon it – I would not dare to intrude any sentiment of my own, nor to disarrange the order of word and thought in the old poem, in an impertinent attempt to make it more pleasing to myself, and perhaps to others. That is not 're-creation' but destruction. [Bodleian Library]

C3: In the third manuscript, this line ended 'hearth-fire glowing'. Tolkien changed this to 'red fire glowing' in the first typescript.

C7–8: In the third manuscript, these lines read:

> Who [has seen the gathered >] shall gather the smoke of the
> dead wood burning?
> [Or seen >] Or behold the flowing years from the Sea returning?

167

Grey as a Mouse · Oliphaunt (1938–54)

Commonly known as *Oliphaunt*, under which title it was reprinted in *The Adventures of Tom Bombadil and Other Verses from the Red Book*, this poem first appeared in Book IV, Chapter 3 of *The Lord of the Rings*, recited by Sam Gamgee. There it is said to be a rhyme that Hobbits have in the Shire:

> Nonsense maybe and maybe not. But we have our tales too, and news out of the South, you know. . . . I've heard tales of the big folk [Men] down away in the Sunlands [Harad]. Swertings we call 'em in our tales; and they ride on oliphaunts, 'tis said, when they fight. They put houses and towers on the oliphauntses backs and all and the oliphaunts throw rocks and trees at one another.

Tolkien composed the verse probably in late April 1944, and sent the finished work with its adjacent chapters to Christopher Tolkien on 30 April, calling it 'a hobbit nursery-rhyme (though [the oliphaunt] was commonly supposed to be mythical)' (*Letters*, p. 111). Its first workings, scribbled on an English examination paper for Navy and Air Force cadets at Oxford issued on 6 September 1943, include already some of its published lines, such as 'Grey as a mouse', but also others which did not survive revision: 'Feet like a lion' (extraordinary, if we read that correctly), 'Ears like a sail | But my little tail', 'But look at my tail', 'And horns for my teeth', 'Poor old oliphaunt'. A second page of rough workings includes parts of four or five different versions of the poem, mostly illegible and the whole firmly struck through, but again with interesting variants: 'Always walking and standing', 'Like a grey hill', 'My legs are like trees'. The work finally came together on a page of the first full manuscript of the chapter (A), though this version too Tolkien ultimately struck through.

[A]

Grey as a mouse,
Big as a house,
Nose like a snake,
I make the earth quake
As I tramp through the grass;

Trees crack as I pass.
With horns in my mouth,
I walk in the South,
Flapping big ears;
Beyond count of years
[I have >] I've stumped round and round,
Never lie on the ground
Not even to die:
Oliphaunt am I,
Biggest of All,
huge old and tall.
If you'd ever met me
You wouldn't forget me,
[*deleted:* As you've never seen me,
You needn't believe me]
If you never do,
You won't think I'm true;
but old Oliphaunt am I,
and I never lie.

In the second manuscript of the chapter, the poem remained the same, except that 'I stump' replaced 'I've stumped' in line 11. The final text appeared in the next (third) manuscript, to which Tolkien added the words immediately preceding the poem as published: 'Sam stood up, putting his hands behind his back (as he always did when "speaking poetry"), and began'. We give here (B) the work as printed.

[B]

Grey as a mouse,
Big as a house,
Nose like a snake,
I make the earth shake,
As I tramp through the grass;
Trees crack as I pass.
With horns in my mouth
I walk in the South,
Flapping big ears.
Beyond count of years
I stump round and round,
Never lie on the ground,
Not even to die.
Oliphaunt am I,
Biggest of all,

Huge, old, and tall.
If ever you'd met me,
You wouldn't forget me,
If you never do,
You won't think I'm true;
But old Oliphaunt am I,
And I never lie.

In his *Nomenclature of The Lord of the Rings*, a guide he prepared in 1966–7 for translators of the work, Tolkien explains that *oliphaunt* is 'an archaic form of *elephant* used as a "rusticism", on the supposition that rumour of the Southern beast would have reached [hobbits in] the Shire long ago in the form of legend' (published in Hammond and Scull, *The Lord of the Rings: A Reader's Companion*, p. 761).

In other books we have described *Oliphaunt* as a reduction, or a later version, of *Iumbo, or Ye Kinde of ye Oliphaunt* (no. 96), but neither statement is precise. Both poems are about the elephant, suggest its size and strength, and were inspired by the medieval bestiary; but Tolkien's purpose in writing *Iumbo* was satire, and he could do as he liked, whereas for *The Lord of the Rings* he needed a poem which prefigured the dramatic appearance of an actual oliphaunt (the Mûmak of Harad) but which was suited to the character of Sam Gamgee, something which could be considered 'traditional' in the Hobbit culture. The result was a work so distinct from *Iumbo* that we chose to present it here as a separate entry rather than (as with the two *Fastitocalon* poems, no. 95) a development of an earlier poem.

As Tolkien said in a letter to his son Christopher, *Oliphaunt* is like a nursery rhyme, more so than one of the moralizing *Physiologus* poems. It also recalls the familiar Eastern parable of the blind men who described an elephant only by touch: the one who felt its trunk said that the animal was like a thick snake; the one who held its ear said that the elephant was like a kind of fan; the one who felt its leg described the beast as like a tree trunk; the one who groped its side said that it was like a wall; the one who grabbed its tail described the animal like a rope; and the one who felt its tusk said that the elephant was hard, smooth, and like a spear.

In 1952 Tolkien made a private recording of the final version of *Oliphaunt*, since commercially released.

A7: 'Horns', i.e. tusks.

A12: In a subsequent manuscript, Tolkien considered whether to change 'lie' to 'lain', but immediately rejected the idea.

168

Out of the Mountain Shall They Come Their Tryst Keeping · *Over the Land There Lies a Long Shadow* (1938–54)

In Book V, Chapter 2 of *The Lord of the Rings*, as the men of Rohan gather to ride in aid of Minas Tirith, Rangers from the North under Halbarad arrive with Elrohir and Elladan, the sons of Elrond, and Elrohir delivers a message from his father: 'Bid Aragorn remember the words of the seer, and the Paths of the Dead'. Aragorn explains that the words Elrond refers to are those of Malbeth, a seer 'in the days of Arvedui, last king at Fornost', and he speaks them in the form of a poem.

In Tolkien's papers, the first version of the prophecy Aragorn recites (A), not yet that of Malbeth, is very different from the published text (see *The War of the Ring*, p. 300).

[A] Out of the mountain shall they come their tryst keeping
at the Stone of Erech, their horn shall blow,
when hope is dead and the kings are sleeping,
and darkness lies over [earth >] world below
Three lords shall come from the three kindreds
From the north at need by the paths of the dead
Elflord dwarflord and lord forwandréd
and one shall wear a crown on head.

In this manuscript of the chapter, it is Halbarad who gives the message to Aragorn, containing the poem in its entirety, not merely a reference to it. Aragorn says that it is 'an old rhyme of Gondor which none have understood; but I think I perceive somewhat of its sense now.' As well he should, with an Elf-lord, the son of the Elven-king of Mirkwood (Legolas), and a Dwarf-lord, one of the royal line (Gimli), among present company. He himself, of course, is a 'lord forwandréd' (forwandered), one who wanders far and wide.

In the next draft, the Rangers 'bid Aragorn remember the dark words of old' (B).

[B] Out of the mountain shall they come their tryst keeping;
At the Stone of Erech their horns shall blow,
When hope is [dead >] lost as the kings are sleeping
and [*deleted:* the] shadow lies on the world below:
Three lords shall come from the three kindreds
from the North at need by the Paths of the Dead,
Elf lord, dwarf lord, and [lord >] man forwandréd
and one shall wear a crown on head.

But Tolkien struck this through, and wrote in a new manuscript 'an old rhyme of my kindred, almost forgotten, never understood' (C).

[C] The Shadow falls; the kings are sleeping.
It is darkling time, all lights are low.
Out of the Mountain they come, their tryst keeping;
at the Stone of Erech horns they blow.
Three lords I see from the three kindreds:
halls forgotten in the hills they tread,
Elflord, dwarflord, Man forwandréd;
from the North they come by the paths of the Dead.

'Why does this point to us, you may ask', Aragorn remarks in this draft; 'and I say it fits the hour too well for chance. Yet if more is needed: the sons of Elrond tell me that ere they left Rivendell their father said to them: "If you find Aragorn bid him remember the Paths of the Dead."' But Tolkien rejected this draft as well. In yet another (fourth) manuscript, the message became (D; see *The War of the Ring*, p. 305):

[D] [The Shadow falls >] The days are numbered: the kings are sleeping.
It is darkling time, the shadow grows.
Out of the Mountain they come their tryst keeping;
at the Stone of Erech horns they blow.
Three lords I see from the three kindreds:
halls forgotten in the hills they tread,
Elflord, dwarflord, Man forwandréd;
from the North they come by the paths of the Dead!

After manuscript D came a typescript, but with changes to the message of the poem and its supporting text. The prophecy was now said by Aragorn to be 'an old rhyme-of-lore among my kindred, almost forgotten, never understood; it is but a broken shard of the rhymes of Malbeth, the last Seer of our folk in the North' (E):

[E] The days are numbered; the kings are sleeping.
It is darkling time, the shadow grows.
Out of the Mountain he comes, his tryst keeping;
At the Stone of Erech his horn he blows.
Three lords I see from the Three Kindreds:
Halls forgotten in the hills they tread,
Elf-lord, Dwarf-lord, and Man forwandred:
From the North they come by the Paths of the Dead.

In the earlier versions of the poem, 'they' who come out of the Mountain are presumably the 'three lords'; in text E, it is not clear who the singular 'he' might be, when the plural 'three lords' are still part of the prophecy.

Now Tolkien almost entirely rewrote and extended the verse in a new manuscript of the chapter (F). 'This', Aragorn says, 'is the word that the sons of Elrond bring to me from their father in Rivendell, wisest in lore: "Bid Aragorn remember the Paths of the Dead, for thus spake Malbeth the Seer"' (see *The War of the Ring*, p. 307).

[F] When the land is dark where the Kings sleep
And long the Shadow in the East is grown,
The oathbreakers their tryst shall keep,
At the Stone of Erech shall a horn be blown:
The forgotten people shall their oath fulfill.
Who shall summon them, whose be the horn?
For none may come there against their will.
The heir of him to whom the oath was sworn;
Out of the North shall he come, dark ways shall he tread;
He shall come to Erech by the Paths of the Dead.

Here the 'Three Kindreds' are abandoned, and it is only Aragorn, Isildur's heir, who comes 'out of the North' – from his home in the North of Middle-earth, and from that direction when he issues from the Paths of the Dead, under the mountain north of the Stone of Erech. The verse is no longer an old rhyme of Gondor, but a prophecy made long ago and specific to an heir of the Northern line. Most importantly, we are introduced to the 'forgotten people', the men of the White Mountains who at the beginning of the realm of Gondor had sworn allegiance to its king, Isildur, at the Stone of Erech, but later refused to join the alliance against Sauron when he rose again near the end of the Second Age. Isildur cursed them to be without rest until they were summoned by his heir to fulfil their oath.

The same text of Malbeth's words as in F also appears in yet another manuscript of the chapter, but is marked to be replaced by a rider. In the latter, Tolkien once again thoroughly rewrote the prophecy, now as alliterative verse, achieving its last and longest version. In the final manuscript it is presented in divided half-lines, thus:

> Over the land there lies   a long shadow,
> westward reaching   wings of darkness.
> The Tower trembles;   to the tombs of kings
> doom approaches. . . .

In typescripts that followed, however, and in the published book (G), the lines are closed up.

[G]

> Over the land there lies a long shadow,
> westward reaching wings of darkness.
> The Tower trembles; to the tombs of kings
> doom approaches. The Dead awaken;
> for the hour is come for the oathbreakers:
> at the Stone of Erech they shall stand again
> and hear there a horn in the hills ringing.
> Whose shall the horn be? Who shall call them
> from the grey twilight, the forgotten people?
> The heir of him to whom the oath they swore.
> From the North shall he come, need shall drive him:
> he shall pass the Door to the Paths of the Dead.

Although a relatively short work, the prophecy of the Paths of the Dead gave Tolkien more trouble than many of the poems in *The Lord of the Rings*. In part this was due to his shifting ideas for this particular section of the book, which are reflected in the 'rhyme of Gondor' and the words of Malbeth. Early on, he decided that Aragorn would have something important to do in southern Gondor, and would come to Minas Tirith unexpectedly, but the details of his journey by the Paths of the Dead, the summoning of the oathbreakers at the Stone of Erech, and much else grew and changed in the telling, largely or wholly in the period between *c.* 23 September 1946 and ?October 1947.

In connection with the present poem, Tolkien altered the message

Gandalf brings to Aragorn from Galadriel after the wizard's return from the dead. Originally this read (from *The Treason of Isengard*, p. 448):

> Elfstone, Elfstone, bearer of my green stone,
> In the south under snow a green stone thou shalt see.
> Look well Elfstone! In the shadow of the dark throne
> Then the hour is at hand that long hath awaited thee.

Of this, Christopher Tolkien writes: 'The green stone in the south was borne on Théoden's brow . . . and it was Éowyn who would stand in the shadow of the dark throne within his hall' – Éowyn who, at that point in the story's development, was to be Aragorn's future bride. But with the introduction of Arwen to the tale, and anticipating the prophecy that would be made plain in a chapter yet to come, Galadriel's message became (Book III, Chapter 5):

> Where now are the Dúnedain, Elessar, Elessar?
> Why do thy kinsfolk wander afar?
> Near is the hour when the Lost should come forth,
> And the Grey Company ride from the North.
> But dark is the path appointed for thee:
> The Dead watch the road that leads to the Sea.

A6, 7: As first written, these lines were reversed in order.

E6: As typed, this was the final line, marked in manuscript to be relocated.

F2: 'Shadow in the East', i.e. the spread of Sauron's power from Mordor.

G3: 'Tower' may mean the Dark Tower, Barad-dûr, Sauron's citadel in Mordor, or any tower in Western lands threatened by Sauron.

G12: Before writing this line, Tolkien wrote, and struck through, 'through the dark Door and the Paths of the Dead'. He also considered incorporating 'narrow roads shall he tread' and 'dark ways shall he dare'.

169

From Dark Dunharrow in the Dim Morning (1938–54)

'On down the grey road' went the Riders of Rohan, led by the King of the Mark, Théoden, son of Thengel, 'beside the Snowbourn rushing on its stones; through the hamlets of Underharrow and Upbourn, where many sad faces of women looked out from dark doors; and so without horn or harp or music of men's voices the great ride into the East began with which the songs of Rohan were busy for many long lives of men thereafter' (*The Lord of the Rings*, Book V, Chapter 3). One such song is *From Dark Dunharrow in the Dim Morning*, begun by Tolkien as rough workings in pencil, overwritten in ink. These begin legibly but soon turn chaotic; a second manuscript, transcribed here as A with revisions made in the course of writing, is similar to the first but more coherent. These and other manuscripts of the poem date from the period between *c.* 23 September 1946 and ?October 1947.

[A] From dark Dunharrow   in the dim morning
fate defying   rode Fengel's son.
To Edoras he came;   the ancient halls
of the Markwardens   mist enshrouded,
golden timbers   were in gloom mantled.
Farewell he bade   to his free people,
hearth and high seat   and the hallowed places
[where deep once he drank   ere darkness fell >]
where long he had lived   ere the light faded.
Forth rode the king,   fear behind him,
fate before him,   [faith compelled him >] fealty kept he:
oaths he had taken,   all fulfilled them
over field ?and   four nights and days
east and onward   rode the Eorlingas
through Folde and Fenmarch   [past Firienlode >] and the Firienwood
six thousand spears   to Sunlending
[to the city of the Sea Kings   in the South Kingdom >]
Mundberg the Mighty   under Mindolluin
Sea Kings city   to the South Kingdom.

foe-beleaguered,   fire-encircled
[fate >] Doom] drove them on.   Darkness took them
horse and horseman;   hoof beats afar
sank into silence   so the songs tell us.

Fengel is Old English 'prince, lord', as is *Thengel*, the name of the father of Théoden in later versions. Edoras is the royal town of Rohan, its name the plural of Old English *edor* (*eodor*) 'enclosure, dwelling', but also 'prince, lord'. The Markwardens are the Kings of the Mark (Rohan). 'Golden timbers' refers to Meduseld, the king's hall, whose pillars gleamed with gold. The Eorlingas are the Rohirrim, the people of Eorl the Young, founder of Rohan (*Eorl* + Old English *-ingas* 'people'). 'Fealty' refers to the oath of friendship in need, to which Théoden was also bound, sworn years earlier by Eorl to Cirion of Gondor. The Folde (from Old English *fold* 'earth, land, country') is the centre of Rohan, where the royal house and its kin dwell. The Fenmarch is a marshy area (*fen* + *march* 'boundary, border') on the south-eastern border of Rohan. The Firienwood (from Old English *firgen-wudu* 'mountain-wood') is the wood around the Halifirien, a beacon-hill near the border of Rohan and Gondor.

The order Folde–Fenmarch–Firienwood traces the route of the Rohirrim riding south-east into Anórien, the lands around Minas Tirith, called in the language of Rohan *Sunlending* (Old English 'sun-land-people'). Minas Tirith itself, the central city of Gondor, is *Mundberg* (later *Mundburg* 'guardian-fortress', from Old English *mundbeorg*), on the side of the mountain Mindolluin. The 'Sea Kings' are the Númenóreans who, coming from the Sea (the island of Númenor), founded Arnor and Gondor, the North and South Kingdoms in Middle-earth; by extension, the name also applies to their descendants.

Tolkien followed manuscript A with a fair copy (within the prose narrative), incorporating most of the revisions he marked on the draft, omitting or overlooking only his intention to change 'four nights and days' in line 13 above to 'five nights and days'. In both the earlier manuscript (as followed in our transcription) and the new version, Tolkien wrote his alliterative verse in half-lines; but in the typescripts that followed, he abandoned explicit metrical breaks. He achieved the final text of the poem in the first typescript of the chapter, altering in manuscript 'four nights and days' to 'five' – allowing a longer time for the Rohirrim to reach Minas Tirith – and altering 'Mundberg' to 'Mundburg'. Here, as B, is the work as published.

[B] From dark Dunharrow in the dim morning
with thane and captain rode Thengel's son;
to Edoras he came, the ancient halls
of the Mark-wardens mist-enshrouded,
golden timbers were in gloom mantled.
Farewell he bade to his free people,
hearth and high-seat, and the hallowed places,
where long he had feasted ere the light faded.
Forth rode the king, fear behind him,
fate before him. Fealty kept he;
oaths he had taken, all fulfilled them.
Forth rode Théoden. Five nights and days
east and onward rode the Eorlingas
through Folde and Fenmarch and the Firienwood,
six thousand spears to Sunlending,
Mundburg the mighty under Mindolluin,
Sea-kings' city in the South-kingdom,
foe beleaguered, fire-encircled.
Doom drove them on. Darkness took them,
horse and horseman; hoofbeats afar
sank into silence: so the songs tell us.

In the context of the story, *From Dark Dunharrow in the Dim Morning* was composed long after the events it relates. But by appearing at this point in *The Lord of the Rings*, as the Rohirrim are beginning their ride to the relief of Gondor, before the battle to come, it conveys aspects of the people of Rohan the reader needs to understand before continuing, in particular their character in regard to the keeping of oaths: to them, even an ancient oath is an obligation. Britain had done much the same as a guarantor of the neutrality of Belgium and Luxemburg in the First World War, under a treaty agreed in 1839, and more recently in Tolkien's day, of Poland when they were overrun by Germany in the Second World War.

Tolkien's verse also foreshadows, implying to the reader that Théoden will not return to Edoras – as the fictional poet knew as a fact of history. With an epic air, but no vain boasting of martial glory, it allows no uncertainty as to the outcome, with its many words and phrases indicating tragedy to come: *mist-enshrouded*, *gloom*, *faded*, *fear*, *fate*, *doom*, *darkness*. Yet it was not so to those who fought in the battle, and may be contrasted with Théoden's cry as the Rohirrim are to begin their charge into battle on the Pelennor Fields (Book V, Chapter 5, contemporary with *Dunharrow*):

Arise, arise, Riders of Théoden!
Fell deeds awake: fire and slaughter!
spear shall be shaken, shield be splintered,
a sword-day, a red day, ere the sun rises!
Ride now, ride now! Ride to Gondor!

(A manuscript of this verse is reproduced in McIlwaine, *Tolkien: Maker of Middle-earth*, p. 360.) Although one could find other examples in the long history of leading men before an enemy, Théoden's speech is perhaps most like the exortation in the Old English fragment 'The Fight at Finnesburg': 'Ac onwacnigeað nu, wigend mine, | habbað eowre linda, hicgeaþ on ellen, | winnað on orde, wesað onmode!' ('But arise now, my warriors, seize your shields, remember your courage, fight in the vanguard, be as one!').

In 1952 Tolkien made a private recording of *From Dark Dunharrow*, and also of the final part of the chapter 'The Ride of the Rohirrim' from which we have quoted Théoden's words to his men; both have since been commercially released.

A2: In the earlier rough draft Tolkien wrote 'fear defying' as a trial, then 'fate defying'. Christopher Tolkien has suggested that his father may have written *Fengel* inadvertently, having already used *Thengel* in earlier draft chapters. *Fengel* appears, however, in several places in the rough workings. Next to its use in A2, Tolkien wrote a query, 'Thengel?'

A7: 'High seat', i.e. throne.

A15: In the earlier rough draft Tolkien wrote 'Fold' rather than 'Folde'. In *The War of the Ring* (1990) Christopher Tolkien speculates that *Firienlode* is 'perhaps the original name of the Mering Stream, which flowed through the Firien Wood' (p. 356); *lode* is an old word for 'watercourse'.

A20: 'Foe-beleaguered fire-encircled', i.e. Minas Tirith is under siege.

170

We Heard of the Horns in the Hills Ringing (1938–54)

The present alliterative poem is a pendant of sorts to *From Dark Dunharrow in the Dim Morning* (no. 169), and was written in the same period. Whereas the Dunharrow verse anticipated the fighting in Book V, Chapter 6 of *The Lord of the Rings*, so the present work recalls, immediately after the event, the tragic losses in the Battle of the Pelennor Fields. 'No few had fallen,' Tolkien writes, 'renowned or nameless, captain or soldier; for it was a great battle and the full count of it no tale has told.' But later, a 'song of the Mounds of Mundburg', of the burial mounds at Minas Tirith, was made by a poet of Rohan.

Little can be drawn from its rough initial manuscript, only a few names and phrases – 'Harding and Grimbold', 'Deorwine the Marshal', 'In the land of stone', 'In the fields of Mundberg', many mentions of 'home' and 'homeward' – but also one complete line which survived into the final poem (with one change of spelling), 'In the mounds of Mundberg under mould they lie'. The next manuscript (A), made probably soon after the fragmented first workings for the poem, brought Tolkien's ideas together, though still with indecision.

[A]

We heard in the hills   the horns ringing,
[*or* We heard of the horns   in the hills ringing,]
of swords shining   in the South-kingdom:
steeds went striding   to the Stoningland
a wind in the morning,   war at sunrise.
There Thengel [*sic*, for Théoden] fell   Thengling mighty
life and lordship   long had he wielded
[*deleted:* To his land returned not]
hoar king and high,   Harding and Grimbold,
Dunhere and [Elfhelm >] Deorwin the marshal.
   [*deleted:* Marculf]
Hirluin the Fair   [from >] to the hills [of >] by the sea,
nor Forlong the great   to the flowering vales
Ever of Arnach   [return ever >] to his own country
returned in triumph   nor the tall bowman
doughty Duinhir   to the dark waters

[*deleted:* under mountain]
meres of Morthond   [and >] under mountain-shadows
Death in the morning   and at day's ending
Lords took and lowly.   Long now they sleep
under grass in Gondor   by the Great River
Red it ran then.   Red was the sunset
the hills under heaven   high snowmantled
blood red burning   blood dyed the earth
In the Field of Mundberg   in the far country.
[*or* in the Stoningland   in the Stone kingdom]

Stoningland and deleted *Stone kingdom* are alternate names for Gondor, as used in Rohan (*Gondor* is Sindarin *gond* 'stone' + *dôr* 'land').

If we interpret correctly the pages of drafting for this poem, Tolkien wrote a prose passage very like that which precedes the elegy in the published book, beginning 'Aragorn and Éomer and Imrahil rode back towards the Gate of the City'; in manuscript this ends with the line we quote above, beginning 'No few had fallen'. Only then, it seems, did Tolkien decide to include a poem at this point (i.e. text A), writing it on a new page. The sentence 'As long after a maker in Rohan said in his song', a continuation of the prose passage, is written immediately above it.

Tolkien next seems to have begun to copy that text onto a fresh sheet, but soon introduced new readings. He was still uncertain about which names to include among the fallen, and struggled with the final four lines of the poem, trying different phrases with the words *red* and *blood*. We give here, as B, as much of this new version as we can make out, before Tolkien revised it further.

[B] We heard in the hills   of horns ringing
[*or* We heard of horns   in the hills ringing]
of swords shining   in the South-kingdom:
steeds went striding   to the Stoning-land,
as wind in the morning.   War they [*the line ends*]
There Théoden fell,   Thengling mighty;
to his golden halls   and green pastures
in the Northern fields   never returning,
high lord of the host.   Harding and Grimbold,
Dúnhere and [Elfhelm >] Deorwin the marshal
fought and fell there   in a far country.
in the Mounds of Mundberg   under mould the[y] lie
with their league fellows   lords of Gondor.

Not Hirluin the fair   to the hills by the sea
nor Forlong the old   to the flowering vales
Ever to Arnach   in his own country
returned in triumph,   nor the tall bowmen
Derufin and Duilin   to their dark waters,
meres of Morthond   under mountain-shadows.
Death in the morning   and at day's ending
Lords took and lowly.   Long now they sleep
under grass in Gondor   by the Great River
Grey runs the flood,   gleaming silver
[*deleted:* Red foamed that day   rolling waters
[*deleted:* ?Foamed Blood ??? bled at]
[*deleted:* Red then Red]
[*deleted:* Red ran the foam there]
[*deleted:* Foam]
[Red ran the lode >] Red then with blood
Blood red ??? ?day   ??? were the loud waters

The text continues like this, without resolution, for more than a dozen lines. In the margins Tolkien tried out other names to replace those he had written: *Guthwin* for *Dúnhere*, *Gulin* for *Guilin*, 'Dunhere & ?Macaulf', 'Herufare & Herubrand', 'Horn and Fastred'. And he pursued this line of thought also on another page (C).

[C] Theoden of Markland   Thengling mighty
Harding and Guthwin
Dunhere and Marculf   Deorwin and Grimbold
Herufare and Herubrand   Horn and Fastred

Grey ran the flood flowing silver
Red it rolled then roaring water
foam dyed with blood flamed at sunset
streams mountains burned in the evening

Tolkien nearly reached the final text of the poem in his next manuscript, a fair copy we will refer to as C^1 in our notes (in *The War of the Ring*, p. 371, Christopher Tolkien calls this 'the first good text' of the poem, that is, more legibly written), and in the first typescript, which we will call C^2, where Tolkien omitted metrical breaks between half-lines. Only in the typescript sent to the printer was the poem at last fully in the form now published (D).

[D] We heard of the horns in the hills ringing,
the swords shining in the South-kingdom.
Steeds went striding to Stoningland,
as wind in the morning. War was kindled.
There Théoden fell, Thengling mighty,
to his golden hall and green pastures
in Northern fields never returning,
high lord of the host. Harding and Guthláf,
Dúnhere and Déorwine, doughty Grimbold,
Herefara and Herubrand, Horn and Fastred,
fought and fell there in a far country:
in the Mounds of Mundburg under mould they lie
with their league-fellows, lords of Gondor.
Neither Hirluin the Fair to the hills by the sea,
nor Forlong the old to the flowering vales
ever, to Arnach, to his own country
returned in triumph; nor the tall bowmen,
Derufin and Duilin, to their dark waters,
meres of Morthond under mountain-shadows.
Death in the morning and at day's ending
lords took and lowly. Long now they sleep
under grass in Gondor by the Great River.
Grey now as tears, gleaming silver,
red then it rolled, roaring water:
foam dyed with blood flamed at sunset;
as beacons mountains burned at evening;
red fell the dew in Rammas Echor.

As might be expected in an elegy composed by a poet of Rohan, the first of the warriors to be named are from among the Rohirrim. But those he lists from line 14 are men of Gondor, and all were named earlier in the catalogue of reinforcements arriving at Minas Tirith near the end of Book V, Chapter 1: 'old Forlong the Fat, the Lord of Lossarnach', 'from the uplands of Morthond, the great Blackroot Vale, tall Duinhir with his sons, Duilin and Derufin, and five hundred bowmen', 'Hirluin the Fair of the Green Hills from Pinnath Gelin'. It is a sign of the bond between the two peoples that the Riders of Rohan and the great of Gondor who fell on the Pelennor were buried together, 'league-fellows' even in death; so it was also for brothers in arms in Tolkien's world when *We Heard in the Hills* was written.

Théoden was not himself buried in the Mounds of Mundburg, but taken to Rohan to lie with his ancestors in the Barrowfield. In

Book VI, Chapter 6 of *The Lord of the Rings*, his funeral becomes an opportunity for another memorial song.

> Out of doubt, out of dark, to the day's rising
> he rode singing in the sun, sword unsheathing.
> Hope he rekindled, and in hope ended;
> over death, over dread, over doom lifted
> out of loss, out of life, unto long glory.

Tolkien's prose introduction to the work is also moving:

> Then the Riders of the King's House upon white horses rode round about the barrow and sang together a song of Théoden Thengel's son that Gléowine his minstrel made, and he made no other song after. The slow voices of the Riders stirred the hearts, even of those who did not know the speech of that people; but the words of the song brought a light to the eyes of the folk of the Mark as they heard again afar the thunder of the hooves of the North and the voice of Eorl crying above the battle upon the Field of Celebrant; and the tale of the kings rolled on, and the horn of Helm was loud in the mountains, until the Darkness came and King Théoden arose and rode through the Shadow to the fire, and died in splendour, even as the Sun, returning beyond hope, gleamed upon Mindolluin in the morning.

Although the mere five lines of the poem are meant clearly to be only a small part of an epic whole, Tolkien wrote no more than these. Presumably they are also meant to recall the words of Éomer in Book V, Chapter 6 (written between 14 August and 14 September 1938), as he saw coming to the city black sails supposed to belong to the Corsairs of Umbar, and prepared to make a last stand:

> Out of doubt, out of dark, to the day's rising
> I came singing in the sun, sword unsheathing.
> To hope's end I rode and to heart's breaking:
> Now for wrath, now for ruin and a red nightfall!

Tolkien's reference to 'the battle upon the Field of Celebrant' is to a victory long ago in which Eorl the Young came to the aid of the armies of Gondor, for which deed Cirion of Gondor gave Eorl the lands that became the kingdom of Rohan.

Tom Shippey has said (in 'Alliterative Verse by Tolkien') that the best of Tolkien's alliterative verse is in *The Lord of the Rings*, in particular the three 'epitaph poems': the present work, *From Dark Dunharrow in the Dim Morning*, and Gléowine's dirge quoted above. These, he argues, are fine as poetry as well as good illustrations of the warrior culture of Rohan. Shippey also singles out Théoden's battle-cry (see poem no. 169), and points to the three lines Éomer speaks as Théoden dies (Book V, Chapter 6), which are both an epitaph and a call to battle:

> Mourn not overmuch! Mighty was the fallen,
> meet was his ending. When his mound is raised,
> women then shall weep. War now calls us!

To this one could add, from the same chapter, even the language of the grave-marker made for the king's horse, also killed at the Pelennor and, by having fallen on the king, indirectly the cause of his death:

> Faithful servant yet master's bane,
> Lightfoot's foal, swift Snowmane.

In 1952 Tolkien made a private recording of the final version of the verse, *We Heard of the Horns in the Hills Ringing*, since commercially released.

A17: 'Morthond' in this context is the vale of Morthond, also called the Blackroot, a river in Gondor.

A21: 'Red was the sunset': Tolkien was concerned to include this image early on, twice writing in drafts 'fire at evening', later 'fire at sunset', 'wild fire in the grass', 'blood red the hills', 'blood red the earth'. Ultimately the river is said to be 'dyed with blood flamed at sunset; | as beacons mountains burned at evening' combining two sources of the colour red, blood and flame.

D3: In C^1 'Stoningland' read 'Stoning-land', changed in C^2.

D4: In C^1 this line ended 'morning: war was kindled', changed in C^2.

D8: In C^1 the last name in this line was 'Guthwin', changed to 'Guthlaf' in manuscript ('Guthláf' only in the printer's typescript).

D9: In C^1 this line read 'Dunhere and Morculf, | | Deorwin and Grimbold'. It was changed to the final form in C^2.

D10: In C^1 the first name in this line is 'Herefare', changed to 'Herefara' in C^2.

D11: In C^1 this line ended with a semi-colon, changed to a colon in C^2.

D16: In C^1 this line read (much as B16) 'Ever, to Arnach | | in his own country'. In C^2 Tolkien changed 'Ever' to 'ever'. The full final reading of the line was reached in the typescript for the printer.

D17: In C^1 'triumph' is followed by a comma (as B17), changed to a semi-colon in C^2.

171

I Sit upon the Stones Alone · In Western Lands beneath the Sun (1938–54)

Our final selection from *The Lord of the Rings* is the song that Sam Gamgee sings in Book VI, Chapter 1. Frodo having been captured by Orcs, Sam is 'weary and feeling finally defeated'; he has the Ring, but cannot find his friend in the Tower of Cirith Ungol, in the cleft of that name within the Mountains of Shadow. To his surprise, 'moved by what thought in his heart he could not tell', he begins to sing. 'He murmured old childish tunes out of the Shire, and snatches of Mr. Bilbo's rhymes that came into his mind like fleeting glimpses of the country of his home. And then suddenly new strength rose in him, and his voice rang out, while words of his own came unbidden to fit the simple tune.' He hears a faint voice singing in reply – he has found Frodo.

Tolkien had it in mind since late 1941, when he wrote a summary of the story beyond its chapters in Lothlórien, that Frodo would be caught by the enemy and taken to a tower, and there Sam would 'do a thing of daring' and sing. '"Troll-song" [poem no. 83] – or some other Hobbit song – or possibly part of the Elves' song *O Elbereth* [see no. 151]. (Yes)' (*The War of the Ring*, p. 333). In the end, working on this late section of his book in August–September 1948, Tolkien chose to write a new song, the present poem. He seems to have realized at once that the 'Troll-song' ('The Lonely Troll he sat on a stone') would have been too comical for singing in an Orc-tower – though it is not out of the question that its first words helped to inspire the original opening of the new verse – and a version of *A Elbereth Gilthoniel* served to encourage Sam in Shelob's lair in Book IV, Chapter 10.

In *Sauron Defeated* Christopher Tolkien comments that the new song was 'much worked on'. He prints in full the version we give below as B, stating that it 'was preceded by rougher but closely similar versions' (p. 27). Among the *Lord of the Rings* papers at Marquette University, however, one finds only a single earlier draft of the poem (A, illustrating revisions in the manuscript), very rough indeed, and to all appearances its initial text, composed within the narrative of the chapter. There it is introduced by the words: 'Quavering and thin his voice sounded in that strong hostile place – ?cert[ainly] a hobbit voice not [the] clear song of [an] Elven-lord. But it gathered a little strength as Sam began to weave words with his tune and thoughts.'

[A] I sit upon the stones alone
The fire is burning red.
The tower is tall the mountain dark
[The >] All living things are dead.

[I sit upon >] In western lands the sun may shine
There flower and trees in spring
Is opening is blossoming
and there the finches sing

But [*above:* While] here I sit alone and think
of days when I was young [*above:* grass was green] of
[*deleted:* and of grass green, and]
and earth was brown and grass was green, [*above:* and I
was young]
they might have never been.
[*deleted:* and I was young and ???]
and ?my hills were ?merry
and of the songs we sang

and you I see go walking free
along the homely road ways
on a bright and windy day
Now here I sit and think of you
and call ???
and ask the empty world
that ??? dark dream
were you hear present ?song

From this beginning, Tolkien developed the following lyrics, sung to 'an old tune that Bilbo used to sing'. Our transcription B represents the text with revisions made in the course of writing. (Compare Christopher Tolkien's transcription in *Sauron Defeated*, p. 27.)

[B] I sit upon the stones alone;
the fire is burning red,
the tower is tall, the mountains dark;
all living things are dead.

In western lands the sun may shine,
there flower and tree in spring
Is opening, is blossoming;
and there the finches sing.

But here I sit alone and think
of days when grass was green,
and earth was brown, and I was young:
they might have never been.
For they are past, for ever lost,
and here the shadows lie
deep upon my heavy heart,
and hope and daylight die.

[*Tolkien changed lines 14–16 to:*]
and buried here I lie,
deep beneath the shadow-sea
where hope and daylight die.

But still I sit and think of you;
I see you far away
walking down the homely roads
on a bright and windy day.
It was merry then when I could run
to answer to your call,
could hear your voice or take your hand;
but now the night must fall.

[The >] And now beyond the world I sit,
and know not where you lie!
[O master dear, will you not hear >]
O Master, will you hear my call
[my voice before we die? >] and answer ere we die

In *Sauron Defeated* Christopher Tolkien indicates that in line 13 of this version his father changed 'past' to 'gone' on the manuscript; this was so, but it was done in pencil, after initial writing in blue ink. Christopher also notes that the end of line 18 was altered on the manuscript to 'the shadows sink'; here too the change, in black rather than blue ink, was made after the fact. These revisions are reflected in the poem as given in the next manuscript of the chapter, following version B except in the penultimate line, which ends 'hear my voice' rather than 'hear my call'. But then, Tolkien chose to discard most of what he had composed, wrote a new, much shorter version (C) next to the old poem which he firmly struck through, and again on a slip of paper, or rider, affixed to the previous text.

[C]

In western lands the Sun may shine;
  there flower and tree in Spring
are opening, are blossoming,
  and there the finches sing.
Or maybe it is cloudless night,
  and swaying beeches bear
the Elven-stars as jewels white
  amid their branching hair.

Though here at journey's end I lie
  in darkness buried deep,
beyond all towers strong and high,
  beyond all mountains steep,
above all Shadow rides the Sun
  and Stars for ever dwell:
I will not say that Day is done,
  nor bid the Stars farewell.

Nearly the same text appears in the typescript of the book given to the printer: there line 13 is 'above the Shadow rides the Sun', and line 15 has 'the Day' rather than 'that Day'. But at the eleventh hour, before type was set, Tolkien marked both the typescript and the manuscript rider with several changes, and thus, with two exceptions (described in our notes), reached the text of the poem as finally published (D).

[D]

In western lands beneath the Sun
  the flowers may rise in Spring,
the trees may bud, the waters run,
  the merry finches sing.
Or there maybe 'tis cloudless night
  and swaying beeches bear
the Elven-stars as jewels white
  amid their branching hair.

Though here at journey's end I lie
in darkness buried deep,
beyond all towers strong and high,
beyond all mountains steep,
above all shadows rides the Sun
and Stars for ever dwell:
I will not say the Day is done,
nor bid the Stars farewell.

In the first version of his song, Sam refers to one tower and one mountain, but although he and Frodo are in a single tower, this is in a wall of mountains, the Ephel Dúath; in text B, the reference is appropriately plural, 'the mountains dark'. Then in C, as Sam becomes more defiant than nostalgic, he shows his courage against all towers – he is threatened also by Minas Morgul and Barad-dûr – and against all mountains, of which there are many in Mordor.

It seems certain, from a reference to 'Richard Coeur de Lion and the minstrel' Tolkien made in a letter to the composer Donald Swann, that the episode of Sam's song was inspired by the legend of the minstrel Blondel de Nesle searching for King Richard I of England after his master was captured by Leopold of Austria while returning from the Crusades and held for ransom. Blondel went from castle to castle, singing one of Richard's favourite songs, until the King joined in, revealing his presence. For Sam it was a simpler matter. Tolkien had earlier, in 'The Silmarillion', used the same motif in regard to the Elf Fingon searching for his imprisoned cousin Maedhros, and to Lúthien looking for Beren in Sauron's Isle of Werewolves.

A musical setting of the poem by Donald Swann appeared in *The Road Goes Ever On: A Song Cycle* (1967), and was performed by pianist Swann and baritone William Elvin on the recording *Poems and Songs of Middle Earth* (1967).

A6: The fourth word appears to be 'trees', plural, though the verb in A7 is singular. The reading is 'tree', singular, in B6.

B30: Tolkien seems to have considered an alternate reading for this line (before revision), 'O will you not hear me, Master dear'.

C6–8: The image is that of stars shining through the branches, fancifully 'branching hair', of a beech tree.

D13: The rider manuscript begins 'above all' as written, the typescript 'above the' as typed, changed in manuscript to 'above all'.

D15: The rider manuscript has 'that Day', without revision, the typescript 'the Day'.

172

Rhyme (1938)

At Christmas 1920 Tolkien began an annual tradition of sending his children a letter written by 'Father Christmas'. These were endlessly creative, illustrated and decorated, arriving in envelopes with special stamps and 'postmarks'. In time, other residents of the North Pole added their own news and comments. The most prominent of these other 'authors' was the North Polar Bear, Karhu (Finnish 'bear'); he was well meaning, but often the cause of trouble, such as when he fell downstairs while carrying too many parcels, or opened a window so that a breeze scattered a desk full of papers. Tolkien's daughter Priscilla described 'N.P.B.' as an *enfant terrible* whose cavalier attitude towards authority appealed to children. His nephews, Paksu and Valkotukka (Finnish 'stout' and 'white-hair'; below, 'P. & V.'), also came to live at the North Pole. Father Christmas's secretary, the elf Ilbereth, in contrast was a much quieter, more mature figure.

By 1938 Priscilla, aged nine, was the only one of the four Tolkien children still young enough to receive greetings from Father Christmas. In the letter for that year, he (that is, Tolkien) wrote that he was 'frightfully sorry that I haven't had time to draw any big picture this year, and Ilbereth (my secretary) has not done one either; but we are all sending you some rhymes instead. Some of my other children seem to like rhymes, so perhaps you will.' We have transcribed the poem below. Written mainly by Father Christmas 'himself' in his distinctive shaky hand, it also has additions by Polar Bear, whose heavy hand (or paw) we have indicated in boldface, and by Ilbereth, whose flowing script is here in italics. Since Polar Bear's nephews could not write, they made bear-shaped blots. Unfortunately, we cannot render the letter's decorations of fir, candles, and ornaments, but they may be found in facsimile in later editions of *Letters from Father Christmas*.

The *Rhyme* – Tolkien wrote this title at the top of its first page – is shamelessly comic, with many of its rhyming pairs intentionally awkward: *verses/worse is*, *news/whose*, *paws/because*, *plates/chocolates*. In lines 5 through 7, Father Christmas suggests that he is not good at writing verse because there is no rhyme for his name in English, indeed the gap after line 3 is meant to show that he was at a loss as to what to write. Polar Bear needles him from the margin, and later suggests that Father Christmas has altered facts to achieve a suitable rhyme. The account of successive crises and dramas in the work is in much the same vein as *Monday Morning* (poem no. 122).

Again this year, my dear Priscilla,
when you're asleep upon your pillow; **BAD rhyme!**
beside your bed old Father Christmas **that's beaten you!**

[The English language has no rhyme
to Father Christmas: that's why I'm
not very good at making verses.
But what I find a good deal worse is
that girls' and boys' names won't rhyme either
(and bother! either won't rhyme neither).
So please forgive me, dear Priscilla, **she won't**
if I pretend you rhyme with pillow!]

As I was saying —
beside your bed old Father Christmas
(afraid that any creak or hiss must How's that? F.C.
wake you up) will in a twinkling **OUT! PB**
fill up your stocking *I've an inkling*
that it belongs, in fact to pater — *Had to help FC out*
but never mind! At twelve, or later, *here. Ilbereth*
he will arrive — and hopes once more
that he has chosen from his store **I did it**
the things you want. You are half past nine; *She is not a clock!*
but still I'll hope you'll drop a line
for some years yet, & won't forget
old Father Christmas and his Pet,
the N.P.B (and Polar Cubs [bear shapes]
as fat as little butter-tubs), blots by P. &V.
and snowboys and Elves — in fact the whole
of my household up near the Pole.
Upon my list, made in December,
your number is, if you remember,
fifty six thousand, seven hundred,
and eighty five. It can't be wondered **weak!**
at that I am so busy, when
you think that you are nearly ten,
and in that time my list has grown
by quite ten thousand girls alone,
even when I've subtracted all
the houses where I no longer call!

You all will wonder what's the news;
if all has gone well, and if not who's
to blame; and whether Polar Bear
has earned a mark good, bad, or fair
for his behaviour since last winter.
Well — first he trod upon a splinter, **just rhyming**
and went on crutches in November; **nonsens: it was**
and then one cold day in December **a nail – rusty too**
he burnt his nose & singed his paws
upon the kitchen grate, because
without the help of tongs he tried
to roast hot chestnuts. 'Wow!' he cried, **I never did!**
and used a pound of butter (best)
to cure the burns. He would not rest, **I was not given a**
but on the twenty-third he went **chance**
and climbed up on the roof. He meant
to clear the snow away that choked
his chimney up — of course he poked
his legs right through the tiles, & snow
in tons fell on his bed below.
He has broken saucers, cups, and plates;
and eaten lots of chocolates;
he's dropped large boxes on my toes, **you need not**
and trodden tin-soldiers flat in rows; **believe all this!**
he's over-wound engines and broken springs, *You need I.*
& mixed up different children's things;
he's thumbed new books and burst balloons
& scribbled lots of smudgy Runes
on my best paper, and wiped his feet
on scarves and hankies folded neat —
And yet he has been, on the whole,
a very kind and willing soul.
He's fetched and carried, counted, packed, **hear, hear!**
and for a week has never slacked:
he's climbed the cellar stairs at least
five thousand times — the Dear Old Beast!

I wish you wouldn't scribble
on my nice rhyme
F.C.

Paksu sends love and Valkotukka —
They are still with me, and they don't look a
year older, but they're just a bit
more wise, & have a pinch more wit.

The GOBLINS, you'll be glad to hear,
have not been seen at all this year,
not near the Pole. But I am told
they're moving South, and getting bold,
& coming back to many lands,
and making with their wicked hands
new mines & caves. But do not fear!
They'll hide away when I appear.

Christmas Day. Postscript by Ilbereth.

Now Christmas Day has come round again —
and poor N.P.B. has got a bad pain!
They say he's swallowed a couple of pounds
of nuts without cracking the shells! It sounds
a Polarish sort of thing to do —
but that isn't all, between me and you;
he's eaten a ton of various goods
and recklessly mixed all his favourite foods,
honey with ham and turkey with treacle,
and pickles with milk. I think that a week'll
be needed to put the old bear on his feet.
And I mustn't forget his particular treat:
plum pudding with sausages and turkish delight
covered with cream and devoured at a bite!
And after this dish he stood on his head —
it's rather a wonder the poor fellow's not dead!

Absolute ROT:
I have not got
a pain in my pot. *Rude fellow!*
I do not eat
turkey or meat:
I stick to the sweet
Which is why
(as all know) I

am so sweet myself,
you thinuous elf!
Good by!

He means fatuous
no I don't you're
not fat but
thin and silly

You know my friends too well to think
(although they're rather rude with ink)
that there are really quarrels here!
We've had a very jolly year
(except for P.B.'s rusty nail):
but now this rhyme must catch the Mail —
a special messenger must go,
in spite of thickly falling snow,
or else this won't get down to you
on Christmas day. It's half past two!
We've quite a ton of crackers still
to pull, and glasses still to fill!
Our love to you on this Noel —
and till the next one, fare you well!

Father Christmas
P.B.
Ilbereth
P & V

4–11: Square brackets are in the original.

8: In the manuscript, 'boys'' is written 'boy's'. We have silently corrected.

15: 'Out!': Polar Bear's judgement uses the language of an umpire in cricket.

17: *Pater* is Latin 'father'. In England, it was customary for children to hang up a parent's sock, as the child's own would not have allowed much room for filling.

28: 'Pole': the 'Father Christmas' letters are full of details of the present-making operation at the North Pole, enlivened occasionally by unwanted visitors: see ll. 82 and following.

31–32: In the letter for 1936, Ilbereth reported that Polar Bear had invented a number system 'so that every child that Father Christmas deals with has a number and we elves learn them all by heart, and all the addresses.'

45: 'Nonsens' is Polar Bear's spelling.

48: 'Kitchen grate', i.e. the grate on a cooker (stove).

50: Roasted chestnuts, i.e. nuts from the Sweet chestnut tree (*Castanea sativa*), are a traditional Christmas food.

71: The 'correction' of 'here' to 'hear' is part of the letter's verisimilitude.

85: Tolkien's reference to Goblins moving South may be an allusion to dark news out of Europe, as a new war with Germany approached.

103: *Plum pudding*, a traditional Christmas dish in Britain, is a boiled pudding made with dried fruit (*plum* in this sense is a raisin). *Turkish delight* is a confection based on a gel of starch and sugar, with chopped date, nuts, etc. There are different varieties. The combination 'plum pudding with sausages and turkish delight covered with cream' is meant to sound vile, and would be.

130: A *cracker* in this sense is a tube wrapped with colourful paper and containing a prize or prizes. It crackles, or snaps, when the ends are pulled apart.

173

Sir Orfeo (1943 or 1944)

The Middle English poem *Sir Orfeo*, composed probably in the late thirteenth or early fourteenth century, is an adaptation of the popular Greek tale of Orpheus and Eurydice. In the new work, when the fair queen Heurodis is abducted by magic, her grief-stricken husband, the English king Orfeo, places his realm in the care of a steward and flees into the wilderness with only a beggar's cloak and a harp he can play with sublime skill. For ten years, he charms the birds and beasts with his music, and occasionally sees the king of Faërie riding by, or others of his kind. One day, he recognizes Heurodis in a group of ladies from the king's retinue, and follows them to the Faërie castle. Posing as a minstrel, he pleases the king with his music and is given a gift of his choice. He claims Heurodis, and returns home with her.

Sir Orfeo does not seem to have been a set text in the Oxford English School when Tolkien was an undergraduate, though he may have read it independently. He was certainly familiar with it by 1919–22, while preparing the glossary (*A Middle English Vocabulary*) for Kenneth Sisam's *Fourteenth Century Verse and Prose*, a collection which includes *Sir Orfeo* in its entirety. In 1943 or 1944, he prepared a version of *Sir Orfeo* in Middle English to be used in courses offered at Oxford to Navy and Air Force cadets; Tolkien served as lecturer and administrator of this programme from the start of 1943. A typescript of Tolkien's edition was reproduced in 1944 by the Academic Copying Office in Oxford, and later reprinted in *Tolkien Studies* (1, 2004). The original printing is not credited to Tolkien by name, though there can be little doubt that it is his work.

Probably around the same time, he also made a Modern English translation of the poem. In his '*Sir Orfeo*: A Middle English Version by J.R.R. Tolkien' (2004), Carl F. Hostetter argues that Tolkien based his edition on that in *Fourteenth Century Verse and Prose*, then for his translation followed his own text for the Oxford cadets. Curtis A. Weyant has shown, however, that the analysis Hostetter provides allows one 'to examine specific lines in Tolkien's translation . . . that either follow Sisam's edition over his own or which diverge from both Middle English editions (Sisam's and Tolkien's) altogether. Doing so reveals Tolkien's translation . . . as a nuanced composition . . .' ('"A Translator Is Not Free": J.R.R. Tolkien's Rules for Translation and

Their Application in *Sir Orfeo*' (2021), p. 78). Addressing the question of dating the translation, Hostetter points out that Tolkien's correct reading of a Middle English word – *aumal* 'enamel' rather than *animal* 'animal' – corresponds to the 1945 revision of his *Vocabulary*; this suggests that the Modern English text, or at any rate this part of the text (line 364), was prepared no later than 1945. We have dated it conservatively to 1943 or 1944, concurrent with Tolkien's work on *Sir Orfeo* in Middle English.

The complete Modern English *Sir Orfeo* (604 lines) may be found in *Sir Gawain and the Green Knight, Pearl and Sir Orfeo*, edited by Christopher Tolkien and first published in 1975. From this, we have made for the present book a selection of sixty-eight lines from the middle of the poem (pp. 129–31), after Orfeo has gone into the wilderness and to the point he sees his wife again and they recognize each other.

A Lord! who can recount the woe
for ten long years that king did know?
His hair and beard all black and rank
down to his waist hung long and lank.
His harp wherein was his delight
in hollow tree he hid from sight;
when weather clear was in the land
his harp he took then in his hand
and harped thereon at his sweet will.
Through all the wood the sound did thrill,
and all the wild beasts that there are
in joy approached him from afar;
and all the birds that might be found
there perched on bough and bramble round
to hear his harping to the end,
such melodies he there did blend;
and when he laid his harp aside,
no bird or beast would near him bide.

There often by him would he see,
when noon was hot on leaf and tree,
the king of Faërie with his rout
came hunting in the woods about
with blowing far and crying dim,
and barking hounds that were with him;
yet never a beast they took nor slew,

and where they went he never knew.
At other times he would descry
a mighty host, it seemed, go by,
ten hundred knights all fair arrayed
with many a banner proud displayed.
Each face and mien was fierce and bold,
each knight a drawn sword there did hold,
and all were armed in harness fair
and marching on he knew not where.
Or a sight more strange would meet his eye:
knights and ladies came dancing by
in rich array and raiment meet,
softly stepping with skilful feet;
tabour and trumpet went along,
and marvellous minstrelsy and song.

And one fair day he at his side
saw sixty ladies on horses ride,
each fair and free as bird on spray,
and never a man with them that day.
There each on hand a falcon bore,
riding a-hawking by river-shore.
Those haunts with game in plenty teem,
cormorant, heron, and duck in stream;
there off the water fowl arise,
and every falcon them descries;
each falcon stooping slew his prey,
and Orfeo laughing loud did say:
'Behold, in faith, this sport is fair!
Fore Heaven, I will betake me there!
I once was wont to see such play.'
He rose and thither made his way,
and to a lady came with speed,
and looked at her, and took good heed,
and saw as sure as once in life
'twas Heurodis, his queen and wife.
Intent he gazed, and so did she,
but no word spake; no word said he.
For hardship that she saw him bear,
who had been royal, and high, and fair,
then from her eyes the tears there fell.

The other ladies marked it well,
and away they made her swiftly ride;
no longer might she near him bide.

In our discussions for poem nos. 34 and 62, in each of which we quote some additional lines from Tolkien's Modern English text, we touch upon *Sir Orfeo* as an analogue or influence on his mythology, a point made at greater length by Tom Shippey in *The Road to Middle-earth*. The 'fusion or kindling-point' of Tolkien's elves, Shippey writes,

> would seem to be some twenty or thirty lines from the centre of the medieval poem of *Sir Orfeo*, itself a striking example of the alchemies of art. In origin this is only the classical story of Orpheus and Eurydice, but the fourteenth-century poet (or maybe some forgotten predecessor) has made two radical changes to it: one, the land of the dead has become elf-land, from which the elf-king comes to seize Dame Heurodis; two, Sir Orfeo, unlike his classical model, is successful in his quest and bears his wife away, overcoming the elf-king by the mingled powers of music and honour. The poem's most famous and original passage is the image of the elves in the wilderness, seen again and again by Orfeo as he wanders mad and naked, looking for his wife, but never certainly identified as hallucinations, phantoms, or real creatures on the other side of some transparent barrier which Orfeo cannot break through. [pp. 58–9]

The passage in question is lines 281–288, given above.

Shippey also remarks that 'many hints' from *Sir Orfeo* 'took root in Tolkien's mind', later finding expression in 'the shadow-army with its echoing horns which was to follow Aragorn from the "paths of the dead"' in *The Lord of the Rings*, and in *The Hobbit* the 'great hunt' the dwarves see passing by in Mirkwood, and 'the fierce, proud, impulsive, honourable elf-king who imprisons Thorin but will take no advantage in the end even of Bilbo'. In addition to these, there is 'the association of the elves with the wilderness . . . and with the music of the harp' (p. 59).

174

A Closed Letter to Andrea Charicoryides (1943)

Charles Williams (1886–1945) wrote poetry, biography, church history, literary criticism, and fantasy novels set in the contemporary world. The first of the latter to be published was *War in Heaven* in 1930, though *Shadows of Ecstasy* (1933) was the first to be written. Williams' works were not widely popular; they are certainly not to everyone's tastes. *Taliessin through Logres* (1938) and *The Region of the Summer Stars* (1944), his two volumes of poetry related to the legend of King Arthur but wrapped within a mythology unique to Williams, are particularly complex. And yet, his work was admired by notables such as W.H. Auden and T.S. Eliot – Eliot called Williams' novels 'supernatural thrillers' – and most enthusiastically by C.S. Lewis.

At the start of war in 1939, Williams moved to Oxford with the London offices of Oxford University Press, where he was an editor. C.S. Lewis persuaded him to join the Inklings, the informal group of authors and academics which also included Tolkien. Lewis and Tolkien together also brought Williams into the Oxford English Faculty, whose numbers were depleted during the conflict. Tolkien's largely disparaging opinion told to Dick Plotz in a 1965 letter, in which he found Williams' works 'wholly alien, and sometimes very distasteful, occasionally ridiculous', is often taken as a measure of his lack of regard for Williams personally during their years together at Oxford, but there is a great deal of evidence to show that they were in fact close friends who enjoyed each other's company and conversation. When Williams died suddenly in 1945, Tolkien was demonstrably sad, as he wrote in a letter to Williams' widow.

Near the end of 1943, Tolkien composed a poem in honour of his friend, which we give below from its printing in *The Inklings: C.S. Lewis, J.R.R. Tolkien, Charles Williams and Their Friends* by Humphrey Carpenter (1978), pp. 123–6. Its excessively erudite title is given in a typescript of the poem held by the Marion E. Wade Center, Wheaton College, Illinois: *A Closed Letter to Andrea Charicoryides Surnamed Polygrapheus, Logothete of the Theme of Geodesia in the Empire, Bard of the Court of Camelot, Malleus Malitiarium, Inclinga Sum Sometimes Known as Charles Williams*.

'Our dear Charles Williams many guises shows:
the novelist comes first. I find his prose
obscure at times. Not easily it flows;
too often are his lights held up in brackets.
Yet error, should he spot it, he'll attack its
sources and head, exposing ramps and rackets,
the tortuous byways of the wicked heart
and intellect corrupt. Yea, many a dart
he crosses with the fiery ones! The art
of minor fiends and major he reveals —
when Charles is on his trail the devil squeals,
for cloven feet have vulnerable heels.

'But heavenly footsteps, too, can Williams trace,
and after Dante, plunging, soaring, race
to the threshold of Eternal Grace.
The limits of all fallen men, maybe,
(or mine alone, perhaps) explain why he
seems best to understand of all the three
Inferno's dark involved geography.

'Geography indeed! Here he again
exerts a subtle mind and labouring pen.
Geodesy say rather; for many a 'fen'
he wrote, and chapters bogged in tangled rhymes,
and has surveyed Europa's lands and climes
dividing her from P'o-L'u's crawling slimes,
in her diving buttocks, breast, and head
(to say no fouler thing), where I instead,
dull-eyed, can only see a watershed,
a plain, an island, or a mountain-chain.
In that gynecomorphical terrain
History and Myth are ravelled in a skein
of endless interchange. I do not hope
to understand the deeds of king or pope,
wizard or emperor; beyond my scope
is that dark flux of symbol and event,
where fable, faith, and faërie are blent
with half-guessed meanings to some great intent
I cannot grasp. For Mount Elburz to me
is but a high peak far beyond the sea
(and high and far I'd ever have it be).

'The Throne, the war-lords, and the logothetes,
the endless steps, the domes, the crowded streets,
the tolls, the taxes, the commercial fleets,
Byzantium, New Rome! I love her less
than Rome the Old. For War, I must confess,
Eagles to me no more than ravens bless,
no more than Fylfot, or Chrysanthemum
blown to a blood-red Sun. Byzantium!
Praise her, ye slaves and eunuchs! I'll be dumb.
To me she only seems one greater hive,
rotting within while outwardly alive,
where power corrupts and where the venal thrive;
where, leeches on the veins of government,
officials suck men's blood, till all is spent.
If that is what by Law and Order's meant,
then any empire's over-lofty crown,
and vast drilled armies beating neighbours down
to drag them fettered through New Order's town,
to me's as good a symbol, or as ill
of Rule that strangles and of Laws that kill,
of Man that says his pride is Heaven's will.
O, buttocks to Caucasia!'
'Tolkien, please!
What's biting you? Dog in the Manger's fleas?
Let others hear, although you have no mind,
or have not seen that Lewis has divined
and has expounded what you dully find
obscure. See here, some thirty lines you've squandered.
You came to praise our Charles, but now you've wandered.
Much else he wrote that has not yet been pondered.'

'Quite true, alas! But still I'm rather puzzled.
There's Taliessin — no, I'll not be muzzled;
I'm writing this, not you; I won't be hustled —
there's Taliessin now: I'd always thought
that in the days of Cymbeline he wrought,
ere Rome was Old or New, and that if aught
is now preserved of what he sang or said,
'tis but an echo times have edited
out of all likeness to his tongue long dead,
the ancient British, difficult and dark,
of a minor minstrel in an Outer Mark.

But here, it seems, a voyage in some swift bark
to that Black Sea (which now is mainly Red)
has much enlarged him, both in heart and head;
but still I understand not aught he said!

'A truce to this! I never meant to do it,
thus to reveal my folly. Now I rue it.
Farewell (for now) beloved druid-poet!
Farewell to Logres, Merlin, Nimue,
Galahad, Arthur! Farewell land and tree
heavy with fates and portents not for me!
I must pass by all else you wrote:
play, preface, life, short verse, review or note
(rewarded less than worth with grudging groat).
'When your fag is wagging and spectacles are twinkling,
when tea is brewing or the glasses tinkling,
then of your meaning often I've an inkling,
your virtues and your wisdom glimpse. Your laugh
in my heart echoes, when with you I quaff
the pint that goes down quicker than a half,
because you're near. So, heed me not! I swear
when you with tattered papers take the chair
and read (for hours maybe), I would be there.
And ever when in state you sit again
and to your car imperial give rein,
I'll trundle, grumbling, squeaking, in the train
of the great rolling wheels of Charles's Wain.'

We have found it convenient to explain the many references or allusions Tolkien makes in the poem in the form of notes, below.

14–19: In 1943 Williams published *The Figure of Beatrice: A Study of Dante*, one of his most significant works of criticism. The Italian poet Dante Alighieri (1265–1321) wrote his great *Commedia*, the *Divine Comedy*, in three parts: *Inferno*, *Purgatorio*, and *Paradiso*. The first of these concerns Dante's journey through Hell, which is said to have nine concentric circles of torment, a 'dark involved geography'.

22: *Geodesy* is the mathematical study of the figures and areas of the Earth. In *The Inklings* Humphrey Carpenter glosses 'fen' as 'the name of a section in Avicenna's *Canon of Medicine*; also used by Chaucer in 'The Pardoner's Tale' (p. 124).

25: In Williams' Arthurian poems, the far country of P'o-L'u, ruled by a headless emperor, is the centre of evil.

26–30: Tolkien is commenting on the 'gynecomorphical' map included in (some editions of) *Taliessin through Logres*, an image of a nude female superimposed on a map of the Empire (Europe, 'Europa' in Tolkien's poem) with the head of the 'woman' over Logres (Britain).

33–34: 'King or pope, wizard or emperor', i.e. four principal figures in Williams' Arthurian poems. The 'king' is Arthur, the 'wizard' Merlin.

36: 'Blent', i.e. blended.

38: Mount Elburz is a mountain in the Caucasus, mentioned several times in Williams' Arthurian poems.

41–44: Byzantium, or Williams' vision of it, figures in his Arthuriad. Carpenter notes that 'the Throne, the war-lords', etc. are 'reminiscent of Williams' poem "The Vision of the Empire" in *Taliessin through Logres*, except of course that to Williams these things are pleasing'. *Logothete* was an administrative title in the Byzantine Empire.

47–48: A *fylfot* is a form of cross (swastika) associated with Anglo-Saxon culture; a variation was adopted by the Nazi movement. Carpenter observes that 'Chrysanthemum | blown to a blood-red Sun' refers to two emblems of the Japanese Empire. Tolkien composed his poem during the Second World War.

64: The phrase 'dog in the manger' refers to a person who spitefully withholds something useless to himself from others who could use it. It derives from the fable of a dog who does not eat grain but prevents a horse, or ox, from eating it.

66: 'Lewis', i.e. C.S. Lewis.

72: Taliessin is the poet of Williams' Arthuriad.

75: 'In the days of Cymbeline': the historical Cymbeline (the form of name used by Shakespeare in his play), or Cunobeline, was a king in pre-Roman Britain in the first century AD. Williams took Taliessin from Celtic legend and set him in a fictional period combining Arthurian Britain and the Byzantine Empire.

81: 'Outer Mark': we presume that Tolkien meant to refer to a distant territory, using *mark* in the sense of *march* (from Old English *mearc* 'boundary'), a word historically used to refer to the parts of England on the borders of Scotland and Wales.

83: 'That Black Sea (which now is mainly Red)': many of the lands touching the Black Sea at the time Tolkien wrote this poem were part of, or associated with, the Communist ('Red') Soviet Union.

88: 'Druid-poet': in *Taliessin through Logres* Taliessin describes himself as 'Druid-sprung', i.e. from a high-ranking class in Celtic cultures.

89–90: 'Logres, Merlin, Nimue, | Galahad, Arthur' are place (Logres) and personal names associated with Arthurian legend.

107: 'Charles' Wain' is a name for the constellation Ursa Major, the Great Bear, also called Arthur's Plough. Tolkien is also playing on *wain* 'wagon'.

175

The Death of St Brendan · Imram
(*c.* 1945–55)

In *Sauron Defeated* Christopher Tolkien comments on the 'elaborate versification' of this poem and describes its complex history: 'no less than fourteen closely-written pages of initial working', followed by 'four finished manuscript texts' and a typescript, and 'much further work on it followed later' (*Sauron Defeated*, p. 295). Only its first workings have been available to us in the original, written quickly and for the most part very rough. The text on the first four pages (as preserved in the Bodleian Library, numbered by Tolkien 1 through 4) is complete and, for the most part, legible with moderate effort. We have transcribed this version as A, incorporating revisions Tolkien made in the course of writing.

[A]

At last out of the deep seas he passed
and mist rolled on the shore,
and loud waves ran under moonlit cloud
as the laden ship him bore
to Ireland home to wood and mire
To the town far away
where the knell of Cluain-ferta's bell
was tolling in green Galway.
Where Shannon down to Lough Derg ran
under a rainclad sky
St. Brendan came at his journey's end,
and his bones in Ireland lie.
'O tell me father, for I loved you well,
if still you have words for me,
of things most strange in the remembering
in the long and lonely sea;
of islands by deep spells beguiled
where dwell the Elven-kind.
In seven years the steep road to heaven
or the Living Land did you find?'

‘The things I have seen the many things
have long now faded far;
but three come clearly back to me
a tree a cloud and a star
We sailed a year and a day and hailed
no field nor coast of men,
no boat nor bird we saw ever afloat
for forty days and ten;
and pale before us hung a misty veil
and the falling sun fell dead
when suddenly afar we heard a thudding
and espied a gleam of red.
Sheer from the leaden seas uprearing
a shoreless mountain stood
its side rose black from the sullen tide
to the red lining of its hood
No cloak nor cloud no burning smoke
no black uplooming thunder
In world of men saw I ever unfurled
as that pall that we passed under
But astern at last it lay and I turned
and that a cloud went bye
a lonely peak of ?towering stone
from sea to sky
and red gold crown of fire.
The tower top of a foundered power
We sailed then on till the wind had failed
and we toiled then with the oar
and hunger and thirst us surely wrung
and we sang our psalms no more
A land at last then with a silver strand
at the end of strength we found
The waves were singing in pillared caves
and pearls lay on the ground
And steeply the shores went upward leaping
To slopes of green & gold
And a stream out of the rich land teeming
through coombs of shadow rolled.
Through gates of stone then we rowed in haste
and passed and left the sea
And silence like a dew fell on that isle,
and holy it seemed to be.

Like a green cup deep in the brim of green
that with wine the white sun fills
was the land we found and we saw there stand
as a land between the hills
A tree more fair than I ever dreamed
might climb in Paradise
Its foot was like a great tower's root
its height beyond men's eyes
So wide its boughs that the least would hide
In shade an acre long
In the silence of that hollowed isle
In the stillness then we sang
but the sound of those soft psalms around us
as organ thunder rang
and from stem to crown the tree then trembled
from the limbs the leaves in the air
like white birds flew in wheeling flight
and the golden boughs were bare.
From the sky came falling down on high
a song yet heard
not voice of men nor angels voices
But maybe there is a third
Fair kindred there in the world yet lingers
beyond the foundered land:
Yet steep are the seas and the waters deep
beyond the White-tree Strand.'
'O say more, father, and do not stay
But two things you have told:
the tree and the cloud; but you spoke of three —
the star in mind you hold?'
'The star! yes I saw it high and far
at the parting of the road,
a light when the sun had sunk from sight
that as burning silver glowed.
Where the round world plunges steeply down
but on the old road goes
as an unseen bridge that on arches runs
to coasts that no man knows. [']
[']But men say father that ere the end
you went where none have been.
I would hear you tell my father dear
Of that land that you have seen.'

'In my mind the star I still can find
    and the parting of the seas
and the breath as sweet & keen as death
    that was borne upon the breeze
But where they bloom those flowers fair,
        in what air or land they grow
what words beyond the world I heard
    if you would seek to know
in a boat then brother far afloat
    you must labour in the sea,
    and find yourself things out of mind
    you will learn no more from me[.']
In Ireland over wood and mire
    in tower tall and grey
the knell of Cluain ferta's bell
    was tolling in green Galway.
Saint Brendan came to his life's end
    under a rainclad sky
?Thus far he ??? by ?cloud
    and his bones in Ireland lie.

The remaining pages of initial workings are comparatively chaotic and frequently illegible, with many deletions and overlapping revisions. It is not clear if any of these represent drafting prior to text A; some are closer in content to the late text C below, and thus may be subsequent to A. For example, here (as B) are workings equivalent to A1–12.

[B] At last out of the deep sea he passed
and mist lay on the shore
and loud the sea ran under moonlit cloud
as the ?laden ship him bore
To Ireland's green woods and mires
Who comes there creeping like a ghost
a grey shadow from the deep
loud the waves run on the shore
but all else lies asleep
A boat that gleams in the mist
I see not s??? ????
and it was ??? in up the beach.

In Ireland's wooded hills and mires;
in the tower far away
the knell of Cluain ferta's bell
tolled in green Galway.
Where Shannon down to Lough Derg ran
under a cloudy sky
Brendan came back and ?had ?his end
his bones in Ireland lie.

The later workings also include matter not found in A:

A pillar vast it stood there still
with red gold rim of fire
the burning island was lifted
then broke
we looked upon its
and we looked upon Mount Doom

Tolkien subsequently revised text A, in places heavily. The following revision is written next to lines 41–46:

we turned away till it lay astern
the burning black and the gloom
Then the smoking cloud asunder broke
and we looked upon Mount Doom
    Tall as a column in High Heaven's Hall
Than all mortal works/mountains higher
the tower top of a foundered power
red and gold crown of fire

Against these, compare lines 41 and following in text C given below. This is the final version, transcribed by Christopher Tolkien from the poem's typescript, as printed in *Sauron Defeated*, pp. 261–4.

[C] At last out of the deep seas he passed,
    and mist rolled on the shore;
under clouded moon the waves were loud,
    as the laden ship him bore
to Ireland, back to wood and mire,
    to the tower tall and grey,
where the knell of Cluain-ferta's bell
    tolled in green Galway.

Where Shannon down to Lough Derg ran
    under a rainclad sky
Saint Brendan came to his journey's end
    to await his hour to die.

'O! tell me, father, for I loved you well,
    if still you have words for me,
of things strange in the remembering
    in the long and lonely sea,
of islands by deep spells beguiled
    where dwell the Elven-kind:
in seven long years the road to Heaven
    or the Living Land did you find?'

'The things I have seen, the many things,
    have long now faded far;
only three come clear now back to me:
    a Cloud, a Tree, a Star.
We sailed for a year and a day and hailed
    no field nor coast of men;
no boat nor bird saw we ever afloat
    for forty days and ten.
We saw no sun at set or dawn,
    but a dun cloud lay ahead,
and a drumming there was like thunder coming
    and a gleam of fiery red.

Upreared from sea to cloud then sheer
    a shoreless mountain stood;
its sides were black from the sullen tide
    to the red lining of its hood.
No cloak of cloud, no lowering smoke,
    no looming storm of thunder
in the world of men saw I ever unfurled
    like the pall that we passed under.
We turned away, and we left astern
    the rumbling and the gloom;
then the smoking cloud asunder broke,
    and we saw that Tower of Doom:
on its ashen head was a crown of red,
    where fires flamed and fell.

Tall as a column in High Heaven's hall,
    its feet were deep as Hell;
grounded in chasms the waters drowned
    and buried long ago,
it stands, I ween, in forgotten lands
    where the kings of kings lie low.

We sailed then on, till the wind had failed,
    and we toiled then with the oar,
and hunger and thirst us sorely wrung,
    and we sang our psalms no more.
A land at last with a silver strand
    at the end of strength we found;
the waves were singing in pillared caves
    and pearls lay on the ground;
and steep the shores went upward leaping
    to slopes of green and gold,
and a stream out of the rich land teeming
    through a coomb of shadow rolled.

Through gates of stone we rowed in haste,
    and passed, and left the sea;
and silence like dew fell in that isle,
    and holy it seemed to be.
As a green cup, deep in a brim of green,
    that with wine the white sun fills
was the land we found, and we saw there stand
    on a laund between the hills
a tree more fair than ever I deemed
    might climb in Paradise:
its foot was like a great tower's root,
    its height beyond men's eyes;
so wide its branches, the least could hide
    in shade an acre long,
and they rose as steep as mountain-snows
    those boughs so broad and strong;
for white as a winter to my sight
    the leaves of that tree were,
they grew more close than swan-wing plumes,
    all long and soft and fair.

We deemed then, maybe, as in a dream,
that time had passed away
and our journey ended; for no return
we hoped, but there to stay.
In the silence of that hollow isle,
in the stillness, then we sang —
softly us seemed, but the sound aloft
like a pealing organ rang.
Then trembled the tree from crown to stem;
from the limbs the leaves in air
as white birds fled in wheeling flight,
and left the branches bare.
From the sky came dropping down on high
a music not of bird,
not voice of man, nor angel's voice;
but maybe there is a third
fair kindred in the world yet lingers
beyond the foundered land.
Yet steep are the seas and the waters deep
beyond the White-tree Strand.'

'O! stay now, father! There's more to say.
But two things you have told:
The Tree, the Cloud; but you spoke of three.
The Star in mind do you hold?'

'The Star? Yes, I saw it, high and far,
at the parting of the ways,
a light on the edge of the Outer Night
like silver set ablaze,
where the round world plunges steeply down,
but on the old road goes,
as an unseen bridge that on arches runs
to coasts than no man knows.'

'But men say, father, that ere the end
you went where none have been.
I would hear you tell me, father dear,
of the last land you have seen.'

'In my mind the Star I still can find,
    and the parting of the seas,
and the breath as sweet and keen as death
    that was borne upon the breeze.
But where they bloom those flowers fair,
    in what air or land they grow,
what words beyond the world I heard,
    if you would seek to know,
in a boat then, brother, far afloat
    you must labour in the sea,
and find for yourself things out of mind:
    you will learn no more of me.'

In Ireland, over wood and mire,
    in the tower tall and grey,
the knell of Cluain-ferta's bell
    was tolling in green Galway.
Saint Brendan had come to his life's end
    under a rainclad sky,
and journeyed whence no ship returns,
    and his bones in Ireland lie.

Tolkien wrote this poem, initially called *The Ballad of St. Brendan's Death*, for the second part of his unfinished novel *The Notion Club Papers* (end of 1945–mid-1946). In the first instance, it draws upon the legend of Brendan, an Irish monk born around A.D. 486 – we have mentioned him already in connection with other poems (see nos. 74 and 95). Ordained a priest at the age of 26, he founded a number of monasteries, notably Clonfert (Cluain Ferta) in Galway where he is buried, and travelled around Ireland and to Wales, Scotland, and the western isles. Monks went far and wide as pilgrims for the love of God, or to escape Viking raids; but Brendan, nicknamed 'the Navigator', became famous for a voyage he and other monks are said to have made into the unknown west in search of a blessed Land of Promise. Only at the end of their voyage do the travellers find the land they seek, and then they are instructed to sail home. Brendan died around 575, and in time was canonized. His tale is recounted in the *Navigatio Sancti Brendani Abbatis* (*Voyage of Saint Brendan the Abbot*), first written down in the ninth or early tenth century and frequently retold. A popular engraved illustration of Brendan's party atop the whale Jasconius first appeared in 1621 in the *Novi Typis Transacta Navigatio* by Philoponus.

During their journey of seven years, the monks saw many marvels, only a few of which Tolkien borrowed or adapted, and rearranged, for his *Ballad*, later retitled *The Death of St. Brendan*. First was a volcanic island, in text A 'a shoreless mountain' with black sides and a crown of fire, in C a 'Tower of Doom' under a 'smoking cloud' and with a sound of drums 'like thunder coming'. In the *Navigatio* the island is 'full of smiths' forges'; Brendan hears 'the noise of bellows' blowing like thunder, and the beating of sledges on the anvils and iron', and concludes that he and his comrades are 'on the confines of hell' (Denis O'Donoghue, *Lives and Legends of Saint Brendan the Voyager* (1994), pp. 160–1). In draft, Tolkien named the place Mount Doom, alluding to the fire-mountain in *The Lord of the Rings*, but chose not to do so in later texts.

In the poem Brendan and company next come to an island 'very grassy, well-wooded, and full of flowers', with a convenient rivulet where they bring in their boat. There they see 'a tree more fair than ever I deemed | might climb in Paradise'. In the *Navigatio* this is called the 'Paradise of Birds': 'a large tree of marvellous width, but no great height, covered over with snow-white birds, so that they hid its boughs and leaves entirely'. These are revealed as angels who, having neither supported nor opposed Satan in his fall, are doomed by God to 'partially see the Divine presence' but 'remain apart from the spirits who stood faithful. We wander about the world, in the air, and earth, and sky, like the other spirits on their missions; but on festival days we take the shapes you see, abide here [on this particular island], and sing the praises of our Creator' (O'Donoghue, pp. 129–30). In Tolkien's hands, the tree is both wide and high, with 'golden boughs', and apparently covered with leaves which only seem to be white birds.

As a traveller's tale, the *Navigatio* has long captured the imagination. It may also be read as a demonstration of faith. Tolkien used only some of its details in his poem in *The Notion Club Papers*, where he merged the Brendan legend with elements of his private mythology. *The Notion Club Papers* purports to be the record of meetings of a group of like-minded Oxford academics (based on the Inklings), some of whom have dream-visions associated with the matter of Númenor, the Atlantis analogue described in connection with other poems; within its narrative, the 'Brendan' poem is composed by Philip Frankley, who 'woke up about four days ago with the thing largely fixed, and the name Brendan running in my head'. He had read the *Navigatio* 'once upon a time, years ago'. That, says 'Arry' Lowdham, another member of the club, seems to be where you got your Volcano and Tree from. But you've given them a twist that's not in your source. You've put them in a different order, I think, making the Tree further west; and your Volcano is not a hell-smithy, but apparently a last peak of some Atlantis. And the Tree in St. Brendan was covered with white birds that were fallen angels. The one really interesting idea in the whole thing, I thought: they were angels that lived in a kind of limbo, because they were only lesser spirits that followed Satan only as their feudal overlord, and had no real part, by will or design, in the Great Rebellion. But you make them a third *fair* race. [*Sauron Defeated*, p. 265]

Whereas Brendan encountered actual angels singing their praise of God, associated with Frankley's (Tolkien's) tree is 'a music not of bird, | not voice of man, nor angel's voice' but that of 'a third fair kindred', whom one would take to be Elves even if the poet had not already mentioned 'Elven-kind' in line 18.

Probably in 1955, Tolkien revised *The Death of St. Brendan*, making numerous changes while slightly reducing its length. Under the new title *Imram* (Celtic 'voyage'), it was published in *Time and Tide* magazine for 3 December 1955. We give this as D, from the printed text in *Time and Tide*, p. 1561.

[D]

At last out of the deep seas he passed,
　　and mist rolled on the shore;
under clouded moon the waves were loud,
　　as the laden ship him bore
to Ireland, back to wood and mire
　　and the tower tall and grey,
where the knell of Clúain-ferta's bell
　　tolled in green Galway.
Where Shannon down to Lough Derg ran
　　under a rain-clad sky
Saint Brendan came to his journey's end
　　to find the grace to die.

'O tell me, father, for I loved you well,
　　if still you have words for me,
of things strange in the remembering
　　in the long and lonely sea,
of islands by deep spells beguiled
　　where dwell the Elvenkind:

in seven long years the road to Heaven
    or the Living Land did you find?'

'The things I have seen, the many things,
    have long now faded far;
only three come clear now back to me:
    a Cloud, a Tree, a Star.

'We sailed for a year and a day and hailed
    no field nor coast of men;
no boat nor bird saw we ever afloat
    for forty days and ten.
Then a drumming we heard as of thunder coming,
    and a Cloud above us spread;
we saw no sun at set or dawn,
    yet ever the west was red.

'Upreared from sea to cloud then sheer
    a shoreless mountain stood;
its sides were black from the sullen tide
    up to its smoking hood,
but its spire was lit with a living fire
    that ever rose and fell:
tall as a column in High Heaven's hall,
    its feet were deep as Hell;
grounded in chasms the waters drowned
    and swallowed long ago
it stands, I guess, on the foundered land
    where the kings of kings lie low.

'We sailed then on till all winds failed,
    and we toiled then with the oar;
we burned with thirst and in hunger yearned,
    and we sang our psalms no more.
At last beyond the Cloud we passed
    and came to a starlit strand;
the waves were sighing in pillared caves,
    grinding gems to sand.
And here they would grind our bones we feared
    until the end of time;
for steep those shores went upward leaping
    to cliffs no man could climb.

But round by west a firth we found
    that clove the mountain-wall;
there lay a water shadow-grey
    between the mountains tall.
Through gates of stone we rowed in haste,
    and passed, and left the sea;
and silence like dew fell in that isle,
    and holy it seemed to be.

'To a dale we came like a silver grail
    with carven hills for rim.
In that hidden land we saw there stand
    under a moonlight dim
a Tree more fair than ever I deemed
    in Paradise might grow:
its foot was like a great tower's root,
    its height no man could know;
and white as winter to my sight
    the leaves of that Tree were;
they grew more close than swan-wing plumes,
    long and soft and fair.

'It seemed to us then as in a dream
    that time had passed away,
and our journey ended; for no return
    we hoped, but there to stay.
In the silence of that hollow isle
    half sadly then we sang:
softly we thought, but the sound aloft
    like sudden trumpets rang.
The Tree then shook, and flying free
    from its limbs the leaves in air
as white birds fled in wheeling flight,
    and the lifting boughs were bare.
On high we heard in the starlit sky
    a song, but not of bird:
neither noise of man nor angel's voice,
    but maybe there is a third
fair kindred in the world yet lingers
    beyond the foundered land.
But steep are the seas and the waters deep
    beyond the White-tree Strand!'

'O stay now, father! There is more to say.
    But two things you have told:
the Tree, the Cloud; but you spoke of three.
    The Star in mind do you hold?'

'The Star? Why, I saw it high and far
    at the parting of the ways,
a light on the edge of the Outer Night
    beyond the Door of Days,
where the round world plunges steeply down,
    but on the old road goes,
as an unseen bridge that on arches runs
    to coasts that no man knows.'

'But men say, father, that ere the end
    you went where none have been.
I would hear you tell me, father dear,
    of the last land you have seen.'

'In my mind the Star I still can find,
    and the parting of the seas,
and the breath as sweet and keen as death
    that was borne upon the breeze.
But where they bloom, those flowers fair,
    in what air or land they grow,
what words beyond the world I heard,
    if you would seek to know,
in a boat then, brother, far afloat
    you must labour in the sea,
and find for yourself things out of mind:
    you will learn no more of me.'

In Ireland over wood and mire
    in the tower tall and grey
the knell of Clúain-ferta's bell
    was tolling in green Galway.
Saint Brendan had come to his life's end
    under a rain-clad sky,
journeying whence no ship returns;
    and his bones in Ireland lie.

Paul H. Kocher provides a lengthy analysis of *Imram* in *Master of Middle-earth: The Fiction of J.R.R. Tolkien* (1972), remarking on Tolkien's selection from the *Navigatio* 'what he regards as a few central incidents from the welter of marvelous events which the Latin prose narrates with so much gusto'. Source and poem diverge, however, in the order and nature of events:

> the cloud and the volcano are both in the *Navigatio*, but there Brendan encounters them at different times and only near the end of his quest. There the cloud, in fact, is not volcanic smoke but a supernatural barrier across the surface of the sea protecting the Land of Promise of the Saints, so thickly that the monks can scarcely see one another while in it.

For *Imram*, the Cloud 'is no longer a screen around the single island of the saints but a boundary between the normal Atlantic and that paranormal area of it in which the ensuing strangeness of the poem occurs. The *Navigatio* needs no such boundary. There the entire Atlantic from Ireland westward is dotted with islands no one of which is ordinary. Its marvels have no geographical beginning' (pp. 204–6). In regard to the 'Paradise of Birds', Tolkien makes a significant change to its topography, no longer green, pleasant, sunlit, and easy to reach, but surrounded by 'cliffs no man could climb' under a dim moonlight, with only one narrow inlet. Kocher points out that the difficult landing found in the *Navigatio* on the rocky island of 'Paul the Spiritual' and the gems connected with the Land of Promise are transferred in *Imram* to the 'Paradise'.

Tolkien's description in *Imram* of the Star, which Brendan sees 'on the edge of the Outer Night | beyond the Door of Days', and of 'the round world' plunging 'steeply down, | but on the old road goes, . . . to coasts that no man knows', will mean much to serious readers of Tolkien today. Kocher, writing before *The Silmarillion* or *The History of Middle-earth* were published, interpreted it as a covert reference to Christ, who in the *Navigatio* is the light that brightens the Land of Promise, though he was also 'reminded of the one star seen by Sam [in *The Lord of the Rings*] shining high above Mordor as the sign of a transcendent beauty that its shadows can never darken' (p. 211). He was not wrong in either respect. Later, though, he might have connected the Star of *Imram* with Eärendil, the mariner turned into a star as a beacon of hope.

Writing of *Imram* in her 1991 essay 'Sailing West: Tolkien, the Saint Brendan Story, and the Idea of Paradise in the West', Norma

Roche identified the great mountain 'grounded in chasms the waters drowned | and swallowed long ago', standing 'on the foundered land | where the kings of kings lie low', as 'the peak of the Meneltarma, all that is left of downfallen Númenor'. She also compared the birds of 'paradise' to Tolkien's Elves 'exiled from the Blessed Realm after they rebelled against the Valar', and the Tree of the poem to 'the White Tree, image of Telperion'. In addition, Roche says, the island of the birds 'probably represents Tol Eressëa', in sight of Valinor as the birds may see, but remain apart from, the Divine (all quotations from p. 17).

The 'old road' and the 'unseen bridge' are arguably references to the changes to the world after the sinking of Númenor, when the Blessed Land (Aman) was removed beyond mortal reach but a Straight Road to it remained, 'as it were a mighty bridge invisible that passed through the air of breath and of flight' (*The Silmarillion*, p. 282). In *The Notion Club Papers*, the members wonder about references in *The Death of St. Brendan* to 'the round world' and 'the old road', and to 'the parting of the ways': Frankley says that 'you cannot really find or see Paradise by ship, you know', and Lowdham adds vaguely: 'Not in the High Legends, not in those that have power. No longer. And it was seldom permitted anyway, even before' (*Sauron Defeated*, p. 265).

Both Norma Roche and Tom Shippey comment on the longing of Men for an earthly Paradise, a compelling desire in fiction long before Tolkien. Shippey notes in *The Road to Middle-earth* that its expression in other poems by Tolkien, such as *The Happy Mariners* (no. 33) and *The Nameless Land* (no. 74), include a strong sense of a barrier. *Imram*, however, which Shippey describes as 'an extremely private poem by Tolkien', includes 'a resolution of hope and prohibition' in the form of the Land of Promise which was still within 'the circles of the world' (pp. 252, 253) and therefore within mortal reach, if one be worthy. In the *Navigatio* Brendan is shown the blessed isle and told that 'when the Most High Creator will have brought all nations under subjection, then will this land be made known to all His elect' (O'Donoghue, p. 175).

A1–10: Tolkien indented these lines thus.

A5: This line originally began 'back to Ireland'.

A7: Tolkien spells 'Cluain-ferta' thus in this line, and 'Cluain ferta' in l. 119.

A9: The Shannon is the chief river in Ireland, the longest in the British Isles. Lough Derg is a long lake in Galway, Clare, and Tipperary, traversed north to south by the Shannon.

A20: 'Living Land' is a reference to the earthly paradise of Celtic mythology: Tír na nÓg, the land of perpetual youth, or Tír na mBeo, the land of everlasting life.

A30: Above 'falling' Tolkien wrote a word which appears to be 'cloudy'.

A40: Tolkien considered whether to change 'pall' to 'gloom'.

A42: In writing out this line, Tolkien left gaps on either side of 'a'. 'Bye' is spelled thus.

A123: This line has defeated us, but may in fact not be coherent as written. Tolkien first wrote, then deleted, 'whence Shannon down to Lough Derg'. Other workings include 'He journeyed whence no boat returns' and, as in text B, 'and journeyed whence no ship returns'.

C47: 'Tall as a column in High Heaven's hall': Tolkien alludes to the ancient image of the mountains of Earth being the 'pillars of heaven', that is, supporting the sky.

C90: In draft, Tolkien had the monks sing the *Laudes Domini*, the psalm beginning 'When morning gilds the skies' (see poem no. 1).

D45: In the original printing of *Sauron Defeated* (1992) this line is incorrectly printed: 'We sailed then on all till winds failed'. The reading was later corrected, i.e. 'till all' not 'all till'.

D107–108: 'The edge of the Outer Night | beyond the Door of Days' recalls Tolkien's early depiction of Arda in *The Book of Lost Tales*, in which the ship of the (setting) Sun left the World through the Door of Night in the west, travelled through the Outer Dark (or void), and reappeared (rose in the east) through the Gates of Morn.

176

Be He Foe or Friend, Be He Foul or Clean (*c*. 1951)

In the *Quenta Silmarillion*, written probably in the mid-1930s, Tolkien described Fëanor's speech to the Noldor after Morgoth killed Fëanor's father, Finwë, and made off with the Silmarils:

> Fëanor was a great orator with the power of moving words. That day he made before the Gnomes [Noldor] a mighty speech that has ever been remembered. Fierce and fell were his words and filled with wrath and pride, and they stirred the people to madness like the fumes of potent wine. His anger was most against Morgoth, yet most that he said was drawn from the very lies of Morgoth himself; but he was distraught with grief for the slaying of his father, and anguish for the rape of the Silmarils. . . .
>
> He bade the Gnomes prepare for flight . . . to pursue Morgoth and war with him for ever. . . . Then he swore a terrible oath. His seven sons leaped straightway to his side and took the selfsame vow together, each with drawn sword. They swore an oath which none shall break, and none should take, by the name of the Allfather, calling the Everlasting Dark upon them, if they kept it not; and Manwë they named in witness, and Varda, and the Holy Mount [Taniquetil], vowing to pursue with vengeance and hatred to the ends of the world Vala, Demon, Elf, or Man as yet unborn, or any creature great and small, good or evil, that time should bring forth unto the end of days, whoso should hold or take or keep a Silmaril from their possession. [*The Lost Road and Other Writings*, p. 234]

A similar account is given in the later *Annals of Aman*, but there the oath is in alliterative verse, giving it a greater sense of immediacy and dramatic effect. The text below is taken from *Morgoth's Ring* (1993), p. 112.

Then Fëanor swore a terrible oath. Straightway his seven sons leaped to his side and each took the selfsame oath; and red as blood shone their drawn swords in the glare of the torches.

'Be he foe or friend, be he foul or clean,
brood of Morgoth or bright Vala,
Elda or Maia or Aftercomer,
Man yet unborn on Middle-earth,
neither law, nor love, nor league of swords,
dread nor danger, not Doom itself,
shall defend him from Fëanor, and Fëanor's kin,
whoso hideth or hoardeth, or in hand taketh,
finding keepeth or afar casteth
a Silmaril. This swear we all:
death we will deal him ere Day's ending,
woe unto the world's end! Our word hear thou,
Eru Allfather! To the everlasting
Darkness doom us if our deed faileth.
On the holy mountain hear in witness
and our vow remember, Manwë and Varda!'

The 'holy mountain' of line 15 is Taniquetil in Valinor, the dwelling of Manwë and Varda.

Tolkien wrote the *Annals of Aman* around 1951. By then he had already detailed, in his earlier 'Silmarillion' writings on the First Age, the terrible deeds of the Fëanorians in consequence of their oath, and their own terrible fates. At the last, the surviving sons of Fëanor, Maglor and Maidros, fell to the lure of the Silmarils recovered from Morgoth's crown after the War of Wrath, but found that they burned in their hands. In despair, Maidros threw himself and one of the Silmarils into a chasm of fire, while Maglor cast the other into the sea and thereafter 'wandered ever upon the shores singing in pain and regret beside the waves' (*The Lost Road and Other Writings*, p. 331).

177

Scatha the Worm (*c.* 1954)

Around 1954, while correcting the final volume of *The Lord of the Rings* for publication, Tolkien made a manuscript note for a 'further correction' desired for Book VI, Chapter 6. There, for the scene in which Éowyn of Rohan gives Merry an ancient horn, he had written: '. . . said Éowyn, and in the deeps of time it was made for our forefathers by the dwarves, and Eorl the Young. . . .' Now he changed this to its final text: '. . . said Éowyn. "It was made by the Dwarves, and came from the hoard of Scatha the Worm."'

In his note, but not in the published book, Scatha the Worm is said to have been 'of Ered Mithrin long ago'. *Ered Mithrin* is an Elvish name for the Grey Mountains north of Mirkwood, identified on *Thror's Map* in *The Hobbit* as the place 'whence came the Great Worms'. Also written on the note, along its edge, is 'Fram took it [the horn] from the hoard'. Fram, son of Frumgar, is said in Appendix A of *The Lord of the Rings* (in 'The House of Eorl') to have slain 'Scatha, the great dragon of Ered Mithrin, and the land had peace from the long-worms afterwards'.

Having written this change to *The Lord of the Rings* and entered it on a galley proof, Tolkien was inspired to compose a short poem about Scatha, whose name derives from Old English *sceaða* 'injurer, enemy, robber'. Immediately below his note is the text transcribed here as A. Above it are the words 'Scatha the Worm', but it is not clear if these were written by Tolkien as a title for what follows, or as practice for his calligraphy – his writing on this page is in several styles.

[A]

Some have great wings like the wind
Some have fire and fierce wrath,
Some have venom on their long teeth
Some have hides like armour, tails
like steel, tongues like spears, eyes
piercing bright: some are great & golden
Some are green; some are red as
glowing iron. Not so was Scatha.
He was grey, he was cold, he was
silent, and he was blind. He crawled
like a slow creeping death, too

horrible to flee from, froze Men with
fear and his icy breath, and then
crushed them, ground them, under
his long white belly.

Taking up a separate sheet, Tolkien then made a new composition (B) based on the first, with substantial change, now boldly headed *Scatha the Worm*. We have transcribed the manuscript as it stood before Tolkien marked it for revision.

[B] He was cold and long [*written below:* long and cold]
greedy of gold
and sharp bright stones
but his bed was of bones:
hands of dwarves
    and skulls of men
that he piled in his den
and licked them white.
Not for him was flight
or the high airs or the tall hills:
a wingless drake.
Not for him was fire
or battle or blazing wrath
    a slimy snake:
as a wild wind on the mountain height
as the forest
or the greenwood as a red pyre
Crawling, crushing, creeping on
like a slow death
Crushing freezing with fear
and his cold breath
Crushing and grinding
under his white belly
Dark was his dwelling
    as a vast tomb

Finally, in a fair copy (C), Tolkien incorporated numerous revisions he marked to manuscript B. For the first ten lines he uses couplets, then writes four lines in the rhyme scheme ABAB, the next four as CDED, and the final lines as FGFG.

[C]

He was blind and cold,
    but he could smell gold.
He was long and rich,
    and eased his belly[']s itch
    with sharp bright stones;
    but his toys were bones:
    hands of dwarves and skulls of men
    that were piled in his den
    licked smooth and white.
Not for him was flight:
    a wingless drake;
Not for him was fire:
    a slimy snake,
    fouler than mire,
Crawling and creeping on
    like a slow death,
Freezing with fear
    and his cold breath,
Crushing and grinding
    under his white womb;
    dark was his dwelling
    as a dark tomb.

Even here, though, Tolkien considered a final revision, in which lines 21–22 would become 'his dwelling stank | like a dark tomb'.

A4: 'Hides like armour' originally read 'armour like iron'.

A11: Tolkien circled 'slow' but made no change. He was also uncertain about the word in text B.

B6: Tolkien's writing in this manuscript is too haphazard to judge with confidence whether a line should be indented or not, except for ll. 6 (most clearly), 14, and 25.

B19: Tolkien struck through 'slow', but above it wrote 'slow', and also wrote 'slow' in the margin. It may be that his thought was to have this read 'slow slow death', but in text C the reading is, again, simply 'slow death'.

178

Wilt Thou Learn the Lore (?1954)

Tolkien seems to have begun to write *The Istari* in summer 1954, as an offshoot of a planned index for *The Lord of the Rings*. It was typical of his way of working to be attracted by a single question and take off in pursuit of an answer. In this case, the question had to do with the concern of the Valar with the fate of Middle-earth after the fall of Númenor, and the background of Gandalf. The resulting essay was too long to fit within the appendices at the end of that book, but Christopher Tolkien included it in *Unfinished Tales*; and there, one finds a related poem in alliterative verse (pp. 395–6):

Wilt thou learn the lore   that was long secret
of the Five that came   from a far country?
Only one returned.   Others never again
under Men's dominion   Middle-earth shall seek
until Dagor Dagorath   and the Doom cometh.
How hast thou heard it: the hidden counsel
of the Lords of the West   in the land of Aman?
The long roads are lost   that lead thither,
and to mortal Men   Manwë speaks not.
From the West-that-was   a wind bore it
to the sleeper's ear,   in the silences
under night-shadow,   when news is brought
from lands forgotten   and lost ages
over seas of years   to the searching thought.
Not all are forgotten   by the Elder King.
Sauron he saw   as a slow menace . . .

Here 'the Five' are the Istari, or 'Wizards'. Only three played any part in *The Lord of the Rings* – Gandalf, Radagast, and Saruman – though in Book III, Chapter 10, Saruman mentions in passing (as an insult thrown at Gandalf) 'the rods of the Five Wizards'. *The Istari* darkly explains that the remaining two, the 'Blue Wizards', passed into the East and were lost to history. 'Only one [of the Istari] returned', Gandalf, and only he remained true to his purpose.

Dagor Dagorath is the final battle at the end of the world, when Melkor (Morgoth) is prophesied to return and Manwë, chief of the

Valar, descends from his mountain. 'The long roads' refers to the paths (discussed in our comments for poem no. 74) that led to Aman in the West ('the West-that-was'), but which were removed when Númenor fell and the world was remade. The 'hidden counsel' of line 6, the final lines concerned with the 'Elder King' – Manwë – and other points mentioned in the poem are explained in the essay proper:

> Emissaries they were from the Lords of the West, the Valar, who still took counsel for the governance of Middle-earth, and when the shadow of Sauron first began to stir again [after the destruction of Númenor] took this means of resisting him. For with the consent of Eru they sent members of their own high order, but clad in bodies as of Men, real and not feigned, but subject to the fears and pains and weariness of earth, able to hunger and thirst and be slain; though because of their noble spirits they did not die, and aged only by the cares and labours of many long years. And this the Valar did, desiring to amend the errors of old, especially that they had attempted to guard and seclude the Eldar [Elves] by their own might and glory fully revealed; whereas now their emissaries were forbidden to reveal themselves in forms of majesty, or to seek to rule the wills of Men or Elves by open display of power, but coming in shapes weak and humble were bidden to advise and persuade Men and Elves to good and to seek to unite in love and understanding all those whom Sauron, should he come again, would endeavour to dominate and corrupt. [*Unfinished Tales*, p. 389]

The Istari serves to answer many questions, but the accompanying poem begs new ones. Who could have written it? It shows more knowledge than would have been available to any inhabitant of Middle-earth, but too little for those in the West. When was it written? Its reference to Gandalf having returned to Valinor ('only one returned') must postdate that event at the end of the Third Age. By having its text trail off (in line 16) in an ellipsis, did Tolkien intend it to be taken as part of a larger, 'lost' work?

179

Cat (?1956)

According to Humphrey Carpenter (*Biography*), Tolkien wrote the poem *Cat* in 1956 to please Joanna (Joan Anne), a daughter of the author's second son, Michael. She was then eleven years old. In 1962 Tolkien selected *Cat* to appear in *The Adventures of Tom Bombadil and Other Verses from the Red Book*, where it is said to be among the 'marginalia' added by Hobbits to the Red Book of Westmarch, and is one of three 'bestiary' poems with *Fastitocalon* and *Oliphaunt* (nos. 95 and 168 in the present book). Here we give the text of *Cat* as printed on p. 48 of the 1962 collection. Comments about differences in an almost identical typescript in the Bodleian Library may be found in our notes.

The fat cat on the mat
    may seem to dream
of nice mice that suffice
    for him, and cream;
but he free, maybe,
    walks in thought
unbowed, proud, where loud
    roared and fought
his kin, lean and slim,
    or deep in den
in the East feasted on beasts
    and tender men.

The giant lion with iron
    claw in paw,
and huge ruthless tooth
    in gory jaw;
the pard dark-starred,
    fleet upon feet,
that oft soft from aloft
    leaps on his meat,
where woods loom in gloom —
    far now they are,
    fierce and free,
    and tamed is he;

but fat cat on the mat
kept as a pet,
he does not forget.

The *pard* in line 17 was, in medieval lore, a distinct species among great cats, parti-coloured and with a lion's mane. Its speed and violence mentioned in the poem have their origin in bestiary manuscripts. Later, *pard* came to be used as a poetic or literary name for 'leopard' or 'panther'.

For the *Bombadil* collection illustrator Pauline Baynes produced a full-page picture of a domestic cat seeming to dream of lions with their prey, and of a fierce lion attacking a horned animal. Tolkien liked the illustration but thought that it missed 'a main point' of the poem 'in not making one of the "thought-lions" engaged in *man*-eating', as in the cat of the East feasting 'on beasts and tender men' (letter to Rayner Unwin, 29 August 1962, Tolkien–George Allen & Unwin archive).

1: In the typescript, this line began with the more personal 'Your fat cat'; Tolkien changed 'Your' to 'The'. In l. 25 the original typed reading was 'on the mat'; this was changed to 'on your mat', but in the final text 'the mat' is correct.

5: In the typescript, this line began a new sentence.

180

You Walk on Grass (?1956)

The earliest manuscript of this brief poem began with a pencilled text, which Tolkien wrote with confidence for a dozen lines before becoming unsure of its direction. We give this initial version as A.

[A]

You walk on grass with gentle tread
no flower do you bend or break
nor set to wither in your hair
its little life will take
But like a flower you breathe the air
and send it forth more sweet;
the sunlight netted in your hair,
the dews upon your feet,
the stars that look into your eyes
there shine more pure and clear
and as you pass before you flies
the shadow of our fear.

One moment as you pass
a world unstained we see / know
One moment bright as bird on wing
we hear — before you go

From line 11, Tolkien wrote revisions in blue and black inks across his pencilled text, or above or beside the lines, and also workings on the back of the sheet, many of which cannot be read clearly. He then carried some of his changes into a second manuscript (B).

[B]

You walk on grass with gentle tread,
no flower you bend or break,
nor, set to wither in your hair,
its little life will take.
But like a flower you breathe the air
and send it forth more sweet;
The sunlight netted in your hair
the dews upon your feet
the stars that look into your eyes

there live and shine more clear
and as you come before you flies
the shadow of our fear.

One moment bright as you pass and sing
bright as a swift bird on wing,
a world unstained we know
and light forgotten falls on us — until you go

For the first twelve lines, text B was a fair copy. Tolkien then began to write the second stanza as he had done the first, with an alternating, ABAB rhyme scheme:

One moment as you pass and sing
a world unstained we know,
One moment bright as bird on wing
—

The dangling dash in the fourth of these lines suggests that Tolkien intended to add 'until you go' (to rhyme with 'know'). Instead, having decided that the final lines should be a pair of couplets, he indicated that 'One moment as you pass and sing' should be relocated to precede a new text (as in B), and to clarify his intention he repeated the lines more neatly at the foot of the page.

In private notes about his father's poems, Christopher Tolkien did not hazard a guess as to the date of *You Walk on Grass*, or to the identity of the 'You' to whom it is addressed. We are inclined to think that Tolkien intended it for his granddaughter Joanna (see no. 179), who in 1956 was elected May Queen at Checkendon Primary School, Reading. We know from her own account, given at a Tolkien Society dinner, that her grandfather wrote to her on that occasion, and according to a note by the South African author Elwyn Jenkins, he also gave her a poem to honour her 'being crowned Queen of the May, with a picture of her dancing around the maypole, a coronet of flowers in her hair' ('Lord of the Letters', 2018).

A14: 'See / know' is written thus; compare 'know' in B15.

181

The Wind So Whirled a Weathercock (?1956–62)

In his preface to *The Adventures of Tom Bombadil and Other Verses from the Red Book*, which as we have seen treats the collection as if it were poems by or gathered by Hobbits, Tolkien states that the fictional Red Book 'contains a large number of verses', some of which 'are written carelessly in margins and blank spaces' (p. 7). Among these, as a good 'example of their general character', is 'the scribble, on the page recording Bilbo's *When Winter First Begins to Bite* [see poem no. 158]:

The wind so whirled a weathercock
He could not hold his tail up;
The frost so nipped a throstlecock
He could not snap a snail up.
'My case is hard' the throstle cried,
And 'All is vane' the cock replied;
And so they set their wail up.

One might expect that the seven lines Tolkien 'quoted' of this poem in his *Bombadil* volume were the extent of the 'scribble', even that they had been dashed off for the preface without an independent existence. In fact, they are only the first part of a longer work, composed at least five years before Tolkien used it for this purpose in 1962.

Largely illegible manuscript workings for the poem are found among Tolkien's papers on both sides of a compliments slip from the London office of the 3M Company, and more coherent lines are on the reverse side of a memo by D.S. Parsons, Sub-Warden of Merton College, Oxford, dated 5 November 1956. We give the latter text here, as best we can decipher it, incorporating a few revisions Tolkien made in the course of writing. He made further changes for the 1962 preface, e.g. 'weathercock' for 'weather-cock' and 'could not' for 'couldn't'.

The wind so whirled a weather-cock,
he couldn't hold his tail up;
The frost so nipped a thrustle-cock
he couldn't snap a snail up.

'My case is hard' the thrustle cried,
and 'all is vane' the cock replied,
and so they set their wail up.

Said a barn owl to a nightingale
one evening in a spinney
[']Shut down! So high up in the scale
Your voice is thin and tinny. [']
'O hoots to you!' she answered. [']Fowl!
To hear me folk who curse an owl
would gladly pay a guinea. [']

Said Master Chaffinch to his wife:
'Tee hee! just look, my darling!
Did you ever see in all your life
such a fat and vulgar starling?'
'Of course! They're all alike', she said:
'billious [*sic*] about and all ill-bred;
they're not worth two a farthing'.

Said Mrs Starling to her mate:
'That's the kind of folk I hate!
Such little prigs with beaks of tin,
so proud of being neat and thin.
The robin's wife has a vest of red
but his has only grey instead.
Do you think he can't afford it[.]
He's mean and likes to lord it
but he daren't tackle a stronger bird.
Let's peck him for being so absurd.'

That this manuscript was made at different times is evident from the first three stanzas having been written with a calligraphic pen and the fourth in biro (ballpoint). There is a difference as well in rhyme schemes: in the earlier stanzas, Tolkien used ABABCCB, but in the fourth he chose couplets (AABB etc.).

Also on this page is the following text, written in biro in the margin next to the second and third stanzas, and probably referring to the starling: 'He wobbles when he walks | and gobbles when he talks | He fights when [he] eats | and hustles all he meets'.

A *weathercock* (or *-cock*) is a weathervane, a decorative instrument, frequently in the shape of a cockerel (rooster), which when mounted on a roof indicates the direction of the wind. Tolkien alludes to this in line 6, when the cock says 'all is vane', a play on 'all is vain'. The *thrustlecock* is the male song thrush (*thrustle* and *throstle* are alternate spellings of a dialect word), which enjoys eating snails after smashing their shells (Tolkien puns on a 'hard case').

In the second stanza, the birds' argument recalls the Middle English *Owl and the Nightingale* (see no. 89), indeed the whole of the present work is in the vein of the medieval 'debate' poem, if fragmented and undeveloped. Another medieval poem of this sort is 'The Thrush and the Nightingale', in which a male thrush slanders women and the nightingale defends them; here are the two birds again, though not faced one against the other.

It is notable that, in the final stanzas, Tolkien does not present a debate so much as two married couples watching each other across a room with social disapproval, as if at a party. Mr Chaffinch thinks starlings vulgar, and indeed they are, in the sense of 'common' (the common starling is *Sturnus vulgaris*), but then so are chaffinches, with robins and wrens among the most prolific birds in England. Mrs Chaffinch, meanwhile, finds starlings 'all alike', which may be true to a casual observer: outward differences between male and female starlings are subtle. Mrs Starling seems to object to the chaffinch being relatively slender ('neat and thin'), but that is no more than its nature. Her complaint that 'the robin's wife has a vest of red | but his has only grey instead' is confusing: both male and female among European robins (*Erithacus rubecula*) have red breasts, while only the male common chaffinch (*Fringilla coelebs*) has reddish underparts, the female of the species having a grey breast. In draft workings for these lines, Tolkien wrote:

> The robin's wife has vest of red
> The chaffinch's has grey instead
> D'ye think she can't afford it

1–7: Tolkien wrote on the manuscript that this stanza was 'published', presumably after the lines were used, or about to be used, in the *Bombadil* preface.

5: This line originally began 'The case is hard'.

10: In the margin next to this line, Tolkien wrote 'tone'.

12: The owl's cry is a *hoot*, hence 'O hoots to you', a rude reply to the nightingale, but also a play on *hoot* 'to assail with shouts or sounds of disapproval, contempt, or derision', and on 'not giving (or caring) a hoot', i.e. not caring in the slightest.

15: This line originally began 'Said a'. The words, struck through, presumably would have continued 'Said a Chaffinch'. In workings, Tolkien wrote 'Said Mr [*or* a *or* Sir] Chaffinch'.

28: In the margin next to this line, Tolkien wrote '?it ?seems he could afford it'.

182

Yénion Yukainen Nunn' ar Anduine Lútie Loar! · *Loä Yukainen Avar Anduinë Sí Valútier* (1958)

In 1957 the Rotterdam booksellers Voorhoeve & Dietrich invited Tolkien to visit Holland, as an opportunity to promote *The Lord of the Rings* in the Netherlands. Publication of his work in Dutch was completed only that year, the first of its now many translations. Tolkien was unable to accept the invitation, however, until early in 1958, when he agreed to attend a reception in Rotterdam on 28 March. That evening, he was the guest of honour, before an audience of 200, at a 'Hobbit Maaltijd', a 'Hobbit Meal' or 'Hobbit Dinner'. A lengthy account of this event is given by René van Rossenberg in 'Tolkien's Exceptional Visit to Holland: A Reconstruction', 1995.

For his brief speech after dinner, Tolkien wrote a parody of Bilbo's farewell at his 'long-expected party' in *The Lord of the Rings*, and included a brief poem in Quenya, with a version in English. His voice on a recording made at the event is unfortunately none too clear, but a manuscript of the speech is preserved in the Bodleian Library. 'It is now exactly 20 years since I began in earnest to compile the history of our revered hobbit-ancestors of the Third Age', he said, and since then 'a great deal has happened. But I feel all the same that this would be the occasion for some poetry.' The preserved manuscript includes three drafts of the poem with prose translations, given here as A, B, and C. For the first two versions, we have illustrated Tolkien's revisions.

[A]

Yénion yukainen nunn' ar anduine lútie
loar! loar aluvallie [sina >] koiveanyo entule
?naina: Ai loar melle yassen ekkennen
haia palantírielya yárier andavanwe yallume
Eldalie enwa marnie endoresse luminke ar laiqavinye
[i alda >] ólar i aldar epeni ilya [*deleted:* hwi hwírie]
[*deleted:* hwire ephe epphenne p] fentane hwirya.
An [sí enn >] sí sinna 'ekkene
opá ni

Years ten and ten have down the Long River floated[,] years years never again
in my life will you come return upstream. Alas beloved years in which looking
afar I saw in the distance the ages long-departed in times when the Eldar
dwelt yet a little while in Middle-earth, and
young green grew to trees, before all ?things began to
wither in the cold breath of the wizards that have
[?no love >] know[n] all but not love, which back to ?years

Here the English text seems to be incomplete. Tolkien wrote additional Elvish workings at the foot of the page, then struck through the whole of A. He wrote text B very quickly in pencil, on the same page he used to draft the final paragraph of his address.

[B] Loa yukainen avar Anduini valútier:
i allume koivienyo eärello nantule
aluvar[.] Ai loar yassen palantírielya
andavanwe yásier — yá tenn' aldar lente
landanóresse ólaner tó sí
ilyama menta hwirya, [*added:* hondoringe] fúmenen
[*deleted:* hondoringe] istarion.

Twenty years have flowed away down the Long River which never in my life
will return from the sea. [Alas >] Ah years in which looking far away I saw
ages long past when still trees grew free in a wide country. For now all begins
to wither in the breath of cold-hearted wizards who hate the green things
?shall ??? and such lordship is destruction.

The final text among the Bodleian papers (C) is in ink, and less rough than the others only by the standard of Tolkien's handwriting. This too has deletions and additions. We have seen no evidence that Tolkien made a typescript, or a manuscript fair copy, for reading at the dinner. In reading aloud, as captured in the private recording from the dinner, Tolkien followed his text but also extemporized as the mood took him. We have described in our notes differences between the written text C and the oral version as presented.

[C] Loä yukainen avar Anduinë sí valútier:
i aluvar koivienyo eärello nantule.
Ai! loär yassen palantírienye
andavanwë yásier — yá tenn' aldar
lente landanóressë ólaner: ai tó sí
ilyama menta hwirya hondoringe fúmenen
istarion.

Twenty years have flowed away down the Long River, that never in my life
will return from the Sea. Ah years in which looking far away, I saw ages
long-passed, when still trees grew free in a wide country. Alas for now all
begins to wither in the breath of cold-hearted wizards: to know things
they break them, and their lordship is in the fear of death.

At the end of his speech Tolkien said: 'I look east, west, north, south and I do not see *Sauron*; but I see that *Saruman* has many descendants. Hobbits have against them now no magic weapons. Yet, my gentle-hobbits, I give you this toast, *ik stel U deze dronk in*: To the Hobbits. May they outlast the Sarumans and see spring again in the trees.' He had already mentioned his love of trees, and had named Saruman, who was evidently on his mind. In B11, 'wizards who hate the green things' recalls Treebeard's comment that Saruman 'has a mind of metal and wheels; and he does not care for growing things, except as far as they serve him for the moment' (*The Lord of the Rings*, Book III, Chapter 4). And in C11–12, 'to know things | they break them' recalls Gandalf's caution to Saruman in Book II, Chapter 2: 'He that breaks a thing to find out what it is has left the path of wisdom'. The verse as a whole echoes Galadriel's farewell next to the Anduin, the 'long river' of Middle-earth (poem no. 162), with sentiments such as 'the years have passed like swift draughts of the sweet mead in lofty halls beyond the West'.

A1: Tolkien wrote 'Loaron' above 'Yénion', anticipating his revision in B. A *loa* is a solar year, a *yén* 'long year' 144 solar years. *Loaron* is the genitive plural form.

B1: Tolkien wrote 'ea' above 'yukainen'.

C3: The final word in this line originally read 'palantírielya'.

C9: Tolkien read the first part of this line as 'will return for me from the Sea'.

C12: Tolkien read the later part of this line as 'their lordship they establish through the fear of death'.

183

To the University of Oxford (*c.* 1959)

Among Tolkien's papers are three manuscripts over which his son Christopher threw up his hands in despair, calling them in private notes 'scarcely interpretable scraps'. The first of these is a haphazard text which could, perhaps, be poetry, but if so, there is at least no rhyme to it – or (as may be) reason. This begins:

> There is no room for Stories in this hall
> the room is far too great and full of men
> of sound of voices saying many things

The second manuscript consists of three lines only – alliteration, at least:

> Witless I wandered walking idly
> down a busy broad street, bare to the sunlight
> through a thoroughfare

The third 'scrap', however, can (we think) be interpreted as a poetic satire of the institution to which Tolkien gave many years of his life; indeed, the scans we received of these three pages of manuscript were labelled 'To the University of Oxford', a title we have used in our heading. The first draft of the work is very rough, nearly illegible, and firmly struck through. The second amounts to a fair copy, though quickly set down and, evidently, abandoned unfinished; we give this text as A. The third – text B below – is either incomplete or reduced to eight lines only; Tolkien wrote this on the back of an invitation card from the Royal Society of Literature, for a meeting to be held on 3 December 1959. By that date, he had retired from the University of Oxford, at the end of Trinity Term 1959 (20 June), and was no longer the Merton Professor of English Language and Literature. He gave an official valedictory address earlier that month to a capacity audience. Even so, Tolkien remained connected to the institution for the rest of his life, and in 1962 and 1963 even returned to teaching, as substitute faculty while his friend C.L. Wrenn was on sabbatical leave.

[A]

So here we are for ill or good
historically clad in hood,—
like cows in clover, pigs in stye
(so those say who love to lie)
we, dons who roll in idle fat
to one another raising hat
but ought to fall on faces flat
before the young incipients
with neither learning, science, nor sense
who came it seems for domination
demonstration, copulation
filth and pharmaco potation.
What kind of new establishment
would these erect, if off we're sent?
What tyrants that their drugs bemuse,
what lords and ladies of the stews?
What teachers would assent to changes
to promulgate their mindless voices
the gas that they at second-hand
inhale from mouth to mouth

[B]

So here we are, so far so good,
though elementarily posed in hood,
with cows in clover, pigs in fat,
while complimentarily raising hat.
It looks like thunder, smells like cheese,
and automatically charges fees.
It's round the corner, underground,
but axiomatically can't be found.

These two fragments seem very much in line, at least in their sentiment or cynicism, with Tolkien's comment in a letter to his son Michael on 1 November 1963:

> I remember clearly enough when I was your age (in 1935). I had returned 10 years before (still dewy-eyed with boyish illusions) to Oxford, and now disliked undergraduates and all their ways, and had really begun to know dons. Years before I had rejected as disgusting cynicism by an old vulgarian the words of warning given me by [his teacher and mentor] old Joseph Wright. 'What do you take Oxford for, lad?' 'A university, a place of learning.' 'Nay, lad, it's a factory! And what's it

> making? I'll tell you. It's making *fees*. Get that in your head, and you'll begin to understand what goes on.' [*Letters*, p. 473]

But there are hints of fatigue also in the earlier valedictory address, given after a long career of teaching and research which surely would have felt more rewarding if not for the politics, rivalries, and bureaucracy which often attend the academic experience, not to mention the vagaries of students as they pursued (or failed to pursue) an education.

> I have heard sneers at certain elementary kinds of linguistic 'research' as mere spelling-counting. Let the phonologist and the orthographer have their swink to them reserved! Of course. And the same to the bibliographer and typographer – still further removed from the living speech of men which is the beginning of all literature. Contemplating the workings of the B.Litt. sausage-machine, I have at times dared to think that some of the *botuli*, or *farcimina*, turned out were hardly either tasty or nourishing, even when claimed to be 'literary'. But, to use a perhaps more apt simile, the twin peaks of Parnassus are approached through some very dim valleys. If scrambling in these, without any climbing, is sometimes rewarded with a degree, one must hope that one of the peaks at least has been glimpsed from afar. [*Valedictory Address to the University of Oxford*, in *The Monsters and the Critics and Other Essays*, p. 226]

'Historically clad in hood' (A2) refers to traditional academic dress. 'Incipients' (A8) are beginners, newly matriculated students. A 'pharmaco potation' (A12) is a drink with a mixture of drugs (*pharmacological*); a further reference is in line 15, 'What tyrants that their drugs bemuse'.

184

Gardeners' Secrets · *Utch! A Gardener's Secrets* (1960)

This curious late poem exists in two manuscripts, the second of them dated by Tolkien to 1960. We give the first, entitled *Gardeners' Secrets*, as A.

[A] I love them very much
 but the three-a-penny dutch
 won't tell you where the merribels are growing.

So I took a crooked crutch
 from my little wooden hutch
 and thought that I would catch 'em at the sowing.

But it's hard to deal with such:
 you may try but never touch,
  from the cock-a-leery light until the crowing;

You may claw and you may clutch,
 but you won't catch very much,
 and before you know the morning will be showing.

Then the three-penny dutch
 will drag you to your hutch,
 and you'll never see a seed that they were sowing

Tolkien marked this copy with numerous changes, as well as lines for an additional stanza or stanzas which we cannot decipher beyond a few words. The second manuscript of the poem (B), now entitled *Utch! A Gardener's Secrets*, incorporates most of Tolkien's revisions to the first version, and also includes further changes.

[B] I loved them very much,
but the three-a-penny dutch
wouldn't tell me where the merribels were growing.

So I took a crooked crutch
from my little wooden hutch,
and thought that I would catch 'em at the sowing.

But it's hard to deal with such:
one may try but never touch,
from the cock-a-leery light until the crowing;

One may claw and one may clutch,
yet never catch a dutch —
before I knew, the morrowdim was showing!

Then they mumbled double dutch,
and they dragged me to my hutch,
and I never saw a seed that they were sowing!

Three-a-penny (or *three-penny*) means 'cheap, inexpensive', but we cannot identify 'three-a-penny Dutch', unless Tolkien was thinking of flowering bulbs, an important Dutch export. *Merribel* seems a fanciful creation; written above this word in text B is *edabels*, perhaps a play on 'edibles'. A 'crooked crutch' could refer to a bent plough handle (*crutch*). *Cock-a-leery* is a dialect word for 'cockerel' (rooster), who would crow at daybreak ('cock-a-leery light') or *morrowdim*, a coinage Tolkien used as the Shire Hobbits' term for the time of dim light before dawn (with *evendim* 'twilight') in *The Lord of the Rings*.

Double dutch (*double Dutch*) means 'incomprehensible language' – in English there are many slang or dialect terms with 'Dutch', few of them having anything to do with the Dutch language or culture. The *hutch* in the second stanza would seem to be a cabinet or cupboard, from which one would fetch a tool, though in the final stanza *hutch* seems to be a place to live, in the sense of a house for a small domesticated animal – could the speaker of the poem be a rabbit?

It may be that the best one can say about this work is that it is chiefly an exercise in rhyming words ending in the sound *-utch*, hence the title on the second manuscript, and need not make perfect sense in the reading. It is also interesting to note that here Tolkien returned to the lilting AAB rhyme scheme of *Goblin Feet* (no. 27).

A11: 'But' originally read 'and'.
A12: 'And' originally read 'but'.
A13: 'Then' originally read 'And'.

185

The Complaint of Mîm the Dwarf (1961 or 62)

In our discussion of *The Hoard* (poem no. 69) we remarked that, by Tolkien's own statement in the *Tom Bombadil* collection, the 'old dwarf in a dark cave' working his fingers to the bone 'with hammer and tongs and anvil-stone', and to whose fingers silver and gold clave, recalls the dwarf Mîm in the 'Silmarillion' story of Túrin Turambar. Tolkien had introduced Mîm in *The Book of Lost Tales* as 'an old misshapen dwarf who sat ever on the pile of gold [of the dragon Glórund] singing black songs of enchantment to himself' (*The Book of Lost Tales, Part Two*, p. 113). There he is killed by Túrin's father, Úrin (later Húrin), activating a curse Mîm had placed on the hoard. In the tale of Túrin as it stood in the late 1950s, Mîm was a Petty-dwarf, whose people had once been hunted like animals by the Elves of Beleriand. The Petty-dwarves 'loved none but themselves, and if they feared and hated the Orcs, they hated the Eldar no less, and the Exiles most of all; for the Noldor [the Exiles], they said, had stolen their lands and their homes'. Mîm was now 'old even in the reckoning of Dwarves, old and forgotten. And in his halls the smithies were idle, and the axes rusted' (*The Silmarillion*, p. 204). At length, whether by design or misfortune (Tolkien was of two minds), Mîm betrayed Túrin, and finding his way to deserted Nargothrond, claimed its treasure. But Húrin, declaring that it was his son Túrin who had freed Nargothrond by slaying the dragon occupying it, and that he knew of Mîm's treachery, killed the dwarf before the gates of the city.

As will be seen, the Mîm of the present poem shares, besides his name, a few characteristics with the varying depictions of Mîm in 'The Silmarillion'. Both were Petty-dwarves; both led a hard life; both were very old; both had skill in craft; both had a love of precious things. But it is hard to fit the story given here, in which Mîm is – barring his burning anger and venomous knife – a largely sympathetic character, with any of those in Tolkien's mythology. One feels that he is badly done by indeed. He is a clever maker of beautiful objects, which are extensions of his being; his treasure chest is his 'hoard of memory and vanished years'. But Men rob him of all that, treating him like a wild beast, and then they debase Mîm's creations by making them into 'trinkets'. His is the anguish of the creative soul: 'If only I could forgive, I might still catch the shape of one leaf at least, of one flower with dew on it as it shone in the spring by Tarn Aeluin when I was young, and the skill first ran down into my fingers.' Tarn Aeluin in 'The Silmarillion' is a lake in the eastern highlands of Dorthonion.

Manuscript workings for the poem are found on two pages among Tolkien's papers, both sides of a sheet of stationery from the Hotel Miramar in Bournemouth, Dorset, where (as we have said) Tolkien often stayed with his wife, from at least the early 1950s. In these his handwriting is certainly from his later years. A draft of the first stanza of the poem is scribbled on the same page as workings for *The Mewlips* (no. 94); as far as we can decipher it, there are few differences with the final text, most notably that Mîm was originally said to be three rather than two hundred years old. On the other page are relatively legible trials for the second stanza, which we give here as A.

[A] Tink-tink-tink tink-donk donk-donk tink!
no time to eat, no time to drink!
no time for sleep! No night no day
tink-donk no time donk tink to play
But gold and [garnet >] red [*deleted:* and] silver and green,
jet and crystal

But silver and gold and small bright stones
and graven silver and wreathéd gold
and small bright stones

under my fingers open and grow
twine and twinkle and red eyes glow
in beasts and birds among the leaves

knock-chip-cut marble and bone
no time to talk, work all alone
carving, chiselling, no time to rest

The association of text A with workings for *The Mewlips* serves to date it to 1961 or 1962, when Tolkien was writing and revising poetry to make up *The Adventures of Tom Bombadil and Other Verses from the Red Book*. Was he inspired to write a separate work about Mîm – if not exactly the same Mîm about which he had written before – when he mentioned the character in his *Bombadil* preface in connection with

The Hoard? But the new 'Mîm' poem was not published until 1987, and then only in a German translation, as *Mîms Klage* (*Mîm's Complaint*), in *Klett-Cotta: Das erste Jahrzehnt 1977–1987, ein Almanach*, an anniversary volume issued by Tolkien's publisher in Stuttgart. The title in our heading, *The Complaint of Mîm the Dwarf*, is that used by Christopher Tolkien in private notes.

The rough workings mentioned above include only part of Tolkien's text. The finished *Complaint* has twenty-six lines of poetry, followed by seven paragraphs of related prose. Tolkien marked both sections for revision. Much later, Christopher Tolkien made a fresh typescript, incorporating the changes his father indicated, for use by Klett-Cotta in their 1987 volume. Here, as B, we give the text as it is in the later typescript, and have described changes from the author's original typescript in our notes.

[B] Under a mountain in a wild land
a cave opened paved with sand.
One evening Mîm stood by its door:
his back was bent and his beard was hoar;
long ways he had wandered homeless and cold,
the little dwarf Mîm, two hundred years old.
All that he had built, all he had made
with axe and chisel, with hammer and spade,
unfriends had stolen; only his life
and small tools he had saved, and a long knife
venom-edged in a sheath under his cloak
ragged and torn. Still red from the smoke
his bleared eyes blinked; for in heather and briar
stuffed in his tunnels they had set cruel fire,
driving him out, to retch and choke.
Mîm spat in the sand, and then he spoke:

Tink-tink-tink tink-donk donk-donk tink!
No time to eat, no time to drink!
Tink-donk no time donk-tink no time to play!
No time to sleep! No night nor day!
Only graven silver and twisted gold
and small hard stones gleaming and cold.
Tink-tink green yellow, tink-tink white blue:
under my fingers opened and grew
long leaves and flowers, and red eyes glowed
in beasts and birds among the brambles and tree-roots

All things that my eyes had seen, while still they were clear, while still I was young and the world dear. How I slaved to make them endure longer than memory! And they grew in my mind, and writhed under my hands, twisting and twining unto strange and beautiful patterns — always growing and changing, and yet rooted in memory of the world and my love of it. Then one day for an hour I stayed, and lifted my head, and my hands rested on the stone bench. I gazed at my work. For it had come out of Mîm, but was Mîm no longer, and he wondered at it. Jewels I looked at gleaming in the light of my little furnace, lying now on my brown hand, old, but still nimble and slim. And I thought 'Mîm was very clever. Mîm worked very hard. Mîm had a fire in him hotter than the furnace. But Mîm let it nearly all go into these things. They belong to Mîm, for without them not much of him would be left.'

So I thought how to keep them in order, like things stored in a wise memory. For they lay all about the floor, or in heaps in the corners, and some hung on pegs on the walls — like the pages of an old dwarvish book of histories that time had gnawed and winds had harried.

Knock-chip-cut! Crush-tap tam-tam-tap! Tack-tack! Wood and bone now. No time to talk. Work all alone. Planing, sawing, carving, chiselling, filing, nailing. No time to rest. So I made my great chest, with shelves and secret drawers. Guarding dragons glared at the lid, twined and trailed up from their great thorny feet on the ground. The hinges were in their sharp teeth. Dwarf-sires with axes stood beside the heavy lock. Knock-knock, tam-tap! hammer and nails tink-donk the key was made and spell-bound. Doom! The great lid was shut and my tired eyes too. Long I would sleep, with my tired head laid upon my treasure-chest, my hoard of memory and vanished years.

Did I sleep long? I know not the reckoning. The furnace fire was dead, but I was choking in smoke. Men came and took all that I had, the unmade metals that I won long ago from the rocks, the little heaps of stones; and they bore away my chest. They smoked me out like a rat, and in their scornful mercy let me run for it, like a wild thing, through the burning briars and heather about my deep house. They laughed when I trod on hot embers; and my curses blew away on the wind. My red eyes could see no path; and all I could save was a bag of small tools, and under an old cloak, ragged and torn, my secret knife, with runes of venom, in its black sheath. Often I have whetted it, spitting on the edges, till it shone under the hard stars in barren places.

So they took all Mîm's memories and the joys and twists of his mind, to make gems on their sword-hilts, rings on greedy fingers, and moons and stars, trinkets dangling on the breasts of haughty women. They bartered them for little kingdoms and wicked friendships; they lusted for them; they murdered for them, and darkened the gold with the blood of kinsmen. There is a fire in the memories of the old dwarves, and a power out of their feeling hands that drives men mad, even when they understand nothing.

But now I am old and bitter, and in my refuge in the wild hills I must labour on again, trying to catch the echo of my memories before they fade utterly. Ay, my work is still good; but it is haunted. It is not fresh, there lies a blur between me and things I would see and make, like forms and lights broken in a mist of tears. I catch glimpses of what I once made, not of what I once saw.

Dangerous they say I am, full of hate and treachery, old Mîm, the petty-dwarf. I bite with black teeth if handled, or stab in the dark, and the wound of my knife cannot be cured. They dare not come near; but shoot at me with arrows from afar, if I dare to come out to look at the sun. It was not so once, and it is not good that it is so now. The patterns grow queer and twisted and mock the world, things crawl up from a dark place, and fear grows under my fingers, not delight. If only I could forgive, I might still catch the shape of one leaf at least, of one flower with dew on it as it shone in the spring by Tarn Aeluin when I was young, and the skill first ran down into my fingers. But Mîm cannot forgive. The embers of his heart still burn him. Tink-donk donk-tink! No time to think!

A8: 'Wreathéd', i.e. twisted (as in B21).

B2–3: Next to these lines in his typescript, Tolkien typed with a red ribbon 'out of a cavern paved with sand | a stream flowed from a deep spring'. Christopher Tolkien did not adopt them as authorized changes, and indeed they seem to be only passing thoughts.

B9: 'Unfriends', i.e. enemies.

B14: In the first typescript, 'set cruel fire' read 'set the cruel fire' before revision.

B15: This line originally read, in the first typescript, 'driving him out, retching and choking'. Tolkien changed it to the current text, and to add a line (16) to form a couplet.

B17: 'Tink-tink-tink tink-donk', etc. presumably is the sound of Mîm hammering.

Prose paragraph 2: 'An old dwarvish book' read in the first typescript, before revision, 'some old elvish book'. In the margin, next to 'dwarvish', Tolkien also wrote 'or Great Dwarves'; it is not clear if he meant that 'Great Dwarves' might replace 'elvish' (struck through) instead of 'dwarvish', or if he had in mind the alternative reading 'an old book of histories of Great Dwarves'. In any case, Christopher Tolkien chose 'dwarvish' as the change in making his revised typescript.

Prose paragraph 3: In the first typescript, before revision, 'work all alone' read 'work on all alone', 'the key was made' read 'the key is made', and 'the great lid was shut' read 'the great lid is shut'.

Prose paragraph 4: In the first typescript, 'from the rocks' read 'from the earth' before revision.

Prose paragraph 5: In the first typescript, before revision, 'and moons and stars, trinkets dangling' read 'and trinkets, like moons and stars, dangling', and 'bartered them for little kingdoms' read 'bartered them for lordships and little kingdoms'.

Prose paragraph 6: In the first typescript, 'labour on again' read 'labour all again' before revision.

Prose paragraph 7: Here 'petty-dwarf' is spelled thus, without a capital letter. In the first typescript, 'it is not good that it is so now' read 'it is not good, if it is so now' before revision.

186

Ho! Tom Bombadil · *The Fliting of Tom Bombadil* · *Bombadil Goes Boating* (1962)

In our discussion of *The Adventures of Tom Bombadil* (no. 121), we mention that Tolkien labelled the manuscript of a short poem the 'germ of Tom Bombadil' and dated it to the 'mid 1930s'. Christopher Tolkien took this note to mean that the 'germ' was the precursor of the first poem to feature the character, the *Adventures*, which was composed apparently around 1931 and first published in 1934. He correctly states that his father made the first (ink) manuscript of the 'germ' late in life, and the accompanying note around the same time as the text (that is, if not at once, then shortly thereafter), but he did not address the question as to exactly when Tolkien composed the poem proper, no earlier manuscript being extant.

As we have said, although there are similarities between the 'germ' and the *Adventures*, the latter seems to have been inspired most directly by the features of the Dutch doll belonging to Tolkien's children, and by a story, or stories, about 'Tom Bombadil' their father told to them. Moreover, there is no physical evidence of the 'germ' developing into that first of the 'Bombadil' poems. On the other hand, it can be established clearly that the 'germ' was the foundation of the sequel to the *Adventures*, ultimately called *Bombadil Goes Boating*, composed in 1962 for inclusion in *The Adventures of Tom Bombadil and Other Verses from the Red Book*. A late pencil manuscript and a typescript preserved in his papers show Tolkien allowing the 'germ' – transcribed below as A – to spark a new 'adventure' for Tom, which quickly grew as he found its measure.

[A]

(Said I)
'Ho! Tom Bombadil,
Whither are you going
With John Pompador
Down the river rowing?'

(Said he)
'Through Long Congleby,
Stoke Canonicorum,
Past King's Singleton
To Bumby Cockalorum —

To call Bill Willoughby,
Whatever he be doing,
And ax Harry Larraby
What beer he [be >] is a-brewing.'

(And he sang)
'Go, boat! Row! The willows [be >] are a-bending,
reeds are leaning, wind is in the grasses.
Flow, stream, flow! The ripples are unending;
green they gleam, and shimmer as it passes.

Run, fair Sun, through heaven all the morning,
rolling golden! Merry is our singing!
Cool the pools, though summer be a-burning;
in shady glades let laughter run a-ringing!'

Tolkien seems to have chosen the names *John Pompador*, *Bill Willoughby*, and *Harry Larraby* solely for their rhythm: each surname has three syllables, like *Bombadil*, and 'Larraby' rhymes with 'Harry' (or, later, clipped ''Arry'). *Stoke Canonicorum* is the medieval name of the present Stoke Canon in Devonshire. We can find no evidence that *Long Congleby*, *King's Singleton*, or *Bumby Cockalorum* are, or were, actual English place-names, though they contain genuine place-name elements. *Long* in *Long Congleby* is derived from Old English *lang*, the length of a piece of land, and *-by* from Old Norse *býr*, *bœr* 'village, homestead'. *King's* appears as an element in English place-names, such as *Kingston*, and English town-names exist with *Singleton*. *Bumby* is a dialect word for 'marshy land, quagmire', and a *cockalorum*, or *cocalorum*, is a self-important little man –Christopher Tolkien told us that his father often used *cockalorum*, possibly to mean 'absurd, elaborate fuss'.

After the ink manuscript A came the pencil manuscript mentioned above (B), written quickly but neatly, without quotation marks or labels for the two speakers.

[B]

Ho! Tom Bombadil,
    Whither are you going,
With John Pompador,
    Down the river rowing?

Through Long Congleby,
    Stoke Canonicorum,
Past King's Singleton
    To Bumby Cockalorum.

To call Bill Willoughby,
    Whatever he be doing,
To ax 'Arry Larraby
    What beer he be a-brewing.

Row, boat, row! The [willows >] trees are a-bending,
    The reeds are leaning, wind is in the grasses.
Flow, stream, flow! The ripples are unending;
    green its gleam and shimmer as it passes.

Run, fair sun, through heaven all the morning
    a-rolling golden. Merry we are singing!
Cool the pools, though summer be a-burning;
    the shady glades with laughter are a-ringing.

Tolkien placed the third stanza of B within brackets, perhaps considering whether to change or delete it. It returned only slightly revised in the next version, a typescript (C). Tolkien now replaced the final two stanzas of B as he began to take the work in a different direction.

[C]

'Ho! Tom Bombadil,
    whither be you going
with John Pompador
    down the river rowing?'

'Through Long Congleby
    and Stoke Canonicorum,
past King's Singleton
    to Bumby Cockalorum.'

‘[Will you tell >] Tell Bill Willoughby
    to mind what he’s a-doing.
And ax Arry Larraby
    what beer he be a-brewing.’

‘Nay!’ said Bombadil.
    ‘We be only rowing,
to smell the water like;
    no errands we be going.
Let old lazy Bill
    do whatever he pleases!
There aint no beer in brew
    and there aint no cheeses
As good as there be Under-hill.
    I’ll be soon returning.
You come to my house
    when the lights are burning.’

‘Ho, ho! cocky Tom!
    It’s wet on river-bottom.
Look out for willow-snags,
    mind the weir at Shotham!’

[‘] Say less, Fisher Blue
    ere your crest be fallen
You’re bright out of doors,
    at home a dirty fellow
Go home and preen yourself
    with the bones of fishes
weed your garden-plot
    and wash [the >] your dirty dishes.
Maybe, ere set of sun
    you’ll have time to hear us,
coming home ere day is done,
    singing songs to cheer us. [’]

At the foot of the sheet for C, Tolkien typed four lines, apparently meant as a continuation:

The old Fisher Blue
    cocked his ear to listen
        heard Tom singing go
    saw the oar-drops glisten

It was at this stage that Tolkien chose to abandon whatever story he had had in mind in the early drafts, with 'John Pompador' and 'lazy Bill', and instead devised a series of episodes with sharp dialogue, such as that between Tom and the kingfisher begun in text C. He set the poem recognizably in Tom's country along the Withywindle, familiar to readers of *The Lord of the Rings*, and once again, as in that work and *The Adventures of Tom Bombadil*, he displayed Tom's assertive personality and his authority over other creatures. In a letter to Rayner Unwin, he remarked that his 'new *Bombadil* poem' – after the *Adventures* – 'for its understanding . . . requires some knowledge of the *L.R.* [*The Lord of the Rings*]. At any rate it performs the service of further "integrating" Tom with the world of the *L.R.* into which he was inserted' (12 April 1962, *Letters*, p. 446).

But the writing of this new thread did not go swiftly. Although much of the content of the poem followed on from one draft to another, Tolkien needed at least six further drafts before he brought it to its final form. Here, as D, is the beginning of the first entirely new text following the 'germ', not yet given a title.

[D] 'Ho! Tom Bombadil! whither be you going,
in that old bobbing boat, down the river rowing?'

'Maybe, to Brandywine along the Withywindle.
Maybe, friends of mine fire for me will kindle
down by the Hays-end. Little folk I know there,
kind at the day's end. Now and then I go there.'

'Take word then to my kin, bring me back their tidings.
Tell me of diving pools, and the fishes' hidings!'

'Nay!' said Bombadil, 'I am only rowing,
just to smell the water like, not on errands going!'

'Ha! ha! cocky Tom! Mind your tub don't founder!
Look out for willow-snags! I'd laugh to see you flounder.'

'Talk less, Fisher Blue! Keep your kindly wishes!
Fly off and preen yourself with the bones of fishes!
Gay king out of doors, you're an idle fellow
living in a sloven house, though your crest be yellow.
I've heard of fisher-kings tail in air a-dangling
To show how the wind is set: that's an end of angling!'

Then old Fisher Blue shut his beak and listened;
watched Tom singing go, as the oar-drops glistened.

'Hoosh! old Bombadil! 'Tis long since last I met you!
Turned water-boatman, eh? What if I upset you?'

'What? young Whisker-lad. I'd ride you down the river,
My fingers on your back would set your hide a-shiver.
I'd give your otter-fell to Barrow-wights. They'd taw you,
then heap you with golden rings. Your mother, if she saw you,
She'd never know her son, unless 'twas by a whisker.
No, don't tease old Tom, until you be far brisker!'

Under bank Whisker Lad out of water peering watched till
Tom departed
with two darkling eyes. Then under water fast back to home he
started

As in the 'germ', text D begins with a question posed to Tom, but now the speaker is identified: 'Fisher Blue', a kingfisher. Naturally it is a 'king' – the word is in its name – and it is 'gay' in the sense of brilliantly coloured, its upper plumage bright blue and its underparts ruddy. It is sometimes idle, like all birds, but when diving for a fish is swift and sure. When at home, it is indeed in a 'sloven [untidy] house', a nest burrowed into an earthen bank, lined with disgorged fish bones and other debris. In later drafts, the bird's crest is scarlet rather than yellow, and remained so until Tolkien learned that no variety of kingfisher in Britain had that feature; but to keep 'scarlet' for the sake of rhyme, he changed 'crest' to 'breast'.

The phrase 'fisher-kings tail in air a-dangling | to show how the wind is set' refers to a folk superstition which holds that a hung kingfisher's skin will turn like a weathercock. In a later draft, Tolkien changed 'tail' to 'beak'. This was, he told Pauline Baynes (see *Letters*, p. 451), a 'donnish' detail added as a private pleasure, a deliberate allusion to Sir Thomas Browne's *Pseudodoxia Epidemica* (*Vulgar Errors*) of 1646: 'That a Kingfisher hanged by the bill, sheweth in what quarter the wind is, by an occult and secret propriety, converting the breast to that point of the Horizon from whence the wind doth blow . . .' (p. 127).

Another detail of this sort is Tom's threat to 'Whisker-lad' – an otter – to give his *fell* (pelt, or skin) to Barrow-wights, who would *taw* it (make it into leather) and 'heap you with golden rings' (later 'smother you in gold-rings'). The latter is an allusion to the Old Norse story of 'Andvari's gold', in which the god Loki kills Otter (Ótr), a shape-changer who has taken otter form to swim and fish, and brings his skin to his father, Hreithmar (Hreiðmarr). Loki is forced to pay compensation to Otter's family with enough gold to cover the otter skin, down to a final gold ring to conceal a whisker.

Tom's exchanges with the kingfisher and otter are called *fliting*, from Old English *flitan* 'strive, quarrel, dispute'. Examples are found in Northern or medieval literature, such as the trading of insults and boasts in *Beowulf* between the title character and Unferth in Heorot. In the poem as developed, Tom is scolded also by a willow-wren, a swan, a group of hobbits, and Farmer Maggot. In each case, he gives as good as he gets. All of the threats uttered on both sides in fact are made in good humour; as Tolkien says in his preface to the *Bombadil* collection, 'Tom's raillery is here turned in jest upon his friends, who treat it with amusement (tinged with fear)' (p. 9). That this was to be the central idea of the poem is reflected in titles given to three of the drafts in succession: *The Fliting of Tom Bombadil*, *The Merry Fliting of Tom Bombadil*, and *The Adventures of Tom Bombadil II: The Merry Fliting*. The last of these was later reduced to simply 'II', and the title *Bombadil Goes Boating* applied only just before publication.

The kingfisher's question remained at the start of the second draft of this new thread. But with the third new draft, Tolkien inserted an introductory stanza:

> Autumn was turning brown; the West Wind was calling;
> Tom caught a beechen leaf in the Forest falling.
> 'I've caught a happy day!' he shouted to the breezes.
> 'I won't wait till morrow-year, but take it when me pleases.
> This morn I'll mend my boat, and journey as it chances
> west down withy-stream, following my fancies!'

Here Tom expresses a folk-belief that good luck follows catching a leaf before it reaches the ground. One superstition (of many) says that each leaf caught will guarantee a happy day in the following year, which seems to be the case here. Tom seizes the day, unwilling to wait 'till morrow-year', and chooses to go down the 'withy-stream', the Withywindle, the winding river bordered by *withies*, or willows (see no. 121).

With the fourth draft, a revision of the introductory lines was followed by an exchange between Tom and a willow-wren (E). For this version we illustrate changes made in the manuscript.

[E] Autumn was turning brown; the West Wind was calling;
Tom caught a beechen leaf in the Forest falling.
'I've caught a happy day!' [he shouted to >] blown me by the breezes.
['I won't >] I'll not wait till morrow-year. I'll take it when me pleases.
This [morn >] day I'll mend my boat and journey as it chances
west down the withy-stream, following my fancies!'

Little Bird sat on twig. '[Willow! >] Whillow, Tom! I heed you.
I've a guess, I've a guess where your fancies lead you!
Shall I go, shall I go, bring him word to meet you?'

'No names, you tell-tale, or I'll skin and eat you,
babbling in every ear things that don't concern you!
If you tell Willowman [where >] that I've gone, I'll burn you,
roast you on a willow-spit: that'll end your prying!'

Willow-wren cocked [his >] her tail, piped [as >] ere [he >] she went flying:
'Catch me first, catch me first! No names are needed.
Down by Mithe, I'll say. The message will be heeded.'
'I'll be there before you.
'Tis long since west-away messages I bore you.
"Down by Mithe", I'll say, "just as sun is sinking."
Hurry up, hurry up! That's the time for drinking.'

Tom laughed to himself: '[Well, I did not send her >] Maybe I will go there.
Other [ways >] paths I might take. Today Tom will row there.'
He shaved oar, patched his boat; from hidden creek he hauled her
through reed and sallow-brake under leaning alder,
then down stream he went, singing: '[Withi willo! >] Silly-sallow!
Flow withy-willow-stream over deep and shallow!'

Tolkien plays on 'willow' with the name of the wren (more commonly called the willow warbler), its cry 'whillow', and a mention of Willowman (Willow-man, Old Man Willow) from *The Lord of the Rings* and the earlier poem, and he shows the playfulness of the bird in its dialogue ('Catch me first, catch me first!').

Tom shaves his oars – makes or adjusts them with a spokeshave or drawing-knife – and mends his cockle-boat, so called because it resembles a cockle-shell. Now he meets the kingfisher and the otter, followed by an episode with 'Old Swan of Elvet-isle' who gives Tom 'a black look' and snorts at him loudly, because Tom is wearing one of his feathers (in the final version of *The Adventures of Tom Bombadil*, 'he wore in his tall hat a swan-wing feather'). It can do no more, because it is mute, or is supposed to be according to the folk belief that swans are voiceless, or at least not musical, until just before death; in fact, even the so-called Mute Swan is not wholly without voice. Here all Old Swan can do is huff its wings and hiss, and it hardly seems fair that Tom should make fun of it.

Tom comes at last to 'Withy-weir', a low dam built across the Withywindle (at the end of the poem, his boat has to be dragged over the weir when being pushed upstream). The water rushes down 'into Windle-reach', a stretch of the Withywindle beyond the weir, which leaves Tom 'spinning like a windfall', like a twig or leaf blown down by the wind. At last he reaches the hythe (landing-place) at Grindwall, where the Withywindle flowing south-west out of the Old Forest joins with the Brandywine. There Tom meets hobbits of nearby villages, Hays-end and Breredon. He calls them 'little fatbellies', alluding to Hobbits' love of food and drink, and receives three arrows in his hat for his insults. But the hobbits nonetheless take him across the Brandywine in their wherry (a light rowing-boat).

In the same draft as text E is found the most heavily worked version of the poem's final stanzas, transcribed below as F. This includes Tom's 'fliting' with Farmer Maggot, known to readers of *The Lord of the Rings* for his aid to Frodo, Sam, and Pippin at his farm in the Marish. It is also, in one of the most delightful passages Tolkien ever wrote, a celebration of the happiness of the rural life – one can't help but wonder if he was recalling the time between summer 1896 and late 1900 or early 1901, when he lived in the idyllic hamlet of Sarehole, with its mill and fields, south of Birmingham. This is followed by a gentle denouement in which the animals Tom has 'flited' – otter, kingfisher, wren, but only in later drafts the swan – have the last laugh. As the section begins, since Tom has not been met at the hythe by Farmer Maggot as expected, he begins to walk south towards Rushey and Maggot's farm, Bamfurlong, along a causeway that ran parallel to the Brandywine.

[F] Tom stumped along the road, as the day was failing.
Rushey lights gleamed ahead. He heard a voice him hailing.
'Woa there!' Ponies stopped, wheels halted grinding.
Tom went plodding [on >] past, never looked behind him.

'Ho there.' [*sic*] beggar-man! tramping in the Marish!
What's your business here? Hat all stuck with arrows!
Someone's warned you off, caught you at your sneaking?
Come back! Tell me now what it is you're seeking.
Shire-ale, I'll be bound, paid from another's pocket!
I'll bid them lock the door, and then in vain you'll knock it!

'Well, well, Muddyfeet! [For >] From one that's late for meeting
Away back by the Shire-mithe that's a surly greeting!
You old farmer fat that cannot walk for wheezing,
cart-drawn like a sack, ought to be more pleasing.
Penny-wise tub-on-legs! a beggar can't be chooser,
or else I'd bid you go, and you would be the loser.
Come, Maggot! Help me up! A tankard now you owe me.
Even in cockshut light [old >] my friends ought to know me!'

Laughing they drove away, in Rushey never halting,
though Trout inn open stood, and they could smell the malting;
[turning down >] they turned down Maggot's lane, rattling and bumping,
[*deleted:* Tom in] the old cart dancing round and jumping.
Stars shone on Bamfurlong, and Maggot's house was lighted;
fire in the kitchen burned to welcome the benighted.

Maggot's sons bowed at door, his daughters did their curtsy,
His wife brought tankards out for those that might be thirsty.
Songs they had and merry tales, the supping, and the dancing;
Goodman Maggot too for all his belt was prancing
Tom did a hornpipe when he was not quaffing.
Daughters did the Springle-ring, Goodwife did the laughing.

When others went to bed in hay, fern, or feather,
Close in inglenook they laid their heads together.
Old Tom and Muddyfeet, [sharing >] swapping all the tidings
from Barrowdowns to Tower Hills: of walkings and of ridings,
Dwarves going to and fro, Grey-elves from the Havens

on strange journeys in the Shire, gatherings of ravens,
[*deleted:* rumours in whispering trees, shadows on the borders]
of wheat-ear and barleycorn, of sowing and of reaping,
[strange >] queer tales from Bree, and talk at smithy, mill, and cheaping;
rumours in [*deleted:* the] whispering trees, south-wind in the larches,
tall watchers by the Ford, shadows on the marches.

Old Maggot slept at last in chair beside the embers
[Morning came >] Ere dawn Tom was gone: a dream that one half remembers,
[part >] some merry, [part >] some sad, [and of dark foreboding >] some of hidden warning.
[*deleted:* None heard Tom depart; footprints quickly fad]
None heard door unlocked [*deleted:* nor the gates closing]; rain showers [at >] in the morning
his footprints washed away;
[*deleted:* footprints in the lane at seven paces faded]

[*Here the text begins anew for three lines:*]

Old Maggot slept at last by the embers sitting.
Ere dawn Tom was gone; no one heard him flitting,
none heard the door unlocked

three [nights >] days his boat lay by Grindwall
and then was gone away up Withywindle.
Otter-folk, hobbits said, came by night and loosed her,
dragged her over weir, and up stream they nosed her.
Fisher king perched on bow, on thwart the wren was singing;
[*deleted:* the last leaves left the boughs and overhead went winging]
merrily [the >] his cockle-boat for Tom homeward bringing
[left it in hidden creek >] back to his hidden creek, but
oars they left behind them.
Many a day they lay at hythe for Tom to come and find them.

Tom's nickname for Farmer Maggot, 'Muddyfeet' (later 'Muddy-feet', in another draft 'Muddyfoot') reflects the moist nature of the Marish – the name is an old form of *marsh* – a district of reclaimed marshland in the eastern part of the Shire. In the Prologue to *The*

Lord of the Rings Tolkien wrote that the Hobbits of the Marish 'were rather large and heavy-legged, and they wore dwarf-boots in muddy weather'. Tom insults his friend for his size: 'You old farmer fat', 'cart-drawn like a sack' – Tom has had to walk from the Mithe while the farmer drove a pony-cart – 'tub-on-legs!' In Book I, Chapter 4 of *The Lord of the Rings* the farmer is described as 'a broad thick-set hobbit with a round red face'. His girth is further emphasized by 'Goodman Maggot too for all his belt was prancing' (F28). Tom's 'penny-wise' comment is meant to counter Maggot's 'paid from another's pocket' (for a drink of Shire-ale); later Tolkien made the connection more explicit by having the farmer remark instead 'you've not a penny'.

The name of Maggot's farm, *Bamfurlong*, is an actual English place-name, probably from *bean* + *furlong*, meaning a strip of land usually reserved for beans. The curious name *Maggot* is meant only to be 'Hobbit-like', not to refer to the English word for 'grub, larva'; in the *Lord of the Rings* Prologue it is said that 'the folk of the Marish . . . had many peculiar names and strange words not found elsewhere in the Shire'

Their social customs, however, appear to have been shared by other Hobbits, such as the *springle-ring*, a dance of Tolkien's own imagining in which the participants often leap up; in the middle of Bilbo's farewell speech in Book I, Chapter 1 of *The Lord of the Rings*, 'Master Everard Took and Miss Melilot Brandybuck got on a table and with bells in their hands began to dance the Springle-ring: a pretty dance, but rather vigorous'. *Springle* is a dialect word for 'nimble, active'.

In his letter of 12 April 1962 to Rayner Unwin, Tolkien wrote also that *Bombadil Goes Boating* 'tickles my pedantic fancy', in part 'because one of the lines comes straight, incredible though that may seem, from *The Ancrene Wisse*', a thirteenth-century guide or set of rules for anchoresses in Middle English on which Tolkien was an expert; his edition of one manuscript of the work was published by the Early English Text Society the same year as the *Bombadil* collection. The line in question in *Bombadil Goes Boating* is 'talk at smithy, mill, and cheaping' (see F39), referring to gossip heard at the local forge, grain mill, and market-place (*cheaping*, from Old English *céap* 'market'). In the *Ancrene Wisse* (or *Ancrene Riwle*) anchoresses – female religious recluses who choose to live out their lives in small cells – are warned against 'idle, unclean, and venomous' speech. It is said (readers of the work are told) that almost every anchoress has an old woman to purvey 'all the talk of the countryside . . . so that there is now a saying: "From mill and from market, from smithy and from anchor-house one hears the news."' Instead, the anchor-house, the home of anchoresses or anchorites, 'ought to be the most solitary place of all', and yet is 'spoken of together with those three places in which there is most gossip' (*The Ancrene Riwle*, translated by M.B. Salu (1955), p. 39).

The phrases 'shadows on the borders' (F37) and 'shadows on the marches' (F41) recall Tolkien's statement in the Prologue to *The Lord of the Rings*: 'At the time when this story begins . . . there were many reports and complaints of strange persons and creatures prowling about the borders [of the Shire], or over them: the first sign that not all was as it should be. . . .' This is emphasized in text F in the 'tidings' exchanged by Tom and Maggot: 'Dwarves going to and fro, Grey-elves from the Havens | on strange journeys in the Shire, gatherings of ravens'. For the final text (G) Tolkien made the 'news' seem less dire though still mysterious. In a letter to Pauline Baynes, he wrote that in contrast to *The Adventures of Tom Bombadil*, which he meant to be 'a hobbit-version of things long before the days' of the events of *The Lord of the Rings*, *Bombadil Goes Boating* 'refers to the days of growing shadow, before Frodo set out' (1 August 1962, *Letters*, p. 451). In his preface to the *Bombadil* volume, however, Tolkien says that the poem 'was probably composed much later and after the visit of Frodo and his companions to the house of Bombadil' (p. 9).

Finally, we present *Bombadil Goes Boating* in full, as it was published in the 1962 collection, pp. 17–21, 23.

[G] The old year was turning brown; the West Wind was calling;
Tom caught a beechen leaf in the Forest falling.
'I've caught a happy day blown me by the breezes!
Why wait till morrow-year? I'll take it when me pleases.
This day I'll mend my boat and journey as it chances
west down the withy-stream, following my fancies!'

Little Bird sat on twig. 'Whillo, Tom! I heed you.
I've a guess, I've a guess where your fancies lead you.
Shall I go, shall I go, bring him word to meet you?'

'No names, you tell-tale, or I'll skin and eat you,
babbling in every ear things that don't concern you!
If you tell Willow-man where I've gone, I'll burn you,
roast you on a willow-spit. That'll end your prying!'

Willow-wren cocked her tail, piped as she went flying:
'Catch me first, catch me first! No names are needed.
I'll perch on his hither ear: the message will be heeded.
"Down by Mithe," I'll say, "just as sun is sinking."
Hurry up, hurry up! That's the time for drinking!'

Tom laughed to himself: 'Maybe then I'll go there.
I might go by other ways, but today I'll row there.'
He shaved oars, patched his boat; from hidden creek he
hauled her
through reed and sallow-brake, under leaning alder,
then down the river went, singing: 'Silly-sallow,
Flow withy-willow-stream over deep and shallow!'

'Whee! Tom Bombadil! Whither be you going,
bobbing in a cockle-boat, down the river rowing?'

'Maybe to Brandywine along the Withywindle;
maybe friends of mine fire for me will kindle
down by the Hays-end. Little folk I know there,
kind at the day's end. Now and then I go there.'

'Take word to my kin, bring me back their tidings!
Tell me of diving pools and the fishes' hidings!'

'Nay then,' said Bombadil, 'I am only rowing
just to smell the water like, not on errands going.'

'Tee hee! Cocky Tom! Mind your tub don't founder!
Look out for willow-snags! I'd laugh to see you flounder.'

'Talk less, Fisher Blue! Keep your kindly wishes!
Fly off and preen yourself with the bones of fishes!
Gay lord on your bough, at home a dirty varlet
living in a sloven house, though your breast be scarlet.
I've heard of fisher-birds beak in air a-dangling
to show how the wind is set: that's an end of angling!'

The King's fisher shut his beak, winked his eye, as singing
Tom passed under bough. Flash! then he went winging;
dropped down jewel-blue a feather, and Tom caught it
gleaming in a sun-ray: a pretty gift he thought it.

He stuck it in his tall hat, the old feather casting:
'Blue now for Tom,' he said, 'a merry hue and lasting!'
Rings swirled round his boat, he saw the bubbles quiver.
Tom slapped his oar, smack! at a shadow in the river.
'Hoosh! Tom Bombadil! 'Tis long since last I met you.
Turned water-boatman, eh? What if I upset you?'

'What? Why, Whisker-lad, I'd ride you down the river.
My fingers on your back would set your hide a-shiver.'

'Pish, Tom Bombadil! I'll go and tell my mother;
"Call all our kin to come, father, sister, brother!
Tom's gone mad as a coot with wooden legs: he's paddling
down Withywindle stream, an old tub a-straddling!"'

'I'll give your otter-fell to Barrow-wights. They'll taw you!
Then smother you in gold-rings! Your mother if she saw you,
she'd never know her son, unless 'twas by a whisker.
Nay, don't tease old Tom, until you be far brisker!'

'Whoosh!' said otter-lad, river-water spraying
over Tom's hat and all; set the boat a-swaying,
dived down under it, and by the bank lay peering,
till Tom's merry song faded out of hearing.

Old Swan of Elvet-isle sailed past him proudly,
gave Tom a black look, snorted at him loudly.
Tom laughed: 'You old cob, do you miss your feather?
Give me a new one then! The old was worn by weather.
Could you speak a fair word, I would love you dearer:
long neck and dumb throat, but still a haughty sneerer!
If one day the King returns, in upping he may take you,
brand your yellow bill, and less lordly make you!'
Old Swan huffed his wings, hissed, and paddled faster;
in his wake bobbing on Tom went rowing after.

Tom came to Withy-weir. Down the river rushing
foamed into Windle-reach, a-bubbling and a-splashing;
bore Tom over stone spinning like a windfall,
bobbing like a bottle-cork, to the hythe at Grindwall.

'Hoy! Here's Woodman Tom with his billy-beard on!'
laughed all the little folk of Hays-end and Breredon.
'Ware, Tom! We'll shoot you dead with our bows and arrows!
We don't let Forest-folk nor bogies from the Barrows
cross over Brandywine by cockle-boat nor ferry.'

'Fie, little fatbellies! Don't ye make so merry!
I've seen hobbit-folk digging holes to hide 'em,
frightened if a horny goat or a badger eyed 'em,
afeared of the moony-beams, their old shadows shunning.
I'll call the orks on you: that'll send you running!'

'You may call, Woodman Tom. And you can talk your beard off.
Three arrows in your hat! You we're not afeared of!
Where would you go to now? If for beer you're making,
the barrels aint deep enough in Breredon for your slaking!'

'Away over Brandywine by Shirebourn I'd be going,
but too swift for cockle-boat the river now is flowing.
I'd bless little folk that took me in their wherry,
wish them evenings fair and many mornings merry.'

Red flowed the Brandywine; with flame the river kindled,
as sun sank beyond the Shire, and then to grey it dwindled.
Mithe Steps empty stood. None was there to greet him.
Silent the Causeway lay. Said Tom: 'A merry meeting!'

Tom stumped along the road, as the light was failing.
Rushey lamps gleamed ahead. He heard a voice him hailing.
'Whoa there!' Ponies stopped, wheels halted sliding.
Tom went plodding past, never looked beside him.

'Ho there! beggarman tramping in the Marish!
What's your business here? Hat all stuck with arrows!
Someone's warned you off, caught you at your sneaking?
Come here! Tell me now what it is you're seeking!
Shire-ale, I'll be bound, though you've not a penny.
I'll bid them lock their doors, and then you won't get any!'

'Well, well, Muddy-feet! From one that's late for meeting
away back by the Mithe that's a surly greeting!
You old farmer fat that cannot walk for wheezing,

cart-drawn like a sack, ought to be more pleasing.
Penny-wise tub-on-legs! A beggar can't be chooser,
or else I'd bid you go, and you would be the loser.
Come, Maggot! Help me up! A tankard now you owe me.
Even in cockshut light an old friend should know me!'

Laughing they drove away, in Rushey never halting,
though the inn open stood and they could smell the malting.
They turned down Maggot's Lane, rattling and bumping,
Tom in the farmer's cart dancing round and jumping.
Stars shone on Bamfurlong, and Maggot's house was lighted;
fire in the kitchen burned to welcome the benighted.

Maggot's sons bowed at door, his daughters did their curtsy,
his wife brought tankards out for those that might be thirsty.
Songs they had and merry tales, the supping and the dancing;
Goodman Maggot there for all his belt was prancing,
Tom did a hornpipe when he was not quaffing,
daughters did the Springle-ring, goodwife did the laughing.

When others went to bed in hay, fern, or feather,
close in the inglenook they laid their heads together,
old Tom and Muddy-feet, swapping all the tidings
from Barrow-downs to Tower Hills: of walkings and of ridings;
of wheat-ear and barley-corn, of sowing and of reaping;
queer tales from Bree, and talk at smithy, mill, and cheaping;
rumours in whispering trees, south-wind in the larches,
tall Watchers by the Ford, Shadows on the marches.

Old Maggot slept at last in chair beside the embers.
Ere dawn Tom was gone: as dreams one half remembers,
some merry, some sad, and some of hidden warning.
None heard the door unlocked; a shower of rain at morning
his footprints washed away, at Mithe he left no traces,
at Hays-end they heard no song nor sound of heavy paces.

Three days his boat lay by the hythe at Grindwall,
and then one morn was gone back up Withywindle.
Otter-folk, hobbits said, came by night and loosed her,
dragged her over weir, and up stream they pushed her.

Out from Elvet-isle Old Swan came sailing,
in beak took her painter up in the water trailing,
drew her proudly on; otters swam beside her
round old Willow-man's crooked roots to guide her;
the King's fisher perched on bow, on thwart the wren was singing,
merrily the cockle-boat homeward they were bringing.
To Tom's creek they came at last. Otter-lad said: 'Whish now!
What's a coot without his legs, or a finless fish now?'
O! silly-sallow-willow-stream! The oars they'd left behind them!
Long they lay at Grindwall hythe for Tom to come and find them.

As noted for *The Adventures of Tom Bombadil*, Tolkien associated both that poem and *Bombadil Goes Boating* in his preface to the *Bombadil* collection with Buckland, because 'they show more knowledge of that country, and of the Dingle, the wooded valley of the Withywindle, than any Hobbits west of the Marish [reclaimed marshland near Buckland, home of Farmer Maggot] were likely to possess. They also show that the Bucklanders knew Bombadil . . .' (p. 9). In Book I, Chapter 7 of *The Lord of the Rings* it is established that Tom had 'recent knowledge' of the Shire from Farmer Maggot, 'whom he seemed to regard as a person of more importance than [the hobbits] had imagined. "There's earth under his old feet, and clay on his fingers; wisdom in his bones, and both his eyes are open," said Tom.'

Tom Shippey in *The Road to Middle-earth* thinks that at the end of *Bombadil Goes Boating* 'there is a suggestion that the whole thing is a dream', from its phrase 'as dreams one half remembers' (G142). 'Even his [Tom's] footprints are washed away, his boat vanishes, and all that is left is a pair of forgotten oars, which by themselves mean nothing. It is as if Tom has gone back to his natural world, leaving Maggot and his mortal friends to meet their own fate, separate from his' (pp. 248–9). Bombadil is of a separate nature from mortals, though he enjoys acting like one, and perhaps it is to be expected that, as a supernatural being, he can vanish without trace. His cockle-boat, however, in the poem is explicitly left at the hythe for three days, and hobbits see it moved upstream by otters. Its oars remain at the hythe even longer, and were not 'forgotten' but 'left behind' – as it seems to us, to pay Tom back for his insults earlier in the poem. Otter's question, 'What's a coot without his legs, or a finless fish now?' is surely another way of saying that a boat is useless without its oars. How

Tom returned home without his cockle-boat is left unsaid, but he had 'other ways'.

After its exchange with Tom early in the poem, the kingfisher flies off, dropping 'jewel-blue a feather'. Tom catches it and – in the final text – puts 'in his tall hat, the old feather casting: | "Blue now for Tom," he said, "a merry hue and lasting!"' In draft F, this stanza read:

> Fisher-King shut his beak, winked his eye, as singing
> Tom passed under bough. Flash! then he went winging;
> dropped down jewel-blue a feather, and Tom caught it,
> stuck it in his old hat: a pretty gift he thought it.
> He rowed on chanting slow with oar-drops glistening;
> and all about river-folk were watching him and listening.

In another draft, Tolkien wrote 'Blue, he said, for merry days, and long may they be lasting'. In *The Adventures of Tom Bombadil* Tom wore a swan's feather, 'the old feather' now discarded. When Tom then meets the swan, he says: 'You old cob, do you miss your feather? | Give me a new one then! The old was worn by weather.' *Bombadil Goes Boating* gave Tolkien the opportunity to explain why Tom wore a swan-wing feather in the earlier poem, but 'a long blue feather' in *The Lord of the Rings* (Book I, Chapter 6) – it was a stray feather dropped by a kingfisher. But Tom's feather was already blue in the early prose story of 'Tombombadil' in the days of King Bonhedig.

A13: *Ax*, in 'ax Harry Larraby', is a dialect pronunciation of 'ask'.

C10, 12: At the end of each of these lines, Tolkien changed a question mark to a full stop.

C19: Here and later, Tolkien spelled 'aint' thus, not 'ain't'.

C28: Like most of the place-names introduced in A, 'Shotham' seems to be a Tolkien invention, perhaps from Old English **scēot* 'steep hill' + *hām* 'village'.

C30: 'Ere your crest be fallen': Tolkien is playing on the words *crest* 'feathers on a bird's head' and *crestfallen* 'dejected, dispirited'.

C32: Tolkien considered alternate text, apparently as a replacement to l. 32 with an additional three lines:

> though your crown be yellow
> yu're [*sic*] a dandy sloven
> Gay king out of doors,
> your house you cannot govern

C34: Tolkien considered whether to change this line to 'bury bones of fishes'.

D1–2: In the next draft, Tolkien revised these lines to read 'Whee! Tom Bombadil! Whither be you going, | bobbing in a cockle-boat, down the river rowing?' 'Whee!' is more bird-like than 'Ho!' if not necessarily kingfisher-like.

D5: Hays-end, where Tom knows 'little folk' (hobbits), is the end of the *hay* or boundary fence of Buckland. See further, note for F52.

D15–16: Tolkien considered whether to change these lines to 'at home you're just a sloven | fish-heads among the weeds! your house you cannot govern'.

E10: 'Tell-tale': the wren, a 'Little Bird' who offers to carry a message to Farmer Maggot, will be a proverbial 'little bird who told me'.

E16: In his preface to the *Bombadil* volume Tolkien glosses *Mithe* as 'the outflow of the Shirebourn', one of the rivers in the Shire, with 'a landing-stage, from which a lane ran to Deephallow and so on to the Causeway road that went through Rushey and Stock', two villages in the eastern part of the Shire (p. 9). The name is derived from Old English *(ge)myðe* 'junction of streams'.

F2: *Rushey*, spelled 'Rushy' on the Shire map in *The Lord of the Rings*, is named for *rush*, the marsh or waterside plant + Old Norse *-ey* 'isle', connoting a patch of hard land in a marsh.

F29–30: These lines were originally in the opposite order.

F35–36: 'Grey-elves from the Havens | on strange journeys in the Shire': the Grey-elves are the Sindar, elves who remained in the coast-lands of the North-west of Middle-earth rather than obey the summons of the Valar to pass over Sea to Aman. The Havens, or Grey Havens, are harbours from which Elven ships, and Frodo and Bilbo among others at the end of *The Lord of the Rings*, set sail into the West.

F38–39: These lines were originally in the opposite order.

F39: 'Queer tales from Bree' recalls the saying 'strange as news from Bree' in *The Lord of the Rings*, Book I, Chapter 9, meaning 'odd tidings'.

F41: 'Tall watchers by the Ford' presumably refers to the Rangers (Men) of the North who in *The Lord of the Rings* kept watch, as at the crossing of the Brandywine at Sarn Ford.

F45: 'Quickly fad': this line ends in the middle of a word.

F52: In his preface to the *Bombadil* collection Tolkien notes that '*Grindwall* was a small hythe on the north bank of the Withywindle; it was outside the Hay [the defensive hedge between Buckland and the Old Forest, at the furthest extent of the Shire to the east], and so was well watched and protected by a *grind* or fence extended into the water' (p. 9).

G43: 'The King's fisher': when Tolkien looked into the word *kingfisher* he found that it 'did not mean, as I had supposed, "a King that fishes". It was originally *the king's fisher*. That links the swan (traditionally the property of the King) with the fisher-bird; explains both their rivalry, and their special friendship with Tom: they were creatures who looked for the return of their rightful Lord, the true King' (letter to Pauline Baynes, 1 August 1962, *Letters*, p. 451).

G49: 'Rings swirled round his boat, he saw the bubbles quiver': the otter's entrance recalls that of Otter in Chapter 1 of Kenneth Grahame's *The Wind in the Willows* (1908), where 'a streak of bubbles' travels 'along the surface of the water' before Otter appears to Mole and the Water Rat. Later, he leaves with 'a swirl of water and a "cloop!"' Here otter-lad departs with a 'whoosh!' and 'river-water spraying'.

G57: *Coot* in current use refers to any black aquatic bird of the genus *Fulica*, but earlier was used generically for a water-bird, especially the guillemot (or willock), a sea-bird whose behaviour can be irrational, hence 'mad as a coot'. Tom is a 'coot with wooden legs', in the otter's opinion, because he is paddling (with wooden oars) his cockle-boat down the Withywindle, by analogy with a water-bird paddling with its webbed feet. At the end of the poem, after the animals have moved Tom's boat to his 'hidden creek' but left its oars at the hythe, otter says, 'What's a coot without his legs, or a finless fish now?' – a coot cannot swim without legs, or a fish without its fins – calling back to his earlier 'coot with wooden legs'.

G67: *Elvet* is an old word for 'swan, from Old English *elfetu*, surviving in place-names such as *Elvetham* in Hertfordshire.

G73–74: 'If one day the King returns': at the time in the history of Middle-earth when the poem is set, before the War of the Ring, Aragorn has not yet become ruler of Arnor and Gondor. *Upping* and 'brand your yellow bill' refer to an annual Crown census conducted in Britain since the twelfth century, of swans owned by the Crown, later in concert with the Worshipful Company of Vintners and the Worshipful Company of Dyers. *Upping* means 'to drive up or together', so that marks of ownership, in the form of nicks, could be cut into the swans' bills. Today, swans do not have their bills cut, but are given foot-rings with identification numbers.

G81: 'Billy-beard': presumably, Tom has a beard like that of a billy-goat.

G82: The village name *Breredon* is derived from Old English *brēr* 'briar' + *dūn* 'hill'.

G88: 'Horny goat', i.e. a goat with horns. Tom is responding to the hobbits' 'billy-beard' remark in H81.

G89: 'Moony-beams', i.e. moonbeams.

G90: 'Orks', i.e. Orcs.

G95: The river Shirebourn flows into the Brandywine. Its name is derived from Old English *scīr* 'bright, clear, pure' + *burna* 'stream'.

187

Rosalind Ramage (1963–4)

In 1963 a young *Hobbit* enthusiast, Rosalind Ramage, wrote to the author enclosing an original poem. Rosalind was the daughter of James Ramage, a former porter at Merton College, Oxford; James later read English at Oxford and became a teacher at the Cathedral School in Wells, Somerset. In his reply to Rosalind, Tolkien praised her poem, in which she rhymed *harp* with *carp*, and he remarked on the beauty of the harp as a musical instrument and of the word *harp* with which there are few rhymes. He was also inspired to write a poem of his own, in which Rosalind herself plays a role. In its first manuscript, written primarily with a fountain pen, Tolkien began 'Once Rosalind | was blown by the wind', but revised the opening in biro (ballpoint pen) to begin 'One spring afternoon'. This first version is given here as A.

[A]

[*added:* One Spring afternoon
like a balloon]
[Once >] fair Rosalind
was blown by the wind,
till she was high
up in the sky.
Then she looked down
and [she >] below saw [*deleted:* there] a town:
very small, very grey
among green it lay.
'What can that be,
I wonder?' said she.
'No use at all
for hobbits, too small
for the tiniest gnomes,
if they wanted homes
up above ground.'
She heard then a sound
from far under of bells.
'Why, that must be Wells,
where the funny clock chimes,
and at meal-times

the swans come and ring!
What a good thing,
at least I now know
where I am! I must go!
It's time for *my* tea.
But, O deary me!
How shall I get there
without ladder or stair?'
'You'll never be missed!'
the cold wind hissed:
only his joke,
for just as he spoke,
he let her gently go,
fluttering slow
like a swan's feather
in the spring weather.
Down she came without damage:
Rosalind Ramage.

Tolkien made a fair copy of his draft as revised, entitled *Rosalind Ramage* and signed 'J.R.R.T.', changing only a few marks of punctuation, and sent it to Rosalind with a letter dated 7 December 1963. On 10 December, Rosalind's mother replied with warm thanks for Tolkien's letter and poem. The fair copy manuscript of the poem, and one page of Tolkien's letter, are reproduced in McIlwaine, *Tolkien: Maker of Middle-earth*, p. 97.

Probably in late 1964, after he was asked by editor Caroline Hillier to contribute work to the anthology *Winter's Tales for Children*, Tolkien made another manuscript copy of the poem, changing line 3 to 'Little Rosalind' and writing line 19 as 'far under of bells'. He also made a typescript of the same text, but perhaps now finding the poem too short, revised and significantly enlarged it by marking up a carbon copy. A typescript of the final text (B) was in the hands of Caroline Hillier by early December 1964, together with copies of *Once upon a Time* (no. 48) and *The Dragon's Visit* (no. 107). Hillier accepted the latter two works for her collection, but not *Rosalind Ramage*.

[B]

One spring afternoon,
like a balloon
little Rosalind
was blown by the Wind
till she was high

up in the sky.
Then she looked down:
Far below was a town;
very small, very grey
among the green it lay.
'What can that be,
I wonder?' said she.
'No use at all
for hobbits, too small
for the tiniest gnomes
if they wanted homes
up above ground.'
Then she heard a sound
from far under of bells.
'Why, that must be Wells!
Where the funny clock chimes
and at meal times
the swans come and ring!
What a good thing
that at least I now know
Where I am! I must go!
It's time for *my* tea.
Mr. Wind!" said she,
'please, do you hear?'
'O yes, my dear.
No tea in the sky.
And as you can't fly,
you won't get it again;
you'll have to drink rain
and live upon air.'
'But away down there
they'll wonder where
in the world I have got.'
'They won't mind a lot:
they'll empty the pot;
more butter they'll spread
on the nice brown bread;
they'll eat all the cake.
Make no mistake,
you'll never be missed!'
So the Wind hissed.
'But that isn't fair

with me up in the air!'
She said in a fright.
'O well, all right,'
he said with a puff,
'If you've had enough
of me, we must part.
But, bless your heart,
it was only my joke!'
Then just as he spoke
he let her gently go
fluttering slow
like a swan's feather
in the spring weather.
Down she came without damage:
Rosalind Ramage!

Tolkien wrote to Caroline Hillier on 10 December 1964 that he was sorry *Rosalind Ramage* would not be included in her book, 'for the little girl's sake, though I can understand its exclusion in what is evidently going to be a tight squeeze. I thought it might seem a little below the general age-level at which you are aiming; and anyway it would take up more room in proportion to content, since printing in very short lines is necessary to its style' (Bodleian Library). The anthology was published in October 1965. That same month, on 26 October, Rosalind wrote to tell Tolkien that she had recently had her eighth birthday, had read *The Lord of the Rings* and bought his *Tree and Leaf*, and was starting to write her poems in a book.

When composing *Rosalind Ramage* Tolkien drew on memories of a visit he made to Wells, a cathedral city and market town, in April 1940. 'Funny clock chimes' refers to a fourteenth-century astronomical clock on the north transept of Wells Cathedral, with performing figures and chimes on the quarters. His other reference is to swans who live in the moat at The Bishop's Palace, Wells, and ring a bell when they want to be fed.

B38: In a manuscript addition to the carbon typescript, Tolkien first wrote 'I can have got to', then revised it to 'in the world I have got to'. In the new typescript, the final 'to' is omitted, for the rhyme with 'lot' and 'pot'.

188

Three Children (?1964)

In private notes, Christopher Tolkien calls *Three Children* a 'very curious little poem, the point of which escapes me' beyond the fact that it is based on a nursery rhyme:

> Come, let's to bed,
> Says Sleepy-head;
> Tarry a while, says Slow;
> Put on the pot,
> Says Greedy-gut,
> We'll sup before we go.

That Tolkien spent much time with this work is shown by its multiple drafts; that it is one of his later poems is shown by two of its earlier draft pages having been written on the reverse of leaves from a weekly engagement calendar for May and June 1964. Also, one manuscript page includes (distinct from the *Three Children* text) the words 'Bimble Bay', another is on a sheet bearing the typewritten title *Rosalind Ramage* (poem no. 187), and a third shares a leaf with workings for *Once upon a Time* (no. 48), all contemporary with Tolkien's submissions of poetry to *Winter's Tales for Children* in 1964. It may be that *Three Children* was an attempt by Tolkien to write a poem tailored for that collection, though in the end he did not submit it.

We have transcribed the earliest, untitled manuscript of the poem as A. The characters' names are italicized (underlined) in the original.

[A]

Three children lived upon a time
  within a little house,
and one went creeping in and out
  as quiet as a mouse:
    They called him *Slo*.

Another liked to lie a-bed
  and wander in a dream,
where trees were very tall and fair
  with blossom white as cream:
    This was *Do*.

The third was round and very fat;
    of pudding and blancmange,
of apple pie and chocolate
    and toffee she was fond:
        This was *Flo*.

Once *Do* a-nidding-nodding said:
    'The fire is burning low —
Let's rake it out and go to bed!'
    'O wait a bit!' said *Slo*,
        to drowsy *Do*.

'O wait a bit, O wait a bit!
    Don't hurry and don't fuss!
It isn't nearly seven yet
    it isn't time for us'
        so said *Slo*.

'Put on again the porridge-pot
    and get a spoon and bowl!
Come stir it up and serve it hot!
    Put on a bit more coal.'
        So said *Flo*.

    [']I am as empty as a hole
I want a bit of supper first
        Before I go to bed[.']
And yet she looked as if she'd burst —
    Her face was very red.
'No!' said *Do*. 'Woa!' said *Slo*.
    [']I am so ver-ee hunger-ee[.']
        So said *Flo*.

In five of the seven stanzas Tolkien marked changes to the names and associated pronouns: for example, in lines 15 and 30 'Flo' became 'Do' ('Do' became 'Flo' in line 10), and 'she' became 'he'. These carried into the second text (B), a fair copy and the only version to include a title, *Three Children*.

[B]

Three children lived upon a time
    who kept a little house;
and one went creeping in and out

as quiet as a mouse —
they called him *Slo*.

Another liked to lie a-bed
and wander in a dream,
where trees were very tall and fair
with blossom white as cream —
this was *Flo*.

The third was round and very fat;
of pudding and blancmange,
of apple pie and chocolate
and toffee he was fond —
This was *Do*.

Once *Flo* a-nidding-nodding said:
'the fire is burning low —
let's rake it out and go to bed!'
'O wait a bit!' said *Slo*,
to drowsy *Flo*.

'O! wait a bit! O wait a bit!
Don't hurry and don't fuss!
It isn't nearly seven yet,
it isn't time for us.'
So said *Slo*.

'Put on again the porridge-pot,
and get a spoon and bowl!
Come, stir it up and serve it hot!
Put on a bit more coal!'
So said *Do*.

'I am as empty as a hole!
I want a bit of supper first,
before I go to bed.'
And yet he looked as if he'd burst;
his face was very red.

'No!' said *Flo*. 'Woa!' said *Slo*.
'I am so veree
hungeree!'
So said *Do*.

The third manuscript of the poem is very like the second, with only small differences, such as 'and kept' for 'who kept' in line 2, and '& this was *Flo*' (with added ampersand) in line 10. In the margin are workings for changes to several lines; for the most part, these are illegible, but we can make out 'once bore yellow fruit' as a replacement for 'were very tall and fair' in line 8, and 'and lovely blossoms cream' for 'with blossom white as cream' in line 9. These revisions became moot, however, with the fourth text (C), a typescript made with a carbon copy (we suspect that Tolkien considered this work too for submission to *Winter's Tales for Children*), in which there are notable differences relative to B, and six rather than seven stanzas. Tolkien no longer emphasized his characters' names, and added an *e* at the end of each, perhaps to make it clear that all were to be pronounced with a long *o*.

[C]

Three children once upon a time
    lived in a little house;
and one went creeping in and out
    as quiet as any mouse:
        and that was Sloe.

Another liked to lie a-bed
    and wander in a dream
where no one cooked or brushed or washed
    or sewed a tiresome seam:
        and that was Floe.

The third was very round and fat,
    for puddings, apple-tart,
butter and cream and sausage-rolls
    were dearest to his heart:
        and that was Doe.

Once Flo [*sic*] a-nidding nodding said:
    'The fire is burning low.
Come! rake it out, and go to bed!'
    'O wait a bit!' said Sloe
        to sleepy Floe.
'Put on again the porridge-pot,
    and get a spoon and bowl!
Come stir it up, and serve it hot!
    I'm empty as a hole!'
        So said Doe.

'I want a bit of supper first
before I go to bed!'
And yet he looked about to burst,
and his face was very red.
'No!' said Floe.
'Woa!' said Sloe.
'But I'm so very hung-er-ee!'
said poor Doe.

This was the last finished text of the poem, but not the end of its evolution. Tolkien filled much of the margin of the typescript with new workings, then wrote additional rough drafts on six pages, becoming rougher as he progressed and in places writing ink over pencil, on paper he had convenient to hand including the calendar leaves mentioned above. We have transcribed as D, as best we can make it out, the most developed of these later manuscripts, incorporating Tolkien's marked changes.

[D]

Three people once (two fat, one thin)
lived in a little house,
And one went quietly out and in
as softly as a mouse;
and that was Sloe.

(But he or she, or Kit or Cat,
I really do not know)

Another liked to lie in bed,
dreaming in a sleep.
Where no one cooked, or washed, or fed;
or had a house to keep
and that was Floe.

(But young or old, or short or tall
there's nothing here to show)

The last was round and really fat,
for cakes and treacle-tart,
And butter cream and chocolate
were dearest to his heart;
and that was Doe.

(That he was he, is plain to see,
so on we now can go)

Once Floe a-nidding-nodding said:
'The fire is burning low.
Come, rake it out, and go to bed!'
[*deleted:* But 'Nooo, why naow?' said Sloe.]
a ????? long ago!'
Why naow said Sloe

????? noise like that

In this text, the 'three children' become 'three people' of indeterminate age. Floe seems to be the most mature: only she thinks about chores ('Where no one cooked, or washed, or fed; | or had a house to keep'); she is an analogue of Firiel in poem no. 141. Doe is now described very like Perry-the-Winkle, who 'grew so fat | through eating of cramsome bread, | his weskit bust' (poem no. 105); with the exception of sausage-rolls in text D, his favourite foods are a menu of the rich sweets children enjoy, or in literature are typically said to enjoy. Tolkien laid on a similar (if more adult) feast in Chapter 1 of *The Hobbit*, when the dwarves descend on Bilbo in the 'unexpected party': 'raspberry jam and apple-tart', 'mince-pies and cheese', 'pork-pie and salad', cakes and eggs, ale, coffee, and red wine.

And yet, if one were to look past details such as the raking of fires and the putting on of porridge-pots, Sloe, Floe, and Doe could just as easily be cats, moving quietly through the house, sleeping, eating – and mewling to be fed.

A1–2: Tolkien used a very similar opening in his earliest draft for the 1930s poem that became *The Wanderers* (no. 142): 'Three children once upon a time | lived in a cottage white'.

A2: Tolkien wrote in the margin, as a replacement for 'within', '& kept'. The different words appear in the third manuscript (only); in the second manuscript Tolkien wrote 'who kept'.

A11–14: Tolkien considered whether to change these lines to:

The third was round and very fat;
on pudding & on tart,
on apple pie and chocolate
and thus she set her heart:

A12: *Pudding* in this context is surely a sweet dessert, like plum pudding, rather than a savoury dish. The word in general (British) use also means 'dessert' of any kind. *Blancmange* is a sweet, glutinous dessert made with flavoured cornflour and milk.

A16: 'A-nidding-nodding' is a dialectal equivalent of 'nodding off'. This line originally read 'When Do was nodding there he said'. We have italicized 'Do'; Tolkien omitted an underline beneath the name, no doubt inadvertently.

A23: This line originally read 'It's hardly six o'clock as yet'.

A29: 'A bit more coal': as we write, coal is still used for heating in some homes in Britain.

D6: 'Kit or Cat', i.e. child or adult (kitten or cat); compare 'young and old', D13.

D11: 'A house to keep', i.e. to manage.

D20–21: Next to these lines Tolkien wrote in pencil: 'It was hardly to be wondered at | that he weighed a [ton >] stone'.

D25–26: In the preceding draft manuscript Doe complains 'Not yet', 'I can't'.

189

Where the Riming Rune-Tree Blows (*c.* 1964)

This late untitled poem is found in three manuscripts. None is dated, but a note by Christopher Tolkien suggests that his father wrote it around 1964, and this would seem to be confirmed by Tolkien's handwriting. The earliest of the three texts is given here as A.

[A]

Where the riming rune tree blows
    by the running water,
Where the foaming Celon flows,
    O my dearest daughter!
In the meads of Míriel
    under mists of *níva*,
by the stony stepping-well
    on the ?slopes of Hríva.
There I'd have you ever roam
    till the world is ended
though I cannot journey home
    till the world is mended:
        O my lonely daughter.

Below these lines, Tolkien wrote further workings in pencil. These include 'There I'd have you ever dwell | o'er the running water | in the meads of Míriel | O my dearest daughter', apparently an alternate opening for the poem. Most of the remainder of the pencil text is illegible, but we can make out 'by the gleaming water', 'there where I met Tinúviel', and 'where long ago Tinúviel' (followed by 'sang'), the latter of which seem to concern the poet's relationship with his wife, whom he associated with the beguiling Elf Lúthien Tinúviel (see poem no. 64).

'Riming' is an archaic spelling of 'rhyming'. *Rune* here does not necessarily mean a letter of an ancient Germanic alphabet, or more generally a secret or mystery, but perhaps most aptly a poem. *Celon* seems to refer to a river, and in 'The Silmarillion' it is indeed the name of one, Sindarin for 'stream flowing down from heights'. *Míriel* is also in Tolkien's mythology, as the name of the Elf who died after giving birth to Fëanor (on the manuscript an alternative name, 'Mirobel', is added in pencil); but in 'the meads of Míriel' it could be read as the name of a place rather than that of its dweller. We are unable to explain *níva*, apparently a place-name, underlined in the manuscript and omitted in the next version; above 'mists' Tolkien wrote 'mountain'. We do not find *stepping-well* in dictionaries, but a *steeping-well* is a pool, or vat, in which something is steeped, or soaked, such as malt or flax. *Hríva* in text A appears to be the name of a mountain, but in the later version ('Hríva's mountain') could be that of an inhabitant or resident spirit; it is likely to be related to Quenya *hrívë* 'winter'. Above '?slopes' in line 8 Tolkien wrote 'steeps', that is, slopes.

The second manuscript of the poem contains several changes relative to the first. Tolkien further revised this text slightly, then wrote out a fair copy in which he made a few additional changes, marking some of these also in the previous copy. We give the final text as B, with alterations described in notes.

[B]

Where the riming rune-tree blows,
    by the gleaming water
where the foaming Ivrin flows
    O my fairest daughter!
In the meads of Máriel
    by the flowering fountain,
by the stony stepping-well
    under Hríva's mountain,
there I'd have you ever dwell
    O my dearest daughter!
There with you I too would roam,
    if the world were mended;
but now I cannot journey home,
    till the world is ended:
        Alas! my lonely daughter!

Here 'Celon' became 'Ivrin'. In 'The Silmarillion' *Ivrin* is the name of the source of the river Narog; in one version of the story of Tuor, it is described as lying in a 'great stone basin carved by falling waters' within 'a tree-clad hollow under the hills' (*Unfinished Tales*, p. 37). One could, perhaps, in the later text of the poem conclude that 'the foaming Ivrin', 'the flowering fountain', and 'the stony stepping-well' in the shadow of 'Hríva's mountain' are three names for the same river-source. There does not seem to be a 'Máriel' in Tolkien's mythology.

Below text B Tolkien added an intriguing note: 'Lines originally arising at a time when deeply anxious about completing my work, &

at the same time in grief at an estrangement from my daughter – now mended'. We cannot place this 'estrangement' in time or explain its nature. If not for this, one could interpret the poem as a minor offshoot of 'The Silmarillion'; but because of the note, the *Riming Runetree* seems to be autobiographical, and at the time of its writing Tolkien was sad that his daughter was absent – physically or emotionally distant. 'There I'd have you ever dwell', he says, and if not, wherever she was 'with you I too would roam'. As a consequence, she must be 'lonely'; Tolkien seems to have felt loneliness himself.

Priscilla did in fact live and work away from Oxford for a number of years, in Bristol, Birmingham, and London, but that was in the 1950s, and even then she took a long holiday in Italy with her father in 1955. (She once said that her decision to go off on her own was due partly to a desire to establish herself as an individual, not only as the daughter of a well known author and scholar.) If the manuscripts of the poem were indeed written around 1964, as we and Christopher think, Priscilla and her father were then both living in Oxford. In any case, the words 'originally arising at a time' suggest that Tolkien added his note at some later date, after the 'estrangement' was 'mended'.

Around 1964, 'The Silmarillion' was the work Tolkien was most anxious to complete. It was wanted by Allen & Unwin to follow *The Lord of the Rings*, but Tolkien realized, as he told a correspondent that January, that the end was still some distance away. Complicating this effort was a series of other tasks, notably in 1964 reading proof for the volume *Tree and Leaf*.

For the cover of *Tree and Leaf* Tolkien provided one of his illustrations of the 'Tree of Tales', which he called the 'Tree of Amalion', whose many leaves and flowers signified poems and legends. It is not impossible that 'the riming rune-tree' is another expression of the 'Tree of Tales', of which Tolkien writes in *On Fairy-stories*, with its 'countless foliage . . . with which the Forest of Days is carpeted' (*Tree and Leaf* (2001), p. 56). Or, considering the imagery that follows in the poem, it may be like Castaly, the fountain of Parnassus sacred to the Muses, whose waters could inspire those who drank them with the gift of poetry. We are also put in mind of the story in the eddic poem *Hávamál*, in which Odin, chief of the Norse gods, learns the secrets of runes and mighty songs by hanging, pierced by his spear, for nine nights from a windswept tree.

B1: Tolkien hyphenated 'rune-tree' with the second manuscript.

B6: In both the second and third manuscripts, Tolkien changed 'and' to 'by', and 'fountains' to 'fountain'.

B9: In the second manuscript 'dwell' is followed by a semi-colon.

B10: In the second manuscript, Tolkien wrote this line after 'till the world is ended' (l. 14), then marked it for relocation.

B11: In the second manuscript this line has no punctuation at its end.

B13: In the second manuscript Tolkien inserted 'now' after 'but'.

B14: In the second manuscript 'ended' is followed by a full stop.

B15: In the second manuscript this line ends with a full stop.

190

Though All Things Fail and Come to Naught (*c.* 1964 or 65)

In private notes, Christopher Tolkien remarked that he could 'cast no light on this extraordinary poem'. It is, at least, from Tolkien's later years, as can be judged from his handwriting. We can try to sense what he was feeling when he wrote this philosophical complaint: it is nothing if not an expression of mood, and not one of happiness. Humphrey Carpenter wrote of Tolkien's habits late in life, after he had retired from Oxford, famous because of *The Hobbit* and *The Lord of the Rings*, his correspondence with readers demanding attention while his publisher wanted him to complete *The Silmarillion*. 'Life is grey and grim', he confessed to himself. 'I can get nothing done, between staleness and boredom (confined to quarters), and anxiety and distraction.' He wrote these comments in a diary he began soon after the death of his friend C.S. Lewis in November 1963, an event which, comparing himself to a tree, felt 'like an axe-blow near the roots' (*Biography*, pp. 241–2).

We have guessed that he composed the present poem around 1964, after Lewis's death and when the weight of fame and expectations is known to have pressed especially upon him. On 28 May 1964 he told Rayner Unwin, in one of the first letters he had written in weeks, that 'the events and troubles of this year have defeated me, and I began to think finally. [But] I am at last recovering health and some kind of mental equilibrium' (Tolkien–George Allen & Unwin Archive, HarperCollins). But then, later in 1964, he was concerned with reading proofs of *Tree and Leaf*, and was asked by Rayner Unwin about his translations of *Sir Gawain and the Green Knight* and *Pearl* (poem nos. 70, 90), and he unsuccessfully tried to write a preface for an edition of George MacDonald's 'The Golden Key', work which led to a new story, *Smith of Wootton Major*; and then, in early 1965, copyright issues with the American editions of *The Hobbit* and *The Lord of the Rings* required him to revise both of those works as a priority, and to petition his American readers to stand with him in support of his rights against what he considered piracy. Carpenter writes that Tolkien

> was saddened by the consciousness of waning powers, and wrote in 1965: 'I find it difficult to work – beginning to feel old and the fire dying down.' Occasionally this plunged him into despair, and in his later years he was particularly prone to the gloom that had always characterised his life; the very sense of retirement and withdrawal was sufficient to bring out this side in his nature,

though he also had 'the capacity for high spirits and good fellowship' (*Biography*, p. 236).

We should also mention another reason for regret that Tolkien began to have in the 1950s. He expressed it at least as early as December 1954, in a letter to a reader, Patricia Kirke, to whom he remarked that the Sacred Canon was now performed in less time than it took to read church notices. In March 1956, he wrote to Kirke of his sadness that the reform of the Catholic liturgy then underway had removed, or significantly changed, the ceremony and modes he had known for most of his life. Perhaps most notably for Tolkien, English was used increasingly in the Mass instead of Latin, to encourage more personal worship by a congregation who could speak in their vernacular; this change was made more formally in December 1963 by the Second Vatican Council, in the *Sacrosanctum Concilium* ('Constitution on the Sacred Liturgy'). Tolkien could read and speak Latin, and continued to use it in responses and prayer. In August 1967 he wrote to his son Michael that 'the Church which once felt like a refuge, now often feels like a trap. . . . I think there is nothing to do but to pray, for the Church, the Vicar of Christ [the Pope], and for ourselves; and meanwhile to exercise the virtue of loyalty, which indeed only becomes a virtue when one is under pressure to desert it.' He admitted that the church 'was not intended by Our Lord to be static or remain in perpetual childhood; but to be a living organism (likened to a plant), which develops and changes in externals by the interaction of its bequeathed divine life and history – the particular circumstances of the world into which it is set' (*Letters*, p. 553). Nonetheless, he was personally unhappy with some of the changes, and at the loss of features which to him were worth preserving.

Here, as A, we have transcribed as best we can the earliest of the three manuscripts of *Though All Things Fail*, written on two elongated leaves, as it seems to have stood as first composed. On its second page (after line 26), the text is less easy to decipher and also more heavily worked, and written around other marks not related to the poem.

[A]

Though all things fail & come to naught,
and all in vain is vainly wrought;
though Time's long lanes stretch lagging on
without a turn, till they are gone,
& all things that must walk that way
have nothing accomplished that shall stay
or be remembered — since all thought
is nothing, of nothing, unto nought;
though even negation — neither night
nor silence is — since voice nor light
nor being is ——— when such an end
is reached by all, as some pretend,
as seems solution truly fit
for an unmeaning tangle knit
by nought for nothing — yet tis hard
for one still in the high walls barred
that pen time's wayfarers so strait
not to believe at least that hate
and folly, hindrance, gasping fret
that all these lanes with anguish set
and made so weary — (never mind the end)
they were so needless grim to wend
that these at least should find some hell
some echo of remorse some fell
indelible imprint that still
when all is over linger will.

before the ?unappeasable ?he
should not before the hunted run
the wrath inexpressible
the ghost of ghosts the might have been

'tis hard indeed not still to think
that everlastingly beyond the brink
the dreadful ghost of what is done
shall not pursued for ever run
the wrath inexpressible
the ghost of ghosts — the might have been

This text is followed by three further, largely illegible lines, each of them struck through. The first reads 'At last that we nor others'.

In the second manuscript, given here as B before further revision, Tolkien changed the earlier half of the text only in small particulars, while consolidating the latter half which had been less developed in A.

[B]

Though all things fail & come to naught,
and all in vain is vainly wrought;
though Time's long lanes stretch lagging on
without a turn, till they are gone,
and all things that must walk that way
have nothing accomplished that shall stay
or be remembered — once all thought
is nothing, of nothing, unto naught;
(though even negation, neither night
nor silence is, for voice nor light
no being have) when such an end
is reached by All (as some pretend;
as seems solution truly fit
for an unmeaning tangle knit
by Naught for Nothing) still 'tis hard,
for one still in the high walls barred
that pen Time's wayfarers so strait,
not to believe at least that hate,
folly and cruelty that beset
all lanes with anguish, or with fret
and misery (never mind the end!
they were so needless grim to wend)
that these at least should find some Hell,
some echo of remorse, some fell
indelible imprint that will,
when All is over, linger still.
'Tis hard indeed not now to think
that everlastingly beyond that brink
the dreadful ghost of what was done
shall not, pursued for ever, run
from the unforgiving wraith unseen
the ghost of ghosts the might have been.

After marking further changes to text B, Tolkien made a fresh manuscript, incorporating his revisions and altering a few marks of punctuation; and on this in turn he marked two words for replacement, only one of which changed in the first typescript; we give this final version of the poem as C. The second typescript, made by Christopher Tolkien, is identical to the first except that it excludes most of five lines: see below.

[C]

Though all things fail & come to naught,
and all in vain is vainly wrought;
though Time's long lanes stretch lagging on
without a turn, till they are gone,
and all things that must walk that way
have nothing accomplished that shall stay
or be remembered — (since all thought
is nothing, of nothing, unto naught,
even negation: neither night
nor silence is, for voice and light
no meaning have) — when such an end
is reached by All, as some pretend
(it seems solution truly fit
for an unmeaning tangle knit
by Naught for Nothing), still 'tis hard
for one yet in the high walls barred
that pen Time's wayfarers so strait,
not to believe at least that hate,
folly, and cruelty that beset
all lanes with anguish or with fret
and misery — never mind the End!
the way is needless grim to wend —
that these at least shall find a Hell
beyond Oblivion, some fell
indelible imprint that will,
when All is over, linger still.
    'Tis hard indeed not to believe
that endlessly without reprieve
the dreadful ghost of What-is-done
shall still pursued for ever run
from the remorseless wraith unseen,
the Ghost of Ghosts, the Might-have-been.

When typing text C, Tolkien seems to have overlooked most of lines 7–11, from '(since all thought' to 'no meaning have', and instead added them at the foot of the page, repeating there the final words of line 11. Christopher Tolkien interpreted a pencil mark his father lightly drew through these appended lines to mean that they were to be deleted from the final poem, hence Christopher omitted them from the second typescript. But enlargement of the first typescript reveals a faint insertion mark in line 7, indicating that the lines typed at the foot of the page, themselves indicated by a pencil stroke, were not to be deleted but restored to their intended place.

A8: 'Nought' is spelled thus here in A; in B Tolkien changed this to 'naught'. Throughout his writing, he used both forms (as shown in the glossary for the present book), both words meaning 'nothing', and both derived from Old English *nawiht* or *nowiht*. Some writers use *nought* strictly to mean the numeral zero, but in general practice there is no distinction.

A11: The dash in this line is especially long in the original.

A30: A 'might have been' (C32, 'Might-have-been') is something which might have happened in different circumstances. The words are usually said with regret that one has not made a different choice or choices, supposing that the alternate outcome would be better than what actually occurred.

B9: Tolkien marked 'though' to be changed to 'not'; in the third manuscript neither word was used, and the line begins 'even negation', as later in C.

B11: Tolkien considered whether to change 'no being have' to 'not being is'.

B15: Tolkien considered whether to change 'still' to 'yet'.

B19–20: Tolkien replaced these lines in the course of writing. Previously they read 'and folly, hindrance, the gasping fret | that all these lanes with anguish set'.

C11: Tolkien changed 'being' to 'meaning' in the typescript.

C22: Tolkien changed 'they were' to 'they are' in the third manuscript, then to 'the way is' in the typescript.

C24: Tolkien changed 'some echo of remorse' to 'beyond Oblivion' in the third manuscript (the revision is marked on the second manuscript as 'beyond oblivion').

C27: Tolkien changed 'not now to think' to 'not to believe' in the third manuscript.

C30: Tolkien changed 'shall not' to 'shall still' in the typescript.

C31: Tolkien changed 'the unforgiving wraith' to 'the remorseless wraith' in the third manuscript.

191

No Longer Fear Champagne (1966)

This poem of seven lines, with no formal title, is found in a manuscript as well as a typescript. The latter, preserved in single ribbon and carbon copies, appears with *My Heart Is Not in This Land Where I Live* (no. 192). We give first (A) the manuscript text.

[A]

No longer fear champagne,
nor burgundy, nor brandy!
From port do not refrain!
Take anything that's handy,
light, sparkling, or heady:
on your eyes will fall no mist,
your legs will still be steady,
if you wear an amethyst.

The typescript text (B) is almost identical to A.

[B]

No longer fear champagne,
nor burgundy, nor brandy!
From port do not refrain!
Take anything that's handy,
light, sparkling, or heady!
On your eyes will fall no mist,
your legs will still be steady,
if you wear an amethyst.

On the manuscript, Tolkien added a note in pencil: 'March 1966. Verses included in jewel-case containing an amethyst brooch (a gift given at our Golden Wedding Feast in Merton College March 22 1966 to Marjorie Incledon)'. A similar note appears on the ribbon copy of the typescript. In private notes, Christopher Tolkien commented that Marjorie Incledon was his father's 'much-loved first cousin. The reference of this poem is to the etymology of the word *amethyst*, Greek negative *a-* and *methustos* 'drunk' from *methustein* 'to intoxicate' (*methis* 'wine'); the amethyst was believed once upon a time to prevent intoxication.'

192

My Heart Is Not in This Land Where I Live (?1966)

This brief work is poetry or prose, depending on how it is presented. It is found in two manuscripts as well as a typescript with *No Longer Fear Champagne* (see no. 191). Probably the earlier of the manuscripts (A) is written with a fountain pen in broken lines, as poetry.

[A] My heart is not in this land where I live:
I am far from home.
I have friends that are dear to me; but
under their voices are echoes, and
beyond their faces are shadows of the
land that was my home.
Longing is on me, for those that I have
lost; and for fields that I shall not
see again: they have been destroyed,
but I cannot forget my home.
Not miles, nor leagues, nor wide waters
lie between us, but days upon days,
years upon years: a journey none
can retrace; and nowhere now in
this world can I find my home.

In its other manuscript, in green biro (ballpoint pen), and in the typescript (B) Tolkien wrote a version of these words, with small differences relative to A, as continuous prose.

[B] My heart is not in this land where I live: I am so very far from home. The people are dear to me, but under their voices are echoes, and beyond their faces are shadows of the land that was my home. Longing is on me for those that I have lost, and for fields that I shall not see again, for my home that I cannot forget. Not miles, nor leagues, nor wide waters lie between us, but days upon days, years upon years, a journey none can retrace; and nowhere now in this world can I find my home.

The text of the prose manuscript differs slightly from that of the typescript, in that 'longing is on me' reads 'longing has come upon me'; 'lie between us' reads merely 'lie between', there is no comma after 'days upon days', and 'retrace' is followed by a comma rather than a semi-colon.

Below the text on the ribbon typescript, probably at a later date, Tolkien wrote: 'for they have been destroyed & the machines have ?destroyed my home'. But at the foot of the carbon typescript is 'for fields that are blasted & for trees that are felled'. To the manuscript text, Tolkien later added an explanatory note, dated '*c.* 1966': 'Lament of an old man for the fair country of his childhood, which has now been utterly destroyed beyond recognition.' The landscape of England had indeed changed greatly since Tolkien was a boy. He recognized this at least by 1933, when he revisited Sarehole, the hamlet near Birmingham where he had lived as a child, and found that much that he had thought idyllic had been lost to urban growth. Military appropriations during the 1939–45 war had also scarred the land: 'The heart has gone out of the Little Kingdom, and the woods and plains are aerodromes and bomb-practice targets', he wrote in 1945, using his name for the part of Oxfordshire in which his story *Farmer Giles of Ham* is set (letter to Stanley Unwin, *c.* 18 March 1945, *Letters*, p. 165).

193

As You Must Admit (?1966)

As You Must Admit seems to be no more than it appears, a work of nonsense made for no more than the pleasure of its words and rhymes. It is found in Tolkien's papers in two manuscripts, the first on two pages, the second on one; neither bears a title. Because the second of these, a fair copy, bears a close resemblance to the earlier copies of *No Longer Fear Champagne* and *My Heart Is Not in This Land Where I Live* (nos. 191, 192), we have assigned the present work also to 1966, if with a query. The first page of its first manuscript is in red and green biro (ballpoint pen), written quickly and clearly with exuberance, but Tolkien wrote the second page with a fountain pen, which may suggest that there was a gap of time between composing one half of the poem (to 'It's very jolly too for the soldier', line 17) and picking it up again.

Each text is very similar to the other, but they differ sufficiently that we have transcribed them both in full, as A and B. In doing so, we have had to make a number of decisions as to whether Tolkien intended a line to be indented, and by how much, as his spacing in these manuscripts is very subtle.

[A]

As you must admit,
    when the captions fit,
it's very jolly too for the soldier:
Away, away from Horniman's bay
with the tinfoil on his shoulder!
Let us call a halt
    by the barrel of salt,
    before we all get older —
Down, down, in Corrigan's town,
    where the marble houses moulder.
So up with your hand
    and start the band
with the cake and the candle-holder
Never say die to a piece of pie,
As I have always told yer!
Away away! from Horniman's bay
    it's very jolly too for the soldier.

Now come what may,
& whatever you say,
the leather-foot can't go further:
Around and round without touching the ground
is simply wilful murther!
So hang, let hang the orang-outang!
for what could be absurder?
Let the trees go blue & ooze with glue,
if I gird you with my girder.
[I'll >] You'll see [you >] me through,
& I'll see you,
And friendship can't go further.
So let them hang the orang-outang
for a capital capital murder!

[B] As you must admit,
if the captions fit,
it's very jolly too for the soldier:
away, away from Horniman's Bay
with the tinfoil on his shoulder!
Let us call a halt
by the barrel of salt,
before we all get older,
down, down on the Corrigan's town,
where the marble houses moulder.
So up with your hand
and start the band
with the cake and the candle-holder!
Never say die to a piece of pie,
as I have always told yer'.
Away, away, from Horniman's Bay
it's very jolly too for the soldier.

Now come what may
& whatever you say,
a leather-foot can't go further:
around and round without touching the ground
is simply wilful murther.
So hang, let hang the orang-outang!
For what could be absurder?
Let the trees go blue and ooze with glue,

if I gird you with my girder,
  You'll see me through,
  and I'll see you;
and friendship can't go further.
But why then hang the orang-outang
  for a capital, capital murder?

One could become exhausted trying to explain such a work. Phrases such as 'very jolly too for the soldier' and 'tinfoil on his shoulder' seem as if they should be lyrics for popular songs, and 'leather-foot' (a soldier with leather boots?) and 'gird you with my girder' (strike with a heavy blow?) candidates for a dictionary of slang. But Tolkien was inventive, and here as elsewhere we suspect that he was giving his imagination free rein while accommodating the needs of his rhymes and alliteration.

'Town' and 'Bay' (originally uncapitalized 'bay'), for example, work well as internal rhymes for 'down' and 'away', let alone – if more outlandish – 'orang-outang' (from the Malay for 'wild man') with 'hang'. There may or may not have been specific sources for 'Corrigan' or 'Horniman', though the first is in Breton folklore (see poem no. 116), and the second was (and is still) a brand of tea. 'Yer' (line 15) is a dialect pronunciation of *you*, and 'murther' (line 22) an archaic spelling of *murder*. A *capital murder* (line 31) is a statutory offence, defined as killing with aggravated circumstances, but Tolkien is also playing on *capital* 'splendid'.

194

'At Last the Time Has Come,' He Said (?1966)

Tolkien wrote the first manuscript of this poem in a rough hand on a scrap torn from a leaf of discarded examination paper. We give its text as A, as it was first set down.

[A]

'At last the time has come,' he said,
'when we are all at sea;
for you are baking gingerbread,
while I am boiling tea!
The world will soon be nine days old
and near the end of wonder,
and all the surface will be sold
for songs or something under.
Then where will little Billy sit
and keep his feet from frost,
while Uncle makes a song of it,
and counts the bitter cost?'
'Right here, right here!' then Billy cried.
[']My feet are in the flame;
though o'er my head go time and tide
I still shall keep my name
I still shall bake or dream I bake
and call for pandemain
Though sea may roar and earth may quake,
I shall not cry in vain

Tolkien marked this text lightly for revision, then made a fair copy (B) which incorporates his changes. Like manuscript A, it has no formal title.

[B]

'At last the time has come,' he said,
'when we are all at sea,
while you are baking gingerbread,
and I am boiling tea!
The world will soon be nine days old,
and near the end of wonder,
and all the surface will be sold

for songs or something under.
Then where will little Billy sit
and keep his feet from frost,
while Uncle makes a song of it,
and counts the bitter cost?'
'Right here, right here!' then Billy cried,
[']my feet are in the flame!
Though over me flow time and tide,
I still shall keep my name;
I still shall bake, or dream I bake,
for you the pandemain;
though sea may roar and earth may quake,
you will not cry in vain.'

'At Last the Time Has Come' immediately recalls 'The Walrus and the Carpenter' from *Through the Looking-glass and What Alice Found There.*

'The time has come,' the Walrus said,
'To talk of many things:
Of shoes — and ships — and sealing-wax —
Of cabbages — and kings —
And why the sea is boiling hot —
And whether pigs have wings.'

But although the present work shares a rhythm and a selection of words with Lewis Carroll's poem, it seems to be more satire than nonsense. The lightness of tone with which Tolkien begins quickly ends, as 'he' begins to speak of the world becoming 'nine days old, | and near the end of wonder', presumably a play on 'nine days' wonder', a phrase at least as old as Chaucer's late-fourteenth-century *Troilus and Creseyde*, meaning a passing phenomenon. What does it mean when one ceases to wonder at the world, an unendingly wonderful place? And what of its 'surface' being 'sold | for songs or something under', that is, for trifling sums, for less than its worth? Tolkien's mood again, as we have seen already among his late work, is one of pessimism. Is this another comment on the destruction of the landscape? 'Where will little Billy sit' if there is no place left for him to do so? And yet Billy is defiant, crying 'Right here', here will he sit – wherever 'here' may be – and vowing to 'keep his name', to go on as he has 'though sea may roar and earth may quake', to bake even though he is only dreaming of baking.

The relationship of 'he' and Billy is not clear, nor is the significance of *pandemain*. This is an early name (in the *Oxford English Dictionary*, *paindemaine*) for soft white bread, a refined product available in medieval times only to the wealthy, as opposed to the less refined brown bread eaten by everyone else. The word seems to have come from Latin *panis dominicus* 'the Lord's bread'. In text B, Billy is baking 'for you', the 'he' of the poem; but in A this line read 'and call for pandemain', with Billy doing the calling, just as in the final line of text A it was he who 'shall not cry in vain', not 'you'.

Tolkien preserved *At Last the Time Has Come* in his papers with the previous few works in this book (nos. 191–193), and manuscript B is very similar in appearance to the later copies of those other poems. For this reason, we have placed them together, dated to or around 1966. It is possible, however, that the first manuscript of the present work was composed earlier. On its back, written by Tolkien in a formal hand squeezed into the margins around a student essay about *Paradise Lost*, are a few sentences connected with his mythology, referring to news of war coming to the forest of Brethil:

> Then when the chieftains had ended their debate and were about to depart, each to his own post and ward, a sudden rumour arose, and the sound of horseman [*sic*] galloping from the North, crying as their [*sic*] came. And a cold fear of they knew not what clutched the hearts of all that heard that cry in the dark. In this way came the tidings of the Nírnaeth to Brethil in the valley of Sirion.

The Nirnaeth Arnoediad, or 'Battle of Unnumbered Tears', was fought in the great war of Elves, Men, and Dwarves against Morgoth (see poem no. 130); in this, most of the Men of Brethil were killed. We have not been able to find this passage among published 'Silmarillion' texts. In private correspondence, Christopher Tolkien remarked that the prose style of the passage 'looks to me more like the later, lengthier prose writings on Túrin or Húrin, early or late 1950s. Sadly it does not seem possible to give a date to this piece.' In any case, this seems to us like so many other examples of writing found on Tolkien's manuscripts unrelated to a primary text, which he made when he was in the mood to practise calligraphy and dashed off whatever came to mind.

195

For W.H.A. (?1967)

In the late 1920s W.H. Auden read English at Oxford. He attended at least one of Tolkien's lectures on *Beowulf*, which he found unforgettable. Much later, having been elected Professor of Poetry at Oxford, he praised the study of Old English in general – much to the dismay of those who objected to it being in the syllabus – and Tolkien's recitation of it in particular. Auden himself was a poor scholar, his aim in reading English having been only to learn about literature as art, so that he might become a great poet – as indeed he was, as well as a distinguished playwright and critic. He gave *The Lord of the Rings* warm reviews, which Tolkien found encouraging, and they had a long correspondence though they sometimes disagreed. 'I regard him as one of my great friends', Tolkien wrote late in life, 'although we have so seldom met except through letters and gifts of his works' (letter to Robert H. Boyer, 25 August 1971, *Letters*, p. 577).

In 1962 Auden contributed 'A Short Ode to a Philologist' to the book *English and Medieval Studies Presented to J.R.R. Tolkien on the Occasion of His Seventieth Birthday* (1962). Tolkien later returned the favour, writing a poem in Old and Modern English, *For W.H.A.*, for the journal *Shenandoah* (pp. 96–7), a special number (Winter 1967) in tribute to Auden on his sixtieth birthday.

Woruldbúendra sum bið wóðbora,
giedda giffæst; sum bið gearuwyrdig,
tyhtend getynge torhte mæðleð;
sum bið bóca gléaw, on bréosthorde
wísdóm haldeð, worn fela geman
ealdgesægena þæra þe úðwitan
fróde gefrugnon on fyrndagum;
sum bið wilgesíð, wǽrfæst hæle,
fréondrǽdenne fǽle gelǽsteð.
Sumne wát ic, secg héahmódne,
þe þissa gifena gehwane on geogoðféore
him ealdmetod éstum gesealde.
Wer wíde cuð Wíhstan hatte,
swilce wæs éac háten on eardgearde

Wǽgmundinga Wígláfes fæder
secga holdestan, and siððan eft
bearn Wíghelmes þe æt beaduwe gecrang
æt Mældúne be his mandryhtne
on gefrǽgan þam gefeohte. He nú forð tela
níwan stefne þæs naman brúceð
him to weorðmynde, Wíhstan úre.
Swa sceal he á mid mannum mǽre wunian,
þǽr sittað searoþancle sundor tó rúne,
snyttrum styriað sóðgied scopa.

Ic þis gied be þé to grétinge
awræc wintrum fród, Wíhstan léofa,
þeah ic þorfte hraðor þancword sprecan.
Rægnold Hrædmóding.

Among the people of earth one has poetry in him,
fashions verses with art; one is fluent in words,
has persuasive eloquence sound and lucid;
one is a reader of books and richly stores
his mind with memory of much wisdom
and legends of old that long ago
were learned and related by loremasters;
one is a mate to choose, a man to trust,
whose friendship's call faithfully answers.
Another I know of noble-hearted,
to whom all these gifts in his early days
the favour of Fate freely granted.
Now wide is his renown. Wystan his name is,
as it once was also of the Wægmunding
in his far country, father of Wiglaf
most loyal of lieges, and in later time
of Wighelm's son who in war was slain
at Byrhtnoth's side by the Blackwater
in the famous defeat. He follows after,
and now anew that name uses
to his own honour. Auden some call him,
and so among men may he be remembered ever,
where as they sit by themselves for solace of heart
the word-lovers, wise and skilful,
revive the vanished voices of makers.

These lines about you I linked together,
though weighted by years, Wystan, my friend:
a tardy tribute and token of thanks.
J.R.R.T.

As Tom Shippey has remarked ('Poems by Tolkien in Other Languages', 2006), Tolkien modelled *For W.H.A.* on the Old English poem known as 'The Gifts of Men' (or 'The Arts of Men'), found in the Exeter Book manuscript. God bestows special gifts to men as He will, the poet says: one may be given worldly treasures, while another is poor in riches but wise in thought; one may have greater strength of body; one may be fair of appearance; one may be a skilled poet, another eloquent with words ('Sum biþ woðbora, giedda giffæst, sum biþ gearuwyrdig'); and so on. According to Tolkien, writing in alliterative verse, Auden has an abundance of gifts, 'the favour of Fate freely granted'.

He also notes that Auden's Christian name, *Wystan*, was borne by Anglo-Saxon heroes (variably *Weohstan*, *Wihstan*): one was a champion, the father of Wiglaf who stood by Beowulf against the dragon when all others had fled, both members of the Wægmundings (the clan to which Beowulf himself belonged); and the other – named in *The Battle of Maldon* as the son of Þurstan and of Wigelin (or Wighelm) – was one of the loyal, doomed retainers of Byrhtnoth at the Maldon (see poem no. 129). (Auden himself was named after the Mercian Saint Wystan, or Wigstan.)

In his essay '"For W.H.A.": Tolkien's Poem in Praise of Auden' (2013) Carl Phelpstead makes a metrical analysis of Tolkien's work, concluding that he 'demonstrates technical accomplishment in his ability to write strictly regular lines of alliterative verse in both Old and modern English'. Phelpstead notes, nonetheless, 'a small number of awkward phrases in the modern English version where the metre appears too obviously to be determining the diction'. He suggests that 'the nature of modern English required Tolkien to depart further from the usual frequency of Old English half-line types in his modern poem than when writing in Old English' (p. 56).

Tolkien signed an Anglo-Saxon equivalent of his name 'Ronald Tolkien' at the end of the Old English version of the poem: 'Rægnold Hrædmóding'. Old English *hrædmōd* means 'hasty', and *-ing* is a suffix indicating a family name (surname).

Appendix I. Limericks and Clerihews

LIMERICKS

Comprising three long and two short lines rhyming AABBA, the limerick is one of the most common types of poetry. Its popularity stems from its brevity, its humour, and its occasional bawdiness (or at least silliness). Many have written limericks, though good ones – like good poems of any sort – are not easy to compose; even Edward Lear, considered the Father of the Limerick, often resorted to repeating the same word or words at the end of both the first and fifth lines, which some consider a cheat. One of Tolkien's earliest poems was a limerick (A), made when he was twelve, and if nothing else it shows an early interest in wordplay. It accompanies a remarkable code letter, or rebus, sent or given by Tolkien to his guardian, the Roman Catholic priest Father Francis Morgan, on 8 August 1904; the limerick itself is in plain language.

[A]

There was an old priest namèd Francis
Who was so fond of 'cheefongy dances'
  That he sat up too late
  And worried his pate
Arranging these Frenchified Prances.

The complete letter was reproduced in colour in the Tolkien fan magazine *Beyond Bree* for October 2020. In a related article, Denis Bridoux suggests that *cheefongy* may be a reference to *chiffon*, a light, diaphanous fabric, and that the word 'Frenchified' may be an early example of the aversion to things French Tolkien expressed much later in life (though we suspect that this antipathy was exaggerated). In the November 2020 number of *Beyond Bree*, Mark Hooker confirmed that *cheefongy* is a dialect word for 'chiffon', and pointed out that in the first part of 1904 the expatriate avant-garde dancer Loïe Fuller was captivating audiences, including one in Birmingham where Tolkien lived, with her renowned 'Radiance Dance'.

A few years later, Tolkien and his cousin Mary Incledon composed a limerick (B) in their invented language 'Nevbosh', or 'New Nonsense'. When in November 1931 he quoted it in his lecture *A Secret Vice*, concerning the invention of languages, it was the only example of Nevbosh he could recall (*The Monsters and the Critics and Other Essays*, p. 203):

[B]

Dar fys ma vel gom co palt 'hoc
Pys go iskili far maino woc?
    Pro si go fys do roc de
    Do cat ym maino bocte
De volt fac soc ma taimful gyróc!'

Humphrey Carpenter offered this translation of the lines in his biography of Tolkien (p. 36):

There was an old man who said 'How
Can I possibly carry my cow
    For if I were to ask it
    To get in my basket
It would make such a terrible row!'

Two further limericks by Tolkien are found with one of his early drawings. We give these as C and D, with the caveat that we are not certain of the final line of D. Limerick C is written below a sketch of a tonsured cleric – possibly illustrating the rhyme – and D is on the back of the same sheet.

[C]

There was an old monk of Algeria
Who of fasting grew wearier — and wearier
    Till at last with a yell
    He jumped out of his cell
And ate up the Father Superior.

[D]

An irascible party of Cofton
Lost her temper distinctly too often
    So great was their rage
    That they purchased a cage
But the last rhyme is round [?bound] to soften.

Cofton is a small village in Devon, whose name conveniently rhymes with *often* (as pronounced with a hard *t*).

See also poem no. 47, *Two-Lieut*, which in each of its two versions is written in the manner of a limerick (or limericks), but does not strictly follow the prescribed five-line form.

CLERIHEWS

All of Tolkien's limericks, as far as we have evidence of them, were written in his earlier years. Later in life, he turned to a different short verse form, the clerihew. This is a comic or nonsensical poem, rhyming (more or less) AABB, typically in two couplets, with lines of unequal length, about an individual with whom the hearer is presumed to have enough familiarity to get the joke. Tolkien's clerihews concern his own acquaintances, in one case himself. The form is named after its inventor, English writer Edmund Clerihew Bentley, and in connection with Tolkien has been thoroughly explored by Joe R. Christopher in 'Tolkien and the Clerihew' (1995).

We have arranged these six efforts alphabetically by subject. The first is from *The Inklings: C.S. Lewis, J.R.R. Tolkien, Charles Williams, and Their Friends* by Humphrey Carpenter, p. 177.

[E]

Mr. Owen Barfield's
Habit of turning cartwheels
Made some say: 'He's been drinking!'
It was only 'conscientious thinking'.

Owen Barfield was a solicitor by profession but a philosopher by preference. His *Poetic Diction: A Study in Meaning*, based on his Oxford B.Litt. thesis, had a profound influence on Tolkien. Carpenter explained (*The Inklings*, p. 177) that the 'cartwheels' of the clerihew 'were of an intellectual sort, and "conscientiously thinking" was one of Barfield's terms for the thought processes related to Anthroposophy', the teachings of Rudolf Steiner which Barfield espoused. Although he attended meetings less often than most, Barfield was a member of the Inklings, an informal group of authors and dons formed by Tolkien and C.S. Lewis.

Another friend and Inkling, Nevill Henry Kendal Aylmer Coghill, was a Fellow of Exeter College, Oxford, and then Merton Professor of English Literature. He made a Modern English version of Chaucer's *Canterbury Tales*, and was responsible for well-regarded theatrical productions with the Oxford University Dramatic Society. Tolkien repeated the clerihew he wrote about Coghill (F), misspelling 'Nevill' and 'doggerel', in a letter to W.H. Auden, 4 August 1965 (*Letters*, p. 501).

[F] Mr Neville Judson Coghill
Wrote a deal of dangerous dogerill. [*sic*]
Practical, progressive men
Called him Little Poison-pen.

Tolkien also wrote in his letter: 'This was at a time when under the name of Judson [Coghill] was writing what I thought very good and funny verses lampooning forward-looking men like Norwood of St. John's' (Sir Cyril Norwood, President of St John's College, Oxford, author of the Norwood report on education). Joe Christopher has suggested that 'Judson' was Coghill's own invention.

Our third clerihew (G) is also from Carpenter, *The Inklings*, p. 177.

[G] Dr U.Q. Humphrey
Made poultices of comfrey.
If you didn't pay his bills
He gave you doses of squills.

Robert Emlyn Havard was a physician who attended both Tolkien and C.S. Lewis. He and Tolkien were fellow Roman Catholics and near neighbours in Oxford after Tolkien moved to Headington, and often sat next to each other at Sunday Mass. 'Humphrey' was a nickname given him by another Inkling, Hugo Dyson, and Lewis's brother, Warren, called Havard a 'useless quack' when he failed to give him a promised lift home – thus, ever after, Havard was also the 'U.Q.' The herb comfrey (*Symphytum*) in fact has well documented medicinal qualities, such as for treating burns or reducing inflammation, when applied externally (internally it is poisonous to humans) as in a poultice or moist mass held on the skin with a cloth; but it is not the sort of treatment one expects from a modern doctor. A *squill* (*Scilla*), or plant terminating in a large bulb, also has a long history of medicinal use, as a bitter diuretic and expectorant.

Father Gervase Mathew, a Roman Catholic priest and fellow Inkling, long resident in Blackfriars, Oxford, made archaeological surveys abroad, lectured regularly on the Oxford Modern History, Theology, and English faculties, and published books on the Reformation and on Byzantine culture. Tolkien's clerihew about him (H) appears in Carpenter, *The Inklings*, p. 186.

[H] The Rev. Mathew (Gervase)
Made inaudible surveys
Of little-read sages
In the dark Middle Ages.

As Carpenter points out, this account 'was entirely true', and as we can see, whimsical. Joe Christopher points out that it is the purpose, and joy, of a clerihew to be silly, or fantastic, *but not accurate*. Tolkien does not seem to have been overly concerned with 'rules' for his poems.

Writing to his friend Amy Ronald on 2 January 1969 (*Letters*, p. 559), Tolkien composed a clerihew about himself (I).

[I] J.R.R. Tolkien
had a cat called Grimalkin:
once a familiar of Herr Grimm,
now he spoke the law to him.

Joe Christopher notes that this violates another rule about clerihews, that the first letter of each line should be capitalized. About *Grimalkin*, he comments that the word usually refers to a cat, especially a female cat; *malkin* is derived from the given name *Matilda*. 'Herr Grimm' is surely Jakob Grimm, who in 1822 described changes in consonants between the Proto-Indo-European and Proto-Germanic languages, known as 'Grimm's Law', which launched Tolkien's field of historical philology. A *familiar* in the supernatural sense is a demon, usually in the form of an animal, supposedly attending a witch or wizard, but the word also can mean 'friend, associate'. Joe Christopher assumes the former, and asks: 'Did the familiar inspire Grimm with the law, or did Grimm teach it to his cat. Given the ambiguous pronouns, did Grimalkin recite the Law to Tolkien or *vice versa*?' (p. 270).

One further clerihew (J) concerns Tolkien's friend Charles Williams (see poem no. 174), from Carpenter, *The Inklings*, p. 187.

[J] The sales of Charles Williams
Leapt up by millions,
When a reviewer surmised
He was only Lewis disguised.

Humphrey Carpenter assumes that this refers to Williams' book *The Figure of Beatrice*, published in summer 1943, but comments that 'this was deliberate nonsense, for the book did not sell vastly and it did not remotely resemble anything [C.S.] Lewis had written' (p. 187). And yet, *The Figure of Beatrice* brought Williams public recognition, possibly because of Lewis's persistent praise.

To these clerihews we will add a poem of similar form but called instead a 'bentley', because it begins with a book title rather than a name. Joe Christopher calls it a 'quasi-bentley' because it, too, does not follow the relevant rules, such as the capitalization of lines. It is quoted in Carpenter's *Biography*, p. 223.

[K]

The Lord of the Rings
is one of those things:
if you like it you do:
if you don't, then you boo!

When *The Lord of the Rings* was first published, reviews tended to be at one of two extremes, giving it high praise or condemning it in no uncertain terms. In some critical circles, this is still the case.

Appendix II. Latin Adages

Late in life, Tolkien wrote a variety of short poems based on Latin adages. Some are found in two or three manuscripts, not always with variation, made at different times. Here we have given priority to the most finished texts, with comments on variations.

[A]

Quod erat demonstrandum!
If you can understand 'em.
They're a piece of cake or a simple fake,
Or an answer made at random.

The Latin, for 'which was to be demonstrated', is often abbreviated to 'Q.E.D.' It is used at the end of an argument, such as a theorem of Euclid, when a stated proposition has been proved.

[B]

Reductio ad absurdam!
If you have ever heard 'em:
they were silly jokes to amuse the mokes
and morons that preferred 'em.

The Latin means 'reduction to the absurd'. It refers to a line of argument in which a premise is proved false by showing that its logical consequence would be absurd or contradictory.

[C]

Abusus non tollit usum —
not even when rather gruesome!
Between me and you the thing to do,
if you want it strong, is to brew some.

The Latin means 'abuse does not cancel use', or misuse of something does not rule out its proper use.

[D]

Audi alteram partem!
as they said in my old kindergarten.
If you will hear or must do — and yet,
    pray do not forget
    it is a certain bet
they won't ever stop once you start 'em.

The Latin means 'listen to the other side'. In an earlier manuscript Tolkien wrote:

[E] *Audi alteram partem!*
Of course if you have the heartem
But don't forget it's a certain bet,
they won't stop once you start 'em.

'Heartem' is simply *heart* extended to rhyme with 'partem' and 'start 'em'. Tolkien considered changing 'They won't' to 'They'll never'.

[F] *Prodit ridiculus mus —*
ridiculiss issimus mus!
But that doesn't say that when mousie would play
an old cata-mountainous puss must.

Translated literally, the Latin means 'the ridiculous mouse comes out – the most ridiculous mouse!' This is probably derived from words by Horace in the *Ars Poetica*, 'Parturient montes, nascetur ridiculus mus' ('Mountains will go into labour, and a ridiculous mouse will be born'), ultimately based on a short poem by Phaedrus. Its moral, more or less, is to not make a mountain out of a molehill, to not make too much of a small matter. Tolkien, however, combines this with a version of a second adage, 'when the cat's away, the mice will play'. With 'cata-mountainous' he plays on both *cat* ('puss'; a *catamountain* is a large wild cat, such as a cougar) and *mountain*.

[G] *Per ardua* (uppards) *ad astra*,
for downwards is dreadful disaster:
a troublesome thought, for those that were taught
there's nothing machines cannot master.

'Per ardua ad astra' means 'through adversity to the stars', and is the official motto of the Royal Air Force. 'Uppards' is a dialect pronunciation of *upwards*. In an earlier manuscript the third line ends 'who were taught'.

[H] I tell you now, *festina lente*!
Is there time? Of course there is plenty;
but don't look and never leap,
though the water looks deep;
just hold your nose while you count twenty.

'Festina lente' means 'make haste slowly' or 'more haste, less speed'. Its earliest use seems to have been by the Emperor Augustus, as attributed by Suetonius. It was also adopted by the Medicis and by the Venetian printer Aldus Manutius (known for the care with which he produced his books), among others. Here again, Tolkien combines one adage with another: 'look before you leap'. In an earlier, working manuscript, the poem reads:

[I] I tell you [*added:* now]: *festina lente*!
Is there time? [O yes >] of course, there is plenty
But don't look and never leap
though it seems very deep:
just hold your nose, while you count twenty

[J] *O caveat, caveat emptor!*
What a heartening thought for a tempter!
It's simply a 'must'; but when it goes bust
You'll find that your pocket is emptier.

'Caveat emptor' means 'let the buyer beware'. In an earlier manuscript, Tolkien is seen working on the final line:

[K] *O caveat caveat emptor!*
What a heartening thought for a tempter!
It's simply a 'must'; but when it goes bust,
what balm in a caveat — emptor!
you're left with a caveat —
you're a caveat still, self *emptor*.

Next to text K, Tolkien wrote in pencil 'You'll find that your pocket is emptier'.

[L] *Praestat difficilius* —
is what they used to say to us:
How well they guessed the poet's plan
to pose a puzzle if he can
So *lectio difficilior*:
to be understood is such a bore.

Translated literally, 'praestat difficilius' means 'makes it more difficult'; a final word usually attached to these is omitted, *lectu*, thus 'makes it more difficult to read'. The reference is to textual criticism, and the difficulties a critic may find in understanding a text when there are competing manuscripts. 'Lectio difficilior' is part of the adage 'lectio difficilior potior', 'the more difficult reading is the stronger', that is, when readings differ between manuscripts, the more unusual one is probably the original. This principle was introduced by the humanist scholar Erasmus, who observed that when copying manuscripts, scribes tended to make difficult texts simpler, rarely the opposite.

In an earlier manuscript of the poem, Tolkien wrote:

[M]

Praestat difficilius —
that's what they used to say to us.
How well they knew the poet's plan
to ?make a puzzle if he can!
So *lectio difficilior*
To be understood is such a bore!

[N]

Pereant qui ante nos
to *nostra* have come pretty close,
or even dared to imitate
posterity, and could not wait
till we arrived in all our pride,
too young, too clever to have died!

'Pereant qui ante nos' is the beginning of a longer Latin adage, 'pereant qui ante nos nostra dixerunt', 'may those perish who have said what we were going to say'. In an earlier manuscript, the fourth line of this poem ends 'who could not wait', and has an alternative reading, 'even daring to pirate'.

[O]

Pecca, pecca fortiter!
When you see your dinner's there,
choose your bib, and peck 'em in,
Chanticlere: you're looking thin.
Pecca, pecca — do not dare,
gobble, gobble *fortiter*.

'Pecca fortiter' means 'sin boldly' (or 'bravely'), and is tied to an idea from the early Church that the greater the sin, the greater the forgiveness – that God forgives a sin if the sinner has faith, and the more boldly one sins, the greater will be the exalting of God's glory. Tolkien extends this, however, by playing on the similar sounds of *pecca* and *peck*, the action of a fowl, such as 'Chanticlere' (a cockerel), in feeding – pecking and eating ('gobble') boldly. In another, very rough manuscript, Tolkien gives the final line as 'pecca pecca do or dare'.

Appendix III. Poem Lists

Tolkien made at least eight lists of his poems, either as records of his work or while planning a collection to be published. All titles in this appendix are spelled, capitalized, and punctuated as in the manuscripts or typescripts.

[A] The earliest list is a manuscript in Blue Poetry Book II (see our Introduction), headed 'Attempts at Verse'. We do not know the significance of the marks Tolkien added next to the numbers of selected titles, but have reproduced them here.

(+)1	Morgen (æsp & ósle)	[*Morning* (*Aspen and Ousel*)]
2	Æfensang	[*Evening*]
+ 3	On néolum dalum	[*The Dale Lands*]
4	Meremenna symbel	[*The Sirens*]
* 5	Oxenaford (of Gifetsleage gesewen)	[*From Iffley*]
+ 6	Nihthelm ofer wegas	[*Darkness on the Road*]
7	Æfenléoht on burgstede	[*Sunset in a Town*]
~ 8	Hréowsung	[?*The Town of Present Sorrow*]
9	Þá sǽflódas	[*The Tides*]
+ 10	Wihta nāthwylc útan	[?*Outside*]
~ 11	Magna dei gloria	
* 12	Éarendeles scipfæreld Ǽfensteorran	[*The Voyage of Éarendel the Evening Star*]
+ 13	Þéostru	[*Dark*]
~ 14	Of ungryndum ic gebidde	[?*The Bidding of the Minstrel*]
15	Spearwena Morgenswég	[*Sparrow-Song*]

Here all but one of the titles (*Magna Dei Gloria*) is in Old English, but written next to no. 11 is also an Old English equivalent, 'Micel is þæs Dryhtnes wuldor'. Next to no. 9 is 'Fyrndaga sǽlćoþ'; compare 'Fyrndagan sæléoþ' below.

Following his list of fifteen poems, Tolkien made a further list of six works, labelled 'Ungefeged inne', i.e. unfit for the purpose. This seems to be contemporary with the preceding list.

*	1	Uncer Lufu	[*As Two Fair Trees*]
*	2	Fyrndagan sæléoþ	[*Sea Chant* (or *Song*) *of an Elder Day*]
	3	Lemmincaignen siþaþ tó Oxenaford	[*Lemminkainen Goeth to the Fords of Oxen*]
*	4	Lemmincaignen færeþ to bróþar sínum on Súþlanden	[*The New Lemminkainen*]
	5	Richard Englenacyning mæþeleþ fore Fyrdum	[*A Fragment of an Epic*]
*	6	Þonne egeliniton féþan on Eastfeldum	[*The Battle of the Eastern Field*]

The latest poems in the initial list are *Dark* and *Sparrow-Song*, both composed in December 1914. In the second list, *As Two Fair Trees* (here *Uncer Lufu* 'Our Love') and *Sea Chant of an Elder Day* both date from January 1915. It may be that Tolkien compiled 'Attempts at Verse' immediately following the 'Council of London' in December 1914, the meeting of the TCBS friends which gave him such impetus to succeed as a poet. It is particularly interesting that he included *The Tides* among works he would include in a collection, but found the *Sea Chant* unsuitable; as seen in our discussion for no. 13, he was dissatisfied with the revision and continued to work at it. *As Two Fair Trees* was 'unfit' presumably because it was too personal. The remaining 'unfit' titles were, by 1915, easily to be considered by their author juvenilia, *jeux d'esprit*, or in retrospect, perhaps absurd.

On the page of his notebook facing A, though it is more of a kind with poems in his primary list, Tolkien wrote the title of a seventh 'unfit' poem, *Wealdielfa geláe* (*Wood-Sunshine*), marked '+'. On the same page, he also wrote 'I 1909: I 1910 I autumn lost', which we interpret to mean that he composed the first listed poem, *Morning*, initially in 1909, then again in 1910, but it was lost that autumn; see our discussion for poem no. 1.

Written by Tolkien above these lists are lines in Old English: 'On þisre béc scop hafaþ gewriten feola léoda | and feola uncúþra gesungen wihta ond geþinga | náles ne dēmaþ ʒe ne forhogiaþ to swíþe netó hraðe'. Roughly translated, they are a plea by the poet, who has written of many people and many strange things, that his readers do not judge him hastily.

[B] A second early manuscript list of poems is found in Blue Poetry Book I, written in pencil. Its first five titles are at the top of the page, followed by the date '1915' written large; it may be that Tolkien wrote the date first, then added the titles. Titles in Modern English, written to the right of those in Old English, were erased, but some are recoverable with photographic enhancement. The latest poem in this list is *The Shores of Faery*, composed 8–9 July 1915.

Fyrndoȝa Sǽléoþ	[*Sea Chant of an Elder Day*]
Þéostru	[*Dark*]
Spearwena Morgenswég	[*Sparrow-Song*]
Swá twégen fægre béamas	[*As Two Fair Trees*]
Se móncyning	[*The Man in the Moon Came Down Too Soon*]
Þá twégen ríderas	[*The Two Riders*]
Þæt Ȝéar onȝinneþ spréotan	[*May Day in a Backward Year*]
Cumaþ þá Nihtielfas	[*Goblin Feet*]
Kôr on ánre byrg forlorennan and déáðan	[*Kôr: In a City Lost and Dead*]
Wit cildru þæt húsincel ærran gamenes	[*You and Me and the Cottage of Lost Play*]
Tinfang wearbela	[*Tinfang Warble*]
Séo Meremennen	[*The Mermaid's Flute*]
Nihthelm ofer wegas	[*Darkness on the Road*]
Morgenléoþ	[*Morning-Song*]
Se strand Ielfalandes	[*The Shores of Faery*]

[C] The first part of list C, also in Blue Poetry Book I, is written in standard pencil, the second part (from the eleventh title) more roughly in blue pencil. The latest work listed, *The Horns of Elfland* (i.e. *The Trumpets of Faery* or *Faërie*) was composed 13–14 July 1915. The numbering, deletions, and blank lines of the list suggest that Tolkien used it to consider the order of poems he would include in a collection.

(a)	æsp and ósle	[*Morning*]
(I)	on néolum dalum	[*The Dale Lands*]
b	meremennena symbel	[*The Sirens Feast*]
2	wealdielfa geláe	[*Wood-Sunshine*]
3	Oxenaford (of Gifetesleage gesewen)	[*From Iffley*]

4	Se nihtstapa	[*Outside*]
5	Éarendeles Scipfæreld ǽfensteorran	[*The Voyage of Earendel the Evening Star*]
6	Fyrndaga sǽléoþ	[*Sea Chant of an Elder Day*]
7	þéostru	[*Dark*]
8	Spearwena Morgenswég	[*Sparrow-Song*]
9	Uncer Lufu (Swá twégen fægre béamas)	[*As Two Fair Trees*]
10	for hwon ástág se Móncyning	[*Why the Man in the Moon Came Down Too Soon*]
11	[*deleted:* Ielfalandes]	
12	[*blank*]	
13	ǽfenleoð	[*Evening*]
14	nihtielfa fél	[*Goblin Feet*]
15	ánre byrg forlorennan and déáðan	[*Kôr: In a City Lost and Dead*]
16	þu and ic (þæt húsincel ǽrran gamenes)	[*You and Me and the Cottage of Lost Play*]
17	[*blank*]	
18	[*blank*]	
19	nihthelm ofer wegas	[*Darkness on the Road*]
20	morgenléoþ	[*Morning-song*]
21	se strand Ielfalandes	[*The Shores of Faery*]
22	[*deleted:* þá bíeman Ielfalandes]	
23	þá bíeman Ielfalandes	[*The Horns of Elfland,* i.e. *The Trumpets of Faerie*]
24	[*blank*]	
25	þá éadigan Sǽlidan	[*The Happy Mariners*]

[D] Tolkien made list D, laid into Blue Poetry Book II, probably at the end of 1915 or the start of 1916, possibly in relation to his proposed book *The Trumpets of Faërie* which he sent, unsuccessfully, to Sidgwick & Jackson in early February 1916. The latest poem in the list is *The Pool of the Dead Year*, composed between late November and early December 1915. Most of the titles in D are abbreviated, and next to each is at least one mark, which we have replicated except for those indicated in notes below. The order of titles is given as first written out, in two columns.

· Kortirion
· Pool of Dead Year

· Aryador
· Dark are the clouds
· Happy Mariners
(Swallow)
· Horns of Elfland
· Princess Ní
· Shores of Faery
·(Morning Song
·(Darkness on Road
· Mermaid's Flute
· L[ay] of Earendel
·((Tinfang Warble
· You and Me
· Kôr
· Goblin Feet
(Completorium)
· May day
·(The Two Riders
· Man in the Moon
· Two Fair Trees
(Sparrow Song

· Dark 14
· Sea Song 14 (12–15)
· V[oyage] of Earendel 14
· Outside 13–14
(Iffley 11
·(Woodsunshine 10
(Dale-lands 10
(Morning
((Sirens

The first four titles, composed between September and December 1915, appear to have been added last, to a list which began originally with *The Happy Mariners* (composed July 1915). Tolkien subsequently marked *Kortirion* and *The Pool of the Dead Year* to be reversed in order, and also *The Pines (Song) of Aryador* and *Dark Are the Clouds about the North*. 'Swallow' is *The Swallow and the Traveller on the Plains*. The last title, *The Sirens*, is struck through. The penultimate title, *Morning*, is redundant, Tolkien having already included *Morning Song*. We interpret the parentheses to indicate his uncertainty about including the titles so marked, and the dots to indicate those titles he chose for a final selection. A large square bracket (not reproduced here) encloses *Morning Song* and *Darkness on the Road*, possibly meant to indicate that the first of these works is to follow the second (among the first four titles in the list, Tolkien marked movement conventionally with curved arrows). Another square bracket is marked next to '(Completorium)' (formerly *Evening*).

At the foot of the sheet, Tolkien wrote '$16^1+4^2+3^2$ add ideas'. We take this to be an attempt to estimate the number of pages the proposed book would occupy: 'sixteen poems, each occupying one page of a printed book, plus four poems each occupying two pages, plus three poems, each of two pages, from works added to the list after it was first written out'. The latter probably refers to some of the works, beginning with *Dark*, written in the second column, next to which Tolkien wrote their years of composition. Below this column are additional figures, '4^1+4^2', presumably 'four poems of one page each, plus four of two pages, not included in the larger calculation'. Discounting repeated *Morning*, there are thirty-one poems in the complete list (16 +4+3+4+4). It seems remarkable that Tolkien should estimate so few pages for some of his poems: *Kortirion*, for instance, would certainly require more than two pages even in a small font, given the usual modest trim size for books of poetry, then as now.

Although there could not have been a great deal of time between lists C and D, Tolkien now chose to include *As Two Fair Trees*, *Sea Song of an Elder Day*, and *Wood-Sunshine*, but to exclude *The Dale-Lands*, *The Sirens*, and others. If this list does pertain to the proposed *Trumpets of Faërie* – and we note that here he gives that poem the title *Horns of Elfland*, perhaps taking R.W. Reynolds' criticism of his preferred title into account (see our general introduction) – Tolkien would have been aware that a suitably modest book could not include too many of his works, and at this time he was reaching new strengths with recent poems such as *Kortirion* praised by his TCBS friends.

[E] Tolkien wrote an informal list in pencil on the first page of Blue Poetry Book I, thus:

Tuor
Sea-chant
Kôr

Cottage of Lost Play

Lonely Isle
Habbanan

Pool of Dead Year
Kortirion
Aryador

L. [i.e. Lay of] Earendel

Shores of Faery
Happy Mariners
Voyage of Earendel
(Mermaid)

Trumpets of Faery
Nî
Tinfang Warble
Over old Hills
Goblin Feet
Man Moon

'Tuor' and 'Sea-chant' presumably refer to the same poem, *Sea Chant* (or *Song*) *of an Elder Day*, i.e. 'the song that Tuor told to Eärendel his son what time the Exiles of Gondolin dwelt awhile in Dor Tathrin the Land of Willows after the burning of their city' (see our discussion for no. 13); and since the list notes this connection ('Tuor'), it must date to no earlier than 1917. '(Mermaid)' is presumably *The Mermaid's Flute*. Most of the poems in list E are related to 'The Silmarillion'.

[F] List F is a typescript made with the purple ribbon associated with Tolkien's years on the English faculty of the University of Leeds (1920–5). As typed, it dates from around the end of that period; the latest poem listed is *Moonshine*, from 1923. To this, in ink and pencil, Tolkien added other poems and (excluded here) notes of publication as late as 1927. Headed 'Contents' and with each poem (in the initial typescript) numbered, it appears to be the table of contents for a collection, perhaps the one Douglas A. Anderson has suggested that Tolkien proposed to the Swan Press, Leeds, or another proposed in 1926 to Basil Blackwell in Oxford. The divisions into four parts are in the original.

1. Kortirion among the Trees
2. Elf-alone
3. May Day
4. Dark
5. The Trumpets of Faery
   [*altered to:* Horns of the Host of Doriath]
6. Goblin Feet
7. Moonshine
8. Tinfang Warble
9. Over old Hills and Far Away
10. Princess Ní
11. Why the Man in the Moon came down Too Soon
12. The Cat and the Fiddle
13. The Ruined Enchanter

14. Iúmonna Gold Galdre Bewunden
[*added:* Light as Leaf on Linden Tree]
15. A Song of Aryador
16. Outside
[*added:* The Nameless Land]

17. Éala! Éarendel, Engla Beorhtast
18. The City of the Gods
19. The Shores of Faery
20. The Happy Mariners
[*added:* The Bidding of the Minstrel]
21. The Mermaid's Flute
22. The Horns of Ulmo [*altered to:* The Horns of Ylmir]

23. Mar Vanwa Tyaliéva, The Cottage of Lost Play
24. As Two Fair Trees
25. The Two Riders
26. Dark are the Clouds about the North
27. The Lonely Isle
[*added:* Wínsele Wéste]
28. The Forest Walker
29. A Dream of Coming Home
30. The Grey Bridge of Tavrobel
31. Evening in Tavrobel

Tolkien also added to the typescript, by hand on the verso of the sheet, 'Iumbo & Whale' and 'Chaucer imitation' (*The Clerkes Compleinte*). Numbers 29 and 31 above (and the same titles in G-IV below) are probably the 'Dream' and 'Two Eves' of the related verses we have discussed as poem no. 48.

[G] Another typescript in Tolkien's papers appears to be a revision of list F. This too was made with a purple ribbon, and to this as well Tolkien later made additions and marginal notes in manuscript. At the head of this sheet is 'Kortirion among the Trees', possibly the general title Tolkien planned for a collection.

I

Kortirion among the Trees
Elfalone
May-day
Dark

II

The Horns of the Host of Doriath
Goblin Feet
Moonshine
Tinfang Warble
Over old Hills and far away
Princess Ní
Why the Man in the Moon came down Too Soon
The Cat and the Fiddle
[*added but struck through:* Knocking at the Door]
The Ruined Enchanter
Iúmonna Gold Galdre Bewunden
Light as Leaf on Linden-tree
A Song of Aryador
Outside
The Nameless Land

III

Éala! Éarendel, Engla Beorhtast
The City of the Gods
[*added:* Last of the [Old] Gods, Brothers in Arms;
added and struck through: Vestr um Haf]
The Shores of Faery
[*added:* Earendel at the Helm]
The Happy Mariners
The Bidding of the Minstrel
The Mermaid's Flute
The Horns of Ylmir
[*added:* Vestr um Haf, Shadowland, The Last Ship
(*Oilima Markirya*)]

IV

Mar Vanwa Tyaliéva, The Cottage of Lost Play
The Two Riders
Dark are the Clouds about the North
The Lonely Isle
1916, Winsele Weste
The Forest Walker
[*added:* The Thatch of Poppies]
A Dream of Coming Home

The Grey Bridge of Tavrobel
Evening in Tavrobel

Below part IV Tolkien added in manuscript:

V Lays

2 Breton Lays
Beowulf

Tolkien also added an 'a' to the second part number ('II' > 'IIa') and wrote in the margin opposite the space between parts II and III:

IIb Bimble Bay a song on the Borders
[*deleted*: A Song of B.B.] The Bumpus
[*deleted*: The Mewlips] The Dragon's Visit
Glip
A Song of B.B. [Bimble Bay]
The Mewlips

With these changes, Tolkien gave list G a rough programme: I, landscape or nature; IIa, faerie or enchantment; IIb, Bimble Bay, i.e. comedy; III, 'The Silmarillion'; IV, a mixture of wartime poems and fantasy; V, lays. Notably in G, Tolkien removed *As Two Fair Trees*, perhaps because he now felt it to be too personal in company with his other works. He had already marked its title on list F with a square bracket, suggesting uncertainty whether to include it.

The two 'Breton Lays' of part V are presumably the two 'Corrigan' poems (no. 116), or the first *Corrigan* and *The Lay of Aotrou and Itroun*, and 'Beowulf' is presumably *The Lay of Beowulf* (no. 117). These poems date from around 1929 and 1930. The latest additions to parts II and III – *The Last of the Old Gods*, *Earendel at the Helm*, *Vestr um Haf*, and *The Last Ship* (*Oilima Markirya*) – were composed around 1931.

It is curious to find *The Mewlips* included with the 'Bimble Bay' poems of added part IIb, as it is not in that series, and evidence suggests that it was not known by that title (but rather, as *Knocking at the Door*) until 1962. This in turn suggests that Tolkien did not add 'IIb' until decades after the list proper and earlier revisions. 'Bimble Bay a song on the Borders' seems to be Tolkien's label for the contents of IIb.

[H] Tolkien wrote manuscript list H first in ink. Later he added in pencil the letter 'P' to indicate that a work had been published, and in such cases, in abbreviated form (but omitted here) the titles of the magazine or collection in which the poem appeared. Four titles were also added in pencil.

i

Kortirion among the Trees
Elfalone
Mayday
Dark

ii.a

The Horns of the Host of Doriath
P Goblin Feet
Moonshine
P Tinfang Warble
Over old Hills & Far Away
P The Princess Ní
P Why the Man in the Moon came down Too Soon
P The Cat and the Fiddle
The Ruined Enchanter
P Iúmonna Gold Galdre Bewunden
P There was a Man who dwelt Alone [*The Shadow Man*]
P As Light as Leaf on Linden-tree
A song of Aryador
Outside
Knocking at the Door
P Looney
[*added in pencil:* Shadowbride]
P Tom Bombadil [*The Adventures of Tom Bombadil*]
P Errantry
[*added in pencil:* Firiel]

ii.b

A song of Bimble Bay
The Bumpus
Glip
P The Dragon's Visit
Old Grabbler
P The Progress of Bimble

iii

Éalá! Éarendel Engla Beorhtast!
P The City of the Gods
The Last of the Old Gods
The Shores of Faery

from the 'Lay of Éarendel' [i.e. *a* and *b*]
a. The Bidding of the Minstrel
b. The Mermaid's Flute
Earendel at the Helm
P The Happy Mariners
The Moon mounted the Mists of the Sea
[i.e. *The Fall of Arthur*]
The Horns of Ylmir
Vestr um Haf
Shadowland
The Last Ship [*Oilima Markirya*]

iv

P The Nameless Land ('Pearl' stanzas)
Mar Vanwa Tyaliéva, The Cottage of Lost Play
The Two Riders
Dark are the Clouds about the North
The Lonely Isle
Wínsele wéste
The Forest-Walker
The Thatch of Poppies
A Dream of Coming Home
P The Grey Bridge of Tavrobel
An Evening in Tavrobel

[*added in pencil:*]

Mythopoeia
P Aotrou & Itroun (Lay)

The existence of lists G and H, so similar in arrangement with a 'programme' of several parts, suggests that Tolkien continued to hope to publish a collection of his poetry despite rejections by Sidgwick & Jackson, et al. If list G, as we think, belongs to around 1931, list H may have been prompted by Tolkien's success in publishing several of his poems later in the 1930s: *Errantry*, *Looney*, and *The Adventures of Tom*

Bombadil appeared in the *Oxford Magazine* between November 1933 and February 1934, and *Firiel* in the *Chronicle of the Convents of the Sacred Heart* in 1934. It is not known, however, if he made any further attempt to interest a publisher at that late date, and in any case from 1936, having come to the attention of George Allen & Unwin, his chief literary concern became *The Hobbit* and *The Lord of the Rings*.

The dating of list H is less straightforward due to the presence of *The Shadow Man* ('There was a man who dwelt alone'). If, as we have supposed in our discussion for poem no. 147, Tolkien wrote this work in the year of its publication, then its inclusion in H dates the list to no earlier than 1936. But if it was composed before 1936 – and lacking extant drafts or other evidence, we must acknowledge the possibility – then in order to date list H one must look instead to the lines beginning 'The moon mounted the mists of the sea': these are associated with the unfinished *Fall of Arthur* (no. 140), the greater part of which Tolkien wrote in ?1933 or 1934. (Their mention of Eärendel, we presume, gained them a place in section iii with other works related to 'The Silmarillion'.) Since Tolkien continued to work on *The Fall of Arthur* as late as 1937, though, one must return to the possibility that list H has a date in line with a 1936 origin for *The Shadow Man*. It could be significant that 'The moon mounted the mists of the sea', as given in H, is the original reading of the line, before Tolkien revised it to 'The moon was fallen into misty caves'.

Tolkien's additions to list H were made at various times and have more determinable dates. For example, a note next to 'The Cat and the Fiddle' and 'As light as Leaf on Linden-tree', 'Rewritten in Magic Ring', refers to the original title of *The Lord of the Rings* in its first phase of writing (1938), and a note at the end states that *The Lay of Aotrou and Itroun* was published in the *Welsh Review* for December 1945. The addition of 'Shadowbride' (after 'Looney') is doubly curious, first because it is redundant with its earlier version (*The Shadow Man*) already on the list, and second because Tolkien seems not to have applied the title *Shadow-Bride* until he revisited the poem in 1961 or 1962 – at least, as far as the archival evidence shows.

Appendix IV. Word Lists

Probably in 1914 or 1915, during his final years as an Oxford undergraduate, Tolkien recorded words and phrases he found of particular interest. Since he credited many of these to the poet and essayist Francis Thompson, we suspect that he compiled them after he purchased, in 1913 and 1914, the three volumes of Thompson's collected works, then recently published. He did not make his lists all at once, though, as one may judge by differences in his handwriting and in the colours and density of his inks.

The longest of his lists (A, below), which he called 'Some Magnificent Words (& Phrases) (and Their Authors)', is in two columns on sheets of lined paper. Together with the other lists given here, it was ultimately laid into Blue Poetry Book II (see our Introduction), but its folds indicate that Tolkien sometimes carried it in his pocket. We have transcribed its contents in the order that he wrote them, divided into six alphabetical groups though not in each group in strictly alphabetical order. Thompson has 97 citations, and it may be that many of the words or phrases not credited, such as *uneuphrasied* and *yester-rose*, also came from his works – at least, one finds them in his poems. Shakespeare is cited fewer than half as many times (43), followed by Chaucer with 19 words and Tennyson with 8. Most other authors are credited only once or twice. We have summarized Tolkien's sources for this and his other lists at the end of this appendix.

Of the 229 words listed (counting variations separately), 52 are preceded by an asterisk. We do not know what Tolkien meant by this mark – certainly not to indicate a word he used in a poem, as some such words appear in the list with an asterisk, and others without. It may be that the asterisked words particularly appealed to Tolkien at that moment. After some of the words, he indicated the part of speech intended: *aj* for adjective, *sb* for substantive (noun), *vb* for verb; we have left these abbreviations as found. Tolkien also shortened, in various ways (e.g. 'F. Thompson', 'F. Th.', 'FT'), the names of his source authors or subjects (Elizabethan, Scientific); we have filled these out and regularized them.

Apropos list A, a stray note among Tolkien's early papers reads, with no further details: 'Compound words in Spenser Shakesp[eare] Byron Wordsworth Tennyson Browning Shelley Keats Fr[ancis] Thompson'.

Tolkien wrote a second list (B), headed 'Some Delightful Dialectal Words (Usable)', on a half-sheet of paper torn from an invitation to a meeting of the Stapeldon Society of Exeter College, Oxford, for Monday, 23 February, i.e. in 1914 (Tolkien himself chaired the meeting). As in A, he provided definitions for only some of the words, and we do not know the significance of asterisks before some of the terms. This list was followed a year later by another, either abandoned quickly or deliberately short (C), entitled 'More Dialectals etc., Words Delightful but Not Grand', made on the back of a notice to Tolkien from his bank (Lloyds, Oxford) dated 10 March 1915.

Finally, we have transcribed, as D, a list Tolkien headed 'From ME [Middle English]', written in the same period on another scrap of paper. This includes some of the 'magnificent' words recorded in A, and others with old spelling, such as 'crisopace' for *chrysoprase*. Despite its title, the list is not one of words strictly in Middle English – *aventail*, *bezant*, and *jesserant* (*jazerant*), for example, come from Old French – though they may, perhaps, be found in Middle English texts. In fact it is not certain that Tolkien meant the title to apply to the complete list transcribed, which is divided into three parts and appears to have been written at different moments (if within a narrow period of time).

We have included a few notes on selected points of interest, out of many which might be glossed.

A. SOME MAGNIFICENT WORDS (& PHRASES) (AND THEIR AUTHORS)

ABC

*	amaranth	Tennyson
	acanthus	Tennyson
	adamantean	Thompson
	arcane	Elizabethan; Thompson
*	amorist	Sidney; Thompson
	antre	Shakespeare; Keats; Thompson
	accipitrine	Thompson
	argentine (*aj*)	Thompson
	amice (*sb*, *vb*)	Thompson
*	ancientry	Shakespeare
	ancient of war	Shakespeare
	bent (slope, or bank)	Chaucer
*	bayard (horse)	Shakespeare
	benison	*passim.*; Shakespeare

	beeves	Thompson; *passim.*
	bate (*vb*)	Thompson; *passim.*
	blanch-amiced	Thompson only
	blushet	Thompson only
	belt (*vb*)	Thompson only
	aureole	
	blossomy	Thompson
	citrine (colour)	Chaucer
	chirk (*vb*) (sound)	Chaucer
	cantel	Chaucer; Shakespeare
	chastain	Chaucer
*	champain	Chaucer; Shakespeare; Thompson
	citole (instrument)	Chaucer; Shakespeare; Thompson; *etc.*
*	cadent	'once in Shakespeare, *King Lear* also in Thompson "cadent rhyme"'
	cymar	Thompson
	cerule (*sb*, *aj*)	*passim.*; Thompson
	caryatid	
	create (*aj*)	Thompson; Elizabethan
	curch	Thompson
	coronal	Thompson
*	circumfluous	Thompson
	conflagrate (*aj*)	Thompson
	cincture	Thompson
	crystalline[1]	Shelley; Thompson
*	carcanet	Earle's *Beowulf*[2]; Thompson
	bleaken(ing)	Thompson
	archimage	Thompson
	candent	Thompson
*	chiton	Thompson
	chlamys	Thompson
	antenatal	Shakespeare; Thompson
	conched	Scientific; Thompson
	campment	Thompson
?*	champartie[3]	Chaucer
*	argosy	
	agaric	
*	augrim (algorithm)	
	aglet	
	amethystine	
	coraline	

	crocean	
	basil (plant)	
	cramasie (scarlet cloth)	Elizabethan
	aquern (squirrel)	
	balas-ruby	

DEF

*	eoan	Thompson
*	euphrasy	Thompson; *etc.*
	dulcitude	Thompson
	dulcet (*aj*)	
*	endiapered	
	diaper(ed)	Chaucer; Shakespeare; *etc.*
	deepmost	Thompson
*	dusk (*aj*)	Thompson
	feat	
	emprise	*frequent*
	enow	
	fortalice	Shakespeare; Thompson; *etc.*
	dreamful	Tennyson
*	empillared	Thompson only
	enclip	Thompson only
	fardel	Thompson; *etc.*
	dispread	Thompson
	(en)vermeil(ed)	Thompson
	enwound	Thompson
	enrondured	Thompson
	englut	Shakespeare; Thompson
	escalade	Thompson
	drouth	Thompson
	dread-bolted (thunder)	Shakespeare
	engrafted	Shakespeare
	darraign	Chaucer; Shakespeare
*	foison	Shakespeare
*	fumiter (furrow weeds)	Shakespeare
	fen-sucked (fogs)	Shakespeare
	dolour	Shakespeare
	enguard	Shakespeare
	disquantity	Shakespeare
	darkling (*aj*)	Shakespeare; *passim.*

⋆	empery	Shakespeare; Thompson
⋆	esperance	Shakespeare
⋆	dittany	Tennyson; Thompson
	devisal	Thompson; Patmore
⋆	deliquious	Thompson
	deific (peaks)	Thompson
	fillibeg (kilt)	
	dayspring, dayrim (dawn)	
	freshet (cool stream)	
	frith (woodland)	
	dwale (deadly nightshade)	

GHIJK

	gast(er) (*vb*)	Shakespeare; *etc.*; Chaucer
	hurricano	Shakespeare
	intrinse, intrinsicate	Shakespeare; Elizabethan
	goldsmith(e)ry	Chaucer
	jape (bejape)	Chaucer
	gelid	Thompson
	intertangled	Thompson
	insculped	Thompson
	imagineless	Thompson
	inchmeal	Thompson
	irradiant	Thompson
⋆	galingale	Tennyson
⋆	incarnadine	Thompson; Shakespeare
	hierophant	Thompson
	illuminous (dark or in Thompson light)	Thompson
	journal (*aj*) (daily)	Thompson
	gold-tesserate	Thompson
	gracile	Thompson
	hyaline (*aj*, *sb*)	Milton; Thompson
	inaureole (*vb*)	Thompson
	knarry	Chaucer
⋆	galleon	Thompson
⋆	gramarie (-rye) (magic)	
	gules	
⋆	gloom	Spenser; Keats; *etc.*
	jacinth (a precious stone of hyacinth colour)	Tennyson

*	honey-fly (bee)	Never as far as I can find used before. I got it out of Meillet! 'mouche de miel'[4]
*	impearled	Keats
	Vale of Hinnom[5]	

LMNO

*	lind(en)	Chaucer
	lichwake	Chaucer
	lovesome	Lodge; Thompson
*	labyrinthine	Thompson; *passim.*
	lowlihead -hood	Thompson
*	lustihead -hood	
*	levin (lightning)	Thompson; *common*
	limn (*vb*)	Thompson
*	moly	Tennyson
	museful	Thompson
*	lucent	Thompson
	lucencies, lucent-weeping	Thompson
	o'ercanopy	
	olds (finny olds)[6]	Shakespeare; *etc.*
*	melodize	Thompson
	melodist	
	monody	
	orfrays (golden tassel work)	
	malachite (green stone of colour resembling mallow leaves *μαλάχη*)	Thompson
	malison	
*	lutanist	Thompson; Johnson
*	miniver (former form of *vair*)	
*	nenuphar (blue waterlily)	
	nectarous	Keats

PQRS

	roseal	Thompson
*	savanna	Thompson
	plenilune	Thompson
	splendent	Thompson
	purfled	Thompson

*	rondure	Thompson
	pilot-star	Tennyson
*	spillth	Earle's *Beowulf*; Thompson; ??? Browning[7]
	repured	Thompson
	plain (*sb* complaint)	Chaucer; Thompson
	steel-clear	Thompson
	orgiac	Thompson
	paludament	Thompson
	rubigiuous	Thompson
*	sennet	Shakespeare
	plight (*sb* pledge)	Shakespeare
	sluggardy	Chaucer
	(ap)paraments	Chaucer
	sarcenet	Shakespeare
	samphire	Shakespeare
	sliver	Shakespeare
	slogan	
	sorrow-wreathen	Shakespeare
	Seven-stars (Pleiades)	Shakespeare
	sallet	Shakespeare
	ravin	
	spoom (fly before wind)	
	spoondrift, spindrift (foam blown by the wind)	
	rebeck, ribible	
	puncheon (cask measure)	
	spinney	
	seldseen	
	rubious	
	ramsons (garlic)	
	pennoncel (pencil, pennon)	
	skerry (rock jutting up into sea)	
	skua (large gull)	
	shagreen (rough leather)	
*	shawm, shalm (reed-pipe, ???)[8]	
	shallop	

T – end

tucket	Shakespeare
unable (weak)	Shakespeare

*	toad-spotted (traitor)	Shakespeare
*	trill (trickle)	Shakespeare
	treacher	Shakespeare
	wide-skirted (meads)[9]	Shakespeare
	vaultages	Thompson
	wassail	
*	wassailous	Thompson
*	threne	Thompson
	whist (*aj*) (wonder whist)[10]	
	viewless	
	uneuphrasied	
	translucencies	
	tenebrous	
	tesserate	
	vermeil (vermill)	Spenser
*	yester-(rose)	
*	uranian	Thompson
	vair (a fur, heraldic)	Mackenzie
	vairy (*aj*) (heraldic)	
*	wieldy	
	vail (droop, let down)	
	vambrace (forearm-armour)	
	twibill	

B. SOME DELIGHTFUL DIALECTAL WORDS (USABLE)

hythe
wain
brant (steep)
caller (fresh fish)
carle
daggle (bail in wet)
fey
garth
howe
* immergoose (Northern Diver)
loon (same [as the Northern Diver but] smaller)
farce
lax (salmon)
lift (air)
mickle
murk

sark (shirt)
scut (rabbit's tail)
skep
* swale (shady place)
tarn
thaft (crossbench in boat)
* tibling (sparrow)
toft (mound where dwelling has once been)
wick (corner – cheek)
fleer (mock)
bing (pile)
dump
ing (low lying meadow)
keld (clear spring)
roke, rawk (low fog)
beck
blaeberry
brandreth (grid)
fell (hillside)
ged (pike)
* gowlan, gollan (marigold)
intake
kilp, kelp (pot hook over fire)
paddock (toad)
scree(s)
seaves (rushes)
spindrift
flittermouse

C. MORE DIALECTALS ETC., WORDS DELIGHTFUL BUT NOT GRAND

angletwitch (earthworm)
twire (peep; [from] Shakespeare)
undern

D. FROM M E [MIDDLE ENGLISH]

Lettow (Lithuania; [from] Chaucer)
Ruce (Russia)
ribible (rebeck; two-stringed lute)
gulch (gulp greedily)
* angrim (magic figures)

algorithm (magic figures)
★ sigaldry (enchantment; magics)
ciclaton (rich (scarlet) cloth)
★ Almain (Germany)

Jewel passage contains (in 'Luue Ron' 93/169 *OE Miscell[any]*)[11]
lectorie (amber)
calcedone (chalcedony)
smaragde (emerald)
crisopace

★ Ipotayns ([from] Mandeville; hippopotami)[12]
wonderly
covetice
Lowis and Beme (in Minoṭ = Louis & Bohemian)[13]
Portingal(l) (Portugal)
★★+Tybalt (Tybert) Prince of Cats[14]
Twire (peep, [from] Shak[e]sp[eare])
aventail
bezant
orfrays
mew
★ Beltane
grail (itin)[15]
jesserant

AUTHORS REFERENCED IN LISTS A–D

Anonymous (*Reynard the Fox*)
Robert Browning, 1812–1889
Geoffrey Chaucer, 1340–1400
John Earle, 1824–1903
Samuel Johnson, 1709–1784
John Keats, 1795–1821
Thomas Lodge, *c.* 1558–1625
Compton Mackenzie, 1883–1972
Sir John Mandeville, 14th century
Antoine Meillet, 1866–1936
John Milton, 1608–1674
Laurence Minot, ?1300–?1352
Coventry Patmore, 1823–1896
William Shakespeare, 1564–1616
Percy Bysshe Shelley, 1792–1822

Sir Philip Sidney, 1554–1586
Edmund Spenser, 1552/3–1599
Alfred, Lord Tennyson, 1809–1892
Thomas, of Hales, 13th century
Francis Thompson, 1859–1907

1. As written, *crystalline* contains acute accents: *crýstallíne*.

2. John Earle (spelled by Tolkien 'Earl') translated the Old English *Beowulf* into Modern English prose, as *The Deeds of Beowulf* (1892),

3. The question mark before *champartie* is Tolkien's.

4. *Mouche de miel* is French for 'honey fly', i.e. honeybee.

5. A curious insertion of a place-name in the list. *Vale* (or *Valley*) *of Hinnom* is the modern name for Genenna (Gehinnom), the valley surrounding ancient Jerusalem.

6. *Old*, i.e. *wold* 'open country', does appear in Shakespeare, as in *King Lear*, 'Swithold footed thrice the old'. 'Finny olds', however, appears to be from the second part (1622) of *Poly-Olbion* by Michael Drayton (1563–1631) in lines referring to the River Mease: 'Her Banks which, all her course, on both sides do abound | With Heath and Finny olds'.

7. Before 'Browning' is writing in pencil we cannot make out, other than an ampersand.

8. We are unable to read the word following 'reed-pipe'.

9. *Wide-skirted* does not mean 'meads', but is an adjective modifying *meads* in a line from *King Lear*, 'With plenteous rivers and wide-skirted meads' (i.e. extensive meadows).

10. 'Wonder whist' appears in John Milton's poem 'On the Morning of Christ's Nativity'.

11. The reference is to the *Luue Ron* ('Love Rune') by Thomas of Hales in the *Old English Miscellany* edited by Richard Morris (1872), a standard textbook for Oxford English School students. (The title of the book refers to 'old' English literature in the sense of 'early', not specifically to Old English texts.) The poem begins on p. 93 of the *Miscellany*; its 'jewel passage', comparing love to a 'jewel more precious than any earthly gems', begins on l. 169.

12. The reference is to the *Travels* (*Itinerarium*), or book of marvels, attributed to Sir John Mandeville.

13. The reference is to Lowis (Louis), kayser (ruler) of Bavere (Bavaria), and the kingdom of Beme (Bohemia) in the work of the fourteenth-century English poet Laurence Minot.

14. In the manuscript this line is not only emphasized with two asterisks and a plus-sign, but also underlined. Tybalt, or Tibert, is a character in the popular story of Reynard the Fox. The name *Tybalt* is also that of a character in Shakespeare's *Romeo and Juliet*, who is called 'prince of cats' after the actual cat in 'Reynard'. We cannot help but be reminded of Tevildo, Prince of Cats, in *The Book of Lost Tales*, the precursor of Sauron in Tolkien's later mythology.

15. We read the word in brackets as 'itin'. If this is correct, it could be an abbreviation for *itinerarium*, and thus a reference to a text by that title, though none that we can confirm.

Appendix V. *Bealuwérig*

The manuscript of this poem by Tolkien in Old English, acquired in 2023 by the Bodleian Library, Oxford from the estate of Walter Hooper via the Arts Council, came to our attention too late to be included in the general part of *Collected Poems*, but is too interesting not to present by itself as an appendix. Tolkien evidently gave it to C.S. Lewis, after whose death in 1963 it passed to Hooper, his literary executor. It is not dated, but from Tolkien's handwriting, and the history of his friendship with Lewis, our best guess is that it was made in the 1930s. In this Tolkien used the Tironian *et* (⁊) for the conjunction *and*, which we have retained along with Tolkien's caesuras, or metrical pauses, shown as wide spaces.

Once again for this poem, we have relied on our friend Arden R. Smith to vet our transcription (A) and provide a translation (B). He has also written most of the linguistic discussion following B.

[A]

Þa wæs swelswoloð.   Slíðe tófas
gurron ⁊ gimbledon   on græswǽfan;
mímsæde murnon   morgengrófas,
⁊ hræðmóman   hlúde grǽfon.

'Beorg þe wiþ Bealuwearg,   byre min léofa,
grápan griple,   góman bitre!
Géo-géowfugol   éac georne bebúg!
Hrúmheortne scuna   Hlóþorlæccan!'

He þa folmum wand   felaworpel sweord,
sóhte mánsceaðan   manchygdigne,
oþþæt he be wambe   wambanbéames
reste hine rúmheort   rǽdes æt ende.

Þá he þǽr húfigmód   hwíle reste,
Bealuwearg arás   — blǽst cóm of éagum! —
hwéos ⁊ hwiflede   þurh holt-tulgas
gnyr-bellende,   gryre unlýtel.

Án æfter ánum   inn þurh-éoden
swengas snicre   snacran méces.
Hrǽw féoll on eorðan.   Hafelan grimne
he þa gelumpenheort   lǽdan éode.

'Ac þu Bealuwearge to banan wurde,
hyse béamlíca?' — he be healse genam —
'Hí lá, hú lá! gehnǽstig dæg!'
ceorl cearclode, ciermde on blisse.

Þa wæs swelswoloð. Slíðe tófas
gurron ⁊ gimbledon on græswǽfan;
mímsæde murnon morgengrófas,
⁊ hræðmóman hlúde grǽfon.

Astute readers may notice in this text, even if they do not understand the language, two features in particular. One is the name *Bealuwearg*, Old English for 'malicious outlaw', which recalls that of Tolkien's fell creature in *The Lord of the Rings*, the *Balrog*, and of the wolf-like beasts in *The Hobbit* called *Wargs*. Among lists he made of Old English equivalents of Elvish names, *Balrog* in fact is related by Tolkien to *Bealuwearg* and *Bealubróga*. For these, he notes: 'O.E. [Old English] *bealu* 'evil', cf. Modern English *bale(ful)*; *wearg* 'felon, outlaw, accursed being' (Old Norse *vargr* 'wolf, outlaw', whence the *Wargs*); *bróga* 'terror'' (*The Shaping of Middle-earth*, p. 209). The title Tolkien gave to the present manuscript, *Bealuwérig*, combines *bealu* 'evil' (also 'harm, destruction, malice') with *wérig* 'weary, sad, unfortunate', thus 'weary of evil'; and in this connection, we cannot resist thinking of *Beowulf* (see no. 88) in which the folk of Heorot endured the repeated violence visited upon them by the monster Grendel.

The other point to make about *Bealuwérig*, and here the clues are in its rhythm and in vaguely familiar words such as 'slíðe tófas' and 'felaworpel sweord', is that it is not an original work by Tolkien, but his translation into alliterative Old English of Lewis Carroll's famous nonsense poem 'Jabberwocky'. That verse was first published in full in 1871, in *Through the Looking-glass and What Alice Found There*, a sequel to *Alice's Adventures in Wonderland*. Its first (and final) stanza, however, had appeared already in 1855 in the private magazine *Mischmasch* produced by Carroll and his siblings, where its author pretended that the lines were a 'Stanza of Anglo-Saxon Poetry' and provided 'glosses' of unusual words. How appropriate, then, that Tolkien should have made 'Jabberwocky', whose initial lines Carroll pretended were Anglo-Saxon, into something more authentically in the Anglo-Saxon tongue, if with a considerable amount of invention to accommodate Carroll's inventions.

It has been said that 'Jabberwocky' was well known to schoolboys in the days of Tolkien's youth, and there is much evidence – we have presented some elsewhere in the *Collected Poems* – that Tolkien was very fond of Carroll's writings in general, not only the stories about Alice. C.S. Lewis seems to have enjoyed reading Carroll as much as Tolkien did: particularly in regard to 'Jabberwocky', in one letter he praised A.A. Vansittart's Latin translation of the poem ('Coesper erat: tunc lubriciles ultravia circum | Urgebant gyros gimbiculosque tophi'), and in another he said that 'no one ever influenced Tolkien – you might as well try to influence a bandersnatch' (*Collected Letters*, vol. 3 (2006), p. 1049). If it is not read, quoted, and loved as much today as in the last century, it deserves to be.

For convenience, we quote 'Jabberwocky' here, from chapter 1 of *Through the Looking-glass*. Later in that book, Alice discusses the poem with Humpty Dumpty, who gives his own interpretations.

'Twas brillig, and the slithy toves
    Did gyre and gimble in the wabe:
All mimsy were the borogoves,
    And the mome raths outgrabe.

'Beware the Jabberwock, my son!
    The jaws that bite, the claws that catch!
Beware the Jubjub bird, and shun
    the frumious Bandersnatch!'

He took his vorpal sword in hand:
    Long time the manxome foe he sought —
So rested he by the Tumtum tree,
    And stood awhile in thought.

And, as in uffish thought he stood,
    The Jabberwock, with eyes of flame,
Came whiffling through the tulgey wood,
    And burbled as it came!

One, two! One, two! And through and through
    The vorpal blade went snicker-snack!
He left it dead, and with its head
    He went galumphing back.

'And hast thou slain the Jabberwock?
    Come to my arms, my beamish boy!
O frabjous day! Callooh! Callay!'
    He chortled in his joy.

'Twas brillig, and the slithy toves
    Did gyre and gimble in the wabe:
All mimsy were the borogoves,
    And the mome raths outgrabe.

In translating Tolkien's Old English 'Jabberwocky' into Modern English, as below, Arden Smith has made no attempt to preserve either Tolkien's alliterative verse forms or Carroll's original rhyme and metre. *Bealuwearg* has been retained in that form as a name. Those words not readily interpretable in Old English have been translated using Carroll's original forms or derivatives thereof, in italics.

[B] There was burn-burning. The savage *toves*
grunted and *gimbled* on the grass-*wabe*;
mim-fully mourned the morning-*groves*,
and the quick-*momes* loudly *grabe*.

'Defend thyself against the Bealuwearg, my dear son,
the grasping grip, the cruel jaws!
Also zealously avoid the *Jubjub* bird!
Shun the soot-hearted *Bandersnatch*!'

He then with hands swung a very *vorpal* sword,
sought the *manc*-minded foe,
until he in the hollow of the tummy-tree
rested himself free from care at the end of his plan.

As he there in *uffish* thought a while rested,
Bealuwearg arose — flame came from its eyes! —
it coughed and *whiffled* through the wood-*tulgs*
grind-bellowing, not a small terror.

One after another inward penetrated
the blows of the *snicker-snack* sword.
The corpse fell on the ground. A fierce head
he then *galumph*-heartedly went carrying.

'And hast thou become the bane of the Bealuwearg,
beamish boy?' — he embraced him about the neck —
'*Callooh, callay*! contentious day!'
the man *chortled*, cried in joy.

There was burn-burning. The savage *toves*
grunted and *gimbled* on the grass-*wabe*;
mim-fully mourned the morning-*groves*,
and the quick-*momes* loudly *grabe*.

In Tolkien's translation, *Swelswoloð* (line A1) is his invention to translate *brillig*, which Carroll connected with 'broiling'. It combines the Old English verb *swelan* 'to burn' with its derivative *swoloð* 'burning heat'. *Swel-* and *swol-* are ablaut variants of the same root; compare the vowel alternation in Modern English *swell* and *swollen*.

Sliðe (A1) is a genuine Old English adjective meaning 'savage, cruel', similar in form (but not meaning) to Carroll's *slithy*, a portmanteau of *lithe* and *slimy*.

Tőfas (A1) stands in for Carroll's *toves*, modified by Tolkien to conform to Old English spelling and grammar. According to Humpty Dumpty in chapter 6 of *Through the Looking-glass*, toves are 'something like badgers', 'something like lizards', and 'something like corkscrews'.

Gurron (A2), the preterite (i.e. denoting the past) plural form of *gyrran* 'to sound, chatter, grunt', translates Carroll's phonetically similar *gyre*. In *Looking-glass*, *gyre* means 'to go round and round like a gyroscope'; in the earlier *Mischmasch*, Carroll's definition was 'to scratch like a dog'.

Gimbledon (A2) is used for Carroll's *gimble* ('to make holes') with an Old English preterite plural ending.

Græswǽfan (A2) is a compound of *græs* 'grass' and *wǽfa* or *wǽfe* (with *-an* ending in the dative case), Tolkien's invented Old English form of Carroll's *wabe*. It could have some connection to *wǽfre* 'restless, wandering', seen in *Ottor Wǽfre*, the original name of Eriol, the Anglo-Saxon mariner in Tolkien's *Lost Tales*. In *Looking-glass*, a *wabe* is said to be 'the grass-plot round a sun-dial', in *Mischmasch* it is 'the side of a hill'.

Mímsæde (A3) is Tolkien's invention to translate *mimsy* ('flimsy and miserable'). The first element *mím* may recall *Mímir* from Norse mythology, but was probably chosen by Tolkien simply for its phonetic similarity. The second element is presumably the adjective *sæd* 'full' with adverbial suffix *-e*, thus 'fully'.

Morgengrófas (A3) is Tolkien's invention to translate *borogoves*. The first element of this word is *morgen* 'morning'; the initial *m-* here is undoubtedly due to the need for alliteration with *mímsæde*. The second element recalls *gróf*, the preterite singular of *grafan* 'to dig, carve'; the initial *gr-* reflects the common mispronunciation of *borogoves* as *borogroves*. In *Looking-glass*, a *borogove* is 'a thin shabby-looking bird with its feathers sticking out all round', in *Mischmasch* 'an extinct kind of Parrot' without wings who made its nest under sundials.

Hræðmóman (A4) is Tolkien's invention to translate *mome raths*, reversing the order of the two elements. The first element is *hræð* 'quick, active', clearly chosen for its phonetic similarity to *rath*. The second element is Carroll's *mome*, modified by Tolkien to conform to Old English spelling and grammar. In *Mischmasch* Carroll defined *mome* as 'grave' and a *rath* as 'a species of land turtle'; in *Looking-glass*, a *rath* became 'a sort of green pig', but Humpty Dumpty was unsure about *mome*. In *The Annotated Alice* (2000 edn., p. 152), Martin Gardner notes that in Carroll's day *rath* 'was a well-known old Irish word for an enclosure, usually a circular earthen wall'.)

Grǽfon (A4), Tolkien's invention to translate *outgrabe*, is clearly preterite plural in form, but is not the preterite plural of any attested Old English verb, although it recalls *grafan* 'to dig, carve'. In *Looking-glass*, *outgrabe* meant 'something between bellowing and whistling, with a kind of sneeze in the middle'; in *Mischmasch* it simply meant 'squeaked'.

Grápan (A6) should be a noun in the accusative case, if this half-line is grammatically parallel with the following half-line. The noun *gráp* 'grasp, grip' fits semantically, but would not have the *-an* ending. Note that Tolkien has reversed the half-lines meaning 'the jaws that bite' and 'the claws that catch'.

Géo-géowfugol (A7) is Tolkien's invention to translate *Jubjub bird*. The word *géo* 'once, formerly' exists in Old English, but *Géo-géow* is more likely just onomatopoeic. It would be pronounced approximately like Modern English *yo-yo*.

Hrúmheortne (A8) is a compound of *hrúm* 'soot' and *-heort* '-hearted', used to translate *frumious* – a portmanteau of *fuming* and *furious*, according to Carroll in *The Hunting of the Snark* – which has a phonetically similar initial syllable. Compare *rúmheort* 'large-hearted, generous, free from care' in line 12.

Hlóþorlæccan (A8) is Tolkien's invention to translate *Bandersnatch*. The first element, *hlóþor*, recalls *hlóþ* 'spoil, booty; band (of robbers)' and *hlóþere* 'robber', i.e. 'bandit'. The second, *læcca* (with suffixed *-n* in the accusative case), derives from the verb *læccan* 'to seize, grasp', i.e. 'to snatch'.

Felaworpel (A9) is a compound of *fela* 'much, very' and *worpel*, Tolkien's pseudo-Old English modification of *vorpal*, a word for which Carroll apparently had no explanation.

Manchygdigne (A10) is Tolkien's invention to translate *manxome* (which to Carroll evidently has no connection with the Celtic name of the Isle of Man). The first element, *manc*, is presumably just a phonetically similar nonsense-word. The second element is *-hygdig* '-minded'.

In *wambe wambanbéames* (A11) Tolkien interprets the *Tumtum* of Carroll's *Tumtum tree* as 'stomach', translating it with *wamb* 'belly, womb', which he also uses to refer to the hollow of the tree. Compare Tolkien's use of 'tumtum' for 'stomach' in poem no. 9. In *The Annotated Alice*, Martin Gardner notes that '*tum-tum* was a common colloquialism in Carroll's day, referring to the sound of a stringed instrument, especially when monotonously strummed' (2000 edn., p. 153).

Húfigmód (A13) is Tolkien's invention to translate *uffish thought*. The first element, *húfig*, appears to have been created for phonetic similarity to *uffish*, but Tolkien may also have had such words as *húf* 'horned owl' and *húfe* 'head covering' in mind. The element *-ig* is a common adjectival suffix, the source of Modern English *-y*. To Carroll, *uffish* suggested a gruffish voice, a roughish manner, and a huffish temper.

Hwiflede (A15) is Tolkien's invention to translate *whiffled* ('came whiffling' in the original poem); this is the preterite singular of a putative verb *hwiflian*. Compare the genuine Old English verbs *hwisprian* 'to whisper' and *hwistlian* 'to whistle'. In *The Annotated Alice* (2000 edn., p. 153), Martin Gardner notes that *whiffling*, not a Carrollian coinage, usually meant in his time 'blowing unsteadily in short puffs'.

Holt-tulgas (A15) is Tolkien's invention to translate *tulgey wood*, reversing the order of the two elements. The first element is *holt* 'forest, wood'. The second is a modification of *tulgey*, converted into a plural noun. Carroll himself could not explain *tulgey*.

Gnyr-bellende (A16) is Tolkien's invention to translate *burbled*, combining *gnyrran* 'to grind the teeth' and *bellende* 'bellowing, roaring'. Carroll explained *burbled* as a combination of *bleat*, *murmur*, and *warble*. Tolkien used the word in this sense ('speak ramblingly') in *The New Lemminkainen* and *Doworst* (nos. 8, 139).

Snicre snacran (A18) stands in for the onomatopoeic *snicker-snack*, modified with Old English spelling and word endings. The old word *snickersnee* means 'to fight with a knife'.

Gelumpenheort (A20) is Tolkien's invention to translate *galumphing*. The first element is a modification of *galumph*, identical in form with the past participle *gelumpen* 'happened, occurred'. The second is *-heort* '-hearted'; see lines 8 and 12. Carroll coined *galumph* as a combination of *gallop* and *triumphant*.

Béamlíca (A22) is Tolkien's invention to translate *beamish*. It could be interpreted as 'tree-like': *béam* 'tree, beam' with suffix *-líc* '-like, -ly'. Martin Gardner notes that *beamish* is traced in the *Oxford English Dictionary* to 1530 as a variant of *beaming*.

Hí lá, hú lá! (A23) are Old English interjections to translate *Callooh! Callay!* The interjection *lá!* is the source of Modern English *lo!*

Gehnǽstig (A23) is Tolkien's invention to translate *frabjous*. It appears to be *gehnǽst* 'conflict, battle' with the adjectival suffix *-ig*. Tolkien may have been equating *frabjous* (*fabulous* + *joyous*) with *fractious*.

Cearclode (A24) is Tolkien's invention to translate *chortled* (*chuckle* + *snort*), probably based on the genuine Old English verb *cearcian* 'chatter, creak, gnash'.

Glossary

These are words and names used by Tolkien in his poems which have an archaic or unusual sense, or otherwise may be less familiar to readers. The list is necessarily subjective: no doubt it includes words well known to some, while others may have been omitted because they are too familiar to the editors. All citations are to *poem number*, and all references are to words *in the texts or titles of Tolkien's poems*, as given in the entries, including quotations from Tolkien's poems within our discussion. We have not glossed unusual words in quotations from other authors or in our own text. In a few instances, it has been useful to include references to words in a familiar sense (e.g. *bar* 'obstruction') to distinguish a less familiar but similar usage (e.g. *bar* 'band of colour, light, or darkness').

The Glossary is in two parts: a general sequence of terms, and a list of those words or names mentioned in poems specific to Tolkien's 'Middle-earth' stories. In general, we have omitted words in languages other than Modern English; only in the second part have we glossed terms in Tolkien's invented languages. In the first part, arrangement is mainly by common element; for example, *balefield* is found with *bale*. We have given most nouns in the singular, with plurals noted when it seemed useful, and most verbs in the infinitive, with different tenses or variants as relevant. We have omitted common poetic contractions, such as *e'en* 'even' and *'neath* (or *neath*) 'beneath'; constructions such as *or . . . or* 'either . . . or'; archaisms such as *goeth* and *moveth* where the meaning is clear; familiar medievalisms such as *doth* 'does'; and coinages by Tolkien such as *pepperdillo* (no. 94) and *gloo* (no. 105), which, however, are mentioned in notes.

Sometimes we have commented more expansively in our text about words listed here (e.g. our discussion of *dale*, *dell*, *dingle*, *hollow*, *vale*, and *valley* for poem no. 2). In the second part, we have assumed that the reader has some knowledge of Tolkien's fiction, or will be able to explore it. For example, the name *Beleriand* is needed in some of our definitions, but does not appear in any of the poems we present, so is not itself defined; however, it is easily found in standard references, such as our *Lord of the Rings: A Reader's Companion*.

To keep the Glossary to a manageable length, we have included in the first part only selected words related to nature, while suggesting Tolkien's broad knowledge of trees, flowers, minerals, etc. through an appendix of specific terms.

acold cold, chilled 18
adamant rock or mineral of legend, surpassing hard, like diamond 20, 128; **adamantine** with the qualities of adamant 20
addle-egg rotten egg 89
adipose fat 96
aëry airy, breezy 45
All Hallows, All-Hallows, Allhallows All Saints' Day (1 November) 40
ammonite extinct marine mollusc with a spiral shell 19
an if 67
anemone marine animal with tubular body and stinging tentacles 19
anon soon 5, 53, 70
apprehend understand, perceive 136
arboreal pertaining to trees 136
archipelago group of islands, or sea with many islands 35, 44, 128
argent silver 16, 24, 128, 157
argosy (as plural **argosies**) large merchant sailing ship (used figuratively) 16, 128
arras tapestry 4
array arrange, order 6, 13, 40, 130, 173; ordered arrangement 7, 173; outfit, dress 7, 70
arrow-reed reed with a spear-like tip 134
arrow-sheen brightness of an arrowhead in flight 22
ash World Tree in Norse mythology (Yggdrasil) 131
assize law court (used figuratively) 139
astern behind the stern (rear) of a ship 175
athanasie tansy 96
athwart across 34
attercop spider 128
atwo in two 7
aught, ought anything 89, 91, 129, 139, 174
aureole halo or heavenly crown 83; **aureoled, inaureoled** with a halo 24, 42
axiomatically relying on a proposition self-evidently true 183
azure bright blue 30, 61

babewin baboon, gargoyle 139
bade old past tense of *bid*, commanded 6, 62, 66, 88, 120, 130; uttered 169

bale injury, pain, death 7, 67; **balefield** battlefield 7; **balesheen** light from funeral pyres 7; **balesong** battle-song 7

balled bald 139

bannock round, flat loaf 105

bantam chicken of a small breed 75

bar band of colour, light, or darkness (as in the sky) 3, 40, 45, 94; obstruction (as in a gate) 18, 28, 30, 48, 51, 62, 66, 92, 128, 136; sandbank, shoal 31, 53, 66, 74, 127, 134; **barred** obstructed 43, 190

bark any kind of ship or boat (as used by Tolkien) 7, 16, 31, 33, 88, 174

barleycorn grain of barley 186

barrow burial mound 58, 129; **barrow-wight** spirit living in a barrow 129; *see also names with* **Barrow** *in part* II *below*

basilisk mythical beast with deadly gaze and breath 96

battailous warlike, bellicose 13

battlement parapet with recesses in a fortification 126

beak projection at the prow of a ship 88, 141; bill of a bird 89, 147, 181, 186

beaker drinking vessel 131

begging-letter letter asking for aid to the poor 122

beguile charm 92, 175

beleaguered *see* **leaguered**

bellying swelling 16, 18

Belmarye generally identified as Benmarin (Morocco) 62

bent grass, or grasslike reeds, rushes, or sedges 37; open, grassy place 40, 74

betake go to 173

bewhiles *see* **whiles**

bewilder *see* **wilder**

bier moveable frame for a coffin or corpse 91, 116

bilious (as **billious**) spiteful, bad-tempered 181

billow wave 7, 13, 18, 128, 133, 141; move or build up in waves 7, 13, 124

bitter bitterness 130, 131

blancmange sweet, glutinous dessert made with flavoured cornflour and milk 188

blazon, emblazon adorn 7, 24; **blazon** heraldic device 116, 157; **blazonry** heraldic devices 7

blent old past tense of *blend* 174

bloater cured herring (used for overweight, unattractive person) 103

blood-fain eager to draw blood 7

board table for serving meals 6, 49, 116, 117; table, as for a council 139; food, meals 143

bob shilling, pre-decimal British coin 8, 103
bogey (as plural **bogies**) evil or mischievous spirit, devil 129, 186
boiling bowl pot for cooking or boiling 108
bole, tree-bole trunk of a tree 4, 48, 50, 66, 96
bone steal 83; **boner** thief 83
bouze booze, drink alcohol to excess 139
bower shady recess, arbour 2; dwelling 3, 33, 69, 88, 92, 116, 128
brake thicket, dense group of bushes or trees 48, 54, 186; broke (old past tense of *break*) 92
bramble thorny shrub 173, 185
brave splendid, showy 2, 24, 88, 107; defy 67; **bravery** splendour, finery 128
bray make a loud, harsh sound 6, 67, 106, 130
brazen made of brass 61; flagrant 69, 139
breaker heavy wave 34, 88, 119, 134, 140, 146
briar prickly bush, especially the wild briar-rose 74, 121, 134, 185; **rose** (i.e. briar-rose) 48, 74, 121
brobdingnagian tremendously large 96
brock badger 121, 134
brolly umbrella 105
buckle gird 2
buckler small round shield 159
bumby marshy land, quagmire 186
burble speak ramblingly 8, 139
burden, burdon low undersong or accompaniment to a melody 13, 14
burg walled and fortified town, city 7, 66
burnish make shiny by rubbing 67, 128, 130
byre cowshed 49, 75
byrnie chain mail shirt 88

cadency cadence, rising and falling of elemental sounds (as of the sea) 13
cadent falling 64
canned drunk 96
canorous melodious, resonant 24
canvas ship's sails 33
capital ornamental head of a pillar or column 30, 66; excellent 193; indicating a statutory offence 193
car cart, chariot 62
carcanet necklace or ornamental collar 42, 128
carcase, carkis body 13, 83, 129

carvel small, fast ship, caravel 128
catchpoll petty officer of justice 139
Cathay China 52
cerement waxed cloth for wrapping a corpse 61
chalcedony (also **chrysoprase**) type of quartz, such as onyx or agate 24, 128
champ make a biting or chewing motion (of a horse) 60
champain open country 40, 44
chanty (as plural **chanties**) sea-song, often spelled *shanty* 103
chaplet wreath, garland 55
charabanc (as **charabang**) coach for tourists 103
charnel charnel-vault, place where dead bodies are stored 139
chasmed, chasméd, chasmic, enchasmed having chasms 20, 35, 53
cheaping marketplace 186
chirrup chirp 89, 121
chop-fallen with one's jaw hanging open 139
chrysoprase *see* **chalcedony**
churching appearance at church, especially by a woman to give thanks after childbirth 116
churl person of low birth 129
cincture girdle or belt 35
clack (as **clackest**) make a sharp sound (as of a hard object striking another) 89
clamant urgently clamorous, noisy 40
clangorous repeated clanging, uproar 13
clap put or place 121
cleave (past tense **clave**) hold fast to 7, 69, 88; divide (past tense **clove, cloven**) 7, 124, 128, 130, 131, 132, 141, 159, 163, 174, 175
clerk, (Middle English) **clerke** person with book learning, scholar 68, 139
clink jail 96
cloister covered passage around a courtyard, as in a college 139; **cloistered** secluded 44
clomb old past tense of *climb* 88
cob male swan 186
cobbled paved with small round stones 103
cock turn attentively (as an ear) 60, 107, 186; raise (as a bird's tail) 186; cockerel, rooster 75, 141, 181; **cock-a-leery** cockerel 184; **cock-a-leery light** dawn 184; **cock-crow** dawn 134
cockalorum self-important little man 186
cockle-boat small boat shaped like a cockle-shell 186

cockshut at twilight 48, 186
cocky saucy, impudent 186
codex manuscript with sequential pages in book form 83
colter cut with the blade of a plough 36
conclave meeting, assembly 44, 46
constellate adorned with stars, like a constellation 33, 53
cony (as plural **coneys, conies**) rabbit 121
coomb combe, deep but usually not large valley 175
coot generically applied to a water-bird 186
copse small group of trees 26, 43, 50
coraline coral red 19
corn cereal grain 139, 146, 165, 166; **cornfield, cornland** 61, 141
corpse-candle lighted candle placed beside a corpse before burial 123
corrigan fay, witch 116
corse corpse, body 88
corslet armour for the trunk of the body 6, 7, 88, 117, 129, 131, 159
cottage garden English informal garden, often with ornamental and edible plants 44
course gallop on horseback 25
crag steep rock 7, 12, 13, 70
crozier curled tip of a young fern 26
cunning of ingenious design, skilled 6, 7, 18, 88, 96, 136; skill, knowledge 69, 92, 131
curstly cursed 142

daddy daddy-long-legs, long-legged fly, i.e. crane-fly 75
daisy moon moon daisy, i.e. ox-eye daisy 2
daisy-string string of daisies with stems threaded or braided together 28
dale valley or hollow 2, 23, 66, 67, 89, 90, 109, 116, 117, 121, 130, 141, 148, 175
damozelle damsel, young unmarried woman 56
dandelion clock children's game of blowing dandelion seeds 48
dark-lantern lantern with moveable panel to hide the light 129
darkling in darkness 6, 64, 66, 69, 116, 128, 129, 130, 134, 140, 142, 163, 168; darkening 7, 16, 19; with a dark countenance 7, 186
dart arrow 7, 130, 174
dauntless intrepid, persevering 7, 67, 128, 131
deem regard, judge 7, 58, 88, 136, 139, 140, 175
dell small, deep valley or hollow 4, 26, 69, 74, 116, 150, 159
derring-do heroic action 128

diadem crown or headband 24, 40
diapered decorated with a repeating pattern 42
dight arrayed, clothed 6, 7, 88
ding kill by repeated blows 139
dingle deep dell or hollow 26, 121, 128
dint blow, stroke 7, 139; dent 136
divination seeking knowledge by supernatural means 136
dole destiny, lot in life 88
don university teacher, especially a senior member of a faculty 139
dotty unsteady, (figuratively) silly 60
doughty brave, resolute 6, 88, 170
down gentle rolling hill 90
draggled dirty, wet, limp 121
drake dragon 177
drave old past tense of *drive* 7
dreadly dreadfully, terribly 7, 67, 131, 136
drift deposits left by retreating ice-sheets 35
drouth thirst 24
druery love, especially sexual love 116
druid member of a high-ranking class in Celtic cultures 174
dudgeon anger, resentment 139
dumbledor, dumbledore bumblebee 99, 128
dun dull, greyish-brown colour 126, 132, 142, 175

earth sett, badger's burrow 121
eaves overhanging edge of a roof 1, 38, 130, 142; edge, margin 116, 121, 134
ebon black, dark, the colour of the wood ebony 128
effluvium stink 75
eld old, past times 7, 53, 88; grow old 116
elvet swan 186
emmet ant 101
emulsion medicinal oil 95
enchasmed *see* **chasmed**
enow enough 70, 89
equipage body of men 7
errand purpose, mission 92, 115, 128, 131, 153, 186; **errander** one with an errand 128
errantry travels, roaming 16, 128
erst long ago, formerly 7, 26, 88
esplanade long open area, typically beside the sea 103
esquadron squadron, body of men 7

evensong church service traditionally held near sunset 12
eyot small island (used figuratively) 48

fag cigarette 103, 106, 174
fain gladly, eager 7, 22, 88, 90, 91, 116; *see also* blood-fain, war-fain; **fainest** favourable 88
fairily in the manner of a fairy 39
fairy ring, fairy-ring ring of grass darker than surrounding grass 28
fallow pale brown or reddish-yellow 67, 116, 128, 146
fane temple 40
fare travel, move 2, 7, 9, 16, 37, 42, 57, 67, 70, 74, 88, 90, 92, 116, 119, 132, 145, 150, 158, 172
farthing pre-decimal British coin, one-quarter of an old penny 181
fastness stronghold, fortress 66, 71, 88, 128, 136
fay fairy 50, 65, 92, 116, 140
fealty allegiance 67, 169
featherbrain silly or absentminded person 128
feathered, feathery husky (of a voice) 34
fell fierce, terrible, evil 7, 40, 88, 96, 116, 139, 140, 169, 190; high, barren landscape 37, 61, 70, 88, 109, 112, 132, 153; animal skin, pelt 186; **felled** covered with skin or fur 66; **fell-hearted** with evil intent 129; **felly** fiercely 88
fen low, marshy land 24, 40, 88, 129, 163
fet fetch 88
fetter shackle, bind 17, 35, 67, 92, 174
fey fated to die 40, 130; otherwordly 129
fief land held by a vassal under a lord 52
filigree like delicate jewel work 24
firmament sky, heavens 16, 20, 31, 35, 53, 136, 151
firstling first to appear 40, 48, 66
firth narrow inlet of the sea, estuary 175
flammifer flame bearer 128
fleet group of ships 40, 174; **fleet, fleeting, fleetly** swift, quick 6, 7, 25, 32, 35, 41, 48, 56, 64, 88, 130, 134, 179; move or pass swiftly 42, 67, 114
flint form of quartz, struck with steel to light fires 129
flittermouse (as plural **flittermice**) bat (flying mammal) 27, 40
flotsam floating wreckage 67
foray attack suddenly, raid 128
ford, fording shallow place to cross a river or stream, or crossing at a ford 9, 10, 70, 90, 134, 139; *see also* **Ford** *in part* II *below*

foreshow foretell 7
fortalice fortress, fortification 13
forwander, forwandre wander far and wide 66, 168
founder sink 18, 35, 74, 128, 129, 130, 132, 175, 186
freke bold man, man 139
fret interlace 30, 35, 44; ornament with carving or embossing 52; rub, chafe 127; worry 190
frond leaf of a fern 26
frore frozen 116, 117, 127, 134, 141
frousty frowsty, stuffy 84
fulsome of a large size or quantity 105
fume odoriferous or noxious vapour 35, 37, 63, 88, 131
furbish remove rust from, polish, burnish 128
furl wrap, take in (as sails) 33; **unfurl** 40, 53, 130, 136, 175
furrow shallow trench made by a plough (also used figuratively) 133, 139
fylfot type of cross, swastika 174

gainsay contradict, oppose 139
galleon any kind of ship (used poetically and figuratively) 16, 35, 40, 53, 88, 140
gallowsfowl person who deserves to be hanged (gallows bird), by extension a scoundrel, villain 131
gallows-weed probably gallow-grass, hemp 94
game lame, crippled 83
gammer old woman 143
gan, 'gan gone 5, 7, 88
garner collect, harvest 7, 118, 134; storehouse, granary 146
garth enclosed yard 67, 165
geodesy mathematical study of the figures and areas of the Earth 174
gird, (old past tense) **girt** surround, encircle 6, 24, 40, 42, 44, 130, 193; **girdle** surround, encircle 32, 35, 46; something which surrounds 32, 40; belt 32, 121; **girdle-seat** waist 92; **girdlestead** waist 24, 42
girth measurement around the middle 96
gladdon iris 134
glade open space in a wood or forest 4, 28, 40, 43, 48, 64, 67, 74, 92, 141, 153, 186
glaive broadsword, or generically any sword 66, 88
glamoury enchantment 64, 128
glee song, tale 129
gleed live coal, ember 41

gleeman minstrel 129
glen narrow valley 50, 67, 160
glim light, as of a fire 95
glister sparkle, glitter 7, 22, 35, 67, 90
gloam, gloaming twilight 18, 26, 50, 56, 66, 106, 113, 121, 128; darkening, becoming dusk 28, 33, 35, 128
glower menace 6, 67
goggle wide open 95; **goggled** wearing goggles 63
gome man 139
gondola ship's boat, or a small boat designed for war 18, 128
gonfanon heraldic flag or banner 88
goodman male title of dignity and respect 91, 186
goodwife female title of dignity and respect 186
gorcrow carrion-crow 94
gorgon frightening or repulsive person 63
gossamer fine cobwebs 32, 40, 128, 158
Goth member of a Germanic people (Ostrogoths, Visigoths), invaders of the Roman Empire in the third to fifth centuries 88, 129, 131; German 139
grabble (in the name *Grabbler*) feel or search with the hand, grope 106
grail cup 6, 175
gramarye arcane knowledge 53
gramercy (as **grammercy**) thank you very much 91
greased bribed 96
greave armour for the lower leg 7
grist ground meal (used figuratively) 134
groat very small sum 174
grot grotto 19, 69, 116
guerdon reward 88, 92
guinea pre-decimal British coin (equal to 21 shillings or £1.05) 181
gunwale upper edge of the side of a boat or ship 133
gynecomorphical concerned with female reproductive anatomy 174

habergeon sleeveless coat of mail 128
hale healthy, strong 7, 116; haul, take forcibly 62, 67, 69, 139
hallow make holy 5, 7, 54, 128, 169; shrine, temple 42, 131
hap luck, fortune 88, 90
hark proceed, go 150; *see also* heark
harlot vagabond, beggar 139
harness armour 7, 69, 88, 173; clothe with armour 7; yoke 7, 128

haró exclamation of distress ('alas') 107

harry, a-harry persistently attack 31, 99, 128

haste hasten 88

hauberk armour for the neck and shoulders 7, 66, 88, 166

hawk (in **a-hawking**) hunt with a bird of prey 173

hay hedge 48; cut and dried grass 186

headland narrow piece of land projecting into the sea 58, 88

heark, hearken, hark, harken listen 1, 13, 16, 18, 19, 24, 34, 39, 64, 66, 83, 88, 89, 103, 114, 129, 130, 131, 146

heath, heathland flat, uncultivated land with low shrubs 8, 11, 38, 110, 118, 134

hedge fence or boundary of closely growing bushes or shrubs (also used figuratively) 14, 27, 89, 106, 130

helm helmet 6, 7, 40, 88, 117, 128, 129, 130, 131, 157, 166; steering mechanism of a ship 124, 160

helter-skelter in disorderly haste 121

hest behest, command 67, 88

hilt handle of a sword 7, 109, 116, 129, 159

hoar, hoary greyish-white 40, 41, 42, 46, 70, 116, 117, 129, 139, 140, 146, 157, 170, 185

hobgoblin *see* **goblin**

holden held 140

hollow echoing, as a sound in an empty space 5, 14, 19, 34, 39, 43, 48; **hollow, hollowed** empty 13, 19, 48, 69, 175; empty space, cavity, depression 13, 19, 50, 64, 67, 142

homing, a-homing leading home 3, 19, 35; going home 18, 26, 37, 49, 56

homophemes different words or phrases which when pronounced are made with the same apparent lip movements, often spelled *homophenes* 85

homuncular human 136

honey moon, honey-moon full moon of June, or last full moon of spring 121

horned having horns 60; shaped like a horn (trumpet-shaped) 48

hornpipe lively dance, usually by one person 186

housefold roof 41

howe small hill 4

huff puff out (as wings) 186

humming-top, hummingtop spinning top at its steadiest 121

Hun member of a warlike Asiatic people who invaded Europe in the fourth and fifth centuries 129, 131

hurry (in **hurrying**) rush (as the wind or rain) 134

hurst small hill or wooded rise 7, 26
hythe landing-place 88, 186

ill evil 3, 7, 36, 89, 129, 183
imagineless inconceivable 18, 74
impearl make pearly, decorate with (or as if) pearls 30
impress characteristic mark (as a footprint) 64
impurpurate purple 24
incipient beginner 183
Ind India 52, 96; **Indic** of India 96
inflood flooding or flowing in 61
inglenook chimney corner, recess adjoining a fireplace 186
insensate unfeeling, stupid 63
involuted complicated, abstruse 136
isléd made an island of; as if it were an island, isolated 13

jacinth blue precious stone, a variety of zircon, or its colour 33, 40
jag short projection of rock 13
jape joke 96, 139
javelin light spear 128
jet dark-coloured mineral 20, 185
jorum drinking-vessel 86

keel lengthwise stablizer along the base of a boat or ship 128
keen sharp, penetrating 33, 54, 55, 62, 74, 89, 93, 116, 118, 129, 139, 140, 141, 142, 157, 165, 175
keep strongest or central tower of a castle 44
ken range of knowledge or sight 10, 16, 44, 129
kine cows 8, 111
kirtle woman's gown or outer petticoat 32
knobbed lumpish (as a sign of age) 69
knoll small hill, hillock 4

lambent light playing on a surface (of fire) 44
Lammas Christian festival (1 August) 40
lampad lamp 40
larn teach 83
lattice with small panes set in diagonal strips (as in a window) 28, 43
laund glade, open area among trees 175
lay lyric or narrative poem 18, 44, 54, 64, 89, 129
lea grassland 33, 44, 45, 54, 70, 116

league measure of distance, by land or sea about three miles 25, 50, 74, 128, 140, 191; cooperative group 67, 176; **league-fellow, league fellow, leaguer** member of such a group 130, 170; **leagued** joined together in a league 53
leaguered, beleaguered besieged 40, 131, 136, 142, 169
leal loyalty 88
lede man, person 139
leech bloodsucking parasite (also used figuratively) 130, 174
lees dregs, sediment 22
leprechaun diminutive supernatural being from Irish folklore 27, 29, 43
levin lightning 128
lewd base, vile, ill-bred 89; crude, offensive 103, 139
liege, liegeman vassal, faithful follower 6, 7, 88, 117, 131, 194
liever more gladly, more willingly 66, 67, 89
lift air, sky 41
lime tree with broad, heart-shaped leaves 48; slaked lime, calcium hydroxide 142; **linden, lind** lime tree 64, 160
limn paint 136
limpid clear 24, 48; serene, untroubled 3, 26
linden *see* **lime**
lintelled having a lintel (horizontal support over a door or window) 18
lissom lithe, supple 64, 74, 92
litany recitation 116
littlemary stomach (used for a dining car) 8
loaden laden 5
lode watercourse 170
logothete administrative title in the Byzantine Empire 174
loom, uploom be ominously close 7, 8, 9, 12, 19, 20, 42, 106, 114, 119, 134, 146, 175, 179; **loom, handloom** apparatus for weaving (also used figuratively) 66, 103, 130, 136
loon simpleton 76, 139, 152
looney lunatic 134
lordly splendid 40, 90, 119; haughty 47, 186
lorn forlorn 62
lourdain idler 139
lout bend, bow 139
louver louvre, aperture in a building to admit light but not rain 132
lower look dark and threatening 3, 175
lubber clumsy person 139
lucent shining, luminous 16, 24, 90

mace heavy club (used figuratively) 134
madrigal short, lyrical love poem 38
mail flexible armour of rings, chains, or plates (also used figuratively) 19, 32, 34, 66, 69, 88, 117, 130, 131, 159; **mail-clad, mail-clad** clothed in mail 19, 88, 131; **mail-rings, rings** rings which make up ring-mail armour 69, 128
malachite bright green mineral 128
malting process of brewing or distilling with malt 186
mandragora mandrake, plant in the nightshade family 96
manifold many and various 89
mantle cloak (also used figuratively) 24, 40, 64, 69, 134, 139, 148, 160; **mantled** covered with a cloak (also used figuratively) 40, 92, 119, 169, 170
march borderland 31, 74, 88, 186
marge, margent margin 16, 31, 46, 74
marsh watery low land 70, 94, 110, 111
marshal high-ranking military officer, chief of a household guard 139, 170; **marshaller** commander 7
marsh-gold, marshgold marsh marigold, showy yellow flower in northern wetlands 2
mayhap perhaps 83
may-pole cut pole representing a tree, symbol of fertility 26
may-tree hawthorn 28
mazement amazement 24
mead, meads meadow(s) 8, 13, 37, 40, 44, 73, 74, 111, 164, 189; alcoholic beverage from fermented honey 80, 98, 117, 129, 162; **mead-hall, meadhall** feasting hall and community center 88
meadow grass, meadow-grass wild annual grass 26
meadowy pertaining to meadows 24
meed reward 67
meet appropriate, fitting 170
meiny retainers, followers 139
melilote fragrant grassland plant, sweet clover, often spelled *melilot* 48
mere lake or pond 13, 19, 38, 40, 42, 43, 74, 93, 111, 116, 134, 142, 161, 170
merryman mermaid 137
meseemed as it seemed to me 48, 139
mete give 67, 88
mew common seagull 13, 128, 160
middle-earth the Earth, the world of mortal Men between Heaven and Hell 127, 141, 146; *compare* **Middle-earth** *in part* II *below*

Midland Sea Mediterranean Sea 52
minaret slender tower 24
mind remember 103
minished reduced, diminished 67
mire marshy or swampy ground (also used figuratively) 21, 24, 69, 70, 75, 129, 152, 175, 177
mirk murk, darkness 35, 129
Mirkwood wooded region in Ukraine, battleground of the Goths and Huns 131; *compare* **Mirkwood** *in part* II *below*
mithered bewildered, bothered, confused 8, 101
moke donkey 105
moly herb which counters enchantment 96
money-spider small spider supposed to bring good luck 32
monition warning 136
moonsheen, moon-sheen moonshine, pale light of the moon 66, 134
moor, moorland open, uncultivated land, heath 61, 88, 103, 117, 153
morass muddy or boggy ground 35
morion open helmet 128
mould upper layer of soil 26, 40, 42, 110, 130, 134, 170; make, fashion 52, 88
mountain-lee shelter by the side of a mountain 160
moveless immovable 7, 13; without motion of the wind 40, 42
mugger broad-nosed crocodile 96
murmurous murmuring 3, 13, 18, 19, 34, 37, 39, 40, 46

nark informer 139
natheless nonetheless 8
neat not mixed with other liquids 96
neb nose, snout 128
nenuphar water-lily 74, 134
nicer, nicor water-demon 18, 117
nidding-nodding (as **a-nidding-nodding**) nodding off, becoming sleepy 188
niggard stingy 88
noisome noxious, offensive 5, 7, 8, 9, 94, 128, 143
nonce moment, time being 139
noodle simpleton 76

Ocean of Almain North Sea 24
Oddsteeth 'God's teeth', Elizabethan oath 83
ogre man-eating giant 70, 88, 105, 140

oliphaunt elephant 96, 167
ope open 1, 62
opiate containing opium (referring to the poppy) 49
opine believe, hold an opinion 139
orbed, orbéd like an orb, spherical 21, 31, 40, 54, 128
ostler groom for horses stabled at an inn 60
ought *see* **aught**
ousel blackbird 1
overweening arrogant, presumptuous 67

painter line attached to the bow of a boat for use in tying up 186
paladin knight errant, champion 128
pale area within determined bounds 16; faint (of music) 5, 18, 19
pall cloth over a coffin 116; dark cloud of smoke or dust, enveloping air of gloom 175
pandemain paindemain, refined white bread 194
panoply suit of armour 13, 128
pard great cat, parti-coloured and with a lion's mane 179
parley meeting to debate points in a dispute 136
pate top of the head 28, 105; brain, Appendix I.A
patent made under patent, manufactured 95
patter manner of speaking to sell a product 139
pavilion tent 128
paynim pagan, heathen 7
pelegrim pilgrim 139
pellucid translucently clear 19, 48
pennon military flag or ensign 7; **pennoned** (as **pennon'd**) with pennons 7
pert bold, impudent 139; evident 139
petreous rock-like 136
phial small glass bottle, vial 48, 116
philtre (as **philter**) love-potion 116
pie magpie 89, 139
pikelet small round teacake 105
pillared built with pillars 9, 18; like a (stone) pillar or pillars 34, 42, 159, 175
pinnacle small ornamental tower 13, 44; jagged peak 66, 130
plaint complaint 70, 89
plank put or set down, plonk 8
plash splash 34, 35, 42, 74
pleasance secluded enclosure or part of a garden 90

Pleiades, Pleiads star cluster in the constellation Taurus 40; **seven stars** 157
plenilune time of the full moon 24, 31, 48, 128
plough break a surface (as soil or water; also used figuratively) 7, 53, 139, 146; fail in an examination 76, 139; **ploughshare** colter, cutting blade of a plough 7, 139; **plowman** one who uses a plough (ploughman), farmer 139
plumbless beyond a depth that can be measured 40
plume tufted top of a plant, tassel, or feather (also used figuratively) 22, 110, 160, 175; feather or feathers used as ornament 7; **plumed** ornamented with a plume or plumes 13, 40
porphyry rock containing crystals of feldspar, beautiful purple stone with a high polish 30, 52
porridge spiced broth 24; cereal, usually oatmeal, boiled in water or milk 128, 188
porringer small bowl or vessel for eating soup, porridge, etc. 128
port harbour 40; gateway, portal 44; fortified wine of Portugal 191
potation drink 183
potter work in a desultory but pleasant manner 139
prep-school preparatory school, i.e. school to prepare pupils for university 139
prink primp, see to one's appearance 95
privily privately 96, 139
proven tested in battle 67, 88, 129
provender food, provisions 128
prow leading part of a ship 88, 124, 128, 134, 141
psychotherapeutics drugs used to treat mental illness 85
puffball fungus with a ball-shaped spore case 134
pyre burning heap of material, especially for burning a corpse 24, 44, 88, 177

quaver sing with trills or shakes 42, 64, 128
quay landing-place for ships, pier 52, 134
quick those who live 116
quicken make faster (as music) 60
quickening growing with life 74
quintessential most perfect 48
quod said 67

rag cheap newspaper or magazine 103, 106
raiment clothing 15, 40, 64, 74, 88, 128, 129, 134, 146, 173
raise reach land from the sea 127

rampart defensive wall, fortification 30, 35, 126, 131
rank line or group (as of soldiers; also used figuratively) 6, 7, 130; foul-smelling 48, 106, 142, 173
ravine deep, narrow gorge 53
ream large quantity 139
reave (and past tense **reft**) steal, take by force 91, 116, 129
reck (in **recking, unrecking**) heed, care 7, 11
rede advice, counsel 116
reed, reedy marsh or pond plant with a tall stem 13, 37, 40, 43, 44, 48, 50, 71, 110, 111, 121, 134, 141, 186; *see also* arrow-reed
repartee conversation with quick, witty replies 96
requite return a favour 116
rerd voice 139
resupine reclined backwards 20
rill small stream, rivulet 7, 54, 66, 74, 134, 159
rings *see* **mail**
rive (in past tense **riven**) split or tear apart violently 13, 131
rivulet small stream 4
roke *see* **sea-roke**
rondure circular form 61; **rondured, enrondured** having a round shape 40
Rood the Holy Cross, on which Jesus was crucified 7, 91
root kick 83
rout disorderly group of people, revellers 7, 101, 173
ruckle make or become creased or wrinkled 122
rude primitive 69
rue regret, pity 83, 139, 174
ruel-bone ivory from a marine mammal 134
rune secret, mystery, counsel or writing of a secret nature, or letter in an early Germanic alphabet 53, 84, 128, 146, 159, 172; poem 189
rush marsh or waterside plant with slender, pith-filled stems 43, 111, 121, 134
russet reddish-brown 42, 141
ruth pity 69, 139; **ruthless** without pity 67, 130, 131, 139, 140, 179

sable black 13, 20, 30, 40, 43, 66, 116, 130
sacring funeral bell 116
sallow willow, especially a low-growing variety 186
samite rich fabric of silk, occasionally interwoven with gold 140
sanguine warm, cheerful 16, 24
sapient wise 136
sapphirine bright blue, colour of the rare mineral sapphirine 40

saraband stately court dance 43
sate old past tense of *sit* 31, 62; fully satisfy 8, 88
sausage-roll sausage meat baked in a roll of pastry 188
scabbard sheath for a sword 128
scarfing covering (as with a scarf) 42
scathe harm (noun) 88
scimitar curved sword of Eastern design 7, 62, 92
scop bard, poet 129
scourge whip, flog 7, 61
scree small, loose stones that form or cover a mountain slope 93, 126
scyther one who cuts (such as grass or grain) with a scythe (a long, curved blade at the end of a pole) 40, 130
sea-roke mist, fog, drizzling rain at sea 13
sea-tassel *see* **tassel**
sea-wrack seaweed cast up or growing on a shore 134
sedge grass-like plant with triangular stems and inconspicuous flowers 89
seed animal descendant, progeny 66, 67, 88, 130, 131, 146
selenite variety of gypsum, usually colourless and transparent 24
seraph of the Seraphim, the highest order of angels 61
sere dried up, withered 42, 139
serpent sea-serpent, specifically (capitalized) the Midgard Serpent of Norse mythology 131, 132; (figuratively) a train 8, 9
serried in rank upon rank 7, 128
seven stars *see* **Pleiades**
shale shell 62
shallop open boat propelled by oars or sail, for shallow waters 33
shanty (as plural **shanties**) crudely-built shack 103; *compare* chanty
share cutting blade, as for a scythe 40; *see also* plough
shave (as of oars) make or adjust with a sharp tool 128, 186
shawm antique double-reed wind instrument 48
sheaf (plural **sheaves**) bundle of items tied together, such as stalks after reaping 48, 49, 64, 134
shend put to shame, confound 88
shere sheer 88
shingle small rounded pebbles, as on a beach 34, 88, 93, 103, 128, 134, 140, 146
shiver break, shatter 7, 113, 121, 129, 131, 154; **shiver, a-shiver, ashiver** tremble, vibrate 18, 19, 40, 134, 136, 186; tremble with cold 5, 19, 100, 128, 139
shoon shine 2, 73; old plural of *shoe* 24
shore old past tense of *shear* 128

shrift confession to a priest 139
shroud line supporting the rigging of a sailing vessel, but used by Tolkien for a sail itself 16, 40, 67, 119; burial cloth (also used figuratively), 134, 139, 140; **shroud, enshroud** wrap in, conceal 1, 40, 53, 119, 131, 169; **unshrouded** not buried, i.e. not in a funeral shroud 129
sidle walk in a furtive manner 94
sigaldry enchantment, sorcery 128
silvan associated with woods 26
silverly with a silvery (clear, melodious) sound 22, 27
silvern silver 18, 26, 66
sire father 44, 88, 131, 146
siren creature who used music to lure sailors into shipwreck 5
sister-son nephew, son of one's sister 129
sith since 88
skein loose bundle of yarn or thread (used figuratively) 174
skerry reef or rocky island 19
skiey of the sky 16
skirt edge, border 20; go around, past the edge of 48
slade valley, dell, dingle 90
slot track of an animal 88, 116
smite (past tense **smote**) strike, hit 7, 13, 67, 90, 128, 129, 131, 139, 159
smithy forge 186; **smithying** forging, working in metal 128
smock casual rural woman's dress 141
snortle snort 107
snuff, snuffle, a-snuffle sniff 69, 121, 125
sooth, soothly true 8, 90, 139; **sooth** soothing 99
sot drunkard 129
soundless without sound 30, 116; incapable of being sounded, i.e. of having its depth measured 42
spangle dot, adorn 16, 34
spar pole used for the mast, yard, etc. of a boat or ship 40, 128
spate large amount, flood 61
speed (past tense **sped**) conclude, be successful 153
spindrift spray or foam driven by the wind 13, 140
spinney small area of trees and bushes 89, 181
spire tapering structure on a tower (also used figuratively) 12, 40, 44, 132, 175; spike 66; **spiry** resembling a spire 40
spoil stolen goods 88
spout-hole whale's blow-hole 134

spray group of branches or flowers 89, 142, 173; liquid flying in small drops 18, 42, 134, 160; throw liquid as a spray 28, 186
spume discharge of foam or froth (also used figuratively) 13, 140; create a spume 124
stalactite spear-like structure formed by minerals dripping from a cave roof 128
stalwart resolute 44, 70
standard distinctive flag of a king, regiment, etc., 130
standing stone menhir, large stone stood upright 150
star-sheen starshine, starlight 134
stark bare 7, 61, 110; sharp 20, 53; strong, rigid 21, 126
starveling ill-fed person 139
stave stanza, verse 129; strong wooden stick or iron pole 139
steep slope 5, 90; sharply inclined 67, 103, 111, 126, 128, 136, 146, 171, 175; soak 2
steeping-well (as **stepping-well**) pool or vat for steeping malt, flax, etc. 189
stellar concerning stars 136
stem most forward element of a ship 18, 88
stepping-well *see* **steeping-well**
steps stepladder 122
stern severe, rear part of a ship 88, 146
stook group of sheaves of grain stood on end 67
storeyed towering, like a building with many storeys 40
strait, straitly confined 62, 190
strand thin length, filament 1, 35, 40, 48, 66, 73; shore 31, 88, 90, 94, 128, 134, 146, 160, 161, 175
sullen dismal, melancholic 7, 40, 53, 66, 175
sutler one who supplies provisions to soldiers 129
sward expanse of short grass 6, 40, 54
swart swarthy, dark-hued 7
swath, swathe broad track (used figuratively) 7, 66, 130
swathe wrap (as in garments) 1, 5, 18, 42, 61
swink labour, toil 139

tabour small drum 173
taffeta lustrous silk or silk-like fabric 128
taper slender candle 40, 116; tapered 18
targe light shield 88
tarry, a-tarry linger, pause, delay 91, 128, 141, 163, 188
tassel tufted top of a plant, plume 40, 110; **tasseled** tufted 26; **sea-tassel** tufted head of an undersea plant 19

taw make hide into leather with a chemical solution 186
tawny yellow- or reddish-brown 30
teen injury, harm 88
tellurian of or inhabiting the Earth 136
temper bring to an ideal hardness (as metal) 9, 140
tendrilous having tendrils (as seaweed) 19
terebinth tree which yields turpentine 96
thane man granted land in exchange for military service 67, 69, 88, 117, 130, 169
thatch weave plant material, or cluster or gathering (of flowers) 28, 49
thickset thickly grown 89
thin slender 19, 39, 40, 45, 64, 66; insubstantial 13, 14, 19, 24, 35, 42, 60, 116; of a sound, weak, feeble, high-pitched, but also capable of travelling far 14, 34, 40, 43, 64, 181
thistle-down short, soft hairs on a thistle 105, 128
thraldom state of slavery or captivation 88
thrall bondage, slavery 118; slave 92, 129; **enthralled** captivated 64
thread make way through a narrow place or difficult passage 16, 53; filament (also used figuratively) 14, 24, 39, 42; interweave 32
three-a-penny, three-penny cheap, inexpensive 184
thresh move violently 107
thrill reverberate 1, 3, 89, 173; wave of emotion 19
throng crowd, multitude 6, 7, 41, 44, 53, 66, 92, 99; come in great numbers 7, 9, 40, 44, 52, 62, 88, 130; *see also* wolfthrong
throstle, thrustle song thrush 181; **throstlecock, thrustle-cock** male thrush 181
thumping pole implement for moving linens, etc. in a container of heated water 108
thwart frustrate, foil 66; rower's seat on a boat 186
tinfoil paper-thin metal sheet, usually aluminium 192
tissue lightweight fabric 128, 136
tithe tax 88; tenth 90
toft homestead 116
tonsure haircut which typically creates a bald spot at the top of the head 139
topaz yellow, colour of the precious stone topaz 24, 40
torque decorative neck-ring 88
totty unsteady, dizzy 60
tourneying attending tournaments (contests between knights) 128
tout persistently attempt to sell 103; one who touts 103; rump 139
treacle thick, sticky dark sugar syrup (U.S. *molasses*) 102, 172, 188

tremulous shaking or quivering 19, 39, 43, 48; (by extension) anxious 48, 57
tress long lock of hair (also used figuratively) 13, 42, 74, 88, 92, 116, 121, 128; arrange (as hair) 19, 35
trillup (and as **trillap**) quavering or vibratory sound 29, 43
trinketry precious objects 88
trip move with light, quick steps 4, 65, 141; stumble 24, 122
troth pledge one's word, or such a pledge 67, 128, 130
trump, trumpet brass instrument with a flared bell (also used figuratively) 6, 13, 34, 39, 44, 55, 57, 62, 96, 130, 159, 173, 175; object shaped like a (flower) trumpet 134
tryst make an agreement 67, 117; appointment for a meeting 168
tun brewer's vat 95
turbid roiled, muddy 67
turret small tower 66
twain two 56
twinkle shine, sparkle 11, 16, 26, 27, 33, 40, 43, 48, 57, 64, 67, 73, 126, 154, 172, 174, 185; move lightly and rapidly 24, 116, 141; tinkle, make a bell-like sound 34, 43; **twinkly** make a bell-like sound 43

umbel flower cluster 48, 64
umbraged shadowing 40
unaneled one who has died without receiving Extreme Unction 36
unhouseled one who has not received the Eucharist 36
unmasticated unchewed 96
unplumbed extremely deep, beyond a depth that can be measured 13, 35, 42, 61
unpressed of a bed, not lain in 43
unsunned without the Sun 42
upping driving up or together (as swans) 186
uranian heavenly, celestial 20
urchin shabbily dressed child 139

vainshrieking shrieking in vain, without success 7
vale dale or valley 2, 10, 37, 40, 42, 44, 61, 66, 74, 88, 89, 90, 109, 125, 126, 130, 170; place of sorrow or misery 88
valiance bravery, valour 55
valiant brave, valorous 66; fine, of quality 88, 128
vassal one subject to command by a lord 6, 7
vasty vast 88
vaulted having an arched roof or roofs 159
vaunteth vaunted, boasted 7

venture go to 9, 128; adventure 31; emerge from 89; suggest 139
verdured (**verdurous**) lush with green vegetation 40
vesture garments, dress 20
viand food 6, 24
viol musical instrument, typically with six strings 46, 71

waif homeless child 88
wain wagon, cart 34, 40, 129, 174
waistcoat, weskit sleeveless garment, usually with buttons (U.S. *vest*) 105
wan, wanly pale 1, 7, 14, 15, 24, 26, 32, 40, 42, 116, 117, 119, 140
wankle unsteady, tottering 106
wanton deliberate, unprovoked 107
war-fain, warfain eager for war 7, 88
warted with protuberances like warts 19
waste, wasteland wild, desolate region 7, 8, 9, 11, 16, 44, 46, 53, 67, 93, 112, 128, 132, 146, 153, 163; **wasted** 44
wax become larger or greater 7, 66, 88; **waxen** grown 40, 142
waylaway sadness, regret 76
wayward wandering 16, 64, 67, 74, 92, 101, 139
weal mark, as if with a rod or whip 139
weasand gullet 84
weathercock, weather-cock weathervane, device on a roof to indicate wind direction, sometimes in the silhouette of a cockerel 181
web woven fabric 32, 128; snare, entanglement 116, 128
weeds garments (also used figuratively) 41, 73, 85, 88, 116
ween think 6, 90, 175
weir low dam across a river, designed to raise water level upstream or regulate its flow 38, 40, 186
weird fate, destiny 7, 67
welkin sky 7
well shaft sunk into the ground for water 32; copious source 33, 68; water-spring 121, 150; flow copiously 34, 64, 92
weskit *see* **waistcoat**
westering (of the sun) nearing the west 37, 39, 48
whelming crushing, overwhelming 61
wherry light boat or barge 67, 186
whetstone stone used to sharpen (whet) cutting tools 40
whicker make a sound like a rushing through the air 24
whiles, bewhiles at times 18, 33, 50, 68, 70

wight spirit, ghost 88, 89, 121, 155; person 139; **barrow-wight** spirit living in a barrow 129; *see also* **Barrow-wight** *in part* II *below*
wilder bewilder, confuse 42, 74; **bewilder** enchant 9, 43, 67, 92, 128; **bewilderment** state of enchantment 128
willowed, willow'd having willows 9, 10
winding, a-winding sounding with music 19, 34, 40, 67
winter-even evening in winter 22
wist *see* **wit**
wit intelligence 107, 139, 146; **wot** old past tense of *wit* 'know' 8, 88, 89; **wist** knew, understood 67, 88
withy willow 186
woad blue dye 89
wolfthrong throng of wolves 7
won reached or obtained by effort 26, 33, 74
wont what is customary 90, 173
wood out of one's senses 139
woof weft, crosswise threads on a loom 116
worm dragon 7, 67, 70, 106, 112, 177
wot *see* **wit**
wrack wreckage, downfall, ruin 7, 16; *see also* sea-wrack
wraith apparition 19, 64, 128, 136, 190
wright maker, builder 103
writhen twisted, contorted 93, 128

yell old form of *aisle* 129
yoke domination, oppression 66
yore former times, long ago 37, 38, 64, 88, 92, 109, 112, 128, 131, 146, 160

NATURE WORDS Tolkien's poetry also contains nearly two hundred names of plants, animals, fish, minerals, and other things to be found in nature, in addition to the general nature-related terms such as *copse*, *corn*, *frond*, and *reed*, and less familiar words such as *ammonite* and *athanasie*, we have included above.

Flowers, shrubs, herbs, spices, fruits, vegetables: arrow-reed, asphodel, barley (as barleycorn), bluebell, box, briar (rose), bryony, buttercup, cabbage, campion, cardamom, cauliflower, celandine, chrysanthemum, clematis, corn (i.e. cereal grain such as oats and wheat), daisy moon (ox-eye daisy), dandelion, fern (also everfern, ladyfern), forgetmenot, furze, 'gallows-weed' (probably hemp), grass, harebell, heather, hemlock, hollyhock, honeysuckle (also woodbine), iris (as flag-lily, gladdon), ivy, kidney bean, lady-smock (meadow cress), larkspur, lavender, leopard's bane, lily, lupin (lupine), maidenhair, mandragora (mandrake), marigold (also marshgold, i.e. marsh marigold), marjoram, marrow, melilote, moly (ancient herb), nemophilë, onion, orange, periwinkle (in the name *Perry-the-Winkle*), phlox, pinks (dianthus), primrose, ragwort, reed, sedge, sloe (blackthorn), snowdrop, Solomon's seal, sorrel, tansy (as athanasie), thistle, thyme, water lily (also nenuphar).

Trees: alder, apple, ash, beech, birch, cherry, chestnut, ebony, elm, fir, hawthorn (or thorn), hazel, larch, lime (also linden), maple, nutmeg, oak, pear, pine, poplar (also aspen), terebinth, upas, willow (also sallow, weeping willow).

Fungi: Earth-star, puffball.

Land animals: armadillo, baboon (as babewin), badger (or brock), bat (or flittermouse), bear, boar, bull, cow, crocodile (as mugger), elephant (as oliphaunt), ferret, goat, hare, leech, moke (donkey), mole, mouse, orang-outang, otter, ox, pig, rabbit (or cony), roe-deer, serpent, snail, vole, water-rat, wolf.

Marine animals: ammonite, anemone, coral, crab, narwhal, polyp, sardine, seal, skipper (sea-pike), sole, sprat, whale.

Birds: blackbird (or ousel), chaffinch, chicken (as bantam), cock (cockerel, rooster), coot, cormorant, crow, dabchick, duck, eagle, falcon, finch, gorcrow (carrion-crow), gull (also mew, seamew), heron, kingfisher, nightingale, owl (also barn owl), peacock, petrel, magpie (as pie), raven, starling, swallow, swan, throstle (song thrush), titmouse, wren (willow-wren).

Insects and arachnids: ant (also emmet), bee (bumblebee, dumbledor/dumbledore, bumble, honeybee), beetle, butterfly, daddy (crane-fly), dragonfly, earwig, flea, fly, ghost-moth, grasshopper, greenfly, spider (also money-spider).

Metals and minerals: amethyst, basalt, beryl, brass, chalcedony (or chrysoprase), diamond (or adamant), emerald, flint, garnet, gold, jacinth (zircon), malachite, moonstone (feldspar), onyx, opal, pearl, porphyry, ruby, sapphirine (for the colour), selenite, silver (or argent), topaz (for the colour).

II. NAMES IN TOLKIEN'S MYTHOLOGY

Identifications of characters and places are given according to Tolkien's mythology as it stood at the timc he wrote the poem in question. For example, Felagund and Finrod were separate characters in the *Lay of Leithian* (no. 92), but became joined later in the development of 'The Silmarillion' (Finrod, called *Felagund* 'cave-hewer' after the establishment of his kingdom in Nargothrond). Alternate names are given after, and cross-referenced to, the most prominent form.

Ælfwine *see* **Eriol**
Aelinuial region of great pools at the confluence of the rivers Aros and Sirion in Beleriand 161
Alalminor, Alalminórë town in Tol Eressëa 40; **Land of Elms** 40; **Land of Withered Elms** 40
Aldalómë *see* **Fangorn**
Allfather *see* **Ilúvatar**
Aman lands in the far West of the world 92, 178; **Blessed Realm** 92; **West-that-was** 178
Ambaróna *see* **Fangorn**
Amon Gwareth hill in Gondolin 66
Amon Hen, Amon-Hen hill above the west banks of the Anduin 163
Amroth Elf, king, lover of Nimrodel 160
Anduin Great River of Wilderland 163; **Great River** 170
Angband fortress of Melko in the north of Middle-earth 67
Arnach area of Gondor, also called Lossarnach 170
Arvernien southern part of Beleriand 128
Aryador *see* **Hithlum**
Avalon *see* **Tol Eressëa**
Azanûl valley below the east-gate of Moria, also called Azanulbizar, Dimrill Dale 159

Baggins, Bilbo Hobbit of the Shire 108
Balrog fire-demon, servant of Melko 66, 67
Bamfurlong farm of Farmer Maggot in the Marish 186
Barahir man, father of Beren 92
Barrowdowns (Barrow-downs) downs with burial mounds east of the Old Forest, haunted by wights 186; **Barrows** 186
Barrow-wight, Barrowwight spirit dwelling in Barrow-downs 121, 186; **barrow-dwellers** 121; *compare* barrow-wight *in part* I *above*
Bauglir *see* **Melko**

Bay of Bel bay on the southern shore of Gondor, more fully the Bay of Belfalas 24
Bay of Faery *see* **Faërie**
Bel, Bay of *see* **Bay of Bel**
Beleriand region in the north-west of Middle-earth in the First Age 130
Belfalas coastal region in southern Gondor 163
Belthil name for Telperion, one of the Two Trees 92
Beren Elf, later man, lover of Lúthien 64, 92
Bilbo *see* **Baggins, Bilbo**
Blessed Realm *see* **Aman**
Bombadil, Tom (the name in full) enigmatic protector of the Old Forest 121, 154, 186
Boromir man, son of Denethor 163
Brandywine river flowing through the Shire, border of Buckland 186
Bree settlement of Hobbits and Men east of the Shire 105, 186
Breredon Hobbit village in Buckland 186
Bronweg Elf, companion of Tuor in seeking Gondolin 66

Calacirian, Carakilian region of Eldamar, near the Calacirya or ravine of light 128
Calen-Bel field near the lake Nen Hithoel, also called Calembel, Parth Galen 163
Carnimírië dead rowan tree in Fangorn Forest 165
Causeway raised road along the Brandywine in the Marish 186
Celegorm Elf, son of Fëanor 130
Celon river in Beleriand 189
Côr *see* **Kôr**
Cristhorn pass in the mountains of Gondolin 66
Cuiviénen waters in Middle-earth where the fathers of Elves awoke 92

Dagor Dagorath final battle at the end of the world 178
Dairon Elf, minstrel of Doriath 64, 92; *see also* Ilverin
Damrod Elf, hunter, son of Fëanor 125
Dark Lord *see* **Sauron**
Delving Michel Delving, chief township of the Shire 105
Denethor man, last Steward of Gondor, father of Boromir and Faramir 163
Déorwine (**Deorwin**) man of Rohan, marshal of the household guard of Théoden 170

Derufin man of Gondor, son of Duinhir 170
Dor Lómin (Dorlómin) *see* **Hithlum**
Dor-na-Fauglith charred desert north of Beleriand, also called Anfauglith 130; **Plains of Thirst** 130
Doriath hidden kingdom of Elves in Middle-earth 34, 64, 66
Dorthonion highland with many pines on the northern borders of Beleriand 164
Duilin man of Gondor, son of Duinhir 170
Duinhir man of Gondor, lord of Morthond, father of Derufin and Duilin 170
Dúnedain Men of Númenor and their descendants in Middle-earth 168
Dungorthin valley in Doriath, entrance to Gondolin 66
Dunharrow refuge of the Rohirrim in the White Mountains 169
Dunhere, Dúnhere man of Rohan, lord of Harrowdale 170
Durin dwarf, eldest of the Seven Fathers of the Dwarves 159

Éarendel, Earendel, Earéndel, Eärendel, Eärendil man, mariner, son of Tuor and Idril 13, 16, 18, 31, 33, 74, 124, 128, 140
Edhil *see* **Eldar**
Edoras royal courts of Rohan 169
Eglamar *see* **Eldamar**
Eglavar *see* **Eldamar**
Elanor small golden, star-shaped flower 161
Elbereth Vala, wife of Manwë, kindler of the stars 128, 151; **Elberil** 151; **Fanuilos, Snow-white** 151; **Gilthoniel** 151; **Gilthonieth** 151; **Varda** 66, 176
Elberil *see* **Elbereth**
Eldain *see* **Eldar**
Eldamar land of the Elves in the distant West of the world 31, 41, 92, 128, 161; **Eglavar** 125; **Evereven** 128; **Faërie, Faery** 66, 69; *see also* Elfinesse, Elvenhome
Eldamar, Bay of *see* **Faërie**
Eldar (singular **Elda**) used variously for *Elves*, in its strictest sense indicating those who left the Great Lands and saw the light of Valinor at Kôr 18, 46, 92, 176, 182; **Edhil** 74; **Eldain** 145
Elder Days, Elder-days days before the drowning of Beleriand, the First Age of the world 92, 128, 159
Elder King *see* **Manwë**
Elessar royal name of Aragorn, son of Arathorn, man, Dúnadan, King of Gondor and Arnor 168
Elfhelm man of Rohan 170

Elfinesse (usually) land of the Elves in the distant West of the world 34, 53, 64, 69, 92; *see also* Eldamar, Elvenhome, Faërie
Elfland, Elvenland, Fairyland (generic) lands in Middle-earth inhabited by Elves 31, 34, 43, 65, 66, 125, 141
Elvenhome (usually) land of the Elves in the distant West of the world 64, 69, 128, 141; *see also* Eldamar, Elfinesse, Faërie
Elwing wife of Eärendil, daughter of the man Dior and the Elf Nimloth 128
Encircling Mountains mountains around the plain of Gondolin, also called the Echoriad 66
Eol Elf, husband of Isfin, father of Meglin, elsewhere spelled Eöl 66
Eorlingas Rohirrim, the Riders of Rohan 169
Erech hill in Gondor 168
Erech, Stone of *see* **Stone of Erech**
Eriol man of early England who sailed into the West 44; **Ælfwine** 74
Eru *see* **Ilúvatar**
Evereven *see* **Eldamar**
Evernight dark region south of Valinor 128; **night (Night) of Naught** 128
Ezellohar mound of the Two Trees in Valinor 92

Faërie, Faery bay on the eastern shore of Valinor, below the mountain Taniquetil 31, 66; **Bay of Faery** 140; also called Bay of Faëry, Bay of Eldamar
Fairyland *see* **Elfland**
Falas shorelands on the west coast of Beleriand, also called Harfalas 128
Fanged Ice ice-field in the North of the world, also called Helkaraksë 66
Fangorn forest beneath the south-eastern Misty Mountains 164; **Aldalómë** 164; **Ambaróna** 164; **Tauremorna** 164; **Tauremornalóme** 164; **Tauremornalómë** 164
Fanuilos *see* **Elbereth**
Fastred man of Rohan 170
Feanor Elf, with whom Fingolfin stood in battle 66
Fëanor Elf, master craftsman 92, 130, 176
Fëanorians sons of Fëanor 128
Felagund Elf, son of Finrod 92
Fengel man, father of Tuor in one account, Tuor himself in another 66; *see also* Thengel
Fenmarch marshy land on the south-eastern border of Rohan 169
Fingolfin Elf, father of Turgon and Isfin 66, 130

Fingon Elf, son of Fingolfin 130
Finrod Elf, father of Felagund 92
Finwë Elf, first High King of the Noldor, father of Fëanor, Fingolfin, et al. 130
Firiel, Fíriel woman of Middle-earth 141
Firienwood wood around the hill Halifirien 169
Flinding Elf, son of Fuilin 67
Folde centre of Rohan, the royal dwelling-place 169
Ford Sarn Ford, on the Brandywine 186
Forlong man of Gondor, lord of Lossarnach 170
Fuilin Elf, father of Flinding 67

Galadriel Elf, daughter of Finarfin, wife of Celeborn, lady of Lothlórien 161
Gar Thurion *see* **Gondolin**
Gate of Kings Argonath, on Anduin above the lake Nen Hithoel, with likenesses of Isildur and Anárion 163
Gelmir Elf, father of Fingolfin in one account 66
Gil-galad, Gilgalad Elf, last High King of the Noldor in Middle-earth 157
Gilthonieth *see* **Elbereth**
Gilthoniel *see* **Elbereth**
Glamhoth, glam-hoth body of orcs 66
Glingal *see* **Laurelin**
Gnome Elf, of the kindred also known as the Noldoli (Noldor) 66, 67, 92; **Gnomish** 130
Goblin *see* **Orc**
Goldberry water-sprite of the Withywindle, daughter of the River-woman, wife of Tom Bombadil 48, 121, 154; **River-daughter, River's daughter, River-woman's daughter, river-maid,** etc. 121, 154
Gondobar *see* **Gondolin**
Gondolin hidden city of the Elves in Doriath 66, 159; **Gar Thurion, Garthurion** 66; **Gondobar** 66, 74; **Gondothlimbar** 66; **Gwarestrin** 66; **Loth** 66; **Loth Barodrin, Loth-a-ladwen** 66
Gondor southern kingdom of the Dúnedain in Middle-earth 170; **South-kingdom, South Kingdom** 169, 170; **Stone kingdom** 170; **Stoningland, Stoning-land** 170; **Sunlending** Gondor 169
Gondothlimbar *see* **Gondolin**
Great Lands lands in Middle-earth east of the Great Sea 44
Great Ocean *see* **Sundering Seas**

Great River *see* **Anduin**
Grey Company company of Rangers, led by Halbarad 168
Grey-elves Sindar, elves who remained in Middle-earth rather than obey the summons of the Valar to Aman 186
Grey Havens harbours in the west of Eriador 127; **Havens** 186
Grimbold man of Rohan 170
Grindwall small hythe on the north bank of the Withywindle in Buckland 186
Guthláf, Guthlaf, Guthwin man of Rohan 170
Gwarestrin *see* **Gondolin**

Hador man, founder of the House of Hador 130
Halfling Hobbit 156
Halog man, servant of Morwen 67
Harding man of Rohan 170
Havens *see* **Grey Havens**
Hays-end Hobbit village in Buckland, at end of the High Hay 186
Herefara, Herufare man of Rohan 170
Herubrand man of Rohan 170
Hirluin man of Gondor 170
Hither Shore(s) *see* **Middle-earth**
Hithlum misty region north-west of Beleriand, also known as *Hisilómë* 67, 130; **Aryador** 37; **Dor Lómin** (**Dorlómin**) 66
Hobbit member of a small race of people in Eriador, related to Men 186, 187
Holy mountain *see* **Taniquetil**
Horn man of Rohan 170
Huor man, father of Tuor 66, 130
Húrin man, husband of Morwen, father of Túrin and Nienor (Níniel) 67, 130; **Thalion** 67; **Erithámrod** 67

Ilmarin home of Manwë and Varda on Taniquetil 128, 161
Ilmarin, Hill of *see* **Taniquetil**
Ilúvatar, Ilu Ilúvatar Supreme Being, Allfather 145; **Eru** 176; **Allfather** 176
Imladris *see* Rivendell
Iron Mountains mountain range in the north of Middle-earth, location of the fortress of Melko (Morgoth) 66
Ilverin alternate name for Dairon, or another minstrel of Doriath 64
Isfin Elf, daughter of Fingolfin, sister of Turgon, wife of Eöl, mother of Meglin 66
Isildur's Bane *see* **One Ring**

Ivrin source of the river Narog in Beleriand 189

Khazad-dûm *see* **Moria**
Kôr, Côr, Cor city of the Elves, and hill on which the city was built, in Eldamar 31, 66; **Tirion** 128, 161; **Tûn** 92

Land of Elms, Land of Withered Elms *see* **Alalminórë**
Lassemista dead rowan tree in Fangorn Forest 165
Laurelin younger of the Two Trees of Valinor 66; **Glingal** 92
Lightfoot horse of Rohan, sire of Snowmane 170
Lockholes Hobbit jail in Michel Delving 105
Lonely Island *see* **Tol Eressëa**
Lords of the West *see* **Valar**
Lórien gardens and dwelling-place of the Vala Irmo (Lórien) in Aman 92; *see also* Lothlórien
Loth *see* **Gondolin**
Loth-a-ladwen *see* **Gondolin**
Loth Barodrin *see* **Gondolin**
Lothlórien refuge of the Elves east of the Misty Mountains 160; **Lórien** 160, 161
Lúthien Elf, daughter of the rulers of Doriath, lover of Beren 64, 92, 125; **Luithien** 125; **Tinúviel** 64

Maggot name of a Hobbit farmer in the Marish, and his family 186
Maidros Elf, eldest son of Fëanor 130
Mailrond man, servant of Morwen 67
Maiar (as singular **Maia**) 'gods', lesser than the Valar 176
Manwë chief of the Valar 130, 176, 178; **Elder King** 128, 178
Marculf man of Rohan 170
Marish reclaimed marshland in the eastern part of the Shire, near the Brandywine 186
Mark-wardens, Markwardens kings of Rohan 169
Markland Rohan 170
Meglin Elf, son of Eol and Isfin, betrayer of Gondolin 66
Melian Maia, queen of Doriath, wife of Thingol, mother of Lúthien 92; **Ar-Melian** 92
Melko *see* **Morgoth**
Middle-earth continent of Arda (the Earth) between Aman in the West (across the Sundering Sea) and the Land of the Sun to the East 95, 127, 128, 141, 176, 178; **Hither Shore(s)** 128, 161; *compare* middle-earth *in part* I *above*
Mîm dwarf, betrayer of Túrin 185

Mindolluin mountain behind Minas Tirith 169
Míriel Elf, mother of Fëanor 189
Mirrormere lake in the valley below the east-gate of Moria, also called Kheled-zâram 159
Mithe outflow of the river Shirebourn 186; **Shire-mithe** 186
Mithril true-silver 128
Mordor, Mor-dor land of Sauron, in the east of Middle-earth 149, 157
Morgoth Vala, enemy of Elves and Men, bringer of death and discord 66, 67, 92, 130, 176; **Bauglir** 67; **Lord of Woe** 67; **Melko** earlier name of Morgoth 66, 145
Moria dwarf city, the Dwarrowdelf 159; **Khazad-dûm** 159
Morthond vale of the Morthond, or Blackroot, river in Gondor 170
Morwen woman, wife of Húrin, mother of Túrin and Nienor (Níniel) 67
Mounds of Mundburg, Mounds of Mundberg burial mounds at Minas Tirith 170
Mountain Wall Pelóri, mountains on the eastern shore of Aman 128
Mundburg, Mundberg Minas Tirith, capital of Gondor 169, 170

Nan Elmoth wood in Doriath 92
Narog river in Middle-earth 67
Nargothrond underground fortress of the Elves built into the banks of the river Narog 67, 159
Narrow Ice ice-bound strait in the remote North between Middle-earth and the 'Uttermost West', the Helcaraxë 128
Nebrachar unidentified place of Goblins 125
Neldoreth forest in the northern part of Doriath 164
Night of Naught *see* **Evernight**
Nimbrethil wooded region of Arvernien 128
Nimrodel Elf, lover of Amroth 160; **Linglorel** 160, 164; **Nimlothel** 160; **Taur-na-neldor** 164
Níniel Nienor, woman, daughter of Húrin and Morwen, sister of Túrin 130
Niphredil flower, like a snowdrop 74
Noldoli *see* **Gnome**
Norland North-west of Arda in the Elder Days, especially Beleriand and adjacent regions 128
Númenor island of Men west of Middle-earth 145; **Westernesse** 128

Oathbreakers men of the White Mountains who broke their oath of allegiance to Isildur 168
Old Man Willow, Willow-man, Willowman, Willow malevolent willow-spirit on the Withywindle 121, 154, 186
One Ring ruling ring of power, made by Sauron 149; **Isildur's Bane** 156
Orc demonic creature, servant of Melko 66, 67, 92, 125, 130; **Goblin** 66, 108
Orfalas unidentified shore 128
Orod-na-Thôn , Orod Thon, Orod Thun, Orod Thuin mountain in Dorthonion 164
Orofarnë dead rowan tree in Fangorn Forest 165
Ossiriand, Ossir region of seven rivers in Beleriand 164
Outer ocean ocean surrounding Arda (the Earth), the Encircling Sea 130; **outer seas** 33

Palúrien *see* **Yavanna**
Paths of the Dead haunted underground passage through the White Mountains 168
Pelóri *see* **Mountain Wall**
Plains of Thirst *see* **Dor-na-Fauglith**

Rammas Echor great wall around the Pelennor 170
Rauros falls on the Anduin below the lake Nen Hithoel 163
Rivendell sanctuary of Elves in the foothills of the Misty Mountains, home of Elrond Halfelven 153; **Imladris** 156
River-daughter *see* **Goldberry**
River-woman, Riverwoman water-sprite of the Withywindle, mother of Goldberry 121
Rohan kingdom of Men (the Rohirrim), the plains north of Gondor 163
Rushey village in the eastern part of the Shire 186

Sarn Ford *see* **Ford**
Sauron evil Maia 178; **Dark Lord** 149
Sea-kings men of Númenor, founders of Arnor and Gondor 169
Shadow *see* **Shadowy Sea(s)**
Shadow-folk lost elves of Aryador 37; **shadow-people** 37
Shadow in the East spread of Sauron's evil from Mordor 168
Shadow meres, Shadow-meres (probably) Aelinuial, the 'Lakes of Twilight', region of great pools at the confluence of the rivers Aros and Sirion in Beleriand 161

Shadowmere, Shadow-mere Luvailin, mere in Eldamar 128
Shadowy Sea(s), shadowy seas waters which concealed Valinor 33, 66, 74, 92, 130, 140; **Shadow** 74
Shire settlement of Hobbits in Eriador 105, 163, 186
Shire-mithe *see* **Mithe**
Shirebourn river of the Shire, flowing into the Brandywine 186
Shrouded Island *see* **Tol Eressëa**
Shrouded Islands *see* **Twilit Isles**
Silmarils jewels crafted by Fëanor containing the light of the Two Trees 92, 128, 176
Silpion elder of the Two Trees of Valinor, later called Telperion 66
Sirion river in Beleriand 125, 130
Snow-white *see* **Elbereth**
Snowmane horse of Rohan, born of Lightfoot 170
Solosimpe third kindred of the Elves, the 'shoreland pipers', later called Teleri 46; **Solosimpi** 54
South Kingdom, South-kingdom *see* **Gondor**
Stone of Erech great black stone on the hill of Erech 168
Stoningland, Stoning-land *see* **Gondor**
Sundering Sea(s), sundering seas ocean between Middle-earth and the Undying Lands in the West of the world 46, 64, 151, 161; **Great Ocean** 151; **Shoreless Sea** 161; **Western Sea(s)** 151, 159
Sunlending *see* **Gondor**
Sunless Year period between the destruction of the Two Trees and the creation of the Sun 151

Taniquetil mountain in Valinor, tallest peak in Arda (the Earth) 31; **holy mountain** 176; **the Mountain** 128; **Hill of Ilmarin** 128, 161
Tarmenel high heaven, region of wind 128
Tasarinan valley of willows in Beleriand 164; **Nan-tasarion** (and variations) 164
Taur Fuin dark forest in Dorthonion, Taur-nu-Fuin (or Taur-na-Fuin) 66
Taur-na-neldor *see* **Neldoreth**
Tauremorna, Tauremornalóme, Tauremornalómë *see* **Fangorn**
Thalion *see* **Húrin**
Thangorodrim mountain range above Angband in Middle-earth 67
Thengel man, King of Rohan, father of Théoden 169, 170; **Fengel** 169; *see also* **Théoden**
Théoden man, King of Rohan, son of Thengel 169, 170; **Thengling** son of Thengel, i.e. Théoden 170

Thingol Elf, king of Doriath, husband of Melian, father of Lúthien 92; **Elu Thingol** 92
Thornsir falling stream below Cristhorn 66
Thousand Caves Menegroth, fortress in Doriath 92
Three Kindreds three 'tribes' of Elves, the Teleri, the Noldoli (Gnomes), and the Solosimpi 67
Thu Maia, chief lieutenant of Melko, elsewhere spelled Thû 66
Tinfang Warble the piper Timpinen 29
Tinúviel *see* **Lúthien**
Tirion *see* **Kôr**
Tol Eressëa, Tol Eressea island of the Valar and Elves near Valinor 46; **Avalon** Tol Eressëa 140; **Lonely Island** 66, 128; **Shrouded Island** 128
Tom Bombadil *see* **Bombadil, Tom**
Tower Hills hills at the western edge of the Shire 186
Tower of Guard Minas Tirith, city of Men in Gondor 163
Tumladin plain of Gondolin within the Encircling Mountains 66; **Tumlad** 125; **Tumledin** 125
Tûn *see* **Kôr**
Tuor man, son of Fengel (later Huor), husband of Idril, father of Eärendel 13, 66
Turgon Elf, king of Gondolin, father of Idril, uncle of Meglin 66, 67, 130
Túrin man, son of Húrin and Morwen, brother of Nienor (Níniel) 67
Twilit Isles islands lying between Tol Eressëa and Valinor in the Shadowy Sea, also called the Enchanted Isles and the Shadowy Isles 33; **Shrouded Islands** 128
Two Trees Laurelin and Silpion (Telperion) 66

Uldor man, Easterling, betrayer of Maidros 130
Ulmo Vala, lord of waters 13, 92; **Ylmir** 13
Ungoliant, Ungoliont gigantic spider, ally of Melko/Morgoth 66, 128

Valar (singular **Vala**) 'gods' created by the One, makers of Arda (the Earth) 92, 176; **Lords of the West** 178
Valinor land of the Valar in the West 31, 66, 92, 128
Varda *see* **Elbereth**

Weathertop hill north-east of Bree 105
West-that-was *see* **Aman**
Western Sea(s) *see* **Sundering Seas**

Westernesse *see* **Númenor**
Wilderland wild lands to the west and east of the Misty Mountains 163
Willowman, Willow-man *see* **Old Man Willow**
Withywindle river, a lesser tributary of the Brandywine, flowing through the Old Forest 121, 154, 186
World's End remote side of Valinor 128

Yavanna Vala, 'Earth-mother', giver of fruits 66; **Palúrien** 66
Ylmir *see* **Ulmo**

Bibliography

I. WORKS BY J.R.R. TOLKIEN

Acta Senatus. *King Edward's School Chronicle*, June 1911, pp. 26–7. Unsigned, but Tolkien's authorship is confirmed.

Adventures in Unnatural History and Medieval Metres, being the Freaks of Fisiologus. *Stapeldon Magazine*, June 1927, pp. 123–7. Includes *Fastitocalon* and *Iumbo, or ye Kinde of ye Oliphaunt*.

The Adventures of Tom Bombadil. *Oxford Magazine*, 15 February 1934, pp. 464–5.

The Adventures of Tom Bombadil and Other Verses from the Red Book. Illustrations by Pauline Baynes. London: George Allen & Unwin, 1962. Also: Expanded edn. Ed. Christina Scull and Wayne G. Hammond. London: HarperCollins, 2014.

The Annotated Hobbit. Ed. Douglas A. Anderson. Rev. and expanded edn. Boston: Houghton Mifflin, 2002.

The Battle of Maldon, together with The Homecoming of Beorhtnoth Beorhthelm's Son and 'The Tradition of Versification in Old English'. Ed. Peter Grybauskas. London: HarperCollins, 2023. Also includes excerpts of lectures by Tolkien.

The Battle of the Eastern Field. *King Edward's School Chronicle*, March 1911, pp. 22–6.

Beowulf: A Translation and Commentary together with Sellic Spell. Ed. Christopher Tolkien. London: HarperCollins, 2014.

Beowulf and the Critics. Ed. Michael D.C. Drout. Rev. 2nd edn. Tempe, Arizona: ACMRS, 2011.

Bilbo's Last Song (At the Grey Havens). Boston: Houghton Mifflin, 1974 (poster). London: George Allen & Unwin, 1974 (poster). London: Unwin Hyman, 1990 (book). The British poster and subsequent book are illustrated by Pauline Baynes.

The Book of Lost Tales, Part One (vol. 1 of *The History of Middle-earth*). Ed. Christopher Tolkien. London: George Allen & Unwin, 1983.

The Book of Lost Tales, Part Two (vol. 2 of *The History of Middle-earth*). Ed. Christopher Tolkien. London: George Allen & Unwin, 1984.

The Cat and the Fiddle: A Nursery-Rhyme Undone and Its Scandalous Secret Unlocked. *Yorkshire Poetry*, October–November 1924, pp. 1–3.

The City of the Gods. *The Microcosm*, Spring 1923, p. 8.

The Clerke's [*sic*] *Compleinte*. *The Gryphon*, December 1922, p. 95. Reprinted in *Arda 1984* (Uppsala, 1988), pp. 1–2, with commentary (pp. 7–8) by T.A. Shippey and a translation into Modern English (pp. 7–8) by Anders Stenström (Beregond) and Nils-Lennart Johannesson. A revised manuscript of the poem was printed in facsimile, with commentary, in 'The Clerkes Compleinte Revisited', *Arda 1986* (1990), pp. 1–13.

Concerning 'The Hoard'. Manuscript, accompanying a letter to Eileen Elgar, 5 March 1964. Heritage Auctions, Dallas, online auction, 16 July 2022. *https://historical.ha.com*.

Doworst. A portion was published in *A Elbereth Gilthoniel!* 2 (?Summer 1978). Newsletter of the Monash University Tolkien fan group, the Fellowship of Middle Earth.

The Dragon's Visit. *Oxford Magazine*, 4 February 1937, p. 342. See also *Winter's Tales for Children 1* below.

Dragons. Lecture, in *The Hobbit, 1937–2017* by Christina Scull and Wayne G. Hammond. London: HarperCollins, 2018. pp. 39–62.

Tha Eadigan Saelidan: The Happy Mariners. See *A Northern Venture* below.

Early Elvish Poetry and Pre-Fëanorian Alphabets. Ed. Christopher Gilson, Bill Welden, and Carl F. Hostetter. *Parma Eldalamberon* 16 (2006), pp. 53–104. Includes *Oilima Markirya*, pp. 53–87; *Nieninqe / Nieninque*, pp. 88–97; and *Earendel*, pp. 98–104.

The English Text of the Ancrene Wisse. Ed. J.R.R. Tolkien. London: Published for the Early English Text Society by the Oxford University Press, 1962.

Enigmata Saxonica Nuper Inventa Duo. See *A Northern Venture*, ed. Leeds University English School Association, in bibliography part II.

Errantry. *Oxford Magazine*, 9 November 1933, p. 180.

An Evening in Tavrobel. See *Leeds University Verse 1914–24* below.

The Fall of Arthur. Ed. Christopher Tolkien. London: HarperCollins, 2013.

Farmer Giles of Ham. Embellished by Pauline Diana Baynes. London: George Allen & Unwin, 1949.

Fastitocalon. See *Adventures in Unnatural History* above.

Finn and Hengest: The Fragment and the Episode. Ed. Alan Bliss. London: George Allen & Unwin, 1982.

Firiel. *Chronicle of the Convents of the Sacred Heart* (Roehampton) 4 (1934), pp. 30–2.

For W.H.A. *Shenandoah*, Winter 1967, pp. 96–7.

From Iffley ('From the many-willow'd margin of the immemorial Thames'). *Stapeldon Magazine*, December 1913, p. 11.

Goblin Feet. In *Oxford Poetry 1915*. Ed. G.D.H. Cole and T.W. Earp. Oxford: B.H. Blackwell, 1915. pp. 64–5. See also Cole and Earp, *Oxford Poetry 1915*; *Fifty New Poems for Children*; and Dora Owen, *The Book of Fairy Poetry*, in bibliography part II.

The Grey Bridge of Tavrobel. *Inter-University Magazine*, May 1927, p. 82.

The Happy Mariners. *Stapeldon Magazine*, June 1920, pp. 69–70.

Henry Bradley, 3 Dec., 1845–23 May, 1923. *Bulletin of the Modern Humanities Research Association*, October 1923, pp. 4–5. Repr. *Tolkien Studies* 12 (2015), pp. 141–8, with commentary by Tom Shippey and Peter Gilliver.

The Hobbit, or There and Back Again. First edn. published London: George Allen & Unwin, 1937. See also *The Annotated Hobbit* above, and John D. Rateliff, *The History of* The Hobbit, in bibliography part II.

The Homecoming of Beorhtnoth Beorhthelm's Son. In *Essays and Studies 1953*. Ed. Geoffrey Bullough. London: John Murray, 1953. pp. 1–18.

Imram. *Time and Tide*, 3 December 1955, p. 1561.

Iumbo, or ye Kinde of ye Oliphaunt. See *Adventures in Unnatural History* above.

Iúmonna Gold Galdre Bewunden. *The Gryphon*, January 1923, p. 130. Rev. version (as *Iumonna Gold Galdre Bewunden*), *Oxford Magazine*, 4 March 1937, p. 473.

The J.R.R. Tolkien Audio Collection. London: Harper Audio/Caedmon, 2001.

J.R.R. Tolkien Reads and Sings His The Hobbit and The Fellowship of the Ring. New York: Caedmon Records, 1975.

J.R.R. Tolkien Reads and Sings His The Lord of the Rings: The Two Towers / The Return of the King. New York: Caedmon Records, 1975.

Knocking at the Door. *Oxford Magazine*, 18 February 1937, p. 403.

I·Lam na·Ngoldathon: The Grammar and Lexicon of the Gnomish Tongue. Ed. Christopher Gilson, Patrick Wynne, Arden R. Smith, and Carl F. Hostetter. *Parma Eldalamberon* 11 (1995).

The Lay of Aotrou and Itroun. *Welsh Review* 4, no. 4 (December 1945), pp. 254–66. See also the Flieger edition below.

The Lay of Aotrou and Itroun together with the Corrigan Poems. Ed. Verlyn Flieger. With a note on the text by Christopher Tolkien. London: HarperCollins, 2016.

The Lays of Beleriand (vol. 3 of *The History of Middle-earh*). Ed. Christopher Tolkien. London: George Allen & Unwin, 1985.
Leeds University Verse 1914–24. Comp. and ed. the English School Association. Leeds: Swan Press, 1924. Includes *An Evening in Tavrobel*, p. 56; *The Lonely Isle*, p. 57; and *The Princess Ní*, p. 58.
The Legend of Sigurd and Gudrún. Ed. Christopher Tolkien. London: HarperCollins, 2009.
Letters from Father Christmas. Ed. Baillie Tolkien. London: HarperCollins, 2023.
Letters of J.R.R. Tolkien. Rev. and expanded edn. Ed. Humphrey Carpenter, with the assistance of Christopher Tolkien; new edn. supervised by Chris Smith. London: HarperCollins, 2023.
Light as Leaf on Lindentree. *The Gryphon*, June 1925, p. 217.
The Lonely Isle. See *Leeds University Verse 1914–24* above.
Looney. *Oxford Magazine*, 18 January 1934, p. 340.
The Lord of the Rings. 50th anniversary edn. Ed. Wayne G. Hammond and Christina Scull. London: HarperCollins, 2004. First edn. published London: George Allen & Unwin, 1954–5.
The Lost Road and Other Writings: Language and Legend before 'The Lord of the Rings' (vol. 5 of *The History of Middle-earth*). Ed. Christopher Tolkien. London: George Allen & Unwin, 1987.
A Middle English Vocabulary. Oxford: Clarendon Press, 1922.
Mîms Klage. In *Klett-Cotta: Das erste Jahrzehnt 1977–1987, Ein Almanach*. Stuttgart: Klett-Cotta, 1987. pp. 302–5. German translation of *The Complaint of Mîm the Dwarf*.
The Monsters and the Critics and Other Essays. Ed. Christopher Tolkien. London: George Allen & Unwin, 1983. Includes (*inter alia*) *Beowulf: The Monsters and the Critics*, pp. 5–48; *On Translating Beowulf*, pp. 49–71; *Sir Gawain and the Green Knight* (1953 lecture), pp. 72–108; *A Secret Vice*, pp. 198–223; and *Valedictory Address to the University of Oxford*, pp. 224–40.
Morgoth's Ring: The Later Silmarillion, Part One: The Legends of Aman (vol. 10 of *The History of Middle-earth*). Ed. Christopher Tolkien. London: HarperCollins, 1993.
The Nameless Land. In *Realities: An Anthology of Verse*. Ed. G.S. Tancred. Leeds: Swan Press, 1927. pp. 24–5.
Narqelion. In 'Narqelion: A Single, Falling Leaf at Sun-fading' by Paul Nolan Hyde. *Mythlore* 15, no. 2, whole no. 56 (Winter 1988), pp. 47–52.
Noel. *The 'Annual' of Our Lady's School, Abingdon* 12 (1936), pp. 4–5.

Nomenclature of The Lord of the Rings. In *The Lord of the Rings: A Reader's Companion* by Wayne G. Hammond and Christina Scull. 3rd edn. London: HarperCollins, 2014. pp. 750–82.

A Northern Venture: Verses by Members of the Leeds University English School Association. Leeds: Swan Press, 1923. Includes *Tha Eadigan Saelidan: The Happy Mariners*, pp. 15–16; *Why the Man in the Moon Came Down Too Soon*, pp. 17–19; and *Enigmata Saxonica Nuper Inventa Duo*, p. 20.

On Fairy-Stories. In *Essays Presented to Charles Williams*. Ed. C.S. Lewis. Oxford: Oxford University Press, 1947. pp. 38–89. See also *Tolkien On Fairy-Stories* below.

Once upon a Time. See *Winter's Tales for Children 1* below.

Poems and Songs of Middle Earth. New York: Caedmon Records, 1967. Readings by Tolkien, and music by Donald Swann and William Elvin.

Poems and Stories. Illustrated by Pauline Baynes. London: George Allen & Unwin, 1980.

Prefatory Remarks on Prose Translation of 'Beowulf'. In *Beowulf and the Finnesburg Fragment*. Tr. John R. Clark Hall. New edn., rev. with notes and an introduction by C.L. Wrenn. London: George Allen & Unwin, 1940. pp. viii–xli. Also published as *On Translating Beowulf* in *The Monsters and the Critics and Other Essays* (above).

The Princess Ní. See *Leeds University Verse 1914–24* above.

Progress in Bimble Town. *Oxford Magazine*, 15 October 1931, p. 22.

The Qenya Alphabet: Documents by J.R.R. Tolkien. Ed. Arden R. Smith. *Parma Eldalamberon* 20 (2012).

Qenyaqetsa: The Qenya Phonology and Lexicon. Ed. Christopher Gilson, Carl F. Hostetter, Patrick Wynne, and Arden R. Smith. *Parma Eldalamberon* 12 (1998).

The Return of the Shadow: The History of The Lord of the Rings, Part One (vol. 6 of *The History of Middle-earth*). Ed. Christopher Tolkien. London: Unwin Hyman, 1988.

The Road Goes Ever On: A Song Cycle. See Donald Swann in bibliography part II.

Roverandom. Ed. Christina Scull and Wayne G. Hammond. London: HarperCollins, 1998.

Sauron Defeated: The End of the Third Age (The History of The Lord of the Rings, Part Four), The Notion Club Papers, and the Drowning of Anadûnê (vol. 9 of *The History of Middle-earth*). Ed. Christopher Tolkien. London: HarperCollins, 1992.

A Secret Vice. See *The Monsters and the Critics and Other Essays* above, and the edition by Fimi and Higgins below.

A Secret Vice: Tolkien on Invented Languages. Ed. Dimitra Fimi and Andrew Higgins. London: HarperCollins, 2016.
The Shadow Man. The 'Annual' of Our Lady's School, Abingdon 12 (1936), p. 9.
The Shaping of Middle-earth: The Quenta, the Ambarkanta and the Annals (vol. 4 of *The History of Middle-earth*). Ed. Christopher Tolkien. London: George Allen & Unwin, 1986.
The Silmarillion. Ed. Christopher Tolkien. London: George Allen & Unwin, 1977.
Sir Gawain and the Green Knight. Ed. J.R.R. Tolkien and E.V. Gordon. Oxford: Clarendon Press, 1925.
Sir Gawain and the Green Knight (the 1953 W.P. Memorial Lecture). See *The Monsters and the Critics and Other Essays* above.
Sir Gawain and the Green Knight, Pearl and Sir Orfeo. Tr. J.R.R. Tolkien. Ed. Christopher Tolkien. London: George Allen & Unwin, 1975. A de luxe edition (London: HarperCollins, 2020) includes a reproduction of a manuscript of *Gawain's Leave-Taking*.
Sir Orfeo. Ed. J.R.R. Tolkien. Oxford: Academic Copying Office, 1944.
Smith of Wootton Major. Illustrations by Pauline Baynes. London: George Allen & Unwin, 1967.
Songs for the Philologists by J.R.R. Tolkien, E.V. Gordon and others. London: Privately printed in the Department of English at University College, London, 1926. Includes thirteen poems by Tolkien (titles thus): *From One to Five*, p. 6; *Syx Mynet*, p. 7; *Ruddoc Hana*, p. 8; *Ides Ælfscyne*, pp. 10–11; *Bagme Bloma*, p. 12; *Eadig Beo Þu*, p. 13; *Ofer Widne Garsecg*, pp. 14–15; *La, Huru*, p. 16; *I Sat upon a Bench*, p. 17; *Natura Apis: Morali Ricardi Eremite*, p. 18; *The Root of the Boot*, pp. 20–1; *Frenchmen Froth*, pp. 24–5; *Lit' and Lang'*, p. 27.
The Story of Kullervo. Ed. Verlyn Flieger. London: HarperCollins, 2015. Includes *On 'The Kalevala' or Land of Heroes*. Materials were earlier published by Flieger as '"The Story of Kullervo" and Essays on *Kalevala*', *Tolkien Studies* 7 (2010), pp. 211–78.
Tinfang Warble. Inter-University Magazine, May 1927, p. 63.
Tolkien On Fairy-Stories. Ed. Verlyn Flieger and Douglas A. Anderson. London: HarperCollins, 2008.
The Tolkien Reader. New York: Ballantine Books, 1966.
The Treason of Isengard: The History of The Lord of the Rings, Part Two (vol. 7 of *The History of Middle-earth*). Ed. Christopher Tolkien. London: Unwin Hyman, 1989.

Tree and Leaf. New edn. Ed. Christopher Tolkien. London: HarperCollins, 2001. Includes *On Fairy-Stories*, *Leaf by Niggle*, *Mythopoeia*, and *The Homecoming of Beorhtnoth Beorhthelm's Son*.
Tree and Leaf, Smith of Wootton Major, The Homecoming of Beorhtnoth Beorhthelm's Son. London: Unwin Books, 1975.
Unfinished Tales of Númenor and Middle-earth. Ed. Christopher Tolkien. London: George Allen & Unwin, 1980.
Valedictory Address to the University of Oxford. See *The Monsters and the Critics and Other Essays* above.
The War of the Ring: The History of The Lord of the Rings, Part Three (vol. 8 of *The History of Middle-earth*). Ed. Christopher Tolkien. London: Unwin Hyman, 1990.
Why the Man in the Moon Came Down Too Soon. See *A Northern Venture* above.
Winter's Tales for Children 1. Ed. Caroline Hillier. London: Macmillan; New York: St Martin's Press, 1965. Includes two poems by Tolkien: *Once upon a Time*, pp. 44–5; and *The Dragon's Visit*, pp. 84, 86–7. Both were reprinted in *The Young Magicians*, ed. Lin Carter. New York: Ballantine Books, 1988.
Words, Phrases and Passages in Various Tongues in The Lord of the Rings. Ed. Christopher Gilson. *Parma Eldalamberon* 17 (2007).

II. OTHER PRINTED WORKS

Alexander, Michael. *The Earliest English Poems*. Harmondsworth, Middlesex: Penguin Books, 1966.
Allen, Richard Hinckley. *Star Names: Their Lore and Meaning*. New York: Dover Publications, 1963.
The Ancrene Riwle. Tr. M.B. Salu. London: Burns & Oates, 1955.
Anderson, Douglas A. 'The Mystery of Lintips'. *Tolkien and Fantasy* (blog), 22 July 2013. *http://tolkienandfantasy.blogspot.com/2013/07/the-mystery-of-lintips.html.*
—— 'Publishing History'. In Drout, *J.R.R. Tolkien Encyclopedia* (2006), pp. 549–50.
——, ed. *The Annotated Hobbit*. Rev. and expanded edn. Boston: Houghton Mifflin, 2002.
Annear, Lucas. 'Language in Tolkien's "Bagme Bloma"'. *Tolkien Studies* 8 (2011), pp. 37–49.
Arduini, Roberto, Giampaolo Conzonieri, and Claudio A. Testi, eds. *Tolkien and the Classics*. Zurich and Jena: Walking Tree Publishers, 2019.

Atherton, Mark. *There and Back Again: J.R.R. Tolkien and the Origins of* The Hobbit. London: I.B.Tauris, 2012.
Barfield, Owen. *Poetic Diction: A Study in Meaning*. London: Faber and Gwyer, 1928.
The Battle of Maldon. Ed. E.V. Gordon. London: Methuen, 1937.
Beare, Rhona. 'The Trumpets of Dawn'. Typescript of unpublished lecture, private archive.
Benedikz, B.S. 'Some Family Connections with J.R.R. Tolkien'. *Amon Hen* 209 (January 2008), pp. 11–13.
Beowulf and the Finnesburg Fragment. Tr. John R. Clark Hall. New edn., rev. with notes and an introduction by C.L. Wrenn. London: George Allen & Unwin, 1940. Includes preface by Tolkien; see bibliography part I.
Beowulf with the Finnesburg Fragment. Tr. C.L. Wrenn. Rev. W.F. Bolton. 3rd edn. rev. London: Harrap, 1973, rpt. 1980.
Bold, Alan. 'Hobbit Verse versus Tolkien's Poem'. In *J.R.R. Tolkien: This Far Land*. Ed. Robert Giddings. London: Vision; Totowa, New Jersey: Barnes & Noble Books, 1983. pp. 137–53.
Bonechi, Simone. 'Tolkien and the War Poets'. In Arduini, Conzonieri, and Testi, *Tolkien and the Classics* (2019), pp. 205–15.
Bowman, Mary R. 'Refining the Gold: Tolkien, *The Battle of Maldon*, and the Northern Theory of Courage'. *Tolkien Studies* 7 (2010), pp. 91–115.
Bridgwater, Sue. '*What Is It But a Dream?* Tolkien's "The Sea-Bell" and Yeats' "The Man Who Dreamed of Faeryland"'. In Eilmann and Turner, *Tolkien's Poetry* (2013), pp. 117–51.
Bridoux, Denis. 'Letting Images Speak for Themselves: Tolkien's Rebus Letter to Fr. Francis Morgan, August 8, 1904'. *Beyond Bree*, October 2020, pp. 1–2. The letter itself is reproduced on pp. 11–12.
Brown, Ivor. *Random Words*. London: The Bodley Head, 1971.
Brown, Josh. 'The Poems of *The Hobbit*'. In *Critical Insights: The Hobbit*. Ed. Stephen W. Potts. Amenia, New York: Grey House Publishing, 2016. pp. 130–44.
Browne, Thomas. *Pseudodoxia Epidemica, or Enquiries into Very Many Received Tenents, and Commonly Presumed Truths*. London: Printed by T.H. for Edward Dod, 1646.
Buck, Percy C., ed. *The Oxford Song Book*. London: Oxford University Press, 1921.
Bullough, Geoffrey, ed. *Essays and Studies 1953*. See *The Homecoming of Beorhtnoth Beorhthelm's Son* in bibliography part I.
Burns, Maggie. '*The Battle of the Eastern Field*'. *Mallorn* 46 (Autumn 2008), pp. 15–22.

Caldecott, Stratford. *The Power of the Ring: The Spiritual Vision behind* The Hobbit *and* The Lord of the Rings. New York: Crossroad, 2012.
Carpenter, Humphrey. *The Inklings: C.S. Lewis, J.R.R. Tolkien, Charles Williams, and Their Friends*. London: George Allen & Unwin, 1978.
—— *J.R.R Tolkien: A Biography*. London: George Allen & Unwin, 1977.
Carroll, Lewis. *The Annotated Alice*. The definitive edition. Introduction and notes by Martin Gardner. New York: W.W. Norton, 2000.
—— *The Complete Works of Lewis Carroll*. New York: Vintage Books, 1936, rpt. 1976.
Cawsey, Kathy. 'Could Gollum Be Singing a Sonnet?: The Poetic Project of *The Lord of the Rings*'. *Tolkien Studies* 14 (2017), pp. 53–69.
Chambers, R.W. *Beowulf: An Introduction to the Study of the Poem with a Discussion of the Stories of Offa and Finn*. 3rd edn., with supplement by C.L. Wrenn. Cambridge: Cambridge University Press, 1959.
Chaucer, Geoffrey. *The Works of Geoffrey Chaucer*. Ed. F.N. Robinson. 2nd edn. Boston: Houghton Mifflin, 1961.
Christie's. *Valuable Books and Manuscripts*. London, 12 July 2023. *https://www.christies.com*.
Christopher, Joe R. 'Tolkien and the Clerihew'. In Reynolds and GoodKnight, *Proceedings of the J.R.R. Tolkien Centenary Conference, Keble College, Oxford, 1992* (1995), pp. 263–71.
—— 'Tolkien's Lyric Poetry'. In Flieger and Hostetter, *Tolkien's Legendarium: Essays on* The History of Middle-earth (2000), pp. 143–60.
Clark, Willene B. *A Medieval Book of Beasts: The Second-Family Bestiary*. Woodbridge, Suffolk: Boydell Press, 2006.
Cole, G.D.H., G.P. Dennis, and W.S. Vines, eds. *Oxford Poetry, 1910–1913*. Oxford: B.H. Blackwell, 1913. Includes introduction by Gilbert Murray.
——, and T.W. Earp, eds. *Oxford Poetry 1915*. Oxford: B.H. Blackwell, 1915. Includes *Goblin Feet* by Tolkien, pp. 64–5 (see bibliography part I); 'Songs on the Downs' by G.B. Smith, p. 60; and three poems by H.T. Wade-Gery, pp. 70–2.
——, W.S. Vines, T.W. Earp, W.R. Childe, and A.L. Huxley, eds. *Oxford Poetry 1914–1916*. Oxford: B.H. Blackwell, 1917. Reprints *Oxford Poetry 1915*.

Coleridge, Samuel Taylor. *The Poems of Samuel Taylor Coleridge*. Ed. Ernest Hartley Coleridge. London: Oxford University Press, 1912, rpt. 1961.

Cossio, Andoni. 'The Unpublished "Mód Þrýþe Ne Wæg" by C.S. Lewis: A Critical Edition'. *Journal of Inklings Studies* 14, no. 1 (2024), pp. 62–8.

Cottrell, G.F. 'Football Retrospect'. *King Edward's School Chronicle*, June 1911, p. 42.

Coward, T.A. *The Birds of the British Isles and Their Eggs*. 1st ser., 5th edn. London: Frederick Warne, 1936.

Davidson, Christine. '*The Sea-Bell*: A Voyage of Exploration'. In *Tolkien, the Sea and Scandinavia: The 11th Tolkien Society Seminar . . . June 15, 1996*. Ed. Richard Crawshaw. Telford: The Tolkien Society, 1999. pp. 11–18.

Deyo, Steven M. 'Niggle's Leaves: The Red Book of Westmarch and Related Minor Poetry of J.R.R. Tolkien'. *Mythlore* 12, no. 3, whole no. 45 (Spring 1986), pp. 28–31, 34–7.

Dickens, Charles. *A Christmas Carol in Prose*. Facsimile edn. 1843; New York: Columbia University Press, 1956, rpt. 1957.

Dickins, Bruce, and R.M. Wilson, eds. *Early Middle English Texts*. New York: W.W. Norton, 1951.

Drout, Michael D.C. 'Reading Tolkien's Poetry'. In Eilmann and Turner, *Tolkien's Poetry* (2013), pp. 1–9.

—— Review of *Beowulf: A Translation and Commentary together with Sellic Spell* by J.R.R. Tolkien. *Tolkien Studies* 12 (2015), pp. 149–72.

——, ed. *J.R.R. Tolkien Encyclopedia: Scholarship and Critical Assessment*. New York: Routledge, 2006.

Eden, Bradford Lee. 'Strains of Elvish Song and Voices: Victorian Medievalism, Music, and Tolkien'. In *Middle-earth Minstrel: Essays on Music in Tolkien*, ed. Bradford Lee Eden. Jefferson, North Carolina: McFarland, 2010. pp. 85–101.

'Editorial'. *King Edward's School Chronicle*, February 1911, pp. 1–2.

Eilmann, Julian. *J.R.R. Tolkien: Romanticist and Poet*. Zurich and Jena: Walking Tree Publishers, 2017.

—— and Allan Turner, eds. *Tolkien's Poetry*. Zurich and Jena: Walking Tree Publishers, 2013.

Ekman, Stefan. 'Echoes of *Pearl* in Arda's Landscape'. *Tolkien Studies* 6 (2009), pp. 59–70.

The Elder or Poetic Edda. Ed. and tr. Olive Bray. London: Viking Club, 1908.

Elliott, J.W., composer. *National Nursery Rhymes and Nursery Songs*. London: George Routledge and Sons, 1871.

'Fantasy That! – A Tolkien Original'. *Monash Review*, July 1975, p. 2.
Fifty New Poems for Children: An Anthology Selected from Books Recently Published by Basil Blackwell. Oxford: Basil Blackwell, [1922]. Includes *Goblin Feet* by Tolkien and 'Romance' by E.F.A. Geach.
Fimi, Dimitra. 'Tolkien and Folklore: *Sellic Spell* and *The Lay of Beowulf*'. *Mallorn* 55 (Winter 2014), pp. 27–8.
Fisher, Jason. 'The Origins of Tolkien's "Errantry"'. *Lingwë: Musings of a Fish* (blog), 25 September 2008; 1 October 2008; 7 November 2008. *http://lingwe.blogspot.com/2008/09/origins-of-tolkiens-errantry-part-1.html, http://lingwe.blogspot.com/2008/10/origins-of-tolkiens-errantry-part-2.html, http://lingwe.blogspot.com/2008/11/origins-of-tolkiens-errantry-part-3.html.*
Fitzgerald, Jill. 'A "Clerkes Compleinte": Tolkien and the Division of Lit. and Lang.' *Tolkien Studies* 6 (2009), pp. 41–57.
Flieger, Verlyn. 'Fays, Corrigans, Elves, and More: Tolkien's Dark Ladies'. In Flieger, *There Would Always Be a Fairy Tale: More Essays on Tolkien*. Kent, Ohio: Kent State University Press, 2017. pp. 165–77.
—— 'Poems by Tolkien: *The Hobbit*'. In Drout, *J.R.R. Tolkien Encyclopedia* (2006), pp. 520–2.
—— 'Poems by Tolkien: *The Lord of the Rings*'. In Drout, *J.R.R. Tolkien Encyclopedia* (2006), pp. 522–32.
—— *A Question of Time: J.R.R. Tolkien's Road to* Faërie. Kent, Ohio: Kent State University Press, 1997.
—— Review of *The Fall of Arthur*. *Tolkien Studies* 11 (2014), pp. 213–25.
—— *Splintered Light: Logos and Language in Tolkien's World*. Rev. edn. Kent, Ohio: Kent State University Press, 2002.
—— and Carl F. Hostetter, eds. *Tolkien's Legendarium: Essays on* The History of Middle-earth. Westport, Connecticut: Greenwood Press, 2000.
Fliss, William M., and Sarah C. Schaefer. *J.R.R. Tolkien: The Art of the Manuscript*. Milwaukee: Haggerty Museum of Art, Marquette University, 2022.
Fontenot, Megan N. '"No Pagan Ever Loved His God": Tolkien, Thompson, and the Beautification of the Gods'. *Mythlore* 37, no. 1, whole no. 133 (Fall/Winter 2018), pp. 45–62.
Foster, Myles Birket. *Birket Foster's Pictures of English Landscape . . . with Pictures in Words by Tom Taylor*. London: Routledge, Warne, and Routledge, 1863.
Foster, Robert. *The Complete Guide to Middle-earth: From* The Hobbit *to* The Silmarillion. New York: Ballantine Books, 1978.

Frank, Roberta. 'Dróttkvætt'. *New Literary History* 50 (2019), pp. 393–8.

Garth, John. '"Francis Thompson": Article for Exeter College Essay Club'. In Drout, *J.R.R. Tolkien Encyclopedia* (2006), pp. 220–1.

—— '"The Road from Adaptation to Invention": How Tolkien Came to the Brink of Middle-earth in 1914'. *Tolkien Studies* 11 (2014), pp. 1–44.

—— *Tolkien and the Great War: The Threshold of Middle-earth*. London: HarperCollins, 2003.

—— *Tolkien at Exeter College*. 2nd edn. Oxford: Exeter College, 2022.

—— *The Worlds of J.R.R. Tolkien: The Places That Inspired Middle-earth*. London: Frances Lincoln, 2020.

Gay, David Elton. 'J.R.R. Tolkien and the *Kalevala*: Some Thoughts on the Finnish Origins of Tom Bombadil and Treebeard'. In *Tolkien and the Invention of Myth: A Reader*. Ed. Jane Chance. Lexington: University Press of Kentucky, 2004. pp. 295–304.

Gilliver, Peter, Jeremy Marshall, and Edmund Weiner. *The Ring of Words: Tolkien and the Oxford English Dictionary*. Oxford: Oxford University Press, 2006.

Gilson, Christopher. '*Narqelion* and the Early Lexicons: Some Notes on the First Elvish Poem'. *Vinyar Tengwar* 40 (April 1999), pp. 6–32.

Goering, Nelson. Comments on 'Dróttkvætt' by Roberta Frank. Tolkien Society Facebook forum, 26 April 2020. *https://www.facebook.com/groups/6522796067/*.

—— '*The Fall of Arthur* and *The Legend of Sigurd and Gudrún*: A Metrical Review of Three Modern English Alliterative Poems'. *Journal of Inklings Studies* 5, no. 2 (October 2015), pp. 3–26.

Gordon, R.K., sel. and transl. *Anglo-Saxon Poetry*. London: J.M. Dent & Sons, 1954, rpt. 1967.

Grahame, Kenneth. *The Wind in the Willows*. London: Methuen, 1908; rpt. 1966.

Greene, William Chase. 'Richard I before Jerusalem: The Newdigate Prize Poem 1912'. *The Harvard Graduates' Magazine* 21 (1912–13), pp. 41–6.

Grybauskas, Peter. 'A Portrait of the Poet as a Young Man: Noteworthy Omission in *The Homecoming of Beorhtnoth Beorhthelm's Son*'. *Tolkien Studies* 17 (2020), pp. 163–78.

Haden, David. *Tolkien and the Lizard: J.R.R. Tolkien in Cornwall, 1914*. Stoke-on-Trent: Burslem Books, 2021. Privately issued by the author as a PDF.

Haggard, H. Rider. *The Annotated* She. Ed. Norman Etherington. Bloomington: Indiana University Press, 1991.

Hammond, Wayne G., and Christina Scull. *J.R.R. Tolkien: Artist and Illustrator*. London: HarperCollins, 1995.

—— —— *The Lord of the Rings: A Reader's Companion*. 3rd edn. London: HarperCollins, 2014.

Hausmann, Michaela. 'Lyrics on Lost Lands: Constructing Lost Places through Poetry in J.R.R. Tolkien's *The Lord of the Rings*'. In *Sub-Creating Arda: World-Building in J.R.R. Tolkien's Work, Its Precursors and Its Legacies*. Ed. Dimitra Fimi and Thomas Honegger. Zurich and Jena: Walking Tree Publishers, 2019. pp. 261–84.

Helms, Randel. *Tolkien's World*. Boston: Houghton Mifflin, 1974.

Hibberd, Dominic, and John Onions, eds. *The Winter of the World: Poems of the First World War*. London: Constable & Robinson, 2007.

Higgins, Sørina. 'An Introduction to "Taliessin through Logres"'. *The Oddest Inkling* (blog), 12 May 2016. *https://theoddestinkling.wordpress.com/2016/05/12/an-introduction-to-taliessin-through-logres/*.

Hillier, Caroline, ed. *Winter's Tales for Children 1*. See bibliography part I.

Hodgson, Geraldine E. *Criticism at a Venture*. London: Erskine Macdonald, 1919.

—— *English Literature: With Illustrations from Poetry and Prose*. Oxford: Basil Blackwell, 1923.

Holdaway, Penelope Anne. *An Exploration of Changing Visions of Faërie through His Non-Middle-earth Poetry*. Ph.D. thesis (School of Critical Studies, College of Arts, University of Glasgow, 2021). *https://theses.gla.ac.uk/83263/*.

Holmes, John. '"A Metre I Invented": Tolkien's Clues to Tempo in "Errantry"'. In Eilmann and Turner, *Tolkien's Poetry* (2013), pp. 29–44.

Homer. *The Iliad of Homer*. Tr. Richmond Lattimore. Chicago: University of Chicago Press, 1961, rpt. 1971.

—— *The Odyssey*. Tr. Robert Fitzgerald. New York: Vintage Books, 1990.

Honegger, Thomas. '*The Homecoming of Beorhtnoth*: Philology and the Literary Muse'. *Tolkien Studies* 4 (2007), pp. 189–99.

—— 'The Man in the Moon: Structural Depth in Tolkien'. In *Root and Branch: Approaches towards Understanding Tolkien*. Ed. Thomas Honegger. Zurich and Berne: Walking Tree Publishers, 1999. pp. 9–76.

Hooker, Mark. 'Annotated Transcription of Tolkien's 1904 Rebus Letter to Fr. Francis'. *Beyond Bree*, November 2020, pp. 2–5.

Hostetter, Carl F. 'Editing the Tolkienian Manuscript'. In Ovenden and McIlwaine, *The Great Tales Never End: Essays in Memory of Christopher Tolkien* (2022), pp. 129–44.

—— '*Sir Orfeo*: A Middle English Version by J.R.R. Tolkien'. *Tolkien Studies* 1 (2004), pp. 85–123.

Hyde, Paul Nolan. 'Narqelion: A Single, Falling Leaf at Sun-fading'. *Mythlore* 15, no. 2, whole no. 56 (Winter 1988), pp. 47–52.

Izzo, Massimiliano. 'In Search of the Wandering Fire: Otherworldly Imagery in "The Song of Ælfwine"'. In Milon, *Poetry and Song in the Works of J.R.R. Tolkien* (2018), pp. 5–28.

Jenkins, Elwyn. 'Lord of the Letters'. *Sunday Times*, 13 May 2018.

Johnston, George Burke. 'The Poetry of J.R.R. Tolkien'. *Mankato State University Studies* 2, no. 1 (February 1967), pp. 63–75.

Judd, Walter S., and Graham A. Judd. *Flora of Middle-earth: Plants of J.R.R. Tolkien's Legendarium*. New York: Oxford University Press, 2017.

Keats, John. *The Poetical Works of John Keats*. Ed. H.W. Garrod. London: Oxford University Press, 1956.

Kilby, Clyde S. *Tolkien and The Silmarillion*. Wheaton, Illinois: Harold Shaw Publishers, 1976.

King, Don W. *C.S. Lewis, Poet: The Legacy of His Poetic Impulse*. Kent, Ohio: Kent State University Press, 2001.

Kipling, Rudyard. *Puck of Pook's Hill*. London: Piccolo, 1975, rpt. 1979.

—— *Rudyard Kipling's Verse, Inclusive Edition, 1885–1918*. Garden City, New York: Doubleday, Page, 1919.

Kippers, Marion. 'Imram: Tolkien and Saint Brendan'. In *Lembas Extra 2009: Tolkien in Poetry and Song*. Ed. Cécile van Zon. Wapenveld, Netherlands: Tolkien Genootschap Unquendor, 2009. pp. 32–47.

Kocher, Paul H. *Master of Middle-earth: The Fiction of J.R.R. Tolkien*. Boston: Houghton Mifflin, 1972.

Kollmann, Judith J. 'How "All That Glisters Is Not Gold" Became "All That Is Gold Does Not Glitter": Aragorn's Debt to Shakespeare'. In *Tolkien and Shakespeare: Essays on Shared Themes and Language*. Ed. Janet Brennan Croft. Jefferson, North Carolina: McFarland, 2007. pp. 110–27.

Kullmann, Thomas, and Dirk Siepmann. *Tolkien as a Literary Artist: Exploring Rhetoric, Language and Style in* The Lord of the Rings. Cham, Switzerland: Palgrave Macmillan, 2021.

Langland, William. *Piers the Ploughman*. Tr. J.F. Goodridge. Rev. edn. Harmondsworth, Middlesex: Penguin Books, 1966.
Larsen, Kristine. '"Diadem the Fallen Day": Astronomical and Arboreal Motifs in the Poem "Kortirion among the Trees"'. In Milon, *Poetry and Song in the Works of J.R.R. Tolkien* (2018), pp. 29–40.
—— '"Following the Star": Eärendil, Númenor, and the Star of Bethlehem'. *Journal of Tolkien Research* 16, no. 2 (2023), article 3.
Lee, Stuart D. 'Great Britain'. In Potter, *A History of World War One Poetry* (2022), pp. 164–81.
—— 'J.R.R. Tolkien and *The Wanderer*: From Edition to Application'. *Tolkien Studies* 6 (2009), pp. 189–211.
—— ed. *A Companion to J.R.R. Tolkien*. 2nd edn. Chichester: Wiley Blackwell, 2022.
—— and Elizabeth Solopova. *The Keys of Middle-earth: Discovering Medieval Literature through the Fiction of J.R.R. Tolkien*. 2nd edn. Basingstoke, Hampshire: Palgrave Macmillan, 2015.
Leeds University English School Association, ed. See *Leeds University Verse 1914–24* and *A Northern Venture* in bibliography part 1.
Lewis, C.S. *Collected Letters*. Ed. Walter Hooper. London: HarperCollins, 2000–6. 3 vols.
Lindop, Grevel. *Charles Williams: The Third Inkling*. Oxford: Oxford University Press, 2015.
'Literary Society'. *King Edward's School Chronicle*, December 1910, pp. 91–2.
Longfellow, Henry Wadsworth. *The Complete Poetical Works of Henry Wadsworth Longfellow*. Boston: Houghton Mifflin, 1893, rpt. 1903.
Lönnrot, Elias. *The Kalevala, or Poems of the Kaleva District*. Tr. Francis Peabody Magoun, Jr. Cambridge, Massachusetts: Harvard University Press, 1963.
—— *Kalevala: The Land of Heroes*. Tr. W.F. Kirby. London: J.M. Dent & Sons, 1907, rpt. 1951. 2 vols.
Macaulay, Thomas Babington. *Lays of Ancient Rome*. London: Longman, Brown, Green, and Longmans, 1842.
MacDonald, George. *At the Back of the North Wind*. 1870; rpt. London: J.M. Dent & Sons, 1973.
—— *The Princess and the Goblin*. 1871; rpt. London: J.M. Dent & Sons, 1973.
McIlwaine, Catherine. *Tolkien: Maker of Middle-earth*. Oxford: Bodleian Library, 2018.
Mahler, Gustav. *Lieder und Gesänge*. Mainz: Schott, 1892.

Malory, Thomas. *Le Morte d'Arthur*. Ed. Janet Cowen. Harmondsworth, Middlesex: Penguin Books, 1969.

Martsch, Nancy. 'Tolkien's Poetic Use of the Old English and Latinate Vocabulary: A Study of Three Poems from *The Adventures of Tom Bombadil*'. In Eilmann and Turner, *Tolkien's Poetry* (2013), pp. 163–76.

Medcalf, Stephen. '"The Language Learned of Elves": Owen Barfield, *The Hobbit* and *The Lord of the Rings*'. *Seven* 16 (1999), pp. 31–53.

Milon, Anna, ed. *Poetry and Song in the Works of J.R.R. Tolkien: Proceedings of The Tolkien Society Seminar 2017*. Edinburgh: Luna Press Publishing, 2018.

Milton, John. *Complete Poems and Major Prose*. Ed. Merritt Y. Hughes. Indianapolis, Indiana: Odyssey Press, 1957, rpt.

Moffat, Alfred, ed. *What the Children Sing: A Book of the Most Popular Nursery Songs, Rhymes and Games*. London: Augener, [1915].

Morris, Richard, ed. *An Old English Miscellany*. London: Published for the Early English Text Society by N. Trübner, 1872.

Morris, William. *The Earthly Paradise: A Poem*. 1868–70; rpt. London: Longmans, Green, 1918.

—— *The Story of Sigurd the Volsung and the Fall of the Niblungs*. 1876; rpt. London: Longmans, Green, 1928.

Murray, Gilbert. 'Introduction'. In Cole, Dennis, and Vines, *Oxford Poetry 1910–1913* (1913), pp. xi–xxi.

Nicholson, D.H.S., and A.H.E. Lee, eds. *The Oxford Book of English Mystical Verse*. Oxford: Clarendon Press, 1917.

O'Donoghue, Denis. *Lives and Legends of Saint Brendan the Voyager*. 1893; rpt. Felinfach, Wales: Llanerch, 1994.

Olsen, Corey. *Exploring J.R.R. Tolkien's* The Hobbit. Boston: Houghton Mifflin Harcourt, 2012.

—— 'The Myth of the Ent and the Entwife'. *Tolkien Studies* 5 (2008), pp. 39–53.

—— 'Poetry'. In Lee, *A Companion to J.R.R. Tolkien* (2022), pp. 152–65.

Opie, Iona and Peter, eds. *The Oxford Dictionary of Nursery Rhymes*. New edn. Oxford: Oxford University Press, 1997.

Ordway, Holly. *Tolkien's Faith: A Spiritual Biography*. Park Ridge, Illinois: Word on Fire Academic, 2023.

—— *Tolkien's Modern Reading: Middle-earth beyond the Middle Ages*. Park Ridge, Illinois: Word on Fire Academic, 2021.

Ovenden, Richard, and Catherine McIlwaine, eds. *The Great Tales Never End: Essays in Memory of Christopher Tolkien*. Oxford: Bodleian Library Publishing, 2022.
Owen, Dora, ed. *The Book of Fairy Poetry*. London: Longmans, Green, 1920. Includes *Goblin Feet* by Tolkien.
The Owl and the Nightingale. Ed. Eric Gerald Stanley. London: Nelson, 1960.
The Owl and the Nightingale, Cleanness, St Erkenwald. Tr. and introduced by Brian Stone. Harmondsworth, Middlesex: Penguin Books, 1971.
Parker, Rennie. *The Georgian Poets: Abercrombie, Brooke, Drinkwater, Gibson and Thomas*. Plymouth: Northcote House, in association with the British Council, 1999.
Patrick, Millar, et al., eds. *The Scottish Students' Song Book: Published for the Song Book Committee of the Students' Representative Councils of Scotland*. London and Glasgow: Bayley & Ferguson, 1897.
Pearl. Ed. E.V. Gordon. Oxford: Clarendon Press, 1953.
Percy, Thomas. *Reliques of Ancient English Poetry*. London: Printed for J. Dodsley, 1765. 3 vols.
Phelpstead, Carl: '"For W.H.A.': Tolkien's Poem in Praise of Auden'. In Eilmann and Turner, *Tolkien's Poetry* (2013), pp. 43–59.
—— 'Myth-making, Sub-creation, and World-building'. In Lee, *A Companion to J.R.R. Tolkien* (2022), pp. 67–79.
—— *Tolkien and Wales: Language, Literature and Identity*. Cardiff: University of Wales Press, 2011.
—— '"With Chunks of Poetry in Between": *The Lord of the Rings* and Saga Poetics'. *Tolkien Studies* 5 (2008), pp. 23–38.
Philoponus, Honorius (Caspar Plautius). *Nova Typis Transacta Navigatio*. [Linz: Printer not known], 1621.
Piechnik, Iwona. 'Finnic Tetrameter in J.R.R. Tolkien's *The Story of Kullervo* in Comparison to W.F. Kirby's English Translation of the *Kalevala*'. *Studia Linguistica Universitatis Iagellonicae Cracoviensis* 138 (2021), pp. 201–20. *https://www.ejournals.eu/pliki/art/20509*.
Porck, M.H. 'Medieval Animals in Middle-earth: J.R.R. Tolkien and the Old English and Middle English *Physiologus*'. In *Figurations animalières á travers les textes et l'image en Europe*. Ed. A. van de Haar and A.E. Schulte Nordholt. Leiden: Brill, 2022. pp. 266–80.
Potter, Jane, ed. *A History of World War One Poetry*. Cambridge: Cambridge University Press, 2022.
Raffel, Burton, tr. *Poems from the Old English*. [Lincoln]: University of Nebraska Press, 1960.

Rateliff, John D. 'Hiawatha Earendil'. *Sacnoth's Scriptorium* (blog), 4 June 2010. *http://sacnoths.blogspot.com/2010/06/hiawatha-earendil.html*.

—— *The History of* The Hobbit. London: HarperCollins, 2007. 2 vols.

—— 'Inside Literature: Tolkien's Explorations of Medieval Genres'. In *Tolkien in the New Century: Essays in Honor of Tom Shippey*. Ed. John Wm. Houghton, et al. Jefferson, North Carolina: McFarland, 2014. pp. 133–52.

—— 'J.R.R. Tolkien: "Sir Topas" Revisited'. *Notes and Queries* 29, no. 4 (August 1982), p. 348.

—— '"That Seems to Me Fatal": Pagan and Christian in *The Fall of Arthur*'. *Tolkien Studies* 13 (2016), pp. 45–70.

Rawls, Melanie A. Letter to the Editor. *Mythlore* 19, no. 3, whole no. 73 (Summer 1993), p. 34.

—— 'The Verse of J.R.R. Tolkien'. *Mythlore* 19, no. 1, whole no. 71 (Winter 1993), pp. 4–8.

Review of *Oxford Poetry 1915*. *New Age*, 30 March 1916.

Reynolds, Patricia. 'Green Rocks: White Ship: *Oilima Markirya* (The Last Ark)'. *Mallorn* 27 (September 1990), pp. 33–5.

—— and Glen H. GoodKnight, eds. *Proceedings of the J.R.R. Tolkien Centenary Conference, Keble College, Oxford, 1992* (= *Mallorn* no. 33, *Mythlore* no. 80). Milton Keynes: Tolkien Society; Altadena, California: Mythopoeic Press, 1995.

Richard of Devizes, and Geoffrey de Vinsauf. *Chronicles of the Crusades: Being Contemporary Narratives of the Crusade of Richard Cœur de Lion* . . . London: Henry G. Bohn, 1848. Includes translation of *Itinerarium Regis Ricardi*.

Ricketts, Harry. *Strange Meetings: The Poets of the Great War*. London: Chatto & Windus, 2010.

Roche, Norma. 'Sailing West: Tolkien, the Saint Brendan Story, and the Idea of Paradise in the West'. *Mythlore* 17, no. 4, whole no. 66 (Summer 1991), pp. 16–20, 62.

Rosebury, Brian. *Tolkien: A Critical Assessment*. Houndmills, Basingstoke, Hampshire: Macmillan, 1992. Rev. as *Tolkien: A Cultural Phenomenon*. Houndmills, Basingstoke, Hampshire: Palgrave Macmillan, 2003.

Ross, Robert H. *The Georgian Revolt, 1910–1922: Rise and Fall of a Poetic Ideal*. Carbondale: Southern Illinois University Press, 1965.

Rossenberg, René van. 'Tolkien's Exceptional Visit to Holland: A Reconstruction'. In Reynolds and GoodKnight, *Proceedings of the J.R.R. Tolkien Centenary Conference, Keble College, Oxford, 1992* (1995), pp. 301–9.

Rossetti, Christina. *The Poetical Works of Christina Georgina Rossetti.* Ed. William Michael Rossetti. London: Macmillan, 1904.
Runciman, Steven. *A History of the Crusades*. Harmondsworth, Middlesex: Penguin, 1965. 3 vols.
Russom, Geoffrey. 'Tolkien's Versecraft in *The Hobbit* and *The Lord of the Rings*'. In *J.R.R. Tolkien and His Literary Resonances: Views of Middle-earth*. Ed. George Clark and Daniel Timmons. Westport, Connecticut: Greenwood Press, 2000. pp. 53–69.
Ruzich, Constance, ed. *International Poetry of the First World War: An Anthology of Lost Voices*. London: Bloomsbury Academic, 2021, rpt. 2022.
Ryan, J.S. 'Henry Bradley, Keeper of the Words of English and His Heroic Passing'. *Quettar* 27 (January 1987), pp. 7–15.
—— 'Homo Ludens: Amusement, Play and Seeking in Tolkien's Earliest Romantic Thought'. In Ryan, *Tolkien's View: Windows into His World*. Zurich and Jena: Walking Tree Publishers, 2009. pp. 47–54.
The Saga of King Heidrek the Wise. Tr. Christopher Tolkien. London: Thomas Nelson and Sons, 1960.
Sayer, George. 'Recollections of J.R.R. Tolkien'. In Reynolds and GoodKnight, *Proceedings of the J.R.R. Tolkien Centenary Conference, Keble College, Oxford, 1992* (1995), pp. 21–5.
Scull, Christina. 'Tolkien's Poetry'. *Amon Hen* 93 (September 1988), pp. 22–4. Report of a talk by Priscilla Tolkien.
——, and Wayne G. Hammond. *The Hobbit, 1937–2017*. London: HarperCollins, 2018.
—— —— *The J.R.R. Tolkien Companion and Guide*. 2nd edn. London: HarperCollins, 2017. 3 vols. (*Chronology*, *Reader's Guide*).
The Seafarer. Ed. I.L. Gordon. London: Methuen, 1960.
Selver, Paul. Review of *Oxford Poetry 1914–1916*. *New Age*, 11 July 1918.
Shakespeare, William. *The Complete Works of Shakespeare*. Ed. Irving Ribner and George Lyman Kittredge. Waltham, Massachusetts: Ginn, 1971.
Shelley, Percy Bysshe. *The Complete Poetical Works of Percy Bysshe Shelley*. Ed. Thomas Hutchinson. London: Oxford University Press, 1934, rpt. 1956.
Sherwood, William. *The 'Romantic Faëry': Keats, Tolkien, and the Perilous Realm*. M.A. thesis (University of Exeter, 2019). *https://ore.exeter.ac.uk/repository/handle/10871/40585*.
Shippey, T.A. (Tom). 'Alliterative Verse by Tolkien'. In Drout, *J.R.R. Tolkien Encyclopedia* (2006), pp. 10–11.

—— 'Boar and Badger: An Old English Heroic Antithesis?' *Leeds Studies in English* 16 (1985), pp. 220–39.
—— *J.R.R. Tolkien: Author of the Century*. London: HarperCollins, 2000.
—— '"King Sheave" and "The Lost Road"'. In Ovenden and McIlwaine, *The Great Tales Never End: Essays in Memory of Christopher Tolkien* (2022), pp. 166–80.
—— 'Poems by Tolkien in Other Languages'. In Drout, *J.R.R. Tolkien Encyclopedia* (2006), pp. 514–15.
—— *The Road to Middle-earth*. 2nd edn. London: Grafton, 1992.
—— *Roots and Branches: Selected Papers on Tolkien*. Zurich and Jena: Walking Tree Publishers, 2007.
—— 'Tolkien and "The Homecoming of Beorhtnoth"'. In Shippey, *Roots and Branches* (2007), pp. 323–39.
—— 'Tolkien's Development as a Writer of Alliterative Poetry in Modern English'. In Eilmann and Turner, *Tolkien's Poetry* (2013), pp. 11–26.
—— 'The Versions of "The Hoard"'. In Shippey, *Roots and Branches* (2007), pp. 341–9.
—— 'William Morris and Tolkien: Some Unexpected Connections'. In Arduini, Conzonieri, and Testi, *Tolkien and the Classics* (2019), pp. 229–45.
Simonson, Martin. The Lord of the Rings *and the Western Narrative Tradition*. Zurich and Jena: Walking Tree Publishers, 2008.
Sisam, Kenneth, ed. *Fourteenth Century Verse and Prose*. Oxford: Clarendon Press, 1922. Also includes glossary by Tolkien, *A Middle English Vocabulary*.
Smith, Arden R. 'Tolkienian Gothic'. In *The Lord of the Rings 1954–2004: Scholarship in Honor of Richard E. Blackwelder*. Ed. Wayne G. Hammond and Christina Scull. Milwaukee: Marquette University Press, 2006. pp. 267–81.
Smith, Geoffrey Bache. *A Spring Harvest*. Ed. J.R.R. Tolkien [and Christopher Wiseman]. London: Erskine Macdonald, 1918.
Smith, William. 'Obituary for Henry Bradley'. In Drout, *J.R.R. Tolkien Encyclopedia* (2006), p. 465.
Smol, Anna. 'Tolkien's King Sheave Story'. *A Single Leaf* (blog), 27 May 2016. *https://annasmol.net/2016/05/27/tolkiens-king-sheave-story/*.
Strack, Paul. 'Q. Oilima Markirya "The Last Ark"'. *Eldamo: An Elvish Lexicon*. *https://eldamo.org/content/words/word-578245545.html*.
Stubbs, Charles William. *Bryhtnoth's Prayer and Other Poems*. London: T. Fisher Unwin, 1899.

Sudell, T.S. 'The Alliterative Verse of *The Fall of Arthur*'. *Tolkien Studies* 13 (2016), pp. 71–104.

Swank, Kris. 'The Poetry of Geoffrey Bache Smith with Special Note of Tolkienian Contents'. *Journal of Tolkien Research* 12, no. 2 (2021), article 2.

—— 'Tom Bombadil's Last Song: Tolkien's "Once upon a Time"'. *Tolkien Studies* 10 (2013), pp. 185–97.

Swann, Donald, composer. *The Road Goes Ever On: A Song Cycle*. Poems by J.R.R. Tolkien. Boston: Houghton Mifflin, 1967. 2nd edn., Houghton Mifflin, 1978. 3rd edn., London: HarperCollins, 2002.

Sweet, Henry. *An Anglo-Saxon Reader in Prose and Verse*. 8th edn., rev. Oxford: Clarendon Press, 1908.

Tennyson, Alfred, Lord. *The Poetical Works of Alfred, Lord Tennyson, Poet Laureate*. New York: Thomas Y. Crowell, 1900.

Thomas, Edward. *The Collected Poems of Edward Thomas*. Ed. R. George Thomas. Oxford: Oxford University Press, 1981, rpt. 1997.

Thompson, Francis. *The Works of Francis Thompson*. Ed. Wilfrid Meynell. London: Burns & Oates, 1913. 3 vols.

Thomson, James. *Autumn: A Poem*. 2nd edn. London: Printed by N. Blandford, for J. Millan, 1730.

Tolley, Clive. 'Tolkien's "Essay on Man": A Look at Mythopoeia'. *Inklings Jahrbuch* 10 (1992), pp. 221–35.

Treharne, Elaine, ed. *Old and Middle English: An Anthology*. Oxford: Blackwell, 2000. Includes selections from the Exeter Book.

Truffelli, Ugo. Comment, 20 May 2020. 'Sir Gawain and the Green Knight Deluxe'. *Tolkien Collector's Guide https://www.tolkienguide.com/modules/newbb/viewtopic.php?post_id=25019#forumpost25019*.

Turner, Allan. 'Early Influences on Tolkien's Poetry'. In Eilmann and Turner, *Tolkien's Poetry* (2013), pp. 205–21.

Tyler, J.E.A. *The Complete Tolkien Companion*. London: Pan Books, 2002.

Vaninskaya, Anna. *Fantasies of Time and Death: Dunsany, Eddison, Tolkien*. London: Palgrave Macmillan, 2020.

Weber, Henry, ed. *Metrical Romances of the Thirteenth, Fourteenth, and Fifteenth Centuries*. Edinburgh: Printed by George Ramsay and Company, for Archibald Constable [etc.], 1810. 3 vols. Vol. 2 includes *Richard Coer de Lyon*.

Weinreich, Frank. 'Metaphysics of Myth: The Platonic Ontology of "Mythopoeia"'. In *Tolkien's Shorter Works: Proceedings of the 4th Seminar of the Deutsche Tolkien Gesellschaft and Walking Tree*

Publishers Decennial Conference. Ed. Margaret Hiley and Frank Weinreich. Zurich and Jena: Walking Tree Publishers, 2008. pp. 325–47.
Wells, H.G. *The Definitive Time Machine: A Critical Edition of H. G. Wells's Scientific Romance*. Ed. Harry M. Geduld. Bloomington: Indiana University Press, 1987.
West, Richard C. 'The Interlace Structure of *The Lord of the Rings*'. In *A Tolkien Compass*. Ed. Jared Lobdell. La Salle, Illinois: Open Court, 1975. pp. 77–94.
—— '*The Lays of Beleriand*'. In Drout, *J.R.R. Tolkien Encyclopedia* (2006), pp. 348–50.
Weyant, Curtis A. '"A Translator Is Not Free": J.R.R. Tolkien's Rules for Translation and Their Application in *Sir Orfeo*'. *Tolkien Studies* 18 (2021), pp. 63–92.
White, T.H. *The Bestiary: A Book of Beasts*. New York: Capricorn Books, 1960.
Williams, Charles. *The Arthurian Poems of Charles Williams: Taliessin through Logres and The Region of the Summer Stars*. Woodbridge, Suffolk: D.S. Brewer, 1982.
Williams-Ellis, Clough. *England and the Octopus*. 1928; rpt. London: CPRE, 1996.
Wilson, A.N. *C.S. Lewis: A Biography*. London: Collins, 1990.
Wordsworth, William. *The Complete Poetical Works of William Wordsworth*. London: Macmillan, 1888, rpt. 1900.
Wright, Joseph. *Grammar of the Gothic Language*. Oxford: Clarendon Press, 1910.
Wright, Thomas, and James Orchard Halliwell, eds. *Reliquiæ Antiquæ: Scraps from Ancient Manuscripts*. London: William Pickering, 1841. 2 vols.
Wynne, Patrick, and Carl F. Hostetter. 'Three Elvish Verse Modes'. In Flieger and Hostetter, *Tolkien's Legendarium: Essays on* The History of Middle-earth (2000), pp. 113–39.
Yates, Jessica. '"The Battle of the Eastern Field": A Commentary'. *Mallorn* 13 (1979), pp. 3–5.
—— 'The Source of "The Lay of Aotrou and Itroun"'. In *Leaves from the Tree: J.R.R. Tolkien's Shorter Fiction*. London: Tolkien Society, 1991. pp. 63–71.
Zimmer, Paul Edwin. 'Another Opinion of "The Verse of J.R.R. Tolkien"'. *Mythlore* 19, no. 2, whole no. 72 (Spring 1993), pp. 16–23.

III. ARCHIVAL SOURCES

We have used, to varying degrees, the Tolkien papers and other archival collections in the Bodleian Library, University of Oxford; the Tolkien Collection of the Archival Collections and Institutional Repository, Raynor Memorial Libraries, Marquette University, Milwaukee, Wisconsin; the E.V. and Ida Gordon archive held by Special Collections & Galleries, Leeds University Library; the collections of the Marion E. Wade Center, Wheaton College, Wheaton, Illinois; the Tolkien–George Allen & Unwin correspondence archive held by HarperCollins UK; and private communications with Christopher Tolkien. We are grateful for permission to quote from specific papers or collections of papers as detailed below.

BODLEIAN LIBRARY, OXFORD Blue Poetry Books I and II, and Verse Files I and II, Tolkien Papers; correspondence between J.R.R. and Edith Tolkien, letters from Dora Owens and R.W. Reynolds, Tolkien's Rotterdam speech and poem, and one version of *Kortirion* (no. 40), Tolkien Family Papers; Tolkien's comments on the translation of poetry, MS. Tolkien A 30/1; Tolkien's letter to Prof. Leyerle, MS. Tolkien A 35; letters written by members of the T.C.B.S., MS. Tolkien F 75; *The Adventures of Tom Bombadil* (1962) poems, MS. Tolkien 19; alliterative *Beowulf* translation, MS. Tolkien A 29/1; *Beowulf and the Finnesburg Fragment* ms. introduction, MS. Tolkien A 17/2; *The Children of Húrin*, MS. Tolkien S 3; *The Death of St Brendan*, MS. Tolkien B 65/2; *The Homecoming of Beorhtnoth Beorhthelm's Son*, MS. Tolkien 5 and MS. Tolkien Drawings 88, fol. 24v; paper on the *Kalevala*, MS. Tolkien A 61; *King Sheave*, MS. Tolkien B 60 (A)/2; *The Lay of the Fall of Gondolin*, MS. Tolkien S 1/XIV; *The Man in the Moon Came Down Too Soon* in the Book of Ishness, MS. Tolkien Drawings 87, fol. 22v; *The Owl and the Nightingale* poem and lecture notes, MS. Tolkien A 9/1; *A Rime for My Boy*, MS. Tolkien Drawings 86, fol. 25r; *The Shores of Faery* in the Book of Ishness, MS. Tolkien Drawings 87, fol. 21v; *The Story of Kullervo*, and early version of *May Day*, MS. Tolkien B 64; *The Trumpets of Faery* and *The Happy Mariners* in the Book of Ishness, MS. Tolkien Drawings 87, fols. 78v–76v rev.; Sidgwick & Jackson papers, MSS. Sidgwick and Jackson; Tolkien material in the papers of Walter Hooper will remain in that archive.

TOLKIEN PAPERS, ARCHIVAL COLLECTIONS & INSTITUTIONAL REPOSITORY, MARQUETTE UNIVERSITY MSS-1/1/21/6–9 (no. 60); MSS-1/1/23/4–5, MSS-1/2/38/11–13 (no. 64); MSS-1/1/21/5, MSS-

1/2/39/3–4, 3/1/24/14, 3/1/42/9–10 (no. 83); 1/1/27/7a, 1/1/51/8a (no. 108); 1/1/27/8a, 1/1/27/9a, 1/1/51/9a, 1/1/51/10a, 1/1/28/1a (no. 109); 1/1/7/7a, 1/1/57/9a (no. 110); 1/1/25/1b (no. 111); 1/1/12/10a, 1/1/65/4a, 1/1/65/5a (no. 112); 1/1/20/1a, 1/1/69/1a, 1/1/69/2a (no. 113); 1/1/31/1b (no. 114); 1/1/31/1a, MSS-1/1/8/2a, MSS-1/1/8/2b, MSS-1/1/8/3a, MSS-1/2/3/13a, 3/8/15/9a (no. 115); MSS-3/1/9/1, MSS-3/1/9/2, MSS-3/1/9/3, 3/3/1, MSS-3/1/11/13–15, MSS-3/1/10/1–4, 3/3/8/8, MSS-3/1/12/4–6, MSS-3/1/13/1–3, MSS-3/1/14/1–2, MSS-3/1/15/1–2, MSS-3/1/16/1–3, MSS-3/1/17/1–2, 3/3/18/15–17, 3/4/1/14–16, 3/4/16/16–19, 3/4/18/11–13, MSS-3/1/18/1–3, MSS-3/1/19/1, MSS-3/1/20/2–5 (no. 128); MSS-1/2/5/7a, MSS-1/2/5/8a, MSS-1/2/5/9a (no. 149); MSS-1/1/8/4b, MSS-1/1/8/5a, MSS-1/1/11/3a, MSS-1/1/10/11a, MSS-1/1/10/12a, 3/8/22/3a (no. 150); MSS-1/1/8/7a, MSS-1/1/8/7b, MSS-1/1/8/8b, MSS-1/1/11/4a, MSS-1/1/10/14a (no. 151); MSS-1/2/9/3a, MSS-1/2/9/3b (no. 152); MSS-1/2/9/6b (no. 153); MSS-1/1/16/8b, MSS-1/1/16/9b, 3/1/16/10a (no. 154); MSS-1/1/20/13a, MSS-1/1/20/13b, MSS-1/1/20/5b (no. 155); 3/1/20/11a, 3/1/20/11b, 3/1/20/12a, 3/1/20/12b, MSS-3/1/32/3a (no. 156); MSS-1/2/38/3a, MSS-1/2/38/4b (no. 157); MSS-2/1/6/4a, 3/3/8/rider (no. 158); MSS-1/2/30/10a, MSS-1/2/30/10b, MSS-2/1/7/3a, MSS-2/1/7/4a, 3/3/10/20a, 3/3/10/20b (no. 159); MSS-2/1/11/9a, MSS-2/1/11/8a, MSS-2/1/11/14a, MSS-2/1/11/17a, MSS-2/1/11/19a, MSS-2/1/11/19b, 3/3/12/6a, 3/3/26/7a, 3/3/26/8a, 3/3/26/9a (no. 160); MSS-2/1/14/21a, MSS-2/1/14/24a, MSS-2/1/14/22a, MSS-2/1/14/23a (no. 161); MSS-2/1/14/24a (no. 162); MSS-2/1/18/4a, MSS-2/1/18/5a, 3/5/1/6a (no. 163); MSS-2/1/22/4a, 3/5/4/8a (no. 164); MSS-2/1/22/11a, MSS-2/1/22/10a, 3/5/4/14a (no. 165); MSS-3/1/33/1a, MSS-2/1/25/2a, 3/5/6/1b (no. 166); MSS-3/2/12/9b, MSS-3/2/12/10a, MSS-3/2/12/12a, 3/6/3/9b (no. 167); 3/7/4/4a, 3/7/3/7b, 3/7/3/9a, 3/7/3/8b, 3/7/9/9a, 3/7/9/10a, 3/7/37/6a (no. 168); MSS-3/1/21/1a, 3/7/19/2b (no. 169); 3/7/19/3a, 3/7/22/6a, 3/7/20/9b, 3/7/20/9a, 3/7/20/10a, 3/7/43/5a (no. 170); 3/8/3/6b, 3/8/1/10a, 3/8/1/11a, 3/8/26/9a, 3/8/35/12a (no. 171).

E.V. & IDA GORDON ARCHIVE, SPECIAL COLLECTIONS & GALLERIES, LEEDS UNIVERSITY LIBRARY MS 1952/2/10 (no. 77); MS 1952/2/4 (no. 78); MS 1952/2/11 (no. 81); MS 1952/2/7 (no. 82); MS 1952/2/9 (no. 83); MS 1952/2/8 (no. 86); MS 1952/2/12 (no. 87); MS 1952/2/15 (nos. 97, 98); MS 1952/2/13 (no. 99); MS 1952/2/16 (no. 120); MS 1952/2/1 (no. 129); MS 1952/2/14 (no. 133); MS 1952/2/18 (no. 143); MS 1952/1/1 (letter from Tolkien to E.V. Gordon, 2 January 1929).

Index

Here our primary focus is on Tolkien's poems and on his career as a poet, as opposed to his fiction, scholarship, or general biography. For the most part, then, we have selected terms which have a weight of importance *in the context of Tolkien's poetry* and which we think useful for its study. We have, however, made some exceptions in regard to his *legendarium* or mythology, chiefly when a place or character is the *subject* of a poem or a character is the *speaker* or *author* of a poem, and we have selectively indexed significant elements in *The Hobbit*, *The Lord of the Rings*, and 'The Silmarillion', such as *Middle-earth* and *Silmarils*. The reader may also consult the second part of our Glossary (from p. 1437), which is a guide to names in the mythology *mentioned in the poems*.

Most of our coverage in the Index comprises (1) titles of the collected poems, with priority given to the title which, in our judgement, is the most familiar or central in a poem's evolution; (2) titles of Tolkien's works in general, including art, mentioned in our commentary, excepting only the collected *Letters*; (3) authors and titles of works noted as sources, inspirations, or analogues for Tolkien's poems, or otherwise related to the poetry; (4) names of critics; (5) selectively, names of other persons, firms, or institutions concerned with Tolkien's life or the writing or publishing of his poems; (6) names of places associated with the poems; (7) topical subjects of poems; (8) names of poetry movements or groups, with poetic forms and metres grouped under 'Poetry'; and (9) names of languages, other than Modern English and including his invented languages, in which Tolkien wrote his poems or which are associated with them. We have not indexed our Chronology, Glossary, or Bibliography, or the final, more procedural pages of the Introduction.

Titles given below refer to works by Tolkien unless qualified. All titles of Tolkien's works, regardless of length or form, are *italicized*. Page numbers of the main entries for individual poems are given in **boldface**. Names beginning *Mac* or *Mc* are uniformly entered as if spelled *Mac*. Citations in Roman numerals are to the Introduction in volume 1, which also contains text pp. 1–448. Pages 449–976 are in volume 2, and 977–1410 in volume 3.